Nutrition, Health, and Safety for Young Children

Promoting Wellness

Nutrition, Health, and Safety for Young Children

Promoting Wellness

Joanne Sorte — Oregon State University

Inge Daeschel — Oregon State University

Carolina Amador — Community Health Centers of Benton and Linn Counties

Boston   Columbus   Indianapolis   New York   San Francisco   Upper Saddle River
Amsterdam   Cape Town   Dubai   London   Madrid   Milan   Munich   Paris   Montreal   Toronto
Delhi   Mexico City   Sao Paulo   Sydney   Hong Kong   Seoul   Singapore   Taipei   Tokyo

Vice President and Editor in Chief: Jeffery W. Johnston
Senior Acquisitions Editor: Julie Peters
Senior Development Editor: Max Effenson Chuck
Editorial Assistant: Tiffany Bitzel
Vice President, Director of Marketing: Quinn Perkson
Marketing Manager: Erica DeLuca
Marketing Assistant: Drew Jameson
Senior Managing Editor: Pamela D. Bennett
Senior Project Manager: Linda Hillis Bayma
Senior Operations Supervisor: Matthew Ottenweller
Operations Specialist: Laura Messerly
Senior Art Director: Diane Lorenzo
Text and Cover Designer: Rokusek Design, Inc.

Photo Coordinator: Lori Whitley
Permissions Administrator: Rebecca Savage
Cover Art: Shutterstock
Art Studio: Rolin Graphics
Media Producers: Autumn Benson and Emily Ryan
Media Project Manager: Rebecca Norsic
Full-Service Project Management: Cindy Sweeney, S4Carlisle Publishing Services
Composition: S4Carlisle Publishing Services
Printer/Binder: Courier/Kendallville
Cover Printer: Lehigh Color/Phoenix/Hagerstown
Text Font: Garamond Book

Notice: Care has been taken to confirm the accuracy of information presented in this book. The authors, editors, and the publisher, however, cannot accept any responsibility for errors or omissions or for consequences from application of the information in this book and make no warranty, express or implied, with respect to its contents.

Credits and acknowledgments borrowed from other sources and reproduced, with permission, in this textbook appear on appropriate page within text.

Every effort has been made to provide accurate and current Internet information in this book. However, the Internet and information posted on it are constantly changing, so it is inevitable that some of the Internet addresses listed in this textbook will change.

Photo Credits: Photo credits appear on page PC-1, which constitutes a continuation of this copyright page.

Library of Congress Cataloging-in-Publication Data
Sorte, Joanne.
Nutrition, health, and safety for young children: promoting wellness/Joanne Sorte, Inge Daeschel, Carolina Amador.
p. ; cm.
Includes bibliographical references and indexes.
ISBN: 978-0-13-234941-3
1. Children—Health and hygiene—Textbooks. 2. Children—Nutrition—Textbooks.
I. Daeschel, Inge. II. Amador, Carolina. III. Title.
[DNLM: 1. Child Nutritional Physiology Phenomena. 2. Child Care—methods. 3. Child Welfare.
4. Child. 5. Health Promotion. 6. Infant. 7. Nutritional Requirements.
WS 130 S714n 2011
RJ101.S655 2011
613.2083--dc22
2009046238

www.pearsonhighered.com

10 9 8 7 6 5 4 3
ISBN-13: 978-0-13-234941-3
ISBN-10:   0-13-234941-8

I extend loving appreciation to my parents, Jean and Burrell Godard, and to my family: Bruce, Cascade, Matt, Caden, Jerry, Misty, Isabelle, and Sally, who have taught me many things about nutrition, health, and safety and the joys of playing outdoors.

Joanne Sorte

I would like to thank my husband Mark and our four children, Ariel, Lea, Kimberly, and Devin, for their love and support throughout the writing of this book.

Inge Daeschel

I extend genuine appreciation to all children, each of whom bring wisdom, courage, and joy to the world. I would like to also extend an extra special thanks to my family: Scott, Lucia, and Oscar, who bring me great peace, joy, and awe.

Carolina Amador

about the authors

From left: Joanne Sorte, Inge Daeschel, and Carolina Amador

Joanne Sorte has been an early childhood professional for more than 30 years. She earned her bachelor of arts degree in child development and family life, and her master of science degree in human development and family sciences at Oregon State University (OSU). She began her early childhood professional experiences as a home visitor for the Home Base program in Yakima, Washington. She then directed a preschool program for Lower Columbia College in Longview, Washington, and worked as the family services coordinator for Head Start. These experiences inspired her commitment to serving families from diverse backgrounds, while raising three children with her husband provided her many opportunities to experience the joys of child development and parenting. She taught in preschool settings for several years, until accepting a position on the faculty of Human Development and Family Sciences at OSU as director of the Child Development Laboratory in the Hallie Ford Center for Healthy Children and Families. She is also director of the OSU Oregon Head Start Prekindergarten Program and an active member of the Oregon Head Start Association. Recognizing the value of the laboratory preschool as a formative experience for children, families, and students, she guided the evolution of a blended early education program model where children from low-income families, children with special needs, and children from the general community attend preschool together in the early education laboratory. She directs the practicum experience for students majoring in early childhood development and education, supervises graduate students, and facilitates research on child development and wellness. She has coauthored an intervention program with Inge Daeschel called *Health in Action: 5 Steps to Good Health*. She enjoys advocating for education and being active with her family.

Inge Daeschel is a licensed and registered dietitian who is board certified as a specialist in pediatric nutrition. She received her bachelor of science degree in foods and nutrition science at Plattsburgh State University in New York. She completed her dietetic internship at Massachusetts General Hospital in Boston and received her master of science degree in nutrition science from the University of Tennessee at Knoxville. She worked at Duke University Medical Center, first as pediatric dietitian clinician and later as assistant chief clinical dietitian. This position was instrumental in developing her interest in helping families understand the nutritional needs of their children.

She and her family relocated to Oregon where she worked at the Corvallis Clinic and later accepted a faculty position as instructor in the department of Human Development and Family Sciences at Oregon State University (OSU) where she is health and nutrition services coordinator of the OSU Child Development Laboratory and the OSU Oregon Head Start Prekindergarten Program. She is also a nutrition consultant providing services to an area hospital, two WIC programs, and the Head Start and Migrant Head Start programs. Her expertise in feeding children is based on personal as well as professional experience, gained raising four children, including one with multiple food allergies. She has coauthored with Joanne Sorte an intervention program called *Health in Action: 5 Steps to Good Health*, which promotes wellness by providing focused messages that address nutrition and physical activity in early childhood programs.

Carolina Amador, M.D., is a board-certified pediatrician. She received a bachelor of education degree in speech pathology at the University of Georgia in Athens. She earned her medical degree from the Medical College of Georgia in Augusta and completed her residency in pediatrics at West Virginia University in Morgantown. She worked as chief resident in pediatrics at West Virginia University where she developed a lactation clinic as well as a focus on advocacy for breast-feeding mothers. She is in the process of obtaining a master's degree in public health from the University of Washington in Seattle with a focus on maternal and child health. She moved with her husband to Corvallis, Oregon, and has worked as a general pediatrician for 7 years and is currently employed by a community health center that serves a large percentage of Hispanics and migrant workers. During these years as a general pediatrician, she has developed professional interests in childhood obesity prevention, health disparities, and Latino health. She has been involved in community events and organizations advocating for children's health including the Oregon State University Head Start Health Advisory Committee, the Benton County Healthy Weight and Lifestyle Coalition, the Benton County Oral Health Coalition, and the Breastfeeding Coalition of Benton County. Throughout her years of education and medical practice, she has participated in several international health experiences in Ecuador, Honduras, Uganda, and Malawi.

preface

This is an exciting time to be an early childhood educator. At the forefront of this excitement is the broad and enthusiastic confirmation that early childhood professionals play an important role in establishing the foundations of wellness for young children. Teachers of young children are experiencing new challenges, including an increasingly diverse population, more identified food allergies, concern about the obesity epidemic, more focus on serving children with special health care needs in classrooms, threats to children's safety, and increased awareness of the environment and the use of sustainable practices in early childhood settings. These issues also present fresh opportunities for teachers to appreciate the interrelationships among nutrition, health, and safety and to share their knowledge with children and their families.

This practical text provides students with a comprehensive understanding of the nutrition, health, and safety needs of young children from birth into school age. Furthermore, it prepares teachers to serve diverse populations of young children in family child care, child care centers, preschools, and elementary school settings. Students are brought into many classrooms through in-text examples and assignable, online video-based exercises on MyEducationLab, which bring concepts to life.

Our intention is to equip students with a strong understanding of wellness concepts, preparing them to implement healthful practices and teach young children ways to contribute to their own wellness. These skills emerge as students gain insight into how to enhance children's well-being:

Partner with children and families and nutrition, health, and safety professionals to promote wellness in young children. Students learn that they will work within a network of support to meet children's nutrition, health, and safety needs.

Implement and model appropriate wellness practices. Students will be able to design and use practices that are fitting for children's age and developmental capabilities in tune with children's developmental, health, and language needs and responsive to family cultural practices.

Recognize the important contributions of nutrition, health, and safety to children's learning and overall well-being. Students will be ready to:
- Provide wholesome nutrition that promotes optimal growth, development, and learning.
- Attend to children's individual health needs and implement healthful classroom practices that build wellness habits to last a lifetime.
- Establish environments and implement practices that ensure children's physical and emotional safety, creating the foundation for exploration, creativity, and discovery.

We extend a warm invitation to students to join the team of early childhood professionals who cherish these important early years and who celebrate each child's potential for a healthy, happy, and productive future. In the following pages, we describe how this text helps students to *understand, see,* and *teach* wellness concepts.

helps students to *understand* wellness concepts

choices in the MyPyramid format for a variety of cultural groups. This information, presented in English, helps teachers understand traditional ethnic food choices.

Teaching English Language Learners

Appropriate teaching practices guide how nutrition concepts are presented for all children, with special consideration given to those who are English language learners. Strategies that promote understanding of the nutrition message include the following:

- Have children learn by participating in hands-on activities, such as cooking activities and taste tests.
- Use a range of foods, recipes, and food preparation and cooking methods to reflect a variety of cultural approaches.
- Base the activity on a bilingual children's picture book with a focus on nutrition.
- Use visuals such as real food, food models, or pictures of food whenever presenting a verbal message.
- Speak clearly. Show and explain concepts in more than one way.
- Invite parents and others to visit the class to demonstrate a nutrition concept, to engage children in a cultural food tradition, and to be role models promoting the value of cultural diversity.
- Plan field trips to local businesses such as ethnic supermarkets, restaurants, and bakeries to experience how traditional foods are made.

Teachers who promote healthful eating from a multicultural perspective need to challenge themselves to explore new ideas and ways of planning appropriate and healthful menus for young children. They should also educate themselves about the nutrition traditions of alternate cultures. The resources that guide teachers and families with important nutritional information provide the structure to guide decision making about the selection and presentation of foods. The actual foods selected, however, evolve from the teacher's knowledge of the needs of all children in the group, including their cultural traditions. This highlights the important role that teachers play in

Figure 3-8 A Food Guide from Mexico

Source: From Fomento De Nutrición Y Salud A.C. Used with permission.

Figure 3-9 A Food Guide Pagoda from China

Fats and Oils, 25g

Milk and Milk Products, 100g
Bean and Bean Products, 50g

Meat and Poultry, 50–100g
Fish and Shrimp, 50g
Eggs, 25–50g

Vegetables, 400–500g
Fruits, 100–200g

Cereals 300–500g

China

Source: Based on an illustration from the Chinese Nutrition Society, http://www.cnsoc.org/asp-bin/EN/?page=8&class=42&id=149.

- Through anecdotes, cases, and authentic examples, the authors use a storytelling approach that helps **contextualize** wellness concepts for students. Chapter opening **scenarios** reveal common situations involving teachers, children, and their families grappling with nutrition, health, and safety issues. These scenarios are woven through each chapter to illustrate the teacher's role.

- Promotes **culturally responsive** teaching of nutrition, health, and safety concepts, including content about vegetarian, religious, and cultural diets and working with diverse families.

- Nutrition Chapters 3 to 8 break complex content down through clear writing, diagrams, and frequent classroom examples.

- Chapter 13 is a unique chapter on **children's mental health.**

- Topical features in each chapter—**Nutrition Notes, Safety Segments, Policy Points,** and **Health Hints**—introduce readers to current issues in health, safety, and nutrition to create awareness and develop sound practices.

Safety Segment

Thimerosal and Vaccines

Thimerosal is a mercury compound that was used until recently as a preservative in vaccines. The U.S. Food and Drug Administration (FDA) requires the use of preservatives with vaccines to prevent their contamination with dangerous organisms. Before preservatives were used, serious illnesses and deaths were reported from contaminated vaccines.

Considerable concern has been raised regarding a suspected association between thimerosal and autism. In 2001 and 2004, the Institute of Medicine conducted reviews focusing on the relationship between thimerosal and the neurodevelopmental disorders of autism, attention deficit/hyperactivity disorder, and speech/language delay. The committee concluded that there is no evidence of a relationship suggesting that

Nutrition Note

Building Interest in New Foods

Children are enthusiastic about cooking activities, and it is also fun for them to taste the results of their cooking projects. Cooking with children provides opportunities to teach about foods: where food comes from, how food smells, tastes, and feels, and how to prepare different kinds of food. Cooking also engages children in activities that help to develop motor skills as they use their arms, hands, and fingers. Children have different developmentally appropriate "kitchen skill" levels depending on their age. Understanding children's skill levels helps teacher to direct students to activities that help them feel successful. Kitchen skills for different age categories of children are listed below.

2-Year-Olds

- **Scrubbing** vegetables and fruits
- **Carrying** unbreakable items to the table
- **Dipping** foods
- **Washing** and **tearing** lettuce

- **Shaking** a drink in a closed container
- **Spreading** butters or spreads
- **Kneading** dough
- **Washing** vegetables and fruits
- **Serving** foods

- **Scrubbing** vegetables (potatoes, mushrooms)
- **Cutting** soft foods with a plastic knife (mushrooms, hard-boiled eggs)
- **Pressing** cookie cutters

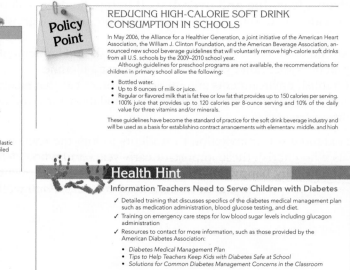

Policy Point

REDUCING HIGH-CALORIE SOFT DRINK CONSUMPTION IN SCHOOLS

In May 2006, the Alliance for a Healthier Generation, a joint initiative of the American Heart Association, the William J. Clinton Foundation, and the American Beverage Association, announced new school beverage guidelines that will voluntarily remove high-calorie soft drinks from all U.S. schools by the 2009–2010 school year.

Although guidelines for preschool programs are not available, the recommendations for children in primary school allow the following:

- Bottled water.
- Up to 8 ounces of milk or juice.
- Regular or flavored milk that is fat free or low fat that provides up to 150 calories per serving.
- 100% juice that provides up to 120 calories per 8-ounce serving and 10% of the daily value for three vitamins and/or minerals.

These guidelines have become the standard of practice for the soft drink beverage industry and will be used as a basis for establishing contract arrangements with elementary, middle, and high

Health Hint

Information Teachers Need to Serve Children with Diabetes

✓ Detailed training that discusses specifics of the diabetes medical management plan such as medication administration, blood glucose testing, and diet.

✓ Training on emergency care steps for low blood sugar levels including glucagon administration

✓ Resources to contact for more information, such as those provided by the American Diabetes Association:

- *Diabetes Medical Management Plan*
- *Tips to Help Teachers Keep Kids with Diabetes Safe at School*
- *Solutions for Common Diabetes Management Concerns in the Classroom*

Sources: Sample Section 504 Plan & Diabetes Medical Management Plan for a Student with Diabetes, June 2007, Alexandria, VA: American Diabetes Association, retrieved October 30, 2009, from http://www.diabetes.org/advocacy-and-legalresources/discrimination/school/504plan.jsp; Tips for Teachers of Students with Diabetes, Alexandria, VA: American Diabetes Association, retrieved October 30, 2009, from http://www.diabetes.org/uedocuments/

helps students to *see* wellness concepts . . . and *apply* them

What if...

a parent asked you to store her child's epinephrine autoinjector (EpiPen) in the classroom for emergency use, but your program's practice is to lock the EpiPen with other medications in the director's office? Is the parent's request legitimate? How would you manage this?

- Reflective **What If. . . . ?** situations place students in the classroom to think about how they would solve possible day-to-day challenges related to nutrition, health, and safety.

What if...

you wanted to support sustainability in early childhood settings? How would you approach this goal? How might teachers' sustainability practices influence young children?

- **MyEducationLab** videos, artifacts, and other resources correspond to text content in assignable exercises throughout the text to help students see how early childhood professionals convey important health, safety, and nutrition concepts to young children.

MyEducationLab

Go to the Assignments and Activities section of Topic 3: Menu Planning in the MyEducationLab for your course and complete the activity entitled *Introducing Children to New Foods*. How does this teacher entice her children to try different fruits and vegetables?

helps students *teach* wellness concepts to children

- Chapter 2, **Teaching Wellness Concepts,** establishes the importance of children's learning through play and an integrated curriculum and also supports students who need to create learning activities in a field experience with a suggested activity plan format.

- Each chapter contains **Teaching Wellness curriculum lesson activities** presented in developmentally appropriate ways for infants and toddlers, preschoolers, and school-age children. Many of these can be viewed online in video-based assignable exercises in MyEducationLab.

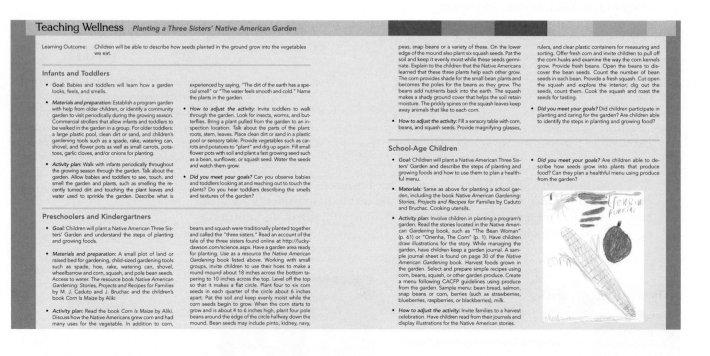

Teaching Wellness *Planting a Three Sisters' Native American Garden*

Learning Outcome: Children will be able to describe how seeds planted in the ground grow into the vegetables we eat.

Infants and Toddlers

- **Goal:** Babies and toddlers will learn how a garden looks, feels, and smells.

- **Materials and preparation:** Establish a program garden with help from older children, or identify a community garden to visit periodically during the growing season. Commercial strollers that allow infants and toddlers to be walked in the garden in a group. For older toddlers: a large plastic pool, clean dirt or sand, and children's gardening tools such as a spade, rake, watering can, shovel, and flower pots as well as small carrots, potatoes, garlic cloves, and/or onions for planting.

- **Activity plan:** Walk with infants periodically throughout the growing season through the garden. Talk about the garden. Allow babies and toddlers to see, touch, and smell the garden and plants, such as smelling the recently turned dirt and touching the plant leaves and water used to sprinkle the garden. Describe what is

experienced by saying, "The dirt of the earth has a special smell" or "The water feels smooth and cold." Name the plants in the garden.

- **How to adjust the activity:** Invite toddlers to walk through the garden. Look for insects, worms, and butterflies. Bring a plant pulled from the garden to an inspection location. Talk about the parts of the plant: roots, stem, leaves. Place clean dirt or sand in a plastic pool or sensory table. Provide vegetables such as carrots and potatoes to "plant" and dig up again. Fill small flower pots with soil and plant a fast growing seed such as a bean, sunflower, or squash seed. Water the seeds and watch them grow.

- **Did you meet your goals?** Can you observe babies and toddlers looking at and reaching out to touch the plants? Do you hear toddlers describing the smells and textures of the garden?

Preschoolers and Kindergartners

- **Goal:** Children will plant a Native American Three Sisters' Garden and understand the steps of planting and growing foods.

- **Materials and preparation:** A small plot of land or raised bed for gardening, child-sized gardening tools such as spade, hoe, rake, watering can, shovel, wheelbarrow and corn, squash, and pole bean seeds. Access to water. The resource book *Native American Gardening: Stories, Projects and Recipes for Families* by M. J. Caduto and J. Bruchac and the children's book *Corn Is Maize* by Aliki

- **Activity plan:** Read the book *Corn Is Maize* by Aliki. Discuss how the Native Americans grew corn and had many uses for the vegetable. In addition to corn,

beans and squash were traditionally planted together and called the "three sisters." Read an account of the tale of the three sisters found online at http://lucky-dawson.com/science.aspx. Have a garden area ready for planting. Use as a resource the *Native American Gardening* book listed above. Working with small groups, invite children to use their hoes to make a round mound about 18 inches across the bottom tapering to 10 inches across the top. Level off the top so that it makes a flat circle. Plant four to six corn seeds in each quarter of the circle about 6 inches apart. Pat the soil and keep evenly moist while the corn seeds begin to grow. When the corn starts to grow and is about 4 to 6 inches high, plant four pole beans around the edge of the circle halfway down the mound. Bean seeds may include pinto, kidney, navy,

peas, snap beans or a variety of these. On the lower edge of the mound also plant six squash seeds. Pat the soil and keep it evenly moist while these seeds germinate. Explain to the children that the Native Americans learned that these three plants help each other grow. The corn provides shade for the small bean plants and becomes the poles for the beans as they grow. The beans add nutrients back into the earth. The squash makes a shady ground cover that helps the soil retain moisture. The prickly spines on the squash leaves keep away animals that like to each corn.

- **How to adjust the activity:** Fill a sensory table with corn, beans, and squash seeds. Provide magnifying glasses,

rulers, and clear plastic containers for measuring and sorting. Offer fresh corn and invite children to pull off the corn husks and examine the way the corn kernels grow. Provide fresh beans. Open the beans to discover the bean seeds. Count the number of bean seeds in each bean. Provide a fresh squash. Cut open the squash and explore the interior; dig out the seeds, count them. Cook the squash and roast the seeds for tasting.

- **Did you meet your goals?** Did children participate in planting and caring for the garden? Are children able to identify the steps in planting and growing food?

School-Age Children

- **Goal:** Children will plant a Native American Three Sisters' Garden and describe the steps of planting and growing foods and how to use them to plan a healthful menu.

- **Materials:** Same as above for planting a school garden, including the book *Native American Gardening: Stories, Projects and Recipes for Families* by Caduto and Bruchac. Cooking utensils.

- **Activity plan:** Involve children in planting a program's garden. Read the stories located in the *Native American Gardening* book, such as "The Bean Woman" (p. 61) or "Onenha, The Corn" (p. 1). Have children draw illustrations for the story. While managing the garden, have children keep a garden journal. A sample journal sheet is found on page 30 of the *Native American Gardening* book. Harvest foods grown in the garden. Select and prepare simple recipes using corn, beans, squash, or other garden produce. Create a menu following CACFP guidelines using produce from the garden. Sample menu: bean bread, salmon, snap beans or corn, berries (such as strawberries, blueberries, raspberries, or blackberries), milk.

- **How to adjust the activity:** Invite families to a harvest celebration. Have children read from their journals and display illustrations for the Native American stories.

- **Did you meet your goals?** Are children able to describe how seeds grow into plants that produce food? Can they plan a healthful menu using produce from the garden?

- The theme of being a good **role model** to children is emphasized throughout.

- **Integrated curriculum** for teaching nutrition, health, and wellness promotes current evidence-based practices.

- Content aligns with **NAEYC** professional preparation and program standards.

instructor supplements

The following instructor tools supplement, support, and reinforce the content presented throughout the text. All supplements are available for download for instructors who adopt this text. Go to www.pearsonhighered.com, click on "Educators," register for access, and download files. For more information, contact your Pearson representative.

Online Instructor's Manual The *Instructor's Manual* provides chapter-by-chapter tools to use in class. Lecture or discussion outlines, teaching strategies, in-class activities, student projects, key term definitions, and helpful resources will reinforce key concepts and applications and keep students engaged.

Online Test Bank These multiple-choice and essay questions tied to each chapter provide students the opportunity to assess their understanding of the chapter content. An answer key is provided.

Online PowerPoint Slides Each slide reinforces key concepts and big ideas presented throughout the text.

Pearson MyTest is a powerful assessment generation program that helps instructors easily create and print quizzes and exams. Questions and tests are authored online, allowing ultimate flexibility and the ability to efficiently create and print assessments anytime, anywhere! Instructors can access Pearson MyTest and their test bank files by going to www.pearsonmytest.com to log in, register, or request access. Features of Pearson MyTest include:

- Premium assessment content
  - Draw from a rich library of assessments that complement your Pearson textbook and your course's learning objectives.
  - Edit questions or tests to fit your specific teaching needs.

- Instructor-friendly resources
  - Easily create and store your own questions, including images, diagrams, and charts using simple drag-and-drop and Word-like controls.
  - Use additional information provided by Pearson, such as the question's difficulty level or learning objective, to help you quickly build your test.

- Time-saving enhancements
  - Add headers or footers and easily scramble questions and answer choices—all from one simple toolbar.
  - Quickly create multiple versions of your test or answer key, and when ready, simple save to MS-Word or PDF format and print!
  - Export your exams for import to Blackboard 6.0, CE (WebCT), or Vista (WebCT)!

Using MyEducationLab with This Book

MyEducationLab

Teacher educators who are developing pedagogies for the analysis of teaching and learning contend that analyzing teaching artifacts has three advantages: it enables new teachers time for reflection while still using the real materials of practice; it provides new teachers with experience thinking about and approaching the complexity of the classroom; and in some cases, it can help new teachers and teacher educators develop a shared understanding and common language about teaching. . . .[1]

As Linda Darling-Hammond and her colleagues point out, grounding teacher education in real classrooms—among real teachers and students and among actual examples of students' and teachers' work—is an important, and perhaps even an essential, part of training teachers for the complexities of teaching in today's classrooms. For this reason, we have created a valuable, time-saving website—MyEducationLab—that provides you with the context of real classrooms and artifacts that research on teacher education tells us is so important. The authentic in-class video footage, interactive skill-building exercises, and other resources available on MyEducationLab offer you a uniquely valuable teacher education tool.

MyEducationLab is easy to use and integrate into both your assignments and your courses. Wherever you see the MyEducationLab logo in the margins or elsewhere in the text, follow the simple instructions to access the videos, strategies, cases, and artifacts associated with these assignments, activities, and learning units on MyEducationLab. MyEducationLab is organized topically to enhance the coverage of the core concepts discussed in the chapters of your book. For each topic on the course you will find most or all of the following resources:

Connection to National Standards Now it is easier than ever to see how your course work is connected to national standards. In each topic of MyEducationLab you will find intended learning outcomes connected to the appropriate national standards for your course. All of the *Assignments and Activities* and all of the *Building Teaching Skills and Dispositions* in MyEducationLab are mapped to the appropriate national standards and learning outcomes as well.

Assignments and Activities Designed to save instructors preparation time, these assignable exercises show concepts in action (through videos, cases, or student and teacher artifacts) and then offer thought-provoking questions that probe your understanding of theses concepts or strategies. (Feedback for these assignments is available to the instructor.)

Building Teaching Skills and Dispositions These learning units help you practice and strengthen skills that are essential to quality teaching. First you are presented with the core skill or concept and then given an opportunity to practice your understanding of this concept multiple times by watching video footage (or interacting with other media) and then critically analyzing the strategy or skill presented.

---

[1] Darling-Hammond, L., & Bransford, J. (Eds.). (2005). *Preparing teachers for a changing world*. San Francisco: John Wiley & Sons.

IRIS Center Resources The IRIS Center at Vanderbilt University (http://iris .peabody.vanderbilt.edu)—funded by the U.S. Department of Education's Office of Special Education Programs (OSEP)—develops training enhancement materials for preservice and in-service teachers. The center works with experts from across the country to create challenge-based interactive modules, case study units, and podcasts that provide research-validated information about working with students in inclusive settings. On your MyEducationLab course we have integrated this content where appropriate to enhance the content coverage in your book.

General Resources on Your MyEducationLab Course The *Resources* section on your MyEducationLab course is designed to help you pass your licensure exam, put together an effective portfolio and lesson plan, prepare for and navigate the first year of your teaching career, and understand key educational standards, policies, and laws. This section includes:

- *Licensure Exams:* Access guidelines for passing the Praxis exam. The *Practice Test Exam* includes practice questions, *Case Histories*, and *Video Case Studies*.
- *Portfolio Builder and Lesson Plan Builder:* Create, update, and share portfolios and lesson plans.
- *Preparing a Portfolio:* Access guidelines for creating a high-quality teaching portfolio that will allow you to practice effective lesson planning.
- *Licensure and Standards:* Link to state licensure standards, national health and education standards, and early childhood education standards.
- *Beginning Your Career:* Educate yourself—access tips, advice, and valuable information on:
  - *Resume Writing and Interviewing:* Expert advice on how to write impressive resumes and prepare for job interviews.
  - *Your First Year of Teaching:* Practical tips to set up your classroom, manage student behavior, and learn to more easily organize for instruction and assessment.
  - *Law and Public Policies:* Specific directives and requirements you need to understand under the No Child Left Behind Act and the Individuals with Disabilities Education Improvement Act of 2004.

Study Plan A MyEducationLab Study Plan is a multiple-choice assessment tied to chapter objectives, supported by study material. A well-designed Study Plan offers multiple opportunities to fully master required course content as identified by the objectives in each chapter:

- *Chapter Objectives* identify the learning outcomes for the chapter and give you targets to shoot for as you read and study.
- *Multiple-Choice Assessment*s assess mastery of the content (tied to each chapter objective) by allowing you to take the multiple-choice quiz as many times as needed. Not only do these quizzes provide overall scores for each objective, they also explain why responses to particular items are correct or incorrect.
- *Study Material: Review, Practice, and Enrichment* gives you a deeper understanding of what you do and do not know related to chapter content. This can be accessed through the *Multiple-Choice Assessment* (after you take a quiz, you receive information regarding the chapter content on which you still need practice and review) or through a self-directed method of study. This material includes text excerpts, activities that include hints and feedback, and media assets (video, simulations, cases, etc.).
- *Flash Cards* help you study the definitions of the key terms within each chapter.

Visit www.myeducationlab.com for a demonstration of this exciting new online teaching resource.

Acknowledgments

We would like to thank the many reviewers whose valuable feedback and insights have helped shape and enhance our manuscript:

Sara Jane L. Adler, Washtenaw Community College

Mary Elizabeth Ambery, Southeast Missouri State University

Tracey Bennett, Vance-Granville Community College

Isela Castanon-Williams, El Paso Community College

Jamie Christensen, Iowa Lakes Community College

Jane B. Dennis, Tarleton State University

Rosanne Dlugosz, Scottsdale Community College

Sherry L. Forrest, Craven Community College

Jane A. Hildenbrand, Ivy Tech Community College

James P. Hinkle, Fayetteville Technical Community College

Jennifer M. Johnson, Vance-Granville Community College

Susan Johnson, Northern Virginia Community College, Louden

Janice Englander Katz, Child Care Consortium, Inc.

Marian Marion, Governors State University

Teresa S. McKay, Ivy Tech Community College

Sherry Nolte, Honolulu Community College

Mary A. Nunaley, Volunteer State Community College

Sandra Poirier, Middle Tennessee State University

Maureen Powers-Maiocco, The State University of New York at Canton

Nicole Reiber, Coastal Carolina Community College

Bernadette Rodriguez, Brookhaven College

Ruth Saur, Lorain County Community College

Rebecca Wardlow, Ashford University

Andrea J. Zarate, Hartnell College

We also extend special appreciation to the students, children, and families of the Child Development Laboratory in the Hallie Ford Center for Healthy Children and Families at Oregon State University and to the teachers and staff for their expert advice: Shahrnaz Badiee, Anna Chase, Amelia Cobarrubias, Dana Crawford, Cris Dogaru, Sandi Hunt, Barb Whitney, Julia Limbrick, Kathleen McDonnell, Wendy McKenna, Rosie Schimerlik, and Jacquie Volkers, and Jaime Williams.

We would also like to thank the following individuals for their contribution to MyEducationLab: Julie Bullard, Greg Castor, Jeanne Czernowski, Ariel Daeschel, Jennifer England, Connie Gassner, John Harris, Ryan Kral, Debra Pierce, Nikki Reiber, Sharon Reid, Gigi Sims, and Dawn Warneking.

We extend special appreciation to the staff of the Community Health Centers of Benton and Linn Counties for enthusiastically serving underprivileged children in our community and for always offering their time and energy to advocate for children and their families.

Finally, we thank our editors, Julie Peters and Max Effenson Chuck, whose encouragement, expertise, and support made this book possible.

brief contents

contents

part 3 Promoting Healthful Practices 285

special features

POLICY POINTS

part 1 | Promoting Wellness

chapter 1 | The Interconnection of Nutrition, Health, and Safety

Learning Outcomes

After reading this chapter, you should be able to:

1. Define wellness and describe how nutrition, health, and safety contribute to children's health and well-being.

2. Identify and discuss some of the contexts in which children grow and develop and provide examples of their impact on children's ability to learn.

3. Identify some of the trends in nutrition that affect children's development and learning.

4. Discuss current issues in children's health and describe how they impact children in the early childhood setting.

5. Describe current safety standards and topics that are important to the early childhood classroom.

6. Summarize the important role teachers play in building a foundation for children's wellness.

It is lunchtime at Kaylee's family child care program. She completed her associate's degree in early childhood 2 years ago, and since then has offered a family child care program in her home as a way to work in her field while enjoying her two young children. The children have washed their hands and gathered in the kitchen. They know the routine of finding their places while Kaylee changes Dominique's diaper, washes his hands, and seats him in his high chair. Kaylee washes her hands too, and then offers the foods family style for the older children. She serves Dominique his "burrito" in small tortilla pieces, and spoonfuls of refried beans and grated cheese, and she provides Nancy a burrito without cheese to address her milk allergy. Then Kaylee sits down to eat with the children. "Beans!" says Dominique. Kaylee gives Dominique a big smile while the children cheer for Dominique's new word.

Across town, Hector is carrying out the recycling and trash from the preschool class. He is tired from the busy day and looking forward to going home soon. As he walks to the side of the building, Hector thinks about Zach, a child who attends the early childhood class in a wheelchair. Zach has a muscle-wasting disease that will continue to worsen. But it is Zach's cheerful spirit that sticks in Hector's mind. Hector recalls that today Zach asked about whales, wondering if whales can live under the ice at the North Pole. Hector doesn't know the answer to this question, but decides to stop off at the library on his way home to find a book about whales that he can share with Zach tomorrow.

In another community, Sharina and Amelia walk together through the children's play yard. The principal for the reservation's elementary school has asked them to participate in a review of the outdoor areas as part of a tribal health initiative to increase children's participation in active play. The teachers could easily be distracted by the views across the grasslands outside the fenced area. Instead they are discussing the safety checklist on their clipboards. They make notes about the need to address the hard-packed ground under the play structures, and they recall that Amy and Tadi asked them to plan a garden area, while Dustin and Winona want enough space to play double-ball.

This is an exciting time to be an early childhood professional! Not only does research on growth and development continue to emphasize the importance of the early years in setting the stage for a child's future capacity to learn, but the important role teachers play in guiding children's development is being given renewed attention and recognition. Early childhood professionals work in many different settings, but like the teachers in the opening scenario, early childhood teachers have much in common. In the examples, each teacher demonstrates special enjoyment of very young children and knowledge of child development. Each participates willingly in the full spectrum of responsibilities associated with caring for children's nutrition, health, and safety, from daily tasks to individualized planning. Each teacher also actively embraces the intriguing challenge of providing purposeful experiences to advance each child's learning. Central to these efforts are each child's nutrition, health, and safety. This chapter describes the links between nutrition, health and safety; offers information about important influences on children's well-being; explores current issues in nutrition, health, and safety; and discusses the important ways that teachers contribute to the development and future potential of young children.

FOUNDATIONS FOR WELLNESS IN YOUNG CHILDREN

Families, early childhood educators, and community members alike envision communities where wellness is a goal for all people. Wellness is a positive state of health and well-being. It is achieved through healthful practices, such as consuming a nutritious diet, exercising, and sleeping well. It also includes access to resources, such as sufficient foods, safe environments, immunizations, and health care. Words such as *healthy*, *happy*, and *thriving* are used to describe the state of wellness. The early childhood years are an important period for building the foundations for wellness. Learning healthful practices during the early years is crucial to children's ability to attain optimal development and establish the capacity to learn.

Understanding the Interrelationship Among Nutrition, Health, and Safety

Children's growth, development, and wellness are established through the building blocks of nutrition, health, and safety. Each makes a specific contribution to optimal development and the child's ability to grow and thrive:

- *Nutrition* encompasses the relationship between the nutrients that are eaten, digested, and absorbed and how they impact growth, development, and health. A child's diet, or the foods and beverages consumed to nourish and support the body and its processes, must meet the child's nutritional demands during the active early years in order for the child to grow appropriately. Serving safe and healthful foods is one way that nutrition is practiced in the early childhood setting.
- *Health* focuses on physical and mental well-being and the absence of disease. It is achieved through a variety of healthful practices that seek to prevent and minimize illness or disease. In the early childhood setting, washing hands and encouraging families to obtain childhood immunizations are common health practices.
- *Safety* refers to keeping children from harm. Safety is increased through practices that reduce the likelihood of unintentional injury or exposure to environmental toxins. Safety is practiced in many ways in the early childhood setting, including establishing safe environments, practicing safety rules, and supervising children for safety.

Nutrition, health, and safety are closely aligned and interrelated. The healthful benefits of one factor affect the positive outcomes in the others. Gaps or challenges in one area negatively affect the others. For example:

A healthy, thriving child is ready to learn.

- In order for foods to be healthful, they must be stored, prepared, and served in a safe and sanitary manner.
- When children consume safe and healthful foods, their bodies are provided with the nutrients needed for optimal development, including learning. A healthful diet also improves the child's ability to fend off illness and to recover from illness and injury when they occur. A healthful diet enhances children's growth and well-being.
- Healthy children grow strong and capable of playing in coordinated and safe ways. Children who are healthy and well nourished are ready to be more attentive in the learning setting and are better able to learn about safety rules and ways to keep healthy through appropriate health practices and by eating healthful foods.

Some interrelationships are complex. Current research reveals a strong interrelationship between factors such as nutrition and risk for disease in adulthood (Barker, 2004; Gluckman, Hanson, & Pinal, 2005). From the moment of conception through early infancy and childhood, children's diet is thought to trigger a predisposition, or tendency, to good or poor health by influencing how specific genes are expressed (Kaput, 2004, 2008). Pregnancy and prenatal development, early childhood, puberty, and old age are times when diet can influence gene function, creating a positive or negative impact on health (Dolinoy, Das, Weidman, & Jirtle, 2007). For example, a mother's diet and rate of weight gain during pregnancy, the birth weight of the infant, and the infant's diet may predict risk for chronic disease by establishing genetic imprinting that increases the likelihood the child will develop obesity, diabetes, heart disease, or cancer (Cutfield, Hofman, Mitchell, & Morison, 2007; Dolinoy et al., 2007; Oken, Taveras, Kleinman, Rich-Edwards, & Gillman, 2007).

Early childhood teachers generally recognize important aspects of the relationship among nutrition, health, and safety, and implement classroom practices to foster positive development. They know that healthy practices need to be learned during early development. Teachers also:

- Share an important responsibility with families to provide the best nutrition possible for infants and children, helping to meet the child's immediate nutritional needs while at the same time protecting the child from future chronic disease.
- Help to promote positive health practices, and may be instrumental in identifying gaps in a child's health services by providing information and referrals to families.
- Work to ensure children's safe experiences in the early childhood setting.

In sum, teachers are significant participants in developing the context of nutrition, health, and safety that surrounds the children they serve. Each of the teachers in the opening case scenario advances the goals of nutrition health and safety in the context of their early childhood programs. Kaylee adapts a nutritious lunch to fit the needs of children according to their age and addresses children's special dietary needs. Hector looks beyond Zach's health concerns, responding to Zach's curiosity by bringing new books into the classroom for exploration and learning. Sharina and Amelia review the playground for safety concerns and the importance of establishing large spaces for highly active play. They also think about studying food and nutrition by creating a gardening space. These teachers are putting wellness approaches into action.

Focusing on Young Children

The early childhood years, birth through age 8, are important years for growing and learning and represent a crucial time for establishing children's wellness. Early childhood is a unique period of development during which growth is rapid and complex. Many physical and emotional changes occur during this time. For example, young children gain strength, coordination, and control over movement. Complex skills such as walking and speech emerge as children become motivated to explore and act on the world around them. The intricacies of social and emotional development play out as children develop trust and attachment to caregivers. Language blossoms and cognitive problem-solving skills are tested and refined. Crucial to this wealth of growth and maturation is healthy brain development.

early childhood
the period from birth through age 8

neurons
the nerve cells of the brain

Early Brain Development

At birth the brain is a relatively immature organ. It continues to grow and develop across the life span, but most significantly during the early childhood years. Brain development is primarily involved with creating connections for communication between the brain's nerve cells, or neurons. Both the number and organization of these connections are important in establishing links between the various parts of the brain. These links influence all aspects of children's functioning and ability to learn, such as recognizing the sounds that form language, coordinating movement to achieve the ability to walk, recognizing shapes and letters, and developing the ability to manipulate math functions, control behavior, and manage social interactions (Hawley, 2000; Massachusetts Institute of Technology, 2006). Children's ability to learn and ultimately to function in society depends on the success of brain development during the early years.

Brain development is guided by a rich interplay between children's genetic makeup and the kinds and quality of children's experiences. Genetics guide the child's physical appearance, pace of development, temperament, and style and set the stage for future learning and development. It is children's experiences, however, that influence, shape,

MyEducationLab

Go to the Assignments and Activities section of Topic 1: Basic Nutrition in the MyEducationLab for your course and complete the activity entitled *Brain Development and Nutrition* to understand how nutrition affects the brain and learning.

and mold the contributions of their genetic makeup. Interesting and rich experiences create and reinforce positive and useful connections among brain regions. The normal process of brain development creates many more potential connections than are typically used. Lack of experience or negative experiences result in closing off or "pruning away" brain connections (Hawley, 2000). This is a "use it or lose it" process that relies on sufficient experience and stimulation to encourage appropriate brain connections.

Teachers who encourage children to touch and explore their world help children use and build skills that lead to understanding and language development. For example, touching water helps children learn and understand the word *wet*. Interactive experiences encourage brain connections to evolve and expand. Children who are restricted from touching and exploring, such as infants who are kept in their playpens with few toys or interaction, lose out on opportunities to gain knowledge about the world and begin to believe that such explorations are fruitless. If this restraint is prolonged, children stop being interested in exploring, brain connections that support curiosity wither, and new brain connections do not emerge. Teachers provide the safe nurturing care and positive experiences children need to promote healthy brain development, ensuring not only children's survival, but reducing the potential for illness while supporting positive, healthful development. In sum, the experiences children have, or don't have, during this formative period establish their capacity to learn and set the course for future development.

There is also increasing evidence that contextual factors can "turn on and turn off" genes, affecting how the genes are expressed. It appears that genes are "turned on and off" by external factors such as diet, abuse, and stress. This line of study is called **epigenetics** (Kauwell, 2008; Poulter et al., 2008; Rodenhiser & Mann, 2006). In addition, unique periods of development, or **critical periods**, may exist during which genetic expression is more likely to be influenced by dietary and other factors. Investigations into these and other theories about influences on growth will continue to inform understanding of how children's brains develop.

epigenetics
the study of how genes are "turned on and off" by external factors such as diet, abuse, and stress

critical periods
unique periods of development

early childhood teachers
all those who provide care and education for young children

context
the environment and circumstances that surround the child and affect the child's experiences

Early experiences enhance brain development and establish children's capacity to learn.

The Impact of Teachers

Teachers of young children (birth through age 8) are second only to families in influencing children's positive experiences and healthful brain development. Teachers spend many important hours with young children providing care and education in a variety of settings: family child care, center child care, kindergarten, after-school care, evening child care, and more. Care and education are intricately intertwined during the early years. Care, by nature, encompasses education, and education is an important part of the caring relationship. For this reason, we refer to all those who provide care and education to young children as **early childhood teachers**.

Early childhood teachers are involved in important work at a time that is crucial for the developing child. They establish safe, nurturing environments that inspire children's curiosity and exploration. They offer inviting and interesting toys and activities that promote problem solving and invention. They introduce vocabulary and ask questions to expand vocabulary and concept development. Early childhood teachers also teach children to interact positively with one another, promoting healthful relationships. The impact teachers have on children's lives is truly momentous.

Viewing Children Within the Context of Home, School, and Community

Children do not grow and develop in isolation. Instead, children's wellness is heavily influenced by the **context** in which the child develops, including the environment and circumstances that surround the child and affect the child's experiences. Teachers come to understand that family conditions—poverty, the health and education of the child's family, cultural beliefs, and many other factors—interact and contribute to the child's development in positive and negative ways. Urie Bronfenbrenner's (1979) ecological systems theory describes and explains these processes and spheres of influence as a way to reinforce the importance of viewing the child's health and well-being within the context of the environment. This theory depicts the child as developing within a nested series of surrounding systems that connect and interact with one another. As shown in Figure 1-1, the ecological systems theory identifies four types of environmental systems that surround the child.

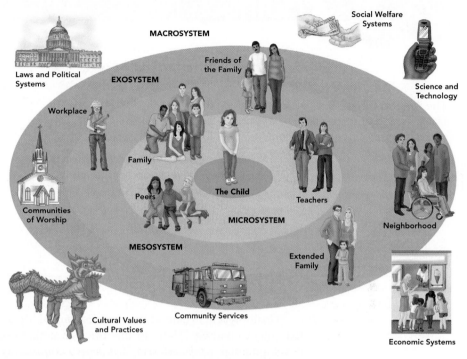

Figure 1-1 Bronfenbrenner's Ecological Systems Theory Describes Child Development in Context

- *Microsystem:* Includes the environments that immediately surround the child, such as the home, the early childhood setting, and school. Safe and nurturing surroundings positively affect children's health and well-being, whereas domestic violence or a poor-quality early childhood setting may interrupt healthy development.
- *Mesosystem:* Refers to the connections and interactions that take place in the microsystem. Family participation and positive relationships with the teacher are examples of positive influences on children's development, whereas disagreements among divorced parents can negatively affect children's well-being.
- *Exosystem:* Involves people and places that provide indirect influences on the child's development, such as the extended family or neighborhood. Children's wellness is supported by safe and healthy neighborhoods, and is negatively affected by unsafe neighborhood environments.
- *Macrosystem:* Includes the influences of the larger social, cultural, political, and economic contexts. For example, children's wellness is supported when society values children's health and access to high-quality early childhood education. Conversely, children's well-being may be threatened in times of economic depression due to reduction in resources such as accessible health care (Bronfenbrenner, 1979).

Early childhood teachers have responsibilities that intersect with all levels of these contextual systems. For example, teachers have direct responsibility for creating and managing the early childhood setting (microsystem). They work to meet the nutrition, health, and safety needs of each child and to ensure that the child's experience is rich with interest and challenge, while protecting the child from dangers. In this way the quality of the early childhood setting directly affects the child's positive outcomes. Teachers also establish important connections between the early childhood setting and the child's home (mesosystem) by building relationships where families and teachers share knowledge and ideas about how to best promote the child's development. Through these relationships, teachers gain information that allows them to develop individualized plans for the care and education of the child. Teachers are able build on child and family strengths that are revealed through this relationship, and often can minimize recognized gaps in children's experience and care. The *Nutrition Note* describes one way in which teachers and families work together to provide a positive model for children in terms of diet.

Nutrition Note

Adults Are Important Models for Healthful Eating

The American Dietetics Association tracks eating practices as a measure of diet trends. A recent survey revealed that adults have increased consumption of these healthy foods in the past 5 years:

- Whole grains.
- Vegetables.
- Fruits.
- Low-fat foods.
- Omega-3 fatty acids.

Overall more adults report that they "have a good attitude toward diet and exercise" and that they "are doing their best to eat healthfully." This is a promising trend for the health and well-being of both adults and children. Families and teachers who model eating nutritious foods and healthful eating practices encourage children's acceptance of wholesome foods and teach positive eating habits. This contributes to children's wellness.

Source: Based on *Nutrition and You: Trends 2008: Report of Results,* presented at the American Dietetic Association Food and Nutrition Conference and Exposition, October 26, 2008.

Finally, teachers extend their professional skills and responsibilities to the larger systems that affect children. They do this through actions such as screening children for special developmental needs, referring families to community services, advocating for the needs of children at school board meetings or community planning commissions, and championing the development of policies that affect children's education, health, and well-being. These contextual systems involve reciprocal relationships, meaning that as well as providing advice and advocacy, teachers are called on to participate in forwarding the goals of local, state, and national initiatives designed to improve outcomes for young children.

National Initiatives Supporting Wellness

Early childhood teachers, families, health professionals, and policy makers are joining together to promote the activities and policies needed to support the foundations of wellness. These efforts are based on public health approaches that seek to identify health issues specific to the community and bring citizens together around disease prevention and intervention. These approaches aim to positively affect both individual and community-wide health practices. They encourage individuals to learn and practice positive health behaviors. In addition, they assign responsibility to all levels of the community for implementing healthful group practices and establishing policies that forward individual and community wellness. Several national initiatives promote these interests. Each places a focus on engaging both individuals and the community in the effort.

Healthy People 2010

Healthy People 2010 is a national initiative established in 1979 to improve the health and well-being of people across the country. Organized around health objectives gleaned from evidence-based practice, the initiative's goals are to help people of all ages to:

- Improve their quality of life and increase the number of years of healthy life.
- Eliminate health disparities (U.S. Department of Health and Human Services [HHS], 2000).

To reach these goals, *Healthy People 2010* organizes 467 objectives within 28 health indicator focus areas. Topics that relate to the care and education of young children include those listed in Figure 1-2.

Healthy People 2010 uses a comprehensive approach that invites the community, from individuals to organizations, to integrate the goals into their daily practices. In this way the

Figure 1-2 *Healthy People 2010* **Topics That Aim to Improve Children's Nutrition, Health, and Safety**

- Access to quality health services
- Maternal, infant, and child health (prenatal exposure to substances, prenatal health care, risk factors, developmental disability)
- Immunizations and infectious disease
- Injury and violence prevention
- Mental health and mental disorders
- Nutrition and overweight (nutrition in schools, food security)
- Oral health
- Physical activity and fitness
- Tobacco use (exposure to second hand smoke)

Source: *Healthy People 2010*, 2nd edition (2 vols.), by the U.S. Department of Health and Human Services, 2000, retrieved August 31, 2009, from http://www.healthypeople.gov/Publications.

project generates multiple approaches to improving the health of young children and their families. *Healthy People 2010* is currently gathering input for establishing the objectives for *Healthy People 2020* (HHS, 2008).

National Call to Action

The National Call to Action is a program of the U.S. Department of Health and Human Services that seeks to advance the health and well-being of Americans by promoting oral health and eliminating disease (HHS, 2003). The initiative developed as a result of a collaboration of public and private partners, who identified oral health as critical to general health and well-being. Oral health refers to all aspects of dental, gum, and mouth health. The U.S. Surgeon General describes unmet oral health needs as a "silent epidemic" affecting vulnerable people, including poor children and those of racial and ethnic minority groups (HHS, 2003). Partners at all levels of society are challenged to improve health and well-being by:

oral health
dental, gum, and mouth health

- Promoting oral health.
- Improving quality of life.
- Eliminating oral health disparities (HHS, 2003).

Action steps focus on encouraging partners to work for improved understanding of the importance of oral health and on overcoming barriers that limit access to oral health care.

Healthy Child Care America

Healthy Child Care America is an initiative coordinated by the American Academy of Pediatrics that seeks to improve the health, safety, development, and well-being of young children through quality child care and early education. The effort calls on families and early childhood and health professionals to work together to support children so they enter school healthy and ready to learn. The initiative's goals aim to:

Oral health is a critical component of health and well-being.

- Maximize resources.
- Develop comprehensive services.
- Nurture children.

Healthy Child Care America serves as a resource for child care providers and families by offering health and safety materials. It works with programs funded through the HHS's Maternal and Child Health Bureau to provide technical assistance and improve children's access to health services (American Academy of Pediatrics, 2007). Central to the Healthy Child Care America initiative is the view that community partners can work as a team to develop comprehensive services that aid children.

National Health and Safety Performance Standards for Child Care

The National Resource Center for Health and Safety in Child Care and Early Education is a program of the HHS's Maternal and Child Health Bureau. The center is charged with promoting health and safety in out-of-home child care settings nationwide. To achieve this goal, the center provides a resource for families and child care providers called *Caring for Our Children: National Health and Safety Performance Standards: Guidelines for Out-of-Home Child Care Programs*. A sample of the resources that promote health and safety in out-of-home care is listed in Figure 1-3. The performance standards guidelines were established in collaboration with the American Academy of Pediatrics and the American Public Health Association. They serve as standards for the direct provision of services to young children, guidelines for state licensing of early childhood programs, and as a resource for policy development.

National Children's Study

The National Children's Study is an investigation into the effects of environmental influences on the health and development of young children. Several federal agencies are collaborating in the project, including the HHS and the U.S. Environmental Protection Agency. The project will follow 100,000 children from across the country from birth to age 21.

The National Children's Study is designed to reveal the effects of natural and human-made environmental, biological, genetic, and psychosocial factors on different phases of children's growth and development to increase understanding of these factors on health and disease. Outcomes from the study will influence the development of health practices and policies that will guide individuals, program practices, and policy development to improve the health and well-being of young children.

No Child Left Behind Act of 2001

Congress established the No Child Left Behind Act (NCLB) in 2001 (Public Law 107-110) directing the U.S. Department of Education to promote the primary goal of improving education across the nation by closing the achievement gap among low-performing and high-performing children and schools. The initiative calls on families, teachers, and community members to take steps to improve children's early literacy skills and to make sure that all children are successful in school. The strategies identified to meet the goals of NCLB include the following:

- Improve accountability for children's educational progress.
- Provide choices for families in selecting schools.
- Enhance local control and flexibility for targeting use of federal funds.
- Put emphasis on use of evidence-based practices, approaches that have been shown to be effective through research (U.S. Department of Education 2001).

Figure 1-3 Health and Safety Resources Provided by the National Resource Center for Health and Safety in Child Care and Early Education

- Guides for families, including selecting child care and indicators of quality early childhood programs
- Guidance publications, such as *Caring for Our Children: National Health and Safety Performance Standards: Guidelines for Out-of-Home Child Care Programs*, that provide standards for typical and special care situations, such as caring for children with special developmental needs, transporting children in child care, and administering medications
- Web-based resources such as *Healthy Kids Healthy Care*
- Links to child care information
- Responses to frequently asked questions
- State licensing information

Sources: *Caring for Our Children National Health and Safety Performance Standards: Guidelines for Out-of-Home Child Care Programs,* 2nd edition, by the American Academy of Pediatrics, the American Public Health Association, and the National Resource Center for Health and Safety in Child Care and Early Education, 2002, retrieved August 31, 2009, from http://www.eric.ed.gov/ERICDocs/data/ericdocs2sql/content_storage_01/0000019b/80/14/0d/14.pdf.

NCLB calls attention to the fact that the early years are important learning years, and recognizes that early childhood education is a key to children's success. The initiative reinforces the need for children's success to be central to parent, teacher, and community education efforts.

Partnership for 21st-Century Skills

The Partnership for 21st-Century Skills was formed in 2002 through the efforts of the U.S. Department of Education, business organizations, and interested individuals. Its mission is to address the gap between the knowledge and skills students learn through the current K–12 educational system and those that are needed to be successful in 21st-century communities and in the workplace. The partnership proposes that a new focus is needed to ensure that students graduating from high school in the United States are capable of succeeding in rigorous higher education coursework and prepared to compete in the global workforce. To address this, the partnership has identified six core elements of a 21st-century education (The Partnership for 21st-Century Skills, 2004):

1. *Core subjects:* including English, reading, or language arts; mathematics; science; foreign languages; civics; government; economics; arts; history; and geography (as identified by the No Child Left Behind Act of 2001).
2. *21st-century content:* such as global awareness; financial, economic, business and entrepreneurial literacy; civic literacy; and health and wellness awareness.
3. *Learning and thinking skills:* skills that build the student's capacity to know how to keep learning throughout life, including critical thinking, problem solving, communication, creativity and innovation, collaboration, and contextual learning.
4. *Information and communications technology* (ICT): refers to the ability to use information and media technology and to contribute to future ICT developments for the 21st-century.
5. *Life skills:* including leadership, ethics, accountability, adaptability, personal productivity and responsibility, people skills, self-direction, and social responsibility.
6. *21st-century assessments:* including better approaches to evaluating what students are learning and what teaching approaches are working.

Although early childhood education is not a formal partner in this movement, many of the skills identified for a 21st-century education align well with the early childhood developmental approach that builds children's capacities to become self-directed learners, establish effective relationships, and participate in their own health and wellness. The National Association for the Education of Young Children (NAEYC) reinforces the benefits of play as the mechanism for achieving these competencies. Through "playful learning" children enjoy focusing on intentionally planned learning topics (NAEYC, 2009b). These intentional experiences build children's learning capacities in child-appropriate ways.

These initiatives have put a spotlight on the early years of development as crucial to children's healthful development and ability to learn across a lifetime. They reinforce the importance of teaching young children. The teachers in the opening case scenario may not be aware that they are part of a committed team of professionals who are dedicated to making a positive difference for young children.

What if . . .

one of your relatives asked you why you wanted to be a teacher of young children? Would you be able to describe the importance of early childhood teachers to children's health and well-being?

COMPLEX INFLUENCES ON EARLY CHILDHOOD EDUCATION

Changing demographics across the nation are altering the makeup of early childhood classrooms. In addition, various factors affect the development of young children and uniquely influence children's experiences in the early childhood setting. These complex influences are important for teachers to consider. Some factors add interest and richness to children's

Figure 1-4 Racial and Ethnic Composition Among Children Under Age 18 in the United States (2008)

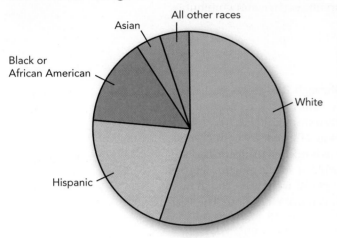

Source: *America's Children in Brief: Key National Indicators of Well-Being, 2009*, by the Federal Interagency Forum on Child and Family Statistics, 2009, retrieved August 31, 2009, from http:// www.childstats.gov/ americaschildren08/index.asp.

experiences, such as the increase in cultural diversity among children in early childhood settings. Others may put children at risk for poor health and development and may compromise their ability to learn, such as the negative impacts of poverty. Recognizing these changes and other influences helps teachers to focus attention on identifying aspects that support children's development and those that may negatively influence their well-being. Teachers who mediate or reduce the negative effects by tending to these children's needs help children attain success that they may not otherwise achieve.

Multicultural Early Childhood Classrooms

Early childhood class groups are becoming more multicultural. Each decade has seen a significant increase in diversity among children under the age of 18 (Federal Interagency Forum on Child and Family Statistics, 2008), with the numbers of children of Hispanic heritage growing in nearly all parts of the country. It is estimated that 22% of children have at least one foreign-born parent. The racial composition of children under age 18 is shown in Figure 1-4.

Nationwide, nearly 20% of children speak a home language other than English. These numbers vary depending on the region, with rates as high as 64% of children in the West, and as low as 11% in the Midwest (Federal Interagency Forum on Child and Family Statistics, 2008). This means a growing number of children in early care and education settings speak a language other than English in their homes and are learning English in the early childhood classroom. These children are recognized as English language learners (ELLs) and may need special focus to support them as they explore early childhood concepts and learn English. Such trends draw attention to influences of racial and ethnic heritage on children's development and well-being. They are also reminders of the importance of early childhood teachers who are sensitive to and competent in embracing cultural diversity and aware of strategies that support teaching children from diverse backgrounds.

Cultural and ethnic practices vary, and their influence on children's development, health, and nutrition affects how children experience and learn in the early childhood classroom. The term ethnic refers to groups with common national, tribal, religious, linguistic, racial, or cultural origins or backgrounds. Cultural and ethnic practices that interface with the classroom may affect diet, food choices, dress, hygiene, comfort with health practices, levels of physical activity, expectations for boys and girls, and other aspects such as how sleeping arrangements are managed at home and how napping is arranged in the classroom. Teachers need to be aware that perspectives on children's nutrition, health, and safety vary among families, and that inviting conversation about practices that may be different between home and the classroom is important.

Teachers themselves have beliefs and expectations that are rooted in their own cultural or ethnic perspectives. Finding ways to negotiate differing perspectives of families and also those of teachers who work together provides an important challenge and an opportunity for new discoveries that will improve the learning opportunities for children.

Diverse Family Structures

The influence of the family on children's well-being is of primary importance, as families are the most important teachers of their children. To understand this influence it is also important to recognize that the traditional family structure is changing. Family arrangements include various combinations of adults caring for children: children raised by teenage mothers or single fathers, grandparents who are the child's legal guardians, children with same-sex parents or who divide their time between the homes of their divorced

English language learners
those who speak a language other than English in their homes and who are learning English

ethnic
groups with common national, tribal, religious, linguistic, racial, or cultural origins or backgrounds

MyEducationLab

Go to the Assignments and Activities section of Topic 2: Feeding Children in the MyEducationLab for your course and complete the activity entitled *Cultural Knowledge.* How do teachers infuse the early childhood curriculum with explorations of family culture?

parents, and children who live temporarily in foster care placements. Trends show increasing rates of children born to unmarried mothers—as high as 38% in 2007, and decreasing numbers of young children with two married parents—68% in 2007 (Federal Interagency Forum on Child and Family Statistics, 2008). The diversity of family arrangements reminds teachers to get to know each child and family as a unique group, with their own special "history" and strengths, and with differing challenges that affect the family's ability to address children's well-being.

Other aspects of the family arrangement influence children's development and well-being. For example, the numbers of families with two working parents is increasing as more mothers join the workforce. More than 50% of mothers with infants and as many as 63% of mothers with children under the age of 6 are working (U.S. Department of Labor, 2008). This trend highlights the busy nature of family life as parents balance work and care for their children. Also, the numbers of children with a parent in either state or federal prison continues to increase. In 2007, nearly 1.7 million children had a parent who was incarcerated, and the numbers of incarcerated mothers more than doubled between 1999 and 2007 (Sentencing Project, 2009). This situation disrupts the child's home life, and results in a long period of separation from a parent, which can have negative effects on a child's development. These trends highlight the need for teachers to be aware of the child's family life and to recognize the challenges families may face in providing for the child's well-being.

Poverty

Poverty creates many conditions that challenge children's development. It threatens the health and well-being of 5.2 million children under the age of 6 in the United States today (Douglas-Hall & Chau, 2008). This number reflects the children who are being raised in families with income below the federal poverty level as established by the HHS. An additional 10.6 million young children are growing up in families whose income is not sufficient to provide for the basic needs of the family (Douglas-Hall & Chau, 2008). The term low income refers to an amount estimated to be less than twice the federal poverty level.

The number of children in poverty continues to increase, meaning teachers are encountering more children affected by poverty's challenges. For example, between 2000 and 2007, the number of children birth to age 6 who were poor increased by 24% (Douglas-Hall & Chau, 2008). Although poverty in and of itself does not cause poor health outcomes, being poor does put children and families at risk for a variety of conditions that challenge children's wellness and ability to learn. Poverty requires families to make difficult choices, such as paying rent or purchasing food. Children may be malnourished because families are compelled to select low-cost foods rather than make nutritious purchases. Families may not be able to afford necessary health care, and living conditions may be substandard. Children affected by the negative effects of poverty enter the classroom with challenges that may prevent their ability to learn and thrive.

Living Conditions

Low-income families often struggle to find affordable and safe housing. Nearly 40% of households in the United States face problems such as inadequate, crowded, or fiscally inaccessible housing (Federal Interagency Forum on Child and Family Statistics, 2008). Inadequate housing suggests all manner of deficiencies, including those that put children at risk, such as older homes that contain dangerous lead-based products or housing that is located in unsafe neighborhoods. Many low-income families face the difficult burden of housing that costs more than 50% of the family's monthly income (Federal Interagency Forum on Child and Family Statistics, 2008). When housing costs require such a large portion of the family income, the family struggles to meet other basic needs, including food and health care. The frequency of moves is also high among low-income families for reasons such as difficulty in making rent payments and seeking to save money by finding more affordable housing options. Factors such as these introduce health risks, contribute to stress, and increase family mobility. School attendance may be irregular as children are moved from one school to

MyEducationLab
To enhance your understanding of how teachers can help families participate in the classroom and become acquainted with one another, go to the IRIS Center Resources section of Topic 7: Chronic Illness/Special Health Care Needs in the MyEducationLab for your course and complete the Module 9: *Collaborating with Families.*

low income
refers to an amount estimated to be less than twice the federal poverty level

another, interrupting learning and social networking. Early childhood teachers must build relationships quickly and work purposefully to reinforce learning opportunities for children who experience such disruptions.

Food Insecurity

food insecurity
not having enough food at all times to maintain an active life; worrying that there may not be enough money to obtain sufficient food

The U.S. Department of Agriculture (USDA) reports that more than 17% of children ages 0 to 17 years live in households that are classified as experiencing food insecurity (Federal Interagency Forum on Child and Family Statistics, 2008). Food insecurity refers to not having enough food at all times to maintain an active life, as well as situations where families worry that they may not have enough money to obtain sufficient food. Families who are food insecure often make changes in their diets, reducing the variety, quality, and desirability of the foods they obtain (Nord, Andrews, & Carlson, 2004). Many rely on community emergency food sources such as food banks or social service agencies.

Food insecurity is reported among one-third of families with incomes below the poverty level (Nord et al., 2008) and is higher among black and Hispanic families possibly because of the higher incidence of poverty among these groups (Federal Interagency Forum on Child and Family Statistics, 2008). Food insecurity may put children at risk for poor diets and related health concerns. Hunger may get in the way of children being able to focus and learn.

Breakfast programs offer an important contribution to the nutrition of children from low-income families.

Teachers should look for signs of hunger. Because many programs and schools provide meals as part of services, teachers can guide children and families to access school lunch programs. In the opening scenario, Kaylee offers a nutritious meal to the children in her family child care. She may be participating in the Child and Adult Care Food Program where she has learned about the importance of recognizing children whose family may be suffering from food insecurity.

Urban and Rural Considerations

Community influences have a significant effect on children's healthful development, introducing both strengths and potential risks to their nutrition, health, and safety. Children in urban settings may be at risk for environmental toxins such as industrial and vehicle contaminants, whereas children in rural settings may be at risk from agricultural sprays. Rates of physical activity are lower among children in urban settings and higher for children living in rural communities (HHS, Health Resources and Services Administration, & Maternal and Child Health Bureau, 2005). However, in spite of this, an increasing trend toward obesity is being seen in rural areas, especially among minority children, children from low-income families, and children from the South (Joens-Matre et al., 2008; Liu, Bennett, Harun, & Probst, 2008). The availability and accessibility of resources such as community-based nutrition and exercise programs, health care facilities, safe bike and walking paths, and grocery stores that offer fresh produce all affect children's health and well-being (Blankenau, 2009). Knowledge of these influences helps teachers to plan developmentally and locality appropriate activities for young children.

In the third opening case scenario, Sharina and Amelia are reviewing the playground for safety issues, but they also consider ways to enhance the educational contribution of the rural outdoor space to promote knowledge of nutrition through the proposed garden plot and to promote physical activity. Teachers in an urban classroom might plan a field trip to a farm where children could learn about how food is grown and harvested. These are examples of ways in which teachers address challenges that may be specific to the urban or rural setting.

What if...

your classroom served a high percentage of low-income children? Many teachers enjoy cooking "community soup," an activity for which each child is asked to bring a food to put in the soup. Would this be a good choice for this classroom?

TRENDS AND INFLUENCES AFFECTING NUTRITION

Awareness is growing about the critical role of good nutrition in promoting health through disease prevention during the early years of development. Teachers in early childhood setting share an important responsibility with families to provide the best nutrition possible for infants and children in their care. Greater attention is being given to guidelines that support healthful diets for young children. Current issues focus on the negative impacts of overweight and obesity and redefining children's diets to support good health.

The Obesity Epidemic

The number of children who are overweight or obese has been increasing at an alarming speed. For example, the obesity rate among preschool children increased from 5% in 1980 to 12.4% in 2006, reaching 31.9% in 2008 among children ages 2 to 19 years (Ogden, Carroll, & Flegal, 2008). The trend described in Figure 1-5 is so serious that it has been labeled an *obesity epidemic*. Serious health consequences are associated with being overweight or obese at such a young age (Fontaine, Redden, Wang, Westfall, & Allison, 2003; Olshansky et al., 2005). In fact, the average life span of those who are obese as children may be shortened by as much as 2 to 5 years. Health experts believe that the adverse consequences of long-term obesity are so powerful that the current generation of children may be the first to have a shorter life span than their parents (Fontaine et al., 2003; Olshansky et al., 2005). These alarming projections highlight the need to understand the causes of obesity and how to prevent them. Teachers have an important role in these efforts. Just as early childhood educators support a preventive approach to health and safety by advocating for immunizations or wearing bike helmets, so too are teachers important to obesity prevention.

Current lifestyle factors related to nutrition and physical activity contribute to the obesity epidemic. Trends in nutrition and eating behaviors include fewer infants being breast-fed, more snacking and eating meals away from home, and larger portion sizes, all of which lead to increased consumption of sugars and fats. In addition, families today have decreased consumption of fruits, vegetables, and whole grains in foods that make a more healthful contribution to the diet. These eating habits have tipped the scales toward less healthful diets that are higher in calories.

Lifestyle factors related to physical activity also contribute to the obesity epidemic. These include an increase in sedentary activities such as time spent sitting while watching television and playing computer games, and reduced activity due to high-density living and inadequate access to safe parks and recreation facilities (Centers for Disease Control and Prevention [CDC], 2008; Council on Sports Medicine and Fitness & Council on School Health, 2006; World Health Organization, 2009). In early childhood settings, teachers report that children are spending more time at table activities and less time playing actively outdoors (Sorte & Daeschel, 2006). Taken together, current trends in nutrition and physical activity add up to poor health outcomes for young children.

Redefining Children's Diets

Recognition is growing among health authorities about the need to address the specific nutritional needs of very young

overweight
an excess of body fat that may lead to obesity; measured by a body mass index score in the 85th to 95th percentile

obese
a medical condition related to the excess accumulation of body fat that may have an adverse affect on health, measured by a body mass index score that is higher than the 95th percentile

Figure 1-5 Trends in Childhood Obesity

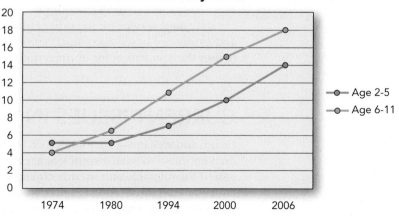

Childhood Obesity Rates

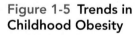

Source: From *Journal of the American Medical Association*, 295:13, p. 155. Copyright © 2006. Republished with permission.

children and promote healthful eating habits during the early childhood years. A variety of resources have been developed to help teachers and families contribute to children's health now and in the future.

Dietary Guidelines for Americans, 2005

The USDA's Center for Nutrition Policy and Promotion promotes good nutrition practices through the *Dietary Guidelines for Americans, 2005* (HHS & USDA, 2005). These address the specific dietary needs of young children and provide key evidenced-based diet and physical activity recommendations to direct attention to healthful practices.

Dietary Reference Intakes

The Institute of Medicine of the National Academies established the Dietary Reference Intakes (DRIs) to address goals for children's nutrient intake and provide advice on recommended intake ranges for vitamins, minerals, and calorie-containing nutrients that are important for children's healthful development (Otten, Pitzi-Hellwig, & Meyers, 2006).

The USDA combines the general guidelines of these two sources to create individualized meals plans using the MyPyramid food guidance system. The MyPyramid system offers suggestions on what and how much to eat from each food group for individuals age 2 years and older (American Dietetic Association, 2005). These food guidance systems help teachers understand what to feed children to support and maintain health and to promote the development of good eating habits.

Feeding Children

Guidelines for creating a positive nutritional environment for young children are also available. Feeding guidelines consider how food is presented to young children, describe the roles and responsibilities of teachers and families, and highlight the child's right to choose what and how much to eat from the foods that are offered. Figure 1-6 lists how different health, professional, and government organizations weigh in on guidelines for feeding young children.

What if. . .

you were assigned to teach 2-year-old toddlers instead of the 3- to 4-year-old preschoolers you normally teach? What aspects of children's nutrition would you explore to prepare yourself to feed toddlers appropriately?

Feeding guidelines such as those shown in Figure 1-6 are important for teachers to understand and know how to implement. Those who teach in Head Start settings or who work in classrooms accredited by the NAEYC are responsible for addressing the standards for feeding children that are promoted by these organizations. In addition, teachers play an important role in setting the tone for healthful nutrition practices in their classrooms. In the opening scenario, Kaylee demonstrates her awareness of feeding children of different age groups in individually appropriate ways. While offering essentially the same menu, she adjusts the ways foods are served to baby Dominique, addresses Nancy's food allergy, and manages a family-style meal service for the other children. Understanding the basic concepts of nutrition and evidenced-based recommendations for feeding young children helps teachers to establish the foundation for optimal nourishment, a vital component of good health.

CURRENT ISSUES IN CHILDREN'S HEALTH

Health and well-being are founded on the prevention and treatment of illness, yet many children continue to have insufficient access to basic health care services. Recent research explored the role of health in early childhood programming, seeking to identify practices that are most effective in linking children and families to the supports and services needed to promote healthy development (Fine & Hicks, 2008). Their findings reveal that "health matters"! Key indicators of health and well-being focus attention on the resources that support children and families to access the services they need.

Figure 1-6 Feeding Guidelines Offered by Health, Professional, and Government Organizations

Feeding Guidelines	USDA CACFP[a]	Head Start[b]	Public Health/Pediatrics[c]	NAEYC[d]	ADA[e]
Clean and safe	√	√	√	√	√
Family-style service	√	√	√	√	√
Adults sit with children	√	√	√	√	√
Child-sized portions (prepare)	√	√	√	√	√
Adults model	—	√	√	√	√
Children regulate intake	—	√	√	√	√
Self-serve	√	√	√	√	—
Integrated part of curriculum	—	√	—	√	√
Allow time	—	√	—	√	√
Child-sized equipment/utensils	—	—	√	√	√
Allow for seconds	√	—	√	√	—
Not forced to eat/resist clean plate	—	√	√	—	√
Avoid using food as reward/punish	—	—	√	—	√

[a]US Department of Agriculture: Child and Adult Care Food Program: Code of Federal Regulations. http://www.fns.usda.gov/cnd/Care/Regs-Policy/226-2004.htm. Accessed March 17, 2005.
[b]US Department of Health and Human Services: *Head Start performance standards. Section 1304.23 Child Nutrition.* 2002. http://www.acf.dhhs.gov/programs/hsb/pf/1304_ALL.pdf. Accessed. March 17, 2005.
[c]American Academy of Pediatrics, American Public Health Association, National Resource Center for Health and Safety in Child Care Program: *Caring for Our Children: National Health and Safety Performance Standards: Guidelines for Out-of-Home Child Care Program.* Elk Grove Village, IL: American Academy of Pediatrics, 2002.
[d]National Association for the Education of Young Children: NAEYC Accreditation Performance Criteria, http://www.naeyc.org/accreditation/standards/standard5/standard5B.asp. Accessed August 10, 2006.
[e]American Dietetic Association: Position of the American Dietetic Association: Nutrition Standards for Child-Care Programs. *J Am Diet Assoc.* 1999;99:981–988. American Dietetic Association: Position of the American Dietetic Association: Benchmarks for Nutrition Programs in Child Care Settings. *J Am Diet Assoc.* 2005;105:979–986.

Source: Reprinted from *Journal of the American Dietetic Association*, 108(2), M. Sigman-Grant, E. Christiansen, L. Branen, J. Fletcher and S. L. Johnson, About feeding children: Mealtimes in child-care centers in four western states. p. 340, Copyright 2008. Used with permission from Elsevier.

Indicators of Well-Being

Since 1997, agencies across the federal government have collaborated through the Federal Interagency Forum on Child and Family Statistics to compile a report on the well-being of children and families called *America's Children in Brief: Key National Indicators of Well-Being* (Federal Interagency Forum on Child and Family Statistics, 2008). These indicators provide insight into the challenges that must be addressed in order to ensure that each child has the opportunity for healthful development. The indicators for health are discussed next.

Health Insurance

Access to health insurance is a significant determinant of whether health care prevention and treatment services are used. The number of children with health insurance coverage has been decreasing significantly during the past decade. In 2006, 8.7 million children ages 0 to 17 had no form of health insurance coverage (Federal Interagency Forum on Child and Family Statistics, 2008). Families who lack health care insurance are more likely to forgo preventive health care due to its high cost and may tend to delay obtaining medical treatment until an illness is in an advanced stage.

Access to a Usual Medical Provider

Families who have identified and can access a usual source for health care services are more likely to obtain the preventive and treatment services needed to ensure good health. Many families do not have an identified source of health care, sometimes called a medical home. In the absence of a usual medical provider, families may obtain services at an

medical home
place where a child obtains preventive health care, sick health care, immunizations, and coordination of medical care needs

emergency room or other sources where medical records and familiarity with the child's health history are not available as a resource (Federal Interagency Forum on Child and Family Statistics, 2008).

Oral Health

Good dental health involves regular brushing and professional dental care. Periodic dental health visits are recommended for children over the age of 1, however many children do not have access to a dentist. In 2006, 25% of all children ages 2 to 8 had not seen a dental care provider in the past year. Children from low-income families were least likely to receive dental care (CDC, 2007). Oral health care is important to overall health, and untreated needs can have a negative impact on children's ability to learn and thrive.

Childhood Immunizations

Obtaining vaccinations for preventable diseases is another indicator of whether preventive health care services are being used. In 2006, 81% of children ages 19 to 35 months received the recommended immunizations. This leaves 19%, or more than 8 million children, without recommended protection from preventable disease (CDC, 2009).

Disparities in Health Care

Disparities or inequities in health care have been identified as a significant challenge to the health and well-being of young children. Throughout this text, when we talk about disparities in health care, we are referring to the fact that some individuals or groups of children are disproportionately at risk for disease and do not have adequate access to health care.

disparities in health care refers to the fact that some individuals or groups of children are disproportionately at risk for disease and do not have adequate access to health care

Children from low-income families or minority groups are at highest risk for health disparities. When compared to children from more affluent families, poor children typically have significantly less access to health insurance and most often do not have a usual health care provider, tend to suffer from oral health care problems, and are less likely to be immunized. Children in families with younger parents are also less likely to have insurance or regular health care (Federal Interagency Forum on Child and Family Statistics, 2008). In addition, trends show that children from low-income families have twice the risk for lead exposure due to living in older homes (Child Trends & Center for Child Health Research, 2004). This is of great concern because the developing brain is highly sensitive to lead. These issues highlight the need to focus on reducing identified health disparities. Teachers have a role in this in that they can share information with families, refer families to available services, and advocate for children in need.

Children's Mental Health

Young children's mental health and social-emotional well-being have emerged as an area that is receiving a great deal of attention. In fact, the incidence of mental health problems among young children is considered to be at a level of crisis in the United States today. As many as 10% of children have a serious mental health disorders with another 10% suffering from mild to moderate concerns (American Psychological Association, 2009). Mental health concerns among young children are often not satisfactorily addressed. Many do not have access to mental health services due either to a lack of health insurance or because of the limited number of mental health consultants with expertise in serving very young children. In addition, some children with poor social and emotional development or mental health concerns exhibit difficult behaviors in the classroom. Families and early childhood teachers report increasing challenges in understanding and managing these difficult behaviors.

Positive early experiences are crucial to decreasing the negative effects of poor mental health and potentially preventing the development of future mental health issues (Cohen & Kaufmann, 2005). Teachers play an important role in fostering children's good mental health by providing support and guidance to each and every child. Teaching children to learn to share materials in the prekindergarten classroom or take turns leading the class to the library in the elementary school setting are examples of ways in which teachers contribute to children's ability to manage their emotions and behaviors effectively. These activities help children build competencies that support learning. Teachers are also important partners with families and mental health professionals in identifying factors that put children at risk for poor mental health and establishing strategies to enhance children's success in the typical classroom.

Teachers partner with mental health professionals to reduce the negative impacts of poor mental health in early childhood.

Inclusion of Children with Significant Health Concerns

Early childhood classrooms are serving more children with special health concerns than ever before. This trend reinforces the importance of training and supporting teachers to effectively manage children's special health care needs. For example, the number of children with significant food allergies has increased by 10% in the past 10 years (Decker et al., 2008). More than 7.5% of children under the age of 4 have been diagnosed with asthma (Dey & Bloom, 2005). More young children with diabetes are being served, as well as many children who have unidentified health needs, such as iron deficiency, obesity, or other health conditions. It is important for teachers to fully understand children's special health needs and know how to appropriately address them in the classroom setting. Having access to health care consultants is an important resource to ensure children's appropriate care. In the opening scenario, Hector demonstrated his comfort with managing Zach's unique health condition. As he reflected on ways to encourage Zach's curiosity about whales, Hector showed he was able to look beyond Zach's health challenge and recognize the child within.

CURRENT SAFETY STANDARDS

One of the primary responsibilities of early childhood teachers is to keep all children safe. Protecting children from unintentional injury requires a special focus on the vulnerabilities of each age group, intentional planning to arrange safe environments, and effective supervision strategies. Safe practices are supported by policies and procedures that guide health and safety routines and that assist teachers to recognize and correct any safety concerns, such as ensuring that electrical outlets are covered or that broken toys are removed.

Teachers are also important participants in keeping children safe from abuse or neglect. Knowing how to recognize and report suspected maltreatment, and supporting children who have suffered from violent events are significant contributions early childhood teachers make to ensure children's safety. Several specific safety topics, such as those discussed in the sections that follow, are being considered in the early childhood community today.

Managing Security

Early childhood teachers and their programs or schools are directing more attention than ever before to security in the early childhood setting. Early childhood education programs and schools are located throughout communities, with some situated in neighborhoods that introduce particular safety challenges. While most programs have some method for controlling entry to the early childhood spaces, some settings choose to address safety risks by installing coded entry locks and other security devices. Such measures, although appropriate for particular settings, have the potential to detract from the welcoming and comfortable environments that are the hallmark of early childhood environments.

Early childhood teachers play an important role in developing program safety measures that are appropriate for the age and development of the children being served. In the opening

What if. . .

in your job as an after-school care provider for first through third graders you discover that a child has a persistent cough that no one seems to be addressing? You suspect that the parent is hoping the illness will go away on its own since the family does not have insurance. What ideas do you have to help the family obtain the care the child needs?

scenario, Sharina and Amelia reflect on the children's requests for play spaces in the outdoor setting. They use this information in concert with their checklist of safety guidelines to create recommendations for playground revisions. In this way they are active contributors to the school's educational and safety plans.

Regulatory Guidelines

The regulations that govern licensed child care and education settings continue to evolve in order to address newly identified risks to children's safety. Topics such as group size, adult-to-child ratio, rules for supervision of children, screening for criminal history, and periodic training in infant and child first aid and cardiopulmonary resuscitation receive periodic review to ensure they adequately address children's safety. Other practices are also scrutinized as new concerns emerge in an effort to improve the quality of children's care and education and to ensure safety.

Hiring practices in children's settings are receiving greater attention. More focus is being directed toward teacher qualifications and training, background checks, and assessment of the applicant's appropriateness for teaching young children. In addition, many states are making available information about validated complaints that have been registered against a licensed program and the nature of such complaints. These efforts invite individuals to report unsafe conditions or problems that may result in harm to children and represent one way in which communities are participants in improving children's safety.

Materials used in children's settings are also being reviewed with renewed vigor. Product safety alerts appear frequently in the news, highlighting the need for teachers to keep aware of potential safety risks in the classroom. Many toys have been removed from the market because they present safety hazards in the form of toxic paints or small parts that pose choking hazards. Newly identified health hazards, such as the dangers related to small magnets if they are swallowed, are also of concern. Teachers should have an action plan in place to remove unsafe toys and materials as soon as problems are identified. The U.S. Consumer Protection Safety Commission is the go-to source for product recalls.

The use of "eco-healthy" toys and thinking "green" in children's settings are newly emerging perspectives that aims to establish safe environments and guide selection of safe toys and classroom materials. This approach focuses on removing toxic products from the environment and reducing waste. The Oregon Environmental Council (2009) provides an Eco-Healthy Child Care Checklist that directs teachers to ensure air quality by not permitting smoking; using nontoxic art supplies, cleaning supplies, and pest prevention methods; and reducing classroom waste. These are excellent topics to explore with families because such discussions help develop a partnership to improve children's safety in both the early childhood and home settings. The *Safety Segment* provides another sample topic for parent and teacher discussion.

The National Resource Center for Health and Safety in Child Care and Early Education is a primary source of information about state-by-state child care licensing regulations. Teachers have an important responsibility to keep aware of changes in regulatory guidelines and to update their practices when new information becomes available.

What if . . .

you wanted to introduce an "eco-healthy" approach in your classroom? How would you encourage the leaders in your children's setting to adopt this perspective? How could you involve families in this project?

Planning for Disasters

Events during the past decade have increased awareness of the impact of disasters on young children and their care and education settings. Natural disasters, such as severe weather, and human-made disasters, such as chemical spills or purposeful attacks, have unfortunately come to the forefront of safety management. Planning proactively to respond appropriately when children's safety is threatened by disastrous events is of utmost importance. Teachers must establish effective strategies to keep children safe if a disaster occurs. These include maintaining emergency supplies, creating effective communication systems, and practicing a disaster management evacuation plan.

Safety Segment

Laws Governing Toy Safety Challenge Innovation

The Consumer Product Safety Improvement Act of 2008 prohibits the sale of toys that contain lead-based products or various chemicals present in some plastics. Manufacturers must prove compliance with the law, which requires testing by independent labs to prove that every accessible toy component meets the guidelines. The laws governing toy safety aim to remove dangerous products present in children's play things, but some say that this will limit toy availability to only mass-produced and marketed items that are often not the kinds of innovative or heirloom materials selected for use in educational settings.

Source: *Consumer Product Safety Improvement Act of 2008* (Public Law 110–314), by the One Hundred Tenth Congress of the United States of America, 2008, retrieved September 1, 2009, from http://www.cpsc.gov/cpsia.pdf.

THE ROLE OF TEACHERS

Early childhood teachers have gained new credibility as active partners in the health and development of young children. There are two reasons for this: new knowledge established by research and recognition of new challenges in children's healthful development (Fine & Hicks, 2008). This has put early childhood and the teachers of young children in the spotlight. Such attention comes with considerable responsibility. To meet this challenge, this text will help teachers of young children gain core knowledge about the contributions of nutrition, health, and safety to children's development and also recognize the important role of the early childhood classroom as a point where health, education, and family support intersect.

evidence-based practices interventions and strategies that have been evaluated through research and established as credible and significant toward reaching a desired goal, such as improving a particular skill, promoting knowledge, or achieving a specific quality standard

Using Evidence-Based Practices

Effective practitioners need to know and understand the interventions and practices that are most successful in providing for children's nutrition, health, and safety: evidence-based practices. Evidence-based practices are the interventions and strategies that have been evaluated through research and established as credible and significant toward reaching a desired goal, such as improving a particular skill, promoting knowledge, or achieving a specific quality standard. Using evidence-based practices means teaching with intention. They guide teachers to *know*—know what to do, how to do it, and why.

Preparing for emergencies is an important responsibility of early childhood teachers.

Evidence-based practices specify the particular underlying principles and activities that lead to effective outcomes. Familiar evidence-based practices for early childhood form the basis for developmentally appropriate practice (DAP) outlined by the NAEYC (2009a). DAP guides teachers to consider three important aspects as they establish environments and interventions to best meet children's needs:

1. The age-related characteristics of children, which allow teachers to predict the activities and experiences that will promote children's development.
2. Individual child characteristics learned through observations and interactions with each child, which inform the teacher about the child's strengths, interests, and approaches to learning.
3. The impacts of the social and cultural contexts in which the children live, which help teachers formulate meaningful and relevant experiences for children (NAEYC, 2009a).

Quality and Accountability

Evidence-based practices are used in many fields as a way to focus attention and efforts on goals and outcomes and to help in measuring success. In the field of early childhood education, the number of requirements has increased for programs that receive public funds, such as Head Start and Early Intervention/Early Childhood Special Education. These requirements compel programs to be accountable for the educational progress of the children they serve. Programs have been guided to use evidence-based practices as one way to improve program quality, increase the effectiveness of teacher and program efforts, and improve the return on investment.

Challenges

Several challenges exist for teachers who aspire to use evidence-based practices. Strain and Dunlap (2006), in their recommended practices guide titled *Being an Evidence-Based Practitioner*, offer the following recommendations:

- *Maintain flexibility.* The fields of education and child development are constantly evolving, and research investigations are revealing new findings and perspectives all the time. Consequently, many evidence-based approaches are in the emerging stages where controversy and discussion are still evident. For example, research on emergent practices for some diverse populations is minimal, limiting the applicability of some promising approaches. Teachers need to keep abreast of such evolutions and maintain a willingness to adapt practices when changes are recommended.
- *Make a commitment.* Using evidence-based approaches in the classroom can be complicated if others in the school, center, or group setting are not supportive of the approach. In addition, some teachers may be concerned that adopting evidence-based practices puts them in a position of having their teaching effectiveness tested. This can make some teachers feel uncomfortable as they wonder how such evaluation would be used.
- *Make informed choices.* Evidence-based practices often inspire the development of new fads by marketers for new curriculum and equipment. Early childhood teachers are prime targets. After all, the early years focus on hands-on exploration and what could be more interesting than a new reading curriculum package with attractive puppets and stickers? Teachers who implement evidence-based practices need to be prepared to make wise choices, selecting the most appropriate new materials and bypassing the others.

Networks of Support

Early childhood teachers often work relatively independently, and sometimes essentially alone, such as in family child care homes or in kindergarten classrooms where the teacher is the only adult. In these settings, the teacher does not have the benefit of a teaching partner to share at-the-moment ideas and reflections. Using evidence-based practices helps teachers feel confident that they are teaching in ways that are consistent with the recommendations of the field (Strain & Dunlap, 2006). In this way, they feel that they are collaborators in the effort to ensure children's optimal nutrition, health, and safety. This ensures their contribution to the positive effects on children's social and educational attainment.

The Office of Head Start lists a variety of evidence-based practices that are encouraged in Head Start classrooms. Other sources have emerged to address the need to support teachers with evidence-based information, such as the Center on the Social and Emotional Foundations for Early Learning, which provides guidance for teachers who work with children who have or are at risk for challenging behaviors.

Guidelines, Standards, and Regulations That Support Best Practices

A variety of resources are available to support teachers as they identify and implement evidence-based practices. Child care licensing standards for health and safety offer basic guidelines. National resource centers, such as the National Resource Center for Health and Safety in Child Care and Early Education and the National Association of Child Care Resource and Referral Agencies, provide research-based and professionally reviewed materials to guide

Health Hint

Emerging Practices in Program Accreditation

The National Association for the Education of Young Children includes Emerging Practices in its program accreditation materials as indicators that particular topics are still under review for appropriate inclusion. The following Emerging Practice relates to health in the early childhood setting:

Standard 5: NAEYC Accreditation Criteria for Health Standard

5. A. 10. Precautions are taken to ensure that communal water play does not spread infectious disease. No child drinks the water. Children with sores on their hands are not permitted to participate in communal water play. Fresh potable water is used, and the water is changed before a new group of children comes to participate in the water play activity. When the activity period is completed with each group of children, the water is drained. Alternately, fresh potable water flows freely through the water play table and out through a drain in the table.

Source: *NAEYC Academy of Early Childhood Program Accreditation*, by the National Association for the Education of Young Children, 2008, retrieved July 2009 from http://www.naeyc.org/academy/primary/viewstandards.

program practices. The three major accrediting bodies for early childhood programs also provide guidelines for appropriate practice:

- National Association for the Education of Young Children.
- National Association for Family Child Care.
- National AfterSchool Association.

These professional organizations also offer a variety of membership benefits and resources through their professional journals and professional development conferences. The *Health Hint* describes an emerging practice for program accreditation by the NAEYC.

Making a Commitment to Professionalism

Early childhood teachers are the standard bearers for the important early years of development. Making a commitment to professionalism is a significant step in taking on the responsibilities of effective teaching. This goes beyond the concept of "do no harm" in that it encourages teachers to purposefully take action to improve children's health and well-being. It means being intentional about the choices made when planning and implementing activities for children, and using evidence-based practices rather than making choices based on myths or "the way it's always been done."

Professionalism encompasses the expectation that teachers develop **dispositions**, or values, beliefs, and attitudes that promote positive outcomes in the children they teach. Teachers' dispositions are evident through their interactions with children, families, and others. Professional dispositions that are of particular importance in teaching include the values of fairness and equity and the belief that all children can learn. Making a commitment to professionalism includes being a reflective practitioner whereby teachers evaluate their success in practicing dispositions that support children's health and well-being. The self-inventory in Figure 1-7 offers a guide for developing professional competencies in nutrition, health, and safety of the young child.

dispositions
the values, beliefs, and attitudes of the teacher that are put into action to promote positive outcomes in children

Professionals should adhere to a code of conduct. Early childhood teachers should implement the *Code of Ethical Conduct* advanced by the NAEYC (2005). The *Code of Ethical Conduct* guides the decisions and actions of teachers, such as recognizing children's vulnerability and reliance on adults and the importance of creating environments that are safe and healthful for children. The code is a beginning point for becoming an advocate for children and families. Being an advocate means supporting actions that promote the well-being of children, such as backing initiatives to provide more healthful meals in

Figure 1-7 Self-Inventory for Wellness Practices

How much do you know about your own health and well-being? How much do you know about the nutrition, health, and safety practices of young children, from birth to age 8?

Personal Practices	Always	Sometimes	Never	Reflections and Comments
I eat vegetables and/or fruits at every meal.				
I drink skim or 1% milk and choose low-fat cheeses.				
Half of the grains I eat are whole grains.				
I am overweight.				
I feel rested when I wake up each day.				
I smoke.				
I get at least 150 minutes of cardiovascular exercise every week.				
I wash my hands with soap and water after I use the bathroom.				
I eat fast food.				
My vaccinations are up to date.				
I have a primary care physician or a "medical home."				
I get a flu shot each year.				
I have a dental checkup at least once each year.				
I wear a seat belt and avoid talking on a cell phone or text messaging when I drive.				
I follow bicycle safety rules when I am riding on the road.				
I wash fresh fruits and vegetables before I eat them.				
I get 8 hours of sleep most nights.				
When I teach children I dress appropriately so I am comfortable playing outdoors with them.				
I recognize signs of illness and stay home when I am ill.				
I develop friendships and enjoy socializing and laughing with others.				
I have friends/family with whom I can consult when I have concerns.				

schools, and supporting efforts to provide safe parks and outdoor areas where children can play and families can socialize. Being an advocate is a lifelong endeavor that develops over the years. A commitment to professionalism encourages early childhood practitioners to take on leadership roles in their program as well as in their community and to collaborate with professionals in nutrition, health, and safety to improve children's well-being. The *Policy Point* describes the importance of advocating for healthy child development.

Finally, a commitment to professionalism requires dedicating time and resources to pursue professional development activities that contribute to the teacher's knowledge

Figure 1-7 Self-Inventory for Wellness Practices *(continued)*

Young Children's Wellness Practices	I Was Aware of This	I Was Somewhat Aware of This	I Was Not Aware of This	Reflective Questions and Things I Want to Learn About
The medical field recommends that, ideally, infants should be exclusively breast-fed for the first 4 to 6 months.				
It is recommended that adults replace infants' use of a bottle and nipple with a cup after 12 months of age.				
Children age 2 and older should drink skim or 1% milk unless they are underweight.				
Children should be served fruits and/or vegetables at meal and snack times.				
Children should be offered but not forced to eat any food including a "no thank-you bite."				
Fresh fruit should be served rather than juice because it adds fiber to the diet.				
Breakfast is a very important meal and enhances learning.				
Children should have their first dental visit by their first birthday.				
Families are children's first teachers, but teachers can have tremendous influence over young children's health and well-being.				
Being outside in cold weather does not, by itself, give a child a cold.				
Play promotes cognitive development.				
Building relationships with nurturing adults promotes children's development.				
Children should be physically active every day.				
TV viewing should be limited to 1 to 2 hours or less per day and children under age 2 should not view TV at all.				
Even very young children can learn ways to keep safe.				

and understanding of excellence in professional practice and emerging trends to enhance quality in early childhood care and education. This effort calls on early childhood teachers to be willing to reflect on their current practices, to identify personal strengths to further enhance, and to identify areas where additional professional development is needed. Successful educators are open to new ideas and approaches that will improve children's abilities to grow and thrive.

Policy Point

ADVOCATING FOR HEALTHY CHILD DEVELOPMENT SUPPORTS STRONG COMMUNITIES

Policies that support healthful child development are founded on scientific research and emerge from the belief that all children can learn. The Center on the Developing Child at Harvard University summarizes this connection in their introductory mission statement:

> The Center on the Developing Child was founded in 2006 on the belief that the vitality and sustainability of any society depend on the extent to which it equalizes opportunities early in life for all children to achieve their full potential and engage in responsible and productive citizenship. We view healthy child development as the foundation of economic prosperity and strong communities, and our mission is to advance that vision by leveraging science to enhance child well-being. . . . in the service of closing the gap between what we know and what we do to support positive life outcomes for children. . . .

Source: The President and Fellows of Harvard College. 2008. The Center on the Developing Child. Retrieved online December 2008 at: http://www.developingchild.harvard.edu/content/about.html.

Summary

Wellness is established on the building blocks of nutrition, health, and safety which work together to increase children's abilities to develop and thrive in the educational setting. Teachers are second only to families in influencing children's healthful development making the study of these wellness components crucial to successful teaching.

However, many complex influences affect children's lives and their ability to learn. A growing multicultural society, diverse family structures, food insecurity, and the impacts of poverty are factors that must be understood in order to establish classroom approaches that are relevant to the needs of young children.

Current trends seek to address emerging challenges. Greater attention is being given to the guidelines for children's nutrition and strategies to tackle the obesity epidemic. More focus is being directed to the conditions that compromise children's well-being, such as disparities in health care. Increased efforts are being made to enhance children's safety through improved regulations and emergency management planning. Recognizing these trends helps teachers promote children's wellness and attain positive educational outcomes.

Teachers assume an important responsibility for meeting children's developmental and educational needs. This text guides teachers to understand the interrelationship of nutrition, health, and safety, and provides background information sufficient for teachers to feel confident in their ability to create learning environments and teaching approaches that will make a significant contribution to children's learning.

Never before has the value of the early learning years been recognized with such enthusiasm and intensity. Teachers offer significant contributions to the health and vitality of children, families and communities making it an exciting time to be a teacher of young children.

Key Terms

Context, p. 6

Critical periods, p. 6

Developmentally appropriate practice, p. 21

Diet, p. 4

Disparities in health care, p. 18

Dispositions, p. 23

Early childhood, p. 5

Early childhood teachers, p. 6

English language learners, p. 12

Epigenetics, p. 6

Ethnic, p. 12

Evidence-based practices, p. 21

Food insecurity, p. 14

Low income, p. 13

Medical home, p. 17

Neurons, p. 5

Obese, p. 15

Oral health, p. 9

Overweight, p. 15

Wellness, p. 3

Review Questions

1. How do nutrition, health, and safety interrelate to affect children's wellness?
2. What are some of the national initiatives that relate to children's health and wellness, and how do these affect teachers?
3. How does poverty impact children's ability to learn?
4. What are the current trends in nutrition, health, and safety and how do they impact the early childhood classroom?
5. How can teachers use their knowledge of nutrition, health, and safety to help children learn?

Discussion Starters

1. Consider the term *wellness*. Make a list of words that describe wellness to you. What would wellness look like in a young child? Share your list with others.
2. Team with two other students to discuss nutrition, health, and safety. Assign each to advocate for one of these three building blocks of children's healthful development. Discuss the contributions of each and attempt to identify which of these components is most significant in promoting children's well-being. Are you able to agree on one primary component or are the three too interrelated to stand alone as most important?
3. Reflect on the complex influences that affect the demographics or class makeup of children in the community where you grew up. How would you describe the typical family in your home community? Were resources available to assist families and provide for the nutrition, health, and safety, of children? Can you identify any community services that benefited you during your early development?
4. Recall a class or group of children you have observed or with whom you have worked. Did you see developmentally appropriate practices being used in the setting? Were you able to observe teachers making adjustments in activities or approaches to meet the needs of the age group or of individual children in the class? Were nutrition, health, and safety considered in the classroom practices?

Practice Points

1. Reflect on an early childhood classroom you have observed. Briefly describe the contexts that surround the child using the ecological systems theory. Identify aspects of each system (micro-, meso-, exo-, and macrosystem) that support children's healthful development and those that challenge development.
2. Gather more information about the National Children's Study. What environmental, biological, genetic, and psychosocial factors are being discussed that may influence different phases of children's growth and development? What connections are being made between these factors and health and disease?
3. Think about your home community and the complex influences that affect children's development. What complicating factors are most prevalent in your community? What resources are available to address those influences? Interview an early childhood teacher and discuss the trends that are seen as most challenging to children's health and wellness.

Web Resources

Healthy Child Care America
www.healthychildcare.org

National Association for the Education of Young Children
www.naeyc.org

The National Children's Study
www.nationalchildrensstudy.gov

MyEducationLab
To assess your understanding of the interrelationship among nutrition, health, and safety in early childhood education settings, go to the Book Specific Resources section in the MyEducationLab for your course, select *Nutrition, Health, and Safety for Young Children*, Chapter 1 of the Study Plan, and then complete the multiple choice questions and activities.

chapter 2 | Teaching Wellness Concepts

Learning Outcomes

After reading this chapter, you should be able to:

1. Describe how children learn.

2. Identify and explain the components of purposeful planning.

3. Plan wellness activities that are appropriate for each age group.

4. Identify resources to support teaching wellness concepts.

5. Plan ways to partner with families in teaching wellness concepts.

Marty, Greg, and Armetha are taking a brisk walk as part of their school's new wellness initiative and also a part of today's staff meeting. They have been asked to walk for 30 minutes while discussing ways to implement nutrition, health, and safety activities in their classrooms. Marty is lead teacher for a prekindergarten class, Greg teaches kindergarten, and Armetha teaches a first- and second-grade mixed-age group. They are enthusiastic about the Walk & Talk time and their ideas flow freely. Marty wants to conduct more cooking activities to introduce children to the science of cooking. She also has some ideas about how to explore cultural aspects through different ways of cooking the same food product—like rice. Greg suggests that his kindergartners are ready to learn about how foods add up to a healthful diet. He wants to explore this using math concepts and by talking about the energy that food provides for the human body. Armetha says she will have her class investigate where various healthful foods are grown. She envisions using food as a way to study climates and geography, as well as to identify the foods that are grown locally. Their walking time is almost up and they are reluctant to stop! They decide to meet before school each Tuesday morning, to walk and talk about more ways to teach wellness.

Putting educational ideas into meaningful action is one of the exciting aspects of teaching young children. It draws on skills that involve both the art and science of teaching. Teachers use creative approaches to interest and expand children's knowledge of nutrition, health, and safety concepts. They base their teaching strategies on evidence-based practices and conduct ongoing evaluation of their approaches to learn how their ideas help children learn.

Including a wellness program as part of the early childhood curriculum helps children establish a foundation of healthful behaviors and instills in them a sense of capability and confidence that they can promote their own well-being. It reinforces the belief that children are partners in their own health and wellness. In this chapter we describe some of the foundations for effective teaching of nutrition, health, and safety concepts and also describe the ways teachers plan, implement, and evaluate meaningful wellness experiences in the early childhood setting.

HOW CHILDREN LEARN

Early childhood is a unique period of development. It is a time when the pace of growth is significantly more rapid than at any other. During the early years children develop the capacity to use their learning "tools," including their senses and their innate curiosity and motivation, to explore and learn to communicate. Teachers, such as those in our opening case scenario, are attuned to how children learn and know how to plan and implement approaches that are most appropriate and effective for each individual child and well as each group of children. They know that learning is a progression through which children begin by attaining basic knowledge and move on to using strategies to solve complex problems. Various aspects of how children learn inform the teacher's understanding of how to teach.

Constructing Knowledge

Children learn when they experience new ideas and gain new information that is added to what they already know. This is called *constructing knowledge*. The process of constructing knowledge was studied by Jean Piaget (1929), Lev Vygotsky (1962), Jerome Bruner (1966), and others. Their theory of how children learn is called the constructivist approach. This approach provides a useful way of thinking about how to teach so children will learn. Piaget explained learning as a cumulative process that involves important processes and challenges, including organization, adaptation, disequilibrium, equilibrium, social interactions, and scaffolding, all of which are discussed next.

constructivist approach
an approach in which children build their own knowledge by fitting new information and ideas with what they already know

mental structures
the ways children understand and think about the world

organization
an inborn capability that allows children to use the simple processes of learning to build complex mental structures

adaptation
the result of assimilation and accommodation; new information becomes part of the child's working mental structures

assimilation
the process of taking in new information and fitting it into existing mental structures

accommodation
the process of taking in new information and creating new mental structures

Organization and Adaptation

Piaget (1929) described learning as the evolution and development of children's mental structures. Mental structures, sometimes called *schemas*, are ways of thinking about the world. Mental structures are like a set of "rules" that children develop as they interact with the world to explain how things work and what things mean. Mental structures involve many different kinds of concepts. Some examples include knowing the routines of the day (get up, eat breakfast, go to school), understanding that people and objects do not just disappear when they are out of sight (called *object permanence*), or learning concepts of measurement. Mental structures are influenced by children's maturation, experience, and social interactions. Children's mental structures guide how information is processed, organized, and adapted to create new ways of understanding.

Organization refers to an inborn capability that allows children to use the simple processes of learning provided by the senses, such as touching, seeing, and hearing, to build more complex mental capabilities such as problem solving and abstract thinking. Adaptation is learning. It is the continual change that occurs within children's mental structures as they interact with and learn from their environment. Adaptation emerges through assimilation as children take in and fit new experiences into their existing mental structures and through accommodation as children modify their mental structures to include new ideas and information.

For example, 3-year-old Charlie has a mental structure for "water." He knows many of the characteristics of water: It is wet, runny, smooth, and sometimes cool and sometimes warm. When he experiences water in different settings, such as in the bathtub, the faucet, in a cup, or in a rain puddle, he is able to assimilate this new information into his mental structure for water. The new information "fits" as an additional characteristic: that water can be present in many places. However, when Charlie first discovers water in the form of ice and is confronted with the properties of freezing and melting, he is faced with new information that does not easily fit into his previous mental structure for water. He is incredulous! He may deny that the ice cube is water, because the notion does not fit with the "rules" of his mental structure. Through experience, such as licking the ice cube, and guidance from his teacher, he learns that ice is a form of water, that it is very cold and hard, and that after a period of time it melts when it sits on the table. To accommodate this information, Charlie must modify his thinking about water: Sometimes it is runny, sometimes it is hard. He must also create new mental structures to organize and manage the information about the ice cube changing from liquid to solid (freezing) and solid back to liquid (melting). He learns new words, and he also learns new concepts.

Adaptation results when the process of accommodation is complete, and the new information is part of the child's new working knowledge. Young children are constantly organizing and adapting new information through the concrete experiences provided by play. To learn, children must act on and participate with the world around them (Piaget, 1929). During play, children are able to follow their own interests, select the toys and materials that intrigue them, and practice and repeat skills that are exciting to them (Bruner, 1966). This freedom to explore allows children to test new ideas, repeat routines to reinforce existing knowledge, assimilate information at their own pace, and accommodate new ways of using the information. Play is the context within which children construct the knowledge base that supports their understanding of the world. This highlights the importance of establishing ample opportunities for children to play in the early childhood classroom.

Play is the child's most effective teacher.

Disequilibrium and Equilibrium

Another aspect of the learning process involves the balance between children's discomfort with new ideas and experience and their comfort with familiar knowledge and events. This entails the experiences of disequilibrium and equilibrium.

Disequilibrium refers to the uneasiness that children experience when faced with new challenges. Unfamiliar experiences and events may cause surprise and make children feel unsure. This "confusion" is an important part of the learning process. Similar to when a teacher asks a question, disequilibrium arouses children's interest and focus and inspires creative inventions as they try to find an explanation for the unexpected event. In most cases disequilibrium encourages children to explore and persist until the unfamiliar situation is tested, studied, and understood. However, disequilibrium can also cause children to feel dismay or frustration, which may cause them to give up and abandon the task. This is likely to occur if children are faced with experiences that are beyond their developmental capability. Planning developmentally appropriate activities that suit the needs of individual learners is crucial to helping children persist when faced with new challenges.

disequilibrium
the uneasiness that children experience when faced with new challenges

Equilibrium, on the other hand, refers to a state of balance or calmness experienced by children during the learning process. It is established as children practice familiar routines and test and reinforce their knowledge. For example, children may enjoy playing "doctor's office" over and over again, reinforcing their knowledge of what happens in a medical office and during a checkup. When the experience affirms what children already know, confidence and sureness are enhanced. Equilibrium also results when children adapt new experiences and information into their mental structures and are capable of using them appropriately. In the earlier example, Charlie feels confident as he tells his family, "Ice is water frozen. It is cold and hard, but when you put it in the sun it melts. Let me show you!"

equilibrium
a state of balance or calmness experienced by children during the learning process

Children need many opportunities to participate in familiar play experiences where they can practice and reinforce their skills and confirm their existing knowledge (mental structures). They also need inviting, and sometimes surprising, play opportunities that introduce new challenges and problems to explore and solve. These experiences help children build strategies for managing new ideas. Ensuring that children have a multitude of familiar and challenging experiences promotes optimal learning.

Social Interactions and Communication

Learning through play does not happen simply by interacting with materials. Important social interactions and communication also occur during play, which peak children's interest and enhance learning (Vygotsky, 1962). Social interaction provides opportunities for children to talk together about what they are doing, give each other ideas and directions, and serve as role models for one another. Vygotsky noted that language is a key element in this learning process. Teachers and families use language to help children focus on the significant aspects of an activity, and make meaning from what they have experienced. For example, teachers offer new vocabulary or ask questions that focus children's attention on what they are doing, such as, with a 2-year-old, "Yes, you noticed that there are bubbles in the sink when you wash your hands. Now they're on the drain. Where do you think the water and the bubbles are going?" or with a 7-year-old, "You were running fast at recess. Is your heart pumping quickly? Can you feel how you are breathing hard? Why do you think your body reacts this way after running?" Vygotsky also contributed the notion that important social aspects of culture are communicated and practiced through social interaction and language. Dramatic play settings are ideal places to observe children practicing the social styles of their culture, as in the roles children develop and the themes they select for play.

Scaffolding

Teachers guide the learning process by structuring experiences that are familiar and of interest to the child and that offer challenges just beyond the child's current level of understanding and ability. This process is called **scaffolding**. It is an essential aspect of the constructivist approach to learning. Just as scaffold equipment provides support during a construction project, scaffolding in teaching supports the child to move into new levels of understanding and the next levels of skill. Figure 2-1 describes the steps involved in scaffolding.

scaffolding
the process of structuring learning experiences around existing knowledge and offering challenge that is just beyond the child's current level of understanding and ability

Figure 2-1 Steps in Scaffolding Children's Learning

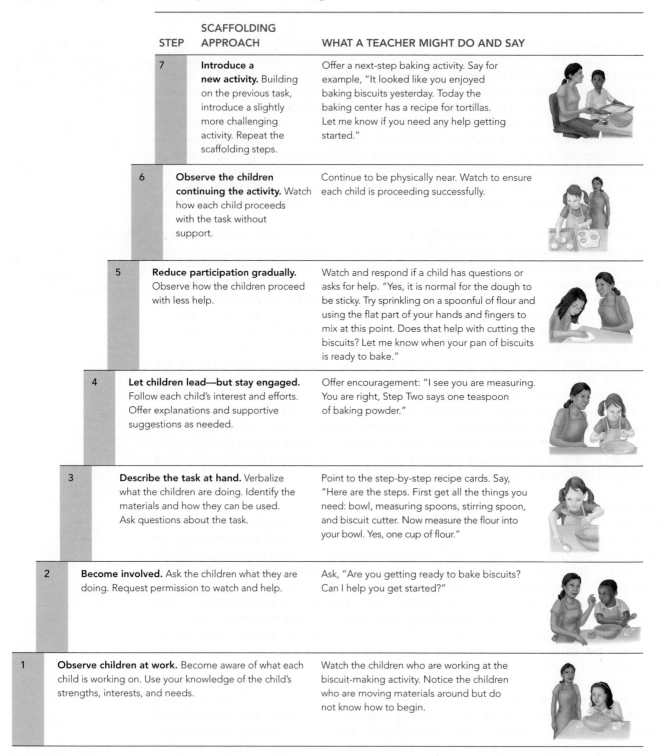

STEP	SCAFFOLDING APPROACH	WHAT A TEACHER MIGHT DO AND SAY
7	**Introduce a new activity.** Building on the previous task, introduce a slightly more challenging activity. Repeat the scaffolding steps.	Offer a next-step baking activity. Say for example, "It looked like you enjoyed baking biscuits yesterday. Today the baking center has a recipe for tortillas. Let me know if you need any help getting started."
6	**Observe the children continuing the activity.** Watch how each child proceeds with the task without support.	Continue to be physically near. Watch to ensure each child is proceeding successfully.
5	**Reduce participation gradually.** Observe how the children proceed with less help.	Watch and respond if a child has questions or asks for help. "Yes, it is normal for the dough to be sticky. Try sprinkling on a spoonful of flour and using the flat part of your hands and fingers to mix at this point. Does that help with cutting the biscuits? Let me know when your pan of biscuits is ready to bake."
4	**Let children lead—but stay engaged.** Follow each child's interest and efforts. Offer explanations and supportive suggestions as needed.	Offer encouragement: "I see you are measuring. You are right, Step Two says one teaspoon of baking powder."
3	**Describe the task at hand.** Verbalize what the children are doing. Identify the materials and how they can be used. Ask questions about the task.	Point to the step-by-step recipe cards. Say, "Here are the steps. First get all the things you need: bowl, measuring spoons, stirring spoon, and biscuit cutter. Now measure the flour into your bowl. Yes, one cup of flour."
2	**Become involved.** Ask the children what they are doing. Request permission to watch and help.	Ask, "Are you getting ready to bake biscuits? Can I help you get started?"
1	**Observe children at work.** Become aware of what each child is working on. Use your knowledge of the child's strengths, interests, and needs.	Watch the children who are working at the biscuit-making activity. Notice the children who are moving materials around but do not know how to begin.

Source: Adapted from *Early Childhood Education Today*, 11th edition, by G. S. Morrison, 2009, Boston, MA: Allyn and Bacon/Merrill Education. Copyright 2009 by Pearson Education. Adapted with permission of the publisher.

The teachers in the opening scenario have unique plans to implement wellness activities related to food for the various age groups they teach. They demonstrate their understanding of the children's interests, and each has identified ways to purposefully promote the exploration of specific concepts, such as the science of food preparation and the cultural aspects of foods. They are prepared to guide children to construct knowledge about the role of food in healthful development.

The Role of Brain Development

Brain development during the early years is crucial to establishing basic patterns for managing information and increasing the capacity for the child's future ability to learn (Shonkoff & Phillips, 2000). At birth, the child has nearly 100 billion neurons, brain cells that are ready to assist with growth and development. Brain growth and development are stimulated by experiences and interactions. During the infant and toddler years, the brain focuses on organizing the information provided by sensory systems, such as sight, touch, taste, smell, and hearing. Children are innately wired to move and explore, and adults should allow them this freedom. From age 3 onward, brain development is highly directed toward growing and refining the neuron connections. Through this development language emerges, cognitive structures are established, and social and emotional capabilities are realized, allowing the child to become a social being who is capable of learning (Center on the Developing Child, 2007). This establishes the early years as an important period for brain development and learning. Loving relationships and interactive communication with teachers and other adults contribute to this growth.

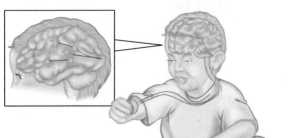

Learning relies on the development of a complex system of neuron connections. As children experience new information, the neurons reach out to one another, interacting and building a network of highly sophisticated connections. These connections are used again and again as the child explores and interacts with the world, establishing the channels for managing information and making sense of experiences and learning. Practicing skills is a primary way of reinforcing brain cell connections. Connections that are not used are pruned away to allow the brain to be more efficient. In this way experience and learning change the "architecture" of the child's brain (Center on the Developing Child, 2007). Figure 2-2 depicts how the brain's complex network of connections evolves through interaction and experience.

Brain plasticity is an important part of this process of making connections. Plasticity refers to the brain's ability to be flexible and change when new information modifies existing connections among the neurons and then expands or replaces previous knowledge. For example, first a young child may learn that a four-legged animal is called a *dog*. The child stores this information, and may conclude that all four-legged animals are dogs. The child modifies this thinking when it is discovered that another four-legged animal (that looks somewhat different) is called a *cat*. This refinement in thinking is continually modified and expanded as the child learns about the unique characteristics and the names of many animals that have four legs. The original lesson about the "dog" remains, while new neural connections are formed to organize the new information. Brain plasticity provides for these modifications and is an important aspect of the child's ability to learn.

brain plasticity
the brain's ability to be flexible and change when new information is learned

Children who are provided rich opportunities for learning benefit by developing highly complex webs of neural connections that support future learning. Children who are deprived of these learning opportunities, or who experience chronic stress or toxic environments, show diminished neuron development in areas of their brains, especially those that control learning and behavior (National Scientific Council on the Developing Child, 2007). The federal Administration for Children and Families (ACF) has recognized the importance of providing a breadth of educational opportunities for children from disadvantaged backgrounds to address this deficit. The *Policy Point* describes a particular ACF initiative to improve children's health and well-being.

The teachers in the opening scenario are planning activities to teach wellness to children across the early childhood age span. This enrichment will promote optimal development among the children in their classes. It is a reminder that teachers play an important role in children's brain development when teaching wellness.

What if. . .

you were asked at a job interview to explain how children learn? Using the information provided as well as examples from your experience, draft an appropriate response. Describe how you use this information to inform your style of teaching.

HEAD START BODY START

The federal Administration for Children and Families of the U.S. Department of Health and Human Services has made a significant commitment to the health and well-being of young children through funding for the creation of *Head Start Body Start: The National Center for Physical Development and Outdoor Play*. The project, a joint effort of the American Alliance for Health, Physical Education, Recreation and Dance (AAHPERD) and the National Association for Sport and Physical Education (NASPE), addresses a key component of the Surgeon General's Childhood Overweight and Obesity Prevention Initiative. The center aims to increase physical activity, outdoor play, and healthy eating among the 900,000 children participating in Head Start programs nationwide. The 4-year project will provide guidance for developing policies and setting national priorities for improving children's health and well-being.

Source: Based on "$12 Million Head Start Grant Awarded to NASPE and AAPAR," retrieved September 3, 2009, from http://www.aahperd.org/aahperd/template.cfm?template=pr08_1010.html.

Domains of Development

developmental domains
areas of development

Learning emerges from experiences in several developmental domains, or areas, including cognitive, language, physical, social, and emotional. Each fosters growth through the contributions of particular learning systems. The commonly recognized development and learning domains are discussed next.

Cognitive Development

Cognitive development involves learning to make meaning from the world. It includes growth and development of the sensory systems that form the basis of perception and the skills to use this information to learn. Cognitive development includes:

- Developing memory and problem-solving skills.
- Thinking logically: "I need to wash my hands after I use the bathroom."
- Using symbols, such as understanding gestures, using sign language, reading signs, drawing, and writing.

Language Development

Language development involves understanding and using language and other forms of communication to gather and exchange information and ideas. This domain includes:

- Listening and speaking.
- Using language to express needs and to make social connections, such as asking for help with putting on shoes or asking for a turn at the swing.
- Building the foundations for literacy skills such as reading and writing.

Physical Development

Physical development includes overall physical health as well as growth and development of the muscle systems. This includes the large muscles of the arms, legs, and whole body to accomplish movement and also the small muscles of the hands, fingers, wrist, toes, and eyes to accomplish fine motor manipulation tasks. Physical development focuses on:

- Developing muscle strength, control, and stamina to accomplish safe and purposeful exploration and manipulation, such as pulling a trike to its storage area.
- Integrating and coordinating movement to accomplish complex tasks, such as an infant crawling or pulling to a standing position, a preschooler learning to climb on playground equipment, or a school-age child learning to dribble a basketball.
- Supporting the general well-being needed for healthful development.

Social-Emotional Development

Social-emotional development involves building the skills needed to interact, work and play successfully with others. This area encompasses how children learn about the world and their place in it. Social-emotional development means:

- Learning to build trusting and caring relationships with others.
- Identifying and expressing feelings in appropriate ways, such as "I miss my mom, but I know she'll come back after work".
- Developing the ability to make choices, take responsibility for own actions and be capable of solving problems in social settings: "OK, you be the red guy and I'll be the blue guy. Next time I get red."

Learning across the various domains is highly interrelated. That is, successful learning in one domain affects, and is also dependent on, successful learning in the other domains (National Association for the Education of Young Children [NAEYC] & National Association of Early Childhood Specialists in State Departments of Education [NAECS/SDE], 2002; National Scientific Council on the Developing Child, 2007). Table 2-1 describes how learning in the developmental domains relates to teaching wellness.

Teaching wellness concepts by planning activities across the developmental domains is an approach that is well suited to the education of young children. Many teachers use methods such as charting activities to encourage their ideas and to coordinate their plans. Figure 2-3 shows one way to plan wellness activities using this approach.

Attention to teaching in the developmental domains is also evident in class groups that use a center-based approach to early education. In a **center-based approach** the classroom environment is designed around particular learning centers, such as the manipulatives or block areas, the science table, dramatic play corner, or library. Learning in the developmental domains occurs and overlaps in each of the classroom centers. For example:

- Manipulative and block areas support fine and gross motor development, cognitive development, and social-emotional development.
- Science corners and game and puzzle centers invite children into cognitive problem-solving situations where fine motor skills are used.
- Dramatic play settings stimulate social-emotional and language development.
- Library areas and listening centers encourage language development and promote sharing and other social-emotional skills.

Teaching children during the early years of development is uniquely different from teaching older children. Focus on the developmental domains is more central to the early childhood approach. Young children should have ample opportunity for playful learning and exploration using their senses, because the information learned in this way is important to building a foundation of knowledge that is used for later learning.

center-based approach approach in which the classroom environment is designed around particular learning centers, such as the manipulatives or block areas, the science table, dramatic play corner, or library

Curriculum Content Areas

Curriculum content areas, or disciplines, include the areas of study that are familiar in the school setting. Familiar curriculum content areas include:

- Literacy.
- Mathematics.
- Science.
- Art.
- Social science.
- Health and well-being.

Successful learning in the curriculum content areas is closely linked to skills acquired in the developmental domains. While learning in the curriculum content areas builds on the capacities established in the developmental domains, it leans more toward

Table 2-1 Developmental Domains and Implications for Promoting Wellness

Developmental Domain	What Might Be Observed	What Teachers Do to Promote Wellness
Ages Birth–2 Years		
Physical	• Dramatic weight gains occur in first 6 to 12 months. Most babies double their birth weight by 4 to 6 months. • By this age, children should express hunger and satiety.	• Watch for cues the child is hungry (fussy, clinging, or crying) or satiated (sleepy, calm). • Hold infants and interact during feedings.
	• Pincer grasp usually appears around 9 months. • Self-feeding skills continue to develop. • Teeth begin to emerge between 4 and 12 months.	• Introduce healthy finger foods. • Introduce a variety of foods. • Introduce oral care; wipe gums and teeth or brush with soft bristle toothbrush (no toothpaste).
	• Mobility increases. • Slower growth and more play results in short feeding periods. Parents may worry that their child "doesn't eat enough."	• Create a safe place for play. • Encourage socially interactive, frequent meals. • No force feeding.
Social-emotional	• Around 4 months, infants become interested in the outside world and may seem distracted while feeding.	• Continue social interactions with feedings and look for satiety cues, such as the child pulling away from the bottle or beginning to play.
Language, cognition, and play	• Language emerges; vocabulary increases exponentially.	• Introduce health and safety words and ideas such as "I am washing your hands to take away germs that can make you sick" or "We are walking in the crosswalks to keep safe."
	• Child does not yet recognize impact of actions (like hitting or biting). • Play is solitary and parallel.	• Establish and reinforce basic guidelines for behavior (no biting). • Ensure toys are appropriate for play; no small items.
Ages 3–5 Years		
Physical	• Brain and body growth slows, corresponding with decreases in nutritional requirements.	• Provide healthful food choices. • Schedule small meals and snacks across the day. • Offer opportunity for child to serve self; encourage recognition of satiety.
	• Wide variation in motor activity and skills. Activities include throwing, climbing, dancing, riding bicycles, or kicking.	• Encourage activity by providing a range of materials and challenges. • Provide many opportunities for children to be active, even when the weather isn't optimal.
Social-emotional	• Mood shifts rapidly between feelings of independence and dependence. • Is highly sensitive to a variety of emotions.	• Avoid using food as a reward for behaviors or to soothe emotions. (A child might associate fast food with love and nurturing.) • Help children recognize emotions of self and others. Use words like *angry, upset, happy, excited, surprised*. • Teach concepts such as acceptance, tolerance, negotiation.
Language, cognition, and play	• Language development is extremely rapid. • Begins to understand cause and effect of behaviors. • Engages in many forms of play including interactive and cooperative play.	• Introduce children to new fruits and vegetables; teach names of foods. • Teach safety skills. • Teach and support appropriate interactions and social skills. Stop bullying or intimidating behaviors.

Table 2-1	Developmental Domains and Implications for Promoting Wellness (Continued)	
Developmental Domain	What Might Be Observed	What Teachers Do to Promote Wellness
Ages 6–8 Years		
Physical	• Growth continues slowly. • Motor strength, coordination, and stamina increase, contributing to the ability to perform complex movements (e.g., play sports). • Children desire to be "normal."	• Allow children to select foods and food portions by offering healthful alternatives. • Offer many opportunities for physical activity. • Guide development of healthy perceptions of body image.
Social-emotional	• Importance of peer relationships increases. • Children seek acceptance (conformity).	• Facilitate healthy social skills. • Teach skills in negotiation. • Support positive peer relationships. • Promote children's individual strengths and skills.
Language and cognition	• Language includes popular peer phrases. • Thinking patterns include concrete as well as logical operations.	• Teach basic explanations of nutrients and how they relate to health. • Teach and practice making healthful choices. • Teach and practice safety behaviors.

Sources: Based on *The Complete and Authoritative Guide: Caring for Your Baby and Young Child; Birth to Age 5,* by the American Academy of Pediatrics, 2005, New York: Bantam Books; and *Child Health Nursing; Partnering with Children and Families* (pp. 129–168), by J. Ball and R. Bindler, 2006, Upper Saddle River, NJ: Pearson Prentice Hall.

Figure 2-3 Wellness Planning Chart

Cognitive Development

- Match real fruits and vegetables to colored construction paper to discover a food rainbow. (Art)
- Conduct cooking activities to sample a variety of foods. Sample the same food prepared in different ways: fresh, juiced, sauced. (Science)
- Create a picture list of different foods. Have children mark the foods they like. Identify most and least liked. (Math)

Social–Emotional Development

- Read the book and provide props for children to dramatize the story *The Very Hungry Caterpillar* (E. Carle). (Literacy)
- Ask parents for ideas about field trips to places where food is grown, processed, or sold. (Social Studies)
- Invite families to come to school to talk about foods from their family tradition. (Social Science)

Wellness Concept

Eat a variety of foods every day.

Physical Development

- Play sorting games using small manipulative toys; define variety; sort matching items; then sort to create groups with variety (no matches). (Fine motor; Math)
- Paint a class mural of foods on butcher paper placed on the wall. (Art)
- Hop to music. Stop the music and ask each child, "What is your favorite: fruit, vegetable, dairy, protein?" (Health and well-being)

Language Development

- Provide a fresh fruit, vegetable, or grain. Ask small groups of children to talk about the food and make a list of different words to describe that food. (Literacy)
- Have children interview their families to learn about each person's favorite foods. (Social Science)
- Create a classroom chart of all the different foods the children eat for a week. (Social Science)

learning specific information rather than developing general capacities for learning. In addition, content information is reinforced when activities and lessons use various developmental approaches to exploration and discovery. Teachers, such as those in our opening scenario, recognize this relationship when they create daily and weekly activity plans. Greg knows that children in his kindergarten class are interested in food. He proposes that discussing the number of servings of food needed from each food group to meet nutrient requirements will also be a good way to practice addition.

Special attention is needed to bridge the transition of intentional teaching from the developmental domain approach in prekindergarten education to the curriculum content areas focus in elementary education. To address this, the NAEYC and the NAECS/SDE (2002) have developed a position statement on early learning standards. The statement underscores the need for prekindergarten and K–3 teachers and curriculum specialists to plan around the common early learning curriculum areas as well as the traditional developmental domains to ensure that children are supported to gain the skills they need to easily transition into kindergarten.

Approaches to Learning

Children each have their own way of learning. Some are visual learners, some are auditory learners, and some learn using a combination of skills and abilities to absorb information. Understanding the learning styles of each child in the class and helping them develop the skills they need to successfully navigate various learning settings are important ways teachers support individual learners. This involves fostering positive approaches to learning, including attributes such as:

- Motivation and curiosity.
- A sense of exploration and discovery.
- Persistence.
- The ability to use new information and concepts in new settings.

Many aspects of developmentally appropriate early education support children's engagement in the learning process. Activities that spark children's interest, invite them into interaction with materials, and allow them to process ideas and concepts at their own pace reinforce positive perceptions about learning. For example, a sensory table full of ice chunks of differing shapes and sizes, measuring spoons and cups, and paints of different colors is an invitation to exploration and discovery. Such experiences build children's ability to focus and extend their attention spans, naturally igniting their curiosity. These types of learning events are crucial to developing positive approaches to learning.

hands-on and experiential using sensory capabilities to inspect, explore, and learn

Hands-On and Experiential Learning

Young children learn best when activities and experiences are hands-on and experiential, meaning the child is able to use all of his or her sensory capabilities and innovative ideas to inspect, touch, manipulate, taste, smell, shake, weigh, and poke. Hands-on activities allow the child to experience all manner of lessons from both the materials being used as well as instructions about how to use them. Showing children a picture of vegetable soup and telling them that this is healthful food is one approach to teaching. But this approach misses too many learning opportunities and would not be considered appropriate in the early childhood setting. A cooking activity that introduces soup as healthful food is an appropriate approach. It provides information about washing, peeling, cutting, measuring, and mixing as well as building self-help skills that can be used in other settings. The sensory experience of smelling the vegetables reinforces the attractiveness and desirability of vegetables as healthful food. The challenge of transforming vegetables into a pleasing soup adds interest to the experience, further reinforcing the

A hands-on cooking activity is an important way for children to learn about healthful food.

lesson. In the opening case scenario, Marty knows that her preschool children will learn best about the science of cooking through hands-on experiences with food. Hands-on and experiential activities are more effective than passive styles of teaching because they allow children to access more details and understand more about the nature of the materials being explored.

Hands-on and experiential activities should comprise the majority of experiences in the early childhood classroom. Such activities provide flexibility because they allow children to approach the experience from their individual age and stage of development. This frees the teacher to observe the child at play and to ask open-ended questions to reinforce health and wellness concepts, such as "I see you are playing dentist office. What kinds of things have you been telling the children about keeping their teeth healthy?" These activities offer opportunity to provide guidance about safety features, saying for example, "I see you know how to steer your tricycle away from the other children. That is a safe way to ride." Hands-on and experiential learning activities increase the pace and quantity of learning.

Intentional and Incidental Learning Approaches

Children learn from every observation, interaction, and experience of every minute of the day. There is no time during the class day when children are not learning! This means the teacher has an important responsibility to offer intentionally planned activities and lessons and to be prepared to guide children when unplanned learning, or incidental learning, opportunities occur. Intentional activities and lessons are purposeful. They are crafted to address specific learning outcomes, and the success of the experience is evaluated. Incidental learning opportunities are more accidental or emergent. They occur when teachers take advantage of situations that occur during the course of the day to teach a particular concept. For example, a planned wellness activity might teach children how to cover their coughs or how to wash their hands. An incidental learning situation might include noticing a child watching the birds at the birdfeeder outside the window and taking advantage of the moment to talk about the foods that birds eat to keep healthy. A balance of planned activities and opportunities for unstructured play where incidental learning opportunities can emerge is important in the daily schedule.

Planned learning provides structure to the teaching of wellness concepts. Some preschool, kindergarten, and elementary programs implement prepared curriculum approaches, whereas others use a self-designed or program-designed approach. Curriculum resources typically support teachers with activity outlines and guides that teachers can adapt for use with their class groups. Purposeful planning ensures that important wellness learning goals are addressed.

Incidental learning allows teachers to follow the interests of individuals or groups of children, taking advantage of learning opportunities that occur in the natural process of the day. Teachers are able to capture the opportunity provided by special moments when the child's curiosity has been aroused and attention is focused on the event, both of which are key elements to learning. Incidental learning situations offer elements of surprise, or opportunities for exploration and discovery that were unanticipated. In the opening case scenario, Greg needs to be prepared to continue the exploration of food energy whenever an incidental opportunity presents. On the playground he might ask a child who has been running with a kite to estimate how much food energy she has used. This question takes advantage of an incidental learning moment, even though the teacher and child may agree to research the answer later in the day during study time. To take full advantage of incidental learning situations, teachers need to be prepared to teach spontaneously and with purpose when learning possibilities emerge.

PLANNING WITH PURPOSE

Teaching is an interactive process that requires purposeful and intentional planning, making it more than a gathering of interesting activities that children enjoy. Informed decisions must be made about how to assemble the environment and how to present activities to

MyEducationLab

Go to the Assignments and Activities section of Topic 13: Wellness Curriculum in the MyEducationLab for your course and complete the activity entitled *Teaching Children Health Lessons.* What different hands-on and experiential learning approaches does this teacher use to teach about oral health?

incidental learning unplanned, accidental, and emergent learning opportunities

What if. . .

the parent of a new child in your class approached you with concern, saying that she noticed that all the children are doing is playing and wondering when you are going to begin teaching? How would you respond?

optimize learning. Purposeful and intentional teaching means teaching with a particular reason and goal in mind. It is this purposeful approach that characterizes high-quality teaching and that is associated with greater academic gains among young children when they enter kindergarten (Howes et al., 2008). In order for teachers to plan purposeful and intentional wellness activities, attention must be given to the basic elements of early education, as discussed next.

Developmentally Appropriate Practice

The purposeful teaching plan must fit children's developmental readiness; that is, it must be developmentally appropriate. Children are most able to learn when the experiences are appropriate for their age, stage of development, and individual maturity level (Piaget, 1929; NAEYC, 2009). Teaching using developmentally appropriate practices matches tasks with the children's level of understanding and skill in order to appropriately scaffold the learning experience. A specific style of learning occurs in each age group or developmental period.

Babies experience their first wellness lessons through a safe and appropriate environment.

Infants

Babies learn foremost through sensory exploration and through movement. Piaget (1929) calls this the *sensorimotor period*. Touching toys, bringing a toy to the mouth and exploring its sensations, and moving arms, legs, hands, head, and torso are a baby's learning experiences. Increasing coordination and motor skill development such as rolling over, crawling and walking, and recognition of an object's permanence (the continued existence of an object even though it is out of sight) are examples of the ways learning is demonstrated. Teaching infants wellness concepts involves:

- Providing safe and appropriate opportunities for babies to freely explore using their sensory and motor skills, such as placing toys in a variety of shapes and textures within reach of the infant's hands and feet.
- Introducing healthful routines, including washing the baby's hands before eating and after diapering.
- Modeling safe interactions, such as guiding the baby to touch another child with gentle motions.

Toddlers and Preschoolers

Children in the 2- to 5-year-old age range tend to use their intuitive curiosity as the motivation and process for learning. While continuing to use their sensory and motor capabilities, these children explore the environment without preconceived notions. They manipulate toys, explore their uses, and begin to organize newly discovered information. For example, a toddler may attempt to sit on a doll house–sized chair, showing awareness of the purpose of the toy, but not yet recognizing the disparity of her size compared to the size of the toy chair. A preschooler may use a block at one moment as part of a road for a toy truck or as a telephone in another play setting. Through play and exploration, children in this group begin to organize their understanding through the use of increasingly complex spoken language and by using symbols to represent ideas, such as drawing pictures of their family or writing their name. Piaget (1929) called this the *preoperational period* in recognition of the child's need to experience the environment in order to begin the process of understanding it. For these children learning relies on the opportunity to experience a wide range of materials and participate in activities. Wellness activities for toddlers and preschoolers include:

- Providing ample opportunity for children to explore their ideas by manipulating materials such as plastic food and utensils and dramatizing wellness scenarios in dramatic play settings such as getting a shot or receiving a bandage "to stop the blood from the accident".
- Offering planned activities that guide children to learn nutrition, health, and safety rules, such as washing hands before eating or sitting down to eat to avoid choking.

- Guiding children by offering language that supports understanding of wellness concepts: "Closing the gate keeps everyone safe" and "Covering your mouth when you cough keeps your friends and teachers healthy."

Early Elementary-Age Children

Children ages 5 to 8 learn best when they can explore ideas in real and tangible ways. Providing actual experiences helps this age group to grasp the facts of an idea. For example, using blocks to explore the math concepts of addition and subtraction helps to ground the concept of quantity in real terms. Collecting the classroom's paper garbage for a week helps children to visualize how much paper is used and clarifies the importance of recycling much more than simply talking about recycling. Planned wellness activities that are rich with hands-on opportunities are important for teaching this group, which Piaget (1929) termed the *concrete operations period*. Wellness activities for elementary school children include:

- Offering individualized activities, such as having children keep a diary of all the foods they have eaten for the day.
- Guiding small group activities, such as using a safety checklist to identify any potential dangers in the classroom.
- Identifying healthful alternatives to less healthful activities, such as snacking on apples instead of potato chips.

Because learning emerges in different ways for different age groups, teachers must establish approaches to teaching about wellness that are not just a simplified activities created "backwards" from curriculum used with older age groups, but activities that are purposeful and appropriate. Figure 2-4 provides an example of a wellness curriculum topic addressing

Figure 2-4 Planning a Wellness Curriculum Topic to Fit Children's Developmental Capabilities

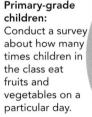

Toddlers: Read books about healthful fruits and vegetables.

Primary-grade children: Conduct a survey about how many times children in the class eat fruits and vegetables on a particular day.

Preschool children: Sort fruits and vegetables by attributes such as color or shape, what grows on a tree, or what grows in the soil.

Kindergarten children: Learn about the ways different families prepare fruits and vegetables.

healthy fruits and vegetables designed to fit children's developmental abilities. The wellness curriculum, or activity plan, should take into account the children's age-related learning characteristics and stage of development. Each group is capable of learning about fruits and vegetables according to their developmental readiness.

Teachers constantly observe how children participate in and respond to the wellness lessons they provide. Adjustments can be made if children are struggling to understand a concept or if they are not interested or engaging in the activity. Observation and evaluation also guide teachers to follow up on activities that are especially enjoyed by children, allowing children's interests and ideas to extend the lesson. Figure 2-5 lists essential elements to consider when teaching wellness concepts to young children.

Process-Oriented Activities

Developmentally appropriate activities in the early childhood setting include process-oriented activities. Process-oriented activities engage children in the manipulation and enjoyment of using and creatively exploring materials. They do not have specifically planned results, but focus on process rather than product. This approach invites children to be self-directed as they create their own plan for interacting with the materials. It fosters curiosity and self-discovery. Process-orientated activities allow children to participate without the stress of achieving a preconceived product. Teaching wellness using the process-oriented approach can be accomplished in many ways. For example, Jenna, a toddler teacher, equips the play house with appropriate wellness props such as pretend soap and towels and play foods to introduce the wellness concepts of hand washing and eating wholesome foods. Wilson offers bike helmets and knee pads in his dramatic play setting for the preschool class, allowing children to

What if. . .

you were planning a wellness lesson to teach during the second week of your kindergarten class? What topic would you select for your first wellness lesson? How would you teach the lesson to fit the developmental capabilities of your group?

process-oriented activities
learning activities that focus on process rather than product

Figure 2-5 **Essential Elements in Teaching Wellness**

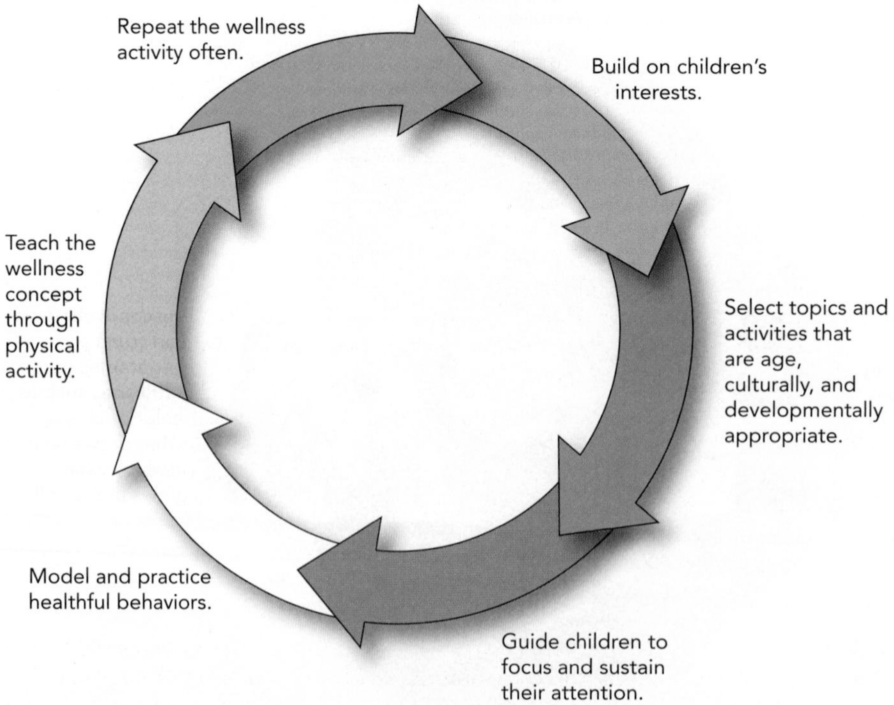

Repeat the wellness activity often.

Build on children's interests.

Teach the wellness concept through physical activity.

Select topics and activities that are age, culturally, and developmentally appropriate.

Model and practice healthful behaviors.

Guide children to focus and sustain their attention.

Sources: *Perspectives: Rich Experiences, Physical Activity Creates Healthy Brains,* by the National Scientific Council on the Developing Child, 2006, retrieved September 2, 2009, from http://www.developingchild.net/pubs/persp/pdf/Physical_Activity_Create_Healthy_Brains.pdf; and *Early Brain Development and Learning,* by K. A. Wesson, 2003, retrieved September 3, 2009, from http://www.sciencemaster.com/columns/wesson/wesson_early_01.php.

explore sporting equipment designed to increase safety. Other ideas include adding figures to the block corner that depict police officers, firefighters, or medical personnel. These approaches involve children in nutrition, health, and safety play that is process oriented.

Everyday Routines

Healthful behaviors are best taught through familiar everyday activities. Teaching wellness through familiar everyday routines allows children to practice a positive behavior, or habit, naturally establishing it as a part of the child's daily rhythm. For example, washing hands before eating is a natural part of the daily routine that is familiar in early childhood settings. Once children have been oriented to this routine, they participate willingly because it is a predictable step before meals. As children mature, teachers reinforce the importance of washing hands by showing children how to thoroughly clean hands to get rid of germs. Teachers plan activities so children learn about how germs that cause illness get on their hands and into their mouths. Older children may study germs under a microscope and learn more about the illnesses that are caused by different germs. Each is a step in establishing the healthful behavior of hand washing.

Child-Selected and Teacher-Directed Activities

Learning in the early childhood setting is organized around child-selected activities, those in which children are active participants in the learning environment, and teacher-directed activities, where children are passive participants. Child-selected play offers children the freedom to choose the activities that are of greatest interest to them and to play at that activity until they are ready to make a change. Child-selected play is self-directed. It inspires children to follow their interests when selecting a play activity and encourages self-management in that play setting. It also promotes individual motivation and persistence with interests and ideas. Child-selected play, often called free playtime or self-selected playtime, typically comprises a large portion of the daily schedule of activities in the early childhood classroom.

Teacher-directed activities are structured and aim to teach a specific skill or involve children in a prescribed process. Teacher-directed activities focus children's attention on important aspects of the activity and lead children through the steps to complete the activity. They teach the skills of listening, responding, and following directions. Teacher-directed activities ensure that meaningful concepts are presented and practiced by all children. Balancing child-selected and teacher-directed activities ensures that children experience a variety of opportunities for learning.

Teaching wellness concepts is managed differently in each approach. During child-selected play, wellness activities are offered as part of the various options. For example, placing a large plastic model of teeth beside a large toothbrush invites children to "practice" brushing teeth. Similarly, placing dental care props in the dramatic play area or putting books on dental care in the book corner invites children to explore the wellness concept of dental health. Teacher-directed wellness activities include inviting a dentist to visit the group and reading a story or leading a song about brushing teeth. Each approach provides valuable information about dental care.

child-selected activities
activities in which children actively develop the course of play

teacher-directed activities
activities in which children are guided by the teacher through each step of the learning process

Project Learning

Project learning refers to activities that grow and evolve across a period of time, as opposed to activities that start and finish within the class time. Project learning sets the stage for children to explore wellness concepts in a step-by-step fashion until the children determine that the topic has been exhausted. A project approach is especially fitting for teaching wellness among older preschoolers and primary-grade children. It allows children to become invested in a topic, supports children's participation in their own learning, and teaches persistence.

MyEducationLab

Go to the Assignments and Activities section of Topic 3: Menu Planning in the MyEducationLab for your course and complete the activity entitled *Introducing Children to New Foods*. What strategies viewed in this video could you expand to create a project learning approach?

Project topics may be proposed by the teacher or may come about from ideas offered by the children. They usually address a particular topic of study. Projects may be process oriented (such as collecting leaves and identifying them) or they may have a specific goal or outcome (such as creating a class collage that includes 100 pressed leaves). Often the direction of the project may emerge and evolve as children collaborate around an idea or common vision.

A first-grade classroom in Kansas put project learning into practice by taking on the project of arranging their classroom environment. The process involved multiple opportunities for discussion, decision making, and collaboration about the floor plan, furnishings, and safety. In this project children learned about safety features by inviting the fire marshal to talk about the importance of arranging furniture to keep pathways open so children can easily move to the exits in case of an emergency. The children also learned how to select materials that do not contain toxic products and those that were constructed in a healthful and sustainable manner. While children were engaged in considering decision-making details, the teacher provided developmentally appropriate support as needed. As well as establishing a close-knit community of learners, the children who were engaged in the Kansas project rated higher in reading achievement when compared to a control group of children who were not involved in project learning (Mester, 2008). The project approach motivates children's interest and encourages children to become self-directed in the learning setting.

In the opening case scenario, Armetha has a plan for a project through which her young elementary-aged children will learn about locally grown foods. To put her plan into action, she will need to guide children through the beginning steps to support them as they take on the project of planning their approach to researching and contacting local growers. Marty will guide her preschool class through the project of preparing a healthful afternoon snack. She will provide support, including helping children to take photographs during each step of the project and serving as scribe to record information the children provide as they work through the steps:

On Day 1 they:

- Negotiate menu planning (fresh fruit and trail mix in a bowl).
- Draft a shopping list of supplies (dry cereal, blueberries, bananas).

On Day 2 they:

- Create a picture outline of directions for preparing the snack (picture drawing of ½ cup cereal, 1 spoonful of blueberries, and ¼ banana).

On Day 3 they:

- Invite the program cook, or a dietitian to talk about healthful food preparation rules: Wash hands before working with food; keep hands away from mouth.
- Draw pictures as reminders of the rules.
- Practice washing their hands.

On Day 4 they:

- Prepare their own snack portions (in their own bowls).
- Eat the snack together and talk about the project and what they learned.

On Day 5 they:

- Assemble the photographs of their snack-making project, arranging them to show the steps of their project.
- Create and display a poster showing their work.
- Meet together to review their poster and talk about the project: what they learned, what they should do next!

All through the project period, the children are thinking about their plans, new ideas are emerging, and the wellness goal is being reinforced.

Teaching across Centers and Learning Areas

Planning wellness activities across centers and learning areas is an important way to ensure that the concepts are practiced and reinforced. Purposeful teaching recognizes that learning does not happen in specific or confined "silos" of activity centers or learning areas (Schickedanz, 2008). Each area offers opportunities for multiple kinds of learning, and learning in one area influences learning in all other areas. For example, in the sensory center, children play at a table filled with water and measuring containers. They gain social skills as they share the space, communication skills as they negotiate division of materials, cognitive awareness as they pour and measure quantities, and physical dexterity as they manipulate the movement of the water.

During project learning, new ideas emerge and wellness goals are reinforced.

Infusing wellness topics across centers reinforces the importance of the wellness topic and fosters the opportunity for children to access the lesson through a different mode, or type, of learning. When teaching safety concepts, appropriate first aid props, such as plastic gloves, bandages, and gauze rolls, can be added to the dramatic play center, while toy people figures such as police officers and firefighters are provided near the trucks, and puzzles with safety themes are displayed at a table. Teaching topics across centers also ensures that all children come into contact with the wellness message. Some children may have a preference for one kind of play, such as blocks or dramatic play and might miss the learning opportunity if the wellness topic is only offered in one area. Planning wellness activities across the centers and learning areas ensures that the concepts are reinforced.

One first-grade teacher uses a classroom newspaper to teach across the centers and learning areas (Sahn & Reichel, 2008). Her project approach guides children to explore wellness topics throughout the day while also practicing social skills, writing, and creative expression. She establishes three topic columns, each with a special focus for investigation and reporting. Children choose a column to focus on for the week. They gather information through various modes of investigation and record their findings in a notebook. On Friday each child creates a story or picture to add to a large template newspaper that is posted for everyone to read. Younger children can be engaged in a similar activity by creating pictures to post on a classroom nutrition, health, and safety wellness bulletin board (see an example in Figure 2-6). This approach allows children to participate according to their individual skill levels (Sahn & Reichel, 2008).

Another approach is to match wellness topics and use them as the theme for a period of time. The *Nutrition Note* outlines an example of nutrition, physical activity, and motor skills topics that can be partnered in the early childhood curriculum and at home to focus on topics that are significant in improving children's well-being (Sorte & Daeschel, 2006). Examples of activities are presented that can be expanded to fit the various classroom centers and learning areas. Sharing the wellness topics with families encourages a partnership and extends the messages of the curriculum plan to the home environment.

Figure 2-6 A Classroom Display of Nutrition, Health, and Safety Pictures Creates a Wellness Newsletter for Everyone to Enjoy

Nutrition Note

Partner Wellness Topics across the Curriculum

Week	Nutrition Topics — plus —	Physical Activity Topics — plus —	Motor Skills Topics
1	Explore low-fat dairy products.	Study how physical activity helps the body to grow.	Play games that include leaping, jumping, and hopping.
	IDEAS: Conduct taste tests of low-fat milks and cheeses.	Read books about active play. Have children brainstorm a list of the kinds of active play they like. Create a poster.	Place cardboard letters on the ground; have children move to the letters of their name.
2	Study fruits and vegetables.	Arrange spaces for active play both indoors and outdoors.	Practice throwing skills: tossing, throwing, and catching.
	IDEAS: Sort fruits by sizes (lime, lemon, orange, grapefruit, melon). Taste each; describe the flavors.	Have children sort pictures of ways to be active into indoor or outdoor or both settings.	Roll socks into balls; toss at various tubs and targets.
3	Talk about eating breakfast every day.	Study different ways to play outdoors every day.	Play games that involve walking, running, galloping, and skipping.
	IDEAS: Provide breakfast-making prop containers in dramatic play: pancake mix, cereals, juice, milk, fruit.	Have small groups of children plan an outdoor game using no toys or equipment and then teach the game to others.	Take a neighborhood "I Spy" walk: Prepare a list of things to look for and check them off when children see them. Move around a baseball diamond: walk to first base, run to second, skip to third, and gallop home.

What if. . .

you were planning to teach a wellness topic in different centers in your preschool classroom? What topic would you choose? How would you teach the topic in different centers or learning areas in your classroom?

Evidenced-Based Practices

Wellness concepts and activity plans should be founded on the best information available about children's nutrition, health, and safety. This means that the information guiding the wellness curriculum should be founded on research and promoted by reputable agencies and groups, such as the National Institutes of Health, Office of the Surgeon General, American Dietetic Association, American Academy of Pediatrics, and Consumer Product Safety Commission. It is important for teachers to stay informed about the practices that are supported by research and professional consensus and to avoid following approaches that are heavily based in opinion and personal preference.

Week	Nutrition Topics — *plus* —	Physical Activity Topics — *plus* —	Motor Skills Topics
4	Learn about basic whole foods (not processed foods).	Explore the toys and equipment needed for different kinds of sports and active play.	Enjoy dancing to music and learning about stretching activities.
	IDEAS: Make a granola mix of whole foods for a snack.	Create "stations" in the outdoor play area with different games to try. Stamp children's hands at each station or provide a "passport" to stamp to encourage children to try each stop.	Provide streamers and scarves; have children bring favorite music. Invite a children's yoga instructor to demonstrate stretching moves.
5	Learn about the importance of eating a variety of foods.	Learn how to play different outdoor games.	Practice coordination skills like balancing.
	IDEAS: Select a food to taste for each color of the rainbow.	Provide different sports equipment for children to try on.	Provide a balance beam; try walking and balancing with a beanbag on head or while placing hands on hips.
6	Study how different families eat meals together.	Learn how children play actively in other countries and cultures.	Invent activity challenges.
	IDEAS: Invite children to take pictures of their family at mealtime for a class poster.	Check out books of games played by children of the world to try, such as *Kids Around the World Play! The Best Fun and Games from Many Lands*, by A. N. Braman (New York: Wiley, 2002).	Create an obstacle course that requires a mix of movements: jumping, crawling, climbing.

Source: Based on "Health in Action: A Program Approach to Fighting Obesity in Young Children," by J. M. Sorte and I. Daeschel, 2006, *Young Children*, 61(3), pp 40–48.

Planning wellness goals for nutrition is a good example. Nearly everyone has an opinion about food and what constitutes a healthful diet. Many cultural values are related to food with respect to what is eaten and how it is prepared. Teachers may have children in the class who do not eat beef or pork. Some may eat vegetarian, vegan, or organic diets or diets that use no processed sugar. Teachers' nutrition messages must address core informational and behavioral practices that are commonly agreed on to advance health and well-being. Core practices can often bridge differing points of view. For example, the wellness concept of "Food should be clean and carefully prepared" is a core practice that everyone would value. Established health and nutrition practices recognize that germs and potential toxins can be found on unwashed fruits and vegetables. Founding the nutrition wellness concepts on evidence-based goals that have been identified by health professionals gives the teacher confidence that the nutrition message is credible.

Culturally Relevant Approaches

To be most effective, wellness activities should be compatible with the child's family and cultural experiences. Children learn best when the early childhood activities and lessons are valued and relevant to their home culture. The NAEYC (2005) reports that "Continuity between home and early childhood settings supports children's social, emotional, cognitive and language development" (p. 1).

Knowledge of the nutrition, health, and safety concerns and perspectives held by families guides teachers to create an appropriate wellness program. For example, learning to take an appropriate serving size during family-style meal service at preschool is one way of practicing healthful eating behaviors. However, a child might be confused by this lesson if their practice at home is for the adult to serve the child. Some families believe that children should eat all that has been served, whereas the classroom approach may be to encourage but never force children to eat. Similarly, thinking about what causes disease or how to manage illness can vary greatly. Families are an excellent source of information about practices at home and cultural restrictions on foods that can be avoided when planning cooking and tasting activities. Engaging in these conversations helps teachers and families find ways to develop a wellness program that is compatible for both home and school.

Children who are English language learners often benefit from learning new concepts in their home language before or alongside learning them in English. The familiarity of the home language adds credibility to the message and ensures that children fully understand complex issues. This is important when teaching safety skills, such as staying away from poisonous products, using playground equipment safely, or not playing near traffic. Teachers need the support of families and language resource personnel to ensure that each child in the class has access to important wellness information in their home language.

Culturally relevant teaching is demonstrated by creating a classroom environment that reflects the backgrounds and traditions of all children in the class (NAEYC, 2005). This includes selecting toys, books, and other learning props that reflect children's home lives and using examples that demonstrate the breadth of cultural perspectives. To promote learning about healthful nutrition, food examples that represent the traditions of the full class group should be available. Inviting into the classroom the community workers in health and safety professions who reflect the diverse makeup of the class is another way of teaching about the many contributions of cultural diversity.

What if. . .

you wanted to learn more about the ways families of the children in your class teach about wellness? How would you begin the conversation?

DESIGNING WELLNESS ACTIVITIES

An exciting aspect of childhood is that *all* experiences are educational. Activities and events at home, in early childhood education settings, and in school all contribute to children's understanding of the world (American Academy of Pediatrics, Committee on Early Childhood, Adoption, and Dependent Care, 2005). In addition, young children are capable of learning healthful behaviors and being participants in promoting their own wellness. Helping children learn about health topics builds knowledge, and participating in health practices builds good habits. These are the desirable and measurable outcomes of the wellness curriculum. An effective wellness program is designed to capture the possibilities of this important period of learning. It is accomplished through an organized approach to teaching about health and well-being. It relies on establishing a curriculum that forwards wellness concepts through appropriate and intentionally designed activities.

Building a Wellness Curriculum

National health and safety goals for children pre-K–12 have been established by the American Association for Health Education to guide the development of a comprehensive program of wellness activities. Figure 2-7 describes the health education goals for children in prekindergarten through grade 5 and gives examples of activities that promote each goal.

The national health and safety goals are promoted in the early childhood setting through a planned wellness curriculum, ensuring that the messages are coordinated and

Figure 2-7 National Health Education Standards and Activity Examples for Pre-K through Grade 2 and Grades 3 through 5

1. Students will comprehend concepts related to health promotion and disease prevention to enhance health.	
Pre-K–2: Children will describe ways to prevent communicable diseases by conducting a puppet show about hand washing.	**Grades 3–5:** Students will identify examples of emotional, intellectual, physical, and social health by creating a poster that gives one example of each.

2. Students will analyze the influence of family, peers, culture, media, technology, and other factors on health behaviors.	
Pre-K–2: Children will identify how peers can influence healthy and unhealthy behaviors by drawing pictures of children showing other children how to be healthy and not healthy.	**Grades 3–5:** Students will describe how the school and community can support personal health practices and behaviors by conducting interviews and creating a health newsletter.

3. Students will demonstrate the ability to access valid information and products and services to enhance health.	
Pre-K–2: Children will identify professionals who can help promote health by sorting picture cards of community health providers (nurse, doctor, dentist) and general community workers (builder, waitress, businessperson).	**Grades 3–5:** Students will locate resources from home, school, and community that provide valid health information by creating a community health resources list researched through Internet and phone book reviews.

4. Students will demonstrate the ability to use interpersonal communication skills to enhance health and avoid or reduce health risks.	
Pre-K–2: Children will demonstrate healthy ways to express needs, wants, and feelings through role-playing activities.	**Grades 3–5:** Students will demonstrate refusal skills to avoid or reduce health risks through skits focused on saying no to drugs and refusing offers to smoke.

5. Students will demonstrate the ability to use decision-making skills to enhance health.	
Pre-K–2: Children will identify situations when a health-related decision is needed by jumping up when a health decision is needed (I am hurt, hungry, sleepy) and sitting down when the decision is not health related (I want to read a story, watch TV, or wear my new shoes).	**Grades 3–5:** Students will analyze when assistance is needed when making a health-related decision.

6. Students will demonstrate the ability to use goal-setting skills to enhance health.	
Pre-K–2: Children will assess personal health practices by placing a mark beside pictures that depict healthful behaviors (brushing teeth, eating fruits and vegetables, playing outside, sleeping).	**Grades 3–5:** Students will set a personal health goal, such as eat healthy snacks, and track progress toward its achievement with a daily journal.

7. Students will demonstrate the ability to practice health-enhancing behaviors and avoid or reduce health risks.	
Pre-K–2: Children will demonstrate behaviors that avoid or reduce health risks, such as practicing safety on the playground or safe management of toys and materials, after these skills have been taught.	**Grades 3–5:** Students will explain the importance of assuming responsibility for personal health behaviors by writing and presenting a short report addressing "How I Can Keep Myself Healthy."

8. Students will demonstrate the ability to advocate for personal, family, and community health.	
Pre-K–2: Children will make requests to promote personal health by writing their family a letter asking for their assistance to help them to improve their family's health by eating well, staying away from tobacco or drugs, or playing actively.	**Grades 3–5:** Students will encourage others to make positive health choices by creating posters for the school encouraging others to eat well, not to smoke or take drugs, and to play actively.

Source: Reprinted with permission from the American Cancer Society. *National Health Education Standards: Achieving Excellence, Second Edition.* Atlanta, GA: American Cancer Society; 2007, www.cancer.org/bookstore.

staged appropriately for each age group and that topics are covered comprehensively rather than randomly. A wellness curriculum includes selected concepts and is put into action through activities that address related topics. For example:

- Wellness concepts are statements or messages that convey an important idea or message about healthful nutrition, health practices, and ways to increase safety.
- Wellness topics are themes, subjects, or issues that teach a wellness concept through an activity or lesson approach.

Examples of wellness concepts and topics are presented in Figure 2-8.

Figure 2-8 Sample Wellness Concepts and Topics

Nutrition Concepts	Nutrition Topics	Health Concepts
• Food is important to grow strong and be healthy.	• Nutrients provided by different foods • Foods that are OK all the time; foods that are OK some of the time • Healthy snacks	• Germs can make you sick.
• Eat a variety of foods every day.	• Different kinds of food groups: fruits, vegetables, grains, proteins, dairy • The rainbow of food colors • Menu planning	• Wash hands to get rid of germs.
• Food should be clean and carefully prepared.	• Wash fruit before eating • Only eat food provided by your teacher or safe adult • How to keep food clean, safe	• Parents, doctors, and dentists can help if you get sick.
• It is important to drink water.	• Where water comes from • When it is important to drink water • Water is important to plants and animals	• It is important to eat, play, and rest to keep healthy.

What if. . .

you are in the process of setting up an activity when you notice a statement on the product label that says "Keep refrigerated"? You realize the product has been sitting out overnight but the class is about to start. What would you do?

Wellness concepts are identified from familiar nutrition, health, and safety messages as well as issues that have particular importance in the community. For example, avoiding germs is an important wellness concept for all children. Staying away from the ocean is an especially important safety concept for children who live along the coast, whereas learning to ride the subway safely is important for children who live in the city. The wellness curriculum should be planned to address both general and location-specific aspects of children's lives.

Wellness concepts are broad statements that are relevant for all children, whereas wellness topics and activities are selected for their appropriateness for the particular age group. The wellness concept "Washing hands is important to wash away germs" is a relevant message for everyone, but is taught using topics and activities that fit the children's age and maturity. For example:

- Infants begin to learn this concept when the teacher washes a child's hands after diapering and before eating. (*Wellness topic:* when to wash hands)
- Toddlers practice this message while washing hands as they sing a favorite song. (*Wellness topic:* how to wash hands)
- Preschoolers explore the idea of germs sticking to hands by painting their hands and then experiencing how much vigorous washing is needed to remove the paint. (*Wellness topic:* challenges in washing germs away)
- School-age children study germs to learn about illnesses that are caused by germs, how children come in contact with germs, and where germs can hide on the hands. (*Wellness topic:* how germs contribute to illness)

The wellness curriculum should outline the wellness concepts that will be taught during the year, including when the concept will be introduced, practiced, and reinforced.

Planning for Safety

All aspects of the wellness curriculum must be safe. It is the teacher's responsibility to review the details of each activity and lesson to ensure that it is safe and appropriate for the children in the class group. This involves making safe selections about what to teach and

Health Topics	Safety Concepts	Safety Topics
• Where germs come from • Where germs hide • Cover your cough	• **Stay away from dangers: fire, traffic, strangers, poison.**	• Fire and evacuation drills • Stranger danger • Poisons
• How to wash hands • When to wash hands	• **Follow the rules to keep safe.**	• Classroom safety • Playground safety • Pedestrian safety • Bus safety
• Visit to the doctor • How to brush teeth • What to do if you get sick	• **Parents and teachers help keep children safe.**	• Community safety workers • Following directions • Asking adults for help • Telling about abuse
• Eat healthful food • Play and be active • When to rest	• **Care for one another.**	• Share and take turns • Helping others • Use words; no hurting • Make friends

how to teach it and supervising children for safety at all times. The *Safety Segment* offers a guide for reviewing activities for safety.

Cooking activities are popular for forwarding nutrition concepts in the early childhood setting. Several approaches improve safety when presenting these activities:

- Maintain a list of recipes that are appropriate for use in class groups where children have milk, egg, nut, or wheat allergies. Avoid known food allergies when conducting food tasting and cooking activities.
- Predict the safest way for children to participate in cooking activities. Identify child-directed activities such as shaking cream to make butter, and recognize the activities that need teacher assistance, such as cutting apples for applesauce. Invite parent volunteers as needed to help conduct cooking activities.
- Purchase supplies from approved food vendors.
- Assemble the environment to avoid risks. As needed, limit the number of spaces for children to participate. This assists with supervision. Ensure that children wash their hands before participating. Allow each child to prepare his or her own food, especially if the food is not to be cooked. Serve the food soon after preparation.

Making purposeful judgments about the safety of each activity in the wellness program is the teacher's responsibility.

Paint takes the place of germs in this wellness experiment about how to wash away germs.

Promoting Physical Activity

Current lifestyles are not providing the healthful levels of activity that children once enjoyed (Hassink, 2006). Even very young children are spending more time than ever before participating in sedentary activities such as playing computer games and watching television. In the classroom, children spend large amounts of time engaged in desk, table, or sedentary floor activities. Physical activity patterns are established during the early childhood years and tend to persist into adult life (Goodway & Robinson, 2006). For this reason, it is critical that early

Safety Segment

Ensure Safety in All Curriculum Activities

Review and consider the credibility of the safety curriculum resource.

- Is the source a reputable group?
- Is the source selling something?

Consider the wellness message being promoted.

- Is the message appropriate for the class?
- Can the message be adapted to fit the age and developmental maturity of the children?

Screen each activity for potential dangers.

- Are the materials used safe and appropriate?
- Are there potential dangers about how children will be involved in the activity?

Supervise the activity and protect children from harm.

- Should any aspects be changed or removed?
- Should any adaptations be made to improve safety?

Source: Based on *New State Report Card on Child Care: States Fall Short in Protecting Children's Safety & in Promoting Learning in Child Care*, by the National Association of Child Care Resource & Referral Agencies, 2007, retrieved September 4, 2009, from http://www.naccrra.org/news/press-releases/31.

Figure 2-9 Characteristics of the Preschool Environment That Influence Physical Activity

The National Association for Sport and Physical Education recommends that all preschool-age children (ages 3–5 years) participate in up to 60 minutes of structured activities *and* 60 minutes of unstructured play every day. Most children's settings do not provide this level of active play. Characteristics of children's environments influence the amount of time children spend in moderate and vigorous physical activity. Children are more active in:

- Higher quality programs, such as those that have wellness policies.
- Settings with large playground spaces where children can run and be active.
- Schools with more portable equipment, such as balls and hoops that encourage children to plan and direct their own active play.
- Settings that limit use of electronic media, which contributes to sedentary play rather than active play.

Sources: "Influences of Preschool Policies and Practices on Children's Physical Activity," by M. Dowda, R. R. Pater, S. G. Trost, M. Joao, C. A. Almeida, and J. R. Sirard, 2004, *Journal of Community Health, 29 Active Start: A Statement of Physical Activity Guidelines for Children From Birth to Age 5*, 2nd Edition, by the National Association for Sports and Physical Education, 2002, retrieved September 15, 2009, at: http://www.aahperd.org/naspe/template.cfm?template=ns_active.html.

childhood and school programs integrate physical activity into their wellness goals and daily routines. Physical activity provides many health benefits, including (Hassink, 2006):

- Improved energy level and ability to handle stress.
- Increased self-confidence and self-esteem.
- Opportunities to make new friends.
- Reduced risk of diabetes, heart disease, and high blood pressure.
- Better concentration in school.

Various characteristics of the early childhood environment influence the quantity and quality of time children spend in physically active play as described in Figure 2-9.

Figure 2-10 MyActivity Pyramid for Kids

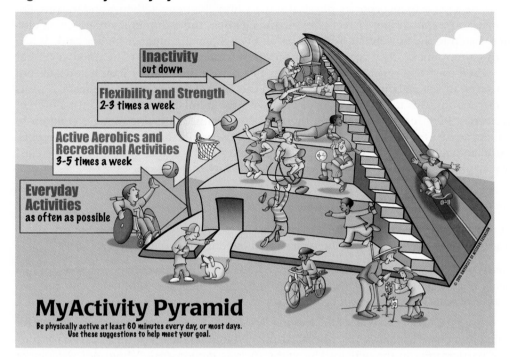

Source: University of Missouri Extension. *MyActivity Pyramid for Kids.* Retrieved November 23, 2009, from http://extension.missouri.edu/publications/DisplayPub.aspx?P=n386.

Young children are typically eager to participate in physical activities that are interesting and appropriately challenging. They enjoy testing their physical skills and discovering their capabilities. To take advantage of this, numerous opportunities must be provided to encourage active play everyday. Teaching games is a good way to introduce children to the enjoyment of physical activity. Games using a brightly colored parachute are universally enjoyed by young children and adults. For example, as the children gather at the edge of the parachute, Andy, the teacher, gives instructions to hold on firmly and listen for directions. Together the children and teachers sweep their arms upward while the parachute fills with air. Then they sit down quickly as they swing their arms down toward the ground, and the parachute gently comes to rest on them. Participating in games like these helps teachers model how to be active and creates an environment that welcomes fun.

Children also need ample opportunity to invent their own active play. Providing movable equipment, such as balls, hoops, and cones, that children can access on their own is a good way to encourage this. The ready presence of such materials inspires children to move about to create their own games and challenges. This naturally results in movement as children toss and chase after the balls or jump from hoop to hoop, or run in and out of a row of plastic cones. Storing this equipment in baskets and buckets provides an additional benefit. The containers help children move the materials from place to place and can be used as props for active play as well. Large climbing and play structures encourage active play, but they are often very expensive and require adequate space for appropriate installation. Providing sufficient movable equipment is the better investment in settings where space and funds are limited.

A planned approach to promoting physical activity ensures that children's needs for movement are being addressed. The *MyActivity Pyramid for Kids,* as shown in Figure 2-10, is a resource for teachers who are establishing wellness programs. It is also a good source of information for families to promote physical activity at home.

General guidelines to consider when developing physical activity programs include the following (Hassink, 2006):

- Recognize that all activities that involve movement are beneficial.
- Provide fun and safe choices for physical activities.
- Support children to feel comfortable. Ensure that children are not teased.

Physical activity often takes place outside or in a gymnasium; however, the classroom can also be a place to incorporate physical activity into children's activities and lessons. For example, to promote number recognition, Julie gathers the group in a circle, telling children to listen to the movement instructions and watch for the number on her card. When she says a movement, they are to repeat the movement as guided by the number on her card. When everyone is ready, Julie holds up a card with the number 7 on it and calls out "Hop seven times!" When she puts the card on the floor everyone stops. Then she repeats the instructions, this time holding up a card with the number 2, and calls out a different movement: "Jump up and crouch on the floor two times." Soon she asks the children to volunteer an idea for movement. The children are active while they learn number concepts. Physical activity can also be incorporated into literacy and science. For example, the class may read about frogs and then explore and practice how frogs move.

Components of Appropriate Activities

Wellness activities need thoughtful and purposeful planning to ensure they are organized and appropriate. Each activity in the plan should include these components:

- *Activity name.*   The name given to the wellness activity helps convey the concept that is being taught. The activity name is used to introduce the lesson and helps cue children about what skills the activity will promote.

- *Activity goal.*   Each activity of the lesson plan should have a specific measurable goal, or learning outcome. The goals describe what the children will learn or be able to do as a result of participating in the activity. Use verbs such as *demonstrate, show, tell, discuss,* or *perform* when writing activity goals. For example, "Children will be able to describe how hand washing takes away germs" or "Children will be able to demonstrate how to cross the street safely." Although most activities foster the development of more than one kind of skill, the unique wellness concept should be clearly identified.

- *Materials list.*   A brief list of materials needed to conduct the wellness activity is important. It helps teachers organize the purchasing of materials and guides assembly and setup. A materials list is also useful when planning adjustments or adaptations for children with special circumstances, such as including adaptive scissors for a child who requires special supports or identifying a variation in a recipe for fruit smoothies for a child who requires a soy-based milk product.

- *Activity plan.*   This component offers a brief but organized summary of what children will do and what the teacher will do when presenting the wellness activity. The plan should describe how the materials will be arranged for children to access on their own or how the teacher will introduce the activity.

- *Adjustments and differentiations.*   Each activity anticipates that children have certain skills or abilities in order to accomplish the identified goal. Special considerations may be needed to plan a successful experience for children who have not yet achieved these skills or for those with advanced skills. Specialized instruction may be needed for children with special developmental needs. The activity plan should describe these accommodations and adjustments.

- *Evaluation.* Successful teaching and learning relies on an assessment of whether the goal of the activity was met, and an evaluation of which aspects worked well and which need to be changed next time. In early childhood settings assessment focuses on observing children when they are participating in the activity, watching what they do and listening for what the children say. These observations cue the teacher to the appropriateness of the activity and provide the feedback needed to understand teaching effectiveness.

A written plan organizes thinking about the purpose for each activity and how the activity contributes to the overall wellness program. Written activity plans are useful when team teaching and help guide volunteers who may assist with setting up the activities and supervising children. Figure 2-11 provides an example of a wellness activity plan.

Figure 2-11 Sample Outline for Wellness Activities

Wellness concept: It is important to drink water.

Activity name: Water Scramble

Learning outcome: Child will recognize when to drink water.

Age group: Preschool and elementary

Goal: Children are able to identify when it is important to drink water.

Materials: Large picture cards showing children engaged in various activities, some that are healthful times to drink water (active play settings such as playing sports, hiking in the sunshine, playing on the playground) and some where drinking water is not as necessary (inactive playtimes such as reading, making a puzzle, building with blocks).

Activity plan: Gather children on the playground or in a large space where children can move freely. Introduce the activity by telling children it is important to drink water after active play or when you are hot, and less important after quiet or inactive play. Guide the children to move to one side of the room if they see a card that shows when it is important to drink water and move to the other side of the room if they see a card showing it is less important to drink water. After children have tried the game once, have one of the children be the leader.

How to add to or adjust the activity: Instead of using pictures, ask the children to call out an activity for the other children to respond to. Guide the children to jump, skip, or walk backward as they move to the side of the room. Adjust the movement direction to fit children's developmental capabilities. If a child moves with a wheelchair, say, "Jump or roll to the wall." Add interesting additions, such as skip and clap, or hop with hands on head.

Did you meet your goal? Can you observe each child responding appropriately to the picture cards? Are children able to identify other times when it is important to drink water?

Written plans also create useful records to support future development of the wellness program. For example, Marty, the preschool teacher from the opening case scenario, may discover that the activity she planned would be more appropriate for Greg's kindergarten children. Because her activity plan is written down, she is able to share it with Greg as a future resource.

IDENTIFYING RESOURCES

Successful teaching depends on the teacher's ability to identify and make good use of supportive resources. Accessing up-to-date resources keeps the wellness curriculum current and relevant to emerging trends. Resources include those that help teachers design wellness activities for all children.

Including All Children: The Individuals with Disabilities Education Act

Many children with developmental challenges participate in today's early childhood classrooms. This has not always been the case. Before the initiation of federal laws ensuring the rights of children with disabilities to a free and appropriate public education, only one in five children with disabilities received early education services. In 1975 Congress enacted the Education for All Handicapped Children Act (Public Law 94-142) enabling young children across the nation to receive early intervention and special education services and to be prepared for further education, employment, and independent living. Since that time the law

What if. . .

you are presenting a wellness activity, but discover that the children want to play with the materials and do not want to proceed through the steps of the activity? What will you do to adapt the lesson?

MyEducationLab

Go to the Assignments and Activities section of Topic 7: Chronic Illness/Special Health Care Needs in the MyEducationLab for your course and complete the activity entitled *Early Intervention*. What benefits do early childhood classrooms offer to children with special developmental needs?

early intervention services
services provided to infants and children, ages birth through 3 years, who have an identified disability, and their families

special education services
services for children with disabilities, ages 3 to 21 years, to support their educational development and preparation for further education, employment, and independent living

individualized family services plan (IFSP)
an educational and family services plan for infants and children, ages birth through 3 years, that describes the child's disability and outlines goals for supporting the child's appropriate development

individualized education program (IEP)
an educational plan drafted by families, special education specialists, and teachers for children ages 3 to 21 to describe the child's disability and outline goals for appropriate education

has been reauthorized, most recently with the Individuals with Disabilities Education Act (IDEA) of 2004. The IDEA has four main objectives (U.S. Department of Education, 2007):

- To ensure a free and appropriate public education for all children with disabilities.
- To protect the rights of children with disabilities.
- To support states to provide special education services.
- To ensure that early intervention programs are effective.

Currently more than 6.5 million children and families receive early intervention and special education services each year (U.S. Department of Education, 2009). The majority of these children participate in classrooms with their typically developing peers.

Early childhood teachers participate with families, physicians, and others in identifying children who may be eligible to receive services through the IDEA. Children with observable developmental delays are referred to the local education agency (LEA), which has the responsibility to provide early intervention and special education services. The LEA conducts assessments to determine the nature of the child's developmental delay and to ascertain if the disability hinders the child's educational progress. Children may be identified for service based on hearing, vision, speech, orthopedic or other health impairments, autism, pervasive developmental delay, or other learning disabilities.

When children are identified for special education services, families, teachers, and special education professionals work together to create an individualized family services plan (IFSP) for infants and children through age 3 or an individualized education program (IEP) for children 3 to 21 years of age. These plans describe the child's disability, including how it affects the child's learning. Goals are listed to support the child's educational progress, and plans are made to select an early childhood placement that offers the least restrictive and most appropriate environment.

The IFSP or IEP is a resource for teachers. It helps teachers identify accommodations that may be needed in the classroom, such as special scissors to support children with fine motor delay, adaptive chairs for children with orthopedic impairments, or open floor plans and furnishing arrangements for children who move with a wheelchair. In some cases children are assigned a special education assistant who supports the child's inclusion in the classroom. Specialized instructional approaches may be also be required to support children's learning, including wellness concepts. Early intervention therapists can offer ideas for teachers about ways to adapt activities to support children's participation and understanding of the wellness message.

Supports for Teachers

Many resources are available to provide ideas about wellness concepts and topics to explore with young children. Each source should be reviewed carefully to ensure that the information is credible and that the message and activities are safe and appropriate for the class group. Some of these resources are discussed next.

Curriculum Books and Internet Resources

Curriculum books and Internet resources offer a range of ideas that help with the identification and development of wellness concepts and topics. Activities can be adapted to fit the needs and maturity of the class. Weighing the activities against the components discussed earlier in this chapter will guide the teacher to make appropriate adjustments as needed. Figure 2-12 provides examples of curriculum resources for a wellness program.

Community Health Professionals

Community health and wellness professionals are another good source of information. These professionals can inform wellness policies, assist with the design of a children's wellness curriculum, provide training for teachers and families, and help teachers to address unique health issues in the classroom when they arise. Providing teachers access to the expertise of health professionals is seen as so important that some states require early childhood programs to establish formal relationships with health consultants such as pediatric

Figure 2-12 Curriculum Resources

Nutrition

- The USDA's *MyPyramid for Preschoolers* and *MyPyramid for Kids*
  www.mypyramid.gov
- USDA/ARS Children's Nutrition Research Center at Baylor College of Medicine
  Nutrition Information and Sites Just for Kids
  www.bcm.edu/cnrc/resources/kids.html
- Kalich, K., Bauer, D., & McPartlin, D. (2009). *Early Sprouts: Cultivating Healthy Food Choices in Young Children.* St. Paul, MN: Redleaf Press.
- USDA Agriculture Library, Food and Nutrition Information Center, Lifestyle Nutrition
  http://fnic.nal.usda.gov/nal_display
- National Dairy Council's Nutrition Explorations
  www.nutritionexplorations.com/educators/main.asp

Health

- SPARK Early Childhood Physical Activity Program and SPARK K–6 Physical Activity Program
  www.sparkpe.org
- Kids Health in the Classroom (Nemours Foundation)
  http://classroom.kidshealth.org
- National Association of Sport & Physical Education
  www.aahperd.org/naspe
- Smith, C. J., Hendricks, C. M., & Bennett, B. S. (2007). *Growing, Growing Strong: A whole health curriculum for young children*, Revised Edition. St. Paul, MN: Redleaf Press.

Safety

- Feigh, A. (2008) *I Can Play It Safe.* Free Spirit Publishing, Inc. Minneapolis, MN.
- O'Brien-Palmer, M. *Healthy Me: Fun Ways to Develop Good Health and Safety Habits.*
- Safe Kids. U.S.A. *Activities for kids!*
  www.usa.safekids.org

nurses or community health providers (Aronson, 2002). Some early childhood settings create health services advisory committees to discuss children's health and wellness and advise about the development of program policies and procedures. Such resources engage informed community members with early childhood teachers, creating a partnership that enhances understanding across the service systems.

Professional Development and In-Service Training

Commitment to continuing education is a quality of successful teachers. Accessing professional development opportunities related to children's health and wellness, attending seminars and workshops, and participating in in-service training are all ways to learn about resources to support effective teaching. All early childhood teachers and most elementary school teachers are required to participate in periodic health and wellness training, such as infant and child first aid and cardiopulmonary resuscitation. These trainings often include updates about nutrition, disease, and injury prevention.

Membership in professional organizations is another way to learn about resources. Membership in the National Association for the Education of Young Children connects teachers to a multitude of resources and information that is directly applicable to the education of young children. The NAEYC conferences are popular venues for learning and exchanging ideas about teaching young children.

> **What if. . .**
> you moved to a new community to teach and wanted to join a professional organization? How would you learn about the groups that were available in your new community?

Appropriate Children's Books

Children's literature is a wonderful way to introduce wellness topics. The colorful presentation and engaging characters focus children's attention on specific messages, such as foods to eat for good health, what happens when you visit the doctor or dentist, and ways

Figure 2-13 Children's Literature to Support the Wellness Curriculum

Nutrition
   The Very Hungry Caterpillar (E. Carle)
   Eating the Alphabet: Fruits & Vegetables from A to Z (L. Ehlert)
   Bread Bread Bread (A. Morris & L. Heyman)
   Everybody Cooks Rice (N. Dooley)
   My Whole Food ABC's (D. Richard)

Health
   Como Cuidar Mis Dientes/Taking Care of My Teeth (T. DeBezelle)
   Those Mean Nasty Dirty Downright Disgusting But Invisible Germs (J. A. Rice)
   My Amazing Body: A First Look at Health and Fitness (P. Thomas)
   Germs Are Not for Sharing (E. Verdick and M. Heinle)
   Bear Feels Sick (K. Wilson and J. Chapman)
   Cuts, Breaks, Bruises, AND Burns: How Your Body Heals (J. Cole)

Safety
   Safety on the Playground; Safety on the School Bus; Safety around Strangers (L. Raatma)
   Franklin's Bicycle Helmet (E. Moore)
   Stop Drop AND Roll (M. Cuyler)
   Dinosaurs, Beware! A Safety Guide (M. Brown)

to keep safe. In response to the growing interest in teaching children wellness concepts, authors and vendors offer picture books on a variety of nutrition, health, and safety topics. As always, teachers need to review these resources to ensure that the message is reflective of current trends in wellness and that the presentation is appropriate for the age and maturity of the children. The teachers in the opening case scenario use their local libraries to find literature resources that will help them reinforce the concepts that they wish to present, such as cultural aspects of foods for Marty's preschool class, food as a source of energy for Greg's kindergarten class, and how and where foods are grown for Armetha's elementary school class. Teachers often develop a list of their favorite books for teaching particular topics, adding to it when new resources are discovered. A sample list of children's literature is offered in Figure 2-13. Other lists of appropriate children's literature for wellness topics can be found on the NAEYC and American Dietetic Association websites.

PARTNERING WITH FAMILIES

Creating partnerships with families is an important part of teaching. Parents, who are the first teachers of the young child, have much to share about how their child learns and the goals they have for their child in the early childhood setting. Teachers also want to share the important outcomes that they are fostering as children participate and learn in the early childhood classroom. Working together, teachers and families create a team to implement mutual goals for children's wellness.

Involving Families in Curriculum Development

Inviting families to participate in the development of the wellness program is an ideal way to gather a variety of ideas about wellness concepts and topics. Such discussions help the teacher identify wellness themes that are of interest and concern to families, which also helps the teacher focus on topics that are relevant to the children. Families are the best resource for sharing ideas about their culture and ways of thinking about wellness. They can offer perspectives the teacher may be unaware of, and often parents will volunteer to help present culturally specific information. Families are one of the best resources for sharing ideas about how to adapt activities to address the needs of children who have particular challenges. These ideas emerge when teachers hold discussion groups where each participant is invited to share personal stories about their family traditions and ways they keep their children healthy. Establishing a wellness program blog or inviting families to e-mail

MyEducationLab

Go to the Assignments and Activities section of Topic 13: Wellness Curriculum in the MyEducationLab for your course and complete the activity entitled *Partnering with Parents to Teach Wellness*. How did the teachers in this classroom involve families in teaching oral wellness?

their ideas is another way to contact families who are not able to attend discussion meetings. The goal is for all families to feel invited to participate. Involving families in planning helps teachers recognize topics for which there may be disagreement and also offers a forum for discussing conflicting points of view.

Reinforcing Wellness Concepts at Home and School

The collaborative relationship built between the teacher and families increases the likelihood that wellness concepts taught at school will be reinforced at home. It serves as an invitation for families to be involved in the process of their child's early childhood education at school, and it provides a mechanism for parents to inform teachers about how families can help promote wellness. Communication and role modeling are important elements of this collaboration.

Families are the best resource for sharing information about their culture.

Communicating about Wellness Activities

Communicating with families in the development of the wellness curriculum is needed for another important reason. Teaching wellness concepts is unique from teaching basic educational lessons. Some wellness topics, especially those that relate to health and safety, have the potential to raise concerns or potentially frighten children. Even a carefully presented lesson about evacuating the classroom for a fire drill may introduce worries in children who are mature enough to recognize that a fire *could* happen and that fire is very dangerous. Ongoing communication is important in order for families to recognize when such activities have been presented, to observe for signs of worry, and to reassure children that parents and health and safety workers will take care of them.

School-to-home communication can be accomplished through posters, newsletters, e-mail messages, and periodic classroom group meetings to share common wellness goals such as those identified by the NAEYC (1999) for school and home:

- Provide nutritious meals.
- Ensure children get sufficient sleep.
- Identify a regular medical provider.
- Obtain recommended immunizations.
- Keep children home when they are sick.
- Encourage physical activity.
- Protect children from harm.

Sharing wellness topics and informing families about the activities that are being conducted also reminds families to practice healthful behaviors at home.

Being Healthful Role Models

Children learn by watching others, including their family and teachers. Helping a child learn healthy habits requires that these important role models have knowledge about wellness practices, a healthful attitude, and physical energy. Being a wellness role model involves making a commitment to a healthful lifestyle. It means letting children see how you work to put your healthy ideas into practice. Here are ways teachers and families set good examples for children (American Academy of Pediatrics, 2007):

- Eat well and stay active.
- Get regular health checkups and recommended vaccinations.
- Join a smoking cessation program if you smoke.

What if. . .

you have just completed a series of activities teaching children to make healthful food choices rather than choosing sweet foods, when a child sees you open your lunch bag and asks you why you are eating doughnuts? How would you respond?

Health Hint

Talking with Families about Children's Health

Sometimes teachers need to communicate concerns about a child's health. When talking with families, remember to:

- Be sensitive; know that most parents really care about their child's health.
- Communicate respectfully.
- Be prepared to carefully and simply state your concern.
- Recognize family challenges.
- Assist with creating strategies for improvement.
- Be a positive member of the child's support network.
- Understand resources in the community to which you can refer the family.

- Ensure positive experiences with food and eating; sit together at meals.
- Participate in physical activities with children. Dance and play together.
- Model healthful behaviors: wash hands, cover coughs, stay home when ill.

What if. . .

you recognized that a child was coming to school hungry? How would you approach the family members and what resources would you tell them about?

Healthy role modeling enhances wellness activities in the classroom. For example, when teachers demonstrate how to use tongs to serve apple slices, children will recognize this as the appropriate way to serve food. When teachers bend and stretch vigorously with musical games, children learn to participate enthusiastically too. When adults wash their hands after sneezing, children see that adults practice the health behaviors they expect of children. Being a healthful role model demonstrates that wellness habits are important.

Guiding Families

Partnering with families to improve children's health and well-being infers several responsibilities. For example, it means that teachers may be asked to provide guidance for families when special situations occur. The teacher may need to talk with parents about a concern for a child's unmet health need or a suspected eating disorder. Teachers are also in a position to recognize when families are experiencing difficulties. For example, parents who experience high levels of stress may be less able to put into action prevention measures to reduce their child's risk of injury or illness (Alemango, Niles, Shafer-King, & Miller, 2008). Engaging in such discussions may be difficult. The *Health Hint* offers guidance for communicating with parents when difficult health concerns must be shared.

Teachers also serve as a resource for families, informing them of community health issues, such as food safety alerts, new immunization requirements, or product safety issues. This means that teachers must keep aware of emergent health issues that could affect both the classroom and the home setting. Having a mechanism in place to communicate important wellness information is helpful, such as establishing a special bulletin board for important news or creating a family e-mail list. The outreach efforts that teachers make are important resources for families (O'Connor, 1999). Teachers play an important role in promoting wellness among children, by assisting families to develop networks of support and by guiding them to access the services children may need.

MyEducationLab

To assess your understanding of how to teach young children and their families about nutrition, health, and safety, go to the Book Specific Resources section in the MyEducationLab for your course, select *Nutrition, Health, and Safety for Young Children,* Chapter 2 of the Study Plan, and then complete the multiple choice questions and activities.

Summary

Teaching young children about health and wellness is an important responsibility of early childhood educators. Young children are capable of learning behaviors that will contribute to their well-being throughout life. To optimize this opportunity, teachers must understand how children learn and how to create a wellness program that is relevant and appropriate for the age and maturity of the children they teach.

Purposeful planning increases the likelihood that the wellness program is organized around meaningful concepts and focused on topics that will interest children. It ensures that the wellness messages are infused across the curriculum, that they reflect current knowledge in nutrition, health, and safety, and that they are considerate of the cultural traditions of each child.

Children's safety is a primary consideration when designing wellness activities. This is best achieved by planning in advance to identify appropriate learning goals and needed materials and to outline the steps of each activity. In this way teachers are prepared to safely address the requirements of children with special developmental needs or who may benefit from adjustments that allow them to better access the wellness message.

Various resources are available to support teachers as they hone their approach to teaching wellness. More are emerging every day due to the high level of concern for children's well-being. Teachers need to take advantage of opportunities to learn more about the nutrition, health, and safety behaviors that make the most difference in children's lives and ensure that such information is provided to children and their families. Teachers and families are partners in the effort to build children's capabilities to live healthful lives. Teaching wellness is a process of discovery that promises positive benefits long after children have grown beyond the early childhood years.

Key Terms

Accommodation, p. 30

Adaptation, p. 30

Assimilation, p. 30

Brain plasticity, p. 33

Center-based approach, p. 35

Child-selected activities, p. 43

Constructivist approach, p. 29

Developmental domains, p. 34

Disequilibrium, p. 31

Early intervention services, p. 56

Equilibrium, p. 31

Hands-on and experiential, p. 38

Incidental learning, p. 39

Individualized education
program (IEP), p. 56

Individualized family services
plan (IFSP), p. 56

Mental structures, p. 30

Organization, p. 30

Process-oriented activities, p. 42

Scaffolding, p. 31

Special education services, p. 56

Teacher-directed activities, p. 43

Review Questions

1. Discuss the constructivist approach to teaching. Describe scaffolding and how teachers use it.

2. Describe the domains of development and learning and provide an example of how children learn in each area.

3. What does it mean to teach wellness "across the curriculum" and why is this important?

4. What does purposeful planning mean and why is it important?

5. Why is it important to partner with families when teaching wellness?

Discussion Starters

1. Identify wellness concepts that would be especially important to teach children in the community where you live and explain why.

2. Discuss different activity approaches including process-oriented activities, hands-on and experiential activities, and projects. Describe why each is important for children to experience.

3. Consider the cultural diversity present in your community. What aspects of each tradition would contribute to the plans for teaching wellness in your area?

Practice Points

1. Select a wellness concept related to nutrition. Brainstorm a list of topics and activities that could be used to teach that concept. Refer to Figure 2-8 to get ideas, but think of an alternate concept and topics.

2. Design a hands-on activity with a health focus for a preschool setting. Write a wellness activity plan that addresses all of the plan's components.

3. Identify a safety topic. Describe how to appropriately teach that topic to each of three age groups: toddlers, preschoolers, and primary school children.

Web Resources

National Association for the Education of Young Children
www.naeyc.org

National Scientific Council on the Developing Child
www.developingchild.net

U.S. Department of Education, Building the Legacy: IDEA 2004
http://idea.ed.gov

Promoting Good Nutrition

part 2

chapter 3 | The Foundations of Optimal Nutrition

Learning Outcomes

After reading this chapter, you should be able to:

1. Discuss nutritional issues faced by children in the early childhood setting as they relate to the changing food environment.

2. Define malnutrition and discuss nutrition issues that lead to under- and overnutrition.

3. Discuss the recommended standards and guidelines that promote healthful eating and how those systems can be applied to early childhood education settings.

4. Describe diverse ethnic educational resources that contribute to healthful diets in the early childhood setting.

Luisa arrives early at preschool with 3-year-old Gabriella. They have just come from a doctor's appointment where Luisa learned that Gabriella is overweight and also has iron-deficiency anemia. The doctor told her this means Gabriella does not have enough iron in her blood for healthy development. Luisa is upset and turns to her daughter's preschool teacher, Cecilia, for advice. She can't understand why Gabriella who is eating enough to become overweight isn't getting enough iron. Cecilia tells Luisa that she will study her resources and talk with her tomorrow.

As Cecilia reviews the materials she has about children's nutrition, she remembers that Gabriella receives a vegetarian diet when she is at preschool, and she is enthusiastic about drinking milk and favors cheese and yogurt. The next day they meet near the computer where Cecilia locates a website that discusses the iron content of foods. Luisa realizes that Gabriella is not eating many of the high-iron foods listed and decides to add more of these to her child's diet. She also recognizes that some of Gabriella's favorite foods, the dairy products, are rich in calcium and vitamin D but are not very good sources of iron.

Cecilia says that she will explore whether the preschool lunch can be changed to offer more iron-rich foods in place of some of the cheese entrées that are being served as part of Gabriella's vegetarian diet. Cecilia copies the information about iron-rich foods and provides Luisa with the telephone number of the local Women, Infants, and Children program where she can get more nutritional advice. Luisa leaves the classroom feeling much more positive about the situation and appreciates the collaborative support provided by Cecilia.

Life cannot exist without nutrition. From the moment babies are fed their first meal, the nutrients they consume affect their growth, development, and well-being. Nutrients are substances found in foods that are essential requirements of life and thus are necessary for survival and growth. Nutrition refers to the relationship between the nutrients found in foods and their influence on the human body. The nutritional environments to which children are exposed both before birth and throughout their early childhood years influence health across the life span (Barker, 2004; Dolinoy & Jirtle, 2008; Gluckman, Hanson, & Pinal, 2005; Mayer-Davis et al., 2006; Scholtens et al., 2008).

Teachers play an important role in creating environments that support children's nutritional health (Hughes et al., 2007; Story, Kaphingst, & French, 2006). Some teachers plan menus, select foods, and manage food preparation and service in the early childhood setting. In settings for older children, teachers are typically much less engaged in direct food service, but are equally involved in recognizing the important health impacts of good nutrition on children's ability to participate, to pay attention to lessons, and to learn. In the chapter-opening case scenario, Cecilia, a busy teacher, takes time to discuss Luisa's concerns about her child's nutrition. When Cecilia learns that Gabriella has a nutritional deficit, she helps Luisa to discover ways to address her child's nutritional needs both at home and at school. Cecilia demonstrates a basic knowledge of nutrition and recognition of the resources that are available to support appropriate planning for children's diets. Her knowledge about the significance of nutrition to good health and learning makes an important contribution.

This chapter introduces the science of nutrition and provides an overview of current nutrition issues faced by children and their families, preparing teachers to recognize and address the diet concerns of young children. We discuss important standards and evidence-based recommendations that form the basis for nutrition guidelines for feeding infants, toddlers,

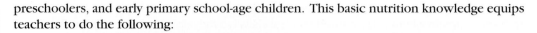

nutrients
substances found in foods that are essential requirements of life and, thus, are necessary for survival and growth

nutrition
refers to the relationship between the nutrients found in foods and their influence on the human body

preschoolers, and early primary school-age children. This basic nutrition knowledge equips teachers to do the following:

- Understand how nutrition impacts children.
- Identify food sources of nutrients.
- Recognize the components of a healthful diet.
- Plan healthful menus.
- Use the various education and nutrition information guidelines.
- Develop personal eating habits that influence teachers' health and enhance their ability to serve as role models for children.

This chapter also presents a summary of food guidance systems created for different populations so that you will understand the rich diversity of ethnic foods served to young children and how they contribute to a healthful diet.

UNDERSTANDING HOW NUTRITION AFFECTS CHILDREN

Optimal nutrition provides children with the building blocks they need for healthful growth and development. Providing optimal nutrition for children in the early childhood setting relies on teachers who have an appropriate understanding of the components of good nutrition and recognition of the factors that sidetrack families from providing the foods that children need for healthful growth and development.

Identifying Optimal Nutrition

phytochemicals
natural compounds found in plants that may protect against disease and support good health

antioxidants
natural compounds found in plants that may protect cells from damage and thereby decrease the risk of cancer

Teachers who understand and support the optimal nutrition of young children help them acquire the nutritional building blocks needed to thrive.

Optimal nutrition refers to the best possible nourishment for children. It is based on access to an appropriate amount and combination of foods in the diet, including dairy products, grains, fruits, vegetables, meats, and beans. Consumption of these foods provides children with the essential nutrients such as proteins and important vitamins and minerals. Optimal nutrition includes eating foods that provide phytochemicals and antioxidants, which are natural compounds found in plants that may protect against disease, and also eating the right combination of energy- or calorie-providing nutrients (the carbohydrates, fats, and proteins) so that the needs of growth are balanced with that of physical activity. Too little energy from food means children will not grow adequately; too much energy from food and children will face problems with obesity.

In the early childhood setting, optimal nutrition revolves around healthful meals that meet the standards set by government and health agencies, and that are offered in appropriate ways and at times of the day to support children's energy needs. It includes carefully selected snacks, the types of foods served at school events, and the recipes used in cooking activities. Finally, good nutrition in the early childhood setting is fostered by teachers who demonstrate appropriate nutrition practices, such as eating healthy foods with children and participating as active role models.

Collaborating with Families

Most parents are genuinely concerned about how their children eat and have a strong commitment to the types of foods they serve at home. Factors such as family socioeconomic status, rural versus urban living, family lifestyle, ethnicity, and religious traditions have some bearing on the foods families give their children to eat. The early childhood program may be the family's first experience entrusting others with the feeding of their children and their first exposure to food provided in group settings. Parents want to know what their child will be eating and want to participate in ensuring that their child is cared for appropriately. Teachers, such as Cecilia, understand these concerns. They invite parents to share important information about the child's needs. They are also prepared to describe the menus and ways foods are offered to children to help parents build confidence in the teacher's ability to appropriately provide for their child's well-being.

Teachers who take the time to describe menus and address the nutritional concerns of children in their programs create a bond of trust with families about the care of their children.

Children come to early childhood classes with unique nutritional needs that are influenced by their age, activity level, genetics, and sometimes the presence of disease or illness. Teachers assume the important responsibility of supporting children's healthful development by appropriately nourishing the children in their care (Hughes et al., 2007; Story et al., 2006). Teachers like Cecilia accommodate the nutritional needs and special diet requirements of each child in their classes and establish a common ground with families to ensure that the meals served are nourishing, mutually acceptable, and, as much as possible, within the constraints of budget and school policy. Creating collaborative relationships with families to meet children's nutritional requirements sets a tone that supports good health and fosters positive food experiences.

Teachers are also important resources for parents when it comes to feeding young children. The early childhood years provide a window of opportunity for establishing habits that lead to a lifetime of healthful eating and wellness (American Dietetic Association, 2005b). During these years children explore flavors and textures and develop comfort and familiarity with foods that are frequently served. They begin to establish preferences for these familiar foods, including how they are prepared and served. They develop confidence that food will be available to them and that they can trust their families and teachers to satisfy their hunger. Consider the following example:

> Twice a month at Linda's preschool program, the meal service catered by the local school district offered Cheese Zombies on Fridays as an entrée. Cheese Zombies are a whole-grain, oblong-shaped roll stuffed with low-fat cheese and baked. The children loved this meal. When a new food service manager was hired, Zombies disappeared from the menu. The children were disappointed and asked Linda on more than one occasion when they were going to have Zombies again. A parent also mentioned as she dropped off her child that he missed the Zombies! Linda decided to call the school district and talk with the new manager, who said she was very willing to put them back on the preschool menu.

Linda acted as an advocate for the children in her program to ensure that menu items they enjoy are available.

Teachers support the development of good eating habits by establishing predictable schedules for food service and relaxed and comfortable mealtimes. Teachers help families learn to be advocates for children's optimal nutrition by encouraging parents to push for schools and early child care programs to serve nutritious foods and to promote physical activity to support good health. For example, when school budget cuts result in decisions that eliminate physical education programs, teachers can provide families with the guidance they need to effectively communicate with school authorities their opinions. Teachers can direct interested families to participate in school health advisory councils and wellness committees so that parents have input into the nutrition and health standards established for their schools and school districts.

What if. . .

a child joined your class who was identified as very underweight and both parents were developmentally delayed? How would you address the nutritional needs of this child and ensure the family understood how to meet the child's needs at home, too?

Recognizing Challenges to Nutrition

Teachers share with parents an important role in shaping the health of young children. They have oversight in feeding children in the early childhood setting. They teach children about food and nutrition, and must be able to address childhood nutrition issues such as occurred in Gabriella's case. To be prepared to effectively manage this complex responsibility, teachers must be able to recognize aspects of the changing food environment that challenge children's diets and learn about ways to work with families to ensure children have the opportunity to experience optimal nutrition.

During the past 30 years, there has been a shift in the way Americans eat. These changes represent challenges to good nutrition and have the potential to compromise children's health.

Disappearing Family Meals

Meals that are prepared at home and served and consumed by the family are important to children's nutrition. Children eat more fruits, vegetables, whole grains, and calcium-rich foods when meals are prepared at home (Spear, 2006). In addition, family meals help children develop a sense of family connection and social support that helps them do well in school (Duyff, 2006). However, sit-down family meals are occurring less frequently. One reason is the time constraint experienced by working parents. Sixty-two percent of families with children have dual incomes, 27% of children in the United States are from single-parent families, and some family members hold more than one job (Sloan, 2009; U.S. Department of Labor, Bureau of Labor Statistics, 2008). These families are strapped for time and often resort to quick mealtime solutions when feeding their children. For example, 50% of mothers surveyed indicate time was the most important criteria for selecting what to prepare for dinner, while only 26% chose healthfulness and 12% cost (Sloan, 2009). Another factor contributing to the decline in family meals is that many young parents raising children lack basic cooking skills because they were raised in homes where minimal "cooking from scratch" occurred (Jarratt & Mahaffie, 2007).

Eating Away from Home

There is a growing trend toward eating meals away from home. Busy families frequently rely on meals provided by fast-food restaurants. Children are attracted to fast-food establishments because of the exciting environment and promotional toys that are offered. Parents are attracted to the low-cost menu items. However, families may not always recognize the high nutritional price they pay for these quick meal solutions. Children who eat fast food receive larger portions than they would consume at home, and fewer options for fruits, vegetables, and milk are available. Fast-food meals also tend to be high in sodium content and higher in total fat (including the less healthy saturated and *trans* fats). In addition, children drink more soft drinks when eating at restaurants. Soft drinks contain 10 to 12 teaspoons of sugar per 12-ounce cup or can and have minimal nutritionally redeeming qualities. This is especially problematic because when soft drinks are consumed they take the place of more nutritious foods and beverages (Meinke, 2009). Researchers have shown that eating frequently at fast-food restaurants can lead to obesity (Mehta & Chang, 2008; Pereira et al., 2005).

In spite of increasing awareness about an obesity epidemic and the recent challenging economic times, families' reliance on fast food for quick, inexpensive meals continues to increase. For example, McDonald's Corporation (2009) reported a 5% increase in sales in the United States in 2008. Teachers may observe families dropping off children with a fast-food breakfast or offering them a fast-food meal or snack when picking them up at the end of the day. While supervising children at play, teachers may observe play themes such as this one:

> Meredith, a preschool teacher, notices Tristan playing in the dramatic play area. He sits in a chair outside the playhouse and leans toward the "window." In an official tone he orders, "A hamburger and fries!" When Tristan's not ordering fast

Because of time and cost, fast food is a convenient and inexpensive way to feed busy families. What are the consequences for today's children?

food at play, he frequently asks Meredith if they are going to have a hamburger and fries at lunch. Later, Tristan's mother tells Meredith that she is worried about Tristan's weight. After talking with Meredith, Tristan's mother decides to limit trips for fast-food meals and to prepare more meals at home.

Using Convenience Foods

Families that choose to eat meals at home often look for convenient and quick ways to pre-pare foods. A survey of U.S. food consumption trends reveals that only 57% of evening meals are made from scratch, while 24% are prepackaged meals that require partial preparation and 8% are frozen or heat-and-serve style foods (Sloan, 2008). Prepack-aged and frozen foods, like restaurant fare, can have high fat, sugar, and sodium content and may lose a portion of their beneficial nutritive properties such as vitamins and fiber during processing.

The reliance on convenience food is also evident in the lunches children bring from home. Children's lunches often include prepackaged lunch meals, store-bought cookies, chips, or soft drinks (Sweltzer, Briley, & Robert-Grey, 2009). Home-packed lunches often do not provide the variety of fruits, vegetables, and dairy products needed to support good nutrition in young children (Sweltzer et al., 2009). Teachers who understand nutrition requirements and standards can provide helpful nutrition education to families to ensure that home-packed lunches are nutritious. The University of California's Lunch Box Program (see Figure 3-1) provides helpful infor-mation for families, in English and Spanish, on how to prepare safe and healthful meals for the lunch box for preschool and school-age children (University of California Cooperative Extension, San Luis Obispo County, 2007).

> ## What if. . .
> you ask a child in your class what he had for dinner the previous night and he says, "The same thing I have every night—fried chicken and French fries."? How would you respond? How might you approach the child's parent or family to discuss more nutritious options?

Identifying New Wellness Opportunities

Emerging interest in wellness has created a heightened awareness around food production and nutrition practices. Many families are paying special attention to the foods they serve, and school settings are focusing on wellness policies.

Growing Interest in Sustainable Food Practices

Some families have made a gradual shift in how they think about food purchased for their children. Many families are interested in supporting sustainable food practices. Supporting sustainable food practices includes for example, choosing pesticide or hormone free food that is grown locally and processed minimally. Foods grown and produced by local meth-ods are increasingly attractive choices for "green" consumers. One study noted that 13% of mothers choose organic foods for their children, and a total of 29% look for *natural* claims on the product label (Sloan, 2009).

Many families are also concerned about global warming and select locally grown foods as much as possible. Some families, such as Gabriella's, are environmental vegetarians, who choose a vegetarian lifestyle because they believe the production of animal foods is not sus-tainable. Parents who select organic or sustainable foods or both may bring this preference to the school setting. They may confront teachers with food requests that are difficult to fulfill in an institutional food service setting where food costs and availability must be factored into menu planning. These situations present an opportunity for collaboration with families. To-gether teachers and families can explore the challenges of meeting new requests and identify opportunities for change. New ideas offered by concerned parents can be the motivating factor for improving menus and providing a fresh look to established mealtime routines.

sustainable food practices
the use of food production methods that protect the environment and the ability of future generations to produce food

environmental vegetarian
individuals who choose a vegetarian lifestyle because they believe the production of animal foods is not sustainable

Increasing Interest in Wellness in the School Environment

Children spend a significant amount of time in early childhood settings and at school, where they may eat breakfast, lunch, and an afternoon snack. As a result they consume a sizable portion of their daily food intake in the education setting (Story, 2009). Health authorities and parents have become increasingly interested in promoting wellness in set-tings that serve young children, which could lead to improvements in the diets offered.

Figure 3-1 Lunch Bag Ideas for School-Age Children The University of California Cooperative Extension, San Luis Obispo County, can be a resource for teachers who want to encourage families to prepare nutritious and safe brown bag lunches.

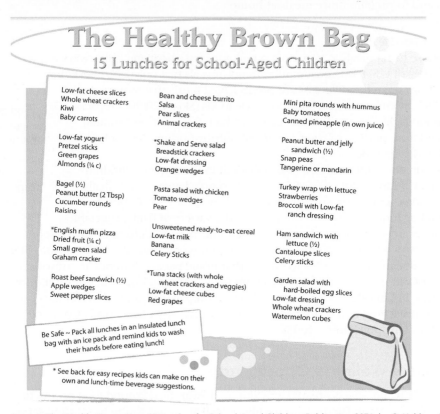

Source: *The Healthy Brown Bag: 15 Lunches for School-Aged Children*, Publication 8371, by C. Kohlen, J. Schouten, and S. Peterson, 2009, Oakland, CA: The University of California Division of Agriculture and Natural Resources, retrieved from http://anrcatalog.ucdavis.edu/pdf/8371.pdf. Used with permission.

competitive foods
foods provided outside the realm of traditional school food service such as foods from vending machines, school stores, à la carte menu options, and foods used for rewards and fund-raising

Improved wellness policies and a heightened level of awareness regarding the negative features of competitive foods (foods from vending machines, school stores, à la carte menu options) and foods used for rewards and fund-raising are welcome trends that are beginning to have an impact on the quality of diets offered to children in schools. A recent study on the nutritional quality of meals offered during the school year reveals that more schools are meeting improvement goals, including guidelines for limiting saturated fats, offering skim or 1% milk, and providing more fresh fruits (Jarratt & Mahaffie, 2007). Much room for improvement remains, however, because many schools still serve foods that are too high overall in fat and sodium and too low in fiber content (Gordon, Crepinsek, Ronette, & Clark, 2009; Jarratt & Mahaffie, 2007).

What if. . .

you were approached by a parent who tells you that their family eats only organic food and requests a "natural foods diet" for their child? How would you respond?

UNDERSTANDING MALNUTRITION

Negative nutritional trends affect the food environment both at home and in the school setting. In fact, overall the quality of the diet consumed by children in the United States does not meet national dietary standards and recommendations for maintaining good nutritional status. As a result many children are poorly nourished (Story, 2009; U.S. Department of Agriculture [USDA] Center for Nutrition Policy and Promotion, 2008). When children's diets do not contain the right combination of nutrient-rich foods, malnutrition can develop. Malnutrition refers to an imbalance in the diet of one or more vital nutrients that support appropriate growth and development (Thomas, 2007). The two types of imbalance are:

- **Undernutrition,** in which children do not get enough calories, protein, or other nutrients.
- **Overnutrition,** in which too many calories are consumed.

In the opening case scenario Gabriella faces both aspects of malnutrition: iron-deficiency anemia due to insufficient iron intake, and obesity due to too many calories in the diet. Researchers suggest that undernutrition and overnutrition can occur simultaneously when children eat foods low in nutrients such as iron, but high in calories (Nead, Halterman, Kaczorowski, Auinger, & Weitzman, 2004; Pinhas-Hamiel et al., 2003).

Gabriella is not alone. The USDA periodically conducts surveys to find out how well people eat. Using a tool called the *Healthy Eating Index–2005,* which attempts to define diet quality, researchers found that all food groups except for grains were lacking in children's diets. The Third School Nutrition Dietary Assessment Study also found that fruits, vegetables, dairy products, and whole grains are deficient in US children's diets. Children are however, consuming higher than recommended amounts of fat, sodium, and calories (Story, 2009). This highlights the need to improve fruit, vegetable, whole grain, and low-fat milk intake and decrease the low-nutrient foods that are high in sugar, sodium, and fat in the diets of young children. (USDA Center for Nutrition Policy and Promotion, 2008). Teachers become part of the solution to this nutritional paradox by understanding the difference between undernutrition and overnutrition and helping families address some of the more common conditions that may occur due to these aspects of malnutrition.

Recognizing Undernutrition

Although diets in the United States include an abundance of food for many people, the nutritional well-being of children can be compromised by nutrient deficiencies, or undernutrition. Undernutrition may be the result of poor dietary choices, serious illness, or lack of financial resources to provide sufficient amounts of healthful foods.

Insufficient Calorie Intake

Some infants and children do not consume sufficient calories to grow properly. They often appear significantly thinner or smaller compared to other infants and children of the same age. Physicians follow growth by measuring weight, length or height, and head circumference and comparing these measurements to standard growth charts. If children vary significantly from established growth patterns, they may be diagnosed with **failure to thrive,** a condition in which a child's growth rate slows down or comes to a halt. Infants or children with failure to thrive experience a drop-off in the rate of weight gain first, followed over time by a faltering of growth in height.

Failure to thrive may also be due to an underlying medical condition, such as heart, lung, or digestive problems. Sometimes growth failure can be related to psychological, social, or financial problems within the family. Undernutrition can occur in families who:

- Experience emotional problems.
- Lack funds due to unemployment.
- Are involved in substance abuse.
- Are homeless.
- Lack knowledge about appropriate feeding.
- Use poor feeding techniques or have established a poor feeding relationship with their child (Block, Krebs, Committee on Child Abuse and Neglect, & Committee on Nutrition, 2005; Satter, 2000; Wright, Parkinson, & Drewett, 2006).

When undernutrition is recognized, teachers work in conjunction with health care providers and families to provide nutrition support to children who

malnutrition
an imbalance of one or more vital nutrients in the diet that support appropriate growth and development, resulting in undernutrition or overnutrition

undernutrition
a type of malnutrition in which individuals do not get sufficient calories, protein, or other nutrients to meet their bodies' needs

overnutrition
a type of malnutrition in which individuals consume too many calories

Identifying undernutrition requires looking beyond the child's height and weight. Consider the child's living situation, economic situation, and whether the child has a history of medical or psychological problems.

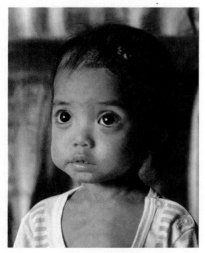

failure to thrive
a condition in which the growth rate slows down or comes to a halt; may be due to an underlying medical condition, such as heart, lung, or digestive problems or related to psychological, social, or financial problems within the family

psychosocial
refers to psychological and social factors that affect well-being

supplemental food programs
federal food programs that provide nutrition assistance for at-risk populations such as children, low-income families, and the elderly

iron-deficiency anemia
a common single-nutrient deficiency of iron that results in the body making fewer red blood cells with less hemoglobin than normal; causes sleepiness, impaired growth and development, and increased risk of infection in young children

are not growing properly. Specially prepared infant formulas, supplemental high-calorie beverages, and nutritious high-calorie snacks may be prescribed. If the problem is psychosocial, teachers can help families access appropriate support services such as those provided by doctors, dietitians, social workers, or qualified mental health advisers. A psychosocial concern refers to psychological or social factors that affect a child's well-being. For example, if a mother does not interact well with her baby because of postpartum depression and, therefore, doesn't respond appropriately to her baby's hunger cues, a psychosocial feeding problem can result.

Teachers can refer parents to supplemental food programs (federal food programs that provide nutrition assistance) such as the Special Supplemental Nutrition Program for Women, Infants, and Children, more commonly known as the WIC program. WIC serves low-income women, infants, and children up to age 5 by providing nutritious foods, such as milk, soy milk, whole-grain starches, eggs, cheese, juice, beans, peas, peanut butter, tofu, fruits, vegetables, baby foods, and formula, to supplement their diets (California WIC Association, 2008). In addition, food resources can be obtained from the Supplemental Nutrition Assistance Program (SNAP), formally called the Food Stamp Program, which helps low-income families buy healthy foods (USDA Food and Nutrition Service, 2009).

Iron-Deficiency Anemia

Iron-deficiency anemia is a condition in which, due to lack of iron in the diet, a person's body does not make enough healthy red blood cells to accomplish the goal of transporting oxygen in the bloodstream. It is one of the more common nutrient deficiencies among children in the United States. Researchers estimate that approximately 18% of high-risk children (Skalicky et al., 2006) and 8% to 10% of children 1 to 3 years of age are iron deficient (Brotanek, Gosz, Weitzman, & Flores, 2008).

The signs of iron deficiency include sleepiness, irritability, difficulty concentrating and maintaining body temperature, brittle nails, a sore tongue, and poor school performance (Halterman, Kaczorowski, Aligne, Auinger, & Szilagyi, 2001). In addition, when children are deficient in iron, their immune system is less able to fight off infections, leading to illness and decreased school attendance. Of greatest importance is the association of iron-deficiency anemia with cognitive, mental, and motor skill developmental delays. When young children do not receive enough iron in their diet, the development of the central nervous system may be significantly delayed and brain development may also be compromised (Beard, 2008). A window of opportunity may be available when these adverse effects can be corrected. The window, however, is age and time sensitive. If left untreated, the health concerns associated with iron-deficiency anemia may be irreversible (Beard, 2008; Lozoff, Jimenez, Hagen, Mollen, & Wolf, 2000).

Sufficient iron in children's diets is also important because it offers protection against lead poisoning. When iron levels are low, lead from the environment is more readily absorbed. The *Health Hint* describes the iron, lead, and calcium connection.

Children ages 1 to 3 are at high risk for iron deficiency if they are at the younger end of the age range, Hispanic, overweight, from low-income families or were bottle fed milk for a long period of time (milk is low in iron and too much prevents toddlers from eating iron-rich foods) (Brotanek, Halterman, Auinger, Flores, & Weitzman, 2005; Brotanek et al., 2008; Skalicky et al., 2006).

What if. . .

you suspected that a child in your class was not getting sufficient food due to the family's economic difficulties? How would you address this issue with the family? What food resources in your community would you recommend to them?

In the opening case scenario, Gabriella faces two risk factors for iron deficiency. She is an overweight child and is of Hispanic descent. Children who are obese are three times more likely to be iron deficient than nonobese children (20% versus 7%) (Brotanek, Gosz, Weitzman, & Flores, 2007). Hispanic toddlers are three times more likely than Caucasian and African American children to be iron deficient (16% versus 5% and 4%). In addition, Gabriella consumes a diet that is low in iron content due to her vegetarian food choices. She prefers cheese and milk products instead of iron-rich beans, peas, lentils, and leafy green vegetables. For Gabriella the risk factors compound, resulting in her iron deficiency.

Teachers are in a good position to watch for the symptoms of iron deficiency. Teachers affiliated with Head Start programs are more likely to be aware of children who have low iron

Health Hint

The Iron, Lead, and Calcium Connection

Industrialized society has created a lead burden that is evident worldwide. Lead is a heavy metal that can have significant health consequences when children are exposed to it in their environment. Urban environments, in particular those with older dilapidated multiple-dwelling buildings, create high-risk situations in terms of lead exposure because lead-containing paints often flake off in the older buildings. Children can get lead poisoning by breathing and swallowing dust that contains lead.

What are some effects of too much lead in children?

- It increases the risk of anemia because it inhibits the production of heme, the oxygencarrying component of hemoglobin in the red blood cells.
- It can cause central nervous system damage in children who are exposed.
- It can result in impaired intellectual function, impacting learning into adulthood.
- It can cause behavioral problems.
- It can damage kidneys and the immune system. (Mayo Clinic, 2007)

How does optimal nutrition prevent lead toxicity?

- Children who are iron deficient absorb more lead.
- When children go a long time without eating (fasting), they tend to absorb more lead.
- A diet high in fat content promotes more lead absorption.
- A high-calcium diet protects by competing with lead for absorption. (Pearse & Mitchell, n.d.)

What can early childhood educators do to protect children from lead poisoning?

- Establish lead-free classroom environments.
- Provide meals that are high in iron and calcium, and low in fat.
- Refer family to a health care professional for a blood lead test, if the child is at risk for iron deficiency or environmental lead exposure.

---

levels because of the Head Start–mandated requirement that medical and nutritional screens be conducted. These screenings often include an evaluation of children's iron status.

Rickets, Vitamin D, and Bone Health

Rickets is a nutritional deficiency caused by a lack of vitamin D. This deficiency can cause bones to form improperly, resulting in severe skeletal deformities. Often considered a nutritional deficiency of the past, health authorities now recognize that rickets has not disappeared, making it an example of a health concern caused by undernutrition.

Milk service is often encouraged in early childhood settings because it helps build strong bones. Milk contains calcium, a mineral that is a building block of bones. It is also fortified with vitamin D, a nutrient that helps the body absorb calcium from the diet. Vitamin D is an unusual nutrient because it comes from dietary sources such as fortified milk, fortified soy milk, fortified yogurt, fortified cereals, and fortified fruit juices. Vitamin D is also produced in the skin in the presence of sunlight. Infants who are breast-fed exclusively and not exposed to sufficient sunlight tend to be at risk for vitamin D deficiency, especially if they live in a temperate climate and are dark skinned (Pettifor, 2004).

Based on new research that looked at the role of vitamin D in health, the dietary recommendation for vitamin D was recently doubled by the American Academy of Pediatrics for infants, children, and adolescents (Wagner, Greer,

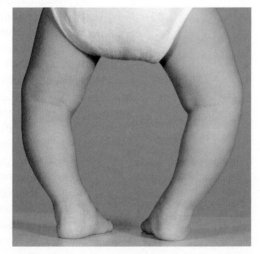

Children with severe vitamin D deficiency develop malformations of skeletal bones, including bowlegs.

rickets
a nutritional deficiency caused by a lack of vitamin D; can cause bones to form improperly, resulting in severe skeletal deformities

vitamin D
a nutrient (fat-soluble vitamin) that aids in calcium absorption; can be obtained from dietary sources such as fortified milk and yogurt, but can also be produced in the skin in response to sunlight

Section on Breastfeeding, & Committee on Nutrition, 2008). Vitamin D may also play an important role in maintaining immunity and preventing diseases such as diabetes and cancer (Wagner et al., 2008). Teachers can contribute to children's health and reduce the risk of vitamin D deficiency in young children by ensuring that children are offered vitamin D–fortified milk or vitamin D and calcium–fortified soy milk at meal and snack times instead of juice that is not fortified or soft drinks. Fortified margarine, eggs, and fish such as salmon, tuna, sardines, and mackerel also provide a rich source of vitamin D in children's diets (Otten, Pitzi-Hellwig, & Meyers, 2006).

Addressing Undernutrition

The U.S. Congress introduced the National School Lunch Act in 1946 as a direct result of the recognition that school meals were needed to help protect against dietary deficiency diseases (Story, 2009). The School Breakfast Program was enacted with the passage of the Child Nutrition Act of 1966. Its goal is to improve the nutritional well-being of children from low-income families (Story, 2009). In 1968 the earliest version of the Child and Adult Care Food Program was established to provide nutritional support to children in child care (US Department of Agriculture, Food and Nutrition Service, 2009). Children who participate in early care and education programs have a lower reported incidence of iron-deficiency anemia (Brotanek et al., 2007). This may be because these settings serve iron-rich foods such as meat, poultry, fish, dried beans, iron-fortified cereal, bread products and grains, peanut butter, eggs, and green leafy vegetables. These programs, guided and supported by child nutrition programs, act as a safety net for young children but are not sufficient to meet all of their growth and development needs. Teachers need to be knowledgeable about the importance of nutrients such as iron in the diet. They also need to understand the urgency of addressing iron deficiency or any form of undernutrition if it is identified so they can help families access resources, as Cecelia did in the opening case scenario.

Recognizing Overnutrition

Excessive consumption of calorie-rich foods also plays a role in the quality of diet and health of young children. Overnutrition is a form of malnutrition caused by an imbalance of calories consumed when compared to calories needed for growth and activity. Overnutrition causes children to become overweight or obese. Today's changing nutrition environment and more sedentary lifestyles are factors in overnutrition and have resulted in an epidemic of obesity in young children. In fact, obesity is the number one form of malnutrition in the United States today, and researchers report the heaviest children are getting even heavier (Meyer-Davis, 2008; Porth, 2007).

Identifying Obesity in Children

Obesity is identified and defined based on measurements of children's heights and weights that are plotted on growth chart. Conducting height and weight screenings during the beginning of a program's year is a procedure than can help screen for children who are underweight or overweight and obese. The Centers for Disease Control and Prevention (CDC) provides growth charts to assist in screening and identifying children who are at risk for overweight and obesity. (See the Book Specific Resources on MyEducationLab for growth charts.) The charts show percentile curves that represent the range of distribution of heights and weights typical in young children in the United States (CDC National Center for Health Statistics, 2007).

In children over age 2 another criterion used to determine appropriate rate of growth is the **body mass index (BMI)**. Although heights and weights give a comparison for norms based on age, the BMI is not age specific. Instead, the BMI assesses body weight relative to height to determine the risk for overweight or obesity (CDC National Center for Health Statistics, 2007a, 2007b). The CDC makes it easy for teachers to calculate and plot BMIs for individual children and also by class with their BMI tool for schools (see the Web Resources listing at the end of the chapter). Figure 3-2 shows different BMI measurements for a 5-year-old boy. This figure illustrates how BMIs are used to identify obesity, overweight, healthy weight, and underweight in young children.

For infants and toddlers under age two growth is also evaluated by monitoring weight, length and weight relative to length. These measurements should be recorded regularly

MyEducationLab

Go to the Assignments and Activities section of Topic 1: Basic Nutrition in the MyEducationLab for your course and complete the activity entitled *Obesity in Children*. What strategies can you use in the early childhood setting to support lifestyle changes that promote healthy weight in young children?

body mass index (BMI)
a calculation that evaluates weight in relation to height to assess whether an individual is obese or underweight. In young children BMI is also a measure of growth. It is calculated by dividing the weight (kg) of a person by the height (m) squared

Figure 3-2 What Is the BMI? This growth chart indicates how children are identified as obese, overweight, healthy weight, and underweight using the BMI calculation.

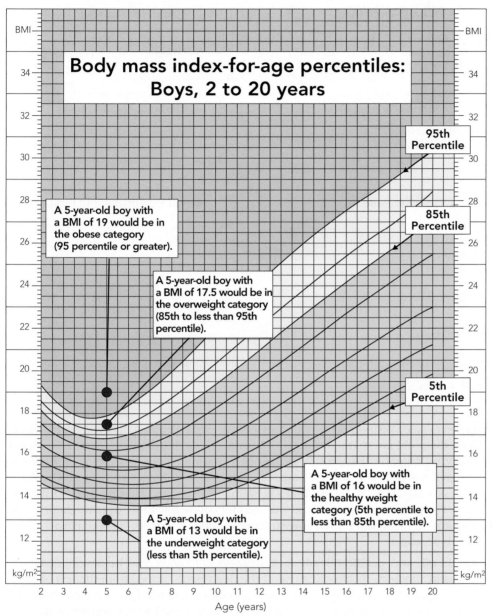

Body mass index-for-age percentiles:
Boys, 2 to 20 years

95th Percentile

85th Percentile

A 5-year-old boy with a BMI of 19 would be in the obese category (95 percentile or greater).

A 5-year-old boy with a BMI of 17.5 would be in the overweight category (85th to less than 95th percentile).

5th Percentile

A 5-year-old boy with a BMI of 16 would be in the healthy weight category (5th percentile to less than 85th percentile).

A 5-year-old boy with a BMI of 13 would be in the underweight category (less than 5th percentile).

Age (years)

Source: Adapted from *Healthy Weight: Assessing Your Weight: About BMI for Children and Teens*, by the Centers for Disease Control and Prevention, 2009, retrieved September 8, 2009, from http://www.cdc.gov/healthyweight/assessing/bmi/childrens_bmi/about_childrens_bmi.html.

throughout the year to ensure that proper growth is occurring. (Growth charts are discussed in more detail in Chapter 10.)

If excessive weight gain is identified, sharing this information with parents can set a course for change and obesity prevention. In dealing with weight issues in young children an "ounce of prevention is truly worth a pound of cure" because children who are obese when young are more likely to grow up to be overweight and obese adults. A fat baby is no longer regarded as a healthy baby, and children do not always grow out of their "baby fat."

The Health Consequences of Obesity

Being overweight or obese during childhood is of great concern because of the immediate as well as the long-term health consequences. Obese children suffer from problems such as

What if. . .

you had a family whose cultural traditions valued heavy babies and young children and who felt that this was a sign of good health? How would you address the sensitive subject of obesity?

Figure 3-3 **Health Problems Associated with Obesity in Children**

Heart-Related Risks	Lung-Related Risks

High blood cholesterol levels
High blood pressure
Increased risk of heart attack or stroke
   as adults
	Asthma
	Obstructive sleep apnea syndrome (a sleep
	   disorder in which frequent breathing
	   interruptions occur during sleep)

Endocrine-Related Risks	**Orthopedic-Related Risks**
Insulin resistance Type 2 diabetes	Bowlegs Slipped capital femoral epiphysis (the ball of the thigh bone slips off the thigh bone) Arthritis
Cancer-Related Risks	**Mental Health–Related Risks**
Breast cancer Colon cancer Cancer of the esophagus Kidney cancer	Depression Low self-esteem
Gastrointestinal-Related Risks	
Nonalcoholic fatty liver disease Gall bladder disease	

Sources: Information from "Policy Statement: Prevention of Pediatric Overweight and Obesity," by the American Academy of Pediatrics Committee on Nutrition, 2003, *Pediatrics, 112*(2), pp. 424–430; and *National Cancer Institute Fact Sheet: Obesity and Cancer: Questions and Answers*, by the National Cancer Institute, 2004, retrieved from http://www.cancer.gov/cancertopics/factsheet/risk/obesity.

sleep apnea
a sleep disorder in which a person's breathing pauses during sleep

sleep apnea (a sleep disorder in which a person's breathing pauses during sleep), asthma, and orthopedic problems that interfere with learning and contribute to a higher incidence of absenteeism (Waters & Baur, 2003). Being obese at a young age and over long period of time can have a significant adverse impact on health and longevity (Flegal, Graubard, Williamson, & Gail, 2005; Fontaine, Redden, Wang, Westfall, & Allison, 2003; Olshansky et al., 2005). Figure 3-3 summarizes the health risks for children who are overweight or obese.

Unfortunately, the health-related consequences of obesity can become self-perpetuating. Consider this scenario:

> At age 8 Colin was significantly obese. During his third-grade year he developed a hip abnormality in which the growing end of the thigh bone slipped from the ball of the hip joint, a condition often linked to obesity. Colin experienced considerable pain and ultimately required surgery to realign the joint. Colin missed school and when he was able to return he used a wheelchair for 6 weeks. During this time he was unable to participate actively in physical education classes. His weight increased because of this inactivity. Although his teacher tried to help him catch up with his class assignments, his condition was painful, making it hard for him to progress in his schoolwork.

In this scenario, Colin's obesity caused both health and learning problems.

The Psychosocial Impact of Obesity

Children who are obese often experience low self-esteem, depression, and poor peer interactions (Nevin-Folino, 2008). Researchers in one study revealed that obesity affected health-related quality-of-life indicators such as physical, psychosocial, emotional, social, and school functioning. The effects were comparable to those reported for children diagnosed with cancer and who were undergoing treatment (Schwimmer, Burwinkle, & Varni, 2003). In addition, obese children were four times more likely than healthy children to do poorly in school (Schwimmer et al., 2003).

The psychosocial consequences become more prevalent as children become older. For instance, by first grade students become sensitized to obesity, preferring nonobese

What if. . .
you observed a child who was obese being bullied? How would you manage this situation?

friends and attributing negative personality traits such as laziness and sloppiness to obese children (Dietz, 1998). Teachers should be particularly attuned to the challenges faced by children who are overweight and obese whose struggles with self-esteem increase as they mature.

The Role of Inadequate Physical Activity

Lack of sufficient physical activity contributes to the other side of the coin of obesity, inadequate energy expenditure (the amount of calories burned), which compounds the problem of overnutrition. Maintaining a healthy weight requires a fine balance between calorie intake and energy expenditure. Some practices in early childhood and school settings may contribute to inadequate physical activity among young children, such as:

- Providing little space for indoor or outdoor active play.
- Offering insufficient quantity and quality of time scheduled for physical activity in daily programming (Finn, Johannsen, & Specker, 2002).
- Devoting most of the school day to academic achievement, as mandated by some school districts, at the cost of time for exercise.
- Neglecting training of teachers in after-school programs who are able to promote and model physical activity (Coleman, Geller, Rosenkranz, & Dzewaltowski, 2008).
- Withholding recess as a form of punishment or as a means to have children catch up on assignments.
- Eliminating physical education classes due to funding constraints, which decreases opportunities for exercise and also decreases the focus on teaching physical activity skills that support active lifestyles.

Teachers are in a good position to encourage activity in young children by increasing the amount of time in the daily schedule devoted to outside play and incorporating physical activity into daily routines, as follows:

- Plan walking field trips and scavenger hunts in the community.
- Include a physical activity center during self-select time.
- Provide activities using portable playground equipment, such as balls and hoops.
- Plan school events with a physical activity theme, such as a field day, sock hop dance, walk or bike to school day, walking club, parent–child activity night.
- Offer fund-raisers that encourage physical activity such as a jog-a-thon, fun run, or family walking obstacle course.
- Promote noncompetitive sports and cooperative games so that all children—regardless of skill level and ability—will want to participate.

The National Association for Sport and Physical Education (NASPE) is a professional organization and national authority on physical education, sports, and physical activity. The NASPE has established general physical activity guidelines for children in two main age divisions: birth to age 5 and ages 5 to 12 (see Web Resources). These age-specific physical activity recommendations give teachers parameters to consider as they strive to achieve physically active environments for the children in their care.) Important standards are listed for each age group. For example, it is recommended that toddlers (1- to 2-year-olds) receive 30 minutes of structured physical activity each day and preschoolers (3- to 4-year-olds) 60 minutes. Toddlers and preschoolers should participate in at least 60 minutes or more of unstructured play per day as well. NASPE also recommends that, unless sleeping, young children should not be sedentary for more than 60 minutes at a time.

Guidelines are also offered on how to promote the physical activity of infants by creating safe settings that do not limit movement, but do stimulate babies to explore their environment (NASPE, 2009). The NASPE website provides links to excellent resources that help teachers incorporate physical activity into the early childhood education setting.

energy expenditure
the amount of energy or calories used by the body during rest and physical activity

MyEducationLab

Go to the Assignments and Activities section of Topic 5: Health Promotion/Policy in the MyEducationLab for your course and complete the activity entitled *Health Activities for Elementary Children*. How do these events support the establishment of health habits that focus on obesity prevention?

Inactive lifestyles contribute to the rising incidence of obesity.

Food Insecurity and Obesity

Food insecurity, or consistently having too little food to eat due to financial constraints, can lead to obesity (Casey et al., 2006; Darmon, Ferguson, & Briend, 2002; Drewnowski & Darmon, 2005; Drewnowski & Specter, 2004). Although it seems contradictory, hunger and obesity can exist side by side. This situation was first described by William Dietz, M.D., who hypothesized that families who lack money are more likely to purchase foods they can afford, which tend to be high in fat content, a contributor to overweight. He also proposed that there may be a "Physiologic adaptation in response to episodic food shortages" (Dietz, 1995, p. 766). In other words, when individuals have suffered from food insecurity, their bodies may undergo physiologic changes that make them more susceptible to gaining weight when they eat.

Children who are obese and who eat larger than normal serving sizes may be reacting to the stress of food insecurity. Teachers need to consider how they will support children who struggle with obesity and food insecurity. Here is how one teacher approached this situation:

> Vanessa, a preschool teacher, carefully supervises Kimberly during mealtime, especially when oranges are on the menu. Kimberly, who is overweight, frequently serves herself more orange wedges than the one-half orange portion planned for each child. This became a problem during the family-style meal service when the other children at the table did not get their share of oranges. Vanessa, who was concerned about Kimberly's weight, mentioned this behavior to Kimberly's father Mark. Mark explained that the family could not afford to buy fresh fruit very often and admitted that Kimberly had never had oranges before coming to school. Vanessa recognized that Kimberly's family was suffering from food insecurity. During the meal service she showed Kimberly how to count out her portion. Then she arranged for Kimberly to have more oranges if she wanted after everyone was served.

Addressing Obesity

Helping children learn healthful eating habits and encouraging enjoyment of physical activity are two ways in which teachers can promote a proactive approach to the challenges of the obesity epidemic. It is important for educators to stay abreast of evidence-based approaches to achieve these goals. Teachers and their early childhood programs are partners with families and communities in promoting healthy lifestyles for children. Classroom approaches that help teachers be proactive in addressing the concerns of obesity include the following:

- Provide an environment that supports wellness, such as offering nutritious meals and providing space and equipment for physically active play.
- Integrate nutrition concepts into program curriculum and activities. For example children can study different kinds of beans, learn how whole-grain bread is made, and participate in growing a vegetable garden.
- Introduce games that promote physical activity, such as "Duck, Duck, Goose" or "Four Square."
- Invite parents to help plan menus, to share ideas about nutrition activities and games, and to promote these wellness approaches at home.
- Be a good wellness role model. Eat with pleasure the healthful meals served to children. Model enjoyment of physical activity and participate in active games with the children.

Teachers who have insight into the challenging and changing nutrition environment in the United States have the tools necessary to formulate a plan for protecting the health and well-being of young children in their care. See the *Policy Point* for information on supporting policy changes that impact obesity.

USING RECOMMENDED STANDARDS TO GUIDE HEALTHY EATING

Knowledge of nutrition is crucial in supporting good health in adults and children alike. Teachers and parents select and plan a healthy diet for the children in their care and, therefore, must understand the components of food that contribute to a balanced diet.

SUPPORTING POLICY CHANGES THAT IMPACT OBESITY

Many teachers feel a strong need to advocate for change in their school or community to fight the obesity epidemic. To start, they need information to "shake things up." To influence decision makers, they need information that relates specifically to their state.

The Oregon Health Sciences University, with support from the U.S. Department of Health and Human Services, developed a website called the Data Resource Center for Child and Adolescent Health at http://www.childhealthdata.org/content/Default.aspx#. This resource offers state-by-state data on the incidence of obesity and discusses what each state is doing to address the obesity epidemic. These powerful facts can provide the impetus teachers need to support change that improves the wellness of young children.

Source: *Childhood Obesity Action Network, State Obesity Profiles,* by the National Initiative for Children's Healthcare Quality, the Child Policy Research Center, and the Child and Adolescent Health Measurement Initiative, 2009, retrieved on March 3, 2009, from http://www.childhealthdata.org/content/07ObesityReportCards.aspx.

Researchers and experts in the field of nutrition have established guidelines and standards to ensure that teachers know how to plan appropriate menus and serve foods that support healthy development.

Understanding Dietary Reference Intakes

The Dietary Reference Intakes (DRIs) established by the Institute of Medicine of the National Academies are one of the important standards used to guide development of a healthful diet. They were developed in phases starting in 1997 through 2005, using the most recent research on nutrition, to establish evidence-based reference values that specify the amount of nutrients needed in the diets of adults, children, and population groups to maintain good health (Otten et al., 2006). (DRIs are listed in Web Resource and can be found in the Book Specific Resources on MyEducationLab). The nutrients covered by the DRI guidelines include those that are considered essential nutrients because they either cannot be made in the body or cannot be made in sufficient quantities to meet the body's needs; consequently, the nutrients must be consumed in the diet.

The Dietary Reference Intakes form the basis for diet recommendations made by health and government authorities. They are used as a foundation for the development of public policies that address the health and wellness of children in the United States. For example, the *Dietary Guidelines for Americans, 2005* and the *MyPyramid for Kids* base their diet recommendations on meeting the nutrient goals established by the DRIs. In addition, the National School Lunch Program, which currently reflects the 1989 Recommended Dietary Allowances, will soon update their standards for menu planning to reflect the new DRIs (Committee on Nutrition Standards for National School Lunch and Breakfast Programs Food and Nutrition Board, 2008).

The Dietary Reference Intakes are the guiding force when researchers assess the nutritional quality of children's diets. Studies that link iron-deficiency anemia to insufficient iron intake could not draw these conclusions without the DRIs, the yardstick for healthy diets. To understand the DRIs, it is helpful to become familiar with how the nutrients are divided into different categories, as discussed next.

Classification of Nutrients

Nutrients are classified into six major categories: protein, fat, carbohydrates, vitamins, minerals, and water (see Figure 3-4). Food provides energy or calories from proteins, fats, and carbohydrates (macronutrients) and essential nutrients such as vitamins and minerals (micronutrients).

Macronutrients Proteins, fats, and carbohydrates are macronutrients that are needed in large amounts in the diet. Carbohydrates and fats are predominantly used as a source of

dietary reference intakes (DRIs)
a listing of daily estimated nutrient requirements; used to assess diets for adequacy at the nutrient level

reference values
a point of reference for nutrient intake levels to help interpret adequacy of intake

essential nutrients
nutrients that either cannot be made in the body or cannot be made in sufficient quantities to meet the body's needs and therefore must be consumed in the diet

macronutrients
nutrient category that includes protein, fats, and carbohydrates; they are the energy- or calorie-providing nutrients and are needed in large amounts in the diet

carbohydrates
macronutrients in the form of sugars and starches that provide the body with energy

fats
macronutrients that provide the most concentrated source of energy for the body; also used to cushion the organs and to insulate the body

Figure 3-4 Classification and Sources of Nutrients

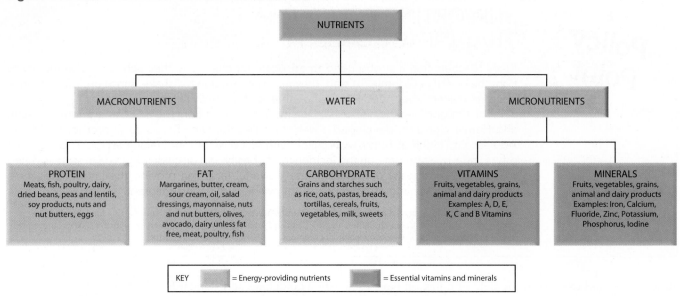

fuel for the body. Proteins can also be used as fuel; however, they are preferentially used to regulate body processes and serve as building blocks for body structures such as muscles, organs, and blood.

The balance of macronutrients in the diet as well as the total amount provided by the diet is very important. Too many calories from the macronutrients will cause excessive weight gain, whereas too little may result in insufficient growth. Macronutrients are found in the typical foods children consume during a day. For example, a tuna sandwich served at lunch contains protein (in the tuna), carbohydrates (in the bread), and fat (in the mayonnaise). Most foods are a combination of macronutrients. Bread contains mostly carbohydrates, but does have some protein, and its fat content can vary considerably as in the case of a high-fat croissant. The milk served at mealtime is also a combination of protein, fat, and carbohydrates unless the milk is fat free.

Micronutrients The micronutrients include vitamins and minerals. The body requires micronutrients in much smaller amounts than macronutrients, but they are essential for children to thrive. It is with the assistance of micronutrients that energy from the macronutrients can be processed. Micronutrients promote growth and development. Each micronutrient has a unique role. Micronutrients are found in all different types of foods but some foods have a higher concentration of certain micronutrients. For example, milk is high in vitamin D and calcium, whereas citrus fruits and kiwis are high in vitamin C.

Water Water is essential for survival because all systems in the body need water to carry on life processes. Water transports nutrients in the bloodstream and flushes the body of wastes. It helps the body maintain proper temperatures through perspiration. Children obtain water from the beverages they drink, but also get water from foods that they eat such as fruits and vegetables.

Components of the Dietary Reference Intakes

The Dietary Reference Intakes include five component parts. The first four components establish recommendations for the consumption of micronutrients. The fifth component establishes guidelines for the macronutrients (Otten et al., 2006). The components are as follows:

- **Recommended Dietary Allowances (RDAs):** Evidence-based nutrient goals that meet the needs of almost all healthy individuals including infants and children.
- **Adequate Intakes (AIs):** Same as the RDAs, but kept distinct because the evidenced-based research is not as strong.

- **Estimated Average Requirements (EARs):** These nutrient recommendations meet the needs of 50% of the population and are used to assess food intakes of groups and provide standards for research conclusions.
- **Tolerable Upper Intake Levels (ULs):** These are the highest nutrient intake levels that pose no risk. They are used to ensure food safety by providing standards for individuals taking supplements or consuming fortified foods.
- **Acceptable Macronutrient Distribution Ranges (AMDRs):** AMDRs provide recommendations for protein, fat, and carbohydrate consumption, expressed as a percent of total calorie needs. AMDRs are used to promote health and decrease the risk of chronic disease by providing guidelines on what proportion of the diet should consist of fats, carbohydrates, and protein.

Young children up to age 3 have a higher AMDR for fats than older children and adults. This is because they have smaller stomachs and a rapid rate of growth, both of which result in a need for higher calorie foods. This influences diet recommendations such as serving whole milk to most children up to age 2, and then switching to skim or 1% milk for children older than 2 years of age (see the *Nutrition Note*).

Some parents, in an effort to provide healthful diets to young children, restrict foods that have higher fat contents. Teachers can share with families that restricting fat excessively in young children's diets can negatively impact their rate of growth. For example, a teacher noticed that a 14-month-old in her program was not gaining weight as well as in the past. In a discussion with her mother, the teacher learned the baby was weaned from breast milk to rice milk when her daughter turned 1 year old. A referral to a dietitian revealed that rice milk was not an ideal choice because of its low fat and protein content. A switch back to whole milk resulted in an improved rate of weight gain.

Other families may worry about picky eaters who make limited food choices and wonder if they are getting enough nutrients. They may wonder if giving them multivitamins is appropriate. The *Safety Segment* describes the importance of using caution when offering multivitamins. Teachers, when asked, should refer concerned parents to their health care providers for recommendations about multivitamin use.

In summary, the Dietary Reference Intakes reflect a variety of goals established by nutrition experts. These goals include ensuring that diets are adequate, but not excessive, in nutrient content and are protective of long-term health (Otten et al., 2006). Although teachers may not need to refer often to the DRIs, familiarity with them, and recognition of the

Recommended Dietary Allowances (RDAs)
evidence-based nutrient goals that will meet 97% to 98% of an individual's daily nutrient requirements; used to assess the nutrient needs of healthy individuals

Adequate Intakes (AIs)
like the RDAs, the estimated amount of nutrients that will meet 97% to 98% of an individual's daily nutrient requirements, but is established when there is not enough evidence-based research to establish an RDA or EAR

Estimated Average Requirements (EARs)
estimated amount of nutrients that will meet 50% of an individual's daily nutrient requirements; used to assess the nutrient needs of populations and as the basis for establishment of RDAs

Tolerable Upper Intake Levels (ULs)
the highest nutrient intake levels that pose no risk; used to ensure food safety by providing standards for individuals taking supplements or consuming fortified foods

Nutrition Note

Fats for Infants

Fat is an important nutrient for infants and toddlers who have high energy needs because of their rapid growth. These young children have a small stomach capacity and can only meet their nutritional needs for growth and development by eating calorie-dense fats. The fat intake requirement of infants is greater than at any other time in life with infants needing 45% to 55% of their calories to come from fat.

Fats serve not only as a source of energy but as an aid in the absorption of the fat-soluble vitamins A, D, E, and K. Fat is also a source of *essential fatty acids*, which are vital in supporting optimal brain growth and development in infants. It is very important for adults who care for infants and toddlers to recognize the important role fat plays in early development.

Sources: "Dietary (n-3) Fatty Acids and Brain Development," by S. M. Innis, 2007, *Journal of Nutrition, 137*(4), pp. 855–859; and "Lipid Requirements of Infants: Implications for Nutrient Composition of Fortified Complementary Foods," by R. Uauy and C. Castillo, 2003, *Journal of Nutrition, 133*(9), pp. 2962S–2972S.

Acceptable Macronutrient Distribution Ranges (AMDRs) provide recommendations for protein, fat, and carbohydrate consumption, expressed as a percent of total calorie needs; used to promote health and decrease the risk of chronic disease by providing guidelines on what proportion of the diet should consist of fats, carbohydrates, and protein

Daily Values (DVs) dietary reference values that are used on food labels and represent the requirements of an "average" individual, unlike Dietary Reference Intakes, which have reference values that represent different age and gender categories

science that is behind such resources, reminds teachers of the importance of nutrition and diet to healthy growth and development.

Evaluating Daily Values and Reading Food Labels

Another nutrient-based guidance system is one that teachers see every day: the daily values (DVs), which are located on the label of almost all foods purchased and consumed. Daily values indicate what percent of the daily recommended amount of a nutrient is met when a portion of a food is consumed. For example, a label may show that a serving of food meets 20% of the daily recommended amount of iron. This means 80% more iron must be consumed in other foods to meet the total daily value. The total daily value is based on a 2,000-calorie diet. Figure 3-5 shows an example of DVs displayed on a food label.

The daily values were established as a standard for measuring the contribution of a food item or supplement to the diet. The daily values are different from the Dietary Reference Intakes in that they are not age and gender specific. Instead, they represent what has been determined to be the average intake range of most people in the United States. The requirements for babies, children, teenagers, adults, pregnant and breast-feeding woman, and the elderly were examined and averaged into one set of values. That is, the daily values are designed for an "average" person; they are a "one-size-fits-all" recommendation. This approach is appropriate to meet the needs of most people; however, some individuals may need less than the DV-recommended amounts of nutrients and some might need more. Infants and young children, for example, would need less than the daily value on the label. Because infants and children have lower nutrient needs than the daily value, teachers need to recognize that meeting 100% daily value is not a goal for them. Rather, daily values can best be used to understand the nutritional composition of a food. For example, a food that contains 5% or less of the daily is low in a particular nutrient. If it contains 20% or more of a nutrient it is considered high source of that nutrient (U.S. Food and Drug Administration [FDA], 2009).

Safety Segment

Keep Children Safe from Multivitamin Overdoses

The Dietary Reference Intakes (DRIs) provide guidance on the amount and types of essential nutrients individuals need to consume to maintain a healthy diet. Sometimes children may not eat as well as they should. Families may consider giving multivitamins to their children to make sure nutrition goals are met. Should children take multivitamins? Most healthy children do fine without dietary supplementation. Their needs are less than those of adults, and they may be consuming foods that are fortified such as breakfast cereals or juices.

Teachers should direct families with concerns to discuss the use of multivitamins with their doctor or dietitian. If they are advised to take multivitamins, they should select ones that are designed for children. Caregivers should be careful about how they are dispensed. Many multivitamins can look and taste like candy, and children who take too many put themselves at risk.

The American Academy of Pediatrics and the American Dietetic Association agree that vitamin and mineral supplements (except for vitamin K in the newborn infant, vitamin D for the breast-fed infant, and non–breast-fed infants, and children who drink less than 4 cups of formula or milk per day, and fluoride in nonfluoridated communities) are not needed for most healthy children and that it is always better to meet nutrient needs with foods rather than in pill form.

Sources: From *Pediatric Nutrition Handbook*, 6th edition, edited by R. Kleinman, 2009, Elk Grove, IL: American Academy of Pediatrics; "Position of the American Dietetic Association: Fortification and Nutritional Supplements," by the American Dietetic Association, 2005, *Journal of the American Dietetic Association, 105*(8), pp. 1300–1311.

Figure 3-5 Sample Label for a High-Fiber Cereal

The nutrient content of a product cannot be assessed without knowing its serving size and how many servings are in a box.

Divide fat calories by total calories × 100 to get %fat calories. Healthy diets aim for more foods that have 30% calories or less from fat.

Information on fat and cholesterol content is particularly important for those concerned about heart health or weight. *Trans* fat and saturated fats and cholesterol should be kept as low as possible. Remember that just because a food announces its *trans* fat free does not mean it is low in saturated fats.

The sodium content of U.S. diets tends to be higher than desirable. A food is considered low sodium if it has 140 mg or less per serving.

The total carbohydrate figure includes fiber and sugar. The sugar includes natural sugars as well as added. This product is higher than some because it is a cereal with raisins. Look for foods that are rich in fiber. High fiber is 5 g or more per serving.

Children and adults should consume a diet rich in these nutrients. This product has been fortified and is a good source of iron. The DV for iron is 18 mg. At 25% this cereal provides 4.5 mg of iron per serving. 5% or less of DV is low and 20% or more is high in a particular nutrient.

Here are the standard intakes by which the %DV is derived. The complete list of the standard nutrients content for a 2,000-calorie diet can be found at: http://www.cfsan.fda.gov/~dms/flg-7a.html.

Ingredients are listed from highest to lowest concentration. Allergy information is provided.

Nutrition Facts

Serving Size 1 cup (59g/2.1 oz)
Servings per Container About 12

Amount per Serving	Cereal
Calories	190
Calories from fat	15

	% Daily Values*
Total Fat 1.5g	2%
Saturated fat 0g	0%
Trans fat 0g	0%
Cholesterol 0mg	0%
Sodium 350mg	15%
Potassium 360mg	10%
Total Carbohydrate 45g	15%
Dietary fiber 7 g	28%
Sugars 19g	
Other carbohydrates 19g	
Protein 5g	

Vitamin A	10%
Vitamin C	0%
Calcium	2%
Iron	25%

*Daily Values are based on a 2,000 calorie diet. Your daily values may be higher or lower depending on your calorie needs

	Calories	2000	2500
Total fat	Less than	65g	80g
Sat fat	Less than	20g	25g
Cholesterol	Less than	300mg	300mg
Total carbohydrates		300g	350g
Fiber		25g	30g

Ingredients: Whole wheat, bran, sugar, raisins
CONTAINS: WHEAT

The daily values are in the process of being updated to reflect the new Dietary Reference Intakes and to take into consideration the nutrient requirements of children and pregnant and breast-feeding women (Committee on the Use of Dietary Reference Intakes in Nutrition Labeling, 2003).

Food Label Requirements

In 1990 the Nutrition Labeling and Education Act (NLEA) established clear food labeling requirements. What was once a system riddled with misleading claims and unrealistic portion sizes is now an organized and accessible nutrition report within a nutrition information facts panel. The content of labels must now include:

- *Portion sizes:* Listed in both the U.S. system of measurement (1/2 cup) and metric amounts (120 mL) or in amounts commonly consumed (6 crackers).
- *Nutrient composition of the food:* Includes calories, fat calories, total fat, *trans* fats and saturated fats, cholesterol, sodium, potassium, total carbohydrates, fiber, sugar, and protein. (**trans fats** are a type of unhealthy fat found in food that promotes heart disease)
- *Specific vitamin and mineral content:* Includes, for example, vitamin A, vitamin C, calcium, and iron.
- *Nutrients:* Listed as a percent (%) of daily values.

trans fat
a type of unhealthy dietary fat that is created when oils are partially hydrogenated; when found in food can promote heart disease

- *Ingredients:* Listed in order of highest to lowest concentration.
- *Warnings:* Lists possible allergens (briefly discussed in next section).
- *Nutrition claims:* Uses a standardized approach, such as what constitutes "low fat" or "high fiber" (see Table 3-1).
- *Health claims:* Claims that have been approved by the FDA for listing on food labels to describe a link between the food and health. (U.S. Food and Drug Administration, 2003b)

Overall, the information provided on food labels helps consumers determine how the food contributes to the daily total nutritional intake and how a food's nutritional content compares to that of other foods. Teachers are likely to use label-reading skills when they comparison shop, looking for nutrient-rich foods to use in any type of food preparation for children, whether for lunch meals, snacks, or food-related school activities.

gluten
a type of protein found in the grains of wheat, rye, and barley that causes symptoms in adults and children with celiac disease. Oats are sometimes avoided as well on a gluten-free diet

Reading Labels for Food Allergens

The Food Allergen Labeling and Consumer Protection Act, approved in 2004 and initiated in 2006, mandates that eight major foods or food groups—milk, eggs, fish, crustacean shellfish, tree nuts, peanuts, wheat, and soybeans—be included on the food label to help people with food allergies recognize products they may need to avoid.

Gluten free is a term that can voluntarily be included on labels. Gluten is a type of protein found in the grains of wheat, rye, barley, and possibly oats. Gluten causes symptoms in

Table 3-1	Understanding Nutrient Content Claims
Nutrient	**Per Serving**
SODIUM	
Sodium free	Less than 5 mg
Very low sodium	35 mg or less
Low sodium	140 mg or less
Reduced sodium	25% lower than regular
CALORIES	
Calorie free	Less than 5 calories
Low calorie	40 calories or less
Reduced	25% lower than regular
FAT	
Fat free	Less than 0.5 g
Low fat	3 g or less
CHOLESTEROL	
Cholesterol free	Less than 2 mg
Low cholesterol	20 mg or less
SATURATED FAT	
Saturated fat free	Less than 0.5 mg
Low saturated fat	1 g or less
Reduced saturated fat	25% less than regular
TRANS FAT	
Trans fat free	Less than 0.5
FIBER	
High fiber	5 g or more

Source: *FDA Backgrounder: The Food Label,* by the U.S. Food and Drug Administration, 2008, retrieved September 8, 2009, from http://vm.cfsan.fda.gov/~dms/fdnewlab.html.

adults and children with celiac disease, a genetic gastrointestinal disorder (FDA, 2003a, 2007). Allergy information is shown on the bottom of a food label (in Figure 3-5 notice the statement "contains").

Special Labeling for Infant/Toddler Foods

The FDA and USDA have established slightly different labeling regulations for foods such as infant cereals and baby foods that are targeted toward children under the age of 2 and children ages 2 to 4 (Kurtzweil, 1995). For example, labels may not contain information about fats and cholesterol. These regulations were developed in recognition of the specific nutrient needs of very young children. Special labeling for children's foods ensures that adults who care for children avoid making the mistake of inadvertently restricting certain nutrients such as fat and cholesterol that are needed for young children to grow properly (FDA, 2003).

Label reading is an important skill for teachers who may be gatekeepers for the types of food schools purchase for their meal service or foods uses for cooking activities. Label reading helps teachers to:

- Make decisions about the nutritional contribution of different foods.
- Ensure children get foods that are rich in healthful vitamins, minerals, and fiber.
- Select foods low in saturated fats, *trans* fats, and cholesterol (if over age 2).
- Avoid foods that are high in sodium.
- Select appropriate foods for children with food allergies or sensitivities, cultural food preferences, and special diets.

celiac disease
a genetic gastrointestinal disorder that is characterized by an immune response to gluten that damages the gastrointestinal tract and leads to malabsorption

What if. . .

a parent informed you that she did not want her child to consume any foods with *trans* fats? How would you negotiate a common ground with the parent and the child who might object to having to eat something different than what the other children in the class get to eat?

Using the *Dietary Guidelines for Americans, 2005*

The *Dietary Guidelines for Americans, 2005* is a collaborative effort of the Department of Health and Human Services (HHS) and the USDA (2005). The guidelines are issued every 5 years to address the needs of people 2 years of age and older, offering recommendations for the general public as well as special populations such as children, the elderly, and pregnant women. The new dietary guidelines are currently undergoing revision and will be available in 2010. The DRIs were introduced in phases starting in 1997 through 2005. The current dietary guidelines are described in Table 3-2.

Table 3-2	Dietary Guidelines for Americans, 2005
Guideline	**Recommendation**
1. Consume adequate nutrients within calorie needs.	Select food rich in nutrients while limiting saturated and *trans* fats, cholesterol, added sugars, and salt.
2. Manage weight.	Balance calories consumed with calories used.
3. Pay attention to physical activity.	Be physically active every day and reduce sedentary activities.
4. Eat foods from all food groups.	Consume more fruits and vegetables, whole grains, fat-free or low-fat milk, and dairy products.
5. Pay attention to fats.	Keep diet lower in fat (20% to 35%) and limit foods rich in saturated and *trans* fats and cholesterol.
6. Select healthful carbohydrates.	Include fiber-rich fruits, vegetables, and whole grains with little added sugar.
7. Consider sodium and potassium.	Limit salt intake and consume foods rich in potassium, such as fruits and vegetables.
8. Ensure food safety.	Practice food safety principles when preparing and serving foods.

Source: *Dietary Guidelines for Americans, 2005*, by the U.S. Department of Health and Human Services and the U.S. Department of Agriculture, 2005, retrieved September 1, 2009, from http://www.health.gov/dietaryguidelines/dga2005/document/pdf/DGA2005.pdf.

Figure 3-6 **Components of a Nutrient-Dense Diet**

Choose Fresh Fruits (or frozen without sugar) such as citrus fruits, mangos, berries, melons, papaya, bananas, kiwis, peaches, nectarines, plums

Choose Fresh Vegetables (or frozen without sauces) such as dark green and deep orange vegetables as well as tomatoes; red, green, and yellow peppers; red cabbage

Select Whole, Basic, Unprocessed Foods

Select Lean Cuts of Meat, Skinless Poultry and Fish, and Use More Alternative Protein Sources such as dried beans, peas and lentils, soy products, and nuts or nut butters

Select Low-Fat Dairy Products such as skim or 1% milk (age 2 and older), low-fat cheeses and plain yogurt with fresh fruit

Select Whole Grains such as oats, brown rice, whole grain breads, rolls and cereals, barley, corn tortillas

The dietary guidelines provide overall lifestyle recommendations in addition to dietary guidance through the following goals:

- To help individuals meet nutrient intake requirements established in the Dietary Reference Intakes.
- To support dietary choices that reduce risks for chronic disease and support optimal growth.
- To provide guidelines for physically active lifestyles.
- To address issues related to food safety (HHS & USDA, 2005).

The dietary guidelines highlight that consuming nutritious foods, rather than supplements, is the foundation for good health. They also stress the importance of making smart choices from all food groups in order to obtain the most nutrients per calorie consumed. Figure 3-6 provides guidelines for selecting foods that are nutrient dense in relation to their calorie content. Nutrient-dense foods are foods that are high in vitamin and mineral content compared to their calorie content. Select unprocessed foods lower in sodium, fat and sugar content. Consider how the dietary guidelines with their focus on nutrient-dense foods were put to use by Kerrin in her family child care program:

nutrient-dense foods foods that are high in vitamin and mineral content while relatively low in calorie content

Kerrin decided to review the dietary guidelines before writing the menus for her child care program. She felt she was doing very well because she chose many nutrient-dense fruits and vegetables to place on her menu. She realized, however, that the guidelines recommended that at least half of the grains offered to children be whole grains. She decided to take steps to increase the whole-grain portions offered on her menus. She switched to the exclusive use of whole-grain bread products, brown rice, and whole-grain cereals. She also decided to combine nutrient-dense foods such as chicken stir fry over brown rice and sweet potato muffins, yogurt, and berry smoothies. These changes enhanced the nutritional quality of the menu and were well received by the children.

Together the dietary guidelines and the Dietary Reference Intakes are the primary contributors to the policies that guide federally supported child nutrition programs. These guidelines can also be used more directly by teachers for:

- Planning menus.
- Implementing good nutrition and health education activities and lessons (see the *Teaching Wellness* feature).
- Developing parent education programs.
- Selecting topics for newsletters, posters, and bulletin board displays.
- Making healthy decisions about what to eat and how to plan their own active lifestyle to enhance health.

Understanding Feeding Guidelines for Infants and Toddlers

Growth during the first 2 years of life occurs at a rate that is faster than any other period of development. This is also a transitional feeding time during which new foods are introduced, and children begin to feed themselves. Parents and teachers may have many practical questions regarding the feeding progression for children in the infant and toddler age group, however, this is the one age group that is not accounted for in the *Dietary Guidelines for Americans, 2005*. To address this, nutrition experts affiliated with the American Dietetic Association and the American Academy of Pediatrics have developed feeding guidelines which can be accessed on their websites. (See Web Resources). These guidelines, which are summarized in Chapter 5, provide advice for caregivers about:

- When babies are ready for complementary foods (liquids, semisolids, and solids that are not breast milk or formula).
- What babies should be fed.
- The signs that babies give when they are hungry or full.
- How to link infant feeding and physical skills with feeding progression.

The infant feeding guidelines summarized in chapter 5, give special attention to the introduction of complementary foods as the young child progresses from consuming only liquids to accepting semisolid and then solid foods. They focus on the addition of foods that contain nutrients that are important during this period of growth and development. and support teachers by providing evidence-based feeding recommendations.

Using the MyPyramid *Food Guidance System*

The MyPyramid *Food Guidance System* is an important publication of the USDA. It combines the specific nutrient recommendations of the Dietary Reference Intakes and the general messages of the *Dietary Guidelines for Americans, 2005* and translates them into practical step-by-step directions for daily meal planning. The MyPyramid system provides information for individuals to achieve personal health and nutrition goals and offers food intake recommendations for young children ages 2 to 5, children ages 6 to 11 years, and adults (USDA, 2009d). The system focuses on the importance of both diet and physical activity to enhance health and is individualized for different age categories of children. For example, Figure 3-7 illustrates recommendations for preschoolers.

What if. . .

a mother in your program asked you to feed her 3-month-old baby cereal? Is this appropriate? How would you address this situation?

complementary foods
liquids, semisolids, and solids that are not breast milk or formula and are introduced into infants' diets in stages based on development

MyEducationLab

Go to the Assignments and Activities section of Topic 1: Basic Nutrition in the MyEducationLab for your course and complete the activity entitled *Using the Food Pyramid.* How is the Food Guide Pyramid used in the cafeteria setting to increase children's knowledge of both nutrition and physical activity in the mix-it-up lunchroom activity?

Teaching Wellness *Eating Fruits and Vegetables Keeps Me Healthy*

Learning Outcome: Children will experience the sensory aspects (taste, smell, and touch) of a variety of fruits and vegetables.

Infants and Toddlers

- *Goal:* Babies who are eating finger foods and toddlers will smell, touch, and taste various fruits and vegetables.

- *Materials and preparation:* Small unbreakable cups. Select fruits and vegetables in a variety of colors: yellow bananas, red strawberries, cut-up purple seedless grapes (**important:** grapes are a choking hazard if not cut up), green beans, white potato cubes, and orange cooked carrot strips. Cook vegetables until soft enough to pierce with a fork. Cut fruits and vegetable into tiny pieces no larger than ¼ inch. Place food on a tray and cover each different food with an unbreakable cup.

- *Activity plan:* Demonstrate for infants that a food is under each cup. Encourage the child to pick up a cup and discover the fruit or vegetable underneath. Say words that convey pleasure, positive appreciation, and interest, such as "I like to eat fruits and vegetables because they taste good." Name the food, and allow the infants to taste, smell, and feel each food.

- *How to adjust the activity:* For toddlers place different foods into the small paper cups. Have them close their eyes and smell the fruits and vegetables. Ask them, "Can you tell me what this is?" With eyes closed have the toddlers stick a hand in the cup and feel the fruit or vegetable. Talk through the process while encouraging the child through each step. Say, "First let's smell this. Does this smell good? What do you call this food?" Then say, "Now let's touch the food. How does this feel?" Then ask the child, "Do you want to taste the food? How does it taste?" Ask them, "Do you know that fruits and vegetables are good for you?" Reinforce each child's effort by remarking, "You are getting to know about fruits and vegetables by smelling, touching, and tasting these foods. That is a good way to learn."

- *Did you meet your goal?* Did the child explore the fruits and vegetables?

Preschoolers and Kindergartners

- *Goal:* Children will identify fruits and vegetables that they like and understand that fruits and vegetables are good for them.

- *Materials and preparation:* The children's book *Eating the Alphabet: Fruits & Vegetables from A to Z*, by Lois Ehlert; fresh fruits and vegetables depicted in the book cut into bite-size pieces and placed in unbreakable cups. Cover each cup with foil; poke a few holes in the foil with a toothpick or fork. Spoons and napkins.

- *Activity plan:* Explain that there are lots of fruits and vegetables—enough for each letter of the alphabet. Read the book *Eating the Alphabet: Fruits & Vegetables from A to Z*. Invite children to name the fruits and vegetables as you read. Explain that fruits and vegetables are an important part of their diet by saying, "Fruits and vegetables are good for us. Eating them helps us feel good and gives our bodies the energy we need to keep healthy so that we can run and play." Set out six to eight covered cups with different fruits and vegetables for a group of four to five children. Ask the children to smell the fruits and vegetables and try to identify them by smell. Have the

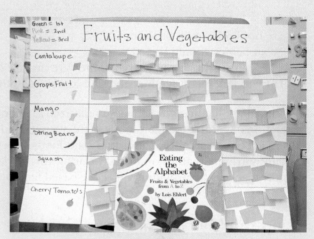

Teachers can integrate math concepts into their nutrition activity by having children vote and tally their favorite fruits and vegetables.

children remove the foil and serve themselves one piece of the food from each cup. Encourage them to describe the smell and taste of each fruit or vegetable, and talk about which they like best. Encourage children's efforts by saying, "You are really exploring these fruits and vegetables by smelling and tasting them."

- *How to adjust the activity:* Have the children gather in a circle. Name a fruit or vegetable from the book. Ask children to jump up high if they like the food that was named. Vary the movement each time a food is named. Invite children to name a fruit or vegetable and ask the other children to respond about whether they like it or not. Create a chart of fruits and vegetables. Have children vote for which fruit and vegetable they like best.

- *Did you meet your goal?* Are children able to identify a fruit and vegetable they like?

School-Age Children

- *Goal:* Children will identify fruits and vegetables for each color of the rainbow and describe why fruit and vegetables are an important part of the diet.

- *Materials and preparation:* Construction paper in rainbow colors, crayons or marking pens, scissors, glue.

- *Activity plan:* Show the children the *MyPyramid for Kids* Poster. Briefly review the different food groups, focusing on fruits and vegetables. Describe the benefits of these foods by saying, "Fruits and vegetable are very high in vitamins, minerals and fiber, components of food that are important for the body to grow." Explain that the most healthy fruits and vegetables are dark green and deep yellow, for example, spinach, broccoli, mangos, papayas, cantaloupe, carrots, and sweet potatoes. Invite the children to make a rainbow using the colored construction paper. Ask them to draw pictures of fruits and vegetables for each color or to write in the names of fruits and vegetables for each color.

- *How to adjust the activity:* Make a MyPyramid recipe for children to take home. Pizza is a food that can be prepared using all of the food groups of the food guide pyramid. Provide a list of ingredients for children to copy and preparation steps they can illustrate. For example:

Ingredients: whole-grain pizza crust, pizza sauce, grated mozzarella cheese, turkey ham strips, pineapple chunks, sliced tomatoes, broccoli, zucchini, sliced olives.

Steps to make Pyramid Pizza:

Step 1: Place crust on pan, spread with pizza sauce.

Step 2: Sprinkle with cheese.

Step 3: Add turkey ham, pineapple, vegetables.

Step 4: Bake at 375 degrees for about 15 minutes.

Did you meet your goal? Are children able to identify a fruit and vegetable for each color of the rainbow? Can they explain why fruits and vegetables are healthy foods?

The MyPyramid guidance system offers a solution to healthy eating that is personalized and positive. According to the USDA, the overall goals of the MyPyramid system are to encourage adults and children to:

- Make informed selections from each food group.
- Balance food and physical activity.
- Select foods that are high in nutrients in relation to the calorie content.
- Stay within daily calorie requirements (USDA, 2009c).

The MyPyramid materials focus on four themes: (1) variety, (2) proportionality, (3) moderation, and (4) activity (USDA, 2009c). They offer recommendations for eating foods from each food group to assist in making the healthiest choices, such as eating whole grains, lean meats, fat-free or low-fat dairy, a variety of fruits and dark green and orange vegetables, and healthful fats. Other resources available on the MyPyramid website include educational materials and lessons that support nutrition and physical activity messages in the classroom setting.

MyEducationLab

Go to the Building Teaching Skills and Dispositions section of Topic 1: Basic Nutrition in the MyEducationaLab for your course and complete the activity entitled *Use MyPyramid to Analyze Children's Diets.* As you work through the learning unit consider why it is important for teachers to become familiar with MyPyramid.

Figure 3-7 **MyPyramid for Preschoolers**

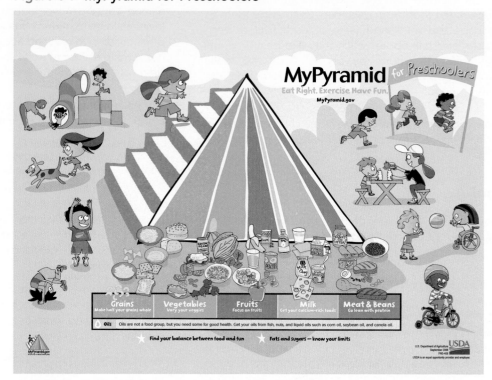

Source: *MyPyramid for Preschoolers*, by the U.S. Department of Agriculture, 2009, retrieved July 6, 2009, from http://www
.mypyramid.gov/Preschoolers.

ETHNIC FOOD GUIDANCE SYSTEMS

The U.S. population is becoming increasingly multicultural. Consequently, teachers must
be responsive to the cultural influences on children's diets as well as other aspects of
school life. Various resources are available to support teachers as they become familiar
with the food guidance systems from other countries. For example, Figures 3-8 and 3-9 illustrate Mexican and Chinese food guides, respectively. Figure 3-10 illustrates a Native
American food pyramid. Many of the recommendations are similar to those of the UDSA
MyPyramid system in that eating a variety of foods in appropriate portions is encouraged.
The foods listed within these guidelines reflect typical food choices of each ethnic group
(Painter & Lee, 2002).

Providing Bilingual Educational Materials

MyPyramid has also been translated into a variety of different languages thanks to the
New Education for New Americans project at Georgia State University (2004). The
"Good Food for Kids," series, found at the same web resource, explains key nutrition
concepts important for young children. These materials are offered at a sixth-grade reading level and presented in English side by side with an alternate language of choice
(36 different languages are represented). These materials are versatile tools teachers can
use when educating families on nutrition related topics. The Canadian government pub-
lishes *Canada's Food Guide,* which is available in 10 different languages (Health Canada,
2008). The Southeastern Michigan Dietetic Association (n.d.) has information on food

choices in the MyPyramid format for a variety of cultural groups. This information, presented in English, helps teachers understand traditional ethnic food choices.

Teaching English Language Learners

Appropriate teaching practices guide how nutrition concepts are presented for all children, with special consideration given to those who are English language learners. Strategies that promote understanding of the nutrition message include the following:

- Have children learn by participating in hands-on activities, such as cooking activities and taste tests.
- Use a range of foods, recipes, and food preparation and cooking methods to reflect a variety of cultural approaches.
- Base the activity on a bilingual children's picture book with a focus on nutrition.
- Use visuals such as real food, food models, or pictures of food whenever presenting a verbal message.
- Speak clearly. Show and explain concepts in more than one way.
- Invite parents and others to visit the class to demonstrate a nutrition concept, to engage children in a cultural food tradition, and to be role models promoting the value of cultural diversity.
- Plan field trips to local businesses such as ethnic supermarkets, restaurants, and bakeries to experience how traditional foods are made.

Teachers who promote healthful eating from a multicultural perspective need to challenge themselves to explore new ideas and ways of planning appropriate and healthful menus for young children. They should also educate themselves about the nutrition traditions of alternate cultures. The resources that guide teachers and families with important nutritional information provide the structure to guide decision making about the selection and presentation of foods. The actual foods selected, however, and the lessons taught about nutrition evolve from the teacher's knowledge of the needs of all children in the group, including their cultural traditions. This highlights the important role that teachers play in

Figure 3-8 A Food Guide from Mexico

Source: From Formento De Nutrición Y Salud A.C. Used with permission.

Figure 3-9 A Food Guide Pagoda from China

Fats and Oils, 25g

Milk and Milk Products, 100g
Bean and Bean Products, 50g

Meat and Poultry, 50–100g
Fish and Shrimp, 50g
Eggs, 25–50g

Vegetables, 400–500g
Fruits, 100–200g

Cereals 300–500g

China

Source: Based on an illustration from the Chinese Nutrition Society, http://www.cnsoc.org/asp-bin/EN/?page=8&class=42&id=149.

Figure 3-10 **Native American Food Pyramid**

KEY

These symbols show fats, oils, and added sugars in foods.

⬤ Fat
(Naturally occuring and added)

▼ Sugars
(added)

A Guide to Daily Food Choices

Fat's Oils and Sweets
use sparingly

Low or Non-fat Dairy Products Milk, Yogurt & Cheese Group
2-3 Servings

Meat, Poultry, Fish, Dry Beans Eggs & Nuts Group
2-3 Servings

Vegetable Group
3-5 Servings

Fruit Group
2-4 Servings

Bread, Cereal Group
6-11 Servings

Rice, Pasta Group
6-11 Servings

Source: From CANFIT, http://www.canfit.org. Used with permission.

What if. . .

a parent from an Asian culture expressed concern that there were not enough menu items that appealed to her child? For example, the parent noticed that rice was not offered very often. How would you respond?

selecting and serving healthful foods in the early childhood setting, and in presenting nutrition wellness activities that assist all children to learn valuable nutrition lessons.

Summary

Good nutrition is the foundation for good health and optimal learning. Yet many young children are poorly nourished. The changing food environment has resulted in decreased time spent sharing family meals and more reliance on fast foods, restaurant dining, and convenience foods. These changes have had a negative impact on the quality of children's diets. In spite of many positive trends, including the goal of supporting more sustainable food practices and the desire to improve the school food environment, children's diets still do not meet MyPyramid recommendations for fruit, grain, and dairy groups and are higher in fat and sodium content than advised by the *Dietary Guidelines for Americans, 2005* (American Dietetic Association, 2008).

Planning a healthful menu and serving appropriate foods are important for children's health and ability to learn. Children who do not eat nutrient-rich foods can face undernutrition, overnutrition, or both—especially if families face food insecurity. Consumption of too few or too many nutrients negatively impacts learning and development and may have lifelong health consequences. In addition, the overconsumption of food coupled with decreased physical activity has resulted in an obesity epidemic among young children that threatens their long-term health and wellness. Recognizing nutritional problems during the early years offers the opportunity for modifications to be made to improve children's health outcomes. This positive contribution involves teachers, families, and health care providers.

The food guidance systems are important resources for ensuring that children receive optimal nutrition. They help teachers create an environment that fosters good nutrition and health. The Dietary Reference Intakes, which are established levels of nutrient requirements, and the daily values found on food labels provide specific information on nutrient requirements to help guide food selection and menu planning. The Dietary Reference Intakes are the basis of the *Dietary Guidelines for Americans, 2005*, which provides general advice on nutrition and physical activity. The MyPyramid interactive educational tool takes the guesswork out of healthful eating by providing detailed guidance on how to construct a nutrient-rich, high-quality diet. Teachers can use this information to establish classroom practices that promote good health and wellness in young children as well as to guide their own personal health goals. The food guidance systems are adaptable to a variety of ethnic food practices, and many are available in languages other than English so that increasingly teachers have tools they need to overcome language barriers and to protect the health of all children in their care.

MyEducationLab

To assess your understanding of the foundation of good nutrition and food guidance systems, go to the Book Specific Resources section in the MyEducationLab for your course, select *Nutrition, Health, and Safety for Young Children*, Chapter 3 of the Study Plan, and then complete the multiple choice questions and activities.

Key Terms

Acceptable Macronutrient Distribution Ranges (AMDRs), p. 81

Adequate Intakes (AIs), p. 80

Antioxidants, p. 66

Body mass index (BMI), p. 74

Carbohydrates, p. 79

Celiac disease, p. 85

Competitive foods, p. 70

Complementary foods, p. 87

Daily values (DVs), p. 82

Dietary Reference Intakes (DRIs), p. 79

Energy expenditure, p. 77

Environmental vegetarians, p. 69

Essential nutrients, p. 79

Estimated Average Requirements (EARs), p. 81

Failure to thrive, p. 71

Fats, p. 79

Gluten, p. 84

Iron-deficiency anemia, p. 72

Macronutrients, p. 79

Malnutrition, p. 70

Micronutrients, p. 80

Minerals, p. 80

Nutrients, p. 65

Nutrient-dense foods, p. 86

Nutrition, p. 65

Overnutrition, p. 71

Phytochemicals, p. 66

Proteins, p. 80

Psychosocial, p. 72

Recommended Dietary Allowances (RDAs), p. 80

Reference values, p. 79

Rickets, p. 73

Sleep apnea, p. 76

Supplemental food programs, p. 72

Sustainable food practices, p. 69

Tolerable Upper Intake Levels (ULs), p. 81

Trans fats, p. 83

Undernutrition, p. 71

Vitamin D, p. 73

Vitamins, p. 80

Review Questions

1. List three ways in which the food environment has changed in the past 20 years and summarize the impact of these changes on children's diets.
2. Define malnutrition as it relates to under- and overnutrition and provide an example of each.
3. Describe how obesity is identified and how it impacts young children in terms of health and psychosocial consequences.
4. Discuss the five components of the Dietary Reference Intakes and how they are different and when they are used.
5. Describe the messages that are conveyed in the *Dietary Guidelines for Americans, 2005* and the MyPyramid system. How are these food guidance systems similar and how are they different? How can they serve as a guide for what teachers serve in school?

Discussion Starters

1. Explain how food insecurity can lead to obesity. How can teachers help alleviate food insecurity if they identify this problem in children's families?
2. How can teachers address the obesity epidemic in their programs?
3. How can teachers implement the principles of the *Dietary Guidelines for Americans, 2005* and the MyPyramid system in their classrooms? How would you do this for toddlers, preschoolers, and school-age children?

Practice Points

1. Gabriella is exactly 4 years old. She weighs 48 lbs and is 44 inches tall. Using the CDC BMI website listed in the Web Resources section, calculate her BMI. Today is 1/1/present year. Her birth is 1/1/present year–4. Using the growth charts in the Book Specific Resources on MyEducationLab (also available on the CDC growth chart web site listed in the Web Resources section), determine what the percentile is for her height, weight, and BMI. What weight classification would you give her? What does this tell us about Gabriella?
2. Suppose you were asked to find out if Gabriella's iron intake was sufficient. Using the information in Question 1 on age, height, weight, and date of birth and the diet recorded below, go to MyPyramid Tracker at www.mpyramid.gov to determine how Gabriella's diet rates. What changes might you recommend?

Breakfast:	1 flour tortilla with 1 ounce of cheese
	½ cup orange juice
	1 cup milk, 2%
Snack:	1 cup milk, 2%
	¼ cup teddy graham crackers
Lunch:	1 slice whole wheat bread with 1 ounce of cheese
	1 cup tomato soup
	1 sliced kiwi
	1 cup of milk, 2%
Snack:	1 apple
Dinner:	½ cup rice, white
	1 ounce cheese
	1 cup salad with 1 tablespoon Italian dressing
	1 flour tortilla
	1 cup apple juice

3. Refer to the breakfast cereal food label shown in Figure 3-5. Explain three nutritional qualities that make this a healthy food choice. What might you be concerned about?

Web Resources

American Academy of Pediatric's Starting Solid Foods
http://www.aap.org/bookstore/brochures/br_solidfoods_2008_sample.pdf

American Dietetic Association's The First Year: Nutrition for Your Baby
http://www.eatright.org/ada/files/First_Year.pdf

CDC Growth Charts and BMI Calculator
www.cdc.gov/GrowthCharts
www.cdc.gov/healthyweight/assessing/bmi/childrens_BMI/tool_for_schools.html

Data Resource Center for Child and Adolescent Health, Childhood Obesity State Report Cards
www.childhealthdata.org/content/ObesityReportCards.aspx

Dietary Guidelines for Americans
www.cnpp.usda.gov/Publications/DietaryGuidelines/2005/2005DGPolicyDocument.pdf

Institute of Medicine of the National Academy, Dietary Reference Intakes
http://www.iom.edu/Home/Global/News%20Announcements/~/media/Files/Activity%20Files/
Nutrition/DRIs/DRISummaryListing2.ashx

The Lunch Box Program
http://cesanluisobispo.ucdavis.edu/Nutrition,_Family_and_Consumer_Science208/
Lunch_Box_Handouts.htm

MyPyramid
www.mypyramid.gov

National Association for Sport and Physical Education
www.aahperd.org/naspe

chapter 4 | The Science of Nutrition

Learning Outcomes

After reading this chapter, you should be able to:

1. Define nutrition science.

2. Identify the steps in the process of digestion.

3. Explain how nutrients are absorbed and identify the accessory organs involved in absorption.

4. Describe the function of carbohydrates, proteins, and fats and the food groups in which they are found.

5. Define the role of vitamins and minerals and their interactions in supporting the growth, development, and health of infants and children.

6. Summarize how the knowledge of nutrients can be used to plan healthful diets for young children.

Jamal is a 5-year-old kindergartner who is noticeably small for his age. During health screening day his teacher, Tonya, notices that his weight falls in the 5th percentile range when plotted on standard growth charts. She puts a notice for his family with his height and weight measurements in his backpack. As she thinks about Jamal, it occurs to her that since the first day of school he has frequently complained of being tired, has been irritable, and often has difficulty concentrating in class. She wonders if there is a connection to his poor rate of growth.

The next day Jamal's mother, Aiesha, tells Tonya she has scheduled an appointment with the doctor to find out why Jamal is so thin. She tells Tonya that she suspects his poor growth is related to his sensitive stomach and that he frequently has bloating and diarrhea. The fact that his growth has recently stalled worries her.

A couple of weeks later, Aiesha shares important news with Tonya. Jamal has been to a specialist where tests reveal he has celiac disease. Aiesha was told that celiac disease is an inherited condition in which an immune response to gluten, a protein found predominantly in wheat, barley, and rye, causes damage to the lining of the small intestine. This damage interferes with digestion and absorption, which is why Jamal is so thin. Aiesha was also told that the cornerstone to his treatment is diet.

Aiesha gives Tonya a list of foods Jamal can and cannot eat. She asks Tonya if the school will be able to provide Jamal with gluten-free meals. She also wonders if he will feel left out at mealtime because he can't eat the same foods as the rest of the children. Tonya reassures Aiesha that there are others in the school who require special diets, including a child in first grade who also has celiac disease. She explains that to accommodate children with special diets, a special allergen-free table is available where children may sit together and get assistance from lunchroom staff. Perhaps Jamal may want to join this group at mealtime.

Tonya then calls the director of food services about the need for a gluten-free diet. She also notes that the classroom parents rotate bringing packaged crackers and fruit for snacks. Aiesha agrees to bring in a couple of boxes of gluten-free crackers to have on hand for Jamal. After her discussion with Tonya, Aiesha feels confidant that her son will receive appropriate and appealing meals at school and that he will begin to gain weight.

DEFINING NUTRITION SCIENCE

Nutrition science is the study of how food provides nourishment to support the growth, maintenance, and repair of the human body. Understanding the science of nutrition helps teachers learn about healthful eating for themselves and the children in their care. The responsibility of feeding young children is important because they are nutritionally vulnerable and dependent on adults to make choices and provide for them. For example, infants and children need more calories for their size compared to adults because they are growing. When they are not consuming the right types and amounts of food, nutritional problems can develop quickly. If children face the additional stress of an illness or disorder such as celiac disease, the nutritional concerns can increase significantly.

The information shared in this chapter explains why the substances found in food are necessary for good health. Step-by-step descriptions explain how the body digests and absorbs food in order to generate the energy needed to function. Sometimes the process of digestion and absorption is complicated by health conditions. We discuss disorders that young children may experience in the process of digestion and absorption so that you, as an early childhood educator, will feel prepared to handle a variety of feeding challenges. In addition, we explain why different food groups are important to maintain a healthful diet and discuss the role of the essential macronutrients (carbohydrates, protein, and fats) and micronutrients (vitamins and minerals). Finally, the information in this chapter will provide you with the background fundamentals you need to teach nutrition concepts to young children and support young children who have digestive disorders.

UNDERSTANDING THE PROCESS OF DIGESTION

nutrition science
the study of how foods provide nourishment to support the growth, maintenance, and repair of the human body

digestion
the mechanical and chemical breakdown of foods into smaller nutrient components to make it available for absorption

digestive system
the gateway for all nutrients into the body; made up of the gastrointestinal tract and other accessory organs that aid in digestion

gastrointestinal tract
the mouth, esophagus, stomach, and small and large intestines; part of the body where foods are digested and changed to nutrients in anticipation of being absorbed

To understand why specific foods are needed in the diet, we need to start at the beginning and look at what happens to food once it is consumed. The overall goal of eating is to take the nutrients found in food and transport them from the outside of the body to the inside, where they are used to maintain body functions. The nutrients found in food are essential for young children because they:

- Provide energy.
- Are necessary for growth.
- Repair and maintain the body.
- Regulate body processes.
- Affect how genes are expressed (turned on or off) and therefore affect overall health.

We turn now to a discussion of the digestion process. Teachers who understand this process will have a better understanding of why nutrients and balanced diets are so important for infants and young children. This knowledge helps develop strategies to ensure all children are well nourished.

The Digestion Process

Digestion is the mechanical and chemical breakdown of foods into smaller nutrient components, making the nutrients available for absorption. Multiple steps take place when turning the cereal with milk served for breakfast at school into the fuel children need to start the day. The process takes place in the digestive system, which is made up of the gastrointestinal tract and other accessory organs that aid in digestion. This multiple-organ system is the gateway for all nutrients into the body.

Problems in the digestive system can have catastrophic consequences for infants and children. Problems result in the required nutrients not being available to the body in the amounts needed to sustain growth and development. For example, Jamal was not getting adequate nutrition because his digestive system was compromised by the celiac disease. Jamal needs the help of his teacher and food service staff to plan meals he can eat at school, using foods that avoid further damage to his gastrointestinal tract. This highlights the need for teachers to understand normal digestion and absorption so they can troubleshoot when issues related to food intake arise in the feeding of infants and children.

The gastrointestinal tract is like a long, tube-shaped conveyor belt with food pushed along the length of it by the wave-like contractions of the intestinal muscles. As Figure 4-1 illustrates, food undergoes both mechanical and chemical changes within the digestive tract to ready it for absorption, which occurs predominantly in the small intestine.

As food moves along this conveyor belt, it is chopped, churned, and mixed with enzymes, acids, and mucus, which slowly change it into smaller absorbable substances. Attached to the gastrointestinal tract are accessory organs, such as the salivary glands, liver, and pancreas, that secrete a variety of components that also aid in the digestion process (see Table 4-1).

Digestion begins in the mouth and proceeds through multiple steps before the food consumed can be used for energy.

The Mouth

The start of all digestive action takes place in the mouth. The mechanical process of chewing physically breaks food down into small pieces. This allows saliva (spit) to begin its work. Saliva released from the salivary glands contains digestive enzymes, which start the chemical breakdown of food. Enzymes are proteins that speed up chemical reactions. Saliva is sometimes formed in the mouth even before food is consumed. For example, children who see an appetizing entrée such as pizza or smell its enticing aroma will begin building up saliva in their mouths. Saliva keeps the tongue moist so that taste buds can work more effectively. The moist chewed-up food forms a mass, which is pushed to the back of the mouth by the tongue, ready to be swallowed. The teacher's role in this first step of digestion is to decide the types of foods to offer children that match their ability to chew. This reduces the risk of choking.

Textures of Foods

Textures of food play a role in children's ability to chew and swallow. This ability depends on the child's age and whether the child has conditions that interfere with chewing. For example, infants who are learning to swallow their first nonliquid foods are offered puréed textures. This provides a gradual introduction of new textures to manage. By around 10 months, teeth begin to appear and side-of-the-mouth chewing develops. Foods with more texture are well received at this time. Food textures may need to be altered for children who have difficulty chewing because of motor development delays. The *Teaching Wellness* feature provides an activity that will help children understand how their mouth helps jump start the process of digestion.

Protecting Teeth

Foods provide both dental risks and benefits. These risks and benefits need to be considered when selecting foods in order to protect the teeth, the greatest tool of the mouth. Although foods provide the nutrition needed to strengthen teeth, some foods can cause

Figure 4-1 The Digestive System

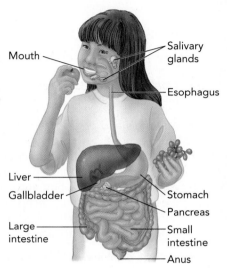

Mouth — Salivary glands — Esophagus — Liver — Gallbladder — Large intestine — Stomach — Pancreas — Small intestine — Anus

enzymes
proteins produced by the body's cells to speed up chemical reactions

Table 4-1	The Parts of the Gastrointestinal Tract and Their Functions

	Accessory Organs	Chemical Secreted	Functions
Mouth	Teeth	None	Mechanically chop food into small pieces.
	Tongue	Ligual lipase	The tongue moves food around in the mouth. The lipase begins fat digestion.
	Salivary glands	Saliva, enzyme amylase	Saliva moistens foods; the amylase begins carbohydrate breakdown.
Esophagus	None	None	Provides passageway from mouth to stomach.
Stomach	None	Gastric juices that include:	The stomach acts as a holding unit for food as it is churned, mixed and produces secretions.
		Acids	Create an acidic environment so that enzymes can work.
		Enzyme pepsin	Causes protein breakdown.
		Mucus	Binds and mixes food, protects stomach.
Small intestine		Intestinal juices and mucus	The secretions cause the chemical breakdown of proteins, fats, and carbohydrates to substances that can be absorbed; protects and lubricates the intestine.
	Liver and gallbladder	Bile	Bile emulsifies fats and helps in fat breakdown.
	Pancreas	Pancreatic juices	The juices cause chemical breakdown of proteins, fats, and carbohydrates to substances that can be absorbed.
Large intestine, rectum, and anus	None	None	Absorb water; stores and eliminate stools.

Sources: Based on *Lubey's Biohelp: The Human Digestive System*, http://users.adelphia.net/~lubehawk/BioHELP!/biotopcs.html; and *Williams' Essentials of Nutrition and Diet Therapy*, (pp. 188–194) by E. D. Schlenker, 2007, St. Louis: Mosby Elsevier.

Teaching Wellness *Digestion Begins in the Mouth*

Learning Outcome: Children will gain an understanding of how tasting and chewing food begins the digestion process.

Older Infants and Toddlers

- *Goal:* To introduce foods of different flavors and textures.

- *Materials and preparation:* A divided food tray with four sections. In one section place chopped plums and strained plums, in another unsalted and salted saltine crackers. In the third, place cooked sweet and white potatoes, mashed and chopped into bite-size pieces, and in the final section ripe bananas (mashed and offered as tiny cubed pieces). Cut fruits and vegetable into pieces no larger than ¼ inch.

- *Activity plan:* Show infant the food on the divided tray. Encourage the child to pick up a piece of food and taste it. Say words that convey surprise and interest, such as "Wow, that plum tastes sour!" or "Doesn't that banana taste sweet?" or "Can you tell which cracker is salty?" When the child has the food in her mouth, say "You are chewing food to make it easy to swallow," or when she chews the cracker, say "That's a really hard cracker. Can you make it soft enough to swallow by chewing?" Name the food and the flavor and allow the infants to taste, smell, and chew each food.

- *How to adjust the activity:* For toddlers, add foods with an increasing variety of textures as well as flavors. For example, serve applesauce and thin sliced apple with the skin removed. Try different types of apples to show the difference in flavor (tart Macintosh, sweet Golden Delicious, sour green apple). Have the children tell you which they think is easier to chew and swallow: applesauce or apples. Try grapefruit or oranges to share the sour flavor. Reinforce each child's efforts by remarking, "You are getting to know how foods taste different and that chewing food makes it soft so you can swallow it," and "You can see that even the same types of food like apples can taste different. Tasting and chewing is a good way to learn about food and what happens to food when we eat."

- *Did you meet your goal?* Did the children explore the taste and textures of different foods? Did they have an opportunity to recognize that some foods take longer to chew than others?

Preschoolers and Kindergartners

- *Goal:* To learn that digestion starts in the mouth and to understand that some foods take longer to chew than others and that foods can taste very different.

- *Materials:* Small plastic dental mirrors or hand mirrors; a variety of foods with different textures and flavors similar to toddler activity but with additional options; the book *The Very Hungry Caterpillar* by Eric Carle.

- *Activity plan:* Explain that many foods taste different. Some are sweet, some are salty, and some are sour. They feel different in the mouth. Some are soft and easy to chew, and some are hard and take longer to chew. Offer some examples. Say to children, "We chew food so that we can swallow it. The food that is chewed goes into our stomach and helps us feel full. The food we eat gives us energy to run, play, and grow." Read *The Very Hungry Caterpillar*. Invite children to name the fruits and vegetables and other foods as you read the book. Ask the children, "Is this a hard food to chew or an easy one?" As you read the book and come across pictures of various foods, ask the children, "How do you think this food tastes? Is it sweet or sour? Is it salty?" See if they recognize that the caterpillar is growing. When the book is finished point out how the caterpillar grew to be a butterfly just like they will grow big and strong. Invite children to explore the different textures and tastes of foods and offers reinforcements as indicated above. Encourage children's efforts by saying, "You are really exploring these fruits and vegetables by chewing and tasting them."

- *How to adjust the activity:* Have the children sit at a table with the dental mirror or hand mirror. Have them open their mouths and look at their teeth. Ask them, "Can you count your teeth? Do you know which are for biting off and which are for mashing and grinding?" Teachers who have large plastic models of teeth can point out the different types of teeth. Hand out one saltine cracker per child. Have them chew the cracker and open their mouth. Ask, "What does the cracker look like? Why is it wet?" Explain how saliva, or "spit," helps us to taste and swallow food. Say "When we chew and swallow food we begin the first stage of digestion."

- *Did you meet your goal?* Are children able to identify that foods have different tastes and textures and that chewing helps them to swallow food?

School-Age Children

- **Goal:** To identify how the nose influences the sense of taste and how the tongue and teeth help us to chew and swallow food.

- **Materials:** Same as for preschoolers. In addition a variety of foods: raw cabbage or broccoli, lemon or lime, ripe pear or peach, pretzels or saltine crackers, apple or pear slices, onion pieces, small cups of vinegar and vanilla extract, the book *Chewy, Gooey, Rumble, Plop* by Steve Alton. Food preparation activity: bananas, stick pretzels, raisins, peanut butter (check for allergies) or whipped light cream cheese if there are allergies, a small piece of broccoli, paper plates, and plastic knives.

- **Activity plan:** Same as preschool activity plan but in addition read the pop-out book *Chewy, Gooey, Rumble, Plop*, focusing on the first pages, which discuss chewing and saliva. Explain to children that food flavors vary. Discuss the different flavors (saltiness, sweet, sour, and bitter). Ask children if they understand why foods taste different and why some children like the taste of some foods and others do not. Explain the role of the taste buds. Say "Children have more taste buds than grown-ups (taste buds "wear out" when you get older) and therefore taste some foods more than adults, especially bitter flavors. That may be why many children don't like the taste of olives or spinach or coffee." Go on to explain that "Some people are born with more taste buds and are more sensitive to flavors." Say "This is why not everyone likes the same foods."

  Have them hold a mirror to their mouth and identify the taste buds. Have them move their tongues around and look under their tongues. Do they see any taste buds? Have them look at the teeth. Ask them if the can identify the teeth for biting and grinding.

  Next have them sample the raw cabbage or broccoli, lemon or lime, ripe pear or peach, pretzels or saltine crackers, and have them identify the different flavors of bitter, salty, sweet, and sour. Have students place a piece of saltine under their tongues. Can they taste it? Now put in on top of their tongues. See if they can chew it without moving their tongues. Take another piece of cracker and place it on the middle of the tongue without chewing. Can they taste it? What happens when they chew it and move it around in the mouth? Explain how saliva moistens the foods and makes it easier to be tasted by the taste buds. Discuss how chewing and swallowing food is the first step of digestion.

- **How to adjust the activity:** Children can create their own hungry caterpillar. Seat four to five children in a group. Place in front of them small bowls filled with pretzel sticks, peanut butter, broccoli pieces, and raisins. Give them each a washed banana. Have them peel the banana and cut it into four or five pieces on a plate with the plastic knife. Spread one side of each piece with peanut butter. Stick the pieces back together. Stick the pretzel sticks into the sides of the banana the pretzel sticks (break each pretzel stick in two) to represent legs and place two into the front piece to represent antennae. Using peanut butter, stick two raisins to the front of the banana to represent eyes. Place a piece of broccoli in front of the caterpillar. While preparing the caterpillar ask children if they can identify the food group of each food used to make the caterpillar. Once they are done, allow the children to eat the caterpillars. Ask them if they can identify the different flavors. If any children in the class have peanut allergies, substitute whipped cream cheese for the peanut butter.

- **Did you meet your goal?** Are children able to identify by taste and name different types of flavors? Can they identify how the tongue, saliva, and teeth work together to make food easier to taste and swallow and that swallowing is the first step in digestion?

What if. . .

you needed to plan the menu for your family child care program, which serves infants through preschool-age children? What modifications of texture might you need to take into consideration? What modifications in texture might you make for an older child? What can you do to ensure modified foods are appealing to all age groups?

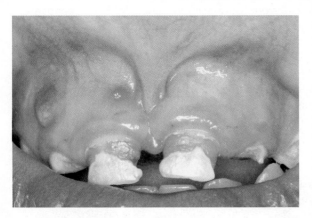

Teaching families about infant dental hygiene and the risks of putting babies to bed with bottles can help prevent baby bottle tooth decay.

MyEducationLab

Go to the Assignments and Activities section of Topic 5: Health Promotion/Policy in the MyEducationLab for your course and complete the activity entitled *Teaching Children about Nutrition.* How can the topic of digestion be introduced to young children?

dental decay. Dental decay is an infectious process in which various plaque-forming bacteria turn the carbohydrates that children eat into acid. This acid causes the loss of calcium from the teeth, resulting in decay.

Protecting teeth starts as soon as they erupt. For infants, this means that babies should not be put to bed with bottles filled with beverages such as milk, formula, fruit juice or fruit drink or allowed to access a filled bottle all day (American Dental Association, 2005). Ongoing, repeated exposure to the sugars contained in these beverages puts infants at risk for baby bottle tooth decay. *Baby bottle tooth decay* is the development of early dental cavities that is extensive and particularly damaging to the front teeth, although any teeth can be involved (American Dental Association, 2005).

Untreated dental decay can cause suffering and pain and affect the ability to eat, speak (impaired language development), and concentrate in the school setting (American Academy of Pediatrics, 2008; Centers for Disease Control and Prevention [CDC], Division of Oral Health, 2009). Nutritional factors that increase the risk of dental decay include a high intake of fruit juices and soft drinks, delayed weaning from the bottle, access to toddler cups throughout the day and the intake of sticky foods such as raisins, granola bars, and carbohydrate foods, such as bread, crackers, and cookies, that get stuck in the teeth. These factors result in prolonged exposure of the tooth surface to the acids that cause tooth decay.

By contrast, the foods that protect teeth include milk and cheese. These dairy products may be helpful in neutralizing acids produced by bacteria in the mouth and also provide calcium, phosphorus, magnesium, and vitamin D, which help to build strong teeth and healthy oral tissues in young children (McBean, 2000). Fluoridated water is another nutrient that protects teeth by making tooth enamel strong and preventing bacteria from making acids that damage teeth (American Academy of Pediatrics, 2008). Well water and bottled water may not be good sources of fluoride. The xylitol found in some sugar-free gums decreases bacteria in the mouth and helps strengthen teeth (Burt, 2006; Ly, Milgrom, & Rothen, 2006).

Teachers help children protect their teeth by teaching them the basics of oral hygiene. Including tooth brushing as part of the daily routine ensures that the first step of digestion is not hampered by dental decay. Teachers are also important resources for families. For example, they can provide guidance to help children receive needed dental services, as described in this example:

Three-year-old Devin attends the Head Start program. Although he attends school regularly, he is often irritable and tired. He does not smile and he does not eat well. One day his teacher, Lea, notices that Devin has a swollen cheek. She is concerned and asks Devin to let her look in his mouth. She sees that Devin's front teeth are visibly decayed, but he says that a back tooth is hurting him.

Lea calls Devin's mother, Andrea, and learns that Devin still takes a bottle to bed. Lea tells Andrea that she thinks Devin is suffering from painful cavities. She strongly encourages Andrea to schedule an emergency dental exam. She helps her locate a dentist who will provide the service at a reduced cost for children enrolled in the Head Start program. The exam reveals that two of Devin's teeth are infected. Devin receives extensive dental treatment. When it is completed, Lea notices that he has an entirely different demeanor. He is happy, smiles, and eats with enthusiasm. He is ready to learn now that he is no longer in pain.

Swallowing and the Esophagus

Next in the process of digestion is swallowing. After the mass of chewed food is swallowed, it enters the esophagus, a tube that connects the mouth to the stomach. The food mass is pushed by wave-like contractions to the stomach. The entrance into the stomach is controlled by a small muscle called the lower esophageal sphincter. The sphincter is like a gate that opens and shuts, letting food in and gas out (as burps), as needed.

Swallowing Difficulties

Swallowing food is a simple process that occurs without effort for most individuals. However, the process of chewing and swallowing uses a multitude of muscles and must be synchronized with breathing. Some children have a condition called dysphagia, which is the inability to swallow foods or liquids easily. Many conditions are associated with dysphagia such as prematurity, developmental disabilities, cerebral palsy, and Down syndrome.

Teachers and families need to be aware that swallowing difficulties can result in significant feeding challenges. Feeding times may be prolonged and the child may choke, cough, or gag, which is unpleasant and frightening for the child and requires the extra attention of teachers. The consequences of dysphagia can include poor nutrition, aspiration (when food or liquids are inhaled into the lungs), and pneumonia (American Academy of Pediatrics [AAP] Committee on Nutrition, 2009; Prasse & Kikano, 2009). Teachers often become part of a team, which includes families, health care professionals, and early intervention staff, to work together to achieve the goals of safe eating and good nutrition. Figure 4-2 provides a checklist for teachers who work with children who have swallowing disorders.

Reflux

Sometimes infants and children experience difficulty keeping food in the stomach. This can happen when the lower esophageal sphincter is relaxed, causing spitting up or gastroesophageal reflux (GER). As many as 67% of children with GER spit up at least once a day after a feeding (Campanozzi et al., 2009). Often called "happy spitters," these infants grow well and do not experience any pain or compromise to their growth. The spitting up peaks around 3 months of age and usually resolves by 12 to 14 months without any negative consequences (Gold, 2007).

When spitting up is chronic and severe, however, it is called gastroesophageal reflux disease (GERD). GERD is a condition that causes the contents of the stomach to back up into the esophagus. GERD can cause pain and heartburn (Nevin-Folino, 2008). Heartburn is a burning sensation experienced when the esophagus is exposed to stomach acids. GERD can cause small amounts of stomach contents to be aspirated or inhaled into the lungs. It can trigger asthma and pneumonia (Yoshida, Kameda, Nishikido, Takamatu, & Doi, 2008). The *Safety Segment* discusses the recommended sleep position for infants with GERD.

Infants who frequently reflux to the point of vomiting may not get enough nutrients, leading to poor growth. Additionally, the esophagus can become irritated, resulting in bleeding that leads to anemia (Samour & King, 2005). The use of specially thickened formulas or the addition of rice cereal or another commercial thickening agent to formula or liquids can sometimes help decrease the incidence of vomiting, thus allowing infants to gain weight (Horvath, Dziechciarz, & Szajewska, 2008). Adding cereals to liquids in bottles is not

dysphagia
a disorder characterized by the inability to swallow foods or liquids easily

aspiration
occurs when food or liquids get into the lungs instead of into the stomach

gastroesophageal reflux (GER)
reflux of stomach contents into the esophagus

gastroesophageal reflux disease (GERD)
severe reflux of stomach contents into the esophagus that causes pain, heartburn, indigestion, and when associated with excess vomiting, can result in poor growth in young children

Figure 4-2 A Teacher's Checklist: Caring for Children with Swallowing Disorders

☐ **Positioning:** Does the child need special positioning and an adaptive feeding chair? The correct position is essential in promoting safe swallowing during feeding.

☐ **Oral aversion:** Is the child involved in a desensitization program to help him overcome aversion to flavors, textures, consistencies, and temperatures of foods? What is the teacher's role?

☐ **Nutrition plan:** Is a modification of food consistency needed? Does special menu planning need to happen before the child can come to school? Are supplements required?

☐ **Adaptive feeding equipment:** Does the child need tube feeding equipment, positioning seats, or special cups, plates, bottles, nipples, or plates?

☐ **Skill building:** Are there exercises that focus on developing oral motor skills and or adaptive swallowing skills? What are the teacher's responsibilities?

Source: Based on *Pediatrics Nutrition Handbook, 5e*, edited by R. Kleinman, 2004, Elk Grove, IL: American Academy of Pediatrics Committee on Nutrition.

Safety Segment

Gastroesophageal Reflux Disease

Infants with gastroesophageal reflux disease (GERD) need special consideration when it comes to sleeping position. Babies with GERD may vomit frequently and choking can be a concern. The American Academy of Pediatrics recommends that infants be placed on their backs to sleep to prevent sudden infant death syndrome (SIDS). Having babies sleep on their stomachs is considered only when the risk of death due to GERD outweighs the potential increased risk of SIDS (Michail, 2007). The baby's medical provider should recommend the appropriate sleeping position. If the reflux is severe enough to warrant the doctor's recommendation that the baby sleep on his stomach, special arrangements should be made:

- Ensure the infant's mattress is very firm.
- Raise the mattress slightly at the head.
- Remove pillows, toys, or excess blankets.
- Position the baby's head so that the mouth and nose are not blocked in any way (University of Maryland Medical Center, 2009).

advised, however, unless recommended by a health care provider because it may displace more vital nutrients in formula (Samour & King, 2005).

Teachers can help reduce some of the symptoms infants experience by supporting the baby in an upright position during and after feeding. Medications can also be prescribed by a physician to help alleviate symptoms and ensure good nourishment. Suggestions for managing GER and GERD and other digestive conditions are listed in Table 4-2.

The Stomach

Once food reaches the stomach, it is mixed with stomach acids, secretions, and enzymes, which begin to break down the protein in the food. The stomach's role is to squeeze and churn the food and move it further along the digestive tract. Although food generally flows from the stomach to the small intestine, sometimes it comes back up when children vomit. Whereas reflux is usually burping of stomach contents, vomiting is a much more violent event. A child vomiting in the classroom always creates a disruption.

The first question that may come to mind for teachers when considering a vomiting episode is "Should this child go home?" Vomiting can be caused by gastrointestinal infections or other factors such as allergies, medications, overeating, and motion sickness. Schools and preschools have policies about illness that are shared with families through parent handbooks or preschool websites. The National Resource Center for Health and Safety in Child Care and Early Education (2009) recommends that if a child has two or more episodes of vomiting within 24-hours, she should be sent home. In practice, since it is often difficult for a teacher to know how often a child has vomited within a 24 hour period, parents are called. A decision as to whether a child should go home is made based on the child's history of illness, the incidence of similar illnesses in the classroom, and whether there was a possible noninfectious source of illness such as twirling too long on the tire swing.

What if. . .

a mother, rushing to go to work, told you that her child vomited before coming to school? The mother is not concerned because she feels it was related to roughhousing with a sibling right after eating breakfast. How might you handle this situation? Would you allow the child to stay?

UNDERSTANDING THE PROCESS OF ABSORPTION

absorption
the transport of nutrients from the small intestine into the circulatory system

The transport of nutrients from the gastrointestinal tract into the body is called absorption. The primary site of absorption is the small intestine. When food has been broken into sufficiently small units, it is ready to be transported into the body via the circulatory system.

| Table 4-2 | Common Childhood Disorders of the Gastrointestinal Tract |

Disorder	Symptoms	Nutrition Risk Factors	Tips for Teachers	When to Call the Health Experts
Celiac disease	Gas, bloating, and diarrhea or constipation, poor appetite, fatigue, weight loss.	Poor growth, malabsorption, anemia, increased risk for osteoporosis (brittle bone disease) due to poor calcium absorption.	Very close attention must be paid to diet. Avoid food containing gluten, such as wheat, barley, rye, and oats (unless the oat are gluten free). A lactose-free diet is sometimes indicated as well. Check with family. Set up meeting with families, teacher and food service staff to recommend the use of special gluten-free products.	When a change in diet does not resolve symptoms.
Constipation	Constipation is the painful passage of stool that is hard and dry.	Poor appetite.	*Infants with constipation:* Refer family to health care professional for advice. *Children with constipation:* 1. Encourage them to drink adequate fluids. 2. Encourage them to be physically active. 3. Encourage them to consume foods high in fiber content such as fruits, vegetables, and whole-grain breads and cereals.	After 3 to 5 days if constipation has not been resolved.
Diarrhea	Watery stools that occur with increased frequency, cause stomach cramping, and are not explained by change in diet.	Dehydration. *Signs of dehydration:* dry mouth and tongue, decreased amount of dark-colored urine, or in babies and young children, no wet diapers for 3 hours or more, dry skin, crying without tears.	Infants and children who are sick with diarrhea should be sent home as soon as possible. Maintaining adequate hydration is important. Small sips of liquids are better tolerated than large amounts. On the return to school provide a regular diet and avoid excess juice/soda intake and foods high in fat content.	If there is blood in the diarrhea or the child is vomiting repeatedly or starts acting very sick or if there are signs of dehydration.
Gastroesophageal reflux disease (GERD)	A baby or child whose stomach contents back up into the esophagus (spitting up or vomiting). Other symptoms include coughing, irritability, and poor feeding and growth.		Thickened formula may be recommended by the child's physician. Infants should be fed in an upright position. Large meals should be avoided. Avoid feeding an infant in a car seat, which tends to result in a slumped feeding position and may actually put more pressure on the gastroesophageal sphincter, worsening symptoms. Burp frequently during feeding. Children can grow out of GERD by the time they are 1 to 2 years of age.	If projectile vomiting occurs in children less than 2 months of age. Difficulty breathing after spitting up.

(Continued)

Disorder	Symptoms	Nutrition Risk Factors	Tips for Teachers	When to Call the Health Experts
Lactose intolerance	Noninfectious diarrhea, gas, and bloating caused by the inability to break down lactose, the sugar found in milk, due to an insufficiency of an enzyme called lactase.	Children on a lactose-free diet may need calcium and vitamin D supplementation if unable to tolerate any dairy products.	Milk intake should be limited or restricted based on individual tolerance. Sometimes small amounts of lactose found in hard cheeses, cream cheese, and cottage cheese may be tolerated. Substitute juice, lactose-free milk, or soy milk in the school setting.	When symptoms do not improve with change in diet.
Swallowing disorders	Coughing or choking during feedings.	Malnutrition, aspiration (getting food or liquids into the lungs), pneumonia, and difficult mealtime behavior.	Assessment of oral motor capabilities by a speech or occupational therapist to provide teacher/families guidelines on positioning, food consistency, etc. Should be included as written guidelines in the IFSP or IEP. It is very important to have a proper feeding chair that supports the swallowing process. *Note:* Funds for special services such as assistance with feeding, special supplements or foods, feeding equipment, or the services of a registered dietitian, special education teacher, or occupational therapist may be available through IDEA.	If there is aspiration of food that results in difficulty breathing.
Vomiting	Vomiting is the forceful emptying of the stomach's contents through the mouth.	Dehydration (see signs of dehydration listed for diarrhea)	Infants and children who experience two or more incidences of vomiting within the previous 24 hours should be sent home as soon as possible. Maintaining adequate hydration is important. Upon return to school, a child can usually go back to a regular diet within 24 hours of the last vomiting episode and can consume a regular diet with avoidance of excess juice/soda and fatty foods.	The child shows sign of dehydration, vomits blood, is confused or difficult to awaken, or the child starts acting very sick.

Sources: Based on *Pediatric Gastroenterology and Nutrition*, MassGeneral Hospital for Children, retrieved September 11, 2009, from http://www.massgeneral.org/children/specialtiesandservices/gastroenterology_and_nutrition/default.aspx; and *Digestive Diseases*, National Digestive Diseases Information Clearinghouse, retrieved September 11, 2009, from http://digestive.niddk.nih.gov/ddiseases/a-z.asp.

The Small Intestine

villi
located on the surface of the folds of the small intestine; is where absorption takes place

When the stomach has completed churning and breaking food into smaller pieces, it releases it into the small intestine. The small intestine is an approximately 20-foot-long tube where the most significant part of chemical digestion occurs (Mahan & Escott-Stump, 2004). It is designed in such a way as to absorb as many nutrients as possible. To accomplish this, the inside of the small intestine has a series folds that are lined with villi. The finger-like villi are,

Table 4-3	Macronutrient Sources and the Breakdown Products of Digestion		
Macronutrient	**Selected Sources**	**Primary Breakdown Products**	**Role of Nutrient**
Protein	Meats, fish, poultry, cheese, milk, eggs	Amino acids	Growth and repair; can be used as energy if necessary
Fats	Oil, margarine, butter, mayonnaise, salad dressing	Fatty acids and glycerol	Stored energy source. Aids absorption of vitamins A, D, E, K
Carbohydrates	Grain products, fruits, vegetables, milk	Simple sugars: fructose, glucose, and galactose	Body's main energy source

in turn, lined with microvilli so that the total area involved in absorption is larger in size than a tennis court (Shills, Shike, Ross, Caballero, & Cousins, 2006).

Intestinal enzymes, acids, bile, and pancreatic juices further digest the major nutrients, breaking down carbohydrates, proteins, and fats and making them ready for absorption. When the nutrients are finally small enough to be absorbed, they enter the circulatory system (National Digestive Diseases Information Clearinghouse, 2008). Once in the circulatory system they are transported to various cells of the body. Table 4-3 shows the food sources and final breakdown products of carbohydrates, protein, and fats. The products that are not absorbed by the small intestine are collected in the large intestine.

microvilli
located on the surface of the villi, further expanding the surface area to enhance absorption of nutrients

The Large Intestine

The large intestine is the last section of the digestive system. Its primary role is to absorb water and some minerals and vitamins from the products not absorbed in the small intestine. Anything that cannot be digested, such as fiber, collects in the rectum until it is expelled via the anus as a bowel movement.

Understanding Problems Related to Absorption

Providing children with a variety of foods from each of the food groups at mealtime is the best way to ensure a healthy, balanced diet. However, children can face nutritional problems in spite of eating a good diet if they have trouble with absorption. These problems can be significant enough to impact a child's growth and development. Teachers are the child's link to responsible care when parents are not available. Understanding factors that impact nutritional health ensures that teachers can effectively care for children with health concerns. Children who are physiologically comfortable will be more apt to learn. Parents feel confident leaving their child in the care of a teacher who understands and is able to respond to their child's unique needs.

Understanding Malabsorption

When the small intestine's lining becomes damaged, it is difficult to absorb nutrients. This condition is called malabsorption and can happen in a number of different circumstances. Diet-related conditions of malabsorption can often be modified by changes in diet.

malabsorption
occurs when damage to the small intestine's lining results in difficulty absorbing nutrients, leading to diarrhea and sometimes weight loss

Celiac Disease This genetic condition is caused by the body's response to a group of proteins referred to as *gluten*. The symptoms of celiac disease vary and the condition is sometimes hard to diagnose. The most common features include malabsorption with resulting gas, bloating, stomachache, and diarrhea. Children can experience weakness, weight loss, joint pain, and loss of appetite. The malabsorption can lead to anemia and increased risk for osteoporosis (weak bones), as well as generalized malnutrition (Kalayci, Kansu, Girgin, Kucuk, & Aras, 2001). As we saw at the beginning of the chapter with Jamal, children with

osteoporosis
condition that results in porous, weak bones that break easily

celiac disease can also experience irritability, mood swings, and depression, which can adversely affect a child's ability to learn (Rashid et al., 2005; Samour & King, 2005).

In Jamal's situation his celiac disease caused damage to his gastrointestinal tract, resulting in an inability to absorb nutrients, which led, in turn, to poor growth. Jamal had to give up gluten-containing bread, pasta, pizza, muffins, and cookies, among other things that he liked to eat. His mother knew it was essential for Jamal to follow a special diet. She also knew that, although it might be difficult for him to make changes in his diet, he would adjust once he began to feel better.

Lactose Intolerance One of the enzymes in the small intestine is called lactase. Lactase helps digest the sugar in milk, called lactose (CDC Division of Oral Health, 2009). Unlike a milk protein allergy, which is an immune response that triggers serious and sometime life-threatening symptoms, children who are lactose intolerant simply do not make sufficient lactase. When they consume too many dairy foods or beverages with lactose they develop gas, bloating, and diarrhea (Guandalini, Frye, Rivera, & Borowitz, 2006).

The degree of lactose intolerance varies. Some children may be able to tolerate up to a cup of milk or yogurt per day. Yogurt with active live cultures and aged cheese are generally better tolerated than milk. Infants who are lactose intolerant can do well with either a lactose-free or soy formula. However, it is important to note that lactose intolerance in children under age 3 is uncommon (Heyman, 2006). The incidence of lactose intolerance is also higher in certain ethnic populations including African Americans, Asian Americans, and individuals of Native American descent (CDC Division of Oral Health, 2009).

Some children can develop a secondary lactose intolerance because of damage to the small intestine, which results in not enough lactase being available to aid in digestion. For example, if children have had gastroenteritis or "stomach flu," they may develop a temporary lactose intolerance until the small intestine heals. It is also not uncommon for children like Jamal who have celiac disease to be lactose intolerant.

The consequences of exposure to lactose are not as dire or dangerous as those of food allergies. Consequently, some children may be willing to suffer the consequences of lactose intolerance in order to eat a food they desire. Teachers and parents should clarify a feeding plan for children with lactose intolerance. It is also important for teachers to understand the effects of lactose intolerance and recognize how they may affect a child. For example:

> Jesse, a third grader, requests a pass to the restroom about a half hour after lunch. He is gone for 15 minutes. When he returns to the classroom the substitute teacher is upset and issues a referral to the principal's office. She assumes Jesse was taking advantage of the fact that she was not his usual teacher and had simply wasted time in the bathroom and halls. Jesse turns beet red and emphatically states, "I was using the bathroom!" He explains to the principal as he sits down to discuss the referral: "The only thing I did wrong was drink chocolate milk. I really like it but it doesn't like me. It gives me a stomachache." A quick look at his health files confirms lactose intolerance. Jesse's referral is immediately rescinded although it takes a little more time for his pride to be restored.

The symptoms of lactose intolerance can be quickly resolved by avoiding foods high in lactose content. Milk is a high-lactose food. Using lactose-reduced milk or vitamin D and calcium–enriched soy milk in place of regular milk will solve most children's problems. A conversation with families helps teachers to understand the degree of lactose sensitivity. Other dairy products such as yogurt, cheese, and ice cream also contain lactose. In addition, less obvious foods that have lactose added include lunch meats, hotdogs, baked goods, margarine, pancake and cake mixes, and instant potatoes (American Dietetic Association [ADA], 2008). Teachers should determine whether these foods must be removed from a particular child's diet as well.

Diet-Related Diarrheas Diarrhea can be caused by factors such as viruses and bacteria, but sometimes children eat or drink something that triggers diarrhea. Diarrhea is characterized by watery stools that occur with increased frequency and stomach cramping.

lactose intolerant term used to define an individual who experiences gas, bloating, and diarrhea because of an inability to break down the lactose found in milk

What if. . . you had a toddler in your program with lactose intolerance whose family was inconsistent in restricting lactose? Because of this, the child was having periodic bouts of diarrhea that were affecting potty training. How would you discuss this subject with parents?

Certain foods can cause diarrhea in young children. For example, many foods contain sugar alcohols (a type of sugar substitute) that are not completely digested and absorbed by the body. Sugar-free gum, candy, and cookies may contain sugar alcohols. These foods pass into the large intestine and are fermented by bacteria, which can cause diarrhea when children eat too much. Food labels list the following terms for sugar alcohols: sorbitol, mannitol, xylitol, maltitol, maltitol syrup, lactitol, erythritol, isomalt, and hydrogenated starch hydrolysates (International Food Information Council, 2008).

Other causes of diarrhea include the following (Ball & Bindler, 2006):

- Excess juice consumption, particularly apple and pear juices, which are naturally high in sorbitol.
- Consumption of drinks with caffeine such as tea or soft drinks.
- Diets that are excessively high in fiber.
- Overfeeding.
- The introduction of new foods that the child does not tolerate.
- Foods that result in malabsoption because of Crohn's disease (a disease that causes inflammation of the digestive tract), or irritable bowel syndrome (a dysfunction of the large intestine).

When a child has a bout of diarrhea, teachers must review the symptoms, consider the classroom incidence of diarrhea, and obtain family input before deciding whether to send a child home or not. Sometimes it is unclear whether a child is ill. Loose stools may not always be indicative of a major gastrointestinal illness; they could instead indicate a mild change in stool patterns. Figure 4-3 provides guidance in determining when to send children home if they have loose stools.

Diarrhea that is caused by viruses or bacteria may also be accompanied by vomiting. This combination creates a more critical condition because dehydration can occur. The infectious causes of diarrhea are discussed in Chapter 11.

> ## What if. . .
> you had a child in your class who complained of stomachaches? How might you manage this problem? What might you discuss in a conversation with the child's parents?

Understanding Constipation

Sometimes too much water is absorbed in the large intestine and constipation occurs. Constipation is the painful passage of stools that are hard and dry. This problem sometimes happens when children feel shy about using the bathroom at the early childhood or school programs. Constipation also can be caused by lack of fiber in the diet, inadequate fluid

Figure 4-3 What to Consider When a Child Has Loose Stools

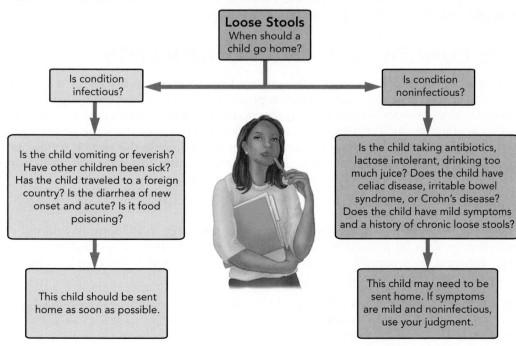

intake, and insufficient physical activity. When the amount of fiber in the diet is insufficient, the waste products of digestion and absorption move more slowly through the large intestine and, consequently, more water is reabsorbed, causing drier stools. Adding fiber and water to the diet allows for easier passage of stools. Physical activity also stimulates the movement of stool through the gastrointestinal tract.

Teachers can help prevent constipation by providing children with:

- Opportunities to drink water between meals, especially on warm days.
- Sufficient time for physical activity.
- Nutritious foods rich in fiber.
- Easy access to toilet facilities.

Aiding Digestion and Absorption

To ensure that children receive the most nutrition from their foods, teachers must create an environment that enhances and supports the natural rhythms of eating. Children feel confident about eating when they know that meals will be presented within a reasonable time frame and include foods they enjoy. The stomach generally empties in 2 to 4 hours. Planning meals and snacks every 3 to 4 hours is appropriate for most children. In fact, the Child and Adult Care Food Program (CACFP), a child nutrition program that is designed to reimburse programs for nutritious meals served to children, requires specific mealtime scheduling so that meals are not served too close together or too far apart.

The sight, aromas, and taste of food can be very important to children. These factors stimulate the production of saliva and gastric juices and can contribute to muscular activity of the gastrointestinal tract, inducing hunger pains. It is essential to provide appealing meals that stimulate the senses and whet the appetite to ensure adequate intake. For some low-income families, the meals provided at school are the best chance for their children to eat healthy, balanced meals. Making sure desirable, appetizing foods are served supports a healthy diet.

Emotional upset can interfere with digestion. This occurs because under stress the body makes fewer digestive enzymes. In addition the wave-like movements of the gastrointestinal tract that move food along are limited by stress. For these reasons, meals should be provided in a calm environment with limited distractions. To avoid stress and anger at mealtimes, plan enough time so that children can eat in a relaxing manner. In the elementary school setting, the timing of meals before outside breaks can result in a rush to finish eating. Planning sufficient time for meals as well as outdoor play provides the best balance for health and nutrition.

What if. . .

at the beginning of the school year, you noticed that your class has been assigned early lunch period, which is right before recess, and you have observed on more than one occasion that your third-grade students were rushing through lunch and throwing food away in an effort to quickly get outside to play? How would you resolve the problem?

THE FUNCTION OF MACRONUTRIENTS

Through the process of digestion, food is converted into components that can be readily absorbed. The macronutrients (carbohydrates, proteins, and fats) as their name suggests, are needed in large amounts because they supply energy (see Figure 3-4 for a review of the classification of nutrients). This energy is used for physical activity and the repair and replacement of cells but also for growth and development in children. In this section we discuss energy as well as the composition of food and macronutrients. This information will help you put into focus the rationale behind diet recommendations for young children.

Understanding Energy

calorie
a unit of measurement of the amount of energy that is released from food when it is metabolized by the body

Food provides energy for the body. Food energy is measured in the form of calories. A calorie represents the amount of energy released from food when it is metabolized by the body. Different macronutrients provide different amounts of calories. The calories per gram of protein, fats, and carbohydrates are as follows:

- Protein   4 calories
- Carbohydrates   4 calories
- Fats   9 calories

Children need energy to run and play as well as to maintain body functions such as breathing and pumping blood. The energy released from these nutrients when they are metabolized provides the fuel needed by the body.

Nutrient Composition of Foods

Food is a complex mixture of carbohydrates, proteins, fats, vitamins, and minerals. When children drink a glass of milk, they are consuming protein, fat (unless it's skim milk), and carbohydrates. The meat in a roast beef sandwich contains protein and fats, whereas the whole-grain bread contains some protein but mostly carbohydrates, as illustrated in Figure 4-4. The mayonnaise on the sandwich is predominantly fat, whereas the lettuce and tomato have small amounts of carbohydrates. When children eat a piece of fruit, they are consuming carbohydrates.

Foods can be grouped together based on similar nutrient composition. The MyPyramid system uses these food groups to explain healthy meal choices (USDA, 2009). Understanding the composition of food can be helpful when working with children who require special diets. For example, when planning meals for children with diabetes, teachers should understand the sources of carbohydrates in the diet. Eating an appropriate amount from each food group ensures that the body has sufficient energy, vitamins, and minerals to sustain life. Achieving the right balance between calories consumed and calories burned is one of the primary goals of healthy eating.

Figure 4-4 **Milk, Meat, and Whole-Wheat Bread Are a Combination of Macronutrients; Mayonnaise is Mainly Fat, and Pieces of Fruit Are Carbohydrates**

Releasing or Storing Energy

The metabolism of nutrients is a balancing act in which energy is either being released for immediate use or stored so that it is available at a later time. This releasing and storing occurs simultaneously from the moment of conception to the end of life. For example, when children play soccer, they use energy to contract their muscles, move their body, pump blood, breathe faster, and perspire to keep cool. When they stop for a snack of orange wedges, they use energy to digest and absorb the oranges. At the same time energy is also being used to maintain and repair the body and build muscles as they exercise. Growth will continue to occur even while children play soccer, provided that there is enough energy available in the diet. If children eat more oranges than they need immediately for fuel, energy will be stored in the liver, muscles, and fat cells for later use.

The releasing and storing of energy cannot be accomplished without the presence of vitamins, minerals, and water. The finely tuned metabolic processes of life are interrelated and codependent. Often vitamins and minerals have more than one role.

Determining Energy Needs

Children's energy (calorie) needs change as they grow and vary depending on age, whether they are boys or girls, and what size they are. Calorie needs also vary according to children's level of activity. Children playing soccer have greater energy needs than do classmates who sit on the sidelines and watch the game. The amount of energy children need depends on many variables; however, most children are able to self-regulate their energy needs and maintain appropriate growth. A closer evaluation of energy needs by health care professionals may be needed when children are underweight or overweight. The baseline of calories needed to sustain life and maintain the body's function such as breathing, pumping blood, and repairing cells, is called the basal metabolic rate (BMR). Calories needed to digest and absorb food and for physical activity are added to the BMR to obtain the total energy expenditure, or the amount of calories a child burns each day. When this information is determined, the child's diet is reviewed to ensure that enough, but not too much, food energy is being consumed in the diet to balance the child's energy needs.

Children have high calorie needs in relation to their size because of the energy requirements for growth. The Dietary Reference Intakes (DRIs) list the calorie requirements

basal metabolic rate (BMR)
a measurement of the baseline calories individuals need to sustain life and maintain the body's functions such as breathing, pumping blood, and repairing cells

total energy expenditure
a measurement of the number of calories needed by individuals; includes the basal metabolic rate plus the calories used for physical activity and the digestion and absorption of food

of children by age (see Web Resources) (Nelms, Sucher, & Long, 2007; Otten, Pitzi-Hellwig, & Meyers, 2006). Other factors that can influence calorie needs are illness and fever. For instance, Jamal's calorie needs are increased because he is experiencing malabsorption and has damage to his intestinal tract. He must also compensate for the loss of nutrients due to diarrhea and use extra calories for repair of his intestinal tract.

Teachers who feed children must take into consideration their differing needs for calories and serve age-appropriate portion sizes. Providing healthful diets and an environment that supports physical activity ensures that the balance of using and storing energy is maintained, and that proper growth and excess weight gain is avoided.

Carbohydrates

Carbohydrates provide the body's most abundant source of energy. They are found in grains, fruits, vegetables, milk products, and sweets. Cultures throughout the world rely on carbohydrates to provide their predominant source of nourishment. Each culture's carbohydrate choice is based on geography, terrain for farming, and cultural traditions. Rice, beans, maize, wheat, potatoes, barley, cassava, and quinoa are just some of the variety of plants that provide inexpensive energy sources for people of the world. These plant sources of carbohydrate are important because they provide an ongoing source of glucose. Glucose, a simple sugar, is the common fuel for all cells and the only source of energy for the brain. The different types of carbohydrates include simple sugars and complex carbohydrates and are illustrated in Figure 4-5.

Figure 4-5 Types of Carbohydrates

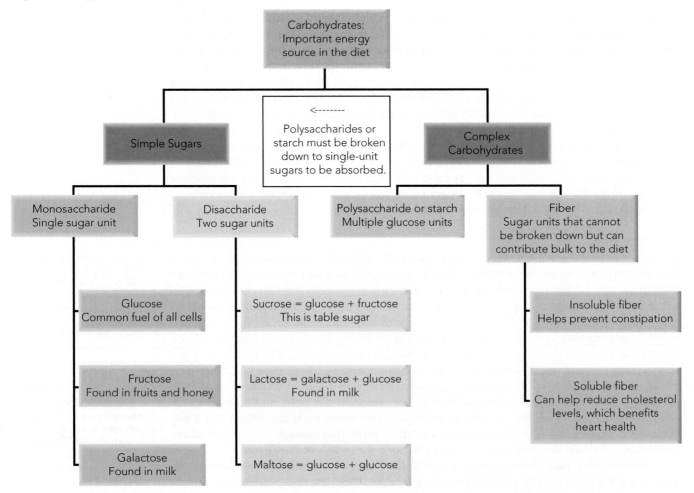

Sugars

Six different sugars play a role in children's diets. They are divided into two groups based on whether they occur as a single sugar unit or are bonded together as two units.

Monosaccharides The simplest type of sugar consisting of single sugar units are mono-saccharides. They include glucose, fructose, and galactose. Glucose and fructose occur naturally in some foods such as fruits and honey. Galactose is a simple sugar made by animals and found in the milk they produce. All sugars and starches must be broken down to mono-saccharides via digestion to be absorbed and metabolized in human cells (Shills et al., 2006).

Disaccharides Two single sugar units, when bonded together, are called disaccharides. They include sucrose, lactose, and maltose. Table sugar is sucrose. It consists of fructose and glucose units that are bonded together. Lactose is milk sugar. It consists of galactose and glucose sugar units. Maltose consists of two glucose units.

Conflicting Role of Sugar in the Diets of Young Children Teachers and families often have very strong preferences about whether sugar should be included in the diets of young children. Teachers must make judgments about how to manage these concerns, as described in the following scenario:

> Hallie, a teacher in a kindergarten/first-grade blended class, has a parent who feels that graham crackers contain too much sugar and should not be offered as a snack in class. Another parent has complained because Hallie does not allow cupcakes to be served for celebrations such as birthdays. A third parent does not permit her child to eat canned fruit at snack time because it contains high-fructose corn syrup. Each parent has strong feelings about sugar. Hallie tries to accommodate their preferences while at the same time considering the school's policies.

Opinions about sugar can be put into perspective by reviewing the recommendations of health authorities and federal guidelines. The Institute of Medicine's DRIs recommend that sugar not exceed 25% of total calories (Otten et al., 2006). Added sweeteners such as sucrose and fructose are generally recognized as safe (known as GRAS) by the Food and Drug Administration (FDA), yet health concerns exist about the increased use of added sugars in the diets of young children (ADA, 2004), as discussed in the *Health Hint*.

The body does not distinguish between a unit of glucose obtained by eating a jelly bean versus a unit of glucose obtained by eating a slice of whole-grain bread when it comes to metabolizing that glucose for energy. However, teachers need to consider other concerns related to the inclusion of foods that contain sugar. For example, a jelly bean is simply calories, whereas the slice of whole-grain bread is rich in fiber, vitamins, and minerals. Eating foods high in sugar may displace needed nutrients in the diet of young children (ADA, 2004; Bhargava & Amialchuk, 2007; Murphy & Johnson, 2003). For example, children who consume "worms in the dirt" (chopped chocolate cookies on top of chocolate pudding and threaded with gummy worms) during a midmorning cooking activity may not eat their lunch of turkey sandwiches with milk, apple, and carrots sticks. Consequently, they will get fewer of the recommended nutrients important for growth and development.

The American Dietetic Association (2004) points out that pushing sugar intake to more than one-quarter of the total calorie intake for the day compromises diet quality. Unfortunately 13% of U.S. children ages 4 to 8 exceed the 25% recommendation. The percentage of total calorie intake for sugar gets even higher as they get older. In addition, frequent exposure to sugary, sticky foods and sweetened beverages is linked to an increase in dental cavities. Health experts are also concerned that drinking too many beverages rich in sugars including soft drinks, and juice may lead to obesity (Malik, Schulze, & Hu, 2006; Vartanian, Schwartz, & Brownell, 2007). Of significance is that even toddlers as young as ages 1 to 3 are consuming soft drinks (Rampersaud, Bailey, & Kauwell, 2003).

monosaccharides
these are the simplest type of sugar consisting of single sugar units and include glucose, fructose, and galactose

disaccharides
these are sugars that contain two single sugar units, which are bonded together. They include sucrose, lactose, and maltose

MyEducationLab

Go to the Assignments and Activities section of Topic 1: Basic Nutrition in the MyEducationLab for your course and complete the activity entitled *Collaborating with Families to Reduce Sugar and Processed Food*. What factors influence sugar intake in young children?

Health Hint

High-Fructose Corn Syrup: Are There Health Risks?

Does high-fructose corn syrup increase the risk of obesity and the chronic diseases associated with obesity because of the way it is metabolized? Some studies suggest this is the case, although research has had conflicting results. High-fructose corn syrup is used in food products such as soft drinks canned fruits, and processed desserts because it is sweeter than sucrose and inexpensive.

Fructose is a monosaccharide that is absorbed slower than glucose in the gastrointestinal tract. When glucose is absorbed it triggers the release of the hormones insulin and leptin, both of which inhibit appetite. This does not occur when fructose is absorbed. There is speculation that this may lead to overeating. Fructose has the ability to stimulate the liver to make fats (triglycerides), which increase in the bloodstream, perhaps contributing to a potential risk for heart disease. However, some confusion surrounds studies about pure fructose versus high-fructose corn syrup. High-fructose corn syrup and sucrose both contain about 50% fructose and 50% glucose. Most researchers agree that high-fructose corn syrup and sucrose produce similar effects on metabolism and they have found no differences in appetite, feelings of fullness, or short-term calorie intake. Can evidenced-based recommendations be made about high-fructose corn syrup? Not yet because research is still ongoing.

In the meantime, teachers can take a judicious approach to high-fructose corn syrup by:

- Not offering soft drinks to young children.
- Serving fresh fruit instead of canned fruit, especially fruits packed in heavy syrup.
- Avoiding processed desserts.

Sources: "Consumption of High-Fructose Corn Syrup in Beverages May Play a Role in the Epidemic of Obesity," by G. A. Bray, S. J. Nielsen, and B. M. Popkin, 2004, *American Journal of Clinical Nutrition, 79*(4), pp. 537–543; *High Fructose Corn Syrup,* by K. Clark, 2009, retrieved September 8, 2009, from http://www.eatright.org/cps/rde/xchg/ada/hs.xsl/nutrition_7883_ENU_HTML.htm; and "Fructose, Weight Gain, and the Insulin Resistance Syndrome," by S. Elliot, N. Keim, J. Stern, K. Teff, and P. Havel, 2002, *American Journal of Clinical Nutrition, 76*, pp. 911–922.

What if . . .

other teachers in your school offered candy as a reward to children who are keeping on task? What if you complained to the principal and were brushed aside? What type of nonfood methods might you use to motivate students?

Taken together, there is concern when children's diets exceed the recommended level for sugar intake. For this reason, schools are taking steps to reduce children's intake of high-calorie soft drinks at school, as discussed in the *Policy Point*.

One concern that can be alleviated is the link between sugar and behavior. Researchers have found that in general there is no link between hyperactivity and sugar intake in the general population of children (Benton, 2008; Nevin-Folino, 2008; Samour & King, 2005; Wolraich, Wilson, & White, 1995). Some research, however, suggests that a small number of children with attention deficit/hyperactivity disorder (5% to 10%) may show improvement of symptoms if sugar in their diet is restricted (Samour & King, 2005).

The goal is for children to consume sugar in moderation and within the context of an otherwise healthful diet. Teachers set the tone in the classroom for healthful eating by raising the level of awareness among parents as well as children. For this reason many children's settings limit foods that are perceived as "sweets." Healthful food choices can include foods that are sweet tasting. Teachers should however select foods with nutritionally redeeming qualities such as sweet potato or carrot muffins, zucchini bread, oatmeal cookies, and frozen yogurt with strawberries. Overall the goal for children and their families is to learn a mindful and moderate approach to eating.

Policy Point

REDUCING HIGH-CALORIE SOFT DRINK CONSUMPTION IN SCHOOLS

In May 2006, the Alliance for a Healthier Generation, a joint initiative of the American Heart Association, the William J. Clinton Foundation, and the American Beverage Association, announced new school beverage guidelines that will voluntarily remove high-calorie soft drinks from all U.S. schools by the 2009–2010 school year.

Although guidelines for preschool programs are not available, the recommendations for children in primary school allow the following:

- Bottled water.
- Up to 8 ounces of milk or juice.
- Regular or flavored milk that is fat free or low fat that provides up to 150 calories per serving.
- 100% juice that provides up to 120 calories per 8-ounce serving and 10% of the daily value for three vitamins and/or minerals.

These guidelines have become the standard of practice for the soft drink beverage industry and will be used as a basis for establishing contract arrangements with elementary, middle, and high school programs. They are applicable to the school setting, including before- and after-school programs they also include all beverages sold outside the context of school breakfast and school lunch programs (i.e., vending machines, snack carts, à la carte menu items).

These guidelines do not cover sporting events, school plays, and so on, where parents are present or are selling soft drinks as boosters. They do not supersede state legislation, school district policies, or local initiatives, which may be more restrictive. For example, schools may choose not to allow sugar-sweetened soft drinks at school plays or other after-school events that include parents.

This initiative is a step in the right direction in that it shows that both schools and industry are making a concerted effort to reduce the intake of calorie-rich, nutrient-poor beverages. Whether the initiative is effective or not, the overall message can only help in our goal to decrease overweight and obesity in children.

Sources: Based on *School Beverage Guidelines: The American Beverage Association & The Alliance for a Healthier Generation*, by the American Beverage Association, 2009, retrieved October 16, 2009, from http://www.ameribev.org/nutrition--science/school-beverage-guidelines/; American Heart Association and Clinton Foundation, retrieved September 9, 2009, from http://www.healthiergeneration.org/schools.aspx.

Complex Carbohydrates

Complex carbohydrates are the second category of carbohydrates. They include two different types: starch and dietary fiber. The *starches*, also called polysaccharides, consist of multiple glucose sugars linked together in chains. Breaking starches down to simple sugars (glucose) through the digestive process makes them available for absorption in the small intestine.

Fiber is a type of carbohydrate that cannot be used as energy because humans lack the digestive enzymes to break it down. However, dietary fiber does provide significant health benefits. The recognized health benefits depend on the type of fiber being consumed: insoluble or soluble (ADA, 2008).

Insoluble Fiber A type of fiber that comes from the structural components of plant cell walls and does not dissolve in water is referred to as insoluble fiber. Wheat bran, rice bran, whole-wheat breads, crackers, and cereals, and the seeds in berry fruits are examples of this insoluble fiber. Eating foods with insoluble fiber aids with digestion. Insoluble fiber acts like a sponge to draw water into the stool. Softer, bulkier stools move through the gastrointestinal tract more quickly, which helps children maintain regular bowel habits and avoid constipation.

Soluble Fiber A fiber that readily mixes with water, forming gels and giving foods a thickened consistency is called soluble fiber. Oatmeal, oat bran, and beans are

polysaccharides
complex carbohydrates that consist of multiple glucose sugars linked together in chains. Also called starch

insoluble fiber
a type of dietary fiber that does not dissolve in water. It comes from the structural components of plant cell walls and is found in wheat bran, rice bran, whole-wheat breads, crackers, cereals, the seeds in berry fruits. This type of fiber prevents constipation

The complex carbohydrates found in dietary sources include starch and fiber.

soluble fiber
a type of dietary fiber that readily mixes with water to form gels. It gives foods a thickened consistency and is found in oatmeal, oat bran, and beans. It can bind with cholesterol, thus inhibiting cholesterol absorption, which can protect against heart disease

examples of soluble fiber sources (ADA, 2008). Soluble fiber offers significant health benefits. It binds with cholesterol in the diet so that less cholesterol is absorbed, protecting children from heart disease. It also delays stomach emptying, making children feel full longer, and may aid in weight control.

Whole grains are a type of carbohydrate in which all parts of the grain, including the germ, endosperm and bran, are consumed. For example, oatmeal, brown rice, whole wheat, and corn are examples of whole grains. Whole grains are healthy for children because they are rich in fiber, vitamins, and minerals and contain naturally occurring antioxidants that reduce the risk for cancer and heart disease (Whole Grains Council, 2009).

Adding more fiber to early child care program menus can be easily accomplished with a few simple adjustments in food selection that focus on whole grains and more fresh fruits and vegetables. Figure 4-6 shows examples of both a high-fiber and a low-fiber breakfast. Chapter 6 provides additional child-friendly strategies for increasing the fiber content of young children's diets.

Proteins

Proteins are the basis of life in humans. Without proteins the body cannot grow, reproduce, or repair itself. Proteins are organic compounds that contain carbon, hydrogen, oxygen, and nitrogen. Proteins are essential in all life processes and are particularly important to young children because they are growing.

Defining the Function of Proteins

Proteins have three primary roles: growth and repair of the body, regulation of the processes within the body, and energy:

1. *Proteins are necessary for growth and repair.* Proteins form structures in the body such as skin, bones, organs, and muscles. Insufficient protein during growth can impede brain development and function (Otten et al., 2006). Proteins consumed in the diet are digested into amino acids, which when absorbed are used to make body protein that needs to be replaced. For example, when a red blood cell dies, a new red blood cell will be made from the amino acids furnished by the diet.

Figure 4-6 A High-Fiber and Low-Fiber Breakfast

Breakfast A	Fiber (grams)	Breakfast B	Fiber (grams)
½ cup Raisin bran	5.5	½ cup Puffed rice	0.2
1 cup milk, skim	0	1 cup milk, skim	0
Whole-grain bread	2.2	White bread	0.6
1 Tbsp peanut butter	1	1 Tbsp cream cheese	0
1 cup strawberries	3.3	1 cup orange juice	1.0
Total	**12 grams**		**1.8 grams**

Source: *USDA National Nutrient Database for Standard Reference, Release 17: Fiber Content of Foods,* by the U.S. Department of Agriculture, 2004, retrieved September 8, 2009, from http://www.nal.usda.gov/fnic/foodcomp/Data/SR17/wtrank/sr17a291.pdf.

2. *Proteins control body functions.*   This is managed through a system of regulatory processes. Enzymes, hormones, antibodies, and red blood cells are just a sampling of the protein-based components that help the body maintain vital functions. When children fight off a cold, antibodies (a type of protein found in the blood that fights infections) come to their rescue. When they eat lunch, protein-based enzymes break the food down for digestion and absorption. The multitude of uses for protein in the body explains why it is so important for children to have sufficient amounts in their diet.

3. *Proteins can be used for energy if need be.*   Protein, however, is a fuel of last resort because of its importance in other body functions such as growth and development. Too much protein in the diets of children is not stored as protein, but instead is converted into body fat.

Understanding Amino Acids

Amino acids are the biological compounds that act as building blocks for all proteins. Twenty different amino acids combine in innumerable ways to build the vast array of proteins found in humans. The process for converting dietary protein into human protein is as follows:

1. Plant or animal protein is consumed.
2. Protein is broken down into amino acids in the small intestine.
3. Amino acids are absorbed and recombined in different sequences according to the type of human protein needed (such as skin cells, hormones, muscle).

amino acids
biological compounds that act as the building blocks for all proteins

Essential, Nonessential, and Conditionally Essential Amino Acids

How well children are able to build proteins for their body depends on whether the right amount and type of amino acids are available. Amino acids can be categorized based on the need to have them provided in the diet:

Eggs, meat, poultry, and beans are excellent sources of protein in the diet.

- Essential amino acids: the nine amino acids the body cannot make. It is "essential" that these amino acids be provided by the diet.
- Nonessential amino acids: the five amino acids the body can readily make.
- Conditionally essential amino acids: amino acids the body is sometimes able to make, but sometimes must be provided by the diet (Otten et al., 2006; Samour & King, 2005).

An example of a situation in which an amino acid is conditionally essential is seen in premature infants who may have limited ability to make certain amino acids. Therefore the diet must be supplemented either by fortifying breast milk or by using specially designed formulas that are higher in protein content (Otten et al., 2006; Samour & King, 2005).

The Quality of Protein All of the essential amino acids must be available in the diet to make the body's protein. If one particular essential amino acid is low in the diet, the body will make protein only until it runs out of this amino acid in spite of the fact that other amino acids are readily available. Similar to missing a link in a chain, if one link is missing the chain simply cannot be put together. When a food is low in a particular amino acid, that amino acid is called the limiting amino acid. The presence or absence of a limiting amino acid determines the quality of the protein:

limiting amino acid
an essential amino acid that is lacking in a dietary protein source, thereby limiting protein synthesis

- *High-quality protein:* Protein that comes from animal sources has all of the essential amino acids or links needed to make human protein chains. These are called high-quality proteins and include milk, eggs, cheese, meats, fish, and poultry. All protein

What if. . .

a parent believed his overweight child needed to follow a low-carbohydrate diet? What are the disadvantages of such a diet for young children? How would you handle this diet request?

Go to the Assignments and Activities section of Topic 3: Menu Planning in the MyEducationLab for your course and complete the activity entitled *Whole Grains*. How can you identify what are whole grains?

complementary protein proteins that are low in different amino acids but can be combined to provide enough total essential amino acids to form all of the amino acids necessary to build human protein

essential fatty acids a type of fatty acid that cannot be made by the body and must be obtained from the diet; needed for growth and maintaining a healthy immune system

Some of children's favorite foods consist of complementary proteins.

from animal sources is high quality except for gelatin. Soy protein is also a source of high quality protein.

- *Lower quality protein:* Some foods provide lower quality proteins because they do not contain much protein or have a limiting amino acid. For example, fruits and many vegetables are generally not good sources of protein. Other foods of plant origin can add significant amounts of protein to the diet, but are limiting in an amino acid. For instance, grains are low in some amino acids and legumes are low in others. However, if they are combined over the course of the day, enough essential amino acids are available to make the necessary links to form the proteins needed by the body (Otten et al., 2006). These foods are said to contain complementary protein because, in combination, they provide all of the amino acids necessary to build human protein.

Traditionally, people from all cultures have learned to match foods that provide complementary proteins. Examples include:

- Red beans and rice.
- Peanut butter and whole-grain bread.
- Bean burritos.
- Falafel (made from chick peas) and whole-wheat pita.
- Hummus (chick peas and ground sesame seeds) and whole-wheat crackers.
- Tofu and rice.
- Soy milk and whole-grain toast.

Supplementing a lower quality protein (one with a limiting amino acid) with small amounts of high-quality animal protein results in a complete protein combination that provides all of the essential amino acids such as serving beans with cheese.

Defining Protein Requirements

The Dietary Reference Intake for protein requirements changes as children grow. For example, children's protein needs are 13 grams per day for 1- to 3-year-olds and 19 grams for 4- to 8-year-olds (Otten et al., 2006). To put this into perspective, 1 cup of milk has about 8 grams of protein on average, a 1-ounce serving of meat/poultry provides 7 grams of protein, and a slice of bread from the grain group provides about 3 grams of protein. Totaled together, 18 grams is enough to meet just about all the protein needs of young children. The typical U.S. diet provides ample protein. The CACFP requires 1.5 ounces of protein to be served for lunch for 3- to 5-year-olds. This represents about 10 grams of protein. To get a sense of what this portion represents visualize a half a deck of cards. Although this may seem like a small portion, for a child it provides more than enough protein.

Fats

The fats are the most concentrated source of calories in the diet. Although too much fat is not beneficial because of its link to obesity, there is a role for healthful fats in children's diets. Fats provide essential fatty acids that cannot be made by the body and must be obtained from the diet. Essential fatty acids are needed for growth and maintaining a healthy immune system (Hark, Deen, & Campbell, 2005; Taylor et al., 2006). Lack of essential fatty acids in infants can result in learning problems and impaired growth and vision (Mahan & Escott-Stump, 2004; Stipanuk, 2006). Fats help with the absorption of the fat-soluble vitamins

A, D, E, and K (Otten et al., 2006) and provide a concentrated source of energy to support growth in infants and young children. Fats also add flavor and satiety to foods. Some fats also promote heart health.

Types of Dietary Fat

Dietary fats are often referred to as "good" fats and "bad" fats. Good fats are those that reduce the risk of heart disease. They include polyunsaturated fats and monounsaturated fats, which come predominantly from plant sources. Both reduce the risk for heart disease by lowering blood cholesterol levels and decreasing inflammation, although there is an ongoing debate as to which one of these two types of fats is more beneficial (Harris et al., 2009; Harvard School of Public Health, 2009a; Jakobsen et al., 2009). Omega-3 fatty acids are a type of polyunsaturated fat that is found in fish as well as plant oils such as canola and flaxseed oil.

The "bad" dietary fats are those that increase the risk of heart disease. They include the saturated fats and *trans fatty acids*. Saturated fats come predominantly from animal sources, but also include coconut oil, palm oil, and palm kernel oil. *Trans* fatty acids are formed during food processing when liquid oils are made solid. Although both types of fat increase the risk of heart disease, *trans* fatty acids are especially harmful (American Heart Association, 2008). Dietary cholesterol is a fat-like substance that is found in foods of animal origin. Cholesterol is also made in the body. Increased levels of cholesterol in the bloodstream are associated with heart disease risk. Table 4-4 lists types of dietary fats and dietary cholesterol, fats, their dietary sources, and their impact on the risk for heart disease.

Dietary Fats and Health

The health impact of dietary fats is linked to how cholesterol and fats are transported in the blood. Just as oil and vinegar don't mix, neither do fats, cholesterol, and blood. To transport fat and cholesterol to where they are needed in the body, the liver packages them in a lipoprotein "coating." One of the most common types of lipoproteins is low-density lipoprotein (LDL), also commonly called LDL cholesterol or "bad" cholesterol. Elevated LDL levels in the bloodstream are a marker for heart disease. LDL accumulates in the arteries, forming plaque, which is fatty deposits made of cholesterol and other fatty compounds

polyunsaturated fats
unsaturated fats with two or more double bonds in their chemical structure that come predominantly from plant sources (such as corn oil, safflower oil), are liquid at room temperature, and reduce the risk of heart disease

monounsaturated fats
unsaturated fats with one double bond in their chemical structure (such as olive oil and canola oil) that also come from plant sources, are liquid at room temperature, and reduce the risk of heart disease

omega-3 fatty acids
polyunsaturated fats that are found in fish and also plant oils such as canola and flaxseed oil; protect against heart disease

saturated fats
fats found predominantly in animal sources that are solid at room temperature and are detrimental to heart health

trans fatty acids
fats formed during the process of hydrogenation where liquid oils are made solid and are especially harmful to heart health

Table 4-4	Types and Sources of Dietary Fats and Dietary Cholesterol	
Types of Fat or Cholesterol	**Dietary Sources**	**How They May Impact Risk for Heart Disease**
Polyunsaturated fats	Corn oil, safflower oil, sunflower oil, soybean oil	Reduce
Monounsaturated fats	Olives, avocados. olive oil, canola oil, peanut oil, and nuts	Reduce
Omega-3 fatty acids	Flax oil, canola oil, soybean oil, fatty types of fish	Reduce
Saturated fats	Cheese, meats, poultry, milk (except nonfat), cream, butter, coconut oil, palm oil, palm kernel oil	Increase
Trans fats	Stick margarine, vegetable shortening, some commercial baked goods such as pastries and doughnuts, fried foods such as French fries	Increase
Dietary cholesterol	Cheese, meats, poultry, milk, butter, eggs, liver	Increase

Source: Reprinted with permission from *Dietary Reference Intakes: The Essential Guide to Nutrient Requirements*, 2006 by the National Academy of Sciences, courtesy of the National Academies Press, Washington, D.C.

dietary cholesterol
a fat-like, waxy substance that is found in foods of animal origin, that plays a role in heart disease risk when consumed in excess

lipoprotein
a fat and protein complex that helps transport fats and cholesterol in the bloodstream

low-density lipoprotein (LDL)
a class of lipoprotein that transports cholesterol in the bloodstream; when elevated, it can increase the risk of heart disease

(Jakobsen et al., 2009). When plaque builds up, it can block blood flow and cause a heart attack or stroke (Harvard School of Public Health, 2009a; National Heart Lung and Blood Institute, 2008; Texas Heart Institute, 2009).

Another common lipoprotein is high-density lipoprotein (HDL). This is called the "good cholesterol" because it protects the heart. HDL picks up excess cholesterol in the circulatory system and brings it back to the liver where is can be excreted. This reduces the risk of heart disease.

The key to a healthy diet is to:

- Substitute good dietary fats for bad fats.
- Avoid *trans* fats.
- Limit the amount of cholesterol consumed so that LDL cholesterol and HDL cholesterol remain within acceptable ranges within the blood (Harvard School of Public Health, 2009a).

Teachers should understand that the biggest influence on blood cholesterol levels is the mix of fats in the diet—more so than the amount of cholesterol found in foods (Harvard School of Public Health, 2009a). The *Nutrition Note* takes a look at the role of saturated and *trans* fats in children's diets.

Nutrition Note

The Role of *Trans* Fats and Saturated Fats in Children's Diets

As of January 1, 2006, the U.S. Food and Drug Administration requires that *trans* fats be listed on food labels. Why might this create problems in children's diets? With the initiation of this labeling law, food companies have been scrambling to find replacements for *trans* fats. Coconut and palm oils are being used as a replacement for *trans* fats in some food products, but those oils are not a healthier alternative given that these are both saturated fats. Labels can state that it is *trans* fat free but still contain saturated fats. Saturated fats, like *trans* fats, stimulate the production of LDL or bad cholesterol.

When checking labels, teachers should look for both *trans* fat and saturated fat content. Review the food labels shown here to compare the fat composition of various types of spreads.

Butter**	Margarine, stick†	Margarine, tub†
Nutrition Facts Serving Size 1 Tbsp (14g) Servings Per Container 32 Amount Per Serving Calories 100 Calories from Fat 100 % Daily Value* Total Fat 11g 17% Saturated Fat 7g ◄ 35% Trans Fat 0g ◄ Cholesterol 30mg ➡ 10%	**Nutrition Facts** Serving Size 1 Tbsp (14g) Servings Per Container 32 Amount Per Serving Calories 100 Calories from Fat 100 % Daily Value* Total Fat 11g 17% Saturated Fat 2g ◄ 10% Trans Fat 3g ◄ Cholesterol 0mg ➡ 0%	**Nutrition Facts** Serving Size 1 Tbsp (14g) Servings Per Container 32 Amount Per Serving Calories 60 Calories from Fat 100 % Daily Value* Total Fat 7g 11% Saturated Fat 1g ◄ 5% Trans Fat 0.5g ◄ Cholesterol 0mg ➡ 0%
Saturated Fat : 7g + *Trans* Fat : 0g **Combined Amt.: 7g**	Saturated Fat : 2g + *Trans* Fat : 3g **Combined Amt.: 5g**	Saturated Fat : 1g + *Trans* Fat : 0.5g **Combined Amt.: 1.5g**
Cholesterol: 10% DV	**Cholesterol: 0% DV**	**Cholesterol: 0% DV**

*Nutrient values rounded based on FDA's nutrition labeling regulations. Calorie and cholesterol content estimated.
**Butter values from FDA Table of *Trans* Values, 1/30/95.
†Values derived from 2002 USDA National Nutrient Database for Standard Reference, Release 15.

Sources: *Food Products and Trans Fat—Staying on Top of Recent Changes*, by C. Biesemeier, 2006, retrieved August 15, 2007, from http://www.eatright.org/cps/rde/xchg/ada/hs.xsl/nutrition_9899_ENU_HTML.htm; and *Trans Fat Now Listed with Saturated Fat and Cholesterol on the Nutrition Facts Label*, by the U.S. Food and Drug Administration, 2006, retrieved September 9, 2009, from http://vm.cfsan.fda.gov/~dms/transfat.html.

Implications of Dietary Fats in Children's Diets

Thinking about heart disease in infants and young children may seem premature. However, as teachers plan what they should feed young children, they must consider the foods that will foster children's healthful growth and development. They also need to consider the importance of nutrition as it relates to disease prevention. It has been estimated that as many as 50% of primary school–age children have one or more risk factors for heart disease (Reed, Warburton, & McKay, 2007). Furthermore, children may inherit a genetic predisposition to elevated blood cholesterol levels.

The type of fat consumed in the diet plays an important role in supporting the health of all children. Consequently, as teachers plan meals and cooking activities, they should focus on the use of healthy fats. For example, when making biscuits with children, teachers should select a recipe that uses oil instead of shortening and, when margarine is used, be sure to select a brand that does not have *trans* fatty acids.

Remember, however, that during infancy and the toddler years, restricting fat and cholesterol is not advised by health care professionals because of the calories these children need for growth. The position of the Institute of Medicine of the National Academies, the American Dietetic Association, and the American Heart Association is that young children should make a gradual transition from receiving 50% of their calorie needs from fat during infancy to 30% to 35% during the ages of 2 to 3 (Nicklas, Johnson, & American Dietetic Association, 2004; Otten et al., 2006; Strathearn, Mamun, Najman, & O'Callaghan, 2009). By the time children are ages 4 and older, a diet closer aligned with the adult requirements of 25% to 35% is recommended (American Heart Association, 2006).

Summary of the Role of Macronutrients

The goal of a healthful diet is to achieve a beneficial balance of macronutrients. Foods are a combination of proteins, fats, and carbohydrates. When children eat foods in a manner that supports MyPyramid recommendations, they are ensured balanced diets that contain an appropriate percentage of calories from carbohdyrates, fats, and proteins. The diet will have sufficient protein for the growth and repair of the body. It will have enough fat to meet calorie needs, but not have too much, thereby decreasing the risk of heart disease and obesity. It will have ample carbohydrates to meet energy needs and provide sufficient fiber for good health.

VITAMINS AND MINERALS AND OTHER IMPORTANT DIETARY COMPONENTS

Vitamins and minerals are components in food that are required in small amounts to sustain body processes. They are referred to as micronutrients. Vitamins and minerals are needed to release and utilize the energy found in protein, fats, and carbohydrates. They help transport oxygen, fight infections, build body structures such as bones and teeth, and keep the body working efficiently and in good repair. Vitamins and minerals also play an important role in preventing chronic diseases such as heart disease and cancer (Harvard School of Public Health, 2009b). The goal of all nutrient guidance systems is to encourage the intake of a varied and balanced diet, thereby ensuring children consume the micronutrients needed to sustain health. It is best to obtain the micronutrients from foods as opposed to vitamin pills, which may not provide all the beneficial nutrients.

Vitamins

The body requires 13 essential vitamins, as listed in Table 4-5. Vitamins are organic compounds found predominantly in the foods we eat. The exceptions are vitamin D, which can be made by the body when the skin is exposed to sunlight, and vitamin K, which is produced by microorganisms in the gastrointestinal tract (Sizer & Whitney, 2006). Vitamins are essential. Without them humans cannot process and use energy from the proteins, fats, and carbohydrates we consume. Vitamins can be categorized into two groups: water-soluble and fat-soluble.

plaque
fatty deposits made of cholesterol and other fatty compounds that clog the arteries of the heart and increase the risk of heart attack

high-density lipoprotein (HDL)
a class of lipoprotein that transports excess cholesterol from the bloodstream back to the liver where it is excreted; lowers the risk of heart disease

Table 4-5 **Vitamins**

	Functions	Good Food Sources*	Symptoms of Excess Intake	Symptoms of Deficiency
Water Soluble				
Thiamin (B₁)	Helps metabolize carbohydrates and some amino acids for energy. It is beneficial for the nervous system and is essential for growth and development	Enriched and whole-grain products (breads and cereals), pork, ham, liver, legumes, and nuts, fortified meat substitutes	None reported	Loss of appetite, weight loss, Leads to beriberi: Symptoms include loss of appetite, weight loss, mental changes, muscle weakness, enlarged weakened heart, heart failure, nerve problems
Riboflavin (B₂)	Helps metabolize protein, fat, and carbohydrates for energy	Milk and milk products, enriched bread products, and fortified cereals	None reported	Sore throat, mouth, and tongue with cracks at the corners of mouth
Niacin (B₃)	As part of a coenzyme it helps with the metabolism of carbohydrates, protein, and fat	Milk, liver, meat, poultry, fish, enriched whole grains, and fortified cereal	Leads to pellegra: symptoms include rash, vomiting, diarrhea, bright red tongue, depression, apathy, and memory loss	Pellegra: symptoms include rash, vomiting, diarrhea, bright red tongue, depression, apathy, and memory loss
Pyridoxine (B₆)	Helps metabolize proteins and glycogen	Meat, fish, poultry, starchy vegetables, noncitrus fruits, fortified cereals, organ meats, fortified soy-based meat substitutes	Neurologic disorders and numbness	Convulsions, loss of weight, depression, confusion, skin problems, microcytic anemia
Pantothenic acid	Part of a coenzyme involved in fatty acid and carbohydrate metabolism	Poultry, meat, fish, eggs, broccoli, tomatoes, potatoes, whole grains, legumes	None reported	Deficiency is rare
Biotin	Functions as a coenzyme; helps break down proteins and carbohydrates for energy	Widely available in foods, especially liver, egg yolk, milk	None reported	Deficiency is associated with intake of raw egg whites over a long period of time (egg whites have avidin, which binds with biotin). Skin conditions, loss of appetite, depression, hair loss
Folate or folic acid	Involved in protein metabolism. Red blood cell formation and DNA synthesis	Yeast, liver, leafy green vegetables, beans, legumes, seeds, fortified breads, and cereals	Excess masks vitamin B₁₂ deficiency, which causes neurologic damage	Macrocytic anemia, poor growth, swollen tongue *Special consideration:* Women of childbearing age require folic acid supplementation to reduce the risk of neural tube defects in infants
Vitamin B₁₂	Functions as a coenzyme; involved in the metabolism of fatty acids and amino acids. Helps form red blood cells	Found only in animal foods, meat, fish, poultry, cheese, milk, eggs, fortified soy products	None reported	Leads to pernicious anemia and neurologic problems Supplementation may be required in individuals with malabsorption, and infants of vegan mothers who are breast-feeding

Table 4-5   **Vitamins** (*Continued*)

	Functions	Good Food Sources*	Symptoms of Excess Intake	Symptoms of Deficiency
Vitamin C	Involved in collagen formation. Improves wound healing, resistance to infection and iron absorption	Fruits and vegetables: especially citrus fruits, tomatoes, potatoes, kiwi fruit, peppers, broccoli, strawberries	Increased incidence of kidney stones, gastrointestinal distress	Leads to scurvy: symptoms include bleeding gums, decreased wound healing, easy bruising, swollen and painful joints
Fat Soluble				
Vitamin A	Important for normal vision, growth, immune function, formation of skin and mucous membranes, reproduction	There are two types: *Preformed:* liver, dairy products, fish, fortified margarine, and milk *Carotenoids:* orange fruits and vegetables (carrots, sweet potatoes, cantaloupe), dark green vegetables	Toxicity only from preformed vitamin A: nausea, vomiting, headache, dizziness, blurred vision, lack of muscular coordination; excessive intake during pregnancy leads to birth defects	Night blindness, blindness, poor bone growth, impaired resistance to infection
Vitamin D	It aids in the absorption and raises the levels of calcium and phosphorus in the blood, which promotes bone formation and bone maintenance	Can be made in the skin in the presence of sunlight. *Food sources:* fatty fish, fortified milk and cereals, infant formula. Breast milk is not a rich source and, therefore, supplementation is recommended in exclusively breast-fed infants	High blood levels of calcium, calcification of soft tissues such as kidneys, blood vessels, nausea, vomiting, and poor appetite	Leads to rickets in children with faulty bone growth and undermineralized bones in adults
Vitamin E	Acts as an antioxidant protecting cell membranes	Vegetable oils, wheat germ, fortified cereals, nuts, fruits, vegetables, meats, poultry, fish, eggs	None reported with naturally occurring vitamin E; excessive supplementation can lead to impaired blood clotting	Rare but can cause hemolytic anemia in premature infants
Vitamin K	Synthesizes protein so blood can clot. Ensures health of bones	Produced by gastrointestinal tract bacteria. Dark green leafy vegetables, broccoli, pork, liver	None reported	Rare, but when it does occur, it can lead to impaired blood clotting as a decreased ability to clot. Vitamin K does not cross the placenta effectively; therefore, infants are provided vitamin K supplementation at birth

*Breast milk and formula are good sources of vitamins unless indicated otherwise.

Sources: Based on *Dietary Reference Intakes: The Essential Guide to Nutrient Requirements*, edited by J. J. Otten, J. Pitzi-Hellwig, and L. D. Meyers, 2006, Washington, DC: National Academies Press; *Manual of Pediatric Nutrition*, 4th edition, edited by K. M. Hendricks, and C. Duggan, 2005, Hamilton, Ontario: B. C. Decker, Inc.; and *Pediatric Nutrition Handbook*, 6th edition, edited by R. Kleinman, 2009, Elk Grove, IL: American Academy of Pediatrics.

Water-Soluble Vitamins

The water-soluble vitamins include all the B vitamins and vitamin C. These vitamins dissolve in water and are absorbed directly into the bloodstream. Unlike fat-soluble vitamins (discussed next), water-soluble vitamins cannot be stored in any significant amount in the body. Because of this the B vitamins and vitamin C should be consumed on a daily basis. Excess water-soluble vitamins are excreted in urine and, therefore, the risk for toxicity from overconsumption is low.

Water-soluble vitamins often act as coenzymes, or partners that help enzymes, to regulate all types of body processes, including those that produce energy (Duyff, 2006). For example, the B vitamins act as coenzymes in the metabolism of proteins, fats, and carbohydrates.

Fat-Soluble Vitamins

The fat-soluble vitamins include vitamins A, D, E, and K. These vitamins dissolve in fat and are stored in the body until needed. This means they do not need to be consumed every day. The absorption of fat-soluble vitamins is enhanced by fat in the diet. For example, vitamin A in a fresh spinach salad is absorbed better when the salad is eaten with an oil-based salad dressing.

Children like Jamal, who experience malabsorption of dietary fats, are more likely to have poor absorption of fat-soluble vitamins. Because fat-soluble vitamins are stored, children are less likely to develop a deficiency of these vitamins. However, they are at more risk for toxicity if overconsumption occurs.

Minerals

Minerals are substances that originate from the earth. Minerals come from plants and animal foods and from water. The minerals in the ground are absorbed by plants and become part of the food chain. Like vitamins, minerals initiate and regulate processes within the body. They are essential for growth because they are part of body structures such as bones and teeth.

Minerals are divided into two groups, the macrominerals and the microminerals, based on how much is required in the diet:

- Macrominerals: calcium, phosphorus, magnesium, sodium, chloride, sulfate, and potassium. The requirement for macrominerals is 100 mg/day or more.
- Microminerals: iron, zinc, iodine, fluoride, selenium, manganese, copper, chromium, molybdenum, and cobalt. The requirement for microminerals is 15 mg/day or less (Mahan & Escott-Stump, 2004).

Table 4-6 illustrates the role of selected macrominerals and microminerals and describes the symptoms that children might exhibit if their bodies do not have enough or receive too much of these important nutrients.

A subcategory of the macrominerals includes the electrolytes. Electrolytes such as chloride, potassium, and sodium play an important role in helping to regulate fluids in and out of the body's cells. These minerals also help transmit nerve impulses. That is, they send messages to the brain for muscles to contract and relax. During gastrointestinal upset, diarrhea and vomiting can cause a loss of electrolytes and water. This can quickly result in dehydration. Dehydration is the dangerous lack of water in the body that can occur when insufficient fluids are consumed or when the body experiences excessive loss of fluids through vomiting and diarrhea.

A diet high in sodium content is not recommended for young children. High sodium intake is associated with high blood pressure in salt-sensitive individuals. The *Dietary Guidelines for Americans, 2005* (U.S. Department of Health and Human Services and U.S. Department of Agriculture, 2005), the American Heart Association (2006), and the American Dietetic Association (Nicklas et al., 2004) all emphasize the importance of not eating too much salt.

What if. . .

you noticed that your program's menu frequently offered a combination of high-sodium menu items such as a ham sandwich served with a pickle slice, chips and canned soup, or hotdogs served with French fries and canned baked beans? What recommendations might you make? Can you think of more healthful substitutions?

Table 4-6   Selected Minerals

	Functions	Good Food Sources	Symptoms of Excess Intake	Symptoms of Deficiency
Macrominerals				
Calcium	Is a component of bones and teeth, important for growth, involved in blood clotting, nerve impulse, muscle contractions	Milk and milk products, sardines, clams, oysters, tofu, kale, broccoli, greens, calcium-fortified orange juice, and soy milk	Decreases absorption of other minerals, impairs kidney function	Increases risk of fractures and osteoporosis
Phosphorus	Involved in the formation of bones and teeth and in energy metabolism, is important in growth and maintenance of tissues, maintains acid-base balance of body fluids, is part of cell membranes and genetic materials of cell	Dairy foods and almost all other foods	Blood levels can become elevated when kidneys are not functioning well or when calcium regulation is dysfunctional	Rare
Magnesium	Involved in bone health and a plethora of enzymatic reactions, including those involved in energy metabolism	Leafy vegetables, whole grains, nuts, legumes, tofu	None from food sources	Rare: hypocalcemia, muscle cramps and seizures, interference with vitamin D metabolism
Sodium and chloride	Maintains fluid balance, regulates blood pressure, involved in the function of nerves and muscles	Salt, cured and processed foods, condiments such as soy sauce, ketchup, steak sauce	High blood pressure in salt-sensitive individuals, which is a risk factor for heart disease, stroke, and kidney disease	Rare: Extreme exercise in hot temperatures can cause sodium depletion with symptoms of confusion, headache, vomiting, and seizure
Potassium	Maintains fluid balance and regulates blood pressure. Is involved in the function of nerves and muscles, maintains heartbeat	Fruits and vegetables	Blood levels can become elevated when kidneys are not functioning well (hyperkalemia) which can lead to cardiac arrhythmia	Hypokalemia (low blood potassium) can occur in people taking diuretics, which can lead to cardiac arrhythmias
Microminerals				
Iron	Involved in the transport of oxygen as part of red blood cells and is a component of proteins such as enzymes	Meat, poultry, fish, fortified breads and cereals, beans, peas, lentils	Acute toxicity, gastrointestinal distress	Iron-deficiency anemia, delayed psychomotor development, increased risk of infection, fatigue, irritability
Zinc	Is essential for growth and development. Is a component of enzymes. Plays a role in wound healing	Red meats, liver, eggs, dairy products, some seafood, vegetables, whole grains	Excess supplementation may cause diarrhea, stomach cramps, and vomiting; can suppress the immune system, decrease HDL cholesterol	Slow growth, poor appetite, slow wound healing, loss of hair, infections, problems with sense of taste and smell

(Continued)

Table 4-6	Selected Minerals *(Continued)*			
	Functions	Good Food Sources	Symptoms of Excess Intake	Symptoms of Deficiency
Iodine	Is an essential component in thyroid hormones, which regulate enzymes and metabolic processes	Seafood, iodized salt, processed foods that use iodized salt	Thyroiditis, thyroid suppression	Goiter, mental retardation, cretinism, hypothyroidism, delay in growth and development
Fluoride	Is necessary for the health of teeth and bones. Protects against dental caries	Fluoridated water	Enamel and skeletal fluorosis	Dental decay
Selenium	Functions as a coenzyme and acts as an antioxidant	Meat, seafood, cereals, dairy products, fruits and vegetables	Hair and nail brittleness and gastrointestinal disturbances, rash, fatigue, nervous system abnormalities	Enlarged heart
Manganese	Involved in the formation of bone and metabolism of amino acids, cholesterol, and carbohydrates	Grain products, tea and vegetables	Results in symptoms similar to Parkinson's disease	Impaired growth and skeletal abnormalities have been seen in animal studies. A diet deficiency is unlikely to occur

Sources: Based on *Dietary Reference Intakes: The Essential Guide to Nutrient Requirements*, edited by J. J. Otten, J. Pitzi-Hellwig, and L. D. Meyers, 2006, Washington, DC: National Academies Press; *Manual of Pediatric Nutrition*, 4th edition, edited by K. M. Hendricks and C. Duggan, 2005, Hamilton, Ontario; B. C. Decker; and *Pediatric Nutrition Handbook*, 5th edition, edited by R. Kleinman, 2004, Elk Grove, IL: American Academy of Pediatrics.

Water

The macronutrients and micronutrients receive a lot of attention when discussing a healthy diet. Little attention, however, is given to the importance of water in the diet. Adults cannot survive more than 3 to 5 days without water, and young children even fewer days. Water accounts for 50% to 60% of the adult's body composition and 70% to 75% of the infant's body (Otten et al., 2006; Samour & King, 2005). Water performs myriad functions:

- Water regulates body temperature through perspiration.
- Water transports nutrients and oxygen as a component of blood.
- All chemical reactions of the body take place in water.
- Water helps to remove waste products from the body (Otten et al., 2006; Sizer & Whitney, 2006).

Decreases in the water content of the body can have immediate consequences. Individuals feel tired, experience headaches, and find it difficult to concentrate. Insufficient water can lead to dehydration and death.

Because of their higher water composition, infants and children are more sensitive to fluctuations in water status. Diarrhea, vomiting, and fever can quickly lead to

Offering water at routine times, especially during warm weather, helps children maintain a healthy fluid balance.

dehydration. Providing a liquid rehydration solution such as Pedialyte can restore fluid and electrolytes. Teachers must make sure that infants and children are well hydrated, especially on warm days when children are active. Providing water as a beverage between meals has the advantage of supplying fluoride (in fluoridated communities), a mineral that protects teeth from the risk of dental decay.

Phytochemicals

Phytochemicals are newcomers to the realm of nutrition science, but preliminary research suggests that these chemicals offer significant health benefits. Phytochemicals are found in fruits and vegetables. Diets rich in these foods offer protection from chronic diseases such as cancer, heart disease, stroke, high blood pressure, and urinary tract infections, to name just a few. The research is still new, however, the following is known about phytochemicals:

- Eating more fruits and vegetables provides vitamins, minerals, and phytochemicals.
- A single food will often contain many different phytochemicals. For example, tomatoes contain two phytochemicals, lycopene and polyphenols, which are both associated with lower cancer risk (Campbell et al., 2004).
- Foods that are rich in color are likely to be rich in phytochemicals. This includes carrots, pumpkins, sweet potatoes, winter squash, spinach, collards, kale, cantaloupe, red peppers, papayas, tomato products, watermelon, and purple grapes.
- Eating a variety of foods will maximize the benefits of phytochemicals.

Children can learn about the importance of food components such as phytochemicals. Consider how Francisco shares the importance of eating a variety of fruits and vegetables rich in phytochemicals:

> Francisco introduces his second-grade class to the concept of phytochemicals by presenting a variety of brightly colored vegetables on the science table. He places child-safe pumpkin cutters on the table with the foods and invites children to "dissect" the vegetables. The children are guided to study the structure and color of each food. Francisco tells them about the new research on phytochemicals and how these chemicals protect the body from disease. Then he guides the children to plan a menu that includes one of the brightly colored vegetables. The children present their menus to the group and tell why they have selected each item on their menu.

Important Vitamins and Minerals for Children

All vitamins are important for children to consume. However, vitamins involved in growth need special consideration. Often times vitamins and minerals work in concert to provide the combination of nutrients needed to perform important roles in the body.

The Teamwork of B Vitamins

The B vitamins work together in important body processes. As discussed earlier, protein is used to produce enzymes that jump-start and speed up the chemical reactions that occur in the body, sometimes by a factor of a million or more (Berg, Tymoczko, Stryer, & Clark, 2002). To do this, the enzymes must join with the molecules involved in a reaction. Coenzymes support them in this role. The B vitamins, in addition to other roles, often act as coenzymes in metabolic processes assisting in the release of energy from the macronutrients. Some of the B vitamins also prevent certain types of anemia. Folic acid helps prevent neural tube defects.

What if. . .

you were taking your class on a walking field trip and the day turned out to be unseasonably warm? How would you ensure each child had access to enough water?

MyEducationLab

Go to the Assignments and Activities section of Topic 1: Basic Nutrition in the MyEducationLab for your course and complete the activity entitled *Folic Acid*. As a teacher, why is it important for you to understand the nutritional benefits of folic acid?

Eating a variety of rich-colored fruits and vegetables provides vitamins, minerals, and phytochemicals.

Vitamin A

Vitamin A is generally recognized for its role in vision. The "old wives' tale" that carrots are good for the eyes is true. Vitamin A, found in carrots, sweet potatoes, and dark leafy green vegetables, will not correct near- or farsightedness, but this vitamin is required for vision. Vitamin A is needed to make a pigment of the eye that is very sensitive to light and aids vision. In addition to its role in vision, vitamin A also supports growth of bones and the overall body and helps maintain a healthy immune system.

Children in developing countries throughout the world still experience deficiencies in vitamin A and the resulting blindness that occurs if left untreated (Ramakrishnan & Darnton-Hill, 2002). Vitamin A deficiency is usually not a problem in the United States, but can occur in children who experience malabsorption. For example, Jamal who has celiac disease is more likely to be at risk for vitamin A deficiency (Alwitry, 2000). Figure 4-7 lists sources of vitamin A that appeal to children.

Vitamin A toxicity is a more likely concern in the United States. This can be caused by well-meaning parents who oversupplement or provide more than the Tolerable Upper Intake Levels (UL) of vitamin A. This is of particular concern because the U.S. food supply consists of many vitamin-fortified foods and beverages. In addition, children who mistake chewable or "gummy" style multivitamins for candy are also at risk for toxicity. Too much vitamin A can cause skin rashes, loss of hair, problems with bones, growth problems, liver damage, and even death (Eledrisi, McKinney & Shanti, 2008; Otten et al., 2006). Because vitamin A is one of the fat-soluble vitamins, excess amounts are stored in the liver, which increases the risk of toxicity.

Vitamin D, Calcium, Phosphorus, and Magnesium

Vitamin D is required for healthy bone development, as are the minerals calcium, phosphorus, and magnesium. Calcium, phosphorus, and magnesium also play a key role in the structure of teeth. These three minerals account for 98% of the body's mineral content (AAP Committee on Nutrition, 2009). They are priority nutrients for children because of their importance for bone growth and maintenance. Vitamin D stimulates the intestinal absorption of calcium and phosphorus. Vitamin D is synthesized in the skin through exposure to sunlight. Certain factors can limit this synthesis. Children for example who are dark skinned or use sunscreen will make less vitamin D (Otten et al., 2006).

Vitamin D deficiency is more common than previously recognized and has been called pandemic by some researchers (Holick & Chen, 2008). A vitamin D deficiency can cause rickets, a condition that results in the softening of bones in young children (see discussion in Chapter 3). Teachers can influence the consumption of these important bone building nutrients by offering milk and dairy products and other foods that are good sources of

Figure 4-7 Child-Friendly Sources of Vitamin A

- **Infants:** pureed peaches, apricots, mangoes, or commercially prepared pureed carrots, sweet potatoes, and squash.
- **Toddlers:** milk, eggs, shredded cheese, diced cooked carrots, mashed sweet potatoes with crushed pineapple, diced peaches, mango or apricot yogurt parfait, diced cantaloupe, steamed broccoli with cheese sauce, vegetable soups made with peas, carrots, sweet potatoes, and/or spinach, pumpkin custard.
- **Preschoolers and older:** milk, eggs, cheese, carrot sticks, carrot raisin salad, spinach and grapefruit salad, sweet potato, pumpkin, or carrot muffins or bread, homemade baked sweet potato fries, mango or peach smoothie, raw broccoli or red pepper strips with low-fat dip, homemade cream of spinach or kale soup, cantaloupe slices, peas and carrots, cottage cheese with cubed peaches, mangos or papaya, salad with dark green leafy lettuces, baked sweet potato, apricots, frozen homemade fruit pops made with peach or apricot nectar.

Vitamin D, calcium, phosphorous, and magnesium. The intake of these nutrients can be increased in children's diets in the following ways:

- Offer cold cereal with milk.
- Prepare hot cereal and cream soups with milk instead of water.
- Offer yogurt.
- Use soy milk or orange juice that is vitamin D and calcium fortified if a milk allergy or lactose intolerance is an issue.
- Make smoothies using milk, yogurt, and fruit.
- Offer fatty fish such as tuna, sardines, and salmon.
- Offer items prepared with eggs: scrambled eggs, egg salad, French toast (Duyff, 2006; National Institutes of Health, Office of Dietary Supplements, 2008).

Iron and Vitamin C

Iron and vitamin C are another important vitamin and mineral team that is linked together in function. In Chapter 3 we discussed how a lack of iron in children's diets results in iron-deficiency anemia, which is a particular concern among older babies and toddlers as they transition from breast milk and formula to solids. Because the consequences of iron-deficiency anemia are linked to adverse effects on both motor and cognitive development, teachers must understand dietary strategies for making the most of the iron found in children's diet (AAP Committee on Nutrition, 2009).

The iron content of a food does not reflect the amount of iron that will be absorbed. Studies show that plant sources of iron (nonheme iron), such as beans, peas, lentils, and green leafy vegetables, are not as well absorbed as the animal sources of iron (heme iron) found in meats, poultry, eggs, and fish.

Certain dietary strategies, however, can help balance meals for better iron absorption. Vitamin C, for example, enhances the absorption of nonheme iron. Figure 4-8 provides some nutritious ideas for pairing iron with vitamin C–rich foods. In addition, just a little bit of meat in a meal containing nonheme iron will enhance overall iron absorption (Hurrell, Reddy, Juillerat, & Cook, 2006). A bean and beef burrito, for example, is a food combination that promotes nonheme iron absorption. Foods can also impede iron absorption. For example, diets that have a very high fiber content and the tannins found in tea can inhibit iron absorption.

Teachers can ensure that young children start off on the right foot when it comes to iron intake by following suggestions such as these recommended by the American Academy of Pediatrics Committee on Nutrition (2009) and Dee et al. (2008):

- Introduce iron-fortified infant cereal or strained meats around 6 months of age.
- Supplement iron for those breast-fed infants who are not able to consume enough iron from foods.

nonheme iron
a type of iron that is not readily absorbed by the body; found in plants

heme iron
a readily absorbed form of iron found in meats

Figure 4-8 Food Combinations That Support Iron Absorption

Vitamin C and Nonheme Iron Combinations
orange juice and enriched cereal
salsa and burritos
tomato sauce and chili beans
sliced strawberries and peanut butter on whole-wheat bread
kiwi and orange and tossed spinach salad

Meat and Nonheme Iron Combinations
ham and pea soup
pork and baked beans
ground beef and bean burrito

- Do not feed infants younger than 12 months regular cow, goat, or soy milk.
- Avoid serving young children excessive amounts of milk, which can decrease their appetite for high-iron foods.

What if. . .

a mother in your program was breast-feeding her 6-month-old and wanted you to provide cow's milk to the baby while in your care whenever she did not have a sufficient amount of pumped breast milk available? What would you advise?

IMPLEMENTING NUTRITION SCIENCE

In Chapter 3 we discussed different food guidance systems such as the Dietary Reference Intakes, *MyPyramid for Kids,* and *MyPyramid for Preschoolers* to provide teachers with an understanding of the standards that form the basis for food recommendations. In this chapter, we supplied basic nutrition information that covers the digestion, absorption, and classification of nutrients. Teachers need to understand this information for several important reasons. Meeting children's nutritional needs is an obvious primary goal. Understanding how diet recommendations impact personal health is also important for teachers. In addition, teachers who understand nutrition can promote nutrition principles across cultural food preferences. Finally, effective teachers need to understand the nutrition principles they are teaching.

Meeting the Nutritional Needs of Children

Teachers who understand the principles of nutrition have a stepping stone to knowing what to feed children. Teachers can best understand how to meet children's needs by evaluating each child's nutrition and health histories with attention directed to:

- Evidence of overnutrition or undernutrition.
- Health conditions that impact nutrition such as celiac disease or diabetes.
- The need for special diets.
- Food likes and dislikes.
- Cultural food preferences.

This type of information used in conjunction with the above-mentioned resources helps teachers plan healthful menus that meet the nutritional needs of all children in their care.

Promoting Personal Health

Teachers work hard and must cope with stress and the time constraints of their profession. In addition, teachers have the added responsibility of making sure children are kept safe while in their care. When teachers don't eat well, exercise, and get enough sleep, they compromise their own resiliency. Teachers need to take care of themselves so that they can provide optimal care and education for children. Teachers who exercise and eat healthfully promote their own wellness and are prepared to be vital educators and positive role models for children.

What if. . .

you were a teacher of a kindergarten/first-grade blended class and planned to teach about dairy products? What nutrition concepts do you feel are appropriate for this age? How would you modify the lesson to take into consideration the age range of children in the classroom?

Understanding Cultural Food Choices

Understanding cultural food preferences and belief systems regarding food choices is an important part of providing nutritional care for children. Minimizing personal cultural biases and preconceived opinions is important in effective communication. For instance, infants starting solids in the United States rely on infant cereals, strained meats, and fruits and vegetables as first foods. They then gradually transition to foods with more texture. Infants from Hispanic families are more likely to be introduced to foods such as rice, soups, tortillas, and beans as early as 6 to 12 months of age (Mennella, Zeigler, Briefel, & Novak, (2006). This is a cultural difference rather than a "wrong way" of feeding infants.

Having respect for a culture while providing nutritional care creates a collaborative approach between teachers and parents that ultimately benefits the child. Understanding basic nutrition principles helps teachers to promote healthful diets that explore and honor cultural preferences. Here is how one teacher puts this philosophy into action:

> Miguel, a 24-month-old, is a selective eater and does not like many of the foods Brittany offers at her family child care program. Brittany asks Miguel's mother, Diana, what types of foods Miguel enjoys. Diana tells Brittany that Miguel's favorite dish at home is caldo de pollo. Brittany is not familiar with the ingredients so Diana explains the recipe for the chicken and vegetable soup. Later that week Brittany serves caldo de pollo for lunch and all of the children, including Miguel, enjoy the nutritious food.

Teaching Nutrition Concepts

Understanding nutrition science helps teachers to effectively teach nutrition concepts, and teaching nutrition concepts is no longer an option when it comes to good health. For example, the California Department of Education feels nutrition is so important that they have drafted nutrition competencies for children prekindergarten through grade 3 (California Department of Education, 2008). These competencies are aligned with the national health education standards. Table 4-7 lists some of the nutrition competencies that relate to understanding basic nutrition. This example highlights the growing expectation for teachers to present activities and lessons that teach nutrition concepts and shows another way in which the understanding of nutrition science promotes effective teaching.

MyEducationLab

To assess your understanding of the science of nutrition, go to the Book Specific Resources section in the MyEducationLab for your course, select *Nutrition, Health, and Safety for Young Children*, Chapter 4 of the Study Plan, and then complete the multiple choice questions and activities.

Table 4-7	State of California's Nutrition Competencies
Nutrition Competency	**Examples of How Competencies Will Be Met**
1. Students will know and understand the relationship between the human body, nutrition, and energy balance.	A. Know the six nutrient groups and their functions. B. Describe how nutritional needs vary throughout the life cycle. C. Know the physiology of the human body as it relates to nutrition and physical activity.
2. Students will know current nutrition and physical activity recommendations and how to apply them.	A. Know nutrition guidelines. B. Assess personal dietary needs. C. Understand the influence of nutrition on health. D. Assess the relationship of physical activity and nutrition to health. E. Establish personal goals and make healthy food and fitness choices.
3. Students will identify and explore factors influencing food choices.	A. Identify influences on food choices. B. Explore factors that contribute to achieving and maintaining a healthy body and positive body image.
4. Students will demonstrate proper food handling and storage to maximize the nutritional quality of food and personal hygiene to prevent foodborne illness.	A. Identify one way of preparing foods for eating. B. Demonstrate proper hand-washing technique before food handling and eating. C. Name ways to store food that helps to keep it clean and fresh.
5. Students will identify valid nutrition information and advocate for positive health policies and practices.	A. Access valid nutrition information and nutrition services. B. Advocate for positive health policy and practices.
6. Students will identify and explore influences of local, national. and global factors on the quantity and quality of food.	A. Identify foods that come from particular regions. B. Understand the factors (local, regional, statewide, national, and global) that influence food availability, production, and consumption.

Note: The competencies are further defined with suggested classroom activities to meet these competencies and link to other curriculum subjects for prekindergarten through grade 12 on the website.

Source: From *Nutrition Competencies for California's Children—Healthy Eating & Nutrition Education*, by the California Department of Education, 2008, retrieved September 9, 2009, from http://www.cde.ca.gov/ls/nu/he/ncccindex.asp. Reprinted by permission from the California Department of Education, CDE Press, 1430 N. Street, Suite 3207, Sacramento, CA 95814.

Summary

Nutrition science is the study of how food provides nourishment to the body to support its growth, maintenance, repair, and reproduction. The consequences of poor nutrition are evident in both-immediate and long term health. Nourishing young children is an important responsibility. Because of this teachers must fully understand and embrace the basic principles of healthful eating. Teachers have a responsibility to impart accurate and unbiased information in their promotion of health and nutrition concepts.

Teachers may find that understanding the science of nutrition is enhanced by an awareness of how food is digested, absorbed, and metabolized. The digestive process can be challenged, however, by a variety of health issues that can result in malabsorption and poor growth. A teacher's understanding of these processes and the potential for disorders helps them partner with parents to provide a calm feeding environment that meets the dietary needs of children.

Food can be categorized into six major groups: proteins, fats, carbohydrates, vitamins, minerals, and water. The energy-providing macronutrients include protein, fats, and carbohydrates. Vitamins and minerals are micronutrients that sustain body processes and are needed to release and utilize the energy found in protein, fats, and carbohydrates. Water is a vital nutrient. It transports nutrients and oxygen as a component of blood, and all chemical reactions of the body take place in water. Phytochemicals are health-promoting substances found in food that offer protection from chronic diseases such as cancer, heart disease, stroke, high blood pressure, and urinary tract infections.

Teachers who learn the principles of nutrition are able to translate recommendations into healthful meals for children and choose healthful diets for themselves. They are also able to take cultural food differences into account when planning meals. Teachers who understand the foundations of nutrition are able to effectively teach nutrition concepts.

Key Terms

Absorption, p. 104

Amino acids, p. 117

Aspiration, p. 103

Basal metabolic rate (BMR), p. 111

Calorie, p. 110

Coenzymes, p. 124

Complementary protein, p. 118

Dehydration, p. 124

Dietary cholesterol, p. 119

Digestion, p. 98

Digestive system, p. 98

Disaccharides, p. 113

Dysphagia, p. 103

Electrolytes, p. 124

Enzymes, p. 99

Essential fatty acids, p. 118

Fat-soluble vitamins, p. 124

Gastroesophageal reflux (GER), p. 103

Gastroesophageal reflux disease (GERD), p. 103

Gastrointestinal tract, p. 98

Heme iron, p. 129

High-density lipoprotein (HDL), p. 120

Insoluble fiber, p. 115

Lactose intolerant, p. 108

Limiting amino acid, p. 117

Lipoprotein, p. 119

Low-density lipoprotein (LDL), p. 119

Macrominerals, p. 124

Malabsorption, p. 107

Microminerals, p. 124

Microvilli, p. 107

Monosaccharides, p. 113

Monounsaturated fats, p. 119

Nonheme iron, p. 129

Nutrition science, p. 97

Omega-3 fatty acids, p. 119

Osteoporosis, p. 107

Plaque, p. 119

Polysaccharides, p. 115

Polyunsaturated fats, p. 119

Saturated fats, p. 119

Soluble fiber, p. 115

Total energy expenditure, p. 111

Trans fatty acids, p. 119

Villi, p. 106

Water-soluble vitamins, p. 124

Review Questions

1. Explain the process of digestion, including the role of each part of the gastrointestinal tract and the breakdown products of foods.

2. Describe the physical characteristics of the small intestine that enhance the absorption of nutrients.

3. Define two conditions/disorders that impact digestion or absorption and how.

4. List the six nutrient categories and explain the difference between macronutrients and micronutrients.

5. Provide three reasons why it is important for teachers to understand nutrition science.

Discussion Starters

1. Imagine that the parents of the second graders in your classroom have complained that the school's food menu has too many processed foods and not enough fiber. How would you address this issue? Who would you involve in this conversation?

2. The process of digestion involves the mechanical and chemical breakdown of food. What are some examples of the mechanical breakdown of food? What are some examples of chemical breakdown? What are the breakdown products of the macronutrients?

3. Select a competency from Table 4-7. After referring to the *Nutrition Competencies for California's Children* at http://www.cde.ca.gov/ls/nu/he/ncccindex.asp explain what levels of expectations you might have for prekindergarten, kindergarten, and third-grade children.

Practice Points

1. What would happen if a child in your program has diarrhea? How would you decide whether she should go home or stay at school? What foods or beverages should she avoid until she feels better and no longer has diarrhea?

2. A 3-year-old who has celiac disease is going to start school soon. Plan a lunch menu and snack menu for his first day at school.

3. Develop a Teaching Wellness lesson for a third-grade class that teaches a concept from the competencies listed in Table 4-7.

Web Resources

California Department of Education Nutrition Competencies for California's Children
   http://www.cde.ca.gov/ls/nu/he/ncccindex.asp

Celiac Sprue Association
   www.csaceliacs.org/index.php

Dietary Reference Intakes
   www.iom.edu/CMS/3788/4003.aspx

National Digestive Diseases Information Clearinghouse
   http://digestive.niddk.nih.gov

chapter 5 | Feeding Infants

Learning Outcomes

After reading this chapter, you should be able to:

1. Explain how and what to feed infants from birth to 6 months of age and describe the importance of establishing a supportive feeding relationship.

2. Discuss how developmental milestones for infants ages 6 months to 1 year guide decision making about the progression of offering solid foods.

3. Describe concerns and methods for feeding infants with special needs.

4. Discuss cultural influences on feeding practices.

Amelia, a family child care provider, has just been introduced to baby Manuel. His mother Lucia is dropping him off at Amelia's house for the first time. Manuel is 3 months old and is being transitioned from breast milk to formula by his mother who is returning to work part time. She feels she may not have the accommodations at her workplace to express (pump) breast milk and has decided to introduce formula. Manuel has just begun to accept the bottle. Lucia admits she wishes she didn't have to use formula because Manuel has such a sensitive stomach, especially since she started cereal 2 weeks ago. She started solids a little early to make sure Manuel has enough to eat when he starts child care. After sharing information about Manuel's normal routine, she nurses him and after he falls asleep, she places him in his assigned crib and goes to work.

Amelia checks on Manuel who naps for almost 3 hours. She begins lunch for the other children. When a toddler cup is knocked to the floor, Manuel wakes up with a start and begins to cry. Amelia is busy feeding another infant. By the time she gets to Manuel he is extremely upset. She tries to give him his bottle, but he is so upset he sputters and chokes on the formula. Halfway through the bottle he throws up and begins to cry again. She tries giving him cereal, but he pushes it out with his tongue. It seems to Amelia that Manuel may be in pain as he pulls his legs up and continues screaming. When Lucia comes to pick him up an hour later she is surprised to see teacher Amelia pacing the floor with her very upset son. She takes Manuel and immediately sits down to nurse him. As Manuel settles down, both Amelia and Lucia admit that he has had a challenging first day.

Early childhood teachers are frequently called on to ease the child's transition into the early childhood group. Knowing about a child's pattern of eating is very important in that process, especially for infants who are less able to communicate about their needs. As demonstrated in the opening case scenario, teachers and families need to work together to plan a successful transition and to continue to communicate about children's nutritional needs.

In this chapter we explore feeding practices for infants, including ways to create positive eating experiences. We also discuss resources that can assist teachers to build child wellness through healthy nutrition in the early childhood setting. We focus on feeding issues that sometimes arise during specific developmental stages and offer strategies to support the optimal nourishment of infants during critical times of growth and development. Understanding the fundamentals of infant nutrition is especially important in the face of the increasing incidence of overweight and obesity in young children. Decisions made about feeding can have ramifications on the rate of weight gain of infants and result in lifelong consequences.

Not every infant can adapt to the standard approach to feeding. Flexibility and accommodations may be needed for babies with special needs. In addition, cultural food practices can sometimes create a need to rethink how teachers feed young children. For example, the progression of infant feeding from breast milk or formula to solids may vary from one culture to another. Understanding these differences ensures that teachers are prepared to manage the nutritional needs of young children in their care.

THE BALANCE OF NURTURE AND NUTRIENTS

Infants need a nurturing feeding relationship and appropriate nutrition in order to grow and thrive. The feeding relationship established between infants and their families and caregivers is an important contributor to successful growth and development. A good feeding relationship is established when teachers and parents are responsive to infants' feeding cues, such as hunger and satisfaction. A warm, caring relationship supports effective feeding. In turn, good feeding supports good nutrition, which is critical during infancy because of the rapid rate of growth that occurs during the first months after birth.

Babies learn about the world through their senses. When infants are talked to and held by their teachers, this verbal and tactile stimulation contributes to the "wiring of their brains," or their neurological development. The combination of holding, talking, and smiling

feeding relationship
the relationship established when teachers and families are responsive to infants' feeding cues; supports effective feeding and good nutrition

at babies while they eat is how babies learn. Later, as foods are introduced, babies learn about their environments through the aromas, colors, tastes, and textures of the foods to which they are exposed. As the opening case illustrates, without an effective feeding relationship, providing nourishment can become a challenge even when a baby is hungry. The feeding relationship is half of the equation that teachers balance when nourishing infants. It is also essential for teachers to understand what to feed infants.

Feeding infants follows a progression that evolves as children develop. The needs of infants are particularly important because the consequences of inappropriate feeding are significant. The nutritional needs of infants are influenced by how well mothers are nourished prior to and during pregnancy. For example, women who gain too much or too little weight during pregnancy may give birth to infants who were over- or undernourished in the uterine environment. Both of these scenarios may cause changes in their metabolism that put these infants at increased risk for obesity later on in life (Kleinman, 2009). Women who have anemia during pregnancy are more likely to have infants with low iron stores (Kleinman, 2009). Iron deficiency may affect the development of the central nervous system and is linked to developmental delays in young children, including deficits in cognitive and motor skills development (Beard, 2008; Lozoff, Jimenez, Hagen, Mollen, & Wolf, 2000).

In addition, some infants, such as those who are born prematurely, have nutrition-related health concerns. The medical complications associated with being born early may prevent babies from growing well while hospitalized, so families need to ensure a healthy rate of growth when premature infants are sent home. The unique feeding and nutritional needs of these children may require teachers to prepare special transitional formulas or offer fortified breast milk that is higher in calories per ounce.

Finally, teachers also assist families of well-nourished infants to maintain feeding practices to help their babies continue to grow and thrive. The special nutrient needs of each infant must be recognized in order to provide an appropriate feeding plan. In this chapter, we discuss the feeding strategies for infants in two age categories: birth to 6 months of age and 6 to 12 months of age.

FEEDING INFANTS: THE FIRST 6 MONTHS

The first 6 months of life are a time of significant growth and development. At birth infants do not have a fully developed gastrointestinal tract, immune system, nervous system, or brain (Gale, Walton, & Martyn, 2003; Kleinman, 2009). Good nutrition is essential to support the continued development of these vital systems. In fact, the development that occurs during the first year is unparalleled by any other time in the child's life. By 5 months of age, most infants have doubled their birth weight. By the end of the first year, birth weight is increased by approximately 200%, length by 55%, and head circumference by 40% (Goran & Sothern, 2006). The size of the brain doubles by age 1 and triples by age 6 (Dangerfield, 1998; Gale et al., 2003). To achieve this rapid rate of growth and provide needed support for optimal brain development, a sufficient supply of calories and nutrients is needed.

Infants need only breast milk or formula for the first 4 to 6 months of life, and because an infant's stomach is small, frequent feedings are needed. Breast milk is ideal because it is easily and quickly digested and provides ideal proportions of essential nutrients.

The Breast-Fed Infant

Breast milk is the gold standard for the nourishment of infants because it contains the perfect combination of nutrients to support optimal growth and development. In a few situations, however, the use of breast milk is not acceptable, such as when mothers are HIV positive or taking illegal drugs or certain prescribed medications (Nevin-Folino, Armorde-Spalding, & Nieman, 2008). Unlike formula, the nutrient content of breast milk changes over time to meet the maturing infant's needs and when fed exclusively to babies will support growth until 6 months of age (Kleinman, 2009).

MyEducationLab

Go to the Assignments and Activities section of Topic 1: Basic Nutrition in the MyEducationLab for your course and complete the activity entitled *Brain Development and Nutrition*. How does good nutrition foster healthy brain development in young children?

Benefits of Breast Milk

The nutritional benefits of breast milk are significant. The type of fat found in breast milk is easily absorbed by the baby and its composition appears to be ideally suited to promote brain and vision development (Kleinman, 2009). The protein composition of breast milk is also more easily digested than that of formula and it provides just the right amount to promote growth. Breast milk also contains enzymes that help in the absorption of the fats, carbohydrates, and protein found in breast milk.

Breast milk is recommended as the infant food of choice by a number of health organizations including the American Academy of Pediatrics (AAP, 2005; Kleinman, 2009), the American Academy of Family Physicians (Mooreland & Coombs, 2000), the Academy of Breastfeeding Medicine (2009), the World Health Organization (WHO, 2003), and the American Dietetic Association (ADA, 2005). The consensus recommendation is to maintain breast-feeding for at least the first year of life. (The WHO encourages breast-feeding until age 2 or older.)

The advantages of breast milk are not limited to nutrition. Various components in breast milk, including antibodies, help prevent illness and infection. The antibodies in breast milk provide a health advantage for breast-fed infants compared to formula-fed babies. Formula-fed infants, for example, have a higher incidence of illnesses such as allergies, eczema, urinary tract infections, stomach flu, type 1 diabetes, earaches, pneumonia, leukemia, and sudden infant death syndrome compared to breast-fed infants (Moreland & Coombs, 2000). Colostrum is the first milk produced by the nursing mother. It is so rich in protective factors that the American Academy of Pediatrics calls it an *infant's first immunization* (see Figure 5-1).

Breast milk may also contain factors that stimulate the development of the gastrointestinal tract, which, as the largest organ of the immune system, helps reduce the risk of recurrent infections, inflammatory diseases, and allergies (Kleinman, 2009; Rees, 2005). The research suggests that breast-fed infants, particularly those born prematurely, perform better on IQ tests administered later in childhood and have overall better cognitive performance than children who do not receive breast milk in infancy (Dee, Li, Lee, & Grummer-Strawn, 2007; Ribas-Fito, Julvez, Grimalt, & Sunyer, 2007; Schanler, 2007). In addition, studies indicate that breast-feeding may protect against developmental delays and support the attainment of gross motor skills and language development (Bates, 2007; Dee et al., 2007; Innis, Gilley, & Werker, 2001; Sacker, Quigley, & Kelly, 2006).

Breast milk also plays a role in maintaining healthful weight of young children. A review of research has shown that breast-feeding reduces the chance of infants becoming overweight by 15% to 30% and that the longer the mother nurses, the greater the protective effect (Centers for Disease Control and Prevention [CDC], 2007b; Mayer-Davis et al., 2006).

Teachers directly benefit from having breast-fed infants in their care. Breast-fed infants are less likely to have colds, ear infections, urinary tract infections, and diarrhea. An additional benefit is that the Child and Adult Care Food Program (CACFP), a child nutrition program designed to reimburse programs to offset the cost of nutritious meals, supports breast-feeding. The CACFP provides reimbursement to programs for breast milk that is fed to infants in a bottle, thereby reducing costs to programs that might otherwise need to purchase formula. A claim to CACFP for reimbursement cannot be made, however, if the breast-feeding mother nurses the baby while at the child care setting (U.S. Department of Agriculture [USDA], Food and Nutrition Service, 2000). Figure 5-2 summarizes the many benefits of breast milk.

Rates of Breast-Feeding

The frequency of breast-feeding in the United States has increased in the past two decades. In 1971, 24% of U.S. mothers began breast-feeding their infants at birth. In 2005–2006 this rate increased to 77%, exceeding the health goals established by *Healthy People 2010*, which aimed for a goal of 75% of all women initiating breast-feeding (McDowell, Wang, & Kennedy-Stephenson, 2008; Ryan, Rush, Krieger, & Lewandowski, 1991; U.S. Department of Health and Human Services [HHS], 2000). In spite of the improvement in the number of infants who are breast-fed at birth, in the United States the number of mothers who continue breast-feeding their infant until age 1 still lags far behind the global average. Globally 79% of infants are

Figure 5-1 The American Academy of Pediatrics Promotes Breast-Feeding

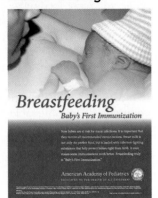

Source: Used with permission from American Academy of Pediatrics Childhood Immunization Support Program and Breast-Feeding Promotion in Physicians' Offices Practices Program, http://www.aap.org/breastfeeding/curriculum/documents/pdf/BFIZPoster.pdf.

colostrum
the first milk produced by the nursing mother; it is rich in antibodies and other protective factors to help keep infants healthy

What if . . .

while you were feeding a 2-month-old baby a bottle of breast milk, the mother arrived at the program and wanted to nurse the baby instead? How would you respond to this request? Could this feeding be counted as a reimbursable CACFP meal? How might you get a definitive answer?

breast-fed until age 1 compared to only 21% in the United States. This rate falls below the *Healthy People 2010* goal of 25% of mothers breast-feeding their infants to age 1 (CDC, 2008; HHS, 2000; WHO, 2003). Lower rates of breast-feeding in the United States occur among mothers who have children in child care at age 6 months, non-Hispanic black women, and mothers of lower socioeconomic status. Except for Hispanics, mothers under age 20 also tend to not breast-feed their infants to age 1 (Li, Darling, Maurice, Barker, & Grummer-Strawn, 2005; McDowell et al., 2008).

Cultural Influences on Breast-Feeding Practices

Cultural perspectives are factors in whether women breast-feed their infants and for how long. Hispanic women living in the United States are more likely to initiate breast-feeding; however, this tends to change depending on the degree of acculturation (Gill, 2009; Harley, Stamm, & Eskenazi, 2007). For example, Hispanic mothers who have spent all of their lives in the United States are 2.4 times more likely to stop breast-feeding compared to Hispanic mothers who have been in the United States for 5 years or less (Harley et al., 2007). Although non-Hispanic black women have lower rates of breast-feeding initiation in the United States, in recent years, this group has shown the greatest improvement going from 36% in 1993–1994 to 65% in 2005–2006 (McDowell et al., 2008). Additionally, more foreign-born mothers living in the United States breast-feed compared to U.S.-born women (Pak-Gorstein, Haq, & Graham, 2009). This reflects the U.S. culture in which breast-feeding, although promoted, may be considered an option rather than the norm for feeding infants.

Culturally specific beliefs can have both positive and negative influences on breast-feeding practices among nursing women. For example, Islamic women aim to breast-feed their infants for 2 years; religious guidance supports them in this practice (Shaikh & Ahmed, 2006). However the traditional garb worn by Islamic women decreases their exposure to the sun, leading to vitamin D deficiency among the mothers. In turn, this may result in vitamin D deficiency among infants who receive breast milk low in vitamin D (Allali et al., 2006; Taylor, Wagner, & Hollis, 2008). Some Hispanic mothers feel that breast milk can be negatively affected by situations that precipitate strong anger (*coraje*) or shock (*susto*) in their lives. They may choose not to breast-feed or to stop breast-feeding for fear the milk will be harmful to the baby. Asian mothers also believe that "vital energy" is required for the production of breast milk and that when the body is "imbalanced" the mother's milk can become unhealthy for the baby (Pak-Gorstein et al., 2009). In Native American cultures the infant's father and maternal grandmother may play a role in influencing the mother's decision about whether to breast-feed (Dellwo Houghton & Graybeal, 2001).

Teachers who learn about the cultural perspectives of breast-feeding that guide families decisions, are better able to understand and support the establishment of healthful feeding practices. This can be accomplished by fostering close communication about the care of infants and approaching varying beliefs and practices with sensitivity and respect. Teachers who include family members in interactive and supportive discussions about breast-feeding may increase the likelihood and length of time mothers choose to breast-feed.

Supporting Breast-Feeding Mothers

Teachers are an important part of the nursing mother's support system. They can have a positive impact on helping nursing mothers continue to breast-feed. The WHO (2003) highlights this influential role in promoting positive infant feeding practices and supporting breast-feeding mothers who return to work. Research shows that women who have a sense of "confident commitment" are more likely to be successful in breast-feeding (Avery, Zimmermann, Underwood, & Magnus, 2009). Teachers who share in the care of infants can offer positive support for this commitment. The National Association for the Education of Young Children (NAEYC, 2009) provides specific guidelines, such as Health Standard 5.B.09, on how to support breast-feeding in early childhood settings. A sample program policy in support of breast-feeding is presented in the *Policy Point* feature. Creating a policy such as this reinforces the program's commitment to families and outlines the responsibilities of teachers and other program staff.

Figure 5-2 The Benefits of Breast Milk

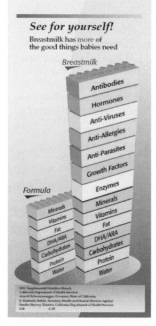

Source: Used courtesy of the WIC Supplemental Nutrition Branch of the California Department of Health Services.

SUPPORTING BREAST-FEEDING IN THE EARLY CHILDHOOD SETTING

Sunshine Child Care Center recognizes the nutritional and health benefits of breast-feeding and is committed to supporting mothers who wish to breast-feed or provide expressed breast milk for their infants. To promote and support this philosophy Sunshine Child Care Center adheres to the following policy:

1. Mothers will be provided a private place to breast-feed or pump breast milk that has access to a comfortable chair, a water supply for hand washing, and an electrical outlet.
2. Mothers will be allowed to keep pumped breast milk in the center's refrigerator. All breast milk will be stored in clean containers and labeled with infant's name and the date milk was expressed.
3. Staff will be trained on the appropriate handling of breast milk using the American Academy of Pediatrics and NAEYC recommendations as outlined in *Health Standard 5.B.09*.
4. Breast milk will be stored no more than 48 hours.
   - Thawed breast milk will be stored no more than 24 hours.
   - Frozen breast milk will be stored no more than 3 months at 0°F (–18°C).
5. All staff will receive training on how to sensitively coordinate infant feeding with the breast-feeding mother's work schedule.
   - Staff will help ease mother and baby's transition to work by developing a feeding plan.
   - Staff will try not to feed baby just before mother arrives.
   - Staff will try not to waste breast milk.
6. Breast-feeding will be supported and promoted by sharing resource information for mothers and posting flyers that highlight the Sunshine Child Care Center's commitment to breast-feeding. The policy will be made available to parents in the parent handbook.
7. The program director will be responsible for maintaining and updating the policy and ensuring compliance standards are met.

Sources: From *Academy for Early Childhood Program Accreditation: Standard 5: NAEYC Accreditation Criteria for Health Standard*, by the National Association for the Education of Young Children, 2008, retrieved June 14, 2009, from http://www. naeyc.org/academy/primary/viewstandards; *Model Health Breastfeeding Promotion and Support Policy for Child Care Programs*, by Public Health: Seattle and King County, 2009, retrieved September 20, 2009, from http://www.kingcounty.gov/ healthservices/health/child/childcare/modelhealth.aspx; and *Ten Steps to Breastfeeding Friendly Child Care Centers*, by the Wisconsin Department of Health Services, 2008, retrieved September 20, 2009, from http://dhs.wisconsin.gov/health/ physicalactivity/pdf_files/BreastfeedingFriendlyChildCareCenters.pdf.

The first step in supporting nursing mothers may occur before babies are enrolled. For families who have made the decision to have their infant attend a program, teachers can provide advice on how to ease baby's transition from nursing at the breast to accepting breast milk in a bottle. Figure 5-3 offers suggestions to help babies become accustomed to drinking breast milk from a bottle as well as breast-feeding.

Breast-feeding support is particularly important for mothers who are returning to work and dealing with new schedules, lack of sleep, and obstacles in the work environment. Although the decision to go back to work does not tend to influence breast-feeding initiation, the timing of when women stop breast-feeding is often linked to their return to their jobs (Kimbro, 2006). Teachers can be a vital source of support during this crucial time. They can help by accommodating the nursing mother's need to breast-feed by arranging a comfortable and private place for mothers to nurse when they drop off and pick up their babies. Welcoming mothers who stop by during the day to nurse during their lunch breaks is also an effective means of assisting mothers in maintenance of their breast milk supply and commitment to breast-feeding. Figure 5-4 provides a checklist of ways that early childhood settings can be supportive of infants and mothers who are breast-feeding.

Linking pregnant and nursing mothers to community organizations and resources that promote and support breast-feeding is another important contribution that teachers make. For example, in the opening case scenario Manuel had a difficult first day because a good

Figure 5-3 Tips to Share with Parents about Transitioning Babies from the Breast to the Bottle

1. **Start early but not too early:** Infants become used to what they know and can develop a strong nipple preference for the breast. At around 4 weeks of age, babies have mastered breast-feeding and the mothers' milk supply is usually well established. This is a good time to try offering a bottle of breast milk as babies are still generally open to this option.
2. **Be consistent:** Offer breast milk in a bottle every day or every other day to keep babies used to the bottle's nipple.
3. **Ask for help:** Babies are more likely to accept a bottle from another family member or friend, rather than the mother.
4. **Choose the right time:** Babies should not be too hungry or too upset.
5. **Be patient; don't let the situation escalate:** Keep offering the bottle using gentle encouragement. Babies will gradually get used to the nipple. If there is too much pressure and tension surrounding this transition, babies may begin to get upset as soon as they see the bottle.

Sources: Based on *Making the Transition from Breast to Baby Bottles,* by W. C. Fries, 2009, retrieved September 20, 2009, from http://www.webmd.com/parenting/baby/bottle-feeding-9/weaning-from-breast; and *Starting Solid* Foods, by the American Academy of Pediatrics, 2008, retrieved December 6, 2009, from http://www.aap.org/bookstore/brochures/br_solidfoods_2008_sample.pdf.

Figure 5-4 Checklist for a Breast-Feeding-Friendly Program

☐ Is a breast-feeding policy included in the program information package?
☐ Does the program support breast-feeding for all teachers and staff?
☐ Are teachers trained in strategies to support breast-feeding families?
☐ Is there a comfortable relaxing space set aside for breast-feeding?
☐ Are procedures and guidelines in place for:
   • Handling and storage of breast milk?
   • Knowing what to do if there is insufficient breast milk?
   • Serving breast milk to infants (temperature, type of bottle, how to hold baby, how to gently mix breast milk)?
   • Providing educational brochures that support and offer advice on breast-feeding?
☐ Are teachers aware of referral resources to provide support for breast-feeding families?

Sources: From *Breastfeeding Friendly Child Care Centers*, by the New York State Department of Health, 2008, retrieved September 20, 2009, from http://www.health.state.ny.us/prevention/nutrition/cacfp/breastfeedingspon.htm; and *Ten Steps to Breastfeeding Friendly Child Care Centers*, by the Wisconsin Department of Health Services, 2008, retrieved September 20, 2009, from http://dhs.wisconsin.gov/health/physicalactivity/pdf_files/BreastfeedingFriendlyChildCareCenters.pdf.

What if. . .

you were caring for a breast-fed infant who was crying and hungry, but you knew the mother was due to arrive within a half hour and liked to breast-feed when she got there? How would you manage this situation?

transition plan was not in place. Amelia and Lucia recognized that they could explore ways to provide Manuel breast milk in spite of Lucia's return to work. Amelia provided the phone numbers for various resources: a lactation consultant, a dietitian, the county Women, Infants, and Children (WIC) office, and La Leche League. She told Lucia that these resources would help her find information and guidance on pumping breast milk for Manuel. She told Lucia that La Leche League also has a website that provides state-by-state information, including laws that promote accommodations in the work site for expressing breast milk (La Leche League International, 2009). They sat down and discussed how to coordinate Manuel's feedings with Lucia's work schedule. Lucia decided to use her half hour break at work to pump breast milk for Manuel so that instead of offering formula, Amelia could feed him expressed breast milk. Lucia also planned to nurse Manuel just before she left and as soon as she came to pick him up at the end of the day. They tried and experienced success with these new strategies. An added benefit was that Manuel's stomach distress went away. All three partners in this feeding relationship were happy with the new plan.

Safe Handling of Breast Milk

Teachers must take special precautions to safely handle, store, and serve breast milk provided by mothers to feed their infant. Teachers need to be sure to wash their hands before handling breast milk. Breast milk should be provided in clean containers, such as sturdy plastic bags designed for storing breast milk that fit directly into the bottle. Breast milk stored in soiled containers should not be accepted. Containers should be clearly labeled with the baby's name and the date that the milk was expressed.

When the infant arrives at the early childhood setting the breast milk should be stored in the refrigerator immediately. Breast milk can be stored in the refrigerator at 39°F (4°C) for 48 hours (some experts allow up to 72 hours) (Kleinman, 2009; NAEYC, 2008; USDA Food and Nutrition Service, 2002b). Once a bottle of breast milk has been offered, any milk that is not consumed should be discarded; do not save it to offer at another feeding. Any breast milk that has set out over an hour or that has been fed over an hour's period of time should be discarded.

Sometimes breast milk is frozen for later use. Breast milk can be stored in the freezer at 0°F (–18°C) for up to 3 months (some experts allow freezer storage for up to 6 months (Kleinman, 2009; NAEYC, 2008; USDA Food and Nutrition Service, 2002b). If breast milk is frozen, it should be thawed by transferring the container to the refrigerator until it is ready to use, by placing it in a container of warm water and turning it often, or by holding it under warm running water. Frozen breast milk should never be thawed or heated in a microwave oven because liquids are often heated unevenly. Uneven heating could easily burn a baby's mouth or damage the milk. In addition, bottles may explode if left in the microwave too long, and excess heat can destroy the nutrient and beneficial health qualities of the expressed milk. Once thawed, breast milk should not be refrozen.

By using safe handling techniques, breast-feeding mothers and caregivers of breast-fed infants can maintain the quality of expressed breast milk and the health of the baby (American Academy of Breastfeeding Medicine, 2004; AAP, American Public Health Association [APHA], & National Resource Center for Health and Safety in Child Care and Early Education, 2002; CDC, 2007a).

Unlike formula, breast milk is not a standard product. Initially when babies are first born, colostrum-rich milk can be pale to bright yellow in color. Mature breast milk can vary in color depending on the foods or supplements the mother consumes and the fat content. The fat in breast milk will rise to the top of the storage container. The amount of fat varies depending on how much fore milk and hind milk is expressed. Fore milk is the watery, nutrient-rich milk that is first released when the baby begins nursing. Hind milk is milk from the back of the breast and is rich in fat and calories and is secreted at the end of nursing or expressing breast milk. Simply shaking the bottle of breast milk gently ensures that the fat is redistributed in the milk and made available to the infant. Mothers should be encouraged to express and save breast milk in small 2-oz volumes as well as larger volumes to provide teachers an option when baby wants just a little more. This helps prevent the waste of this valuable food.

Nutrients of Importance for Breast-Fed Infants

Although breast milk is a perfect form of nutrition designed to meet the needs of most healthy infants, some dietary considerations when using breast milk require special attention as the infant matures.

Vitamin D Breast milk is not a rich source of vitamin D, an important vitamin that enhances calcium absorption and facilitates the building of strong bones and teeth. Vitamin D is produced in the body when skin is exposed to sun. However, infants and young children, particularly those who have minimum exposure to sunlight and those who are dark skinned, are at risk for developing rickets, a deficiency disease associated with abnormal bone mineralization and development. Therefore, the AAP recommends providing 400 IU vitamin D supplements for all breast-feeding infants (Kleinman, 2009).

Vitamin B$_{12}$ A lack of vitamin B$_{12}$ can be a concern for infants of breast-feeding mothers who are vegan (vegetarians who do not consume any foods of animal origin including dairy products or eggs). This can result in a form of anemia as well as impaired neurological development. Vegan mothers are encouraged to take vitamin B$_{12}$ supplements (Wagnon et al., 2005).

> ## What if. . .
> you noticed that a bottle of breast milk in the refrigerator was not labeled by the mother who dropped it off with the date it was expressed? What would you do?

fore milk
the watery, nutrient-rich breast milk that is first released when the baby begins nursing

hind milk
milk from the back of the breast that is rich in fat and calories and is secreted at the end of nursing or expressing breast milk

MyEducationLab

Go to the Assignments and Activities section of Topic 2: Feeding Children in the MyEducationLab for your course and complete the activity entitled *Breast Feeding*. After listening to breast-feeding and formula-feeding mothers, what is your perspective on feeding infants?

Iron Prior to birth babies lay down stores of iron in their liver. In addition, the iron in breast milk is easily absorbed and is sufficient until around 6 months of age. But by 6 months of age (or earlier in premature infants), an infant's iron reserves are depleted. Insufficient iron can negatively impact growth and cognitive development. Babies who are iron deficient or anemic are likely to be tired and cranky and are at increased risk for illness due to a compromised immune function. For these reasons, it is important to introduce iron-rich foods such as iron-fortified cereal and meats to supplement the infant's dietary intake of iron from breast milk. Introducing whole cow's milk at this age is not recommended because it can cause intestinal bleeding, which also increases the risk of anemia (Irwin & Kirchner, 2007).

Zinc Zinc is an important mineral for growth and a well-functioning immune system. Zinc in breast milk is easily absorbed and meets the needs of infants until about 6 months of age. The older breast-fed infant's needs for zinc can be met with the introduction of strained meats and zinc-fortified cereals (Kleinman, 2009).

Note that the infant's need for iron and zinc coincides with the typical introduction of solid foods. Delaying introduction of solids can result in suboptimal intake of these nutrients.

The Formula-Fed Infant

Some babies receive their nutrition through formula, which is a manufactured product used as a substitute for breast milk. Although breast milk is the best form of nourishment, babies can also thrive on infant formulas. Mothers may choose to use infant formula for several reasons. For example, women who are infected with HIV or have active tuberculosis should not breast-feed (Bray, Nielsen, & Popkin, 2004). Although many medications women take are acceptable, some are unsafe and can pass into the breast milk and have a negative impact on the baby. In these cases mothers should be advised to consult with their health care provider to discuss their concerns.

Some mothers also worry that breast milk may contain possible contaminants such as chemicals and pesticides and, therefore, may choose not to breast-feed. A recent study suggests that more than three-quarters of breast-feeding mothers who were interested in knowing if their breast milk was contaminated said they would wean early if they learned their breast milk contained a harmful substance (Geraghty, Khoury, Morrow, & Lanphea, 2008). The *Safety Segment* provides reassuring background information regarding the relative risks of breast milk contamination. However mothers choose to feed their infants—through breast-feeding, infant formula feeding, or some combination—they should be supported in their decision.

Types of Infant Formula

Like breast milk, infant formula is designed to meet the nutrient needs of infants until 6 months of age. A variety of infant formulas are available. Infant formulas may differ in the type of carbohydrate, protein, and fat they contain. Several of the different types of infant formula are discussed next.

Modified Cow's Milk–Based Formulas Modified cow's milk is the most commonly used commercial formula. It is comprised of cow's milk that has been altered to provide the best composition of protein, fat, and carbohydrates in an easily digested form. Some cow's milk formulas are lactose free, to support the feeding of the rare infant who is lactose intolerant. This product is not appropriate for infants who are allergic to milk because it contains cow's milk protein. Thickened cow's milk–based formulas are available for infants who suffer from gastroesophageal reflux disease. These products contain added rice starch that when exposed to stomach contents thickens, which may reduce the spitting up and help the baby keep the formula down (Adler & Dickinson, 2009).

Soy-Based Formulas Soy-based products were developed in the 1960s for infants who are allergic to cow's milk or have lactose intolerance. The substitution of soy formula for infants with a cow's milk allergy is less accepted these days based on research that reveals

Safety Segment

Breast Milk and Environmental Contaminants

Breast milk is the ideal form of nutrition for infants and is recommended by leading health authorities. However, mothers and caregivers may wonder if breast milk is safe considering the potential risk for contamination from environmental pollutants. Pollutants can be found in the air, water, and food supplies. Mothers consume foods or beverages that contain these contaminants, which can be stored in the body and transferred via breast milk to the infant during breast-feeding.

The health risk of these contaminants is not clearly understood because of the difficulty in determining whether the pollutants are related to prenatal exposure before a baby is born or after a baby is born and breast-fed. Fortunately, the levels of these contaminants have been decreasing in the environment with the advent of regulatory restrictions on their production and use that began 30 to 40 years ago. In 2001 the Stockholm Convention, an organization focused on decreasing global environmental pollution, created an international treaty that brings worldwide cooperation to solving these problems. These actions have had positive results. In recent studies, Swedish women showed a significant decline in the amount of breast milk contaminants and U.S. pregnant women also showed decreased levels of exposure to these types of contaminants.

In spite of the concern about environmental pollutions, breast-feeding is strongly recommended by the World Health Organization because the tremendous benefits of breast-feeding far outweigh the potential risks.

Sources: "Persistent Organochlorine and Organobromine Compounds in Mother's Milk from Sweden 1996–2006: Compound-specific Temporal Trends," by S. Lignell, M. Aune, P. O. Darnerud, S. Cnattingius, and A. Glynn, 2009, *Environmental Research, 109*(6), pp. 760–767; "Environmental Contaminants in Breast Milk," by K. Nickerson, 2006, *Journal of Midwifery & Women's Health, 51*(1), pp. 26–34; *Fact Sheet: What Is the Stockholm Convention?* by the Stockholm Convention, 2009, retrieved August 1, 2009, from http://chm.pops.int/Convention/Media/Factsheets/tabid/527/language/en-US/Default.aspx; and "Serum Concentrations of Selected Persistent Organic Pollutants in a Sample of Pregnant Females and Changes in Their Concentrations During Gestation," by R. Y. Wang, R. B. Jain, A. F. Wolkin, C. H. Rubin, and L. L. Needham, 2009, *Environmental Health Perspectives, 117*, p. 1244.

as many as 20% to 60% of infants allergic to cow's milk formula (the type of allergic response that causes enterocolitis, or inflammation of the small intestine and colon) are also allergic to soy formula (Nevin-Folino et al., 2008; Samour & King, 2005). Soy-based formulas are often used by families who are vegetarian.

Hypoallergenic Formulas Hypoallergenic formulas contain protein that has been broken down into smaller components such as peptides and amino acids, making them less likely to cause an allergic response and easier to absorb. These products were developed for children with cow's milk or soy allergies and for infants who have gastrointestinal or liver disease that results in problems with absorption.

There are two types of hypoallergenic formulas. The protein hydrolysate formulas have the protein broken down into amino acids and small peptides, whereas the amino acid–based formulas designed for extremely sensitive infants contain only amino acids. These formulas are very expensive and are only selected with careful consideration by health care providers. Another type of formula contains partially hydrolyzed protein. The protein in this type of formula is not broken down extensively and, therefore, should not be used when infants have a cow's milk protein allergy (Kleinman, 2009).

Premature Formulas These formulas are designed to support the increased nutritional needs of the premature infant. They provide higher calories, more protein, and increased levels of some vitamins and minerals per ounce compared to standard formulas (*Nourishing the Very Low Birth Weight Infant*, 2007). For example, standard formulas and breast milk contain 20 calories per ounce, whereas premature formulas contain 22 to 24 calories per ounce. Some very low birth weight infants may need to consume a more concentrated formula or a formula to which additional ingredients such as carbohydrate and fat have been added to increase the caloric density. When preparing formula in any way that deviates from standard mixing directions on the label, a prescription from the health care provider is needed.

Enhanced Infant Formulas Since 2002 most cow's milk–based formulas have been supplemented with the substances DHA (docosahexaenoic acid) and ARA (arachidonic acid), also called omega-3 fatty acids, because they are thought to be important building blocks for the development of the baby's brain and eyesight (Chao & Vandenplas, 2007). These fatty acids, found naturally in breast milk, can be made by babies from other essential fatty acids found in formula but not, perhaps, in optimal amounts. Although research is ongoing, there are good indications that addition of these supplements to formula is beneficial for cognitive development and visual acuity (Abad-Jorge, 2008; Auestad et al., 2003; Cheatham, Colombo, & Carlson, 2006; McCann & Ames, 2005).

Follow-Up Infant Formulas These formulas are designed to meet the needs of older infants and toddlers (9 to 24 months) who have begun to eat solids but may not be eating enough to meet all of their nutritional requirements. Although nutrient content varies depending on brand, the follow-up formulas tend to be higher in iron, calcium, and vitamins than whole milk. The AAP states that although these products are nutritionally adequate they do not have a significant advantage over breast milk or formula in combination with a healthy diet (Kleinman, 2009).

All infant formulas undergo scrutiny by the U.S. Food and Drug Administration (FDA). The vitamin and mineral content of formula is standardized based on FDA regulations that specify the nutrient level requirements to ensure that all formulas fed to infants are safe and nutritionally complete (FDA, 2009). Selection of the infant formula is made by the infant's family in consultation with their health care provider. The decision is guided by identifying formula that is most appropriate for the baby. Infants should receive the same type and form of formula in the early childhood setting that is used in the home setting.

Formula Intolerance

formula intolerance results when infants have difficulties and symptoms that appear to be related to the formula they are consuming

Formula intolerance occurs when infants have difficulties and symptoms that appear to be related to the formula they are consuming. Teachers need to keep families informed when babies show signs of excessive gas, bloating, diarrhea, abdominal pain, vomiting, excessive crying, rash or allergic symptoms.

It is often challenging for families and teachers to recognize when babies are unable to tolerate their formula. Normal infant behavior includes crying, vomiting, gas, and diarrhea. Often well-meaning mothers will switch formulas in an attempt to solve these perceived problems. A recent study showed that mothers were more likely to switch formulas based on perceived formula intolerance as compared to physicians, indicating that sometimes mothers will make unnecessary and sometimes expensive changes in formula use that may not be warranted (Berseth, Mitmesser, Ziegler, Marunycz, & Vanderhoof, 2009). Over time, teachers gain experience with many infants. They are able to reassure families about normal infant behavior and direct them to health care providers if they have concerns about formula intolerance.

Forms of Infant Formula

Infant formula is available in three different forms:

- *Ready-to-feed:* This is usually the most expensive form and requires no preparation.
- *Canned concentrate:* This formula requires water to be added to a concentrate.
- *Powdered:* This is the least expensive form of formula and requires a powder to be mixed with water.

The type of formula is selected based on need for convenience and cost considerations. For example, a child care program may have a policy of only offering ready-to-feed formulas if they participate in CACFP or do not have adequate space for formula preparation.

Safe Preparation of Infant Formula

Safe and sanitary procedures must be used when preparing infant formula. Formula and water must be measured exactly. Inaccurate measurements can lead to dangerous problems. If formula is prepared with too much water, it will be too low in calories and nutrient concentration to meet the needs of the baby, resulting in poor growth. If the formula is too concentrated, diarrhea and dehydration can result and may cause excess calorie intake. Figure 5-5 provides general guidelines for preparing formula. If powered formula is used, it is important to use the scoop provided in the can because scoops can vary slightly in size depending on the brand or type of formula.

The National Resource Center for Health and Safety in Child Care and Early Education is a valuable resource for early childhood education programs. It provides an online book on health and safety standards entitled *Caring for Our Children: National Health and Safety Performance Standards: Guidelines for Out-of-Home Child Care Programs*, Second Edition (AAP, APHA, & National Resource Center for Health and Safety in Child Care and Early Education, 2002). This re-source provides guidance in establishing policies and procedures within the early childhood setting including guidelines for infant formula preparation as well as many other aspects related to providing nutritious meals for children.

What if. . .

you noticed a coworker in the infant class not properly measuring formula when preparing it for infants in her care? How would you handle this? What risks are involved with this practice?

Understanding the Feeding Relationship

One of the many pleasures in caring for children is feeding young infants. Their complete satisfaction is rewardingly apparent as they suck and swallow the breast milk or formula offered to them. This is an important time for teachers and infants to connect, one on one,

Figure 5-5 Guidelines for Safe Preparation of Infant Formula

1. Wash hands using appropriate hand washing procedures.
2. Only serve formula that comes in factory-sealed containers and is the same brand and form that is served at home.
3. Prepare formula using manufacturer's directions. When preparing powdered formula *use the scoop that comes with the can* because the size of scoops can vary among different brands or types of formula.
4. Use water from an approved source.
   - Water sources should be approved by the local health department. Children's programs that use well water should have the water tested for safety.
   - Families should use water sources approved by the baby's health care providers.
5. Prepare the water for use. The American Academy of Pediatrics and the Food and Drug Administration recommend using tap or bottled water that has been brought to a rolling boil for 2 minute and then allowed to cool before adding to the infant formula powder or concentrate. Some well water hazards are not eliminated by boiling. Contact the local health department for advice.
6. Use cold tap water that has been allowed to run for 2 minutes. This reduces the risk of excess lead content. Warm water or water that has sat in pipes for a period of time can contain lead.
7. Use sanitary equipment. All equipment used to prepare and serve formula should be clean and sanitized. Bottles and nipples should be washed with dish detergent and clean water or in the dishwasher if available. Check with the child's family to determine if sterilization of bottles and nipples is necessary.
8. Wash off the top of canned formula and open with a clean can opener.
9. Store appropriately. Prepared formula or an opened can of concentrate that is covered can be stored up to 48 hours in the refrigerator.
10. Warm the formula for use. Formula can be warmed by holding the bottle under running warm tap water or by placing it in a container of hot water no warmer than 120°F (49°C). Formula should not be heated in a microwave oven because it can heat unevenly and hot spots can scald the baby's mouth.
11. Serve within 1 hour. Formula is safe for feeding up to 1 hour; past this time a new bottle should be prepared.
12. Discard leftover formula. Any formula left over after a feeding is contaminated by the baby's mouth and should be discarded.
13. Do not freeze infant formula.
14. Develop and use a system for monitoring the temperature of the refrigerator where infant formula is stored.

Sources: Based on *Caring for Our Children: National Health and Safety Performance Standards: Guidelines for Out-of-Home Child Care Programs*, 2nd edition (Chapter 4, "Nutrition and Food Service"), by the American Academy of Pediatrics, American Public Health Association, and National Resource Center for Health and Safety in Child Care and Early Education, 2002, Elk Grove Village, IL: American Academy of Pediatrics; Washington, DC: American Public Health Association, retrieved August 31, 2009, from http://www.eric.ed.gov/ERICDocs/data/ericdocs2sql/content_storage_01/0000019b/80/14/0d/14.pdf; and *Guidelines for Bottlefeeding*, by H. Darlene Martin and Nancy M. Lewis, 1994, National Network for Child Care, Urbana-Champaign, IL: University of Illinois Cooperative Extension Service, retrieved September 20, 2009, from http://www.nncc.org/Nutrition/guide.bottlefed.html#anchor111745.

A close feeding relationship between teacher and child enhances the baby's growth and development.

in a relaxed and comfortable setting. Designate a special place to feed infants such as a rocking or comfortable chair to enjoy the time socializing with the baby. Looking into infants' eyes and allowing them to gaze back at you builds positive bonds of trust and appreciation. It is during this interaction that teachers learn to recognize the feeding cues babies give to indicate when they are hungry or full.

Feeding Cues

Teachers should be able to recognize feeding cues in order to satisfy the needs of the infant. Although developmentally, infants share common traits, they also exhibit a wide variety of individual characteristics and rates of maturation that affect cues, making each feeding relationship a unique experience. Infants are born with the instinctual ability to cry when they are hungry. However, babies cry for a variety of reasons. The caregiver must learn the nuances of the message the baby is trying to convey. This understanding is important because babies are completely reliant on the adults in their lives to meet all of their physical and emotional needs.

Signs of Hunger and Satiety

Successfully reading hunger and satiety (fullness) cues can reduce infants' stress and enhance the feeding relationship. A baby's inability to verbalize means the teacher must rely exclusively on body language and behavior to recognize any needs. Although each infant will have unique ways of expressing needs, a variety of common signs may suggest when babies are hungry or full. Table 5-1 provides a list of common behaviors associated with hunger and fullness in infants.

Some babies become very anxious when hungry. They can work themselves into such a spell of frustrated crying that when they finally receive the breast or their bottle they may

Table 5-1	Understanding Hunger and Fullness Cues in Infants
Hunger Cues	**Fullness Cues**
EARLY CUES	EARLY CUES
Alert and looking at caregiver	Stops sucking
Increased arm and leg motions	Seals lips together
Mouthing lips, fingers, or fists	Turns face away
Rooting	Spits out or plays with nipple
Grunting sounds	Falls asleep
Opens mouth wide	Limbs are relaxed
Fussing	
LATE CUES	LATE CUES
Appears tense	Baby arches back and turns face away
Frantic crying	Baby gets irritable with repeated attempts to offer bottle
Trembling	Crying

Sources: Adapted from *Infant Nutrition and Feeding: A Reference Handbook for Nutrition and Health Counselors in the WIC and CSF Programs*, by the National Agricultural Library, 2008, retrieved September 20, 2009, from http://www.nal.usda.gov/wicworks/Topics/Infant_Feeding_Guide.html#guide; and *Child of Mine: Feeding with Love and Good Sense*, by Ellyn Satter, 2000, Boulder, CO: Bull Publishing Company.

sputter or gulp air, which in turn leads to gas, stomach distention, spitting up, and even more crying. Recall in the opening case scenario that Manuel became very upset on his first day because he woke up in a new environment and had his feeding delayed. On top of that, he wanted the breast for comfort and was offered the unfamiliar bottle with formula instead. He worked himself into such a frenzy

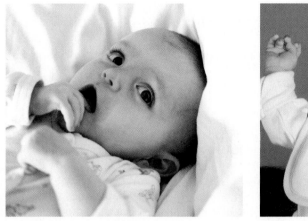

that he swallowed air, causing him to spit up. The best way to avoid such frantic behavior is to be attuned to and respond quickly to early feeding cues. If Amelia had been able to respond to Manuel immediately, he may have been more accepting of the bottle.

Recognizing babies' early signs of hunger prevents the need for them to use later signs of hunger: crying.

Similarly babies' fullness cues should not be disregarded in an effort to have them finish a bottle or clean a plate. This can cause infants to fuss and struggle. If the conflict persists, it will likely result in poor eating habits (over- or undereating) and compromise the feeding relationship (Abad-Jorge, 2008). In turn, a teacher's or parent's lack of sensitivity to infants' fullness cues can result in overfeeding, setting the stage for excess weight gain and obesity (Worobey, Medina, & Martin, 2007; Worobey, Lopez, & Hoffman, 2009). With time and experience, as well as input from families, teachers and infants settle into a routine and an effective feeding relationship ensues. The *Teaching Wellness* feature provides examples of ways in which teachers can help older infants and young children identify their signs of hunger and fullness.

Feeding Infants from a Bottle

Infants should always be fed on demand. It is inappropriate to impose a feeding schedule on infants in an early childhood setting unless this has been authorized by a health professional for medical reasons. Teachers should not put infants in a crib with a bottle. Bottle-propping puts babies at risk for choking, earaches, and dental caries. It also decreases time spent in bonding and socializing. Instead, teachers should feed one baby at a time so they can easily and quickly interpret and be responsive to feeding cues.

Formula or breast milk is often accepted better if warmed, but this is not necessary. The USDA Food and Nutrition Service in their infant nutrition and feeding guide (2002b) provides guidance for caregivers who feed infants breast milk or formula from a bottle (see Web Resources). They advise that teachers should wash hands before feeding infants. Babies should be held comfortably, positioning them so that their heads are held higher than their trunks and they are facing the teacher. This helps prevent choking and promotes the opportunity for social interaction. The bottle should be tilted so that the milk moves into and fills the nipple. Keeping

Figure 5-6 **Examples of Different Types of Nipples**

the nipple full helps prevent the infant from swallowing excessive air. Touching the nipple to the infant's mouth stimulates the sucking reflex as feeding begins. There are many types of nipples that families can select based on personal preference or need as illustrated in Figure 5-6.

Periodically, babies need to take a break to be burped. This is accomplished by holding the baby upright against the teacher's shoulder and gently patting on the baby's back until air has been expelled (Abad-Jorge, 2008). Feeding continues until babies provide cues that they are full. This time should be calm and comfortably paced, not rushed. Spitting up after a feeding is

Flat-topped nipple

Standard nipple

Orthodontic nipple

Haberman or special feeder nipple

Teaching Wellness   *I Feel Hungry, I Feel Full*

Learning Outcomes: Children will be able to communicate when they are hungry and when they are full.

Infants

- *Goal:* To introduce the child to recognizing and communicating feeling hungry and feeling full.

- *Materials:* Pureed fruits and vegetables of different colors for young infants who have recently started solids, or small mashed pieces of fresh fruit and cooked vegetables such as banana and cooked carrots for older infants. Sign language glossary that includes terms for *full* (bend elbow and hold hand and arm straight across the body; keep hand and arm parallel and lift up under the chin) and *hungry* (shape hand as if holding a cup; place hand on upper chest with palm facing chest, and slide it downward). Web Resource: Babies and Sign Language, Free Baby Sign Language Dictionary and Glossary, www.babies-and-sign-language.com/glossary-photos.html.

- *Activity plan:* Talk to the baby while preparing the meal. Ask baby, "Are you hungry? Do you want to eat?" Use sign language hand motions for hunger. Just before putting the meal on the baby's tray use the sign language for hungry again. Serve baby the meal. Allow baby to help self-feed if appropriate. When the baby stops eating (closes mouth, turns away head, or acts disinterested in eating), ask the question "Are you full?" while at the same time making the sign for feeling full. Do this routinely before and after mealtimes helping the baby to grasp the concept.

- *How to adjust the activity:* Once baby has mastered hunger and full signs, use the sign language glossary/dictionary to add more sign language terms that can aid in mealtime communication such as *eat*, *finish*, *thirsty*, and different foods or beverages.

- *Did you meet your goal?* Could you observe the infant attending to your words and motions as you talked and made the signs for hungry and full?

Toddlers, Preschoolers, and Kindergartners

- *Goal:* To be able to recognize and describe the signs of hunger and fullness while enjoying healthful foods.

- *Materials:* The children's book *Lunch* by Denise Fleming, three or four different types of fruits and vegetables that are referred to in the book (watermelon, blueberries, peas, carrots cut into pieces that are age appropriate), paint of various colors, large sheet of white mural-sized paper, flat trays, tubs with water and paper towels for washing feet.

- *Activity plan:* Talk with children about how it feels to be hungry and full. Share the sign language hand motions for hungry and full. Ask children to describe how they feel when they are hungry (growling, rumbling stomach, watery mouth) and full (stomach that feels bigger, no more growling and rumbling). Read the book *Lunch*. Discuss how the mouse is feeling at the beginning of the book and at the end using sign language terms for hungry and full. As you read the book identify the healthful qualities of the foods and their colors.

  Place the mural-sized paper on the ground with trays of paint the colors of the foods used for the activity. Have children remove shoes and socks. One at a time, have children identify their favorite fruit or vegetable while looking at a tray of cut-up fruits and vegetables. Ask the child to step in a tray with paint the color of his favorite food. Assist the child to walk across the paper just as the mouse did in the book. Provide a tub of water and paper towels and assist children to wash and dry their feet and put socks and shoes on. Use clean water to wash each child's feet. Eat lunch together. As you wait for the food, ask children, "Is your stomach growling?" Just before the end of the meal have children stop and listen to their stomachs again. Ask, "How does your stomach feel now?" Display the mural in the classroom.

- *How to adjust the activity:* Provide paintbrushes of varying sizes, so that children who struggle with fine motor skills will find a brush that works for them. Reinforce the verbal discussion with picture cue cards for hungry and full. Create a song to include the concepts of hungry (growling stomach) and full (stomach says "Ahhhh.") This helps children who have difficulty focusing and paying attention stay on task. Have each child paint a picture of her or his favorite food as inspired by the book. Encourage older children to draw a picture of a very hungry or very full mouse. Post pictures in the classroom.

- *Did you meet your goal?* Were children able to describe the sensations of hunger and fullness?

This toddler shows she is hungry by reaching and crying. She is happy when she receives her food and is able to use sign language to indicate when she is full.

School-Age Children

- *Goal:* To be able to recognize signs of hunger and fullness while learning about the digestive system.

- *Materials:* The book *Chewy, Gooey, Rumble, Plop* by Steve Alton, masking tape, stethoscopes.

- *Activity plan:* Read the book *Chewy, Gooey, Rumble, Plop.* Review why we eat food and what happens to food once it's eaten. Review the steps in digestion. Discuss how the body sends signals when it is time to eat and when it is time to stop eating. Have children reflect on these signals, what they are, and how they make them feel. With masking tape divide the room into three lanes. Identify the lanes as "hungry," "not hungry or full," and "full." Ask children to go to the lane that best describes how they feel. Ask children in the hungry lane why they are hungry. Did some skip breakfast? Does being hungry make it hard for them to concentrate? Ask children in other lanes why they are not hungry. Using the stethoscopes, have children listen to their stomachs and talk about the sounds they hear. Talk about why it's important to pay attention to hunger and fullness signals.

- *How to adjust the activity:* Ensure enough space so that children who move with a wheelchair can navigate successfully into a "lane." Provide picture cards to depict hungry, neither hunger or full, and full. Use these to assist children who have difficulty following verbal directions, such as those who are hard of hearing or others who may attend better with this approach, such as children with autism. Have children prepare a snack such as popcorn or muffins or any food that smells good while it's being prepared. Ask children how the smell of food impacts their feeling of hunger. Ask them what attributes of food make them more hungry. What makes them not want to eat a food?

- *Did you meet your goal?* Are children able to identify hunger and fullness signs?

normal. However, if there is projectile vomiting or vomiting of large volumes of breast milk or formula, the family should be encouraged to obtain advice from their health care provider.

Communicating with Parents

Communicating with parents is an important teacher responsibility. A baby's behavior cannot be fully understood unless it is put into the context of the child's most recent experiences. For example, it is important for parents to share information such as how well the baby is sleeping at night, when the baby was last fed and changed, and if a baby is teething. This helps the teacher understand the infant's needs. Teachers cannot effectively read the signs of the infant if they don't know "what's up." For instance, in the opening case scenario, it might have been an easier first day for Manuel and Amelia, his caregiver, if his mother Lucia had mentioned that Manuel had slept poorly and been up a good part of the night before.

Similarly, teachers need to share information such as what and how much the infant eats and the frequency of diaper changes so the family feels informed. One way to ensure detailed communication is to send home a note with families at the end of each day. Figure 5-7 provides an example. Another effective communication approach is to use a notebook with a section for writing comments back and forth between the teacher and family.

How Often and How Much to Feed a Baby

What if. . .

you had a mother who was consistently behind schedule when dropping off her infant and frequently left without sharing important details such as when her baby was last fed? How might you ensure better communication?

Teachers feel more secure that they can meet infant needs if they have a general idea of how often and how much babies should be fed. Babies usually develop a routine for eating that is influenced by their weight, age, whether they receive breast milk or formula and whether they are eating solids. In general, newborns who are breast-fed tend to eat every 1½ to 3 hours or about 8 to 12 times per day for the first 6 weeks. By the time they are 4 to 6 months old, they consume greater volumes of breast milk, and feedings gradually decrease to 5 or more feedings per day (Kleinman, 2009). Newborns receiving formula typically need 8 to 12 feedings per day, although some will be hungry less often because formula takes longer to digest than breast milk. By 4 to 6 months the number of formula feedings decreases to 4 to 6 or more

Figure 5-7 Sample Parent Update Form

Baby's Day at Sunshine School

Baby's name _____

Baby slept from _____to_____   Baby's mood was _____
_____to_____   _____

Today:

Baby drank _____ bottles or ounces of formula   Baby ate the following solids: _____

Baby drank _____ bottles or ounces of breast milk   _____

Baby drank _____ bottles or ounces of _____

Baby was last fed _____ (what baby had) at _____AM or PM (time)

Baby had diaper changed at_____ AM/PM   Baby had diaper changed at _____ AM/PM
• wet   • wet
• stool   • stool
• both   • both

Baby had diaper changed at _____ AM/PM   Baby had diaper changed at _____ AM/PM
• wet   • wet
• stool   • stool
• both   • both

Baby needs the following items:

Baby wipes   Diapers   Formula   Breast milk

Extra clothes   Other _____

Additional comments: _____

Source: Based on *Infant Toddler Daily Communication Form*, by North Dakota Child Care Resource and Referral, retrieved from http://www.ndchildcare.org/ providers/supporting-children-families/docs/Written%20Daily%20Communication.pdf.

Table 5-2	Feeding Guidelines				
	Feeding Guidelines for Formula-Fed or Breast-Milk-Fed Infants[a]		CACFP Meal Plan for Formula-Fed or Breast-Milk-Fed Infants[b]		
Age	Number of Formula Feedings/Day	Range of Intake (oz)/Day	Breakfast (oz)	Lunch/Dinner (oz)	Snack (oz)
Newborn	8–12	18–24	4–6	4–6	4–6
1–4 mo	6–8	18–32	4–6, increasing to 4–8 oz at 4 mo	4–6, increasing to 4–8 oz at 4 mo	4–6
4–6 mo	4–6	28–45	4–8	4–8	4–6
6–9 mo	3–5	24–32	4–8, increasing to 6–8 oz at 8 mo	4–8, increasing to 6–8 oz at 8 mo	4–6, decreasing to 2–4 or 2–4 fruit juice at 8 mo
9–12 mo	2–4	24–32	6–8	6–8	2–4 or 2–4 fruit juice

[a]Formula and breast milk contain the same amount of calories per ounce; therefore, expressed breast milk's range of intake is comparable to that of formula.
[b]Recommendations do not include solid foods. See the Appendix for the complete meal plan.

Sources: Adapted from *The American Dietetic Association Complete Food and Nutrition Guide*, 3rd edition, by R. L. Duyff, 2006, Hoboken, NJ: John Wiley & Sons; *Formula Feeding FAQs: How Much and How Often*, by Kids Health, 2009, retrieved September 20, 2009, from http://kidshealth.org/PageManager.jsp?lic=1&ps=104&article_set=45609#; and *Child and Adult Care Food Program: Meal Patterns*, by the U.S. Department of Agriculture, Food and Nutrition Service, 2002, retrieved September 20, 2009, from http://www.fns.usda.gov/CND/Care/ProgramBasics/Meals/Meal_Patterns.htm#Infant_LunchSupper.

bottles per day as infants mature and are able to hold greater volumes in their stomachs (Duyff, 2006). With the introduction of solid foods, infants begin to need less breast milk or formula.

This information provides general feeding guidelines. However, it is important that infants be fed on demand. This means they are provided breast milk or formula whenever they are hungry. A rigid schedule for feedings only creates stress for both babies and caregivers. In addition, infants experience growth spurts, at which time the demand for formula or breast milk may increase. Table 5-2 provides information on the typical feeding expectations for infants, illustrating the wide range of feedings per day and amount of milk consumed.

The expectations for infant meal quantities outlined by the CACFP are also shown in Table 5-2, demonstrating the range of breast milk and formula intake on a per meal basis (Duyff, 2006; Hendy & Raudenbush, 2000).The CACFP provides this information as a guideline for meeting reimbursement requirements (Duyff, 2006; Hendy & Raudenbush, 2000. CACFP supports demand feeding, however, by allowing flexibility in when the feeding is served (when the baby is hungry) and how much is offered (feed until the baby is full).

Inappropriate Infant Feeding Practices

Teachers work closely with families. At times, teachers may learn that families are not feeding infants in ways that are healthy and appropriate. In this case, teachers can take the opportunity to gather resources and educate families about safe and healthy feeding practices. Providing and reviewing educational materials on infant feeding are positive ways to introduce these concerns. The family's medical provider is also a valuable resource. The following sections illustrate some of the common poor feeding practices.

Putting the baby to bed with a bottle can result in increased risk of cavities and choking. It is also a missed opportunity for socializing.

Grandparents are often vital members of the team of adults caring for infants and can provide valuable information to teachers when they drop off their grandchildren.

Adding Cereal to Formula in the Bottle

Sometimes families feel that the addition of infant cereal to formula in the bottle will increase a baby's likelihood to sleep through the night. Research has shown that this is not the case and can create problems (Macknin, Medendorp, & Maier, 1989). For example, cereal in the bottle can lead to choking. The early introduction of solid foods, including cereals, also increases the risk of acquiring allergies. When infants are ready for solid foods, they are ready to learn to eat from a spoon. Putting cereal in a bottle delays this natural developmental opportunity. Putting cereal in the bottle also throws off the balance of nutrients in the feeding by displacing the nutrients of breast milk or formula with infant cereal. This may result in the intake of excessive calories, putting the baby at risk for overweight and obesity.

When researchers delved into the reasons mother's added cereal to the bottle, some reported that they did not recognize cereal as a solid. Others indicated that feeding decisions were influenced by grandparents (Black, Siegel, Abel, & Bentley, 2001; Heinig et al., 2006). These reasons provide opportunity for discussion and problem solving to identify the practices that are best for babies. The *Nutrition Note* discusses the influence of grandparents in feeding infants and offers suggestions on how teachers can collaborate with grandparents to support healthful infant feeding practices.

Finishing the Bottle

Some parents and teachers may encourage a baby to finish the bottle to avoid wasting formula or breast milk. This disrupts the infant's ability to self-regulate intake by altering responsiveness to internal cues of hunger and satiety, putting them at risk for developing obesity (Bergmann et al., 2003). The infant's feeding cues should be respected. When the baby is full, the feeding is stopped and the extra formula or breast milk is discarded.

Using Honey in the Bottle or on the Pacifier

infantile botulism
a serious illness that results from ingesting *Clostridium botulinum* spores that germinate and release a deadly toxin in the gastrointestinal tract

The inappropriate feeding practice of putting honey in a baby's bottle can have very severe outcomes. A serious foodborne illness called infantile botulism can occur in infants as a result of consuming honey (California Department of Public Health, Division of Communicable Disease Control, 2004; Farmularo, 2009). This illness occurs because infants' digestive systems are not fully developed. This allows the botulism spores to grow, and eventually releases a potent toxin causing illness. This rare foodborne illness can cause a progression of symptoms that lead to paralysis and death if not identified early and treated.

Avoiding honey is imperative until after the baby's first birthday (Cox & Hinkle, 2002; Tanzi & Gabay, 2002). This includes foods that contain honey such as yogurt with honey, honey graham crackers, and breads and cereals that contain honey. Older children and adults have more mature gastrointestinal tracts and do not experience harm from honey.

Although honey has been considered the culprit for infant botulism, note that in most cases no source of the botulism illness can be found. In these cases it is believed that the illness was acquired through swallowing invisible airborne dust that contains the botulism spores (California Department of Public Health, Division of Communicable Disease Control, 2004). This emphasizes the importance of keeping pacifiers and other items young babies put in their mouths clean, especially when they are dropped on the ground.

Many cultures consider honey an acceptable source of nourishment to be given to babies to cleanse the system shortly after birth and before the initiation of breast-feeding

Nutrition Note

Grandparents and Infant Feeding Decisions

Parents have the ultimate responsibility for making decisions regarding the care and feeding of their infants. Grandparents play a wonderful and important role in the lives of their grandchildren, but sometimes can exert significant influence on feeding decisions, especially when parents are young or inexperienced. Many grandparents may share child-rearing responsibilities and be involved in dropping off and picking up children.

Grandparents have a natural interest in the child's well-being, but may not be aware that guidelines for feeding infants have changed since they were parents. For example, grandparents may have introduced solids earlier with their children than is currently recommended by health care professionals. Adding cereal to the bottle was a more common practice in the past. Grandparents may feel a heavy baby is a healthy baby. Grandmothers may not be supportive of breast-feeding if they did not breast-feed themselves. Parents may make appropriate decisions about feeding that are not supported by grandparents, creating tension that can spill into the early childhood setting. For example, a grandparent may admit to feeding strained meat to an infant whose parents are vegan.

It is important for teachers to respect boundaries and recognize that, unless grandparents have legal custody or guardianship of their grandchildren, the parents have the final say about what to feed their children. However, teachers can help manage these influences by creating a strong bond of communication among all the family members involved in the infant's care. Teachers can provide sources of information for grandparents on feeding and food safety such as the following web resources:

WIC Works Sharing Center at http://www.nal.usda.gov/wicworks/Sharing_Center/statedev_statelist.html where the following handouts are available:

- *Grandparents Play an Important Role*
- A Special Message for Grandparents

North Dakota State University Education and Extension Service also has a handout entitled *Seniors and Food Safety: When Grandparents Take Care of Grandchildren* at http://www.ag.ndsu.edu/pubs/yf/foods/fn703.pdf

These messages also help guide grandparents to be part of the infant's support team:

✓ Learn and follow new child care practices and recommendations, especially those that relate to infant feeding.
✓ Support the infant's family in their efforts to provide the best nutritional options for your grandchildren.
✓ Follow infant hunger and fullness cues. Allow infants to decide when they want to eat and how much.
✓ Give infants the gift of healthful diet. As they begin their transition from breast milk or formula to solids, offer only nutritious foods and beverages.
✓ Spoil your grandbabies with loving attention instead of rewarding them with food.
✓ Share the message of good nutrition with other family members.

or as a component of foods offered as babies get older (Pak-Gorstein et al., 2009). Teachers can create awareness of the risk by providing access to educational materials. The California Department of Public Health's Infant Botulism Treatment and Prevention Program has created a brochure that explains the risk factors associated with this rare but deadly food poisoning (California Department of Public Health, Division of Communicable Disease Control, 2004).

Offering Alternate Milks

Families may choose to feed their babies with a product other than breast milk or infant formula. This is not advised because only breast milk and infant formula can meet the nutritional needs of infants. Researchers estimate that even though cow's milk is not recommended for young infants approximately 17% of families give infants cow's milk by the time they are $10\frac{1}{2}$ months of age (Grummer-Strawn, Scanlon, & Fein, 2008). Milk produced by cows should not be served until a baby has reached 12 months of age. Consuming cow's milk can lead to iron-deficiency anemia. This occurs because the content of iron in cow's milk is low, and cow's milk can cause intestinal blood loss in some infants. Cow's milk is also too high in protein, sodium, and potassium for infants, which puts stress on the kidneys. Finally, cow's milk is not supplemented with vitamins and minerals that babies need (Kleinman, 2009; Nevin-Folino et al., 2008; Samour & King, 2005).

Goat's milk should also not be used for the same reasons. In addition, goat's milk is very low in folic acid, which can lead to a form of anemia (Otten, Pitzi-Hellwig, & Meyers, 2006; Samour & King, 2005). Alternative vegetarian beverages designed for consumption by adults such as soy beverages, rice beverages, and other vegetarian milk substitutes are not acceptable for infants. These beverages may be too low in fat and they are not supplemented appropriately to meet the vitamin and mineral needs of infants. The protein content of rice milks and other vegetarian milk substitutes, except soy milk, is also very low (Nevin-Folino et al., 2008). It is important for teachers to offer guidance if parents suggest the use of alternative milks before a baby reaches his or her first birthday.

FEEDING THE INFANT: 6 MONTHS TO THE FIRST BIRTHDAY

Between 6 and 12 months of age, babies' bodies and diets undergo a significant transformation. The maturation of the gastrointestinal tract allows the infants' diet to evolve from the exclusive intake of liquids to the consumption of adult-like solid foods. Babies are gradually exposed to myriad aromas, flavors, and textures that come with the introduction of complementary foods. Complementary foods are any foods or beverages introduced to babies' diets that are in addition to breast milk or formula.

Introducing Complementary Foods

Babies should begin eating when they demonstrate developmental signs of readiness, usually between 4 and 6 months of age.

As infants grow their need for additional vitamins and minerals requires the introduction of additional foods and beverages. However, the ideal time for infants to start complementary foods has been a topic of ongoing discussion among different health organizations (AAP Committee on Nutrition, 2004; Butte et al., 2004; Samour & King, 2005). Introducing solids too early can result in increased risk for choking, eczema, and food allergies. Early introduction of solids may also displace the valuable nutrients found in breast milk and formula with the less needed nutrients found in the complementary foods, thus interfering with proper growth and decrease the duration of breast-feeding (Tarini, Carroll, Sox, & Christakis, 2006; USDA Food and Nutrition Service, 2002b; Grummer-Strawn et al., 2008).

The "window of opportunity" for introducing complementary foods *and* advancing flavors and textures occurs somewhere between 4 and 6 months of age through 10 months of age. Providing a gradual transition in food textures during this time frame decreases the risk of rejection of foods with more texture and consistency at a later date (Butte et al., 2004). Infants who are exposed to a variety of foods and textures are more accepting of new textures and new foods than those who are not (Blossfied, Collins, & Delahunty, 2007). For example, offering a baby pureed commercial infant bananas first, then well-mashed ripe bananas, and finally ripe bananas cut up into ¼-inch pieces is an example of a progression of textures. If this advance in texture does not occur, as babies get older, they may refuse more lumpy textures.

When introducing complementary foods, offering infants many different flavored foods such as pureed peas and commercially prepared carrots or green beans may increase their willingness to try new foods as they get older. Interesting too is research that suggests infants whose mothers eat a variety of foods during pregnancy tend to be more open to trying new foods. Changes in the flavor of the amniotic fluid that surrounds the baby before birth promote greater food acceptance when the baby begins eating solid foods. Breast-fed infants are also more likely to try different foods. This is because breast milk flavor changes with the types of food mothers consume (Beauchamp, 2009; Mennella, Jagnow, & Beauchamp, 2001). Pregnant and breast-feeding women who eat a healthy diet with a variety of foods keep their infants well nourished and contribute to success when the infant begins to eat solid foods.

Reflect back on the opening case scenario. The stomach pain and gas Manuel experienced were related to the switch from breast milk, which is easily digested, to formula. Manuel was also started on cereal at 3 months of age. This was too early for his immature digestive tract. The diet changes left him gassy and fussy. His situation illustrates the impacts of starting babies on solid foods too soon.

The World Health Organization (2009) recommends exclusive breast-feeding for the first 6 months of life and adding solids when the baby is 6 months old. The American Academy of Pediatrics and the American Dietetic Association agree with this recommendation but also acknowledge that infants can be developmentally ready to begin solids between 4 and 6 months of age (Butte et al., 2004; Nevin-Folino et al., 2008; Kleinman, 2009). Ultimately the decision to start complementary foods is linked to the infant's physiological and nutritional needs. A baby's gastrointestinal tract and kidneys are ready to handle solids by around 4 to 6 months (Butte et al., 2004). Up-and-down chewing and moving food around in the mouth with the tongue enhance the jaw and muscle development needed later for speech. Teachers and families can use signs of infant readiness as guidelines. In sum, the progression to solid foods can best be linked to the infant's developmental skills.

Linking Developmental Skills to Feedings

Transitioning from liquids to pureed solids, from pureed solids to textured foods, and then to the self-feeding of table foods are all eating achievements linked to developmental milestones. Infants are born with the instinctual skills that help them to survive. They know to turn reflexively toward the breast or bottle when their mouth or cheek is brushed by the nipple (rooting reflex) and will begin to suck when something touches the roof of their mouth (sucking reflex). When the lips are touched, the tongue comes out of the mouth (tongue thrust reflex) (USDA Food and Nutrition Service, 2002b). These reflexes help to ensure infants can latch onto a bottle or breast. In addition, infants possess a gag reflex, which is activated when food is placed in the back of the mouth and results in the ejection of the food.

Infants' development and growth can help determine when to initiate semisolid foods. For example, it is time to introduce complementary foods when infants develop the oral motor skills to consume semisolid foods safely (Samour & King, 2005). The tongue thrust and gag reflexes gradually start to diminish. Infants are able to move food around in the mouth with their tongues and they begin to use an up-and-down chewing motion (USDA Food and Nutrition Service, 2002b).

Table 5-3 provides helpful information for determining the types of foods to introduce based on developmental milestones. It shows the link between the developmental stages and appropriate progression of foods and texture types for infants and toddlers. The physical and eating skills are provided as a guide to selecting complementary foods. A visual relationship between the introduction of complementary foods and the transition in food texture and feeding styles is illustrated in Figure 5-8. This figure offers guidance on when to change textures and when to introduce finger foods and the use of cups.

The ability of an infant to grasp cereal with his hand (palmar grasp) and pick up individual oat cereal rings with the thumb and index finger (pincer grasp) indicates he is ready to try new textures and should be given opportunities to self-feed.

Table 5-3 | Infant Feeding Guidelines: Birth to 12 Months

Age	Developmental Milestones	Key Recommendations	Infant Feedings	Textures
Birth to 4 months	Infants are: born with sucking and rooting reflexes and know how to suck-swallow-breathe while feeding; head control develops.	The American Academy of Pediatrics (AAP) recommends exclusive breast-feeding for a minimum of 4 months but ideally up to 6 months of age. Breast-fed and formula-fed infants require 400 IU of Vitamin D/day until consuming 32 oz of formula or (after 12 months of age) 32 oz of milk.	Breast milk and/or formula.	Liquid
4–6 months	Infants can: hold head up, sit with support and push up on arms, move food in the mouth with tongue to aid in swallowing, remove food from spoon with lips, indicate hunger by moving toward food and fullness by turning head away. Tongue thrust reflex may initially be present but decreases with time.	Introduction of solid foods can start between 4–6 months. Infants who are born smaller or consume low amounts of breast milk may need the earlier introduction of solids. Single ingredient new foods are introduced one at a time. Observe for allergies. Wait 3–5 days before offering another new food. Iron-fortified cereal and pureed meats provide good sources of iron and zinc. Juice is not advised. Introduce a cup without a lid.	Breast milk and/or formula. Iron-fortified infant cereal, fruits, vegetables. If iron is needed, health care providers may recommend the addition of meats, egg yokes and legumes.	Pureed
6–8 months	Infants can: sit without support, chew using up and down movements and use tongue to move food to the side of the mouth for chewing, pick up and eat finger foods.	Juice is not needed but if offered, use only 100% juice and limit to 2–4 ounces per day. Begin the introduction of finger foods around 7–8 months (see Figure 5–11). Avoid foods that pose a choking risk.	Breast milk and/or formula. Iron-fortified infant cereal, fruits, vegetables, meats, egg yolks, and legumes.	Pureed and mashed foods, finger foods
8–12 months	Infants can: use pincer grasp to pick up food, and hold cup but still spills, crawl and pull selves to stand. Later infants can: stand alone, pull selves to standing and begins taking first steps. Up and down chewing is established. Infants want to feed themselves.	Offer more finger foods and soft cooked foods from the table. Offer at least three types of food per meal for variety. Adding extra sugar, fat or salt to foods is not necessary. Never use honey. Avoid foods that pose a choking risk.	Breast milk and/or formula. Iron-fortified infant cereal, fruits, vegetables, meats, egg yolks, and legumes.	Pureed, mashed, ground, or finely chopped foods, finger foods

Sources: *Pediatric Nutrition Handbook*, 6th edition, edited by R. E. Kleinman, 2009, Elk Grove Village, IL: American Academy of Pediatrics; *Pediatric Manual of Clinical Dietetics*, 2nd edition, edited by N. L. Nevin-Folina, 2008, Chicago, IL: America Dietetic Association; *The First Year: Nutrition for Your Baby*, by the American Dietetic Association, 2009, Chicago IL: American Dietetic Association; "The Start Healthy Feeding Guidelines for Infants and Toddlers," by N. Butte, K. Cobb, J. Dwyer, W. Graney, and K. Rickard, 2004, *The Journal of the American Dietetic Association, 104*(3), pp. 442–454; and *Infant Nutrition and Feeding: A Reference Handbook for Nutrition and Health Counselors in the WIC and CSF Programs, Appendix D: Guidelines for Feeding Healthy Infants, Birth to 1 Year Old*, by the U.S. Department of Agriculture, Food and Nutrition Service, Special Supplemental Food Programs, 2008, Washington, DC: U.S. Department of Agriculture.

It is helpful for teachers to share their observations of developmental signs of readiness and refer families to their health care professional if families express feelings of uncertainty about introducing new food experiences. In general, babies are ready to begin eating pureed foods when:

- They are able to hold their head steady and can sit with support.
- They are able to push up on straightened arms when lying on their stomach.
- They can draw in the bottom lip as a spoon is removed from the mouth.
- They can keep food in the back of the mouth and swallow rather than push it out with tongue.
- They can turn their head away when they are full (Butte et al., 2004; USDA Food and Nutrition Service, 2002b).

What if. . .
you had limited experience with babies and were assigned to provide care in an infant class? What questions might you have about feeding babies? What situations might cause you to worry? What resources could you turn to for advice?

Figure 5-8 Relationships Between the Introduction of Complementary Foods and the Transition in Texture and Feeding Styles

Age of Infant By Month	Birth 1 2 3	4 5 6	7 8	9 10 11 12
Age Grouping	Birth through 3 months	4 months through 6 months	6 months through 8 months	8 months through 12 months
Sequence of Introducing Foods	Breast milk or Infant Formula	Complementry Foods[a]		
Texture of Complementary Foods		Strained/Pureed (thin consistency for cereal)		
			Mashed	
				Ground/Finely Chopped
				Chopped
Feeding Style	Breastfeeding/Bottle Feeding			
		Spoon Feeding		
		Cup Feeding		
				Self Feeding/Finger Foods

Special note: ▇ represents the age range when most infants are developmentally ready to begin consuming complementary foods. The American Academy of Pediatrics section on breastfeeding recommends exclusive breastfeeding for the first 6 months of life. The AAP Committee on Nutrition recommends that, in developed countries, complementary foods may be introduced between ages 4 and 6 months. This is a population-based recommendation and the timing of introduction of complementary foods for an individual infant may differ from the recommendation.

[a]Complementary foods include infant cereal, fruits, vegetables, and meats and other protein-rich foods modified to a texture appropriate for the infant's developmental readiness.

Source: From *Infant Nutrition and Feeding: A Reference Handbook for Nutrition and Health Counselors in the WIC and CSF Programs*, National Agricultural Library, 2008, retrieved September 20, 2009, from http://www.nal.usda.gov/wicworks/Topics/Infant_Feeding_Guide.html#guide.

Understanding What to Feed Infants

Communication between families, teachers, and health care providers becomes important during infants' transition to solids. It is the family's responsibility to introduce new foods gradually into the baby's diet. Research does not support the introduction of complementary foods in any specific order. However, the American Academy of Pediatrics recommends infant cereals and pureed meats as important first foods because they introduce key nutrients, iron and zinc, which are important minerals in the diets of breast-fed infants (Devaney, Ziegler, Pac, Karwe, & Barr, 2006; Kleinman, 2009; Krebs, 2000).

The current practice for caregivers who feed infants is to introduce pureed meats late in babies' diet. When pureed meats are served, they are often mixed in commercial infant dinners. These combination meals have far less zinc and iron than pureed meats alone. A large survey of the dietary patterns of infants and toddlers showed that less than 10% of 7- to 11-month-old infants consumed pureed meats as a single-ingredient food (Krebs & Hambidge, 2007). Teachers can share with families the benefits of introducing fortified cereals and meats earlier in their babies' diets especially if they are breast-fed. Formula-fed infants receive the iron and zinc they require because these nutrients are included in the formula.

Single-ingredient foods should be introduced into infants' diets one at a time with a wait period of 3 to 5 days before introducing the next new food. This way if an allergy develops it is easier to identify the food that has caused it (Kleinman, 2009; Nevin-Folino et al., 2008). For example, after introducing rice cereal and offering it with success for 4 days, an infant might then progress to another cereal. Once all of the cereals have been introduced, meats might be a logical next step for breast-fed infants. A notebook entry or chart check-off system in which parents communicate the acceptability of a new food to the caregiver can be a helpful way to share which foods have been introduced. Figure 5-9 provides an example.

Fruit juices that are 100% juice can (but need not) be added to the diet at approximately 6 to 8 months of age. It is recommended that not more than 2 to 4 ounces be provided to infants per day. Juice should be introduced in a cup rather than a bottle. Commercial infant fruit desserts or pudding desserts, unlike pureed single-ingredient fruits, often contain added starches and sugar (sometimes in the form of concentrated fruit juice) and should be avoided (Nevin-Folino et al., 2008).

Figure 5-9 Infant Food Checklist

Baby's name _____

General guidelines to remember:
- Introduce the new food.
- Offer it for approximately 3 to 5 days before introducing another new food.
- Watch for signs of allergic reaction.
- Remember: Babies do not need fat, sugar, spices, or salt added to foods.

Check the appropriate boxes when you want your baby's teacher to begin a new food at school that the baby has been exposed to at home and tolerates.

Infant Cereal
- ☐ Rice cereal   ☐ Barley cereal   ☐ Oatmeal

Strained Meats/Poultry
- ☐ Strained chicken   ☐ Strained turkey   ☐ Strained beef or veal

Strained Vegetables
- ☐ Green beans   ☐ Sweet potatoes   ☐ Peas
- ☐ Squash   ☐ Carrots   ☐ Spinach

Strained Fruits
- ☐ Peaches   ☐ Prunes   ☐ Guava
- ☐ Applesauce   ☐ Apricots   ☐ Papaya
- ☐ Pears   ☐ Mango   ☐ Prunes
- ☐ Bananas
- ☐ Finger foods _____

_____

_____

Figure 5-10 Making Baby Food

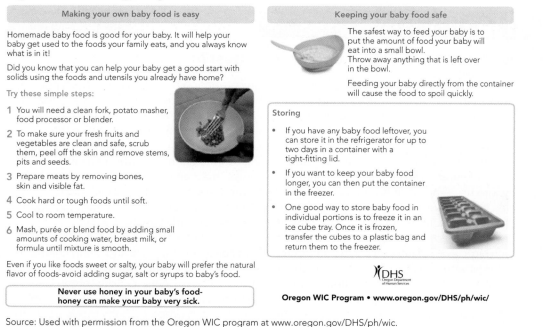

Making your own baby food is easy

Homemade baby food is good for your baby. It will help your baby get used to the foods your family eats, and you always know what is in it!

Did you know that you can help your baby get a good start with solids using the foods and utensils you already have home?

Try these simple steps:

1 You will need a clean fork, potato masher, food processor or blender.

2 To make sure your fresh fruits and vegetables are clean and safe, scrub them, peel off the skin and remove stems, pits and seeds.

3 Prepare meats by removing bones, skin and visible fat.

4 Cook hard or tough foods until soft.

5 Cool to room temperature.

6 Mash, purée or blend food by adding small amounts of cooking water, breast milk, or formula until mixture is smooth.

Even if you like foods sweet or salty, your baby will prefer the natural flavor of foods-avoid adding sugar, salt or syrups to baby's food.

> Never use honey in your baby's food- honey can make your baby very sick.

Keeping your baby food safe

The safest way to feed your baby is to put the amount of food your baby will eat into a small bowl.
Throw away anything that is left over in the bowl.

Feeding your baby directly from the container will cause the food to spoil quickly.

Storing

• If you have any baby food leftover, you can store it in the refrigerator for up to two days in a container with a tight-fitting lid.

• If you want to keep your baby food longer, you can then put the container in the freezer.

• One good way to store baby food in individual portions is to freeze it in an ice cube tray. Once it is frozen, transfer the cubes to a plastic bag and return them to the freezer.

DHS
Oregon Department of Human Services

Oregon WIC Program • www.oregon.gov/DHS/ph/wic/

Source: Used with permission from the Oregon WIC program at www.oregon.gov/DHS/ph/wic.

Some caregivers, with a goal to providing nutritious basic whole foods for babies, choose to make home-prepared baby food. This is an acceptable alternative that is cost effective and offers increased flexibility regarding types of ingredients and textures; however, food safety is an important consideration (Clemson Extension, 2009). Home-prepared infant foods should be made from fresh ingredients, cooked until soft and tender, pureed, and stored promptly. Food safe methods of food preparation and storage are particularly important in preparing foods for infants. (See Chapter 8 for guidelines on cooking, cooling, and storage of food.) Figure 5-10 provides guidelines on preparing and storing baby food that can be shared with families. The *Health Hint* describes some of the precautions to consider when preparing infant foods.

In summary, health experts have reached a general consensus on the following key points about introducing complementary foods:

• There is no evidence to support introducing foods in a particular order.
• There is no nutrition-related rationale to adding complementary foods before age 4 months.
• There is support for adding pureed meats or iron and zinc–fortified cereals to the diets of breast-fed infants at 4 to 6 months (Butte et al., 2004; Kleinman, 2009).

Understanding How to Feed Solids to Infants

An important goal for teachers and families is to create a feeding experience that continues to foster the feeding relationship. Feed babies at a pace that is comfortable for them. When feeding infants solid foods, consider the following practical recommendations:

• The teacher's hands should be washed before preparing and serving the meal, and the infant's hands should be washed before eating.
• Teachers should have space identified for feeding infants that includes high chairs with removable trays that can be easily sanitized.
• Babies should have specifically assigned and labeled high chairs.
• Babies should be placed in a high chair when fed unless they have special needs or disabilities. Sitting up straight with feet supported promotes proper swallowing and helps reduce the risk of choking.
• Use plastic-coated baby spoons with food placed on the tip of the spoon to make it easier to access and swallow.

MyEducationLab

Go to the Assignments and Activities section of Topic 2: Feeding Children in the MyEducationLab for your course and complete the activity entitled *Developmentally Appropriate Mealtimes for Infants.* How does the teacher ensure a positive mealtime experience for the infant in her care?

Health Hint

Is Homemade Baby Food Always Best?

Many families and early childhood teachers enjoy preparing baby food from fresh ingredients. They like the idea of knowing exactly what the infant is eating. They may make this choice because they prefer organic ingredients, have an abundance of fresh produce from home gardens, or want to save money. Making baby food is a healthful choice; however, adults who care for young children must be aware that chemicals, called *nitrates*, are found in some foods and water. Nitrates can be toxic to infants. Infants who consume unsafe levels of nitrates develop a type of anemia known as "methemoglobinemia" or "blue baby syndrome." The nitrates impact hemoglobin, a component of red blood cells, so that oxygen is not picked up as readily. The lack of oxygen in the blood causes a bluish cast to the skin. Babies younger than 3 to 6 months of age are particularly susceptible.

Where do the nitrates come from? Formula prepared with well water contaminated with high levels of nitrates can be the source of this condition. Families and family child care settings with wells should be sure to check the nitrate level in their well water. Some vegetables tend to be high in nitrate content. These include beets, carrots, green beans, spinach, turnips, collard greens, and squash. Preparing infant foods using these vegetables should be avoided during the first year of life. Commercially prepared baby foods are monitored for nitrate content and do not pose a risk. Additionally, infants do not receive high levels of nitrates in breast milk regardless of a mother's diet.

Sources: From *Starting Solid Foods,* by the American Academy of Pediatrics, 2008, retrieved December 6, 2009, from http://www.aap.org/bookstore/brochures/br_solidfoods_2008_sample.pdf; "Infantile Methemoglobinemia: Reexamining the Role of Drinking Water Nitrates," by A. A. Avery, 1999, *Environmental Health Perspective, 107*(7), pp. 583–586; "Infant Methemoglobinemia: The Role of Dietary Nitrate in Food and Water," by F. R. Greer, M. Shannon, Committee on Nutrition, and Committee on Environmental Health, 2005, *Pediatrics, 116*(3), pp. 784–786; and "Methemoglobinemia Caused by the Ingestion of Courgette Soup Given in Order to Resolve Constipation in Two Formula-Fed Infants," by F. Savino et al., 2006, *Annals of Nutrition & Metabolism, 50*(4), pp. 368–371.

- Place food in a small bowl for serving. Don't feed babies directly from a jar because this will contaminate the baby food.
- Always supervise the baby in the high chair. Never leave baby unattended.
- Remember, babies have small stomachs and, therefore, require small but frequent meals and snacks.

The CACFP provides other helpful guidelines on suggested meals and snack routines for infants (see the Appendix, CACFP Meal Pattern Requirements for Infants and Children).

Offering Finger Foods

The introduction of finger foods gives infants an opportunity to practice their developing fine motor skills. Finger foods can be introduced into diets when infants have developed the **pincer grasp** (the ability to pick up items using the thumb and forefinger). In addition, oral motor skills such as using the jaw to mash foods and moving food around from side to side in the mouth, are indicators that babies are ready to eat finger foods. This generally occurs between 7 and 8 months of age. Finger foods should be soft enough for babies to chew using their gums.

Cooperation between teachers and families is important as the infant is exposed to new textures, shapes, and sizes of food. A system should be in place to track what finger foods the infant has been fed. Cooked fruits and vegetables can be excellent first finger foods. NAEYC guidelines (2008) recommend cutting foods for infants into pieces no larger than ¼-inch squares to prevent choking. Teachers are also encouraged to evaluate each baby's chewing and swallowing skills when preparing and offering finger foods (NAEYC, 2008). As babies grow older and are exposed to wheat and milk, breads, cereals, and small pieces of cheese can be

pincer grasp
the developmental ability of infants to pick up items using thumb and forefinger

Figure 5-11 Examples of First Finger Foods

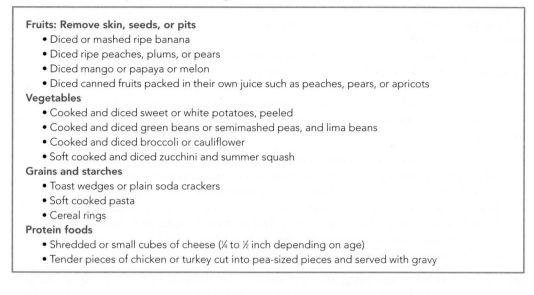

Fruits: Remove skin, seeds, or pits
- Diced or mashed ripe banana
- Diced ripe peaches, plums, or pears
- Diced mango or papaya or melon
- Diced canned fruits packed in their own juice such as peaches, pears, or apricots

Vegetables
- Cooked and diced sweet or white potatoes, peeled
- Cooked and diced green beans or semimashed peas, and lima beans
- Cooked and diced broccoli or cauliflower
- Soft cooked and diced zucchini and summer squash

Grains and starches
- Toast wedges or plain soda crackers
- Soft cooked pasta
- Cereal rings

Protein foods
- Shredded or small cubes of cheese (¼ to ½ inch depending on age)
- Tender pieces of chicken or turkey cut into pea-sized pieces and served with gravy

added to the diet. Some examples of finger foods are listed in Figure 5-11. When serving finger foods, the teacher can promote social interaction and introduce cognitive and language skills by for example, counting the pieces of food or identifying their colors or flavors.

Feeding Concerns in Older Infants

Older infants accomplish the transition from a milk-based diet to regular soft foods over an amazingly short period of time. Sometimes during this transition infants are challenged when the adults who care for them make inaccurate assumptions about the types of foods or beverages that should be offered. Teachers can share with families feeding practices that keep their babies healthy and safe.

Reducing the Risk of Choking

When planning meals for infants, it is particularly important to consider whether the food prepared might pose a choking risk. Although Chapter 8 discusses choking risks in young children and provides a list of high-risk foods to avoid, this section addresses the specific choking concerns of infants. Infants are new eaters and are developing oral motor skills at different rates.

Learning how to swallow solids and manipulating a challenging array of foods within the mouth are aspects of infants' developmental growth and maturity. It is important for teachers to be vigilant when textured foods are introduced. Teachers can reduce the risk of choking by ensuring infants are fed in a calm environment with limited distractions. For example, wiping off infants' faces before they swallow their last bite or putting food into their mouths while they are crying or laughing places babies at risk for choking. Likewise, medications for teething pain should not be applied before meals because gums, mouth, and throat can become numb. This can make swallowing more difficult.

Foods items used for teething can pose a risk too. For example, chicken bones, raw carrots, frozen bananas, bagels, and whole apples are not recommended. The following foods have characteristics that cause concern about choking in infants:

- Slippery foods that are round such as grapes and cooked carrots.
- Easy to inhale foods such as sunflower seeds, peanuts, raisins, popcorn, and corn kernels.
- Sticky, chewy foods such as peanut butter, fruit leathers, and gummy candy.
- Firm food that can wedge in the throat such as hotdogs, whole bananas, and bagels.
- Hard, dry foods such as pretzels and chips.

As older infants advance their eating skills, textured foods can be mixed with softer foods to aid in swallowing. For example, adding pureed carrots to rice, pureed sweet potatoes to finely diced turkey, or pureed peaches to alphabet pasta provides healthful, easy-to-swallow combinations.

Teachers may experience family members who don't support or understand the risks of specific foods. For instance, a parent might say, "Oh my baby does fine with grapes. She knows how to chew them" or "I always give him popcorn and he never chokes on it." It is an important responsibility of teachers to inform families if they notice feeding practices that put young infants at risk. For example, consider the following situation:

> Brittany, an 11-month-old baby, had not been coming to Patty's program for the past week. Her mother called to inform Patty that although Brittany was home and doing well, she had spent the past week in the intensive care unit being treated for pneumonia. Brittany had inhaled a sunflower seed that she grabbed from a bowl at a family picnic a couple of weeks before. Her mother thought Brittany had coughed it out, but the seed had remained in her lung and became a source of infection. A pediatric surgeon was able to remove the seed.

Brittany was lucky that she did not die. Because of the hazards of choking, early childhood programs should establish policies that prohibit foods that are choking risks from being served. The policy should include a descriptive list of foods that are not acceptable to serve to infants due to choking risk.

Introducing Foods That Are Low in Nutritional Quality

Eating habits are established early, and infancy is a critical time for starting these habits off right. However, sometimes adults who care for infants introduce solids that are low in nutritional quality or foods that are high in calories in relation to the nutrients they offer. A better choice is to offer foods that have high nutrient density. Nutrient density describes foods that have a high percentage of nutrients per serving size, but are not excessively high in calories. For example, mashed bananas are nutrient dense because they are a rich source of vitamin C, potassium and fiber and are low in fat and salt. Single-ingredient pureed infant foods are nutrient dense. The CACFP reimburses for only the use of infant foods that contain a single ingredient such as 100% fruit, and 100% vegetables with the exception of pureed meats, which can contain gravy but cannot be offered in a mixed commercial infant dinner (Oregon Department of Education, 2009).

high nutrient density describes foods that have a high percentage of nutrients per serving size, but are not excessively high in calories

Studies conducted on the eating habits of U.S. infants provide some astounding trends. As many as 50% of infants are exposed to French fries, candy, cookies, or cake by 1 year of age. In addition, 15% were consuming sweetened drinks such as soda or juice drinks (Grummer-Strawn et al., 2008). Introducing these foods at such a young age may establish preferences that contribute to excess fat and calorie intake among young children. These figures reveal that families need positive reinforcement and guidance in helping their infants establish healthful eating habits. Teachers play an informative role in helping families navigate the introduction of solid foods into the diet of babies and encouraging the introduction of age-appropriate soft cooked and pureed or mashed whole foods such as fruits, vegetables, and unprocessed meats and poultry. Program policies and procedures and CACFP guidelines set the tone for early childhood settings and create a nutritional ambiance that can favorably impact families' perceptions about foods.

Infants Learning about Food and Eating

Eating is a learning process. Infants learn about food if they are allowed to examine it. This may mean feeling the food by looking, touching, poking, squishing, smelling, and tasting it. Through these explorations infants are learning how to move food in their mouth, to chew, and to swallow. Allowing babies to self-feed when they indicate readiness is also a learning experience. It is also important not to force the intake of any foods. Babies are cautious about new foods and it may require up to 10 to 15 exposures before a new food is accepted (Butte et al., 2004). This learning process requires adults to be understanding and patient as new foods are introduced and to respect the baby's feeding cues for hunger and fullness. (Refer to Table 5-3 earlier in the chapter for feeding guidelines.)

An important part of the learning process is to expose infants to a wide variety of foods. This increases the likelihood that they will be open to eating new foods and learn to enjoy a balanced diet as they grow older. It is very important for teachers to model good eating behaviors because babies and children learn from what they see teachers do and what they hear teachers say. Consider the following scenario:

> Mary is in charge of the infant class. She takes a sip of the soft drink she has sitting on her desk. Jeremy an 11-month-old points to her can of soft drink but Mary says, "No, this is not for you Jeremy." Jeremy starts crying just as Rosalie, his mother, comes in to pick him up. Mary explains why Jeremy is crying. Rosalie replies, "Well I always share my soft drink with him. He loves it." What can Mary say?

Setting a good example and being a good role model are not always easy tasks. It requires a great deal of personal reflection and introspection to recognize when the behaviors modeled in front of children and families are not ideal. The best approach is to learn from situations like the one Mary experienced, and identify a better approach for next time.

Babies should be allowed to fully experience the food they are fed. Let them play with the food. The feel of food as well as the taste and smell of food all contribute to babies' learning experiences.

FEEDING INFANTS WITH SPECIAL HEALTH CARE NEEDS

Infants with health-related conditions sometimes face significant feeding challenges that can impact growth and development. These conditions may include developmental disorders and physical disabilities. Teachers and families along with health care professionals form a team in helping infants with health issues maintain a nutritious diet with sufficient calories for growth. They also strive to help infants acquire eating skills and behaviors that support good nutrition.

Infants with Feeding Problems

Infants are born with the instinctual ability to obtain nourishment from the breast or bottle by latching on, sucking, swallowing, and breathing in a synchronized manner. Infants with developmental delays, however, may not always be effective eaters. Feeding problems become apparent as they struggle with nursing or bottle feedings and perhaps fail to gain weight appropriately. Feeding problems are defined by the American Academy of Pediatrics as developmental disorders related to the mouth (Kleinman, 2009). Swallowing problems, discussed in Chapter 4, are abnormalities in the swallowing process. An infant who struggles with liquids and coughs or chokes during meals has symptoms of a swallowing disorder. Infants who gag on foods that need to be chewed, have a strong preference for smooth or crunchy foods, and but have no problems with liquids also show symptoms of a feeding problem (Kleinman, 2009).

Feeding problems can be either sensory or motor based (Kleinman, 2009). For example, some babies may have issues with oral sensitivity. Infants with oral hyposensitivity have less feeling within the mouth and are, therefore, less conscious of where food is once it is placed inside their mouths. Oral hypersensitivity, on the other hand, describes a condition in which infants are overly aware of foods placed in or near their mouths. For these babies, food brought near or into the mouth can cause a gag or bite-down reflex. These conditions can make mealtimes challenging for both baby and caregiver (Children's Hospital at Westmead, 2003).

feeding problems
developmental disorders related to the mouth

oral hyposensitivity
an oral motor condition is which infants have less feeling in the mouth and are not entirely aware of where food is when it is placed within the mouth

oral hypersensitivity
an oral motor condition in which infants are overly aware of foods placed in or near their mouths

oral motor delay
a developmental delay that can result in weak oral muscles and tongue movement such that difficulties occur in chewing

Babies with oral motor delays may have difficulties chewing due to weak chewing muscles. They may also have problems moving food around within the mouth due to uncoordinated tongue movement. This can result in choking or gagging (Kleinman, 2009). Teachers who suspect feeding issues or have concerns about an infant's ability to consume solids should confer with families and consider referral to an early invention team and the infant's health care provider. Collaboration with speech, physical, or occupational therapists can help identify and provide assessments of infants' feeding issues (University of Washington Center on Human Development and Disability, 2001).

Feeding Premature Infants

Premature infants may have special feeding needs. Infants are considered premature if they are born before 37 weeks of gestation. These fragile infants may have different nutritional requirements than the baby born full term. Premature infants should receive breast milk if possible. Breast milk offers immunological protection and improved developmental outcomes compared to formula. In premature infants (but not necessarily near-term infants), expressed breast milk can be fortified with special milk fortifiers to meet the higher protein, vitamin, and mineral requirements of growth (AAP, 2005; Kleinman, 2009; Samour & King, 2005). Premature infants who are not breast-fed are given special formulas developed to meet the higher nutrient needs necessary for appropriate growth.

corrected age
the number of weeks a baby is born early subtracted from the baby's current age in weeks

cleft lip
a birth defect in which the lip does not grow together

cleft palate
a birth defect that consists of an opening in the roof of the mouth

If families want teachers to prepare the formula in any way that deviates from standard mixing directions on the label or to add fortifiers to breast milk, a prescription from the health care provider with a clearly written out recipe is required. In some cases a demonstration by the parent on how to prepare formula may be helpful. Teachers should rely on the guidance of health care providers and parents on when to introduce solid foods for premature infants. As a rule, the introduction of solids for these infants should be based on developmental readiness, which may need to be based on of the baby's due date or corrected age as opposed to date of birth. A baby's corrected age is the number of weeks the baby was born early subtracted from his current age in weeks. For example, an infant who enters a child care center when he is 3 months old but was 3 weeks premature would have a corrected age of 2 months 1 week, or 9 weeks old. Generally infants who are premature begin solids by the time they are 6 months old corrected age and when they weigh about 13 to 15 pounds (Texas Department of Health/Nutrition Services, 1994). Premature infants are at greater risk than full-term infants for developing iron-deficiency anemia because their bodies have lower stores of iron. They should be fed a variety of foods rich in iron content when they are ready.

Figure 5-12 Position for Feeding a Baby with Cleft Lip or Cleft Palate

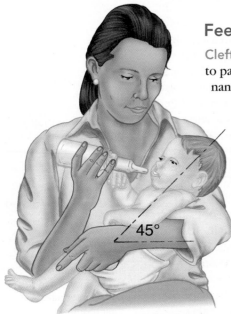

45°

Feeding Infants with Cleft Lip and Cleft Palate

Cleft lip and cleft palate are birth defects of the lip and mouth that contribute to particularly complex swallowing problems. During the first few weeks of pregnancy, the sides of the lip and mouth begin developing and eventually come together. In some cases the sides of the mouth or lips do not fuse properly, creating a cleft palate or cleft lip or both. A cleft lip is generally not problematic for babies because they can generally still suck and swallow. A cleft palate, however, consists of an opening in the roof of the mouth. Babies with a cleft palate cannot produce enough negative pressure to suck successfully (Christensen & Saal, 2005). This problem can be overcome with the use of special bottles that allow formula or breast milk to be squeezed into the infant's mouth. Elongated nipples can also be used to help with sucking and swallowing (see Figure 5-6, The Haberman or special feeder nipple). Figure 5-12 illustrates how to position a baby with cleft lip or cleft palate when feeding. Feeding in the upright position prevents breast milk or formula from getting in the nose.

A cleft lip is surgically closed at about 3 months of age and a cleft palate is repaired at about 9 months; therefore, caregivers should make

Figure 5-13 **Tips for Teachers: Feeding an Infant with a Cleft Lip or Cleft Palate**

- Have parents demonstrate the use of special feeding equipment. If an elongated nipple with flexible bottle is used, practice squeezing the bottle in the sink to get an idea of the correct rate of flow.
- Have parents present the first time you feed the infant.
- Feed infants in an upright position to prevent milk from going up into the nose and ear canals (see Figure 5-12).
- Select a comfortable seat and try to reduce distractions. Infant feeding may take longer.
- Pay extra attention to burping because more air may be swallowed while feeding.
- Be supportive of the mother who pumps and feeds the baby breast milk.
- Remember: The progression of solids in babies with cleft lip or cleft palate is the same as for comparably aged infants.

sure infants are well nourished prior to surgery (Christensen & Saal, 2005). Children with cleft lip and palate can be fed an adequate diet with the use of a few simple strategies such as those outlined in Figure 5-13.

FEEDING INFANTS FROM DIFFERENT CULTURES

The introduction of solids into the diets of infants is an important and celebrated event in many cultures. For example, one of children's first rites of passage in the Hindu religion is *annaprashana*. This ceremony celebrates the baby's first taste of solid food, a sweet rice dish prepared with milk. The baby sits in the lap of a family member and is fed the rice dish in a celebratory event that includes family and friends (Gazetteers Department, Government of Maharashtra, 2006). Families of the Jewish faith may also participate in a weaning celebration. This is a family affair that occurs at home and can include a religious blessing and songs. Someone other than the mother, such as the father, a sibling, or grandfather, has the honored role of feeding the baby solids for the first time (Diamant, 2005). In the United States, families might honor the start of feeding solids in a more casual way by taking photos of their baby's first bite of solid food and writing an entry about the event in the child's baby book or blog.

These types of meaningful celebrations create emotional connections to special foods. Many families subsequently have strong preferences for the traditional foods they prepare and those preferences extend to the food they choose to offer infants. For example, U.S. infants are traditionally offered dried infant cereal as the first solid food choice. This is followed by an orderly progression of pureed vegetables, followed by pureed fruits, and finally pureed meats and poultry. This was considered best practice until recent evidenced-based research revealed that there is no reason to introduce solid foods in any particular order and that pureed meats with their zinc and iron content have particular benefits for breast-fed infants (Kleinman, 2009). This example points out that all cultures can have traditions that include healthful and less than healthful trends.

In general, most cultures have traditional first foods that include some type of grain mixed with water, broth, or milk to create a gruel or porridge that is fed to infants (Encyclopedia of Food & Culture, 2006). Asian families, for example, may prepare congee, a thick rice-based soup to which a variety of ingredients can be added (Ramachandran, 2004). Hispanic families may choose to offer bean broth with small pieces of soaked tortilla, mashed beans, rice, and broth-based soups (Mennella, Ziegler, Briefel, & Novak, 2006). In the United States, rice, barley, and oatmeal are commercial baby cereals that are offered as traditional first foods.

Cultural food choices can have an impact on the health of infants. For example, in Lebanon, where sesame is a traditional component of the diet, allergies to this seed can be more severe than peanuts, leading researchers to ask, "Is sesame the 'Middle Eastern' peanut?" (Irani, Germanos, Kazma, & Merhej, 2006). Mercury poisoning was found in Chinese infants residing in Australia who were consistently fed contaminated fish in a traditional fish congee (fish mixed with a rice porridge) as an infant complementary food (Corbet & Poon, 2009). Some cultural

What if. . .

you had a family in your class that came from a country where food resources were very limited and they became upset when you allowed their baby to play with his food? How would you manage this?

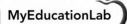
MyEducationLab
To assess your understanding of issues regarding infant feeding, go to the Book Specific Resources section in the MyEducationLab for your course, select *Nutrition, Health, and Safety for Young Children*, chapter 5 of the Study Plan, and then complete the multiple choice questions and activities.

traditions involve the adult chewing foods until it becomes gruel-like in composition, making it easier for babies to swallow. There have been rare reports of hepatitis B and HIV transmitted by this practice (CDC, 2009; Gaur et al., 2009).

These cultural practices point out the need for teachers to understand and respect the basis of food choice in different cultural groups. At the same time teachers have an important responsibility to ensure the safety and nutritional quality of foods offered to the infants in their care. Both families and teachers share a common goal, which is to support the optimal health and development of the infants in their care.

Summary

The impact of good nutrition during infancy is profound. Infants who receive too much or too little nourishment can suffer consequences that are immediate and long term. Growth and development can be negatively impacted, increasing the risk of chronic disease in adulthood.

Breast-feeding is the preferred feeding of choice and should be supported in early childhood education settings. Infant who are breast-fed should be introduced to fortified infant cereal and pureed meats and poultry between 4 and 6 months of age to help meet their needs for dietary sources of zinc and iron. Formula-fed infants can be fed one of several different types of formulas that run from standard to highly specialized products. Selecting which formula to use as well as the time at which to introduce solids is a decision shared by families and their child's health care provider.

When feeding infants breast milk, formula, or solid foods, the teacher needs to develop a supportive feeding relationship. Teachers need to be sensitive to feeding cues and recognize signs of hunger and fullness. The social-emotional development of infants is fostered by caring interactions with adults who are responsive to infants' emotional and physical needs. Feeding is a time for cuddling and chatting with babies. It should not be associated with negative feelings or events or linked to anger or frustration. A nurturing relationship between teachers and infants helps create a climate of understanding and trust, which in turn supports effective feeding.

Teachers help infants develop healthy attitudes toward foods by being sensitive to their feeding cues and supporting self-regulation of food intake. This means teachers allow infants to dictate when and how much they eat. Teachers also promote healthful eating habits by routinely exposing infants to a wide variety of nutritious foods. Teachers encourage infants to experience healthful eating by permitting them to use all their senses when they eat: to see, touch, smell, taste, and even play with food during meals and snack times.

Teachers have an important responsibility to work with families and their health care providers to accommodate infants with special needs. They also must make conscientious efforts to understand different cultural practices related to feeding infants. Close communication between teachers and families is the cornerstone of collaborative care and facilitates the optimal nourishment of infants.

Key Terms

Review Questions

1. Discuss the benefits of breast-feeding and how teachers can support the breast-feeding mother.

2. Describe the characteristics of different types of formula and explain how they are safely prepared, stored, and fed to infants.

3. Provide examples of infant feeding cues and describe how they relate to a trusting feeding relationship.

4. Explain the progression of infant foods and how this progression relates to infants' developmental skills.

5. Provide an example of an infant's special need that may cause a feeding problem. Describe how to meet the infant's nutritional needs.

Discussion Starters

1. How would you support a nursing mother who is returning to work but has a position with an inflexible schedule and a boss who is unsympathetic to the mother's breast-feeding goals?

2. A mother is hearing contradictory advice from friends, relatives, and health care professionals about introducing solid foods in her infant's diet. How would you help this mother without adding to the confusing advice she has already received?

3. A mother is feeding her infant a cultural dish that contains honey. How do you manage this situation in a culturally sensitive way while considering the safety of her infant?

Practice Points

1. Baby Matt is 6 months old. He is currently being exclusively breast-fed. His mother Jenna is wondering how to begin solids. This is her first baby and she doesn't want to make any mistakes. She is returning to college and will be leaving Matt at his teacher Fran's home child care program four mornings per week. Jenna asks Fran for advice. Using your knowledge of infant nutrition discuss how you will decide on an infant feeding progression that will meet Matt's needs. List the questions you might ask Jenna as you gather information for developing a feeding plan.

2. Using CACFP meal patterns for infants found in the Appendix, design a menu for a 10-month-old infant.

3. You are responsible for developing an activity for an infant class. You want the focus to be on exploring the tastes, colors, and texture of foods. Your class has a 6-month-old, an 8-month-old, and two 10-month-old infants. Plan an activity and explain the decisions you made as you prepared this lesson.

Web Resources

American Academy of Pediatrics
www.aap.org

Feeding Infants: A Guide for Use in the Child Nutrition Programs
www.fns.usda.gov/tn/resources/feeding_infants.html

Infant Nutrition and Feeding: A Guide for Use in the WIC and CSF Program
http://www.nal.usda.gov/wicworks/Topics/FG/CompleteIFG.pdf

La Leche League
www.llli.org

National Resource Center for Health and Safety in Child Care and Early Education
http://nrc.uchsc.edu

Feeding Toddlers, Preschoolers, and School-Age Children

chapter 6

Learning Outcomes

After reading this chapter, you should be able to:

1. Define the nutritional needs of toddlers and discuss how to manage eating issues typical of this age group.

2. Describe three strategies that enhance how preschoolers learn about nutrition.

3. Define how to create a quality nutritional environment for school-age children.

Laura, a teacher in the toddler class, is concerned about Michaela, an 18-month-old who attends her child care program. Michaela is a petite child who was born 4 weeks premature and has a history of poor growth. Her mother Hanna has strong ideas about what and how much Michaela should eat. She insists that Laura make sure Michaela eats all of her school lunch. She tells Laura, "Unless I watch her like a hawk she won't eat and the doctor says she needs to gain weight." Laura has tried a variety of ways to get Michaela to eat. She has used stickers on a chart. She has offered a special dessert if Michaela eats her entire meal. Michaela is often resistant and mealtimes have become stressful. Laura doesn't feel good about this, but she understands how important it is for Michaela to eat enough to gain weight. She is concerned that sometimes the only nourishment Michaela will consume is her milk.

The situation comes to a head when Michaela, in a fit of frustration, throws her lunch plate to the floor. Laura, with Hanna's enthusiastic agreement, requests a meeting with their program's dietitian, Christina, who oversees their food service. Christina recognizes that in spite of everyone's good intentions, Michaela is not eating well. She also knows that using forceful techniques for getting children to eat during mealtimes often backfires. She commends both Hanna's and Laura's efforts on behalf of Michaela to provide her with a healthful diet, but points out the missing link for success—allowing Michaela to decide what she is going to eat and how much. Hanna is very worried that this approach won't work but agrees to a trial period. At first Michaela does eat less but as she sees that both her mother and teacher are not pressuring her to eat, she begins to feel free to explore her food. Michaela is still not a big eater but things are improving. Laura feels better about the approach and mealtimes are less stressful. Hanna is pleased that her relationship with her daughter is better because they are no longer battling about food.

Children undergo tremendous growth and developmental change during their first year of life. They enter the toddler years having completed the transition from a single-ingredient, liquid-based diet to a multitude of solid foods, from being fed to self-feeding, and from basic instinctual communication to increasingly determined and directive requests for food. Their nutritional needs are in transition, too. Toddlers, preschoolers, and school-age children are not growing as rapidly as infants and, therefore, their eating style changes from a somewhat indiscriminant ingestion of calories to a more selective mode of eating in which preference plays an increasingly important role. Preschoolers continue to advance in the textures and complexity of foods they consume because better chewing skills allow them to eat most foods found in adult diets. School-age children learn to make independent food choices and put into practice the eating habits they acquired when younger.

The multitude of steps taken by caregivers to positively influence children's nutritional well-being can be sabotaged if children are given messages that undermine the nutritional care and guidance they have previously received. For example, children receive confusing mixed messages when they come to school sporting events where soft drinks, candy bars, and chips are served after learning about making healthful nutrition choices from their teachers and school food service staff.

To address these issues, we focus this chapter on the nutritional requirements unique to three age groups: toddlers, preschoolers, and school-age children up to age 8. We review child nutrition programs that are implemented in the school setting and discuss how they set the stage for healthy diets. We also describe methods for managing the unique challenges that can complicate feeding and impact children's nutritional status. Finally, we provide strategies for using the classroom and cafeteria environments to support healthful nutrition messages. These approaches ensure that wholesome nutrition habits and patterns take firm root, providing children with a lifelong foundation of healthful eating.

Toddlers do best when they are provided an array of healthful foods offered in a supportive manner. Allow toddlers to feed themselves but offer assistance when needed.

FEEDING TODDLERS

Feeding toddlers (children from 12 to 36 months) is different from feeding infants. The complacent attitude of infants with their easy acceptance of food can change when these children become toddlers. Appetites that were once consistent in infants become sporadic and selective in toddlers. In addition toddlers establish their autonomy by asserting themselves at mealtimes. Toddlers, like Michaela, are often ready and willing to do battle about what they will and will not eat. The wise caregiver remains neutral, does not overreact, and continues to offer nutritious foods in a supportive, nonconfrontational manner.

According to the American Dietetic Association (Nevin-Folino, 2008), caregivers should:

- Allow toddlers to explore foods as they become increasingly independent in their food choices.
- Promote pleasure and success while eating.
- Avoid succumbing to unreasonable demands.

Caregivers are also responsible for providing a healthful balanced diet that meets the nutritional needs of toddlers. To accomplish these goals, teachers need to understand the nutritional needs of toddlers, recognize characteristics of toddler diets, and know how to feed toddlers in culturally appropriate ways.

Understanding the Nutritional Needs of Toddlers

Toddlers need the same variety in their diets as adults. They have made the transition from strained infant foods to soft table foods. To address these changes, some adjustments to texture and size of pieces need to be made so that foods are easy and safe for toddlers to eat. As the amount of solid food eaten increases and begins to provide more of the nutrient needs of the toddler, the role of milk in the diet decreases. However, breast-feeding still has an important role, so teachers should support the mother who is committed to breast-feeding.

Supporting Extended Breast-Feeding

Mothers who continue to nurse their toddlers after their first birthday give their child the precious gift of time. Time is a commodity that is often hard to come by for women who work or go to school. Extended breast-feeding allows mothers and toddlers to reconnect after being apart and contributes to toddlers' social and emotional well-being by providing a special peaceful time of comfort and reassurance.

The health benefits of breast-feeding outlined in Chapter 5 continue to provide advantages to toddlers. In addition, breast milk develops a greater concentration of immunological components as babies mature. This may reflect natural adaptations in breast milk to accommodate the greater likelihood of toddlers being exposed to infections as they grow older (Stein, Boies, & Snyder, 2004). The *Safety Segment* provides an example of the benefits of breast-feeding during a flu pandemic. These are important reasons for teachers to support the efforts of breast-feeding mothers.

extended breast-feeding practice of mothers who continue to nurse their toddlers after they have reached 1 year of age

Balancing Toddler Diets

Often the quality of toddlers' diets will vary from day to day based on their food preferences and what they choose to eat. Caregivers can enhance the likelihood of toddlers eating well by planning meals that include a variety of wholesome foods. Fruits and vegetables in an assortment of rich colors are more likely to add nutrients such as vitamins A and C to the diet. Meats, poultry, and fish are rich sources of iron and zinc, and dairy products are excellent sources of vitamin D and calcium. A balanced diet for toddlers includes high-iron foods as well as fruits and vegetables rich in vitamin C, which aids in iron absorption.

What if. . .

you noticed, as a mother came to pick up her toddler, that he wanted to nurse but she was feeling awkward about her child's request? How would you respond?

Safety Segment

Breast Milk Protects during Flu Pandemics

Teachers may not recognize the true gift they provide infants and toddlers in their care when they support mothers who are breast-feeding. Even mothers may not fully understand how fortunate they are to be breast-feeding their babies and toddlers when infectious disease strikes because breast milk offers immunological protection for infants. It is so beneficial that the Centers for Disease Control and Prevention (CDC) encourages mothers to nurse their children even if they become ill with influenza. In addition, they recommend that mothers who are too sick to nurse use a breast pump to express and feed the breast milk to their child. The CDC makes the following recommendations for breast-feeding mothers who are sick with H1N1 influenza virus:

- Do not stop breast-feeding if you are ill because a mother's milk is made to help her child fight diseases.
- Breast-feed often and limit formula feeding if your child takes supplemental formula.
- Be careful not to cough or sneeze in your child's face.
- Wash your hands often with soap and water.
- Your health care provider may request that you wear a mask to keep from spreading influenza to your child.
- Provide pumped breast milk even if you are too sick to feed your child.

Source: *What Should Pregnant Women Know about 2009 H1N1 Flu (Swine Flu)*, Centers for Disease Control and Prevention, retrieved October 7, 2009, from http://www.cdc.gov/h1n1flu/guidance/pregnant.htm.

Understanding Portion Sizes for Toddlers

Children's appetites should dictate portion size. One rule of thumb to follow when deciding how much to serve at meals is that children need about 1 tablespoon of food from each food group per year of age (Hunter & Cason, 2008). The Child and Adult Care Food Program (CACFP) provides specific guidance regarding appropriate portion sizes for toddlers. Figure 6-1 provides a sample menu for toddlers using the CACFP guidelines for children ages 1 to 2. The menu includes foods rich in vitamins and minerals for meals and snack times. Menu planning is discussed in more detail in Chapter 7.

Teachers are often surprised at the small portions recommended for children. Usually these amounts are sufficient for most children; however, the CACFP recommendations describe minimum portions and some children may require or desire more food. It is important to serve enough food so that children feel satisfied. In the opening case scenario, Michaela's mother, Hanna, was very concerned about how much her daughter was eating. A helpful strategy that Laura might use is to show Hanna examples of the normal portion sizes for toddlers. This way Hanna's expectations for Michaela will be reasonable.

Recognizing Characteristics of Toddlers' Diets

Teachers who care for toddlers must make decisions about what foods are nutritious and also safe for children to eat. Even when teachers do not plan the menus, they must be in tune with characteristics that influence the diets for toddlers. This includes considering the

Figure 6-1 Sample Breakfast, Lunch, and Snack Menu Using CACFP Guidelines for Toddlers

MEAL	PORTION SIZE
Breakfast	
Oatmeal	¼ cup
Mixed berries	¼ cup
Milk, whole	½ cup
Lunch	
Milk, whole	½ cup
Simmered diced turkey with au jus	1 ounce (the size of a small matchbox)
Mashed sweet potatoes	2 tablespoons
Diced kiwi	2 tablespoons
Whole-grain bread	½ slice
Trans-fat-free margarine	½ teaspoon
Afternoon Snack	
Pizza muffin:	
Whole-wheat English muffin with tomato sauce and	¼ muffin
	1 tablespoon
cheese, shredded	½ ounce
Water	

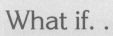

textures and consistency of food served, timing meals appropriately, and understanding the impacts of development on children's diets and eating capabilities.

What if. . .

you sat down to eat and someone served you a mixing bowl full of cooked rice? How would you feel? How do you think toddlers feel if very large servings are offered to them?

Modifying Food Textures and Consistency

The textures and consistencies of food need to be adjusted for toddlers, especially as they begin to master table foods. Meats, poultry, and other foods need to be chopped into small bite-size pieces no larger than ½ inch for toddlers through age 2 (National Association for the Education of Young Children [NAEYC], 2009, Standard 5.B.14a). The skin should be removed from fruits, and soft, easy-to-mash foods should be offered. Extra sugar, salt, and spices are not necessary.

Mixing textured foods with foods that have smoother consistencies can make them easier for toddlers to swallow. For example, young children do well with casseroles, stews, and spaghetti sauces over pasta. Choosing soft foods that don't fall off spoons such as cooked cereal, refried beans, cottage cheese, and yogurt can help toddlers feel more successful when they eat. Foods that fall off the spoon easily such as peas and gelatin should be avoided.

Timing of Meals

Toddlers still have small stomachs. They are, however, ready to shift from the demand feeding of infancy to more scheduled meals. Offering three meals plus snacks every 2 to 3 hours provides toddlers ample opportunity to refuel. This routine is also helpful because of toddlers' variable appetites. In fact, the NAEYC recommends that meals and snacks be least 2 hours but not more than 3 hours apart (NAEYC, 2008). This is helpful information to share with families whose toddlers are selective eaters. In the opening case scenario, one strategy Laura can use to reassure Hanna about her daughter's eating habits is to explain the toddlers' need for frequent meals and snacks. This way Hanna will know that even if Michaela doesn't consume very much at mealtime, she will soon have another opportunity to eat. Michaela may be more motivated by hunger to eat her snack later on.

Teachers need to evaluate the eating skills of children and make decisions about the appropriateness of food served. This 19-month-old has no problems managing the zucchini sticks.

Understanding Impacts of Development

Children's developmental skills influence their ability to negotiate biting, chewing, and swallowing certain foods. For example, a 14-month-old toddler will have different eating skills than a 19-month-old. The 19-month-old may have no problems managing thinly cut zucchini sticks, whereas the 14-month-old will do better if the zucchini is steamed and cut into small pieces. Toddlers' willingness to eat also changes as they grow and develop. This willingness is impacted by a variety of factors, including the child's growth rate, preference for "sameness," and changes in the child's perceptions of taste.

Decrease in Growth Rate A toddler's rate of growth is slower than during the infant period. Because of this the child's food intake decreases. This natural decrease in eating is sometimes seen as having a poor appetite or being picky.

The Need for "Sameness" Toddlers are busy maturing, developing, changing, and learning many new skills. Sometimes routine foods provide comfort and security during times of rapid change and development (Zero to Three, 2009). Toddlers may feel secure and comfortable with their mashed potatoes mixed with peas and want to hold off on trying new foods.

Changing Taste Perceptions Taste buds are located on the roof of the mouth, the cheeks and tongue. Toddlers perception of bitter tastes is more sensitive than infants whose taste buds are not fully matured and adults whose sensitivity to taste has begun to decrease with age. Research suggests that there are variations in the ability to taste bitter. Some children may taste bitter more strongly than others and therefore their food preference is not within their control (Bell & Tepper, 2006). Spinach, broccoli, brussels sprouts, cabbage, and grapefruit may have flavors that are too strong for some toddlers. Teachers need to be patient and understand that eating patterns are influenced by a toddler's stage of development.

Understanding How to Feed Toddlers

Toddlers experience significant developmental transitions as they strive to establish their independence. They are increasingly mobile and may occasionally show their autonomy through challenging behavior. "No" may become a well-used word in their vocabulary. Teachers recognize that these responses are natural expressions as toddlers begin to learn to make their own decisions. Sometimes these first steps in learning to make choices show up in the realm of eating. Teachers are better able to help promote positive eating habits if they recognize and anticipate potential feeding challenges and are prepared to address them.

Selective Eaters

Selective eaters are children who accept a very limited variety of foods, eat small portions, and may not be very interested in eating (Chatoor, 2009). This eating pattern is sometimes called picky or finicky. Selective eating, however, is relatively common in the toddler age group and is considered normal.

Before labeling children as selective eaters, teachers should reflect on normal toddler eating behavior and recognize that children's previous eating patterns are undergoing changes as they mature. Some selective eaters limit food choices to such an extent that teachers may become concerned about the nutritional adequacy of the child's diet. The best way to determine if the problem is a significant issue is to assess the child's growth patterns using a growth chart. If children are growing at a normal rate, then they are getting sufficient calories to grow and develop in spite of their selective eating habits. For many toddlers choosy eating is a temporary phase. For some it can become a long-term pattern that may require intensive intervention using a team approach that includes health care providers, families, and teachers (Williams, Hendy, & Knecht, 2008).

selective eaters
children who make very limited food choices

Food Neophobia

Food neophobia refers to fear of new foods. Toddlers are often suspicious of new foods. This fear may be an adaptive behavior that has historically protected young children from eating poisonous substances (Cooke, Haworth, & Wardle, 2007). In two different studies that looked at pairs of twins and their fear of new foods, a strong genetic tendency toward food neophobia was observed. The inheritability rate ranges from 66% to 78% (Cooke et al., 2007; Knaapila et al., 2007). In other words, children may inherit their fear of new foods from their relatives. A mother, for example, may very well be accurately assessing the situation when she states, "He eats just like me. I was always a picky eater."

In spite of this likely genetic tendency, if children are introduced to a variety of new foods early on and given ample exposure to these new foods, it can help overcome their hesitations about trying something new. Teachers understand that various and repeated exposures to any new concept help children to learn. The same holds true for learning to accept new foods. It may take 10 to 15 exposures or more before young children are confident enough to try new foods (Ellyn Satter Associates, 2009). Toddlers also benefit from having role models (teachers or peers) who demonstrate pleasure in eating a variety of foods (Wardle & Cooke, 2008).

food neophobia
term used to describe fear of new foods

Another strategy is to offer new foods along with foods toddlers already like. For example, 2-year-old Shawn, who attends a family child care program, does not like many vegetables. When his teacher Ruby offers him vegetables she also offers diced soft fruits because she knows Shawn really likes fruit. This takes the pressure off of Shawn because there is something available that he likes to eat. He is able to try the new food without the pressure of hunger. Figure 6-2 provides additional ideas for teachers to help remove pressure while giving toddlers time to learn and get used to new foods.

Figure 6-2 Strategies for Encouraging the Selective Eater

Strategies for the eating challenge "I don't like vegetables!"
✓ Seat the child next to a child or teacher who likes vegetables.
✓ Offer vegetables with familiar foods; for example, add grated carrots to spaghetti sauce.
✓ Provide enjoyable opportunities to explore foods: classroom gardens, taste tests, cooking projects.
✓ Serve vegetables with condiments: for example, low-fat ranch dressing or yogurt.
✓ Serve vegetables in child-friendly ways; for example, make a smoothie using fruits and vegetables.

Strategies for the eating challenge "I don't like meat!"
✓ Add meat to combination dishes: ham with macaroni and cheese, beef and bean burrito.
✓ Offer high-protein alternatives: peanut butter, beans, peas and lentils, tofu, tempeh, and eggs.
✓ Offer fork-tender meats such as braised beef or pork or chicken stew with gravy.
✓ Serve meats with condiments: ketchup, barbecue sauce, salsa, cheese.

Strategies for the eating challenge "I don't like milk!"
✓ Serve milk cold and with a straw.
✓ Provide yogurt or cheese as calcium-rich alternatives.
✓ Serve flavored milk.

Strategies for the eating challenge "I refuse to eat a meal!"
✓ Ask child to sit at the table and visit with the group; allow children to eat the amount they want (even if the amount is nothing).
✓ Do not offer alternatives to the meal (except for required special diets).
✓ Do not offer any food until the next snack or mealtime.

Strategies for the eating challenge "I will only eat certain favorite foods (food jag)!"
✓ Continue to offer the basic program menu food items.
✓ Avoid rewards for eating particular foods.
✓ Be patient. Food jags usually go away.

Food Jags

food jag
the persistent eating by young children of a limited number of favorite foods for a period of time

A food jag occurs when toddlers select a very limited number of favorite foods to eat and reject all others, including foods they liked in the past. Sometimes a well-loved favorite will suddenly no longer have appeal and another food will take its place. Teachers and families who recognize a food jag should try to focus on what the children are still eating rather than focusing on what they are no longer eating. It may become evident that, although the child's food selections are limited, there may be three or four choices from each food group that the child still accepts. Teachers should not draw attention to this eating behavior because it may prolong the food jag. Just as in the case of the selective eater, it is important to offer a variety of foods from each of the food groups.

Teachers may be concerned about conflicts with CACFP recommendations and reimbursement guidelines when children experience food jags and refuse to eat a particular food group. The *Policy Point* discusses how to navigate the CACFP when children are selective eaters or during a food jag.

Families and teachers may also become concerned that the quality of the child's diet is inadequate. Families who are concerned about a prolonged food jag can obtain advice and reassurance from the child's health care provider.

Division of Responsibility in Feeding

Responsibility for healthful eating is shared between teachers and children. Teachers are responsible for what children eat, when they eat, and where they eat. Children are responsible for whether they eat and how much (Satter, 2000). Teachers provide leadership and structure in eating, while keeping a focus on the nutritional quality of the diet. Children's responsibility relies on their innate ability to select and eat the amount of foods needed to maintain growth and a healthful weight (Satter, 2000).

What if. . .
you had an older toddler in your classroom who consistently refused to sit at the table for breakfast? How would you handle the situation? What if the program director was pressuring you to have all of the children sit down together so the meals can be counted for CACFP reimbursement purposes?

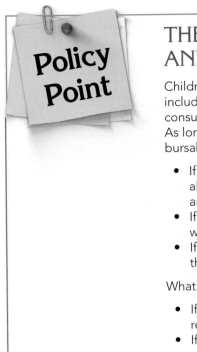

Policy Point

THE CHILD AND ADULT CARE FOOD PROGRAM AND THE PICKY EATER

Children's programs can obtain CACFP reimbursement only if all of the required food groups, including milk, are offered at each meal. Teachers may be concerned that children need to consume foods from all food groups in order to receive reimbursement. This is not the case. As long as the appropriate foods are served, programs are able to count the meals as reimbursable. But what if a child can't drink milk?

- If a child has a medical reason for not drinking milk, such as lactose intolerance or milk allergy, a health authority can provide documentation that allows the program to make an appropriate substitution and still receive CACFP reimbursement.
- If the child simply doesn't like milk, programs can still claim a reimbursement if the milk was offered but refused.
- If, however, families request that no milk be served and ask that juice be offered instead, the program cannot get CACFP reimbursement for that meal.

What about the child who refuses to eat a meal?

- If the child sits down and is offered a meal but chooses not to eat, the program can still receive reimbursement for this meal.
- If the child refuses to sit down at the table for a meal, the program cannot receive reimbursement.

When teachers seek to impose their will on children, negative repercussions may result. Children may become compliant and potentially overeat, or display defiance and not eat enough. Children should not feel pressured to try a new food. Teachers may be surprised to learn that this means not even requiring children to take a "no thank-you bite" or clean their plate. Allowing children to regulate their own food intake preserves the feeding relationship and helps children become competent eaters. Competent eaters are children who feel positive about foods and eating, are able to accept an increasing variety of different foods, and understand their internal food cues. Competent eaters know when they are hungry and when they are full (Satter, 2007).

In the opening case scenario, Hanna and Michaela had not established a division of feeding responsibility. This was because Hanna did not trust Michaela to eat enough and the doctor confirmed her fears. In her well-intentioned goal of trying to get Michaela to eat, she applied pressure and was met with resistance. Laura contributed to the problem too by taking on Hanna's role as food enforcer when Hanna wasn't there. With input from the dietitian, Laura and Hanna were able to pull out of the food battle and allow Michaela the freedom of choice. Figure 6-3 provides a summary of how teachers can support the division of feeding responsibility in the early childhood and school settings.

Weaning from the Bottle

Some toddlers struggle with the transition to solid foods. They find comfort in the bottle and prefer to get their calories from milk or juice. Excessive milk or juice consumption, however,

The division of feeding responsibility allows children to master the acceptance of a new food on their own time line.

Figure 6-3 Division of Responsibility in Feeding

Teachers' Responsibilities: What, When, and Where
- Provide young children with structure when eating meals.
- Meals should be routine and include snacks in between meals.
- Meals and snack should be consumed in a designated area.
- Avoid menu substitutions or "short-order cooking" unless there is a medical reason.
- Serve family-style meals with the teacher socializing and modeling healthful eating.
- Avoid food or drinks between meals or snacks except for water.
- Minimize distractions so teachers and young children can enjoy eating together.

Children's Responsibility: How Much and Whether
- Allow children to self-serve while assisting them to take what they will realistically eat. Do not restrict how much they eat except as it relates to fair distribution of food between all children at the table. There should be enough food available however to allow them to have more of any food if they want it.
- Avoid the "no thank you" bite which is a control tactic that interferes with food acceptance because it takes away the child's joy in mastering a new food and puts pressure on the child.
- Let children decide what they would like to eat.
- Let children decide how much they want to eat from the food adults have put on the table.

Source: Adapted with permission from *Child of Mine: Feeding With Love and Good Sense.* Copyright © 2005 by Ellyn Satter, MS RD LCSC BCW, owner Ellen Satter Associates. www.EllynSatter.com.

What if. . .

you observed a colleague pressuring a child to eat? What if the colleague said she was unconvinced of benefits of the division of feeding responsibility approach? How would you respond?

can blunt the appetite for solid foods. In the opening case scenario, a contributing factor to Michaela's poor food intake was her reliance on milk. Her preference for milk and her mother's concern that Michaela consume some form of nutrition prevented Michaela from taking interest in her food. Although milk is a rich source of nutrients, including calcium, it does not meet all of the vitamin and mineral needs of young children. For example, milk is not a good source of iron. Children who drink too much milk may not eat enough nutritious foods rich in iron, which can lead to anemia.

It is also important for children to wean from the bottle to reduce the risk of dental cavities and avoid a lag in the development of appropriate feeding skills. The American Academy of Pediatrics recommends weaning children from a bottle by 12 to 15 months of age (Kleinman, 2009). Teachers can help support weaning by collaborating with families and making sure a consistent message is sent to toddlers both in the home and program setting. Figure 6-4 provides strategies teachers and families can use to support the weaning process.

Delayed weaning from the bottle creates risks for dental cavities because of the constant exposure of teeth to beverages that contain sugar.

Switching to Whole Milk

It is very important for infants to receive breast milk or formula during their first year of life. Once they reach their first birthday, they are ready to make the transition from formula to whole milk. Breast-fed toddlers may also be offered whole milk, however mothers may choose to continue to breast-feed. The CACFP and Women, Infants, and Children (WIC) programs recommend that toddlers receive whole milk until 2 years of age (U.S. Department of Agriculture [USDA] Economic Research Service, 2002; USDA Food and Nutrition Service, 2009e). Skim, 1%, and 2% milk may be too low in fat content to support an adequate rate of weight gain and growth. The fat and cholesterol in whole milk may support neurological development. The fat in whole milk also aids in vitamin A and D absorption. However, points of view differ concerning the fat content in milk provided to toddlers. The *Health Hint* describes some of the questions raised by health authorities regarding the type of milk that should be offered to toddlers.

Figure 6-4 Strategies for Weaning from the Bottle

When:
Offer formula or breast milk from a cup starting at 6 months and begin the weaning process by around 12 months.

How:
1. Select one meal or snack time to introduce a cup. Use the cup at this meal for 1 week. Discuss with parents which meal to start substituting a cup for a bottle.
2. Every week substitute a cup for a bottle at another meal. Coordinate with parents which meal and what type of cup to use.
3. Assist the child to hold the cup and sip the liquid.
4. A toddler may still need assistance with self-comfort measures. Offer alternatives such as a pacifier, soft blanket, stuffed animal, and extra hugs and cuddles.
5. A consistent approach should be used at home and school.

Source: Based on *UCSF Children's Hospital's Baby Bottle Weaning*, Copyright © 2002–2007, by The Regents of the University of California, at http://www.ucsfhealth.org/childrens/edu/bottleWeaning.html.

Health Hint

The Fat Content of Milk: What's Best for Children?

The general consensus among health authorities is that when children reach 2 years of age, the fat content of the milk they consume should be gradually decreased from whole milk (4% butterfat content) to skim or 1% milk. This goal is promoted in an effort to introduce a heart-healthful diet and prevent obesity in children. But recommendations become less clear for toddlers between 1 and 2 years of age. Issues under consideration include the following:

- Some health authorities discourage low-fat (2% or 1%) or skim milk because it is believed that fat and cholesterol in a child's diet is beneficial for central nervous system development and provides adequate calories for growth.
- The American Academy of Pediatrics suggests that when infants have a family history of overweight, obesity, or heart disease, it is appropriate to serve 2% low-fat milk.
- The American Heart Association, whose mission is focused on preventing coronary artery disease, also advises 2% milk for children after age 1.

Teachers should follow the guidelines provided by governmental agencies and the recommendations of the USDA Food and Nutrition Service and be open to individualizing practices for toddlers as advised by the child's health care provider and in collaboration with families.

Sources: "Dietary Recommendations for Children and Adolescents: A Guide for Practitioners: Consensus Statement from the American Heart Association," by the American Heart Association, 2006, *Pediatrics, 117*(2), pp. 544–559; "The Start Healthy Feeding Guidelines for Infants and Toddlers," by N. Butte et al., 2004, *Journal of the American Dietetic Association, 104*, pp. 442–454; "Lipid Screening and Cardiovascular Health in Childhood," by S. R. Daniels, F. R. Greer, and the Committee on Nutrition, 2008, *Pediatrics, 122*(1), pp. 198–208; and *Dietary Guidelines for Americans, 2005*, by the U.S. Department of Health and Human Services and U.S. Department of Agriculture, 2005, retrieved September 1, 2009, from http://www.health.gov/dietaryguidelines/dga2005/document/pdf/DGA2005.pdf.

Exploring Cultural Differences in Feeding Toddlers

Teachers, families, and the children who attend early childhood programs come from a wide array of cultural backgrounds. Teachers who are familiar with their own cultural perceptions and seek out information and knowledge about other cultures are better able to understand and support the differences in how children are introduced to food. They are also

Children's cultural practices may influence how they eat and when they are served meals.

better able to appreciate the family eating habits. For example, people eat food with their hands in Bangladesh, India, Nepal, and Pakistan, whereas people in Asian countries use chopsticks and spoons (Luitel, 2006). Some cultures sit on the floor to eat meals or serve themselves from a communal bowl. Understanding family eating practices helps teachers recognize these influences on toddlers' feeding skills and behaviors at mealtimes.

Nutrition practices in food selection can vary as well. In China and in Western African cultures, milk is not used as a beverage and limited milk is used in cooking (Sizer & Whitney, 2006). This places toddlers at risk for vitamin D deficiency. In Hispanic cultures milk is often considered an ideal food and it is believed that children can never drink too much milk. Weaning from the bottle is often delayed, putting Hispanic children at risk for iron-deficiency anemia (Brotanek, Schroer, Valentyn, Tomany-Korman, & Flores, 2009).

Teachers need to use culturally sensitive approaches when discussing family food practices and agree on the approaches that will be used in the school setting. Teachers should also support healthful traditional food practices and find ways to incorporate diverse foods in the children's menu at school. This can be accomplished by planning menus that include foods that reflect cultural preferences or special cultural occasions, and planning social events such as potlucks where families can share special cultural dishes to promote cultural awareness.

What if. . .

a 2-year-old child from India in your class wouldn't use eating utensils? What would you do?

Understanding the Teacher's Role in Promoting Healthful Eating Habits

The foremost nutrition goal for feeding toddlers is to establish a foundation of eating habits that supports immediate growth and long-term health. Teachers can achieve this goal by linking developmental skills to feeding skills and by being good role models.

Linking Developmental Skills to Feeding Skills

Teachers develop a keen understanding of child development. They assess and recognize signs of readiness for advancing skills in all realms of children's lives including eating. They understand that children develop eating skills at different rates. Being attuned to children's development helps teachers make decisions about what and how to feed toddlers. It also prepares teachers to use a variety of strategies to encourage healthy eating habits. Table 6-1 describes the link between physical, social–emotional, and intellectual development and approaches to feeding toddlers. The *Teaching Wellness* feature provides specific examples of ways teachers can help children experience new foods while they learn about nutrition.

Teachers as Role Models

Toddlers seek to imitate the adults in their lives. This means that teachers are important role models, and that children are watching what you eat. Teacher behaviors influence the choices they make. In addition, modeling pleasant interactions during mealtime introduces toddlers to appropriate eating behaviors. Providing opportunities for toddlers to self-feed and self-serve promotes competence and accomplishment.

Teaching Toddlers about Nutrition

Toddlers are curious and learn best when abstract concepts are a part of everyday tangible experiences. Some of the diverse ways that toddlers learn about food and eating occur when they are exposed to healthful, colorful meals rich in aromas, tastes, and textures.

MyEducationLab

Go to the Building Teaching Skills and Dispositions section of Topic 2: Feeding Children in the MyEducationLab for your course and complete the activity entitled *Analyze the Developmental Appropriateness of Children's Mealtime Experiences*. As you work through this learning unit, consider what differences you see in the children's feeding capabilities in the different classroom settings.

Table 6-1   Developmental Influences on Toddlers' Eating and Relevant Teacher Strategies

Development	Feeding Strategies for 12- to 24-Month-Olds
PHYSICAL	
Rate of growth decreases.	Toddlers are more selective and eat less than infants. Offer variety and age-appropriate portions.
Toddlers tend to eat frequently throughout the day.	Smaller frequent meals are more common. Snacks are desirable and necessary. Avoid daylong access to bottles or toddler cups filled with calorie-containing beverages. This can cause problems with dental decay and decrease appetite for food.
Most begin walking by 14 months.	Attention span can be short when it comes to eating as toddlers desire to practice new motor skills. Distractions should be kept to a minimum. They are expending calories as they move and grow, and adequate calorie intake is important.
Most feed themselves but still spill on occasion.	Toddlers should be given a cup and spills should be expected. They should be allowed to self-feed but assistance should be available when they need it.
SOCIAL-EMOTIONAL	
Toddlers want to do things independently.	Allow them to select what they want to eat. Offer choices but not too many. Allow them to practice eating skills and to select age-appropriate foods from a healthful array offered by caregivers.
Frustration can lead to temper tantrums.	Provide gentle guidelines for mealtime behavior. Do not pressure toddler about which food to eat or force food intake. Never feed a crying child. Offer meals that are easy for toddlers to eat to promote feelings of success rather than frustration.
They enjoy independent play rather than playing with other children.	Although meals are increasingly social, toddlers will focus on meeting their own needs.
Sharing is still challenging and most are very possessive.	Each child should have his or her own highchair and when old enough to sit at the table his or her own space and place setting. Family-style meal service helps toddlers learn to take turns and share food from a common serving bowl.
Remembering rules is still not possible.	In a positive manner remind about mealtime rules such as washing hands, sitting down together, not licking the serving spoon, etc.
They become more self-aware and start to feel emotions such as jealousy, affection, pride, and shame.	Help them to feel proud of their eating skills. Do not offer blame when spills occur. Recognize eating skill achievements such as "You are learning to drink from a cup."
They become more fearful.	Toddlers may be afraid to try new foods. Offer food without pressure. It takes many exposures before toddlers will accept a new food. Offer a new food along with a food that they like.
They benefit by having routines and schedules.	There should be a schedule for when and how meals and snacks are served. Mealtime procedures should follow a typical beginning, eating, and ending sequence of events.
INTELLECTUAL	
Toddlers are curious.	Offer many different types of foods with various flavors, textures, tastes, and smells. Allow them to touch, taste, squeeze, drop, and overall experience the food. Food may go in the mouth and out again. Toddlers learn through these exploratory activities.
When they want something, they will point to it.	Be responsive to toddlers' communication attempts. When they point at a food, verbalize their request: "You are pointing at the yogurt. Do you want yogurt?" Teaching basic sign language can help toddlers communicate when they are hungry and when they are full.
They can identify familiar objects by name and begin to use two-word sentences.	Identify foods, eating utensils, and other toddlers sitting at the table by their names to facilitate language skill development. Use typical words associated with mealtimes such as *please* and *thank-you*.
No is an important word in their vocabulary.	Set reasonable limits. Redirect negative emotions such as "You don't want that bread but you really like the carrots."

(Continued)

Table 6-1	Developmental Influences on Toddlers' Eating and Relevant Teacher Strategies (Continued)
Development	**Feeding Strategies for 12- to 24-Month-Olds**
They can name familiar pictures.	Read children's books that have themes in which children can identify different types of food.
They begin to use items for their intended function.	Demonstrate for toddlers how to use spoons and forks. Assist them when they drink beverages from a cup. Offer them a napkin to wipe their face.
They have a short attention span.	Limit distractions such as TV and parents who arrive to pick up children near mealtime.
Toddlers are very active.	Toddlers cannot sit for very long. Mealtimes vary but 20 to 30 minutes provides time for eating while not stretching mealtime beyond toddlers' limits. Do not allow toddlers to leave the table with food (either in the mouth or carried in the hand) because this can pose a choking risk.

Source: Development portions of this table from The National Network for Child Care—NNCC, by C. Malley, (1991). University of Connecticut Cooperative Extension System, *Toddler Development (Family Day Care Facts series). Amherst, MA: University of Massachusetts. Used by permission.

Participating in family-style meal services helps toddlers to establish positive mealtime behaviors and develop social skills such as sharing, passing food, and saying "please" and "thank-you." Mealtime in the classroom provides opportunities for toddlers to practice fine motors skills, such as spreading, pouring, and grasping foods with tongs. Mealtime is also an important time to introduce diverse foods and familiar foods prepared in different ways. Helping with cleanup fosters self-help skills as children put dishes into a tub and wipe their place at the table after they eat.

Classroom activities provide opportunities for children to have direct hands-on experiences with food-related topics. Activities that introduce toddlers to nutrition concepts include simple food preparation tasks that allow them to stir, cut soft foods, pour ingredients into a bowl, wash fruits and vegetables, and knead dough. These experiences allow toddlers to taste, smell, and touch different foods. Children's books with food-related themes, dramatic play with food props, and creative activities that include food topics are all appropriate ways to teach toddlers about foods and nutrition. These approaches help toddlers to establish positive eating habits that support them as they move into the preschool years.

Children learn about food through dramatic play. This little boy has also learned about food safety and is appropriately wearing gloves while pretending to handle fresh produce.

FEEDING PRESCHOOLERS

Franklin is 4 years old. During the health screening at preschool, it was determined that he is overweight. His teacher, Madeline, shares this information with his family by sending home a note that reports his height and weight measurements. The following day Franklin's mother, Lenora, stops to talk to Madeline. She is very concerned. Several people have commented on Franklin's weight and she feels frustrated. The note from the health screening is the final straw. Lenora vows to start Franklin on a diet the next day. She insists Franklin not receive any more snacks. Madeline understands Lenora's frustration. She obtains Franklin's growth chart from his school file and brings it to the meeting to share with Lenora. The chart shows that Franklin is at the 90th percentile but he has been growing at the same rate during the past 2 years. Together they identify some resources that Lenora can review, and Madeline recommends that Lenora check with Franklin's health care provider before making any drastic changes in his diet. Lenora feels reassured by Madeline's practical approach. She decides to check with the medical care provider at Franklin's next well-child checkup. In the meantime she will focus on making sure the choices offered at home model the types of healthful foods provided at school.

During the eager-to-please preschool years, children experience a decreased rate of growth that can result in unpredictable eating behaviors. Children's body fat naturally decreases as they leave the toddler years and enter the preschool years. This means that preschooler children's appetites, like those of toddlers, can be sporadic. Preschool children may eat well one day but need encouragement to sit and eat the next. As their experience with foods expands, they also develop distinct preferences. To support preschoolers in their efforts to develop positive eating habits, teachers need to understand the nutritional needs and characteristics of the diets of this age group, understand how to create positive mealtime experiences, and be prepared with strategies to teach children healthful nutrition concepts.

Understanding the Nutritional Needs of Preschool Children

Preschool-age children rely on a high-quality diet to support growth and development. The goal is to balance their nutrient needs with their calorie requirements and energy expenditure. This is best accomplished by providing a variety of foods rich in tastes, colors, and textures while establishing habits that promote an active lifestyle. Teachers can find dietary advice about feeding preschool-age children from several sources including the federal government's MyPyramid for Preschoolers food guidance system (USDA, 2009b), the CACFP, and the *Dietary Guidelines for Americans, 2005* (U.S. Department of Health and Human Services [HHS] & USDA, 2005). Each of these sources encourages the provision of a variety of foods from each of the five food groups and is discussed in more detail in Chapter 7. The *Dietary Guidelines for Americans* (HHS & USDA, 2005) offers a series of recommendations about diet choices for individuals age 2 through adulthood, such as:

- Start each day with breakfast.
- Ensure that half of the grains offered are whole grains.
- Include a variety of colorful fruits and vegetables, and limit juice.
- Offer low-fat or fat-free milk or cheese.
- Offer lean or low-fat meats that are baked, broiled, or grilled.

Preschool children also need to consume foods that provide all needed nutrients including vitamins and minerals. Studies that look at the nutrient content of meals served in child care centers and family child care programs often reveal that the minerals iron, zinc, and magnesium are present at low levels (Roberts & Heyman, 2000; Walls, Hertzler, & Miller, 2001). Because these nutrients are particularly important for brain development, planning for adequate dietary sources in snacks and meals is essential (American Dietetic Association, 2005). Meals for preschool children should include foods such as meats, poultry, beans, nuts, seafood, whole grains, fortified breakfast cereals, and green leafy vegetables that are good sources of these minerals.

The MyPyramid for Preschoolers system (USDA, 2009b) is also an excellent resource for understanding the nutritional needs of young children (see Chapter 3 and the Web Resources section at the end of this chapter). The USDA provides sample menus for meals and snacks that are appropriate for preschool-age children (see Figure 6-5). The MyPyramid site provides good information for teachers and families. For example, in the preschool case scenario the resources that Madeline shares with Lenora include the menu guidelines shown in Figure 6-5 as well as information that describes the portion sizes recommended by the CACFP. In addition, Madeline points out that health care providers generally do not place young children on weight-loss diets but instead stress the importance of following healthy eating guidelines and being physically active. Lenora begins to feel more confidence in the way she feeds Franklin and the way Franklin eats when she examines these resources.

Learning Outcome: Children will accept a variety of foods.

Infants and Toddlers

- *Goal:* Older infants will practice selecting and tasting different fruits and vegetables.

- *Materials:* Two muffin tins that have space for six muffins, brightly colored fruits and vegetables. For younger infants, select strained fruits and vegetables. Older infants can have soft cooked and mashed fruits and vegetables. Food selections for an older infant might include:
  - *Yellow:* mashed banana or creamed corn.
  - *Orange:* cut-up peaches or mangoes.
  - *Green:* mashed green peas or cut-up soft green beans.
  - *Red:* small pieces of strawberries or cut-up watermelon or cut-up cooked beets.
  - *Blue:* mashed blueberries.

- *Activity plan:* The teacher's and infant's hands should be washed before beginning. Fill both muffin tin spaces with prepared fruit. Place one muffin tin in front of the teacher and one in front of the baby. (If baby is likely to dump tin onto the floor, select a divided plate with suction cups to keep it in place.) Allow baby to eat. Talk about the colors of the different foods. Have teacher model tasting foods, commenting on flavor and color. Say words that convey pleasure and interest, such as "I like these orange mangoes" or "This red watermelon makes me happy because it tastes so good." Encourage tasting, but do not force.

- *How to adjust the activity:* For toddlers, provide more variety of texture. Cut fruits and vegetables into very small pieces. Model enjoyment of all the different tastes and flavors. Ask toddlers to point to the foods they like. Count the pieces of fruit and vegetables and talk about the colors. Describe what the child is doing. Say, "You are trying different fruits and vegetables. That is a good way to find out what they taste like."

- *Did you meet your goal?* Is the toddler exploring, choosing, and tasting new foods?

Preschoolers and Kindergartners

- *Goal:* Children will explore different forms of tomatoes and tomato products, choose products to taste, and identify which ones they like.

- *Materials:* The book *I Will Never Not Ever Eat a Tomato* by Lauren Child. Different types of tomatoes such as a grape or cherry tomato, Roma tomato, and traditional-shaped tomato cut up into small pieces (especially the grape and cherry tomatoes, which can be choking hazards), baked tortilla chips. Other tomato-based foods such as ketchup, salsa, heat-and-serve tomato soup, spaghetti sauce. Spoons, 2-ounce paper cups, paper napkins, serrated knife for cutting tomatoes, small plastic cutting board. Poster paper and markers.

- *Activity plan:* Set up a tomato taste-testing center. Place the different varieties of fresh tomatoes and the different tomato products in paper cups to sample. Provide the cups of tomato products for children to sample. Place the poster paper on the wall. Create columns on the poster; label one column for each tomato product. Have children sample the different types of tomatoes and tomato products. Use baked tortilla chips on a paper plate for dipping into sauces. Guide children to write their name in the column for each tomato and tomato product they like. At group time gather the children and read the book. Talk about the tomato tasting test and review the chart. Identify the products that more children liked. Have children describe why they liked certain tomatoes and tomato products.

- *How to adjust the activity:* Explore other fruits and vegetables such as red, green, and yellow pepper strips or red, yellow, or green apple slices, applesauce, and apple juice. Children who have hearing or vision impairments or are learning English should sit near the teacher. Consider children's food allergies and avoid problem foods.

- *Did you meet your goal?* Did children explore, choose, and taste different tomato products?

School-Age Children

- *Goal:* Children will be able to sort foods into categories based on food groups and nutritious and less nutritious qualities and tally how many vegetables their table eats at lunchtime.

- *Materials:* Paper, crayons, MyPyramid poster, 3-inch × 3-inch card stock, magazines, glue, tape, butcher paper, *My Food Pyramid* by DK Publishing.

- *Activity plan:* Have one child lay down on the butcher paper. Have two other children draw around the child's body. As an alternative provide a pre-drawn body image. Invite children to cut out pictures from magazines or draw pictures of different foods onto paper cards. Place the picture cards in a basket. Gather children together. Introduce the concept of food groups. Read the book and review the MyPyramid poster. Talk about the different food groups and the importance of a healthful diet. Describe the qualities of foods that make them nutritious or less nutritious. Define "junk food." Tape the body outline poster on the wall. Have children select four or five food picture cards from the basket. One at a time have children identify the food group depicted on the card. Then have them tape the cards depicting foods that are nutritious inside the body design, and tape pictures of "junk food" outside the body design.

- *How to adjust the activity:* Have children sort the picture cards into food groups. Count the number of picture cards for each food group.

- *Did you meet your goal?* Are children able to describe food groups and foods that are nutritious and less nutritious? Were they willing to try new foods such as vegetables in the cafeteria?

Later that month when Lenora takes Franklin to his health care provider she learns that although Franklin is above average in size, because he is growing steadily rather than excessively his growth rate is actually fine.

Recognizing Characteristics of Preschool Children's Diets

Preschool-age children have developed many eating skills and are able to eat most of the foods that adults eat. They enjoy socializing at mealtimes and are eager to participate in serving themselves. They develop confidence as they master tasks such as spreading jam on a slice of bread and pouring milk from a small pitcher into a cup. As teachers promote these skills, various aspects of the preschool diet need to be considered to ensure that children receive safe and nutritious meals. The textures and consistencies of foods still play a part in the preschool diet. Appropriate scheduling of meals, attention to portion sizes, and establishing approaches that encourage children to accept new foods are all important areas of focus when feeding preschool children.

Food Textures and Consistencies

Preschool children have completed the teething process and are ready to eat most solid foods. But chewing and swallowing skills are still developing, so special attention must be given to foods that could represent a choking hazard. Foods that are difficult to chew, such

Figure 6-5 Sample Menu Using MyPyramid for Preschoolers

These patterns show one way a **1200 calorie MyPyramid Plan** can be divided into meals and snacks for a preschooler. Sample food choices are shown for each meal or snack.

Notes for using the Meal and Snack Ideas.

Breakfast	Breakfast Ideas		
1 ounce Grains ½ cup Fruit ½ cup Milk*	Cereal and Banana *1 cup crispy rice cereal* *½ cup sliced banana* ½ cup milk*	Yogurt and Strawberries *½ cup plain yogurt** *4 sliced strawberries* 1 slice whole wheat toast	Applesauce Topped Pancake *1 small pancake* *¼ cup applesauce* ¼ cup blueberries ½ cup milk*

Morning Snack	Morning Snack Ideas		
1 ounce Grains ½ cup Fruit	1 slice cinnamon bread ½ large orange	1 cup toasted oat cereal ½ cup diced pineapple	Frozen Graham Cracker Sandwich *2 graham crackers (4 squares)* *½ cup mashed banana*

Lunch	Lunch Ideas		
1 ounce Grains ½ cup Vegetables ½ cup Milk* 1 ounce Meat & Beans	Open-faced Chicken Sandwich and Salad *1 slice whole wheat bread* *1 slice American cheese** *1 ounce sliced chicken* ½ cup baby spinach (raw) ¼ cup grated carrots	Soft Taco (meat or veggie) *1 small tortilla* *½ cup salad greens* *¼ cup chopped tomatoes* *¼ cup shredded cheese** *1 ounce cooked ground beef or ¼ cup refried beans*	Bagel Snake *1 mini whole grain bagel* *¼ cup sliced cherry tomatoes* *¼ cup diced celery* *1 ounce tuna* ½ cup milk*

Afternoon Snack	Afternoon Snack Ideas		
½ cup Vegetables ½ cup Milk*	½ cup sugar snap peas ½ cup yogurt*	½ cup veggie "matchsticks" (carrot, celery, zucchini) ½ cup milk*	½ cup tomato juice 1 string cheese*

Dinner	Dinner Ideas		
1 ounce Grains ½ cup Vegetables ½ cup Milk* 2 ounces Meat & Beans	Chicken & Potatoes *2 ounces chicken breast* *¼ cup mashed potato* ¼ cup green peas 1 small whole wheat roll ½ cup milk*	Spaghetti & Meatballs *½ cup cooked pasta* *¼ cup tomato sauce* *2 meatballs (2 ounces)* ½ small ear corn on the cob ½ cup milk*	Rice & Beans with Sausage *½ cup cooked brown rice* *¼ cup black beans* *¼ cup bell pepper* *1 ounce turkey sausage* ¼ cup broccoli ½ cup milk*

*Offer your child fat-free or low-fat milk, yogurt, and cheese.

Source: From MyPyramid.gov at http://www.mypyramid.gov/preschoolers.

as meats, still need to be cut up into small pieces to avoid choking. Round cherry tomatoes or grapes, because of their shape, present a choking risk. However, by chopping fresh tomatoes or quartering the grapes, this risk is avoided. Cutting raw vegetables, such as carrots, into thin strips makes them easier for children to bite and chew safely. Supervision at mealtime is crucial. Teachers may need to remind preschool children to stay seated when they eat to decrease the risk of choking.

Scheduling Meals and Snacks

Preschool children become accustomed to eating meals and snacks at predictable times. As with toddlers, providing three meals and three snacks at intervals of every 2 to 3 hours provides active preschoolers with a consistent energy source throughout the day. Snacks should be planned to provide important nutrients and also be low in added fat and sugars. For example, a corn, bean, and salsa dip served with whole-grain corn tortillas or baked tortilla chips provides a rich assortment of nutrients compared to cookies and a fruit punch drink.

Avoiding Portion Distortion

Teachers may unknowingly offer children larger portions than desirable in an effort to make sure children have sufficient food for growth. This is problematic and potentially unhealthy. Researchers have found that children consume more calories when large portions are offered, especially as they enter the preschool years (Fisher, Liu, Birch, & Rolls, 2007). Infants and toddlers are very in tune with their internal cues for hunger and satiety. They will eat when they are hungry and stop when they are full (Fox, Devaney, Reidy, Razafindrakoto, & Ziegler, 2006).

As children enter their preschool years, they are influenced by environmental cues such as the presence of desirable food, the time of day, and the portion size (McConahy, Smiciklas-Wright, Mitchell, & Picciano, 2004; Rolls, Engell, & Birch, 2000). When children are allowed to serve themselves they choose smaller portions and may consume as much as 25% fewer calories (Orlet Fisher, Rolls, & Birch, 2003). Providing the opportunity for preschool children to serve themselves through family-style meal service may help prevent excess calorie intake, thereby reducing the risk of obesity. Using child-sized plates and bowls also prevents portion distortion. (See Figure 6-6 for examples of how portions have increased in recent years.)

What if. . .

a child in your class seems to always put more on his plate than he can eat? What would be a good strategy to address this?

Creating a Child-Friendly and Healthful Diet

Creating a child-friendly diet focuses on selecting and preparing foods that encourage children to try a variety of foods. The Food Guide Pyramid, CACFP, and the *Dietary Guidelines for Americans* provide advice about number of servings as well as how to balance the different food groups. However, creativity is needed to select and prepare foods that children will accept while at the same time teaching them about nutrition.

To address this, teachers can focus on offering new foods at a specific meal, selecting foods from the different food groups, and paying attention to particular nutrients. For example, teachers might focus on the role of fiber in the menu. They can influence the consumption of high-fiber foods by reviewing menus, rethinking snacks, and planning cooking activities that use fiber-rich foods. They can plan ways to enhance preschoolers' acceptance of these foods by frequently exposing children to foods high in fiber. In addition, they can increase the likelihood that children will try new foods by incorporating this nutrition concept into a variety of class activities. For example:

- Observe what happens to dried beans (which are high in fiber) when they are left in water. *Concept:* Fiber is good for us because it holds water and keeps us regular.
- Study celery and onion skins through a magnifying glass to observe fiber. *Concept:* Plants provide us with fiber.
- Taste different high-fiber breads and cereals. *Concept:* Fiber is found in grains and tastes good.
- Prepare a fruit salad of apples, pears, melons, and berries. *Concept:* Fiber is found in the skin and seeds of fruits.
- Sample a variety of different tomatoes. *Concept:* Fiber is found in vegetables and sometimes there are many types of the same vegetable to taste and try.

Figure 6-6 Portion Distortion

Bagel
Calorie difference: 210 calories

3-inch diameter
140 calories

6-inch diameter
350 calories

Cheeseburger
Calorie difference: 257 calories

333 calories

590 calories

Soda
Calorie difference: 165 calories

6.5 ounces
85 calories

20 ounces
250 calories

French Fries
Calorie difference: 400 calories

2.4 ounces
210 calories

6.9 ounces
610 calories

Source: From www.nhlbi.nih.gov/health/public/heart/obesity/wecan/learn-it/distortion.htm

Understanding the Teacher's Role in Creating a Positive Mealtime Experience

A positive mealtime experience enhances children's comfort and offers a relaxed environment for eating and trying new foods. Teachers help create this positive environment by creating a comfortable space and establishing routines that children can be a part of. Mealtimes should be considerate of cultural traditions and should encourage visiting and conversation. Teachers are important role models during mealtimes.

Arranging the Mealtime Environment

A comfortable physical environment supports meal service and enhances the eating experience. Space for children to eat should be adequate without being crowded. Chairs and tables should be child sized so that children can sit comfortably and focus on eating. Silverware, cups, plates, and serving utensils should be sized to match the children's motors skills (American Dietetic Association, 2005).

The environment should be free of hazards such as food warming units, electrical cords, and large containers of hot foods. Tables should be properly sanitized before and after use. The food served should be visually appealing and prepared in such a way as to promote children's success when eating. Decorate the setting with a changing array of posters or food-related displays that convey nutrition education messages while adding color and interest to the space.

Children learn about fiber by going to the Farmer's Market and seeing different types of fruits and vegetables. They also learn that there can be many types of the same vegetable to try and they often have different flavors.

What if. . .

you wanted to focus on encouraging breakfast in your program? How would you implement a child-friendly breakfast menu and teach preschoolers about the breakfast meal?

MyEducationLab

Go to the Assignments and Activities section of Topic 2: Feeding Children in the MyEducationLab for your course and complete the activity entitled *Cultural Knowledge*. How is this teacher's explanation of cultural differences relevant to feeding children?

Establishing Comfortable Routines

Teachers set the tone for mealtimes by establishing routines that convey appropriate expectations and help the meal service to flow easily and enjoyably. Children learn to predict their responsibilities and tasks, which provide them with a sense of security and comfort about mealtime. For example, children can wash their own hands, help set the table, serve themselves family style, and help with cleanup.

Considering Cultural Traditions

Mealtimes are important for nourishing children, but they also convey social and cultural values. Mealtime practices vary across different social groups in terms of how children participate, the timing of meals, the items served, and the sequence of food presentation. Children obtain cultural knowledge about food and eating by their active observation and participation in mealtime routines and socialization (Ochs, 2006). Teachers should be aware that children's cultural traditions and experiences may differ from the practices in the classroom setting. In the United States a cultural norm at mealtimes is that everyone sits down together before anyone starts to eat. Children who start to eat before everyone is seated are reprimanded and considered impolite. This practice is reinforced by the CACFP program guidelines, which state that everyone must be seated at the table with the adult present and all food components available before eating starts (Oregon Department of Education, 2009). In China, however, older generations are often served before younger generations, and in formal social occasions children may be excluded until older adults are finished eating (Ochs, 2006).

Encouraging Conversation

Another very important aspect of meals is the opportunity they provide for language development. Talking and visiting during mealtime helps children learn new vocabulary and how to listen and tell stories. It is also an important way children acquire command of culturally relevant knowledge, and conversation contributes to the language and cognitive skills that support children's ability to learn to read and write (Snow & Beals, 2006). Teachers encourage visiting by actively listening to children, restating and elaborating on what children have said, and asking probing questions during mealtime conversations. How would you include children who are English learners in conversations while eating?

Being a Good Role Model

Preschooler children watch and copy the behaviors of their teachers—a reminder of the importance of being a good role model. An important aspect of modeling for preschool children involves helping children learn to make decisions about food by providing opportunities for children to serve themselves and choose what and how much they eat. This provides the practice children need to support good decision making during the school years when the selection and eating of food becomes less supervised. It is important for teachers to remember that forcing a child to eat a food can create food aversions. Even teachers trying to be good role models may not be able to eat all of the foods that are offered because of food restrictions, allergies, previous negative experiences, or preferences. Consider this situation:

> Mac, a 68-year-old retiree, volunteers 3 days a week in a Head Start classroom. He confesses to the teacher, Mindy, that he finds eating lunch with the children a challenge. Mindy is surprised because the children generally interact well with Mac during mealtimes. He quickly reassures her that it isn't the children he finds challenging, it's eating the vegetables! He says vehemently, "I just can't eat cabbage, broccoli, or cauliflower. I know I should be a better role model but my mother forced me to eat them when I was a kid and I just can't do it." Mindy reassures him that no one, including volunteers, is pressured to eat something they don't like.

Children may notice that a teacher does not eat a certain food and ask why. Food allergies are a factor of health and safety and should be explained to children as clearly as possible by saying, "My doctor has helped me to learn that my body cannot accept eating peanuts. This is only true for some people, not everyone." Food restrictions related to cultural or religious practices can be explained by stating, "In my culture we choose not to eat cheese." When teachers do not like a food that is served they might respond by saying in a neutral way, "I don't care for broccoli when it is cooked. I like it better raw." These examples are a reminder that teachers are people, too.

Being a good role model is not always easy, and teachers must learn how to navigate situations where their personal preferences challenge their ability to be the perfect role model. Sharing information simply and clearly and modeling how to try and eat as many foods as possible communicate an attitude of being open to new flavors and experiences.

Teaching Preschoolers about Nutrition

Preschoolers are full of questions and want to master new experiences. The most effective learning opportunities are those in which children are active participants. Nutrition concepts should be integrated into the daily routine. Certain themes can teach children a breadth of information about nutrition.

Learning about the Origins of Food

Preschool children may not have a clear understanding of where food comes from. When asked, they may say that food comes from the kitchen, restaurant, or grocery store. Concepts such as the origin of food, how seeds grow into plants, where milk comes from, how food gets from the farm to the table, or how grains of wheat become loaves of bread may be new. Teachers can introduce these concepts in many ways such as through field trips, school gardens, and classroom cooking activities.

Field Trips Taking preschoolers outside of the classroom extends learning to real-life situations and experiences. Field trips, because of their novelty, often create very memorable moments that enhance acquisition of knowledge. A trip to the dairy barn, milk processing plant, and grocery store shows children the sequence of steps involved in getting milk from the farm to the table. Tasting different types of milk (whole, low-fat, skim, or goat's milk) while discussing the nutrients they contain and their health benefits is meaningful because children get to experience a lesson through multiple senses.

School Gardens Planting and growing a school or classroom garden provides an opportunity for children to experience the surprise and delight of pulling a carrot out of the ground or picking and shelling a fresh pea for the first time. Children are better able to develop a clear picture of the origin of food when they plant seeds, watch them grow, tend to the plants, and then have the pleasure of eating what they have produced.

Food and nutrition concepts are brought to life as children learn about plants, insects, and rain, and also learn about cooperating, persevering, and waiting for food to grow. Gardens foster learning about the cycle of life and sustainability through composting, compatible planting, and careful use of water. Whether the facility offers space for a garden plot, raised garden bed, or a garden planted in large containers at the edge of the playground, city and country dwellers alike learn about nature, the environment, and healthful nutrition through participation in school gardens.

Classroom Cooking Activities Cooking activities teach many concepts and are of great interest to children because they get to sample what they have made. Literacy is promoted as children view simply illustrated directions and sequential steps. Math skills are practiced through measuring and weighing foods. Science concepts are introduced as children see how ingredients interact when mixed together. The origin of a food item is enhanced when

MyEducationLab

Go to the Assignments and Activities section of Topic 2: Feeding Children in the MyEducationLab for your course and complete the activity entitled *Early Childhood Mealtime Experiences*. What are the teacher's roles in these mealtime settings?

Field trips extend learning to real-life situations.

children experience the steps of food preparation. For example, making corn tortillas by grinding dried corn, mixing, and baking offers opportunity to study where the corn was grown and how it was dried.

Activities That Support Nutrition Education

Activities that teach children about food and nutrition are popular in the preschool classroom. They can be infused in many activities. Themes can be reinforced by offering related activities at various learning centers. Pizza is an example of a food that uses products from each food group. The activities listed below relate to pizza, a five-food-group food.

- *Dramatic play props for an Italian restaurant:* chef's hat, aprons, pizza delivery boxes, pizza pans, plastic pizza cutters, checkered tablecloth, plastic food models of pizza, spaghetti, salad, milk.
- *Math props:* a cash register and play money.
- *Literacy props:* menu, paper to record "pizza orders," telephone to receive take-out orders.
- *Creative materials to "make" pizza:* colored paper to cut and paste to make paper pizzas with a tan crust, green and red peppers, brown mushrooms, yellow pineapple and cheese, black olives.
- *Blocks to create a food group pyramid:* magazines with food pictures for children to cut and paste to boxes, creating one box for each food group (grains, fruits, vegetables, dairy, meat), and stacking to create a pyramid.
- *Science exploration center with ingredients to make pizza:* whole-wheat flour, yeast, salt, and warm water, measuring cups and spoons, bowls, and pizza sauce and toppings.

What if. . .

you wanted to extend the pizza theme by planning a manipulative activity and a game that promotes large motor skills? What activities would you develop?

FEEDING SCHOOL-AGE CHILDREN

It is "Sock Hop" dance night for the children of Locust Grove School and Paul and Jose, two third-grade boys, are having a fantastic time at this 1950s-style event. The Parent–Teacher Association (PTA) has obtained donations for the cake-walk contest. Soft drinks, cotton candy, and buttered popcorn are available for all to eat. The PTA is also selling candies and gift wrap as a fund-raiser. Paul has won a whole iced cake that he proudly shows to his teacher Anne, who is supervising the dance. Anne is a member of the School Health Advisory Council, which includes the principal, teachers, and parents with interest in nutrition and wellness. Anne is exasperated by the excess of "junk food" at the dance. She tries to respond positively to Paul but feels the school's wellness goals are not always being met. She wonders how she will be able to convey her health and nutrition concerns to other staff and families. As she reminds Paul to be careful walking with that big cake, she comes up with a great idea. She will invite a member of the PTA to join the School Health Advisory Council. This will help create a connection between these groups who have the best interests of kids in common.

Primary school-age children become captains of their own ships when it comes to eating. They are now in a larger environment and experience less supervision at mealtimes. A school cafeteria is rife with activity and throwing away parts of a packed lunch or choosing not to select or eat certain components of a school lunch menu are decisions that primary school-age children can make. Here is where they get to practice all of the nutrition-related decision-making skills they learned in their home and early childhood programs.

In spite of this newfound freedom, teachers continue to have important responsibilities to positively influence children's ideas and decisions about food. Teachers need to understand the nutritional needs of this age group and recognize the characteristics of diets that support growth and development. They also need to understand how to create a positive nutritional environment and know how to teach nutrition and wellness concepts.

Understanding the Nutritional Needs of School-Age Children

School-age children's rate of growth is slow and steady compared to infancy, preschool, and the adolescent years that are yet to come. Their nutrient requirements increase with their increasing size and are reflected by larger portions in the MyPyramid food guidance system's recommendations. Children are able to accommodate longer time periods between meals.

The school-age years are a time when children's food choices are increasingly influenced by peer groups and media advertising. Maintaining a steady rate of growth can be hampered by societal influences such as decreased opportunities for physical activity, increased time in front of TVs and computers, and increased exposure to processed, easy-to-prepare convenience foods, fast foods, and snack items that can lead to excess weight gain. Understanding these influences helps teachers understand the challenges that children face related to eating and being active.

Recognizing Characteristics of School-Age Children's Diets

School-age children have usually worked out the kinks of eating and experience fewer food-related feeding problems than toddlers and preschoolers. During this time children become more responsible for selecting their own foods. If they are not pressured school-age children can manage their internal hunger and satiety cues sufficiently to support growth and maintain normal weight. This success relies on an environment that supports healthful eating and avoids pressures related to food acceptance. Teachers contribute to this positive environment by being alert to the timing of meals and recognizing the importance of breakfast and the school lunch program.

Timing of Meals

A pattern of three meals with three snacks per day is still advised for school-age children. In most kindergarten and first-grade classroom settings, children consume snacks in the morning at school. By the time children are in second and third grade the morning snack is discontinued. Teachers should be sensitive to the hunger cues among children in their class-room to determine whether to plan snacks as part of the morning routine. Nutrient-dense snacks that are low in fat and sugar continue to make a positive contribution to children's nutrient needs. Studies show that midmorning snacks may help children concentrate and may also improve memory (Benton & Jarvis, 2007; Muthayya et al., 2007).

The Importance of Breakfast

Some school-age children eat breakfast at home while others participate in the School Breakfast Program. Other children may skip breakfast because of hectic family lifestyles, early morning time constraints, or the family's lack of familiarity with the School Breakfast Program. It is estimated that approximately 10% to 30% of children skip this "most important meal of the day" (Rampersaud, Pereira, Girard, Adams, & Metzl, 2005). Eating breakfast boosts children's intake of key vitamins and minerals, improving the chances that children will meet their daily nutrient requirements (Food Research and Action Center, 2009; Rampersaud et al., 2005). Children who skip breakfast may be more at risk for obesity because by the time they are able to eat they are so hungry they may make poor choices and overeat. In addition, prolonged fasts, such as occur when the breakfast meal is skipped, may increase the insulin response to food offered later in the day, promoting fat storage and weight gain (Rampersaud et al., 2005; Zeratsky, 2009).

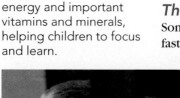

Breakfast provides energy and important vitamins and minerals, helping children to focus and learn.

School Breakfast Program The School Breakfast Program (SBP) is a child nutrition program administered by the federal Food and Nutrition Service that offers cash subsidies from the USDA for every meal served by participating school districts (USDA Food and Nutrition Service, 2009c). Participating schools must provide one-quarter of the Recommended Dietary Allowance for school-age children of protein, calories, vitamin A, vitamin C, iron, and calcium and adhere to principles of the *Dietary Guidelines* that include keeping fat at 30% of total calories or less (USDA Food and Nutrition Service, 2009c).

The SBP is an important program that becomes even more valuable during difficult economic times when families may struggle to afford meals for their children. Some children are not hungry when they first wake up. The SBP gives them another opportunity to eat a nutritious meal a little later in the morning (Food Research and Action Center, 2009). The SBP and lunch program are available free of charge to children whose family income is 130% or less than the federal poverty level. A reduced-price option is also available to families whose income is between 130% and 185% of the established federal poverty level (USDA Food and Nutrition Service, 2009c). This makes the SBP accessible to many children and families.

Impact of Breakfast on Learning Breakfast is a significant meal not only because it helps children maintain a balanced diet, but also because it can impact learning. Studies show that children who eat breakfast experience benefits such as:

- Increased math and reading scores.
- Improved speed and memory in cognitive tests (Food Research and Action Center, 2009; Rampersaud et al., 2005).
- Improved school behavior and attentiveness, which supports the overall educational environment (Benton & Jarvis, 2007).

Children who do not eat breakfast are at a disadvantage academically. Teachers need to share this important information with families, and help them explore options for providing morning meals for their school-age children.

In the school-age case scenario, Anne is the teacher representative for the Health and Wellness Council at her school. She brings her concern to one of the monthly meetings. She has noticed that many children, regardless of family income level, are skipping breakfast and coming to school hungry. The school district food service manager, also a member of the committee, decides to offer the children a free breakfast once a month as a way to increase families' awareness of the School Breakfast Program. The committee decided to coordinate this with walk and bike to school events so that children can take advantage of a healthy breakfast when they arrive at school. This is an excellent way to convey the message that nutrition and physical activity are both important components of wellness.

> **What if. . .**
>
> you noticed a child was consistently coming to school hungry in the morning and you suspected there were financial concerns at home? How would you address this problem?

Providing School Lunch

Lunch is usually the largest meal offered when children are at school. It plays a major role children's diets through programs such as the National School Lunch Program.

National School Lunch Program   The National School Lunch Program (NSLP) is a child nutrition program offered by the USDA Food and Nutrition Service that provides nutritious lunches for children attending school. To receive federal subsidies, school lunches must provide at least one-third of the Recommended Dietary Allowances for protein, iron, calcium, and vitamins A and C and keep fat at 30% of total calories or less (USDA Food and Nutrition Service, 2009b). Many children benefit from the nutritious meals provided by the NSLP. Currently the Committee on Nutrition Standards for National School Lunch and Breakfast Programs of the Institute of Medicine of the National Academies is working on revising standards that were last updated in 1995. The new standards will reflect changes in the *Dietary Guidelines for Americans* and Dietary Reference Intakes (DRIs) and will address the obesity epidemic (Stallings, 2009).

Like the School Breakfast Program, the NSLP is available free of charge to children whose family income is 130% or less than the federal poverty level and at reduced price to families whose incomes are between 130% and 185% of the established federal poverty levels. The USDA also provides a variety of other programs to support the nutritional health and wellness of school-age children:

- *Team Nutrition:* This program provides technical support and training for food service employees at school as well as nutrition education opportunities for children and teachers (USDA Food and Nutrition Service, 2009d).
- *HealthierUS School Challenge:* This program promotes and recognizes positive change in school nutrition and health environments. It provides guidelines for improving nutrition and physical activity in the school setting. When schools comply with these recommendations, they are certified as Bronze, Silver, Gold, or Gold of Distinction Schools (USDA Food and Nutrition Service, 2009a).
- *Afterschool Snack Program:* This program provides children with a nutritious snack when they participate in after-school programs where they can take part in planned, enriching activities in a safe and supervised setting (USDA Food and Nutrition Service, 2009b).
- *Summer Food Service/Seamless Summer Programs:* These programs continue to provide nutritious school lunches throughout the summer break in communities where 50% or more of the children served are eligible for free or reduced meals year around, ensuring that low-income children have access to nutritious meals (USDA Food and Nutrition Service, 2009b).

Teachers make a positive impact on children's nutrition and the wellness climate of schools by endorsing and participating in initiatives such as these.

School Lunch: Before or After Recess?   The timing of school lunch has become an issue of importance in many schools. The predominant practice in primary schools is to eat lunch and then participate in outdoor recess. For example, fewer than 5% of primary

Figure 6-7 Benefits of Recess Before Lunch

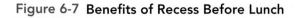

What is a
Recess Before Lunch
Policy?

Where students go to
recess first, then eat lunch.

Montana schools are reaping
the benefits:

★ Improved student behavior on
the playground, in the cafeteria
and the classroom.

★ Students waste less food and
drink more milk. This leads to
increased nutrient intake.

★ Improved cafeteria
atmosphere.

★ Children are more
settled and ready
to learn.

Tips For Getting Started:

★ Build support within your
community and school staff.

★ Realize that adapting the
schedule is a work in progress.

★ Develop a hand washing routine.

★ Schedule adequate time for
students to eat (at least
25-30 minutes.)

★ Decide where to store cold
lunches for easy access.

★ Take care of lunch money prior
to recess.

★ Practice this new routine with
the students. Spend as much
time in the lunchroom as possible during first few weeks.

★ Be committed, even through a
trial period, to stick with it.
Expect some resistance.

Source: Used with permission from http://www.opi.mt.gov/schoolfood/recessBL.html, Montana Team Nutrition Program, Montana State University and School Nutrition Programs, Office of Public Instruction, Helena, Montana, 2009.

schools schedule lunch after recess (Rainville et al., 2006). Yet research shows that children who eat lunch after recess eat better and waste less food (Rainville. Wolf, & Carr, 2006). Many children rush through lunch to go outside to play. For children from low-income families, this can mean missing a vital opportunity for a nutritious meal. Teachers may consider advocating for offering lunch after recess if they notice children are coming back from recess hungry (see Figure 6-7).

Understanding the Teacher's Role in Creating a Quality Nutrition Environment

Perspectives about the quality of children's nutritional environment have shifted in recent years. Increased concern about the health of children in the United States due to increasing rates of childhood obesity and decreasing rates of activity have led to a greater awareness of the need to provide more healthful meals, more physical activity, and foods that are produced and purchased in more sustainable ways. This thinking has led to the development of a school wellness movement. These initiatives have been supported by a number of recently enacted programs and initiatives that place a high degree of importance on good nutrition and physical activity.

School Wellness Policy

In 2004, the Child Nutrition and WIC Reauthorization Act was signed into law. This act made it mandatory for schools to establish a school wellness policy by January 2006 (Centers for Disease Control and Prevention & National Center for Chronic Disease Prevention and Health Promotion, 2009). With the advent of this requirement, a new mind-set was put into place related not only to the foods being served but also to the overall quality of the school environment in supporting health practices. This law has shifted the focus of food service from not only providing adequate nutrient intake but also to providing meals that promote healthful eating habits in an effort to prevent chronic diseases such as obesity, diabetes, high blood pressure, heart disease, and stroke. As a result, federally sponsored school nutrition programs have made major strides to revamp their menus to address the new health and nutrition guidance systems.

The school wellness policy must also address the importance of physical activity for improving the health climate of the school setting. The importance of physical education classes, recess, and before- and after-school opportunities to participate in sports activities are reemphasized in this approach. Figure 6-8 summarizes the requirements for physical activity that must be included in the school wellness policy. Overall the message is clear: Schools must enhance the school environment to promote healthy food choices and increase levels of physical activity. Nutrition and physical activity are two sides of the same coin; without one or the other, children's health and wellness are compromised.

In addition, school wellness policies must address the provision of food that occurs outside of the realm of traditional school food service. Food is served in a variety of situations

Figure 6-8 School Wellness Policy Guidelines for Addressing Physical Activity

- Students are given opportunities for physical activity during the school day through physical education (PE) classes, daily recess periods for elementary school students, and the integration of physical activity into the academic curriculum.
- Students are given opportunities for physical activity through a range of before- and/or after-school programs including, but not limited to, intramurals, interscholastic athletics, and physical activity clubs.
- Schools work with the community to create ways for students to walk, bike, rollerblade, or skateboard safely to and from school.
- Schools encourage parents and guardians to support their children's participation in physical activity, to be physically active role models, and to include physical activity in family events.
- Schools provide training to enable teachers, and other school staff to promote enjoyable, lifelong physical activity among students.

Source: From *Healthy Schools: Setting Physical Activity Goals,* by the USDA Food and Nutrition Service, retrieved October 7, 2009, from http://teamnutrition.usda.gov/Healthy/wellnesspolicygoals_physicalactivity.html.

in the school setting. For example, food is commonly available at after-school programs and school social and sporting events. Food is often used as a reward in the classroom setting as well. The case scenario highlighted some of the problems associated with providing foods at school events that contradict school wellness policy goals. Teachers, administrators, and parents need to develop policies that are supportive of healthy eating. The *Nutrition Note* gives an example of how teachers can replace using food as a reward for classroom activities. Guidelines from the Food and Nutrition Service for establishing policies that address these issues

What if. . .

you noticed groups of children sitting on the bench during recess? What ideas do you have to encourage them to be more active?

Nutrition Note

Avoid Using Food as a Reward

Rewarding children with food to reinforce behavior or reward academic achievement is not good practice and the repercussions are not always obvious. Negative consequences of using food as a reward include the following:

- *Creating value for the food being used for reward:* Children begin to think "This candy must be very special if it's used by my teacher to get me to do something."
- *Encouraging children to eat when they are not hungry, creating a link between food and behavior rather than food and hunger:* This promotes a pattern of children rewarding or comforting themselves with food and predisposes them to obesity in the future.
- *Sabotaging children's diet:* Children may be less likely to eat a healthy lunch or snack.
- *Promoting eating between meals and snack times:* This increases the risk for obesity and dental caries.
- *Exposing children to high-fat and -sugar, low-vitamin and -mineral foods:* This creates a taste for these foods.

More effective and healthful ways to acknowledge positive behaviors include:

- Assigning children a leadership opportunity, such as passing out books or leading a song.
- Allowing children to choose the story at group time.
- Offering a walk with the teacher.
- Providing an extra 5 minutes of outside playtime.

Figure 6-9 Wellness Policy Guidelines for Food and Beverages Served at School

✓ The school district sets guidelines for food and beverages sold in:
- á la carte sales in the food service program on school campuses.
- Vending machines, snack bars, school stores, and concession stands on school campuses.
- School-sponsored fund-raising activities.

✓ The school district sets guidelines for refreshments served at parties, celebrations, and meetings during the school day.

✓ The school district makes decisions on these guidelines based on nutrition goals, not on profit making.

Source: From *Healthy Schools: Setting Nutrition Guidelines for All Foods and Beverages Available on School Campuses During the School Day*, by the USDA Food and Nutrition Service, retrieved October 7, 2009, from http://www.fns.usda.gov/tn/Healthy/wellnesspolicygoals_guidelines.html.

are offered in Figure 6-9 and can help teachers to envision how they can foster good nutrition in all settings of the school environment.

Children with Special Needs All children are entitled to wellness. Some children with special developmental or health needs may experience challenges that make achieving wellness particularly relevant. Some may have conditions that predispose them to being underweight, whereas others will be more prone to obesity.

Teachers must communicate with families and health care providers to determine how to best meet children's goals for healthful weight. Some children may follow special diets to manage health conditions. On occasion, attending to these medical needs can compromise the overall quality of the child's diet. For example, meeting the nutritional needs for calcium in a child with a milk, egg, and soy allergy may prove difficult. Children on gluten-free diets may not be offered enough variety at school to ensure they eat enough. Teachers cannot make medical recommendations but they can encourage collaboration among families, school nutrition personnel, and health care providers to ensure that children's special nutritional needs have been appropriately addressed. Teachers can also step back from the details and determine whether routine wellness goals are being met.

What if. . .

the physical education teacher in your school did not feel appropriately trained to include a child with cerebral palsy in her class? What ideas would you have to offer?

Children from Culturally Diverse Backgrounds Promoting wellness goals benefits all children but may be particularly important for children from diverse cultural backgrounds. Some ethnic groups suffer disproportionately more from chronic health conditions related to nutrition and obesity. For example, when using body mass index as an indicator, the incidence of obesity is estimated at 31.2% among American Indian/Native Alaskan children, 22% for Hispanics, 20.8% for blacks, 15.9% for whites, and 12.8% in Asians (Anderson & Whitaker, 2009). Efforts to promote wellness among all children must be addressed in culturally appropriate ways. Strategies include:

- Communicating school wellness goals, policies, and educational materials in the home languages of children attending the school.
- Incorporating healthful ethnic dishes in the school menu.
- Providing translation services at parent education seminars.

The Cafeteria as a Learning Lab

Part of the technical assistance offered to schools to support the implementation of school wellness policies is access to resources that help teachers learn about and effectively convey nutrition and health messages. This includes taking advantage of the school cafeteria as a learning lab. Resources, education materials, and ideas to support nutrition education in the cafeteria are provided by the *Healthy Meals Resource System* (USDA, 2009a). Activities that use the cafeteria as a learning center include:

- Offering taste tests of new foods and recipes.
- Displaying food sculptures.

- Conducting nutrition poster contests.
- Providing cafeteria kitchen tours.
- Preparing healthful recipes.
- Inviting important guest visitors to promote good nutrition and physical activity.

Understanding the Teacher's Role in Promoting Healthful Eating Habits

Teachers continue to be an important influence in supporting good eating habits in school-age children. They enhance their influence by sharing nutrition information with families and advocating for the children in their care.

Communicating with Families

Teachers and school administrative staff have responsibilities to share nutrition and health information that supports healthful eating in the home environment. This can be accomplished by providing nutrition and health-related articles in school newsletters or on the school menus sent home with children. Schools can post the lunch menu on the school website and provide nutrient analysis for menu items. Information about carbohydrate content for children with diabetes, and alternative menu options for children with special nutritional needs or preferences can also be provided. Teachers and schools can offer parent education programs on nutrition and sponsor family events that promote physical activity. These activities promote a partnership approach to helping school-age children eat healthy and be active.

The school cafeteria becomes a learning lab when children are exposed to nutrition-related activities such as creating food sculptures.

Teachers as Advocates

Teachers are important advocates for healthy school environments. They promote healthful nutrition and wellness among school-age children by advocating for nutritious menus and supporting the school breakfast and lunch programs. Teachers continue to serve as role models for healthful eating and physical activity behaviors. Eating school lunch with children and participating in physically active games and events during recess send important messages to young children.

In the case scenario Anne did not criticize Paul's prize of a large cake. Instead she encouraged him to put the cake aside and join her and the other children on the dance floor where he had fun while exercising. The next day when Paul came back to school Anne asked him if his family was excited about the cake. He told her he'd had one piece of cake, but it didn't taste good. His mother gave him permission to throw it away if he wanted to and he did. At the next School Health Advisory Council meeting Anne asked members to consider devising policies specific to social events at school and it was agreed to ask a PTA member to serve on their School Health Advisory Council.

Participating in school committees that support healthy eating and physical activity provides opportunities for teachers to advocate for policies and programs that fit the developmental learning of school-age children while fostering healthy habits that contribute to children's health and wellness.

Helping Families Access Nutrition Services

Sometimes children have nutritional needs that cannot be solved easily. Families may need to obtain consultation with health care providers who have expertise in the field of nutrition. The scrutiny of children's weight by health care authorities in face of the obesity epidemic has brought the issue of overweight into the spotlight for many families (see Chapter 3 for a discussion on obesity). Families may turn to teachers with their concerns. Teachers can direct families to appropriate health care providers and support their recommendations in the early childhood setting.

anorexia nervosa
an eating disorder that is caused by a distortion of body image, characterized by the severe restriction of food intake resulting in significant, and sometimes life threatening, weight loss

bulimia nervosa
an eating disorder that entails periods of binge eating followed by purging activities such as vomiting, using laxatives, or excessive exercising

The focus on the obesity epidemic has revealed another health care concern relating to weight: eating disorders. Eating disorders represent an extreme dysfunction in eating habits that develop gradually and eventually become an uncontrollable conflict about food consumption that can negatively impact the growth, development, and the health of children (Kleinman, 2009). Two commonly recognized types of eating disorders include anorexia nervosa and bulimia nervosa. Anorexia nervosa is caused by a distortion of body image and is characterized by the severe restriction of food intake resulting in significant weight loss. Bulimia nervosa entails binge eating followed by purging activities such as vomiting, using laxatives, or excessive exercising. Although typically eating disorders are considered an adolescent issue, more young children are being identified with eating disorders at earlier ages (Tanofsky-Kraff, Faden, Yanovski, Wilfley, & Yanovski, 2005). These are psychological disorders that result in medical complications that can be life threatening (Nevin-Folino, 2003; updated 2008). Dieting, a society that values thinness, and mass media influences appear to be common precipitators of eating disorders (Field et al., 2008; Rome et al., 2003). Some of the warning signs or risk factors associated with the development of eating disorders include a history of dieting, a preoccupation with weight, and the preference for solitary eating (Field et al., 2008; Martinez-Gonzalez et al., 2003).

It is important for teachers to support nutritious diets to promote good health and avoid focusing on weight or appearance when discussing healthful eating with children. For example, it is appropriate to comment on healthful food choices such as, "It's great to see you drinking water instead of soda, Waverly" while on the other hand it's detrimental to state, "Maria, if you drink that soft drink you're going to get fat." It is paramount that children develop a positive body image. A moderate approach that puts more emphasis on some foods and less emphasis on others and that avoids rigid restrictions of any food teaches children how to eat well and with enjoyment.

Learning about the different food groups provides children with an understanding of basic nutrition concepts.

Teaching School-Age Children about Nutrition

The school-age years are an important time for teaching children about nutrition and wellness. The 2004 Child Nutrition and WIC Reauthorization Act focuses on nutrition education by requiring school wellness policies to include a systematic approach to nutrition education. Figure 6-10 provides a summary of the components of the school wellness policy that addresses the requirements for providing nutrition education in schools.

Nutrition education needs to be integrated into all aspects of the school environment. Nutrition messages should be incorporated into math, reading, and health curricula. Teachers may be concerned that teaching nutrition will require a new curriculum and take time from the daily schedule to teach a new subject. Instead this perspective requires a shift in mind-set (Huber, 2009). Any lesson plan can integrate physical activity and nutrition concepts. It is a matter of looking at lesson plans through a wellness lens. Many helpful resources are available such as the website developed by the Iowa State University Extension, which contains a database of nutrition education and physical activity curricula (see the Web Resources section).

Teaching Basic Nutrition Concepts

A useful curriculum for teaching basic nutrition concepts to school-age children is the federal government's MyPyramid for Kids program. This resource is available for three different

Figure 6-10 Requirements for the Nutrition Education Component of a School Wellness Policy

- **Grades pre-K–12 receive nutrition education** that is interactive and teaches the skills they need to adopt healthy eating behaviors.
- **Nutrition education is offered in the school dining room** as well as in the classroom, with coordination between the food service staff and teachers.
- **Students receive consistent nutrition messages** throughout the school, classroom, cafeteria, home, community, and media.
- **Nutrition is integrated** into the health education curricula or core curriculum (e.g., math, science, language arts).

Source: From *Healthy Schools: Setting Nutrition Education Goals*, by the USDA Food and Nutrition Service, retrieved October 7, 2009, from http://www.fns.usda.gov/tn/Healthy/wellnesspolicygoals_nutritioned.html.

age levels to serve children in grades 1 through 6. Free of charge, the materials include lesson plans, a CD with music, reproducible worksheets, and Go Fish game cards. The MyPyramid lessons introduce the concept of food groups and teach students to identify the foods they eat in their diets. Understanding these basic nutrition concepts helps children to categorize foods and understand the role of food in maintaining good health.

Using an Integrated Nutrition Curriculum

Many nutrition and health curricula support an integrated approach to learning. For example, the North Carolina Nutrition Education and Training Program developed an integrated curriculum called *Food for Thought* (see the Web Resources section). Lesson plans are available for kindergarten through grade 5 on nutrition-related topics. These lessons focus on integrating healthy eating and physical activity with math and English language arts. The lesson plans include objectives, teacher resources, and teacher input sections that help teachers organize their nutrition lessons.

Another curriculum called *Cooking with Kids* addresses goals established by a local student nutrition advisory council to improve school food (see the Web Resources section). The bilingual curriculum introduces the concepts of food and culture through taste testing and cooking lessons. The cafeteria participates too by serving *Cooking with Kids* recipes throughout the school year. The cooking lessons focus on preparing recipes from five different regions of the world. Each lesson begins by using a map to identify where the recipe originated from and then provides the history of the foods and how they are grown, as well as the nutritional contributions of the ingredients used in preparing the recipe.

Teachers have access to a tremendous amount of support from a variety of resources as they strive to promote nutrition and health messages in the school environment. The extent of these resources emphasizes the importance placed on nutrition issues as health and education authorities team up to help solve the obesity epidemic and promote wellness.

Teaching about Sustainable Nutrition

Sustainable nutrition is the consumption of food that is grown in such a way as to protect the environment. Sustainable nutrition practices focus on encouraging the use of foods that have had minimal processing, packaging, and transportation, thereby decreasing the energy used in their production. In addition, careful sustainable growing practices are used to protect soil and water resources. Children are increasingly concerned about the environment. Teachers have the unique role and responsibility of helping children develop the collective skills to create a sustainable community. Teaching about sustainability empowers students. It also helps them understand the connection between the careful management of the environment and its impact on the economy and the livability of their community. Teachers can integrate sustainability concepts throughout the nutrition lessons they teach and relate these ideas to the school environment as well as the community at large.

MyEducationLab

Go to the Assignments and Activities section of Topic 5: Health Promotion/Policy in the MyEducationLab for your course and complete the activity entitled *Teaching Children about Nutrition*. What instructional strategies does this teacher use to teach children about nutrition?

MyEducationLab

To assess your understanding of issues related to feeding toddlers, preschoolers, and school-age children, go to the Book Specific Resources section in the MyEducationLab for your course, select *Nutrition, Health, and Safety for Young Children*, Chapter 6 of the Study Plan, and then complete the multiple choice questions and activities.

Sustainability as a core practice has been successfully adopted by a number of schools. For example, in Vermont, two pilot schools are participating in the *Sustainable Schools Project*. This foundation funded project is:

> [a] dynamic new model for school improvement and civic engagement. The program helps schools use sustainability as an integrating context for curriculum, community partnerships, and campus practices. (Sustainable Schools Project, 2008)

The project supports teachers by providing assistance with curriculum consultations and training and linking teachers to community partners and projects. It also helps them identify funding sources. This type of support can greatly enhance teachers' ability to foster an in-depth and meaningful approach to sustainability.

Summary

The diets of toddlers and preschool-age children are in transition as eating skills develop. Children learn about foods through experience and repeated exposures. A varied and balanced diet is important to promote positive eating habits and to help children explore and accept a wide range of foods. Toddlers are busy acquiring new eating skills. Teachers support these efforts by understanding toddlers' nutritional requirements and knowing how to feed them to address selective eating patterns, food neophobia, and food jags as toddlers learn about eating.

Preschool-age children have mastered many new eating skills and do well with routinely scheduled meals and snacks. The division of feeding responsibility helps preschool children learn to become autonomous eaters. This is supported by teachers who understand feeding responsibilities: Children choose whether they eat and how much, while teachers are responsible for what children eat, when, and where. Teachers need to understand general nutrition concepts and be familiar with the food guidance systems that support appropriate feeding practices such as the Child and Adult Care Food Program and MyPyramid for Kids.

Children in kindergarten through third grade are still growing at a steady pace and need healthy, balanced diets that meet their growth needs. Teachers need to advocate for each child to receive breakfast at home or school and to support the school lunch program. School-age children have more freedom than younger children to make their own decisions when eating in the school setting, so nutrition education, eating practices, and being physically active continue to be important wellness messages.

Teachers are also important advocates for school-age children. As advocates, teachers contribute to school wellness policies by encouraging healthful practices related to food and physical activity across the school environment and in all school-related activities. Teachers continue to be powerful role models for children of all ages. Demonstrating healthful eating and physical activity behaviors and environmental responsibility makes a positive contribution to children's future health.

Key Terms

Anorexia nervosa, p. 196

Bulimia nervosa, p. 196

Extended breast-feeding, p. 170

Food jag, p. 174

Food neophobia, p. 173

Selective eaters, p. 173

Review Questions

1. Feeding toddlers can sometimes be challenging. Discuss three challenging feeding situations a teacher might experience when providing meals to toddlers.

2. Discuss the types of developmental skills that must be considered when serving foods to toddlers.

3. Explain three strategies for teaching preschoolers about food and nutrition.

4. Explain how a teacher becomes an advocate for wellness in school programs.

5. Describe how to integrate nutrition, physical activity, and sustainability into planned curriculum.

Discussion Starters

1. Describe how you would encourage a child who is a selective eater and has multiple food allergies to broaden his food choices.

2. Outline plans for a field trip to help preschool children learn where bread comes from. Where would you take the group? What aspects of bread production would you focus on?

3. Imagine that your elementary school has decided to embrace the concepts of sustainability. Discuss how to incorporate this into classroom routines as well as lesson plans.

Practice Points

1. Using the CACFP guidelines for toddlers in the Appendix, plan menus for a breakfast, a lunch, and a snack.

2. Using MyPyramid recommendations for preschoolers who require 1,000 calories per day, plan a lunch menu. Are there significant differences between the CACFP and MyPyramid guidelines?

3. Create a math lesson for second-grade children that integrates nutrition and sustainability concepts.

Web Resources

CDC Local Wellness Policy Tools and Resources
www.cdc.gov/HealthyYouth/healthtopics/wellness.htm

Cooking with Kids Curriculum
http://cookingwithkids.net/About_Us/index.html

Ellyn Satter's Division of the Responsibilities of Feeding
www.ellynsatter.com

Food and Nutrition Information Center: Toddler Nutrition and Health Resource List
www.nal.usda.gov/fnic/pubs/bibs/gen/toddler.pdf

Iowa State University Extension: Database of Nutrition Education Curriculums
www.extension.iastate.edu/nutrition/search.php

MyPyramid for Preschoolers
www.mypyramid.gov/preschoolers/index.html

North Carolina Nutrition Services Branch of North Carolina Division of Public Health: Food for Thought Curriculum
www.nutritionnc.com/ResourcesForSchools/index.htm#fftConnection

Zero to Three
www.zerotothree.org/site/PageServer?pagename=homepage

chapter 7 | Menu Planning

Learning Outcomes

After reading this chapter, you should be able to:

1. Explain the four phases of menu planning.

2. Describe menu planning requirements for early child care settings.

3. List three broad program goals that support the development of healthful menus.

4. Explain the procedure for building a menu.

5. Discuss strategies for managing young children's special dietary considerations.

Jeanine places a set of old menus on her kitchen table and begins the process of planning a new set of menus for the upcoming week. Feeding 3- to 5-year-olds has its challenges. Every week she plans menus, shops, and prepares food for a group that includes one finicky eater, a child who is allergic to milk, another who is overweight, and one who for religious reasons does not eat pork. Included in the mix is a 3-year-old vegetarian whose well-intentioned mother makes many menu suggestions that Jeanine tries to accommodate even though it puts a strain on her food budget. Jeanine participates in the Child and Adult Care Food Program, a federal child nutrition program that provides funding to offset the cost of meals and snacks. This helps but completing the paperwork to meet the program's reimbursement requirements is time consuming.

Jeanine wants to plan nutritious meals but there are so many recommendations to consider she wonders where to start. She recalls how last week none of the children ate the mashed sweet potatoes she served and thought with regret of all that wonderful vitamin A going down the kitchen disposal. Such waste is also not cost effective! Jeanine realizes she needs to rethink her approach to menu planning. Her goals are to plan nutritious menus that are appealing to children, meet families' expectations, and fit her food budget constraints. At the same time she wants to streamline her menu planning process and make sure she meets the unique needs of each child in her program. She organizes her materials and begins.

The best health recommendations are useless unless they can be applied easily to daily life routines. This is true when creating routines for early childhood programs as well. For example, in the case scenario Jeanine struggles with the weekly planning of healthful menus for a small group of young children who have a wide range of nutritional needs. If you were responsible for Jeanine's program, how would you translate diet guidelines into menus that promote healthful eating and obesity prevention in young children? How would you feed this group of 3- to 5-year-old children nutritious meals that meet all of their needs? First you need a plan.

In this chapter we describe a systematic way to develop appropriate menus. We begin by discussing the resources available for developing menus that meet quality recommendations and are appealing to children. We discuss how to establish and promote broad program-wide nutrition-related wellness goals through effective menu planning. We detail a step-by-step procedure for writing and implementing menus and define strategies for purchasing, storing, and preparing foods to keep menus cost effective. All of this work is for naught, however, if children don't eat what is offered. To address this, we discuss strategies that support children as they explore new foods. We also provide tactics for adapting menus for children with special dietary needs and religious or cultural preferences. Taken together, this information will help you plan menus that support appropriate growth and development in young children.

HEALTHFUL MENU PLANNING

The menu forms the foundation of nutritional health in the home and guides many other aspects of food management in the children's setting, such as food purchasing, storing, preparation, and service. Developing a healthful, cost-effective menu requires an understanding of nutrition goals, evidence-based nutrition practices, and food budgeting. The task of menu planning may seem daunting as these many aspects are addressed and balanced. A good menu, however, can save time and money and—as with any other skill—menu planning becomes easier with practice. Menu planning is made simpler by using a four-phase approach:

- *Phase 1:* Understand child nutrition and food program requirements.
- *Phase 2:* Establish broad program nutrition goals.
- *Phase 3:* Write menus using a step-by-step approach.
- *Phase 4:* Adapt menus to support special dietary needs or food preferences.

The first phase of menu planning includes understanding specific program requirements. Teachers need to be aware of existing nutrition, licensing, and funding directives when planning menus in early childhood settings. For example, the *Dietary Guidelines for Americans* and the Recommended Dietary Allowances (RDA) are food guidance systems that form the foundation for federal food program recommendations, including the Child and Adult Care Food Program, the National School Lunch Program, the School Breakfast Program, and the After School Snack Program (U.S. Department of Agriculture [USDA] Food and Nutrition Service, 2008b). These established requirements provide teachers direct guidance in menu planning.

The second phase of menu development focuses on determining how well menus address nutrition wellness goals established for the early childhood setting. In the opening case scenario, Jeanine is committed to offering many different fruits and vegetables in her class. Based on her familiarity with the *Dietary Guidelines for Americans*, she understands the importance of offering a wide variety of fruits and vegetables to children when they are young. She chooses *Tasting the Fruits and Vegetables We Read About* as a theme in her curriculum that focuses on learning about the foods discussed in different children's books and plans to start with *Eating the Alphabet* by Lois Ehlert.

The third phase of menu planning involves the steps associated with menu writing and implementation, putting the concepts of the previous two phases into action. This is a creative process in which teachers are encouraged to take into consideration the flavors, textures, colors, and aromas of foods when designing menus that tempt the palates of young children.

Finally, the fourth phase of menu development focuses on how to adapt menus to support alternative or special diets so that all children, regardless of health concerns or cultural preferences, receive a healthy balanced diet. These four phases of menu planning provide teachers with an approach to creating healthful, appealing menus that are easy to use and cost effective.

UNDERSTANDING REQUIREMENTS FOR MENU PLANNING

Young children grow and develop quickly during the early childhood years. They rely on their families and teachers to ensure that they get the nutritious foods they need every day. Planning healthy meals that appeal to children and accommodate their needs is a key component of this responsibility. This goal is considered so important in early childhood settings that a variety of established requirements must be met for licensed programs and those funded by state or federal agencies. Failure to provide healthy menus may jeopardize children's nutritional needs and may also put the children's program or school at risk for having its license revoked or funding rescinded. Therefore, early childhood educators must:

- Understand the teacher's role in menu planning.
- Determine the types of guidelines and how to apply them to menu planning.
- Develop a system to organize these resources so that they are easily accessible.

These steps ready teachers for actual menu writing. But first teachers must consider their specific program and the role they play in the menu planning process.

Identifying the Teacher's Role

The teacher's role in menu planning varies depending on the style of the early childhood setting. Most settings offer snacks and meals or supervise children as they eat food brought from home. Teachers who work in large child care centers and primary school settings are usually not responsible for writing menus. Such organizations usually rely on food service professionals to plan menus. In contrast, teachers in family child care settings and small child care centers are often involved in menu planning.

Although teachers may not always be directly involved in preparing menus, an understanding of the concepts and requirements for menu planning helps teachers reinforce healthful eating practices and educate children and their families about nutrition. The menu is a focal point for teaching children about foods and nutrition and can provide families with a tool for their own menu planning.

Understanding healthful menu planning has other benefits. Teachers are often the link between children with special food-related concerns and food service staff. Recognizing how special food needs impact the menu helps teachers know how to advocate for accommodations. They can make sure the correct menu items are served to all children, especially those who require special diets. If teachers plan classroom cooking activities in which the food prepared replaces a meal or snack, they need to know how to make appropriate menu substitutions. Teachers in primary schools typically have direct responsibility for planning and supervising snacks served in the kindergarten or early primary classes where young children often get hungry between meals. All teachers benefit by being prepared to plan appetizing, nutritious menus.

Understanding Menu Planning Resources

Many resources are available to guide menu planning for young children. Some agencies, such as funding authorities, provide a list of nutritional requirements that food service in children's settings must meet to secure financial reimbursement. Health organizations offer diet advice based on evidenced-based research, which is summarized in guidelines. Food safety is another factor covered by various licensing requirements. These requirements and guidelines direct the types of food choices teachers make when planning menus. A successful menu is appealing to children and in compliance with the regulations for meeting children's nutritional needs. Examples of the different types of authorities and the agencies and programs that fall under their oversight are found in Table 7-1. By adhering to the authorities' recommendations and regulations, teachers can understand the parameters that guide menu writing.

Understanding Funded Menu Planning Systems

Two agencies provide the template for menu planning in early childhood settings: the Child and Adult Care Food Program, which guides menu planning for prekindergarten programs, and the National School Lunch Program, which guides menu planning for schools. Each offers information on how to prepare menus that meet the federal assisted meal program prerequisites for reimbursement.

The Child and Adult Care Food Program (CACFP)

The CACFP is a federal child nutrition program funded by the Food and Nutrition Service of the USDA. The CACFP aims to increase the quality and affordability of early childhood programs by providing funds for nutritious meals and snacks. Participating programs are eligible to receive reimbursement for either two meals and one snack per day or one meal and two snacks. The funds allow participating programs to provide nutritious meals to low-income children (USDA Food and Nutrition Service, 2008b). Early childhood education programs can participate in CACFP if certain eligibility criteria are met.

Eligibility for Participation Licensed or approved nonprofit public or private child care centers, Head Start programs, family child care homes, after-school programs, and homeless shelters are eligible to participate in the CACFP. Participating programs enter into an agreement with the state agency in charge of administering the CACFP to receive reimbursement for some of the costs involved in providing snacks and meals for children. Many child care programs, unlike primary school setting, do not charge separately for meals. The amount of reimbursement to programs is determined using guidelines that are based on the household income of each enrolled child.

The classification of families' income as eligible for free, reduced, or paid meals, therefore, does not reflect what families are charged but rather determines the degree of reimbursement the program receives from the CACFP funding authority. For-profit child care programs may be

Table 7-1	Menu Planning Resources	
Types of Authorities	**Types of Agencies**	**Types of Programs**
Health authorities	Government agencies, health care organizations	Maternal and Child Health Bureau American Public Health Association American Academy of Pediatrics USDA Food and Nutrition Service • *USDA Dietary Guidelines for Americans*, 2005 • MyPyramid American Dietetic Association American Medical Association
Licensing authorities	State child care licensing agencies, Food and Drug Administration, Public Health Service, state public health divisions, county health departments	National Resource Center for Health and Safety in Child Care and Early Education Local, state, and federal regulators who inspect programs that are involved in food service using the FDA Food Code, which contains food safety rules
Accreditation authorities	National agencies that set professional standards for early childhood education programs	National Association for the Education of Young Children (NAEYC) National Association for Family Child Care (NAFCC) National Early Childhood Program Accreditation (NECPA) Commission National AfterSchool Association (NAA)
Funding authorities	Federal or state agencies that provide funding for early childhood education programs, child nutrition programs, Administration for Children and Families, Office of Head Start	Child and Adult Care Food Program (CACFP) National School Lunch Program (NSLP) School Breakfast Program (SBP) After School Snack Program (ASSP) Federal and state Head Start and Early Head Start programs

Sources: Based on *Caring for Our Children: National Health and Safety Performance Standards: Guidelines for Out-of-Home Child Care Programs*, 2nd ed., by American Academy of Pediatrics, American Public Health Association, and National Resource Center for Health and Safety in Child Care, 2007, Elk Grove, IL: American Academy of Pediatrics; and *U.S. FDA/CFSAN FDA Food Code*, 2005, Washington, DC: U.S. Food and Drug Administration, retrieved June 1, 2008, from http://www.cfsan.fda.gov/~dms/foodcode.html.

What if. . .

a child in your program refused to drink milk? What would you do? How do you think this would impact CACFP reimbursement?

eligible to participate in the CACFP if 25% of the children enrolled qualify for free or reduced-price meals or subsidized child care payments (Title XX of the Social Security Act funding) (USDA Food and Nutrition Service, 2008b). All Head Start children are eligible for free meals regardless of family income level (USDA Food and Nutrition Service, 2008a). To receive CACFP reimbursement, participating programs must maintain accurate records, including menus planned, foods purchased and served, and numbers of children who ate at each meal. Teachers must record exactly how many children eat at each meal while the meal is served, which is called a point-of-service meal count. The CACFP reimbursement is paid directly to programs.

Family child care providers may also be eligible for participation in the CACFP, which has established two tiers of reimbursement rates. If family child care providers are located in low-income neighborhoods or have personal incomes that are at or below 185% of the federal poverty level they are eligible for Tier I reimbursement rates, which are greater than Tier II levels (USDA Food and Nutrition Service, 2008b).

Benefits of CACFP CACFP helps offset food and food service administrative expenses, making child care more affordable. The CACFP also provides yearly training for teachers to learn about nutrition for infants and children, and also menu planning. The CACFP's system for menu planning helps teachers understand which food groups need to be served and in what amounts for each specific age group to meet children's nutritional requirements. Even programs that do not participate in the CACFP find that the CACFP guidelines provide an excellent framework for drafting menus.

Breakfast Meal Pattern	Day 1	Day 2
1 grain/bread	⅓ cup cornflakes	½ slice whole-grain bread
1 fruit/vegetable	½ cup sliced banana	½ cup cubed cantaloupe
1 milk	¾ cup 1% milk	¾ cup 1% milk

Figure 7-1 Sample Menu: CACFP Breakfast Meal Pattern for 3- to 5-Year Olds

CACFP Program Requirements The CACFP guides meal-by-meal menu planning with specific requirements for infants and young children. Also called meal patterns, these meal-by-meal breakdowns provide menu planning templates for three age group categories for infants and three age group categories for children. The meal patterns outline the food groups, or components, that need to be offered and the amounts of each food required to qualify as a CACFP-approved breakfast, lunch, supper, or snack. The food group components for children's meals include milk, grains/breads, meats/meat alternates, and fruits/vegetables. It is important for teachers to remember that the CACFP portions represent the minimum portion to serve. Very active children and older children usually need larger portions to satisfy their hunger. Sufficient food should be available to meet these needs.

Meal pattern requirements for infants are very specific. They outline the minimum amounts of breast milk or formula and other age-appropriate infant foods that must be served to meet CACFP guidelines. The infant meal patterns show teachers the progression of how foods are introduced and served to infants over the first year of life. They also offer guidelines about how much breast milk or formula infants generally consume. The Appendix provides meal pattern requirements for infants and children participating in the CACFP.

Teachers should easily recognize the value of these meal service patterns as they plan menus. Planning healthy menus is not left up to chance in programs that use CACFP guidelines. For example, a teacher who is planning the morning meal for 3- to 5-year-old children can refer to the CACFP breakfast meal pattern for the 3- to 5-year-old age category as shown in Figure 7-1. Peanut butter, a protein alternate, can be used on day 2 to enhance flavor and acceptance of the slice of bread; however, a meat or meat alternate is not essential for the breakfast meal to meet CACFP requirements.

CACFP Creditable Foods High-quality food is a priority of the CACFP. For example, CACFP guidelines recommend that foods from the grain group be either enriched or whole grains. These guidelines also mandate that 100% fruit juice be served at snack time only. If a food does not meet these specifications it is not considered a creditable food. A creditable food is one that meets CACFP guidelines and is eligible for reimbursement. A noncreditable food does not meet the CACFP's quality standards and is not eligible for reimbursement. (See the Book Specific Resources on MyEducationLab for a list of creditable and noncreditable starch/grain foods.) Incentives to use both creditable foods and accurate menu planning tactics are strong. When programs use noncreditable food items in place of creditable foods or make mistakes in menu planning, they cannot claim reimbursement for that meal. See Figure 7-2 which shows two meals. The meal on the right does not meet CACFP standards because juice was served at lunch. Milk is required at breakfast and lunch meals.

The National School Lunch Program (NSLP) and School Breakfast Program (SBP)

The NSLP and SBP are programs of the USDA that are designed to improve children's health and well-being by providing access to nutritious meals (see Chapter 6). All public and private schools and residential child care institutions

meal patterns
a guide to inform menu planners which food groups, or components, need to be offered and in what amounts for breakfast, lunch, supper, and snack for infants and children

components
term used by the CACFP to describe food groups; includes milk, grains/breads, meats/meat alternates, and fruits/vegetables

creditable food
food that meets CACFP guidelines and is eligible for reimbursement

noncreditable food
food that does not meet quality standards established by the CACFP and when served in place of a creditable component makes a meal or snack ineligible for reimbursement

Figure 7-2 CACFP Standards Require That Milk Be Provided with Breakfast and Lunch

Figure 7-3 Menu Planning Options and Requirements for the National School Lunch and School Breakfast Programs*

✓ **Traditional Food-Based Menu Planning System**
  - Schools must *offer* at least five food items for lunch and four food items for breakfast.
  - Quantities of milk, meat/meat alternates, fruits/vegetables, and grains are specified.

✓ **The Nutrient Standard Menu Planning System**
  - Reimbursable meals must contain a minimum of three menu items and must include an entrée, fluid milk, and one side dish at lunch and fluid milk and two side dishes for breakfast.
  - Menus must provide an average of one-third of 1989 Recommended Dietary Allowance (RDA) for protein, calcium, iron, vitamin A, and vitamin C at lunch (one-quarter the RDA for breakfast) and provide appropriate levels of calories for the age/grade group.
  - Menus must be consistent with the 1995 *Dietary Guidelines for Americans* by limiting the percent of calories from total fat to 30% of the actual number of calories offered, limiting the percent of calories from saturated fat to less than 10% of the actual number of calories offered, and contain acceptable levels of sodium and cholesterol and dietary fiber.

*Nutrition standards and meal requirements are currently undergoing revision.

Sources: From *Dietary Guidelines for Americans, 2005 and the New Dietary Reference Intakes: Potential Implications for the NSLP and SBP Meals* (PowerPoint presentation), by Jay Hirschman and Clare Miller, 2008, Alexandria, VA: USDA Food and Nutrition Service, retrieved August 24, 2009, from http://www.fns.usda.gov/ora/menu/Presentations/DGAsandDRI.pdf; and School Breakfast Program Menu Planning, USDA Food and Nutrition Service, 2009, retrieved September 25, 2009 from http://www.fns.usda.gov/CND/Breakfast/Menu/sbp-menu-planning.htm

are eligible to participate in the NSLP program if they agree to offer a nonprofit school lunch program that meets all federal regulations and is available to all children (USDA Food and Nutrition Service, 2009). The NSLP and SBP are managed by the each state's education authority, which establishes agreements with schools, institutions, and other facilities.

Primary grade school teachers are generally unlikely to plan menus. However, they should be aware of the type of menu planning system in place at their schools so that they can support goals that promote the development of positive eating habits. Teachers who support the NSLP and SBP help create a healthful school nutrition environment and enhance opportunities for nutrition education.

NSLP menu planning follows either a traditional food-based or a nutrient standard menu planning system (USDA, 2007). Similar to the CACFP, the traditional food-based menu planning system identifies food groups that must be offered in specified amounts at each mealtime. The nutrient standard menu planning approach uses a computer analysis system that evaluates menus while they are being prepared. This method offers some flexibility in daily menu planning, because the analysis of nutrients is summed over the course of the week rather than on a daily basis. Figure 7-3 provides guidelines that must be met to receive funding via the NSLP and SBP.

Teachers can participate in school district wellness committees where input on menus is sought. Individual schools may also have school health advisory committees or councils that discuss menu options, wellness policies, and opportunities for nutrition education. These opportunities bring teachers, families, and school food service personnel together to discuss health and nutrition issues, including goals for menu planning. Supporting healthful practices is everyone's responsibility.

Head Start/Early Head Start Programs

Head Start is another federal agency that provides funding conditional on meeting specific nutrition standards. Head Start is administered by the Office of Head Start (OHS), Administration for Children and Families (ACF), and the U.S. Department of Health and Human Services (HHS) (2008). Head Start and Early Head Start grantees are guided by the Head Start Performance Standards, which outline performance measures for all aspects of the program. Teachers who work with menus in the Head Start setting must become familiar

---

traditional food-based menu planning system menu planning approach for National School Lunch Program that is similar to the CACFP approach in that specific food groups called components must be offered at mealtimes

nutrient standard menu planning system computer-based menu planning approach for the National School Lunch Program that analyzes the specific nutrient content of menu items automatically while menus are being planned; also called *NuMenus*

Head Start Performance Standards federal regulatory guidelines that provide oversight on all aspects of Head Start and Early Head Start program administration not only with CACFP guidelines, but also with the Head Start standards for menu planning. A section in the Head Start Performance Standards entitled *Child Nutrition* (Title 45 Chapter XIII, Part 1304, Sec. 1304.23) outlines the standards that relate to program nutrition services. A few of these are summarized below:

- All children's nutritional needs must be met, including those with special diets and children with disabilities.
- Programs must serve foods that broaden a child's food experience, including cultural and ethnic foods.
- One-third of a child's daily nutritional needs must be met in part-day programs and one-half to two-thirds in full-day programs.
- Programs must participate in the CACFP and portion sizes must meet CACFP guidelines.
- Foods served must be high in nutrients and low in fat, sugar, and salt (HHS Administration for Children and Families, 2006).

In general, the CACFP guidelines support the Head Start Performance Standards. However, some foods that the CACFP allows on occasion such as cookies, doughnuts, and sweet rolls conflict with Head Start standards on serving foods that are low in sugar and fat content. In this situation, the more stringent Head Start Performance Standards must be followed by Head Start and Early Head Start programs.

USDA *Schools/Child Nutrition Commodity Program*

The Food and Nutrition Service of the USDA manages the distribution of commodity foods through the USDA Schools/Child Nutrition Commodity Program (USDA Food and Nutrition Service, 2008c). Commodity foods are foods that the federal government has legal authority to purchase from American farmers and distribute to support farm prices. The food is made available to state agencies and Indian Tribal Organizations and is distributed through a variety of venues including the CACFP. Early childhood programs participating in CACFP are eligible to receive these foods. Commodity foods typically include some fresh but predominantly canned and frozen fruits, fruit juices, and vegetables, frozen or canned meats, poultry and tuna fish, cheese, dry and canned beans, peanut butter, vegetable oils, rice, pasta products, flour, cornmeal, and oats (USDA Food and Nutrition Service, 2008c). Programs using commodity foods should have a list of these foods on hand when planning menus.

commodity foods
foods that the federal government has legal authority to purchase from American farmers and distribute to support farm prices. These foods are used to support nutrition assistance programs including child nutrition programs

Organizing Resources

Remembering the many details of menu planning is not necessary if resources are well organized and accessible. In the opening case scenario, Jeanine recognizes the need to improve her approach to writing menus. She starts by compiling recommendations and regulations for meals service and menu planning in a notebook. She also creates a computer "folder" to organize her electronic resources. She finds it helpful to review and refer to these resources while she drafts her menus. Jeanine's resource files include information that pertains to her family child care program and to the age group she serves:

- An electronic bookmark to the federal government's MyPyramid for Preschoolers.
- A copy of the *Dietary Guidelines for Americans, 2005* (HHS & USDA, 2005).
- Position paper of the American Dietetic Association, *Benchmarks for Nutrition Programs in Child Care Settings* (American Dietetic Association, 2005).
- State licensing guidelines for food preparation and service (American Academy of Pediatrics, American Public Health Association, & National Resource Center for Health and Safety in Child Care, 2007).
- CACFP guidelines (USDA Food and Nutrition Service, 2008b).
- A link to the Special Supplemental Nutrition Program for Women, Infants, and Children (WIC) Works Resource System where there are guidelines for feeding children from infant to age 5, information on ethnic foods, and food preparation advice including thrifty recipes (WIC Works Resource Team, 2009).

MyEducationLab

Go to the Building Teaching Skills and Dispositions section of Topic 3: Menu Planning in the MyEducationLab for your course and complete the activity entitled *Develop Children's Meals that Conform to National Guidelines.* As you work through this learning unit, consider whether each of these menus meets necessary standards.

MyEducationLab

Go to the Assignments and Activities section of Topic 1: Basic Nutrition in the MyEducationLab for your course and complete the activity entitled *Using the Food Pyramid*. How do you see this school program implementing MyPyramid's recommendations?

Teachers who are drafting menus for their Head Start program might also include this item in their notebooks:

- Head Start Performance Standards for Nutrition (HHS Administration for Children and Families, 2007).

A program serving infants and toddlers benefits by including:

- The USDA Food and Nutrition Service, *Feeding Infants: A Guide for Use in the Child Nutrition Programs* (see the Web Resources in Chapter 5).

A teacher in a large child care center involved in menu planning will also need:

- A copy of the National Association for the Education of Young Children (NAEYC) Health Standards 5A (*Promoting and Protecting Children's Health and Controlling Infectious Disease*) and 5B (*Ensuring Children's Nutritional Well-Being*), which provide standards for feeding infants, food safety, timing of meals and snacks, and guidance on foods that cause choking (NAEYC, 2009).
- The contact number for a registered dietitian who can evaluate menus if the program does not participate in the CACFP (NAEYC, 2009).

In her menu planning, Jeanine uses the USDA's MyPyramid for Preschoolers to find out that girls and boys between the ages of 3 and 5 who participate in a moderate rate of physical activity each day (30 to 60 minutes) need between 1,200 and 1,400 calories (see Figure 7-4) (USDA, 2009). She selects the 1,400-calorie level to determine age-appropriate amounts for the children her program serves. She learns that preschool-age children need 5 ounces of grains (half of which should be whole grains), 3 cups of fruits and vegetables, 2 cups of fat-free milk, and 4 ounces of lean protein per day.

Figure 7-4 MyPyramid Meal Pattern for a 1,400-Calorie Level

Based on the information you provided, this is your daily recommended amount from each food group.

GRAINS 5 ounces	VEGETABLES 1 1/2 cups	FRUITS 1 1/2 cups	MILK 2 cups	MEAT & BEANS 4 ounces
Make half your grains whole	**Vary your veggies** Aim for these amounts each week:	**Focus on fruits**	**Get your calcium-rich foods**	**Go lean with protein**
Aim for at least **2 1/2 ounces** of whole grains a day	**Dark green veggies** = 1 1/2 cups **Orange veggies** = 1 cup **Dry beans & peas** = 1 cup **Starchy veggies** = 2 1/2 cups **Other veggies** = 4 1/2 cups	Eat a variety of fruit Go easy on fruit juices	Go low-fat or fat-free when you choose milk, yogurt, or cheese	Choose low-fat or lean meats and poultry Vary your protein routine–choose more fish, beans, peas, nuts and seeds

Find your balance between food and physical activity	**Know your limits on fats, sugars, and sodium**
Be physically active for at least **60 minutes** every day, or most days.	Your allowance for oils is **4 teaspoons a day.** Limit extras–solid fats and sugars–to **170 calories a day.**

Source: From *USDA MyPyramid Steps to a Healthier You* at http://www.mypyramid.gov.

Jeanine needs to know how much total food she will require for children attending her program. She learns from the American Dietetic Association's position paper titled *Benchmarks for Nutrition Programs in Child Care Settings*, which references Head Start Performance Standards, that children in part-day programs (4 to 7 hours) should be served meals that meet one-third of their daily nutrient needs, while those in full-day programs (8 hours or more) should receive at least half to two-thirds of their daily requirements (American Dietetic Association, 2005; Code of Federal Regulations, 1998). Jeanine also decides to check the National Resource Center for Health and Safety in Child Care and Early Education website (American Academy of Pediatrics et al., 2007) to refresh her memory on national and state health and safety performance standards. She is reminded that in her home state she is required to participate in a food safety course to obtain a food handler's card and that her menus should follow CACFP guidelines.

Having these requirements easily accessible helps teachers like Jeanine streamline their menu writing, create a menu that successfully meets the nutrient needs of young children, and support the reimbursement requirements for federally funded child nutrition programs.

What if. . .

you were not responsible for menu planning in your preschool program and noticed that the portions provided were often very large? What might be your concerns? What resources would you use to understand appropriate portion sizes for the children you serve?

ESTABLISHING PROGRAM NUTRITION GOALS

Menu planning and the selection and service of foods reflect the early childhood setting's goals for wellness and nutrition. Using nutrition as a way to improve health and prevent illness and disease is a common theme. When endorsed by teachers and supported by the total program environment, this goal can promote healthful lifestyles and dietary changes that are sustainable into adulthood. Healthful nutrition is especially important during early childhood when lifelong eating and physical activity patterns are being established. Teachers are uniquely positioned to have a significant impact on beneficial eating habits in young children that support wellness and health.

Promoting Healthful Eating Habits through Menu Planning

Early childhood education programs influence many aspects of children's lives. For example, research demonstrates the effectiveness of the elementary school setting as a means of preventing and achieving improvement in overweight and obesity in children (American Dietetic Association, 2006; Katz, O'Connell, Yanchou Njike, Yeh, & Nawaz, 2007). In response to the increasing incidence of childhood obesity, the American Dietetic Association states there is a need to "broaden the focus of dietary guidance to address children's overconsumption of energy-dense, nutrient-poor foods and beverages and physical activity patterns" (American Dietetic Association, 2008c). Teachers who plan menus need to carefully consider not only the nutrient requirements of meals but also the dietary practices that protect children's health.

Health authorities have been considering these issues and look to research to establish evidence-based recommendations (see Chapter 1). Evidence-based practices shift the basis of decision making from historical practices to those supported by the best available science. A good example of evidence-based guidelines and a starting point for teachers to consider when establishing program nutrition wellness goals is the *Dietary Guidelines for Americans, 2005* (HHS & USDA, 2005). Using the dietary guidelines as a guide, there are concrete things programs can do to promote healthful eating in the early childhood classroom.

Offering Children More Fruits and Vegetables

Fruits and vegetables are rich in vitamins, minerals, and fiber and, with a few exceptions, are low in fat and always cholesterol free. Consequently, eating fruits and vegetables can lead to lowered total fat, saturated fat, and cholesterol intake and a higher intake of nutrients

MyEducationLab

Go to the Assignments and Activities section of Topic 3: Menu Planning in the MyEducationLab for your course and complete the activity entitled *Introducing Children to New Foods.* How does this teacher entice her children to try different fruits and vegetables?

protective against heart disease, high blood pressure, obesity, and cancer (American Dietetic Association, 2008a, 2008b; Dauchet, Amouyel, Hercberg, & Dallongeville, 2006; Riboli & Norat, 2003; Steffen et al., 2003; Tucker et al., 2005). Fruits and vegetables are also rich in vitamin A, which helps maintain and protect healthy vision (Harvard School of Public Health, 2008). Teachers who identify the goal of adding more fruits and vegetables to menus sometimes face a dilemma. How do they get children to eat what's good for them?

Enticing Children to Eat More Fruits and Vegetables   The flavor of foods is the primary basis by which young children decide whether or not to eat or drink something (Mennella & Pepino, 2005). Children respond to certain tastes differently than adults because their sensory system for taste is not yet fully developed. Infants and young children tend to like sweet-tasting foods more than adults and bitter-tasting foods less (Mennella & Pepino, 2005). Infants, however, may not be as discriminating between tastes and are more accepting of the introduction of new foods than toddlers or preschoolers (Birch, Gunder, & Grimm-Thomas, 1998). This information can be used to advantage. Teachers and families should be partners in making sure infants are exposed to a wide variety of fruits and vegetables when they are young to create an acceptance that will last into older years (Guidetti & Cavazza, 2008).

Toddlers and preschoolers may be less accepting of the introduction of new foods such as vegetables than when they were infants (Nicklaus, Boggio, Chabanet, & Issanchou, 2005). In response to this reluctance, teachers and families may begin to limit the types of foods offered to those that children like, as a way to ensure that children get enough to eat. Young children, however, learn through experience. By offering foods repeatedly, children will learn over time to accept a new food (Birch et al., 1998; Satter, 2005; Wardle et al., 2003). It is always important to remember to offer different foods, but not force children to eat them. Forcing causes stress and tension around mealtime and may end up creating food aversions (Satter, 2005).

Menu Planning Strategies to Include More Fruits and Vegetables   Teachers can use a variety of strategies in menu planning to increase children's interest in fruits and vegetables. Consider these tactics:

- Plan to serve fruits and vegetables with flavors, textures, and smells that appeal to children. For example, overcooked broccoli has a less desirable texture and aroma than raw broccoli, so children may do better with raw broccoli.
- Serve foods that are visually appealing. Salads with lots of color are more desirable than ones prepared with plain iceberg lettuce.
- Offer various forms of fruits and vegetables. Fresh, frozen, canned, and dry varieties all count toward good nutrition.

Whole foods are foods that have undergone minimal food processing and have no ingredients added to them that detract from a healthful diet.

- Plan menu items into which shredded or pureed vegetables or fruits can be added such as pizza, spaghetti, chili, meatloaf, quick breads, and muffins.
- Serve foods using different methods of preparation such as shredded carrot raisin salad, steamed carrots, mashed carrots, carrot soup, or carrot muffins.
- Select menu items that combine various vegetables or fruits such as soups, stir-fried vegetables, or fruit salads.
- Introduce a new fruit or vegetable frequently, and serve it along with familiar foods. Realize that it can take up to 10 to 15 exposures before children accept new foods (Satter, 2005).
- Use classroom cooking activities to introduce children to new fruits and vegetables.
- Add dips that have nutritious qualities to the menus to increase the likelihood that children will try them:
  - Serve sliced vegetables with salsa, ketchup, or low-fat ranch dip.

- Serve sliced fruits with yogurt or peanut butter.
- Dip graham crackers into applesauce.
- Dip whole-grain toast wedges or low-fat string cheese into pureed strawberries.

It is always important to focus on nutrition by offering variety when planning menus. Teachers can follow the USDA Food and Nutrition Service (2007c) suggestions:

- Offer a daily a fruit or vegetable rich in vitamin C such as citrus fruits, kiwis, strawberries, mangoes, red peppers, and tomatoes.
- Include dark green or deep orange vegetables on the menu three or four times per week. Varieties include broccoli, dark green leafy vegetables such as spinach, leaf lettuce, carrots, sweet potatoes, and winter squashes.
- Include potassium-rich fruits and vegetables such as bananas, prunes, prune juice, raisins, oranges, orange juice, tomatoes, tomato juice, potatoes, cantaloupe or honeydew melon, dried apricots, and dried peaches.

These strategies help set the stage for getting children to try more fruits and vegetables. There is one tactic, however, that is easy and costs next to nothing to implement. Teachers and families simply need to eat their fruits and vegetables at mealtimes, too. Modeling, especially with enthusiasm, is a very effective strategy for improving children's willingness to try new foods (Addessi, Galloway, Visalberghi, & Birch, 2005; Guidetti & Cavazza, 2008; Hendy & Raudenbush, 2000a; Wardle et al., 2003).

Encouraging Whole Basic Foods

Whole basic foods are important contributors to health and should replace highly processed foods on the menu whenever possible. Whole basic foods are foods with only one ingredient. Milk, fresh fruits and vegetables including dried beans, peas, and lentils, whole grains, nuts, fresh meats, poultry, and fish are all basic nutrient-rich foods to which no salt, sugar, or fat has been added (Sizer & Whitney, 2006). Whole foods are foods that have undergone minimal food processing and have no ingredients added to them that detract from a healthful diet. For example, consider a fresh potato. It is naturally rich in potassium, vitamin C, and fiber. When it is turned into a potato chip, it loses its vitamin C and fiber and gains excess sodium and fat. Compared to a fresh potato, the potato chip is a less-than-desirable food choice.

Eating Whole Foods Promotes Health Whole foods such as whole grains and fresh fruits and vegetables are rich in fiber, a dietary substance that is only found in the plants consumed as food. Some types of fiber prevent constipation. Other types of fiber help reduce cholesterol levels, which makes these foods heart healthy (see Chapter 4). Whole grains are foods that contain all parts of the grain kernel including the bran, endosperm, and germ, even after the grain is milled. Whole grains are rich in essential vitamins, minerals, and fiber. They also contain high levels of antioxidants, which are helpful in reducing the risk for cancer, heart disease, and other diseases (American Dietetic Association, 2007). In contrast, refined grains have had the bran and germ removed in the milling process, which reduces the fiber and nutrient content. Examples of refined grain products include white bread, pasta, and white rice.

Sometimes some of the nutrients that were lost during processing, such as the B vitamins and iron, are added back into the product. When this is done, the grain is referred to as an enriched grain. In addition, sometimes grain products are fortified. Fortified means the grains have had extra nutrients added to support good health. For example, bread products are fortified with folic acid, a B vitamin.

A good rule of thumb to remember when purchasing whole-grain breads is to look for products that list "whole" or "whole-grain" before the ingredient's name on the nutrition facts label and that also state they are 100% whole grain. Another way to determine whether a food contains whole grains is to look for a stamp developed by the Whole Grains Council (2008). This stamp is assigned to food items that contain 16 grams of whole grain or more, which is considered one serving of a 100% whole-grain product. Not all whole-grain products contain this label. Table 7-2 shows the Whole Grains Council stamp and lists the number of servings of whole grains recommended for boys and girls.

whole basic foods foods with only one ingredient such as milk; fresh fruits and vegetables, including dried beans, peas, and lentils; whole grains; nuts; eggs; fresh meats; poultry; and fish. Whole foods have undergone minimal food processing

whole grains grains that contain all parts of the grain kernel including the bran, endosperm, and germ after the grain is milled

refined grains grains that have the bran and germ removed during the milling process, which reduces the fiber and nutrient content

enriched grains refined grains that have some of the nutrients that were lost during processing, such as B vitamins and iron, added back into them

fortified grains grains to which extra nutrients have been added to support the good health of the general population

Table 7-2	Daily Recommended Servings of Grains and Whole Grains Based on Calorie Needs of Inactive Children					
	Total Servings Grains per Day		Minimum Recommended Servings of Whole Grain		Estimated Grams of Whole Grains	
Age (years)	Girls	Boys	Girls	Boys	Girls	Boys
2–3	3	3	1.5	1.5	24	24
4–8	4	5	2	2.5	32	40

Sources: Adapted from *Inside the Pyramid: How Many Grain Foods Are Needed Daily*, http://www.mypyramid.gov/pyramid/grains_amount.aspx; and logo courtesy Oldways and the Whole Grains Council, wholegrainscouncil.org.

Whole grains can be included in menus with the addition of foods such as brown rice, whole wheat (bulgur, cracked wheat, wheat berries, and whole-wheat flour), oats and oatmeal, corn including whole cornmeal and corn tortillas, barley, and quinoa.

Menu Planning Strategies to Include Whole Foods Adding whole foods to program menus may require revising current menus to minimize highly processed foods. Strategies for adding more whole foods to menus include the following:

- Plan to use whole-grain breads, whole-grain English muffins, bagels, hamburger buns, and whole-meal cornbread. (For children who resist brown breads, use white whole-wheat breads that look and taste similar to white bread but are whole grain.)
  - Serve side dishes that are whole grains such as brown rice, bulgur, whole-wheat tortillas, and whole-wheat pasta.
  - Serve fresh fruit in place of juice or canned fruits.
  - Serve fresh or plain frozen vegetables in place of canned vegetables or frozen vegetables with sauces.
  - Serve turkey burgers instead of processed chicken patties. Make chicken strips using chicken and whole-grain bread crumbs.
  - Serve homemade soups to which barley or brown rice is added.
- Plan whole-grain cooked and cold cereals for breakfast. Whole-grain cereals can be used for snacks either served with milk or as part of a trail mix.
- Add kidney beans to salads, serve vegetarian chili, and include bean or peas in soups. Serve frijoles with whole-grain tortillas or hummus with whole-grain pita bread.

The goal of adding whole foods to the menu is to increase options that appeal to children's taste and also fit into the program's budget and the kitchen's food preparation capacity.

Limiting High-Fat Foods When Planning Menus

Young children are growing and have high calorie needs. Fats can be part of a healthful diet when used to meet these needs. However, fats affect health in diverse ways. A high intake of saturated fats, *trans* fats, and cholesterol may increase the risk of heart disease. A high intake of fat also makes it more challenging to avoid consuming excess calories, which leads to an unhealthy rate of weight gain (HHS & USDA, 2005) (see Chapter 4).

With some thoughtful consideration the menu can become an ideal tool for keeping the dietary fat content of meals within recommended ranges. The menu needs to be planned to achieve a balance between low-fat and high-fat foods. In addition, the menu should substitute the more healthful unsaturated fats for saturated fats. Several strategies help to accomplish this:

- Switch to skim or 1% milk (age 2 and older).
- Offer low-fat dairy products such as low-fat cheeses and fat-free yogurts.

What if. . .

you wanted to introduce whole foods into children's diets? What whole grains might appeal to young children? What other whole foods would you choose to introduce?

MyEducationLab

Go to the Assignments and Activities section of Topic 3: Menu Planning in the MyEducationLab for your course and complete the activity entitled *Making Sense of Whole Grains*. What are some ways to ensure that children consume whole grains?

- Use more heart-healthy oils, including olive, canola, and peanut oils, and select foods that contain heart-healthy fats. For example:
  - Substitute oil and vinegar or Italian salad dressing for blue cheese dressing.
  - Use avocados as condiments on salads, to spread on sandwiches, or as a dip.
  - Use nut butters and nuts on menus (unless children in the class have nut or peanut allergies).
  - Use broth-based soups instead of cream-based soups.
  - Use oven-baked fries or sweet potato fries made from fresh potatoes tossed with a small amount of olive oil.
- Avoid the *trans* fatty acids found in many commercial margarines, shortenings, crackers, cookies, pies, doughnuts, some chips, and French fries.
- Serve heart-healthy fish on the menu such as tuna, salmon, and sardines.

When teachers use these strategies to plan menus they set standards of practice that support excellence in menu planning.

Creating Menus That Support Sustainability

Interest in the use of sustainable practices and sustainability is growing. This idea has relevance to menu planning and food service. Sustainable practices are those that meet current needs without compromising the ability of future generations to meet their needs (United Nations Department of Social and Economic Affairs Division for Sustainable Development, 2009). Sustainability also encompasses the interconnectedness of human and natural systems. It is the linking of social, economic, and environmental goals to create practices that support the perpetuation of these systems.

In selecting foods and planning menus, the concept of sustainability involves asking questions such as "What are the environmental consequences of using this product, this procedure, or this vendor when making decisions about menus?" or "Does my choice negatively affect other systems or people?" There is general consensus that many human activities are not sustainable. Early childhood programs make a commitment to health and wellness, not just for the present, but also for the future. This commitment to well-being is naturally attuned to concepts of sustainability. The following sections discuss sustainable practices in relation to menu planning and food service.

> **What if. . .**
> you wanted to support sustainability in early childhood settings? How would you approach this goal? How might teachers' sustainability practices influence young children?

Using Locally Grown Produce

One way to support sustainability when planning menus is to purchase foods that are grown locally. This means identifying and purchasing from growers located within a 150-mile radius of the program (Shuman, 2005). Foods should also be cultivated using sustainable agricultural practices that are environmentally friendly and socially responsible. This means foods are produced with soil and water conservation, pesticide reduction, and wildlife habitat conservation in mind. They are also produced in environments that support safe and fair working conditions and that provide healthy and humane care of livestock (Shuman, 2005).

Selecting Environmentally Responsible Products

Along with the foods selected during menu planning are all of the products used to implement meal service. Selecting cleaning products that are environmentally friendly is a desirable sustainable practice. For example, sanitizers used for cleaning tables and other surfaces should be safe, leave no harmful residue for children, and should not cause negative impacts on the environment when washed down the drain. Selecting reusable food service materials is another sustainable practice. Disposable plastic silverware and Styrofoam plates are less desirable than reusable products. Products that come wrapped in individual packaging are less desirable because of the quantity of packaging material. Purchasing items in bulk is more sustainable.

Recycling

Recycling and composting are practices that contribute to sustainability. For example, establishing recycling stations in classrooms or cafeterias for milk cartons contributes to sustainability and is a good way for children to be involved with this concept. Children can participate in recycling activities and learn about the phases of production that end with

Learning Outcome: Children will be able to describe how seeds planted in the ground grow into the vegetables we eat.

Infants and Toddlers

- *Goal:* Babies and toddlers will learn how a garden looks, feels, and smells.

- *Materials and preparation:* Establish a program garden with help from older children, or identify a community garden to visit periodically during the growing season. Commercial strollers that allow infants and toddlers to be walked in the garden in a group. For older toddlers: a large plastic pool, clean dirt or sand, and children's gardening tools such as a spade, rake, watering can, shovel, and flower pots as well as small carrots, potatoes, garlic cloves, and/or onions for planting.

- *Activity plan:* Walk with infants periodically throughout the growing season through the garden. Talk about the garden. Allow babies and toddlers to see, touch, and smell the garden and plants, such as smelling the recently turned dirt and touching the plant leaves and water used to sprinkle the garden. Describe what is

experienced by saying, "The dirt of the earth has a special smell" or "The water feels smooth and cold." Name the plants in the garden.

- *How to adjust the activity:* Invite toddlers to walk through the garden. Look for insects, worms, and butterflies. Bring a plant pulled from the garden to an inspection location. Talk about the parts of the plant: roots, stem, leaves. Place clean dirt or sand in a plastic pool or sensory table. Provide vegetables such as carrots and potatoes to "plant" and dig up again. Fill small flower pots with soil and plant a fast growing seed such as a bean, sunflower, or squash seed. Water the seeds and watch them grow.

- *Did you meet your goals?* Can you observe babies and toddlers looking at and reaching out to touch the plants? Do you hear toddlers describing the smells and textures of the garden?

Preschoolers and Kindergartners

- *Goal:* Children will plant a Native American Three Sisters' Garden and understand the steps of planting and growing foods.

- *Materials and preparation:* A small plot of land or raised bed for gardening, child-sized gardening tools such as spade, hoe, rake, watering can, shovel, wheelbarrow and corn, squash, and pole bean seeds. Access to water. The resource book *Native American Gardening: Stories, Projects and Recipes for Families* by M. J. Caduto and J. Bruchac and the children's book *Corn Is Maize* by Aliki

- *Activity plan:* Read the book *Corn Is Maize* by Aliki. Discuss how the Native Americans grew corn and had many uses for the vegetable. In addition to corn,

beans and squash were traditionally planted together and called the "three sisters." Read an account of the tale of the three sisters found online at http://lucky-dawson.com/science.aspx. Have a garden area ready for planting. Use as a resource the *Native American Gardening* book listed above. Working with small groups, invite children to use their hoes to make a round mound about 18 inches across the bottom tapering to 10 inches across the top. Level off the top so that it makes a flat circle. Plant four to six corn seeds in each quarter of the circle about 6 inches apart. Pat the soil and keep evenly moist while the corn seeds begin to grow. When the corn starts to grow and is about 4 to 6 inches high, plant four pole beans around the edge of the circle halfway down the mound. Bean seeds may include pinto, kidney, navy,

recycling. Programs or schools should consider the purchase of *Earth Tubs* or other composting units used to compost cafeteria food waste (Green Mountain Technologies, 2009). Children can see how compost changes over time and can be used to enrich gardens.

Planting School Gardens

A school garden is an excellent way to contribute to sustainability, while offering a range of other learning opportunities. Planting a garden provides opportunities to discuss climate, weather, soil, growing practices, insects, growing cycles, and food. When children tend gardens they are physically active, which reinforces health goals. Eating homegrown fruits peas, snap beans or a variety of these. On the lower edge of the mound also plant six squash seeds. Pat the soil and keep it evenly moist while these seeds germinate. Explain to the children that the Native Americans learned that these three plants help each other grow. The corn provides shade for the small bean plants and becomes the poles for the beans as they grow. The beans add nutrients back into the earth. The squash makes a shady ground cover that helps the soil retain moisture. The prickly spines on the squash leaves keep away animals that like to each corn.

- *How to adjust the activity:* Fill a sensory table with corn, beans, and squash seeds. Provide magnifying glasses,

rulers, and clear plastic containers for measuring and sorting. Offer fresh corn and invite children to pull off the corn husks and examine the way the corn kernels grow. Provide fresh beans. Open the beans to discover the bean seeds. Count the number of bean seeds in each bean. Provide a fresh squash. Cut open the squash and explore the interior; dig out the seeds, count them. Cook the squash and roast the seeds for tasting.

- *Did you meet your goals?* Did children participate in planting and caring for the garden? Are children able to identify the steps in planting and growing food?

School-Age Children

- *Goal:* Children will plant a Native American Three Sisters' Garden and describe the steps of planting and growing foods and how to use them to plan a healthful menu.

- *Materials:* Same as above for planting a school garden, including the book *Native American Gardening: Stories, Projects and Recipes for Families* by Caduto and Bruchac. Cooking utensils.

- *Activity plan:* Involve children in planting a program's garden. Read the stories located in the *Native American Gardening* book, such as "The Bean Woman" (p. 61) or "Onenha, The Corn" (p. 1). Have children draw illustrations for the story. While managing the garden, have children keep a garden journal. A sample journal sheet is found on page 30 of the *Native American Gardening* book. Harvest foods grown in the garden. Select and prepare simple recipes using corn, beans, squash, or other garden produce. Create a menu following CACFP guidelines using produce from the garden. Sample menu: bean bread, salmon, snap beans or corn, berries (such as strawberries, blueberries, raspberries, or blackberries), milk.

- *How to adjust the activity:* Invite families to a harvest celebration. Have children read from their journals and display illustrations for the Native American stories.

- *Did you meet your goals?* Are children able to describe how seeds grow into plants that produce food? Can they plan a healthful menu using produce from the garden?

and vegetables helps children learn where food comes from and inspires them to try the fruits and vegetable they helped to grow.

At Sunnyside Environmental School, an inner-city school located in Portland, Oregon, every grade level has its own garden. The first- and second-grade classes create a "snacking" garden of vegetables that can be picked and eaten for immediate gratification (Anderson, 2009). The school's focus integrates academics with hands-on learning about horticulture, outdoor education, and the environment, giving inner-city children an opportunity to learn in the natural setting. The *Teaching Wellness* feature discusses planning a school garden with children of different ages.

Health Hint

Building Health in the Classroom and at Home through Menu Planning

Everyone has opinions and ideas about food. Harnessing this interest and energy can be empowering for children's programs and families alike. It can also contribute to health in the classroom and at home through a shared partnership approach. Strategies to accomplish this include the following:

- Match menu offerings with curriculum activities in the classroom. For example, focus on including milk, yogurt and low-fat cheese on the lunch menu and explore where dairy foods come from by taking a trip to a dairy and watching cows be milked. Taste test different types of dairy products. Serve a salad made with a variety of lettuces and invite children to paint a portrait of the various lettuce leaves. Prepare a snack where all foods offered are circles (apple circles, cucumber circles, cracker circles) then study circles in class (sponge paint circles, cut circles, trace circles) and at outdoor play time (play circle games around the parachute).
- Ask children to offer ideas for menu items. Encourage children to name favorite fruits, vegetables, grains, dairy products, and meats. Invite children to name foods they would like to try.
- Invite families to participate on a menu review committee. Involving families in the development of menus invites them to contribute ideas and recipes that reflect their culture and family eating practices.

Through a menu planning partnership, children, families, and teachers learn about food preferences, gain knowledge of family cultural and eating practices, and discuss the health benefits of certain foods. Families learn about nutrition by working with teachers who are adhering to nutritional guidelines and requirements. When families are part of a menu planning partnership they are empowered with the knowledge they need to make nutritious food choices at home that support good health for the entire family.

Partnering with Children and Families

Obtaining ideas from children, their families, and other program staff is another important resource for menu planning. Teachers have the opportunity to observe meal service in the classroom, which provides insight into details that are helpful for selecting menu items. By noticing children's response to menu items and the amount of food left on their plates, teachers become aware of trends. This insight can be used to develop or revise menus that will enhance food acceptance. Talking with other teachers to find out what they see as successful versus less successful menu items in another useful source of information. The *Health Hint* describes the partnership between teachers, families, and children in planning menus. Whether teachers are creating a brand-new menu from scratch or revising a menu currently in place, input from these sources can be invaluable.

WRITING MENUS

With a good understanding of the requirements for children's menus and knowledge of nutrition wellness goals, teachers are ready to gather the tools they need and begin to make decisions about the menu.

Gathering Tools for Menu Planning

Once teachers envision the type of menu they wish to produce, it is helpful to organize and review the resources discussed in the previous section that help support menu writing. Other useful resources to include in a menu planning notebook are:

- Old menus and cost analysis of the menus, if available.
- Menu templates (see Figure 7-5).
- A list of foods that reflect the food preferences of culturally diverse populations within the program (see Table 7-3).
- A list of the special diets and food allergies of children in care.
- Recipes and recipe templates (from the program's previously used recipes, USDA website, etc.).
- A list of commodity foods.
- Price lists for suppliers or sales flyers for local grocers.
- A grocery shopping list template.

Once these tools have been gathered, teachers are ready to schedule a block of uninterrupted time to plan menus.

Deciding on the Type of Menu

The type of menu selected influences many aspects of food service. How much food needs to be purchased and stored, the required food service equipment, and the labor needs for implementing menus are all determined by the type of menu teachers select. Two types of menus typically guide menu planning (Martin & Conklin, 1999):

- A static menu is one in which the items on the menu remain the same every day. This type of menu is commonly seen in restaurants or hospitals and has a variety of choices to satisfy most preferences.
- A cycle menu offers new foods every day and is planned for a week or longer and then repeats.

static menu
menu on which the items remain the same every day; commonly seen in restaurants or hospitals

cycle menu
menu that offers new foods every day, is planned for a week or longer, and repeats itself

Figure 7-5 Sample CACFP-Compatible Menu Template

Week 1	Monday	Tuesday	Wednesday	Thursday	Friday
Breakfast Milk Fruit/Vegetable Bread/Grain Meat/Meat Alternate (optional)					

Lunch
Milk
Meat/Meat Alternate
Fruit/Vegetable
  (either two of one
  or one of each)
Bread/Grain					

Snack **(any two components)** Milk Fruit/Vegetable Bread/Grain Meat/Meat Alternate					

Table 7-3	Culturally Diverse Food Preferences		
Culture	Protein Sources	Grain Sources	Fruit and Vegetable Sources
Asian	Fish, pork, poultry, shellfish, dried beans, tofu, nuts	Rice, cereals, breads, noodles	Cabbage, kimchee, hot peppers, fruit juice
African American	Pork, ham, beef, fish, legumes, dried beans, peas	Rice, cereals, breads, biscuits, corn products such as hush puppies, cornbread, grits	Greens such as collard greens, kale, cabbage, turnips, beets, onions, okra, succotash, carrots, potatoes, yams, sweet potatoes, corn, peaches, melons, apples, bananas
Middle Eastern	Beef, lamb, chicken, lentils, chick peas, pistachios, almonds, fish, black beans, yogurt	Couscous, millet, pita, rice, bulgur	Onions, spinach, cucumbers, artichokes, potatoes, green beans, cabbage, eggplant, okra, squash, olives, figs, apples, apricots, plums, grapes, melons, bananas, tangerines, lemons
Mexican	Beans, poultry, beef, pork, eggs, goat, fish, shellfish, chorizo, menudo	Rice, tortillas (corn and flour), breads	Tomatoes, jicama, yams, cactus, salsa, chilies, sweet potatoes, squash, onions, corn, tomatillas, guava, mango. bananas, oranges, cherimoya, limes

Sources: Based on *Cultural Diversity*, by the National Food Service Management Institute, 2002, retrieved June 15, 2009, from http://www.olemiss.edu/depts/nfsmi/Information/Newsletters/Mealtime_memo_index.html#2002; and *Ohioline, Food: Cultural Diversity-Eating in America* Ohio State University, College of Food, Agriculture, and Environmental Sciences, retrieved June 15, 2009, from http://ohioline.osu.edu/lines/food.html.

A repeating 4- to 6-week cycle menu is often used in early childhood settings and schools. Cycle menus are time and cost effective. Once written, the cycle menu is available to use repeatedly. Establishing a cycle menu creates a familiar system for shopping and food preparation. Through experience teachers learn how much to purchase and prepare, thereby reducing food waste. Cycle menus can be created to incorporate seasonal foods. For example a 4- to 6-week cycle can be offered in the summer to use seasonal produce such as watermelon, peaches, and berries. A winter cycle menu would focus on readily available foods such as oranges, apples, and carrots. Cycle menus can be easily adjusted for variety and flexibility to reflect holidays or other special events.

Teachers need to decide how often to rotate their menus and must consider how to balance familiar well-accepted foods with new food options that broaden taste experiences. For example, in the chapter-opening scenario, Jeanine decides to improve her menu planning practices by switching to a 4-week cycle menu. Although the cycle menu will take time to write initially, in the long run she knows that it will save her time and effort once it is complete. She plans to include some of the favorite foods she has used in the past, but will expand the menu to offer a greater variety of fruits, vegetables. and whole grains.

Creating a Budget for Menus

The menu implements the program's food service goals including providing safe, healthful, and appealing meals to young children. The menu also directs the cost of meal service. For example, a menu that includes entirely fresh fruits and vegetables may cost more than one that relies on fresh, canned, and frozen produce. The way to understand the impact of these costs to the overall operation of an early childhood program is to develop a budget. A budget is a plan that designates the financial reserves available for purchasing, preparing, and serving foods. It is an itemized summary of expected food service–related expenses matched with the estimated income to cover these expenses. Teachers planning menus must stay within the constraints of the budget allotted for food service expenses.

budget
plan that designates the financial reserves available for food purchasing, preparation, and service of meals

Determining Income Sources for Menu Implementation

The income to support food service operations costs comes from a variety of sources depending on the children's program or school funding design. These sources include:

- Family fees for care and education.
- Child care subsidies for eligible low-income children.
- CACFP reimbursements for meal service.
- Public school district funding.
- Grants such as Head Start funds provided for programs that serve low-income families (Oliviera, 2005).

Sufficient funds are needed to implement an early childhood food program, including the costs of food, equipment, and the salaries of food service staff. The percentage of income needed is estimated to range from 6% to 19% of the total budget (Child Care, 2001). If the costs for food service exceed 19% of the total program income, teachers should review their menu planning, food purchasing, and food preparation practices and look at ways to control costs.

Using Cost Control Strategies

Cost control strategies must consider all aspects of food program expenses. Besides direct food purchasing expenses, other costs related to food service over which teachers can exert some control include the use of disposable supplies (napkins, straws, dish detergent) and durable items (dishes, silverware, cooking utensils, and food service equipment). Sometimes a very simple change can make a significant difference. For example, consider the following situation:

> Sunshine Preschool food service staff must wear hairnets during food service. One of the teachers noticed that sometimes employees would use as many as three to four hairnets each day, discarding them whenever they left the kitchen for breaks and putting new ones on when they returned. She talked with the program's food service manager about this wasteful practice. The manager reviewed the kitchen supplier's catalogue and found out that each hairnet cost about 25 cents. She realized that with five food service employees, the program was spending at least $5 per day on hairnets. The manager looked into the cost of institution caps and found out that they cost $16 each. She ordered five caps at a total cost of $80. She realized that with this switch to caps instead of hairnets, the program would soon experience cost savings because the expense of the new caps would be repaid in just over 2 weeks.

Considering these types of details helps keep costs within the constraints of the budget. Cost control strategies involve teachers evaluating the menu planning process from its inception all the way to the actual serving of meals.

Control of food service costs can make or break a program's budget. Any expenses that are unnecessary take funds away from other vital areas of the early childhood program. The fundamental basics for food purchasing entail estimating food requirements based on the menu, creating a shopping list, pricing foods to obtain the best bargain, and purchasing food from either large suppliers, wholesale clubs, or local retail grocers.

A budget for purchasing foods for classroom and program activities is also important. A teacher may want to offer an activity that teaches children how orange juice is made using fresh oranges. A cooking activity may form the basis of a family meeting, or refreshments may be served at a family social or staff meeting. Procedures should be in place to communicate the budget available for these activities. Guidelines are also needed to ensure that teachers communicate with food purchasers in a timely manner so that adjustments can be made to the weekly shopping list. This avoids the need for last minute purchasing, which often results in less attention to cost.

The USDA publication *Building Blocks for Fun and Healthy Meals—A Menu Planner for the Child and Adult Care Food Program* (USDA Food and Nutrition Service, 2000) recommends the following strategies to help contain food service costs:

- Keep good food records especially as they relate to food costs.
- Be a bargain hunter when it comes to buying foods:
  - Purchase locally and know what's in season.
  - Use commodity foods when available.
  - Shop from a grocery list.
  - Study flyers and coupons.
  - Shop at large discount stores.
  - Compare the cost of packaged items with the cost to purchase in bulk.
  - Purchase reusable food service supplies rather than disposable when possible. (This strategy supports sustainability as well as budget goals.)
  - Prevent food waste through spoilage by using proper storage strategies.
- Use standardized recipes. Standardized recipes are tried-and-true recipes that leave less room for error.
- Aim to prepare exactly what is needed. This helps avoid excess leftovers and costly substitutions if food runs out and helps to ensure CACFP guidelines are met so that full reimbursement can be claimed.

standardized recipes recipes that have been tested for quality, accuracy, and yield, which results in a consistent, predictable food products

Building Menus

An organized approach is important when making food selections. Deciding on menu choices and serving sizes requires the planner to consider the age and nutritional needs of children in the program. For example, will the menu serve older infants and toddlers as well as preschool-age children? Can food items be altered to accommodate the younger eaters? How will food be apportioned? Can the menu accommodate children on special diets? These types of questions guide menu development.

Starting the Day with Breakfast

Foods traditionally offered at breakfast contribute significantly to the total day's intake of vitamins, minerals, and fiber and overall can enhance the quality of a child's diet. Breakfast foods include fortified cereals, enriched and whole-grain breads, fruits, and milk. When breakfast is skipped it is very difficult to make up these nutrients at other meals (Affenito, 2007; Rampersaud, Pereira, Girard, Adams, & Metzl, 2005). In addition, research has shown that eating breakfast is a simple practice that may have a positive effect on how well children do in school (Rampersaud et al., 2005). For example, one study revealed that when breakfast was consumed, children showed an increase in cognitive function, attention, and memory (Wesnes, Pincock, Richardson, & Hails, 2003). In spite of its many benefits, not all programs serve breakfast because it is assumed that children have eaten before coming to school. Instead many programs serve a midmorning snack. Programs eligible to participate in the CACFP may find it cost effective to switch from serving a morning snack to serving breakfast. The reimbursement for the breakfast meal is larger than that for the morning snack, and with a few changes in the menu the switch can be easily accomplished.

The breakfast menu can be constructed following CACFP guidelines. Selections are made from the three required components: milk, fruits/vegetables, and starches/grains. Teachers involved in menu planning can support nutrition-related goals by offering a variety of menu items such as whole-grain fortified cereals and whole-grain breads. Milk service is required by CACFP, therefore, many menus include fresh, frozen, or canned fruits instead of juice for breakfast. Offering whole fruits or vegetables is desirable whenever possible. Figure 7-6 provides a breakfast template that includes a 1-week menu for preschool-age children. This template provides guidance on portions to be served to meet CACFP requirements as well as information on the amount of food is needed to serve a class of 20. This menu uses simple to prepare foods that can be used in a program with limited capacity for extensive cooking.

Figure 7-6 Sample Breakfast Menu

Fall Menu Week: 3 of 6	Monday	Tuesday	Wednesday	Thursday	Friday
BREAKFAST MENUS	Wheat flakes cereal Milk, nonfat Grapefruit, half	Whole-grain wheat bread Milk, nonfat Sliced kiwi Low-fat cream cheese	Whole-grain bread sticks Orange quarters Milk, nonfat	Oat rings cereal Milk, nonfat Banana	Warmed corn tortilla Black bean and corn salsa Canned pineapple Milk, nonfat
REQUIRED FOOD AMOUNTS	1/3 cup cereal 3/4 cup milk 1/2 grapefruit	1/2 slice bread 3/4 cup milk 1/2 kiwi 1 tsp cream cheese	1/2 bread stick 2 orange quarters 3/4 cup milk	1/3 cup cereal 3/4 cup milk 1/2 banana	1/2 corn tortilla 1/2 ounce shredded low-fat cheese 1/4 cup black bean and corn salsa 1/2 cup canned pineapple 3/4 cup milk
OPTIONAL FOODS		Cream cheese			Can decrease pineapple to 1/4 cup
SPECIAL DIRECTIONS	Cut grapefruit in half and section		Warm bread sticks in oven		Prepare following standardized recipe
TOTAL AMOUNT OF FOOD TO SERVE PER CLASS BASED ON A 20-CHILD CLASS	7 cups of cereal or 1 10-oz box 1 gallon of milk	10 slices of bread 1 gallon of milk 10 kiwis 1/2 cup cream cheese	10 bread sticks 1 gallon of milk 10 oranges	7 cups cereal or 1 10-oz box 1 gallon of milk 10 bananas	10 corn tortillas 10 oz of shredded cheese 5 cups black bean and corn salsa 1 #10 can of pineapple 1 gallon of milk
Special diets: 1 lactose-free diet in Room 115 1 no citrus fruits in Room 117 (oranges, grapefruit, or lemons)	Substitute soy milk for milk. Substitute apple half for grapefruit.	Substitute juice for milk. Use jam instead of cream cheese.	Substitute juice for milk. Substitute sliced peaches for oranges.	Substitute soy milk for milk.	Substitute juice for milk. Substitute cubed ham for cheese.

Selecting the Main Entrée for Lunch

The lunch meal is the largest meal offered at most programs and contributes significantly to children's overall energy and daily nutrient intake. A meat/meat alternate selection is needed to establish a CACFP-compatible lunch meal. The main entrée is often selected first because this menu item tends to be the highlight of the meal and is usually the most expensive menu item. The following considerations are useful when planning a cycle menu for lunch:

- How often should a particular entrée be served during the menu cycle?
- If an entrée is offered more than once a month, how can the side dishes be changed to ensure variety?
- How often will hot versus cold entrées be served? During the summer, sandwiches and chef's salads might be well received, whereas stews and soups may be preferred during the winter months.

commercially prepared entrée
a processed main course item to which ingredients may have been added

If a **commercially prepared entrée** (a processed main course item to which ingredients may have been added) is chosen for the menu, it must be identified by the Child Nutrition (CN) Labeling Program. This is a voluntary federal program that supports labeling disclosure for the Child Nutrition Programs (USDA Food and Nutrition Service, 2007a). A CN label is required by the CACFP on foods that contribute to the meat/meat alternate component of the menu for reimbursable meals. Processed foods such as breaded fish and chicken products, frozen hamburger patties, pizzas, burritos, and garden burgers are examples of foods that require a CN label. A CN label clearly identifies how a product can be counted in the CACFP meal component requirements. Figure 7-7 provides an example of a CN label. Notice how the CN label communicates how much is needed of a processed product to meet protein equivalents when planning meals that adhere to CACFP requirements.

Consider the decisions a teacher might make while selecting an entrée for the menu. To meet CACFP requirements, the lunch menu requires a protein source for the entrée. Spaghetti is a versatile and nutritious choice. Even toddlers are able to eat this main dish without difficulty. The sauce for the spaghetti can be made with ground turkey, a more economical protein choice compared to ground beef. Lean ground turkey is also low in fat and rich in iron. In addition, the tomato sauce is an excellent source of vitamin C, which helps with iron absorption. Children will consume lots of vegetables with this entrée if green peppers, mushrooms, and chopped zucchini and summer squash are added to the tomato sauce. This menu item is also easy to adapt for children with special diets. For example, spaghetti is acceptable for children following milk-free diets if the sauce is prepared without cheese. Some sauce can be reserved and prepared without ground turkey for children following vegetarian diets. Adding 1.5 ounces of shredded mozzarella cheese provides an appropriate protein source for the vegetarian. The addition of fat, sugar, and salt should be keep to a minimum as recommended by the *Dietary Guidelines for Americans, 2005* (American Dietetic Association, 2005).

Selecting Side Dishes for Lunch

After the entrée is selected, the side dishes such as starches/grains, fruits, and vegetables need to be chosen to round out the menu. Side dishes contribute to the menu's balance both in nutrition and sensory appeal. Variety in the selection of the side dishes is important to ensure that children get all of the nutrients they need for good health. It is also important to consider whether the flavors and textures within a meal are varied and complementary. When too many similar flavors, such as strong, spicy, or sweet, are offered in the same meal "mouth boredom" can occur. For example, a lunch with many sweet components, such as peanut butter and jelly, spiced apples, carrot raisin salad, and milk may be unappealing even to children with the most tenacious sweet tooth.

Figure 7-7 A Sample Child Nutrition Label

```
─────────────── CN ───────────────
                                    000000
    This 3.00 oz serving of raw beef patty provides when
CN  cooked 2.00 oz equivalent meat for Child Nutrition Meal   CN
    Pattern Requirements. (Use of this logo and statement
    authorized by the Food and Nutrition Service, USDA 05-84.)
─────────────── CN ───────────────
```

Source: From *Building Blocks for Fun and Healthy Meals—A Menu Planner for the Child and Adult Care Food Program*, by the U.S. Department of Agriculture, Food and Nutrition Service, 2000, retrieved March 26, 2008, from http://teamnutrition.usda.gov/Resources/buildingblocks.html.

Figure 7-8 Variety and Contrast in Flavor, Texture, and Visual Appeal Inspire a Good Appetite

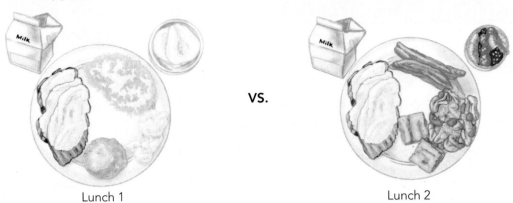

Lunch 1   VS.   Lunch 2

Visual balance is important too. Menu selections should represent food components that look appealing as evidenced by a variety of colors, shapes, and sizes. Figure 7-8 shows two different planned lunches. The contrast of colors in Lunch 2 is more likely to encourage the appetite in both children and teachers. This is desirable because it is much easier for teachers to model good eating behaviors when they truly enjoy the meal.

Side dishes, such as the starches/grains and fruits and vegetables, can often be used to introduce children to new foods. Young children may be leery of unfamiliar foods do better when new foods are offered with familiar favorites. However, children often require repeated exposures before they are willing to try a new food (Cooke, Haworth, & Wardle, 2007; Harris, 2008; Wardle et al., 2003). Children who have an opportunity to prepare foods in classroom cooking activities are more likely to try something new. The *Nutrition Note* describes ways to build children's interest in new foods. In addition, when teachers and peers consume a new food, it enhances children's willingness to try something different, too (Hendy & Raudenbush, 2000a, 2000b; Wardle & Cooke, 2008).

Grains/Starches Variety in the type of starch or grain side dish selected is important at mealtimes. For example, if spaghetti is offered one day followed by lasagna the next, the menu becomes boring. The menu needs to alternate the presentation of whole-grain breads, brown rice, and whole-wheat or corn tortillas to provide enough variety to maintain interest.

Fruits and Vegetables When selecting fruits and vegetables for the menu, vary the way the food is prepared and served. Some vegetables, such as broccoli, cauliflower, spinach, carrot sticks, and pepper strips, may be better accepted if they are served raw with low-fat dip. If shopping is done once a week, perishable fresh produce should be served early in the weekly menu. Some flexibility may be needed; for example, if the bananas are green on Monday and the kiwi fruit is hard on Tuesday, they should be used later in the week.

Selecting Beverages

Beverage selections are also important to the nutritional value of meals. The beverages that meet the requirements for CACFP reimbursement are milk for breakfast and lunch, and either milk or juice (but not both) for a snack. Milk alternatives should be available for children who are lactose intolerant or allergic to milk. Although not part of menu planning, it is important to ensure that children have unlimited access to water throughout the day. Water should also be available for events such as walking trips, field days, and family social events. In addition, it is important for children to stay hydrated in the winter months when heavy clothing and strenuous outdoor activities coupled with heated inside environments can increase the need for fluids.

What if. . .

you were planning the side dishes to accompany a spaghetti entrée for lunch? What type of whole foods (fruits, vegetables, whole grains) and beverages would you select?

Nutrition Note

Building Interest in New Foods

Children are enthusiastic about cooking activities, and it is also fun for them to taste the results of their cooking projects. Cooking with children provides opportunities to teach about foods: where food comes from, how food smells, tastes, and feels, and how to prepare different kinds of food. Cooking also engages children in activities that help to develop motor skills as they use their arms, hands, and fingers. Children have different developmentally appropriate "kitchen skill" levels depending on their age. Understanding children's skill levels helps teacher to direct students to activities that help them feel successful. Kitchen skills for different age categories of children are listed below.

2-Year-Olds

- **Scrubbing** vegetables and fruits
- **Carrying** unbreakable items to the table
- **Dipping** foods
- **Washing** and **tearing** lettuce and salad greens
- **Breaking** bread into pieces

3-Year-Olds

- **Pouring** liquids into batter (help children measure first)
- **Mixing** batter or other dry and wet ingredients together

- **Shaking** a drink in a closed container
- **Spreading** butters or spreads
- **Kneading** dough
- **Washing** vegetables and fruits
- **Serving** foods

4- and 5-Year-Olds

- **Juicing** oranges, lemons, and limes
- **Peeling** some fruits and vegetables (bananas, onions)
- **Mashing** soft fruits and vegetables (bananas, cooked potatoes, sweet potatoes)

- **Scrubbing** vegetables (potatoes, mushrooms)
- **Cutting** soft foods with a plastic knife (mushrooms, hard-boiled eggs)
- **Pressing** cookie cutters
- **Measuring** dry ingredients
- **Cracking** and beating eggs
- **Setting** and **clearing** the table
- **Wiping** up after cooking

Sources: Adapted from *Cooking with Children*, by the California Department of Health Services, retrieved from http://www.wicworks.ca.gov/education/nutrition/kidsRecipes/cooking_w_index.htm; and http://www.cdph.ca.gov/programs/wicworks/Pages/WICNECookingwithChildren.aspx. Used with permission.

Rounding Out the Day with Snacks

The snack is an important meal for young children. Snacks provide a "second chance" to obtain nutrients missed at meal times. The CACFP requires that snack menus include two components from any of the four food groups (milk, fruits/vegetables, cereals/grains, and protein/protein alternate) to meet reimbursement requirements. To ensure that children are meeting MyPyramid recommendations, the snack menu should center on serving fruits and vegetables as much as possible. Although 100% fruit juice may be served as part of a healthy snack, priority should be given to fresh fruits and vegetables, which provide added fiber and nutrients and are more likely to help children feel full longer. Figure 7-9 provides examples of easy-to-prepare, child-friendly snacks that include at least two food groups. Snacks are more likely to be prepared and served under the direction of teachers than any other meal. As with lunch and breakfast, a variety of factors influence the choice of snacks, including the age of the children in the program and the availability of kitchen space and staff for food preparation. Which components are used in these snack combinations?

What if. . .

you were planning snacks for your program? What types of healthy and appealing snacks might you consider for infants, toddlers, preschoolers, and school-age children?

Transitioning to New Menus

Once the cycle menu for breakfast, lunch, and snacks has been completed, a systematic evaluation of the menu is conducted to ensure that menu planning goals have been met. Figure 7-10 provides a checklist for reviewing the menus and determining if they are ready

Figure 7-9 Nutritious Snack Combinations

Low-fat cheese and whole-grain crackers
Peanut butter on sliced apples
Cereal with banana and 1% milk
Whole-grain waffles topped with applesauce
Fruit smoothies (milk blended with fruits)
Whole-grain English muffin mini pizza
Baked potato topped with low-fat cheese and broccoli
Cheese quesadilla topped with corn/black bean salsa
Whole-grain raisin bread with sliced Swiss cheese
Banana dipped in yogurt and crushed cereal
Ham and low-fat cheese rollup served with baby carrot sticks
Fruit salad topped with vanilla yogurt and low-fat granola cereal

Note: Cheese, although a dairy product, is considered a meat/protein alternate when counting food components for CACFP. Also, only two components in any combination are required for snacks.

to be implemented. Staff involved in food preparation and service should participate in the menu review at this point. A food service employee might recognize a potential problem with equipment or food storage. A cook might recognize a food preparation procedure that takes more time than is advisable. This input provides the opportunity to revise the menu plan as needed before it is put into use.

Implementing a new menu can initially create some "bumps in the road." Food purchasing may involve a bit of trial and error as amounts of food needed for new recipes are estimated and tried. Opportunities to try out new recipes before they are used in the new menu can be very helpful but may require some additional start-up time. The transition to the new menu can be eased by:

- Notifying families of the new menus in advance.
- Modeling an adventuresome attitude while trying new foods.
- Observing children's reaction to new menu options.

Through careful planning the new menu can set the tone for healthy eating habits and have a beneficial impact on the nutritional status of children and teachers alike.

Using Meal Service to Enhance Menu Acceptance

Learning to eat is a developmental process that is acquired over time. Infants are entirely dependent on adults to provide what is best for them nutritionally. As children mature the teacher's role shifts from making food decisions for children to supporting them as they strive to achieve eating independence. This is accomplished by supporting children's development of eating skills and by providing an environment in which children are able to make their own healthful food selections within the context of the nutritious options provided by well-planned menus.

Supporting the Development of Eating Skills

The menu also makes important contributions to children's opportunities to gain eating and self-help skills. Appropriate menu items encourage children to learn to feed themselves. Finger feeding is an important developmental stage in learning to self-feed. As children learn to manipulate a spoon and fork, the menu must reflect foods prepared in ways that children can manage. Eating oatmeal with a spoon is a good first step. Peas may be too challenging for toddlers and preschoolers to eat with a fork.

When planning menus for a wide range of ages (infants to preschoolers), the adaptability of foods served should be considered. For example, apple wedges are a good choice for toddlers and older, whereas unsweetened applesauce would be a better choice for an 8 month old infant. Teachers should allow children to feed themselves as much as they are

What if. . .

you observed that children were disinterested in the menu offerings because they were the same every week? What suggestions might you make to the director or food service authority at your program? What resources could you use to support your point of view?

Figure 7-10 Sample Menu Evaluation Checklist

Sunshine Preschool Program

Date: 4/1/2011

Menu planner: *Michelle*

Age of students: *3- to 5-year-olds*

Are food components/food groups being met?

☐ Breakfast (first three components required)
  ☐ Milk component/group
  ☐ Fruit or vegetable component/group (no juice)
  ☐ Grains or breads group
  ☐ *Optional foods:* meat/meat alternate group, *trans* fatty acid–free margarine, jam, jelly, low-fat cream cheese

☐ Lunch (first four components required)
  ☐ Meat/meat alternate group
  ☐ Fruit/vegetable group (1/2 cup total); no juice
  ☐ Grains or bread group
  ☐ Milk group
  ☐ *Optional foods:* salad dressing, low-fat vegetable dip, mayonnaise, salsa, ketchup

☐ Snacks contain two of four components.

☐ There is wide variety within the components groups.

☐ Menus contain a variety of flavors, contrasting colors, shapes, textures, temperatures, and forms.

☐ Menus are culturally appropriate.

☐ Menus are able to accommodate special diets.

☐ Menus reflect input from children, parents, and staff.

☐ Menus support sustainability when possible (local seasonal foods, foods from program garden).

☐ Special occasions are represented.

☐ Menu items can be accommodated by the food preparation staff, equipment, and facilities.

☐ Menu items are foods appropriate for the age group.

☐ Recipes are available.

☐ Breakfast, lunch and snack menu items avoid repetition of foods on any given day:
  ☐ Nutritional goals that support dietary guidelines and recommendations are met.

☐ Three different fruits and five different vegetables are offered weekly.

☐ A dark green or orange vegetable or fruit rich in vitamin A is offered three or more times per week.

☐ A fresh fruit or raw vegetable is offered daily.

☐ A good source of vitamin C is offered each day.

☐ A whole-grain food is served daily.

☐ At least four different entrées are offered each week and they are moderate in fat content

☐ Dishes that include cooked dried beans or peas are offered once a week or more.

☐ Two or more sources of iron are offered each day.

☐ Low-fat or nonfat milk is available daily.

Sources: Adapted from "USDA Child and Adult Care Food Program Center Manual," by the Oregon Department of Education, 2006, retrieved August 24, 2009, from http://www.ode.state.or.us/services/nutrition/cacfp/pdf/2006_center_manual.pdf; and *HealthierUS School Challenge: Recognizing Excellence in Nutrition and Physical Activity*, USDA Food and Nutrition Service, retrieved August 24, 2009, from http://www.fns.usda.gov/tn/HealthierUS/index.html.

able even though this is sometimes a messy business. Spills are to be expected and should be treated in an unconcerned manner. Teachers should respond with encouragement as children try new foods or textures or learn a new self-feeding skill. Planning meals that challenge children to learn new skills without frustration is an extra dimension in menu planning.

Eating utensils, tables, and chairs should be age appropriate in size. Children should be able to sit with their feet touching the ground. The table should be at a comfortable height and there should be ample room at the table for children to maneuver. The room should be at a pleasant temperature with good lighting and distractions should be minimized. Parents coming in to pick up children after lunch should be encouraged to avoid entering the room until meal service is done. If there is a television in the family child care home, it should not be on during meal service. Teachers should not be talking on the phone during meal service but rather at the table interacting with children.

Enhancing the Social Experience for Children

Mealtimes should be relaxed and enjoyable. Teachers create this comfortable atmosphere by establishing guidelines for acceptable eating behavior. This includes offering meals on a routine schedule and allowing enough time so meals are not rushed. The expectations for eating etiquette should be introduced and reinforced, such as washing hands before eating, helping set the table, waiting until everyone is seated before beginning to eat (if age appropriate), and helping clean up after the meal. Mealtimes are also important social times as children talk and visit with each other and their teachers.

Selecting a Type of Meal Service

Meal service can be accomplished in a variety of ways in the early childhood or school setting, including the following:

- *Restaurant-style meal service* involves portioning food out on plates before it is served to children at the table. This is an efficient method that guarantees each child receives the correct portion and may help contain costs by minimizing food waste.
- *Cafeteria-style meal service* entails children making food choices while moving through a cafeteria line. This method allows children to select what they want to eat, but does not allow them to determine the amount. This style of service is common in the primary school setting.
- *Family-style meal service* involves placing foods and beverages in serving containers on the table. Children serve themselves, choosing what they will eat and how much. In this approach, teachers sit with children to model appropriate eating behaviors, assist with meal service when needed, and provide conversation as well as educational activities focused on foods (Connecticut State Department of Education, 2005).

The advantage of family-style meal service is that it involves children in the process of food service and uses mealtime as an educational experience. Family-style meal service is also a comfortable and nonthreatening way to introduce new foods. It provides opportunity for teachers to introduce the food choices of the day and to model how children may serve themselves. This gives children time to decide what to select based on their preferences. Children find the assurance they need to try new foods by observing what other children and teachers are eating. Family-style meal service also allows children to make their selections based on how hungry they feel. They learn to recognize hunger and satiety cues because they can take a small serving size with the knowledge that they can have more if they so desire (HHS, 2000). Family-style meal service also helps children to practice fine motor skills as they dish out foods and pour beverages. Children learn to make choices, take turns, share, and "not lick the spoon."

Some programs may combine restaurant-style service with family-style service in an effort to get the best of both methods. For example, the entrée may be served to children restaurant style while the salad, fruit, and beverage are served family style. This ensures that all children get the desired portion of the main entrée but still provides the opportunity for children to make food choices and practice serving themselves. Regardless of the type of meal service, it is important for teachers to sit with children, modeling healthy eating practices and encouraging social interactions.

Managing Foods from Home

Many children's programs ask families to provide the foods for snacks or have children bring their own lunches from home. Teachers may find it difficult to manage the food children bring to school. Part of the challenge faced when children bring food from home is the inconsistency in what is provided and how it impacts the program's nutrition. For example, what should teachers do if families send soda pop in their child's lunch box or perishables that may pose a food safety risk? Developing policies and procedures for home-prepared meals helps establish a partnership with families to support the healthful eating environment teachers wish to create for all children.

One helpful resource is the NAEYC's standards for program accreditation. The NAEYC recommends that foods brought from home to be shared with other children must consist of whole fruits or commercially prepared packaged foods (NAEYC, 2008). Home-baked items may be delicious and healthful, but can pose food safety risks if appropriate food preparation and storage practices are not followed. Children with allergies are also put at risk when there is no list of ingredients for teachers to read. It is important to communicate

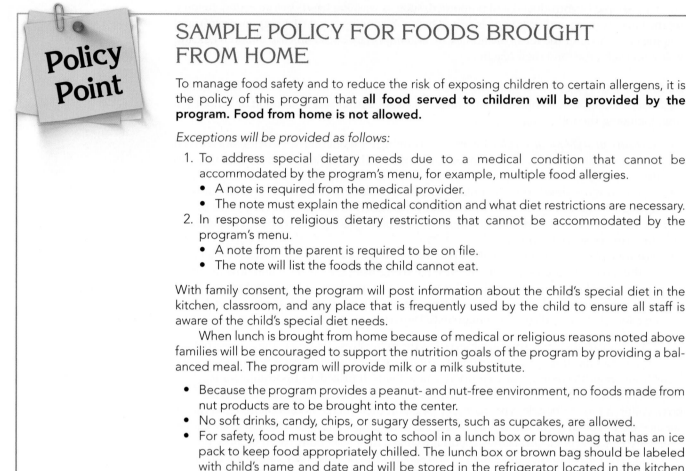

Policy Point

SAMPLE POLICY FOR FOODS BROUGHT FROM HOME

To manage food safety and to reduce the risk of exposing children to certain allergens, it is the policy of this program that **all food served to children will be provided by the program. Food from home is not allowed.**

Exceptions will be provided as follows:

1. To address special dietary needs due to a medical condition that cannot be accommodated by the program's menu, for example, multiple food allergies.
   - A note is required from the medical provider.
   - The note must explain the medical condition and what diet restrictions are necessary.
2. In response to religious dietary restrictions that cannot be accommodated by the program's menu.
   - A note from the parent is required to be on file.
   - The note will list the foods the child cannot eat.

With family consent, the program will post information about the child's special diet in the kitchen, classroom, and any place that is frequently used by the child to ensure all staff is aware of the child's special diet needs.

When lunch is brought from home because of medical or religious reasons noted above families will be encouraged to support the nutrition goals of the program by providing a balanced meal. The program will provide milk or a milk substitute.

- Because the program provides a peanut- and nut-free environment, no foods made from nut products are to be brought into the center.
- No soft drinks, candy, chips, or sugary desserts, such as cupcakes, are allowed.
- For safety, food must be brought to school in a lunch box or brown bag that has an ice pack to keep food appropriately chilled. The lunch box or brown bag should be labeled with child's name and date and will be stored in the refrigerator located in the kitchen until meal service.
- The program will provide the family with the Child and Adult Care Food Program guidelines for snacks and lunches to assist with planning healthful food from home meals.

Source: *Standard 5: Health Topic 5.B: Ensuring Children's Nutritional Well-Being, Criterion 5.B.02 and Criterion 5.B.05, 2009,* Washington, DC: National Association for the Education of Young Children.

What if. . .

a parent arrived at school with a plate full of homemade cupcakes to celebrate a child's birthday? How would you handle this? How would you draft a program policy to address this issue?

with families the goals for maintaining the safety of food brought from home and the kinds of food allergies or food restrictions that are present in the class group. A sample policy is described in the *Policy Point*. Reviewing the food from home policies with families before children start the program helps families make healthful choices for foods sent from home. A list of recommended foods is useful to guide food selections when families are asked to contribute to the snacks for the classroom. This provides an opportunity to reinforce the program's food safety and nutrition goals. These approaches ensure that foods brought from home contribute to the nutritional well-being of children and protect children who for cultural or health reasons cannot eat the traditional foods brought in for snack times.

CREATING MENUS THAT SUPPORT ALTERNATIVE OR SPECIAL DIETS

Some children cannot consume the standard infant formula or the typical menu offered at a program or school. They may have food allergies, special medical conditions, or cultural, religious, or philosophical beliefs that require a special diet. Acting in partnership with families, teachers, food service staff, and administrative staff need to find ways to accommodate children's special diet needs.

Planning Menus for Children with Food Allergies

Managing special diets can be challenging especially when children must follow allergen-restricted diets. It is estimated that about 4% of the U.S. population has food allergies. The incidence is higher in young children where 1 in 17 children under the age of 3 has allergic reactions (Food Allergy Anaphylaxis Network, 2007). Each classroom is likely to have one or two children with food allergies.

Understanding Food Allergies

Allergies occur when the body's immune system responds inappropriately when exposed to typically harmless proteins found in certain foods. Once these proteins are identified as foreign bodies, or allergens, the body produces antibodies called immunoglobulin E (IgE). When the food is consumed again, the immune cells located throughout the body recognize the allergen and release chemicals, including histamine, into the bloodstream. These chemicals cause the myriad of symptoms associated with allergies (Krishnaswamy, Ajitawi, & Chi, 2006). Some of these reactions to food allergens are immediate and some are delayed.

anaphylaxis
a severe, life-threatening reaction that can lead to a drop in blood pressure, loss of consciousness, and death if untreated

contact dermatitis
a rash that occurs when an allergen comes in contact with the skin

- *Immediate reactions* occur within minutes or up to 2 hours. Symptoms include hives, rash, swelling of the mouth, throat, red and tearing eyes, wheezing, difficulty breathing, vomiting, diarrhea, and anaphylaxis. Anaphylaxis is a severe life-threatening reaction that can lead to a drop in blood pressure, loss of consciousness, and death if untreated.
- *Delayed reactions* occur within 2 hours up to about 48 hours. Symptoms include contact dermatitis, a rash that occurs when an allergen comes in contact with the skin (American Academy of Pediatrics Committee on Nutrition, 2004; Sampson et al., 2006; Simons et al., 2007).

A summary of food allergy symptoms is provided in Figure 7-11.

The only way to prevent allergic reactions is to avoid the offending food. This means that special menu decisions must be made to omit foods that contain allergens from the diet of children with that particular food allergy. In addition, teachers need to be prepared to manage a severe food allergy reaction in the event that an accidental exposure occurs. A food allergy action plan must be developed by the family and health care provider for emergency response at school (see the Food Allergy and Anaphylaxis Network Web Resource). A food allergy action plan identifies symptoms and specifies how to treat the allergic reaction in case of an emergency. Epinephrine is the product used most often to manage anaphylaxis. It is administered by injection (see Figure 7-12). Early childhood teachers in family child care settings must have a plan for the care of other children while the teacher provides care for a child experiencing an allergic reaction.

An excellent resource for families and teachers is the Food Allergy and Anaphylaxis Network (FAAN). The FAAN website provides a sample *Food Allergy Action Plan* (FAAN, 2007). It also lists the responsibilities of schools, families, and children for managing food allergies and creating a safe environment for children with allergies.

Figure 7-11 Common Signs and Symptoms of an Allergic Reaction

- Hives, rashes
- Itching of the mouth, ears, throat, face, or any part of the body
- Swelling of the lips, tongue, throat, or any part of the body
- Red, watery, irritated eyes
- Runny nose
- Nausea, vomiting
- Diarrhea
- Stomach cramps
- Change of voice
- Coughing
- Wheezing, difficulty breathing
- Trouble swallowing, tightness in the throat
- Problems with breathing, wheezing, asthma
- Dizziness
- Fainting or loss of consciousness
- Slurred speech
- Anxiety and feelings of doom

Source: Adapted from *Medline Plus Medical Dictionary: Anaphylaxis*, http://www.nlm.nih.gov/medlineplus/ency/article/000844.htm.

Figure 7-12 Epinephrine Injector

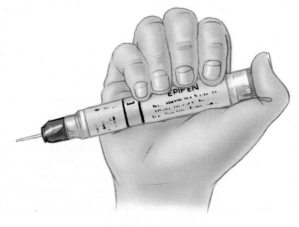

Feeding children with allergies is a serious responsibility. The consequences of making a mistake with their diet can be life threatening. It is important for families to share information about children's allergies with teachers and food service staff before the child attends the program. This provides time to make appropriate adjustments to the menu, an important aspect in creating a safe environment. Teachers may be very busy during meal service in the early childhood classroom, and in elementary settings teachers are usually not present when children eat. In addition, food products are used in a variety of other ways in early childhood programs. It is important to be aware of times when an allergen exposure might occur. If everyone involved in food service is informed about a child's food allergy, the likelihood that a food service error will happen is reduced. The *Safety Segment* provides an example of how one preschool program communicates about special diet requirements for children with food allergies. It is also important to listen to children who have life-threatening allergies. Even very young children are often well aware of what they can and cannot eat.

Infants with Food Allergies

Individuals involved in menu planning usually adapt the daily menu to accommodate children with food allergies. How menus are adapted varies depending on the age of the child. Allergies may begin to appear in infants when solid foods are introduced, and they

Safety Segment

Communicating about Allergy Diets

Special diets need careful planning. Foods need to be handled safely to avoid cross contamination, and the foods need to be distributed to the correct child. Good communication and safety checks along the way help prevent food "accidents." Below is an example of the steps involved in managing peanut allergies.

Sunshine Preschool receives food through an agreement with a vendor. The vendor is the local school district's food service. Food is prepared offsite and sent via heated and chilled carts to the preschool program. One classroom has two children severely allergic to peanuts. What can the teacher do to ensure that these children are safe from potentially life-threatening allergens?

1. *School district food service:* The teacher or preschool dietitian contacts the school district kitchen who provides food for the center. Information about a child's food allergy is communicated prior to the child attending the class. A peanut-free menu is requested and all labels and recipes are checked for peanut-containing products. The school district kitchen ensures that containers and packaging for special peanut-free diets are labeled.
2. *The preschool:* The preschool decides to implement a peanut-free program. No peanuts or peanut products will be served on the menu. Staff members are asked to not bring peanut products to school. The peanut-free plan is shared with families who are asked to not send their children to school with any peanut products. A list of children on special diets and their classroom is posted on the kitchen bulletin board. Staff is oriented to not make any substitutions for the peanut-free diet without prior approval from the dietitian. Staff members receive training on how to administer a rescue medication via an epinephrine injector.
3. *The classroom:* Assistant teachers are assigned to be in charge of serving and supervising service of special diets. The assistant teacher is asked to sit with the children who have food allergies at mealtime. Children with special diets are served first. A Food Allergy Emergency Protocol is developed by the child's health care provider and is posted in the classroom near the phone so that all staff will know what to do and who to call in case of an emergency.

are exposed to new foods. Families that are concerned about allergies may delay the introduction of solids until their infant is 6 months of age (American Academy of Pediatrics Committee on Nutrition, 2004; Butte et al., 2004; Greer, Sicherer, Burks, & Committee on Nutrition and Section on Allergy and Immunology, 2008a). Foods should be introduced one at a time, waiting for 3 to 5 days before the next new food is offered. In this way, if allergy symptoms develop, it is easier to identify the offending food (American Academy of Pediatrics, 2008). Families should provide teachers with a list of foods that have successfully been introduced. It is important for this list to be updated periodically to add new foods the infant tolerates (National Resource Center for Health and Child Care and Early Education, 2009). Menus planned for infants emerge from the list of well-tolerated foods. If a food allergy is identified, the offending food is eliminated from the infant's diet.

The teacher must closely follow recommendations from the family and health care provider for elimination of food allergens. This information should be documented in an individualized care plan. Families should be closely involved in identifying appropriate menus for infants with allergies. The family should approve the menu and, with the family's consent, the child's special diet should be posted where it is easily accessible in areas where food is prepared and served and any other area that the child typically uses

MyEducationLab

Go to the Assignments and Activities section of Topic 3: Menu Planning in the MyEducationLab for your course and complete the activity entitled *Accommodating Food Allergies*. What precautions do these programs enforce to ensure that children with food allergies are safe?

Checklist for Managing Food Allergies in the Classroom

Activities or lesson plans:
- ☐ Do any cooking activities use foods with potential allergens?
- ☐ Are food items with potential allergens used in other activities (sensory tables with corn meal, pasta, or rice, sorting and stringing pastas, made-from-scratch play dough)?

Field trips:
- ☐ Are allergen-free foods available for lunch and snacks?
- ☐ Does the emergency kit include children's medications (i.e., epinephrine injector) and an up-to-date Food Allergy Action Plan?
- ☐ Does everyone know who is carrying the child's medication?
- ☐ Does someone have a cell phone?

Lunchroom procedures:
- ☐ Is there a plan in place for assuring the child receives the correct food from food service?
- ☐ What practices are used to remove all traces of allergens during cleanup?
- ☐ Are kitchen staff informed and trained on food allergies?
- ☐ Is there sufficient supervision of the child with allergies during meal service to ensure that the correct food is selected and served and that children are not sharing food?

Social events:
- ☐ Are foods with allergens coming into the classroom from outside sources for classroom celebrations, picnics, etc.?

Teacher's absence:
- ☐ Is there a plan in place to ensure allergen safety when the teacher is absent?
- ☐ Is backup staff trained to supervise food service for children with allergies?

Classroom environment:
- ☐ Does more than one class use the same classroom (AM and PM classes)?
- ☐ Are both teachers aware of the allergies of each other's students?

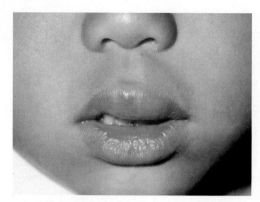

Children with allergies often have symptoms such as hives, a rash, and swelling of the mouth and throat.

(*Standard 5: Health Topic 5.B: Ensuring Children's Nutritional Well-Being, Criterion 5.B.05*; NAEYC, 2008). It is also imperative to carefully read food labels. Foods selected for purchase for infants should be single-ingredient foods to prevent inadvertent exposure to an allergen. Some infant foods that might appear to be single-ingredient products can have hidden sources of potential allergens. For example, some infant meats and poultry are prepared with gravy that contains cornstarch, a potential allergen (U.S. Food and Drug Administration, 2006).

Supports should be provided for breast-feeding mothers (*Standard 5: Health Topic 5.B: Ensuring Children's Nutritional Well-Being, Criterion 5.B.09*; NAEYC, 2008). This is especially important because breast-feeding may offer protection from the development of food allergies. Breast-fed infants who have a family history of allergies are less likely to develop skin rashes or a milk allergy in the first 2 years of life compared to infants who drink regular formula (Greer, Sicherer, Burks, & Committee on Nutrition and Section on Allergy and Immunology, 2008b). Sometimes breast-fed babies become exposed to allergens in mother's breast milk. If this occurs the mother may have to restrict consumption of certain foods (Greer et al., 2008b). In these situations teachers must be sure to not offer stored breast milk that predates the start of the mother's elimination diet.

Extra care is also needed when preparing infant formula to avoid cross contamination. Strategies to avoid cross contamination include the following:

- Formula should be prepared in specifically identified containers, using specific mixing utensils.
- Bottles should be cleaned with specific bottle brushes and thoroughly rinsed.
- Special hypoallergenic formulas should be labeled so that bottles are not inadvertently given to the wrong infant. The label on the formula should be double-checked before feeding the infant.

Toddlers, Preschoolers, and Primary-Grade Children with Food Allergies

The challenge in planning menus for children with food allergies is ensuring that the foods offered are allergen free while still meeting nutritional recommendations. In addition it is important to create enough variety so that children do not become bored with the substitutes offered. Using whole basic foods instead of processed foods may reduce the risk of allergen exposure for children who have multiple allergies. For example, children who have egg and wheat allergies can consume fresh baked chicken without fear of allergen exposure, whereas prepared chicken strips or nuggets will most likely contain these allergens.

As with infant diets, food for young children should be prepared and served to avoid cross contamination. Food purchased for children with allergies should be labeled with the child's name and date and properly stored. In addition, special diet items must be labeled when served so that children receive the correct allergen-free foods (see Figure 7-13). Menus for children with allergies should be approved by families and posted so that all staff involved know what children with special diets will be served. During meal service, young children should be supervised so that they do not inadvertently consume other children's food. School-age children should be cautioned about sharing lunches.

It is important to alert staff members and families to not bring in foods that can trigger severe allergic reactions in children. This request should be translated for families who are not English speakers. When the menu is carefully planned to accommodate food allergies and food service safety checks are a routine part of food service and preparation, teachers minimize the risk of accidental exposure to food allergens. If exposure does occur teachers can be confident that there is an allergy action plan in place.

Figure 7-13 Example of Labeling Special Diet Items

Planning Menus for Children with Type 1 Diabetes

Children with diabetes have special dietary needs that require close coordination between families and teachers. They must be served meals and snacks that meet their nutritional needs and at the same time maintain appropriate blood sugar levels. Teachers who have children with diabetes in the class need specialized training by a diabetes educator about the effects of physical activity, diet, and insulin on blood glucose levels. They also must be trained in the treatment of diabetes emergencies (American Diabetes Association, 2008).

Understanding Type 1 Diabetes

Type 1 diabetes is a chronic medical condition that results in the inability of glucose to get from the bloodstream into the cell where it can be used as energy. It is predominantly the carbohydrates (starches/grains, fruits, milk, and sweets) in a diet that are broken down to glucose during digestion and then absorbed into the bloodstream to be transported to the cells where it is used as energy. The hormone insulin is required to allow glucose into the cell. Children with type 1 diabetes require insulin injections to meet this need. (More details about diabetes are provided in Chapter 12.)

type 1 diabetes
a condition that results in the inability of glucose to get from the circulatory system or bloodstream into the cell where it can be used as energy; requires insulin to correct

Understanding the Diet for Type 1 Diabetes

Children with diabetes generally do not require special foods although sugar substitutes and sugar-free beverages are helpful to have on hand (Howell & National Food Service Management Institute, 2003). A very important aspect to consider when planning menus and providing meal service for children with diabetes is the amount of carbohydrate-containing foods served at meal and snack time. In addition, because the goal is to balance blood glucose or sugar levels with the need for insulin, the timing of meals and snacks is very important. Regular meal and snack times help prevent high or low blood sugar levels.

The special diets of children with diabetes vary depending on the child's age and their calorie requirements. Teachers will know how much to serve and when based on the child's meal plan. A child's meal plan is developed and reviewed by health care professionals such as dietitians to help children with diabetes. This individualized plan reflects the child's food preferences, eating habits, and financial considerations (Nevin-Folino, 2008). The family receives the meal plan instructions and is typically the resource for communicating the meal plan to the teacher. In addition, the management of all aspects of a child's diabetes including diet are outlined in Diabetes Medical Management Plan and the 504 Plan. (See Web Resources.) To accommodate children who have diabetes, families need to:

meal plan
a diet guidance tool developed by health care professionals such as dietitians to help children with diabetes and their families know what amount of carbohydrates they should eat and when so that their blood sugar level stays within an acceptable range

- Communicate which meals the child will consume at school.
- Provide the meal plan, which typically includes educational materials on the carbohydrate content of foods such the *Exchange Lists for Meal Planning* (American Dietetic Association & American Diabetes Association, 2003).

For their part in accommodating children with diabetes, teachers need to:

- Learn the carbohydrate content of foods offered on the menu and understand the portions that are allowed per the child's meal plan.
- Ensure regular mealtimes. If a meal is delayed, a backup plan for providing food is necessary to prevent the child with diabetes from having a low blood sugar reaction.
- Review foods planned for special events and receive approval from families about the particular food items and amounts that should be served.
- Plan appropriate foods for meals away from the program, such as picnics or field trips.
- Develop strategies and obtain guidance from families on what to do if a child refuses to eat.

What if. . .

a child in your class has diabetes and the lunch meal is late? You wonder if you should provide the child with diabetes an emergency snack while the other children continue to wait. How would you manage this? How would you explain this to the other children?

Close monitoring of a child's blood sugar level is accomplished by pricking the finger and using a glucose meter to determine if the blood sugar is within an acceptable range.

- Obtain training and guidance on what foods to feed or medication to administer (glucagon) if the child's blood sugar levels get too low.
- Make provisions in case the teacher is absent. A substitute teacher must be trained in diet and diabetes management (American Diabetes Association, 2008).

Teachers may be called on to check children's blood sugar levels, make decisions about the amount of food to serve based on the child's blood sugar level, and administer insulin. All information pertaining to these types of decisions is included in the Diabetes Medical Management Plan and the 504 Plan.

Planning Menus for Children Who Are Overweight or Obese

A healthful menu requires little modification to accommodate children who are overweight. Most children identified as overweight or obese will continue to eat from the regular menu unless a physician has determined a specially structured diet is a medical necessity (Davis et al., 2007). Children who are significantly obese may be referred to a multidisciplinary obesity care team. In this case, families may provide more specific diet recommendations from their health care team. Only a select group of children with significant obesity-related health issues will require this type of intervention (American Medical Association, 2007; National Initiative for Children's Healthcare Quality, 2008).

Many of the strategies available for managing overweight or obesity among children also address prevention. Attention is given to improving health rather than focusing only on weight. This protects both the physical and social/emotional well-being of young children (Society for Nutrition Education, Weight Realities Division, 2002). A well-planned menu is an effective tool for implementing nutrition recommendations and teaching children and their families what constitutes a balanced meal. The American Academy of Pediatrics and the American Dietetic Association recommend the following evidence-based nutrition practices for preventing and treating overweight and obesity:

- Limit the intake of sugar-sweetened beverages, soft drinks, and juice.
- Encourage the intake of sufficient fruits and vegetables.
- Eat breakfast daily.
- Provide appropriate portion sizes (American Dietetic Association, 2009; Davis et al., 2007).

Other helpful tactics to consider when adjusting menus to meet the needs of children who are overweight or obese include:

- Serve low-fat entrées and lean meat, fish, or poultry without the skin.
- Select fresh fruit instead of juice or canned fruit.
- Use low-fat condiments such as low-fat salad dressing and mayonnaise.
- Serve skim or 1% milk to children age 2 and older.
- Offer whole foods and whole-grain foods high in fiber content.

In the chapter-opening scenario Jeanine's goal was to create a system for menu planning. Developing a 4-week cycle menu was the first step in her plan. She then found that by switching to skim milk, adding more fruits and vegetables, and limiting juice, she was able to create a more healthful nutrition environment for all the children, including the child in her class who was overweight.

Planning Menus for Children with Special Needs

Children with medical conditions or special developmental needs may also have special diet requirements. Children with special developmental needs may be at increased risk for nutritional problems. For example, a survey of children birth to age 3 participating in an early intervention programs revealed that 79% to 90% had one or more nutritional risk factors (American Dietetic Association, 2004). In addition, these children may have unique feeding concerns, such as problems with chewing

What if. . .

you had a child attending your program who had a special diet with which you were unfamiliar? What strategies would you use to ensure you fully understood the diet? What steps would you take to make sure a menu was planned that met the needs of this child?

and swallowing. This highlights the need for careful discussion of menus and the adjustments that may be needed to ensure that the child's dietary needs are well understood. Directions for meeting the child's nutrition and feeding needs in the classroom setting should be obtained from the child's health care provider.

In some situations teachers may require specialized training. For example, if a child requires tube feedings, teachers will need to be trained in tube feeding administration before the child attends. With tube feeding, a liquid supplement is fed via a tube that enters the stomach or small intestine. This method is used when a child is not able to eat solid foods or the amount that can be eaten is insufficient in volume for the child to achieve adequate nutritional intake. Training would be provided by a qualified health care professional. In some cases the medical professional may provide written approval for a family member to provide the training. A medical statement needs to be on file documenting the need for the special diet and describing the recommended feeding practices. Figure 7-14 is a sample form that can be used for any child requiring a special diet (USDA Food and Nutrition Service, 2001).

tube feeding
a method of feeding used when eating solid foods is not possible or insufficient in volume to achieve adequate intake. A liquid supplement is fed via a tube that goes into the stomach or small intestine

There are many factors to consider when adapting menus for children with special health and development needs. Children with special needs may have varying requirements for calories to maintain an appropriate rate of growth. Some children may find it difficult to eat enough calories to support growth because of increased calorie requirements, oral-motor problems, or developmental delay of feeding skills, while other children may face increased risk for obesity due to poor muscle tone or decreased physical activity. In addition, drugs prescribed for the special health need may interfere with nutrient absorption or appetite. Some children may experience diarrhea or constipation (Samour & King, 2005). Table 7-4 provides a summary of the nutritional and related health concerns of several developmental disorders and syndromes.

Adjustments to the way food is offered may also be needed. These include:

- *Food texture:* Food may need to be ground or pureed.
- *Food consistency:* A commercial thickener may need to be added to liquids.
- *Special equipment:* Special equipment such as a feeding chair or special plate and eating utensils may be necessary.
- *Commercial supplements:* Supplements may be used to boost calorie intake or for tube feeding.
- *Calorie level:* High-calorie or low-calorie foods may be needed.
- *Mealtimes:* More time may be needed for consuming meals.

Families and early intervention specialists are good resources for guidance about managing children's eating concerns. During mealtimes teachers should observe children with special eating concerns carefully, watching for chewing, swallowing, and other eating problems. The NAEYC (2009) recommends that staff keep a daily record documenting the type and amount of food consumed by children with special needs and provide this information to families. Any concerns should be shared because children may need to be referred to a feeding clinic that offers the services of a physician, an occupational or speech therapist, and a pediatric dietitian.

Planning Menus for Children with Vegetarian Diets

A vegetarian diet is one in which the child's primary source of nutrition comes from plant foods. There are different types of vegetarian diets. Teachers need to understand which type of vegetarian diet a child requires so that they understand the type of substitutions to make on program menus. Table 7-5 describes four types of vegetarian diets and the foods that are avoided and consumed.

Infants with Vegetarian Diets

The age of a child influences vegetarian menu planning decisions. A vegetarian diet can safely meet the nutritional needs of infants. At first infants are either breast-fed or provided regular formula. Soy formula is an option for infants whose families avoid all animal sources of food

Figure 7-14 Eating and Feeding Evaluation: Children with Special Needs

PART A			
Student's Name		Age	
Name of School	Grade Level	Classroom	
Does the child have a disability? If yes, describe the major life activities affected by the disability.		Yes	No
Does the child have special nutritional or feeding needs? If Yes, complete Part B of this form and have it signed by a licensed physician.		Yes	No
If the child is not disabled, does the child have special nutritional or feeding needs? If Yes, complete Part B of this form and have its signed by a recognized authority.		Yes	No
If the child does not require special meals, the parent can sign at the bottom and return the form to the school food service.			
PART B			
List any dietary restrictions or special diet.			
List any allergies or food intolerances to avoid.			
List foods to be substituted.			
List foods that need the following change in texture. If all foods need to be prepared in this manner, indicate "All." Cut up or chopped into bite size pieces: Finely ground: Pureed:			
List any special equipment or utensils that are needed.			
Indicate any other comments about the child's eating or feeding patterns.			
Parent's Signature		Date:	
Physician or Medical Authority's Signature		Date:	

Source: From *Accommodating Children with Special Dietary Needs in School Nutrition Programs—Guidance for Food Service Staff*, p. 34, 2001, Alexandria, VA: USDA Food and Nutrition Service, retrieved August 25, 2009, from http://www.fns.usda.gov/cnd/Guidance/special_dietary_needs.pdf.

including milk. Solid foods are introduced gradually, following the same guidelines recommended for nonvegetarian infant diets. In place of animal protein sources, protein-rich vegetable foods such as pureed legumes, tofu, soy yogurts, and dairy products such as pureed cottage cheese and yogurt are offered. Infant cereal is particularly beneficial especially for breast-fed infants because it is rich in iron and zinc, nutrients generally found in meat products. Infants following a vegan diet require specific attention to maintain adequate nutrient

Table 7-4   Nutritional Concerns of Select Developmental Disorders and Syndromes

Developmental Disorders and Syndromes	Altered Growth Concerns	Feeding Problems	Other Health Concerns	Implications for Teachers
Attention deficit/hyperactivity disorder (ADHD)	Some children may experience slower rate of weight gain and growth	Depressed appetite due to medications	N/A	Provide calorie-dense, nutrient-rich foods if child is underweight. Offer three meals and three snacks. Feingold diet is not considered effective although perhaps 3% respond to diet. Sugar intake is not linked to ADHD.
Autism	N/A	Limited food selections, strong dislikes, ritualistic eating (i.e., the way food is arranged and the sequence in which it is served).	Medications may impact vitamin and mineral status; pica (the eating of nonfood items such as clay, dirt, or paper)	Provide diet recommended by parents and health care provider. Gluten- and casein (milk)-free diet may be requested by parents although this diet is not evidenced based.
Cerebral palsy	Poor growth; failure to thrive if child has oral motor problems; if not, there is increased risk of overweight when physical activity is limited	Oral/motor problems	Medication/nutrient interactions; gum disease; constipation	If underweight: Provide calorie-dense, nutrient-rich foods. If overweight: Provide low-energy diet. Adjust textures as needed. May require special feeding assistance, extra time to feed, or tube feeding. Encourage oral hygiene.
Down syndrome	Poor growth initially due to poor suck and/or congenital heart disease; risk for obesity increases later on	Poor suck in infancy	Gum disease and dental problems due to decreased salivary flow; increased risk of congenital heart disease and osteoporosis; constipation	Watch for adequate growth the first year; later provide low-energy diet to prevent obesity. Encourage oral hygiene and the intake of adequate dairy products. Provide fiber-rich diet and adequate fluids.
Epilepsy and seizure disorder	N/A	N/A	Medication/nutrient interactions; seizures; constipation	Some children may need special diets for seizure control that are coordinated with family and health care providers.
Fetal alcohol syndrome	Poor growth; failure to thrive	Poor suck and difficult to feed	Mild to moderate mental retardation; poor coordination; hyperactivity in childhood	Offer calorie-dense, nutrient-rich foods. May require tube feeding.
Muscular dystrophy	Slow weight gain; sometimes obesity	Swallowing problems	Vitamin/mineral deficiencies; constipation	Monitor weight and provide appropriate calorie intake. May need feeding assistive devices.
Spina bifida	Risk for obesity	Swallowing problems	Urinary tract infections; may develop latex allergies; constipation	Provide low-energy, high-fiber diet to prevent obesity. When latex allergy exists, children should avoid bananas, kiwi, water chestnuts, and avocados.

Sources: Adapted from Journal of the American Dietetic Association, 104(1). Providing Nutrition Service for Infants, Children, and Adults with Developmental Disabilities and Special Health Care Needs. Copyright 2004. Reprinted with permission from Elsevier; with information obtained from "Nutrition Management of Developmental Disabilities," p. 202, Chapter 15 in Pediatric Manual of Clinical Dietetics, 2nd updated edition, edited by Nancy Nevin-Folino, Karen Amorde-Spalding, and Leisje Nieman, 2008, Chicago: American Dietetic Association; Pediatric Nutrition in Chronic Diseases and Developmental Disorders: Prevention, Assessment and Treatment, 2nd edition, edited by Shirley W. Ekvall and Valli K. Ekvall, 2005, New York: Oxford University Press; "Muscular Dystrophy Campaign: Nutrition and Feeding in Individuals with Neuromuscular Conditions," by A. Bagnell and T. Davies, retrieved November 17, 2007, from http://www.muscular-dystrophy.org/assets/0000/7842/Nutrition_and_feeding.pdf

Table 7-5	Types of Vegetarians	
Type of Vegetarian	**Avoids**	**Consumes**
Lacto-ovo	Meats, poultry, fish	Eggs, milk and dairy products, foods of plant origin
Ovo-vegetarian	Meat, poultry, fish, dairy	Eggs, foods of plant origin
Lacto-vegetarian	Meat, poultry, fish, eggs	Milk and dairy products and foods of plant origin
Vegan	Meat, poultry, fish, eggs, and dairy	Only foods of plant origin

Source: Based on "Nutrition for the Vegetarian Child," p. 100, Chapter 8 in *Pediatric Manual of Clinical Dietetics*, 2nd updated edition, edited by Nancy Nevin-Folino, Karen Amorde-Spalding, and Leisje Nieman, 2008, Chicago: American Dietetic Association.

intake. A feeding progression chart for infants on vegan diets is provided in Table 7-6. Nut or peanut butter are good vegetarian foods, but should not be given by the spoonful to children younger than 4 years of age due to the risk of choking (American Academy of Pediatrics, 2007). Bread and peanut butter can form a glob in the roof of the mouth, which can make it difficult to swallow.

Toddler, Preschool, and Primary-Grade Children with Vegetarian Diets

Young children whose vegetarian diet includes milk, other dairy products, and eggs receive a diet that supports growth. It can be more challenging to meet the nutrient needs of children on vegan diets. Sometimes the fiber content of a plant-based vegan diet provides so much bulk that children become full before their nutrient needs are met. One way to ensure sufficient calories and protein for growth is to provide nutrient- and calorie-dense foods. This is especially important for children who are selective eaters. Food products that increase calories in the diet include nut butters (assuming there are no allergies), oils, and avocado. Whole soy milk should be offered rather than fat-free or low-fat milk, and it should be fortified with calcium and vitamin D. Rice milk and nut milks are not recommended for toddlers because they are typically lower in protein and fat. It is important to compare labels and make informed decisions when selecting beverages.

Several aspects are important to consider when planning menus to meet vegetarian diet needs:

- Select vegetarian protein products that are fortified with calcium, iron, vitamin D, zinc, and vitamin B_{12}.
- Serve calcium and vitamin D fortified soy milk (whole soy milk for children under age 2) when a cow's milk substitute is needed.
- Use meat substitutes such as soy burgers, vegetarian deli slices, bean loaves, soy sausage, nut butters, and tofu to maintain variety in the menu.
  - Avoid gelatin products made from pork, such as marshmallows, gummy candies, and gelatin desserts.
    - Plan healthful vegetarian snacks, such as crackers with nut butters, fruit smoothies made with milk or soy milk, cheese sandwich, or yogurt or cottage cheese mixed with fruit.

Respecting the philosophical beliefs of families and providing them with the means for sustaining these practices in early childhood programs are important.

Planning Menus to Reflect Cultural Preferences

The traditions associated with eating are some of the most deeply ingrained behaviors of life. Many cultural traditions, customs, and beliefs are associated with food practices and affect the family's preferences for their child's diet in the early childhood setting. Making

MyEducationLab

Go to the Assignments and Activities section of Topic 3: Menu Planning in the MyEducationLab for your course and complete the activity entitled *Culturally Relevant Menus That Meet Nutritional Guidelines.* What are some key considerations that these teachers take into account when planning menus?

What if. . .

children in your class noticed that a child was being served a special diet? How would you respond to their questions?

Table 7-6	Suggested Feeding Schedule for Vegan Infants			
Food	4–6 Months	6–8 Months	9–10 Months	11–12 Months
Milk	Breast milk or soy formula	Breast milk or soy formula	Breast milk or soy formula	Breast milk or soy formula
Cereal and breads	Iron-fortified infant cereal (can be delayed until 6 months)	Infant cereal, crackers, toast, unsweetened dry cereal	Infant cereal, crackers, toast, unsweetened dry cereal, soft bread	Infant cereal, crackers, toast, unsweetened dry cereal, soft bread, rice, pasta
Fruits	None	Strained fruit, fruit juice	Soft or cooked fruit, fruit juice	Soft, canned, or cooked fruit, peeled raw fruit, fruit juice
Vegetables	None	Strained vegetable, vegetable juice	Soft, cooked, mashed vegetable, vegetable juice	Soft, cooked pieces of vegetable, vegetable juice
Legumes	None	Tofu, pureed legumes, soy yogurt can be added at 7–8 months	Tofu, pureed legumes, soy cheese, soy yogurt	Tofu, mashed legumes, soy cheese, soy yogurt, bite-sized pieces of soy burger, tempeh

Note: Some infants may developmentally be ready to eat additional solids at 4-6 months. See Table 5-3, Infant Feeding Guidelines: Birth to 12 Months.

Source: Reprinted from *Journal of the American Dietetic Association*, 6, pp. 670–677. Considerations in planning vegan diets: infants by Ann Reed Mangels and Virginia Messina. Copyright 2001. Reprinted with permission from Elsevier.

adjustments to menus for children based on family cultural practices requires close communication with families.

Each culture's food practices can have health and nutrition advantages and disadvantages for children. For example, traditional Asian meals are low in meats and rich in vegetables, which contributes to a reduced incidence of heart disease, bowel cancer, and breast cancer (Hill, 2008). Middle Eastern diets are high in olive oil, which contributes to that population having, in general, lower blood pressures (Nolan, 2008; Stein, 2004). Ethnic and cultural diets can also have negative features. For example, a study of Mexican American preschoolers showed that children's intake of calories, fat, and saturated fat exceeded recommendations, putting them at risk for obesity and its associated health risks such as diabetes (Mier et al., 2007). This may reflect a degree of acculturation to mainstream American dietary practices because traditional Hispanic diets are low in fat and high in fiber (Kulkarni, 2004). African American "soul food" is rich in green leafy vegetables such as collards, kale, mustard, and turnip greens and high-fiber beans such as black-eyed peas and red beans. However, the diet also relies on fried and seasoned meats and whole-milk products, resulting in a higher than recommended fat and sodium intake (Edwards, 2003; Kulkarni, 2004).

Teachers also need to be aware that infant feeding practices vary among different cultural and ethnic groups. For instance, in one study, 6- to 11-month-old children of Hispanic heritage were more likely than white infants to be eating fresh fruits, baby cookies, and foods such as soups, rice, and beans that are traditional foods in their culture (Mennella, Ziegler, Briefel, & Novak, 2006). Feeding practices may also differ from the goals of the early childhood setting. For example, some cultures give sugar water to infants or add other foods to bottles of formula (Nevin-Folino, 2008). When planning to meet cultural preferences, teachers need to work closely with families to identify foods from the cultural tradition that can be included in the menu while also meeting the goals for healthful menus.

cultural competency
the respectful understanding and appreciation of cultural differences and similarities among groups and the ability to use this understanding to effectively interact with people across cultures

Planning menus that reflect the cultural backgrounds of children in the class or school is one way of demonstrating cultural competency. Cultural competency refers to the respectful understanding and appreciation of cultural differences and similarities among groups and the ability to use this understanding to effectively interact with people across cultures. Strategies to support cultural sensitivity in the early childhood setting include the following:

- Plan menus that include culturally diverse food options.
- Offer classroom cooking activities for children to prepare and taste foods that represent a variety of traditions.
- Offer opportunities for parents to learn about healthful ethnic cooking by using a grain staple, such as rice, in a variety of ethnic recipes.
- Provide information, such as menus, in the various home languages of children present in the class.
- Read children's books on eating that reflect culturally diverse settings.
- Conduct field trips to grocery stores, supermarkets, and bakeries, including visits to culturally diverse establishments.

Teachers are respected sources of authority and information in many cultures. In response to this respect, teachers should provide accurate information about diet and nutrition that is reputable and culturally sensitive.

Planning Menus to Address Religious Beliefs and Practices

What if. . .

you wanted to include activities that explored cultural diversity in your class curriculum? What themes would you use? What foods could you include on the menu to reinforce your theme?

Religious beliefs, customs, traditions, and practices hold deep meaning to the families who adhere to them. In some cases religious belief systems and practices influence the diet choices of children. For example, some religious groups refrain from eating certain meats. Hindus do not eat beef, and people of Islamic and Jewish faiths may avoid pork and pork products. Devout Seventh Day Adventists avoid all meats. Teachers need to work closely with families to identify food restrictions and preferences based on religious customs or practices. Table 7-7 summarizes common religious food practices among eight different religious groups.

The Islamic Religion

Adherents to Islam follow religious writings that recommend a mother breast-feed her infant until 2 years of age if possible (Nevin-Folino, 2008). Modesty is an important aspect of this religion. Providing a private location for Islamic mothers who are breast-feeding helps support them in maintaining this feeding relationship. The traditional dress and head covering of Islamic women cover most of their body. This puts them and their infants at risk for vitamin D deficiency if the infants are exclusively breast-fed.

Many Muslims consume a *halal* diet, which means they consume foods that are lawful or permitted according to the Quran (Islamic Food and Nutrition Council of America, 2008). Only the flesh of animals or poultry killed in a humane way while speaking the name of God can be eaten, such as beef, veal, turkey, chicken, goat, and lamb. The Halal diet avoids pork and pork products such as the gelatin used in marshmallows, gummy candies, and gelatin desserts.

The Jewish Religion

The Jewish religion also has rules about how animals are butchered. According to Jewish law all blood must be drained from the meat for it to be considered *kosher*. Kosher symbols are used on processed foods to designate that they have been prepared in accordance with dietary laws. Milk and meat cannot be consumed at the same meal. The term *pareve* on a label indicates foods that contain neither meat nor dairy products. These foods are therefore considered neutral and can be served with either meat

| Table 7-7 | Common Religious Food Practices |

Food or Food Practice	Seventh-day Adventist	Buddhist	Eastern Orthodox	Hindu	Jewish	Mormon	Muslim	Roman Catholic
Beef		A		X				
Pork	X	A		A	X		X	
All meat	A	A	R	A	R		R	R
Eggs/dairy	O	O	R	O	R			
Fish	A	A	R	R	R			
Shellfish	X	A	O	R	X			
Alcohol	X				A	X	X	
Coffee/tea	X					X	A	
Meat/dairy at same meal					X			
Leavened foods					R			
Ritual slaughter of meats					+		+	
Moderation	+	+				+	+	
Fasting*		+	+	+	+	+	+	+

X = prohibited or strongly discouraged; A = avoided by the most devout; R = some restrictions regarding types of foods or when foods are eaten; O = permitted, but may be avoided at some observances; + = practiced

*Fasting varies from partial (abstention from certain foods or meals) to complete (no food or drink).

Source: From KITTLER/SUCHER, Food and Culture, 5e. © 2008 Brooks/Cole, a part of Cengage Learning, Inc. Reproduced by permission. www.cengage.com/permissions

or milk. Pareve foods include eggs, fish, grains, fruits, and vegetables. Pork and pork products are not permitted in the kosher diet. Fish with fins are permissible, but shellfish are not. Eggs and fish can be eaten with either milk or meat. During food preparation and service, the cooking and eating utensils are also kept kosher. This means that those of the orthodox faith have available two sets of serving ware and cooking utensils for the separate preparation of meat and milk.

The restriction that prohibits drinking milk and eating meat in the same meal is in conflict with the Child and Adult Care Food Program and the School Lunch Program requirements for milk and meat components served at lunch and supper. To address this, the USDA Food and Nutrition Service provides three options for Jewish schools, institutions, and sponsors to select from and still be in compliance with regulations:

Option I: Serve an equal amount of 100% juice in place of milk with lunch or supper. Programs operating 5 days per week may substitute juice for milk twice per week for lunches and twice for suppers, but no more than once each day.

Option II: Serve milk at an appropriate time before or after the meal service period, in accordance with applicable Jewish dietary law.

Labeling of foods makes it easier to determine if a food is acceptable for a child following Jewish or Muslim dietary laws.

MyEducationLab

To assess your understanding of how to build healthy menus, go to the Book Specific Resources section in the MyEducationLab for your course, select *Nutrition, Health, and Safety for Young Children,* Chapter 7 of the Study Plan, and then complete the multiple choice questions and activities.

Option III: Serve the supplement (snack) juice component at lunch or supper. Serve the lunch milk component as part of a supplement (snack) (USDA Food and Nutrition Service, 2007b).

When planning menus it is helpful to determine a local source for special dietary products such as kosher or halal foods.

The Seventh Day Adventist Religion

This religion encourages the lacto-ovo vegetarian diet. Eggs and dairy are permitted although egg yolks are limited to three per week. The use of whole grains is encouraged. This diet is healthy for children as long as there are not too many high-fiber foods to interfere with the consumption of adequate calories. Menu planning for these children would follow the guides for the lacto-ovo vegetarian diet (see Table 7-5).

Summary

A well-planned menu is the foundation for creating a healthful nutrition environment in early childhood settings. An organized approach to menu planning ensures that nutritious meals are designed. This involves writing menus that demonstrate understanding of food program requirements and program nutrition goals and that support alternative and special diets. Many resources are available to assist teachers and food service personnel to plan nutritious meals that meet the recommendations of health, licensing, accreditation, and funding authorities. Program nutrition goals ensure that children receive appropriate foods and take into consideration quality-of-life issues such as sustainability.

A cycle menu is typically selected for early childhood settings. This helps organize the process of menu development, purchasing, and food service. It also helps family child care settings, programs, and schools establish and maintain cost-effective practices. The process of menu development includes selecting entrées, side dishes, and beverages that offer variety in taste, texture, and visual appeal. Once established, the basic menu is adjusted to accommodate special dietary needs.

Careful menu development is important. Children receive a large portion of their daily requirement of nutrients in the early childhood setting. They rely on adults to help them learn about making good food choices. Mealtime offers opportunities for children to participate in relaxed social discussions and guides children to learn self-help skills such as serving their own food and clearing their dishes. Children with special dietary concerns or cultural or religious preferences depend on their teachers to ensure they receive the appropriate meal. Families who send food from home also benefit from the information provided by programs that helps them make healthful choices for the child's lunch and snacks. Overall, careful menu planning contributes to children's health and wellness, and establishes healthful eating practices that children can sustain throughout life.

Key Terms

Review Questions

1. What is the four-phase approach to planning menus?
2. What types of resources should a teacher have on hand when planning menus?
3. How would you use CACFP guidelines to plan a breakfast, lunch, and snack menu?
4. What types of health conditions require a special diet?
5. What adjustments to the menu might be needed to accommodate religious or cultural traditions?

Discussion Starters

1. Discuss the following situations. How would you deal with each scenario in such a way that a child's accidental exposure to an allergen is avoided?
   a. A young child might trade or share foods with a child who has allergies.
   b. Food service staff forget to prepare the special diet.
   c. Cross contamination of foods occurs such that some allergen gets into an otherwise acceptable food.
   d. The teacher is absent. How would the substitute know who has allergies and special dietary requirements?
   e. Foods from home are brought in for a celebration and a toddler with allergies is reaching for something he should not have.

2. A group of parents is upset about the school lunch menu. Some are concerned that there are too many processed foods, not enough whole grains, and too much canned fruit instead of fresh fruit. How would you approach this dilemma?

3. A 4-year-old in your program is obese. His mother tells you she has placed him on a diet and he can only eat the foods she packs for him from home. The boy cries during lunch because he can't eat what the other children are eating and he is hungry. How do you handle this situation?

Practice Points

1. You have been asked to join the School Health Advisory Council to develop a policy concerning beverages sold in vending machines at the school. Write a policy that addresses beverages available at school during the day and at after-school events and fund-raisers. Cite evidence-based recommendations to support your policy.

2. Using the MyPyramid menu planner, design a menu that meets Child and Adult Care Food Program requirements as well as MyPyramid recommendations for a 5-year-old girl. (*Hint:* Use the Appendix to determine CACFP requirements. Go to the MyPyramid.gov website and link to the MyPyramid menu planner.)

3. Using the four phases of menu planning, list two program requirements, establish two broad program goals, and develop a 1-day menu that will meet the needs of a preschool Head Start program that includes Hispanic children.

Web Resources

American Diabetes Association:
Diabetes 504 plan
https://www.diabetes.org/uedocuments/ad-504-adanasndredf-2007.pdf

Diabetes Medical Management Plan
https://www.diabetes.org/uedocuments/DMMP-finalformatted.pdf

Food Allergy and Anaphylaxis Network's Food Allergy Action Plan
http://www.foodallergy.org/actionplan.pdf

Institute of Medicine of the National Academies: Dietary Reference Intakes
www.iom.edu/CMS/54133.aspx

National Food Service Management Institute: Measuring Success with Standardized Recipes
www.nfsmi.org/ResourceOverview.aspx?ID=88

U.S. Department of Agriculture: MyPyramid
www.mypyramid.gov

U.S. Department of Agriculture Food and Nutrition Service Child Nutrition Programs
www.fns.usda.gov/CND, which includes links to:
Child and Adult Care Food Program
National School Lunch Program
School Breakfast Program

U.S. Department of Health and Human Services: *Dietary Guidelines for Americans, 2005*
www.health.gov/DietaryGuidelines

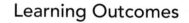

chapter 8 | Food Safety

Learning Outcomes

After reading this chapter, you should be able to:

1. Discuss the contaminants responsible for foodborne illness.

2. Define the role of federal, state, and county food safety standards and their impact on food service in the early childhood setting.

3. Explain how to implement a food safety system in the early childhood setting using the principles of the Hazard Analysis and Critical Control Point system and standard operating procedures.

4. Describe how to minimize food contamination risk during purchasing, storage, preparation, and service of meals in the early childhood setting.

5. Explain food safety precautions that need to be considered during an emergency and define strategies for managing food defense.

6. Learn how to teach concepts of food safety to young children.

Lacey's class of preschool children enjoys an eventful day. Lacey and Joan, teachers at Sunshine Preschool, have scheduled a field trip for their class groups to an area supermarket. They observe how meat is ground and packaged. They watch as bread and rolls are made and baked in large ovens in the bakery. At the end of the visit, they get to sample fresh warm bread and sliced oranges. When the children return to preschool, they eat lunch (turkey sandwiches, green salad, sliced watermelon, and milk), which was prepared in the school kitchen. Just as lunch is ending, Lacey is surprised by Kimberly's mother who arrives bearing a platter of homemade frosted cupcakes in celebration of Kimberly's fourth birthday.

The next morning Lacey gets the first inkling that something is wrong. A third of the children in the class are absent. Several parents call in reporting similar symptoms: vomiting, stomach cramps, and diarrhea. Lacey talks to the director, Jill, who decides to notify the health department of a suspected outbreak of a foodborne illness.

The health sanitarian begins to investigate the situation. The trip to the supermarket is determined to not be the source of the problem. The supermarket manager and workers have food safety training certification; they follow state and federal food safety guidelines and have consistently passed local sanitation inspections. The children who had toured the area where meat was prepared had washed their hands before eating the snacks. Also the children in Joan's class have not gotten sick.

The food service at the preschool is also reviewed. The director of food service shows the sanitarian their Hazard Analysis and Critical Control Point food safety plan where documentation confirms that proper safety procedures have been used in preparing the lunch. This confirmation and the fact that only the children in Lacey's class are experiencing symptoms similarly rules out the preschool food service as the source of the problem. Next the sanitarian interviews Kimberly's mother. Ultimately the homemade cupcakes are identified as the culprit in this outbreak of foodborne illness. It is discovered that the frosting on the cupcakes was made with raw egg whites. Salmonella food poisoning was later confirmed by laboratory tests.

Lacey is upset that this has occurred in her class. She takes pride in providing a healthy, safe environment for the children in her care. She constantly sanitizes surfaces and carefully supervises children as they wash their hands before meals. She had been caught unaware when Kimberly's mother brought in the cupcakes and had allowed them to be served against her better judgment. After this event she learns that serving food made in a home kitchen is against the preschool policy. She decides that she needs to rethink her practices on food safety. She is glad to learn that Jill intends to follow up by offering a food safety in-service training for both teaching and food service staff.

Food is a source of nutrition, however, in some situations it can also become a source of illness. **Foodborne illness** is the sickness that results from the consumption of contaminated foods. It is estimated that foodborne illnesses account for approximately 76 million illnesses per year (Marriott, 2006). According to the Centers for Disease Control and Prevention (CDC) the incidence of key foodborne diseases is greatest in children less than 4 years of age (CDC, 2009). Understanding how foods become contaminated and the hazards they pose in the early childhood setting helps teachers prevent situations that put children and staff at risk for a foodborne outbreak. Infants and young children are particularly at risk for food poisoning because their immune systems are not yet fully developed (CDC, 2008b; Field, 2005; Imhoff et al., 2004; Monterrosa et al., 2008b). In addition, their bodies produce fewer stomach acids compared to adults. Stomach acids offer protection from some infectious microorganisms (Ohio State University Extension, 2003). For these reasons young children are at greater risk than adults for becoming sick when exposed to contaminated food, and the illness can become severe and even life threatening. In fact, one of the risk factors identified by the CDC for certain specified bacterial illnesses is attendance at a child care center (CDC, 2008b; Jones et al., 2007; Marcus, 2008).

Part of teachers' daily routines often involves the handling of food for children. This entails special responsibilities. In the opening case scenario, Lacey followed food-safe

foodborne illness
an illness caused by eating food that has been contaminated by biological, chemical, or physical contaminants

practices in the classroom. However, the weak link that resulted in foodborne illness occurred when oversight of food preparation was left to an individual who was outside the umbrella of the program's food safety procedures. The scenario illustrates the importance of the teacher's role in making informed decisions about food preparation within the program setting and with *any* risky situation that may lead to foodborne illness. Children may be at risk when served food prepared by an individual who has not received food safety training in a home kitchen that has not been inspected and approved by an appropriate health regulatory agency.

In this chapter we provide information to help you understand how to effectively manage food safety. We discuss the nature of foodborne illness. We also describe the food safety requirements mandated by federal and state regulations that provide the foundation you need to develop and implement an evidenced-based food safety program. We also discuss food safety related to emergencies and food defense to help you be prepared to deal with unplanned events. Finally, we discuss how teachers can help young children learn food safety concepts.

IDENTIFYING HAZARDS THAT CAUSE FOODBORNE ILLNESS

contamination
occurs when something hazardous to health is present in food or drink

Contamination occurs when something hazardous to health is present in food or drink. Food and beverages can become contaminated by a variety of agents including those that are biological in origin, such as germs. Chemical agents such as pesticides and cleansing agents can accidentally end up in food and pose a health risk as well. Physical hazards to food safety include items that fall into foods such as fingernails, insects, metal shavings, and glass (McElhatton & Marshall, 2006; McSwane, Rue, & Linton, 2005; National Food Service Management Institute [NFSMI], 2002). A review of the different types of food hazards provides insight into the causes of foodborne illness.

Recognizing Biological Hazards

biological hazards
living microorganisms that contaminate food and cause foodborne illness

The majority of biological hazards are germs or microorganisms that grow on food and cause serious illness when consumed. These germs include bacteria, viruses, and parasites. (U.S. Food and Drug Administration, Center for Food Safety and Applied Nutrition [FDA/CFSAN], 2006b). Germs that contaminate food are by far the greatest hazard to health and occur more often than chemical and physical contamination (National Restaurant Association [NRA], 2008).

Understanding how microorganisms create illness prepares teachers to identify risky food safety situations and prevent foodborne outbreaks from occurring. Microorganisms damage the human body in three different ways: via infection, intoxication, or toxin-mediated infection (McSwane et al., 2005).

Teachers who work with children often handle food, so they must understand the food safety risks associated with feeding young children.

Infection

Infection is most familiar because it is a process that occurs routinely in the early childhood setting. Children "catch a cold" or a "flu bug" and the infection runs its course. A foodborne illness that is classified as an infection is similar in that there is an exposure to germs. The exposure, however, occurs via food instead of by coughing or sneezing. The germs grow in the body and create symptoms (see Figure 8-1) until the body's immune system destroys the germs and children are once again healthy.

Table 8-1 defines the three different categories of foodborne illness and provides some examples of microorganisms that cause sickness as well as steps teachers can take to prevent an outbreak from occurring. *Salmonella*, the microorganism responsible for the outbreak in Lacey's class, falls into the infection classification. Because the egg white in the frosting was not cooked, *Salmonella* bacteria were able to proliferate, especially because the cupcakes were stored at room temperature.

Intoxication

Intoxication refers to foodborne illness caused by microorganisms that grow on the food and release toxins (poisons) into it. This in turn produces the symptoms of illness. This type of food poisoning can be very dangerous when the toxin is not destroyed by cooking or the toxin is highly lethal. For example, the microorganism responsible for the foodborne illness called *botulism* creates a toxin that causes paralysis and is considered one of the most dangerous biological hazards known to man (CDC, 2008a; McSwane et al., 2005). Strategies teachers can use to avoid the production of toxins in food are listed in Table 8-1.

Toxin-Mediated Infection

The final classification of foodborne illness is the toxin-mediated infection, which has features of both infection and intoxication. When food containing a harmful microorganism is consumed, the germs begin to reproduce and then release toxins in the gastrointestinal tract (Clemson University Department of Food Science and Human Nutrition, 2008). *E. coli* O157:H7 is a microorganism that produces a toxin-mediated infection and has gained media attention because of the outbreaks associated with unpasteurized juice, ground beef, and spinach (CDC, 2005; FDA, 2007b; U.S. Department of Agriculture [USDA], Food Safety and Inspection Service, 2009). When food containing *E. coli* is cooked to appropriate temperatures, the microorganisms are destroyed and foodborne illness does not occur. The risk of illness, however, remains for food that is not cooked prior to meal service. Fresh fruits and vegetables have increasingly been identified as sources of foodborne outbreaks of *E. coli* (Lynch, Tauxe, & Hedberg, 2009; Noah, 2009).

Food irradiation can be used to control spoilage and eliminate germs that cause foodborne illness (U.S. Environmental Protection Agency [EPA], 2009a). In August 2008 the FDA (2008d) approved the use of irradiation as a means to make fresh iceberg lettuce and fresh spinach safer from microorganisms such as *E. coli*. Labels must indicate when food has been irradiated by displaying the irradiation logo (EPA, 2009b).

Irradiation of food is a controversial method of food preservation. Some consumers are concerned that irradiated food may become radioactive and, therefore, dangerous to eat. However, the source of radiation used in food preservation is too low to add radioactivity to foods and has been determined by the FDA to be safe. Remember that irradiation is just one tool in the arsenal of options available to fight foodborne illness. The FDA emphasizes that, "no preservation method is a substitute for safe food handling procedures" (EPA, 2009a).

Recognizing Chemical Hazards

Chemical hazards are contaminants in foods that pose a health risk when consumed. Chemical contamination can occur during the growing, harvesting, processing, and storage of foods. Examples of chemical contaminants that come in contact with food during growing and harvesting include pesticides and fertilizers. During processing chemical contaminants in food include lubricants, cleansing detergents, and sanitizers (Lelieveld, Mostert, Holah, & White, 2003). Chemical contamination can also occur when food is not appropriately stored. In the early childhood setting, a potential risk for chemical contamination occurs when cleaning agents are stored near food. Chemical agents can spill onto foods causing contamination. There is also a chance for mistaken identity when cleaning agents are stored in containers that look similar to items of food (see Figure 8-2).

Recognizing Physical Hazards

Physical hazards are items that get into foods that may cause injury or illness. Examples include glass, rocks, metal shavings, staples, bandages, insects, hair, fingernails, and jewelry. In a children's program physical contaminants might include beads, glitter, or beans

---

Figure 8-1 Common Symptoms of Foodborne Illness

- Stomach cramping
- Vomiting
- Diarrhea
- Headache
- Fever
- Chills

Sources: *Food-Safe Kitchens*, by A. Marchiony, 2004, Upper Saddle River, NJ: Pearson Prentice Hall; and *Bacteria and Foodborne Illness*, National Institute of Diabetes and Digestive and Kidney Diseases, 2007, retrieved September 16, 2009, from http://digestive.niddk.nih.gov/ddiseases/pubs/bacteria/#2.

What if. . .

food arrived in the classroom from the kitchen and you noticed the hamburgers appeared pink in the center and undone? What would you do to ensure children do not get a foodborne illness? What would you do if a child has already taken a bite?

MyEducationLab

Go to the Assignments and Activities section of Topic 4: Food Safety in the MyEducationLab for your course and complete the activity entitled *Causes and Prevention of Foodborne Illness*. What did you learn from this video that you will use when serving food to young children?

chemical hazards
unnatural chemicals that are present in foods and pose a health risk when consumed

physical hazards
items that fall into foods that may cause injury or illness

Table 8-1		Foodborne Illness and Prevention Strategies for Teachers	
Methods by Which Microorganisms Cause Foodborne Illness	Explanation	Common Microorganisms That Cause Illness and Food Sources	Prevention Strategies for Teachers
Infection	The micro-organism is present on the food, the food is eaten, the organism grows in the body (primarily in the gastrointestinal tract) and causes illness.	**Microorganisms:** *Salmonella* (bacteria) **Foods:** Poultry, eggs, dairy products, and produce such as fresh spinach, lettuce, and melons	1. Poultry and eggs must be cooked to appropriate temperatures (see Figure 8-9) 2. Teachers need to prevent cross-contamination: • Consider preparing salad or other produce to be served fresh before handling poultry. • Sanitize surfaces after handling poultry. • Wash hands thoroughly (see hand washing procedure in Figure 8-14). • Buy produce from reputable sources and rinse it before handling and serving. 3. Teachers or other food handlers must not come to work when ill. 4. Children should not handle raw eggs in class cooking activities. Substitute pasteurized cholesterol-free egg substitute. 5. Frozen poultry must be thawed in a refrigerator rather than on a counter.
Infection		**Microorganisms:** *Norovirus* (virus) **Foods:** Shellfish and prepared foods that have been exposed to contaminated water or handled by an infected food handler who transfers germs by touching the food or the equipment with which food comes in contact	1. Teachers and food handlers must practice good personal hygiene: • Wash hands thoroughly (see hand washing procedure in Figure 8-14). • Wear gloves when slicing fruits or preparing salads, sandwiches, and other ready-to-eat food. 2. Keep a sanitized food preparation and service area including children's dining tables. 3. Teachers' strategies to limit the spread of germs: • Report an outbreak to the local health department. Get their advice and recommendations. • Consider the use of paper products to minimize transfer of germs for a temporary period of time. • Have separate staff handle dirty and clean dishes and wear gloves to prevent cross-contamination of clean dishes. • Ramp up cleaning and sanitizing in the classroom setting. • Reinforce the message to food handlers: Don't come to work if sick. • Ensure that all staff and children don't come back to school until 72 hours after the last episode of vomiting or diarrhea. 4. Purchase foods from reputable sources. 5. Provide staff training and education.

Methods by Which Microorganisms Cause Foodborne Illness	Explanation	Common Microorganisms That Cause Illness and Food Sources	Prevention Strategies for Teachers
Infection		**Microorganisms:** Hepatitis A (virus): **Foods:** Shellfish and prepared foods that have been exposed to contaminated water or handled by an infected food handler who transfers germs by touching the food or the equipment with which food comes in contact	Same recommendations as for *Norovirus*.
Infection		**Microorganisms:** *Listeria monocytogenes* (bacteria): **Foods:** Ready-to-eat foods such as cold cuts, hotdogs, unpasteurized soft cheeses, smoked seafoods, and raw meat Grows in cool, moist environments	1. Teachers need to make sure that food is discarded after its "use by," or expiration, date. 2. Raw meats should be cooked to proper temperatures (see Figure 8-8). 3. Pregnant teachers or staff should avoid consuming these foods unless thoroughly heated because this germ causes miscarriage and serious illness in newborns. 4. Only pasteurized dairy products should be used in programs. 5. Teachers should use strategies to prevent cross-contamination (see *Salmonella* entry above).
Intoxication	The microorganism grows on food and releases a toxin, which when consumed causes illness.	**Microorganisms:** *Staphylococcus aureus* (bacteria) **Foods:** Meat and meat products, poultry and egg products, salads such as egg, tuna, chicken, potato, and macaroni, bakery products that are cream filled, sandwich fillings, and milk and dairy products	1. Washing hands after touching hair (use hair restraints), nose, face, and body is important because staph germs are harbored on the body. 2. Wounds on hands and arms must be covered by teachers or staff preparing food. 3. The toxin produced by this germ is not destroyed by heat; therefore, careful food preparation, cooling, and reheating are necessary and food should not be left in the temperature danger zone. 4. During cooking activities children should not handle food that remains uncooked unless it is for their own consumption. For example: • Peeling ingredients for a cooked soup for the class is allowable. • Chopping celery for tuna salad for the class is not. • Chopping celery for a single serving of tuna salad to be eaten by the child preparing it is allowable.

(Continued)

Methods by Which Microorganisms Cause Foodborne Illness	Explanation	Common Microorganisms That Cause Illness and Food Sources	Prevention Strategies for Teachers
Intoxication		**Microorganisms:** *Clostridium botulinum* (bacteria) *Note:* In infants under 12 months of age it acts as a toxin-mediated infection. **Foods:** Incorrectly home-canned foods; dented, leaking, or bulging canned foods	1. Teachers should not serve home-canned foods. 2. Do not purchase or serve food that comes in dented, leaking, or bulging cans or cracked jars. 3. The toxin produced by this germ is not destroyed by heat; therefore, careful food preparation, cooling, and reheating are necessary and food should not be left in the temperature danger zone
Toxin-mediated infection	The micro-organism grows on food, the food is ingested, and the microorganism grows in the body and releases a toxin in the body.	**Microorganisms:** *Clostridium botulinum* in infants **Foods:** Predominantly honey, which contains spores that, because of the low acidity of infants' stomachs, proliferate in the gastrointestinal tract and release a toxin	Teachers should not feed infants less than 12 months of age honey or any honey-containing products such a honey yogurt or honey-flavored cereals or crackers.
Toxin-mediated infection		**Microorganisms:** *Clostridium perfringens* (bacteria) **Foods:** Meat, poultry, and improperly cooled foods	1. Teachers should make sure food is properly cooked, cooled, and reheated. 2. Foods should be held at proper temperatures. 3. Foods should only be reheated once.
		Microorganisms: Shiga toxin-producing *Escherichia coli*; also known *as E. coli* O157:H7 (bacteria) **Foods:** Uncooked beef, contaminated produce, unpasteurized apple cider	1. Teachers should make sure food is cooked to proper internal temperatures. 2. Never serve unpasteurized juice. 3. Teachers should use strategies to prevent cross-contamination (see *Salmonella* entry above). 4. Children should never handle raw beef.

Sources: *Disease Listing: Botulism General Information*, Centers for Disease Control and Prevention, 2008a, retrieved September 14, 2009, from http://www.cdc.gov/nczved/dfbmd/disease_listing/botulism_gi.html; *Food-Safe Kitchens*, by A. Marchiony, 2004, Upper Saddle River, NJ: Pearson Prentice Hall; *Essentials of Food Safety and Sanitation*, 4th edition, by D. McSwane, N. R. Rue, and R. Linton, 2005, Upper Saddle River, NJ: Pearson Prentice Hall; and *Servsafe coursebook*, 5th edition, National Restaurant Association Educational Foundation, 2008, Upper Saddle River, NJ: Pearson Prentice Hall.

and rice from sensory tables that are mistakenly returned to a food preparation area. Wearing caps or hairnets, removing jewelry when preparing and serving food, maintaining kitchen equipment, and practicing pest control are on-site strategies that can minimize the risk of physical contaminants in foods. In addition, teachers should carefully clean tables that are used both for school activities and eating before and after any type of meal service to avoid the chance of introducing physical contaminants to food.

Understanding the type of contaminants found in food reveals the number of ways food can become unfit for human consumption. Fortunately, the United States has one of the safest food supplies in the world (McSwane et al., 2005). This is due in part to federal, state, and local agencies that oversee regulations that keep foods wholesome and safe. These regulatory agencies also step into action when food products from other countries are found to be unsafe. For example, in September 2008, infant formulas produced in China were found to contain melamine, a contaminant that causes kidney stones, kidney failure and in some cases death. (World Health Organization, 2008). The Food and Drug Administration (FDA) immediately released a health information advisory clarifying that infant formula producers in the United States do not use imported formula or milk products from China and confirming that the nation's formula supply is safe. (Food and Drug Administration, 2008a and b). The FDA requires all companies in the United States that produce infant formulas to register with the FDA and adhere to clearly defined nutrition and labeling requirements. Companies must also undergo annual inspections of their manufacturing plants (FDA, 2008a). These types of careful regulations support food safety for the most vulnerable segment of our population: infants.

This logo indicates that this food has been irradiated as a method of food preservation.

Figure 8-2
Food and cleaning agents should not be stored together because of the risk of chemical contamination and the potential for mistakenly using the wrong product

Recognizing Allergens as a Special Type of Hazard

Some children face an additional food safety risk that is unique to them and harmless to most others: food allergies. Children with food allergies are at risk for exposure to allergens, which can have life-threatening consequences. In Chapter 7 you learned about the various aspects of food preparation and menu planning that must be taken into consideration for children with food allergies. Food allergies are also a food safety issue. Teachers must read food labels carefully to determine if the allergens are present in the foods being offered to the child with allergies. Although the Food Allergen Labeling and Consumer Protection Act (FALCPA) requires that the eight major food allergens (milk, wheat, egg, soy, fish, shellfish, peanuts, tree nuts) be listed on food labels, there are more than 160 known food allergens that can trigger allergic reactions Careful label reading is especially important for children who suffer less common allergies (FDA/CFSAN, 2004b, 2006a). For example, consider the following situation:

> Jan, a teacher in a toddler classroom, discovered how important it is to check on potential food allergens. A 2-year-old in her class has a mild allergy to cranberries. The toddler began to display irritability and stomach discomfort. The child's father believed it was caused by something eaten at school. Jan asked the food service manager to check the labels of all products used to prepare meals for any form of cranberries. The next day the food service manager reported back. In an effort to use up extra cranberry sauce, the cook had been mixing it with grape jelly and was serving it with breakfast. The vendor stopped this practice when its effects were identified.

Children with celiac disease can also face a food safety risk. Celiac disease is an intolerance to gluten-containing foods such as wheat, rye, barley, and possibly oats. For

What if. . .

you were to look at your hands and wrists? Do you wear jewelry that could be a potential contaminate? What if you were preparing food for your kindergarten classroom and you noticed that a gem from your ring was missing? What would you do?

What if. . .

you had a new child entering your program who needed a gluten-free diet? What information would you need to gather before the child enters your program? What would you do if you were unsure whether a food item contained gluten?

these children consuming gluten-containing foods causes damage to the lower gastrointestinal tract. Although not as potentially life threatening as food allergies, careful label reading is still important. In August 2008, voluntary labeling identifying gluten content went into effect, making it easier to identify gluten in some foods (FDA/CFSAN, 2004b).

Reading labels is just one aspect of ensuring food safety for children who require special diets. Teachers must also be watchful for cross-contamination. Cross-contamination in the context of food allergies occurs when a nonallergenic food comes into contact with an allergen during cooking, baking, or meal service. For example, if ham is sliced on the same slicing machine used to slice cheese, this will create a situation of cross contamination that puts children allergic to milk at risk when they eat the meat. Cross-contamination can also occur if children share eating utensils, bottles, cups, or food. Teachers who are careful label readers and use safe practices when preparing food for children with allergies and celiac disease create a safe food environment for all children in their care.

cross-contamination
the transfer of harmful microorganisms from one food to another food or from an infected person to food. It can also refer to food contaminated with an allergen

UNDERSTANDING FOOD SAFETY REGULATIONS AND GUIDELINES

Rules to keep food safe originated in ancient times. For example, some of the religious food laws and practices discussed in the previous chapter may have had their foundations in food safety. Rules and regulations that govern food safety protect children from illness and harm and are especially important in settings that serve this vulnerable age group. Food safety is regulated by federal, state, and county agencies. For example, it is not only convenient but a requirement that all establishments in which food service occurs must have hand washing sinks (Nash, 2002).

Federal, State, and County Roles in Food Safety Regulations

Federal food safety laws are established by Congress and implemented through regulations imposed by federal agencies. These regulations outline specific legal requirements related to various categories of food safety (Marriott, 2006). The federal food safety regulations provide the model for state and county guidelines for all establishments that serve food, including early childhood settings. Figure 8-3 summarizes the roles of federal agencies in overseeing the safety of the U.S. food supply. The predominant responsibility for monitoring and investigating foodborne illness, however, rests with state, territorial and county health agencies (Hoffman et al., 2005).

State agencies work with the FDA and other federal agencies to implement food safety standards for foods produced within the state's borders. State or county health agencies conduct inspections at restaurants, grocery stores, retail food establishments, child care centers, and schools (Food Safe Schools, 2004).

MyEducationLab

Go to the Assignments and Activities section of Topic 4: Food Safety in the MyEducationLab for your course and complete the activity entitled *Food Safety Standards.* How can being aware of food safety standards help teachers like Casey avoid committing food safety violations?

Impact of Food Safety Regulations

Federal food safety regulations have a direct impact on early childhood programs. For example, the Child Nutrition and WIC Reauthorization Act of 2004 mandates that all schools participating in the National School Lunch or School Breakfast Program must obtain food safety inspections twice a year (USDA Food and Nutrition Service, 2005). In addition, funding sources such as Head Start and the Child and Adult Care Food Program have food safety standards in place such that if a program receiving their funds is not in compliance, the program risks losing its funding. Child care licensure by state agencies is contingent on passing health inspections that include an evaluation of food production

Figure 8-3 The Roles of Federal Programs That Oversee Food Safety

---

Environmental Protection Agency (EPA):

- Prevents air, water, and land pollution.
- Helps avert chemical contamination of foods through its regulation of the use of toxic substances such as pesticides and sanitizers.
- Sets standards. The FDA and the USDA enforce these legal requirements.

Food and Drug Administration (FDA):

- Oversees the safety of all foods except for meat, eggs, and poultry.
- Inspects all aspects of food processing ensuring that food shipped through interstate commerce is safe, wholesome, unadulterated, and accurately labeled.
- Implements food recalls if a food is determined to be hazardous.
- Provides, in conjunction with the U.S. Public Health Service, a set of national food safety standards called the Food Code.

U.S. Department of Agriculture (USDA):

- Oversees and sets the standards for the safety, wholesomeness and quality of meats, egg products, and poultry.
- Investigates and makes recommendations for recalls related to any meat, poultry, or egg product that is deemed hazardous for consumption.

Sources: "Capacity of State and Territorial Health Agencies to Prevent Foodborne Illness," by R. E. Hoffman, J. Greenblatt, B. T. Matyas, D. J. Sharp, E. Esteban, and A. K. H. Liang, 2005, *Emerging Infectious Diseases, 11*(1), pp. 11–16; *Principles of Food Sanitation*, 4th edition, by N. G. Marriott, 1999, Gaithersburg. MD: Aspen Publishers; *Essentials of Food Safety and Sanitation*, 4th edition, by D. McSwane, N. R. Rue, and R. Linton, 2005, Upper Saddle River, NJ: Pearson Prentice Hall; FDA *Food Code,* U.S. Food and Drug Administration, 2009, retrieved September 15, 2009, from http://www.fda.gov/Food/FoodSafety/RetailFoodProtection/FoodCode/default.htm; and *About Food Safety and Inspection Service*, U.S. Department of Agriculture, 2008, retrieved September 14, 2009, from http://www.fsis.usda.gov/About_FSIS/index.asp.

sites. Efforts such as these implement food safety regulations and improve the quality of food service in children's settings.

Teachers and others who prepare and serve food in school settings must be familiar with the agency that monitors food safety in the child's setting. In most cases this agency is the local health department. The health department is a program's ally in creating a food safe environment. Creating a strong working relationship with the county health department sanitarians has many benefits because:

- They assist programs in developing effective food safety policies and standard operating procedures.
- They are a resource for food safety and foodborne illness related questions and issues.
- They conduct inspections that support school goals for promoting food safe environments.
- They investigate foodborne illness outbreaks and assist programs in developing steps to control the spread of infection.
- They help programs identify when a foodborne outbreak needs to be reported to state or federal health agencies (Food Safe Schools, 2004).

Teachers and health department personnel have a common goal: children's health and safety. A close working relationship reduces the likelihood of food safety problems. If a concern is identified, health department personnel can provide timely expert advice to limit an illness outbreak. In the opening case scenario, the health department was a key resource. With the sanitarian's help the program was able to identify the source of illness. The *Health Hint* provides an additional example of the benefits of collaboration between the health department and children's programs or schools when the potential for illness threatens.

Health Hint

Managing a Foodborne Illness Outbreak

An outbreak of Norwalk virus was linked to a local fast-food establishment where a recently ill employee had handled lettuce without gloves. Within days, a number of families in the preschool classroom reported their child had been diagnosed with Norwalk virus. One child spent the night in the hospital due to dehydration.

The teacher called the health department for advice. In addition to providing information about the symptoms of Norwalk virus and methods of transmission, the following preventive steps were recommended:

- Inform all staff not to come to work if they are sick.
- Direct food service and other kitchen staff to take extra precautions when handling dirty dishware and remind them to wash their hands frequently.
- Wash and sanitize toys and surfaces in the classroom using a chlorine bleach solution.
- Remind teachers and children about washing hands after using the toilet and changing diapers and before eating or preparing food.
- Send home an illness notice explaining the signs and symptoms of Norwalk virus. Notify families that no child or staff should return to the program until 72 hours after their last symptoms.

Although a few additional cases occurred in the program, the spread of the illness was limited due to the health department's expert advice and the teacher's quick action.

Source: From *Making the News in Benton County: Norwalk-Like Virus Health Alert,* by the Benton County Health Department, April 27, 2006, retrieved September 16, 2009, from http://www.co.benton.or.us/read_article.php?d=&p=72.

Developing a Food Safety System

What if. . .

there was a suspected foodborne illness in your program? Who would you contact? What additional training would you need to be able to identify the signs of a potential foodborne illness? How would you try to minimize the spread of illness?

Hazard and Analysis Critical Control Point (HACCP) system
a proactive food safety system that identifies potentially hazardous foods and evaluates food safety risk during food preparation and service

Program inspection by regulatory agencies helps create an environment of knowledge and accountability, which is necessary to support food safety goals. However, an even more important goal for programs is to develop a system of self-inspection that implements the most up-to-date food safety recommendations and monitors the safety of foods. The regulations that pertain to food safety are ever-changing based on new technologies and public demand in response to food safety events. For example, after an *E. coli* 0157:H7 outbreak in 1993, that occurred in the Pacific Northwest as a result of hamburgers that were not cooked to proper internal temperatures (the outbreak caused 400 illnesses and four deaths) a more evidenced-based approach to food safety was demanded, resulting in the development of the Hazard Analysis and Critical Control Point system approach (USDA, 2008).

The FDA is responsible for the development of the Hazard and Analysis Critical Control Point (HACCP) system (USDA, 2008). The HACCP is a proactive, preventive system for tracking food through the many phases of production, processing, preparation, and service and evaluating the potential for exposure to contamination. The origin of HACCP has its roots in the U.S. space program where scientific principles were used to ensure that foods fed to astronauts during space missions were absolutely safe (Goodrich, Schneider, & Schmidt, 2005; USDA, 2008). The FDA and the USDA require the use of HACCP procedures in certain food processing industries. For example, the use of HACCP is mandatory in plants processing seafood, fruit juice, meat, and poultry (USDA, 2008).

HACCP procedures can be adapted to any establishment that is involved in food service, including schools. In fact, the Child Nutrition Reauthorization Act of 2004 required the HACCP food safety system to be implemented in all school district food services by 2006 (Iowa State University Extension, 2007; USDA Food and Nutrition Service, 2005). Schools represent the first retail food service establishment in which HACCP was mandated.

Currently early childhood programs such as child care centers can voluntarily participate in HACCP food safety programs and use the state and local health departments to understand local food safety requirements (FDA/CFSAN, 2006b). Understanding and implementing HACCP also supports the National Association for the Education of Young Children (NAEYC) accreditation goals for food safety as described in Health Standard 5.B.03 (NAEYC, 2009).

Some early childhood programs contract with local school districts to provide their food. Food received from public school kitchens has been prepared using HACCP food safety recommendations. Whether a program receives meals through a contracted meal service, prepares food on site, or serves meals prepared in a home kitchen, it is important to understand and implement HACCP food safety recommendations.

HACCP Overview

A quick overview will help you understand the overall concepts of HACCP. This overview is followed by a more in-depth explanation of the HACCP principles that will assist teachers in understanding how HACCP is applied in the early childhood setting.

HACCP is a system for organizing safety measures to ensure that all feasible strategies are used to keep food safe. If, for example, a cook called in sick and a teacher was pulled from the classroom to prepare lunch for 50 children, how would the teacher know what to do to make sure food was safely prepared? If a HACCP system is in place, all of the procedures involved in preparing a meal (cooking, serving, and cooling foods) have been analyzed and hazardous foods identified. Any risky steps in food preparation have been labeled *critical control points*. This designation is a warning that extra attention is needed to maintain food safety. This warning comes with guidelines, or *critical limits*, that list specific criteria that must be met for food to remain safe (i.e., the temperature a food must reach before it can be served).

To make sure that the HACCP guidelines are consistently met, a monitoring system must be in place that can be verified as effective. This monitoring system outlines what needs to be done when guidelines are not met (corrective actions) and includes procedures for documentation and record keeping. Figure 8-4 summarizes the seven principles of HACCP. The strategies of each principle are discussed in more detail next.

Understanding HACCP Principles

The HACCP system is designed to assess and monitor any potential hazards to food from the point of origin to the point of consumption. The goal is to prevent foodborne illness. Staff at an early childhood program or school are responsible for keeping food safe from the time it enters the program until it is served. Teachers are a part of the system of accountability.

In a large establishment, the HACCP program is usually implemented by a hazard analysis team. In an early childhood setting this might include the food service manager, program director, teachers, and parents. The team develops a plan of action for food safety. To do so, they must first understand the seven principles that form the foundation of this food safety system (Jay, Loessner, & Golden, 2005; McSwane et al., 2005; NRA, 2008; U.S. Food and Drug Administration, 2008c).

Principle 1: Hazard Analysis

The first principle of hazard analysis involves evaluating hazards that might cause safety issues with specific foods. Actions for this step entail reviewing the menu and identifying foods that are most likely to be hazardous because of their ability to sustain microbial growth if contaminated.

Potentially Hazardous Foods Foods that can readily support the growth of microorganisms that cause spoilage or illness when improperly handled are called potentially hazardous foods. Preventing the growth of bacteria in food is critical because this type of microorganism

potentially hazardous foods
foods that readily support the growth of microorganisms that cause spoilage or illness if food safety practices are not in place

Figure 8-4 The Seven Steps of HACCP

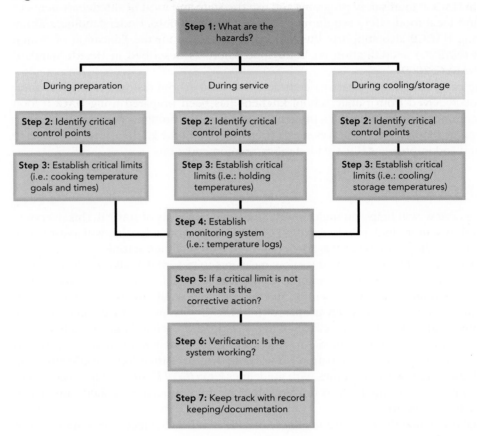

Figure 8-5 Potentially Hazardous Foods

- Cooked meat and poultry.
- Milk and egg products such as custards and cream fillings.
- Shellfish and seafood.
- Cooked starches such as rice, pasta, potatoes, and beans.
- Melons such as cantaloupe.
- Raw sprouts.
- Unprocessed garlic and oil mixtures.
- Foods with sufficient water content to support microbial growth.

Sources: *Essentials of Food Safety and Sanitation*, 4th edition, by D. McSwane, N. R. Rue, and R. Linton, 2005, Upper Saddle River, NJ: Pearson Prentice Hall; *NEHA Training: Food Safety First Principles*, by C. Nash, 2002, Canada: Chadwick House Group Limited; and *Chapter 2: Current and Proposed Definitions of "Potentially Hazardous Foods,"* U.S. Food and Drug Administration, Center for Food Safety and Applied Nutrition, 2004, retrieved September 16, 2009, from http://www.fda.gov/Food/ScienceResearch/ResearchAreas/SafePracticesforFoodProcesses/ucm094143.htm.

causes more cases of foodborne illness than any other hazard (McSwane et al., 2005). Bacteria need certain conditions to flourish, such as moist foods that are rich in protein or carbohydrates and are not too acidic. Microbial growth occurs within a certain temperature range and time period of exposure to that temperature range (usually about 2 to 4 hours for bacteria).

Some potentially hazardous foods are listed in Figure 8-5. Recognizing which foods are potentially hazardous is important, so that appropriate management strategies for monitoring food safety can be established. For example, some of the foods served for lunch in Lacey's classroom in the opening case scenario were potentially hazardous. The turkey on the sandwich, the watermelon, and the milk are foods that require careful management. Foods less likely to cause illness are the orange slices and bread served at the supermarket during the field trip because oranges are acidic and bread is low in moisture content. Teachers can prepare to monitor potentially hazardous foods by circling them on the menu so that they can quickly identify which foods need to be observed more closely (McSwane et al., 2005) (see Figure 8-6). When establishing a HACCP policy, the procedures for dealing with potentially hazardous foods should be established by working through the menu in a stepwise fashion to identify the hazardous foods and account for their handling.

Figure 8-6 Lunch Menu with Potentially Hazardous Foods Identified

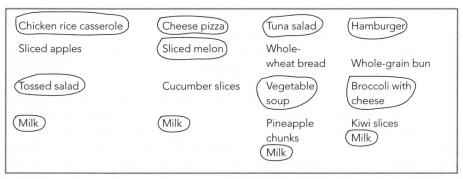

The Process Approach In an effort to promote food safety in all types of establishments where food is consumed, the FDA created a simplified variation of the HACCP food safety system that the USDA promotes for use in schools. It is called the process approach. This approach establishes guidelines for the processes different foods undergo when being prepared (USDA Food and Nutrition Service, 2005, 2008). The USDA identifies these food processes as follows:

- Food preparation with no-cook process: The food is not cooked and does not enter the temperature danger zone. Examples of foods that are subject to this process include cold cuts, tuna salad, and cheese.
- Food preparation for same-day service: The food is heated and served the same day and goes through the temperature danger zone once. Examples include hamburgers, French toast, and scrambled eggs.
- Food preparation using complex food preparation: Food is cooked, chilled, and re-heated, going through the temperature danger zone two or more times (USDA Food and Nutrition Service, 2008). Examples include soups, spaghetti sauce, casseroles, and dried beans (that are cooked, chilled, and later used in a burrito recipe).

Each food item has a different type of risk associated with its preparation process. Risk is related to the number of times the food item moves through the temperature danger zone, the temperature at which microorganisms such as bacteria are more likely to grow, 41 to 135 degrees Fahrenheit (5 to 57 degrees Celsius) (see Figure 8-7) (USDA Food and Nutrition Service, 2005).

The overall goal of the process approach is to minimize the time food spends in the temperature danger zone, thereby decreasing the risk of foodborne illness. The process approach allows menu planners to categorize foods according to the method of preparation and service so that strategies can be developed to manage food safety risks (Food and Nutrition Service of the USDA, 2008).

Food service personnel are responsible for overseeing the process approach for foods served in early childhood centers and schools. Family child care providers, and those serving children in occasional groups, need to identify hazardous foods as well as the process used in preparation to minimize food safety risks when planning menus or cooking activities that use food in the classroom setting. Teachers also support the process approach by ensuring that food delivered to the classroom has been held at appropriate temperatures prior to service and is served immediately to children.

Principle 2: Identify the Critical Control Points

Critical control points (CCPs) are points in the procedure of food processing, preparation, and service at which food handlers can control, or reduce, food hazard risks (McSwane et al., 2005). The points at which control can be established occur during the critical steps in preparing recipes or when holding food prior to meal service. Tools used to manage CCPs include thermometers, refrigerators and refrigeration carts, freezers, ovens, warming carts, and steam tables. For example, a critical control point for a program that receives food from an off-site kitchen includes taking the temperature of the delivered food and only accepting it if it is

process approach
the process of grouping menu items by the method of food preparation into three different processes that are distinguished by the number of times the food item goes through the food temperature danger zone

no-cook process
food is not cooked and does not enter the temperature danger zone

same-day service process
food is heated and served the same day and goes through the temperature danger zone only once

complex food preparation process
food is cooked, chilled, and reheated, going through the temperature danger zone two or more times

temperature danger zone
the temperature range between 41° and 135°F (5° and 57°C) at which microorganisms such as bacteria are likely to grow

critical control points (CCPs)
points in time during food processing, preparation, and service at which control can be exerted to minimize the development of a food hazard risk

Figure 8-7 Food Temperature Danger Zone

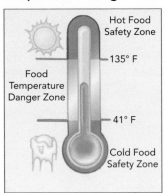

delivered at an appropriate temperature. The temperature of food is measured at the time of delivery to ensure that it is still safe to eat.

Principle 3: Establish Critical Limits

To ensure safety, critical limits (CLs) must be identified for each CCP identified in food processing. The CL is an indicator of whether the control measure is actually managing the identified food safety risk. Critical limits must be measurable, accurate, realistic, and based on evidenced-based research (Schmidt & Newslow, 2007). CLs include the temperatures and times for cooking, holding, cooling, and reheating foods and ingredients in a recipe. For example, the food handler who receives food, such as burritos, delivered from an off-site kitchen needs to know the appropriate temperature for holding this particular food. Figure 8-8 illustrates a recipe developed by the USDA that includes critical control points as well as critical limits.

The CL represents the highest and lowest range for a food safety standard established for a critical control point. This information is available in the Food Code. The Food Code is a set of food safety guidelines established by the FDA and the USDA to promote food safety (FDA, 2009a). For example, the code identifies the critical limit for baking chicken as follows: It must reach an internal temperature of 165°F (74°C) for 15 seconds and maintain a temperature above 135°F (57°C) until the chicken is served (FDA, 2009a). Figure 8-9 shows appropriate cooking and holding temperatures for foods. The USDA website provides standardized recipes for child nutrition programs that offer guidance on food preparation steps and also identifies CCPs and their recommended CLs (USDA, 2006).

Principle 4: Establish a Monitoring System

A monitoring system is needed to ensure that food is checked during all aspects of its flow through the processing system; from delivery through storage, food preparation, and service. Examples of monitoring methods include recording the temperature of foods at delivery and during cooking, cooling, and reheating. The temperature maintained by heating and cooling equipment is also measured. A monitoring system is a crucial aspect of the HACCP plan because deviation from an established critical limit, such as food temperatures during cooking, needs to be identified and action taken to avoid a potentially hazardous food safety situation.

Principle 5: Establish a Corrective Action Plan

A corrective action plan outlines the steps that must be taken immediately if there is a lapse in the identified critical limit for a particular menu item's critical control point. In the early childhood setting, for example, it might be discovered that the hot food holding cart had been unplugged and the bean burritos had not been held at the required temperature. The corrective action would be to discard the burritos.

Principle 6: Establish Procedures for Verification

Verification procedures are needed to verify, or make sure, that the food has been managed according to the five principles listed above. This step ensures that the HACCP plan is working. Conducting inspections observing food storage, production, and service procedures are all methods of verification. The program director can accomplish this by doing spot checks when foods are delivered to see if food handlers are taking temperatures or by monitoring temperature logs.

Principle 7: Maintain a System of Record Keeping

Record keeping is an important aspect of the HACCP process. Written records confirm that each required step is conducted appropriately. For example, in the opening case scenario, the sanitarian was able to rule out the school food service as a source of infection in Lacey's class

Figure 8-8 Example of a Bean Burrito Recipe That Uses HACCP With Critical Control Points and Critical Limits

Ingredients	Amounts for 50 Servings
Dried kidney beans	7 pounds
Onions, chopped	1 cup
Tomato paste	3 cups
Chili powder	3 tablespoons
Cumin	2 tablespoons
Pepper	2 teaspoons
Low fat cheese, shredded	3 pounds
Tortillas	50

Directions:

1. Soak beans overnight in 12¼ quarts of water. Cover and refrigerate
2. Drain beans and add again 12¼ quarts of water and 1 tablespoon salt.
3. Boil gently for 2 hours until tender.
4. Use immediately or cool to 70°F (21° C) within 2 hours and from 70°F (21° C) to 41°F (5° C) or lower within an additional 4 hours.
5. Combine onions, tomato paste, chili powder, cumin, and pepper. Blend and simmer for 15 minutes.
6. Puree beans until smooth in consistency. Combine with ingredients in step 5 and shredded cheese.
7. Steam tortillas until warm
8. Place ½ cup beans onto tortilla and fold.
9. Place on a pan, seam side down.
10. Heat to 165°F (74°C) or higher for at least 15 seconds.
11. Hold for hot service at 135°F (57°C) or higher

Note: Red indicates a critical control point or a step in the recipe that deserves careful attention. Blue indicates a critical limit or standard that must be met for the food to remain safe. If beans are chilled and used at a later time to make the bean burritos, this represents a complex process of food preparation.

Source: Adapted from *Guidance for School Food Authorities: Developing a School Food Safety Program Based on the Process Approach to HACCP Principles,* by the U.S. Department of Agriculture, Food and Nutrition Service, June 2005, retrieved September 15, 2009, from http://www.fns.usda.gov/cnd/CNlabeling/Food-Safety/HACCPGuidance.PDF.

by looking at HACCP logs and records. Taking the temperature of foods at delivery and recording the temperature on a temperature receiving log or on the delivery invoice are also methods that ensure this step is conducted.

Any teacher who consistently handles and prepares food must participate in a food safety plan. In some settings, teachers may not work directly with food and may not need to routinely consider the HACCP procedures. However, understanding how the food safety system works in the early childhood setting or school ensures that teachers are prepared to be a vital link in the chain that supports food safety and protects young children.

Understanding Standard Operating Procedures

Although the HACCP system provides specific strategies for handling foods to prevent foodborne illness, the system cannot be effective if certain general food safety practices are not part of the routine procedures of the food service operation. For example, policies for maintaining a clean kitchen, wearing head coverings during food preparation, sanitizing the kitchen work surfaces and children's eating surfaces, and basic hand washing guidelines are all examples of general food safety procedures that support safe food handling. In the HACCP food safety system, these are called **standard operating procedures (SOPs)** (Iowa State University Extension, 2007).

standard operating procedures (SOPs)
written procedures related to food service tasks that help to maintain food safety

Figure 8-9 Cooking and Holding Temperatures for Foods

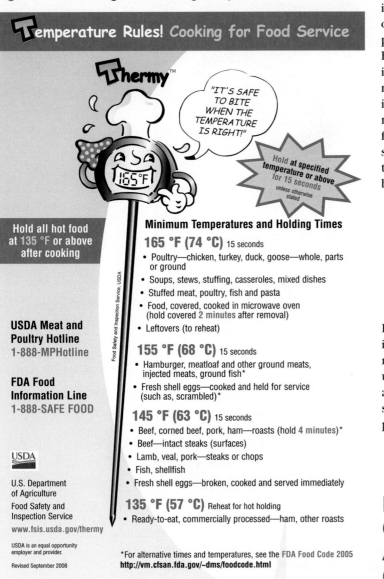

Source: Used with permission from Iowa State University Extension, Iowa State University, 2008.

Standard operating procedures are important in early childhood settings. Programs and schools often have policies and procedures based on best practices that address food safety and sanitation. However, SOPs differ from general school policies in that they are written in a consistent HACCP format, which includes a description for monitoring, implementing corrective action, verification, and record keeping. In a review of trends that affect food safety in retail food service, including schools and child care centers, researchers found that the three most common risk factors for foodborne outbreaks are:

- Improper holding times and temperatures of foods.
- Poor personal hygiene.
- Cross-contamination (the transfer of harmful germs from one food to another or from an infected person to food).

Establishing food safety programs and complying with basic SOPs eliminate these types of risk factors (Sneed & Strohbehn, 2008). In the upcoming section we review general food safety and SOPs that apply to the early child care setting by evaluating the flow of food within a program.

PREVENTING CONTAMINATION AT EACH STAGE OF FOOD HANDLING

Teachers directly involved in the purchase, storage, preparation, and service of foods, such as those who work in the family child care setting, require a detailed commitment to ensuring food safety. All teachers who handle food for young children need to understand the risks associated with each phase of food flow. *Food flow* refers to everything that happens to food from the moment it is purchased and delivered to a program until it is ready to be served (see Figure 8-10) (McSwane et al., 2005).

What if. . .

you observed a staff member who is sick working with food? How would you manage this situation? What types of cross-contamination can occur in the classrooms you have observed?

Minimizing Contamination Risk during Food Purchasing

Purchasing food is the first step in bringing food into the early childhood setting. Although teachers in the family child care setting have more direct responsibility for food safety when purchasing foods for their programs, there may be times when teachers in child care centers or schools also purchase food for classroom cooking activities, snacks, and special social events. All teachers need to consider food safety issues when they buy food for the classroom. A very important

Figure 8-10 An Example of Food Flow

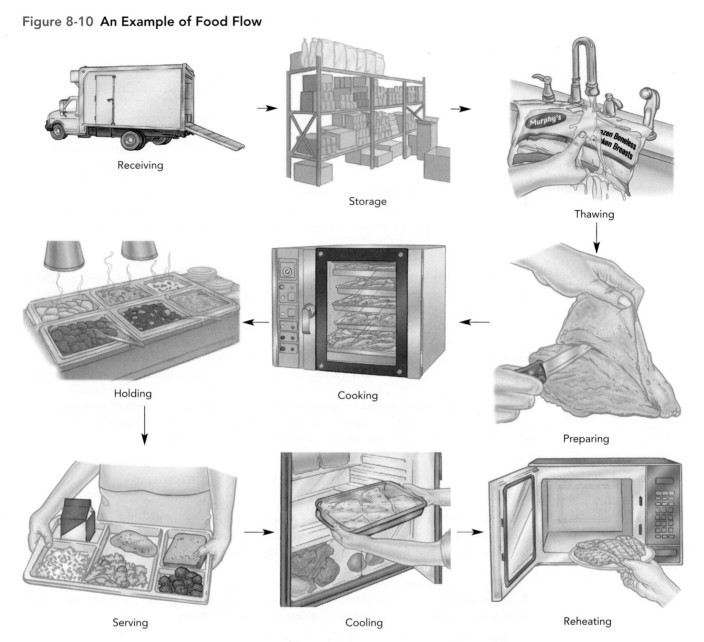

Receiving

Storage

Thawing

Holding

Cooking

Preparing

Serving

Cooling

Reheating

Source: Based on an illustration from TrainCan, Inc.: BASICS.fst ® *Food Safety Training and Certification*, 2004, http://www.traincan.com. Used with permission.

consideration is whether the food comes from an approved source (McSwane et al., 2005). The following tips provide guidance on determining whether foods come from acceptable sources:

- Food must come from a supplier that carries USDA-inspected and -approved meats and poultry and other FDA-approved processed foods.
- Food must be transported in such a way that perishable foods are kept safe.
- Food cannot be home canned.
- Food cannot be prepared in a kitchen that has not been inspected by the health department (McSwane et al., 2005).

Allowing families to bring food from home to share with all children introduces a food safety risk because the home kitchen is not an approved source of food. The intentions of families who bring homemade treats to school, such as the mother who brought cupcakes in the case scenario at the beginning of the chapter, are well meaning. However, these

Figure 8-11 Food Safety Checklist for Purchasing Food

☐ The amount of food purchased can be safely stored.
☐ Perishables (meats, poultry, milk, frozen items) have been placed in the cart last.
☐ Raw meats or poultry have been placed in a plastic bag so that drippings will not contaminate other foods.
☐ Raw meats and poultry have been kept separate in the cart and in a separate grocery bag during checkout.
☐ Labels have been checked to avoid purchasing foods that are past their recommended date of use.
☐ A cooler with ice is available to transport foods from store to home if traveling long distances.
☐ The trip has been planned so that additional stops once food has been purchased are avoided.
☐ Foods have been stored as quickly as possible after purchase.

Source: Used with permission of The Ohio State University Extension, 2120 Fyffe Road, Columbus, OH 43210.

foods pose a safety risk and must not be allowed in the early childhood classroom. In addition these foods can undermine the healthful school food environment that early childhood programs strive to achieve.

Families can be included in the sharing of foods in other ways. Families may offer recipes for inclusion in the program or school menu. Additionally, children's programs can arrange for a family member to prepare a recipe using food purchased by the program from approved sources in the program's kitchen under the supervision of a worker who has a food handler's card.

Preventing foodborne illness requires a proactive approach. A variety of strategies assist teachers when purchasing groceries for their programs. Figure 8-11 provides a checklist of safety tips that support safe practices when shopping for food.

Minimizing Contamination Risk When Receiving and Storing Food

When food arrives at an early childhood program either as a bulk delivery of goods or as cooked meals from a vendor, it must be carefully inspected to determine if the food is fresh and wholesome and free from spoilage. As discussed earlier, testing the temperature of foods is a critical aspect of this inspection.

A food thermometer is an important tool for food safety. To be effective, the thermometer must be routinely calibrated to ensure accurate readings are obtained. You can calibrate a thermometer by using the ice-point method, as follows:

- Insert the thermometer probe into a cup of crushed ice.
- Add enough cold water to remove any air pockets that might remain.
- Allow the temperature reading to stabilize before reading temperature.
- Temperature measurement should be 32°F ($\pm$2°F) (or 0°C [$\pm$1°C]).

Figure 8-12 illustrates the ice-point method of calibrating thermometers. Temperatures should be taken as soon as food arrives to ensure foods sent are heated or chilled to appropriate temperatures.

In early childhood settings and schools, meals are often delivered from a contracted source called a vendor. The food service operations of a school district often act as vendors for early childhood settings in the community, and the school kitchen has the primary cooking responsibility. A key element to ensuring that safe food is sent by the vendor involves creating a detailed contract in which conditions and expectations specify food safety responsibilities, as discussed in the *Policy Point*.

In addition teachers must communicate with vendors about special diet requirements so that children receive the correct menu item. For example, a child in teacher Jaime's class is vegan (eats no animal foods) and another child has a milk and soy allergy. Jaime must make sure that the vegan child receives soy milk and the child with allergies is given rice milk.

**Figure 8-12
Calibrating a
Thermometer Using
the Ice-Point Method**

Policy Point

FOOD SAFETY AND VENDED MEAL SERVICE

An early childhood program that contracts for vended meal service shares responsibility for food safety with the vendors providing the meals. Teachers who work within this setting must support food safety goals to ensure that children are served food that is wholesome. The teacher is the last responsible individual to inspect the food before it is given to children to eat. To ensure that there is a mutual understanding of food safety responsibilities, it is important for programs to establish food safety stipulations within the contract. The contract should include the following:

✓ A specific time and receiving process is designated for delivery of food.
✓ The conditions for delivery of food are outlined, including the use of a sanitary truck with appropriate warming and chilling containers.
✓ The age group to be served is indicated within the contract.
✓ The vendor is in compliance with all federal, state, and county health and sanitation requirements and HACCP principles.
✓ A time is designated for a review of upcoming menus.
✓ Food temperatures at delivery are designated for hot and cold foods.
✓ Conditions for rejection and substitution of unsafe foods are included in the contract.
✓ Production records for total amounts and portion sizes are made available.
✓ Requirements for food labeling of special diets are stipulated.
✓ Access to the following information is included within the contract:
  • Standardized recipes.
  • Nutrition and CN labels for processed foods.
  • Nutritional analysis for each school week if needed.

Source: Excerpted from *Guidelines for Contracting for Vended Meals,* with permission from the Wisconsin Department of Public Instruction, 125 South Webster Street, Madison, WI 53702; 800/243-8782.

Because both milk products appear the same once they are poured into glasses, Jaime will only serve them if they are clearly labeled.

Once food has arrived, been inspected and accepted, staff involved in food preparation must give a high priority to prompt and proper storage. Potentially hazardous foods that sit in the receiving area or a kitchen for an extended period of time can quickly spoil and become unsafe to eat. Such foods must be stored under the correct conditions as soon as possible.

Three types of storage that require special consideration are refrigeration, freezer, and dry goods storage. Figure 8-13 describes factors to consider for each of these storage situations. The length of time a food should be stored is an important consideration. Germ growth is dependent on the amount of time the food product remains within the temperature danger zone. For example, in the case scenario at the beginning of the chapter, both time and temperature factors came into play when cupcakes covered with an egg-based frosting were allowed to sit at room temperature overnight. Potentially hazardous food should not be left at room temperature for more than 2 hours or 1 hour if the temperature is 90°F (32°C) or above (USDA Food Safety and Inspection Service, 2006). The National Resource Center for Health and Safety in Child Care and Early Education provides guidelines for the length of storage of common refrigerated and frozen foods (American Academy of Pediatrics, American Public Health Association, & National Resource Center for Health and Safety in Child Care and Early Education, 2007).

The informal storage of foods that are not menu related should also be monitored. For example, teachers may store crackers, coffee, hot chocolate, nondairy creamer, and other similar foods in a cupboard for social events or staff meetings. These foods can pose a risk because there is generally no system for monitoring dates of expiration. Food that sits in cupboards for long periods of time can become a source of rodent or insect infestation.

Figure 8-13 **Food Storage Recommendations**

Refrigeration Storage

- Perishable foods should be stored at 41°F (5°C) or colder.
- The temperature in refrigerators should be checked daily and recorded on a temperature log.
- All foods should be labeled and dated.
- Special diet items should be labeled with both the date and the child's name.
- Refrigerator shelves should be cleaned weekly.
- Raw meats and poultry should be stored on the bottom shelves and separate from other foods.
- Medications that require refrigeration should be stored away from food in a locked box within the refrigerator.
- Refrigerators in food service areas should be used exclusively for storing foods for children. (Staff should not store personal foods in the refrigerator.)

Freezer Storage

- Foods that are frozen should be stored in moisture-proof wrap, bags, or containers at temperature of 0°F (–18°C) or colder.
- Freezer temperatures should be measured daily and recorded on a temperature log.
- Frozen food items should be thawed in the refrigerator.

Dry Goods Storage (Canned, Jarred, or Packaged Items)

- Dry storage should be located in a room that is cool, dry, and has a room temperature that is maintained between 50° and 70°F (10° and 21°C).
- Food should be keep 6 to 8 inches off the ground.
- Food should be rotated so oldest items are used first.

Sources: *Caring for Our Children: National Health and Safety Performance Standards: Guidelines for Out-of-Home Child Care Programs*, 2nd edition, 2007, Elk Grove Village, IL: American Academy of Pediatrics; *Essentials of Food Safety and Sanitation*, 4th edition, by D. McSwane, N. R. Rue, and R. Linton, 2005, Upper Saddle River, NJ: Pearson Prentice Hall; and *Mealtime Memo for Child Care: Safe Food Storage*, National Food Service Management Institute, 2005, retrieved September 16, 2009, from http://www.olemiss.edu/depts/nfsmi/Information/Newsletters/meme2005-4.pdf.

What if. . .

your school sponsored a yearly potluck picnic? What food safety challenges does the potluck-style social raise? How might you arrange the picnic to increase food safety? Who is responsible for the safety of the food that is eaten?

first in, first out (FIFO) inventory system in which foods that were previously purchased are rotated and newly purchased foods are stored such that older foods are used first

The amount of time a food is in storage affects both food safety and food quality. A system of food rotation needs to be in place to ensure that previously purchased foods are used first. A common method used in the food service industry is first in, first out (FIFO). Newly purchased foods are stored and older products are rotated so that they are used first. For example, consider the teacher shopping for her family child care program. She has in her cart perishables such as eggs, milk, cheese, and fresh produce. In addition she has frozen foods such as peas, waffles, juices, canned corn, tomato sauce, and canned fruits. Once she returns home she evaluates what she currently has on hand and discards any food that is past its expiration date. When storing the newly purchased foods, she labels foods with the date of purchase. She has a food storage rack in her pantry that helps her rotate her canned foods. New food is placed behind previously purchased food making it easy for her to remember which food to use first.

Minimizing Contamination Risk during Food Preparation

Every foodborne illness is preventable. Prevention is a key aspect of keeping food safe during preparation. Three important concepts that support food safety during food preparation and service are maintaining personal hygiene, preventing cross-contamination, and avoiding the temperature danger zone.

Maintaining Personal Hygiene

The human body harbors many microorganisms, which are usually harmless. They live in our lower gastrointestinal tract, mouth, nose, and scalp. These microorganisms usually do not make us sick but can contaminate foods and, if conditions are right, grow exponentially to create a foodborne illness. It is very important for teachers who work with food to maintain consistent and scrupulous personal hygiene. One of the most important aspects of personal hygiene is hand washing.

Hand Washing Hand washing is the simplest and most effective way to decrease the incidence of foodborne illness. Researchers conducting a review of 30 studies on hand washing, 19 of which involved children age 5 and under, found that improvements in hand washing procedures reduced gastrointestinal illness by 31% and respiratory illness by 21% Aiello, Coulborn, Perez, & Larson, 2008). Hand washing education in combination with the use of non-antibacterial soap had the best results. Use of antibacterial soap showed little added benefit (Aiello, Coulborn, Perez, & Larson, 2008). These findings clearly support the importance of frequent hand washing by both teachers and children as an effective means of reducing the risk of foodborne illness and any infectious disease.

Teachers involved in the care of infants need to be particularly careful with hand hygiene. For example, in a family child care setting, in a short span of time teachers may change diapers, wipe runny noses, prepare formula, and organize meals for young children. Hands that are not properly washed become a source of biological contamination of food and increase the risk of foodborne illness.

Hand washing specific to food safety is one of the standard operating procedures recommended by health authorities to support HACPP in the school food service environment (NFSMI, 2005a). Figure 8-14 provides an example of a standard operating procedure for hand washing for staff working with food.

In addition, sinks designated for hand washing only are required to minimize the potential for cross-contamination (American Academy of Pediatrics et al., 2007; FDA, 2009a) (see Figure 8-15). For example, consider the potential for contamination if lettuce is washed in the same sink that was just used by a teacher who changed an infant's diaper. Hands should be dried using a single-use (disposable) paper towel or hand dryer. Drying hands on cloth towels or aprons is not acceptable because these can become soiled and are a potential source of cross-contamination.

Wearing Appropriate Attire Appropriate attire is important for maintaining food safety. Teachers who handle food should not wear jewelry, watches, or rings during food preparation because of the risk of biological contamination. Even with proper hand washing, microorganisms remain on the surface and crevices of these personal items. In addition, gemstones, backs of earrings, and jewelry clasps can come apart and become a physical contaminant of food.

Appropriate attire includes easy-to-clean clothes and head coverings such as a cap or hairnet to contain hair. Long hair should be restrained with a clip. An apron can help protect clothing from getting soiled with food or germs from food preparation activities. Sufficient aprons should be available so that when contamination occurs such as when working with raw meat and poultry, a food handler can easily change into a clean apron before working with other foods such as fruits and vegetables.

Ready-to-eat foods should not come in contact with bare hands (FDA/CFSAN, 2006b). Disposable gloves and serving tongs, ladles, or spoons are appropriate food service tools when working with ready-to-eat foods. Disposable gloves are a useful food safety tool, however:

> You must treat disposable gloves as a second skin. Whatever can contaminate a human hand can also contaminate a disposable glove. Therefore, whenever hands should be washed, a new pair of disposable gloves should be worn. (McSwane et al., 2005, p. 94)

Reporting Infectious Disease One of the primary methods for cross-contamination or transferring germs in food preparation is an infectious staff member who comes to work when sick and contaminates food during the food-handling process. This is an extreme health hazard.

Legal requirements are in place for reporting about food service workers who have a confirmed illness or have been exposed to *Salmonella typhi, Shigella, E. coli* O157:H7,

Figure 8-14 Standard Operating Procedure for Hand Washing

PURPOSE: To prevent foodborne illness by contaminated hands.

SCOPE: This procedure applies to staff who handle, prepare, and serve food.

INSTRUCTIONS:

1. Train program staff on using the procedures in this SOP.
2. Follow state or local health department requirements.
3. Post hand washing signs or posters in a language understood by all food service staff near all hand washing sinks, in food preparation areas, and in restrooms.
4. Use designated hand washing sinks for hand washing only. Do not use food preparation, utility, and dishwashing sinks for hand washing.
5. Provide warm running water, soap, and a means to dry hands. Provide a waste container at each hand washing sink or near the door in restrooms.
6. Wash hands:
   - Before starting work.
   - During food preparation.
   - Before putting on or changing gloves.
   - After using the toilet.
   - After changing diapers or assisting children with toileting.
   - After sneezing, coughing, or using a handkerchief or tissue or wiping children's noses.
   - After touching hair, face, or body.
   - After smoking, eating, drinking, or chewing gum or tobacco.
   - After handling raw meats, poultry, or fish.
   - After any cleanup activity such as sweeping, mopping, or wiping counters, putting away toys, sanitizing children's tables.
   - After touching dirty dishes, equipment, or utensils.
   - After handling trash.
   - After taking a break.
   - After handling animals.
7. Follow proper hand washing procedures:
   - Wet hands and forearms with warm, running water at least 100°F (38°C) and apply soap.
   - Scrub lathered hands and forearms, under fingernails with a nail brush, and between fingers for at least 20 seconds. Rinse thoroughly under warm running water for 5 to 10 seconds.
   - Dry hands and forearms thoroughly with single-use paper towels.
   - Turn off water at the faucet using paper towels when touching the faucet.
   - Use paper towel to open door when exiting the restroom.
   - Double hand washing by early childhood staff who handle food should occur after coughing, sneezing, having contact with body fluids, or using the bathroom. After using the bathroom or assisting a child in the bathroom, the first hand washing will take place in the restroom; the second at the designated hand washing sink in the work area before continuing work with food.

MONITORING:

Administrative staff will visually observe the hand washing practices of the staff involved in food service during all hours of operation.

CORRECTIVE ACTION:

1. Retrain any staff member found not following the procedures in this SOP.
2. Ask staff members who are observed not washing their hands at the appropriate times or using the proper procedure to wash their hands immediately.

VERIFICATION AND RECORD KEEPING:

The administrator will observe staff and document whether hand washing procedures are being effectively used.

DATE IMPLEMENTED: _____ BY: _____

Sources: Based on AMC-HACCP *Publications and Reports: Double Hand Washing with a Fingernail Brush* HACCP, by the Hospitality Institute of Technology and Management, 2005, retrieved September 16, 2009, from http://www.hi-tm.com/Documents/Handflow.html; and *Food Safety Standard Operating Procedures (SOPs)*, by the National Food Service Management Institute, 2005, retrieved September 15, 2009, from http://www.nfsmi.org/ResourceOverview.aspx?ID=75.

hepatitis A, or norovirus or who have symptoms such as vomiting, diarrhea, jaundice, sore throat, or infected cuts, pimples, or boils (FDA, 2009a). Food service workers or teachers who have been ill or exposed to the illnesses listed above must report this to the program director who, depending on state requirements, will share this information with local health authorities. Food service workers and teachers who have contracted the above illnesses should not return to work until they have written approval from a medical provider.

Figure 8-15 Teachers Must Wash Hands in Designated Hand Washing Sinks

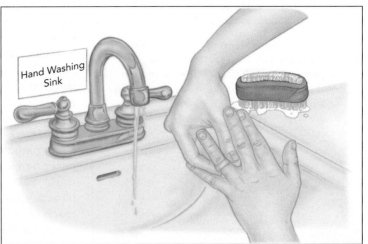

Preventing Cross-Contamination

Using sanitizing methods during food preparation helps to minimize cross-contamination. Cleaning and sanitizing have distinct purposes:

- **Cleaning** refers to the removal of dirt, grime, and food particles using soap, water, and scrubbing. Although cleaning reduces the risk of biological contamination, it does not destroy all germs.
- **Sanitizing** involves the use of heat or sanitizing solutions to reduce the risk of contamination by killing microorganisms (NRA, 2008). After surfaces and equipment have been cleaned, they are then ready for sanitizing.

Methods of Sanitizing Typically, in the kitchen setting items sanitized by food handlers include food preparation and service surfaces, dishware, cookware and utensils, thermometers, food service equipment, and door knobs and handles. Sanitizing is accomplished by:

- Washing dishware, cookware, and utensils in hot water (171°F [77°C] or hotter for 30 seconds or more for manual hand washing).
- Using chemical sanitizers such as bleach or other chemical products approved by the EPA (American Academy of Pediatrics et al., 2007; McSwane et al., 2005).

Both sanitizing methods are used when washing dishes in a three-compartment sink. The three-compartment sink procedure is described in Figure 8-16. The three-sink method is used when a facility does not have an appliance that washes and sanitizes dishes.

Preparing and Using Bleach Solutions Sanitizing with bleach solutions is often done because it inexpensive, kills most germs, can be used in many different situations and in appropriate concentrations, and does not leave a residue that needs to be washed off (American Academy of Pediatrics et al., 2007; McSwane et al., 2005).

The Food Code recommends bleach solution dilutions of between 50 and 100 parts per million (about 1 tsp bleach per gallon water) for cleaning food service surfaces. Health authorities generally agree that leaving the bleach solution on the surface for 2 minutes significantly reduces microbial contamination (American Academy of Pediatrics et al., 2007; FDA, 2009a). A stronger dilution is recommended for sanitizing

cleaning
the removal of dirt, grime, and food particles using soap and water and friction with the goal of reducing risk of biological, physical, and chemical contamination

sanitizing
process used to reduce the risk of contamination by reducing microorganisms to safe levels by heat or sanitizing solutions

Figure 8-16 Procedure for Sanitizing Dishware Using the Three-Sink Method

1. Wash items in water that is at least 110°F (43°C).
2. Rinse in water that is at least 110°F (43°C).
3. Sanitize in hot water (171°F [77°C] for 30 seconds or chlorine bleach solution for at least 60 seconds).
4. Air dry.

Wash   Rinse   Sanitize

Sources: HACCP *in Your School*, by A. Fraser, October 2007, retrieved October 29, 2009, from http://www.foodsafetysite.com/resources/pdfs/schoolhaccp/SchoolHACCPManual.pdf; and *Essentials of Food Safety and Sanitation*, 4th edition, by D. McSwane, N. R. Rue, and R. Linton, 2005, Upper Saddle River, NJ: Pearson Prentice Hall.

spills of body fluids such as blood, feces, urine, and breast milk. For this purpose, a mix of ¼ cup of 5.25% sodium hypochlorite bleach to 1 gallon of water (or 1 tablespoon to 1 quart of water) with 2 minutes of contact time for sufficient sanitizing is recommended (American Academy of Pediatrics et al., 2007). Figure 8-17 provides directions for preparing a bleach sanitizing solution that falls within the 100 parts per million range using regular (5.25% sodium hypochlorite) unscented bleach.

The correct concentration of bleach solution should be maintained to ensure consistent sanitizing. The concentration can be monitored with a kit that uses test strips. Bleach should never be mixed with ammonia or any other cleaning agents because toxic fumes can result. For safety, bottles containing bleach solutions must be clearly labeled and stored out of the reach of children.

A sanitizing routine is needed to ensure that surfaces and equipment are safe for food. It is not sufficient to clean and sanitize when a piece of equipment "looks" soiled. For example, a can opener can appear clean even though the blade may have been exposed to food multiple times during the day. A cleaning schedule, such as the one shown in Table 8-2, helps create an appropriate routine.

Avoiding Contamination during Food Preparation

Biological contamination is a risk during all phases of food preparation such as thawing, cooking, holding, and cooling, and the risk increases substantially when temperature abuse occurs. Once again, temperature control plays an important role in ensuring food safety.

Thawing Food Foods should be thawed overnight in the refrigerator in a drip-pan. Food can also be thawed in the microwave but only if it is going to be cooked immediately (American Academy of Pediatrics et al., 2007; NFSMI, 2009). Food being thawed should never reach temperatures above 41°F (5°C) (FDA, 2009a).

Preparing Food Food safety relies on careful preparation. Cross-contamination is one critical aspect to avoid. An important strategy is to keep raw meats, poultry, eggs, and seafood separate from ready-to-eat foods. Jan, a teacher who cares for children in her home, uses color-coded cutting boards. She uses a red cutting board for preparing raw meats, and a green one for fresh produce. When she prepares salad she doesn't have to worry that her lettuce will come in contact with bacteria from the hamburger patties she prepares on the red cutting board. She also knows it is not a good idea to "eyeball" a food to see if it looks done. One in four hamburgers turns brown before it reaches an internal temperature that kills germs (Partnership for Food Safety Education [PFSE], 2006). Jan uses a thermometer to check the internal temperature of foods. She also refers to the USDA standardized recipes because they tell her what temperatures her foods must reach to minimize the risk of foodborne illness.

Using microwave ovens to cook food may be convenient, but additional factors must be considered. Microwave ovens vary, and heating is not always consistent. To make sure there are no cold spots in food that might harbor bacteria, food should be covered, rotated, and stirred during heating and then allowed to sit for indicated stand times (PFSE, 2006).

Figure 8-17 Directions for Preparing Sanitizing Solution

Sanitizing Solution

Remember: All surfaces must be **CLEAN** before you sanitize or the sanitizer will not work!

100 ppm bleach:

- ¼ tsp. bleach in 1 quart of cool water
- 1 tsp. bleach in 1 gallon of cool water
- Check concentration with chlorine test strips

Bleach
100 ppm

Source: Used with permission from State of Alaska Department of Environmental Conservation, 2006.

Table 8-2	Sample Cleaning Schedule

	How Often?				
Cleaning Activity	After Use	Before and After	Daily	Weekly	As Needed
STOVE					
Clean burners	•				
Clean outside			•		
Clean inside				•	
Clean hood				•	
REFRIGERATOR AND FREEZER					
Defrost/clean					•
Wipe outside			•		
Wipe inside				•	•
FOOD PREPARATION SURFACES					
Clean			•		
Sanitize			•		
SINKS					
Clean	•				
Scrub			•		
CUPBOARD AND OTHER STORAGE AREAS					
Wipe/organize					•
EATING SURFACES					
Clean			•		
Sanitize			•		
KITCHEN EQUIPMENT					
Can opener, mixer, blender, etc.	•				
TRASH					
Nonrecyclable			•		
Earth tub compost			•		
Recyclables			•		•

Source: Adapted with permission from Graves, D.E., Suitor, C.W. & Holt, K.A. (eds.), *Making Food Healthy and Safe for Children: How to Meet the National Health and Safety Performance Standards: Guidelines for Out-of-Home Child Care Programs*. Arlington, VA: National Center for Education in Maternal and Child Health: 1997.

Cooling Food Sometimes food is prepared ahead to serve on another day. Food that is prepared in advance must be chilled in a timely manner so that it does not stay in the temperature danger zone for an excessively long period of time. Consider this example:

Rosalind stays late to prepare soup for the family social event that will be held the following day. Although she uses a USDA-approved standardized recipe, she does not follow proper cooling instructions before refrigerating the soup. The next morning, the health inspector makes an unexpected visit to her children's center. The inspector measures the temperature of the refrigerated soup and finds that it is still 50°F (10°C). The health inspector tells Rosalind that the soup has not been chilled quickly enough for it to be safe and, therefore, the soup must be discarded. The inspector makes some recommendations for the future, telling her that soup can be cooled using shallow 2- to 4-inch-high steam table pans with an ice paddle (a hollow plastic paddle that can be filled with water) and frozen and then placed in the soup to chill it quickly (Fraser, 2008).

Reheating Food Methods for reheating foods are also important to food safety. Reheated foods must reach an internal temperature of 165°F (74°C), which should be sustained for at least for 15 seconds to kill bacteria. The time it takes to reheat foods should not exceed 2 hours. Longer reheating times increase the risk of microorganisms proliferating.

Practices related to keeping and reheating leftover food for service in children's programs is governed by state and local health authorities. If local health regulations allow leftovers to be served, a careful management plan is needed. Any food that is being stored as leftovers should be carefully labeled, including the name of the food, the amount prepared, and the date of preparation. Leftovers should only be reheated once and should also reach an internal temperature of 165°F (74°C) (Fraser, 2007). The same time and temperature rules apply for reheating with microwave ovens although microwave-heated food should be allowed to set for an additional 2 minutes to finish the cooking process before being served (NFSMI, 2005c).

Minimizing Contamination Risk during Food Service

Ensuring safety during food service in the children's settings offers special challenges. Keeping heated food sufficiently hot prior to meal service is important. In school settings children often pass through a lunch line where food is served onto trays by food service workers. This format allows the food in the cafeteria to be held in heating units such as steam tables. This food must be monitored to make sure proper temperatures are maintained. Salad bars also create a food safety risk. Purchasing equipment that contains sneeze guards or food shields reduces the risk of contamination from coughs or sneezes. Salad ingredients are highly perishable and must be keep at 41°F (5°C) or below for proper cold holding.

Children's programs also use family meal–style service, which provides the opportunity for children to gain important self-help skills such as selecting and serving their own food. This approach requires that teachers supervise children to avoid cross-contamination as they serve themselves and pass the serving dishes. It is not usual for children to want to lick the serving spoon, use the same serving spoon for different menu items, or put their used forks into a serving dish when they want another serving. This can result in biological contamination and also put children with food allergies at risk.

It is also important to monitor how long food is maintained at room temperature while waiting to be served. To ensure food safety at the time of service, meals are planned on a regular schedule, with routines that help children to be washed and ready to eat when food is ready, and meal tables have been cleaned and sanitized. It is also important to ensure that food is not too hot for consumption. For example, foods that are heated in a microwave oven can have hot spots that may cause burns to the mouth. Soups and stews may be hot and could pose a burning risk if spilled.

Another aspect of food service safety involves ensuring that children on special diets receive the correct meals. Having a system in place for serving children with special diet requirements is helpful because mealtimes can be very busy. For example, Elisa, a preschooler teacher, finds it helpful to serve the children with special diets first. She posts a list in the classroom that includes the children's names and their special diet needs. The program's dietitian has provided a menu that lists special diet substitutions and Elisa always double checks to make sure the correct foods are being served.

Understanding the food safety risks related to each phase of the flow of food through a program from purchasing and storage to food preparation and service helps teachers to minimize the chances of a foodborne illness. Figure 8-18 provides a checklist that can be used by teachers to make sure all aspects of food safety are being considered on a routine basis.

Figure 8-18 Food Safety Checklist

Date_____ Observer_____

Directions: Use this checklist daily. Determine areas in your operations requiring corrective action. Record corrective action taken and keep completed records in a notebook for future reference.

PERSONAL HYGIENE	Yes	No	Corrective Action
• Effective hair restraints are properly worn.	☐	☐	_____
• Fingernails are short, unpolished, and clean (no artificial nails).	☐	☐	_____
• Jewelry is limited to a plain ring, such as wedding band and a watch and no bracelets.	☐	☐	_____
• Hands are washed properly, frequently, and at appropriate times.	☐	☐	_____
• Burns, wounds, sores or scabs, or splints and water-proof bandages on hands are bandaged and completely covered with a food service glove while handling food.	☐	☐	_____
• Hand sinks are stocked with soap, disposable towels, and warm water.	☐	☐	_____

FOOD PREPARATION	Yes	No	Corrective Action
• All food stored or prepared in facility is from approved sources.	☐	☐	_____
• Food equipment utensils, and food contact surfaces are properly washed, rinsed, and sanitized before every use.	☐	☐	_____
• Preparation is planned so ingredients are kept out of the temperature danger zone to the extent possible.	☐	☐	_____
• Procedures are in place to prevent cross-contamination.	☐	☐	_____
• Food is handled with suitable utensils, such as single-use gloves or tongs.	☐	☐	_____
• Food is cooked to the required safe internal temperature for the appropriate time. The temperature is tested with a calibrated food thermometer.	☐	☐	_____

HOT HOLDING	Yes	No	Corrective Action
• Temperature of hot food being held is at or above 135°F (57°C).	☐	☐	_____

COLD HOLDING	Yes	No	Corrective Action
• Temperature of cold food being held is at or below 41°F (5°C)	☐	☐	_____

REFRIGERATOR, FREEZER, AND MILK COOLER	Yes	No	Corrective Action
• Thermometers are available and accurate.	☐	☐	_____
• All food is properly wrapped, labeled, and dated.	☐	☐	_____
• The FIFO (first in, first out) method of inventory management is used.	☐	☐	_____
• Ambient air temperature of all refrigerators and freezers is monitored and documented at the beginning and end of each shift.	☐	☐	_____

FOOD STORAGE AND DRY STORAGE	Yes	No	Corrective Action
• Temperature of dry storage area is between 50° and 70°F (10 and 21°C) or state public health department requirement.	☐	☐	_____
• The FIFO (first in, first out) method of inventory management is used.	☐	☐	_____
• Chemicals are clearly labeled and stored away from food and food-related supplies.	☐	☐	_____

CLEANING AND SANITIZING	Yes	No	Corrective Action
• Three-compartment sink is properly set up for ware washing.	☐	☐	_____
• Dish machine is working properly (such as gauges and chemicals are at recommended levels).	☐	☐	_____
• Water temperatures are correct for wash and rinse.	☐	☐	_____
• If heat sanitizing, the utensils are allowed to remain immersed in 171°F (77°C) water for 30 seconds.	☐	☐	_____
• Smallware and utensils are allowed to air dry.	☐	☐	_____
• Wiping cloths are stored in sanitizing solution while in use.	☐	☐	_____

Source: Used with permission from HACCP-*Based* SOPs: *Food Safety Checklist,* by the National Food Service Management Institute, 2005, retrieved September 16, 2009. For a complete list, go to http://sop.nfsmi.org/Records/FoodSafetyChecklist.pdf.

Understanding At-Risk Situations in Early Childhood Settings

Although rules and regulations exist that govern food preparation in schools at any age level, feeding young children poses unique challenges. Children's physical and social-emotional development provides the basis for making many decisions that relate to feeding and safe nourishment. In addition, early childhood teachers may work with children from a variety of age groups and must understand children's needs in a variety of settings. It is important to recognize that some food safety issues are unique to the early childhood setting.

Food Safety and Feeding Infants

Infants have a special need for a safe food supply because the immaturity of their immune system puts them at greatest risk for foodborne illness. Infants under 6 months of age rely on breast milk or formula to provide them with optimal nutrition. Infant feeding and handling and storage of breast milk were discussed in earlier chapters. Some additional food safety guidelines to consider when feeding infants are listed below:

- Discard breast milk or formula that has been left out at room temperature 2 hours or more (U.S. FDA, 2009).
- Check formula and baby food to make sure they have not exceeded their "use by" dates.
- Discard any jar of baby food if the safety button on the lid has popped.
- Do not heat breast milk, formula, or baby food in the microwave oven because uneven heating can lead to hot spots, which can burn the baby's mouth and throat. In addition, microwaving can destroy protective immunological components of breast milk (Neifert, 2009).

Nutrition Note

Feeding Breast Milk to Another Mother's Baby

Breast milk is considered the gold standard for infant nutrition. Teachers who support mothers who chose to breast-feed provide an invaluable service to both mother and baby. Breast milk, however, must be handled appropriately to avoid food safety problems.

Teachers who follow proper procedures for handling breast milk will rarely feed a baby the wrong bottle of breast milk. However, a bottle can be put down by one infant and picked up by another. If a baby consumes another infant's bottle of breast milk, this must be treated as an accidental exposure to a potential HIV-containing body fluid.

The National Resource Center for Health and Safety in Child Care and Early Education recommends that the teacher notify the parents of the baby who consumed the wrong milk, the infant's medical provider, and the mother whose breast milk was consumed. The medical provider may recommend that the baby who consumed the wrong milk and that baby's mother have a baseline test for HIV and a follow-up test 6 months later. The mother whose milk was consumed by the wrong child should be asked if she has had an HIV test and if she would be willing to share this information with the family whose

infant was exposed. If she has not been tested for HIV, she should be asked if she would be willing to take a test and follow-up test 6 months later and share the results with the baby's family.

Although the risk of transmission of HIV in breast milk is very low, the follow-up procedures and testing that occur as a result of feeding the wrong breast milk to an infant highlight the importance of following careful food safety procedures when feeding babies breast milk.

Source: Used with permission of the American Academy of Pediatrics, *Caring for Our Children: National Health and Safety Performance Standards: Guidelines for Out-of-Home Child Care Programs*, 2e. Copyright 2002.

- Do not feed baby directly from the jar. This introduces germs from the baby's mouth into the jar of food creating a food safety risk if food is refrigerated for later use.
- If making homemade baby food, be sure the food is thoroughly cooked.
- Do not feed babies honey until age 1 and older due to the risk of botulism.

In addition, the Mississippi State University Extension Service (2005) makes the following recommendations for storing opened jars of strained food:

- *Strained fruits and vegetables:* 2 to 3 days in the refrigerator and 6 to 8 months if frozen.
- *Strained meat and eggs:* 1 day in the refrigerator and 1 to 2 months in the freezer.
- *Combination meals with meats and vegetables:* 1 to 2 days in the refrigerator and 1 to 2 months in the freezer.

Ensuring that infants receive their own mother's breast milk is another important component of food safety when feeding infants. The *Nutrition Note* discusses this topic and offers guidance on what to do if an infant drinks the wrong milk.

Food Safety and Feeding Toddlers and Preschoolers

Choking is a potential hazard for young children. Specific foods introduce safety risks for young children because they are round and large enough to obstruct an airway (FDA, 2005). The American Academy of Pediatrics (2007) recommends that the following foods be avoided for children under age 4:

Hot dogs
Nuts and seeds
Large pieces of meat or cheese
Grapes
Hard, gooey, or sticky candy
Popcorn
A large serving size of peanut butter
Raw vegetables
Small, dried fruits such as raisins
Gum
Hard pretzels.*

Food offered to toddlers and preschool-age children should be cut into age-appropriate pieces of a ½ inch or less. Children should be seated while eating and teachers should supervise mealtimes closely. NAEYC *Standard 5.B.14* provides guidance on foods that pose a choking risk (NAEYC Academy for Early Childhood Program Accreditation, 2009).

Food Safety and Children with Special Needs

Some children with special developmental needs may have food preparation and service requirements that are different than other children. These differences may create unique food safety concerns. For example:

- Children with developmental impairments may be at increased risk for choking and require alternative food textures and/or thickeners added to beverages.
- Children with special needs may require tube feeding, which requires careful handling.
- Service of foods to children with special developmental challenges may take longer as the child negotiates the eating process.
- During meal service temperatures of foods may enter food temperature danger zones longer or more often due to the need to transport special single-serving portions, which are harder to maintain at appropriate temperatures, and prolonged feeding times. Reheating of foods may be more common to support meal service (Krueger, 2007).

As with all food service, specialized equipment used in food preparation for children with special needs such as blenders or food processors must be properly cleaned and sanitized.

---

*Used with permission of the American Academy of Pediatrics, from "Parenting Corner Q&A: Choking Prevention," http://www.aap.org.

Any special feeding devices such as adaptive eating utensils, plates, and bowls must also be properly cleaned and sanitized.

Some children with identified special developmental needs may require a medical statement or guidance from a medical provider, describing the disability and how it affects the child's diet, including what to omit and what to substitute (Krueger, 2007). Teachers may need to obtain training to know how to respond if a child's disability interferes with swallowing or if choking is a potential concern. Teachers need to ensure that all children have access to quality, balanced, wholesome meals that meet their unique requirements. Teachers also need to make sure they understand any required diet modifications.

Food Safety and Food Brought from Home

Some families may ask to bring their child's food from home rather than have meals prepared by the early childhood program. Such a request may be made for children whose diet restrictions are complex. In considering such a request, teachers need to be aware of the health regulations in their area. Many state and local health authorities discourage or prohibit sending meals from home. Foods from home may increase the risk of foodborne illness. Where permitted, a written agreement between families and the children's program should be established (American Academy of Pediatrics et al., 2007). Guidelines for families who choose to bring food from home include the following:

- Food should always be sent in lunch containers that have frozen ice packs.
- Food should be labeled with the child's name, the date, and the type of food.
- Food should not be shared with other children in the program (American Academy of Pediatrics et al., 2007).

What if. . .

you observed a child sharing food from his lunch box with other children? Isn't a child who shares doing something commendable? How might you explain the safety risks to this child?

Families may wish to share food from home with all children in the program. Programs must carefully weigh the pro and cons of allowing food to be brought from home and be proactive in prevention of foodborne illness by devising policies that support safe food and meet state and county regulations. As discussed in an earlier chapter, the NAEYC accreditation standards recommend that foods brought from home to share with other children must consist of whole fruits or commercially prepared packaged foods (NAEYC Academy for Early Childhood Program Accreditation, 2009). Remember too the consequences that occurred in the case scenario, when homemade cupcakes were brought into Lacey's classroom.

Food Safety and Cultural Considerations

Teachers who support cultural traditions in the selection of food for early childhood programs create a respectful enriching environment for all children and their families. However, some cultural food traditions may create a dilemma in terms of food safety. For example, the food traditions of the First Nations people of British Columbia include wild foods such as moose, deer, salmon, rabbit, dried berries, and seaweed (B.C. First Nations Head Start, 2003). Their Head Start programs took steps to ensure that traditional foods served met food safety regulations such as consulting with their health inspectors and making sure meats were processed in approved plants and prepared in inspected kitchens.

Some cultural food choices may be associated with increased risk for foodborne illness. For example, some soft Mexican-style cheeses have been linked to Listeriosis, an uncommon foodborne disease which can cause high fever, severe headache, neck stiffness, nausea and sometimes death (Boggs, Whitwam, Hale, Briscoe, & Karhn, 2001; FDA, 2009b). Sushi, a Japanese dish made with rice, seaweed, vegetables, and often raw fish, has also been linked to foodborne illness. If made with raw fish, this menu item should never be served to young children (Colorado State University Extension, 2006). Teachers can honor cultural food traditions, but this must be done within the context of food safety policies and regulations.

Safety Segment

Food Safety on Field Trips

Taking foods on field trips requires careful planning to keep food safe.

1. *Menu planning:* Field trip menus should include foods with low risk for spoiling. Some safe foods to take along on field trips include:
   - Boxed juices
   - Whole fruit
   - Individual canned or plastic fruit cups
   - Dried fruit (if age appropriate)
   - Whole-grain crackers, breads, bread sticks, and rolls
   - Peanut butter sandwiches (if there are no peanut allergies)
   - Nuts (if there are no allergies and this snack is age appropriate)
   - Trail mix (if age-appropriate ingredients are used)
   - Dry cereal
   - Baked whole-grain chips
2. *Storing food:* Foods must be maintained at proper temperatures. Store foods that need to be chilled in coolers filled with ice or plastic frozen gel packs. Freeze juice boxes and use them to keep other food cold. Place a thermometer in the cooler to make sure temperatures remain under 41°F (5°C). Foods that need to be chilled include:
   - Meat, poultry, fish, or egg salad sandwiches
   - Milk
   - Cheese
   - Yogurt
   - Fruits or vegetables that have been peeled or cut
   - Salads
3. *Hand washing:* Remember to wash hands and have children wash hands before eating. Premoistened hand wipes are not a substitute for hand washing, but can be used if no soap and running water are available.

Sources: *Caring for Our Children: National Health and Safety Performance Standards: Guidelines for Out-of-Home Child Care Programs,* 2nd edition, 2007, Elk Grove Village, IL: American Academy of Pediatrics; *Food Safety Standard Operating Procedures* (SOPs), National Food Service Management Institute, 2005, retrieved September 15, 2009, from http://www.nfsmi.org/ResourceOverview.aspx?ID=75; and *Food Safety for Home Child Care Providers: Chill,* New Mexico State University Cooperative Extension Service, 2004, retrieved September 16, 2009, from http://www.childcarefoodsafety.com/chill/chill.html.

Food Safety on Field Trips

When children go on a field trip, special challenges must be addressed when serving food away from the school program. These challenges have to do with maintaining proper temperatures and personal hygiene. The *Safety Segment* provides advice on acceptable foods for a field trip.

Food Safety and Classroom Cooking Activities

Children learn about food by touching, tasting, and smelling it. They are often more likely to want to try new foods when they have helped with preparation. Safety management considerations for classroom cooking activities include the following:

- *Raw foods:* Avoid handling raw foods that contain infectious microorganisms. Children making cookies using a recipe that calls for eggs are at risk for salmonella food poisoning. Using a pasteurized egg substitute eliminates this problem.

MyEducationLab

Be Food Safe

Go to the Assignments and Activities section of Topic 4: Food Safety in the MyEducationLab for your course and complete the activity entitled *Food Safety Activities for Children.* What activities from this booklet would you use in your class to teach children about food safety?

- *Foods that will not be cooked:* If children participate in preparing foods that will not be cooked, they should only eat the food they have prepared and handled. For example, if the teacher plans an activity where children make salad, each child should be given the ingredients to make his or her own salad.
- *Potential food allergens:* Teachers must make sure that children with allergies or food intolerances are not involved in activities that lead to exposure. For example, covering a pinecone with peanut butter and bird seed would be a risky project for children with peanut allergies. Making playdough from wheat flour would be hazardous to children with celiac disease.

THE EMERGENCY PLAN AND FOOD DEFENSE

Emergencies cannot be predicted, but children's programs and schools can prepare in advance for potential emergencies. Two aspects of food safety guide planning for emergencies: ensuring that there is a safe supply of food and water in case of a natural disaster, and making sure that foods are not tampered with or intentionally contaminated as an act of terrorism.

Developing an Emergency Food Plan

An emergency food plan is needed in the event an emergency requires that children and teachers are not able to return to their homes, but must take shelter in the facility. The Homeland Security Department (2009), the Federal Emergency Management Agency (FEMA, 2009), the American Red Cross (2009), and other agencies (Pennsylvania Emergency Management Agency, 2008) provide guidelines on what foods and how much food and water to store. A 3-day supply of food and water is recommended.

Whereas an effective emergency food plan ensures that children will have access to safe food and water if supplies are interrupted, even an emergency food supply can pose a food safety risk if it is not properly monitored. The FIFO method of food rotation discussed earlier in this chapter is one way to ensure that food on hand is safe. Figure 8-19 lists a variety of emergency foods and the FEMA guidelines for the length of time they should be stored. The emergency food supply should include foods appropriate for the age group of the children served and should include options for children with food allergies and other food restrictions.

Figure 8-19 Food Safety and Storing Emergency Foods

The following provides some general guidelines for replacement of common emergency foods.

Use within six months:
- Powdered milk - **boxed**
- Dried fruit
- Dry, crisp crackers
- Potatoes

Use within one year, or before the date indicated on the label:
- Canned condensed meat and vegetable soups
- Canned fruits, fruit juices, and vegetables
- Ready-to-eat cereals and uncooked instant cereals
- Peanut butter
- Jelly
- Hard candy and canned nuts
- Vitamins

May be stored indefinitely (in proper containers and conditions):
- Wheat
- Vegetable oils
- Dried corn
- Baking powder
- Soybeans
- Instant coffee, tea, and cocoa
- Salt
- Noncarbonated soft drinks
- White rice
- Bouillon products
- Dry pasta
- Powdered milk—**in nitrogen-packed cans**

Sources: Used with permission from *Food and Water in an Emergency*, Federal Emergency Management Agency and American Red Cross, August 2004. Retrieved September 16, 2009, from http://www.fema.gov/pdf/library/f&web.pdf.

Planning for Food Defense

food defense
practice of ensuring that foods are not tampered with or intentionally contaminated as an act of terrorism

The Homeland Security Department has raised awareness that food service establishments may be at risk for intentional contamination of foods by terrorist groups. To provide food defense, which is the assurance that foods are not tampered with or intentionally contaminated as an act of terrorism, food service handlers are the "front line in protecting our food supply" (New York State Department of Health, 2006). For teachers and food services workers, this means being vigilant about who has access to the food that is stored and served to children. Children's programs can implement these strategies:

- Allow only authorized individuals to receive, store, and have access to food preparation areas.
- Know the food delivery personnel and always have someone available to directly receive food.
- Make sure self-service food items are placed in an area that can be supervised by staff.
- Keep buildings and grounds secure by locking doors n delivery, storage, and food preparation areas when not in use and allowing only key or code access.
- Discourage loitering in the program setting or school. Install alarm or video surveillance systems if security problems are an issue.
- Conduct employee background checks to ensure employment of safe teachers and food workers.
- Train employees on food defense and food safety and on how to recognize potential security risks.

These recommendations from the New York State Department of Health's *Food Defense Strategies* website (2006) can heighten awareness of threats to food safety, decreasing the risk that early childhood programs will become targets for deliberate contamination. It is unfortunate that issues of this type need to be considered in the early childhood setting. However, children are vulnerable and have been targeted in the past. It is every program's and school's responsibility to consider all aspects of safety.

TEACHING FOOD SAFETY TO CHILDREN

Although program administrators and teachers bear the responsibility of ensuring a safe food supply, children are capable of helping to create a safe food environment. Teaching children about food safety includes a progression of ideas from basic ideas to more advanced concepts.

Routines in the school setting often are established to keep children safe. These routines also teach children expected behaviors that relate to food safety. Children learn about food safety through these everyday practices, especially if teachers explain the rationale behind the routines. Leading questions are appropriate for preschool-age children and older and could include these:

- We wash our hands because....
- We sneeze into our elbow and not our hands because....
- We pick up the fork by the handle when setting the table because....
- We can put our forks in our mouths, but not the serving spoon, because....
- We share most things, but we only eat or drink our own food because....
- We put milk in the refrigerator because....
- We wash the tables before and after eating because....

Activity-based exploration of food safety topics is appropriate for all children. For example, teaching food safety tips while preparing and sampling food keeps children interested. Singing the "ABC" song once while washing hands teaches children how long to wash their hands in a way that holds their interest. The *Teaching Wellness* feature offers ideas about how to incorporate food safety lessons such as hand washing into the daily curriculum.

Being a good role model and combining simple explanations with consistent reminders help children establish food safety habits that benefit them now and into the future.

What if. . .

you were in charge of creating an emergency food plan? How would you plan for children with special diet needs? What might you include in your emergency food supply to address various special diets?

What if. . .

you were asked to teach food safety topics to children in your class? What topics would you select? How would you create a child-directed activity for a food safety topic? What teacher-directed topic would you teach?

Teaching Wellness *Washing Hands Keeps Me Healthy*

Learning Outcome   Children demonstrate how to prevent the spread of germs by washing their hands before mealtime.

Infants and Toddlers

- *Goal:* Babies are willing to have their hands washed and toddlers are able to wash and dry their hands with help.

- *Materials:* Small tub of warm water, soap, paper towels.

- *Activity plan:* For infants, demonstrate hand washing in the tub of shallow warm water. Say words that convey pleasure, positive appreciation, and interest, such as "I like to wash my hands because it makes them feel so clean. Let's wash and dry our hands before we eat." Dip the baby's hand in the water and use gentle friction to wash hands, allowing the infant to touch and splash about.

- *How to adjust the activity:* For toddlers: Model washing hands at a sink. Talk through the process while modeling and encouraging the child through each step. Say, "First let's get our hands wet, next we add some soap. Now let's sing Happy Birthday two times. Here we go . . . happy birthday to you (etc.). Now let's rinse and dry our hands and then we will be ready to eat." Reinforce the child's efforts by remarking, "You are really scrubbing all parts of your hands. That is how we wash away the germs. This is a good way to clean our hands."

- *Did you meet your goal:* Can the child imitate the steps in appropriate hand washing? When asked, is the child able to identify hand washing as "How do we get rid of germs?"

Preschoolers and Kindergartners

- *Goal:* Children demonstrate appropriate hand washing techniques and can tell teacher one reason hand washing is important.

- *Materials:* Sink with running water, paper towels, liquid soap, the children's book *Those Mean Nasty Dirty Downright Disgusting But . . . Invisible Germs* by Judith Rice, crayons and paper.

- *Activity plan:* Read the book *Those Mean Nasty Dirty Downright Disgusting But . . . Invisible Germs* using a variety of fun voices and hand gestures. Talk through the steps of clean hand washing using pictures or drawings. Invite children to wash their hands at the sink. Reinforce the steps of hand washing:
  - Turn on the water and wet hands.
  - Use one squirt of liquid soap.
  - Wash hands for 20 seconds (sing the ABC song once).
  - Rinse hands including between fingers, palms, backs of hands, and wrists.
  - Dry hands with paper towel.
  - Use paper towel to turn off water.

- *How to adjust the activity:* Show children pictures of germs (microbes). Have children use crayons to draw their favorite germ from the book. Talk about how germs can make people sick and that it is important to wash germs off before eating to stay healthy. Talk about other times its good to wash hands such as after sneezing, petting an animal, or going to the bathroom.

- *Did you meet your goal:* Are children able to wash hands appropriately? When asked, are children able to identify times when it is important to wash hands?

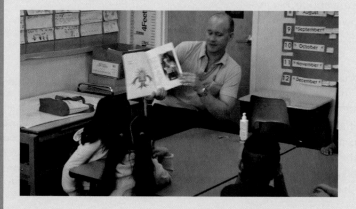

MyEducationLab

To watch how one teacher shows children why hand washing is so important to good health, go to the Video Examples section of Topic 4: Food Safety in the MyEducationLab for your course and watch the video *Health Lessons: Washing Hands.* Note all the ways in which the teacher reinforces this health lesson.

School-Age Children

- **Goal:** To recognize that hand washing removes germs that can cause illness.

- **Materials:** Sink with running water, liquid soap, paper towels, magnifying glass, vegetable oil and dark-colored spice such as cinnamon powder (check for food allergies) or use a disclosing lotion and a UV lamp.

- **Activity plan:** Have a small group of children look at their hands with a magnifying glass. Ask the children to describe what they see. Talk about how you can see dirt but you cannot see germs because they are so small. Describe how germs can hide in the cracks and crevices of the hand and explain why germs can be harmful. Place oil in a pump bottle and put a drop of oil in one hand of each child. Have them sprinkle on cinnamon powder. Show how germs are spread by having children shake a clean hand with a "germy" hand. Have them touch some surfaces and ask "Did the germs spread?" Have children rinse hands for 2 to 3 seconds. Ask "Are the germs gone?" Have children wash hands in a sink for 20 seconds using the steps outlined above. Ask them to observe what happened when they washed their hands carefully. Have children explain why it is important to wash hands.

- **How to adjust the activity:** Obtain pictures of germs that are associated with different illnesses. Have children make posters showing the germs, with statements about why hand washing is important. An alternative option is to create a "Know, Wonder, and Learn Chart" before teaching the lesson. The chart is useful in stimulating group discussion and tapping into students' prior knowledge about hand washing.

It gives them an opportunity to think about what they want to learn about and also helps them keep track of new knowledge.

- **Did you meet your goal:** Are children able to describe why hand washing is important?

- **Accommodations:** Partner children who are learning English, with a peer (preferably bilingual) student. Be sure that the demonstration can be clearly observed. Provide a step-by-step chart with picture directions for children who need extra visual supports. If children have a disability that prevents them from standing by a sink, provide a plastic tub with water and liquid hand soap.

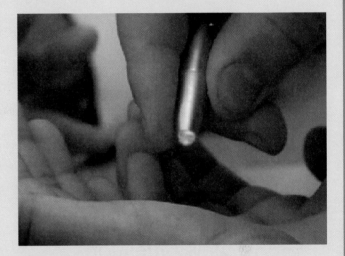

Children can see how much time it takes to wash hands thoroughly by using a disclosing lotion and UV lamp before and after washing hands.

Summary

Food safety is the responsibility of all staff involved in the purchase, storage, preparation, and service of food to young children. Young children have immature immune systems and are at risk for illness or death when exposed to biological, chemical, and physical contaminants or allergens. Understanding the sources of food contamination that can cause foodborne illness is the first step in creating a food safe environment.

Federal, state, and local health authorities are responsible for establishing and regulating food safety in licensed children's programs and schools. These agencies are a good source of information to guide program-level policies regarding food safety. Teachers need to understand the food safety requirements mandated in their area. The county health department and food safety inspectors are a vital link and valuable resource in maintaining food safety in early childhood programs.

Reducing the risk for foodborne illness is accomplished through the development of a consistent food safety plan. The Hazard and Analysis Critical Control Point (HACCP) system consists of seven principles that guide the food safety program for any establishment that serves food. Schools use an adapted version of HACCP called the process approach. The HACCP process approach provides strategies for preventing contamination of food at each stage of food handling. From the time food is purchased until meals are served, food service workers and teachers have important responsibilities to keep food safe and reduce the risk of foodborne illness.

Food safety is an important consideration for managing potential emergencies and natural disasters. In addition, teachers should be aware of the need to monitor for food defense and prevent potential intentional contamination of food.

Children are partners with teachers and families as they learn about food safety and ways they can participate in keeping food safe in their classroom. Teaching children about food safety helps create a safe food environment. Food safety habits are supported by consistent routines that are offered in age and developmentally appropriate ways, with ample opportunity for hands-on exploration.

Key Terms

Biological hazards, p. 248

Chemical hazards, p. 249

Cleaning, p. 269

Complex food preparation, p. 259

Contamination, p. 248

Corrective action plan, p. 260

Critical control points (CCPs), p. 259

Critical limits (CLs), p. 260

Cross-contamination, p. 254

First in, first out (FIFO), p. 266

Food Code, p. 260

Food defense, p. 278

Foodborne illness, p. 247

Hazard and Analysis Critical Control Point (HACCP) system, p. 256

No-cook process, p. 259

Physical hazards, p. 249

Potentially hazardous food, p. 257

Process approach, p. 259

Same-day service, p. 259

Sanitizing, p. 269

Standard operating procedures (SOPs), p. 261

Temperature danger zone, p. 259

Verification procedures, p. 260

Review Questions

1. Discuss three different types of hazards that can impact food safety.

2. Explain the seven principles that form the basis of the HACCP system and why this system is important for maintaining food safety.

3. Explain the methods to prevent contamination at each stage of food handling.

4. Describe how to maintain a safe food environment while children participate in cooking activities in the classroom and while going on a field trip.

5. Discuss how to develop an emergency food plan.

Discussion Starters

1. You have been asked by the director of your preschool program to participate on a hazard analysis committee with the goal of developing a food safety system using HACCP. Explain how you would determine the potential hazards and what steps you would take to develop a food safety system.

2. You are preparing a vegetable soup recipe with the preschool-age children in your class. Explain how you would incorporate a food safety message throughout the activity.

3. Explain the precautions and food safety concerns that need to be addressed during the receiving, storing, preparing, and serving of foods in an early child care setting.

Practice Points

1. Using the sample breakfast menu found in Chapter 7 (Figure 7-6) identify the foods that are potentially hazardous and the ideal temperatures at which they should be maintained.

2. Using Figure 8-9, identify the critical control points and critical limits in the following recipe:

Arroz con Queso

Ingredients	Serve 50
Enriched white rice, medium grain	2 lbs 13 oz.
Water	3½ cups
Fresh onions	1 quart
Canned green chilies, mild	12 oz.
Canned jalapeno pepper, chopped	½ cup
Granulated garlic	1 Tbsp + 1 tsp
Low fat plain yogurt	1 quart +1½ cups
Low fat milk, 1%	1 quart + 1 cup
Salt	2 tsp
Reduced fat Monterey jack cheese, shredded	1 lb
Reduced fat cheddar cheese, shredded	1 lb
Canned pinto beans	2 quarts + 1¼ cups
Fresh tomatoes	1 lb 8 oz.
Reduced fat cheddar cheese, shredded	1 lb 3 oz.

Directions	Critical Control Point (yes or no)	Critical Limit
1. Place rice and water in a stockpot. Bring to a boil. Cover and reduce heat to medium heat. Simmer for 12 minutes or until tender.		
2. Combine onions, chilies, jalapenos, granulated garlic, yogurt, milk, salt, reduced fat Monterey jack cheese, reduced fat cheddar cheese, and pinto beans. Add to rice. Spread 5 lbs 18 ounces in each steam table pan (12″ × 20″ × 2½″); will need two pans.		
3. Bake in conventional oven at 350°F for 35 minutes.		
4. Sprinkle 12 oz. of diced tomatoes and 9½ oz. of reduced fat cheddar cheese over the top of each pan and bake for 5 minutes until cheese is melted.		
Bonus question: What if dried pinto beans were used and cooked in advance to be used the next day—would there be any critical control points and, if so, what would they be?		

Source: Recipe used with permission from the USDA Recipes for Schools page located at the National Food Service Management Institute's website, updated 2006.

Note: For assistance with this Practice Point, refer to the National Food Service Management Institute at http://www.olemiss.edu/depts/nfsmi/Information/ school_recipe_index_alpha.html.

3. Your first-grade class is going to the pumpkin patch to select pumpkins. You arranged to have your school food service provide brown bag lunches for this field trip. A mother has volunteered to make pumpkin cookies to bring along. The pumpkin patch farm will demonstrate how apples are turned into fresh cider and will offer children a taste. What are the food safety risks and how would you manage them?

MyEducationLab

To assess your understanding of food safety issues in early childhood education settings, go to the Book Specific Resources section in the MyEducationLab for your course, select *Nutrition, Health, and Safety for Young Children,* Chapter 8 of the Study Plan, and then complete the multiple choice questions and activities.

Web Resources

FDA Food Code
www.fda.gov/Food/FoodSafety/RetailFoodProtection/FoodCode/default.htm

USDA Team Nutrition Healthy Meals Resource System
http://healthymeals.nal.usda.gov/nal_display/index.php?tax_level=1&info_center=14&tax_subject=221

USDA Team Nutrition Healthy Meals Resource System: Child Care Providers—Food Security and Emergency Preparedness
http://healthymeals.nal.usda.gov/nal_display/index.php?info_center=14&tax_level=3&tax_subject=264&topic_id=1269&level3_id=5264

Promoting Healthful Practices

part 3

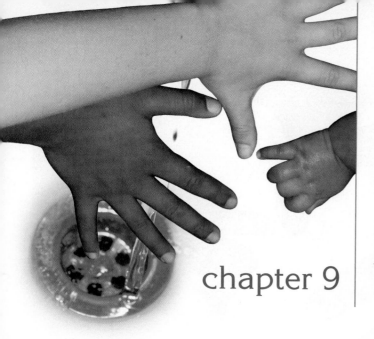

Creating a Climate of Health and Wellness

chapter 9

Learning Outcomes

After reading this chapter, you should be able to:

1. Define health and wellness and describe how they interrelate.

2. Identify the components of health and describe the determinants that affect health and illness.

3. Identify resources that inform the development of health policies in children's programs and schools and describe the components of a written health policy.

4. Describe health disparities and discuss strategies that teachers can use to promote acceptance and tolerance in the early childhood setting.

Cooper is a 7-year-old boy who was born with cystic fibrosis, a hereditary disease that affects the lungs and causes progressive disability in various body systems. He is a pleasant and hard-working child, and his teacher Deanie gets to know him well. She notices in particular that Cooper enjoys drawing pictures of alligators.

Cooper's mother, Alicia, lovingly and tirelessly cares for him. To provide for her family, Alicia works at a job that disqualifies her for Medicaid eligibility. Her employer does not offer health insurance, and because she is unable to afford frequent preventive health care visits and medications for Cooper, he does not receive the care he needs. Instead, his health care is fragmented and usually consists of urgent care visits.

Cooper's school environment is one of the most consistent aspects of his life. Alicia often turns to Deanie to help her cope with her home situation and for assistance with obtaining affordable health care services for Cooper. Deanie is glad that Alicia is open to discussions about Cooper's needs. It encourages her to learn more about ways she can support Cooper in the classroom. Reflecting on the challenges that Alicia faces, Deanie is inspired to plan a children's art show as part of the school open house. Alicia enjoys seeing her son's alligator drawings posted with the classroom display. Deanie takes advantage of the event to introduce Alicia to other parents during the parent meeting. Deanie presents her plans to conduct special health promotion activities in the classroom and then asks the parents for their ideas.

"Every child deserves to be born well, to be physically fit, and to achieve self-responsibility for good health habits" (National Center for Education in Maternal and Child Health [NCEMCH] & Georgetown University, 2008). These goals highlight the importance of creating surroundings that promote and nurture health and wellness in young children. The study of health and wellness is an important component in the professional development of teachers. Children spend a large portion of their day under the care and guidance of their teacher, and they rely on teachers for significant educational support and attention to their health and well-being. Teachers such as Deanie welcome the opportunity to significantly impact the lives of all children by creating healthy classroom environments. They also work to establish a positive and accepting atmosphere that helps each child feel valued and welcome. Together, a healthy environment and an accepting atmosphere create a climate of health and wellness.

In this chapter we introduce the foundations for establishing a climate of wellness. We begin the process by defining health and wellness and discussing the components of health that impact the lives of children. We present strategies for supporting the development of optimal health in young children, and explore the influences of health and culture on children's well-being. Creating a climate of health and wellness is an important teaching goal. The information explored in this chapter will assist you in achieving positive health outcomes for children.

HEALTH AND WELLNESS IN THE EARLY CHILDHOOD YEARS

Health and wellness are concepts that combine to create an overarching sense of well-being. They are interrelated, but different. Understanding the components and the determinants of health helps teachers to recognize that all children do not have the same opportunity for healthful outcomes. The environments in which children live make a significant impact on children's health.

Defining Health and Wellness

Health is a state of complete physical, mental, and social well-being, not merely the absence of disease or infirmity (World Health Organization [WHO], 2003a). Health is influenced by aspects such as genetic makeup, family history of disease, and age.

health
a state of complete
physical, mental, and
social well-being and
not merely the absence
of disease or infirmity

Wellness on the other hand is broader in perspective. It refers to optimal health and the vitality to enjoy life. Wellness is largely determined by lifestyle choices. These lifestyle choices encompass activities such as selecting healthful foods, obtaining preventive health services and following up with health care when needed, and experiencing safe environments.

Individuals cannot change some aspects of their health, but they can improve their health outcomes by making positive lifestyle choices and focusing on wellness goals. In this way health and wellness are interrelated, and the words are often used interchangeably to reflect a positive state of well-being.

Components of Health

Health is established through positive growth, development, and well-being in two major component areas: physical health and mental health. In young children, physical and mental health are essential to overall health and wellness. Each of these components influences the other.

physical health
level of functioning and
well-being individuals
feel with respect
to their bodies

Physical Health

Physical health refers to the condition of the body. It is established through a diet that provides appropriate nutrition, adequate exercise, and sufficient rest. When these conditions are addressed on a daily basis, children are supported in their efforts to develop good physical health.

acute conditions
medical conditions that
have a sudden onset
and short duration

Children's physical health may be compromised by either acute or chronic conditions. Acute conditions are those that have a sudden onset and short duration. Examples of acute illnesses include infectious diseases, such as upper respiratory infections, or childhood injuries, such as bone fractures or sprains. Chronic conditions have a long duration and require ongoing evaluation or treatment. Examples include malformations that are present at birth, called congenital conditions, genetic diseases, and autoimmune disorders. Many children with chronic illnesses are also susceptible, that is, at risk for or prone to acute illnesses. In the opening case scenario, for example, Cooper has a chronic condition called cystic fibrosis, which retards growth and causes frequent lung infections (such as upper respiratory infections and pneumonia), and premature death. His physical health is also likely to affect his mental health, as well his ability to learn and have healthy relationships in school.

chronic conditions
medical conditions that
have a long duration
and require ongoing
evaluation and/or
treatment

congenital conditions
physical defects or
malformations that are
present at birth

susceptible
at risk for or prone to

cystic fibrosis
chronic health condition
that causes growth
retardation and
frequent pulmonary
(lung) infections
and may lead to
premature death

Mental Health

Mental health is the ability to participate, communicate, and function in developmentally appropriate ways with respect to self, family, and peers (NCEMCH & Georgetown University, 2008). Mental health is enhanced by positive social and emotional development. For example, relationships that are loving, stable, and trusting promote positive mental health and wellness in children (NCEMCH & Georgetown University, 2008). Healthy relationships with caregivers and teachers also play a significant role in children's sense of social and emotional well-being. Mental health and wellness are discussed in more detail in Chapter 13.

mental health
the capacity to
experience and manage
emotions, form close
and secure
relationships, and learn
from and experience
the environment

Physical and mental health have an impact on one another. For example, the presence of a special physical need, such as decreased mobility due to an injury or a physical impairment, may negatively influence a child's mental health. On the other hand, children with mental health conditions, such as depression, may develop unhealthy habits that lead to problems in their physical health. In this chapter's case scenario, Cooper is unable to play actively with his peers because of his severe lung disease. This separation from typical physical play and interaction may predispose him to depression.

Determinants of Children's Health and Illness

determinants of health
risk factors or causative
factors that are
associated with a
health problem

Determinants of health are risk factors or causative factors associated with health and disease (Turnock, 2004). Understanding how these factors either cause or contribute to disease is important for developing treatment or intervention programs and for promoting health and wellness in the classroom. Both biological and social factors are determinants of health, as demonstrated in Figure 9-1.

Physical and mental health are interrelated and influence one another.

Biological Determinants of Health and Illness

Biological determinants of health are biological factors that are either present at birth or acquired. They include gene defects, infectious agents, and congenital malformations that can cause disease or contribute to its onset or severity. For example:

- Chronic illnesses, such as cystic fibrosis or Down syndrome, are present at birth because they result from a gene defect.
- Strep throat, bacterial meningitis, and chicken pox are acquired conditions, as all are infectious diseases.
- Congenital malformations such as malformations of the brain or other organs can result in lifelong medical problems affecting both physical and mental health.

Illnesses resulting from environmental toxins and physical injuries are also examples of biological determinants. For example:

- Health problems in children such as those that might result from lead poisoning or secondhand smoke exposure (Bortz, 2005) have clear biological causes.
- A child's physical health can be impacted from injuries sustained on the playground, such as a child who breaks a leg while falling off the climbing bars.

Social Determinants of Health and Illness

Social determinants of health are aspects of the social environment in which children live that influence health or disease (WHO, 2003b). These include race, ethnicity, socioeconomic status, poverty level, education level, housing conditions, and health behaviors. Among these, poverty has the most serious adverse impact on children's health and illness. Although poverty

biological determinants of health
biological factors that either cause a disease or contribute to its onset or severity

social determinants of health
aspects of the social environment related to people's lifestyles and conditions in which they live that contribute to health or disease

Figure 9-1 Biological and Social Determinants of Health

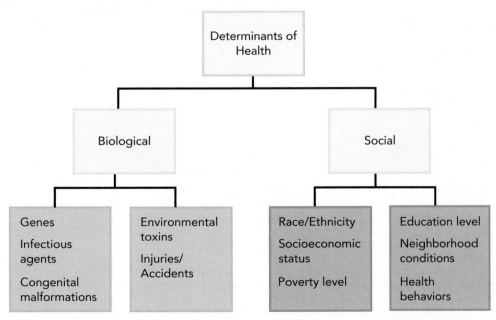

Source: Based on *Social determinants of health: The solid facts*, 2nd edition, by R. Wilkinson and M. Marmot, 2003, Copenhagen, Denmark: World Health Organization.

MyEducationLab

Go to the Assignments and Activities section of Topic 5: Health Promotion/Policy in the MyEducationLab for your course and complete the activity entitled *Meeting the Needs of Children from Low Income Households.* Consider all the ways in which Head Start programs promote health and wellness for young children.

is often thought of with respect to families or adults, children are actually the poorest group in the United States. More children are impoverished now than ever before (Ball & Bindler, 2006).

Children growing up in low-income families have disproportionately more risk factors that negatively impact physical and mental health than do children from higher income families (Fass & Cauthen, 2009). For example, children from low-income families are more likely to experience hunger or food insecurity. As a result, they may be susceptible to physical problems such as fatigue and abdominal pain, which, in turn, may impact their ability to focus on school activities and to learn. These children are much less likely to have had a doctor's visit or a dental visit in the last year (48%) compared to peers who are not poor (70%) (Stebbins & Knitzer, 2007). They are more likely to have physical health problems such as unmet health needs, stunted growth, and lead poisoning, as well as difficulty in school (Ball & Bindler, 2006). Impoverished children also are more likely to experience inadequate immunizations, higher rates of obesity, and more mental health problems (Emerson, 2009).

Poverty-related health problems are evident in the classroom because they encompass both physical and mental health. These negative effects may be observed in children who have suffered from periods of inadequate nutrition, who are overwhelmed by the activity of the classroom, or who lack sufficient energy to function appropriately in the group through the full day. Children may also react to the stress of the impoverished home environment by showing anxiety and difficulties with transitions or changes in routines. A summary of common health problems in children raised in low-income families and implications for teachers is shown in Table 9-1.

Table 9-1	**Common Health Problems Affecting Children Living in Poverty**	
Common Health Problems	**Possible Outcomes**	**Possible Solutions for Teachers**
Inadequate immunizations	• At risk for infectious disease. • Puts other children in classroom at risk.	• Refer to local health clinics, health department, or Community Health Centers.
Common infectious diseases	• School absences. • Increases spread of disease in group setting.	• Promote measures that prevent spread of diseases, such as hand washing.
Sleep deficits	• Difficulties learning. • Problems with attention.	• In child care and preschool, have quiet sleep time. • In school-age children, educate families and refer as needed.
Vision and hearing problems	• Learning problems.	• Conduct screenings. • Refer as needed.
Nutritional deficits	• Physical complaints. • Learning problems.	• Register children for school breakfast and lunch programs. • Refer to community resources.
Dental problems	• Increased risk for pain. • Problems with self-esteem.	• Teach and promote oral hygiene. • Promote screening. • Refer to dental programs.
Injuries		• Teach safety. • Refer to community resources for bike helmets, car seats, etc. • School absences. • Potential disability.
Mental illness	• Problems with self-esteem and peer relationships.	• Encourage extracurricular activities. • Provide links to services.

Source: Ball, Jane W., Bindler, Ruth, McGillis, W., *Child Health Nursing; Partnering with Children and Families.* (1st ed.). © 2006. Reproduced with permission of Pearson Education, Inc., Upper Saddle River, New Jersey.

Children's Health in the Context of Their Environments

The ecological systems theory described in Chapter 1 highlights the health impacts of the environments in which children develop (Bronfenbrenner, 1979). In the microsystem, families directly contribute to children's optimal health and development by meeting children's need for nourishment, providing immunizations, and correcting unsafe conditions in the environment. Positive communications between families and teachers (mesosystem) contribute to the continuity in children's care and provide opportunities for parents and teachers to align teaching approaches in the home and school settings that support children's well-being. Maintaining sanitary conditions in the neighborhood (exosystem) contributes to children's health and well-being. A commitment to health goals for all people in the larger community and social systems (macrosystems) ensures the development of public policies that provide for access to health care. Each aspect of the ecological system contributes to the climate of health and wellness that is crucial to children's optimal development and the attainment of good health.

The early childhood setting and schools play an important role in creating climates of health and wellness through the contexts of Bronfenbrenner's microsystem and mesosystem. When teachers create these healthful environments and develop positive relationships with families, they help to surround children with positive environments in which their needs can be recognized and services can be identified.

Influencing Health and Wellness in the Early Childhood Setting

Learning the skills that promote wellness is a lifelong process that begins when children are very young. Young children depend on adults to make healthy choices for them and to teach them to make choices for themselves (American Academy of Pediatrics [AAP], American Public Health Association [APHA], & National Resource Center for Health and Safety in Child Care and Early Education, 2002). Because children are in a continuous state of absorbing information and learning, they are particularly receptive to aspects in their environment that facilitate learning about health and wellness. At the same time they are also vulnerable to the forces that can obstruct their health. These include challenges such as a poor level of wellness in the family, unsafe communities, and an inability for society to create health policies that support all children (Prilleltensky & Nelson, 2000).

Families and teachers are children's sources for establishing lifestyles that promote wellness. The early childhood years are a time in which children learn the self-help behaviors that positively impact health, such as washing hands and eating a variety of healthy foods. Behaviors that encourage a healthy lifestyle, such as playing actively and getting sufficient sleep, are also introduced and practiced during the early years, setting the stage for health-promoting behaviors across a lifetime. Attention to these responsibilities is important because children in the early years have an increased susceptibility to certain infectious diseases and illnesses.

In addition, many chronic, or ongoing, conditions seen in adulthood such as obesity, heart disease, cancer, and mental health problems have their roots in early childhood (Wilensky & Satcher, 2009). Parents and teachers play an important role in teaching children lifestyle habits that minimize the potential of such diseases occurring. This is a remarkable and exciting opportunity for teachers to positively affect children's lifelong development. This chapter's *Policy Point* describes how characteristics of the preschool environment can influence physical activity.

In the opening case scenario, Cooper comes to the classroom with complex medical problems. In addition, certain individual and environmental variables influence the severity of his illness. Some characteristics of Cooper's life are risk factors, aspects that suggest he is at high risk for disease, whereas others are protective factors, aspects that promote health. For example, being uninsured and having inconsistent health care are risk factors that negatively affect his health; yet having a supportive, loving mother and consistently caring and responsible caregivers are protective factors that positively affect his health.

Understanding the biological and social determinants that impact children guides teachers to establish protective approaches in the classroom. For example, growing up in a poor neighborhood where children are often not free to play outdoors because of unsafe

risk factors
biological or social aspects of health that increase risk of illness or disease

protective factors
biological or social aspects that promote health and wellness

CHARACTERISTICS OF THE PRESCHOOL ENVIRONMENT THAT INFLUENCE PHYSICAL ACTIVITY

The National Association for Sport and Physical Education recommends that all preschool children (ages 3 to 5 years) participate in up to 60 minutes of structured activities *and* 60 minutes of unstructured play every day. Most children's settings do not provide this level of active play. Characteristics of children's environments influence time spent in moderate and vigorous physical activity. Children are more active in:

- Higher quality programs, such as those that have wellness policies.
- Settings with large playground spaces where children can run and be active.
- Schools with more portable equipment, such as balls and hoops that encourage children to plan and direct their own active play.
- Settings that limit the use of electronic media, which contribute to sedentary play rather than active play.

Sources: Based on *Policies and characteristics of the preschool environment and physical activity of young children* by M. Dowda, W. Brown, Karin A. McIver, J. Pfeiffer, C. O'Neill, et al., 2009, Pediatrics, 123, e261–e266; and *Active start: A statement of physical activity guidelines for children birth to five years,* by the National Association for Sport and Physical Education, 2002, Reston, VA: Author.

conditions may compromise children's physical health. Teachers address this by providing opportunities for children to play actively in safely supervised outdoor environments. Overall, children who live in disadvantaged neighborhoods often benefit even more than children living in higher income neighborhoods from school health screenings, classroom activities relevant to health promotion, and referral to needed community resources, simply because access to these services outside of the school setting is inadequate due to the impacts of poverty and lack of access to usual health care. The *Health Hint* describes how characteristics of neighborhoods influence children's health.

Although children may come to the classroom with circumstances that are out of the teacher's control, teachers promote children's health by giving them tools to protect

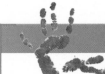

Health Hint

Neighborhoods and Children's Well-Being

Living in poor and racially isolated neighborhoods negatively influences children's health. Disadvantages that affect children include:

- Poorly performing schools.
- Higher rates of crime.
- Substandard housing.
- Limited access to grocery stores and healthy food choices.

Higher neighborhood poverty rates are associated with worse measures of children's well-being:

- The number of children who are read to at home decreases.
- The ability to participate in school outings decreases.
- The number of caretakers with poor mental health increases.
- Negative behaviors increase.
- School engagement decreases.

Sources: Based on *Poor Neighborhoods Create Health "Double Jeopardy" for Minority Kids,* by T. English, March 11, 2008, Washington, DC: Center for the Advancement of Health, retrieved September 23, 2009, from http://www.cfah.org/hbns/archives/getDocument.cfm?documentID=1674; and *How Does Family Well-Being Vary Across Different Types of Neighborhoods?* by M. Turner and D. Kaye, 2006, Washington, DC: The Urban Institute.

themselves, such as warding off germs, practicing safety procedures, or communicating appropriately about their worries and frustrations. Teachers observe children throughout the day and are often the first to know when a child's hunger or thirst is getting in the way of learning. They have the authority to make sure children get outside daily to run and be active, and can institute a policy of teeth brushing after lunch. These practices counterbalance some of the negative factors existing in children's lives. By incorporating practices in the classroom that focus on physical, mental, and emotional health, teachers help children learn behaviors that optimize their long-term health outcomes (Wilensky & Satcher, 2009).

Teachers also contribute to children's healthful development by getting to know each family's social circumstances and the challenges that may impact children's wellness. Teachers arrange opportunities to:

- Promote the development of positive relationships between teachers and parents.
- Increase parental knowledge of children's cognitive and emotional needs.
- Encourage children's healthy social development and behavior.
- Prevent child abuse.

CHILD HEALTH POLICIES

A climate of wellness in the early childhood and school setting is founded on supportive health policies. Health policies are guidelines that define a desired health outcome, such as promoting healthy behaviors or preventing the spread of disease. These policies ensure that safe and appropriate health practices are in place. They also help to guide decision making about how to manage confusing or difficult situations. Health policies in the early childhood and school setting demonstrate that children's health is recognized as a vital aspect of well-being. Developing health policies with goals for optimal nutrition, health, and safety builds a climate of wellness in which children can thrive.

Developing Policies to Promote and Protect Health

Health policies are developed to address common health and safety issues in early childhood and school settings. Specific policies are required by national, state, and local agencies that license children's programs. In addition, national agencies that promote quality standards for children's programs make policy recommendations to improve services for children. Accrediting organizations also outline minimum standards for programs they endorse. These groups compel children's programs to develop policies and practices that are designed to achieve health and safety goals.

Resources for Health Policy Development

A variety of resources are available to guide the development of relevant program health policies. The resources discussed next aim to improve services to young children by establishing best practice goals.

The National Resource Center for Health and Safety in Child Care and Early Education

The National Resource Center for Health and Safety in Child Care and Early Education (NRC) takes the lead in communicating standards that inform child health policies. The NRC is funded by the Maternal and Child

> **What if. . .**
> you were teaching in an area with low-income families? What are some health risks that children in your classroom might encounter? Can you think of some useful activities that you could implement in your setting to positively contribute to their health and well-being?

health policies
guidelines that define a desired health outcome, such as promoting healthy behaviors or preventing the spread of disease

Health and safety policies help teachers establish healthful environments and implement safe practices in the classroom.

Health Bureau of the U.S. Department of Health and Human Services (HHS). The NRC website provides a variety of resources that support health and safety in out-of-home care and education settings:

- *Health and safety standards:* The primary information needed to develop policies that promote health and safety in children's programs is available through the publication *Caring for Our Children: National Health and Safety Performance Standards: Guidelines for Out-of-Home Child Care Programs* (AAP, APHA, & NRC, 2002). This resource presents the rationale for policies that guide health practices and sets the standards for quality in healthful programming.
- *Licensure regulations:* The licensing regulations of the 50 states, the District of Columbia, Puerto Rico, and the Virgin Islands are available for review and comparison. The minimum policies that must be established in licensed family child care and early education programs are presented.
- *Standards-based resources:* User-friendly materials on specific subjects provide information for the development of policies such as how to administer medications in children's settings and when to exclude sick children from care.

Health policies are a requirement for licensed programs. Licensing requirements are established and managed by each state and, in some cases, by counties or cities. Written policies demonstrate how the children's program will meet the health and safety licensing requirements. More importantly, they describe the program's commitment to health and safety.

Decisions about policies are generally managed by program directors, principals, or school district managers. Some programs collaborate with community health providers and have their policies reviewed by a health services advisory committee. However, teachers should be familiar with the licensing requirements and well aware of the policies that guide practice in their setting. The NRC's guidelines for health and safety in children's programs are a ready resource.

Office of Head Start

The Office of Head Start provides the *Head Start Performance Standards* (HHS Administration for Children and Families, 2007), which outline a variety of nutrition, health, and safety policies for Early Head Start, Head Start, American Indian/Alaska Native, and Migrant Seasonal Head Start programs nationwide. Head Start programs are required to develop policies and practices related to:

- Child health and development.
- Child health and safety.
- Child nutrition.
- Child mental health.

National Association for the Education of Young Children

The National Association for the Education of Young Children (NAEYC) is a professional organization committed to increasing the quality of programs that serve children from birth through age 8. They offer several systems of accreditation (endorsement) to acknowledge programs that meet national standards of quality.

accreditation endorsement or acknowledgment of programs that meet national standards of quality

NAEYC accreditation assesses quality in 10 program standards. Topic areas in the health standards include:

- Promoting and protecting children's health and controlling infectious disease.
- Ensuring children's nutritional well-being.
- Maintaining a healthful environment.

School Wellness Policies

In 2004, Congress passed the Child Nutrition and Women, Infants, and Children (WIC) Reauthorization Act. As previously discussed in Chapter 6, this act requires that all school districts with federally funded school meal programs develop and implement school wellness policies. The responsibility of developing specific wellness policies is placed on the school districts so that each can address its own unique challenges. The wellness policies must address the following (Centers for Disease Control and Prevention, 2009):

- Goals for nutrition education, physical activity, and other school-based activities designed to promote wellness.
- Guidelines for all food available on school property.
- Guidelines for reimbursable school meals.
- Plans for community involvement including parents, students, and representatives of the school food authority, school board, school administrators and the public in the development of the school wellness policy.
- Plans for measuring implementation of the wellness policies.

Table 9-2 summarizes examples of policies that are conducive to health and wellness in the early childhood setting.

Table 9-2	Developing Policies That Promote Health and Wellness
Policy Topic	**Examples**
NUTRITION	
Appropriate eating environments	• Provide clean, safe enjoyable eating environment for meals. • Encourage students to participate in school meal programs and protect the privacy of students who eat free or reduced-price meals.
Healthful eating schedule	• Provide adequate time to eat. • Schedule recess before lunch.
Avoiding the use of food and physical activity as reward or punishment	• Use of food as reward or punishment should be prohibited. • Restricting or denying time in physical activities should be prohibited as a form of discipline or homework makeup time.
School activities and environment that promote consistent messages about food and activity	• Fund-raising activities should be supportive of healthy eating. • Teachers should practice healthy eating and serve as role models. • Foods provided in vending machines and offered at school events should meet nutrition goals.
HEALTH	
Hand washing	• Children will wash hands at arrival. • Teachers and children will wash hands at appropriate times: after toileting or diapering, before eating, before and after playing in the water table.
Control of disease	• Children will have up-to-date immunizations before entry into the classroom. • Teachers will teach children about covering their mouths when they cough and when to wash hands. • Information will be provided to help parents recognize when children should stay home from school.
Cleaning	• Restrooms will be cleaned daily and during the day as needed. • Toys will be cleaned whenever they are put into children's mouths or once per week.
SAFETY	
Enrollment	• Obtain emergency contact, health history, and immunization records before children enroll. • Orient families to arrival and departure procedures.
Supervision	• Supervise children by sight and sound. • Establish play spaces to support appropriate supervision.
Outdoor play	• Review the play area for safety every day. • Ensure that gates are closed. • Provide appropriate surfacing under play equipment.

MyEducationLab

Go to the Assignments and Activities section of Topic 5: Health Promotion/Policy in the MyEducationLab for your course and complete the activity entitled *Developing Health Policies and Goals*. What goals have these teachers established to promote health and wellness in their school?

Components of Health Policies

Written health policies need to be clearly and briefly stated and easy to understand and follow. Guidelines for writing health policies include the following:

1. *State prevention goals.* Policies are developed to prevent problems. They are usually written in the form of goals that promote positive health outcomes. For example: *Health checks will be conducted daily* or *Children will be supervised by sight and sound.*

2. *Identify steps to achieve the policy goals.* List the steps, or procedures, to take to implement the policy. Procedures should be specific and identify who will do what. For example: *The lead teacher will greet children at the door and conduct a 20-second health check. Identified concerns will be discussed with the parent.*

3. *Guide response to difficult situations.* Policies must also direct appropriate response to challenging situations. In the health check example, this might include: *If signs of illness are observed, communicate kindly but firmly that the parent must take the child home.*

4. *Ensure procedures are practical and specific to the setting.* Lists of policies established for early childhood and school settings will be similar. However, the procedures for implementing each policy may be different to accommodate the particular setting. Health checks in a preschool setting may be conducted as children and parents arrive. Health checks in the school setting may be conducted during an opening circle activity after children have arrived on the bus.

An important health policy area concerns food allergies. The *Nutrition Note* provides an example related to nut allergies.

Nutrition Note

Policies Relevant to Nut Allergies in Young Children

Peanut allergies are of particular concern to children's health because of the potential for serious, life-threatening reactions. Many early childhood and school settings have developed policies to address this issue:

- A "no nut" policy may be an appropriate approach for settings that serve children with known nut allergies. This means no nuts of any kind or products prepared with nut oil will be served.
- A policy of "no food sharing" is also important so that children with food allergies do not inadvertently eat foods that contain the allergens.

Studies report that two-thirds of fatal allergic reactions occur at school. The situations when children are most at risk for exposure to nut products include:

- Break times, when snacks might be shared.
- Lunchtimes, when foods may be traded.
- Parties, where festive foods made with nut products may be brought into the setting.
- School trips, where children may share snacks or lunches.
- Cooking projects, art, and science activities, where supplies for projects introduce nut products.

With the increasing prevalence of allergies and the severity of reactions, it is critical for children's settings to have policies that define the symptoms related to acute reaction and procedures for what to do if an allergic reaction occurs. Teachers need to be given training on how to identify and respond to nut allergy emergencies.

Source: Based on "Nut Allergies in Schoolchildren: A Survey of Schools in the Seven NHS Trust," by J. Watura, 2002, *Archives of Disease in Childhood, 86,* pp. 240–244.

Safety Segment

Accessing Health and Safety Advice

Planning policies and implementing procedures that promote children's health requires attention to safety details. It is important that health policies do not introduce risks or over-look opportunities to improve children's safety. Obtaining advice from knowledgeable individuals helps teachers improve their classroom practices. Program health and safety policies should be reviewed from a variety of health perspectives, including those of:

- Parents.
- Community health providers.
- Dietitians.
- Sanitarians.
- Child care licensing workers.
- Community safety workers.

Ensuring Policies Are Appropriate for the Setting

Some programs serving young children invite local health consultants to advise on the development of health policies. For instance, Head Start programs convene a Health Services Advisory Committee of parents and professionals to participate in developing and reviewing health policies. This ensures that wellness goals are based on current knowledge and practice. The *Safety Segment* describes how to access the types of people who can provide health and safety advice.

Obtaining the advice of community health workers also helps to identify policies that are needed to address health and safety concerns unique to a certain community. For example, a preschool situated in an area where air quality may pose a health risk should develop a policy related to outdoor play. The policy should describe how the program will determine when air quality is at an unhealthy level (if a smog alert has been issued) and where the children will play if an alert has been announced (AAP, APHA, & NRC, 2002). A school in a metropolitan area where violence is frequently reported might develop policies related to teaching a violence prevention curriculum. The policy would state what curriculum approaches would be used and how often the prevention interventions would be conducted. Health policies should be reviewed periodically, and new policies should be developed when necessary to improve program services.

Policies Promoting Oral Health

Childhood tooth decay, or dental caries, is the most common and preventable chronic disease in childhood (Gehshan & Wyatt, 2007; Lapin & Smith, 2008). Research shows that proper dental care and oral hygiene can significantly decrease dental problems that lead to tooth decay, infection, and illness (Lapin & Smith, 2008).

Young children are capable learners, making the early childhood setting uniquely suited to promoting oral health. Schools can promote oral health through education and dental care services. For children who lack health insurance and are very unlikely to receive usual, regular dental care, such as Cooper at the beginning of the chapter, school-based oral health promotion is the only access to dental care available to protect the health of their mouth and teeth.

dental caries
tooth decay; is the most common and preventable chronic disease in childhood

Oral Health Education

Policies that direct teachers to offer oral hygiene education and encourage toothbrushing after meals contribute to better oral health. Teachers are responsible for planning and implementing these health education activities. The goals for oral health education include helping children understand why their teeth are important and how brushing and seeing a dentist help keep teeth healthy (California Dental Association, n.d.).

MyEducationLab

Go to the Assignments and Activities section of Topic 13: Wellness Curriculum in the MyEducationLab for your course and complete the activity entitled *Teaching Children Health Lessons*. What strategies does this teacher use to reinforce the importance of brushing teeth?

Collaboration with community partners is helpful. In Boyd County, Kentucky, a school collaborated with a local dentist who hosted video conferences explaining how to maintain a healthy mouth. Teachers provided articles and newsletters on good oral health to parents (Lapin & Smith, 2008). Teachers of toddlers and preschool-age groups might read books about taking care of teeth or dramatize a trip to the dentist using puppets. Preschool settings may also provide toothbrushes and toothpaste for children (Lapin & Smith, 2008).

The NAEYC (2005) has identified an emerging practice guideline for accredited early childhood programs that relates to early dental care for infants. The guideline describes how oral health education begins in infancy. The guideline states:

> NAEYC Accreditation Criterion 5.A.13: After each feeding, infant's teeth and gums are wiped with a disposable tissue (or clean soft cloth used only for one child and laundered daily) to remove liquid that coats the teeth and gums. (p. 21)

Proper nutrition also contributes to the prevention of tooth decay. Teaching proper nutrition and serving meals rich in whole grains, fruits, and vegetables are ways to promote oral health. Teachers in Independence, Missouri, designated Friday as "Nutrition Day." Teachers incorporated fruits and vegetables into the regular classroom activities. Newsletters were sent to parents with recipes and activities to promote healthy nutrition (Lapin & Smith, 2008). The *Teaching Wellness* feature describes ways to teach children about the importance of brushing teeth.

Dental Care Services

Oral health in children has become a priority for early childhood health. The Office of Head Start initiated the Head Start Oral Health Initiative for Young Children in 2005, providing supplemental funding for programs to improve their oral health services for enrolled children. School policies that implement dental care services are of great benefit to children. Strategies to provide dental care services in schools include screening for dental problems, promoting school-affiliated or school-based dental care services, and providing fluoride varnish or dental sealants (Gehshan & Wyatt, 2007; Lapin & Smith, 2008).

A variety of dental services can be provided at school-based health clinics or school-affiliated clinics. In Bridgeport, Connecticut, the local health department operates a school-based health center that provides comprehensive dental services once a week including sealants, fillings, and minor extractions. In Little Rock, Arkansas, collaboration between the school district and the Head Start program provides fluoride varnishes to all preschoolers (Lapin & Smith, 2008).

What if . . .

you wanted to teach oral hygiene in your kindergarten class by having the children brush their teeth each day after their snack? What procedures would you need to consider to prevent the spread of germs during toothbrushing? Would you offer toothpaste? Why or why not?

Policies Preventing Disease

Health policies are needed to prevent the spread of disease in the children's setting. Infectious diseases are illnesses that are spread from one child to another through various modes of physical contact. Infectious diseases are commonly spread in any group setting including child care and school settings. To prevent the spread of disease in preschools or primary classroom settings, teachers can employ policies regarding hand washing, room sanitation, and exclusion of children who are ill. Infants and toddlers are particularly vulnerable to infections and, in childhood settings, can have repeated exposures (Wittmer & Peterson, 2006).

infectious diseases
diseases caused by microorganisms that spread from person to person or animal to person by eating contaminated food or water, or other exposure

HEALTH PROMOTION AMONG DIVERSE POPULATIONS

Acknowledging the value and belief systems of children and families from culturally diverse backgrounds is a critical aspect of understanding and promoting health and wellness. An individual's race, culture, and ethnic background influence how they perceive health and illness throughout the life span (Spector, 2009). As discussed in Chapter 1, the demographics of infants and children enrolled in schools and early childhood settings has changed significantly during the past several decades. The cultural composition of families in the United States is becoming increasingly diverse. With more children from a variety of backgrounds in schools today, it is important to understand and acknowledge differing perspectives related to health and health promotion.

Disparities in Quality of Health Care and Quality of Health

Not all families experience the same quality of health care or even the same quality of health. These differences are called health disparities. The roots of health disparities are complex, but can be due to differences in resources and opportunities to obtain needed health care. Examples of disparities in health care include differences in access to immunizations and preventive health care. Some children who are new immigrants to the United States may have experienced substandard medical care resulting in undiagnosed and untreated medical conditions. Children from certain areas of the United States may have been denied health care because of inadequate community health services. Some families have ready access to health care through insurance programs, and they are comfortable using these resources. Others delay accessing medical treatment until health conditions become dire because they do not know how to access the care or cannot afford the cost.

Language may be a barrier for some families. Teachers gain a needed perspective about the potential challenges the families face when they build relationships with each child's family. This knowledge guides teachers to understand the contexts in which the children live and ways the teacher can support the family with information and guidance on health matters. Teachers are usually not health professionals. However, teachers are important links to the resources that are available in the community. Health care professionals and teachers should be aware that these disparities exist and work to help all families access the help they need.

Disparities in the quality of health are more deeply related to social causes. For example, children's early nutrition can influence health outcomes as they grow. Children who experience malnutrition will have worse health outcomes. Children whose families are exposed to discrimination may have adverse health outcomes. Children living in unsafe neighborhoods or in impoverished living conditions will have a higher risk of health problems. Again, teachers may not be able to directly influence a child's living conditions or prior history of malnutrition but, through family support and health promotion, the chances of the child having better health will be greater.

Recognizing Stereotypes and Prejudice

Disparities exist in health care but also in other settings that serve diverse racial, cultural, and socioeconomic groups, such as classrooms. Teachers come to classrooms with their own backgrounds, beliefs, and past experiences. Although they may be conscious of discriminatory practices and work to avoid them, there are other subtle ways in which children and families of diverse backgrounds are treated differently. Stereotyping and prejudice often lead to intolerance:

- **Stereotyping** results when individuals are labeled based on certain characteristics such as racial or ethnic heritage, age, gender, or socioeconomic background. An example of stereotyping is evident when teachers make the assumption that "all" boys prefer to play with trucks, or "all" children of a particular racial group are good at math or are more expressive. Often individuals are not conscious of the way they stereotype others.
- **Prejudice** refers to a negative attitude toward an individual based on group membership (Institute of Medicine [IOM], 2003). Prejudice is fueled by intolerance. It is

> ## What if. . .
> you are a preschool teacher for a culturally diverse population and you encountered a family that used unusual home remedies to treat a chronic cough? What would be your initial impression of this decision? What health issues would you be concerned about? How would you handle your concerns with the family?

health disparities
differences in health outcomes and quality of health and health care experienced by people of different incomes, races, or education levels

stereotyping
the labeling of others based on certain characteristics such as racial or ethnic heritage, age, gender, or socioeconomic background

prejudice
a negative attitude toward an individual based on group membership

Teaching Wellness   *Brushing My Teeth Keeps My Smile Healthy*

Learning Outcome: Children will learn how to brush their teeth.

Infants and Toddlers

- *Goal:* To promote children's willingness to have their gums wiped and teeth brushed.

- *Materials:* Damp washcloth or gauze, toothbrushes with pea-sized dab of toothpaste, paper cups, and paper towels.

- *Activity plan:* For infants without teeth, gently wipe the gums with a damp cloth. Describe what you are doing by saying, "You are keeping your mouth open while I help clean your gums." Say words that convey interest and pleasure, such as "I like to brush my teeth because it makes them feel so clean and healthy."

- *How to adjust the activity:* For infants with teeth, use a small, soft toothbrush to brush teeth and gums. For toddlers, model toothbrushing with a toothbrush. Do not use toothpaste until toddlers are 2 years of age. Talk through the process while modeling and encouraging the child through each step. Say, "First let's brush the front of the tooth, then the sides and then the back." Help children by guiding their hand and when needed by brushing their teeth. To keep them interested sing a song such as the "ABC Song" twice or a tooth song that you make up. For example, sing this to the tune of "Row, Row, Row Your Boat": "Brush, brush, brush, your teeth, brush them twice a day. This will keep them clean and white and help prevent decay." When the children have brushed sufficiently say, "Now let's spit into the cup."

- *Did you meet your goal?* Were children willing to have their gums wiped or teeth brushed? Did the toddlers imitate the steps in appropriate toothbrushing?

Preschoolers and Kindergartners

- *Goal:* To learn to brush teeth appropriately and know that toothbrushing is important.

- *Materials:* Toothbrushes with a pea-sized drop of toothpaste, paper cups, sink with running water, paper towels, a children's book, model of large teeth and a large toothbrush, the book *Clarabella's Teeth* by An Vrombaut.

- *Activity plan:* Have children sit in a circle at a round table. Place a toothbrush and a paper cup with a dab of toothpaste on the edge beside each child. Read the book *Clarabella's Teeth*. Talk about why it is important to brush teeth (to remove food particles that can cause cavities). Show the steps of brushing teeth by demonstrating with the model teeth and large toothbrush. Reinforce the steps of toothbrushing by having children brush their teeth:
  - Have children dab the toothbrush against the toothpaste.
  - Hold the toothbrush at a 45-degree angle; brush front, back, sides of each tooth.
  - Hold the brush flat on top of the teeth and brush them too.
  - Gently brush the tongue.
  - Spit toothpaste into the cup.
  - Rinse toothbrush and return to the child's place in the toothbrush rack.

- *How to adjust the activity:* Obtain and sanitize a Styrofoam egg carton. Cut the egg cups from the carton in strips of 3 egg cups in a row; these strips will be the children's "pretend teeth." Place these in a sensory table with puffs of shaving cream and large toothbrushes. Have the children practice brushing the pretend teeth. Talk about why it is important to brush teeth. Discuss when toothbrushing is important, such as after eating, before going to bed, and when getting up in the morning.

- *Did you meet your goal?* Are children able to brush teeth appropriately? When asked, are children able to tell why it is important to brush teeth?

School-Age Children

- *Goal:* To learn how to carefully brush teeth and understand that toothbrushing removes germs that cause cavities.

- *Materials:* Toothbrushes, paper cups with dab of toothpaste, paper cups with water, disposable dentist mirror, plaque-disclosing tablet, sink with running water, monthly calendar printed on a white sheet of paper, crayons or marking pens.

- *Activity plan:* Have children sit around a table. Discuss how to brush teeth. Have children brush teeth and spit toothpaste into a cup. Ask the children to look at their teeth with a disposable mirror and describe what they see. Do they see any germs? Talk about how you cannot see germs because they are so small. Describe how germs can hide in the cracks and crevices of the teeth and explain why germs can be harmful to the teeth. Point out that germs cause plaque and when plaque sticks to the teeth it causes cavities. Demonstrate to children how to use the plaque-disclosing tablet:
  - Chew on tablet first on one side of the mouth and then on the other. Spit into a cup.

- Have children use their mirrors to look at their teeth again. Do they see red and pink? Say to them, "This is plaque that didn't come off your teeth and can cause cavities." Have them brush their teeth until the color is removed. Look again with their mirrors. Is the color removed? Have children rinse their toothbrushes and return them to the toothbrush rack. Talk about what happened when they brushed their teeth after using the plaque-disclosing tablet. Have children explain why it is important to take their time when they brush their teeth.

- *How to adjust the activity:* Have children decorate a monthly calendar with pictures of teeth and smiles. Post the calendar on the wall. Have children place a mark on the calendar each day that they brush their teeth at school.

- *Did you meet your goal?* Are children able to show how to brush teeth carefully and describe why brushing teeth is important?

evident when teachers group children according to certain characteristics rather than by an understanding of each individual child's skills and needs. For example, the teacher may create a seating arrangement that places the low-income children at the front of the room based on her perception that they will not pay attention if they choose their own seats.

Stereotyping and prejudice can result in discrimination or inequality and unfair treatment. Discrimination exists in health care, education, housing, employment, and other aspects of society. Exposure to discrimination is associated with poor health outcomes (IOM, 2003). Not only must teachers embrace children and their families' differences, they should also ensure that there is acceptance and tolerance among all children in their classrooms.

When the quality of health care delivered to families is substandard, teachers can serve as advocates to support families. The following is an example of the teacher as an advocate:

Anadelia, a child in Shauna's first-grade class, is missing a needed immunization. Her mother, Consuelo, tells Shauna that she has taken her daughter twice to the local clinic to obtain the shot. Both times they were turned away by the receptionist who told them Anadelia did not need any more shots. Consuelo is concerned because the school nurse has told her that Anadelia will be excluded from class if the immunizations are not brought up to date. Consuelo asks Shauna for help.

Shauna and the school nurse collaborate to help Consuelo obtain an appointment to discuss vaccination details with a nurse or doctor. Consuelo returns

What if . . .

a child in your program has recently arrived from a different country? The child's family does not speak English well and does not have health insurance. What will you do to support the family to get the health care they need? Who would you contact? How could you help them gain access to the resources they need?

to the physician's office where Anadelia receives the needed immunization. Shauna reflects on the situation, and feels frustrated that this family was not given sufficient encouragement to sort out the child's needs on the first visit. Was it because the family is Hispanic?

Promoting Acceptance in the Classroom

Teachers set the standard for acceptance and tolerance in the classroom and among children's families. This is demonstrated when teachers strive to interact equitably with all children and families, regardless of their backgrounds and unique characteristics. Teaching children to understand and appreciate differences is one way to promote acceptance. Activities to introduce this complex concept should begin simply and become more detailed, as shown in the following examples:

Sandi offers toddlers and preschoolers many opportunities to sort and classify objects while introducing the concepts of "same" and "different." To begin, she offers items that have only one aspect that is different, such as square blocks of the same size, in two different colors. Children learn to sort by color. Next she increases the challenge by offering both square blocks and small balls in two colors. In this task children are able to sort by color and shape. Activities such as these engage children in interesting discovery of how objects can have characteristics that are the same and at the same time have aspects that are different: Red blocks and red balls are the same color, but have different shapes.

Al engages older children in exploration of personal characteristics that may be the same (Who has five fingers?) and those that may be different (Who has brown hair?). He and the children make lists of the many ways children in the class are the same and different. They begin to understand that a great variety of similarities and differences exist among people. On another day he has the children move to two areas of the room, sorting themselves into groups according to his directions. He offers them choices, such as these: Move to the window if you like to play soccer best or move to the door if you prefer basketball.

He offers a variety of different choice pairs and asks the children to notice who is in their group each time. At the end of the activity, he gathers the children to review what they have learned. The children are able to notice that each time they sort according to their preferences the resulting groups vary. Although each group is usually comprised of several children who made the same choice (sameness), the groups are usually a different combination of children (difference).

Learning about how objects are the same and different is a first step in recognizing and accepting differences in people and ideas.

From these activities children begin to recognize that personal characteristics and personal choices are sometimes the same and sometimes different. Lessons like these plant the ideas that help children to resist stereotyping: Not all people are the same and not all people like the same thing. They also help children learn to oppose prejudice, as the children begin to see themselves as sometimes members of one group (the group that loves soccer, for example) and sometimes members of another group.

Learning to recognize and enjoy differences and to develop a tolerance of differing points of view is a lifelong process. Teachers who model accepting behaviors and who encourage children to explore these topics offer children the opportunity to develop skills of negotiation, problem solving, and appreciation of the rights of self and others.

Supporting Families Who Do Not Speak English

Communication between teachers and parents is critical to children's well-being. Teachers need to be able to discuss the child's educational progress, describe any observed health concerns, and share information about behavioral or social issues. Likewise parents need to be able to inform teachers of any health issues or other concerns they may have about the child. As discussed in Chapter 1, a growing percentage of children come from family's whose first language is one other than English. This means that teachers need a plan to overcome language barriers when communicating with families.

For casual conversations or communicating with families about everyday classroom activities, teachers may be able to involve other family members or even older children as interpreters. When discussing sensitive or confidential issues, however, including health issues, teachers may need to seek the assistance of interpreters to establish needed communication with families. Using English-speaking family members may be a convenient alternative, but it does have some disadvantages. Family members may not be objective and may filter information instead of translating exactly what has been said. This is particularly troublesome in situations involving details of the child's health or behavior. Confidentiality may be compromised when family members are used as interpreters (AAP & Migrant Clinician Network, 2000). Older children who speak English are sometimes used as interpreters. In terms of obtaining medical histories or conveying health information, however, this practice places inappropriate responsibility on the child and has been shown to seriously affect the quality and quantity of information obtained.

Trained interpreters offer an appropriate but expensive option. When this is a viable option, trained interpreters should have the following skills, which are extremely helpful in communicating important information (AAP & Migrant Clinician Network, 2000):

- Demonstrated fluency in both languages being spoken.
- Recognition of colloquial differences among people who speak the same language but are from different countries. Families from Mexico, for example, may use special phrases that are different from Spanish speakers from Chile or Spain.
- Understanding of cultural differences that impact the communication process.
- Clarity about their role and awareness so they do not filter information.
- Recognition of their limitations.
- An understanding of the importance of confidentiality.

When teachers do not have ready access to the assistance of trained interpreters, alternative strategies are needed. These may include:

- Prioritize when trained interpreters are most needed, such as to assist with family conferences or meetings to plan services for children with special developmental needs.
- Identify workers at community health service agencies who are bilingual. Establish connections to support families that you refer to those agencies.
- Create or obtain simple printed bilingual messages related to common early childhood situations to share with parents, such as *Your child appeared ill today* or *Several children in this class have become ill with the flu. Please remember to keep your child home when she is sick.*
- Advocate within the early childhood or school setting for the hiring of bilingual teachers who can assist everyone to improve communication with families who are not English speaking.

Although using family members or children as interpreters may be appropriate for much of the information that needs to be conveyed to families such as future early childhood activities and family responsibilities, this practice should be reconsidered when handling information about any aspects of a child's health.

MyEducationLab
To assess your understanding of how to promote health and wellness in early childhood settings go to the Book Specific Resources section in the MyEducationLab for your course, select *Nutrition, Health, and Safety for Young Children,* Chapter 9 of the Study Plan, and then complete the multiple-choice questions and activities.

Summary

Many factors in children's home, school, and community environments influence their health and well-being. Biological and social factors contribute to children's health, whereas lifestyle factors affect wellness. Health determinants contribute to or challenge children's well-being. Understanding these aspects of health and wellness helps teachers create a climate of health and wellness in the classroom.

Policies that guide health practices in the early childhood and school settings are promoted by licensing and accreditation agencies. The guidance provided by these groups ensures that children have safe and healthy experiences. Policies outline the procedures that create consistency and continuity in health and wellness program services. The presence of policies and procedures reflects the teacher's commitment to health and wellness in the early childhood setting.

As the nation's classrooms become increasingly diverse, teachers must plan health promotion activities that are culturally sensitive and honor differences among families. Health promotion is accomplished through activities and curriculum that introduce children to healthful behaviors. Health-promoting activities can be incorporated into any early childhood experience. Teachers are important role models demonstrating for children what healthy practices look like.

Teachers should understand that racial, cultural, and socioeconomic backgrounds may influence how families respond to health and illness. Families may have different nutritional desires, and they may have different values and beliefs about health and health care. Teachers must understand these differences and build comfortable relationships with families to promote communication about children's health and wellness. Planning activities in the classroom that teach children about differences and how to negotiate different viewpoints makes a positive contribution to children's social and emotional health. Learning to make healthful choices about food and exercise and building social skills are important aspects of health and wellness.

Key Terms

Accreditation, p. 294

Acute conditions, p. 288

Biological determinants of health, p. 289

Chronic conditions, p. 288

Congenital conditions, p. 288

Cystic fibrosis, p. 288

Dental caries, p. 297

Determinants of health, p. 288

Health, p. 287

Health disparities, p. 299

Health policies, p. 293

Infectious diseases, p. 298

Mental health, p. 288

Physical health, p. 288

Prejudice, p. 299

Protective factors, p. 291

Risk factors, p. 291

Social determinants of health, p. 289

Stereotyping, p. 299

Susceptible, p. 288

Review Questions

1. Define *health* and *wellness*. Describe how these terms are linked and how they are different.

2. List the components of health. Describe two determinants of health and illness.

3. Define health promotion and provide examples of ways that children can participate in promoting their own wellness.

4. Define health disparities and give an example that could impact the health of young children.

5. Describe the goals of school wellness policies with respect to nutrition and physical activity.

6. Provide examples of ways teachers can promote children's understanding and acceptance of differences.

Discussion Starters

1. What is your social and cultural background? How do you think your background has affected your quality of health and your access to health care?

2. How can teachers address health disparities in our society?

3. Think about low-income families you have known or worked with in the past. What are some of the challenges they have faced? In what ways do you think children from low-income families are at a disadvantage in our society? Can you think of any advantages or strengths that children might gain from growing up in a low-income family?

Practice Points

1. Examine the community in which you live. What is the incidence of poverty in your area? What resources are available to families with low incomes? What gaps in local services may limit the involvement of children from low-income families in school activities?

2. Imagine that you are in charge of a dental health promotion event for your school. What oral health concepts would you focus on? What resources would you tap to obtain expertise? What ideas do you have to include both children and parents in this learning experience? How would you ensure that this event reaches non-English-speaking families in your school?

3. Create a lesson that promotes physical activity for preschool-age children. Make adjustments for children who have special needs that pertain to mobility. How would you teach this lesson to children who speak predominantly Spanish?

Web Resources

Center for Health and Health Care in Schools: Tools and Documents to Support Immigrant and Refugee Children
   www.healthinschools.org/Immigrant-and-Refugee-Children/Tools-and-Documents.aspx

Model School Wellness Policies
   www.schoolwellnesspolicies.org/

National Center for Child Poverty
   www.nccp.org

National Resource Center for Health and Safety in Child Care and Early Education
   http://nrckids.org

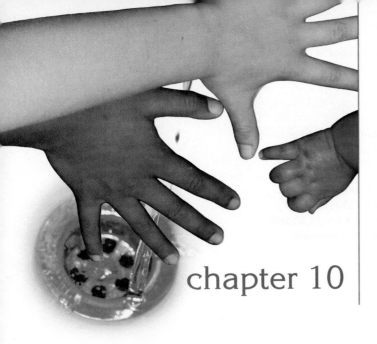

chapter 10 | Health Screening and Assessment

Learning Outcomes

After reading this chapter, you should be able to:

1. Discuss each component of a comprehensive health history.

2. Explain the purpose of immunizations for young children and discuss some of the common concerns families have regarding vaccinations.

3. Describe how to gather and manage confidential health history information.

4. Explain what types of gaps in the health history are frequently identified by teachers.

5. Describe various health screenings and why they help ensure children are able to learn.

6. Explain how teachers monitor children's health in the classroom.

Adelina is a bright 9-month-old infant. Her family has recently immigrated from Mexico. Adelina is being enrolled in an infant child care program, and her family is pleased to have a chance to visit with the teacher, Maria. Maria explains that during their visit she will ask some questions to learn about Adelina's health and development. As they all get settled Maria takes the opportunity to talk and smile with Adelina who is sitting on her mother's lap. After a few moments of visiting, the family provides the records they brought showing that Adelina received her first set of vaccinations in Mexico and additional vaccinations in Texas. As they talk, Maria learns that Adelina had a serious illness at 3 months of age that the family describes as an "infection of the brain." They report that Adelina was hospitalized for several weeks, but has otherwise been healthy.

Maria goes through the health history and enrollment materials, gathering information and explaining about the program. They talk about Adelina's feeding plan and discuss how the mother's breast milk should be transported to the center and how it will be stored. Maria asks if the family has any concerns about Adelina's development. The family reports that Adelina has not started making sounds or using other vocalizations appropriate for her age. They are worried because this is different from their experiences with their older children. Together Maria and the family decide that this should be evaluated further. They record their concerns on a referral form. The family also reports that they have recently moved out of an older home that was very run down. They have heard that a physician can do a simple blood test to determine if the baby was impacted by the presence of lead in the older home. Maria records that suggestion as well.

By the end of the visit Adelina is reaching out to pat Maria's hands and offer her toys. They say good-bye and the family leaves with the referral form to follow up on the issues that they discussed. They feel excited about their daughter's new care setting, and are pleased that Maria is so helpful and easy to talk to. After they leave Maria reflects on their conversations. She makes a note to check back with the family in a week to see what they have learned from their follow-up plan.

Children come to early childhood classrooms with varied health and development experiences. Learning about these aspects of a child's background is an important part of the transition into the classroom. Children's health and development information guides the creation of the care and education plan. It ensures that teachers are aware of children's individual health needs. It also focuses attention on concerns such as allergies or hearing or vision problems so that children do not miss important opportunities to learn.

In this chapter we discuss the significance of evaluating children's health to ensure they are ready to learn. We highlight the importance of managing health information and communicating it appropriately. We explore the common ways in which children are assessed and screened for health and development concerns that might impact learning. Finally, we offer suggestions about how daily health assessments can be conducted in the classroom to efficiently and effectively monitor and improve children's health and well-being.

EVALUATING CHILDREN'S HEALTH AND DEVELOPMENT

Early childhood programs and schools are part of children's health and wellness network. Health evaluation tools are used in early childhood programs and schools because these settings provide an important opportunity to assess children at an early age and determine who needs further assistance or referral for services. The early childhood setting may be the first time that some children have had attention

Evaluating and addressing health concerns at an early age set children on a course for optimal development and learning.

health evaluation
an assessment of a child's overall health and well-being

health screening
an evaluation using specific tools to detect potential health concerns

health assessment
an evaluation of health or a description of an aspect of health

daily health checks
visual assessment of a child's apparent health conducted at arrival

continual observation
consistent observation for signs of impending illness

given to aspects of health and development that influence learning. In this way early childhood programs provide an important contribution to children's future development and opportunity to learn.

Understanding Health Evaluations

A health evaluation is an assessment of a child's overall health and well-being. It is a multifaceted process that reviews and considers the many factors that influence children's health. Health evaluations are conducted for several specific purposes:

1. To understand a child's health status so that teachers can make necessary accommodations.
2. To identify known medical conditions or risk factors for illness or injury.
3. To identify children who benefit from further evaluations or referrals.
4. To help families learn about the health of their child and to understand potential hazards to their child's health.
5. To identify gaps in the family's access to needed resources.

The health evaluation process is an important part of early childhood and school services. In order for children to develop and learn optimally, health problems need to be identified and addressed. The approaches to collecting information to inform an overall health evaluation are discussed in this chapter. Each approach provides guidance for collecting and managing health information.

Health evaluation involves both initial and ongoing approaches. Initial approaches include health screenings and assessments. Health screenings are specific methods used to identify health conditions or risk factors for health problems. Reviewing children's immunization records is a familiar screening practice. Some children's settings and schools offer health fairs or special health screening events where children's hearing, vision, and oral health are evaluated to detect potential problems. Another aspect of screening involves a review of the health history looking for information that, for example, suggests risk factors associated with lead poisoning or dietary habits that put children at risk for anemia or obesity.

Health assessments are evaluations of overall health. In early childhood settings this assessment includes descriptions of each child's general health. Health assessments also focus on particular aspects of health by evaluating children in relation to others. An example is evaluating children's growth through height and weight measurements that are plotted on growth charts.

Ongoing assessment approaches include daily health checks and continual observation for health and illness indicators. Daily health checks involve visual reviews of children soon after they arrive at the classroom. Continual observation refers to consistent and thoughtful recognition that children display observable signs that cue teachers to impending illness. Together these approaches ensure that potential problems are identified so that any needed interventions can be implemented.

Managing Health Information Appropriately

Health information is personal and private information. It must be obtained respectfully, used appropriately, and managed confidentially. In 1996, Congress enacted Public Law 104–191, the Health Insurance Portability and Accountability Act, often referred to as HIPAA. The purpose of this legislation was to improve the effectiveness of the health care system and to maintain the privacy of individual health care information. The act requires that safeguards be in place to ensure that individual health information is managed confidentially and communicated appropriately.

HIPAA requirements are directed primarily to health care providers and insurance agencies. These groups are considered *covered entities*, that is, they are required to follow the HIPAA rules. Child care providers and teachers are not included in the definition of covered entities. However, teachers do come into contact with individual health information and may work with health care providers. For example, collecting health history information as part of the enrollment process provides information about the child's past and current health issues. Details are also gathered about immunizations and results of tests for diseases, such as tuberculosis (TB). As they receive this information, teachers and their programs interface with HIPAA-covered entities. Because of this teachers must ensure that the privacy of child and family health information is protected. This means that children's settings and schools must have policies that describe how confidential information is to be managed and communicated. Health records should be accurate, complete, confidential, and shared appropriately. Policies should provide details about the safeguards to be put in place to maintain confidentiality. Guidelines for appropriate safeguards include the following:

Health information must be managed privately and confidentially.

- Provide a private space for teachers and families to discuss health issues without being overheard.
- Keep all written documents out of view when in use; store documents in a secure and locked file.
- Ensure that information stored on computers is password protected, and that computer screens are turned away from public view when in use.
- Require the signature of the parent or other person authorized by the parent for the release of children's health information (Kentucky Cabinet for Health and Family Services, 2009).

Defining the Health History

Each child's early development and health experiences are unique. A health history is a summary of the child's previous health experiences. It includes the child's medical history, immunization records, information about previous injuries, and a history of the child's development. The health history provides an overall view of the child's physical and mental health and development. A comprehensive, or complete, health history includes the following information and topics that, taken together, create a thorough picture of children's health experiences:

health history
a summary of a child's previous health experiences

- Basic details such as the child's name, birth date, names of the parents or guardian, and family contact information.
- A listing of diseases the child has experienced.
- A summary of any chronic, or continual, health conditions.
- The child's record of immunizations; that is, vaccines given and when.
- A history of significant injuries or accidents the child has had.
- A summary of the child's behaviors or personal style that might make the child more prone to accidents.
- Information about the health and wellness of the child's family, including medical and mental health conditions and challenges.
- A summary of the child's developmental history, such as a timeline of when the child achieved key developmental milestones.
- Information about the child's mental health, including social and emotional well-being.
- Information about the child's nutritional background, to identify nutritional risks such as over- or undernutrition and access to healthy balanced meals.
- A summary of the child's oral and dental health history.
- A summary of resources the family is currently using, and gaps in access to needed medical care.

Knowing these details of children's early life helps teachers to be watchful for aspects that may have negative consequences for growth, development, and learning. Requirements

MyEducationLab

Go to the Assignments and Activities section of Topic 6: Health Appraisals/Screening in the MyEducationLab for your course and complete the activity entitled *Comprehensive Health History*. How will Ashley's forthcoming responses help inform her teacher's instruction for her?

for obtaining health histories within early childhood programs vary according to the type of program and the age of the children in the program. Head Start standards for obtaining health histories represent a comprehensive model that best exemplifies how to obtain information and promote health. Not all teachers will obtain all components of a health history. However, it is important to understand why each component, discussed next, is important to the health and wellness of a child.

Early Development

Prenatal and early development set the stage for later development. The health history briefly explores this information, identifying significant aspects that may continue to influence the child's development.

Pregnancy and Birth History   Information about the mother's pregnancy and birth history helps identify risks for children's development. Questions include whether the mother had any health problems during the pregnancy or during delivery. Some maternal medical conditions cause congenital defects in children. For example, babies of mothers with diabetes are at risk for heart defects. Mothers who contract rubella, a serious viral infection, during pregnancy are at risk for having a baby with a hearing loss. Drug and alcohol use and smoking during pregnancy can also affect a child's development.

> **rubella**
> a viral infection that can cause fetal defects when contracted during pregnancy

> **premature infant**
> an infant born more than 3 weeks early, or less than 37 weeks' gestation

The health history also explores aspects related to the child's birth to learn if the child was a premature infant (born more than 3 weeks early) or if the child experienced any problems at birth or during the first few days of life. A child's birth weight is also of interest. Low-birth-weight babies are at risk for developmental delays, poor school performance, seizures, and hearing or visual impairments. High-birth-weight babies tend to have more traumatic deliveries, which can result in long-term problems. Figure 10-1 provides sample questions to ask when exploring health issues related to pregnancy and birth.

> **developmental milestones**
> physical abilities or tasks that most children are able to achieve by a certain age range

Developmental History   A comprehensive health history includes discussions that help teachers learn about the child's progress with respect to developmental milestones. Developmental milestones are physical abilities or tasks that most children are able to achieve by a certain age range. For example, most children are able to walk on their own by age 2. A few children may walk as early as 9 months. Many children are walking at 1 year of age. Some children show a pattern of reaching developmental milestones earlier than the typical age range. Some develop quickly in some areas of development and more slowly in others. Here are two examples:

- Hal reports that his child began speaking at a very young age, but did not begin to walk until well after the first birthday. He has noticed that the child is more interested in reading and less interested in playing outside.

Figure 10-1 Pregnancy and Birth History

Asking questions about health problems during pregnancy and delivery helps identify potential problems with children's growth and development. Questions include the following:

1. Did the mother have any health problems during pregnancy or during delivery?
2. Did the mother receive prenatal health care?
3. Was the child born outside the hospital?
4. Was the child born more than 3 weeks early or late?
5. What was the child's birth weight?
6. Did the child have any problems at birth or in the first days of life?
7. Did the child or mother stay in the hospital longer than usual due to medical reasons?

Source: Adapted from *Head Start Child Health Record*, by the U.S. Department of Health and Human Services, Administration of Children and Families, retrieved July 31, 2009, from http://eclkc.ohs.acf.hhs.gov/hslc/resources/ ECLKC_Bookstore/Child%20Health%20Record.htm.

- Kayla describes her child as very coordinated and active. She remembers that her child was running around the house at 9 months of age and still prefers to play all ball games rather than doing homework.

Understanding the individual child's pace and pattern of development helps teachers anticipate how to structure learning activities so each child will thrive in the classroom.

Information from a developmental history also helps detect the possibility of developmental problems or delays. The signs of developmental disability are highly variable depending on cause, type, and severity of the delay. Some developmental delays are apparent soon after birth. Others emerge during early childhood and into the early elementary years. Teachers spend many hours with children. They become acquainted with the range of behaviors that are typical for certain age ranges, and often recognize gaps in development through observation of the child in the classroom. Using a developmental milestones checklist is another way to engage families in discussion about a child's developmental history. Checklists, like the one shown in Figure 10-2, guide families to recognize possible indicators of developmental delay.

History of Illness and Disease

The health history helps teachers and families identify and discuss any serious diseases that require special health care or that would affect participation in the classroom. Plans for managing chronic illnesses in the classroom can then be developed and discussed.

Illnesses and Hospitalizations   Significant illnesses and hospitalizations are important aspects of children's health experiences. Some may have long-term consequences. Illnesses such as meningitis may cause hearing loss or cognitive delays. In the opening case scenario

Figure 10-2 Indicators of Developmental Delay

Age 3 to 6 Months

- Excessive stiffness of muscles.
- Floppy or very loose muscle tone.
- Does not turn towards sounds outside of view by 4 months.
- Does not show interest in faces.

Age 6 to 12 Months

- No babbling by 9 months.
- Does not turn in response to name by 12 months.
- Does not exchange facial expressions.
- Does not show interest in objects by pointing.

Age 12 to 24 Months

- Does not follow one-step commands.
- Not walking by 18 months.
- No pretend play by age 2.
- Does not mimic actions or words by age 2.

Age 24 to 36 Months

- Does not follow two-step commands.
- Does not point to or show objects of interest to others.
- Difficulty with nonverbal forms of communication such as eye contact, facial expressions, and gestures.

- Looks for familiar objects when asked.
- By age 3, has made no progress in self-care or toilet training.

Age 3 to 4 Years

- Does not show interest in playing with other children.
- Seems withdrawn on a consistent basis.
- Shows violent behaviors such as hitting or biting.
- Is exceedingly shy or fearful around other children.

Age 4 to 5 Years

- Exhibits overly impulsive behavior when angry or upset.
- Unable to stack a tower of six to eight blocks.
- Unable to accurately give her first and last name.
- Does not talk about daily activities.
- Exhibits extremely fearful, timid, or aggressive behavior.

Age 5 to 8 Years

- Does not recognize letters of the alphabet by the end of kindergarten.
- Not reading by the end of first grade.
- Often is sad, worried, or afraid.
- Difficulties with keeping up physically with peers.
- Often speaks negatively of self.

Sources: From *Early Language Development and Language Learning Disabilities* by K. Grizzle and M. Simms, 2005, Pediatrics in Review. August 2005; 26, pp. 86–95; *Recognition of Autism Before Age 2 Years* by C. Johnson, 2008. Pediatrics in Review. March 2008; 29, pp. 86–96; http://www.firstsigns.org/healthydev/milestones.htm; and *What to expect & when to seek help: A bright futures tool to promote social and emotional development in early childhood*, by R. Mayer, J. M. Anastasi, E. M. Clark, 2006, Washington, DC: National Technical Assistance Center for Children's Mental Health, Georgetown University Center for Child and Human Development, in collaboration with the National Center for Education in Maternal and Child Health.

Adelina's mother reported that her child had been hospitalized for an "infection of the brain." This may have been meningitis. The description of this illness along with the mother's report that Adelina made very few vocalizations might indicate that the child suffers from hearing loss. Serious injuries also have the potential to cause developmental problems. For example, a child who has experienced a serious leg fracture may have damaged the growth center in the bone, resulting in growth retardation of the leg and causing physical limitations.

Chronic Health Conditions The health history should explore chronic or persistent health conditions such as allergies, asthma, or digestive issues. These are important aspects of a child's health that may need special attention in the classroom setting. For example, a teacher should specifically ask if the child has ever been diagnosed with asthma or has had a history of breathing problems or chronic cough. Asthma is one of the most common chronic medical conditions in childhood. It causes inflammation in the lungs in response to environmental agents such as cigarette smoke, pollens, or infections. Although it is generally not diagnosed during infancy, many infants begin exhibiting symptoms of asthma such as frequent infections or chronic cough. Chronic conditions may require specific treatment plans that involve administering medications in the classroom. Discussing this aspect of the health history helps reveal these needs so plans can be established.

Medications and Treatments This aspect of the health history directs teachers and families to discuss and document any medications the child is taking. If medications need to be given when children are in the classroom, special documentation, training, and procedures are needed. Directions from the child's health care provider must be obtained that outline the timing and dose of medications needed and how the medications are given. Any time medications are administered, teachers must document what was given, when, and whether there were any side effects. This information should be available to the family.

Immunization Status

Immunization records are an important part of the health history. Immunizations are important because they prevent the incidence and spread of disease. This is of special significance as children enter group settings where infections frequently occur.

Immunization Requirements An advisory committee at the government's Centers for Disease Control and Prevention (CDC) outlines the immunizations that are recommended for children and adults. The recommendations include the age at which a vaccine should be given, the number of doses, the time between doses, and safety measures related to the administration of the vaccines. Individual states are responsible for establishing laws that outline the specific immunization requirements for children who participate in child care or school settings. These requirements vary from state to state (CDC, 2009). The majority of vaccinations are required during the first 6 years of life. After age 6 additional immunizations are not required again until age 12. A yearly flu shot may be recommended but not required. The family should obtain a document of the child's immunization status and provide it to the early childhood program or school well in advance of attendance. Immunization records are then reviewed by the staff to determine if the child's immunization status meets state requirements and, therefore, if the child is eligible to begin school.

Family Concerns about Immunizations Some families are more concerned about the side effects of vaccines than the risk of the disease they are designed to prevent. These worries have resulted in a drop in immunization rates in some communities and an increase in rates of disease. Some of the most common misconceptions about vaccinations are presented in Figure 10-3.

Several factors contribute to concerns or objections to immunize (American Academy of Pediatrics [AAP], 2009):

- Insufficient information about the vaccine or immunizations, or information that is given at an inconvenient time, for example, just before a vaccination is given when it is difficult to fully explore concerns.

asthma
the most common chronic medical condition in childhood causing chronic inflammation in the lungs in response to environmental agents such as cigarette smoke, pollens, or infections

immunizations
vaccinations are given to individuals to trigger the person's immune response, which helps prevent infection

Figure 10-3 Common Misconceptions about Immunizations

Why should children be immunized when most of these diseases have been eliminated from the United States?

Although the number of these diseases has decreased dramatically in the United States, a number of them remain common in other areas of the world and could easily be reintroduced into the United States.

Do immunizations work? Haven't most people who get a vaccine-preventable disease been immunized?

There are very few people who do not respond well to vaccines, but most vaccines are more than 90% effective. A child who has not been immunized is at much greater risk of acquiring the disease and at greater risk for more severe disease. The immunity obtained from vaccinating is very similar to the natural immunity acquired from having the disease.

Isn't giving children more than one immunization at a time dangerous?

Extensive studies have demonstrated that multiple vaccinations can be given safely to children. The immune system is able to recognize and respond to numerous germs at once. Vaccine trials require that all new vaccines be tested along with existing vaccines to ensure safety.

Do vaccines cause autism?

The concern about the possible association between thimerosal-containing vaccines and autism or the MMR vaccine and autism has been studied extensively. All scientific evidence rejects either association.

Source: Based on *Red Book: 2009 Report of the Committee on Infectious Diseases*, 28th edition, edited by L. K. Pickering, C. J. Baker, D. W. Kimberlin, and S. S. Long, 2009, Elk Grove Village, IL: American Academy of Pediatrics.

- Information that is delivered in a way that does not address the family's concerns.
- Mistrust of the source of information and difficulty sorting out the variety of opposing information from various sources such as antivaccination groups, religious groups, and alternative providers.
- Concerns regarding the number of injections required.
- Not perceiving vaccination risk accurately.
- Lack of appreciation of the severity of vaccine-preventable diseases.

Families may express their concerns about immunizations to their child's teacher. Teachers should be prepared to give accurate information or refer families to an appropriate resource. One concern that families often express relates to the presence of thimerosal in vaccines. Thimerosal is a mercury compound that was widely used until recently as a preservative in vaccinations. The *Safety Segment* discusses some of the concerns families have had about immunizations containing thimerosal. Many studies have evaluated the potential associations of thimerosal with autism and the measles/mumps/rubella (MMR) vaccine with autism. Evidence from these studies does not support these associations (AAP, 2009).

Potential Reactions Following Vaccination Some vaccines can produce adverse reactions—or side effects. Three types of vaccine side effects have been identified (CDC, 2008):

1. Local reaction: This is the most common side effect. Local reactions are characterized by pain, swelling, and redness at the site of the injection. The symptoms generally occur within a few hours after the vaccine and are more common with certain vaccinations, such as Diphtheria, Tetanus, acellular Pertussis (DTaP).
2. Systemic reaction: This reaction is characterized by generalized symptoms including fever, malaise, fatigue, muscle pain, headache, and loss of appetite. These symptoms can occur because of the vaccine or because of a concurrent viral

thimerosal
a mercury compound that was widely used as a preservative in vaccinations

adverse reactions
side effects

local reaction
the most common type of side effect after vaccination; characterized by pain, swelling, and redness at the site of the injection

systemic reaction
a type of reaction following vaccination; characterized by generalized symptoms such as fever, malaise, fatigue, muscle pain, headache, and loss of appetite

Safety Segment

Thimerosal and Vaccines

Thimerosal is a mercury compound that was used until recently as a preservative in vaccines. The U.S. Food and Drug Administration (FDA) requires the use of preservatives with vaccines to prevent their contamination with dangerous organisms. Before preservatives were used, serious illnesses and deaths were reported from contaminated vaccines.

Considerable concern has been raised regarding a suspected association between thimerosal and autism. In 2001 and 2004, the Institute of Medicine conducted reviews focusing on the relationship between thimerosal and the neurodevelopmental disorders of autism, attention deficit/hyperactivity disorder, and speech/language delay. The committee concluded that there is no evidence of a relationship suggesting that thimerosal causes these conditions. They further stated that the benefits of vaccinations are clear and evident, while the concerns related to the use of thimerosal are unfounded. Vaccinations provide a much greater benefit than risk. Meanwhile, the FDA is making efforts to reduce exposure to thimerosal and other forms of mercury in vulnerable populations.

Source: *Thimerosal in Vaccines*, by the U.S. Food and Drug Administration, Department of Health and Human Services, 2005, retrieved July 31, 2009, from http://www.fda.gov/cber/vaccine/thimerosal.htm.

allergic reaction
rare but life-threatening reaction following vaccination

infection. Systemic reactions are sometimes seen after immunizations that use live vaccines such as MMR and varicella (chicken pox). Live vaccines often produce an immune response that is similar to a mild form of the natural disease. These reactions can be very difficult to distinguish from infections that may be contagious, so it is reasonable to seek the advice of a medical professional if a child shows a systemic reaction.

3. Allergic reaction: Allergic reactions are very rare but can be life threatening. They occur in less than 1 in 500,000 doses (CDC, 2008). Signs of allergic reaction to immunizations may include trouble breathing, weakness, wheezing, hives, and swelling of the throat. If any of these reactions is noticed, emergency medical assistance should be obtained immediately.

It is likely that teachers will interact with children who have recently received vaccinations. If a child is ill or if teachers have concerns about any symptoms such as fever, fatigue, lack of appetite, or skin rashes, a follow-up appointment with the child's health care provider should be scheduled.

What if. . .

on the first day of preschool a late-enrolling child arrived with immunization records in hand that were not up to date? How would you handle this situation?

Child Safety and Risk-Taking Behaviors

Gathering information about the child's style and behavioral characteristics helps identify the child's potential for injury. Injuries are the single leading cause of death among children older than 6 months (Farel & Kotch, 2005). In a classroom setting, it is the teacher's responsibility to ensure that each child is safe and secure. Knowing about the child's safety behaviors guides planning for the types of activities offered and helps identify any special supervision the child may require. Asking about the child's physical activity habits includes questions such as these: Does the child tend to take risks? Has the child had any major accidents, fractures, or head injuries that were associated with risk-taking behavior? Conversations with families about child safety behaviors also provide an opportunity to talk about ways to promote health and safety at home. Questions to explore with families include the following:

- Is the family car equipped with appropriately installed car seats or booster seats?
- Are all medications or poisons such as cleaning supplies or chemicals stored out of the child's reach?
- Does the home have a swimming pool, lake, irrigation canal, or other open water source nearby? Have appropriate measures been taken to prevent unsupervised entry into these areas?
- Does the family feel safe in their neighborhood?
- If the family owns guns, are all guns locked up and unavailable?

Nutrition Screening

The nutritional health history identifies aspects of children's dietary habits and special needs that must be addressed in the early childhood setting. Here are some important aspects of the nutritional health history discussion:

- Are there barriers to providing the child healthful foods?
- Is the child's diet nutritious and appropriate for the child's age?
- What are the child's eating habits?
- Does the child have any special dietary needs or food restrictions?
- Is the child growing appropriately?

Discussing the family's ability to provide healthful food for the child may reveal challenges the family faces. This provides an opportunity for teachers and families to explore community resources that may be of support. Such conversations also identify whether a child has suffered from periods of malnutrition (overnutrition and undernutrition) that may have interrupted normal growth and development.

Health Issues Related to Nutrition Other health issues related to nutrition are also discussed, such as diabetes and how it should be managed in the class setting. Some children have challenges related to the physical aspects of eating, such as chewing and swallowing. Food allergies are also an important consideration. Food allergies must be carefully explored so teachers have all the information they need to implement a safe environment. These issues are discussed and strategies are developed for safety at mealtime.

The history also addresses children's individual and age-appropriate feeding needs. It provides an opportunity for families to describe what the child typically eats, how much, and the usual eating schedule. Figure 10-4 provides sample questions to ask when gathering information about children's history and to promote conversations about children's dietary needs.

Special Diets and Food Preferences The nutritional history also informs teachers about family preferences for special diets or food restrictions that they follow for religious and cultural reasons. As teachers gather nutritional histories, they may learn that the family has recently moved to the United States. An exploration of the family's eating patterns and food preferences may reveal the impacts of acculturation. Acculturation refers to the social, psychological, and behavioral changes that are associated with moving to and living in a new country (Elder, Broyles, Brennan, Zuniga de Nuncio, & Nader, 2005). Relocation can influence a family's health behaviors, including the way in which they adjust to dietary changes. Some families may struggle to find familiar foods in the groceries and supermarkets in their new community. They may also be impacted by unhealthy dietary habits of their new environment. The *Nutrition Note* provides more information about the influence of acculturation on family nutrition. Discussing these topics helps teachers be supportive of the family's dietary goals. For example, Su Lin wants her children to learn to enjoy eating rice, and Catalina wants her child to eat only organic dairy foods. Families want to be sure their children are not teased about what they bring for lunch. These discussions, inspired by the nutritional history, inform teachers of concerns they can address through activities that teach children that people eat many kinds of foods.

What if. . .

a parent described their family hobby of riding all-terrain vehicles (ATVs) and indicated that their 4-year-old child drove his own ATV? What would this tell you about this child's risk-taking behaviors? What topics might you discuss with the parent?

acculturation
the social, psychological, and behavioral changes associated with relocation

Figure 10-4 Sample Nutrition Screening Questions

For Infants

✓ Is the baby breast- or bottle feeding?
  • If breast-feeding, will you provide breast milk for your baby?
  • If bottle feeding, what type of formula?
✓ How often does your baby eat?
✓ If formula feeding, how much does your baby eat?
✓ If formula feeding, is your baby on a special formula and are there special directions
  for preparing it?
✓ How long does it usually take to feed your baby?
✓ How does your baby let you know when she is hungry?
✓ How does he let you know when he is full?
✓ Does your baby eat anything other than breast milk or formula? If so, what and how often?
✓ Does your baby have any problems when feeding?
✓ *If age appropriate:* Has your baby had any problems with the introduction of solid foods?

For Preschool and School-Age Children

✓ What foods does your child like? What foods does your child dislike?
✓ Are there any foods your child should not eat for medical, religious, or personal reasons?
✓ Is your child on a special diet?
✓ What is your child's usual meal schedule?
✓ Does your child eat breakfast?
✓ How much and what type of milk does your child drink?
✓ How much juice does your child drink?
✓ Have there been any recent changes in your child's diet?
✓ Does your child have trouble chewing or swallowing?
✓ Does your child eat or chew things that aren't food?
✓ Do you have any concerns about your child's eating?
✓ Do you eat meals at home together as a family?

Source: Adapted from *Head Start Child Health Record*, by the U.S. Department of Health and Human Services, Administration of Children and Families, retrieved July 31, 2009, from http://eclkc.ohs.acf.hhs.gov/hslc/resources/ECLKC_Bookstore/Child%20Health%20Record.htm.

Oral Health History

Gathering information about the child's oral health provides opportunity to explore dental problems the child has experienced. It explores the answers to questions such as these:

- Has the child had any dental surgery or other procedures?
- Has the child ever had a dental examination or screening?
- Is the child under the care of a dentist?
- Does the child brush her or his own teeth?

The oral health history also identifies whether the child may be at risk for dental disease. For example, infants who are fed juice and young children who drink soft drinks are at high risk for developing cavities because of the high sugar content in these beverages. This is especially problematic if babies are put to bed with bottles containing juice.

The oral health history also identifies the family's water source and whether the water is a good fluoride source. Fluoride is a mineral recommended for children 6 months to 6 years of age. Fluoride helps to prevent dental disease. Some public water systems are naturally fluoridated, whereas others have fluoride added to the water system. If the child is drinking well water or water from another nonpublic source, the child may not be getting the fluoride needed to prevent dental disease. In some cases a physician will prescribe fluoride drops as a preventive measure.

What if. . .

you discover that a 5-year-old in your class has never seen a dentist? When you explore this with the family you learn that it is the parents' fear of the dentist that keeps them from making an appointment. What guidance can you provide to ensure the child gets the oral health care that is needed?

fluoride
mineral recommended for children 6 months to 6 years of age for the prevention of dental disease

Nutrition Note

The Effects of Acculturation on Family Nutrition

Acculturation refers to changes in behaviors and ways of thinking that occur when families join a new culture. For example, acculturation impacts eating behaviors and the use of traditional foods. This impact on the diet is more pronounced the longer the family lives outside of their native country. Changes due to acculturation on the diets of Hispanic families who have immigrated to the United States include:

- A decrease in the use of traditional foods.
- An increase in the use of traditional foods in a new way.
- An increase in the use of foods from the host country.

For many Mexican families, dietary acculturation has replaced a diet rich in beans, fruits, vegetables, and grains with a diet comprised of highly processed, sugary foods. Some studies suggest that as acculturation increases, BMI and unhealthy eating habits have increased.

Acculturation also influences infant feeding practices. Breast-feeding rates vary significantly according to race and ethnicity. For example, the rates of breast-feeding among Hispanic mothers in the United States are similar to the national average. However, these rates are markedly lower than the breast-feeding rates of mothers in Mexico. In fact, the longer Hispanic families reside in the United States, the less likely mothers are to breast-feed their infant. For those who do breast-feed, the duration of exclusive breast-feeding (feeding only breast milk for first 6 months of life) is also shorter.

These trends suggest that acculturation can be a risk factor for unhealthy eating behaviors. Early childhood teachers promote healthful nutritional practices by preserving healthy traditional behaviors. They also support children's wellness by assisting families to choose positive dietary options as they integrate aspects of the American diet.

Sources: "Preschooler Feeding Practices and Beliefs; Differences Among Spanish- and English-speaking WIC clients," by J. Greenberg et al., 2007, *Family and Community Health*, 30(3), pp. 257–270; and "The Effect of Time in the U.S., on the Duration of Breastfeeding in Women of Mexican Descent," by K. Harley, N. Stamm, and B. Eskenazi, 2007, *Maternal and Child Health Journal*, 11, pp. 119–125.

Mental and Emotional Health History

Assessing children's social and emotional development through a mental health history is an important part of ensuring a child's overall health and well-being. Social and emotional problems that go unrecognized can persist into adulthood, interrupting normal development. Early identification of problems and early interventions can put children on a course for more positive development (Squires, 2003). The mental health history focuses the discussion on a variety of social and emotional health indicators:

- The child's ability to interact positively with others.
- The child's ability to control emotions, such as aggression.
- The child's interest in playing with other children.
- Ways the child copes with change and stress.
- Problems or worries the child may have.

One common topic in the mental health history involves discussing the child's style when transitioning into a new environment. Three behavior styles are often discussed (Thomas & Chess, 1977):

- *Easy and adaptable:* Describes children who adapt readily to new situations.
- *Difficult and emotional:* Describes children who display high levels of emotion in new situations.

Figure 10-5 Sample Questions for a Mental Health History

✓ Does your child sleep less than 8 hours or have trouble sleeping at night?

✓ Is your child learning to use the toilet? Or, does your child manage toileting by herself?

✓ Can your child dress and undress herself?

✓ Does your child have any worries or fears?

✓ Does your child enjoy playing with children her age?

✓ Does your child experience temper tantrums or have any challenges controlling behavior?

✓ Does your child enjoy fantasy play? Is your child able to recognize the difference between fantasy and reality?

✓ Have there been any changes in your child's life in the last 6 months such as a move, family divorce, or death in the family?

✓ Are you or your family having any problems that might affect your child?

✓ Is your child interested in new experiences?

Sources: Adapted from *Head Start Child Health Record*, by the U.S. Department of Health and Human Services, Administration of Children and Families, retrieved July 31, 2009, from http://eclkc.ohs.acf.hhs.gov/hslc/resources/ ECLKC_Bookstore/Child%20Health%20Record.htm; and *The Complete and Authoritative Guide: Caring for Your Child; Age Birth to Age 5*, by the American Academy of Pediatrics, 2005, New York: Bantam Books.

- *Slow to warm up:* Describes children who withdraw from new situations at first and instead spend time observing before they gradually adapt.

Discussions about these behavior styles help identify the kinds of supports a child may need when beginning in the early childhood setting and when learning the daily classroom routine. Families can also describe other aspects of the child's style or temperament such as the child's adaptability, typical moods, intensity of reaction, and activity level. These characteristics guide teachers to fit their teaching and management approaches to the individual needs of the child.

The mental health history also includes exploration of ways the family soothes the child when the child is worried or hurt. In programs that care for infants, questions should focus on the infant's patterns such as whether the child cries frequently or has fussy periods. Teachers should also ask families about the strategies they use at home. It is common to ask questions about the child's habits during the mental health history. Examples of questions to spark conversation about social-emotional development are shown in Figure 10-5.

Family Health and Wellness

Health and wellness practices within the family impact children's health. Understanding the context that surrounds the child provides clues to the child's healthful development. It also offers an opportunity for teachers and families to discuss resources the family may need and ways the classroom environment can contribute to the child's healthy development.

Family Medical History It is important to know when a parent has a chronic medical condition because these are sometimes inherited or passed down to a child. Teachers should also be aware of situations when families who are ill have difficulties caring for their child. It may be necessary to provide referrals and support for families to obtain the services they need.

Home Environment Aspects of the home environment help identify conditions that may be unhealthy for children. Children who live with or are exposed to smokers are vulnerable to the effects of secondhand smoke. Drug production and drug use exposes children to toxic products and puts children in dangerous situations. Older houses introduce risk for lead exposure from paint and other deteriorating building products that contain lead. Water sources that are not monitored may also put children at risk for unsanitary drinking water. Unsafe neighborhoods surround children with dangers that may, among other things, limit the child's ability to play outside.

MyEducationLab

Go to the Building Teaching Skills and Dispositions section of Topic 6: Health Appraisals/Screening in the MyEducationLab for your course and complete the activity entitled *Inform Families about Effects of Health Practices on Children's Development*. As you work through this learning unit, consider your role in educating families about ways in which they can promote good health for their children as well as themselves.

Family Dynamics The relationships that exist among family members impact children's mental health. The presence of domestic violence and extremely punitive parenting styles surround children with stress that is associated with negative mental health (Bayer, Hiscock, Ukoumunne, Price & Wake, 2008). Dynamics associated with poverty, job loss, and homelessness also contribute negative risk factors. Teachers are an important resource for families who face such needs. Referrals to resources and local support programs are a crucial component of the family support network. Teachers should be aware of such resources and ready with flyers and brochures to share in case this assistance is needed.

OBTAINING CHILDREN'S HEALTH HISTORY

Health information is sensitive information. It is important for teachers to obtain health-related details with understanding and tact. Information should be gathered in an efficient way and should be meaningful and useful for the setting. It should be used to establish individualized care and service and to inform the development of wellness activities in the classroom.

What if. . .

a mother disclosed to you that her husband sometimes used a back room to cook "meth"? She says she doesn't want her child to be near that, but she doesn't have anywhere else to go. How would you respond? What child health and safety questions might this information suggest? What resources would you refer this mother to?

Gathering Health History Information

In some settings the health history is obtained by having the family complete a written form and return it with a record of the child's immunizations. Written forms may be brief and concise or more detailed. In other settings, teachers, health staff, or program directors might meet with families to discuss and record health information. Some programs conduct home visits where teachers and families talk in the home setting. Regardless of how the information is collected, attention to details ensures that an appropriate health history is obtained and that the information is used to improve the child's experience in the classroom. Here is how one teacher prepared for the health history visit:

> Dashay knows that families are sometimes nervous about meeting with the teacher to share health information. He works to create a welcoming environment. He moves a small table near to the window where a group of houseplants offers home-like comfort. He positions two chairs at the table but has others nearby in case many family members come to participate. On the floor nearby he places a tub of brightly colored toys. He sets several out onto the rug with some picture books about "going to school" and some pillows for children to sit on. Dashay likes to offer an herbal tea when he has visitors, and he has a pitcher of water and cups nearby. He is ready when the family arrives, and greets them with a big smile.

Often the process of gathering and discussing the child's health history is completed quickly. If a child has no unusual health or development concerns, the discussion may be very brief. Some children may have health issues that are addressed easily and for whom a plan is developed with no further follow-up needed. A few children may have more complex health considerations that require special discussions, planning, and training. For these children it is important to provide sufficient time to establish a thorough health and safety plan. For each child, the health history sets an important course of action for safe and appropriate services.

Selecting Purposeful Questions

The health history information that is gathered needs to be easy to understand and specific so that useful information is discovered. When only one general question is asked about the child's health, the response may not reveal needed information. For example, if asked, "Does your child have any medical problems," the parent may simply answer, "No" even when the child might have asthma or frequent breathing problems, allergies, or a history of seizures. A child with one of these conditions may be stable and not experiencing any current problems, so the family may not raise it as a concern.

Using a series of questions can prompt the family to recall past or ongoing health problems. A standard comprehensive health history form is used in many settings, such as Head Start programs, to ensure that specific information is gathered. Children's programs may adapt information to create their own health history format including special questions that have relevance in the particular community or with the specific group of children and families served.

What if. . .

a family failed to inform the director or teacher about their child's seizure disorder until the first day of school? What if the parent brought along medication that the child needed to take in the event of a seizure? How would you handle this situation?

Gathering Information Before Children Attend

Ample time should be provided to gather and discuss a child's health history *prior* to the child's attendance. Sometimes this may mean slowing down the enrollment process so all important information can be shared and discussed. Families may need to be reminded that the teacher needs to know about the children's health in advance so that adjustments to the program can be made if needed. Gathering all health information before a child attends is a safety measure. It ensures that important discussions occur and are not overlooked.

Building Comfortable Relationships

Families need to feel comfortable in order to fully share information about their child. This is especially true if the child's history is sensitive or if traumatic events have occurred in the past. Spending a few minutes explaining the purpose of the health history helps everyone focus on the goals of the discussion:

- To share important information about the child's health.
- To identify whether special arrangements are needed to assist the child in the classroom.
- To ensure that appropriate strategies are planned.

Documenting Information Accurately

health literacy
the ability to obtain and understand basic health information in order to make appropriate health decisions

Health history information needs to be recorded clearly and objectively. Families may not know the medical name of a condition or infection. They may use a description rather than a medical term. For instance, in the opening case scenario, Adelina's family reported that the child had an "infection of the brain." The *Health Hint* discusses the importance of health education and health literacy.

Health information should be recorded just as the family reports it. Teachers should not add their own speculation or guesses about the condition the family describes. This way the health record documents the facts as the family understands them. This allows teachers to formulate an understanding of the child's health status based on what is known. Then the teacher may ask the family to obtain additional information from the health care provider to clarify what is not understood.

Asking for Clarifying Information

Teachers should be sure they understand the information shared about the child's health. For example, if a child was hospitalized recently, the teacher might ask if the child has had a follow-up review by the medical provider. It is important to know if health issues have been resolved or if treatment is continuing. Further discussion also reveals needed details. It is helpful to know how a child's chronic health issues are being managed in the home. It is important to know if a food restriction is related to preference or an allergy that could cause a dangerous reaction. Teachers listen carefully to the information that is provided by the family and reflect on how the child's health needs can be managed in the classroom.

Health Hint

Health Literacy

Health literacy is important to consider when gathering health histories, administering health assessments, and promoting wellness practices. Health literacy refers to the family's ability to gather, process, and understand health information, which influences making appropriate health decisions. Skills learned in early childhood will help children be better able to navigate their health care as they get older. Learning, thinking, and life skills as described in the Partnership for 21st Century Skills will contribute to health literacy. The Institute of Medicine estimates that as many as 90 million Americans lack sufficient health literacy skills to function in the current health care system. This means that many families of young children may struggle when managing their child's health care.

Reasons for low health literacy include limited education, language barriers, cognitive impairment, and emotional disorders. To ensure that all families are able to access health messages, teachers should:

- Understand the families being served.
- Recognize the languages spoken by the families, the typical age of families, and ways information is accessed.
- Ensure written materials are concise and limit the number of words.
- Use simple and clear explanations and avoid complex vocabulary.
- Illustrate points with graphics.

Overcoming the obstacles that contribute to low health literacy will improve teachers' ability to promote children's health and well-being.

Source: Information from *Health Literacy in Primary Care: A Clinician's Guide*, by G. G. Mayer and M. Villaire, 2007, New York: Springer Publishing Company.

Identifying Impacts on the Child's Participation

As the details of the health history are discussed, implications for the child's participation in the classroom are noted and a detailed plan is developed. For example, if the child needs to receive medication during the day, a plan for administering the medication must be developed. This usually involves:

- Obtaining instructions from the child's health care provider.
- Training the teacher to identify when and how to administer the medication.
- Establishing protocols for storing medication and recording when the medicine was given.

Similarly, plans for managing allergies, special health care situations, and emergencies should be discussed.

Confirming Who May Access Health Information

Because children's health information is private, it is important to clarify with families who is allowed to have access to the records. In children's programs, this would typically include the classroom teachers and appropriate program staff such as the dietitian, nurse or health consultant, and those who manage children's records. To confirm this, a consent form is signed by the appropriate family member, and the form is stored in the child's file. A sample of such a consent form is shown in Figure 10-6.

Promoting Health and Wellness

Discussing children's health provides a good opportunity for teachers to share information that promotes family well-being and supports children's participation in the

Figure 10-6 Sample Consent to Access Child Health Information

---

Evergreen Children's Center PARENT/GUARDIAN CONSENT FORM

Child's Name _____

Birth Date _____ Gender _____

Parent/Guardian Name _____

Evergreen Children's Center may share health and medical records, and educational development information about my child with:
• **Community Early Intervention/Early Childhood Special Education**
• **Local School District**

(Please initial below)

_____ I have discussed with my child's teacher how and why information about my child may be provided to the agencies listed above.

_____ I understand that my child's information will only be released to the agencies listed above.

_____ I understand that my child's information will be used by staff within the Evergreen Children's Center to provide appropriate services.

_____ I understand that I may revoke this consent at any time.

_____ I have received a copy of this completed form.

My child's teacher has discussed this consent form with me. I understand what has been discussed and I give my permission for my child's information to be shared as described above.

Parent/Guardian Signature _____Date_____

Printed Name _____

Teacher Signature _____Date _____

Printed Name _____

Source: Based on Permission to Share Information form from the Office of Health and Human Services, Massachusetts; and U.S. Department of Education, Family Education Rights and Privacy Act (FERPA).

setting. Many health promotion topics are appropriate for all families, especially as children prepare to transition into a program or school. Teachers are attuned to the topics that are helpful to address when gathering health history information such as the following:

- Offering healthful food at meals and snack times.
- Feeding children breakfast or arriving early to participate in the school breakfast program.
- Ensuring children obtain a full night's sleep.
- Providing sufficient opportunity for active play.
- Dressing children appropriately for the weather and for active play.
- Encouraging the use of sunscreen during outside play.
- Decreasing screen time (television and computers).
- Increasing time spent reading together.
- Teaching children to brush their teeth.
- Teaching children to be safe pedestrians.

Other health promotion topics are situation specific and emerge during the health history discussions:

- Reducing children's exposure to violence and ways to accomplish this among families who live in challenging neighborhoods.
- Reducing children's exposure to stress in families where job loss or adult illness adds difficulties.
- Creating smoke-free environments for children if family members smoke.

Health and wellness promotion is accomplished by partnering with families. Teachers and family members are important role models for children. Together they create a team approach to improving health and wellness in the home and classroom.

Identifying Missing Information

The health history discussion between the early childhood program or school staff member and the appropriate family member concludes with a brief referral summary that highlights any gaps in needed information. In some cases, the family may need to pursue additional immunizations or obtain directions from the child's medical provider about administering a needed medication in the early childhood setting. The family may need to seek clarification about restrictions for a food allergy, or training and guidance about developing a protocol for serving a child with diabetes. The referral summary should clearly list the specific information required and when it is needed.

REVIEWING THE HEALTH HISTORY

Once the health history has been obtained, it is reviewed to identify aspects that impact the child in the classroom. This review should be conducted by an individual trained to recognize gaps in information or aspects that need follow-up or further assessment. Some early childhood settings may have a dietitian or health consultant conduct this review. Others may train teachers or program personnel to manage this responsibility.

Screening Immunization Reports

Children's immunizations records are compared to the list of vaccinations required for the child's age by the particular state. This review can be done by an individual who is familiar with the terminology and the local requirements. Table 10-1 illustrates the standard federal immunization schedule for young children.

If a child is missing a needed vaccination, the program or school contacts the family and guides them to obtain the immunizations before the child attends the early childhood setting or school. Some immunizations are offered as a series of several shots that must be spaced over specified intervals of time. As guided by the health professional, children may begin receiving a vaccination series before entering the early childhood program, and then complete the series at the recommended intervals while attending. The child's immunization record at the school should be updated as additional vaccinations are received to document that the needed series has been completed.

Many states have strict policies regarding children who have not had up-to-date immunizations.

Exclusion Dates

Most states require that all children enrolled in child care and schools have up-to-date immunizations. In an effort to increase the number of children who are protected by immunizations, some states establish immunization exclusion

Table 10-1   Childhood Vaccination Schedule

Recommended Immunization Schedule for Persons Aged 0 Through 6 Years—United States • 2009
For those who fall behind or start late, see the catch-up schedule

Vaccine▼ Age►	Birth	1 month	2 months	4 months	6 months	12 months	15 months	18 months	19–23 months	2–3 years	4–6 years
Hepatitis B[1]	HepB	HepB	see footnote1			HepB					
Rotavirus[2]			RV	RV	RV [2]						
Diphtheria, Tetanus, Pertussis[3]			DTaP	DTaP	DTaP	see footnote3	DTaP				DTaP
Haemophillus influenzae type b[4]			Hib	Hib	Hib[1]	Hib					
Pneumococcal[5]			PCV	PCV	PCV	PCV				PPSV	
Inactivated Poliovirus			IPV	IPV		IPV					IPV
Influenza[6]						Influenza (Yearly)					
Measles, Mumps, Rubella[7]						MMR		see footnote7			MMR
Varicella[8]						Varicella		see footnote 8			Varicella
Hepatitis A[9]						HepA (2 doses)				Hep A Series	
Meningococcal[10]										MCV	

Range of recommended ages

Certain high-risk groups

This schedule indicates the recommended ages for routine administration of currently licensed vaccines, as of December 1, 2008, for children aged 0 through 6 years. Any dose not administered at the recommended age should be administered at a subsequent visit, when indicated and feasible. Licensed combination vaccines may be used whenever any component of the combination is indicated and other components are not contraindicated and if approved by the Food and Drug Adminisiration for that dose of the series. Providers should consult the relevant Advisory Committee on Immunization Practices statement for detailed recommendations, including high-risk conditions: http://www.cdc.gov/vaccines/pubs/acip-list.hlm. Clinically significant adverse events that follow immunization should be reported to the Vaccine Adverse Event Reporting System (VAERS). Guidance about how to obtain and complete a VAERS form is available at http://www.vaers.hha.gov or by telephone, 800-822-7967.

Source: *Recommendations and Guidelines: 2009 Child & Adolescent Immunization Schedules*, by the Centers for Disease Control and Prevention, 2009, retrieved September 29, 2009, from http://www.cdc.gov/vaccines/recs/schedules/child-schedule.htm

dates. If a child's immunization record does not document full completion of the required immunizations, families receive a warning letter from the state immunization registry. The letter alerts families that the child will be excluded from school on a certain date if documentation of immunization is not provided. Teachers may have the unpleasant responsibility of turning children away from child care or school if the immunizations are not completed in advance of the exclusion date.

Exemptions

For the vast majority of children, vaccinations are given according to a prescribed schedule. This typical immunization schedule ensures that children will have all of the required immunizations in time for early childhood or school entry. However, a small percentage of children may be on a modified immunization plan.

State laws also regulate modifications and exemptions to the immunization requirements based on certain circumstances. Three types of immunization exemptions are available: *medical*, *religious*, and *philosophical*. All 50 states allow medical exemptions; all states except West Virginia and Mississippi allow religious exemptions; and only 20 states allow philosophical exemptions (National Conference of State Legislatures [NCSL], 2009). Families can request a modification or exemption from the immunization requirements under these options.

Medical Exemptions Children who are being treated with certain medications or who have particular illnesses should not receive certain vaccinations. This applies to children who are taking an oral steroid medication to treat asthma. Children with medical conditions such as a history of cancer or disease that affects a child's immune system also require a

MyEducationLab

Go to the Assignments and Activities section of Topic 6: Health Appraisals/Screening in the MyEducationLab for your course and complete the activity *Purpose of Immunizations*. What are your thoughts about Dr. Burns' perspective on vaccinating children?

modified immunization schedule. A vaccine can also be excluded from a children's immunization schedule if they have had a severe allergic reaction. Modifications or delays in vaccinations for medical reasons are allowed when recommended by a health care provider. Such exemptions should be documented in the child's health record.

Religious Exemptions Some families claim exemption for religious reasons. The religious exemption laws are intended for families who hold sincere objections to vaccinations based on their religious beliefs. The specific religious exemption requirements vary from one state to another. For example, some states require families requesting a religious exemption to be members of the First Church of Christ or Christian Scientists.

Philosophical Exemptions These exemptions are intended for families who have personal or moral beliefs that contradict immunizing their children (NCSL, 2009). States who allow these exemptions have higher rates of vaccine-preventable diseases such as whooping cough, which is a highly contagious respiratory infection that can be fatal to infants and young children (Omer et al., 2006).

Ensuring Children Have a Medical Home

The review of the health history may reveal that a child does not have an identified medical home. The term *medical home* refers to the location where the family obtains regular health care for their child, including regular checkups, immunizations, and care when the child is sick. Typically, the medical home provider is a physician, nurse practitioner, or physician's assistant. These providers are accustomed to collaborating with child care centers, preschools, and schools and they welcome referrals. Ideally, the medical home provider offers family-centered services that are accessible and culturally attuned (National Center of Medical Home Initiatives for Children with Special Needs, 2007). Families that have health insurance and access to health care are able address children's health needs when they occur.

Under some circumstances, teachers may have the opportunity to assist families in finding medical care services if needed. A list of medical providers in the community is a helpful resource. In addition, teachers can guide families to overcome any obstacles they may face in trying to obtain necessary health care. Obstacles may include the family's lack of health insurance, cultural and language barriers, or a limited number of providers who serve families with Medicare.

Many communities have community health centers or clinics that provide comprehensive primary health care regardless of the patient's insurance status or ability to pay. These clinics are often designed to serve a high-need community or a medically underserved population and can be an excellent medical home resource. Teachers may also collaborate with medical consultants, school nurses, or other community resources to help families.

Confirming Children Have Well-Child Exams

The health history is also reviewed to identify if the child has had regularly scheduled well-child checkups with the health care provider. The focus of well-child exams is on preventive health care. Well-child care involves:

- A review of the child's health history.
- Screening tests.
- Examinations.
- Treatments to prevent disease, including immunizations.
- Education and counseling to promote health.

Families of children who have not had periodic well-child exams should be encouraged to schedule a checkup as part of the enrollment expectations. Head Start Performance Standards require that programs support families to obtain comprehensive health exams for their child. Table 10-2 lists the recommended timing for well-child visits for all children.

What if . . .

a family in your program has misplaced their child's immunization records? They don't want to bother searching for the documentation, so they tell you that they want to claim a religious exemption. What issues does this approach raise? How would you manage this situation?

whooping cough
a highly contagious respiratory infection that can be fatal to infants and young children

well-child checkups
health care visits provided for children to ensure that health and development are progressing normally

Table 10-2	Well-Child Checkup Schedule	
Infants (0–12 Months)	**Children Older Than 1 Year of Age**	
✓ Newborn visit	✓ 15 months	
✓ 2 months	✓ 18 months	
✓ 4 months	✓ 2 years	
✓ 6 months	✓ 3 years	
✓ 9 months	✓ 4 years	
✓ 12 months	✓ 5 years and yearly thereafter	

Making Referrals

When gaps in the child's health care are discovered, follow-up is initiated through the **referral** process. Referrals are recommendations that direct families to needed resources. Common reasons for making referrals include encouraging the family to get a well-child exam, follow up on missing immunizations, or obtain an oral health exam. Another frequent referral in the early childhood setting is referring families to agencies that provide early intervention assessment for suspected developmental delays. Families may also raise questions about children's health that are beyond the scope of the teacher's knowledge and expertise. Any time a concern is identified that requires outside assistance, a referral is appropriate.

referral
process of obtaining assistance for a family after identifying a need

Teachers are an important referral resource when families face difficulties providing sufficient housing, food, or transportation. Sharing information about community support services benefits the family and contributes to the child's well-being. In addition, teachers who recognize that families are facing such difficulties are better able to understand how to support the family and care for the child's well-being in the classroom. Families also benefit from social resources, such as a supportive network of family and friends. Teachers help build social networks among families in the class by sponsoring family socials, game days, and parent and child community service activities. These social networking activities contribute to positive outcomes for children.

Health and development referrals are made in collaboration with families.

Referrals are made in collaboration with families. Together, the teacher and family member identify and record the specific aspects of concern. A written summary supports families when they take their questions to the health care provider. For example, in the opening case scenario Maria and the family have identified two areas for possible follow-up. The observation that Adelina is not making vocalizations concerns both Maria and the family, suggesting that an evaluation of Adelina's hearing is needed. The family has also described living in an older home that was in poor condition. They are aware that building materials in older homes often contain lead, a product that is harmful to young children. They decide to ask that Adelina be evaluated for possible lead poisoning. Together, the teacher and Adelina's family summarize their concerns and the family is prepared with specific goals as they follow up with their medical provider.

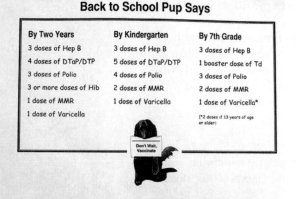

CONDUCTING OTHER HEALTH EVALUATIONS

In addition to the health history, additional health evaluations are conducted to screen for normal health and development. These include physical health, mental health, and developmental evaluations. Some evaluations are conducted for all children. Others are done to follow up on specific concerns. Some evaluations are offered at the children's setting or school by teachers or trained volunteers. Others require the expertise of those with specialized skills, including medical professionals, dietitians, and counselors. In addition, evaluations of children's health include input through growth measurements, vision screenings, and assessment for risk of lead poisoning. All contribute to the understanding of the child's health status and the design of the teaching environment.

Growth Measurements

Growth is one of the most important indicators of normal health and development in children. Height, weight and body mass index are the most important growth measurements. These measurements can be done by a teacher or specialist using reliable measuring devices. Because many children lack access to regular health care, the growth measurements obtained in the school may become an essential resource for identifying health concerns.

Height and Weight

The most common measurements taken are height and weight. In infancy, height is often referred to as *length*. Growth is reviewed by plotting height and weight measurements on standard growth charts. These charts are easily obtained from the CDC's website as well as many other online resources.

Standardized growth charts are available for children ages 0 to 36 months and ages 2 to 20 years. Growth charts for boys and girls can be found in the Book Specific Resources on MyEducationLab. The charts are designed as a tool to determine if growth is within the normal range. If there is any question that a growth measurement is below or above the normal range, the child should be referred to a health care provider for additional evaluation.

Body Mass Index

Body mass index (BMI) is a measure of body fat. It is calculated based on height and weight. BMI is an inexpensive, reliable method used to screen for weight categories, such as obesity, that are risk factors for health problems. BMI is calculated by multiplying weight in pounds by 703 and dividing by height in inches squared. This number is then plotted on BMI charts, which are provided for boys and girls ages 2 to 20 years. The chart shows the categories that determine if the child is underweight, normal weight, overweight, or obese. Children whose BMI falls in the underweight, overweight, or obese categories should be referred for evaluation by a medical professional. BMI charts for boys and girls can be found in the Book Specific Resources on MyEducationLab. In addition, many BMI calculators for children and adults are available online.

The use of the BMI measurement is being explored as a tool to screen for risk for obesity and to encourage schools to focus on teaching and modeling healthy lifestyles. The AAP and CDC recommend the use of BMI as a screening tool for children beginning at age 2. The *Policy Point* discusses controversies involved with BMI screening in schools.

Oral Health Assessments

Conducting oral health assessments in the early childhood setting or school is highly beneficial for children who do not have access to dental care. Dental caries or cavities are one of the most common chronic diseases in childhood. Dental caries are the formation of cavities or tooth decay caused by abnormal growth of bacteria in the mouth. Identification and treatment of dental caries in early life are important to overall physical health. It is recommended that all children have a dental visit by their first birthday and continue regular visits every 6 months for routine care (American Academy of Pediatric Dentistry, 2009).

Many children do not receive these recommended dental examinations. These include children in low-income families, children with special health care needs, and certain racial/ethnic groups such as blacks and Hispanics (Child and Adolescent Health Measurement Initiative, 2003). The federal Head Start program ensures that enrolled children receive comprehensive health care screenings including dental screenings. Head Start serves as a model for supporting early childhood programs to provide the health assessments young children need. The funding that supports Head Start assures that children from low-income families, who often have the greatest need for dental care, are able to receive this service (Gupta et al., 2009).

Many children's programs are able to arrange with a local dentist or dental hygienist to conduct dental screenings at the children's setting. For some children these may be the only dental examinations they receive over the course of many years. If additional care is identified,

Policy Point

CONTROVERSIES SURROUNDING BMI SCREENING IN SCHOOLS

Schools in the United States are mandated to screen for hearing and vision. However, there are no national guidelines regarding measuring children's body mass index (BMI) even though obesity is so widespread among children.

In the United States, some states have passed legislation related to measuring BMI. The Arkansas legislature mandated schools to measure BMI and send home a BMI report card. Tennessee passed legislation allowing schools to do this but did not require it. Some health care experts argue that a single measurement of BMI without incorporating the child's medical, nutritional, and family history may result in mislabeling children as overweight. Others argue that the purpose of a *screening* is to identify all children who may be at risk for a health-related condition, such as obesity. The CDC convened an expert panel to discuss BMI screening in schools. They concluded that there was insufficient evidence to make a recommendation to mandate screening in all schools.

Conducting health screenings, including BMI, may have unintended consequences. What will families do with this information? One study explored parent response when a BMI report card was sent home along with health education materials. The materials that were sent to the families emphasized the importance of not "dieting" but focusing instead on eating healthier and promoting physical activity. Despite this guideline many families reported that they intended to control their child's weight by dieting or limiting food intake. Because most pediatric experts agree that dieting is not recommended in children, the parental reaction was of serious concern and highlighted the need for better health education.

Source: Based on "BMI Screening in Schools: Helpful or Harmful," by J. Ikeda, P. Crawford, and G. Woodward-Lopez, 2006, *Health Education Research, 21*(6), pp. 761–769.

children are referred to their dental provider or community services for further evaluation and intervention.

Accessibility to dental services is often a problem for low-income children. Teachers can share with families options for obtaining dental treatment. For example, "Give Kids a Smile" is an annual component to National Children's Dental Health Month and is observed on the first Friday in February. "Give Kids a Smile" is an American Dental Association event that draws on the volunteer services of dentists to provide dental treatment to low-income children who do not have access to care (American Dental Association, 2009). Many school districts also make arrangements for dental van services where children receive dental examinations and cleanings as well as other forms of treatment for dental caries.

Oral health assessments also provide opportunities to educate children and families about caring for their teeth. Families are notified in advance and permission is obtained for children to participate in dental screenings conducted in the children's setting. Once completed families are provided a report of the findings. This is a good time to share information with families about how to promote oral health and prevent dental caries.

Hearing and Vision Screenings

Specific tools are also used to screen for hearing and vision disorders. Hearing and vision screenings are often conducted in school settings where large numbers of children can be evaluated. Optimal development and

Screenings are highly effective ways to identify children with treatable hearing or vision conditions.

learning are influenced by the child's ability to accurately hear and see. Screening for hearing and vision loss is an important aspect of assisting children to be able to learn.

Hearing Screening

Hearing loss is the most common congenital condition in the United States, affecting 33 infants born every day (National Center of Medical Home Initiatives for Children with Special Needs, 2007). Hearing loss can occur in both ears or just in one ear. It can be mild, moderate, severe, or profound. Milder forms of hearing loss are more difficult to detect because children often compensate by using other sensory stimuli such as watching the environment closely for cues.

Because hearing loss is difficult to detect during the first few months of life, universal hearing screenings for newborns were implemented through the Early Hearing Detection and Intervention (EHDI) program. Most newborns have a hearing screen within the first few days of life before leaving the hospital (U.S. Preventive Services Task Force, 2008). Before this program was implemented many children with hearing loss were not recognized for many months or even years. Children born outside of the United States or children born at home may not have received a hearing screen at birth.

Vision Screening

Vision disorders are common in childhood and can lead to long-term disabilities. It is estimated that 5% to 10% of preschoolers have some type of vision problem (Tingley, 2007). Vision screening is an efficient and cost-effective way to identify children who need further evaluation. For this reason, vision screening has been mandated as a part of federal programs including the Early Periodic Screening, Diagnosis, and Treatment (EPSDT) Program and Head Start. Vision screening is important because when detected early, vision problems can be treated. Vision problems that go untreated can lead to vision loss or blindness. Vision screening detects children at risk for certain conditions including these (Tingley, 2007):

- Amblyopia: a condition that causes unfocused vision; sometimes called lazy eye.
- Strabismus: a condition in which the eyes are not aligned with one another.
- Refractive disorders: conditions that cause problems with focusing; usually corrected with glasses.
- Colorblindness: the inability to distinguish between some colors.

Vision screening done as part of a health care exam includes assessing how well the child tracks movement, fixates on a point, and responds to light. Familiar methods in the early childhood and school setting include having a child cover one eye while looking at a chart with symbols. The child is asked to match or identify the symbol, such as a letter or picture on the chart. These screening methods include directions for how to conduct the screening and indicators that suggest the child be referred for additional vision assessment. In addition to this form of vision screening, teachers can detect visual problems by noticing and reporting symptoms of visual disturbances. Signs of visual problems that teachers may notice include these (Prevent Blindness America, 2005):

- Rubbing eyes frequently.
- Tilting head to look at items.
- Holding objects close to eyes or trouble reading.
- Blinking more than usual.
- Squinting eyes or frowning.

If teachers notice these symptoms, they should refer the child's family to a health care provider for further evaluation. The activities in the *Teaching Wellness* feature contribute to children's learning about hearing and vision.

MyEducationLab

Go to the Assignments and Activities section of Topic 6: Health Appraisals/Screening in the MyEducationLab for your course and complete the activity entitled *Hearing and Vision Screening*. How do the teachers and the health screening administrator put the children at ease while teaching them about the purpose of these screenings?

amblyopia
a disorder that involves abnormal interaction between the eyes causing unfocused vision

strabismus
malalignment of the eyes

refractive disorders
visual conditions that cause problems with focusing

colorblindness
the inability to distinguish between some colors

Teaching Wellness *Health Care Checkups*

Learning Outcome: Children will be more comfortable with the idea of visiting a medical provider and will know what to expect during a checkup.

Infants and Toddlers

- **Goal:** To introduce information about health care checkups and visiting the doctor.

- **Materials:** *Time to See the Doctor* by Heather Maisner and Kristina Stephenson (2004, Kingfisher Publications).

- **Activity plan:** Read the book to the children. Point to aspects in the pictures that show what is found in the doctor's office. Talk about the child who is worried about the checkup and how he becomes more confident. Talk about what the doctor does and why.

- **Did you meet your goal?** Are the young children interested in the book? Do they follow along and anticipate the story? Do they talk about the activities that occur during the checkup? Can they answer, "What is the doctor doing?"

Preschoolers and Kindergartners

- **Goal:** To reduce children's worries about health care checkups through dramatic play exploration.

- **Materials:** Dramatic play props for the health care setting, including a doctor's kit with stethoscope, thermometer, blood pressure gauge, reflex hammer, bandages, and examination gloves.

- **Activity plan:** Provide the props and space for the children to create a doctor's office and conduct imaginative play. Provide picture books about visiting the doctor, such as:
  - *Biscuit Visits the Doctor,* by Alyssa Satin Capucilli (2008, HarperCollins Publishers)
  - *Corduroy Goes to the Doctor,* by Don Freeman and Lisa McCue (2005, Penguin Group)
  - *My Friend the Doctor,* by Joanna Cole and Maxie Chambliss (2005, HarperCollins Publishers)
  - *Elmo's World: Doctors!* by Naomi Kleinberg (2008, Random House Children's Books)
  - *La Doctora Maisy* (Spanish-language edition), by Lucy Cousins (2005, Lectorum Publications)
  - *Going to the Doctor,* by Anne Civardi, Michelle Bates, and Stephen Cartwright (2006, EDC Publishing)
  - *Doctor Ted* by Andrea Beaty and Pascal Lemaitre (2008, Atheneum Books for Young Readers).
  - *Going to the Hospital,* by Fred Rogers (1997, Putnam and Grosset Group)

- **How to adjust the activity:** Invite a medical provider to visit the classroom and talk about what to expect. Take pictures of children playing in the dramatic play area. Create a picture board and have children describe what happens when you visit the doctor. Have children talk about their experiences.

- **Did you meet your goal?** Observe children at play in the dramatic play area. Do they dramatize their experiences at the doctor's office? Do you hear them talking about worries or comforting their "patients"? When asked, are children able to describe with accuracy the kinds of things that happen at the exam?

School-Age Children

- **Goal:** To learn about the work that doctors and other medical providers do and communicate it to others.

- **Materials:** Materials to make posters such as large paper, marking pens, paints. Library books that describe the work of doctors and other medical providers, such as:
  - *What Does a Doctor Do?* by Felicia Lowenstein Niven (2005, Enslow Publishers)
  - *A Day in the Life of a Doctor,* by Heather Adamson (2004, Capstone Press)
  - *Keeping You Healthy: A Book about Doctors,* by Ann Owen (2004, Picture Window Books)
  - *Médico,* by Heather Miller (2003, Heinemann Library)
  - *If You Were a Doctor,* by Virgina Schomp (2001, Benchmark Books)

- *Activity plan:* Provide picture books and other library resources. Ask children to research information about the different things that doctors do. Have individuals or small groups of children create a poster to display describing how medical workers help us.

- *How to adjust the activity:* Have children create posters to share with preschool-age children and send them to early childhood programs. Take a field trip to a nearby preschool program. Have the children describe their posters to the preschoolers.

- *Did you meet your goal?* Do children display their knowledge of the work of medical providers through their posters and conversations? Do the posters effectively communicate this information?

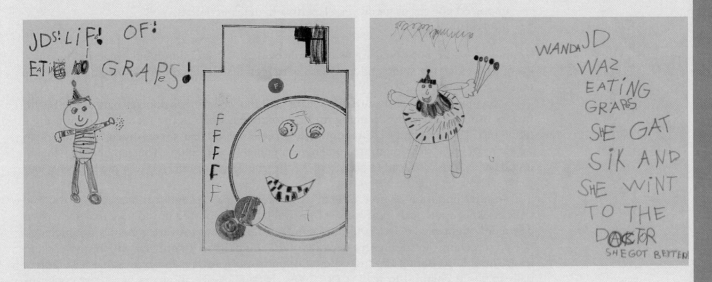

Screening for Communication Disorders

Children with communication disorders have better outcomes if they are diagnosed and treated early (Heward, 2009). Formalized screening for communication disorders varies among different types of early childhood programs. Some school districts have speech-language pathologists screen all kindergarten children for communication disorders (Owens, Metz, & Haas, 2007). Regardless of standard screening practices in early childhood programs, input from families and teachers is a critical component of identifying children with communication disorders. (Communication disorders include conditions that affect speech and language and are discussed in greater detail in Chapter 12.)

For a child whose first language is not English, the teacher must attempt to ascertain if a communication disorder is actually present or if the child functions normally in his or her own native language. When assessing children for disabilities, the Individuals with Disabilities Education Act (IDEA) requires that the assessment be conducted in the child's native language (Heward, 2009).

Lead Screening

Lead is a chemical element commonly found in the environment. It is a component of vehicle emissions and lead paint. In the 1970s, lead poisoning, or lead toxicity, was identified as a common illness among children (Laraque & Trasande, 2005). Lead toxicity can cause permanent neurological damage. Though the prevalence of lead in the environment has decreased, it is still a public health problem, primarily affecting children in urban settings.

The major source of lead exposure is the lead-based paint present in buildings constructed before the 1940s. As many as 25% of children may live in dwellings with deteriorating lead paint and be at risk for lead poisoning (Laraque & Trasande, 2005). Lead-based paint is most dangerous when the paint is deteriorating, and paint flakes and dust are introduced into the environment. It is ingested via a hand-to-mouth route or it can be inhaled. Inhalation is especially a problem when homes containing lead are being remodeled. Here are some other sources of lead exposure:

- Soil and dust.
- Toys.
- Jewelry.
- Exposure to the fetus *in utero.*
- Breast milk.
- Lead plumbing.
- Imported pottery or metal vessels with a high lead content.
- Industrial sources.

Symptoms of lead poisoning are usually only evident when children have ingested high levels of lead. However, some children with very high lead levels do not show any symptoms (Laraque & Trasande, 2005).

Screening for lead exposure in the early childhood setting is done as part of the health history using a checklist. Screening for lead toxicity is done in the medical setting using a blood test. The AAP and CDC recommend targeted blood lead level screenings (American Academy of Pediatrics Committee on Environmental Health, 2005). That is, children who are found to be at risk for lead exposure using the checklist are referred to a medical provider to be screened using the blood test.

Another important source of lead exposure in more recent years has been toys. The risks of exposure to lead in toys exist for toys that are imported or old toys that are passed down or bought used (CDC, 2009). Specific questions about toys are generally not included in lead screening questionnaires because of the difficulty in identifying which toys contain lead. The U.S. Consumer Product Safety Commission issues recalls on toys that have potentially exposed children to lead (CDC, 2009). If families or caregivers have *any* concerns about possible lead exposure, regardless of the lead screening questions, the child should be referred to a health care provider for lead testing.

Children who participate in Head Start programs and are eligible for Medicaid services receive blood lead tests as part of Medicaid's standards of well-child care. This is supported by Head Start Performance Standards (U.S. Department of Health and Human Services, Administration of Children and Families, n.d.). Teachers and programs that use lead screening checklists should have policies in place to refer those children who are at risk of exposure for further evaluation. Figure 10-7 is an example of a checklist to use in screening for lead exposure.

Developmental Screening and Assessment

Detecting developmental problems early in life is important so that intervention strategies can be implemented. Developmental screening is a service to children and families that is conducted to discover if the child's development is progressing as expected. Screening activities are provided soon after the child joins the early childhood program or school.

A plan should be in place to implement screening activities thoroughly and effectively. The screening plan should be (Early Head Start National Resource Center, 2009):

- *Systematic:* purposefully conducted.
- *Comprehensive:* include observations and discussion of developmental history.
- *Sensitive:* considerate of family characteristics, relationships, and other environmental or situational factors.

Screening tools for developmental progress should be considered as part of the larger process of evaluation. Teachers have access to another powerful assessment tool: their ability to conduct meaningful observations. The early childhood setting offers an environment where children's development can be seen in a natural setting. Teachers take advantage of this opportunity by conducting observations of children at play and in interactions with

MyEducationLab

Go to the Assignments and Activities section of Topic 6: Health Appraisals/Screening in the MyEducationLab for your course and complete the activity *Newborn Screening.* Why is it important to ask about whether a child had been screened as an infant as part of the health screening?

Figure 10-7 Lead Screening Checklist

If the answer is yes to any of these questions, the child is considered to be at risk of excessive lead exposure and should be referred to a medical provider for blood lead test screening.
Does your child:

☐ Spend time in buildings built before 1950 with peeling or chipping paint, including child care centers, preschools, or the homes of babysitters or relatives?

☐ Live in or regularly visit buildings built before 1950 with recent, ongoing, or planned renovation or remodeling?

☐ Have a brother or sister, housemate, or playmate being followed up or treated for lead poisoning?

☐ Frequently come in contact with an adult whose job or hobby involves exposure to lead, such as construction, auto repair, batteries, welding, pottery, or other trades?

☐ Live near an active lead smelter, battery recycling plant, or other industry likely to release lead?

☐ Does your family use pottery or ceramics for food or drink that are made in other countries?

☐ Has your child used any traditional or imported home remedies such as Azarcon, Alarcon, Greta, Rueda, Pay-loo-ah, or Kohl?

☐ Was your child adopted from or did your child live in another country?

Source: Adapted with permission from *Lead Poisoning Prevention Program*, by the Oregon Department of Human Services, retrieved September 28, 2009, from http://www.oregon.gov/DHS/ph/lead/docs/parentquest.pdf

others. Knowing about developmental milestones allows teachers to identify behaviors that may benefit from further evaluation.

Both screening and observational assessment are conducted by teachers, or other program personnel, who are familiar to the child and who have received orientation and training on appropriate approaches. Developmental screenings and assessments are conducted using tools that have been validated and are culturally appropriate. The process involves families by first discussing identified concerns. Next, teachers obtain permission from the family to conduct a formal screening and assessment.

When information has been gathered the teacher and family need to decide how to use the information. They discuss the findings and identify the next step. If a developmental concern is suspected, the child is referred to a developmental specialist for additional evaluation. The screening and assessment process also includes identifying the child's strengths and competencies and ways to promote the next steps in development. In this way developmental screening serves two purposes:

1. To identify possible developmental delays early so that intervention strategies can be planned and implemented.
2. To identify children's strengths and needs to inform the development of appropriate classroom curriculum.

Screening and assessment of infants and toddlers is especially challenging. Children in this age group are growing and maturing at a fast rate, and the tools used to conduct developmental assessments are variable in quality. Other challenges are present when assessing this age group, including these (Early Head Start National Resource Center, 2009):

- Developmental areas are closely connected, making it difficult to separate and identify the source of specific concerns.
- Developmental delays in this age group are very subtle.
- Infants and toddlers have limited ability to express themselves or to tell what they think and know, which limits the ability to identify delays through expressive language.

These challenges make ongoing observation especially important. Documentation of developmental observations provides a method for tracking concerns and recognizing when growth occurs or when it is delayed.

What if. . .

you notice a child who has difficulty speaking so others can understand him? What kinds of special observations might you make? How would you approach the family with your concerns? What referrals would you make? What resources in your community would you utilize?

Recognizing normal developmental patterns and milestones for each child is important for all ages. By knowing and understanding typical developmental patterns, teachers are prepared to recognize abnormal behaviors and patterns that fall outside of expected development. Like *red flags*, recognition of behaviors that do not align with expected development attracts the teacher's attention and highlights the need for further exploration.

In many cases, the early childhood teacher is the first person to mention to families that their child may be experiencing a developmental delay or concern. Families may have strong emotional reactions to this information. Teachers should be sensitive to these feelings and prepare carefully for such meetings. Teachers are partners with families in supporting child development wherever the child is on the continuum of developmental skills and competencies. Developmental screening and assessment provide information for purposeful curriculum planning. Teachers are *not* responsible for diagnosing developmental delays; however, they are important sources of referral and support for families if developmental concerns are suspected.

Conducting Daily Health Checks

Keeping attuned to children's health every day is a part of the teaching process that also includes continual observation and reflection. Daily health checks are a natural part of this process. The daily health check is a planned approach to direct teacher attention to the child's health. Teachers conduct these checks to determine if the child shows signs of illness, injury, or other health concerns. The American Academy of Pediatrics, American Public Health Association, and National Resource Center for Health and Safety in Child Care and Early Education (2002) recommend that daily health checks include the following:

- Changes in behavior or appearance from the previous day.
- Skin rashes, itchy skin or scalp.
- Signs of elevated body temperature.
- Complaints of pain or not feeling well.
- Other signs or symptoms of illness.
- Reports of illness or injury.

Daily health checks can be done efficiently and accurately during the greeting time. They are typically conducted by the teacher as the child arrives in the classroom or soon thereafter. The process involves:

- Stopping briefly to focus attention on the child.
- Looking at the child, observing for signs of illness or disease.
- Listening to the parent and child, paying special attention to information that suggests illness.

A description of this kind of approach is outlined in Figure 10-8.

During the health check the teacher watches for signs of good health such as pink skin, bright eyes, and easy breathing. The teacher also observes for indications of health problems such as irritability and asks the family if there are any concerns. If the child appears ill, the teacher needs to be prepared to explain to the family members the symptoms that are observed and discuss arrangements for the child to be taken home.

The daily health check and any symptoms of illness or concerns regarding a child's health should be recorded on a tracking chart. The *National Health and Safety Performance Standards* (AAP et al., 2002) recommend that the daily health check be charted in a way that is convenient for teachers to use, and that provides a picture of the overall class group's health. Two sample formats are shown in Figure 10-9. These charts make it easy to notice the pattern of symptoms of illness and subsequent absences. As total classroom attendance numbers drop due to illness, the chart also demonstrates the rate of disease spread among the children. These charts should be kept for at least 3 months to help track the spread of communicable diseases. They also provide the teacher and program with information to reflect on the effectiveness of disease prevention strategies, such as extra cleaning and sanitizing of the classroom.

Figure 10-8 **Stop-Look-Listen Daily Health Check**

Stop

Greet each child at arrival and take a moment to really observe the child.
Have a small conversation. Ask kind questions, such as "How are you feeling?"
"Did you sleep well last night?" "Did you eat breakfast today?"

Look

Observe these aspects:

	Signs of Good Health	**Possible Signs of Illness**
☐ Skin color	Pink and fresh; typical skin color for individual child	Flushed, feverish, or pale?
☐ Skin appearance	Smooth and calm	Rashy with sores or swelling?
☐ Eyes	Bright and alert	Red with discharge or dull with dark circles?
☐ Nose	Clear and clean	Dripping with nasal discharge?
☐ Ears	Does the child look comfortable	Rubbing and holding ears?
☐ Hair	Clean and combed	Unclean and badly tangled?
☐ General appearance	Does the child look interested in play	Droopy, listless, irritable, or restless?

Listen

Pay attention to what you hear:

	Signs of Good Health	**Possible Signs of Illness**
☐ Breathing pace	Even breathing	Fast breathing or panting?
☐ Breathing sounds	Quiet and smooth	Coughing, spitting, or congested?
☐ Parent reports	No concerns are mentioned	Child has been given medication before school?
		Child would not eat breakfast or has had a stomachache?
		Child has had diarrhea or has vomited recently?
		Child is acting unusually weepy?
		Child has been injured?

FOLLOW UP by asking more about any concerns.
DECIDE if the child is healthy. If signs of illness are present, child should return home.

Ongoing Observation

Observing children and monitoring them for signs of illness is the second part of continual health evaluation in the classroom. Through observation, teachers establish an understanding of each child's typical appearance and style of behavior so that signs of illness are more easily recognized. Signs of illness that are identified through observation include unusual fussiness and crying, listlessness or sleepiness, disinterest in food, paleness, or flushed cheeks. Observation is also important once an illness has been identified. In this situation, the teacher pays special attention to signs of illness spreading to other children.

The observations of children's health that teachers provide are important to families. Families rely on teachers to share feedback about how their child is doing in the class group when they are not present. They need to know if the teacher has detected signs of illness. Sometimes signs of illness are sudden, and require teachers to contact the family member to take the child home due to illness. Other times the cues of potential illness are shared with families at the time of departure. A clear description of the signs of illness is important so the family can continue to monitor the child at home. Ongoing observations respect the needs of young children to have teachers who are their advocates for health and wellness.

Figure 10-9 Daily Health Check and Attendance Tracking Chart

Option 1: Attendance and daily health check information overlap.

Month: *February*	Date									
Child's Name	1	2	3	4	5	6	7	8	9	10
Asma M.		SL	C,V	A	A					
Shay R.					C			A		
Liliana T.					C,V			A	A	A
Riki H-G.								C,V	A	A

Option 2: Attendance and daily health check are recorded separately.

Month: *February*	Date									
Child's Name	1	2	3	4	5	6	7	8	9	10
Asma M.				A	A					
		SL	C,V							
Shay R.								A		
					C					
Liliana T.								A	A	A
					C, V					
Riki H-G.									A	A
								C,V		

Attendance:

Mark if present

Mark if absent   A

Codes for Symptoms:

B = behavior change	I = report of injury	ST = sore throat
CP = chicken pox	L = lice	SR = skin rash
C = coughing	P = complaint of pain	T = suspected temperature
D = diarrhea	SL = sleepy or withdrawn	V = vomiting

Sources: Based on *Caring for Our Children: National Health and Safety Performance Standards: Guidelines for Out-of-Home Child Care Programs*, 2nd edition, American Academy of Pediatrics, American Public Health Association, and National Resource Center for Health and Safety in Child Care and Early Education, 2002, Elk Grove Village, IL: American Academy of Pediatrics; Washington, DC: American Public Health Association. Retrieved August 31, 2009, from http://www.eric.ed.gov/ERICDocs/data/ericdocs2sql/content_storage_01/0000019b/80/14/0d/14.pdf.

Summary

Health evaluation is an important aspect of early childhood development and education. Whether caring for infants and toddlers, nurturing the needs of preschoolers, or supporting school-age children, the teacher–child relationship involves being aware of children's health and wellness. Incorporating health screenings into the children's settings is a highly effective and efficient way to access large numbers of children. Identifying and addressing health and development problems early sets children on a course for improved outcomes and optimal learning.

Health screenings and assessments are initial steps in the process of health evaluation. They provide important information about the wide range of influences on children's health and contribute to an understanding of gaps that may exist in health care.

Collecting children's health history offers an opportunity to obtain health information in partnership with families. The information that is discussed guides the plan of services for the child in the classroom and provides opportunities to promote wellness in the family setting. Conducting assessments such as growth measurements, hearing and vision screenings, nutrition screenings, and developmental assessments ensures children get help for identified needs.

Health information is private and sensitive. It should be gathered and managed confidentially and appropriately. Understanding the status of children's health, promoting health and wellness in the family, and referring children to needed services improves physical and mental health outcomes for all children.

MyEducationLab
To check your understanding of how to assess and monitor children's health and wellness in early childhood settings, go to the Book Specific Resources section in the MyEducationLab for your course, select *Nutrition, Health, and Safety for Young Children*, Chapter 10 of the Study Plan, and then complete the multiple choice questions and activities.

Key Terms

Acculturation, p. 315
Adverse reactions, p. 313
Allergic reaction, p. 314
Amblyopia, p. 329
Asthma, p. 312
Colorblindness, p. 329
Continual observation, p. 308
Daily healthchecks, p. 308
Developmental milestones, p. 310

Fluoride, p. 316
Health assessments, p. 308
Health evaluation, p. 308
Health history, p. 309
Health literacy, p. 320
Health screenings, p. 308
Immunizations, p. 312
Local reaction, p. 313
Premature infant, p. 310

Referral, p. 326
Refractive disorders, p. 329
Rubella, p. 310
Strabismus, p. 329
Systemic reaction, pz 313
Thimerosal, p. 313
Well-child checkups, p. 325
Whooping cough, p. 325

Review Questions

1. Who should know the details about a child's medical history?
2. Describe the three types of exemptions to the required immunizations that are legally allowed in some states.
3. What are the symptoms of visual problems in children?
4. Describe risk factors for lead poisoning.
5. Explain how to perform a daily health check in an early childhood program.

Discussion Starters

1. A significant percentage of families in the United States lack affordable health insurance. Furthermore, even families with public health insurance have difficulty finding regular health care. How might lack of regular medical care influence health screenings in the early childhood setting?
2. Early childhood educators may interact with families who have concerns about vaccinating their children. How might a child who has not been completely vaccinated influence the health of other children in the early childhood setting?
3. As more schools incorporate BMI measurements into health screenings, some children will be identified as overweight or obese. When families are notified about their child's BMI, how do you think they will respond to these screenings? How do you feel about schools using obesity screening tools? Do these screenings have any unintended consequences?

Practice Points

1. A 5-year-old child enrolling in kindergarten in your state is unvaccinated. The family has applied for a religious exemption. Find the laws in your state about vaccinations. Determine what vaccinations are required and if religious exemptions are allowable.

2. Various formats are used to obtain health history information. Contact early childhood programs or the school district in your community to learn how they collect this information. Explore the Internet for sample health history formats and compare them.

3. Conduct the Stop–Look–Listen Daily Health Check (see Figure 10–8) with a child or peer teacher. Are you able to determine potential health concerns using this format?

4. Research information about conducting classroom vision screenings. What materials are available? What is the cost? Is special training required to use the materials? If possible, obtain vision screening materials and conduct a vision screening with a peer teacher or friend.

Web Resources

Centers for Disease Control and Prevention, About BMI for Children and Teens
www.cdc.gov/healthyweight/assessing/bmi/childrens_BMI/about_childrens_BMI.html

Childhood Immunization
www.nlm.nih.gov/medlineplus/childhoodimmunization.html

Children's Vision Screening
www.preventblindness.org/vision_screening/childrens_vision_screening.html

Health and Mental Health Services, School Health Screening Programs
www.nationalguidelines.org/guideline.cfm?guideNum=4-18

Immunization Action Coalition, State Information
www.immunize.org/laws

National Network for Immunization Information, Immunization Issues
www.immunizationinfo.org/immunization_issues.cfm

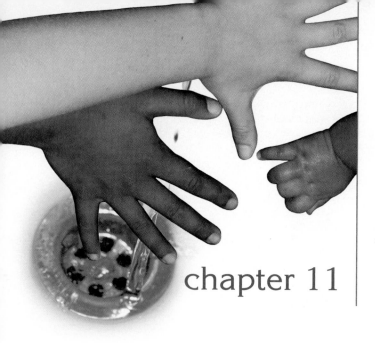

chapter 11 | Managing Infectious Disease

Learning Outcomes

After reading this chapter, you should be able to:

1. Describe the infectious disease process, including route of transmission.

2. Describe common symptoms of illness seen in children and how these are managed in early childhood programs.

3. Describe classroom practices that prevent or minimize the spread of infections.

4. Identify some of the more common infectious diseases and describe when children should be excluded from school because of them.

5. Describe some of the unique health challenges of children who are internationally adopted or refugees.

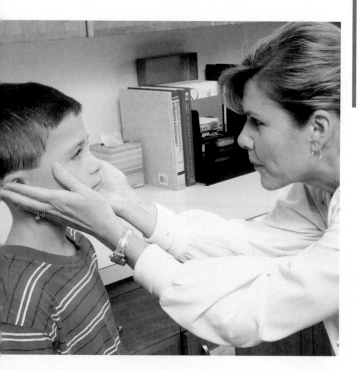

Mark is a healthy and vibrant 6-year-old who usually plays very actively during recess. Today his first-grade teacher, Mary Beth, notices that Mark is unusually quiet and not playing. She asks him if something is bothering him. He says he does not feel well and that his "tummy hurts." Mary Beth tells the other playground monitors that she is going to take Mark to the school office. The school nurse evaluates him and finds he has a fever. She notifies Mark's family who come to take him home. The nurse recommends that Mark be evaluated at a health clinic.

The next day Mark is absent from school. His mother calls and tells Mary Beth that Mark has been diagnosed with strep throat and that he will be out of school for a few days. Mary Beth knows that strep throat is highly contagious, but she is not sure if she should report this to the other families in the class. She e-mails the school nurse for advice. The nurse returns a notice for families alerting them to the signs of strep throat.

At story time Mary Beth talks with the children about ways to keep healthy. She reads *Germs Make Me Sick!* by Melvin Berger to help explore the topic. Mary Beth demonstrates how the children can cover their coughs by coughing into the crook of their arms. They also talk about how to carefully wash their hands and when to wash their hands to keep germs away. At the end of the day Mary Beth hears Calvin declare, "When Mark gets back let's tell him about how to be healthy!"

Children are exposed to numerous illnesses during the early childhood years. Illness is especially common for children who participate in group settings because of the potential for spreading germs. Young children are also especially vulnerable to certain infectious diseases because their immune systems are still developing. Also, because of their small size, they may experience illness more strongly than adults. Children are naturally curious, and their exploration of the world involves touching and handling toys and surfaces. These investigations cause them to put their hands and objects in their mouths, creating easy entry for germs. For all of these reasons, teaching young children naturally involves caring for children when illness occurs in the school or early childhood setting.

Teachers like Mary Beth become familiar with individual children and are able to recognize changes in the child's behavior or appearance that may be clues to sickness. They also know that they are responsible for assisting children when illness occurs, supporting families to get the medical help the child needs, and teaching children ways to keep themselves healthy. To help prepare you for these important aspects of teaching, this chapter describes the basic process of disease transmission and ways to prevent illness from spreading. We discuss some of the symptoms of common diseases and how to manage them in the early childhood setting. Some children such as children who are internationally adopted or who have recently immigrated to the United States may face special health concerns. These needs are also discussed.

Throughout the chapter, when we refer to *disease*, we are talking about illnesses, infections, viruses, and other maladies that cause children to get sick. Teachers are not trained medical professionals and should not offer diagnoses or treatment for health care problems. However, the guidance that is provided here contributes to the specialized set of skills that prepares teachers to care appropriately for children when illness occurs at school.

UNDERSTANDING THE INFECTIOUS DISEASE PROCESS

Diseases caused by infections can interrupt the body's functioning. Usually, the body is able to call into action the intricate biological responses of the immune system to detect and fight off disease. In the process of fighting off infections, a child can become ill and manifest a wide array of symptoms in response to infections. Infectious diseases are illnesses or conditions caused by germs, and they can cause symptoms related to many body systems.

Infectious diseases are quite common in childhood and can be a worrisome aspect of teaching. Children rely on their teachers to comfort and nurture them, and their classmates depend on the teacher to help keep them from getting sick. Teachers who understand the disease process are better able to address these responsibilities by reducing the frequency of disease and minimizing its impact.

The Causes of Disease

germ
an organism or infectious agent that can potentially cause disease

Diseases are caused by microscopic organisms that are present in huge numbers throughout the environment. They include viruses, bacteria, fungi, and parasites that invade the body and cause illness. Each of these organisms exists in one form or another virtually everywhere on earth. In their infectious forms, each is a cause for disease and potentially, death. We commonly refer to these infectious agents as germs.

Viruses

virus
a type of infectious germ that invades human tissue and causes illness

A virus is a type of infectious germ that invades human tissue and causes illness. The body's immune system is highly effective at killing off most viruses. However, illness results when a virus is able to get past the defenses of the immune system. Illnesses caused by viruses include chicken pox, measles, the common cold, influenza, and human immunodeficiency virus (HIV). Usually diseases caused by viruses are allowed to improve on their own. Through this healing process the body's systems develop a certain level of immunity to similar viruses in the future.

Bacteria

bacteria
infectious germs that invade human tissue and cause illness; sometimes treated with antibiotics

Like viruses, bacteria are infectious germs that invade human tissue and cause illness. Some bacteria are useful in digestion and in certain familiar processes such as making yogurt from milk, but other bacteria are pathogenic, meaning they cause disease. These harmful bacteria are the cause of many respiratory illnesses, such as bacterial pneumonia and tuberculosis, and diseases such as tetanus. Bacteria are a major cause of disease and death worldwide. Bacterial infections are often treated through the use of medications such as antibiotics.

Fungi

fungi
a type of germ that can commonly cause skin infections or allergic reactions

Fungi are germs that are the cause of common illnesses such as ringworm or athlete's foot. Other examples of fungi are mushrooms, mold, and baker's yeast. Other fungi are used to grow special molds for making cheese. The spores of some fungi can cause allergies.

Parasites

parasite
infections that invade the body and live within human tissue for extended periods of time

Parasites are present in all ecosystems on the earth. They are infectious agents that feed on or enter the body tissue. They can live on and within human tissue for extended periods of time. Examples of parasitic diseases include head lice, scabies, intestinal worms, malaria, and parasites such as *Giardia*, which are contracted from drinking contaminated water.

communicable diseases
infections that are spread from one person to another

mode of transmission
the route by which an infection is spread

How Disease Is Spread

Disease is caused by viruses, bacteria, fungi, and parasites—commonly referred to as germs.

Infectious diseases are spread from person to person or from an animal or insect to a person. The most frequent infections among young children are communicable diseases, which are spread from one person to another. Disease is spread in different ways, called modes of transmission (see Figure 11-1). Most infections are transferred by one of the four common modes of transmission, as discussed next (American Academy of Pediatrics [AAP], 2009).

Figure 11-1 Common Modes of Transmission

Droplet Transmission

Airborne Transmission

Fecal-oral Transmission

Bloodborne Transmission

Direct Contact and Droplet Spread

Some diseases are spread through direct contact with infectious skin lesions or through contact with body fluids such as the respiratory droplets of another person. Direct contact and droplet spread are common modes of transmission in early childhood settings where children play close together and touching is frequent. For instance, babies tend to crawl across one another when they are playing. They might also offer one another a toy they have been sucking on.

Exchange of germs and droplets also occurs indirectly when the infected droplets land on surfaces that are touched by other children who unintentionally transfer the germs to their mouths. Typical actions such as these occur in everyday play and provide the opportunity to spread disease. For example, Cherice, who is coming down with a cold, may sneeze directly onto Aiden while they are playing with blocks. Or she may turn away and sneeze onto some blocks that are touched a few minutes later by Karl, who has just joined the play. When Karl picks up the blocks and later scratches his nose or puts his fingers into his mouth, the germs are transmitted to him.

Airborne Transmission

Airborne transmission involves the spread of germs through the air and occurs when an infected person sneezes or coughs, spraying droplets of saliva or mucus into the air. Another person may then inhale the droplets and become infected. Infections spread by airborne transmission can spread infections over a much wider area than infectious droplets transmitted by direct contact (Yale Center for Public Health Preparedness, 2006).

airborne transmission
occurs when infected particles are sneezed or coughed into the air and inhaled by another person

Fecal–Oral Transmission

Fecal–oral transmission occurs when microscopic amounts of infected feces are transferred directly from one person to another person's mouth. This occurs either directly, by touching feces, or indirectly, by touching soiled surfaces or objects and then touching the mouth. This method of disease transmission is especially problematic in settings where young children are wearing diapers. Disease can be transmitted by poorly washed hands after changing diapers or after helping children at the toilet.

fecal–oral transmission
occurs when microscopic amounts of infected feces are transferred to another person's mouth either directly or indirectly (surfaces, objects, etc.)

Bloodborne Transmission

Bloodborne transmission occurs through contact with contaminated blood. In this situation, the infection can be transmitted only if the infected blood comes into contact with an uninfected person's bloodstream through a wound. This might happen if a child comes into contact with infected blood from a wound such as a bite, nosebleed, bleeding from excessive scratching of irritated skin, or injury (AAP, 2009). This mode of transmission is very uncommon in early childhood and school settings.

The Incubation Period

Illness does not always occur immediately after contact with an infectious germ. Sometimes illness is not evident until a few hours, days, or even up to a few months in rare cases. The time between the child's first exposure to an infectious agent and when the first symptom of illness appears is called the incubation period.

Each infectious agent has its own typical incubation period. Recognizing that the incubation period for familiar diseases may vary provides important information. For some diseases, the incubation period is the time when the child is most infectious to others. When an illness has been diagnosed, teachers who are knowledgeable about the illness's incubation period are then able to identify other children who may have been exposed to the disease. Knowing about incubation periods also helps teachers know how long to watch for the spread of the disease and to recognize when the potential risk for additional cases is likely to be over.

In the opening case scenario, Mary Beth understands that other children may have been exposed to strep throat. She takes steps to counteract the possible spread of the disease by teaching the children how to cover their coughs and wash their hands carefully. She also shares information with parents about the symptoms of strep throat. In addition, Mary Beth will also watch for signs of strep throat over the next 2 to 5 days, the typical incubation period for this disease.

The period of contagiousness can also vary and be different or similar to the incubation period. Local health departments and health care providers can be excellent resources for teachers when potential outbreaks or questions arise. Table 11-1 outlines modes of transmission, incubation periods, and symptoms associated with the infectious diseases discussed in this chapter.

Symptoms of Disease

Just before disease becomes evident, various warning signs occur. These symptoms or signs of disease alert teachers to impending illness. They guide teachers to be watchful and ready to take appropriate action to care for the child. Symptoms that are frequently associated with disease include the following:

- *Fever*, which may be evident by the child's brightly flushed cheeks.
- *Cough*, especially if the cough is new.
- *Rash*, such as a newly emerging flush on the skin.
- *Vomiting*, especially when vomiting occurs with no other likely explanation.
- *Changes in the child's typical behavior*, such as being very quiet or not engaging in typical play.

In the opening scenario, it was Mark's atypical behavior that caught his teacher's attention. Following her observations, and after talking with Mark, Mary Beth detected that it was highly likely he was becoming ill. She felt reasonably confident that it was in Mark's best interest to see the school nurse for further assessment. Most children's programs do not have a nurse available to assist with determining a course of action for a child who gets sick at school. In these settings, teachers must use their best judgment to determine if the child can be cared for in the setting or if the parent should be contacted.

Table 11-1   Childhood Infections: Mode of Transmission, Incubation Period, and Symptoms

Infectious Disease	Mode of Transmission	Incubation Period	Symptoms
Chicken pox	Airborne, droplet	10–21 days	Fever, cough, rash
Common colds	Droplet	Variable	Fever, runny nose, cough, congestion
Conjunctivitis (pinkeye)	Droplet	Variable	Eye drainage, redness of eyes
Coxsackie virus (hand, foot, and mouth disease)	Droplet	3–5 days	Fever, blisters in the mouth, refusal to eat, rash on palms and soles
Croup	Droplet	Variable	Fever, barky cough, runny nose
Ear infections	Not communicable	Variable	Fever, earache
Fifth disease	Droplet	4–28 days	Fever, headache, muscle aches, rash
Group A strep (strep throat)	Droplet	Several hours to 4 days	Fever, sore throat, rash
Haemophilus influenzae type b (Hib)	Droplet	Unknown	Fever, upper respiratory infection, meningitis
Head lice	Direct contact	10–14 days	Itching of scalp
Hepatitis A	Fecal–oral	15–50 days	Fever, nausea, abdominal pain
Hepatitis B	Bloodborne	45–160 days	Inflammation of the liver
Hepatitis C	Bloodborne	6–7 weeks	Inflammation of the liver
Human immunodeficiency virus (HIV)	Bloodborne	12–18 months	Wide range of symptoms
Influenza	Airborne or droplet; depends on the strain	1–4 days	Fever, muscle aches, sore throat, cough, headache
Measles	Airborne, droplet	7–18 days	Fever, pinkeye, runny nose, rash
Methicillin-resistant *Staphylococcus aureus* (MRSA)	Direct contact	Variable	Skin infections
Pertussis (whooping cough)	Droplet	4–21 days	Initial: fever, runny nose, cough Later: Numerous bursts of cough, sometimes with the characteristic whoop
Pinworms	Fecal–oral	Variable	Itching around anus
Respiratory syncytial virus (RSV)	Droplet	2–8 days	Fever, runny nose, cough, difficulty breathing
Ringworm	Direct contact	Unknown	Rash
Rotavirus	Fecal–oral	1–2 days	Fever, vomiting, diarrhea
Scabies	Direct contact	4–6 weeks	Rash, itching
Streptococcus pneumonia	Droplet	1–3 days	Ear infections, pneumonia, meningitis
Tetanus	Direct contact through open wound	4–21 days	Severe muscle contraction, spasm, seizures
Tuberculosis	Droplet, airborne	2–12 weeks	Chronic cough

Sources: Based on *Red Book: 2009 Report of the Committee on Infectious Diseases*, 28th edition, edited by L. K. Pickering, C. J. Baker, D. W. Kimberlin, & S. S. Long, 2009, Elk Grove Village, IL: American Academy of Pediatrics; and *Epidemiology and Prevention of Vaccine-Preventable Diseases*, 10th edition, edited by W. Atkinson, J. Hamborsky, L. McIntyre, and S. Wolfe, Washington DC: Public Health Foundation.

A description of the symptoms the teacher observed provides helpful information for families and medical providers. It is not appropriate for the teacher to suggest a medical diagnosis or offer a plan of treatment. However, it is appropriate for the teacher to provide a summary of the symptoms that were observed, to inform the family of the intensity of those symptoms, and to recommend that the parent seek medical evaluation. Symptoms provide clues to help medical providers diagnose the disease and create an appropriate treatment plan.

Symptoms for Common Infections

Among the many diseases that children may experience, three groups of infections are most common. These include infections with symptoms of diarrhea, respiratory illness, or skin infections and rashes.

Acute Infectious Diarrhea

diarrhea
the frequent and excessive discharge of watery feces

Diarrhea is the frequent and excessive discharge of watery feces. It is experienced in young children as discomfort and soiled diapers or clothing or as a frequent need to use the bathroom. Infectious diarrhea is caused by both viruses and bacteria. The infection is transmitted from person to person usually by a fecal-oral route. Infectious diarrhea outbreaks are 2 to 3 times more common among children who participate in early childhood group settings than among those who do not. Children are three times more likely to experience infectious diarrhea during their first month in the group setting than at any other time. Children who wear diapers are 17 times more likely to experience infectious diarrhea than nondiapered children. Infectious diarrhea is often spread to family members as well (Shane & Pickering, 2008).

Because of this frequency of occurrence and the potential for the spread of infectious diarrhea, its management and prevention are especially important. Frequent hand washing is critical for children and teachers. If a child develops diarrhea, the teacher should inform parents how many episodes the child experienced. It is particularly important to notice if any blood is present in the child's stool. Other symptoms such as fever, vomiting, or rash should also be reported.

What if. . .

several children in your class developed diarrhea? What policies would you implement to minimize further spread of the illness? What resources in your community would you turn to for assistance if it became a large outbreak of infectious diarrhea?

Respiratory Tract Illnesses

pharyngitis
infection of the throat

sinusitis
sinus infection

pneumonia
lung infection

Symptoms of respiratory tract illnesses involve the nose, sinuses, ears, throat, and lungs. Respiratory diseases are extremely common in young children. Familiar respiratory infections include the common cold, ear infections, **pharyngitis** (an infection of the throat), **sinusitis** (a sinus infection), and **pneumonia** (a lung infection).

Respiratory illnesses may be caused by viruses, bacteria, or fungi. They are most often spread by sneezing, coughing, or drainage from the nose. Symptoms of respiratory tract illness include fever, nasal congestion, runny nose, sore throat, ear pain, cough, or difficulty breathing. Some of these infections are associated with skin rashes as well. Studies report that 89% of illnesses among children in child care settings are respiratory tract illnesses, and the incidence of ear infections is significantly higher among children attending group care (Shane & Pickering, 2008).

Frequent hand washing and teaching children how to cover their coughs are important ways to prevent the spread of respiratory infections. Families should be contacted and children should be referred to their medical provider if they exhibit signs of stress such as uncontrolled coughing, difficulty breathing, or wheezing (American Academy of Pediatrics, American Public Health Association, & National Resource Center for Health and Safety in Child Care and Early Education, 2002). During the initial days of respiratory illness, children may be uncomfortable or in pain. Although they may be receiving treatment and do not have a fever, they should stay at home simply because they are not feeling well and are unable to participate in normal school activities.

The symptoms of runny nose and cough are not uncommon in young children, especially during the winter months. These symptoms alone should not exclude children from attending early childhood programs. If teachers have concerns, parents should be notified. Collaboration with a health care provider may be helpful to determine if exclusion is necessary. Many of these children can safely be included.

Skin Infections and Contagious Rashes

Skin infections are caused by viruses, bacteria, and fungi. They are a common symptom of several diseases. Sometimes respiratory tract infections are associated with skin infections.

Chicken pox is one example. Initially, the disease starts with mild upper respiratory symptoms, then progresses to the characteristic skin rash.

It is not known if skin infections occur more frequently in child care or school settings. Inclusion or exclusion of children with skin rashes depends on the underlying cause. Teachers may need to rely on the recommendations from the child's health care provider when determining if exclusion is appropriate. Frequent hand washing helps minimize potential spread.

PREVENTING AND CONTROLLING INFECTIOUS DISEASE

Children who participate in group settings have the potential to be exposed to a wide range of diseases. This makes it especially important for teachers to be purposeful in implementing strategies to reduce the incidence of illness. Strategies include the following:

- Recognizing national public health policies.
- Complying with medical interventions, such as required immunizations.
- Following recommended practices for the classroom that are provided by licensing and accreditation agencies.
- Establishing and practicing prevention strategies that are established and implemented at the local level by the children's program or school.

We now look at some of the more common prevention strategies: immunizations, health assessments for teachers, and classroom practices to reduce the spread of disease.

Immunizations

The immunizations that are required for entry and participation in early childhood and school settings are put in place to stop the spread of potentially dangerous diseases. Requirements for children's immunizations are typically regulated by federal or state agencies that have oversight for early childhood settings and schools. Immunization requirements are useful to teachers because they help in establishing healthful environments for young children. Immunizations have been proven to be the most effective method of disease prevention among groups of children.

Health Assessments for Teachers

Preemployment and ongoing health appraisals for teachers help reduce the potential for spread of disease between teachers and children and assist in keeping teachers healthy. Health assessments assist in detecting infectious disease that teachers may introduce into the classroom. For example, some infectious diseases such as tuberculosis can be "silent," meaning the adult has no symptoms. The *National Health and Safety Performance Standards* recommend that teachers obtain a health assessment before employment and then every 2 years (AAP et al., 2002). A health assessment for teachers might include these items:

- *Health history:* to establish an understanding of the adult's general state of health.
- *Physical and dental exam:* to screen for illness and to recognize if dental decay is evident. The germs that cause dental decay are infectious and can be communicated to young children.
- *Vision and hearing screening:* to identify the need for glasses or hearing assistance.
- *Tuberculosis* (TB) *screening:* to identify whether the teacher is a potential carrier of TB. Standards related to TB screening are specific to regional health recommendations depending on the risk of TB in the local area. Many programs require a TB test prior to employment and again if the teacher has a known exposure.
- *Review of occupational health hazards:* to clarify risks to the teacher in the children's setting and to identify any accommodations that might be needed.

- *Assessment of limitations:* to identify issues that may require modifications in the workplace, such as regular break times for a teacher who needs to test and manage her own insulin treatment for diabetes.

An assessment of the teacher's immunization history is also important. Immunizations protect the teacher from contracting childhood diseases introduced by the children. The following immunizations are of particular importance for teachers:

- *Hepatitis A:* a viral infection that causes diarrhea and inflammation of the liver.
- *Hepatitis B:* a viral infection that can cause chronic inflammation of the liver that can lead to liver cancer.
- *Tetanus:* a bacterial infection acquired through wounds that can cause severe muscle spasms and death.
- *Influenza:* a respiratory infection that can cause fever, cough, vomiting, and diarrhea.
- *Chicken pox and measles:* viral infections that can cause fever and rash.
- *Pertussis or whooping cough:* a respiratory infection that can cause severe respiratory distress, especially in infants, and prolonged cough.

Some infections, such as hepatitis A and chicken pox, are common among children and can easily be spread to an adult. These infections are often more serious for adults than children.

There is an increasing prevalence of whooping cough (pertussis) among older children and individuals whose immunity from previous vaccination is waning. For this reason the tetanus booster vaccine for adults now includes pertussis vaccination (TdaP). Teachers should receive TdaP instead of the former tetanus booster (dT) (Centers for Disease Control and Prevention [CDC], 2006).

Yearly influenza vaccination is also important for teachers. The flu vaccination is especially important for teachers who work with children younger than 2 years of age and any children who have chronic medical conditions or special health care needs (AAP, 2009). Teachers need to be concerned about their own health. Teachers who may be pregnant should be aware that some childhood illness can have negative impacts on the unborn child. The *Safety Segment* addresses these situations.

Finally, teachers are not only susceptible to infection, but they can spread infection, just as children can. When certain symptoms are present such as fever or vomiting, teachers should stay home and avoid exposing others. If a specific diagnosis has been made, such as strep throat, teachers should follow the same recommendations that are made for children.

Safety Segment

Addressing the Risk of Infectious Disease during Pregnancy

Teachers need to be alert to their own health care. This is especially important for women who become pregnant while teaching young children. Some common infectious diseases introduce risks to the growing fetus, including abnormal development and even death. Infections that spread from the mother to the unborn baby include chicken pox, hepatitis B, coxsackie virus, herpes, and fifth disease.

Teachers who are pregnant or planning to become pregnant should consult with their health care provider. A health history and record of immunizations will help the physician evaluate the need to update immunizations, such as tetanus, diphtheria, and influenza. Teachers who are exposed to infectious disease during pregnancy should contact their health care provider for guidance.

Sources: Based on *Caring for Our Children: National Health and Safety Performance Standards: Guidelines for Out-of-Home Child Care Programs*, 2nd edition, American Academy of Pediatrics, American Public Health Association, and National Resource Center for Health and Safety in Child Care and Early Education, 2002, Elk Grove Village, IL: American Academy of Pediatrics; Washington, DC: American Public Health Association, retrieved August 31, 2009, from http://www.eric.ed.gov/ERICDocs/data/ericdocs2sql/content_storage_01/0000019b/80/14/0d/14.pdf; and "Implications for the Fetus of Maternal Infections in Pregnancy," by E. L. Ford-Jones and G. Ryan, in *Infectious Diseases*, 2nd edition, edited by J. Cohen and W. G. Powderly, 2004, New York: Elsevier.

Classroom Practices for Controlling the Spread of Disease

Purposeful health practices that are routinely followed in children's settings can significantly decrease the frequency of infections. These include such practices as hand washing, conducting daily health checks, sanitizing toys and classrooms, following careful diapering and toileting policies, implementing universal precautions when needed, and teaching children preventive health practices.

Hand Washing

Hand washing is the single most important way to reduce the spread of disease. Unwashed or improperly washed hands are the primary source for the spread of disease (AAP et al., 2002). Numerous studies have demonstrated that simple hygiene measures such as hand washing can significantly reduce the spread of disease (Kotch, 2007).

When to Wash Hands All children and teachers should wash their hands at routine times during the day, such as at arrival or before eating, as well as at other times when germs can be transmitted. Children and teachers should wash their hands at the following times:

MyEducationLab

Go to the Building Teaching Skills and Dispositions section of Topic 8: Infectious Diseases in the MyEducationLab for your course and complete the activity entitled *Prevent the Spread of Infection.* As you work through the learning unit, consider your role in preventing the spread of infection.

- On arrival at school, when coming in from outdoor play, and when returning from a field trip.
- When moving from one classroom to another, for example, when a teacher moves from leading one group to another.
- Before:
  - Eating or feeding a child.
  - Whenever handling food.
  - Giving medication to a child.
  - Playing in the water table, or other water play where more than one child is participating.
- After:
  - Using the toilet.
  - Diapering or helping a child use the toilet.
  - Assisting children to wipe or blow their noses.
  - Contacting body fluids such as mucus (from sneezing), blood, vomit.
  - Providing first aid or care for sores or wounds.
  - Handling animals [see the *Health Hint*].
  - Playing in the water table or sandbox.
  - Handling uncooked food, especially raw meat or poultry.
  - Cleaning or sanitizing.
  - Handling garbage.*

Supporting Children to Wash Their Own Hands Children are capable of washing their hands effectively if the appropriate supports are available. This includes providing a child-sized sink or an appropriate step stool so children can reach the water. Warm, running water is needed to encourage scrubbing and to remove soil and germs. Liquid soap should be provided because it is easier for children to use (see Figure 11-2). Disposable towels are recommended to avoid the spread of germs. Children should be taught to turn the faucet off with a paper towel because this helps reduce the spread of germs from the faucet back to the child's hands. Some studies have shown that faucet handles are one of the most contaminated sites in a child care setting (Kotch, 2007).

Assisting Children with Hand Washing Once children have been taught how to effectively wash their hands, the teacher's role is primarily to supervise for safety. Some children may not be able to wash at a sink with running water. When washing a baby's hands,

---

*Used with permission of the American Academy of Pediatrics, *Caring for Our Children: National Health and Safety Performance Standards: Guidelines for Out-of-Home Child Care Programs,* 2e. Copyright 2002.

or assisting children who cannot stand at a sink or who are too heavy to hold at the sink, the following approach is appropriate (AAP et al., 2002):

- Use a moist paper towel with a small amount of liquid soap to wipe the child's hands. Throw the paper towel away.
- Wet a clean paper towel and use it to wash the child's hands, wiping away any soap. Throw away the paper towel.
- Use a clean paper towel to dry the child's hands. Throw this towel away.

Teachers should wash their own hands after assisting children.

Conducting Daily Health Checks

Daily health checks (as discussed in Chapter 10) are an important way to prevent the spread of disease. Teachers should be prepared to conduct the daily health check as soon as possible after the children arrive. The purpose of the check is to identify children who are ill and who may be need to be excluded from participation. Monitoring for skin rashes, fever, and other signs of disease are important ways teachers help prevent the spread of infections (AAP et al., 2002). For example, teachers should monitor the class group for 2 weeks (the incubation period) following a confirmed case of chicken pox. Teachers should document the findings from the daily health checks to assist in tracking and monitoring illnesses in the classroom.

Cleaning and Sanitizing

Cleaning and sanitizing are important actions in preventing the spread of disease. Young children touch and share many objects throughout the day. Children frequently place their fingers, hands, and toys in or close to their mouths and noses. They deposit germs either directly onto others or indirectly onto surfaces and objects. Because of this, any surface that a child can reach, including floors, should be sanitized regularly to minimize contamination with infectious germs.

Cleaning products should be safe for use in the classroom setting. The bleach and water solutions for cleaning and sanitizing discussed elsewhere in this text are appropriate for use in children's settings. Table 11-2 describes the frequency schedule for sanitizing objects and surfaces in the classroom.

Teachers carry the primary responsibility for a healthy classroom environment. This requires teacher's commitment to ensuring clean and sanitary spaces and equipment. It also

MyEducationLab

Go to the Assignments and Activities section of Topic 8: Infectious Diseases in the MyEducationLab for your course and complete the activity entitled *Sanitizing the Classroom*. Why do you think this process is so important in preventing the spread of infectious diseases?

Figure 11-2 Hand Washing Is the Single Most Important Way to Reduce the Spread of Disease

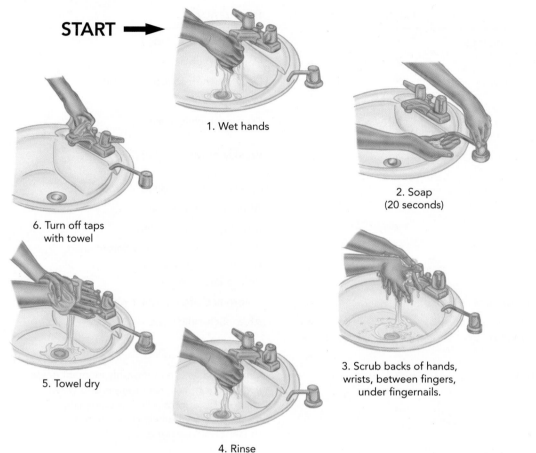

START ➡️

1. Wet hands

2. Soap
(20 seconds)

3. Scrub backs of hands,
wrists, between fingers,
under fingernails.

4. Rinse

5. Towel dry

6. Turn off taps
with towel

Source: Based on steps from LaCrosse County Environmental Health, Wisconsin.

means that teachers need to have a positive disposition toward what can sometimes be a tedious task: cleaning. Several approaches can help:

- Post a cleaning and sanitizing reminder chart to ensure that the schedule is achieved.
- Provide a "wash me" bucket for collecting toys that have been in children's mouths. The toys in the bucket are then sanitized after class.
- Stock the cupboard with disposable towels for wiping doorknobs and cupboard handles.
- Obtain laundry bags for gathering dramatic play clothing at the end of each week so the clothing can be laundered.
- Be prepared to increase the frequency of cleaning and sanitizing when the number of children with illness is unusually high.

Diapering and Toileting

Sanitary practices are especially important when changing diapers or assisting children at the toilet. Settings that provide care for children who wear diapers typically require the use of disposable diapers. Exceptions may be made for children who have a medical reason, such as an allergic reaction to disposable diapers. Figure 11-3 describes appropriate diaper changing procedures. This procedure should be posted in all diaper changing areas. A child should **never** be left unattended on the changing table.

Settings that serve children who are learning to use the toilet are discouraged from using potty chairs because sanitation is difficult. If potty chairs are used, the contents should

Table 11-2	Cleaning and Sanitizing Schedule		

Area	Clean	Sanitize	Frequency
Classroom countertops and tabletops	X	X	Daily or when soiled
Toileting and diapering areas	X	X	Daily or when soiled
Door knobs and cabinet handles	X	X	Daily or when soiled
"Cubbies" or coat areas	X		Weekly
Toys that go into the mouth or have been in contact with saliva or body fluids	X	X	After each child's use
Toys that are not contaminated with body fluids	X		Weekly or when soiled
Dress-up clothes	X		Weekly or when soiled
Hats	X		After each child's use
Blankets, sleeping bags	X		Monthly or when soiled
Cribs and crib mattresses	X		Weekly, before use by different child, whenever soiled or wet
Food service carts	X	X	Before and after each use
Food preparation & service surfaces	X	X	Before and after contact with foods
Utensils and surfaces that have been in contact with saliva or body fluids	X	X	After each child's use
Floors	X	X	Daily and when soiled
Carpets and large area rugs	X		Vacuum daily. Clean monthly in infant areas, every 3 months in other areas and when soiled. Use approved carpet cleaning method only when children will not be present until carpet is dry.

Source: NAEYC. 2005. *NAEYC Early Childhood Program Standards and Accreditation Criteria: The Mark of Quality in Early Childhood Education.* Washington, DC: Author. Adapted with permission from the National Association for the Education of Young Children.

be emptied into a toilet. The potty chair should be placed in a utility sink, to be sanitized after each use (AAP et al., 2002). Ideally, settings serving children ages 2 to 5 should provide child-sized toilets. This makes children more comfortable and helps them learn to manage their own toileting.

When assisting children with toileting, teachers should guide the child in removing their garments and help them use the toilet. Teachers should assist with wiping as needed, remembering to wipe from front to back. Young children may need help with arranging and fastening their garments. Then both the child and the teacher should thoroughly wash their hands. Sinks and toilets should be cleaned and sanitized daily.

Using Standard Precautions

Standard Precautions
a set of guidelines defined by the CDC for use in hospitals and other health care centers to prevent the spread of disease through blood and body fluids

The Standard Precautions are a set of guidelines created to prevent the spread of infections from exposure to blood and body fluids that may contain blood. They have been established by the CDC for use in hospitals and other health care settings. The basic principle is that all blood, body fluids, secretions, excretions (except sweat), nonintact skin, and mucous membranes potentially contain germs that can cause infections (CDC, 2007b).

Figure 11-3 Diaper Changing Procedures

1. **NEVER** leave the child unattended at the changing table.
2. Have all needed supplies available at the changing table. Wash hands.
3. Place the child on the changing table, avoiding contact of soiled diaper with surrounding surfaces.
4. Unfasten soiled diaper, leaving it under child. Clean the child's diaper area and genitalia using appropriate wipes. Clean from front to back. Use a fresh wipe each time removing urine or stool.
5. Remove soiled diaper without contaminating surfaces. Enclose the diaper in a disposable bag.
6. Slide the fresh diaper under the child and fasten.
7. Wash the child's hands and return the child to the supervised area.
8. Clean and sanitize the diaper changing area.
9. Wash your hands. Record diaper change in child's daily log.

Source: Used with permission of the American Academy of Pediatrics, *Caring for Our Children: National Health and Safety Performance Standards: Guidelines for Out-of-Home Child Care Programs,* 2e. Copyright 2002.

Standard Precautions include two important practices relevant to early childhood settings (AAP et al., 2002):

1. Using barriers, such as disposable gloves, when caring for children where blood or body fluids as stated above may be present.
2. Cleaning and sanitizing surfaces to prevent the transmission of infections by touching surfaces that have been contaminated by blood.

Teachers should wear gloves whenever an injury involves blood, such as a cut, scrape, or bloody nose. Once the bleeding has been stopped, any surfaces that have been exposed to blood must be sanitized. Consider this scenario:

> Tom is in the play yard bouncing a ball to Lena. He hears a crash and looks to see that Jimmy has tipped over on the trike. Tom moves quickly to Jimmy who has crawled out from under the trike. He can see that Jimmy's lip is bleeding. As he hurries to Jimmy, Tom reaches into his pocket and pulls out a pair of disposable gloves. He puts them on as he arrives at Jimmy's side. "Hey Jimmy," Tom says as he crouches down to gently hug Jimmy. "That looked like a pretty big bump! Let's go inside and take a good look at it."

Tom was prepared for this accident, and he knew immediately to use Standard Precautions. Many teachers find it useful to place a pair of gloves in their pocket for emergencies such as this. Another strategy is to tape pairs of gloves at various locations on the classroom wall, and in logical locations in outdoor play areas. Each classroom should have a ready supply of disposable gloves as well as disposable toweling and appropriate sanitizing solutions. Even when gloves are used to manage injuries that involve blood, hand washing is still crucial. After use, the gloves should be removed and discarded in a sanitary manner, and hands should be washed.

Teaching Children Preventive Health Practices

Teachers help children be partners in disease prevention by guiding them to develop self-help skills and by teaching age-appropriate and developmentally appropriate prevention practices. Teaching disease prevention practices has a dual purpose: It helps to reduce the spread of disease immediately and educates children about ways to improve their wellness in the future. The *Teaching Wellness* feature offers examples for the classroom.

As discussed in Chapter 2, infusing the daily curriculum with health messages is the best way to engage and educate children about wellness. This includes offering activities that have a health focus. It also means purposefully teaching age-appropriate disease prevention

Learning Outcome: Children will learn how germs spread and how to stop them.

Infants and Toddlers

- *Goal:* To introduce the child to the concept of germs.

- *Materials:* Paint, paintbrush, and paper; paint smocks as appropriate.

- *Activity plan:* Make handprints on paper. Have the toddler paint her hand and pat it against a piece of paper. Keep making handprints until there is not enough paint to make a mark on the paper. Talk about how germs are so small we cannot see them, but that they stick to our hands like paint and spread to others. Have the child look at her hand to see if any paint can still be seen. Talk about how children can wash their hands to take germs away just as washing removes paint.

- *How to adjust the activity:* Have children carry a basket of small blocks ("germs") and "spread" them to places around the room. Tell them these are the germs. When all have been spread around the room, ask the children to "clean" the germs away by gathering them back into their baskets.

- *Did you meet your goal?* Were children able to experience how germs can be spread like paint is spread? Listen to what children say about the activity to assess if children are beginning to discover the concept of germs and their spread.

Preschoolers and Kindergartners *and* School-Age Children

- *Goal:* To learn how germs are spread and ways to stop them.

- *Materials:* Paint, paintbrush, paper towels.

- *Activity plan:* First, talk with children about how germs are spread by touching. Then have a small group of children stand in a line. Have one child paint his hand. Then ask that child to shake hands with the next child in line. Have this child shake hands with the third child in line, continuing until each child has shaken hands. Have the children compare their hands to see how many handshakes continued to pass along the paint. Review the concept of spreading germs by touching.

- *How to adjust the activity:* Have the children paint their hands, spreading the paint on generously. Then have the children wash their hands at the sink. Provide paper toweling for each child. Have the child bring their paper towels to the circle. Have each child show their paper towel. Do any show signs of paint? Talk about how much hand washing is needed to appropriately and thoroughly wash away germs.

- *Did you meet your goal?* Were children able to experience and understand how germs are spread through touching? Were children able to experience and understand how hand washing can reduce the spread of germs, and that careful and thorough hand washing is needed to completely clean away germs?

practices and ways that children can help reduce the spread of germs. Topics for teaching prevention messages include:

- How and when to wash my hands.
- How to blow my nose.
- How my body gets sick.
- How my body tells me I am sick.

- How to cover my cough.
- How to keep my sickness to myself.
- How to take care of myself when I am sick.

Topics such as these should be explored in different ways, through literature and activities. They should be repeated at appropriate intervals to reinforce the ideas. Activities like those suggested in the *Teaching Wellness* feature help children explore concepts, such as how germs are spread, in ways that are appropriate and relevant.

Partnering with Parents

Parents are also important participants in disease prevention and management. To be effective partners, they need teachers to provide them with information about program health practices and ways that parents help keep children and classrooms healthy. Several practices support this effort:

- To begin the partnership, provide preenrollment information about immunization requirements and advise parents to obtain health and dental screenings for their child.
- Communicate the program's commitment to health and wellness in parent handbooks, bulletin boards, and so forth.
- Ensure that families provide contact information and let them know how they will be contacted in case their child becomes ill at school. This information should be updated regularly.
- Orient families to classroom health practices, such as having children wash their hands at arrival and conducting daily health checks. Tell families how they will be notified of illnesses in the classroom.
- Provide information about when to keep children home from school due to illness.
- Inform families about how the program will care for children who become ill at school.

Managing Challenges

Illness in the classroom can be disruptive as teachers work to continue the daily routine and activities while caring for a sick child. Being prepared for such situations is important as a management strategy, but also to ensure that germs and disease are not unnecessarily spread. Obtaining supportive supplies in advance and having resources readily available are important ways to prepare to appropriately care for sick children. Programs should have policies that address situations like epidemics or pandemics as discussed in this chapter's *Policy Point*.

Establish an Isolation Area

Sick children need to be removed from the general class group activities to prevent spread of germs and to allow them to rest appropriately until a family member or emergency contact person can come to get them. An isolation area should be identified in the program facility or in a quiet area of the classroom. A pad and blanket should be readily available to provide a comfortable place to rest. These items should be clean and ready for use, and they should be cleaned and sanitized after use. Ill children should be supervised at all times while they are resting. In some settings this may mean that the isolation area is simply a corner of the room where the teacher can supervise the ill child as well as other children in the space. When children leave the class, they should be "signed out" on a sign-in/out sheet to document who picked them up and when.

Record Illness Information

It is helpful to have an illness recording form available for immediate use. Such forms help to document the child's illness and release from school. The teacher should follow the program or school protocol for recording the child's illness. Helpful information to record includes:

- Child's name.
- Date and time of day.

MyEducationLab

Go to the Assignments and Activities section of Topic 6: Health Appraisals/ Screening in the MyEducationLab for your course and complete the activity *Monitoring Children's Health.* How does the teacher assess whether the child should be isolated from her classmates?

EPIDEMIC? PANDEMIC? WHO SETS POLICY IN DISEASE EMERGENCIES?

Teachers know to call 911 when there's an emergency in the early childhood setting. But where do teachers get information when disease threat is widespread? Epidemics (situations where the incidence of disease is higher than expected) and pandemics (situations where infectious disease becomes geographically widespread) have the potential to impact programming in children's settings and schools. Emerging diseases can spread across the world with great speed. When this happens health authorities must work quickly to identify the infectious agent, discover medical treatment to reduce its effect, and communicate methods to prevent spread of disease.

In recent years, concern about avian flu prompted health authorities to plan management strategies for a potential pandemic health crisis. The H1N1 flu (swine flu) outbreak of 2009 tested the strength of such plans. Early childhood programs have taken steps to model their own policies for disease prevention and communication after these efforts. However, when health crises are emerging, teachers and parents need to know where to turn for current information. Several important resources are available:

- The World Health Organization (WHO) monitors the worldwide incidence and spread of disease. The WHO provides updates as emergencies develop and offers guidance for individuals and communities (www.who.int/en).
- The Centers for Disease Control and Prevention is the national agency for up-to-date information on pandemic disease. The CDC provides information about how to plan for pandemic health emergencies and guidance about what schools and child care programs need to do when pandemic disease is occurring (www.cdc.gov).
- Local health authorities are the go-to agencies for providing local updates and advice for an emergency response to health crises. During pandemic events public health agencies will make recommendations on prevention strategies and will ultimately direct decisions related to program and school closures. Local health authorities also have personnel available to answer questions and provide individualized advice.

These resources usually provide opportunities for individuals to subscribe to online communications to keep abreast of health information.

Children's programs also need to do their part by establishing program and school-level policies for health emergencies. Policies should include:

- How health crisis information will be communicated to families.
- How program or school-level decisions related to closures will be made.
- How families will be notified in the event of a school closure.
- How decisions related to reopening the program will be made.

Teachers who are prepared become part of the network of disease prevention efforts that is needed to protect the health of young children and their communities.

- Symptoms observed.
- Who provided care for the child.
- Who was contacted to pick the child up.
- Who picked up the child from care or school and when.

Be Prepared to Send Sick Children Home

A child's illness can cause disruption in the family work schedule. Some families may not have a backup plan to care for an ill child at home. Families may be stressed about losing their job if they take time off to care for their child. These are realistic concerns that families need to manage. It is helpful to orient families to the program policies related to sick children, so they are alerted in advance to the need to pick up and care for their child if illness occurs.

Teachers should be understanding about the challenges families face, but be firm when children are too ill to attend. If families bring a child back to school too soon following an illness, the daily health check assists teachers to recognize if the child is still too ill to attend school. Some programs have sufficient staff to receive children who are no longer contagious but still recovering from illness. Sometimes families request that their child rest in the classroom rather than go outside for recess or play time. These decisions are made at the program level depending on the capacity to provide individualized supervision.

Have Illness Notifications Available

When children are diagnosed with an infectious condition, teachers need to communicate with other families to alert them to the illness. These notices also guide families in how to monitor their own child for symptoms of the disease. Having basic health alert flyers on hand is an important time-saver for teachers who want to distribute correct information as soon as possible. Figure 11-4 provides a sample health alert for pinkeye.

RECOGNIZING AND MANAGING INFECTIOUS DISEASE

Preventing and controlling infections in early childhood settings requires teachers to have a basic understanding of communicable diseases that are common among young children. Although teachers are not responsible for diagnosing illnesses, those who are able to identify the symptoms of disease are better prepared to understand and control its spread. Teachers can also help families obtain health evaluations when necessary. Infectious diseases can be categorized as either vaccine-preventable diseases, which should occur infrequently, or other infections that are not vaccine preventable and are more common in the children's setting. Rarely, teachers will care for a child who has a bloodborne disease. In this section we briefly describe these diseases and offer insight into whether children should be excluded from the children's setting.

What if. . .

a family brought a child who was visibly struggling with a bad cold, but who the family said was well enough to attend? How would you decide if the child was well enough for school or needed to return home? What clues would you look for?

Figure 11-4 Sample Health Alert for Parents

HEALTH ALERT for Parents: Pinkeye

Please observe your child for pinkeye (conjunctivitis).
Pinkeye has been identified in our classrooms. Pinkeye can be alarming because it may make the eyes extremely red and can spread rapidly. Pinkeye (conjunctivitis) can be caused by infections (such as bacteria and viruses), allergies, or substances that irritate the eyes. It is a fairly common condition and usually causes no long-term eye or vision damage. **But if your child shows symptoms of pinkeye, it's important to contact your doctor.**

Avoid the spread of pinkeye at home. Children get pinkeye by touching an infected person or something an infected person has touched, such as a used tissue. If pinkeye is diagnosed in one eye, it can also spread it to the other eye by touching. Teach and help your child to wash his or her hands often with warm water and soap.

If you think your child has pinkeye, it's important to contact your doctor to try to determine what's causing it and to learn how to treat it.

Vaccine-Preventable Diseases

Vaccine-preventable diseases are those that are prevented by immunization (CDC, 2007a). These diseases have decreased in prevalence during the past several decades because of efforts to increase the number of children who are immunized. For this reason, teachers may never see a child with one of the vaccine-preventable diseases. However, many vaccine-preventable diseases are highly contagious, and some can cause very serious disability or death.

epidemic
situation in which the incidence of disease is substantially higher than what is expected in that population

Outbreaks of these diseases that do occur may result in clusters of individuals being struck with the illness. More expansive outbreaks are labeled epidemics. An epidemic is declared when the number of people with the infection is substantially higher than what would normally be expected in that population.

Next we provide brief summaries of these diseases to help teachers learn to recognize them in the rare event that they occur in the children's setting. Teachers are on the front line of care and service to children. They may be the detectives that discover an outbreak of a vaccine-preventable disease.

Pertussis (Whooping Cough)

pertussis
a bacterial upper respiratory infection that is highly contagious and can be fatal to infants and young children; also called *whooping cough*

Pertussis, also known as *whooping cough*, is a highly contagious and dangerous bacterial disease especially for infants. Symptoms include bursts of uncontrolled coughing and wheezing that create the characteristic "whooping" sound. During these coughing spasms the child may turn blue. When the coughing is severe young children and infants may require hospitalization.

The symptoms of whooping cough often last several weeks. Children diagnosed with pertussis should be excluded from school, and the community health authority should be notified. The immunity provided by the pertussis vaccine tends to fade as individuals age. Therefore, periodic booster shots are required. Teachers should check with their health care provider, and obtain the pertussis booster along with the tetanus booster shot. Any teacher diagnosed with pertussis should be excluded from the classroom until a course of antibiotics has been completed. Unfortunately, the incidence of pertussis has been increasing in spite of effective vaccines. Here is an example scenario:

> Mary Jean is an observant teacher. She pays close attention to the health and well-being of the children in her class. On this day while working in the teacher's room, she surprises herself as she listens to her coworker cough. She remarks, "Michael, if I didn't know better, I would say that you are suffering from whooping cough!" This remark is enough to send Michael to get a checkup at the Immediate Care Clinic. He calls in later to report that he has been diagnosed with whooping cough.

Strong evidence demonstrates that protection provided by the pertussis vaccination wanes over time. In fact, older children or adults who have not received recent boosters are the source of most infections in children (AAP, 2009).

Haemophilus influenzae Type b

Haemophilus influenzae **type b (Hib)**
a bacterial infection that can cause severe respiratory problems or meningitis

meningitis
severe infection of the membranes covering the brain

Haemophilus influenzae type b (Hib) causes meningitis, a severe infection of the membranes covering the brain. It occurs most commonly among infants. It can also cause other serious life-threatening respiratory infections.

- If a case of Hib infection is reported within an early childhood program, the families of each child should be notified as well as the local health authority.
- Children who have not been immunized due to special exceptions should be excluded from school until health authorities determine there is no longer a risk for infection (AAP et al., 2002).

Chicken Pox

Chicken pox is a common childhood condition, especially in unvaccinated children. The chicken pox rash usually progresses from the head to the toes. The majority of the pox, or lesions, appear on the trunk (CDC, 2009). The rash is characterized by itchy red bumps that rapidly progress to fluid-filled lesions. Teachers may notice the bumps on the back of the child's neck or on the cheeks.

- Children with chicken pox should be excluded from school until all the lesions have dried and crusted over.
- Rarely, chicken pox can cause severe complications that require intense medical treatment (CDC, 2009).
- Teachers should share with parents that *aspirin not be used to treat infants and children for chicken pox influenza (or any other suspected viral illness)*. Aspirin use is associated with a serious complication called Reye's syndrome. Reye's syndrome can cause inflammation of the brain and liver and is potentially fatal.

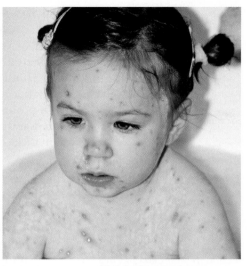
Child with chicken pox.

Measles

Measles is an acute, highly contagious infectious disease. The measles rash begins on the face and head and spreads to the body. It typically lasts for 5 to 6 days (CDC, 2008a). If a case of measles is confirmed, the child should be excluded from the classroom until a medical provider approves the child's return to the classroom.

Tetanus

The tetanus bacteria form spores that are deposited in soil where they can survive for months or even years. The spores are also found in the intestines and feces of many animals, including horses, sheep, cattle, dogs, cats, rats, guinea pigs, and chickens (CDC, 2009). The bacteria usually enter the body through a puncture wound caused, for example, by stepping on a contaminated nail.

- Children should be guided to wash their hands after playing in the dirt and after visiting ranches, farms, and fairs where they may come into contact with infected animal feces.
- In case of injuries causing puncture wounds or cuts, documentation of an updated tetanus vaccine should be confirmed.
- Teachers should periodically receive a tetanus booster to maintain their own immunity.

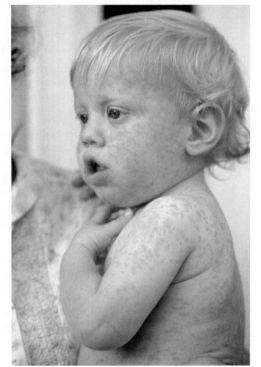
Child with measles.

Influenza (The Flu)

Influenza, also simply "the flu," is a respiratory disease that is caused by a virus. Symptoms include fever, sore throat, muscle aches, and fatigue. The flu can cause complications and many young children are hospitalized each year due to the flu (CDC, 2009).

- Children should be excluded until the symptoms of the flu resolve.
- Hand washing and sanitization practices in the classroom should be monitored.
- Because they are a higher risk group, the CDC now recommends that children between the ages of 6 months to 6 years be given a yearly flu vaccination.
- Teachers should also protect themselves from the disease by obtaining a yearly flu vaccination.

chicken pox
viral infection that causes fever and rash

Reye's syndrome
severe inflammation of the brain and liver caused by giving aspirin to children with certain viral infections

measles
an acute, highly contagious infectious disease that causes fever, rash, and pinkeye

tetanus
a bacterial infection acquired when wounds or lacerations are contaminated with soil that contains the infectious germ

Hepatitis A

Hepatitis A is an acute infection of the liver. Symptoms include fever, diarrhea, abdominal pain, or yellow discoloration of the skin (jaundice). Some children may be exposed and infected with this disease but do not develop symptoms. This is most common among children younger than 6 years of age (CDC, 2009). These children are called *carriers* because they can expose others to the disease even though they do not display the symptoms. The use of standard policies for diapering and toileting when caring for children and following hand washing procedures helps to interrupt the spread of this hidden disease.

Rotavirus

Rotavirus is a virus that causes infectious diarrhea. Symptoms include fever, vomiting, and watery diarrhea. It is spread through the fecal–oral route, making it especially contagious among children under the age of 2 and in settings where children wear diapers. Children infected with rotavirus shed viral particles in the stool before, during, and after they show symptoms of the disease (Bresee, 2008).

Streptococcus Pneumonia

Streptococcus pneumonia is a bacteria that commonly causes respiratory infections, ear infections, pneumonia, infection of the bloodstream, and less commonly, meningitis in young children. The symptoms associated with this bacteria depend on the type of infection. It is transmitted by repiratory droplets. The prevalence of disease has decreased since widespread vaccination was instituted in children in 2000 (CDC, 2009).

What if...

a child in your class has just contracted a second bout of illness involving vomiting and diarrhea? The child's parent has called you to ask why her child is sick again. She wants to know why you have not stopped the spread of this illness. How would you respond?

influenza
a highly infectious virus that causes fever, muscle aches, sore throat, cough, and headache; also called simply "the flu"

hepatitis A
a viral illness of the gastrointestinal tract that causes fever, malaise, nausea, abdominal pain, and, in some individuals, dark urine and jaundice

rotavirus
a common cause of infectious diarrhea in children; symptoms include fever, vomiting, and diarrhea

streptococcus pneumonia
a bacterium that causes respiratory infections that can lead to invasive or more serious infections such as pneumonia or meningitis

common cold
upper respiratory infection that is generally caused by viruses and will not respond to treatment with antibiotics

Other Common Communicable and Infectious Diseases of Childhood

Many diseases of childhood are not vaccine preventable. These infections are common in settings where children have frequent and prolonged contact with one another such as child care, preschool, and classroom settings. Each of the common infectious diseases has its own set of characteristics and implications for management in the children's setting. Exclusion recommendations vary for each disease, as described in Table 11-3.

Common Colds

Common colds are upper respiratory infections that are caused by more than 200 viruses. Viruses causing the common cold are spread by respiratory modes of transmission, such as sneezing. Colds are also spread through direct contact from nose blowing or contact with germs on surfaces. Some cold viruses can survive on contaminated objects for up to several days.

Young children experience between two and eight colds per year, causing a significant number of missed school days (Pappas & Hendley, 2008). Teachers often experience frequent respiratory illnesses during the first few years that they teach young children.

- The best way to interrupt the cycle of infection is to wash hands frequently in the classroom and to ensure that toys and surfaces are sanitized.
- Teachers should also wash their hands immediately when they return to their homes to help reduce the spread of the cold virus.

Conjunctivitis (Pinkeye)

Conjunctivitis, also called *pinkeye*, is a condition in which the lining of the eye becomes inflamed. It is caused by bacterial and viral infections, allergies, chemicals, or trauma. Bacterial and viral infections usually cause white or yellow discharge from the eye, which may cause

Table 11-3   Exclusion Guidelines

Condition	Length of Time Child Should Be Excluded
Fever	When fever has ended or when health care provider recommends
Symptoms of severe illness: lethargy, uncontrolled coughing, inexplicable crying or irritability, difficulty breathing, wheezing, other unusual signs for the child	When health care provider recommends
Diarrhea, not contained by child using toilet	When diarrhea resolves or when health care provider recommends
Blood in stool unless cleared by a health care provider	When health care provider recommends
Vomiting illness	24 hours after last bout of vomiting; when health care provider recommends
Persistent or intermittent abdominal pain	When pain resolves; when health care provider recommends
Mouth sores with drooling	When health care provider recommends
Rash with fever or behavior change	When health care provider recommends
Purulent (draining) conjunctivitis (pinkeye)	After treatment is initiated
Head lice	After first treatment
Scabies	After treatment is completed
Tuberculosis	When health care provider recommends
Impetigo	24 hours after treatment is initiated
Streptococcal infection (strep throat)	24 hours after treatment is initiated
Chicken pox	When all sores are dried and crusted
Pertussis (whooping cough)	5 days after treatment has been completed; when health care provider recommends
Mumps	9 days after onset of salivary gland swelling; when health care provider recommends
Hepatitis A	One week after onset of jaundice and/or illness; when health care provider recommends
Measles	4 days after onset of rash; when health care provider recommends

Source: Used with permission of the American Academy of Pediatrics, *Caring for Our Children: National Health and Safety Performance Standards: Guidelines for Out-of-Home Child Care Programs*, 2e. Copyright 2002.

the eyelids to stick together in the morning. Pinkeye can also be caused by viruses, such as measles, or by the presence of foreign objects in the eye. When a child has symptoms of pinkeye, teachers should:

- Contact the child's parents and refer the child to a health care provider.
- Monitor other children and teachers for signs of pinkeye.
- Disinfect any contaminated articles.
- Notify parents to watch for signs of pinkeye.
- Ensure that proper hand washing procedures are being followed.
- Exclude children with symptoms until they have been seen by a health care provider and approved for readmission.

Pinkeye is a common infection among children.

Croup

Croup is a common upper respiratory infection that causes fever, cough, and in some cases, difficulty breathing. It can also cause noisy breathing called **stridor**. Many different types of

conjunctivitis
condition in which the lining of the eye becomes inflamed due to bacterial or viral infections, allergies, chemicals, or trauma; also called *pinkeye*

croup
a viral upper respiratory infection causing fever, runny nose, and barky cough

stridor
noisy breathing

group A strep infection
infection with bacteria that causes three common infections in childhood: strep throat, scarlet fever, and impetigo

acute rheumatic fever
a serious complication of strep infection that affects the heart

scarlet fever
a type of strep infection characterized by fever, sore throat (not always), and a scarlet rash that has a texture like sandpaper

impetigo
a type of strep infection that causes a skin rash marked by pustular lesions

viruses cause croup. Incubation periods vary according to the virus, but will be in the typical range of 1 to 3 weeks. Its mode of transmission is droplet.

The cough associated with croup is very distinctive and described as *barky* or similar to the sound of a seal. Stridor and difficulty breathing most often occur during the night, but teachers should watch for these symptoms and notify families if they are noted. Children should only be excluded based on the presence of fever or other reasons that prevent the child from participating comfortably, such as breathing difficulty.

Group A Strep Infections

A group A strep infection is caused by bacteria that cause three common infections in childhood: strep throat, scarlet fever, and impetigo. Transmission occurs by direct contact with infected respiratory secretions. The virus is most contagious when children are acutely ill. Symptoms generally include fever, sore throat, and possibly a rash. Children should be excluded from school until they have been treated with antibiotics for 24 hours and no longer have a fever (AAP, 2009). It is especially important to recognize strep throat because, if left untreated, other serious complications can occur such as acute rheumatic fever, a serious complication that affects the heart.

Scarlet fever is a condition characterized by fever, sore throat, and a scarlet rash that has texture like sandpaper. Scarlet fever is often treated with antibiotics. Impetigo is a skin rash comprised of blisters with honey yellow scabs. Impetigo spreads in children's settings through direct contact with infected individuals or from toys. Children with impetigo should be excluded from the classroom or early childhood setting until 24 hours after treatment has started. Exposed lesions should be covered (AAP, 2009).

Ear Infections

Ear infections are common infectious diseases of childhood. Bacteria or viruses that infect the eardrum cause ear infections. Infants and children younger than age 3 are at highest risk. Two-thirds of all children will experience an ear infection before their first birthday. Ear infections occur more often among boys (Kerschner, 2007). Ear infections are not contagious. Therefore, children with ear infections and that accompanying earaches do not need to be excluded from school unless they are too ill to participate in normal activities. If other symptoms such as fever are present, the child may have another illness that is contagious. The child should be separated from the group and parents should be notified.

Fifth Disease

Fifth disease is so called because it is considered the "fifth" of the six common infectious childhood diseases with symptoms of a "breakout" rash. The others include measles (first), scarlet fever (second), rubella (third), fourth disease (not recognized today), and roseola (sixth). Symptoms of fifth disease include fever, head and muscle aches, and the characteristic skin rash. Fifth disease is recognized by its intensely red rash, which appears on the cheeks. This is sometimes called "slapped-cheek" rash. As the illness progresses, the rash becomes more diffuse and has a lacy pattern that appears on the trunk. By the time the rash appears, the child is no longer contagious and should not be excluded from the early childhood setting (AAP et al., 2002).

Ear infections are one of the most common infectious diseases of childhood.

ear infections
infections of the eardrum; some of the most common infectious diseases of childhood

Pinworms

Pinworm infection is a common intestinal parasitic infection in young children. Usually if a child is infected with pinworms, others in the family are infected as well. Transmission occurs by ingesting microscopic eggs by either the fecal–oral route or by contact with contaminated objects such as toys, bedding, clothing, or toilet seats. Symptoms include itching around the anus, vulva, or genital area, although some children have no symptoms

(AAP, 2009). Pinworm infections can be difficult to control in early childhood settings. Hand washing is the most effective way to prevent its spread.

Respiratory Syncytial Virus

Respiratory syncytial virus (RSV) is a viral upper respiratory infection that causes fever, runny nose, cough, and possibly wheezing in some children. Transmission is through contact with contaminated secretions. Contaminated droplets can live on surfaces for several hours. The incubation period is 2 to 8 days. Most children have an initial RSV infection during their first year of life. It is common for children to become reinfected later (AAP, 2009). RSV in older children and adults looks more like a common cold. Most healthy children with RSV have an uncomplicated upper respiratory infection. Younger infants and premature infants are at higher risk for developing breathing difficulties and requiring hospitalizations for complications (AAP, 2009).

RSV occurs in epidemics during the winter and spring. Careful cleaning of surfaces and frequent hand washing are the best ways to prevent infection. Exclusion and notification of parents should occur in children with a fever or with breathing difficulties.

Tuberculosis

Tuberculosis (TB) is a potentially harmful lung infection. It is spread through respiratory and airborne transmission when tiny droplets are propelled through the air from coughing or sneezing. Symptoms include fatigue, fever, and chills. Children are most often exposed to TB from infectious adults. For this reason, many children's programs and schools require that teachers be screened for TB as a requirement of employment.

Infections and Acute Illnesses Involving the Skin

Some infections that are highly contagious in children's settings and schools primarily affect the skin. Head lice, scabies, and ringworm are examples of skin-related infectious diseases. Skin infections are often distinguished by the type and color of the rash they cause.

Head Lice

Head lice is an infestation of the hair and scalp that often causes skin discomfort. It is transmitted most commonly by direct contact with the hair of an infested person. Less commonly, lice are transmitted by sharing personal belongings such as combs, hairbrushes, and hats. Lice can survive for up to 2 days away from the scalp.

Adult lice or nits are usually most visible behind the ears and near the nape of the neck. Itching is the most common symptom of head lice, but many children have no symptoms at all. Head lice should not be considered a health hazard and are not responsible for the spread of other disease (AAP, 2009).

Although head lice do not represent a serious health problem, this infection often causes disruption in the classroom. When an incidence of head lice is discovered, teachers are faced with trying to contain the spread. Parents may respond with disgust when they learn of the presence of lice. To attain better control of this infection, some health authorities have recommended a *no-nit* policy for early childhood programs. This approach requires that children must stay out of school if they have any lice, eggs, or nits in their hair. Nits are the egg casings that may contain a developing louse or they may be empty and not infectious. They can remain visible for up to 6 months on the hair shaft. Consequently, many children have been incorrectly diagnosed with an ongoing head lice infestation and excluded from the classroom. They may have also received unnecessary repeat treatments of *delousing* pesticides. Each year 12 to 24 million school days are lost due to lice exclusion policies (Mumcuoglu, 2006). No-nit policies have not been shown to be effective in controlling head lice infestations and are currently not recommended (AAP, 2009). It is

fifth disease
viral illness characterized by fever, headaches, and muscle aches followed by the skin rash

pinworms
a common intestinal parasitic infection in young children

respiratory syncytial virus (RSV)
a common upper respiratory infection that occurs in children and adults most commonly during the winter and spring months

tuberculosis (TB)
an infection that is transmitted by air droplets and can affect many different parts of the body, most commonly causing lung infections

head lice
an infestation of the hair and scalp that is transmitted most commonly by direct contact with the hair of infested people

Head louse and nit.

also important to remember that over-the-counter and prescription treatments for head lice can be quite toxic and are actually considered pesticides.

Rather than excluding children for head lice, early childhood programs and schools are gaining a new perspective on this annoyance. These thoughts are useful when establishing a policy related to head lice (Mumcuoglu, Meinking, Burkhart, & Burkhart, 2006; Sciscione & Krause-Parello, 2007):

- Head lice are a health annoyance rather than a health emergency.
- Head lice are not associated with poor hygiene and poverty. They are opportunistic, moving from head to head without regard to socioeconomic status.
- Conducting periodic "head checks" at school is a good way to watch for head lice and reduce the spread if they are present. Periodic checks also help change the perspective of head lice away from something to fear to a condition to manage.
- If head lice are discovered, children do not need to be sent home immediately; a few hours at school will not make a significant difference.
- Families of infected children should be notified so treatment can be implemented. All other families should be notified so they can monitor their children for evidence of lice.
- Treatment for head lice can be started by families using over-the-counter shampoos and other hair treatment products designed to kill head lice. If head lice persist despite this treatment, parents should be encouraged to call their child's health care provider for advice.
- Children can return to school when treatment has been completed.
- Teachers should remove all play clothing that touches heads and help ensure that children's coats do not touch in "cubby" coat hanging areas.

Some families may refuse to treat their child for head lice. This may be due to a lack of understanding of how to obtain and use lice treatment procedures or lack of funds to purchase the products. Some families may not want to treat their child with chemical pesticides. Teachers should try to help these families access information and guidance. Community health authorities or pharmacists may be able to guide them to use treatment methods that meet their needs. Ultimately, the negative impact of missed school days may be more problematic than head lice.

Scabies

scabies
a skin infection caused by adult female mites that burrow into the skin, causing an intensely itchy, red, bumpy rash that is seen in a snake-like pattern

Scabies is a skin infection caused by adult female mites that burrow into the skin, causing an intensely itchy, red, and bumpy rash. The rash typically occurs between the fingers, on wrists and elbows, waistline, thighs, genitalia, and buttocks (AAP, 2009). Scabies is transmitted through prolonged, personal contact. Children should be excluded until they have received treatment. Any bedding and clothing the child has used should be washed, including dramatic play clothing. Usually the environment does not need to be specially treated (AAP, 2009).

Ringworm

ringworm
an infection of the skin caused by a fungus

Ringworm is a skin infection caused by a common fungus. It appears as a red and scaly skin rash that has a raised circular shape with healthy skin in the middle. No worm is involved in this condition. It is the shape of the rash that gives the infection its name. Ringworm is transmitted by direct contact with infected humans, animals, or objects. It can occur on the scalp, causing hair loss. Treatment usually involves application of an antifungal cream for several weeks. Children infected with ringworm do not need to stay home from school. Hand washing and maintaining cleanliness in the environment are the most effective ways to prevent spread of the infection.

Coxsackie Virus (Hand, Foot, and Mouth Disease)

coxsackie virus
a common childhood respiratory virus causing fever, mouth sores, and skin rash

The coxsackie virus, also called *hand, foot, and mouth disease,* causes blisters on the hands, feet, and mouth. It is spread through contact with hands and surfaces that are contaminated with infected droplets from the mouth and nose. Symptoms include fever, loss of appetite, and sore throat, followed by sores in the mouth and gums. A nonitchy rash appears first on the hands and soles of the feet.

The virus spreads easily, but exclusion is not usually recommended because exposure to others has already occurred by the time symptoms are recognized. Children should stay home if the symptoms are painful and they are not able to fully participate with the class. Hand washing and sanitizing surfaces are the most important management strategies.

Bite Wounds

Bite wounds are included here because of their potential to cause infection. Bite wounds are relatively common in children's settings. Bites that do not break the skin should be managed with comfort care and guidance to address the cause of the bite. Bites that break the skin are more serious. Around 10% to 15% of human bites become infected (AAP, 2009). Teachers should carefully wash the bite wound, using Standard Precautions, and monitor the child's behavior. Parents should be contacted and encouraged to seek medical evaluation. Bite wounds should be monitored for signs of infection including increasing tenderness, pain, redness, and swelling.

Staph Infections

Staph refers to a multitude of bacteria that cause infections and disease. Thirty different types of *Staphylococci* (staph) can infect humans. Many of these bacteria are naturally found in the mouth and nose and most often do not cause infection. However, sometimes breaks in the skin allow the bacteria to enter the body and cause a staph infection. Methicillin-resistant *Staphylococcus aureus* (MRSA) is a potentially dangerous type of bacterial skin infection that is resistant to many types of antibiotics. It is spread through direct contact and by touching items that have touched an infected wound (CDC, 2008a, 2008b).

MRSA skin infections are characterized by red, swollen, and painful pimples or boils that usually drain pus. Frequent skin-to-skin contact and potential for children to touch contaminated surfaces makes early childhood classrooms likely settings for the spread of infections such as MRSA (CDC, 2008a, 2008b).

- Teachers should be watchful for signs of infection on children's hands and arms.
- Any skin cuts and scrapes should be kept clean and dry. Infected wounds should be covered.
- Children should not share clothing if an infection is suspected.

Special attention to hand washing practices is important, and disposable towels should be used. Children who have an identified MRSA infection should not be excluded unless it is not possible to cover the wound. It is not necessary to inform other families unless there has been accidental contact with the wound (CDC, 2008a, 2008b).

Bloodborne Infections in the Early Childhood Setting

Bloodborne infections such as hepatitis B or C and HIV are not common in early childhood. The risk of transmission even with contact with blood is low. However, because of the seriousness of these diseases, teachers must have a general understanding of precautions for preventing transmission. Consider this scenario:

> During the middle of the kindergarten year, a new child joins the class. Natasha has been teaching for many years, but this is the first time a child has been accompanied by the school nurse and two other people. They stay through the first full day and tend to drop in to observe the child now and then. The child also has a special health emergency protocol that requires Natasha to contact the school nurse and parents anytime a child in the class is diagnosed with a communicable illness. Natasha wonders if the child has some kind of serious disease. She feels uncomfortable but doesn't know why.

What if. . .

a child in your toddler group bit another child, creating a bloody wound on the skin? How would you respond to the child who did the biting? What strategies would you use to reduce the risk of this child biting in the future?

staph infections
  potentially dangerous a type of bacteria that is normally found in the skin but can cause infections under certain circumstances

Methicillin-resistant *Staphylococcus aureus* (MRSA)
  a potentially dangerous type of bacterial skin infection that is resistant to many types of antibiotics

Some diseases tend to cause a great deal of alarm. To address such concerns, teachers need to gather information and learn more about the risks of infection. Using Standard Precautions when managing injuries where blood is present is an important way to increase safety and prevent the spread of bloodborne diseases. In this section we discuss some of the bloodborne diseases that, although uncommon, may occur among young children in child care and school settings.

Hepatitis B

hepatitis B
a virus that causes chronic inflammation of the liver and can lead to cancer of the liver

Hepatitis B is a virus that causes chronic inflammation of the liver and can lead to cancer of the liver. Some children who are infected with hepatitis B experience few symptoms but are carriers of the disease. This is more common in children who were not born in the United States.

The virus is spread through contact with blood and body fluids. It can be transmitted from an infected mother to her baby through labor and delivery. Children infected with hepatitis B should not be excluded from the early childhood setting unless they demonstrate high-risk behaviors. Behaviors and situations that may cause spread of the virus include the following (AAP et al., 2002):

- Aggressive behaviors (biting, frequent scratching).
- Dermatitis (weeping skin lesions).
- Bleeding problems.

Children infected with hepatitis B who exhibit these high-risk behaviors or medical risk factors should be assessed individually by their primary care provider who, together with the program director and local public health authorities, can determine the appropriateness of having the child participate in the early childhood setting. If either the child who bites or who has been bitten is known to have hepatitis B and one of the children is incompletely immunized, both children should be evaluated further by a health care provider (AAP, 2009).

Hepatitis C

hepatitis C
a virus that causes chronic inflammation of the liver that is transmitted through blood and body fluids

Hepatitis C infection in children is very rare. It is a virus that causes chronic inflammation of the liver, and it is transmitted through blood and body fluids. Exclusion of children from early childhood programs is not recommended (AAP, 2009). The risk of transmission by exposure through a skin wound is greater than that of hepatitis B but less than that of HIV (AAP et al., 2002).

Human Immunodeficiency Virus

human immunodeficiency virus (HIV)
a virus that is transmitted through blood and body fluids; most common form of transmission in children is from mother to fetus or baby

Human immunodeficiency virus (HIV) is a virus that is transmitted through blood and body fluids. Modes of transmission include sexual contact, use of contaminated needles, and mother-to-child transmission during pregnancy or the birth process (AAP, 2009). More than 90% of children with HIV in the United States acquired HIV through their mother. Child sexual abuse can be another way children are infected with HIV.

Children infected with HIV pose a challenge in the early childhood setting because management and treatment of their disease is often complex. The infected child is susceptible to infection and steps should be taken to ensure the health and safety of all children so that transmission is prevented. The *National Health and Safety Performance Standards* recommend that the admission of children with HIV be considered on a case-by-case basis, depending on the health, behavior, development, and immune status of the child (AAP et al., 2002). The AAP (2009) outlines the following specific recommendations for children with HIV in the school setting:

- School-age children should be allowed to participate without restrictions except in rare cases where the child has an increased likelihood of exposing others. In these situations, children should be evaluated individually.
- The only people who need to know that the child has HIV are the parents, other guardians, and the physician. The number of people who are aware of the child's

condition should be kept to a minimum. The parents have the right to decide whether or not to inform the school.

- All early childhood programs should adopt routine policies for handling blood and blood-contaminated fluids.
- Children with HIV are at increased risk for serious infections or complications from infectious diseases. The child's family should be notified immediately if the child is exposed to an infectious illness.
- More specific guidelines exist for children with HIV participating in athletics.

Although adults with HIV may work with children, Standard Precautions should be taken. The affected adult should also be cautious about possible exposures to infectious diseases. No cases of transmission of HIV from caregiver to child have been documented (AAP, 2009).

INFECTIOUS DISEASES IN IMMIGRANT AND INTERNATIONALLY ADOPTED CHILDREN

In 2005, more than 22,000 children were adopted from outside of the United States. More than 80% of those adoptions were children from five countries: China, Russia, Guatemala, Korea, and Ukraine (Staat, 2008). In addition, a much smaller group of children came to the United States as **refugees**, immigrants who cannot return to their country due to persecution. Little may be known about the health histories of these children. However, these children may have unique risk factors for infectious disease.

refugees
noncitizen immigrants who cannot return to their country due to persecution

Unknown Health History

Certain infectious diseases and illnesses should be ruled out in children with unknown health histories. Although children born in the United States may also have unknown health histories, the health history of children from international backgrounds is more often incomplete and sometimes unknown. Therefore, these children should have regular medical care where common diseases can be evaluated and addressed.

Having an unknown health history can complicate entry into early childhood programs. Children who come to the United States through international adoption must have a medical examination in their country of origin before coming to the United States. A physician designated by the U.S. State Department must perform the examination, which screens only for selected infectious diseases and serious physical or mental defects that would prevent the issuing of a permanent visa (AAP, 2009). Also, children who are adopted internationally are not required to have documentation showing basic immunizations. Adoptive parents must pledge to obtain basic immunizations for their new children.

Children who are refugees are required to obtain comprehensive medical screening tests prior to their entry into the United States (Staat, 2008). However records of immunization and history of family disease may not be available. This lack of information can pose a problem for enrollment in an early childhood setting or school. Parents who are adopting children and those who are supporting refugee families need the support and guidance of a medical provider. The health professional will ensure the child receives a full medical evaluation and plan for obtaining the immunizations needed for entry into the children's program.

Common Diseases among Immigrant and Internationally Adopted Children

Many internationally adopted children are diagnosed with infectious diseases. This is due to the wide array of infectious agents and diseases to which children from international backgrounds may have been exposed. Across the world, nutrition, living conditions, prevalence of various diseases, and access to health care vary greatly. Teachers should be aware that these children may have unique health challenges that go undetected. For example, many children from international backgrounds may have no symptoms associated with an infectious disease, making diagnosis more difficult.

Figure 11-5 Common Diseases among Internationally Adopted Children

Bacterial diseases:
- Salmonella
- Syphilis
- Tuberculosis

Viral diseases:
- Typhoid fever
- Cytomegalovirus
- Hepatitis A, B, and C
- HIV

Other diseases:
- Lice
- Scabies
- Intestinal worms (parasites)
- Giardia
- Malaria
- Impetigo

Source: Based on "Infectious Diseases in Refugee and Internationally Adopted Children," by M. Staat, pp. 32–37, Chapter 4 in *Principles and Practices of Pediatric Infectious Diseases*, 3rd edition, edited by S. Long, 2008, Philadelphia: Churchill Livingstone.

A list of infectious diseases that are seen among children from international backgrounds is shown in Figure 11-5. Descriptions of some of these illnesses are given next to assist teachers in recognizing infections among children from international communities.

Viral Hepatitis

The prevalence of hepatitis B infection in internationally born children ranges from 1% to 5%. It is most prevalent in children from Asia, Africa, some countries in Central and Eastern Europe, and the independent states of the former Soviet Union. Vaccination is highly recommended unless the child's health care provider has deemed it medically unnecessary. Also, many internationally born children have acquired hepatitis A earlier in life; however, it is recommended that these children also obtain the vaccine unless testing determines it is not needed.

Intestinal Infections

The prevalence of intestinal infections varies depending on the child's age and country of origin (AAP, 2009). These infections are caused by bacteria, viruses, and parasites. When teachers notice any unusual symptoms related to abdominal pain, abnormal appetite, or abnormal stools, parents should be notified and encouraged to have the child evaluated. For the vast majority of these infections, treatment is effective and simple.

Tuberculosis

The prevalence of tuberculosis among internationally born children varies tremendously, from 0.6% to as high as 30% (AAP, 2009). All children who were not born in the United States should be screened for tuberculosis.

HIV Infections

The risk of HIV among internationally born children depends on the country of origin and individual risk factors. It is recommended that all immigrant children should have an HIV test, even if they have had one in their country of origin.

Skin Infections

It is not uncommon for children born outside of the United States to arrive with various skin infections such as impetigo, scabies, or fungal infections. Teachers should be observant for signs of infection, and children should be referred for medical treatment.

Other Infectious Diseases

Outbreaks of certain infections, such as measles, have been reported among internationally adopted children. Often, adoptions from the orphanages where children were living are temporarily suspended until the outbreak is controlled. Typically these illnesses are resolved before these children enroll in child care, preschool, or school.

Children from international backgrounds may have special health risks.

Culture and Management of Infectious Diseases

Families from diverse cultures often have culturally based perspectives about the cause and treatment of infections and disease. For example, Native American families may view illnesses as a result of a disruption of the spirits and may not identify germs as the cause of infections (Ball & Bindler, 2006). Families may turn to religion, herbs, acupuncture, and a variety of other traditional healing practices for illnesses. It is important for teachers to communicate with families in order to protect the health of the child, control disease spread, and honor the family's beliefs.

Regardless of race or ethnicity, each family has its own set of personal and philosophical beliefs about treatment of disease. Personal preferences and beliefs may lead families to use nontraditional forms of medicine. Complementary and alternative medicine (CAM) refers to the use of healing practices that are not considered part of conventional medical practices. Estimates of the use of CAM practices with children range from 20% to 40%. These rates are considerably higher in children with special health care needs. CAM is used less commonly in Hispanic and Black families (Kemper, Vohra, & Walls, 2008).

The use of CAM is typically integrated with traditional medical practices. Examples of CAM that teachers may see with respect to infections are the use of herbal remedies such as eardrops for ear infections or supplements like echinacea or vitamin C for common colds. If families ask teachers to administer any supplement or medications, regardless of the type, the proper procedure for the administration of medicines should be followed in each case.

Complementary and alternative medicine (CAM)
healing practices that are not considered part of conventional medical practices

What if. . .

a parent provided you with a baggie of supplements to give their child at lunch time? How would you begin a conversation with the family about their request?

Summary

Young children are especially vulnerable to infectious disease. They need to explore and touch their environments as they learn about their world. This is their natural style of study. But frequent touching of toys, objects, and surfaces may introduce children to germs that can cause infection. Children rely on their teachers and families to protect them from disease when they can, and to care for them if sickness occurs.

Diseases can be caused by infectious agents that are transmitted easily in early childhood and school settings. Some infections cause symptoms such as diarrhea, respiratory illness, rashes, fever, and vomiting, and these symptoms may be experienced when children are in the classroom. Teachers who recognize these signs of illness are prepared to separate children from the group and care for them until their family is contacted. Teachers also need to be aware of their own risk for contracting infections and take steps to keep disease free.

A variety of preventive practices help teachers to reduce the spread of disease in the classroom. Immunizations, hand washing, and daily health checks are just a few of the ways that teachers help to control infections. Standard Precautions, involving the use of gloves and careful cleaning and sanitization practices, are important strategies to protect children from bloodborne and other diseases. Teachers also have an important responsibility to teach children how they can be participants in keeping themselves healthy. This is an important goal of wellness and provides children with healthful skills that they can use in the future.

Although teachers are not usually medical professionals and should not be diagnosing disease or offering recommendations for treatment, it is important for them to be aware of the many infections that commonly occur among young children. Recognition of symptoms of disease helps teachers plan management strategies in the classroom that interrupt the spread of disease. Some children may be at greater risk for disease. Children from international settings may have been exposed to diseases that are less frequent in the United States. Teachers become keenly aware of children's typical behaviors and may be the first to recognize when illness is developing. They are important participants in the process of caring for children when infections occur.

Overall, infectious disease is a common occurrence during the early years. When teachers participate in reducing the spread and incidence of disease, they are contributing to children's health and well-being. Fewer days ill results in more days of exploration and learning for young children.

MyEducationLab

To assess your understanding of how to recognize and prevent the spread of infectious diseases in early childhood settings, go to the Book Specific Resources section in the MyEducationLab for your course, select *Nutrition, Health, and Safety for Young Children*, Chapter 11 of the Study Plan, and then complete the multiple choice questions and activities.

Key Terms

Acute rheumatic fever, p. 362

Airborne transmission, p. 343

Bacteria, p. 342

Bloodborne transmission, p. 344

Chicken pox, p. 359

Common cold, p. 360

Communicable diseases, p. 342

Complementary and alternative medicine, p. 369

Conjunctivitis, p. 360

Coxsackie virus, p. 364

Croup, p. 361

Diarrhea, p. 346

Ear infection, p. 362

Epidemic, p. 358

Fecal–oral transmission, p. 343

Fifth disease, p. 362

Fungi, p. 342

Germs, p. 342

Group A strep infection, p. 362

Haemophilus influenzae type b (Hib), p. 358

Head lice, p. 363

Hepatitis A, p. 360

Hepatitis B, p. 366

Hepatitis C, p. 366

Human immunodeficiency virus (HIV), p. 366

Impetigo, p. 362

Incubation period, p. 344

Influenza, p. 359

Measles, p. 359

Meningitis, p. 358

Mode of transmission, p. 342

Methicillin-resistant *Staphylococcus aureus* (MRSA), p. 365

Parasite, p. 342

Pertussis, p. 358

Pharyngitis, p. 346

Pinworms, p. 362

Pneumonia, p. 346

Refugees, p. 367

Respiratory syncytial virus (RSV), p. 363

Reye's syndrome, p. 359

Ringworm, p. 364

Rotavirus, p. 360

Scabies, p. 364

Scarlet fever, p. 362

Sinusitis, p. 346

Standard Precautions, p. 352

Staph infections, p. 365

Streptococcus pneumoniae, p. 360

Stridor, p. 361

Tetanus, p. 359

Tuberculosis (TB), p. 363

Virus, p. 342

Review Questions

1. Describe the four modes of transmission for infections. Name two infections that are transmitted by each mode.

2. Describe strategies teachers can use to control the spread of disease.

3. Influenza is still seen in early childhood settings despite vaccination. Describe the mode of transmission and symptoms for this infection.

4. How are head lice transmitted? What policies in early childhood can minimize disease spread?

Discussion Starters

1. As discussed in Chapter 1, we know that the quality of child care has an impact on children's overall health and wellness. What impact do you think the quality of child care has on the control of infectious diseases?

2. Opinions vary related to allowing children to attend school when they have head lice. What are the policies related to head lice in the early childhood and school programs in your area? Do you think a "no-nit" policy should be imposed?

3. HIV is an infectious illness that harbors a significant amount of stigma even in children. Although confidentiality is well established for this illness, a family may choose to be open about their child or a school-age child may discuss his or her infection with friends. How do you think this might influence the child's relationships with his or her peers? How do you think teachers or other staff members would react to the news that a child with HIV is in the classroom?

Practice Points

1. Explore the child care licensing requirements in your area. Are preemployment health assessments required for teachers?

2. Call the local health authority to learn about the requirements for teachers with respect to screening for tuberculosis. Is the TB skin test required?

3. Imagine that a child in your Head Start classroom has been sent home with a fever and is diagnosed with chicken pox a few days later. Draft a policy that addresses notification of parents and as well as controlling the spread of this infectious disease.

Web Resources

Centers for Disease Control and Prevention, Influenza
www.cdc.gov/flu

Centers for Disease Control and Prevention, National Center for Infectious Diseases, Infectious Disease Information: Childhood Diseases
www.cdc.gov/ncidod/Diseases/children/diseases.htm

chapter 12

Teaching Children with Special Health Care Needs

Learning Outcomes

After reading this chapter, you should be able to:

1. Explain special health needs and discuss how these needs affect children's health, functional status, and family dynamics.

2. Identify the goals of inclusion and describe how educating classmates about children's special health care needs helps to create a climate of welcome for all children.

3. Describe the kinds of information needed before teachers administer medications in the early childhood setting.

4. Discuss how partnering with families supports both children and teachers in the inclusive classroom.

5. Identify at least five special health care needs and discuss general strategies teachers can use to support children in the classroom.

Jeremy is a 5-year-old African American boy who will join Mary's kindergarten class in the fall. His medical history is significant and complex. He was born extremely prematurely, at 25 weeks gestation, with a birth weight of less than 2 pounds. He stayed in the hospital for nearly 2½ months after his birth. The ventilator was required for 6 weeks to assist him with breathing and he had bleeding around his brain, which was significant but not uncommon for his degree of prematurity. As a result of his premature birth, Jeremy now has several medical problems that impact his learning. He has cerebral palsy, which mainly affects his lower limbs. He also has asthma and a visual impairment requiring corrective lenses, and he has recently been diagnosed with attention deficit disorder.

Mary has had experience with many children who have special developmental needs, but Jeremy's health history is unique. She wonders how his medical problems will impact his learning in the classroom. She wonders what resources are available through the school to learn more about his various health conditions. She wants to learn more about Jeremy so she can start planning how to help him adjust to the classroom setting. Mary makes notes of her questions. Then she gathers her notebook and walks down the hall to the school library where Jeremy's kindergarten transition meeting is scheduled in a few minutes. One school year is ending, but Mary is already starting to think about next fall and the important experience that is ahead for this young child.

Teaching young children is an exciting profession that combines the enjoyment of helping young children grow and discover their world with the responsibility of ensuring children's health and well-being. This responsibility adds challenge and focus to the endeavor. For many teachers like Mary, the most rewarding aspect of their work comes from crafting individualized approaches that support the learning of children with unique needs.

In this chapter we will discuss children's special health care needs and explore the ways in which a child's exceptional health care needs affect his or her development and the context of the family. We will also discuss laws related to children who have special health needs and briefly explore treatments that are used to improve children's health outcomes. Finally, we will describe the various health needs and discuss some of the ways these conditions are managed in the early childhood and school setting. Understanding children's special health care needs and making purposeful adjustments to the classroom setting are crucial aspects of teaching that characterize the teacher's role in helping children reach their full potential.

UNDERSTANDING CHILDREN'S SPECIAL HEALTH CARE NEEDS

More children with chronic medical conditions are enrolled in early childhood programs and included in school classrooms than ever before. Nearly every early childhood classroom includes children with special health care needs. This highlights the need for teachers to be prepared to serve children who have a variety of medical needs and to prepare their classrooms and curriculum to support these learners.

Defining Special Health Care Needs

Children with special health care needs are those who "have or are at risk for a chronic physical, developmental, behavioral, or emotional condition and who also require health and related services of a type or amount beyond that required by children generally" (U.S. Department of Health and Human Services, Health Resources and Services Administration, Maternal and Child Health Bureau [HHS/HRSA], 2008, para. 1). This definition encompasses a

**children with special
health care needs**
children who have or are
at risk for a chronic
physical, developmental,
behavioral, or emotional
condition and who also
require health and related
services of a type or
amount beyond that
generally required

wide assortment of medical diagnoses with a range of symptoms and severity. In addition, special health care needs can have an impact on educational development.

Meeting the needs of children with special health conditions is a high national priority as reflected in *Healthy People 2010* (HHS, 2000). To support children with special health care needs so they can develop to their full potential, their health care and educational needs must be widely addressed: at home, at school, and in the community. Children's special health care diagnoses, treatments, and educational interventions and outcomes are unique for each child and change as the child grows and develops.

Teachers make a significant contribution to the education and development of children with special health care needs. They do this by being:

- *Capable and willing*—to learn about the child's unique health care and educational needs.
- *Adaptable and able*—to envision and implement appropriate adjustments in the classroom and curriculum.
- *Reflective and responsive*—to identify successful educational interventions and put them into practice when needed.

In the opening case scenario, Mary demonstrated these engaging and proactive characteristics. When she learned she would be teaching a child with special health care needs, she quickly began to outline the kinds of information she would need to be effective as Jeremy's teacher.

MyEducationLab

Go to the Assignments and
Activities section of Topic 7:
Chronic Illness/Special
Health Care Needs in the
MyEducationLab for your
course and complete the
activity entitled *Inclusion in
an Early Childhood
Classroom*. What are
important aspects of setting
up the classroom that will
meet the needs of all
children?

Prevalence of Children with Special Health Care Needs

In 2005–2006, 13.9%, or more than 10 million U.S. children, had a special health care need. Nearly 22% of U.S. households had at least one child with a special health care need (HHS/HRSA, 2008). The two most common special health conditions are asthma and allergies. The increase in the number of children with special health care needs in classrooms is due to both increased inclusion as well as a growing prevalence of certain conditions. Inclusion of children increased significantly after the Individuals with Disabilities Education Act (IDEA) was adopted (as described in Chapter 2).

The incidence of some health conditions has increased as well. For example, the prevalence of premature infants like Jeremy in the opening case scenario is increasing. Although the survival rates for premature infants are higher, some of these babies are left with medical conditions such as cerebral palsy, intellectual disabilities, or other disabilities that will impact the child's ability to learn.

Children with special health care needs (CSHCN) represent a diverse group. Special health care needs are present in families of all income levels, races, ethnicities, religions, and cultures. Black, non-Hispanic children have higher rates of special health care needs than children of other ethnicities, as do boys of any race or ethnicity compared to girls (Newacheck,

Many children with
special health care needs
participate in early
childhood classrooms.

Kim, Blumberg, & Rising, 2008). Prevalence rates for some health conditions vary according to geographic areas. The West generally has fewer children with special health care needs than other areas of the United States (Newacheck et al., 2008). In the southeastern United States, sickle cell anemia is much more common than in West Virginia, where cystic fibrosis is a more prevalent condition.

The incidence of some health conditions varies based on rural or urban settings. For example, asthma rates are usually higher in metropolitan areas compared to rural settings. The prevalence rates are higher in households that have at least one smoker, parental unemployment, or are headed by single parents. Low-income families

have higher rates of children with asthma, developmental problems, and behavioral/conduct problems (Newacheck et al., 2008).

Functional Status

Functional status is an important outcome for CSHCN. Functional status describes the characteristics that are most important to parents and teachers: how well a child can function in the community, in the classroom, and in relationships. The World Health Organization advocates for emphasizing children's functional status and capabilities rather than focusing on children's limitations and disability. This puts the focus on the child and not on the special health care condition or disability. One way this is addressed is through simple vocabulary. When discussing children who have special medical conditions the child's name is used first, followed by the identifying characteristic. The phrase *children with diabetes* reinforces the concept of thinking of children as people with many complexities, qualities, and abilities. The phrase *diabetic children*, by comparison, puts more (and unnecessary) focus on the medical condition and limitations.

To achieve positive functional status, children with special health care needs may require specialized health care services. These services include prescription medications, special diets, or frequent use of health care services (Ball, Bindler, & Cowen, 2010). Specialized services may be offered within the health care system or through special educational services. Here are some examples of specialized health care services:

- Specialist care (pediatric cardiology, pulmonology, neurology).
- Mental health care.
- Dental care.
- Physical therapy, occupational therapy, speech therapy.
- Preventive care.
- Eyeglasses/vision care.
- Prescription medications (HHS/HRSA, 2008).

Ongoing health care issues include a wide spectrum of physical and mental health problems. Nearly 41% of children ages 0 to 5 years with health conditions have problems with breathing, swallowing or digestion, circulation, vision, hearing, or chronic pain (HHS/HRSA, 2008). Despite needing additional health care services, nearly 10% of families of children with special medical conditions report having unmet health care needs. More than 47% of families report *not* having a medical home, or regular medical provider, for their child. Poverty and lack of insurance are risk factors for having unmet health care needs (HHS/HRSA, 2008). The most common unmet special health care needs are mental health and dental health (Jackson Allen, 2004).

When children have unmet health care needs, many aspects of their lives are affected. A child with Down syndrome, a genetic condition that causes intellectual and physical challenges, needs regular vision care because of the high likelihood of needing corrective lenses or other treatment. Without these interventions, the child's health, wellness, and learning are negatively impacted.

Many CSHCN have limited capability to participate in the activities of daily living. These challenges are called functional limitations. Nearly 61% of children ages 0 to 5 with special health care needs have limitations in activities involving self-care, movement, using hands, learning, paying attention, or communication (HHS/HRSA, 2008). Functional limitations are one reason why normal, everyday health promotion is sometimes overlooked in children with special health needs. The *Health Hint* discusses the important role of teachers in promoting physical activity among children with disabilities.

Impact on Families

Special health care needs can add complexity to family life, depending on the type and degree of the child's challenges. Some families may be better able to cope than others depending on socioeconomic status and other family stressors. Families with children who

functional status
term used to describe the characteristics that are most important to parents and teachers: how well a child can function in the community, in the classroom, and in relationships

Down syndrome
a genetic condition that causes mental and physical challenges

functional limitations
challenges that limit a child's ability to participate in activities of daily living

Health Hint

Promoting Physical Activity in Children with Disabilities

All children benefit from physical activity. Sports and recreation are especially important for children with special needs because they promote inclusion, enhance conditioning, and improve overall well-being. Physical activity also fosters positive self-esteem and independence. It can be an excellent way to address many of the issues that challenge children with disabilities. Unfortunately, children with special needs do not always experience the benefits of physical activity. Children with special needs often have lower levels of participation and fitness and higher levels of obesity than children without disabilities.

Teachers are in a position to be leaders in creating collaborations with families, other professionals in the school system, and local health care providers to improve participation in physical activity for children with disabilities. Some aspects to consider when promoting the participation of children who experience disabilities include the following:

- Consider the child's overall health status.
- Consider the child's individual activity preferences.
- Seek to meet activity goals for participation in sports and recreation.
- Ensure safety.
- Advocate for available programs and equipment.

By collaborating with other professionals and encouraging children to participate, teachers make a positive impact on physical activity for children with special needs.

Source: Based on "Promoting the Participation of Children with Disabilities in Sports, Recreation, and Physical Activities," by N. Murphy and P. Carbone, Council on Children with Disabilities, 2008, *Pediatrics, 121*(5), pp. 1057–1062.

have special health needs have added financial stress even if health insurance is available. These stresses have an impact on children's education.

Financial Issues

Financial problems often pose additional challenges to families with CSHCN. Approximately 18% of families with CSHCN report financial difficulties (HHS/HRSA, 2008). Financial problems exist among uninsured and privately and publicly insured families, although it is more common among uninsured and publicly insured families. Additional financial stress may present itself if one of the family members cuts back or quits work because of the child's health. Financial challenges influence the family's ability to obtain medicine, health care services, and other health care needs.

One-third of families of CSHCN who are insured still report that their health insurance does not meet their child's needs (Blanchard, Gurka, & Blackman, 2006). For example, not all prescription medications and therapies are covered by insurance. The consequences of these challenges can be apparent in schools. For example, a child with asthma who does not have an inhaler because her family could not afford it could have symptoms in school that affect her participation and learning.

Educational Impact

Children with special health care needs face several educational challenges. Health conditions often keep children from participating in early childhood education. Families of CSHCN are more likely to have difficulty arranging child care because some children's facilities are reluctant to enroll children with chronic medical conditions or with behavioral

What if . . .

a child in your classroom shows symptoms of asthma? The family has not accessed medical advice, so you have no guidance about how to manage the child's needs in the classroom. You have called the child's family to pick him up early from school, but this means the family member had to leave work and will lose pay because of the missed time. How will you manage this situation? What resources are available to you?

problems (Blanchard et al., 2006). This limits the child's access to quality learning experiences and creates difficulties for family members in maintaining employment.

Attendance is also a problem. Special health challenges disrupt children's ability to attend school regularly. Among school-age CSHCN, more than 14% miss 11 or more days of school per year (Child and Adolescent Health Measurement Initiative, 2008). Irregular attendance places children at a disadvantage in the classroom where learning builds on previous lessons the child may have missed. These issues double the negative impact on learning for children with special health care needs: The health challenge itself may impact the child's ability to learn and also reduce the child's participation and attendance. Special attention is needed to build on the child's capacity to learn and to address gaps that may occur with irregular attendance.

PLANNING INCLUSIVE CLASSROOMS

Children with medical conditions bring special health-related issues and needs to the early childhood setting. These needs include a range of activities such as administering medications and making accommodations in the classroom environment. Because children's health care needs permeate all aspects of their lives, it is important for teachers to understand them and learn how best to address each situation so that children will have more positive health outcomes.

Ensuring Access to Education

The federal Individuals with Disabilities Education Act describes the requirements regarding provision of services to children with disabilities across the nation (U.S. Department of Education [DOE], 2004). Children with special health care needs are identified for service through the IDEA when their health condition interrupts their ability to learn. The IDEA ensures that children with disabling conditions are able to participate in and be supported to progress in general education. The IDEA describes other health impairment as follows:

> Other health impairment means having limited strength, vitality, or alertness, including a heightened alertness to environmental stimuli, that results in limited alertness with respect to the educational environment, that—
> - Is due to chronic or acute health problems such as asthma, attention deficit disorder or attention deficit hyperactivity disorder, diabetes, epilepsy, a heart condition, hemophilia, lead poisoning, leukemia, nephritis, rheumatic fever, sickle cell anemia, and Tourette syndrome; and
> - Adversely affects a child's educational performance (DOE, 2004)

Three specialized plans describe the services available:

- *Individualized family services plan* (IFSP): This early intervention plan for children ages 0 to 3 years is intended to support and provide services that are targeted to improving the child's developmental progress.
- *Individualized education program* (IEP): This plan is for children in the school setting ages 3 to 21 years who need special education services due to cognitive, motor, social, and communication impairments.
- *Individualized health plan* (IHP): This plan is developed for students who have medical conditions that require management or treatment in the school setting. The IHP may be written as a component of the child's IEP.

Early childhood teachers and schools rely on the support of the local education agency (LEA) charged with administering and overseeing the implementation of the IDEA in the state or locality. This is often the public board of education or other authority that is responsible for evaluating children for participation in early intervention services and for providing needed services. This agency participates with families and schools to create a plan that meets the child's educational needs and addresses the impact of special health conditions.

MyEducationLab

Go to the Building Teaching Skills and Dispositions section of Topic 7: Chronic Illness/Special Health Care Needs in the MyEducationLab for your course and complete the activity entitled *Develop Inclusive Classrooms*. As you work through the learning unit, consider what you can do to help create an inclusive classroom for all children.

Policy Point

THE ROLE OF SCHOOL NURSES FOR CHILDREN WITH SPECIAL HEALTH CARE NEEDS

One of the goals of *Healthy People 2010* is to ensure that schools have one school nurse for every 750 students. Even more nurses are recommended for schools enrolling a high number of children with special health care needs. School nurses are directly involved with children's existing and potential health problems. They provide screening and referral for health conditions. School nurses also provide case management services and collaborate with family and community members regarding children's health. Most importantly for children with special health care needs, the school nurse is the health expert for the teams developing the individualized education program (IEP).

School nurses support teachers regarding services for children with special health care needs by:

1. Assessing health complaints. This is particularly important for children who are at risk for acute illnesses such as asthma, cystic fibrosis, and diabetes.
2. Administering medications.
3. Identifying and managing children's health care needs that affect educational achievement.

Recent economic constraints have reduced the number of nurses assigned to schools, hindering the *Healthy People 2010* goal. Early childhood professionals and administrators are important advocates for this service and other forms of school health care support.

Source: Based on "Role of the School Nurse in Providing School Health Services," by Council on School Health, 2008, *Pediatrics, 121*(5), pp. 1052–1056.

Some early childhood programs benefit from training provided by the LEA to implement the child's education and health plan. The guidance of a medical consultant is also beneficial. Some school districts have school nurses available to see children and advise teachers in the care of a child with special health needs in the school setting. The *Policy Point* discusses the role of school nurses as a resource for children with special health care needs, their families, and teachers.

Supporting Appropriate Inclusion

The trend for providing services to CSHCN has moved to an inclusion model. Inclusion focuses on educating children to the greatest extent possible in typical classrooms. The goals of inclusion are access, participation, and support (Division for Early Childhood & National Association for the Education of Young Children, 2009).

Federal laws do not require inclusion, but the IDEA does require that children be educated in the least restrictive environment appropriate to meet their unique needs (DOE, 2004). Teachers are important participants in making placement decisions for children with special health care needs. Along with families and the representatives of the LEA, each classroom is evaluated as a potential educational placement. Decisions are based on the needs of the child, her or his peers, and the classroom's ability to meet those needs.

tracheostomy tube a surgically placed tube that allows air and oxygen to enter the lungs through the neck

gastrostomy tube a tube placed through the abdominal wall into the stomach in order to feed children who are unable to eat orally

Teachers may be asked to monitor the child's health status and provide individualized care. Some needs may address making relatively minor changes in the environment. Others may include changing diapers, suctioning a **tracheostomy tube** (a surgically placed tube that allows air and oxygen to enter the lungs through the neck), or feeding a child with a **gastrostomy tube**, a tube placed through the abdominal wall into the stomach in order to feed children who are unable to eat orally.

Most teachers have not received education about serving children's health needs and may need specialized training to build confidence. They need access to resources to turn to for consultation. In addition, they need to be oriented to strategies that can help support children's access to the environment and participation in the learning activities. Teachers are part of a service team that plans, implements, and evaluates the effectiveness of services provided for children with special needs. They follow the guidance provided by the medical professionals and most often have either daily or periodic support of early intervention specialists and therapists. One aspect of inclusion that falls under the teacher's responsibilities is creating an environment where all children are welcomed and encouraged to thrive.

Administering Medications

More than 78% of children with special health care needs are given prescription medications. They may require medications during the school day. To safely manage this, early childhood settings should have a written policy describing how medications are to be administered. Some programs may choose to designate a person to administer all medications such as a school nurse or a director. Teachers or other staff who administer medications should receive appropriate training to ensure safety. Recommended standards are available to guide best practice procedures for medication administration. For example, the *National Health and Safety Performance Standards* recommend that medication administration be allowed when a health care provider prescribes a medicine or recommends an over-the-counter product and when permission is given by the parent or guardian (American Academy of Pediatrics [AAP], American Public Health Association, & National Resource Center for Health and Safety in Child Care and Early Education, 2002). The medical provider should provide clearly written instructions that explicitly describe what, when, how, to whom, and for what reason a medicine should be administered.

Because medication errors can occur easily, all schools and child care facilities should use a standard form that explains the details of medication administration. A standard form for this purpose is shown in Figure 12-1. Guidelines for the administration of medications include the following (AAP et al., 2002):

- Read and understand the directions on the medication label. Understand the appropriate dose, frequency of administration, and other directions such as taking the medication with food.
- Double check that the name of the child written on the medication is the same as the child receiving the medication.
- Administer the medication according to the prescribed methods and the prescribed dose. Some medications are given on a schedule while others are given as needed.
- Observe and report any reactions or side effects from medications.
- Document the time and amount of medicine given, and the name of the person administering the medication.

Partnering with Families

Communicating with families is essential to appropriate education and care of children with special medical conditions. Developing partnerships with families has a positive impact on children's education and well-being. When children have special health care needs, communication is of even greater importance. Establishing a good working relationship starts when children with health needs are enrolled and are preparing to join the class. Enrollment materials gather many details about a child's condition and special health considerations. Review of the health history further clarifies aspects of the child's need. However, discussing the plan for the child's entry into the early childhood environment directly with a family member is the most important component of a successful transition.

MyEducationLab

Go to the Assignments and Activities section of Topic 7: Chronic Illness/Special Health Care Needs in the MyEducationLab for your course and complete the activity entitled *Medication Administration*. What would be the first thing you do when administering medication to a young child?

Families need reassurance that their child with special health care needs will be safe in the early childhood setting.

Figure 12-1 Medication Administration Permission Form

Medication Permission and Administration Permission Form

The staff of the King Avenue Child Development Center has been asked by

(Parent/Guardian) _____ to administer medication to

(Child) _____ during the school day.

In order to comply with this request and in accordance with our state law, we need the following information from you.

MEDICAL PROVIDER INFORMATION

Health care provider signature _____ Date _____

Health care provider name _____

Address_____ Phone_____

_____ Fax _____

DIRECTIONS FOR ADMINISTRATION OF MEDICATION

Child's name _____ Date of birth _____

Name of medication_____

Purpose of medication _____

Starting date _____ Ending date _____

Dosage _____

When to give medication _____

Time(s) to be given _____

How medication is given: By mouth _____ By injection _____ Other _____

Special instructions _____

Signs or symptom(s) to watch for _____

Possible side effects or reactions _____

Adaptations suggested for the classroom _____

When to call the parent or health care provider regarding symptoms or if the child fails to respond to treatment

_____

_____

Signs that urgent care is needed _____

_____

PARENT PERMISSION

I request and authorize the King Avenue Child Development Center to administer this medication in accordance with the instructions provided by my child's medical provider.

_____

_____

Parent or Guardian Signature   Date

_____   _____

_____

Parent or Guardian Name   Phone

_____   _____

_____

Families may understandably have many worries about their child with special health care needs. They need to feel assured that the teacher is aware of their child's condition and is ready to assume responsibility for the child's safety and well-being. Direct conversation helps to build trust between the family and the teacher. It also contributes to a greater understanding of the relevant issues and strategies. Language and culture are important considerations when building this trusting relationship. Sometimes teachers may tend to communicate less with families who are not English speakers. Some parents may struggle to explain their child's complex health condition and needs. Teachers are responsible for ensuring that every family has the support they need to fully discuss their child's special health care needs. For example, it is not appropriate to use other children in the family as interpreters, so arranging for translation services or encouraging the family to invite a trusted friend to assist with the discussion are examples of ways to ensure full communication and to build an effective partnership.

Once children are enrolled, teacher and family communication focuses on exchanging information about the child's health and well-being during the school day. Families of children with asthma need to know if the child has been coughing, having difficulty with physical activity, or refusing to use the inhaler. A family whose child has **muscular dystrophy**, a genetic condition that causes progressive weakness, needs to know if the child is experiencing emotional problems due to his challenges. Similarly the teacher needs to be informed about any changes in the child's health status or experiences at home that might impact the child's participation in classroom activities.

To facilitate communication with families in her preschool, Janna creates a small notebook for each child with special health care needs. The notebook is placed in the child's cubby-locker. At orientation she describes how the notebook is used by both the teacher and the family to record notes for the other. When Janna wants to communicate a health-related message she writes a note in the log. When the family picks up the child, they check the notebook to read the teacher's message. Similarly the family can leave a message for the teacher. This method helps Janna remember to tell the family about important health observations. Karin uses a different approach. The children in her second-grade class ride the bus, so she does not see families very often. Karin communicates with families about children's special medical needs through e-mail.

muscular dystrophy
a progressive disease of the muscles causing progressive weakness, susceptibility to pulmonary infections, and premature death

Educating Classmates

Some children's medical conditions are apparent, others may not be obvious. When teachers realize, however, that classmates are aware of a child's special health care needs, they plan activities to educate classmates about the medical condition. Young children may view aspects that are unique about a child's appearance, behavior, or interaction in the classroom as "different" or "strange." This is due to children's natural interest and curiosity in things that are different and the potential to be confused and possibly frightened by new situations. Children may be naturally curious about why a child receives medication or a special diet or why a child does not participate in running games. They may also have fears and wonder, "Could that happen to me?" When curiosity or fear is displayed in a negative way, the child with special health care needs may suffer socially.

The potential for negative social interactions is an important reason for educating classmates about a child's medical condition and special needs in the classroom. Sometimes classmates pester or make fun of children with medical conditions. They might imitate the child's movements or laugh at the child's efforts. Teachers need to be aware of these potential reactions and be prepared with strategies to address them.

Children who begin to wear corrective lenses while they are attending the early childhood program may become the center of interest and attention. Sometimes this interest takes a negative tact. For example, another child may reach out to grab at the child's new glasses. Or children may call the child names or say the child looks "weird." Teachers must anticipate and intervene in such situations, describing how corrective lenses help the child to see and explaining that the glasses are precious and important tools for the child. Teachers might have a pair of corrective lenses available to let the other children touch and try on. This approach addresses children's curiosity and invites conversation and questions about vision problems and how they are managed.

In a similar way young children are capable of learning about other medical conditions. When the mystery is removed, children become accustomed to the management of the health need in the classroom; the novelty of the disability wears off, and children are more likely to treat the child with the special health care need in a typical way. Talking with classmates about a child's special health needs helps to address curiosity, lack of understanding, and fear and builds the desired sense of normalcy. This is an important aspect of creating class groups that are caring communities.

Educating classmates about children's special health care needs requires attention to developmentally appropriate messages. Very young children require short and clear explanations such as "I am helping Jax to feel better" or "D'shay needs to take this medicine to help him feel better. You can watch if you want." Older children are capable of learning more details about a condition and the activities that support the child in the classroom. Strategies to support such discussions include the following:

- Begin by discussing experiences that are familiar to the classmates. Ask children if they have ever been sick. Talk about what that felt like. Help children identify ways their family helped them to feel better, such as resting, eating healthy foods, or taking medicine.
- Show the connection between children's common experiences and the child's special health care need. Name the child's medical condition and briefly explain what it is and how it is somewhat similar to other children's health experiences. Talk about how the chronic condition is managed or treated. Identify the ways you help the child care for his or her condition in the class. Explain how the treatment helps the child.
- Talk about how the child developed the special medical condition. Explain if the child was born with the condition or if it was the result of an accident. Clarify whether the condition is contagious.
- Invite children to ask questions. Treat each question as an expression of legitimate interest and concern. Help children learn how to form questions about health.
- Discuss inappropriate interactions with the child if any have been observed. Talk about ways that children can advocate for appropriate treatment of those who have special conditions.
- Include the child with the special health care needs as a leader in the discussion if appropriate. Help the child with special health needs gain strategies and skills for describing and talking about her or his own medical conditions with others.
- Engage family members in classroom discussions. Many families may choose to lead the discussion about their child's needs. You can assist in this process by ensuring that the family member is familiar with appropriate ways to communicate complex information to the particular age group.
- After holding such discussions, observe children's interactions in the class. Reflect on whether the classroom discussion was helpful in supporting positive interactions among the children with special health care needs and their classmates.

Educating classmates about a child's medical condition addresses children's curiosity and increases understanding of the activities used to manage the special health care need in the classroom.

When communicating about a child's special health care need, teachers should avoid drawing undue attention to the child's limitations. Rather the goal is to reinforce the similarities that help children to befriend one another. For example, Paula has cerebral palsy. In the classroom she moves with the support of her walker. When the class takes a field trip to the library, Paula's classmates take turns pulling her in a wagon. Paula sits near the back of the wagon to make room for the bag of books the class is returning to the library. As they travel, they talk together about their favorite books and the topics they want to explore next. When they return to the classroom with their new bag of books, Sam turns to Paula and says, "Thanks for carrying the books." The *Teaching Wellness* feature provide other ideas to support recognition of sameness among classmates.

Supports are available to help teachers guide discussions about particular medical conditions. Picture books are a good way to introduce conversation about children's special medical conditions. Reading books such as those suggested below as part of the year-round reading options reinforces the message that special health care needs are part of the everyday world, just like caterpillars and butterflies! Here are some examples of books for young children with special health needs:

- *Lara Takes Charge* (for kids with diabetes, their friends and siblings) by Rocky Lang and Sally Huss.
- *Taking Asthma to School* (Special Kids in School, Vol. 2) by Kim Gosselin.
- *Taking Food Allergies to School* by Ellen Weiner, Kim Gosselin.

MANAGING SPECIAL HEALTH CARE NEEDS

Learning about chronic health conditions in early childhood equips teachers to be attuned to their impact on children's health and learning. Familiarity with the causes and impacts of special health needs also supports teachers in enrollment conversations with families. It prepares teachers to identify information they need to support the child's positive transition and participation in the classroom.

In the following sections we provide an overview of a variety of medical conditions that affect young children. The conditions are grouped according to their impact on the child's ability to function in the classroom. Examples of strategies used to manage each medical condition in the classroom are provided as a first step in understanding the many ways teachers support children with special health care needs. These suggestions do not replace the guidance provided by health care providers and early intervention specialists. Because most teachers do not have medical training, teachers work in partnership with medical providers, early intervention specialists, and families. This partnership carries the responsibility of planning, implementing, and monitoring appropriate management strategies to support the appropriate inclusion of children with special health care needs in the classroom environment and to address health needs that arise in the early childhood setting.

Conditions Related to the Immune System

Children's immune systems are responsible for controlling infections and responding to foreign substances that enter the body. Dental caries, asthma, environmental allergies, and eczema are common health conditions associated with the immune system.

Dental Caries

Dental caries affect 59% of children, the highest percentage of any chronic disease in children (CDC, 2009). This condition is caused by an interaction between bacteria, carbohydrates, and individual factors including the child's teeth and saliva (Selwitz, Ismail, & Tellex, 2007). Both primary and permanent teeth are affected and can be destroyed by the decay. Dental caries are associated with several risk factors (Selwitz et al., 2007):

- Inadequate salivary flow or composition.
- High number of cavity-causing bacteria.
- Insufficient exposure to fluoride through treatments.
- Gum line recession.
- Genetic factors.

Transmission of cavity-causing bacteria plays a major role in dental caries. The major way in which this bacterium is transmitted is from mothers or other caregivers kissing their babies or through other contact with saliva or oral secretions (Selwitz et al., 2007).

MyEducationLab

Go to the Assignments and Activities section of Topic 6: Health Appraisals/ Screening in the MyEducationLab for your course and complete the activity *Early Intervention*. What are the benefits of early intervention for children with special health care needs and their teachers?

immune system
  responsible for controlling infections and responding to foreign substances that enter the body

Teaching Wellness *Same and Special*

Learning Outcome: Children will be able to identify characteristics of similarity and aspects of uniqueness.

Infants and Toddlers

- *Goal:* To introduce the concepts of *same* and *different*.

- *Materials:* Typical classroom manipulative toys, the book *It's OK*, by Todd Parr (Little, Brown Kids, 2004).

- *Activity plan:* Take advantage of incidental learning opportunities to describe the concepts of same and different. For example, when playing with cube blocks, set aside a pair of green cube blocks and one red cube block. Place the green cube blocks together and say, "Look. These are the same." Then pair a red and green block, and say, "These are different. See? One is green and this one is red."

- *How to adjust the activity:* As children become familiar with the concepts of same and different, ask them to choose a matching item from a group. Hold a blue block and ask the child to find one that is the same. Then ask the child to find one that is different. Read and talk about the book *It's OK*.

- *Did you meet your goal?* Did the children listen to the questions? Can the children find objects that match?

Preschoolers and Kindergartners

- *Goal:* To explore the concepts of *same* and *different* and to discuss the concept of uniqueness and the notion of being special.

- *Materials:* Provide an array of creative materials such as yarn pieces, fabric scraps, magazine pages, construction paper, scissors, glue; the book *We Are All Alike, We Are All Different*, by the Cheltenham Elementary School Kindergartners and Laura Dwight (Scholastic, 2002).

- *Activity plan:* Offer the creative materials during free exploration time. Let children know that you will invite them to show their creations at group time. During group time ask each child to talk about his or her creation. Then lay the pictures on the floor next to each other. Standing around the pictures, invite the children to talk about what is the same and what is different. Talk about aspects of uniqueness and describe how being different is a way of being unique or special.

- *How to adjust the activity:* Read the book *We Are All Alike, We Are All Different*. Use the book to introduce a discussion about same/special characteristics among people. As children dictate, make lists of all the things children can identify that are the same about people and all the things that are different. Talk about ways being the same is interesting and ways that being unique is interesting. Use other books to explore more aspects of same and special:
- *Why Am I Special?* by Melissa Langer (2006)
- *The Family Book,* by Todd Parr (Little, Brown Young Readers, 2003)

384

- *Me I Am!* by Jack Prelutsky and Christine Davenier (Farrar, Straus and Giroux, 2007)
- *I Am Special,* by Charlotte Lisi and David Ortega (Trafford Publishing, 2006)

- *Did you meet your goal?* Are children able to recognize and identify characteristics that make things the same and different? Are children able to list characteristics of similarity and difference among people?

School-Age Children

- *Goal:* To explore the concepts of *same* and *different* and to discuss the concept of uniqueness and the notion of being special.

- *Materials:* Colored plastic mosaic tiles of various shapes, colors, and sizes; the book *This Is My Hair*, by Todd Parr (Little, Brown, 2000).

- *Activity plan:* Provide colored plastic mosaic tiles of various shapes. Invite a small group of children to sort all of the colored tiles by attribute: all of the yellow triangles here, all of the blue squares there, and so on. Ask the children to take one of each shape (or if there are enough take two or more of each shape) to create a design. When children have finished, ask them to look at each other's designs. Are they the same? Different? Talk about how each child had the same shape, color, and number of tiles but each creation is unique and special.

- *How to adjust the activity:* Read the children's book *This Is My Hair*. Have the children draw a picture using the author's illustrative style that depicts their unique style. Display the drawings and conduct an "Illustrator's Interview": Ask each child to describe aspects of their drawing that are similar to others, but to also identify aspects that are unique. Talk about same and special characteristics among children in the class. Provide other books to read about these concepts:
  - *We're Different, We're the Same,* by Bobbi Kates (Random House Books for Young Readers, 1998)
  - *It's OK to Be Different,* by Todd Parr (Little, Brown Young Readers, 2004)

- *I Just Am,* by Tom Lambke and Bryan Lambke (Five Star Publications, 2006)
- *I Am Special,* by Linda Schwartz (Creative Teaching Press, 1978)

- *Did you meet your goal?* Are children able to describe characteristics that make things the same and different? Are they able to discuss aspects of unique and special?

My life with Deaf Sister's-by Brad

Growing up with Deaf sisters a Great and amazing experience so far. I got to learn language called sign-language. I learned many sign's. But the one we use the most in our family is the love sign.

Sometimes I don't know what in the world their saying so I ask my mom for help and if she doesn't know they teach me what that sign mean's. Growing up with. Growing up with deaf sister's it took me awhile to understand them.

All their friends who aren't Deaf love learning sign's. Even though my sister's may get a little crazy at times I still love them and always will.

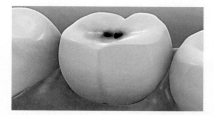

Dental caries are common and an important health condition of early childhood.

Other risk factors include problems accessing dental care. Families living in poverty experience more tooth decay and are less likely to have it treated than those not living in poverty (Psoter, Pendrys, Morse, Zhang, & Mayne, 2006). Lack of access to dental care is a widespread problem among families with young children. Even children covered by Medicaid have low rates of receiving adequate preventive dental care. Fewer than one in five children with Medicaid has a preventive dental visit every year (CDC, 2009).

Racial disparities also exist. Some ethnic minority groups, including Hispanics, are at increased risk for caries (Psoter et al., 2006). For children ages 2 to 5 years, 18% of White children have caries, whereas 40% of Hispanic and 29% of African American children have caries (Vargas & Ronzio, 2006). Children in minority groups also have more severe disease and are more likely to have untreated caries (Vargas & Ronzio, 2006).

Improving oral hygiene and dietary habits can stop the progression of dental caries. Changing unhealthy practices such as frequent consumption of refined sugars and inappropriate infant feeding methods (e.g., putting the child to bed with a bottle of milk) helps improve oral health (Selwitz et al., 2007).

Classroom Management Strategies The CDC has recommended a number of strategies to combat the problem of dental caries, including implementation of school-based programs. Teachers play a role in this prevention effort by (Selwitz et al., 2007; AAP et al., 2002):

- Serving appropriate foods and using feeding practices that support good oral health. These include serving fruit juices only at meals, putting children to bed with bottles that contain only water, and not serving carbonated beverages to children younger than 30 months.
- Wiping the gums and teeth of infants and providing appropriate opportunities for children to brush their teeth at least once during the school day.
- Educating children and their families about plaque, dental caries, and the importance of fluoride treatment and good oral hygiene practices such as brushing at least twice a day and flossing at least every other day.

Asthma

Asthma is a respiratory disease characterized by intermittent attacks of difficult breathing. It causes chronic inflammation of the small airways within the lung, resulting in a narrowing or obstruction of the airways. This narrowing causes children to cough or experience shortness of breath. Children with asthma may also *wheeze*, creating a high-pitched whistling sound while breathing.

Asthma is one of the most common chronic illnesses of childhood. It occurs in 12% to 13% of young children (Akinbami, 2006). The incidence of asthma varies by geographic region, sex, race, and ethnicity. The highest rates are in the northeastern United States. Asthma is more common among boys, and boys have a higher death rate due to asthma than girls. Non-Hispanic black and Puerto Rican children have the highest rates of asthma. Black children have dramatically higher mortality rates from asthma than White children (Akinbami, 2006).

Additionally, although the incidence of asthma increases with age, the highest health care use is by young children. Asthma affects many aspects of children's lives, such as their ability to play, learn, and sleep (Akinbami, 2006). It is the most common reason for missed school days (Child and Adolescent Health Measurement Initiative, 2008). The triggers that cause the symptoms of asthma vary and in many children are unknown. Common triggers are listed in Table 12-1.

Classroom Management Strategies Teachers may be asked to assist children with asthma by administering medications. Two categories of medications are commonly used to treat asthma. One type is used *as needed* to open the airways when the child has symptoms at the onset of an episode, or as a rescue medicine. *Albuterol* is an example of an as-needed medication. This type of medication is used by nearly all children with asthma. The frequency of use depends on the severity and control of the child's illness. The other type of medication is used daily even when the child is not having symptoms to *prevent*

wheeze
a high-pitched whistling sound made while breathing; commonly occurs in children with asthma

albuterol
medication commonly used to open the airways when children have symptoms of asthma at the onset of an episode or as a rescue medicine

inhaled steroids
a type of medication used to prevent episodes of asthma attacks; is used daily even when the child is not having symptoms

nebulizer
a small, electric device that is used to distribute medication as aerosolized droplets for inhalation by the child

episodes. Inhaled steroids are examples of *prevention* medications.

Asthma medications are administered either as a solution with a nebulizer or with an inhaler and spacer. A nebulizer is a small electronic device that distributes a solution into aerosol droplets, or spray, for the child to inhale. An inhaler with a spacer also administers medication to be inhaled but requires more coordination on the part of the recipient. To use an inhaler, the child must be able to put the inhaler in her or his mouth and inhale.

Typically, nebulizers are used more often for infants and toddlers, and inhalers are used for preschoolers and older children. To most effectively receive the medication, inhalers should *always* be used with a spacer. A spacer is a plastic tube that attaches to the inhaler and holds the aerosolized medication in a confined space while the child breathes in the droplets. Asthma medications may need to be administered several times per day.

Children with asthma may receive more than one medication and the frequency of use may change. Periodic communication with the child's family and health care provider may be necessary to understand any changes in the prescribed plan.

In addition to administering medications, management of asthma involves participating with others to address the child's education needs. This includes activities such as these (HHS & DOE, 2003):

- Consult with others, such as the school nurse and families, on children's asthma plans and program policies and procedures for supporting children with asthma.
- Understand the teacher's role in children's asthma management plan.
- Develop clear plans regarding missed schoolwork (for primary school–age children).
- Report if children's asthma symptoms are interfering with their participation in the classroom or learning.
- Encourage children with controlled asthma to participate in physical activities.
- Plan field trips and other activities so that children with asthma can participate.

Teachers are also important sources of recognizing when a child's asthma is uncontrolled and when a child is experiencing an asthma attack. Symptoms of uncontrolled asthma and asthma attacks are similar. Figure 12-2 lists symptoms for both circumstances. Asthma attacks can be life threatening. Even when receiving treatment for asthma, a majority of children will experience attacks (Akinbami, 2006). If symptoms of uncontrolled asthma or an asthma attack are observed, emergency treatment as directed by the child's medical provider should be followed immediately, and the family should be notified as soon as possible.

Table 12-1	Common Asthma Triggers
Indoor allergens	Animal dander Dust mites Cockroaches Molds
Seasonal allergens	Pollens from trees, grasses, weeds Molds
Outdoor allergens	Air pollutants Farm and barn exposure Cold air, dry air
Other irritants	Tobacco smoke Strong odors and fumes from paint, hair spray, perfumes
Other health conditions	Cold, flu, viruses Sinus infections Nasal allergies Reflux
Physical exercise	Especially in cold weather

Source: "Asthma," by A. Liu, R. Covar, J. Span, and D. Leung, pp. 953–970, Chapter 143 in *Nelson Textbook of Pediatrics*, 18th edition, edited by R. Kliegman, R. Behrman, H. Jenson, and B. Stanton, 2007, Philadelphia: Saunders Elsevier.

spacer
a plastic, hollow tube that attaches to an inhaler and holds aerosolized medication in a confined space while the child inhales the medication

A nebulizer is used to treat asthma in infants, toddlers, and young preschool children.

Figure 12-2 Symptoms of Uncontrolled Asthma and Asthma Attacks

Symptoms of uncontrolled asthma:	Symptoms of an asthma attack:

• Cough that lingers after a cold.
• Persistent cough during the day or coughing a lot in the mornings.
• Cough or shortness of breath during or after physical activity, especially in cold weather.
• Reluctance to participate in physical activity or low level of stamina.
• Coughing or shortness of breath even after using asthma medications.
• An increase in the use of asthma medications.
	• Changes in breathing
	  • Early signs: coughing, chest tightness, throat tightness, breathing through the mouth.
	  • Later signs: wheezing, shortness of breath, rapid breathing.
	  • Students may have clipped speech or choppy breathing.
	• Verbal complaints
	  • "My chest is tight" or "My chest hurts."
	  • "I can't catch my breath."
	  • "My mouth is dry."
	  • "My neck feels funny."
	  • "I don't feel well" or "I feel tired."
	  • "My chin (or neck) hurts."

Source: *Managing Asthma: A Guide for Schools*, by the U.S. Department of Health and Human Services and U.S. Department of Education, 2003 retrieved October 9, 2009, from http://www.nhlbi.nih.gov/health/prof/lung/asthma/asth_sch.pdf.

asthma attack
episodes of asthma in which symptoms worsen and require immediate treatment to control breathing; characterized by shortness of breath, fast breathing, or worsening cough

Inhalers and spacers are used for preschoolers and older children.

Environmental Allergies

Environmental allergies occur as a result of a complex interaction between environmental exposure and genetics. They are often referred to as hay fever or seasonal allergies, although they can be due to seasonal or year-round causes. The list of potential stimuli or triggers for allergies is very long. Common examples are tree and grass pollens, dust, mold and mildew, and pet dander. Environmental allergies are a common health problem, affecting 20% to 40% of children. The incidence has been increasing most significantly in urban areas and to a lesser extent in rural areas (Milgrom & Leung, 2007). This trend is not yet well understood. Theories suggest that the increase in exhaust emissions is introducing more allergens into the air, and the effects of global warming are causing certain trees to distribute pollen into the air for more days during the growing season. The risk of developing allergies increases with early exposure to foods or formula during infancy (Milgrom & Leung, 2007) as described in the *Nutrition Note*.

Because of their very high prevalence, chronic allergies impact many children's quality of life. Common symptoms of environmental allergies include runny nose, watery eyes, cough, headache, and fatigue. These symptoms limit children's daily activities, interfere with sleep, and contribute to missed school days (Milgrom & Leung, 2007).

Classroom Management Strategies One of the most important ways teachers can aid children with allergies is to help them avoid known triggers. Adjustments can be made for indoor and outdoor activities. Keeping the indoor environment clean to reduce dust and dry to discourage mold, and mildew, reduces these triggers. Children who have an allergy to grass can be encouraged to play in the area of the playground that has mulch instead of grass or to run and walk in the grassy area rather than sitting on or touching the grass.

Eczema

Eczema is a condition that causes inflammation and itching of the skin. It is characterized by chronically dry skin with periodic episodes of more intense skin rashes that are red, peeling, and very itchy. The most common areas for the rash are the face, backs of hands and feet, and skin folds (back of knees and in front of elbows). Children with eczema may scratch constantly and have difficulty sleeping because of itching. Infants with eczema may be irritable and move about as they are trying to fall asleep. Children with eczema are prone to skin infections because the integrity of the skin is compromised.

Eczema varies in severity and is more easily controlled in some children than others. It is quite common, affecting 17% of infants and children (Ball et al., 2010). Most children who have eczema develop it in the first 6 months of life. Eczema can be triggered by food or environmental stimuli. Triggers include dust mites, pet dander, pollens, soaps, detergents, abrasive clothing, and emotional stress.

Classroom Management Strategies Management of eczema involves avoiding known triggers and judiciously keeping the skin moist with lotions recommended by a medical provider. Teachers may be asked to apply creams or lotions if children experience a flare-up. It is also important to reduce children's contact with strong soaps or detergents by selecting appropriate soap for children to use at the sink.

Conditions Related to the Nervous System

Many chronic health conditions in childhood affect the nervous system or are caused by disorders of the nervous system. Although the effects of these conditions vary, they all have some effect on health and wellness in childhood.

Children with eczema are more likely to contract skin infections.

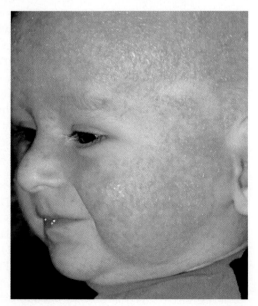

Attention Deficit Disorder and Attention Deficit/Hyperactivity Disorder

Attention deficit disorder (ADD) and attention deficit/hyperactivity disorder (ADHD) are conditions characterized by children having difficulty paying attention and being impulsive or hyperactive. Their causes are not completely understood, however, it is estimated that genetic factors contribute to 80% of cases (Turnbull, Turnbull, & Wehmeyer, 2010). Other health conditions are strongly associated with ADD/ADHD, including structural brain abnormalities and prenatal exposure to toxins. Children with ADD/ADHD tend to have higher rates of other psychiatric or behavioral conditions (Stein & Perrin, 2003). ADD/ADHD can interfere with the attainment of normal developmental milestones. It can also affect the attainment of academic and fine motor skills as well as social and adaptive skills. As a result, children with ADD/ADHD often experience school failure, poor family and peer relations, low self-esteem, and emotional, behavioral, and learning problems (Leslie, 2002; Raishevich & Jensen, 2007).

Estimates of school-age children exhibiting ADD/ADHD range from 5% to 10% (Raishevich & Jensen, 2007). It is one of the common chronic disorders seen in childhood. Of children with special health needs, it accounts for 30% of all diagnoses (Child and Adolescent Health Measurement Initiative, 2008). Boys are three times more likely than girls to be identified (Stein & Perrin, 2003). Children born prematurely are also at increased risk for acquiring ADD. This could be due to any brain abnormality, such as the intracranial hemorrhage Jeremy's mother reported in the case scenario, or there could be subtle developmental effects on the infant's neurological system.

Three types of conditions fall under the ADD and ADHD categories: *predominantly inattentive* (ADD), *predominantly hyperactive-impulsive* (HD), and *combined* (ADHD) (Turnbull et al., 2010). Specific diagnostic criteria exist for each of these types, as described in Table 12-2. In addition to frequently displaying these symptoms, the symptoms should be observed in two or more settings, such as at school and at home. In addition, the symptoms must be seen as impairing social or academic functioning. It can sometimes be difficult to distinguish between normal childhood behaviors and ADHD. Children with ADHD may also share some traits associated with giftedness.

Children with ADD often have other conditions that affect learning and behavior such as learning disabilities, behavioral disorders, or depression. Symptoms of these conditions, such as inconsistent performance or poor organization and time management, may be inappropriately attributed to laziness or lack of motivation (Leslie, 2002). The percentage of children with ADD/ADHD who also have learning disabilities is estimated at 20% (Turnbull et al., 2010). Children with ADHD typically have normal intelligence; however, they often have problems with memory, motivation, and behaviors that are goal directed.

Children with ADD are eligible for development of a behavioral management plan under the IEP process. In 1991, the DOE confirmed that ADHD is considered within the scope of the IDEA (Turnbull et al., 2010). Children with ADHD may also qualify for special education services under the diagnosis of emotional disturbance, which requires a comprehensive evaluation that meets federal and state requirements. This is typically provided by the public school system (Hannah, 2002). Children who do not qualify for services under the IDEA may be eligible under Section 504 of the Rehabilitation Act. ADHD is considered a disability under Section 504 when the child is substantially limited in a major life activity.

Classroom Management Strategies Teachers provide a variety of supports for children with ADD/ADHD. They may be asked to respond to questionnaires that evaluate the child's symptoms in the classroom setting. Adjustments for primary school–age children may include placement in a smaller class group, tutoring supports, or modifying homework (Hannah, 2002).

Behavioral therapies may be recommended to assist children to function effectively in the classroom. Some children will also be prescribed medications such as stimulants that may need to be administered during the day. These medications are used to increase focus and decrease distractibility in the hopes of improving school performance and relationship

stimulants
medications used to increase focus and decrease distractibility for improving school performance and relationship building in children with ADHD

Table 12-2	**Characteristics of ADD and ADHD**

Attention Deficit Disorder: For diagnosis children must exhibit at least six of the following characteristics often:

- Fails to pay close attention to details and often makes mistakes.
- Cannot sustain attention in play or tasks.
- Does not seem to be listening when he/she is spoken to.
- Does not follow through with specific instructions and often does not finish school work or chores.
- Cannot organize themselves when planning tasks or activities.
- Avoids engaging in tasks that require sustained effort mentally.
- Loses things that are necessary for activities.
- Distracted by external stimuli.
- Forgetful during daily activities.

Hyperactive-impulsive type: For diagnosis children must exhibit at least six of the following characteristics often:

- Fidgets with hands and feet.
- Leaves seat when it is expected that they should remain seated.
- Runs or climbs inappropriately.
- Has difficulties participating in leisurely activities.
- Always moving.
- Talks excessively.
- Answers questions before they are completed.
- Cannot wait his/her turn.
- Interrupts or intrudes.

Source: Reprinted with permission from the *Diagnostic and Statistical Manual of Mental Disorders, Text Revision,* Fourth Edition (Copyright 2000). American Psychiatric Association.

building. Extensive literature demonstrates that the use of these medications is safe and effective (Dopheide & Pliska, 2009). Several trials of different dosages, medications, and timing intervals may be necessary before identifying the best treatment for an individual child.

Autism

Autism is the most common condition in a group of developmental disorders called the *autism spectrum disorders* (ASDs). Autism is a condition that involves impaired social interactions, communication problems, repetitive behaviors, and in some circumstances, a restricted range of interests. Other conditions in the ASDs include Asperger's syndrome and pervasive developmental disorder (PDD). The cause of autism is unknown although it appears to have a strong genetic component (Shah, Dalton, & Boris, 2007).

Symptoms Children with autism exhibit a wide spectrum of symptoms. Many experience abnormalities in cognitive functioning, learning, attention, and sensory processing (CDC, 2007). Most have difficulties with joint attention or pretend play. Joint attention is a method of sharing experiences with others by pointing or making eye contact. This skill is typically developed by 18 months of age (Shah et al., 2007). However, children with autism often avoid making eye contact.

The kind and quality of a child's speech is another highly variable symptom. Some children have little to no understandable expressive language, whereas others have extensive speech abilities and may even repeat long segments of songs or movies. Children with autism may also exhibit difficulty with the *quality* of their speech. They may use unusual tones or rhythms and repeat many words or phrases.

Repetitive movements such as hand flapping, head banging, or rocking are hallmarks of autism. In addition, children with autism often have a narrow range of interests in their play. They may spend much of their time in solitary play (Shah et al., 2007).

autism
neurological condition characterized by impairments in social interaction and communication as well as restrictive, repetitive, or stereotypical patterns of behavior

pervasive developmental disorder (PDD)
disorder associated with developmental delays, abnormal or delayed social interactions, and in some circumstances, a restricted range of interests

joint attention
method of sharing experiences with others by pointing or making eye contact

Table 12-3	Criteria for the Diagnosis of Autism

Diagnosis requires a total of six indicators from Sections 1, 2, and 3, with at least two from Section 1, and one from each of Sections 2 and 3.

1. Impairment in the quality of social interactions as manifested by at least two of the following:
   - Impairment in use of nonverbal behaviors such as eye contact, facial expression, body postures, and gestures.
   - Failure to develop age-appropriate peer relationships.
   - Does not seek to share enjoyment, interests, or achievements with others.
   - Lack of social/emotional reciprocity.

2. Impairment in quality of communication as manifested by at least one of the following:
   - Delay or lack of language development.
   - In those who speak, impairment in ability to initiate and sustain conversations.
   - Repetitive use of language.
   - Lack of varied, spontaneous pretend or age-appropriate social imitation play.

3. Repetitive or stereotypical behaviors as manifested by one of the following:
   - Preoccupation with certain interests that is abnormal in intensity or focus.
   - Inflexibly adherent to nonfunctional routines or rituals.
   - Repetitive motor mannerisms such as hand flapping.
   - Preoccupation with parts of objects.

4. Delays in at least one of the following areas with onset prior to age 3:
   - Social interaction.
   - Language used in social communication.
   - Symbolic or imaginative play.

5. Delays are not explained by other pervasive developmental disorders.

Source: Reprinted with permission from the *Diagnostic and Statistical Manual of Mental Disorders, Text Revision*, Fourth Edition (Copyright 2000). American Psychiatric Association.

Diagnosis Diagnostic criteria for autism include impairments in social interaction and communication as well as restrictive, repetitive, or stereotypical patterns of behavior (Shah et al., 2007). Although a physician makes the diagnosis of autism, we have included the diagnostic criteria in Table 12-3 because it includes an important list of symptoms or characteristics that are seen. The diagnosis is typically made after a parent, caregiver, and/or teacher first raises concerns about development or behaviors.

Asperger's syndrome
neurological disorder characterized by normal intelligence, poor peer relationships, lack of empathy (similar to, but milder than, autism), language skills that are generally stronger than other types of PDDs, and a tendency to overfocus on certain topics or objects (planets, geography)

One of the ASDs is called **Asperger's syndrome.** Children with Asperger's typically have normal intelligence. They display poor peer relationships and lack of empathy (similar to, but milder than, autism), have language skills that are generally stronger than other types of PDDs, and a tendency to perseverate on certain topics or objects (planets, geography) (Shah et al., 2007). These behaviors may be observed by teachers in the classroom, which can assist in the diagnositic process.

Diagnosis and treatment of autism have undergone a transformation since autism was first identified as its own condition in the 1950s. It was once considered to be a very rare disorder for which only severely affected children were identified. An alarming increase in the prevalence rates of autism has been of concern to teachers, parents, and public health officials. Determining the cause of this increase has been extremely difficult. Currently autism is seen in 2 to 10 per 1,000 children. It is four times more common in boys than girls (CDC, 2007).

Controversy exists regarding the cause of the increase in cases diagnosed. Some believe that more frequent diagnosis is due to better recognition of the condition, and that children with the condition in the past were misdiagnosed as being mentally retarded. Others are of the opinion that the rates of autism are increasing. The CDC is conducting ongoing surveillance studies to track prevalence rates to better clarify this issue.

The onset of autism occurs during the first 3 years of life; typically children are diagnosed by age 3. Therefore, many children with autism have been diagnosed by the time they enter the public school system. Children with mild autism or Asperger's syndrome, however, may not be diagnosed until the elementary years.

Classroom Management Strategies   The diagnosis of autism is often made over time, creating a stressful and anxiety-provoking anticipatory period for families. Teachers are part of the support system for families during this evaluation period. Providing information about autism and offering opportunities for families to discuss their concerns are ways in which teachers can lend support. When children are diagnosed, teachers are important partners in developing an effective IEP. The goals of the IEP are to reinforce children's desirable behaviors, improve social skills and communication, and reduce nonadaptive behaviors such as aggressive or angry outburst behaviors. Regular routines and a predictable schedule are important, as well as supporting children when schedules vary.

Visual cues are often an effective way to support verbal directions for children with autism.

Strategies involve teaching children communication skills, such as helping Mike recognize when Alan is asking to share a toy by saying, "Mike, turn your head to look at Alan. He has a question for you." Teaching children imitation skills is another step in helping children recognize social cues (Schwartz, Billingsley, & McBride, n.d.). Supporting the child to play Follow the Leader games is a familiar example of teaching imitation in the early childhood setting. Providing visual cues such as picture cards or pointing to posters that depict an action are often effective ways to support verbal directions. The greatest success occurs when these strategies are consistently used both at school and at home.

Teachers are also an important link to connect families to resources to help them learn to cope with the challenges of autism. There is no cure for autism. However, strategies are available to reduce the impact of symptoms and to improve children's functioning. Interventions provided during the early childhood years are considered critical to improving the symptoms of autism.

Learning Disabilities

Learning disabilities are defined as a specific and persistent failure to learn age-appropriate academic skills despite normal intelligence, conventional teaching, and adequate sociocultural opportunities. The main characteristic of learning disabilities is a discrepancy between the expected academic achievement based on the child's IQ, which is normal, and the actual achievement (Heward, 2009). Between 5% and 10% of children are reported to have a type of learning disability (Lagae, 2008).

Learning disabilities include a number of specific disabilities reflecting difficulties in learning reading, writing, and/or mathematics skills. The most common one is dyslexia, a disorder of reading in which children frequently omit, insert, reverse, or substitute words or sounds. The causes are generally unknown, although there is a strong genetic component for certain types of learning disabilities such as dyslexia.

Problems commonly seen in the classroom in children with learning disabilities include the following (Heward, 2009):

- Reading difficulties or learning how to read later than expected.
- Problems with written language including spelling.
- Problems with math.
- Problems with social skills (occurs in about 75% of children with learning disabilities).
- Problems with attention and hyperactivity.
- Behavioral problems.

Classroom Management Strategies   The least restrictive environment as described by IDEA applies to children with learning disabilities. Research demonstrates mixed results with inclusion of children with learning disabilities in the general classroom and some

learning disabilities
term used to describe a condition in which there is a specific and persistent failure to learn age-appropriate academic skills despite normal intelligence, conventional teaching, and adequate sociocultural opportunities

dyslexia
a disorder of reading where children frequently omit, insert, reverse, or substitute words or sounds

controversy exists (Heward, 2009). All major groups advocating for children with learning disabilities are opposed to full inclusion and have published position papers clearly stating that there is a spectrum of possibilities for partial inclusion depending on the child's strengths and needs (Heward, 2009).

Besides specific teaching strategies related to inclusion, input from teachers plays an important role in identification of children with learning disabilities. There is no one test that is diagnostic. Generally, it is a compilation of information gained from parents and teachers along with testing done by the school system that aids in the diagnosis made by specialists.

Cerebral Palsy

Cerebral palsy (CP) is a condition that affects movement and posture. It is caused by problems that occur in brain development before, during, or after birth. Most cases of cerebral palsy are a result of problems that occur before birth and involve anatomical or structural abnormalities of the brain. CP occurs in 1.5 to 2 per 1,000 infants (Ball et al., 2010). Being born prematurely or small for gestational age are risk factors for developing CP.

Children with CP have problems with movement that affect muscle tone and with the signals that promote movement and coordination. Some children have minimal challenges, whereas others experience extensive challenges. Children with CP often experience developmental delays and frequently have other health conditions such as visual problems, hearing loss, speech problems, seizures, and feeding difficulties. About 75% have learning disabilities or intellectual disabilities (Ball et al., 2010). Children with CP may move with a walker or use a wheelchair. They may have trouble with small motor coordination, making it difficult to hold small items and learn to write. Children with CP may experience difficulties with speech. Different classifications of CP are based on the type of movement difficulties and the part of the body that is affected.

Classroom Management Strategies Children with cerebral palsy experience a wide variety of type and severity of symptoms. Teachers should learn about the child's needs for adjustments in the classroom environment to accommodate the child's movement in the setting. Understanding how the child communicates is also important because children with CP may use various communication methods such as a picture board, digital communication device, or keyboard. Many children with CP are supported in the classroom by an educational assistant who works with the lead teacher to manage any medical interventions and to modify the learning environment appropriately. Speech and physical therapists are usually partners in supporting the child's educational plan.

Fetal Alcohol Syndrome

fetal alcohol syndrome (FAS) a neurological condition causing a range of physical and developmental outcomes that occur as a result of fetal exposure to alcohol

Fetal alcohol syndrome (FAS) is a neurological condition caused by exposure to alcohol during pregnancy (Green, 2007). Alcohol consumption during pregnancy is known to have lifelong, severe effects on the fetus, affecting a child's physical, emotional, and neurological development. The prevalence of FAS is reported to be 9.1 per 1,000 (Green, 2007); however, it is estimated that the incidence of FAS is considerably underreported (Niccols, 2007). FAS is the most common cause of intellectual disability and occurs more often than Down syndrome and spina bifida. Fetal alcohol syndrome is characterized by (Green, 2007):

- Abnormalities in the structure of the face.
- Growth deficiency.
- Central nervous system abnormalities including small head circumference, neurological problems, cognitive/developmental deficits, and behavioral/emotional deficits.

philtrum the fold typically seen between the nose and upper lip

The facial abnormalities seen in FAS include a smooth philtrum (the fold typically seen between the nose and upper lip), a thin upper lip, and small eyes, which may be obvious in some individuals or very subtle in others. Central nervous system abnormalities range from severe structural abnormalities of the brain to mild cognitive deficits.

Some children exposed to alcohol do not meet the full criteria for FAS. The term *fetal alcohol spectrum disorders* is used to encompass the range of disabilities associated with exposure to alcohol *in utero*, and includes the diagnosis alcohol-related neurodevelopmental disorder (ARND). The ARND diagnosis is often used when there is a history of alcohol exposure, but the child does not meet all of the official criteria for FAS.

Children with FAS often struggle with attention, memory, and learning, which leads to difficulties in school. Nearly 85% of children with FAS exhibit hyperactivity during the preschool period (Niccols, 2007). A wide range of other symptoms may also be present such as emotional disorders, problems with social skills, abnormal habits, sleep disorders, and behavioral problems such as aggression, inappropriate sexual behavior, delinquency, or self-injury (Green, 2007). As children mature and enter the school years, diagnoses such as ADHD, conduct disorder, depression, oppositional defiant disorder, anxiety disorder, obsessive-compulsive disorder, and bipolar disorder are all common among children with FAS. Consequences of exposure to alcohol during prenatal development include (Green, 2007):

- Deficits in basic cognitive functioning.
- Difficulties in planning, organization, and attention.
- Failure to learn from consequences.
- Memory deficits.
- Speech/language problems.
- Visual problems.

Children with FAS often have subtle characteristics such as a smooth philtrum and a thin upper lip.

As a result, children with FAS are often described as "lazy, defiant, intentional, and manipulative" (Green, 2007, p. 106). Early diagnosis is important. Studies report that children diagnosed before age 6 often do not develop as many behavioral problems (Green, 2007).

Classroom Management Strategies   In spite of the wide range of potential behavioral challenges, many children with FAS are described as outgoing, friendly, and socially engaging. Most children with FAS do not qualify for special education services. As they plan to successfully teach children with FAS, many teachers find evaluation of children's executive functioning to be helpful. Executive functioning refers to children's ability to function in a school setting. The basic tasks involved in executive functioning are planning, organization, and attention.

Teachers focus on teaching skills that build children's self-help skills to navigate through the daily routines of the classroom. Detailed visual cues and prompts are used to make abstract concepts more concrete and to reinforce directions, such as "Time to clean up" or "Time to wash hands." Teachers work to reduce distractions and to help children with FAS focus on tasks and skill-building activities. Teachers also provide immediate feedback for appropriate and inappropriate behaviors.

Intellectual Disability

Intellectual disability is the most common developmental disability. This condition has previously been referred to as cognitive disability or mental retardation, a term that is no longer used because of stigmatization. It is characterized by a significantly below-average score on a test of intellectual ability and by limited ability to function in the tasks of daily life such as self-care, communication, and managing social interactions. Intellectual disability can result from genetic conditions and developmental causes before birth, as well as injury, infection, or illness occurring at birth or during childhood. The most common causes of intellectual disability are Down syndrome, fetal alcohol syndrome, or Fragile X syndrome.

Intellectual disabilities are often associated with environmental or biological causes. Environmental causes tend to be exhibited through mild expressions of disability, whereas severe disease is more likely linked to biological causes. Children with mild intellectual disability are much more likely to have mothers who did not complete high school, linking

alcohol-related neurodevelopmental disorder (ARND)
   neurological condition covering a spectrum of symptoms that can occur with fetal exposure to alcohol; diagnosis is often used when there is a history of alcohol exposure, but the child does not meet all of the official criteria for FAS

executive functioning
   a set of cognitive skills involved in planning, inhibition, concept formation, and reasoning

intellectual disability
   significantly subaverage intellectual functioning, existing concurrently with deficits in adaptive behavior and manifested during the developmental period; adversely affects a child's educational performance; previous term used was *mental retardation*

the disability to genetics and to environmental influences such as poverty and other social issues. Biological causes are typically more severe. They include syndromes or abnormalities in brain development. The cause of intellectual disability is identified in fewer than half the cases of children with mild disease, whereas definite causes for severe disease are determined in 75% of cases (Shapiro & Batshaw, 2007). Social factors and racial disparities are related to this condition. Poverty is more highly associated with intellectual disability than any other social factor. African American children are twice as likely to be diagnosed with an intellectual disability than Caucasians (Turnbull et al., 2010). Table 12-4 lists some conditions that are associated with intellectual disabilities. More than 1.1 million children nationwide are reported as having intellectual disabilities, which accounts for more than 11% of children with special health needs (Child and Adolescent Health Measurement Initiative, 2008).

Children with intellectual disabilities exhibit a wide range of challenges. Adaptive behaviors are challenging for children with intellectual disabilities. Adaptive behaviors refer to the skills children learn in order to function in everyday life. These include language skills, social skills, such as taking turns and sharing, and self-help skills relevant to activities of daily living, such as dressing, bathing, and brushing teeth. Difficulties also include problems with memory, generalization, and motivation (Turnbull et al., 2010). Generalization is the ability to transfer knowledge learned from one activity to another activity in different settings.

Many children with intellectual disabilities also have problems with short-term memory, the information that is stored for a few seconds to a few hours. For example, in the kindergarten classroom Rachel has been teaching 5-year-old Zane to count by pointing to each block and saying the counting words, "One, two, three, four, five." At the end of the counting session, Zane is able to point and count to five. When asked, "How many blocks all together?" Zane responds, "Five!" The next day, when Rachel prepares to practice the counting lesson using toy animals she discovers that Zane is unable to repeat the counting task from the previous day. She recognizes that Zane associates the counting task with blocks, but he cannot generalize the process when using new props.

Classroom Management Strategies Children with intellectual disabilities vary greatly in the supports needed for successful inclusion in the classroom. Some children may need assistance with many aspects of their participation and to ensure that they are sufficiently supervised for safety. A classroom education assistant may be needed to individually support

---

adaptive behavior
skills children learn in order to function in everyday life including language, social skills, and skills relevant to activities of daily living

generalization
the ability of students to transfer knowledge learned from one activity to another activity in different settings

short-term memory
information stored for a few seconds to a few hours

Table 12-4	Conditions Commonly Associated with Intellectual Disabilities
When Did the Trauma Occur?	**Conditions**
Prenatal (before birth)	• Syndromes such as Down syndrome • Maternal illnesses/maternal malnutrition • Parental age • Drug or alcohol use during pregnancy
Perinatal (at birth)	• Prematurity • Birth injury • Neonatal disorders • Lack of access to health care services during birth
Postnatal (after birth)	• Brain injuries • Meningitis • Seizure disorders • Family poverty • Lack of adequate stimulation • Child abuse/neglect • Inadequate early intervention services and family support

Source: *Mental Retardation: Definition, Classification, and Systems of Supports.* 10th edition by Ruth Luccason. Copyright 2002 by American Association on Intellectual Developmental Disabilities. Reproduced with permission of AAIDD in the formats Textbook and Other Book via Copyright Clearance Center.

and teach the child in the larger class group. Children with milder intellectual disabilities may require more modest assistance and can be supported by adapting the typical curriculum. Adaptations may include offering a slower pace for children to explore and try new concepts and providing more specific guidance to ensure directions are understood.

For very young children the focus in the classroom is on developing social interaction and self-help skills. This includes providing specific guidance or age-appropriate modeling and "lessons" about topics such as how to ask for help, how to express needs, how to share a toy, and how to wash hands and serve food. For older children the focus in the class moves toward developing communication and personal care skills and academic skills such as reading, writing, and basic math.

Lead Poisoning

Lead poisoning is a condition caused by swallowing an object that contains lead or breathing in dust that contains lead. Lead is toxic to most body systems including the nervous system. Lead can build up in the body over time, causing lead poisoning which can lead to subtle cognitive impairment in young children. Most children with lead poisoning have subclinical disease, the presence of disease without symptoms. Less common are children who have clinical disease, or disease with symptoms. Symptoms include gastrointestinal complaints such as loss of appetite, nausea, vomiting, abdominal pain, or constipation. At high levels of exposure, lead poisoning can be lethal and result in encephalopathy, brain injury due to a toxin or infection.

The most adverse effect of lead poisoning is its effect on cognition and intelligence. Loss of IQ points has been documented with low or borderline levels of lead in the blood. For this reason, during the past few decades the CDC has lowered the acceptable threshold of levels of lead in the blood (Laraque & Trasande, 2005) stating that no level of lead in blood is safe and the primary focus should be on prevention (CDC, 2005).

Prevention involves recognizing and avoiding sources of lead exposure. The most common sources of lead exposure are lead-based paint and lead-contaminated dust and soil. More recently identified sources include both imported and domestically manufactured toys, eating and drinking utensils, cosmetics, and traditional medicines. Other products that may contain lead include drinking water from lead-lined teapots or lead pipes, food grown in contaminated soil or stored in lead-soldered cans, waste from battery manufacturing, hobby materials used for stained glass work or pottery making, or certain types of candy made in Mexico (Ball et al., 2010).

Young children are at risk for lead exposure because of their mouthing behaviors and because they spend time playing on or close to the ground (Laraque & Trasande, 2005). Children who are not well nourished and have nutritional deficiencies, such as a child with an iron deficiency, may be at increased risk for lead poisoning. Lead poisoning is diagnosed through blood testing that is conducted because of some concern that the child was at risk for exposure.

Classroom Management Strategies Early childhood settings can contribute to prevention of lead poisoning primarily by:

- Establishing classroom environments that reduce exposure to lead.
- Administering lead exposure questionnaires to identify children who may be at risk for lead exposure.
- Educating families about the dangers of lead exposure.

Children identified as having had potential exposure to lead sources should be referred to their primary care provider or public health center for further evaluation.

Spina Bifida

Spina bifida is a defect of the vertebral column or spine that causes the contents of the spinal cord nervous tissue to protrude. It occurs very early in prenatal development, just weeks after conception. The degree to which spina bifida affects children's overall health

subclinical disease
the presence of disease without symptoms

clinical disease
disease with symptoms

encephalopathy
brain injury due to a toxin or infection

spina bifida
a defect of the vertebral column or spine causing the contents of the spinal cord/nervous tissue to protrude

depends on the location of the defect: the higher the defect is in the spinal column, the more severe the effects.

Common health issues associated with spina bifida include (Heward, 2009):

- Hydrocephalus (too much fluid in the chambers of the brain requiring a shunt).
- Seizures.
- Varying degrees of paralysis of lower limbs.
- Varying degrees of bladder and bowel control; some children may require intermittent catheterization of the bladder, a process in which a small tube is placed by the caregiver or child through the urethra into the bladder to remove urine.

Spina bifida occurs in 1 of every 2,000 births. Prevalence rates vary according to race and geography. The incidence is highest among Hispanics, especially those in Texas. Prevalence rates have decreased since identifying folic acid as a recommended supplement for women during the childbearing years, as well as the addition of folic acid into a large variety of cereal and bread products (Turnbull et al., 2010).

Children may require surgery to close the gap in the spine soon after birth. Surgery may also be needed to manage problems with the feet, hips, or spine. Some children may need assistive supports for walking, such as crutches, leg braces, or wheelchairs. Children with spina bifida may experience ADHD, and some may have trouble with bladder and bowel control. They may experience problems with perceptual motor skills; cognitive skills such as attention, memory, sequencing, and organization; and hyperactivity impulse control.

MyEducationLab

Go to the Assignments and Activities section of Topic 6: Health Appraisals/Screening in the MyEducationLab for your course and complete the activity *Raising a Child with Spina Bifida*. What does a teacher need to know about spina bifida in order to be able to help the child and his or her classmates?

Classroom Management Strategies Supporting children with spina bifida in the classroom requires that teachers have an understanding of the child's strengths and needs, medical support requirements, and strategies that support inclusion. Details of a child's condition are often determined through psychological and neuropsychological evaluations. Findings of these assessments guide the development of the child's IEP. Teachers work in partnership with the child's medical provider, early interventionists, and families to identify goals and to plan adjustments in the classroom.

The physical spaces need to be reviewed to ensure children will be able to move throughout the classroom and access the outdoor play area. Children may need to be carefully oriented to the schedule and routines and provided extra time and support when changes in the routine must be made. Some medical supports may be required, such as periodic catheterization to ensure children's bladder health.

The IEP provides focus for teaching, such as needed skills in verbal communication, social skills and behavior management, motor skills, and academic areas. As with all children with special health needs, the focus in the classroom is on assisting the child to experience positive social interactions with other children and to be a part of all classroom activities.

Conditions That Are Genetic

Genes influence most aspects of health. For example, children with certain genes are more prone to develop allergies or asthma. Other health conditions are caused by defects in specific genes. These conditions may or may not be inherited. In this section we discuss some of the conditions that have strong genetic connections, including cystic fibrosis, sickle cell anemia, diabetes mellitus, and others.

Cystic Fibrosis

Cystic fibrosis (CF) is an inherited disease that affects the lungs and digestive system. It occurs because of a defective gene that causes the body to create thick, sticky mucus that clogs the lungs and obstructs the digestive process. This results in progressive respiratory and nutritional problems that lead to severe respiratory infections and premature death. In addition to the chronic respiratory problems, children with CF tend to exhibit poor growth and malnutrition due in part to insufficient pancreatic function.

The abnormal CF genes are most common among Caucasians where the disease is seen in 1 in 3,200 live births. Among African Americans, CF occurs in 1 in 15,000 births, among

Asians the rate is 1 in 31,000, and in Hispanics 1 in 7,000 (Ball et al., 2010). Cystic fibrosis is often diagnosed during the early childhood years; 70% of cases are diagnosed by age 2 (Ball et al., 2010). In the 1950s, few children with CF lived to attend elementary school (Heward, 2009). Now almost all children with CF live to complete primary and secondary school. Children with CF display a number of symptoms:

- Persistent coughing, occasionally spitting up thick mucus.
- Shortness of breath and wheezing.
- Frequent lung infections.
- Poor growth and delayed weight gain.
- Difficulty with bowel movements or frequent greasy stools.

Children with CF typically undergo therapy during which the chest is vigorously thumped to dislodge mucus. This kind of treatment may be required during the day.

In spite of a good appetite, children with CF need to consume a large number of calories to keep up with nutritional requirements. They are typically treated with medications, including inhalers to improve breathing and pills that help them digest food.

Classroom Management Strategies Most children with CF are eligible for services under the IDEA. Teachers work in partnership with medical providers, early interventionists, and parents to support the inclusion of children with CF in the classroom. Understanding the effects of the disease helps to identify appropriate supports. For example, it is important to recognize that children with CF need to cough frequently are highly susceptible to respiratory infections.

Administration of medication may be required. Time should be provided to administer or to allow the child to take medications and to conduct activities or treatments to clear the airway. An appropriate space should be identified to help the child feel comfortable.

An emergency medical response plan should be drafted to guide appropriate response when needed. Regular attendance may be an issue for children with CF depending on the severity of the disease. For school-age children, teachers work with families to optimize learning by arranging appropriate homework to make up missed work.

Sickle Cell Anemia

Sickle cell anemia is a genetic condition that is inherited from both parents. It affects the integrity of red blood cells, causing them to have a much shorter life span than they would normally and to be *sickle* shaped, hence the name of the condition. The condition leads to anemia, chronic pain, and susceptibility to infections. It is most common in African American children with a prevalence of 1 in 500 and Hispanics with a prevalence of 1 in every 1,000 to 1,400 children born (Ball et al., 2010).

sickle cell anemia
an inherited disorder of red blood cells that causes chronic anemia, pain, and susceptibility to infection

The severity of the disease varies and has improved with earlier diagnosis due to newborn screening, antibiotics, and parent education. The chronic anemia that occurs with sickle cell anemia can lead to developmental delays if not carefully managed. The disease is also characterized by acute pain crises that can be precipitated by dehydration and cold weather. The symptoms include pain, swelling of joints, or abdominal pain (Ball et al., 2010). A child with a sickle cell crisis needs urgent medical attention. Many children require blood transfusions and hospitalizations to treat complications of the condition.

Classroom Management Strategies Teachers' main involvement will be to report any complaints of pain or other physical health problems to the parents and school nurse, if appropriate. Children with sickle cell anemia may also miss school days due to illness or hospitalizations, and special considerations should be made to help them make up work. In addition, chronic pain can cause poor peer relationships and problems with self-esteem. Teachers can be an important support system for children and families.

Diabetes Mellitus

Diabetes mellitus is a chronic medical condition that occurs when the body does not produce or appropriately use insulin. Insulin is a hormone that breaks down sugars, starches, and fats into food energy. The body's failure to produce insulin results in elevated blood glucose levels, which has detrimental impacts on the body's organ systems. Left untreated or poorly managed, diabetes can result in many long-term health consequences, including nerve damage, loss of vision, kidney failure, heart problems, circulatory problems that may require amputation, and early death (Thobro, 2007).

insulin
hormone secreted by the pancreas that is essential for the metabolism of glucose and fat

Type 1 Diabetes Type 1 diabetes is brought about by a combination of genetics and immunity. Individuals with certain types of genes are prone to develop diabetes. The condition develops when these individuals experience an autoimmune condition that causes them to develop antibodies against their own pancreas, resulting in the destruction of cells that produce and secrete insulin. Without sufficient insulin, body cells are not able to use glucose (sugar) to fuel the body. Children with type 1 diabetes require administration of insulin through injection or through an insulin pump.

autoimmune condition
causes individuals to secrete antibodies against their own organs

Children who develop diabetes tend to become ill very quickly. Symptoms include:

- Frequent urination.
- Excessive thirst.
- Fatigue.
- Irritability.
- Blurred vision.

In the early childhood setting, children with diabetes may have a noticeable increase in frequency of urination, requiring more frequent diaper changes, or urinary accidents.

Careful management of diabetes and a healthy lifestyle reduce the impact of the disease and improve children's long-term outlook. Type 1 diabetes is typically treated by testing blood sugar levels, administering injections of insulin, and offering a specialized diet and exercise program. A nutritionally balanced diet is needed, and aspects of the diet must be monitored, such as the kinds and amounts of foods eaten and the timing of meals and administration of insulin injections.

After diagnosis, children with diabetes and their families require a good deal of support and education about the disease. It can sometimes take several weeks to months to establish a treatment regimen, which may be frustrating for families and caregivers. Additionally, as children grow, their regimen will change based on changes in their caloric intake, physical activity, and rate of growth. For these reasons, children with diabetes require careful monitoring by their medical provider as well as a specialist in diabetes management.

Type 2 Diabetes Type 2 diabetes results from the body's inability to properly use insulin. This type of diabetes is less common among young children than type 1. Type 2 diabetes typically occurs in later childhood and among older people who are obese and who have a strong family tendency toward type 2 diabetes. Type 2 diabetes is influenced by a family history of diabetes, obesity, and sedentary lifestyle. Some racial groups are at greater risk for developing type 2 diabetes, including African Americans, Hispanic/Latino Americans, American Indians, and some Asian Americans and Native Hawaiians or other Pacific Islanders.

Establishing healthy nutritional and physical activity habits early are prevention efforts that may reduce the incidence of type 2 diabetes. Although this condition is uncommon during the early childhood years, it is important for teachers to understand that the habits and sequence of events leading to the condition begin in early childhood. Not only is the prevalence increasing in children, the average age of onset of type 2 diabetes is becoming younger (Shah, Kublaoui, & White, 2009).

Classroom Management Strategies Children with diabetes typically require no special adjustments for participation in the classroom and academic success. The medical management of the disease in the classroom is the most important area of focus. Management of diabetes requires a clear understanding of the child's medical protocols. Teachers require training on how to test blood sugar levels, how to adjust the kinds and quantities of food served, how to administer insulin injections, and how to recognize and manage emergencies, such as administering glucagon treatments. These practices must be directed by a medical provider. Teachers should receive formal training and supervision as they implement the child's medical plan. Two complications are important to recognize for management of diabetes:

- **Hypoglycemia** occurs when the blood sugar level is low (less than 50 to 60 mg/dL). It can be caused by missed or delayed meals, taking too much insulin, or strenuous exercise (Heward, 2009). Symptoms include faintness, dizziness, blurred vision, drowsiness, nausea, and irritability. Treatment entails giving the child concentrated sugar such as a sugar cube or a glass of fruit juice.

- **Diabetic ketoacidosis (DKA)** is a common, but life-threatening, complication of diabetes. It occurs when blood sugar levels remain high over a period of time as a result of insufficient insulin or sometimes due to illnesses. Symptoms include elevated blood sugars, excessive thirst and urination, unusual odor to breath (smells like acetone/nail polish remover), and lethargy or weakness. Emergency medical personnel should be contacted immediately if DKA is suspected.

hypoglycemia
a low blood glucose level measuring less than 50 to 60 mg/dL

diabetic ketoacidosis (DKA)
a fairly common, life-threatening complication of diabetes that occurs when blood sugar levels remain high over some period of time as a result of insulin deficiency

The demands of diabetes often influence children's social and emotional well-being, affecting their learning and peer relationships. Table 12-5 summarizes some of the issues experienced by children with type 1 diabetes and discusses possible actions to be taken to resolve them. Some of the strategies listed in the table can also be applied to other types of health conditions.

Down Syndrome

Down syndrome is one of the most common causes of intellectual disability (Heward, 2009). Down syndrome is also known as trisomy 21, because it occurs when the child has an extra 21st chromosome. Children with this condition usually have some degree of cognitive impairment, reduced muscle tone, and characteristic facial features, such as almond-shaped eyes, small chin and flat nasal bridge. Children with Down syndrome often suffer from associated health problems, including (Descartes, 2007):

- Congenital heart disease.
- Gastrointestinal abnormalities.
- Leukemia.
- Alzheimer's disease at an early age.
- Immune problems.
- Thyroid problems.
- Diabetes.
- Problems with hearing and vision.

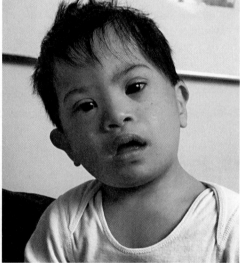

Children with Down syndrome have characteristic facial features.

Children with Down syndrome are typically very social and friendly. They usually experience delays in speech and communication. Although children may understand much of what they hear, their ability to articulate a response and produce understandable speech may be impaired. Motor skill development is also typically delayed. Cognitive challenges related to problem solving and reasoning are evident.

Classroom Management Strategies Children with Down syndrome are eligible for services through the IDEA. Often an educational assistant is assigned to support the child with Down syndrome along with other children with special needs in the classroom. Teachers should be well oriented to the child's IEP goals and strategies for successful inclusion. Children with Down syndrome benefit from inclusive learning activities that are social and interactive. The use of visual cues is another important strategy to guide children to develop self-help skills and to reinforce verbal messages. Activities should be planned to help children build fine motor skills and to improve gross motor coordination.

Children with Down syndrome are often exceptionally sensitive to the visual cues and responses of others. They may be quick to recognize disapproval and are sensitive to failure, which may cause them to avoid situations that may be difficult. Teachers should provide tasks with appropriate challenge and supportive encouragement.

What if. . .

a child in your classroom has Down syndrome? How would you go about planning ways to educate the class about this child's condition? What resources would you use to guide your planning? What would be your goals for this activity?

Table 12-5   Children with Type 1 Diabetes: Issues and Actions to Be Taken by School Systems

Issue	Action to Be Taken by School System
Emotional and social difficulties encountered by the family	• Involve guidance counselor with child and/or family. • Assess family difficulties and implement strategies.
Circumstances that may create challenges for the family (poverty, insurance access, single parent, health literacy issues)	• Obtain educational and supportive resources. • Become a source of support for the family.
Cultural variables that may influence way family views health care system or school system	• Promote environment free of judgment and bias. • Address language barriers and find ways to decrease barriers. • Implement IEPs that incorporate families' cultural views. • Discuss with family their perception of the school's role in their child's diabetes.
Frequent school absences	• Create an IEP ensuring that needs are met including policies for sending work home or giving additional support when missing school days.
Unable to take part in usual school activities (PE, field trips)	• Adapt school activities if possible. • Educate and train school personnel to adequately adapt to children's needs.
Children are bullied or teased because of their condition	• Create strict guidelines about bullying with strict, consistent consequences. • Teach personnel how to intervene with bullying. • Involve guidance counselor if necessary. • Educate other students about diabetes and its management.
Parents' feeling of protection and separation anxiety	• Create and discuss thorough plan of care with family.
Emotional and social reactions of siblings of children with diabetes	• Be aware of difficulties siblings may have. • Involve school counselor.
Communication between parent and school regarding child's illness	• Parents and school personnel should set up specific times to discuss child's condition. • Design a plan for the child, along with family, to ensure that the child's needs are being met.
Communication between school and health care provider	• Set up times to call or meet with health care provider. • Establish rapport and continue relationship with health care provider.
School staff not sufficiently trained or knowledgeable about child's condition	• Implement regular trainings. • Follow up with discussions to address issues that may come up. • Increase amount of time school nurse is available.
Handling emotional needs of children with type 1 diabetes	• Discuss emotional difficulties child may be experiencing. • Involve guidance counselor.
Staff may not know how to discuss illness with peers or handle reactions from peers	• School staff should be aware of and address peers' reactions. • Consult with student and parents to determine how they would like topic of illness to be presented to peers. • Ensure that child's teacher is knowledgeable about illness and is willing to explain condition to others. • Respect child's right to privacy.
Teachers may need to spend too much time attending to needs of child and less time with other children in classroom	• Create resource contacts in the school system.

Source: "Addressing Social and Emotional Issues of Children with Diabetes," by J. Thobro, 2007. Reprinted with permission of *Northwest Public Health*, a publication of the University of Washington School of Public Health.

Muscular Dystrophy

Muscular dystrophy (MD) refers to a group of genetic diseases that cause deterioration of the muscles resulting in progressive weakness, susceptibility to pulmonary infections, and premature death. It is a relatively rare disease that is diagnosed in 500 to 600 newborns each year. The most common type of MD is Duchenne's. It results from a genetic mutation that is linked to the X chromosome, causing the absence of a protein needed to maintain the integrity of muscle. Only males are affected by MD, although females can be carriers of this gene defect.

Initial symptoms of MD are weakness of the lower extremities, which becomes evident in early childhood, usually by 2 to 6 years of age (Heward, 2009). Families or teachers may notice the child has enlargement of the calf muscles, walks on the toes, falls more than other children his age (Ball et al., 2010), or has difficulty with climbing stairs (Heward, 2009). Typically, by the middle of the teenage years, the child is unable to walk. Life expectancy is in the 20s.

Treatment for MD focuses on maintaining as much function as possible. Physical, respiratory, and speech therapies may be offered. Assistive devices are used to support mobility. Some drug therapies may be used.

Classroom Management Strategies Teachers work with early intervention specialists and families to identify the IEP goals for children with MD. Attention to the physical environment is important to allow the child to move easily about the classroom and play yard. Adaptive equipment may be used to support the child's movement. Here is an example:

> Lyle moves with the assistance of an electronic wheelchair. His teacher, Nancy, rearranges the furnishings in her classroom to open pathways for Lyle to move to each activity area. She creates a large open area in the center of the classroom so he can participate easily at group time. At age 3 he is very efficient navigating through the space. His wheelchair has a special attribute that allows him to lower the seat so that he is sitting on the floor. This makes it easy for him to build block structures with his friends and to be at the same height as the other children during group time.

Despite physical health problems, children with MD should receive regular physical therapy and exercise. Outdoor play areas that have firm surfacing are especially important for children who have mobility problems. Teachers are cautioned to never lift these children by the arms because of the increased likelihood of joint dislocations (Heward, 2009). The teacher should provide small motor activities with pieces that come in a range of sizes. This allows the child to select the objects that best fit his ability to grasp and move. Encouraging activities such as hand washing, brushing teeth, and gathering pictures and personal belongings at the end of the day help the child develop organizational and self-help skills.

Seizure Disorders

Seizures are a sign of a brain problem. They occur when the electrical activity in the brain is abnormal. Seizures are the most common pediatric neurological disorder, and they are caused by high fevers, medicines, injuries to the head, and some diseases. Most seizures are relatively harmless, lasting from a few seconds up to 2 minutes. Seizures that last more than 5 minutes are a medical emergency. The types of seizures vary (Major & Thiele, 2007):

- **Partial seizures** are caused by abnormal activation of a limited number of neurons. Children may have twitching or jerks of only part of their body, one extremity, or the face. These seizures may or may not impair consciousness.
- **Generalized seizures** involve a global, or total, abnormal activation of all neurons. These seizures do impair consciousness. In the past these were called *grand mal seizures*.
- **Absence seizures** cause frequent, abrupt, but brief losses of consciousness often accompanied by eyelid flickering. In the past these were referred to as *petit mal seizures*.

partial seizures
seizures caused by abnormal activation of a limited number of neurons; symptoms typically are related to where the focus is located

generalized seizures
seizures caused by global abnormal activation of all neurons

absence seizures
frequent, brief, abrupt losses of consciousness that are often accompanied by eyelid flickering

myoclonic seizures
seizures that result from
brief contractions of a
muscle, muscle group, or
several muscle groups

- **Myoclonic seizures** consist of brief contractions of a muscle, muscle group, or several muscle groups. Abrupt actions, bright lights, percussion instruments, or being startled can provoke these seizures.

febrile seizures
seizures caused by fever

Febrile Seizures Some seizures, such as febrile seizures, may not represent a seizure disorder. Febrile seizures are caused by fever and occur with the sudden rise in body temperature associated with acute illnesses. They are usually brief, lasting less than 1 to 2 minutes, and are more common among children between 6 months and 3 years of age with a peak incidence of 18 months (Ball et al., 2010). Febrile seizures typically occur in 3% to 4% of children under the age of 6. Children who experience febrile seizures usually have a family history of such occurrences. One-third of children who experience one febrile seizure have a recurrence (Johnston, 2007).

Although most febrile seizures do not indicate an underlying problem or serious infection, they can be a frightening experience for teachers and families. Families should be notified immediately if a child experiences a febrile seizure. A clear description of the event is important for families and medical providers. Because of the risk of recurrence, it is extremely important to control any future fevers. Febrile seizures tend to diminish with age and prognosis is excellent.

epilepsy
a chronic seizure disorder
that is defined by having
two or more unprovoked
(not febrile) seizures

Epilepsy A chronic seizure disorder known as epilepsy is defined by having two or more unprovoked, not febrile (fever), seizures. Epilepsy may be caused by problems in brain development, illness or injury, but in some cases the cause is not known. Table 12-6 summarizes the most common causes of epilepsy in newborns, infants, and children. Epilepsy occurs in about 1% of the population.

Epilepsy has no cure, but seizures can usually be managed using medication and other treatments. Many children with epilepsy also have other health conditions. Mental health or behavioral difficulties are experienced by 30% to 50% of children with epilepsy, and 50% experience learning difficulties (Major & Thiele, 2007).

Classroom Management Strategies A seizure care plan needs to be in place for any child with seizure disorders. A seizure care plan should include the following information:

- Type and description of the child's seizures.
- Current treatment regimen including medications, schedule, doses, route of administration, and side effects.
- Restrictions from activities including those that could be dangerous to the child should the child have a seizure during the activity and any activities that could precipitate a seizure.
- How to recognize a seizure and recommendations for first aid should a seizure occur.

Table 12-6	Most Common Causes of Epilepsy in Infants and Children
Infants	**Children**
• Brain malformations • Infections • Metabolic disorder • Brain asphyxia (lack of oxygen to the brain) • Intracranial hemorrhage (more common in premature infants) • Familial neonatal convulsions	• Inherited metabolic or developmental diseases • Genetic syndromes • Infections

Source: Based on "Seizures in Children: Determining the Variation," by P. Major and E. Thiele, 2007, *Pediatrics in Review, 28*(10), pp. 363–372.

- Guidelines on when emergency medical help should be obtained for the child.
- Plan to document seizures if they occur including type/frequency of seizures, how the seizure was managed, any relevant observations.
- Plan to support the family of a child with epilepsy.*

Teachers also need to be oriented to any medications that need to be given, and a medication administration plan must be in place. Often, medication is not given unless the seizure lasts a certain amount of time, typically minutes. This should be defined by the child's health care provider.

Valium is a medication that is often used for acute seizures. It is administered rectally. Teachers follow the protocol for contacting emergency medical services as directed by the medical provider. Management of a seizure disorder may change frequently, especially in young children, requiring the care plan to be reviewed and updated.

valium
a medication that can be given rectally in the case of acute seizure

Conditions Affecting Communication, Hearing, and Vision

Some medical conditions involve the ability to communicate and the use of the hearing and vision sensory systems. Communication refers to the exchange of ideas, feelings, needs, and desires (Heward, 2009). It occurs through a variety of avenues including verbal language, facial expressions, written language, body language, and sign language. Effective communication is necessary for all aspects of daily life. Children begin communicating as young infants and progress rapidly in the first few years of life. It is during this time that communication disorders may become apparent.

A communication disorder, as defined by the American Speech-Language-Hearing Association (ASHA), is "an impairment in the ability to receive, send, process, and comprehend concepts or verbal, nonverbal and graphic symbols systems" (Heward, 2009, p. 303). Conditions affecting hearing and vision can have an adverse impact on aspects of communication. A child born with hearing loss may have difficulty with normal language development. A child with visual problems may not be able to effectively express some forms of nonverbal language. Although many conditions discussed in other sections of this chapter, such as Down syndrome, may involve communication problems, here we focus on children who have disorders specifically affecting communication, hearing, and vision.

communication
the exchange of ideas, feelings, needs, and desires

communication disorder
an impairment in the ability to verbally or nonverbally exchange ideas, desires, or needs

Speech and Language Impairments

Speech is the aspect of language that is produced verbally. Language is a formal code developed by groups of people for the purpose of communication (Heward, 2009). Impairments in the speech and language systems interfere with communication. Communication disorders can be caused by damage to a specific organ or part of the body. More commonly, the cause cannot be attributed to any physical condition and some researchers believe that environmental influences may play a role in some communication disorders (Heward, 2009).

Estimates of the prevalence of speech and language impairments vary widely. Current estimates suggest that 2.5% of school-age children receive special education services for speech and language impairment. Additionally, more than half of children receiving special education services for other diagnoses also receive speech and language services (Heward, 2009).

speech
the aspect of language produced verbally

language
a formal code developed by groups of people for the purpose of communication

Speech Impairments The term *speech impairment* refers to problems in producing verbal speech. Three types of speech impairments are recognized (Heward, 2009):

- *Articulation disorders* affect the production of specific speech sounds. Articulation problems make it difficult to understand children's speech.
- *Fluency disorders* affect the rhythm or flow of speech. Stuttering is an example of a fluency disorder.

---

* Used with permission of the American Academy of Pediatrics, *Caring for Our Children: National Health and Safety Performance Standards: Guidelines for Out-of-Home Child Care Programs*, 2e. Copyright 2002.

- *Voice disorders* cause problems with the quality or use of the voice. Voice disorders can cause chronic hoarseness or abnormalities in the air coming through the nasal passage. These disorders are less common in young children.

Language Impairments Language impairments are typically classified as receptive or expressive:

receptive language disorders
impairments in the understanding of language

expressive language disorders
impairments in the expression of language

- Receptive language disorders are impairments in understanding language. Children with receptive language disorders may have difficulties following directions or understanding spoken language.
- Expressive language disorders are impairments in the expression of language, or the use of language to communicate. Expressive language disorders may cause children to incorrectly use words or phrases.

Children with language impairments often have difficulty in school and with social development and peer relationships. They also tend to have more difficulties reading and writing (Heward, 2009).

Classroom Management Strategies Teachers play an important role in identifying children with speech and language impairments. Through interaction and observation, teachers are often able to identify speech and language problems that families may not recognize. In the home it is not unusual for family members to understand the meaning of children's communication by using contextual cues and nonverbal styles of communication. In the classroom setting, a child's challenges with communication may be more evident. Figure 12-3 lists a number of red flags to watch for that cue teachers to recommend that children receive further evaluation for potential communication disorders.

Children with speech and language problems may be eligible to receive early intervention services. Teachers can integrate speech and language goals into the daily curriculum with the help of speech-language pathologists. Consider this example:

> Nephi sets out a display of plastic snakes on the table. He invites Angie to come inspect the toy snakes. First they count the snakes, discovering that there are "seven snakes." Next they inspect the designs on the toy snakes. Some have stripes and some have spots. They count the striped and spotted snakes and find there are "four striped snakes and three spotted snakes." Through this game Nephi helps Angie practice articulating the "s" sounds. They continue to add descriptive words that use the letter "s" sounds, such as "slithering snakes and silly snakes." As other children join the group Nephi suggests that Angie tell the others how to play the counting game using the toy snakes.

Figure 12-3 Identifying Speech and Language Problems

The following indicate that a child needs further evaluation for a speech and language problem:

- Mispronounces sounds and words that are not typically mispronounced for age.
- Omits word endings (such as –s in plural words).
- Uses immature vocabulary. Has difficulty recalling words.
- Has difficulty comprehending new concepts or words.
- Has difficulty with sequence of events.
- Has difficulty following directions.
- Has difficulty answering questions.
- Conversations often off topic or inappropriate.
- Remembers little of what is said when he or she seems to be paying attention.

Source: From Robert E. Owens, Jr., *Language Disorders: A Functional Approach to Assessment and Intervention*, 4e, (Table 12.3, p. 373). Copyright © 2004 by Pearson Education. Adapted by permission of Pearson Education, Inc.

Hearing Impairment

Hearing impairment is a general term that describes a decrease in ability to hear and discriminate among sounds. Although it is a frequently used term, many people in the Deaf community prefer deaf or hard of hearing. Two kinds of hearing impairment are most common:

- *Conductive hearing loss* refers to the type of hearing loss resulting from problems with the middle ear or eardrum and is usually milder than a sensorineural hearing loss. This kind of hearing loss results from problems with the middle ear or eardrum and is usually milder than a sensorineural condition. Conductive hearing loss is most often treated with medications or surgical methods.
- *Sensorineural hearing loss* refers to damage to the acoustic nerves that connect the ear to the brain, or to the inner ear organ called the cochlea. The cochlea is the organ responsible for hearing. This type of hearing loss is permanent and more difficult to treat. The sound of speech from children who have sensorineural hearing loss is often distorted.

Hearing impairment is one of the most common birth defects. Three in 1,000 babies born in America are diagnosed with permanent hearing loss (Ross et al., 2008). Hearing loss can also develop during childhood and later in life. In the United States nearly half of children with a diagnosed hearing impairment are from racial or ethnic minority populations (Gallaudet Research Institute, 2008). Hearing impairment can be caused by various factors including genetics, illness experienced by the mother during pregnancy, illness during childhood, and injuries. The use of certain medications may cause hearing loss and some environmental conditions can negatively impact hearing. The *Safety Segment* discusses noise-induced hearing loss.

Safety Segment

Noise-Induced Hearing Loss in Children

Noise is an important preventable cause of hearing loss in children. Noise exposure destroys cells in the ear that are essential for hearing. Once lost these cells cannot be regenerated. Noise is a growing concern because of the increasing prevalence of portable music and gaming devices used by children. Other sources of noise include concerts, power equipment, and guns.

Research demonstrates that 12% to 15% of school-age children have some degree of hearing loss due to noise exposure. Although the degree of the hearing loss tends to be mild to moderate, it can create challenges for school-age children, particularly in noisy settings like classrooms. In classrooms even mild hearing loss may reduce how much a child hears and understands directions and lessons. Teachers can make an impact by:

- Recognizing when a child may be having trouble hearing, and referring the child for evaluation.
- Advocating for and implementing policies restricting the use of portable devices and the use of earphones at school.
- Educating parents about noise as a prevalent and preventable cause of hearing loss.

Source: Based on "Noise-Induced Hearing Loss in Children: A 'Less than Silent' Environmental Danger," by R. Harrison, (2008), *Paediatric Child Health*, 13(5), pp. 377–382.

Early identification of hearing loss is important. Research demonstrates that children who are identified with hearing impairment prior to 6 months of age, and who receive appropriate interventions, have a better chance of developing normal speech and language. The exceptions are children who have profound hearing loss in both ears (Haddad, 2007). Because the early years are so important for the development of speech and language, most babies receive a universal newborn hearing screen prior to hospital discharge (Heward, 2009; U.S. Preventive Services Task Force, 2008). Currently 46 states and the District of Columbia have implemented federally legislated early hearing detection and intervention programs to screen newborns for hearing loss (American Speech-Language-Hearing Association, 2009).

Medical definitions of hearing impairment classify the degree of hearing loss on a spectrum from mild to profound. The following degrees of hearing loss describe the lowest range a child can hear. The following decibel level ranges describe degrees of hearing loss (Ball et al., 2010):

- 0–25 decibels (dB): No hearing loss is present.
- 26–40 dB: Mild hearing loss.
- 41–60 dB: Moderate hearing loss; most conversational speech sounds are missed.
- 61–80 dB: Severe hearing loss; no speech sounds can be heard at conversational levels.
- 81–90 dB: Profound hearing loss; no speech sounds heard.
- >90 dB: Deaf; no sounds heard.

Even children with mild hearing loss may miss up to 50% of conversational speech, putting them at high risk for school failure (Ball et al., 2010).

After the newborn period, children typically do not receive a hearing screen at preventive health care visits until 4 or 5 years of age. Some early childhood programs incorporate hearing screenings as part of their health services for children and families.

Observation in the early childhood classroom is another way that children may be identified. Teachers may notice symptoms of hearing loss or difficulties in the child's speech development that may suggest hearing impairment. Table 12-7 lists behaviors that suggest hearing loss in infants, preschoolers, and school-age children. It is also important to remember

universal newborn hearing screen
hearing test done soon after birth that detects hearing loss in newborns

Table 12-7	Signs of Potential Hearing Impairment
Age Group	**Behavior**
Infant	• Diminished or absent startle reflex to loud sound • Awakens only when touched, not when environment is noisy • Does not turn head to sounds by 3 to 4 months • Does not localize sound by 6 to 10 months • Babbles little or not at all
Toddler/preschool	• Unintelligible speech, monotone • Communicates through gesturing • Does not respond to doorbell or telephone • Prefers to play alone and with objects rather than people • Focuses on facial expressions rather than verbal communication
School-age child	• Asks to have statements repeated frequently • Answers questions inappropriately except when looking at speaker's face • Inattention, daydreaming • Poor school performance • Monotone speech • Sits close to TV or turns it up • Prefers to play alone

Source: Ball, Jane W.; Bindler, Ruth McGillis W. & Cowen, Kay J., *Child Health Nursing: Partnering with Children and Families*, 2nd, © 2010. Reproduced with permission of Pearson Education, Inc., Upper Saddle River, New Jersey.

that some children with hearing impairments may not manifest symptoms early in life and can exhibit typical development. This is why screenings are so important. However, if a teacher observes any of the behaviors listed in Table 12-7, the family should be informed and the child referred for evaluation.

Classroom Management Strategies Educational definitions of hearing impairment focus on the impact the hearing loss has on the development and use of speech and language as well as its effects on educational performance. The IDEA identifies two categories under which children may be eligible for services:

- *"Hearing impairment* means impairment in hearing, whether permanent or fluctuating, that adversely affects a child's educational performance but that is not included under the definition of deafness" (DOE, 2004). A child with a hearing impairment can usually hear and respond to auditory stimuli including speech.
- *"Deafness* means a hearing impairment that is so severe that the child is impaired in processing linguistic information through hearing, with or without amplification, and that adversely affects a child's educational performance" (DOE, 2004). A child with deafness is prevented from receiving nearly all forms of sound.

Children identified for services by the local education agency may enter the early childhood program with an outline of goals identified in the IEP. The child's IEP and the early intervention team will outline the focus for services in the classroom. The teacher needs to know the style of communication the child is using. Oral approaches include Listening and Spoken Language, visual and gestural systems include Cued Speech, and American Sign Language. Some children use a total communication method that combines spoken language and American Sign Language (ASHA, 2009). The use of sign language also supports the language development of typically developing children.

Families often have strong preferences for a particular mode of communication. Some may prefer the Total Communication method, which allows the child to be "bilingual"; that is, able to communicate with both spoken and signed language (Katz & Schery, 2006). Teachers also need to know how to check the child's amplification system (hearing aids) *daily* to ensure that it is working appropriately.

Sometimes the disability of the child with hearing impairment can be "invisible." Hearing loss cannot be seen, and often children with hearing impairments blend into the classroom so easily that the teacher may forget the child's special health care need. Common strategies used to teach all young children are also appropriate for teaching children with hearing impairments. The focus on seeing and doing and activity-based learning are characteristic learning modes in early childhood that are also appropriate for children with hearing impairments.

Children with hearing impairments rely on their other senses, such as vision, to support learning. Because of their reduced ability to hear, they do not benefit from incidental conversations in the room. A review of the classroom noise level may be necessary to identify ways to reduce background noises. Facing the child when speaking and getting the child's attention before giving directions help to address this challenge. Speaking clearly and simply in a usual tone and volume and avoiding overly long and complex sentences are useful tactics when giving directions. Using appropriate facial expressions and gestures also helps to reinforce verbal messages, as do real-life pictures. The teacher's face and mouth should be clearly visible to the child who may support understanding by reading lips.

Some children struggle with new vocabulary and the complexities of spoken English. It is important to provide these children with appropriate challenges to continue their learning. Asking "why" and "what will happen if?" questions and providing time for children to consider and prepare an answer are ways to build communication skills. Some children may use American Sign Language to communicate. Teachers can learn basic signs to connect with the child and to ease the child through the daily routines (Dennis & Azpiri, 2005).

Vision Impairments

visual impairment
an impairment in vision that adversely affects a child's educational performance, even with correction

The term **vision impairments** refer to conditions in which vision is reduced even when corrected with glasses or contact lenses. Genetics, birth defects, and eye disorders, as well as age-related eye disease, can cause vision impairments. Some of the common causes are refractory errors (nearsightedness and farsightedness), amblyopia, and strabismus. The prevalence of any visual impairment is quite common. Between 5% and 10% of preschoolers and 20% to 30% of school-age children have vision problems (Ball et al., 2006). Of the children who have vision impairments, nearly two-thirds also have at least one other developmental disability, such as mental retardation, cerebral palsy, hearing loss, or epilepsy.

visual acuity
a measure of how well a child can distinguish forms or discriminate details

Two kinds of vision impairment are typically recognized: low vision and blindness. These are identified using a test of **visual acuity**, a measure of how well a child can distinguish forms or discriminate details. This is typically assessed by having a child read letters, numbers, or symbols on an eye chart. The measure provides a pair of numbers that compare what the child can see against what a normal eye can see at 20 feet.

- A *normal eye* is scored at 20/20.
- *Low vision* is the term used for measures between 20/70 and 20/400.
- Blindness is identified at measures of 20/400.
- *Legal blindness* is measured at 20/200.

blindness
vision of 20/200 or worse even with the best possible correction

For example, a child with low vision (20/70) must stand 20 feet away from an object that a child with normal vision could see clearly at a distance of 70 feet.

Classroom Management Strategies Children with low vision may not be identified for services by the local education agency. Children with more significant vision loss and blindness are likely to be identified for service and will enter the early childhood classroom with an IEP. These children are likely to receive support services from a vision specialist in addition to the early childhood program, and the specialist may serve as a consultant for the child's teacher.

Children with visual impairments rely on their other senses to support learning. Children with low vision are able to use sight for some activities and also use sound and tactile exploration. For these children it may be useful to assess the lighting in the classroom. Reducing glare and providing color contrasts in some materials may assist the child to visually discriminate among objects. Children who are blind rely primarily on tactile and auditory stimuli.

For children with both types of vision challenges, direct interaction with materials and objects is important to support learning. Sensory activities that allow them to gain vocabulary based on tactile stimuli are good choices. Placing ice cubes in the sensory table where children can feel them melting in warm water is a good way to introduce a discussion of temperature, melting and freezing, solids and liquids, and floating. It is important to maintain appropriate expectations for children with vision impairments so they can be as independent as possible. Other ideas for support include these:

Children with visual impairments rely on their tactile and auditory senses to support learning.

- Speak the child's name when addressing them in the classroom. Children with visual impairments may have a difficult time noticing eye contact.
  - Name specific items and events rather than using pronouns like "this" or "that."
  - Give verbal warnings prior to handing something to the child.
  - Provide appropriate supports for mobility in the classroom.
  - When physically showing a child how to do something, put the child's hand over yours rather than the other way around.
  - Assign the child appropriate and meaningful classroom "jobs."
  - Encourage cooperative group activities so that peer socialization skills can be learned.
  - Remember safety while being careful not to overprotect the child.

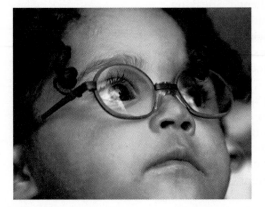

Children with vision impairments may begin learning tactile codes such as Braille along with their early reading activities in elementary school. Specialized instruction of this kind is usually done by a teaching specialist.

Summary

Many children have special health care needs. The range of medical needs varies broadly, from the young child with mild environmental allergies to the child with severe cerebral palsy that affects multiple aspects of daily living. Special health care needs can affect the immune system, neurological system, and communication system. Some have more impact on daily living and learning than others. Even those conditions that do not impact cognition may still influence learning, depending on the health and functional status of the child. Teachers work in partnership with others to address the needs of children with health problems.

With the increasing prevalence of children with special medical diagnoses and improved federal regulations that ensure education for all children regardless of their special health care needs, more children are being cared for in early childhood settings at younger ages. This requires the children's program or school to have certain supports in place. Establishing policies and procedures for administration of medications and emergency response protocols are some of the ways programs prepare to serve children with special health care needs. Working as members of the child's educational team provides a network of supports for the child, family, and teachers. Teachers are important resources when identifying goals for inclusion and planning strategies to address these goals in the classroom. Inclusion approaches include creating spaces that are physically and educationally accessible, that invite children to participate as fully as possible, and that support the needs of children with a wide spectrum of medical and educational challenges. Accommodations may also involve making adjustments to the daily routines and how activities are presented so the special learning styles of children with special health needs are addressed.

Children with special health care needs are first of all, children; they are young people interested in being part of a social group where interesting learning activities are available to stimulate their curiosity. Many of the common teaching methods are appropriate for children with special health care needs. For example, activity-based approaches that provide many hands-on experiences are ideal for all children. More specific teaching strategies are designed to fit the needs of individual learners. Together, teachers, families, medical providers, early intervention specialists, and therapists are a part of the community that welcomes and supports children with special health needs.

MyEducationLab

To assess your understanding of how to teach children with special health care needs in early childhood settings, go to the Book Specific Resources section in the MyEducationLab for your course, select *Nutrition, Health, and Safety for Young Children*, Chapter 12 of the Study Plan, and then complete the multiple choice questions and activities.

Key Terms

Absence seizures, p. 403

Adaptive behavior, p. 396

Albuterol, p. 386

Alcohol-related neurodevelopmental disorder (ARND), p. 395

Asperger's syndrome, p. 392

Asthma attack, p. 387

Autism, p. 391

Autoimmune condition, p. 400

Blindness, p. 410

Catheterization, p. 398

Children with special health care needs, p. 373

Clinical disease, p. 397

Communication, p. 405

Communication disorder, p. 405

Diabetic ketoacidosis (DKA), p. 401

Down syndrome, p. 375

Dyslexia, p. 393

Encephalopathy, p. 397

Epilepsy, p. 404

Executive functioning, p. 395

Expressive language disorders, p. 406

Febrile seizures, p. 404

Fetal alcohol syndrome FAS, p. 394

Functional limitations, p. 375

Functional status, p. 375

Gastrostomy tube, p. 378

Generalization, p. 396

Generalized seizures, p. 403

Hydrocephalus, p. 398

Hypoglycemia, p. 401

Immune system, p. 383

Inhaled steroids, p. 386

Insulin, p. 400

Intellectual disability, p. 395

Joint attention, p. 391

Language, p. 405

Learning disabilities, p. 393

Muscular dystrophy, p. 381

Myoclonic seizures, p. 404

Nebulizer, p. 387

Partial seizures, p. 403

Pervasive developmental disorder (PDD), p. 391

Philtrum, p. 394

Receptive language disorders, p. 406

Short-term memory, p. 396

Sickle cell anemia, p. 399

Spacer, p. 387

Speech, p. 405

Spina bifida, p. 397

Stimulants, p. 390

Subclinical disease, p. 397

Tracheostomy tube, p. 378

Universal newborn hearing screen, p. 408

Valium, p. 405

Vision impairment, p. 410

Visual acuity, p. 410

Wheeze, p. 386

Review Questions

1. How do children's special health care needs affect other aspects of their health and functional status?

2. What are the federal laws that protect the health care needs of children and how do they apply to specific health care needs?

3. In whom and in what geographic regions is asthma more common? What aspects of this illness may be manifested in the early childhood setting?

4. What symptoms would a preschool teacher notice in a child with autism?

5. What aspects of development are affected by fetal alcohol syndrome?

6. How are hearing impairments typically detected?

Discussion Starters

1. How might teachers be able to alleviate stressors that families experience when they are caring for a child with a special health care need?

2. As a teacher of a toddler-age group, you notice a child displaying possible symptoms of autism. How do you approach the family with your concerns? How do you prepare for the meeting? To whom do you make a referral?

3. As a teacher in a second-grade classroom, you are teaching a child with a hearing impairment who requires hearing aids. He is able to speak, but the quality of his voice is obviously affected. Other children notice and ask why he sounds different than they do. How do you handle this situation?

Practice Points

1. Imagine that a child with type 1 diabetes has enrolled in your third-grade classroom. You know that she checks her blood sugar during the day and receives insulin injections. What other information do you need as she begins attending? Who might you collaborate with in addition to her parents?

2. Oftentimes, children who are suspected as having ADHD are evaluated by the school system before being evaluated by a medical professional. Who evaluates children in your school district? How is the diagnosis made?

3. Call your local health department and ask about the prevalence of lead poisoning in your area. Do preschools in your area conduct lead screening? If so, how?

Web Resources

Children and Adults with Attention Deficit/Hyperactivity Disorder
www.chadd.org

Managing Asthma in Schools
www.epa.gov/iedweb00/schools/asthma.html

National Survey of Children with Special Health Care Needs
www.cshcndata.org/Content/Default.aspx

Right Under My Nose: A Book for Children with Spina Bifida
www.myspinabifidabook.org

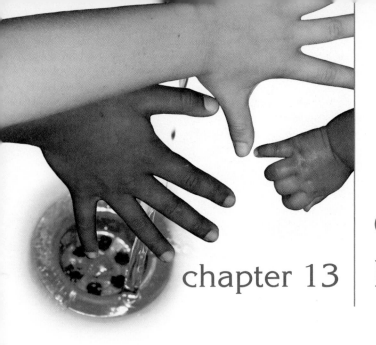

chapter 13 | Children's Mental Health

Learning Outcomes

After reading this chapter, you should be able to:

1. Define mental health and discuss the biological, environmental, and developmental factors that influence mental health in young children.

2. Describe the stages of social and emotional development in children ages birth to 8 years of age.

3. Discuss ways in which children's social and emotional development is fostered in the early childhood classroom.

4. Explain how mental health problems are recognized and identify the most common types of mental health problems seen in young children.

5. Discuss strategies used when teaching children with mental health problems and challenging behaviors.

Parent and teacher conferences have been scheduled for the 2- to 3-year-old class group. Meegan is preparing to meet with Heather's parents. She has made a special effort to schedule the conference late in the day to be sure that there will be enough time to discuss her concerns. Meegan is worried about how to talk about the behavior concerns she has observed. Heather is struggling with her social and emotional development. Her aggressive behaviors with the other children have not stopped in spite of Meegan's efforts to guide and teach her. Meegan has intervened more than once when Heather grabbed another child around the neck. One time Heather picked up a large block and hit the assistant teacher on the head, and during group time she saw Heather hit Arturo in the face with her hand without even turning to look at him.

Meegan believes the parents have also been experiencing difficult behaviors at home because they have shared that they always take the baby to the grandmother's house if they need to leave Heather at home with a caregiver. To prepare for the conference, Meegan has done some reading about social and emotional development and behavior and explored some of the services that are available in the community. She is uncomfortable about sharing the unpleasant observations she has made, but she feels prepared and hopes that the conversation will go well so that she and the family can develop a plan to help Heather.

Sometimes children struggle as they learn to participate in early childhood settings and classrooms. They may experience problems developing typical social and emotional skills and, as a result, exhibit significant behavior problems in the classroom. These may be signs of delayed social and emotional development, or unrecognized mental health issues. Teachers like Meegan are committed to children's positive growth in all developmental domains. They recognize the importance of emotional health to children's well-being and ability to grow and thrive. They are concerned when children display significant behavior difficulties and need guidance about how to effectively address them.

In this chapter the terms *social and emotional development* and *mental health* are used interchangeably to represent a *positive* state of mental and emotional wellness. This highlights the understanding that just as teachers support children's physical health through purposeful practices, teachers also foster children's mental and emotional health through intentionally established environments and positive relationships and experiences that encourage healthful social and emotional development.

In this chapter we focus on ways that teachers contribute to children's mental health. First we define the terminology we will use to discuss children's mental health and describe the impacts of mental health on children's growth and development. We then provide an overview of healthy social and emotional development and discuss the challenges that occur if development goes off course. Next we describe how social and emotional development is related to learning and success in school and explore how children's mental health is promoted in the early childhood classroom. Finally, we review some of the more common mental health disorders and provide guidance for partnering with families and mental health professionals to design successful interventions when children need special help. Focusing on children's mental health is an important teacher responsibility that builds foundations for children's future success and happiness.

UNDERSTANDING MENTAL HEALTH

The early years are a significant period for establishing wellness habits and patterns. This includes fostering children's emotional health as well as their physical health and wellness. Teachers are best prepared to positively impact children's emotional health by understanding mental health, what influences it, how it develops across the early years, and how to recognize typical social and emotional development.

Defining Mental Health

Mental health refers to children's abilities to understand and manage their emotions and behaviors, to function positively with others in age-appropriate and developmentally appropriate ways, and to form meaningful relationships. It encompasses the capacities to enjoy life and to be flexible, adaptable, and resilient (U.S. Public Health Service, 2000). Just as physical health refers to the presence of bodily wellness and absence of disease, mental health is a positive term that refers to the presence of mental or emotional wellness and the absence of mental illness.

The competencies associated with mental health are observable. For example, in her infant and toddler class, Sharina recognizes healthy social and emotional development, or "good" mental health, when she observes Caitlin laughing and crawling over to interact with Lin Lin. Caitlin shows appropriate interest, enjoyment, and curiosity and expresses this through developmentally appropriate emotions and actions. To Sharina this observation is similar to the height and weight measurements she takes to understand children's physical health. While physical measurements give clues to physical health, observations of child interactions help teachers understand children's mental health.

Social and emotional development is a familiar domain of human development. It is also linked to, and considered part of, the **continuum of mental health**. Most early childhood sources consider social and emotional development and mental health to be synonymous, or one and the same (Zero to Three, 2009). This is helpful in guiding teachers to implement classroom practices that promote social and emotional development and, hence, children's mental health. Teachers should recognize, however, that poor social and emotional development does not automatically suggest that children have mental illness. The continuum of mental health includes behaviors that:

continuum of mental health
the range of behaviors associated with positive social and emotional development, mental health problems, and mental illness

- *Demonstrate positive social and emotional development,* suggesting the children are on course for positive outcomes.
- *Indicate problems with social and emotional development,* also called *mental health problems,* suggesting that further attention is needed to guide the child to more positive mental health habits.
- *Imply potential underlying mental disorders,* or *illness,* suggesting that the child be evaluated by a medical professional for possible mental health diagnosis and services.

Positive experiences and interactions in the early years help children to form close and secure interpersonal relationships.

Exhibiting behaviors that are typical for the child's age and developmental level indicates that social and emotional development is on course. Behaviors that are not typical are more challenging to understand. They may indicate that a child is simply slower in this area of development or that the child has not had sufficient experiences to practice and attain typical social and emotional skills. This may be due to negative influences in the home environment or may be signs of undetected mental health disorders (National Scientific Council on the Developing Child [NSCDC], 2008). The boundaries of what behaviors constitute appropriate and inappropriate development are further clouded based on the expectations of social behaviors in different cultures and neighborhoods. For example, behaviors one group considers aggressive may be viewed by another group as a sign of strength.

These issues demonstrate the challenge of knowing "when to worry" (NSCDC, 2008, p. 7). However, in spite of the difficulties associated with defining what behaviors suggest mental health problems, teachers are responsible for managing children's behavior and advancing children's development. In this chapter we explore these issues and offer a range of ways teachers play a role in fostering children's social and emotional development. Teachers do not do this work alone. They keep informed of emerging information, partner with families, collaborate with mental health specialists if needed, and design and implement interventions to promote positive mental health.

Current Focus on Children's Mental Health

Recently children's mental health has gained special attention because the number of children displaying significant behavioral challenges in the classroom appears to be increasing. This has raised awareness that mental health problems are evident even among very young children. In 2001, the U.S. Surgeon General released a report on the critical nature of the state of mental health in children in the United States. The report notes that growing numbers of children are experiencing social-emotional difficulties and mental health disorders. Of even more concern is the increasing number of children with these problems who receive no mental health evaluation or treatment. In the report, the surgeon general acknowledged that mental health is a vital component of children's general health and crucial to their capacity for learning. The report (U.S. Public Health Service, 2000) highlights the need to:

- Increase awareness of childhood mental illness.
- Reduce the stigma of mental disorders.
- Strengthen frameworks for the recognition, diagnosis, and treatment of mental disorders and eliminate disparities in mental health.

Early childhood teachers interact with many children and need special understanding about how mental health develops and ways to support positive outcomes.

Influences on Children's Mental Health

Children's mental health is influenced by a variety of dynamics that can be apparent even in infancy. These include biological, environmental, and developmental factors.

Biological Factors

Biological factors are traits or characteristics that are specific to the individual child and are present at birth. Biological factors include (Zeanah, Nagle, Stafford, Rice, & Farrer, 2005):

- *Genetics,* or hereditary factors such as those that influence physical size and appearance, and pace of development.
- *Temperament,* or the child's style and personality, often described as "easy," "slow to warm-up," or "difficult".
- *Physical and health attributes,* such as physical anomalies and prematurity.

These factors influence development and play a role in how the caregiver responds to the child. Caregivers include parents, other family members such as grandparents, child care providers, and teachers. Early relationships with caregivers train children's minds about how to interact with others and what to expect (Gallagher, 2005; Schore, 2001; Shore, 1997). For example, parents may respond positively to a child who is precocious (advanced in development), while responding less favorably to a child who is slower in development. When caregivers respond positively, children experience a boost to social and emotional health and, in turn, behave in desirable ways. When caregivers respond negatively to undesirable traits or difficult behaviors, such as crying, children are likely to respond with more negative behaviors, such as more crying until they are able to learn what is expected.

Jenna, who teaches infants, knows that some people get frustrated with babies who cry. But she has a special affinity for infants and enjoys trying a variety of approaches to create a strong and positive bond with each child. She is usually highly successful in helping babies establish a strong attachment and develop alternative ways of communicating.

caregiver
parents, other family members such as grandparents, child care providers, and teachers

Environmental Factors

Children's social and emotional development is extremely vulnerable to environmental factors such as these:

- Family life situations, including stress, poverty, abuse, neglect, parental drug use or mental illness, the quality of the nurturing relationship, and cultural influences on parenting.

- Community well-being, including community violence, accessible health care, and social service resources.
- Environmental toxins including chemicals such as mercury and secondhand smoke.

Environmental factors that introduce stress into family life can exert a strong negative influence on children's social and emotional development because anything that affects the parent-child relationship affects the child. Stresses associated with poverty, such as food insecurity, poor housing conditions, or unmet health needs, are examples of factors that add challenge to family life and put children at risk for poor social and emotional development (Zeanah et al., 2005). Teachers can help by providing families with ways to cope with the stresses of poverty, including parenting strategies to try at home, and by encouraging parents to build strong and positive relationships with their children.

Developmental Factors

Brain development significantly influences children's mental health. Although the development of the brain begins at conception and does not end until adulthood, the fastest rate of growth is from the last third of pregnancy until the child's second birthday (Zeanah et al., 2005). During this period, an incredible amount of information is learned, and the structures for future learning are established.

Brain development is influenced by experience with people and the environment. Interactions that are comfortable and nurturing encourage brain cell development and refine brain cell connections, which set the foundation for future learning (Gallagher, 2005; Schore, 2001). Persistent stressful experiences damage normal brain function, interrupting development and causing problems with learning, behavior, and physical and emotional health (NSCDC, 2007).

Understanding the Impacts of Mental Health on General Development

Social and emotional development is closely linked to all other forms of development including physical, cognitive, language and communication, and interpersonal relationships (Cohen et al., 2005). When typical milestones in social and emotional development are not achieved, children tend to also have significant challenges in other aspects of development. Social, emotional, and behavior problems during the early years get in the way of learning, and lead to higher incidences of academic problems, aggression, delinquency, and crime in school-age children and adolescents (Boyd, Barnett, Bodrova, Leong, & Gomby, 2005).

Children with significant social and emotional challenges are often not able to form close friendships, and ultimately may not be capable of assuming the tasks of adulthood, such as maintaining relationships, caring for their own children, and keeping a job (Boyd et al., 2005). If undetected and untreated, mental health challenges tend to persist as children get older. Concerns about the potential of long lasting negative impacts on children's mental health have led to the development of principles that guide mental health services. These are outlined in Figure 13-1.

In the opening scenario, Meegan doesn't know if Heather's behaviors are an indication of a mental health problem. But she does know that Heather is experiencing challenges that are getting in the way of learning. She hopes that discussing these challenges will open up conversation with Heather's family about ways to help Heather at home and at school.

Characteristics of Social and Emotional Development

Social and emotional development begins at birth and progresses actively during the preschool years. It is highly dependent on interactions and relationships with people including family members, teachers, and peers (Boyd et al., 2005). Various factors influence and shape children's social and emotional development such as the child, family, and community characteristics described in Figure 13-2.

Children's social and emotional development occurs in a relatively predictable pattern across the early years. These skills are not learned all at once. They emerge through children's many interactions with their family, teachers, and classmates, and according

MyEducationLab

Go to the Building Teaching Skills and Dispositions section of Topic 10: Mental Health in the MyEducationLab for your course and complete the activity entitled *Support Development of Children's Social Skills*. As you work through the learning unit, consider how the situations depicted in these videos foster social-emotional development.

Figure 13-1 Principles of Children's Mental Health

- Warm, nurturing, protective, and consistent relationships are the building blocks of children's mental health.
- Behavioral indicators of mental health include emotion regulation, the ability to communicate feelings to caregivers, and active exploration of the environment.
- Children's mental health is influenced by the values and beliefs of the family, ethnic and cultural group, and professional perspective.
- Mental health is supported by approaches that focus on relationships, use evidence-based practices, and engage families.
- Teachers need training and supervision about meeting the social and emotional needs of children and families.
- Children can experience mental health disorders in the first 3 years of life.
- A continuum of services is needed to address prevention and treatment of children's mental health concerns.

Source: *Addressing Social-Emotional Development and Infant Mental Health in Early Childhood Systems* (Building State Early Childhood Comprehensive Systems Series No. 12), by P. Zeanah et al., January 2005, Los Angeles: National Center for Infant and Early Childhood Health Policy.

to their developmental readiness. Table 13-1 lists social and emotional milestones of infants from birth to 12 months of age. Characteristics of children 1 to 8 years of age are listed in Table 13-2. Overall, social and emotional development shows a progression from self-centered thinking to a greater understanding of being in relationships with others. Understanding the characteristic steps of social and emotional development helps teachers recognize behaviors that are age and developmentally appropriate, providing information to guide the creation of focused and purposeful activities in the classroom.

Infants

Even in the first few months, infants develop signs of healthy social and emotional development. Characteristics typical of the first year of life include (American Academy of Pediatrics [AAP], 2005):

- Developing a social smile.
- Imitating movements and facial expressions.
- Expressing communication with face and body.
- Enjoying playing with other people.

Figure 13-2 Factors That Influence Social and Emotional Development

Child characteristics:
- Overall physical health.
- Temperament.
- Experience of abuse or neglect.
- Experience in early childhood programs.
- Exposure to violence in the home or community.

Family and community factors:
- The quality of the parent–child relationship.
- The parent's ability to cope with parenting demands.
- Family stress and coping mechanisms.
- The family's access to community support and resources.

Source: *Social and Emotional Development of Children*, California Childcare Health Program, 2006, San Francisco: University of California, San Francisco School of Nursing. Retrieved October 11, 2009, from http://www.ucsfchildcarehealth.org/pdfs/Curricula/CCHA/15_CCHA_SocialEmotional_0406_v2.pdf

After 3 to 4 months of age, infants start becoming less interested in basic needs such as eating and sleeping and more interested in the world around them, providing more opportunities to strengthen relationships with caregivers. These signs of healthful development evolve from children's sense of safety and security. A sense of security emerges from the consistent caregiver's warm, affectionate tone, familiar routines, and positive social interactions.

During infancy, differences in children's temperaments may become more apparent and require that caregivers adjust their interactions for each individual child. Babies of all temperaments need to experience loving, responsive adults, but the manner in which the adults interact with them may be slightly different. For example, more energetic babies may need more patience and gentle guidance from caregivers, whereas calm, sensitive babies may need to be eased into contact with adults and other children (AAP, 2005).

Table 13-1	Social and Emotional Characteristics of Infants Birth to 12 months
Age	**Characteristics**
Birth to 6 Months	• Begins to focus on sights, sounds and interactions • Communicates needs through expressions, sounds and movements • Smiles and enjoys playful interaction • Needs support to learn to soothe and calm self • Develops attachment when needs are met
6 to 12 Months	• Seeks interaction • Enjoys initiating and imitating sounds and actions • Responds positively to encouragement • Prefers familiar routines • Has preference for parent and regular caregivers • May be shy or anxious with strangers

Interruptions in normal development can result in significant problems during infancy. For example, infants who experience hardships or difficulties in attachment with the caregiver during this critical period are more likely to demonstrate abnormal expressions of emotions, inattention and distractibility, disruptions in feeding and sleeping patterns, and developmental delays (Zeanah et al., 2005). This highlights the need to focus on ensuring that infant's establish a sense of safety, trust, and security as crucial elements of social and emotional development during the first year of life.

One to Two Years

During the second year of life, children develop an image of their social world, which includes family, friends, caregivers, and acquaintances. Children at this age view themselves to be at the center of the world. This view is described as being **egocentric**. Although other people interest them, children at this age have no idea how these other people think or feel (AAP, 2005). For example, 1- to 2-year-old children may play alongside others, but they do not yet interact with purpose or play cooperatively. Characteristics of social and emotional development during the second year of life include (AAP, 2005):

egocentric
the child's view of self as the center of the world

- Imitating behaviors of others.
- Being increasingly aware of self as separate from others.
- Being increasingly excited about being around other children.
- Demonstrating increasing independence.
- Beginning to show defiant behaviors.
- Showing more separation anxiety until midyear when it fades.

Interest in exploration is a characteristic of children in the toddler years, creating a "pushing and pulling" situation that can seem confusing. These children desire more independence and may express defiance when exploration is hindered, while at the same time needing to be confident in the caregiver as a source of security. Exploration in toddlers can be encouraged by providing safe, adequate play areas, encouraging children's participation, and using language to label objects, pictures, and ideas. It is important to invite these young children into free exploration within established limits.

Children in this age group need clear and consistent guidance. Typical 2-year-old behavior includes challenges such as aggression. However, these interactions need to be redirected appropriately because 2-year-olds who have persistent behavior challenges such as aggression tend to develop abnormal peer relationships and difficulties later on in school (Zeanah et al., 2005). Focused approaches to guidance build on children's natural curiosity and tendency to explore while teaching appropriate boundaries.

MyEducationLab

Go to the Assignments and Activities section of Topic 10: Mental Health in the MyEducationLab for your course and complete the activity entitled *Enhancing Children's Competence and Self-Esteem*. Why is it important that teachers understand children's emotional and cognitive capacities at different ages and developmental levels?

Table 13-2	Social and Emotional Characteristics of Children Ages 1 to 8 Years
Age	**Characteristics**
1–2 years	• Communicates through both words and actions • Uses increasingly complex vocabulary • Identifies and communicates likes and dislikes • Expresses wide range of emotions • May struggle with emotions and behaviors in new settings • Enjoys interacting with toys • Sometimes cooperates; sometimes seeks to be independent • Plays alone and alongside others
3–5 years	• Begins to identify and talk about own emotions • May express fears or be concerned about "monsters" • Enjoys humor including silly words and word games • May be self-centered but beginning to show empathy for others • Responds well to routines; may need support to make changes • Engages in detailed make-believe play; may struggle with fantasy and reality • Expresses self through singing, dancing, arts and crafts • Seeks interaction with other children
6–8 years	• Uses language to share information and describe stories and events • Seeks independence, but still has fears • Develops a sense of right and wrong • Enjoys companionship with adults but prefers to play with other children • Wants to be liked and accepted by peers • Expresses personal interests and preferred play • Develops and repeats intricate play themes and rules of play • Plays cooperative games with designated rules

Teaching children the parameters for play, establishing clear limits for behavior, and guiding children appropriately without harsh punishment or scolding are important strategies that enhance social and emotional development (California Childcare Health Program, 2006).

Two to Three Years

During the third year of life children continue to be concerned about their own needs. They are still developing awareness of others, and may not understand how others feel. Characteristics of social and emotional development for this age group include:

- Exhibiting more sense of individuality.
- Demonstrating more advanced memory in certain areas.
- Growing in emotional understanding.
- Increasing interest in friendships.
- Increasing development of conscience (sense of right and wrong).

Playing imitation and pretend games are important to social development for this age group. Children 2 to 3 years of age tend to participate in parallel, or side-by-side, play unless they want to play with a toy that is being used by another child. These situations create important opportunities for children in this age group to explore concepts such as sharing and taking turns.

Children at this developmental age seek autonomy and exhibit self-assertion and behaviors related to negotiation, compromise, delay, and ignoring (Ewing Marion Kauffman Foundation, 2002). These are complex challenges, and it is natural for children to struggle to maintain emotional balance. Negotiating a plan to share a toy may begin well, but when it comes to deciding who gets the toy first, the negotiation may result in frustration and impatience. A child might exclaim, "I *AM* sharing, but I want to play with the truck first!" Emotionally, the 2- to 3-year-old period is characterized by mood swings, which are an indication that the child is trying to learn how to control actions, impulses, and feelings (AAP, 2005).

It is natural for children in this age group to test limits and occasionally lose control. Managing their emotional impulses is difficult, thus, anger and frustration may turn quickly into crying, hitting, or screaming (AAP, 2005). Understanding that such behaviors are part of children's natural struggle to gain social and emotional resiliency and competency in difficult situations is important as teachers implement guidance strategies.

Teachers can help children of this age develop healthy emotional skills by setting reasonable and consistent limits that allow children to understand the boundaries for actions and behaviors and begin to take charge of their actions. Offering appropriate encouragement and reinforcement for appropriate behaviors is important. Teachers also need to be prepared to redirect inappropriate behaviors and to help children begin to understand how negative behaviors affect the children around them.

In the chapter opening scenario, Meegan knows that Heather's aggressive behaviors in the classroom won't just go away. She understands that it is her responsibility to identify specific strategies to guide Heather to more appropriate behaviors. At the same time Meegan knows she must try to recognize and understand the challenges that may be limiting Heather's healthful development.

Learning to share is a stage in social and emotional development. Even when very young children agree to share, they still may want the toy first!

Three to Four Years

At ages 3 to 4 years, children's sense of identity and security is stronger and they become more interested in developing relationships with others. Characteristics of social and emotional development for 3- and 4-year-olds include:

- Exhibiting increased interest in interacting with others.
- Using language to communicate wants, needs, and ideas.
- Demonstrating greater ability to manage emotions and regulate behavior.
- Following rules and showing an interest in pleasing others.
- Continuing interest in having a strong relationship with the teacher.

Children in this age group are increasingly interested in associative play, or playing alongside other children and engaging in a similar focus. For example, 3-year-olds might be observed building blocks side by side. They share the same materials and talk about what they are doing, but their play is essentially individual. During this time children start to become more aware of the feelings and actions of others. They notice if another child is upset and can begin to recognize the consequences of their actions.

For example, when Lindsay asks Ben what will happen if he keeps pushing his truck against Karen's block tower, Ben is able to say, "It will fall down." Lindsay follows up by asking, "What do you think Karen thinks about that?" Three-year-olds are becoming more able to take turns, trade toys, and use fewer tactics such as grabbing, whining, and screaming to get what they want (AAP, 2005). A vivid imagination begins to develop during this period, enabling children to explore a wide range of emotions including love, anger, protest, and fear. Imaginary friends are common and children may shift rapidly from fantasy to reality. Children continue to need the support of teachers to understand the expectations of behavior and to help them learn to be flexible and resilient (Gallagher & Mayer, 2006).

Four to Five Years

Children become very social at ages 4 to 5 years. They begin to enjoy an active social life and may even have a *best* friend (AAP, 2005). Friendships should be encouraged because

MyEducationLab

Go to the Assignments and Activities section of Topic 10: Mental Health in the MyEducationLab for your course and complete the activity entitled *Supporting Children's Uniqueness*. What are some ways in which teachers in this video promote positive social-emotional health?

these are key opportunities for children to practice the social and emotional skills that are involved in building and maintaining relationships. Characteristics of social and emotional development for this age group include:

- Focusing on social interactions.
- Practicing taking leadership roles.
- Exhibiting an increasing ability to understand the perspective of others.
- Demonstrating ability to focus on projects.
- Being literal with rules and needing support to understand flexibility.

Four- and 5-year-old children begin to engage in cooperative play in which elaborate games and rules are established, roles are assigned, and the course of play involves negotiation and give-and-take situations. During this time, children develop increased sensitivity for the feelings of others. They are increasingly able to identify feelings and recognize the impact of their behaviors. Self-confidence is also developing, and children are ready for responsibilities that build their sense of competence such as setting a table or cleaning a play area. This age group continues to need the support and guidance of teachers to ensure that all children are included in play and to find security in consistent expectations about behavior.

Five to Eight Years

Children in kindergarten and elementary school enter a time of industrious exploration of their world and interest in greater independence. Characteristics of social and emotional development for this age group include:

- Increasing interest in autonomy and independence.
- Continuing to judge self on how adults value and respond to what they do.
- Beginning to rely on peers for feedback about what is good and bad.
- Demonstrating individual skills and competencies.
- Communicating emotions, ideas, wants, and needs.

Children in this age group tend to become very involved in projects and enjoy working on them over a period of days, seeing them through to completion. It is also a time in which children begin to build friendships and social connections outside of the family, developing friends in the neighborhood and class group.

Cooperative play evolves to a high level as 5- to 8-year-old children carry play themes over from one day to the next. A child may have several good friends, most often children of the same sex, and enjoy frequent contact and "play dates." This is also a time during which children may have heated disagreements that emerge and "blow over" quickly; the child who is an "enemy" on one day may be a "best friend" on the next. Children are growing in their ability to understand the feelings of others. They are able to nurture younger children while looking up to older children as role models.

This age range is also a challenging "between" age. On the one hand, children ages 5 to 8 years are seeking greater independence and find pride in their emergent skills, which may be displayed by tattling when others break the rules, or "pushing back" and showing resistance when given guidance. At the same time, they may still have youthful fears such as death, rejection, or failure, and they can be very sensitive to feedback.

> ## What if. . .
> you observed a 4-year-old child's social and emotional behaviors and noted that some were characteristic of a 2-year-old while others were more typical of a 5-year-old? How might you explain this variation?

PROMOTING SOCIAL AND EMOTIONAL DEVELOPMENT

Growing numbers of children spend many hours in early childhood settings during their early years, providing significant opportunities for teachers to promote positive social and emotional development. Creating appropriate environments, establishing positive relationships, and implementing strategies that specifically encourage social and emotional development equip children with the skills they need to be successful in kindergarten and build capacities that support children's mental health.

Creating Supportive Environments

Establishing environments that are welcoming and attuned to children's development sets the stage for appropriate social and emotional development. Many studies have suggested that children's social and emotional development is encouraged in early childhood environments that meet specific quality standards. These include (Boyd et al., 2005):

- *Small group size and favorable adult–child ratios* to ensure children receive individualized care and support.
- *Partnership with parents* to improve communication about children's needs and how to address them.
- *Curriculum that is developmentally appropriate* to invite children into explorations that are suitable, thus improving learning outcomes.
- *Well-prepared teachers and low teacher turnover* to improve consistency, ensuring that teachers are attuned to children's social and emotional development as they create environments and positive relationships to support learning.

Programs that address these quality indicators have a positive influence on all children; however, the greatest benefits occur among children who are negatively affected by the impacts of poverty, abuse, or challenges due to developmental delay or language acquisition (Ewing Marion Kauffman Foundation, 2002).

Teachers are responsible for creating the welcoming spaces where children play, learn, and thrive. They do this by creating a sense of safety and security, and by arranging the space to avoid unnecessary conflicts, such as providing space for block play and construction that is not in the walkway of the dramatic play center. Other aspects include creating social and quiet areas that allow children to select the setting that meets their needs, and encouraging self-sufficiency by providing toileting areas that allow children to be self-sufficient when age appropriate and labeling tubs and shelves for toys so children can help at cleanup time. Young children recognize environments that are child oriented and child friendly. These attentions to the physical space communicate that children are welcomed and valued.

What if. . .

you were asked to arrange a classroom environment that was welcoming to children? What details in the classroom space would you plan to build children's comfort in the space? Would your children's space have a theme? Special colors? Use plants?

Establishing Caring Relationships

During the early years the child–caregiver relationship has the most important environmental influence on a children's mental health. This relationship exerts positive influence on a child's development when the relationship is responsive and nurturing. Conversely, the relationship can have a negative influence when the relationship is harsh, punitive, or insecure. As a result the quality of the relationship children have with their caregiver can be either a protective factor or a risk factor for social and emotional development.

Recent research has highlighted the value of the teacher–child relationship as making unique contributions to children's development and learning (La Paro, Pianta, & Stuhlman, 2004; Rimm-Kaufman & Chiu, 2007). These include (La Paro et al., 2004):

- *Emotional support,* such as the positive or negative climate of the classroom, teacher sensitivity and responsiveness, interest and regard for the child.
- *Classroom organization,* including management of children's behavior, effective use of routines and learning time, and ways the teacher engages children in learning.
- *Instructional support,* such as modeling and using language, encouraging children's thinking, and giving children feedback.

In the classroom these contributions are put into action through close and nurturing interactions between children and their teachers that demonstrate commitment to building strong and positive reciprocal relationships.

Nurturing Relationships

Building nurturing relationships is a primary component of healthy teacher–child interaction. It encompasses the essential elements of the teacher's contribution to children's positive mental health: respect, responsiveness, appropriate guidance, and positive expectations. For example:

- Providing interesting challenges and encouraging children's natural interests to explore and discover communicates respect, which enhances each child's feeling of worth.
- Recognizing children's strengths and needs, and responding by purposefully planning activities and experiences to meet those needs, shows value for children and promote a mutually trusting relationship.
- Communicating appropriate limits and guiding children to positive interactions help children learn how to be positive members of the group and how to build friendships, demonstrating faith in their capabilities.
- Supporting and caring for children through challenging circumstances, and persisting in helping children to learn, expresses confidence in children's competency.

Teachers also serve as models for children regarding how to manage difficult situations. When teachers face challenges with ease, children learn coping strategies rather than defeat. Some children are born with conditions that influence their overall health such as prematurity or heart defects that may challenge their social and emotional development. The effects of these conditions on children's mental health can be modified by the teacher–child relationship. If a child is born very premature, the teacher can provide high-quality stimulation and attention in order to maximize that child's potential. This focused interaction communicates to the infant a sense of being valued, demonstrates commitment and love for the child, and models a positive approach to managing challenges.

Teachers help young children gain social and emotional skills by setting reasonable limits and providing clear guidelines for behavior.

In her Head Start classroom, Jan tries to model appropriate interactions when she conducts home visits for families of toddlers who have identified special developmental needs. She helps families recognize their child's abilities and accomplishments as they unfold, and encourages them to enjoy their child's unique personality.

Building Attachment

Attachment refers to the bonds of trust, care, understanding, and safety that develop between children and their caregivers. Attachment is a springboard for exploration and future learning. Children who experience the positive bonds of attachment are able to explore and learn with confidence. They know that their caretaker is close and accessible if needed. Without the confidence provided by secure attachment relationships, children may be afraid or remain passive and be unable to initiate and appropriately participate in learning. Children who form strong attachment relationships are better able to manage separation from their families as they enter the early childhood setting, and ultimately are supported to understand themselves as unique human beings (Balaban, 2006; Bowlby, 1969). They tend to be more resilient, have more positive relationships, and perform better in school.

Secure attachments also build children's perceptions of value and self-worth, which are components of personal safety. For example, children who feel valued are better able to understand the concept of safety rules for themselves and others. The *Safety Segment* describes the positive impacts on mental health of children's ability to form attachment relationships. The ability to develop an attachment relationship is considered a hallmark of emotional wellness.

attachment
the ability to form close relationships; to bond with others

What if. . .

a mother of a child in your care blamed family problems on her child's poor social development? How might you explain more healthful ways to approach the child and family's challenge? What ideas do you have to help the parent find support for the family problems mentioned?

Safety Segment

Positive Impacts of Attachment on Children's Mental Health

Strong attachment relationships are crucial to children's safety. Attachment relationships increase children's abilities to care for their own personal safety and be capable of having compassion and empathy for others. When children form attachment relationships, they learn that:

- They are worthy of being taken care of, which leads to children's understanding of how to meet their own needs while recognizing the needs and rights of others.
- They are competent, which builds children's confidence in being able to manage and master challenges.
- They can rely on their teacher (family and community) to be there when they need them, which connects children to others, creating interest and compassion for the well-being of their family and community.

These understandings increase children's ability to care about their personal safety and know who to turn to when they need help.

Source: *Addressing Social-Emotional Development and Infant Mental Health in Early Childhood Systems* (Building State Early Childhood Comprehensive Systems Series No. 12), by P. Zeanah et al., January 2005, Los Angeles: National Center for Infant and Early Childhood Health Policy.

Providing Unstructured Play

Free and unstructured play contributes to children's cognitive, physical, creative, expressive, and social and emotional development. It is considered so important to childhood that the United Nations Commission on Human Rights has identified play as a *right* of childhood (Ginsburg, 2007). Children's involvement in play is one aspect of social and emotional development that is easily observed. Through play children are immersed in dynamic interaction and exploration with the objects and people of their world. Play provides opportunities for children to participate in enjoyable activities, use their imaginations, test ideas, practice dexterity, explore outcomes, and gain mastery. Unstructured play, or play that is not directed by adults, is especially important. It allows children to be self-directed in determining the rules and procedures involved in their play themes. This inspires an individual experience of direction and mastery and also encourages social interaction and problem solving. These activities result in a sense of accomplishment and competence (Ginsburg, 2007; Lucich, 2004). The confidence and resiliency that children develop through child-directed play builds capacities that support them in new situations and challenges. They learn of their abilities to impact the world and apply decision making to outcomes. The *Teaching Wellness* activities provide ideas for setting the stage for children's understanding of their own competencies.

Play also brings children into contact with other people and provides opportunities for them to experience useful social skills such as taking turns, waiting, negotiating, compromising, and sharing (Ginsburg, 2007; Lucich, 2004). Unstructured play allows children to explore according to their own interests and at their own pace. Children who are less verbal, who are learning English, or who have special developmental needs are equally able to engage in and benefit from play when they are allowed to set their own pace and follow their own interests.

Through play, children learn to use words to express emotion and experience the reactions of others. For example, two 4-year-old girls might begin their friendship in this way:

> Sophia hears the teacher introduce Althea. "Hey!" said Sophia. "Althea! That sounds like Sophia! I could be your friend!" Althea thinks for a minute and says, "Sometimes my mom calls me 'Thea.'" Sophia exclaims, "Sometimes my mom calls me 'Phia!' I could be your friend forever!"

MyEducationLab

Go to the Assignments and Activities section of Topic 10: Mental Health in the MyEducationLab for your course and complete the activity entitled *Facilitating Peer Interactions*. How does this teacher show support to both children and encourage interaction?

Teaching Wellness   *I Can Do Things*

Learning Outcome: To develop children's recognition of their own competence by guiding them to realistically identify themselves as people who can do things.

Infants and Toddlers

- *Goal:* Children experience the teacher describing the child's abilities.

- *Materials:* No materials are needed.

- *Activity plan:* Use everyday activities and experiences to encourage, name, and describe the infant and toddler's emergent skills. Use phrases such as "You are drinking milk from the bottle. You know how to drink milk!" or "I see you are looking at the book. You know how to turn the pages."

- *How to adjust the activity:* Describe the actions of adults, pointing out what the grown-up can do, such as

"Your mommy knows how to pack your lunch" or "Your dada knows how to zip your coat." As children begin to develop language, spend some quiet time talking with the child and remembering all the things the child did during the day. Summarize the list, saying, "You colored on some paper, you ate your snack, you took your nap. You know how to do many things."

- *Did you meet your goal?* Does the infant enjoy the friendly conversation? Does the toddler begin to respond when the teacher describes "what" the child can do? Does the child provide examples when asked, "Sasha, what do you know how to do?"

Preschoolers and Kindergartners

- *Goal:* Children can identify skills they have and skills they desire.

- *Materials:* Magazine or clip-art pictures showing people doing many different kinds of activities, some of which depict skills children can typically accomplish and some that take training or practice. Be sure to select pictures that show a range of skill activities, people of varying ages, those with special developmental needs, and other features that would be familiar to the children in the group.

- *Activity plan:* Guide the child to look at each picture and place it in the "I can do this now" pile or the

"I would like to learn to do this" pile. Invite the child to describe one of her skills in detail (such as brushing teeth or cutting a banana slice). Help the child imagine how she could learn a skill that is in her "like to learn" pile (such as riding a bicycle or baking muffins).

- *How to adjust the activity:* Play a "Can you do this?" game. Take turns asking, "Do you know how to . . . jump?" or ". . . take care of a goat?" Add some silly options: ". . . how to give a hippopotamus a bath?"

- *Did you meet your goal?* Can children realistically identify their current skills?

School-Age Children

- *Goal:* Children are able to identify many personal skills.

- *Materials:* Paper, pens, stapler.

- *Activity plan:* Guide the children to construct an *I Can Do Things* book that includes drawings and stories about skills they have.

- *How to adjust the activity:* Work with the children to identify different kinds of skill "chapters" for their book, such as Caring for Myself, Caring for Others, and Caring for My World. Periodically encourage children to add to their book.

- *Did you meet your goal?* Is each child able to draw and write about many skills?

Table 13-3	Stages of Play

Stages of Play	Examples
Solitary	Playing independently, following own interests
Observing	Watching other children, asking questions, but not involved in play
Parallel	Child playing alongside another child using the same materials, but not interacting
Associative	Child playing with another, using same materials, but play is unorganized—each child follows own interests
Cooperative	Child playing with others in an organized way; interacting and establishing themes, negotiating rules and roles

Source: Adapted from *The Value of Play* (Health & Safety Notes), by M. Lucich, 2004, San Francisco: California Childcare Health Program, retrieved October 10, 2009, from http://www.ucsfchildcarehealth.org/pdfs/healthandsafety/valueplayen_adr.pdf; Reprinted with permission from California Childcare Health Program (CCHP). © Copyright 2004. Copying of any portion of this material is not permitted without written permission of CCHP.

From individual exploration to games that involve rules and negotiation, children practice and learn many social skills through different types of play. Table 13-3 describes many of these types of play.

Open and unstructured playtime is important throughout the early years. In some settings, however, free playtime is being reduced due to pressures to promote academic skills in both in the home and in the early childhood and school setting. Academically oriented activities have clear benefits for children's learning. When adult-planned and academically focused activities dominate, children's days may become overscheduled, causing children to feel hurried. Some children can thrive with busy schedules and directed focus on academics at home and in school. Others may suffer from lack of opportunity to play, reacting with anxiety and other signs of stress (Ginsburg, 2007). The trends that promote attention to academic learning rather than play and social interaction are problematic. Free and unstructured play provides many stress-reducing benefits that contribute to children's resilience and help build social and emotional wellness. When such opportunities are not available, children's mental health can suffer.

Contributing to School Success

Healthy social and emotional development significantly contributes to children's future academic success. It also eases the transition from preschool into the new environment of kindergarten. During the early years teachers help children develop the foundational skills to be successful learners. Understanding the skills that support school success, recognizing the challenges that some children face, enhancing self-regulation, and fostering positive approaches to learning are important teacher contributions.

Healthful social-emotional development helps children approach learning with curiosity and enthusiasm.

Skills for School Success

Enhancing children's social skills prepares them to be successful in school. This involves helping children to develop the capacities to (Ewing Marion Kauffman Foundation, 2002):

- Understand their own feelings and those of others.
- Cooperate with peers and adults.
- Resolve conflicts successfully.
- Be resilient.

Enhancing these social and emotional skills is important because children who can take turns and get along with others, and who can listen, pay attention, and be persistent, are also likely to be successful in reading, mathematics, and other academic skills (Shore, 2002). In addition, strong social-emotional skills contribute to children's language development (Ewing Marion Kauffman

Foundation, 2002). Children who are socially and emotionally healthy will be ready to start school, participate in relationships, and fully experience learning.

Understanding Problems

Most children transition successfully into kindergarten. They are ready to manage the new routines and navigate the new expectations. However, some children are not prepared for the changes they will experience. Surveys of kindergarten teachers report that more than half of the children lack the skills and social-emotional competence necessary to function and learn in the school setting (Webster-Stratton, Reid, & Stoolmiller, 2008).

These findings are particularly important because children who do not have the needed social and emotional skills are often the most difficult to teach. They tend to not be interested in learning, lack confidence in their success, and have difficulties cooperating and establishing self-control (Ewing Marion Kauffman Foundation, 2002). They may also display behavior problems as they struggle in the school environment. This is of concern because kindergarten teachers tend to manage classes that are larger than prekindergarten groups and often do so with little or no assistance. Supporting children who struggle and managing their challenging behaviors may strain the kindergarten teacher–child relationship, causing problems later on in school. Studies have shown that children who do not have successful relationships with their kindergarten teachers have more academic and behavior problems at least through eighth grade (Hamre & Pianta, 2001). In addition, when teachers spend so much time managing behavioral problems, they have less time for teaching (Boyd et al., 2005).

Identifying concerns early on, and finding ways to address them, is important, especially for children who are at risk for behavioral and school problems. An increasing number of children are growing up in stressful circumstances that are associated with negative social and emotional development and its consequences, including low achievement, inattentiveness, psychiatric problems, grade retention, and depressed cognitive development (Ewing Marion Kauffman Foundation, 2002). Teachers can help offset some of these risks by creating opportunities for children to experience success. Here is an example:

> Maxwell invites families to participate at reading time in his second-grade class. He models how to enjoy a book with school-age children, and helps children and families practice reading to each other as a way to strengthen their mutual interest in learning and encourage families to appreciate their child's developing skills.

Enhancing Self-Regulation

Self-regulation refers to the ability to manage one's own behavior, which is important to a child's success in group settings. Self-regulation involves the capacity to resist impulses and stay focused even when there are more enticing activities available (Boyd et al., 2005). It is natural for very young children to struggle with delaying gratification (that is, waiting for what they want). However, as children prepare to enter kindergarten, they are expected to develop the capacity to regulate their impulses according to the rules of the new setting. For example, with a few gentle reminders, children in kindergarten are expected to learn to raise their hands and wait to be called on rather than calling out an answer to a question. Learning in the school setting relies on children being able to listen to and follow directions given by the teacher rather than rushing forward with the task.

Early childhood teachers can plan many activities to help children learn and practice self-regulation skills during the preschool years. For example, Su Lin recognized at the beginning of the year that many children in her class would run with excitement from one activity to another. She found that providing clear instructions and a predictable daily routine helped the children understand expectations. When they heard the 5-minute warning bell, they were more able to stop their play and participate in cleanup time in order to move on to the next activity of the day. Su Lin continued to offer specific instructions about appropriate behaviors to reinforce her expectations. Over the year she noticed remarkable improvement. Children's ability to self-regulate enabled them to successfully manage the tasks associated with learning and to develop positive social relationships.

self-regulation
child's ability to manage his or her own behavior

Fostering Positive Approaches to Learning

Children's success as learners also depends on the attitudes, habits, and learning styles they bring to the learning process. These are called approaches to learning. They include the various qualities, characteristics, and dispositions that help children approach new information and manage new tasks. Qualities associated with positive approaches to learning include (Egertson, 2006):

approaches to learning
the attitudes, habits, and learning styles children bring to the learning process

- Curiosity and openness.
- Persistence and focus.
- Reflection and interpretation.
- Imagination and invention.
- Cognitive problem solving.

What if. . .

you were asked to be on an early childhood advisory committee for your community? What ideas could you offer to help promote children's success in school? What strategies might you offer to address the gap in social and emotional development experienced by some children?

Children who approach learning with interest and enthusiasm, and who have practice forming questions and focusing on outcomes, are better able to acquire new information and apply new concepts to future settings. These are signs of positive social and emotional adjustment that contribute to children's success in school. Teachers foster these qualities in many ways, such as by offering a variety of opportunities for children to explore new materials and take on appropriate challenges, and by guiding them during unstructured play with intentional and open-ended questions that require reflection and speculation.

ADDRESSING CHALLENGES TO CHILDREN'S MENTAL HEALTH

Most children experience normal social and emotional development. They gradually develop interpersonal skills and learn to manage their emotions within the broad range of typical development. However, growing numbers of children are experiencing delays and challenges in social and emotional development that are exhibited through significant behavior problems in the classroom (Cohen et al., 2005). Understanding the prevalence of these concerns, how they are identified, and the types of mental health problems that may be experienced by young children assists teachers to better understand and address children's needs.

Understanding the Prevalence of Mental Health Problems

Young children can, and do, experience mental health problems (NSCDC, 2008). Children's social and emotional behavioral difficulties are a common concern for parents and teachers. More than 14% of parents with children over the age of 3 have talked with either a health care provider or a member of school staff about their concerns. More than 5% have been prescribed medications to treat them (Simpson, Cohen, Pastor, & Reuben, 2008). Behavior concerns are reported more frequently for boys and older children than for girls and younger children (Simpson et al., 2008).

In recognition of a growing concern about children's significant behavior issues, diagnostic criteria for identifying early forms of mental health problems among young children have been refined. These tools have been useful in diagnosing mental health problems in more than 15% of children ages 2 to 5 years, and 25% of children ages 8 to 17 years (Egger & Angold, 2006). Mental health problems include serious emotional disorder, anxiety disorder, disruptive behavior disorder, autism, attention deficit/hyperactivity disorder, and depression. In addition, some children experience multiple mental health problems. Consequently, the National Advisory Mental Health Council (2001) predicts that childhood mental health disorders will be one of the top five causes of sickness, disability, and death among children by the year 2020 (Brennan, Bradley, Ama, & Cawood, 2003).

Recognizing Consequences

Mental health problems that begin in early childhood can develop into serious disorders as children age. Mental health problems influence the architecture of the child's developing brain, impairing their capacity for learning and developing social relationships (NSCDC, 2008). In essence, children whose mental health problems go undetected and untreated are at risk for mental health disorders that may persist for a lifetime.

Even seemingly minor mental health problems can impact children and families. Children with mental health problems often have problems with self-esteem, learning, and relationships with others. They are more likely to experience other health conditions that impact their daily activities and increase their absence from school. Unaddressed behavior concerns are also a problem. Nationally, preschool-age children are expelled from their early childhood setting three times more often than children in K–12 school settings (Gilliam, 2005). Expulsion interrupts learning time, and does not help to resolve children's behavior problems. Families are also affected by children's mental health problems. In a national survey, parents of children with mental health problems reported diminished health and quality of life (Centers for Disease Control and Prevention [CDC], 2005).

Access to help and treatment for mental health problems is also a concern. Children from racial and ethnic minority groups have less access than Caucasian children to mental health services (Brennan et al., 2003). Hispanic children in particular are more than 2.5 times more likely than white or black children to have unmet mental health needs (Katoaka, Zhang, & Wells, 2002). These inequities put some children at greater risk.

Recognizing delays in social and emotional development and related problems when children are young is important because it provides opportunities for intervention and support. If left undetected and untreated, the effects of poor social and emotional development can be costly and require long-term interventions that may or may not be successful (Bricker, Davis, & Squires, 2004). Teachers who are attuned to this are better able to advocate when they suspect a need for mental health services.

Identifying Challenges

Children are at risk for mental health problems when their early experiences are negative and threatening and when they do not have adults who are attentive to mediating their fears. Although teachers cannot change children's home environments, they can help children by providing a safe and nurturing school environment and by acknowledging that children face risks to their social and emotional development. For example, as children age, their sense of value and their self-worth are increasingly affected by interactions with peers, sometimes in negative ways. Teachers can help children learn to *test* the reality of negative comments said to them by other children. For example, the *Health Hint* discusses how childhood obesity can be a risk factor for poor social and emotional development.

Observing for Mental Health Problems

Children's difficult behaviors are often the first indication that a problem with social and emotional development may exist. But recognizing behaviors that suggest a mental health problem may not be straightforward. For example, Bob, a teacher in the young preschool room, frequently observes 3-year-old Sasha acting aggressively such as pushing other children in the play yard or knocking over other children's block structures. Bob has been unsuccessful in managing these behaviors and is unsure if they indicate a lack of communication skills or are signs of more serious mental health concerns. He is not alone in wondering how to interpret such behaviors.

Difficult behaviors are a common and natural experience in early childhood classrooms. Even typical behaviors can be difficult to manage, and most children will display inappropriate behaviors at one time or another. For young children, understanding how to participate appropriately in the group setting requires learning the rules and cues for appropriate social interaction. Testing limits as children gain this social knowledge is normal. A core responsibility of early childhood teaching involves guiding children through these aspects of social and emotional development and helping them learn to interact appropriately.

Appropriate behaviors are related to normal growth and development; they are behaviors that are expected of most children based on their age and developmental maturity. Behaviors that are considered appropriate change as children age. What is understandable behavior for a 2-year-old is not expected behavior for a 5-year-old. In addition, children who

Health Hint

Body Image and Children's Mental Health

Being overweight continues to be a social stigma that is difficult for children to understand, and some children who are overweight may develop mental health problems. Many have trouble with low self-esteem and some show symptoms of depression. They may have trouble developing social relationships and display externalizing behaviors such as aggression and conduct problems, or internalizing behaviors such as withdrawal, anxiety, or physical complaints. Children who are overweight also often have more health problems that interfere with attendance and may negatively affect academic achievement.

Issues related to body image begin in childhood and tend to increase as children get older, especially as they start to enter the middle childhood years (after age 8). To foster healthy social and emotional development, teachers guide children to:

- Develop positive peer relationships by pairing children to accomplish a task such as interviewing classmates and creating a poster on the kinds of pets children have.
- Recognize their competencies by having children keep a journal of things they like, things they can do, and things they would like to learn to do.

On occasion, teachers may recommend that the family seek mental health consultation if the child's social and emotional development is significantly impacted by being overweight.

Sources: "Childhood Overweight and Parent- and Teacher-Reported Behavior Problems," by A. Datar and R. Sturm, 2004, *Archives of Pediatrics and Adolescent Medicine, 158,* pp. 804–810; and "The Relationship between Body Mass Index and Behavior in Children," by R. Bradley et al., 2008, *Journal of Pediatrics, 153,* pp. 629–634.

experience special developmental delays may demonstrate behaviors that are understandable given their developmental maturity, but are not age appropriate. For example, 6-year-old Sam, who has a developmental disability, may kick another child who is taking a turn on the bicycle—a behavior commensurate with Sam's special developmental condition, but not typically expected of a 6-year-old. Teachers need to weigh the behaviors that are observed with children's individual age and maturity. Other aspects such as children's culture and nutritional health can also impact behavior.

Understanding Cultural Influences

Children's cultural backgrounds can impact the kinds of behaviors that are considered appropriate. What might be considered appropriate behavior in one culture may not be understood in another. For example, a Korean American child may be taught to hide his emotions, causing his teacher to worry that the child is not capable of expressing and managing his emotions, a possible sign of problems in social and emotional development.

Cultural values also influence family reactions to children's behaviors. For example, parents may allow certain behaviors in the home environment that are not considered appropriate in the early childhood setting. To better understand the cultural framework that influences children's behavior, teachers should discuss these issues with families. This helps everyone understand whether particular behaviors have a recognizable source or whether they indicate signs of problems.

Identifying Sleeping and Eating Habits

Behaviors can also be influenced by children's sleeping and eating patterns. Children who do not receive sufficient rest may show behavior extremes in the classroom. What children eat can also influence the way they behave in the classroom, as described in the *Nutrition Note.* For example, children who have not eaten breakfast or who receive a poor diet may

Nutrition Note

Children's Behavior May Be Influenced by What They Eat

What children eat may influences their physical and mental health possibly impacting their behavior. Although the long-term influence of junk food on behavior problems and mental health is still unclear, it is apparent that junk foods can decrease the quality of children's diets. Diets containing high amounts of sugars and processed foods ("junk foods") can displace the consumption of more nutritious foods. As a result, children may to have lower intakes of vitamins and minerals and healthy fats such as omega-3 and -6 fatty acids, which contribute to healthy brain development.

Teachers are in a position to suggest and promote healthful food choices for snacks and meals brought from home and program social events. These efforts promote overall health and may contribute to children's abilities to better moderate their behavior in the classroom.

Source: "'Junk Food' Diet and Childhood Behavioural Problems: Results from the ALSPAC Cohort," by N. Wiles, K. Northstone, P. Emmett, and G. Lewis, 2009, *European Journal of Clinical Nutrition, 63(4)*, pp. 491–498.

demonstrate behaviors such as inability to concentrate, lethargy, and persistent fatigue. Understanding children's sleeping and eating routines can help teachers understand the source of behavioral issues.

Recognizing Warning Signs

To establish successful class groups, teachers must develop a wide range of behavior management approaches and techniques. Sometimes teachers focus so closely on managing behaviors as they occur that they miss the signs that may indicate a problem may be more complex. To assist teachers to recognize behaviors that have an understandable cause and those that suggest the potential for social and emotional problems, special focus must be given to observing the child's behavior in the classroom setting. Through careful observation teachers look for behaviors that are extreme, such as excessively aggressive or withdrawn behaviors, and for emotional responses that are not age appropriate or that seem atypical. Signs of problems in social and emotional development are demonstrated through behaviors that are:

- Inappropriate or dangerous.
- Frequent and reoccurring.
- Persistent.

Figure 13-3 provides a checklist of signs that may indicate mental health problems.

Making Referrals

A small percentage of children may experience significant behaviors that persist in spite of efforts to guide and manage the behavior concerns. These children may benefit from assessment and evaluation by a behavior specialist or mental health consultant. However, determining when efforts to manage children's behaviors are not making progress and when additional support is needed can be difficult. For example, Hal feels like he is not doing his job as a teacher when Mandy's behavior is not solved by his careful efforts. He feels like the principal will question his teaching skills because the problems persist—in fact, they may be increasing—but he is also struggling because every day is getting harder.

Figure 13-3 **Behavioral Warning Signs**

✓ Mood swings (anger or sadness) or sudden behavior changes
✓ Frequent out-of-control and excessive behaviors, such as fighting, shouting, or other aggressive behaviors
✓ Behaviors that are unusual and not age appropriate
✓ Hurtful or destructive behaviors to self or others
✓ No interest in sights, sounds, touch; is difficult to soothe (infants)
✓ Little emotion, or extreme emotions such as fearfulness or sadness
✓ Absence of language or communication by preschool age
✓ Difficulty forming positive relationships with others
✓ Inability to calm or comfort self
✓ Inability to play with others or objects

Sources: *Social and Emotional Development of Children*, by the California Childcare Health Program, 2006, San Francisco: University of California, San Francisco School of Nursing, retrieved October 11, 2009, from http://www.ucsfchildcarehealth.org/pdfs/Curricula/CCHA/15_CCHA_SocialEmotional_0406_v2.pdf; and Raver, C. C., & Knitzer, J. (2002, July). Ready to enter: *What research tells policymakers about strategies to promote social and emotional school readiness among three- and four-year-old children.* New York: National Center for Children in Poverty. Retrieved October 11, 2009, from http://www.nccp.org/publications/pdf/download_108.pdf.

When well-planned intervention strategies are not successful in redirecting children to more positive behaviors, additional supports are needed for both the child and the teacher. To evaluate progress, teachers, families, and others who may be teaming to address the child's needs discuss questions such as these:

- Have the frequency and intensity of the child's behaviors improved?
- Is the child able to successfully navigate most of the activities during the day with relatively little support or does a teacher need to be nearby to prevent aggressive acts or injury?
- Is the child demonstrating more positive behaviors?
- Is growth evident?

Responses that indicate that problems are continuing mean that more information and support are needed. Referring the child to special services is the next step. Assessment and evaluation services are provided by community health services or mental health counselors in private practice. Some schools may have counselors or behavior management specialists who provide these services.

The teacher's role in making referrals is to provide concrete descriptions of the behaviors that are problematic and information about what is working. Even after referrals are made, the teacher's responsibility to the child continues, through additional efforts to manage and guide behavior. In the example above, Hal finds that talking with other teachers about strategies and support resources is one way for him to boost his confidence and maintain his motivation. Advocating for additional training or the temporary assistance of an aide are other ways that teachers obtain support to better teach children with mental health problems.

Types of Mental Health Disorders

Teachers are an important source of information for parents and health care providers regarding the child's social behaviors and any problems that may be impacting the child's ability to learn and participate effectively in the classroom. However, the diagnosis of mental health disorders is made by medical professionals. Making a definitive diagnosis of mental health problems is complex. It involves a broad review of biological and environmental factors, children's age and development, and assessments of how children function in the school and home environment.

Understanding some of the mental health disorders that may occur during the early years provides teachers with a general understanding of the range of conditions that may affect children's mental health and behaviors in the classroom. The more common mental health disorders identified among young children are discussed in the following sections.

Attention Deficit/Hyperactivity Disorder

Attention deficit/hyperactivity disorder (ADHD) is a condition characterized by restlessness, persistent lack of attention, impulsiveness, and hyperactivity. Behaviors that are associated with ADHD include those that:

- Affect the child in more than one setting, such as at home and at school.
- Are persistent, lasting for a considerable length of time.
- Impair academic or social functioning (Hirsch, 2008).

ADHD affects a small percentage of very young children. Prevalence rates and more discussion of symptoms and treatment are included in Chapter 12. Treatment for ADHD includes classroom modifications and medications; however, the appropriateness and effectiveness of treatment strategies continues to be researched.

Anxiety Disorders

Anxiety is a common emotional response, but when it is persistent and experienced with great intensity, it is considered a problem. It is estimated that about 15% of children experience anxiety disorders at some time (Beesdo, Knappe, Pine, 2009). Signs include being excessively tired, irritable, tense, and experiencing sleep disturbance. Treatment for anxiety disorders may include cognitive problem solving and behavior therapies. Cognitive problem solving might include discussing the potential realities of a fear and identifying ways children can manage them, such as helping a child explore a fear of the red light on the smoke detector. Behavior therapies involve having children gradually face their fears, such as helping a child practice making changes in routines. Medications are also sometimes used. The various types of anxiety disorders are described next.

Separation Anxiety Although common in infants and children up to 18 months of age, separation anxiety diminishes as children age and is not considered typical of older children. It is characterized by an extreme need to be near the parent or home. Behaviors may include inability to sleep alone or fear associated with separating from the parent when being left in the early childhood setting.

General Anxiety Disorder Children with general anxiety disorder express excessive worry about many things including future events, potential dangers such as earthquakes, or being on time. In the early childhood setting this may be seen when practicing for a fire drill. For example, Cathy, a 4-year-old, may begin displaying anxiety as soon as she sees her teacher bring out the home-style smoke alarm that he will use at group time when they will practice evacuating the classroom. Cathy worries about the loud noise made by the smoke alarm. Her teacher notices her discomfort and sets the alarm in a cupboard until group time. Then he asks Cathy if she would like to push the button to make the alarm sound, putting her in control of the situation, or if she would like to cover her ears, giving her an option to reduce the sound of the alarm.

Social Phobia Children with social phobia suffer from extreme shyness and discomfort in social situations, and they may selectively choose to not speak. Often children with social phobia will speak in the family setting, but not in public. Families can often shed light on this situation. Special sensitivity is needed to build the child's comfort with speaking in the classroom setting. Providing opportunities for the child to "talk" with puppets in a small group setting may be helpful.

Obsessive-Compulsive Disorder Children with obsessive-compulsive disorder (OCD) display obsessive and repetitive behaviors, such as repeated hand washing; insistence on routines, such as having the teacher stand in a certain place at the door during arrival and departure; and having things in their place. Teachers may also notice that children use nonsense words or sounds and that they describe reoccurring thoughts and themes for much longer than they would normally be of interest to most children.

Post-Traumatic Stress Disorder Post-traumatic stress disorder (PTSD) occurs after children have experienced or been exposed to a traumatic experience, such as extreme violence in the home or neighborhood or frequent instances of maltreatment. As a result children may be extremely worried, vigilant, and tense. This can be observed as the child watches others from the edge of play. The teacher might also notice that the child constantly keeps her eye on the teachers and parents as they come and go, noticing the details of what everyone is doing. Children who suffer from PTSD have difficulty relaxing and enjoying their play. Teachers assist by building children's sense of security, as in this example:

> Helena, teacher of the class for 3-year-olds, knows that Zack has experienced violence in his home. Zack and his mother now live in a "safe" house for women and children who have suffered from domestic violence, and he does not get to play outside very often due to their current living situation. Zack appears tense and unable to enjoy playing in the preschool. Helena makes arrangements with her coteachers to take Zack outside to play for 10 minutes on his own at the beginning of every day. She runs and plays ball with him and encourages him to climb and swing. After a few days of this routine, she sees that Zack is relaxing. They agree to invite a small group of children outside to play with him on the next day.

Approaches such as this acknowledge children's struggles and provide an option for working through fears in acceptable ways.

Mood Disorders

Mood disorders occur among very young children. They are complex and are treated with a variety of therapies. Mood disorders include bipolar disorders and depression.

Bipolar Disorder Extreme fluctuations in mood and energy are characteristics of bipolar disorder. Children with bipolar disorder may have long periods of normal behavior, and then swing to highly depressive behaviors and then to extreme manic episodes (high-energy swings) (Ball & Bindler, 2006). The types of behaviors and how they may be exhibited in the classroom are described in Table 13-4.

It is estimated that a very small percentage (<1%) of young children less than 8 years have bipolar disorder (Substance Abuse and Mental Health Services Administration, 2009). Bipolar disease is thought to be associated with an underlying biological condition;

bipolar disorder
a mental health condition characterized by extreme fluctuations in mood and energy

Table 13-4	Behaviors Associated with Bipolar Disorder	
Behaviors	**Description**	**Classroom Examples**
Depressive behaviors	• Passivity • Difficulty sleeping or eating • Feeling worthless • Unpredictably switching to manic behavior	• Child shows little interest in toys or other children. • Child appears excessively tired; is not interested in snacks or meals. • Child expresses self-doubt; can't be encouraged to participate.
Manic behaviors	• Excessive high energy • Risky behavior • Unpredictably switching to depressive behavior	• Child makes unusual movements, running, jumping, calling out, moving from activity to activity wildly. • Child tests boundaries; climbs and uses toys and equipment without regard to safety.

Source: *Bipolar Disorder* (NIH Publication 08-3679), U.S. Department of Health and Human Services, National Institutes of Health, and National Institute of Mental Health, 2008, retrieved October 11, 2009, from http://www.nimh.nih.gov/health/publications/bipolar-disorder/complete-index.shtml

however, it is difficult to pinpoint a specific cause. Treatment for bipolar disorder includes medication and various therapies such as cognitive and behavior therapies and family therapy, which are often combined with medications.

Teachers may be involved in logging children's behaviors in the classroom to help inform medical providers and mental health specialists about the child's participation. Teachers also support children with bipolar disorder by establishing familiar routines and guiding them to manage extreme behaviors by offering appropriate choices.

Depression A mental health disorder that causes disturbances in mood is known as depression. Children with depression can display a wide range of behaviors including sadness, irritability, anger, changes in appetite, fatigue, and recurring unexplained physical complaints (Prager, 2009). Depression can affect many aspects of health and wellness including growth and development, behavioral problems, academic performance, and relationships (Ball & Bindler, 2006; Prager, 2009).

The estimates of depression in young children are about 1% to 2%, and it occurs equally among boys and girls (Prager, 2009). Determining the actual cause of depression in young children can be very difficult because no definitive test is available. Evidence suggests that underlying biological causes, such as changes in brain chemistry, might affect a child's mood. Depression can also occur in response to environmental situations such as parental depression and child abuse or neglect (Ball & Bindler, 2006), parental substance abuse, family problems, low socioeconomic or education levels, and loss of a parent or sibling (Prager, 2009). About half of children with depression also have other mental health disorders (Ball & Bindler, 2006).

Medical professionals diagnose depression, giving careful attention to the child's medical history as well as details related to behavior, peer relationships, and behavioral symptoms. The length of time the child's daily functioning has been impaired and the presence of specific symptoms such as sleep disturbance, change in appetite, or thoughts of death are also considered. Sometimes families ask teachers for advice and guidance when they have worries about a child's behaviors, such as the potential for depression. Figure 13-4 illustrates how a teacher recognizes a child who is showing concerning symptoms. Although teachers do not make diagnoses, they do have a responsibility to support families by discussing their concerns, referring them to professional assistance, and working to address children's issues in the classroom.

depression
a mental health condition that causes disturbances in children's relationships; also affects eating and sleeping

What if. . .

it is early in the school year and you realize that one of your second graders, Raymond, spends the opening class meeting time staring at the floor. He never participates and when you try to engage him, he shakes his head, indicating that he doesn't want to speak. What can you do to help Raymond engage with you and his classmates?

Figure 13-4 Children's drawings may provide clues to how they are feeling. Other observations are needed to determine if this is a sign of depression

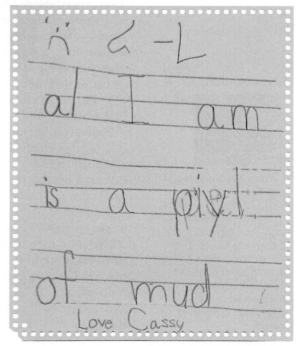

TEACHING CHILDREN WITH MENTAL HEALTH PROBLEMS

Children who experience mental health problems sometimes display significant behavior challenges. These are behaviors that are problematic, out of the ordinary, frequent, persistent, and sometimes dangerous. Children preschool age and younger may demonstrate frequent and persistent behaviors such as hitting, kicking, biting, and throwing toys or furnishings at other children and teachers. School-age children may display aggressive behaviors such as harming animals, starting fires, or fighting, bullying, and other forms of hostile physical or emotional interactions. Teaching children with these behaviors can be very difficult, because they introduce distress, discord, and upset in the classroom.

Significant behavior challenges require a great deal of the teacher's attention and energy to manage while at the same time trying to maintain a learning environment for the larger

Teachers use many strategies when managing children's challenging behaviors, including helping children recognize appropriate ways to interact.

group of children. Sometimes teachers feel that they are only "containing" children's behaviors and not helping them to move on to more positive ways of showing emotions and interacting. Teachers need a range of supports including ways to promote appropriate behaviors, approaches to manage them when they occur, and strategies to direct children from inappropriate to appropriate behaviors. They need to understand the resources that are available to them, such as families and mental health professionals.

Understanding Successful Integration

Many children with mental health problems participate successfully in early childhood classrooms. This success is founded on the attitudes and supports provided by the early childhood setting and teachers, as well as the candid involvement of families.

Characteristics That Support Success

Several characteristics describe programs that support the successful participation in the classroom of children with mental health issues. These include fostering positive attitudes toward the involvement of children with mental health problems and promoting strategic classroom practices by teachers who have competency in working with children who have these special needs (Brennan et al., 2003).

Successfully including children with mental health problems also requires that teachers, families, and program staff all see value in the participation of such children. This requires special efforts to create a common commitment to all children. Teachers are important in promoting this sense of community and acceptance among all children in the class. To accomplish this, they must address two issues. They must establish open and candid communication with the families of children who have mental health problems, and they must encourage other families to be welcoming to children with social and emotional concerns.

Supports Needed from Families

Teachers need the support of families whose children are experiencing mental health problems. These families need to be openly communicative and candid about their child's strengths and challenges so teachers will know how to plan for successful integration (Brennan et al., 2003). Both teachers and parents may have fears related to the participation of the child in the classroom. They may worry about difficult behaviors that will be hard to manage, or that the child will be unsafe, or not accepted by other children (Brennan et al., 2003). Parents of children with mental health problems need reassurance that their child will not be seen as a "bad child" and be "kicked out."

Planning a parent–teacher conference before the child joins the class, or soon after, provides the opportunity for families to provide a full description of the child's challenges, how those challenges have been successfully managed in the past, and clarification about any medical treatments that are in place. This sets the stage for open communication and offers opportunity for teachers to describe how they will help the child be successful in the classroom setting.

The successful involvement of children with mental health problems also relies on the positive attitudes of families whose children are typically developing. Creating a classroom motto that "everyone is welcome" is one way to introduce the concept that all children have a place in the early childhood setting. Offering social events that focus on helping families get acquainted builds a sense of common experience and togetherness. Families may be more resilient or "forgiving" when they occasionally observe a child displaying challenging behaviors if they know and appreciate one another.

MyEducationLab

Go to the Assignments and Activities section of Topic 10: Mental Health in the MyEducationLab for your course and complete the activity *Stress in Childhood*. Why is it important for families to communicate with teachers when a child is experiencing stress at home?

Finally, all families need to be able to see the concrete ways in which teachers are working to build cooperation and harmony in the classroom. Age-appropriate class group meetings where children discuss classroom rules or make a listing of appropriate behaviors demonstrate that teachers are working to educate all children about how to be an appropriate member of a community.

Strategies for Managing Significant Behavior Challenges

Early childhood programs and schools use a number of different strategies to address the significant behavior challenges that may be exhibited by children with mental health problems. These strategies are most effective when teachers address behavioral concerns as part of a continuum of approaches used for all children. A public health model provides the structure for thinking of behaviors along a continuum, and functional assessment approaches assist in identifying details of children's behaviors.

Using a Public Health Model

A public health model is a useful approach for managing significant behavior challenges in the classroom. The public health model focuses on promoting positive behaviors and interactions, preventing problems from occurring, and intervening when needed. The model identifies a three-level approach (Fox & Smith, 2007):

1. *Proactive strategies,* which promote appropriate development. These strategies are used for everyone. They include activities such as creating nurturing environments and establishing strong teacher and child relationships.
2. *Secondary strategies,* which are prevention oriented. These strategies are used for everyone, but are especially focused on children at risk for poor social and emotional development. Activities include conducting special social skills curriculum activities about building friendships and knowing about appropriate behaviors.
3. *Tertiary strategies,* which are intervention focused. These strategies are used for children who have signs of problems such as persistent and significant behavior challenges. Activities include conducting a functional analysis (described later) and implementing child-specific interventions.

The pyramid design depicted in Figure 13-5 highlights the perspective that most behavior challenges can be managed by proactive and prevention strategies, and that fewer behavior challenges rise to the level that requires use of focused interventions, or tertiary strategies.

The public health model is especially useful in early childhood settings because it uses a common approach to teach general social and emotional skills for all children while addressing situations when behaviors indicate that positive development is going off course. For this reason early childhood teachers plan activities and curriculum from two points of view (Brennan et al., 2003): implementing strategies that promote appropriate behaviors and strategies that transform or change inappropriate behaviors to more acceptable interactions.

Promotion Strategies Healthy social and emotional development and developmentally appropriate behaviors are fostered by using carefully planned promotion strategies. These strategies are used for all children, including those who are experiencing problems. Promotion strategies provide models of appropriate interactions and behaviors. Examples of promotion strategies that are useful for classrooms serving children with challenging behaviors are provided in Table 13-5.

> **What if. . .**
> a parent did not disclose that her child had a mental health disorder until after the child was enrolled in your class? Would this influence your relationship with the child or parent? Upon learning of the disorder, how would you respond?

promotion strategies strategies used to promote healthy social and emotional behaviors

Figure 13-5 A Public Health Model for Managing Behavior Challenges

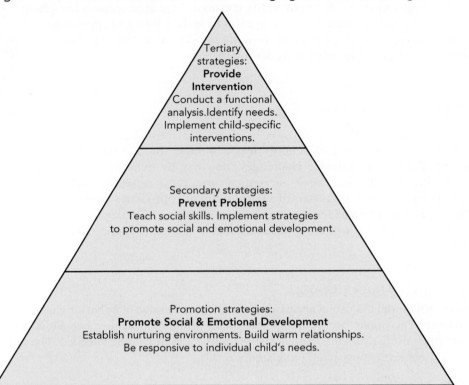

Tertiary
strategies:
**Provide
Intervention**
Conduct a functional
analysis. Identify needs.
Implement child-specific
interventions.

Secondary strategies:
Prevent Problems
Teach social skills. Implement strategies
to promote social and emotional development.

Promotion strategies:
Promote Social & Emotional Development
Establish nurturing environments. Build warm relationships.
Be responsive to individual child's needs.

Source: Adapted from *Promoting Social, Emotional and Behavioral Outcomes of Young Children Served under* IDEA (Policy Brief), by L. Fox and B. Smith, January 2007, Tampa, FL: Center for Evidence-Based Practice: Young Children with Challenging Behavior.

Other promotion strategies specifically targeted to children with behavior challenges include the following:

- Reviewing the ways transitions are managed in the classroom and developing supports for children who display challenging behaviors during this time. Teachers plan transition activities such as "follow my movement" games and singing songs and play word and rhyming games to help children focus and follow directions (Ostrosky, Jung, & Hemmeter, 2008).
- Setting clear boundaries and expectations for conduct. Teachers involve children in establishing classroom rules, talk about positive social behaviors, and provide consistent schedules with interesting choices (Brennan et al., 2003).
- Providing leadership opportunities. Teachers assign pairs of children to manage important tasks in the classroom, such as being the class "greeters" at arrival and departure time, passing out snack items, or being in charge of excusing other children from group time. This team approach builds children's individual sense of control and confidence, and guides children to practice interpersonal relationships (Bovey & Strain, 2008).
- Teaching empathy and responsibility. Teachers provide opportunities for children to care for animals and plants and to show care for other children (Brennan et al., 2003).

transformation strategies
strategies designed to manage negative emotions and change challenging behaviors

Transformation Strategies Children's negative emotions and challenging behaviors are guided to more appropriate actions by using transformation strategies. They involve teaching children to recognize what is wrong or inappropriate with the behavior they are exhibiting. For example, a teacher may tell a child that crying and

Teachers	Peers	Environment

Promotion Strategy #1: Build Relationship with Each Child

- Build relationship with each child based on trust and respect.
- Develop peer relationships with all children in classroom.
- Structure activities so that teachers and children interact frequently and positively.
- Provide one-on-one time as available when child first enrolling.

Promotion Strategy #2: Team with Families

- Encourage consistency between home/school.
- Learn about child's home culture.
- Determine goals family has for child.
- Peers should not be present when adults discuss challenges.
- Children participate in diverse cultural experiences.
- Make time for communication between staff and family.
- Document children's notable experiences.
- Ensure that activities and expectations are culturally appropriate.

Promotion Strategy #3: Work with Knowledge about Each Child's Individual Challenges

- Know what works at home for parents.
- Know key events in child's life.
- Plan for therapeutic activities when appropriate.
- Develop individualized activities that support children with challenges.
- Incorporate therapeutic activities.

Promotion Strategy #4: Use a Developmentally Appropriate Curriculum

- Curriculum should meet needs of all children at the center.
- Engage in common activities that include all children.
- Classroom activities are appropriate for all children.

Promotion Strategy #5: Balance Consistency and Flexibility

- Create a consistent, predictable day while maintaining flexibility.
- Peers model normal behavior.
- Peers receive rewards for healthy social behavior.
- Provide small, structured classroom areas.
- Ensure consistent schedules with choices.

Promotion Strategy #6: Assist Children in Feeling Safe and Calm

- Teach self-soothing behaviors.
- Use artistic expression of feelings.
- Remove child to quiet space when overstimulated.
- Peers withdraw to safe place when feeling anxious.
- Maintain appropriate levels of stimulation.
- Allows important work to be accomplished in small groups.
- Environment and space should promote safety and security.

Promotion Strategy #7: Use Multiple Sensory Channels

- Use physical guidance and touch.
- Attach words to positive feelings and actions using illustrations.
- Peers also use varied sensory activities.
- Non–English-speaking children learn English more rapidly.
- Provide visual schedules.
- Adults should be within reasonable physical proximity.

Promotion Strategy #8: Support Children Through Times of Transition

- Warn children about transitions.
- Spend time with child at drop-off.
- Model appropriate affect and behavior during transitions.
- Build stable staff and consistent staffing patterns.
- Provide transitional objects when appropriate.

Promotion Strategy #9: Promote the Social and Emotional Development Necessary for Learning

- Give opportunities for children to master behavior necessary for learning.
- Consider family cultural context when establishing literacy skills.
- Seek consultation when behavior is interfering with learning.
- Peers model behavior that promotes learning.
- Engage older children in activities such as being a "reading buddy."
- Make books available written in family's home language.
- Use activity kits that promote learning at home.
- Consultants assist with acquisitions of behaviors necessary for learning.

Source: *Setting the Pace: Model Inclusive Child Care Centers Serving Families of Children with Emotional or Behavioral Challenges*, by E. M. Brennan, J. R. Bradley, S. M. Ama, and N. Cawood, 2003, Portland, OR: Portland State University, Research and Training Center on Family Support and Children's Mental Health. Used with permission.

Table 13-6   Transformation Strategies for Managing Difficult Behaviors

Strategies for Teachers and Parents	Examples
Engage in preemptive planning.	• Watch for buildup of negative emotions in children. • Family communicates challenges recently experienced at home.
Develop formal behavior plans through consultation.	• Document incidents. • Use supervision and consultation. • Involve family in planning.
Encourage and assist child to use verbal self-expression.	• Enlist help from speech therapists. • Use signs with children with low verbal skills.
Substitute more appropriate behavior.	• Suggest alternative behaviors in positive terms. • Use art as a vehicle of expression. • Use drawings to illustrate desired behaviors and to indicate negative behaviors.
Foster problem solving.	• Talk through issues with verbal children. • Use drawings to illustrate working through issues. • Use action figures to act out situations.
Employ redirection.	• Use alternate, positive activity to distract child from distressing emotion. • Use alternate physical activity.
Focus attention appropriately.	• Learn behaviors children use to gain attention. • Comfort victims of aggression or children displaying positive behaviors.
Plan for safety of children.	• Plan strategies to keep children safe from their own behaviors and that of others.
Work as a team to address negative behavior.	• Other staff should back teacher up and provide relief. • Use team meetings to plan strategy.
Establish limits and set consequences for negative behavior.	• Emphasize choice with school-age children.
Regulate own emotions.	• Work to not feed children's anger. • Other staff provide back up when necessary.
Engage the school-age child in working through challenges.	• Engage child and family in planning process.

Source: *Setting the Pace: Model Inclusive Child Care Centers Serving Families of Children with Emotional or Behavioral Challenges*, by E. M. Brennan, J. R. Bradley, S. M. Ama, and N. Cawood, 2003, Portland, OR: Portland State University, Research and Training Center on Family Support and Children's Mental Health. Used with permission.

hitting is not appropriate, but asking for a toy is appropriate. As children mature, discussions may include setting goals for increasing appropriate behaviors, as in this example:

Anita, a preschool teacher, talks with 4-year-old Ted each morning reviewing their discussions about playing kindly, without hitting or pushing. During the day she acknowledges Ted's appropriate interactions with a smile, a wink, or pat on the shoulder. If problems occur during the day, Anita steps in to name them and she and Ted identify better choices. At the end of the day, they briefly summarize, "What went well today?" This requires a good deal of Anita's focus, but she is beginning to see progress over time.

Table 13-6 provides a list of transformation strategies. The suggestions include strategies that teachers can use to help change children's emotional reactions and challenging behaviors.

Conducting a Functional Assessment

When a child's significant behavior challenges are recognized, teachers use a focused process to reflect on, describe, and define what is occurring. This is called functional assessment. The Center on Social Emotional Foundations for Early Learning at Vanderbilt University promotes the use of functional assessment to facilitate understanding of children's social and emotional problems and how to address them (Fox & Duda, 2008; Homer, Albin, Sprague, Storey, Newton, 1997). Features of functional assessment include (Fox & Duda, 2008):

functional assessment
a process used to reflect on, describe, and define challenging behaviors

- *Describing the child's behaviors:* What? When? Where? How often? Intensity?
- *Recognizing events surrounding the behavior:* What tends to affect the behavior, such as changes in the routine and schedule, sleep challenges, or medical needs?
- *Identifying predictable events:* In what situations are the problem behaviors likely to occur?
- *Summarizing the child's play abilities:* What successes and difficulties does the child experience in play?
- *Understanding the function of problem behaviors:* What does the child get, or avoid doing, because of the behavior?
- *Reflecting on the effectiveness of the problem behavior:* What response does the child get? How quickly?

The goal of functional assessment is to determine the purpose of the problematic behavior, to design interventions to prevent the problem behavior, and to teach the child appropriate skills.

A functional assessment may be conducted individually by the teacher, or with a team that may include family members, behavior specialists, or counselors. Teachers conduct and record observations of the child's behavior and keep data to look for patterns of behavior. The team meets to learn about the family's experiences with the child's behavior, to discuss what was observed in the classroom, and to plan appropriate interventions.

This approach is successful in helping teachers and families work together to plan ways to prevent problem behaviors and to increase the effectiveness of managing the behaviors in the early childhood setting and home. Remembering the opening case scenario, Meegan may find that the functional assessment process would be a good next step to explore with Heather's family to address Heather's behavior concerns.

What if. . .

you have been hired to teach the kindergarten class? At the end of 2 weeks you find that a great deal of your attention is spent managing a child who displays extremely aggressive behaviors toward another child. Is the behavior unusual? What may be affecting the child's behaviors? How will you address this concern?

Engaging Families

The process of conducting a functional assessment is a reminder that engaging families of children who have mental health problems is key to creating a consistent behavior management plan. Promoting social and emotional development and enhancing children's skills for school success are part of the teacher and family partnership. Teachers invite family participation by teaching about approaches that prevent and address problems in children's social and emotional development, such as the following (Ewing Marion Kauffman Foundation, 2002):

- Modeling adult–child interactions that enhance the overall well-being of children, including making eye contact, addressing children by name, giving children warnings before activities are about to change, and verbally recognizing children's feelings.
- Supporting families to implement parenting approaches that encourage children's social and emotional development, such as providing appropriate opportunities for children to develop independence and autonomy and by using age-appropriate and developmentally appropriate guidance and supervision strategies.
- Inviting families to participate in training to expand competencies related to managing and preventing social and emotional problems.

When meeting with families teachers should encourage communication about parental expectations for guiding children's behaviors and expectations for their children in the classroom. Parenting styles, expectations of personal boundaries, and gender roles are all aspects that influence family expectations for children's behaviors. These need to be carefully explored and understood to facilitate an appropriate interpretation of behaviors. It can be challenging to navigate situations where the teacher observes problematic and possibly dangerous behaviors that the family views as "typical" and appropriate. Consider this example:

> Hector has been teaching 3-year-old Davonne to interact with the other children in the class without pushing and hitting. Davonne is beginning to control his impulse to hit by using his words. Davonne's dad arrives to pick him up from the play yard. Davonne's friend Karl runs by and pushes Davonne saying, "Try to catch me!" Davonne clenches his fists and says, "No pushing!" Hector is sorry that Davonne has been pushed, but he is happy to see that Davonne responded appropriately. Before he can get close enough to comfort and encourage Davonne, Davonne's dad grabs up his son and gives him a shake saying, "When someone hits you, you hit them back!" As Hector approaches the pair, quickly trying to summon the words to explain the behavior plan he has been working on, he realizes that Davonne's dad has been left out of the discussion.

When children have social and emotional challenges at school, families are impacted. Families may be surprised when the teacher identifies a cluster of behaviors as problematic, and not "just being a kid." Some families may feel embarrassed by their child and ashamed, isolated, or shunned. Here is an example:

> Rena, a second-grade teacher, observed Parker saying rude things to another child as he and his mother Kay left the building. Kay did not say anything, but put her hand on Parker's shoulder and quickly walked him to the car as some of the other parents stood by and watched. Rena knows that she needs to support Kay by talking about ways she and Kay can help Parker interact more positively.

Planning intentionally to engage with families and supporting them when problems occur are two ways to improve children's mental health.

Planning Intentionally

Early childhood settings that have been successful in including children with social and emotional needs report that facilitating family participation has been critical to their success (Brennan et al., 2003). This requires making intentional efforts to interact with families every day—not just when a child is having a behavior problem. This occurs through frequent informal contact such as when parents drop off and pick up their children, as well as through organized events such as special classroom visit days, family socials, field trips, and sporting events. Interacting with families on a regular basis builds relationships of mutual trust that are supportive when difficult subjects need to be discussed.

Demonstrating Sensitivity

Parents are often hesitant to discuss mental health issues. Some may feel that mental health issues are not as "real" as physical health issues and believe that people should be able to "fix" their own problems. Families want their children to be accepted by others; they may feel dismayed and embarrassed when their child displays behaviors that are out of the ordinary, aggressive, or problematic. If a mental health issue is identified, parents may wonder if they are to blame. They may find it difficult to reveal this situation to others, and they may not know what to do about it.

Active and supportive communication that includes being sensitive to unique family experiences and perspectives is key to successfully navigating discussions of children's mental health challenges. At times special creativity and problem-solving strategies are needed. For example, language barriers can make communication about children's mental health problems more complex. Discussions may use words and language that are not typically part of everyday communication. Special efforts are needed to ensure clear communication, such as obtaining the support of bilingual family members or qualified interpreters.

At other times teachers may need to approach situations with flexibility, good humor, and understanding. Some children with mental health problems have difficulty being flexible or adapting to rules that are different in different settings. For example, a child may arrive at class wearing a Halloween costume even though the teacher has specifically asked families *not* to send their child to school in costume. The parent may report that the child insisted on wearing the costume, stating that this was the only way they could get the child to school. It is easy to be frustrated when it seems that parents, too, are not "following the rules." However, in this situation, recognizing the challenges the family faces in managing the child's difficult behaviors, and drawing on good humor and understanding rather than frustration, helps the teacher and family negotiate the issue together. This builds a bond of mutual understanding and joint problem solving.

Being Accessible

Engaging with families also requires that teachers be open and approachable when families have questions and need help, and accessible when children's mental health concerns are challenging. Being accessible can be difficult because teachers are usually busy in the classroom during work hours and may not wish to share their telephone number or invite after-hour contacts. Alternative ways to be accessible and responsive to families while maintaining appropriate boundaries include providing a classroom e-mail address or creating a phone or note message system whereby families can ask the teacher to call them. Committing to making contact when such requests are made is an important obligation that teachers need to agree to if such arrangements are offered.

These activities help support the good working relationships that are needed when teachers and families work together to address a child's mental health concern. One teacher offered this summary of accessibility by reporting:

> My classroom parents know they can e-mail me when they have concerns about their child. I spend 15 minutes every evening before I go home answering e-mails. This helps us keep in touch, and the families tell me it makes them feel comfortable when they can share their concerns.

One goal of accessibility is to ensure that families are provided supports to help them cope with their child's challenges. This may involve talking about their concerns, finding other supportive people, and helping the family to recognize that the mental health concern is just one of many characteristics of their child.

What if. . .

a child arrived in your classroom wearing a Halloween costume, even though you had specifically reported to families that costumes would not be appropriate? What would be your approach to managing this situation with the child and family?

Collaborating with Mental Health Professionals

Collaboration with mental health professionals, such as behavior specialists, counselors, nurses, or physicians, provides an important benefit to children who are at risk for or have been diagnosed with a mental health disorder (Ewing Marion Kauffman Foundation, 2002). Consultation supports teachers and families when they are not able to understand children's behaviors and symptoms and need help managing concerns in the school and home. Together, teachers, families, and mental health professionals can usually design an appropriate management plan to address the challenges and assist children to develop coping strategies.

Services provided by mental health consultants include conducting observations of children in the classroom and home setting. Consultation is provided to sort out ways to foster healthy social and emotional development and to manage behavior challenges. The consultant is also an important resource for understanding services that may be available to the child and family in the community, such as public or private family counseling and behavior management "safety net" programs that teach parenting skills and provide respite for families as needed. The mental health consultant may also play a role in helping children's programs and schools develop policies and procedures to promote children's mental health (Brennan et al., 2003).

Early childhood settings also offer a supportive environment for meetings between families and mental health consultants. Children's programs are trusted and familiar places for accessing mental health services. Other benefits to linking families with mental health consultants through the early childhood program include opportunities for mental health professionals to (Ewing Marion Kauffman Foundation, 2002):

- Have brief but frequent interactions with children and families. This is efficient for families and allows the mental health professional to see children in their natural environment.
- Address the needs of all children in the program, not only the child at risk, to participate in prevention efforts and to address problems when they arise.
- Participate in team meetings with teachers and families.
- Advise teachers and families about how to establish environments that foster good mental health.

Providing mental health services in the early childhood setting is a prevention effort that benefits the many children who are enrolled. In this way early childhood teachers and their programs contribute to public health by ensuring that children's social and emotional needs are recognized and addressed. In addition, having access to a behavioral consultant supports teachers to implement successful strategies and greatly reduces the number of children who are expelled from preschool (Gilliam, 2005).

Unfortunately, few early childhood teachers have access to mental health consultants and not all schools have counselors or behavior specialists on staff. Community resources may be available to provide some assistance. Local early intervention services for children with special developmental needs or community health services may offer some supports.

Pursuing professional development training related to children's mental health and advocating for resources to access occasional mental health consultation are other important ways teachers build skills and raise awareness of the importance of children's mental health. Teachers are in a good position to engage in advocacy efforts that bring attention to the need for mental health services for young children. The *Policy Point* describes advocacy features that teachers and families can support and that young children need.

Policy Point

TEACHERS AS ADVOCATES FOR CHILDREN'S MENTAL HEALTH POLICIES

Teachers are in a unique position to recognize children's mental health challenges and to advocate for policies to support services that:

Promote social and emotional development by:

- Raising awareness about children's mental health.
- Increasing focus on social and emotional development.

Prevent mental health problems and address their consequences by:

- Increasing training and professional development to support teachers who work with young children.
- Providing access to mental health consultants who are knowledgeable about challenging behaviors.
- Making mental health supports available to families.

Treat mental health concerns by:

- Improving screening and assessment for mental health problems among young children.
- Supporting children and families who have been affected by substance abuse, child abuse and neglect, and other forms of violence.

Source: *Helping Young Children Succeed: Strategies to Promote Early Childhood Social and Emotional Development* (Early Childhood: Research and Policy Report), by J. Cohen, N. Onunaku, S. Clothier, and J. Poppe, 2005, Denver, CO: Zero to Three and National Conference of State Legislatures. Retrieved October 11, 2009, from http://www.ncsl.org/programs/pubs/summaries/016168-sum.htm.

Summary

Social and emotional development and mental health are synonymous. They refer to children's capacities to manage and express appropriate emotional responses and behaviors, to form close relationships, and to explore and learn. Children who are supported to develop these capabilities are able to adjust successfully to new situations and build positive future relationships. They are also more likely to experience success in school.

Social and emotional development is influenced by various factors including children's experiences in the home and early childhood environment. In the classroom, teachers foster children's social and emotional development by creating supportive environments, by nurturing strong attachment relationships, and by providing ample time for children to explore social relationships through unstructured play.

Sometimes children experience mental health problems that are revealed through significant behavior challenges. Working with families and mental health professionals, teachers help to identify strategies to manage children's difficult behaviors in the classroom and promote more appropriate behaviors and interactions. Young children can, and do, experience mental health disorders. Identifying these conditions is important because early intervention can improve emotional and behavioral outcomes and positively affect learning.

MyEducationLab

To assess your understanding of how to teach children who may be experiencing mental health issues, go to the Book Specific Resources section in the MyEducationLab for your course, select *Nutrition, Health, and Safety for Young Children*, Chapter 13 of the Study Plan, and then complete the multiple choice questions and activities.

Key Terms

Approaches to learning, p. 430

Attachment, p. 425

Bipolar disorder, p. 436

Caregiver, p. 417

Continuum of mental health, p. 416

Depression, p. 437

Egocentric, p. 420

Functional assessment, p. 443

Promotion strategies, p. 439

Self-regulation, p. 429

Transformation strategies, p. 440

Review Questions

1. Describe biological and environmental factors that contribute to children's mental health.

2. What essential skills do children need to form positive relationships?

3. Describe characteristics of early childhood programs that can have a positive impact on social and emotional health.

4. What aspects of social and emotional development contribute to school readiness?

5. What are some strategies teachers can use when working with children who exhibit challenging behaviors?

Discussion Starters

1. Think of a child of any age who you know or have worked with who exhibited difficult behaviors. Do you know of any risk factors the child had such as poverty or coming from a single-parent household? Can you think of any specific warning signs?

2. Consider a child in the early childhood setting who has been exposed to a significant amount of violence and is displaying severe aggression in the classroom. Can you apply the principles of inclusion described in the chapter? How do you feel about including these children in the classroom? Can you describe advantages and disadvantages to inclusion?

3. Based on what you have read about risk factors that contribute to poor mental health in children, can you think of national policies that either contribute to these risk factors or that help alleviate the stress of these factors on children? What services available in your community help families who are at risk?

Practice Points

1. Teachers have endless opportunities in the classroom to promote social and emotional development through establishing healthy relationships and promoting healthy play activities. Can you develop ways in which teachers can engage families in promoting healthy social and emotional development?

2. Mood disorders can interfere with healthy social and emotional development. Can you think of specific ways to help children with mood disorders establish healthy relationships with their peers in the classroom?

3. Develop a list of resources and agencies in your community that can help early childhood programs manage challenging behaviors.

Web Resources

Children and Mental Health Fast Facts
http://mentalhealth.samhsa.gov/publications/allpubs/fastfact5/default.asp

National Center for Child Poverty: Mental Health in Children
http://www.nccp.org/publications/pub_687.html

Zero to Three: Early Childhood Mental Health
http://www.zerotothree.org/site/PageServer?pagename=key_mental

Promoting Safety

part 4

chapter 14 | Ensuring Physical and Emotional Safety

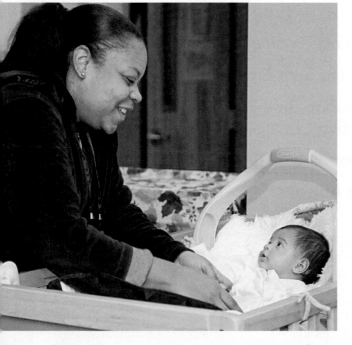

After reading this chapter, you should be able to:

1. Define different aspects of safety and explain the influence of safety on children's growth and development.

2. Identify the most frequent causes for unintentional injury and fatal injury in young children and describe some of the risk factors that affect children's potential for injury.

3. Describe some of the safety standards promoted by licensing regulations and give examples of how they impact children's safety.

4. Compare the different responsibilities that early childhood program leaders and teachers are in charge of and describe how each activity contributes to safety in the children's environment.

5. Describe how teachers demonstrate their commitment to children's physical and emotional safety.

Cass and her husband Everett are looking for child care for their 2-year-old son, Caden. Their friends child attends Sunshine Child Development Center, and they have spoken highly about the program, so Cass and Everett schedule a visit. They have been reading online about how to select a quality program and are prepared with a checklist of questions. Barb, the classroom teacher, greets them, gives them a tour of the classrooms and play yard, and describes the curriculum.

Cass likes the colorful environment and the buoyant involvement of the children. Everett is impressed by the pretend tide pool touch table and the way the teacher is exploring the display with the children by dabbling her hands in the water and talking about the oceans. The class looks inviting and fun. However, they have concerns. They have never left Caden in a setting without individual attention and they worry about whether he will be safe. Cass asks tentatively, "Are you and the other teachers trained in first aid?"

Barb realizes that this young family needs reassurance that the Sunshine Center will take excellent care of Caden. She describes the training and required certifications of the teachers and explains the program's safety policies. They sit for a few minutes in the classroom for 2-year-olds where she gives some specific examples of how teachers are assigned to supervise a particular group of children, and she points out decisions made about the room arrangement that help ensure child safety. As they watch, Cass and Everett observe a teacher holding a child who has fallen down. They like the way she comforts the child and then treats the hurt, using gloves and speaking calmly. When they leave they feel confident that they have found a setting that will be a good fit for Caden and for them.

Families today are concerned about choosing a quality early childhood program and have many questions about safety when they select a setting for their child. Even families who are less aware of safety and quality indicators use their first impressions to determine whether the program is right for their child. They observe the security of the facility and watch how the teachers and children interact. Sometimes families simply have a "feeling" about a program's safety features. They need information and reassurance that their child will be supervised and kept safe. Teachers need to understand these concerns and be prepared to describe the safety practices of their classroom.

Ensuring children's **safety** is a fundamental responsibility of early childhood teachers. Threats to children's safety exist in all parts of the physical and emotional environments in which children grow and learn. This means teachers need to be proactive and prepared in order to keep children safe. Safety in the early childhood setting *is no accident!* It is established when teachers merge knowledge of child growth and development with recognition of the potential risks to children's safety. Teachers learn to pay attention to the possibility for accidents and are prepared to take the steps needed to reduce risk. Understanding and acting on this information is an important part of the process of becoming a teacher and early childhood professional.

A variety of hazards present risks to children's safety. Among these are accidents caused by risks in the environment, poor supervision and safety management practices, weather and other natural disasters, and violence in the community and in the home. In this chapter we introduce information to begin the process of building the knowledge and confidence that teachers need to ensure children's safety. We describe the importance of safety to children's healthful growth and development and discuss the accidental injuries that occur most frequently during childhood. We explore the safety standards and regulations that guide the creation of safe early childhood classrooms and safety management practices. Finally we clarify the responsibilities of early childhood programs and teachers that create the safety net for children in early childhood settings.

In the chapters that follow we will discuss in detail how to create safe environments, implement safety practices, and build teachers' abilities to respond effectively to emergencies and support children who may be experiencing abuse and neglect.

Families want to know about safety features when they make decisions about enrolling their children in early childhood classrooms.

safety
protection from harm or danger

Keeping children safe is an important responsibility. Understanding the risks to safety and learning ways to reduce the potential for accidental injury is the first step in effective safety management.

ENSURING PHYSICAL AND EMOTIONAL SAFETY

Young children grow and mature quickly during the early years. Because of this, teachers need to understand the role of safety in children's typical growth and development. Teachers also need to recognize the influence of development on children's physical ability to navigate safely in the world and their emotional maturity to make safe decisions.

Understanding the Impact of Safety on Healthful Development

Although ensuring children's safety is naturally focused on avoiding harm and pain, it is also a foundational requirement for children's healthful development. Safety is crucial to children's ability to grow, thrive, and develop to their full potential. This involves meeting children's basic needs and addressing their physical and emotional safety requirements.

Maslow's Hierarchy of Needs

Safety is a basic requirement upon which all healthy human development depends (Maslow, 1954). This perspective describes human development as having a hierarchy, or ladder, of needs. Maslow's hierarchy describes the five levels of need that are required by the developing person in order to grow healthfully and to achieve his or her full potential. Figure 14-1 illustrates Maslow's theory as it relates to healthful child development.

The first level describes the physiological (bodily) needs for air, food, and drink. These needs are crucial for basic survival. The second level includes safety needs such as security (protection) and psychological (emotional) well-being. Next are needs related to love and belonging (need for care and nurturing from others), self-esteem (a need for a sense of personal competence and social acceptance), and finally self-actualization (the need to use cognitive knowledge, problem solving, and creative expression).

Maslow (1954) proposed that optimal human development requires each level of need to be satisfied before children can then go on to meet their needs at the next higher level in the hierarchy. Children's security at the first levels builds the foundation on which the more advanced aspects of development depend. When children are in out-of-home care settings, the task of meeting these needs falls to the teachers and early childhood program. It is a reminder of the important contribution that teachers make to young children's physical and emotional safety, essential aspects of children's well-being. This relationship is depicted in Figure 14-2.

Physical Safety

Attending to children's physical safety involves protecting them from bodily harm and injury, such as bumps, bruises, cuts, and scrapes. Any injury that harms children's bodies is a violation of their physical safety. Physical safety is considered in all aspects of program planning for nutrition, health, and general safety practices. For example, safety is a concern when selecting foods and drafting menus for snacks and meals, and when determining the infant feeding practices or meal presentations for older children. It is a key consideration when establishing practices to promote healthy development, such as providing ample time for children to play actively, and to avoid the spread of germs that may lead to disease and illness.

Consideration of children's physical safety is also foremost when designing facilities and selecting toys, materials, and equipment for the classroom. Many aspects of the environment can introduce risks to children's physical safety, such as toxic products used in making toys, broken toys or equipment, or play equipment that is too challenging for children's age and developmental capabilities. Teachers are generally accustomed to planning for and supervising children to avoid physical harm, and they know that this is a very important part of the teaching responsibility. But physical safety is only one important aspect of a child's well-being that must be considered. Emotional safety is another significant element of a child-safe environment.

Emotional Safety

Emotional safety refers to children's internal sense of safety, including being protected and sheltered and free from threat—either real or perceived. Children who feel emotionally safe are able to be attentive to their environment and open to learning from experiences. They are better able to be responsive to the guidance of the teacher and to follow safety rules. Emotional safety is a component of positive mental health that enables children to establish a sense of personal value or worthiness (Cohen, Onunaku, Clothier & Poppe, 2005). It provides children the foundation from which positive social interactions can be built (Shonkoff & Phillips, 2000). Whereas physical safety refers to protection from bodily injury, emotional safety refers to protection from experiences that damage the child's spirit and sense of personal value or worth.

Emotional safety is achieved by providing children with experiences that are free from anxiety and fear; experiences where they feel free to develop trust and confidence (Cohen et al., 2005). Emotional safety is supported through developmentally appropriate programming such as offering a favorable teacher-to-child ratio, establishing reliable and predictable schedules, and offering developmentally appropriate activities. It is also encouraged by planning activities that help children develop attachment to the teacher and class group.

For infants, emotional safety is established through responsive and caring relationships and safe sensory experiences such as sounds that are soothing, touch that is kind, and food that is provided on a regular schedule. Preschoolers and older children experience emotional safety when teachers guide them to learn appropriate ways of interacting and when teacher's step in to ensure that no child experiences bullying or intimidation (National Association for the Education of Young Children [NAEYC], 2005; Shonkoff & Phillips, 2000).

In the opening case scenario, Cass and Everett wanted to know how the teacher will keep their 2-year-old physically and emotionally safe. But they may not use these exact words. Instead they may ask, "How do you keep the classroom secure from intruders?" "What do you do if a child hits?" or "How will you protect my child from bullying?" Teachers need to be prepared to offer concrete examples and confident descriptions of how physical and emotional safety will be supported in the classroom.

Creating a Refuge for Children

Early childhood classrooms are a refuge for children. They offer spaces where children can be free from worry about their physical and emotional safety, which allows them to relax and learn. As depicted in Figure 14-3 some children face many challenges in their daily lives

Figure 14-1 Maslow's Hierarchy Highlights the Importance of Safety

The need for
SELF-ACTUALIZATION
Creativity, spontaneity, problem solving, lack of prejudice

The need for
ESTEEM
Respect, confidence, social acceptance

The need for
LOVE and BELONGING
Care and support
from family and friends

The need for
SAFETY
Physical and emotional security,
protection from violence and aggression

The need to meet
PHYSIOLOGICAL Requirements
Basic bodily needs for air, food, water, shelter

Source: Maslow, A. H. *Toward a psychology of being* (2nd ed.) (1968). New York, New York: Van Nostrand Reinhold.

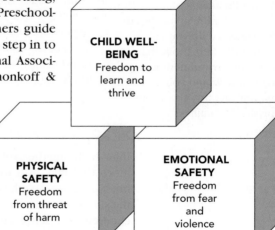

CHILD WELL-BEING
Freedom to learn and thrive

PHYSICAL SAFETY
Freedom from threat of harm

EMOTIONAL SAFETY
Freedom from fear and violence

Figure 14-2 Physical and Emotional Safety Serve as Supports for a Child's Well-Being

Figure 14-3 The Classroom Is a Refuge from Threats to Children's Physical and Emotional Safety

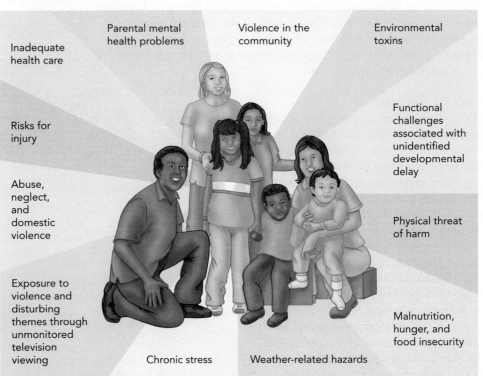

Source: Based on *From neurons to neighborhoods: The science of early childhood development*, edited by J.P. Shonkoff and D.A. Phillips, 2000, Washington, DC: National Academy Press, retrieved October 12, 2009, from http://www.nap.edu/openbook.php?isbn=0309069882

What if. . .

you taught a class of 5-year-olds that included children who live in a violent neighborhood? What steps would you take to help the children know that the classroom environment is a safe place? How would you communicate this classroom approach to families?

outside of the early childhood classroom. Some of these involve negative experiences that can harm children's brain development, such as violence, abuse, and unsafe living conditions (Shonkoff & Phillips, 2000).

Teachers who create classroom environments that protect children from threats and ensure their physical and emotional safety introduce a vision of a healthy lifestyle that supports children in two ways. First, children are provided a direct opportunity to rest, be nurtured, and learn within the secure environment. Second, seeds are planted for the future; children are given concrete experiences of safe and healthy living that gives them hope and broadens their understanding of what their futures can be.

Recognizing Unintentional Injuries

unintentional injury
injury from accident

Injuries during the early years range from incidental accidents and "ouches" to significant injuries that may lead to lifelong disability or even death. These are called unintentional injuries. They include the familiar bumps and tumbles that occur as toddlers learn to walk, the skinned knees that seem to come with the preschool years, and the scrapes and bruises children experience during the early elementary years as they move around their environments and follow their natural curiosity to explore and discover. Unintentional injuries also include severe accidents that have potentially disabling outcomes.

Many children suffer from unintentional injuries each year. During 2008, nearly 4 million children were treated in hospital emergency rooms for unintentional injuries (Centers for Disease Control and Prevention [CDC], 2007). The number of unintentional injuries is probably higher, however, because many are never reported or treated in formal

Table 14-1	National Estimates of the Ten Leading Causes of Nonfatal Injuries, United States, 2007, Highlighting the Three Leading Causes of Injury		
Rank	**Birth–1 year**	**1–4 Years**	**5–9 Years**
1	Fall 120,316	Fall 828,773	Fall 599,540
2	Struck by or against 32,970	Struck by or against 370,572	Struck by or against 399,262
3	Bite or sting 11,787	Bite or sting 134,641	Cut or pierce 111,914
4	Foreign body 11,508	Foreign body 125,000	Cycling 95,871
5	Fire and burns 10,378	Overexertion 83,099	Bite or sting 84,977
6	Other 7,980	Cut or pierce 82,804	Overexertion 80,799
7	Suffocation 6,297	Other specified 60,323	Motor vehicle (occupant) 60,068
8	Unspecified 6,138	Fire and burns 51,651	Foreign body 53,679
9	Overexertion 6,011	Unspecified 46,823	Other transport 45,527
10	Cut or pierce 5,863	Poisoning 41,737	Unspecified 43,323
Total	**219,401**	**1,825,423**	**1,574,960**

Source: *National Estimates of the 10 Leading Causes of Nonfatal Injuries Treated in Hospital Emergency Departments, United States, 2007,* by the Centers for Disease Control and Prevention, National Center for Injury Prevention & Control, Office of Statistics and Programming, retrieved October 2009 from http://www.cdc.gov/ injury/Images/LC-Charts/10lc%20-%20Nonfatal%20Injury%202007-7_6_09.jpg

settings. Overall, it is projected that unintentional injuries affect 10% of young children each year (CDC, 2008). This highlights the importance of vigilance and keeping children safe. Knowing about the causes of injury and their impacts is a good first step.

Causes of Unintentional Injury

The incidence and causes of unintentional injuries are tracked by the CDC. Table 14-1 summarizes the 10 most frequent causes of unintentional injury among babies (up to age 1), toddlers and preschoolers (ages 1 to 4), and primary school–age children (ages 5 to 9). Some causes of childhood injury are relatively familiar, such as burns, whereas other causes are less familiar, such as overexertion.

The majority of unintentional injuries for all age groups are caused by three major types of injury (CDC, 2007):

- **Falls:** Falls are the leading cause of injury in children under the age of 9. In 2007, over 1.5 million children nationwide were treated in hospital emergency rooms due to accidental falls: from cribs, high chairs, beds, chairs, bath tubs, and playground climbing equipment. The risk for falls is the single most important concern for child safety.
- **Struck by or against injury:** Being struck or striking against objects is the second most frequent cause of treated injury for young children, accounting for almost a quarter (22%) of the unintentional injuries for the age group. These injuries occur when babies

fall
injury received when a person descends abruptly due to the force of gravity and strikes a surface at the same or a lower level

struck by or against injury
resulting from being hit or by hitting against an object

pull objects over onto themselves, toddlers wobble into the edge of table tops, or preschoolers and early elementary children accidentally hit each other with toys or sports equipment. The world around young children provides many risks for injury by striking.

- **Bite or sting injury:** Bites and stings are the third most frequent cause and account for more than 6% of unintentional childhood injuries. Bites or stings include human, animal, or insect bites, as well as insect, jellyfish, or plant stings.

Accidents due to these three causes accounted for more than 2.6 million treated injuries in 2007 (CDC, 2007).

Identifying Injury Patterns

Unintentional injuries also appear to occur in recognizable patterns within certain age groups. For example, in children under the age of 2 (Agran et al., 2003):

- The incidence of battering and neglect is highest among babies birth to 5 months old.
- The numbers of babies falling from stairs is highest among babies 6 to 12 months old.
- Hot liquids injure more children ages 12 to 17 months than any other age group.
- Poisoning by medications occurs most frequently among 21- to 23-month-old children.
- Children ages 15 to 17 months experience the highest overall injury rate for any age group under the age of 15.

Teachers need to be generally knowledgeable about the causes of unintentional injury and understand the potential risks for each age group. This information helps to focus attention on preventive actions.

Costs Due to Childhood Injuries

Unintentional injuries also involve a variety of medical and indirect costs. The medical costs related to treatment of unintentional injuries in children are estimated at $17 billion a year (Danseco, Miller, & Spicer, 2000). This direct cost for injury care is staggering, but it is probably a low estimate because many childhood injuries are cared for in the home or early childhood setting and are never reported.

Indirect costs associated with childhood injury include lost income by parents who must leave work to care for their injured child or the child's own loss of future income as a result of a disabling injury (Danseco et al., 2000). The long-range impact of disabling injury can be significant.

The costs for long-term care and management of the disability can be very difficult for families, causing disruptions and challenges that can have negative impacts on the child and family. Providing high standards of safety is one way that teachers make a long-term health contribution to the children they teach and an economic contribution to their communities.

Defining Fatal Injuries

Some unintentional injuries ultimately lead to death. These are called fatal injuries. Table 14-2 discusses the most frequent causes of fatal injuries among young children. For teachers the possibility of a child dying from an injury sustained while in the early childhood setting is unthinkable. But the early years are a time of fast growth and rapid change that increases children's vulnerability. Their ability to put themselves at risk can often outpace their judgment. Children rely on the adults in their lives—families and teachers—to keep them safe. One way to be proactive is to recognize the causes of fatal injuries and to take action to reduce children's risk.

Falls are the leading cause of injury among children under the age of 9.

Table 14-2	Ten Leading Causes of Injury Death by Age Group, United States, 2006, Highlighting the Four Leading Causes for Death Due to Injury		
Rank	**Birth–1 Year**	**1–4 Years**	**5–9 Years**
1	Unintentional suffocation 843	Motor vehicle and traffic 471	Motor vehicle and traffic 515
2	Homicide 179	Drowning 458	Drowning 142
3	Motor vehicle and traffic 139	Fire and burns 202	Fire and burns 118
4	Homicide: other specified 75	Homicide: unspecified 166	Homicide: firearm 62
5	Drowning 51	Unintentional suffocation 137	Unintentional: other land transport 50
6	Undetermined: suffocation 42	Pedestrian 113	Unintentional suffocation 50
7	Homicide: suffocation 36	Homicide: other 51	Homicide: unspecified 24
8	Fire and burns 28	Homicide: firearm 42	Unintentional: other transport 22
9	Three sources tied: Unintentional falls, undetermined, unspecified 23	Fall 38	Pedestrian 22
10	Three sources tied: Unintentional falls, undetermined, unspecified 23	Natural/Environment 37	Two sources tied: firearm and poisoning 18
Total	**1,437**	**1,715**	**1,023**

Source: *10 Leading Causes of Injury Death by Age Group Highlighting Unintentional Injury Deaths, United States, 2006*, Centers for Disease Control and Prevention, National Center for Injury Prevention and Control. Office of Statistics and Programming, retrieved October 2009, from http://www.cdc.gov/injury/Images/LC-Charts/10lc%20-%20Violence%20Related%202006-7_6_09.jpg

Incidence of Fatal Injuries

Fatal injuries are the leading cause of death for children ages 1 to 9 years (CDC, 2006); that is, more deaths are caused by fatal injuries than by disease or congenital defects. In 2006, nearly 4,000 child deaths were attributed to unintentional injury. Deaths due to injury occurred most often in the 1- to 4-year-old age group (toddlers and preschoolers), followed by school-age children (5 to 9 years of age) and infants (birth to 1 year) (CDC, 2006).

Causes of Fatal Injury

Four primary causes of fatal injury have been identified by the CDC (2006):

- *Motor vehicle and traffic accidents* are the leading cause of death due to injury for children ages birth through 9 years, accounting for 1,125 deaths in 2006.
- Suffocation is ranked second, accounting for 1,030 deaths for children under age 9 in 2006. The majority of death by suffocation occurs among infants.
- Drowning is ranked third, causing over 650 child deaths in 2006. The majority of the deaths due to drowning occurred in the 1- to 4-year-old age group. Sources of drowning

suffocation
inhalation, aspiration, or ingestion of food or other object that blocks the airway, causing suffocation

drowning
suffocation (asphyxia) resulting from submersion in water or another liquid

fatalities include standing water in buckets, toilets, wading pools, home swimming pools, and pool covers that collect rainwater.

- Burns are ranked fourth. These injuries caused 348 child deaths in 2006.

Recognizing Risk Factors for Unintentional Injury

A range of factors influence the incidence of injuries and fatalities due to injury among children (Danseco et al., 2000). These include children's age, developmental maturity, sex, race, family income, location of residence (urban or rural), and children's individual risk profile. Figure 14-4 depicts some of these influences. Their influence on actual risk for injury for a particular child is a matter of speculation, as described next.

Children's Age and Developmental Maturity

Children's age and maturity greatly influence risk for injury. Along with growth and physical maturation come new motor skills that introduce a key risk for injury. Children who are less mobile may be unable to move away from dangers. This makes suffocation the number one cause of death for children under the age of 1 year. As children become more mobile, they are able to put themselves into dangerous situations because their mobility may exceed their maturity for recognizing and avoiding danger. For example, physically adept 1- to 4-year-olds may put themselves into danger of drowning by exploring water sources. This age group also experiences high numbers of injuries due to falls and being struck or striking against objects as children test their emerging climbing and movement skills. Children in the 5- to 9-year-old age group gain opportunities to move about more freely, such as walking and bicycling near traffic, which can also introduce new dangers. These factors highlight the importance of adult supervision.

Although the numbers of injuries tend to be higher among preschoolers and young primary age children, more deaths (75%) due to injury occur among infants and preschoolers (CDC, 2006). The high fatal injury rate for babies includes the large number of infants who die as result of sudden infant death syndrome (SIDS). SIDS is the sudden and unexplainable death of a young child and is the leading cause of death of children under the age of 1 year (National Institute of Child Health and Human Development [NICHHD], 2006). Fatalities for the 1- to 4-year-old age group are largely due to traffic and pedestrian causes, as well as drowning and fire injuries (CDC, 2006).

As children age and mature, the risks for some injuries decrease. For example, the rates for death from pedestrian causes drop as children age. This suggests that children become more able to understand dangers and be responsive to educational guidance about staying away from traffic (CDC, 2006).

Children's Sex

A higher fatality rate due to injury is seen among boys than girls (Danseco et al., 2000). This may be because boys are often encouraged to take risks and may be allowed to test their skills more freely, or they may receive less supervision.

Children's Race

Injury rates are higher among white children than among children from other racial backgrounds. However, fatal injuries occur more often among Black and American Indian/Alaskan Native children than White children (Danseco et al., 2000; Pressley, Barlow, Kendig, & Paneth-Pollak, 2007). Black children are twice as likely and American Indian infants are three times more likely to die

Figure 14-4 Individual Risk Factors for Unintentional Injuries

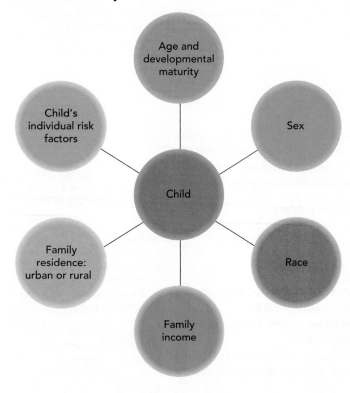

of SIDS than White infants (NICHHD, 2006). These higher mortality rates due to injury may suggest exposure to more severe injuries or less access to follow-up health care or both.

Family Income

Children from families with very low incomes (below $5,000 per year) tend to have the highest numbers of unintentional injuries (Danseco et al., 2000). Reasons for this may include unsafe conditions in the home due to limited resources, or the community surrounding the low-income housing may introduce more dangers.

Location of Child's Residence

Injury rates as well as numbers of fatal injuries are higher for children living in rural areas than for children living in cities (Danseco et al., 2000). Although the numbers of fatal injuries in agricultural settings has decreased in recent years, the number of unintentional injuries has increased (American Academy of Pediatrics [AAP], 2001). Children who live in rural areas are exposed to a variety of risks, including the presence of large animals and farm machinery. These children may be allowed to assume responsibilities that exceed their developmental maturity for understanding safety risks, such as feeding large animals or using equipment, or they may receive less supervision.

The risk for injury is high among children who live in rural areas where a variety of risks, including water sources, large animals, and farm machinery, are present.

sudden infant death syndrome (SIDS)
under the age of 1 year the sudden and unexplainable death of a young child

Individual Child Risk Profile

Individual children also have their own unique patterns and characteristics that form his or her risk profile, or individual potential for injury (Wrigley & Dreby, 2005). This includes aspects of the child's style, such as how the child approaches a new situation or responds to direction, that might affect their safety in the early childhood setting.

When families enroll their children in a program, they often share information that alerts the teacher to aspects of a child's style that may need special attention for safety. A parent might report that the child "Always climbs on things" or say that "He runs away a lot" or "She always puts toys in her mouth." Teachers use this information along with direct observation and interaction with the child to develop an awareness of the child's pattern, temperament, and style. This information is used to recognize potential risks that may be significant for that particular child.

Identifying Risk Factors for Unintentional Injury

Most reported injuries to young children occur in the home setting (Danseco et al., 2000). Out-of-home child care and early childhood settings are generally considered to be safe environments for young children (Wrigley & Dreby, 2005). Child injury in early childhood settings accounts for only about 15% of the total reported injuries of young children (Currie & Hotz, 2004). However, accidents do occur and some children's settings are safer than others (Wrigley & Dreby, 2005).

A detailed study was conducted to examine the numbers of fatal injuries reported in child care settings across the United States (Wrigley & Dreby, 2005). The review looked at the numbers of fatal injuries reported from three types of early childhood settings: child care centers, family child care homes (usually smaller groups of children in the provider's home setting), and in-home child care (care provided for children in the child's home). Of the nearly 1,400 fatal injuries reviewed, the fewest (110) occurred in child care centers. The most fatalities occurred in family child care homes where more than 700 child deaths were reported. In-home child care reported 320 deaths.

It was postulated that fewer fatalities occurred in child care centers because of the more open nature of the environment and the presence of two or more teachers. In addition,

What if. . .

you learned during the enrollment process that a 3-year-old child had experienced two visits to the emregency room as a result of climbing on high shelving in the family's home? In addition, you are told that one time the child was pinned under a television that he had pulled over. How would this information affect your planning? What steps would you take to increase the safety of this child in your classroom?

teachers in child care centers are easily observed, allowing supervisors and other teachers to provide advice regarding safety practices, assist with challenges, and offer support when needed. The safety standards required for licensed children's centers are also likely to reduce the frequency of child injury and death. By contrast, teachers in family child care homes and in-home settings usually work alone or with relatively little support. In-home and family child care home settings may also have environmental dangers that are not present in center-based settings.

During the next decade the numbers of children under the age of 5 who participate in out-of-home care and education settings is expected to increase rapidly (U.S. Department of Labor, Bureau of Labor Statistics, 2009). As the number of two working-parent families and single head of household families continues to increase, the demand for child care in general, as well as the demand for child care during the evening and weekend hours are also expected to grow. In addition, some states are implementing universally accessible prekindergarten programs, which will also boost the numbers of children in early childhood settings.

With more children spending more time in out-of-home care, the need for vigilance will increase. This makes early childhood program safety practices and safety training even more important. Teachers need to keep aware of emerging safety trends to ensure that the children's environments continue to be safe.

What if . . .

you were asked to describe the childhood accidents that are most typical for your community? How would you respond? Where might you find this information?

MyEducationLab

Go to the Assignments and Activities section of Topic 11: Safe Environments in the MyEducationLab for your course and complete the activity entitled *Meeting the Safety Needs of Children at Different Developmental Levels.* What does the plant in this video tell you about the developmental level of the children in this classroom?

Implications for Teachers

Understanding the causes and risk factors for injury equips teachers with important information about the hazards that children face. The next step is to put this information to use by approaching situations with alertness and being ready to assess the situation and take action in relevant ways. At the core, the actions teachers take to ensure children's safety include the following:

- *Review the setting for potential risk.* Do the classroom or play areas have locations that could allow children to fall? Are play spaces crowded with objects children could strike against? Could any of the furniture or materials be pulled over onto a child? Are there animals or insects present in the setting that could pose a risk for bites?
- *Consider the age group and specific children in the setting.* Does the group include children who like to climb or who are especially daring? Do any of the children have known allergies to bites or stings?
- *Identify strategies to reduce risk.* Ensure all animals in the setting have received appropriate inoculations and care from a veterinarian. Are changes needed to make the environment or equipment safer? Is adult supervision organized and sufficient? Is more information needed when children enroll? Do children need to be guided to interact more appropriately?
- *Put appropriate safety strategies into practice.* Are safety responsibilities clear? Do teachers know how to create safe environments, plan safe activities, correct situations that are unsafe, and take action when accidents occur?

Actions such as these involve making a variety of informed decisions and implementing intentionally planned strategies to keep children safe. Safety standards and regulations are helpful resources.

USING REGULATIONS TO IMPROVE SAFETY

Early childhood programs and teachers have access to a variety of resources that guide the development of safety policies and practices. These include professional organizations, research institutes, and the state and local regulatory agencies that have oversight for the safety standards that guide programs serving young children. Licensing requirements and accreditation standards help teachers implement the essential elements of safe early childhood classrooms.

Implementing Safety Regulations

A primary resource for safety in early childhood programs is the publication *Caring for Our Children: National Health and Safety Performance Standards: Guidelines for Out-of-Home Child Care Programs.* This 2002 publication is a joint effort of the American Academy of Pediatrics, the American Public Health Association, and the National Resource Center for Health and Safety in Child Care and Early Education. It provides a comprehensive listing of safety standards and recommendations developed from a review of research and the debates and discussions of individuals and associations with concern for child safety. A key recommendation directs each state to establish by law a regulatory agency with authority to protect children through mandatory licensing of all out-of-home care settings. The recommendation advocates for mandatory licensing of all children's programs including both part-time and full-time settings.

The Role of the Regulatory Agency

In 2005, the National Association for Regulatory Administration (NARA), in collaboration with the National Child Care Information and Technical Assistance Center (NCCIC, a service of the Child Care Bureau, Administration for Children and Families, U.S. Department of Health and Human Services), conducted a child care licensing study to guide the development of policies for the regulation of child care. As a result the role of regulation was defined as providing a basic level of health and safety protection for children in out-of-home care settings by reducing risk of disease, fire, injury, and impairment. Each state's regulatory agency is responsible for providing this protection by enforcing minimum standards for safety.

All 50 states and the District of Columbia regulate child care. The placement of these agencies within state government and the structure of oversight vary from state to state. For example, all states except Idaho have regulatory agencies that provide statewide oversight (NARA, 2005). In some states, larger cities such as New York City and Anchorage, Alaska, have regulatory agencies and certification standards for their specific area. Some states, such as Florida and Idaho, provide this regulatory role through larger counties. Regardless of these differences, all child care regulatory agencies are directed by legislation to:

- Establish standards for out-of-home child care.
- Implement monitoring strategies.
- Enforce the child care regulations.

Licensing Criteria

The criteria that identify when a program must be licensed vary from state to state. Most regulatory agencies identify the following determining factors for mandatory licensing:

- *Group size:* the number of children to be served.
- *Length of the service day:* to separate child care from residential or 24-hour care.
- *Location of care:* centers, family child care homes, and in-home child care.

Regulated child care settings include child care centers and school-based child care settings, family child care homes, and in-home child care. All 50 states regulate child care centers. All but three states (Idaho, Louisiana, and New Jersey) regulate family child care settings in some way (NARA, 2005). In-home child care is not regulated.

In addition, many other children's programs and facilities may be exempt from the regulatory requirements. These include recreation programs, day camps, and programs where the child's parent is on site, such as sports clubs and child care in faith-group settings. NARA (2005) estimates that more than 9 million child care slots are regulated nationwide. These are located in approximately 336,000 licensed early childhood settings. The majority (nearly two-thirds) are licensed family child care settings.

Identifying Common Licensing Requirements

Licensing covers a range of requirements that create the basic and minimal foundation for safety of young children in out-of-home care. Child care licensing requirements address licensing applications and fees, facilities, program design and operation, teacher qualifications and orientation, children's education programming, and nutrition and health requirements.

Licensing Application and Fees

Child care programs that are required to be licensed must apply for a license before starting services. About half of the states require a fee for the license. The fee for center-based care programs is usually based on the number of children in care. Family child care is most often charged a flat licensing fee. Most licenses are valid for a 1- to 2-year period (NARA, 2005).

Facility Requirements

Facilities and indoor and outdoor environments must be inspected. These inspections are typically conducted by a designated agency such as the city or county fire inspector or health department sanitarian. Children's environments are reviewed for safety such as fire hazards, health and sanitation concerns (water, heat, toileting facilities), emergency facility supports (emergency exits, emergency lighting, evacuation plans), and adherence to local building codes. Facilities are also reviewed for minimum square footage, cleanliness, and condition and maintenance of equipment. The durability and appropriateness of furnishings is considered and food preparation and service areas are inspected.

Program Design

Standards for program design and operation are outlined in the licensing requirements. Guidance is provided for determining child age groupings, class group size, and teacher-to-child ratios. Policies for supervision of children, guidance and discipline policies, and plans for safe supervision in special settings, such as field trips, transportation, water activities, naptime, and specialty care, are required. Table 14-3 describes recommendations for maximum group size and teacher-to-child ratios for licensed early childhood programs.

Program Operations

Requirements for general program operations include standards for developmentally appropriate programs. Safety systems such as emergency preparedness plans, fire, earthquake, and evacuation drills, and lock-down procedures are required. Systems to support safety in the program are mandated, such as child attendance records, arrival and departure procedures, and practices for monitoring visitors in the centers. Requirements may include guidance for the provision of services such as transportation, vehicle safety, and use of car seats.

Teacher Qualifications and Requirements at Hire

Licensing regulations dictate minimum qualifications for teachers and the program director, including minimum age, education, and experience as well as requirements for ongoing training. Table 14-4 shows the recommendations for early childhood staff qualifications.

Criminal background and reference checks are required before hire, and many states require a preemployment health assessment to rule out the presence of a communicable disease such as tuberculosis or other conditions that cannot be managed through safety practices.

Table 14-3	Class Size and Teacher-to-Child Ratios for Children in NAEYC-Accredited Programs	
Child Age Groups	**Maximum Class Size**	**Teacher-to-Child Ratio**
Infants (birth to 15 months)	6	1:3
	8	1:4
Toddlers (12 to 38 months)	6	1:3
	8	1:4
	10	1:4
	12	1:4
Toddlers and Twos (21 to 36 months)	8	1:4
	10	1:5
	12	1:6
Preschoolers (2.5- and 3-year-olds)	12	1:6
	14	1:7
	16	1:8
	18	1:9
Preschoolers (4- and 5-year-olds)	16	1:8
	18	1:9
	20	1:10
Kindergartners and young school-age children (5- to 9-year-olds)	20	1:10
	22	1:11
	24	1:12

Source: Based on *Leadership & management: A guide to the NAEYC early childhood program standards and related accreditation criteria*, (p. 29), edited by S. Ritchie and B. Willer, 2005, Washington, DC: National Association for the Education of Young Children.

New Staff Orientation

Regulations also outline expectations for orientation and preemployment training on emergency procedures, procedures for reporting suspected child abuse and neglect, and other safety topics. Regulatory agencies require records to be on file documenting that these standards have been achieved. Licensing requirements may describe other topics that must be covered in new staff orientation such as expectations related to child guidance, strategies to implement family-style meal service, and health policies. Figure 14-5 provides a sample checklist that summarizes the kinds of information that is shared during orientation for new teachers. A signed copy is typically placed in the teacher's personnel file to document completion of this licensing requirement.

Children's Program

Licensing standards outline expectations related to the enrollment of children, including requirements for identifying emergency contacts and obtaining guidance from families about children's care in case of emergencies, child health and nutrition needs, the provision of age-appropriate and developmentally appropriate activities, selection of equipment and materials, family access to the classroom, and parent involvement and communication.

Table 14-4

National Health and Safety Standards Recommendations for Early Childhood Staff Qualifications

DIRECTOR
For programs serving 60 children or less:
- 21 years minimum age
- Bachelor's degree in early childhood education, child development, social work, nursing or other related field or a combination of college course work and experience including:
  - Minimum four courses in child development and early childhood education
  - Two years experience teaching at the same age level
  - Course work in business or early childhood administration or 6 months training in an administrative position
- Certification in pediatric first aid and CPR
- Knowledge of and ability to refer families to community resources and to build community collaborations
- Skill in facility operations
- Ability to design appropriate curriculum
- Ability to communicate effectively both in speaking and writing
- Demonstrated experience in working with children and families in multiple settings

For programs serving more than 60 children:
- The director must demonstrate the qualifications listed above plus at least 3 years experience teaching children of the age group served by the program, and at least 6 months experience in administration.

EDUCATION COORDINATORS, LEAD TEACHERS, TEACHERS
- 21 years minimum age
- Bachelor's degree in early childhood education, child development, social work, nursing, or other related field or a combination of experience and college course work and experience
- One year minimum experience teaching the same ages of children
- Training to meet the child's needs and create a nurturing environment
- Certification in pediatric first aid and CPR
- Ability to recognize and address health and safety hazards and protect children from harm
- Knowledge of normal growth and development
- Knowledge of atypical development and the special needs of children with disabilities
- Ability to appropriately address children's needs through a variety of opportunities for learning and to engage in social experiences
- Ability to communicate effectively both in speaking and writing

ASSOCIATE TEACHERS
- 18 years minimum age
- Associate's degree in early childhood education or child development and 6 months of experience in child care

ASSISTANT TEACHERS
- 18 years minimum age
- High school diploma or GED

The program is to provide orientation and training about child developmental needs and access to consultation and supervision.

AIDES AND VOLUNTEERS
- 16 years minimum age

The program is to provide orientation and training about child developmental needs and consultation and supervision.

CAREGIVERS IN FAMILY CHILD CARE HOMES
- 21 years minimum age
- Accreditation by the National Association for Family Child Care and college certificate demonstrating a minimum of 3 credit hours of family child care leadership or master caregiver training, or hold an associate's degree in early childhood education or child development
- Certification in pediatric first aid and CPR
- Training in health management in child care and the ability to recognize safety hazards and illness in the child care setting
- Knowledge of atypical development and the special needs of children with disabilities
- Ability to appropriately address children's needs
- Ability to communicate effectively both in speaking and writing
- One year experience serving the ages of the children in the family child care setting

Source: Adapted from *Caring for Our Children: National Health and Safety Performance Standards: Guidelines for Out-of-Home Child Care Programs*, 2nd edition, Copyright 2002. Used with permission of the American Academy of Pediatrics.

Figure 14-5 Sample Staff Orientation Checklist Including Safety Topics

Program History and Context

___ Mission
___ Philosophy
___ Program services

___ Our families
___ Licensing rules
___ NAEYC accreditation

Professional Commitment

___ Criminal background check
___ Transcripts/verification of qualifications
___ Reporting child abuse/neglect
___ Confidentiality
___ Infant/child first aid and CPR
___ NAEYC Code of Ethical Conduct
___ Position description

___ Probationary period
___ Pre-employment health screen
___ Professional behaviors and dispositions
___ Professional development expectations
___ Tracking training hours
___ Grievance procedures

Nutrition, Health, and Safety Policies

___ Developmentally appropriate practices
___ Reviewing the environment and reporting hazards
___ Emergency procedures
  • Fire emergency
  • Dental emergency
  • Earthquake
  • Lock down
  • Evacuation
___ Food service procedures
  • Snacks and meals
  • Classroom activities
  • CACFP and Civil Rights training

___ Child guidance policy
___ Drug, alcohol, tobacco policy
___ Health procedures
  • Daily health checks
  • Hand washing
  • Sick child care
  • Illness and exclusion policy
  • Immunization requirements
  • Protocol for administering medications
  • Bloodborne pathogen
___ Field trip procedures
___ Policy and procedure manual

Please initial above indicating your understanding of the topics discussed.

Employee signature _____   Date _____

New employee orientation given by: Signature _____   Date _____

Child Nutrition Requirements

Regulations list expectations for the nutrition and feeding of children in child care. They encompass provision of nutritious snacks and meals, food selection, storage, cleanliness, and processes for food preparation and service. Requirements address protocols for food prepared on site and catered foods that are delivered.

Plans for meeting the feeding needs of children of differing age groups are also outlined. This is especially important in an era where the incidence of children's food allergies is on the rise. As described in the *Nutrition Note*, awareness of children's food allergies requires that keeping children safe from food allergens extends to all aspects of the curriculum.

Children's Health Requirements

Regulatory standards typically mandate health practices to reduce the spread of disease and to ensure child safety in the program setting. These include recommendations for child health exams before enrollment and a listing of immunizations children must have before they can participate. The *Health Hint* describes the many ways in which immunizations keep children safe from the effects of disease.

Rules related to the administration of medications, care of mildly ill children, recording and reporting accidents, hand washing, and diapering procedures are also covered. Many other

Nutrition Note

Monitor Food Allergies for Safety

Pediatricians have documented an increase in the numbers of young children with food allergies. During the past 10 years, research has revealed that an estimated 6% to 8% of children under the age of 3 have food-related allergies. Food allergies often cause skin rashes, and they are the most common cause of anaphylactic shock, which if untreated can lead to death.

When families report that their child has a food allergy, teachers must consider what that means for both food service and classroom activities. This means that early childhood teachers must think broadly about ways children may come into contact with food allergens in all aspects of the curriculum. This kind of comprehensive thinking keeps children safe.

Common Food Allergens	Crafts and Activities That May Bring These Allergens into the Classroom
Eggs	• Cooking and baking activities • Eggshells and cartons used for pasting activities
Cow's milk	• Cooking and baking activities involving milk products (making butter, baking bread, whipping cream, making ice cream) • Taste tests with milk products (cheese, yogurt, ice cream)
Peanuts	• Peanut butter used in making pinecone and birdseed bird feeders • Peanuts and shells used for sensory table, pasting, as dramatic play props, or for trucks to "carry" • Peanuts used to carry on a wooden stick or roll with the nose for a race • Peanut butter play dough
Wheat	• Cooking and baking activities • Wheat berries used in the sensory table or for gluing • Play dough • Flour used in the sensory table
Soy	• Soybeans purchased for use in the sensory table, for gluing and making mosaics, as the "sound ingredient" for making shaker cups or tambourines

Source: Based on "Symposium: Pediatric Food Allergy," by S. H. Sicherer et al., 2003, *Pediatrics*, *111*(6), pp. 1591–1594, retrieved October 23, 2009, from http://pediatrics.aappublications.org/cgi/content/abstract/111/6/S2/1591?maxtoshow=&HITS=10&hits=10&RESULTFORMAT=&fulltext=S.+H.+Sicherer+&andorexactfulltext=and&searchid=1&FIRSTINDEX=0&sortspec=relevance&resourcetype=HWCIT

important policies, such as smoke-free environments, restrictions related to alcohol and drug use, control of hazardous substances, presence of firearms in the setting, and restrictions related to animals in the children's program are outlined to improve children's health and safety in child care.

Monitoring for Compliance

Each regulatory agency is responsible for ensuring that licensed programs meet the mandatory standards at the time the license is approved and that compliance is maintained on an ongoing basis. Monitoring for compliance and instituting clear sanctions for noncompliance are important aspects of health and safety in early childhood programs.

Health Hint

Immunization Keeps Children Safe from Disease

Parents of young children know that immunizations are a regular part of the well-child checkup. But do they recognize that immunizations keep children safe from disease? The American Academy of Pediatrics pays close attention to the incidence of hospitalization and death for many early childhood diseases. They want parents and early childhood teachers to know the facts about immunizations and safety:

- Immunizations save lives and prevent illness from infectious disease.
- Nearly 100 people die each year from chicken pox. The chicken pox vaccine protects most children from getting the disease.
- Hepatitis A is one of the most vaccine-preventable diseases. Immunization has reduced the incidence of hepatitis A to the lowest numbers ever.
- *Haemophilus influenzae* type b (Hib) used to affect more than 20,000 people each year. Since the introduction of the childhood vaccine, only a few hundred cases are identified per year.
- Many childhood diseases are active in countries around the world. Travelers may unknowingly bring these diseases to the United States where they could spread quickly. Immunization keeps children safe.

Sources: *Why Immunizations Are Important,* by the American Academy of Pediatrics, 2000, Common Myths about Immunizations, retrieved October 23, 2009, from http://www.cispimmunize.org/fam/fam_main.html?http&&&www .cispimmunize.org/fam/myths.html; and "Prevention of Hepatitis A Through Active or Passive Immunization Practices: Recommendations of the Advisory Committee on Immunization Practices," by A. E. Fiore, A. Wasley, and B. P. Bell, May 19, 2006, *MMWR, 55*(RR07), pp. 1–23, retrieved October 13, 2009, from http://www.cdc.gov/mmwr/preview/mmwrhtml/ rr5507a1.htm?s_cidrr5507a1_e.

Conducting Site Visits

Child care licensing agencies monitor programs through site inspections, classroom observations, and review of records. Site inspections are conducted as part of the original application for license. Other periodic inspections are conducted either through prearrangement or as unannounced site visits. Most licensing agencies conduct inspections once each year during the license renewal process (NARA, 2005). Inspections focus on identifying problems that put children at risk for injury or disease. The most common licensing violations identified include (NARA, 2005):

- *Exceeding licensed capacity,* such as enrolling too many children for the room and group size.
- *Violating licensing requirements,* including not conducting fire and other emergency evacuation drills or ensuring hygienic food preparation and service.
- *Lack of suitable staff,* such as hiring teachers who do not meet the minimum required qualifications or violating the teacher-to-child ratio.
- *Poor care of children,* including gaps in supervision or providing inappropriate activities for children.
- *Poor administration and record keeping,* such as incomplete emergency records.

Site visits are also used as opportunities to advise and provide technical assistance to the program to help program staff meet and exceed the minimum licensing requirements. In this way, the regulatory agency builds the capacity of early childhood settings to provide safe and appropriate care for young children.

Investigating Complaints

Child care regulatory agencies are responsible for investigating complaints about licensed child care settings. Complaints may come from the general public or from families of children in care. Common complaints include (NARA, 2005):

- Too many children in care.
- Poor supervision and management of child behavior.
- Problems related to children's health, safety, and nutrition.

The licensing agency documents all complaints and decides how to follow-up based on the agency's knowledge of the early childhood setting and the immediacy of the concern. Unannounced site visits and interviews with the program administrator might be conducted to explore the validity of the complaint.

Some regulatory agencies are now making information about verified complaints and the agency's actions available to the general public through the agency website. This step confirms the seriousness with which regulatory agencies view their role in increasing safety in early childhood settings, and provides the public with information to consider when selecting a children's program. It also highlights the importance of the need for teachers to monitor their own classrooms and practices to ensure that licensing regulations are put into practice every day.

Responding to Licensing Violations

When licensing violations are discovered, the licensing agency must determine a course of action. The agency considers whether the violation is of a kind that can be quickly remedied, such as posting emergency procedures, or if it constitutes a serious problem, such as not conducting criminal background checks on program staff. Managing violations always takes into account the immediate safety of the children in the setting. Once the nature of the violation is understood, the regulatory agency determines the appropriate consequence.

What if. . .

you were teaching in a children's program that was found to be in violation of a licensing requirement related to the teacher-to-child ratio? How would you work with your program leaders to create a plan to meet the requirements? What ideas would you have for maintaining the needed ratios while teachers are taking their break?

Understanding Consequences for Licensing Violations

Repercussions are determined based on the severity of the violation. Consequences might include putting the program on probation until the violation has been remedied, withholding licensing or not renewing the license application, or closing the facility. In some cases programs may have to pay a fine for violating important health and safety requirements.

In a few cases the violation may be of significant severity that criminal prosecution and imprisonment are the outcome (NARA, 2005). Enforcing health and safety standards is an important way in which the regulatory agency provides for the safety of young children in out-of-home care and education settings.

Implications for Teachers

Understanding health and safety standards and the regulations that guide licensed children's programs is important for teachers. Familiarity helps teachers understand the importance of the standards in ensuring that appropriate health and safety practices are followed in the classroom. It helps teachers recognize that program safety policies are designed specifically to increase children's safety. It also equips teachers with the information they need to explain to families how the program works to increase children's safety. This was an important part of the conversation in the opening case scenario. Caden's family needed reassurance that the program implemented health and safety practices and that the teacher could confidently describe specific ways she takes action to increase safety.

Knowing about licensing regulations also helps teachers understand that they are not working alone to ensure children's well-being. They see that they are part of a network of safety provided for young children, and they recognize that safety standards and the regulatory agency are resources for improving safety in children's settings.

Moving beyond Minimum Standards

Public systems to ensure the safety of children in out-of-home care settings are still evolving. The current licensing and regulatory activities, while meeting the basic safety needs of children in child care, may still fall short of the goals for a thorough and effective licensing system. Although research data on strategies that improve child safety are becoming more readily available, regulatory standards do not always keep up. For example, the "Back to Sleep" safety campaign has reduced death due to SIDS by 50% for infants below the age of 1 (NICHHD, 2006). In spite of the success of this practice only half of the states currently require that child care centers place infants on their backs to sleep (NARA, 2005). This represents a gap in systematically applying research findings to safety practices.

The NAEYC (1998) issued a position statement calling for improvements in child care licensing nationwide. The association pointed to gaps in the regulatory system that compromise the safety of young children. Among their concerns were reports about the large numbers of children's programs that were not licensed and the potential for some of the programs to be harmful (Galinsky, Howes, Kontos, & Shinn, 1994; Helburn, 1995). NAEYC (1998) called for improvements in this safety system through:

Placing infants on their backs to sleep has greatly reduced the incidence of SIDS.

- Mandatory licensing requirements for all programs that serve young children.
- More comprehensive regulations regarding the skills and education of those working with children.
- Greater focus on research-guided policies.
- More vigorous enforcement of mandatory requirements.

Individual programs can take leadership for implementing practices that move beyond the minimum as suggested by NAEYC. One way programs can take a step beyond the minimum for safety is to achieve program accreditation.

Program Accreditation

The NAEYC (2005) provides a comprehensive system for accreditation that challenges programs to raise the quality of care in early childhood settings. Accreditation is an endorsement by a professional organization that the children's setting and program practices meet important quality standards. Program accreditation is a voluntary system.

The process of becoming accredited moves programs through a system of self-study and program improvement toward high standards of quality, health, and safety. The process includes development of program and classroom portfolios to document ways the program addresses quality standards. A program visitation is scheduled during which a trained individual reviews materials and conducts classroom observations to validate the findings of the program report. This information is used to inform the accreditation decision. All children's settings can voluntarily use the materials provided by the accreditation process to identify aspects of service that can be improved.

Increasing Safety in Other Ways

Individuals and programs can also take other voluntary steps to increase children's safety in early childhood settings. Moving beyond the minimum standards for health and safety that are required for licensing should focus on strategies that have been established by research as significant for increasing children's well-being. These include improving teacher-to-child ratios decreasing teacher turnover, requiring higher teacher qualification standards, and improving training about safety.

Improving Teacher-to-Child Ratios The teacher-to-child ratio is considered to be a significant indicator of quality and a factor for increasing safety in the early childhood setting

(NAEYC, 2005). Most licensing requirements describe a minimum teacher-to-child ratio and minimum number of teachers for a group of a particular size. Improving on this minimum ratio would involve adding another teacher to the classroom. This step provides for increased supervision of children and improves the potential that hazards will be recognized, thus reducing the risk for accidents. Improving teacher-to-child ratios is challenging for programs, because the cost of providing additional teachers can be significant.

Decreasing Teacher Turnover Teacher turnover refers to the number of teachers who have left their teaching position during a particular time period. Frequent teacher turnover has the potential to disrupt children's physical and emotional safety. Teachers develop a keen understanding of the health and safety needs of children in their class. They know which children need to be especially well supervised and which have allergies or special health needs. They also build nurturing relationships that support children through emotional difficulties. This information is not easily transferred during teacher changes, which introduces the potential for children's safety needs to be overlooked.

Frequent teacher turnover may be a sign that the children's program needs to find ways to make the teaching position more desirable by improving pay and offering benefits. Unfortunately, these strategies involve new costs. For example, the median preschool teacher salary in the United States in 2006 was $22,680, whereas the median income for teachers in classes serving older children was around $46,135 (Bureau of Labor Statistics, 2009) . In addition, teachers who have specific skills, such as those who are bilingual, are in demand and competition among programs can also contribute to high teacher turnover rates.

Programs can be most immediately effective by improving practices around teacher transition to ensure that children's safety needs are appropriately addressed. Teachers make key contributions to this process by passing along important child health and safety information when they leave a teaching assignment, and by focusing on quickly learning about children's needs when assuming new positions.

What if. . .

you were offered the opportunity to assume a new teaching position in another early childhood setting? You want to take on the new responsibilities, but are worried about the children in your class who have bonded closely with you. How would you tell the children and families? How would you arrange a smooth transition?

Increasing Staff Educational Qualifications Increasing the qualifications expected for program directors and teachers is another strategy that may improve child safety. NAEYC is moving this way by requiring more specific educational qualifications for administrators of accredited programs. The Office of Head Start and the field of early childhood as a whole have been debating the benefits of increasing the educational requirements for early childhood teachers in an effort to promote better outcomes for children.

The effects of increased educational requirements on child safety tend to vary. Research has revealed that requiring directors to have more education reduces the risk for injury and fatality in the early childhood setting (Currie & Hotz, 2004). This finding reinforces the importance of the program director's role in designing safety practices that improve children's well-being. Interestingly, however, while an increased education level for teachers is found to support gains in children's cognitive growth, it does not appear to improve child safety (Currie & Hotz, 2004). Teachers in the study had varying levels of education, but all apparently had the basic skills needed to keep children from harm. Therefore, while requiring teachers to have higher levels of education has benefits for children's educational progress, efforts to improve children's safety may be managed in other ways. Safety training workshops and focused instruction on creating safe environments and implementing appropriate supervision practices may be more effective.

Providing Enhanced Safety Training Programs may choose to offer staff training beyond the minimum requirements for infant and child first aid and CPR (cardiopulmonary resuscitation). Additional trainings should be selected based on the identified needs of particular children and on trends recognized in the area. For example, training on when and how to use an epinephrine autoinjection (EpiPen) to treat anaphylactic shock from bee stings is reasonable given the number of unintentional injuries due to bites and stings.

Learning how to avoid exposure to bloodborne pathogens equips teachers to keep themselves and children safe in the event of blood spills.

Knowing how to respond to seizures and to asthma attacks are other beneficial training topics that move beyond the required minimum standards for health and safety in licensed programs. Sometimes programs also need to weigh in on debates about health and safety rules that are not yet part of the regulatory requirements. The *Policy Point* describes the debate about use of helmets for children riding tricycles.

Recognizing the Implications of Increasing Regulations

Mandatory licensing and regulations governing the care of young children are designed foremost to improve the health and safety of children in out-of-home care settings, to reduce disease and injury, and to increase child well-being. It is particularly difficult then to recognize that stricter standards designed to increase the quality and safety of children's settings have the potential to push some children into more risky situations. How does this happen?

Implementing more rigorous safety standards carries hidden costs. Improving teacher-to-child ratios, increasing teacher education requirements, providing safety training, and implementing more frequent monitoring visits all are projected to improve

Policy Point

EMERGING SAFETY PRACTICES— DO WE NEED A POLICY?

Sometimes early childhood settings are challenged to make policy decisions that are at the forefront of emerging practices, especially when the best practice approaches are not yet clear. Developing a new policy and putting it into practice require a team approach. The steps identified to put the policy into practice need to be appropriate to the setting and realistic to implement. Steps and an example for developing new policies include:

1. **Define the question or problem.**
   Helmets vs. head lice: Which is a more significant risk to health and safety?
   - Head injuries due to bicycle accidents are a significant safety concern.
   - Sharing helmets may increase the risk of spreading head lice.
2. **Involve teachers, families, and informed community members in the discussions and decision making.**
   - We will create a Helmet Safety Review Team of two teachers, two family members, and a health or safety professional.
3. **Identify the anticipated costs (child health and dollars) and the potential benefits (child health and safety).**
   - *Costs:* Cost of helmets and cleaning supplies; storage is an issue; sharing a few helmets and cleaning them between use would be hard; more head lice means more program cleaning and management.
   - *Benefits:* Teaches children about safety; helps them develop the habit of wearing a helmet; might save future injury; although head lice are a health annoyance, they are not deadly.
4. **Make a decision.**
   - Children will wear helmets when riding tricycles, scooters, or bicycles at preschool.
   - We will invite families to voluntarily send a helmet labeled for their child to use.
   - We will provide four classroom helmets for children to share.
   - We will place cleaning materials on the shelf by the door.
5. **Implement the new plan for a defined trial period.**
   - We will try the new plan for 6 months.
6. **Reflect on how the new approach is working; make suggestions for potential revision of the new policy.**
   - The safety team will meet in 6 months to review how the new policy is working.

children's safety. But these steps will ultimately increase the cost for care. As a result some families may no longer be able to afford to enroll their children in licensed care settings. They may be compelled to seek alternative settings that cost less, which may include settings that are not licensed or regulated. Children's risk for injury may be greater in these unregulated settings (Currie & Hotz, 2004). As a result, the efforts made to increase safety for children in child care may result in more children being placed in unsafe settings.

This also aggravates a current social problem. Affluent families may be able to afford more costly early childhood settings that meet quality, health, and safety standards. However, increasing the costs of programs that meet new regulatory standards makes access to quality early childhood settings even more difficult for low-income families. As regulatory agencies consider stricter standards, and programs work to achieve higher quality, the relative costs and benefits must be explored and reasonable changes implemented.

TAKING RESPONSIBILITY FOR SAFETY

MyEducationLab

Go to the Assignments and Activities section of Topic 11: Safe Environments in the MyEducationLab for your course and complete the activity entitled *Creating Safe Indoor Group Environments*. What do these photos tell you about creating safe environments for young children?

Ensuring children's physical and emotional safety requires careful planning and preparation at the program and classroom levels. At the program level safety depends on strong leadership that prioritizes safety and demonstrates a commitment to increasing safety in all aspects of program services. In the classroom, teachers have specific responsibilities to ensure children's safety in the environment and through interactions. The responsibilities listed in Figure 14-6 demonstrate the different roles taken on by program leaders and teachers. Together program leaders and teachers establish the services and practices that create a context of safety for young children.

Understanding Program Responsibilities

Early childhood program leaders, including directors, coordinators, principals, and other administrators, are responsible for the overall health and safety of children and staff in the early childhood setting or school. They carry primary responsibility for the overarching aspects of safety provided at the program level including physical facilities and program services, policies, and practices. Decisions are also made based on the interrelated nature of program operations. For example, providing safe facilities is important, but is not sufficient if the processes surrounding food storage, preparation, and service are not similarly managed to ensure food safety. These decisions are program leader responsibilities.

Teachers who work in center-based or school settings can rely on their program leaders to establish the systems that help keep children safe. Teachers in family child care or small-group settings often manage both the program-wide aspects of safety as well as those that advance safety in the classroom.

Figure 14-6 Creating a Context of Safety: Program and Teacher Responsibilities

Program Responsibilities	Teacher Responsibilities
• Establish safe facilities.	• Follow program safety practices.
• Create safe program services.	• Create safe classroom environments.
• Hire safe teachers and staff.	• Build strong and caring relationships.
• Develop program safety policies.	• Model safe behaviors.
• Provide insurance.	• Teach safety skills.
• Monitor for safety.	• Supervise children at all times.
• Provide safety training.	• Take immediate action when needed.
	• Advocate for safety.

Providing Safe Facilities

Safe facilities make a significant contribution to children's physical and emotional safety. Program leaders are responsible for providing secure and accessible environments that meet building construction and safety codes. They do this by creating spaces to support program activities, such as safe food storage and preparation areas and safe play yards. They also arrange for needed utilities and monitor and correct safety hazards in the indoor and outdoor settings.

Creating Safe Program Services

Program leaders are in charge of designing services that increase children's safety. This includes monitoring for safety in food service and collecting information about children's allergies and special health care needs in order to provide safe health services. It also involves arranging collaborations with other agencies, for example, to access support to ensure the safe participation of children with special developmental needs or to identify sources for translation services to support communication among teachers and families when language is a barrier.

Hiring Safe Teachers

Safe program services also include ensuring that the people who work in the children's program are safe and appropriate. This involves ensuring that criminal background checks are conducted for all program staff, and that effective monitoring systems are in place to confirm that teachers are using safe practices with children.

Developing Safety Policies

Program leaders are responsible for creating the policies and procedures that guide teachers and other staff as they implement safe services for children. Program leaders also need to be responsive to current issues and concerns. For example, if a particularly contagious flu virus has emerged as a new health concern, a safety policy must be developed to include plans for communicating with families about the symptoms of the flu and when to keep children home, and directing teachers about safe and healthy management of children if symptoms become evident while at school.

Procedures also need to be relevant and appropriate for the setting. For example, if a classroom is supervised by two teachers, the procedures related to meal service must be designed to be accomplished by two people. Table 14-5 provides examples of program-level responsibilities for establishing safety policies in early childhood settings.

Obtaining Insurance and Legal Counsel

Early childhood leaders are responsible for envisioning and planning for events that may impact children's health and safety. An important way that program leaders support their program, the children, families, and staff is through the selection and purchase of accident and liability insurance and hiring a legal counselor if necessary.

Insurance for Accidental Injury and Death Accident insurance provides backup coverage for some of the medical costs involved in treating injuries that occur while children attend the early childhood program. Depending on the details of the selected plan, accident insurance assists families to pay medical costs as a backup to the family's insurance. Note, however, that in some cases the program accident insurance may be the child's only insurance coverage. Programs obtain basic accident insurance coverage as a part of their safety service plan.

Liability insurance Liability insurance is provided to insure the program and its workers against lawsuit. In the event of a tragic injury or death, parents or their insurance agencies may present claims against the program or individual teachers claiming that they have been careless or negligent in their duties. Claims related to child care can be made years after the child was enrolled in the program.

Table 14-5	Sample Program Responsibilities and Actions for Safety

- *Responsibilities:* Aspects for which program leaders are in charge and accountable.
- *Actions:* Concrete ways program leaders implement safety-related responsibilities.

Responsibilities	Actions
Facility and environment	• Monitor safety requirements for indoor and outdoor spaces. • Ensure all spaces are accessible to persons with disabilities. • Plan periodic inspections for fire, health, and sanitation.
Program services	• Set guidelines for child groupings, group size, and teacher-to-child ratios. • Establish recruitment and hiring practices for teachers. • Establish services to support the safety of children with special developmental needs.
Classroom practices	• Establish arrival and departure transition procedures. • Identify health and safety steps for conducting cooking projects in the classroom. • Direct how to arrange visits by pets in the classroom. • Identify steps for planning field trips.
Nutrition practices	• Establish guidelines for selecting, purchasing, storing, preparing, and serving foods. • Outline how to document and communicate about children's food allergies and food restrictions.
Health practices	• Create guidelines: when to have children wash hands, when children should stay home from school due to illness. • Provide diaper and toileting procedures. • Direct teachers about when and how to report incidence of communicable disease.
Safety practices	• Establish guidelines on how and when to practice emergency drills. • Create emergency procedures. • Provide directions about how to manage unauthorized entry of stranger in the building or classroom. • Create system for reporting unsafe conditions.
Training and professional development	• Establish requirements for new teacher orientation on child safety. • Provide guidance on yearly training requirements. • Provide directions on documenting participation in training.
Monitoring	• Establish classroom record-keeping and reporting requirements: attendance, illness, accidents, evacuation drills. • Outline steps for conducting classroom and play yard safety checks.

Source: Based on the information from the Child Care Division of the Oregon Employment Department, 2001.

Programs should purchase the most insurance coverage they can afford (Wyatt, 2001). Lawsuits have been known to award large amounts of money in response to credible suits for loss of a child's life or disability due to injury. Liability insurance is purchased to support the program and teachers in the event that a court of law determines they have been negligent in the care and supervision of children (Maine Bureau of Insurance, 2006).

Obtaining Legal Counsel Program leaders need to know who to turn to for legal guidance. Making arrangements for legal counsel provides the opportunity for program leaders to obtain advice that can be helpful in creating safe policies and in knowing how to respond in case of tragic events (Perri, 2006). This also provides program leaders with the confidence that legal guidance is only a phone call away.

Providing Safety Training
Program leaders are responsible for providing orientation and training for new staff on health and safety procedures. Common topics include infant and child first aid and CPR, how

to respond to incidents that involve bloodborne pathogens, and general program emergency response procedures.

Leaders are also responsible for ensuring that teachers receive ongoing training on relevant and emergent safety topics. These might include training on EpiPen use for children with severe allergies, blood sugar management for children with diabetes, appropriate responses for children with asthma, orthopedic impairments or other health concerns, and how to address challenging and unsafe behaviors.

What if. . .

you were asked to complete a survey on topics you would like to study in a safety training workshop? What topics would be most helpful to your safety skill development?

Conducting Periodic Drills

Program leaders are responsible for ensuring that emergency drills are understood and regularly practiced. Teachers and other early childhood program staff feel more confident about their ability to respond to unintentional injury or fatality when they have had a chance to test their knowledge of the emergency action plan. Just as emergency drills are beneficial in establishing an organized response when evacuating classrooms, teachers benefit from acting out the steps for other potential emergency events.

Monitoring for Compliance

Program leaders are ultimately responsible for ensuring that the systems of safety designed for the children's setting are effectively implemented. Periodic review and monitoring are crucial aspects of this process. Monitoring activities include review of:

- *Program staff reports,* such as accident reports and food service temperature records.
- *Teacher reports,* such as child and teacher attendance reports (to confirm safe teacher-to-child ratios), the dates of emergency drills, and records of participation in safety training.
- *Family and teacher safety team reports,* such as the results of classroom and play yard safety checklists.
- *Classroom observation visits* to review the physical and emotional safety of children in the classroom and understand the effectiveness of the teacher's supervision.
- *Licensing site visit reports,* which describe compliance with health and safety practices, fire safety requirements, and program health and safety reports from the county sanitarian.
- *Family questionnaires,* which are designed to collect feedback about various aspects of program services.

Information learned through these various monitoring activities must be reviewed and evaluated in order to establish action plans for program safety improvement.

Clarifying Teacher Responsibilities

The classroom is the teacher's sphere of influence for education and safety. Teachers are responsible for ensuring children's safety in the classroom and during all class-related activities. This responsibility requires that teachers understand and follow program safety policies, know how to manage safety in the classroom, be skilled in teaching children safety skills, and take emergency action when necessary. Each of these activities links the program-level safety policies to safety at the classroom level, building a comprehensive system of safe care for young children. Table 14-6 illustrates teacher responsibilities and actions that foster safety.

Implementing Program Safety Practices

Teachers are responsible for learning and implementing the safety policies and procedures of the program. Program-level policies and procedures are useless without concerned follow-through by teachers at the classroom level. A true children's safety team blends the administrative design of policies with thoughtful implementation by teaching professionals.

Table 14-6   Sample Teacher Responsibilities and Actions for Safety

- *Responsibilities:* Aspects for which teachers are in charge and accountable every day.
- *Actions:* Concrete ways teachers implement safety-related responsibilities.

Responsibilities	Actions
Know program safety policies.	• Know safety policies and procedures. • Understand the teacher's responsibility for children's safety. • Know where to find program policies; review them periodically. • Participate in safety training workshops.
Provide a safe classroom environment.	• Do not allow toxic products in the classroom. • Keep fire exits cleared and open. • Review indoor and outdoor areas for safety problems every day. • Teach children to interact appropriately; stop bullying.
Build caring relationships.	• Greet children and families individually at arrival. • Get to know each child's style and individual risk for safety. • Teach children social skills: how to be a friend, how to ask for what they need.
Model and teach safe behaviors.	• Teach children safety rules. • Teach pedestrian safety skills. • Model and teach appropriate vocabulary related to safety. Instead of saying, "No!" say, "Let me show you the safe way to do that."
Supervise children at all times.	• Supervise children by sight and sound. • Keep alert and be purposeful when observing children. • Be especially vigilant during field trips.
Take immediate action as needed.	• Keep current on emergency training. • Be ready to respond to emergencies at all times. • Check first-aid supplies at least once a month.
Advocate for strong safety policies.	• Offer ideas when safety practices need improvement. • Report recurring facility safety problems. • Be involved. Don't just leave safety to someone else.

MyEducationLab

Go to the Assignments and Activities section of Topic 11: Safe Environments in the MyEducationLab for your course and complete the activity entitled *Developing Safety Policies and Procedures.* Have you noticed evacuation plans posted in schools?

Many program policies are outlined in detail, providing specific steps for implementation. These must be followed with care to achieve the desired safety outcome. For example, an evacuation procedure may be very specific about who does what and when. Kyra, the first-grade teacher, is notified to prepare the children to respond to the school fire alarm when it sounds. She is directed to lead the children to a designated gathering spot, take a head count to determine whether all children are accounted for, and return to the building when the all-clear bell rings. At the end of the day, Kyra is required to record information about the drill on a prescribed form and return it to the office. These procedures are conducted by all teachers and classes. This approach ensures that the safety policy is systematically practiced and provides an opportunity for program leaders to confirm that the evacuation plan works for large groups of children.

In some cases teachers may have more latitude when it comes to implementing a safety policy at the classroom level. Talea teaches in a preschool setting. She is directed to conduct an evacuation drill once per month, but is allowed to decide when the drill will occur and how the drill will be introduced and carried out. She must notify her supervisor of when she will conduct the drill, and she must keep a record of each drill to document that she has met the monthly practice requirement. When Talea plans her drill, she does so as part of a larger unit on safety. She invites the local firefighter education team to visit her class. The firefighters show children the fire truck, talk about their safety equipment, and teach children what to do in case of fire. After the firefighters leave, Talea guides the children to pair off and follow the assistant teacher while she activates a home smoke alarm. This way she combines the program requirement to conduct an evacuation drill with a classroom safety education theme, reinforcing the message about why evacuation is important. This approach provides an appropriate mechanism for teachers of very young children to design a drill format that fits the children's developmental understanding.

Organizing Safe Environments

Teachers have considerable control when it comes to organizing a safe classroom. They are responsible for ensuring children's physical and emotional safety and are entrusted to assume this role to the best of their ability. This includes arranging the classroom to reduce risk to safety, establishing an atmosphere of security and trust, and helping children to manage difficult interpersonal interactions. No two classrooms look alike, but each is established with safety in mind.

Enhancing Emotional Safety through Relationships

Teachers have close and frequent contact with children. This helps them make significant contributions to children's experience of both physical and emotional safety. Children gain a sense of security when they know the teacher is watching out for them. Teachers focus on developing caring relationships with each child, and assist children to build social bonds with one another, extending a sense of inclusion to all children in the class. These activities build the strong teacher and child relationships that support children's willingness to follow safety guidance and respond to safety directions.

Preschool and older children practice and learn ways to keep safe in case of fire.

Supervising Children

Children's safety depends on appropriate supervision. Teachers have the moral and ethical responsibility to recognize children's vulnerability and dependency on adults and to provide consistent and thorough supervision without fail (NAEYC, 2005). Children should be supervised by sight and sound at all times (Copple & Bredekamp, 2009). Except when formally released from duty (for breaks, or other prearranged times), teachers have direct responsibility for monitoring the care and safety of each child. Supervising children at all times is the single most important way to keep them safe from harm.

What if. . .

you were asked to describe how you supervise children? How would you explain your strategies to ensure that children are always within sight and sound, even in a large space such as the play yard?

Modeling and Teaching Safe Behaviors

Teachers are important role models and as such must ensure that their actions always convey the appropriate health and safety message. This includes doing what they expect children to do. For example, responding appropriately in emergency drills, using an appropriate ladder to stand on rather than a chair to reach objects that are on high shelves, chewing foods carefully, and using words to demonstrate how to ask for help.

Teachers are also responsible for teaching children safety skills. With very young children this might include redirecting a child to keep him from hitting on the window with a block while saying, "Blocks are for building not for hitting. Show me how you can build with blocks." Preschool and school-age children are taught about pedestrian safety by reading a book about how to safely cross the street and then by practicing with their teacher. Examples of ways to teach children about pedestrian safety are provided in the *Teaching Wellness* feature. Being intentional about teaching children skills for pedestrian safety can make a significant impact in helping children avoid the hazards associated with walking near traffic (Agran et al., 2003). Modeling and teaching about safety are ways teachers are intentional about conveying important safety concepts.

MyEducationLab

Go to the Assignments and Activities section of Topic 9: Emergencies and Injuries in the MyEducationLab for your course and complete the activity entitled *Pedestrian Safety*. How can you model pedestrian safety practices for children in your care?

Learning Outcome: Children will learn the steps to cross the street safely. Children will know that they should always cross the street with a grown-up.

Infants and Toddlers

- *Goal:* Infants and toddlers will participate in walks, experiencing the rhythm associated with safely crossing the street.

- *Materials:* Baby carrier, backpack, or stroller for one or more children.

- *Activity plan:* Take a walk in the neighborhood near the children's setting. Have toddlers hold hands with a teacher. Select an area that is not too busy or noisy. Spend time walking along the sidewalk. Talk with the children, describing what you are doing. Say, "We are walking safely along the sidewalk. The sidewalk is the place for people to walk along the street." Next, prepare to cross the street: Stop at a crosswalk. Say, "Now we are getting ready to cross the street. First we stop. We watch the light to know when it is time to move. Do you see the green 'Walk' sign glowing?

That means it is time for us to walk right across. We keep watching to make sure it is safe from cars. There, we are across the street. That was a safe way to cross."

- *How to adjust the activity:* Practice using a pretend street in the play yard. Go to a park or quiet neighborhood and practice crossing at corners that do not have lighted or controlled crosswalks. Talk about stopping, looking both ways for cars, trucks, buses, and bicycles that could be dangerous. Remind children to listen for vehicles. Practice waiting until it is safe to cross, then practice walking right across the street until you are safely on the other side.

- *Did you meet your goal?* Did children participate in the walk? Did they listen to the descriptions of safe crossing? Did you see the toddlers stop, look, and listen?

Preschoolers and Kindergartners

- *Goal:* Children will be able to name the safety cues: stop, look, listen, and cross the street with a grown-up.

- *Materials:* Toy cars, trucks, buses, bicycles, people figures, small street signs (stop, no crossing, yield), blocks, masking tape, paper, pens or crayons, and scissors.

- *Activity plan:* Create a "neighborhood." Place masking tape on the floor in rectangular shapes to resemble neighborhood blocks. Use the tape to mark off a roadway, showing the stripe in the middle of the road. Place blocks, toy vehicles, figures, and small street signs around the neighborhood. Provide the paper, pens or crayons, and scissors at a table nearby. Introduce the activity as a town where the people are learning to move about safely; the vehicles are learning to stop at the stop signs, and the

people are learning to cross the street safely. Invite children to create the town, using blocks to build houses, stores, gas stations. Point out the supplies that could be used to make signs for the street or for the stores. Watch as children play. Ask children questions such as "How will this lady get to the store? Does she know how to cross the street safely?" Later, at group time talk about always crossing the street with a grown-up. Use story books or a puppet character to quiz the children about what they know about pedestrian safety.

- *How to adjust the activity:* Take a neighborhood walk with children. Take turns allowing a child to be the leader. Ask the leader to help you guide the children through the steps of stop–look–listen. Depending on the neighborhood, point out how children can activate the pedestrian crossing light by pushing the

Taking Action in Emergencies

Teachers are responsible for responding immediately if they see children in a dangerous situation or if an accident occurs. Teachers are most empowered to assume this role when they have received emergency response training and are able to practice using potential emergency scenarios. If an emergency occurs, teachers must put the program's emergency response plan into action. They must assume their role in caring for the injured child. Program-level procedures provide backup support for teachers in child care centers and pedestrian crossing button. If children in the class use alternate methods to move about, such as wheelchairs, use inclusive words. Say, for example, "move" along the street, and "move" through the crosswalk instead of "walk."

- **Did you meet your goal?** Are children able to identify the steps for safely crossing the street? Can you observe children practicing the stop–look–listen cues when you are practicing? Are children able to say why it is important to always cross with a grown-up?

School-Age Children

- **Goal:** Children will be able to name the safety cues: stop, look, listen when crossing the street, and describe how to safely walk along the street and cross at the corner.

- **Materials:** Construction paper, scissors, pens, glue tape.

- **Activity plan:** Provide materials for making pedestrian safety books. Discuss the safety cues stop–look–listen and the message for children to cross the street with an adult. Invite children to make a book to read to the others in the class. Guide the children to create a character (a person or animal) that learns about how to walk along the sidewalk safely and how to cross the street. Ask first-grade children to draw and write their stories. Provide models for spelling the words *stop*, *look*, and *listen*. Encourage invented spelling. For second graders, provide pages ready to assemble into a book. On each page

offer a step in the story for children to illustrate and add to, such as "Always walk on the sidewalk," "Stop at the crosswalk," "Look both ways for cars, buses, trucks, and bicycles," "Listen for the sounds of the traffic," or "When it is safe, walk across the street." For third-grade and older children, invite children to elaborate on the basic messages discussed above. Encourage children to depict their neighborhood in their illustrations.

- **How to adjust the activity:** Provide an opportunity for older children to read their books to a younger class group as part of a lesson about pedestrian safety. Have children make bookmarks with the safety cues. Give the bookmarks to a younger class group or place them in the library for others to use.

- **Did you meet your goal?** Are children able to identify the safety cues? Can you observe from their stories that children understand the safety concepts?

school-based settings. Teachers in family child care settings need to have a plan for obtaining support from others in case of emergency.

Advocating for Children's Safety

Teachers are often the first to recognize gaps or problems in program safety procedures because of their firsthand knowledge of the children and classroom and the frequency with which they use safety and emergency practices. Recognizing problems in the environment and in the safety procedures and advocating for improvement are important professional responsibilities of those who teach young children.

Involving Program Staff

Teachers in center-based programs and schools do not work alone when responding to emergency situations. These settings have the benefit of a staff comprised of various program personnel who contribute to children's safety in specific ways. For example:

- Directors and other program leaders ensure safe facilities, hire safe personnel, and implement carefully crafted program safety policies.
- Administrative assistants and office support staff monitor security and access to the building and store confidential information safely.
- Teachers establish safe environments, supervise children for safety, and teach children safety skills.
- Health personnel, such as school nurses or program health coordinators, design safe health practices and ensure that first-aid kits are well stocked and easily at hand.
- Nutrition personnel, such as dietitian consultants, cooks, shoppers, and other food service personnel, make safe food selections and store, handle, and serve food safely.
- Custodians keep facilities safe, clean, and sanitary.
- Bus drivers provide safe transportation.

As program leaders design safe program services and create emergency response plans, the specific roles and responsibilities of program staff should be clarified. Periodically all program staff should participate in making recommendations to program safety procedures. This ensures that the perspectives of those closest to potential emergencies are included.

Teachers in family child care homes and other smaller settings often work alone or with few supporting staff members. The safety procedures and emergency response plan for these settings must be resourceful in accessing needed support. Family members and neighbors can be contacted in advance to identify ways they can provide assistance. This might include reviewing the family child care setting for safety as part of a safety preparedness activity, coming to help supervise children if an emergency occurs, being available to flag down emergency vehicles, or providing support for the early childhood teacher after an emergency event is over. Arranging for such supports ahead of time helps build a community of support and contributes to teachers' confidence as they prepare for emergency events.

Collaborating with Families and Community Members

Young children are vulnerable and need the support of everyone in the community to keep them safe.

Families and community safety workers are also part of the context of safety that surrounds young children. Families and community members bring unique perspectives and have a vested interest in children's safety. Families offer key reminders about the vulnerability of young children and are able to describe how their children might respond in emergency settings. Families also bring suggestions about efficient ways to communicate with them in event of child injury or program emergency.

Community safety personnel have expertise in emergency management and response and are aware of resources that can guide emergency planning. For example, public safety workers may be able to conduct a review of the children's classrooms to identify potential hazards in case of an earthquake or to make recommendations about emergency food supplies the children's setting should have on hand. The participation of families and community members also builds connections among children's programs, teachers, and community agencies to increase awareness about children's safety.

Safety Segment

Sample Safety Updates for Families

The American Academy of Pediatrics recommends these family safety updates:

- **Be cautious with hot liquids.** Hot cooking or drinking liquids cause many burns. Children are burned from spills when taking hot beverages out of the microwave oven and by older children who are carrying hot liquids. Be sure to supervise your child around hot liquids.
- **Most poisonings involve products that have child-resistant packaging.** Remember to store drugs, vitamins, cleaning products, and other dangerous products out of the reach of children.
- **Child shopping cart seats are a source of injury.** Many children are treated in hospital emergency rooms every year because of shopping cart–related injuries. Use the shopping cart safety belts and be sure to carefully supervise your child when shopping.
- **Bath tub and shower injuries are common especially for children ages 4 and younger.** Slips, trips, and falls cause face, head, and neck injuries. Provide nonskid safety mats in the bottom of the tub and shower to help prevent these injuries.
- **Mini-trampolines are dangerous for children.** Many children have suffered severe head injuries from mini-trampolines. Experts recommend not using them.

Sources: "Preventing Unintentional Scald Burns: Moving beyond Tap Water," by G. Lowell et al., 2008, *Pediatrics, 122*(4), pp. 799–804; "Unintentional Child Poisonings Treated in United States Hospital Emergency Departments: National Estimates of Incident Cases, Population-Based Poisoning Rates, and Product Involvement," by R. L. Franklin and G. G. Rogers, 2008, *Pediatrics, 122*(6), pp. 1244–1251; "Improving Safety-Restraint Use by Children in Shopping Carts: Evaluation of a Store-Based Safety Intervention," by G. A. Smith, 2006, *Pediatrics, 118*(2), pp. 739–745; "Injuries Associated with Bathtubs and Showers among Children in the United States," by S. J. Mao et al., 2009, *Pediatrics, 124*(2), pp. 541–547; and "Comparison of Minitrampoline- and Full-Sized Trampoline-Related Injuries in the United States, 1990–2002," by B. J. Shields et al., 2005, *Pediatrics, 116*(1), pp. 96–103.

Making a Professional Commitment to Safety

Becoming a teacher means assuming a professional. This involves assisting families to improve children's safety at home. Teachers also keep attuned to new information about safety and need to share it with families. The *Safety Segment* provides a sample of how teachers can summarize safety information and share it with families. This is part of the teacher and family partnership that is a characteristic of early childhood programs. Working together, teachers and families can reduce the potential for injury and make positive contributions on children's physical and emotional health and safety.

The National Association for the Education of Young Children is the professional organization for those who teach children ages birth to 9 years. Members of NAEYC adhere to the guidelines of the NAEYC Code of Ethical Conduct and Statement of Commitment (NAEYC, 2005) as a way of demonstrating their professional obligation to provide for the health and safety of young children. The primary principle of the NAEYC Code of Ethical Conduct states:

> Above all, we shall not harm children. We shall not participate in practices that are emotionally damaging, physically harmful, disrespectful, degrading, dangerous, exploitative, or intimidating to children. (NAEYC, 2005, p. 3)

Teachers put these principles into practice by taking a proactive stance to safety in the classroom. They view safety as a primary professional responsibility and structure their

What if. . .

you were asked to address the families at your school's curriculum night? The request asks you to describe your professional commitment to children's safety. How would you respond? What aspects of planning and teaching about safety would you describe as the most compelling parts of your commitment?

teaching and care on safety principles. Assuming a professional identify also involves contributing to program and community to efforts to improve safety for children and families. To accomplish this, teachers need to keep current about the risks and causes of injury to young children and know how to identify safety strategies that can make a difference. Advocating in this way requires teachers to study the recommendations of reputable resources and know how to adapt such information to solve problems in the classroom and community.

Summary

Ensuring children's physical and emotional safety is a fundamental responsibility of teachers. It involves recognizing how safety influences children's healthful development and considering its impact on all aspects of teaching. The classroom is an important refuge for children, where they can relax and focus on growing and learning. To create this safe environment and be most effective in their work, teachers need to know about the most common causes of unintentional injury and fatality in young children. In combination with an understanding of individual risk factors for injury, teachers should be prepared to design and implement safe practices in the classroom.

Children's settings and schools are generally safe environments for young children, but accidents can, and do, happen. In response, program leaders and teachers work together to meet or exceed safety standards. Program leaders establish safe facilities and design program policies to ensure children's safety in all program services. Teachers create safe classroom environments, implement safe management practices, and learn to respond when children's safety is threatened. As participants in these safety efforts, families and community members contribute an intimate understanding of their children and professional knowledge, respectively.

Making a commitment to children's physical and emotional safety is an important aspect of professionalism. Teachers demonstrate this commitment by reducing the risks for injury. They establish safe environments, implement safe management practices, supervise children and take action when needed, and advocate for the safety of children in all settings.

Key Terms

Bite or sting injury, p. 456

Burns, p. 458

Drowning, p. 457

Falls, p. 455

Fatal injuries, p. 456

Safety, p. 451

Struck by or against injury, p. 455

Sudden infant death
  syndrome (SIDS), p. 458

Suffocation, p. 457

Unintentional injuries, p. 454

Review Questions

1. Discuss Maslow's hierarchy of needs and explain how physical and emotional safety affect children's growth and development.

2. Identify the most frequent causes of unintentional injury among young children and provide example scenarios of how each cause of injury could occur in an early childhood setting.

3. Describe the individual risk factors that influence a child's potential for unintentional injury.

4. Identify three of the common licensing requirements that contribute to children's safety. Discuss how each affects safety in the early childhood setting.

5. Identify some of the responsibilities and actions taken by early childhood program leaders and teachers to create a context of safety for children in early childhood settings and schools. Discuss how each of these responsibilities contributes to children's safety.

Discussion Starters

1. Reflect on a children's classroom you have taught in or observed. What policies and actions were in place to ensure children's safety? How would you describe these to prospective parents to help them feel their child would be secure in the environment?

2. Consider the aspects of children's age and developmental maturity that influence children's risk for injury. Discuss ways teachers should adapt their supervision practices for each of the following age groups: infants, children ages 1 to 4 years, and children ages 5 to 9 years. Because of the differences in developmental skills, should children be grouped by age? Can a mixed-age class group be safe?

3. Review the various responsibilities teachers have for children's safety. Which responsibility do you feel is most central? Which responsibility do you think is most important to families?

Practice Points

1. Go to the Centers for Disease Control and Prevention web page titled "Injury, Violence & Safety" at http://cdc.gov/InjuryViolenceSafety. Select three topics to explore. Read the "Quick Facts" and "Injury Prevention Tips for Parents and Children." Discuss how this information can guide you as you plan your classroom environment and establish safe supervision practices.

2. Log on to the National Child Care Information and Technical Assistance Center website at http://nccic.acf.hhs.gov/topics/topic/index.cfm?topicId=2. Explore health and safety topics related to facilities, ratios and group size, and staff qualifications. Identify the requirements for liability and auto insurance for small and large family child care and center-based programs in your state.

3. Consider your responsibilities as a teacher for children's safety. Create a list of safety practices that you feel you are ready to assume. Identify at least three concerns you have related to keeping children safe in your classroom. Identify resources that can help you gain the information and skills you need. What actions will you take to improve your competencies and confidence in each of these areas?

Web Resources

Centers for Disease Control and Prevention
   www.cdc.gov

National Association for the Education of Young Children: Code of Ethical Conduct and Statement of Commitment
   www.naeyc.org/positionstatements/ethical_conduct

National Child Care Information and Technical Assistance Center
   http://nccic.acf.hhs.gov

MyEducationLab
To assess your understanding of how to create safe environments for young children, go to the Book Specific Resources section in the MyEducationLab for your course, select *Nutrition, Health, and Safety for Young Children*, Chapter 14 of the Study Plan, and then complete the multiple choice questions and activities.

chapter 15 | Creating Safe Environments

Learning Outcomes

After reading this chapter, you should be able to:

1. Describe some of the aspects that guide planning for children's facilities and discuss strategies for increasing security in children's environments.

2. Plan and create safe indoor environments for young children.

3. Design and establish safe outdoor environments for young children.

4. Select safe and appropriate toys and equipment for young children.

Leah has recently moved to a rural community where she has been hired to lead the local expansion of her state's prekindergarten program. Leah recognizes that the choices she makes will have lasting importance and she is unsure if she has all the information she needs to create an early childhood setting that is safe and appropriate for her new community.

Leah gathers information from the town's website and then schedules a visit with Gerald, the city manager, to learn more about the community. Gerald talks about the population characteristics of the community, identifying the numbers of families with young children and the diversity of cultures in the area. He describes the local industries and the role of agriculture, and shares information about the employment rate and average income of families in the community. He also shares his thoughts about local support for education and describes some of the public service agencies that partner with projects for children and families. Leah asks about specific issues such as the crime rate and incidence of child abuse and neglect. Later Leah gathers resources that make recommendations for equipping early childhood classrooms. When she sits down to plan, Leah has confidence that the facility and classrooms will be appropriate for the children and the community.

Establishing environments that support children's physical and emotional safety is an important task of teaching. Early childhood environments serve the needs of children and families and contribute to the social fabric of communities. They need to be designed and arranged to reduce potential for injury and to support healthy, safe, and appropriate care and education of young children. This involves making many thoughtful decisions, including selecting appropriate locations for children's programs, establishing safe classrooms, and outdoor facilities, and providing safe toys. Teachers like Leah are responsible for ensuring children's safety in the children's environment, which includes the physical facilities and the materials used to facilitate learning (National Association for the Education of Young Children [NAEYC], 2005). The task can be challenging, given the variety of facilities and schools where young children are typically served.

Children's environments are created in many settings, including family child care homes, centers, schools, after-school settings, and camps. In this chapter we discuss the variety of settings that are established for early education and explore how decisions are made to ensure safety. We describe some of the critical attributes of safe facilities, outline how to set up safe classrooms and provide detailed information about how to select safe toys. With this knowledge, teachers like Leah are prepared to create safe environments for any age group.

PLANNING APPROPRIATE EARLY CHILDHOOD ENVIRONMENTS

Establishing facilities to serve young children requires attentiveness to the contexts of the community and neighborhoods as well as an awareness of the family needs that the program is striving to meet. Some communities require safe after-school care for school-age children to keep them safe in the afternoons. Many families may require full-day child care while others are seeking part-day socialization opportunities for their children. Early childhood programs established to address these needs have several factors in common: the need to create safe environments that recognize and value the developmental requirements of young children and appropriate spaces to provide care and education.

Meeting the Need for Safe Spaces

Early education facilities currently provide out-of-home care and education for a large number of young children. The U.S. Census Bureau reports that in 2002 nearly 11.6 million children under the age of 5 participated in some kind of care and education arrangement (Overturf Johnson, 2005). In addition, 15 million children ages 5 to 14 years received some kind of regular care in addition to their school attendance (Overturf Johnson, 2005).

children's environment
the early childhood space
in which children grow and
learn; includes the
building facility, indoor
and outdoor spaces,
toys, equipment,
materials, and people

universal
prekindergarten
public early childhood
education programs
accessible to all 4-year-old
children

Family needs for child care and interest in early education drives much of the involvement of children in early childhood settings. Community goals also play a role. For example, many states are exploring how to provide universal prekindergarten, public early childhood programs that would be accessible to all 4-year-old children, in recognition of the importance of early education in closing educational achievement gaps. Such initiatives increase the need for safe and secure early childhood classroom spaces.

Facility Challenges

Although state and federal support for early childhood services has been growing through programs such as Head Start and Early Head Start, the physical facilities that house such programs have not received as much attention. To date, most early childhood operations have not had the finances to construct new facilities and have had to make do with rented, borrowed, or renovated spaces that were not designed to serve young children. Attention is needed to finance, design, and construct appropriate spaces to serve young children.

Capacity Challenges

Finding ways to address the need for more early childhood facilities is a challenge. Teachers and other early childhood professionals have little training about how to design an appropriate facility or how to manage real estate and loan decisions in order to finance their construction. National facility development policies and regulations are needed to guide the development of safe and appropriate early childhood facilities (Sussman & Gillman, 2007).

Facility Design and Development Resources

Various sources are available to guide the construction and renovation of safe educational facilities. The U.S. Department of Education's National Clearinghouse for Educational Facilities and the U.S. General Services Administration's (GSA's) Public Buildings Service, Office of Childcare (GSA, 2003), offer guidance for the construction of federally funded child care settings.

The NAEYC's accreditation standards and the National Resource Center for Health and Safety in Child Care and Early Education provide guidelines such as those described in Figure 15-1. In addition, some states offer helpful information (see, for example, New Jersey Department of Education, 2004) as well as local government building codes. When teachers like Leah have dual responsibilities for teaching and program management they can access these resources to ensure that facility safety regulations are addressed.

Teaching Children in Many Settings

Nearly every community has an early childhood setting tucked into the framework of the neighborhood. Whether in a residential area, beside the beach or ski area, within an indus-

Figure 15-1 Requirements for the Construction of Safe Early Childhood Facilities

Design Requirements:

- Design meets children's age, developmental, and educational needs
- Minimum 35 square feet usable interior space per child

Construction Requirements:

- Use of nontoxic building materials and lead-free paint
- Appropriate use of nonflammable materials
- Shatterproof glass used at doors
- Appropriate barriers for stairs, landings, decks
- Child-appropriate emergency escape routes

- Clearly marked and lighted exits
- Safe electrical outlets with childproof covers
- Appropriate lighting: shatterproof covers over lightbulbs and fluorescent lights

Systems Requirements:

- Water
- Electrical
- Sewage
- Heat
- Site drainage
- Air quality

Sources: Based on *NAEYC Early Childhood Program Standards and Accreditation Criteria: The Mark of Quality in Early Childhood Education*, 2007, Washington, DC: National Association for the Education of Young Children; Adapted from *Caring for Our Children: National Health and Safety Performance Standards: Guidelines for Out-of-Home Child Care Programs*, 2nd ed., Copyright 2002. Used with permission of American Academy of Pediatrics; National Association for the Education of Young Children. (2008). Overview of the NAEYC early childhood program standards. Retrieved January 12, 2010, from http://www.naeyc.org/files/academy/file/OverviewStandards.pdf.

trial complex, in a high-rise office building, or near a public school, child care and education facilities come in different shapes and sizes. This diversity of spaces highlights the benefits and challenges faced by the early childhood profession when creating safe environments. No single overarching agency governs early childhood services nationwide. Therefore, even within the guidelines of local building codes and the standards of child care licensing regulatory agencies, early childhood professionals are able to make significant decisions about where facilities are located and how classroom are arranged. This flexibility makes it possible for programs to reflect the culture and style of the community.

In order to ensure that environments are safe for children, teachers need to be individually aware of safety standards especially for the classroom and outdoor play areas. Teachers must be prepared to use the resources available to them to envision and create safe classrooms in a great variety of settings. In the long run, for the benefit of young children in the future, early childhood professionals need to participate in guiding the creation of responsive policies for facilities and environments that serve young children. The *Policy Point* discusses deliberations about where state-supported prekindergarten settings should be located: in public schools or community settings?

Policy Point

WHERE SHOULD STATE-SUPPORTED PREKINDERGARTEN BE LOCATED?

Public School Settings

Benefits

✓ State departments of education already have systems for streaming funds to communities through the school district.

✓ New policies could use this existing system to direct funds for the purpose of creating early childhood spaces.

✓ Public school sites have credibility as professional locations for education that may not be as evident in community-based settings.

Challenges

• Creating prekindergarten spaces in school settings has the potential to divert preschooler enrollment from community providers, creating problems for local child care businesses. If large numbers of preschool children leave the community setting, the cost of care for infant and toddler slots would likely increase.

• Prekindergarten programs are typically in session for only part of the day. If the prekindergarten is located in the public school, who will provide the extended-hour services and where?

Community Settings

Benefits

✓ Community settings are already established and ready to serve children and families.

✓ Community settings are highly attuned to child and family needs. This history of service supports programming that addresses the needs of the whole child, not just the child's educational needs.

✓ Community programs have a strong family orientation.

✓ Community settings are set up to provide full-day needs for care.

Challenges

• A system of streaming funds to community programs is not currently established. This may cause organizational challenges.

• Community early childhood programs do not have the history of credibility that the public school setting provides. Some parents may be more confident having their children attend a public school setting.

• Community programs may differ greatly in quality. What quality standards would guide the selection for providing state-funded services?

Source: Based on *Building Early Childhood Facilities—What States Can Do to Promote Quality* (NIEER Preschool Policy Report), by Carl Sussman and Amy Gillman, 2007, New Brunswick, NJ: National Institute for Early Education Research. Retrieved January 13, 2010, from www.nieer.org/resouces/research/Facilities.pdf.

Creating Spaces That Value Children

Decisions made about the design and arrangement of children's spaces are influenced by beliefs regarding the value of children, how children learn, and the role of the teacher and environment in promoting children's growth and development. These aspects reflect a **philosophical perspective** about the connection of the space to the actions that will occur within them. In early childhood settings the child is the primary consideration when designing and arranging safe environments (NAEYC, 2008). The following aspects of environments reflect this child-centered approach:

> **philosophical perspective** attitudes, ideas, and ways of thinking about children: their value, how they learn, the role of the teacher, the role of the physical environment

- *Providing space for child-oriented play.* Spaces should be appropriately sized for the age of the children and the size of the group.
- *Creating a sense of welcome.* Children should feel "at home" in the space.
- *Honoring the work of young children.* Familiar toys and materials should be available and children's art work should be prominently displayed.
- *Recognizing the importance of transition.* Comfortable family-centered entry spaces should be provided to ease the transition into the care setting.

Environments that promote these values provide settings where children's physical and emotional well-being are supported. The creation of such environments has been influenced by several key approaches, such as the Montessori and Reggio Emilia models discussed below.

Maria Montessori

Attention to the arrangement of early childhood environments was promoted by the work of Dr. Maria Montessori (1870–1952). Key to the Montessori approach is the belief that children are capable learners (Montessori, 1966). As a result Montessori-oriented classrooms are orderly environments that invite exploration and promote children's independent learning. Child-oriented spaces are organized to encourage both individual and group exploration. The use of child-sized furnishings is central.

Toys and materials are carefully arranged on low, open shelving, allowing children to choose what they need and be responsible for returning materials to their place after use. Teachers are guided to "follow the child" when arranging spaces and planning activities because children are the center of learning and are valued and respected for their work.

Reggio Emilia

Another model that has influenced the early childhood community is the Reggio Emilia approach. The village of Reggio Emilia, Italy, embraces the ideal that children are of equal value in the community and are the responsibility of the collective group (New, 1993). The community approach is evident in facility design decisions that link children to each other, by providing common spaces and plazas, as well as to their community and world, through large windows and classroom doorways that connect children to the outdoors (New, 1993). Displays of children's artwork, lovely furnishings, and a liberal use of mirrors attract child and adult attention to enjoyment of the indoor and outdoor environments and invite exploration (Edwards, Gandini, & Forman, 1993; Katz & Cesarone, 1994). A hallmark of this approach is the idea that the environment is an additional teacher (New, 1993).

Confronting Challenges

Children's environments in the United States often show limited expression of a purposeful philosophical perspective of value for the work of young children. Most are housed in adapted spaces, where financial challenges limit the opportunity to create innovative and beautiful environments. Sometimes early childhood classrooms appear to put the focus on what teachers do in the setting rather than what children experience (Tarr, 2001). One report claims that U.S. early childhood classrooms tend to be overly busy and crowded spaces (Tarr, 2001), where children are separated from each other and disconnected from the outside world (Greenman, 2005). Some spaces that serve children under the age of 5 have the look of miniature elementary school classrooms where rows of desks or tables dominate (Tarr, 2001), suggesting that young children are not able to be self-directed explorers and learners.

These criticisms invite teachers to revitalize their energy around creating safe environments that enhance development and learning without closing children off from the world.

Envisioning Appropriate Environments

Appropriate environments are established with consideration for children's age, size, and developmental needs (Moore Johnson, 2006). They demonstrate recognition of the ways in which children use their senses to experience and learn from the visual, auditory, aromatic, and tactile attributes of their surroundings. They are also welcoming, comfortable, beautiful and inspirational. Appropriate environments encourage creativity and exploration and build children's confidence to learn (Greenman, 2005). In sum, children's spaces should:

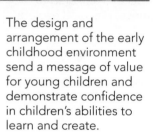

- Support physical safety and emotional security.
- Be welcoming and child and family friendly.
- Address children's age, developmental, and educational needs.
- Be culturally appropriate and developmentally accessible.
- Inspire exploration and discovery.
- Support teaching and learning.

Environments that are appropriate for children offer important attributes that are good for teachers, too. Teachers need comfortable spaces that provide flexibility for creative room arrangement, support curriculum delivery, and offer adequate storage (Moore Johnson, 2006). Appropriate environments for teachers contribute to teacher satisfaction, which may reduce the rate of teacher turnover and thus improve the quality of programming for young children.

The design and arrangement of the early childhood environment send a message of value for young children and demonstrate confidence in children's abilities to learn and create.

Addressing Variety in Children's Environments

Appropriate environments are created to address a range of care needs. Sometimes spaces are assigned for a specific purpose; sometimes shared-use spaces are established. The task of creating a responsive environment depends on the particular need.

Short-Term Child Care

Short-term care settings are established for occasional use, such as child care provided for families while they attend a meeting. Teachers must arrange the environment to accommodate the needs of a range of age groups. This involves identifying and correcting any safety concerns, such as covering electrical outlets, blocking off stairways, or closing off shelves that contain toys inappropriate for the age group. Teachers in short-term care settings arrange the space, provide care, and open and close the children's environment over a matter of hours.

Drop-In Services

Drop-in services are usually provided in prearranged environments where the specific group of children in attendance may vary from day to day or even from one hour to the next. Drop-in care may be provided at the sports club, shopping mall, or in faith group settings. Teachers need to adjust the environment for safety to address the needs of the particular children in attendance.

Full-Day Care and Education

Full-day programs are typically offered in well-established spaces. Children's participation is prearranged and scheduled in settings such as family child care, preschools, child care centers, elementary schools, before- and after-school programs, camps, and enrichment classes. In these settings teachers create environments for a specific purpose in order to serve a particular age group. In these settings teachers can establish and adjust an environment to be safe for an expected age group of children.

Children's environments need to offer sufficient space for children to move, play, and explore.

Addressing Space Needs for Program Services

Children's programs have specific space needs, including classrooms and outdoor play areas, as well as spaces for storage, food preparation, meetings, janitorial supplies, and offices. Children's centers and schools typically separate the areas provided for children from spaces that serve other program activities. Family child care homes often designate special spaces for the children's program while conducting other activities such as meetings with families or business within the general family household areas. Carefully planned and clearly identified spaces increase safety by avoiding overcrowding and unsafe storage habits that may contribute to accidents. A checklist of spaces needed to provide general program services is shown in Figure 15-2.

Meeting Requirements for Usable Floor Space

usable square footage
the amount of floor space that is open and accessible to children

Classroom square footage is considered to be the single most important characteristic of a safe and appropriate children's environment. Usable square footage refers to the floor space that is not covered by furnishings but is open and accessible. This measurement is used as a basic guide to determine the number of children that may be present in the space at one time. As a result, classroom square footage, along with the furnishings plan, determines the group size for any room in the early childhood setting.

State licensing standards and NAEYC accreditation standards have traditionally identified that each indoor classroom should provide a minimum of 35 usable square feet per child. However, this space may be too small, and efforts are under way to increase the recommended square footage per child. The GSA (2003) requires a minimum of 45 square feet of usable floor space per child for federally constructed early childhood facilities. The Head Start Technical Assistance Center (National Head Start Facilities Information Services, 2002) and the *National Health and Safety Performance Standards* (American Academy of Pediatrics [AAP], American Public Health Association, & National Resource Center for Health and Safety in Child Care and Early Education, 2002) recommend 50 square feet per child.

Figure 15-2 Typical Space Needs for Early Childhood Settings

Teacher and General Classroom Space Needs

✓ Sufficient square footage for group size
✓ Durable and easy-to-clean floors, walls, and counters
✓ Emergency exits
✓ Child-sized and adult toileting and hand washing areas
✓ Water fountain or access to fresh drinking water
✓ Food storage, preparation, and service areas
✓ Storage space

Infant Classroom Space Needs

✓ Diaper changing and hand washing area
✓ Space for children's belongings (diapers, clothing)
✓ Sufficient space for cribs and high chairs
✓ Movable dividers to separate mobile and nonmobile infants
✓ Refrigeration for breast milk, infant formula, medications

Toddler Classroom Space Needs

✓ Diaper changing and toileting area
✓ Hand washing area near diapering area

✓ Storage for children's belongings (diapers, clothing, blanket)
✓ Refrigeration for breast milk, infant formula, medications

Preschooler Classroom Space Needs

✓ Coat cubbies; space for child belongings
✓ Space to store cots for napping
✓ Space to store projects
✓ Refrigeration for medications

School-Age Child Space Needs

✓ Lockers for belongings
✓ Appropriate access to gender-specific toilets
✓ Space to store projects

Children with Special Developmental Needs

✓ Accessible toilets, sinks, and furniture
✓ Appropriate floor surfacing, acoustics, and lighting
✓ Storage for adaptive equipment
✓ Sound and light-flashing alarm system

Health Hint

Classroom Space Dilemma

Many early childhood professionals feel that the 35-square-foot guideline for children's indoor spaces is not sufficiently based on research of children's behaviors and instead relies too heavily on adult assumptions about space needs. Some are concerned that small spaces negatively influence children's mental health. They note the following:

- Children participating in facilities that provide 35 square feet per child exhibit greater stress and anxiety than children participating in facilities with more space per child.
- Thirty-five square feet is equivalent to a space 5 feet by 7 feet in dimension, or only slightly more than the square footage of two playpens.

Most programs fall back on the minimum square footage space requirements because of limited space availability and cost challenges. They say that:

- Increasing facility square footage would add significantly to the cost of facility construction.
- Increasing the square footage per child would decrease the number of children that could be served in a particular space, thereby reducing program cash flow.
- Some children may be pushed out of quality care settings to settings with less quality if the space requirement is increased.

How should teachers weigh-in on this issue?

Sources: Based on "Designing Settings for Infants and Toddlers," by Anne Rui Olds, pp. 117–138, in *Spaces for Children: The Built Environment and Child Development*, edited by C. Weinstein and T. David, 1987, New York: Plenum; and *The Great 35 Square Foot Myth*, by Randy White and Vicki Stoecklin, 2003, Kansas City, MO: White Hutchinson Leisure & Learning Group, retrieved October 24, 2009, from http://www.whitehutchinson.com/children/articles/35footmyth.shtml.

These variations highlight the trend toward larger space requirements per child. This has implications for the number of children that can be served in a particular setting as well as the cost of providing care and education services. These issues are discussed in the *Health Hint*.

Ensuring Accessibility

Early childhood programs need to be accessible to children with special developmental needs as described in the requirements of Section 504 of the Rehabilitation Act of 1973 and the Americans with Disabilities Act (ADA). These guidelines ensure that people with disabilities have access to the buildings, classrooms, play areas, and toilets and sinks. Considerations should also be given to meeting the needs of persons who have special health or developmental needs. For example, children who have hearing impairments are supported when classrooms are constructed with soft surfaces to control for noise and are equipped with fire alarms that signal emergencies with a flashing light in addition to the sound of the alarm. Accessibility guidelines are best addressed as facilities are developed and classrooms are furnished. This way the environment is prepared ahead to include all children.

Understanding Building Codes and Facility Requirements

Local building codes specify the requirements for facility construction and renovation. Many regulations address safety features. These include details such as building materials and construction techniques to provide safe and sturdy structures for the climate, and requirements for appropriate handrails and barriers around porches and decks to avoid potential falls. Certain restrictions must be addressed for spaces that serve young children in group care settings. Examples include the following (AAP et al., 2002):

- Building materials must be sturdy and free from hazardous products such as mold, dust, or toxic products.
- Basement spaces may not be used to provide services for children under the age of 2.

MyEducationLab

Go to the Assignments and Activities section of Topic 7: Chronic Illness/Special Health Care Needs in the MyEducationLab for your course and complete the activity entitled *Inclusion in an Early Childhood Class*. How does this classroom promote an inclusive and safe environment?

- Children must be cared for in a ground floor space if the building is constructed of wood.
- Glass windows and doors should use safety glass or be covered with metal mesh safety guards for at least 36 inches from the floor.

Teachers who work in facilities that have been approved by the local building inspector and licensed by the local child care licensing agency must continue to be vigilant to watch for and correct aspects that are not safe.

Providing Appropriate Utility Services

Programs that serve young children are also required to provide appropriate utility services. These services are typically reviewed during child care licensing site visits:

- *Water:* An approved water supply, such as a public water system, must be provided to ensure that children are safe from waterborne illnesses caused by bacteria, parasites, or other infectious agents. Salmonella, *E. coli,* and dysentery are three familiar bacterial agents that can be found in contaminated water. Children's settings that use well water must have the quality of the water tested periodically to ensure a safe water supply.
- *Sewer:* A reliable sewer system is important to avoid contaminating the facility and grounds with sewer seepage that can introduce disease.
- *Electrical services:* Sufficient lighting is important for safe management of children during the program day and in the event of an emergency. Emergency lighting systems at exits and in hallways and stairways help teachers guide children out of the building in case evacuation is needed. Sufficient electrical outlets are also required to avoid overloading the electrical system and to be sure that electrical cords are not laid across the floor, causing tripping hazards.
- *Heating, cooling, and airflow systems:* A system that maintains appropriate temperature and humidity and controls for air pollution is important for health and safety. Fresh air is needed to maintain healthy indoor air quality and to reduce the incidence of respiratory problems (AAP et al., 2002).
- *Garbage services:* Periodic removal of garbage is needed to control for insects, rodents, and other pests that may introduce disease in the children's environment.
- *Communication systems:* Telephones or other communication systems are needed to contact emergency services or families in case of child illness or injury.

Providing these utility services is a safety issue. If services fail due to mechanical failure, weather, or other conditions, children are put at risk and program services may need to be suspended.

Establishing Safe Spaces around the Building

Creating a safety zone around the building supports safe access. Safe entrances and exits, bicycle parking, and loading zones all contribute to safety as children come to school.

Providing Safe Entrances and Exits Designating walkways into the building and clearly marking exits increase safety as children move in and out of the building, as well as during emergency evacuation. As they approach the building children may be at risk from drivers who speed in the nearby streets and parking lots. Walkways should protect children from areas used by cars. Pathways should accommodate strollers, baby carriages, and wheelchairs and be kept clear.

Addressing Parking Lot Safety Parking areas are busy locations that can be a source of danger to young children. Nearly one-third of child pedestrian deaths occur when a child darts out from between two cars into the street or parking lot (Savage, Kawanabe, Mejeur, Goehring, & Reed, 2002). Teachers sometimes need to walk children across parking lots to access outdoor play areas. The area needs to be kept visually open by trimming shrubs and marking walkways through the parking lot with painted stripes, brightly colored traffic cones, flags, or signs. Teachers should also teach children and families about how to move safely across the parking lots.

Marking Emergency Exits Emergency exits are passageways to the outdoors. They should be clearly marked and visible from all areas of the classroom. Access to the exit doors should be kept clear and open at all times. In settings where the exit doors open into a parking lot or other potentially dangerous area, door alarms should be installed to alert the teacher if a child is trying to open the door (AAP et al., 2002).

Establishing Bicycle Parking Areas Bicycle parking spaces should be provided to encourage this healthy form of transportation. This keeps bikes from being propped near the doors, which can introduce a tripping hazard.

Creating Bus Lanes and Passenger Loading Areas Some programs and schools provide bus transportation. Bus loading areas must be identified to ensure that children move directly from the bus onto a sidewalk rather than into a parking lot, which is dangerous.

Children and families need safe access into the children's setting or school.

Marking Emergency Vehicle Parking Zones Programs may be required to designate parking zones for emergency vehicles. These spaces are identified with painted stripes and are usually located immediately outside an entrance.

Designating School Zones Marking the streets near the early childhood facility as a *school zone* is a good way to warn drivers of the presence of young children. Such signs are usually seen near elementary schools. Teachers and families of younger children may need to contact the local traffic planning office or department of transportation to learn if a school zone designation can be established near a preschool or child care center. If this formal designation is not available, early childhood settings often find ways to announce the presence of children by placing signs or decorative flags to mark the site as a children's area.

Managing Security

The security of early childhood facilities is another important aspect of safety. Security involves keeping children safe from contact with inappropriate or unsafe persons. Families want assurance that teachers are going to keep their children safe from intruders, and teachers want support in case an intruder enters the facility. Security plans help to address these concerns.

Significant attention has been given to ensure that children *stay in* the early childhood facility—that they are protected from being able to wander off. Focus must also be directed to ensure that potential intruders *stay out*—that only approved persons have access to the children's facility and classrooms. Security approaches seek to address both of these concerns without unduly constricting children's opportunities to explore, take on challenges, and learn (Greenman, 2005).

To avoid barricading children from the outside world, teachers look to strategies that are appropriate for the setting. These include identifying security concerns within the local neighborhood, recognizing family issues that may introduce security concerns, and controlling access to the building and classroom. In the opening scenario, Leah is seeking to understand these issues as she plans the prekindergarten program environment. Even with these approaches, being alert to the activities and people in the children's environment and supervising children at all times are the key to providing security.

Identifying Neighborhood Security Concerns
Teachers such as Leah in the opening case scenario are often called on to create safe children's classrooms in unfamiliar settings. They are expected to establish spaces that are a refuge from any neighborhood dynamics that threaten the children's safety and well-being.

What if. . .
you observed a child running in and out of parked cars in the parking lot while the parent was talking with another parent? What would you do?

security
keeping children safe from contact with inappropriate or unsafe persons

However, what works in one area may not be appropriate or safe in another. Factors to consider when identifying neighborhood safety concerns include nearby traffic patterns, the presence of community services such as police and emergency medical care, drug or gang-related issues, and the general crime rate. These issues help to prioritize facility and classroom safety goals and the strategies needed to address security issues.

Understanding Family Security Concerns

Sometimes families have circumstances that may threaten the security of the child or other family member that may spill over into the classroom. For example, domestic violence may compel a parent to move to a confidential safe location and obtain a restraining order against the threatening partner. The threatening partner may seek to regain contact at the child's classroom. Teachers need to ask for a copy of the restraining order so that program staff can be alerted to help with security if needed. A special response plan should be created if needed, including when the security response is needed and who to call for support.

Controlling Facility Access

Controlling access involves managing who comes in and out of the facility and who has access to the classroom, as well as controlling for perceived threats, such as harassment and views of violence. Managing access is a familiar security management approach, but it can be complicated because early childhood programs have a responsibility to ensure that parents and legal guardians have access to their children at any time. This requires a confident understanding of who is approved to enter.

Approaches used to control access depend on the style of the facility and types of security concerns that may be present in the local neighborhood. Strategies include:

- Restricting entry to one doorway and providing a lobby with locked doors into the program service areas beyond which only approved individuals may enter.
- Requiring employees to wear identifying uniforms.
- Requiring all persons in the facility to wear employee or visitor identification tags.
- Installing an electronic keyless entry system with passkeys or passwords available only to approved individuals.

Systems like these communicate attentiveness to security and build a climate of watchfulness. However, it is difficult to determine if they are as effective as hoped in actually improving security. When the security system relies heavily on one identified entryway for the building, attention might be diverted from other potential access areas such as doors that are propped open as supplies are moved in and out or windows that provide access into the building. It is important to identify the level of security that is reasonable for the setting. Here are some examples:

- *Setting 1:* A 4-foot-tall play yard fence meets licensing requirements and adequately prevents children from leaving the play area. In this neighborhood the threat of intruders is considered to be low so the 4-foot fence is sufficient. Teachers pay special attention to supervision at the periphery of the play yard.
- *Setting 2:* A 6-foot-tall solid fence is needed to screen out views of gang activity on the street. Although the solid fence closes off visual access, it also limits the teacher's ability to see if there are potential intruders loitering on the other side of the fence. Teachers consider this as they supervise in the play yard.
- *Setting 3:* Special barriers are planned to screen out the high-rise buildings that surround the play area and overlook the space. Teachers advocate for covered areas to be constructed at strategic locations to screen children from view and the potential of being hit by objects tossed from the buildings. They conduct a walk-through of the playground each day before it is used to ensure that the space is clean and no hazardous debris has been introduced.

Security in children's spaces is reinforced by teachers, families, and program staff who continually observe the children's areas for inappropriate people or potential threats.

Implications for Teachers

Teachers may not be in charge of facility design and management, but they do interface with all aspects of facility safety when teaching young children. For example, teachers supervise children when moving through the building to the library, play yard or bus stop. Like children, teachers are affected by the classroom temperature and air quality, and their safety is impacted if the fire alarm does not work. Teachers also rely on food service personnel to deliver safe food, and janitors to keep the rooms clean and sanitary. When concerns for children's safety and security are recognized, teachers are responsible for helping to make corrections by reporting issues and persisting until the concerns are corrected.

Safety is everyone's responsibility. Program leaders, teachers, and families can partner to periodically review the facilities for unsafe conditions and to assess the effectiveness of

Figure 15-3 Facility Safety Checklist

General Facility Overview			
Yes	No	Safety Feature	Follow-Up and Correction
		Facility is accessible; no entrance or exit routes are blocked. Electrical outlets are covered whenever not in use. All lightbulbs are covered. Water source and supply and distribution system are approved and properly maintained. Drinking fountains are properly cleaned, maintained, and provided with adequate water pressure. Sewage system is in good working order. Garbage and refuse are collected and properly disposed of at least weekly. Classrooms receive fresh air; air flow is satisfactory. Heating and cooling systems are sufficient and in good repair. All classroom materials are stored properly. Storage areas are maintained in a safe uncluttered manner. Storage is free from rodent, insect, and vermin infestation. Windows and doors are screened. Other:	

Children's Spaces			
Yes	No	Item	Follow-Up and Correction
		Space provides at least 35 usable square feet per child. Children's spaces are clean and orderly. First-aid supplies are properly stored. Location is marked. Pathways to exit doors are clearly marked and not obstructed. The telephone numbers for poison control, fire, and emergency medical care are posted by each telephone. Classroom equipment is clean and in good repair. Classroom cabinets contain no lotions, bleaches, cleaning solutions, or other potentially hazardous substances. Furnishings are stable or attached to the walls. Stairs have appropriate barriers. Smoke detectors and fire alarms are in working order. A diapering area is designated; equipment keeps children safe; hand washing sink is nearby; area is easy to clean. Toilet rooms are clean, in good repair, well lighted, free from odor, and well ventilated. Hand washing sinks are located near diaper changing and toileting areas. Soap and paper towels are available. Other:	

(Continued)

Figure 15-3 Facility Safety Checklist *(Continued)*

Food Preparation and Service Areas			
Yes	No	Item	Follow-Up and Correction
		Plumbing is in good working order. There is adequate water pressure.	
		Food preparation surfaces are clean and cleared.	
		Stove hoods and filters are clean and properly operating.	
		Refrigeration units are at or below 45°F (7°C) and are equipped with a red/alcohol-filled thermometer.	
		The dishwashing and sanitization equipment is working according to manufacturer specifications; or the three-sink washing and sanitization method is working properly.	
		Garbage storage receptacles are covered with close-fitting lids.	
		Equipment and utensils are clean and in good repair.	
		Food is acquired from an approved source.	
		Food and drink are free from spoilage and harmful substances.	
		Food is prepared and handled to maintain cleanliness and safety.	
		Readily perishable food is stored below 45°F (7°C) or above 145°F (63°C) except when being prepared.	
		Food and drink are properly stored.	
		Food storage is at least 8 inches off the floor, except where storage is on a wheeled platform or stored on a sealed base.	
		Opened containers of food (flour, sugar, cornmeal) are stored properly in sealed containers with appropriate labeling.	
		Utensils and other items are always stored in a clean, dry place protected from contamination.	
		Other:	

Source: Based on "Rules for the Certification of Child Care Centers," Child Care Division of the Oregon Employment Department, 2001.

security protocols. Figure 15-3 provides a sample checklist to use when reviewing the environment for safety. Checklists like these help identify safety hazards so they can be corrected.

ESTABLISHING SAFE INDOOR ENVIRONMENTS

Safe classrooms are important for children to grow and thrive. Teachers are responsible for creating and maintaining these safe spaces. Safety is accomplished through effective classroom arrangement, furnishings that address children's developmental needs, safe storage of toys and equipment, and removing potential hazards.

Organizing the Classroom

Children's spaces are arranged with definite purposes and goals in mind. During the planning process, each part of the available space is assigned to support an important classroom activity, such as arrival and departure, toileting and hand washing, and snack and meal service. Areas are also defined to provide specific activities that promote developmental goals. For example, a reading area is often established to support early literacy. Some spaces will overlap, and furnishings may be adjusted during the day to allow flexibility and variation in the activities conducted. Organization is supported by creating a plan for the classroom and identifying the needs of each age group.

space use plan
a map or diagram of a children's space showing how the space will be used and the locations of desired activities, furniture, entrances and exits, and so on

Creating a Space Use Plan

A space use plan is essentially a map of the children's environment that shows how the space will be arranged and the locations of desired activities. Planning usually starts by identifying basic requirements and then adding the details of activity areas and furnishings. This

Figure 15-4 Preschool or Kindergarten Classroom Space Use Plan

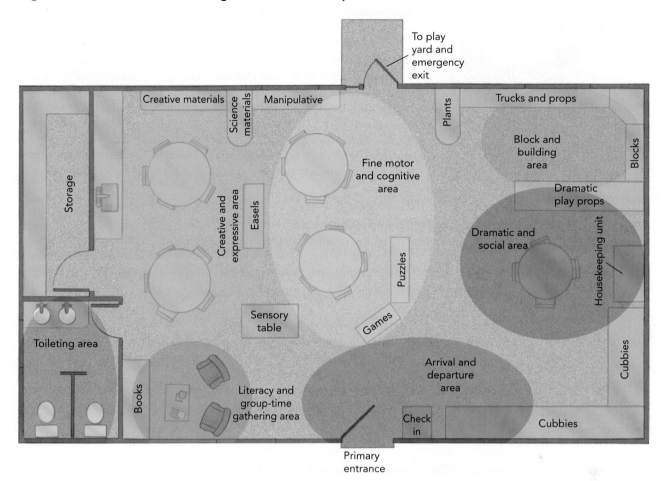

can be accomplished by drawing the basic layout of the space on a large piece of paper, and using smaller circles of paper to identify program needs, activity areas, and furnishings. These can be moved around as the space plan develops. Figure 15-4 provides an example of a preschool or kindergarten classroom space use plan.

Aspects to consider when creating a space use plan vary depending on the size of the space and services to be provided. Examples include the following:

- *Identify a doorway for arrival and emergency exits.* It is important to create open gathering areas inside the entry and exit doors. This ensures that children can be supervised appropriately at arrival and departure. These spaces also offer locations for coat cubbies, bulletin boards, the check-in and -out notebook and the traveling emergency first-aid backpack. Passageways through the classroom to the emergency exit need to be clear of furniture.
- *Arrange pathways through the room.* Passageways may be needed for food service delivery. Access to the toilets and hand washing areas should be kept open and obvious.
- *Provide space for small- and large-group activities.* Space to assemble the children for small-group and large-group activities should be large enough for children to move and participate in games and dancing.

MyEducationLab

Go to the Building Teaching Skills and Dispositions section of Topic 11: Safe Environments in the MyEducationLab for your course and complete the activity entitled *Identify and Eliminate Safety Hazards in Indoor Environments.* As you work through the learning unit, consider the risks to children when teachers do not adhere to strict safety guidelines.

Attaching furniture to the wall prevents tipping hazards.

- *Group activity areas logically.* Activity areas should be planned to avoid unnecessary conflicts. Active areas that involve blocks and trucks should be located away from more quiet areas, such as the reading corner.
- *Take advantage of windows.* Activity areas should be located so natural light is used to best advantage. Placing the dramatic play or creative arts areas near a window where seeds are sprouting may encourage play themes related to the natural environment.
- *Locate furniture.* Low shelves serve a dual purpose when placed in the interior of the room to divide the space. Tall furniture (such as cubbies or shelves) needs to be placed against the wall and attached for safety. Area rugs can designate play spaces and provide variety in color and texture.

Planning for Activity Centers

Early childhood classrooms are often arranged by activity centers, where materials are assembled to support a particular kind of play. Teachers need to consider the specific space needs of each center when setting up the environment. The space needs of typical activity centers are described in Figure 15-5.

What if. . .

you noticed children climbing on a tall shelf to reach the paper supplies? You have reported that the tall shelf is a safety hazard for tipping, but no one has attached it to the wall. What would you do next?

Providing Culturally Relevant Spaces

Environments send a message about who the people are that use them and what they value. This is communicated by what is in the space and what is not (York, 1991). Embracing aspects of culture can be a challenge. Teachers have their own experience and knowledge to draw on, but it is easy to overlook ways the environment can reflect the cultural traditions of the children and families who are

Figure 15-5 **Classroom Centers and Space Needs**

Creative and Expressive Development

- Hard surface flooring to ease cleanup
- Sink for paint and dough mixing and cleanup
- Area to set up a paint easel and drying rack
- Child-accessible storage shelves for supplies

Dramatic and Social Development

- Area for housekeeping or multiuse furnishings
- Child-accessible storage bins for dress-up and props
- Space to move props about

Fine Motor and Manipulative Skills

- Area for a sensory bin table
- Floor and table space for play
- Area for storage shelving and bins

Cognitive and Problem Solving

- Child-accessible storage bins for supplies
- Display area
- Area to store ongoing projects

Language and Literacy Development

- Child-accessible book shelving
- Space for couch or soft chairs
- Space for writing tables

Block and Building Area

- Firm floor surface for building
- Sufficient space for several children to build
- Child-accessible shelving for blocks and props

Large Motor and Movement Area

- *Infants:* Open space appropriate to roll, creep, pull to standing, toss and reach; space that is kept clean from dirt and debris from shoes
- *Toddlers:* Open space to crawl, pull to standing, cruise along sturdy furniture, roll balls, and walk with pull toys
- *Preschoolers:* Open space to dance, balance, build, toss and catch, reach
- *School-age children:* Open space to dance, stretch, balance, build, toss and catch, reach

Group-time Gathering Area

- Rug or carpeting for comfort
- Sufficient space to gather class group

participating. Teachers need to work together with families to gather ideas and put them into action.

One approach is to select visual materials or pieces of artwork to display, such as paintings, weavings, pottery, and tile work. Choosing work from local artists helps make a connection to the community and the local culture. Displaying children's artwork adds another unique expression. Color choices for wall paint and furnishings can convey cultural meaning, and the arrangement of furnishings can help support local customs. For example, placing benches in the lobby or chairs near the door creates a place for families to gather and visit, acknowledging customs that view arrival and departure as important social times. Partnering with families to create culturally relevant spaces communicates that all children and families are welcomed and valued.

Selecting Classroom Furniture

Furniture is an important aspect of the children's environment. It needs to be selected carefully to ensure that it is durable and appropriate to support the needs of the group.

Selecting Child-Sized Furniture

When children enter rooms equipped with furniture that "fits" them, they know they are in a space made for kids, and they respond with interest and enthusiasm. This helps smooth the child's transition into the classroom and sets the tone for a positive experience.

Child-sized furniture includes chairs that children can back up to and sit in without climbing, tables that are approximately waist height where children can stand and play with toys without straining, and shelves that allow children to reach toys without stretching. Child-sized toilets allow children to be more self-sufficient with their toileting needs, and child-sized sinks make it easy for children to reach the water faucets and wash their hands on their own. Furniture that is child-sized encourages the development of self-care skills, providing an example of how the equipment and furnishings of the children's environment support development.

Each age group has special requirements for the kinds of furniture needed. Choices must be appropriate to children's varying sizes to ensure safety.

Infants Furniture for infant spaces should support individual care needs. A crib and high chair should be provided for each baby. Changing tables should be sturdy, easy to sanitize, safe for babies, and comfortable for teachers to use. Each room should provide two comfortable adult-sized chairs to use when feeding babies. Rocking chairs should be selected to avoid pinch hazards. Firm carpeting or area rugs that are easily cleaned add color and softness to the infant environment. Small tubs are helpful for assembling toys. Low room dividers may be useful for dividing spaces for mobile and nonmobile infants.

Mobile Infants and Toddlers Furniture for toddlers and newly mobile infants needs to be low, solid and sturdy. It should not slip as children pull themselves to a standing position. Chairs for toddlers are typically 10 inches high at the seat. They should be designed to avoid the potential of having them slip out from under toddlers as they sit down. Table height should match toddler-sized chairs. Play kitchens and cubbies with coat hooks should be low and sturdy. Shelves with rolling casters on the legs should be avoided unless the casters can be locked to avoid rolling. Toddler spaces also need to provide cots for naptime. These should be comfortable, easy to sanitize, and stackable for efficient storage.

> **What if. . .**
>
> you were new to the community and, like Leah, wanted to learn more about the cultural backgrounds and interests of the children and families you were going to serve? How would you go about getting information directly from children and families?

Child-sized furniture supports children's development of self-help skills and independence.

Preschoolers Furniture for preschool classrooms should fit children of various sizes. A selection of chairs ranging from 10 to 14 inches high at the seat offers choices for seating. Tables of varying heights or with adjustable legs provide flexibility. Shelves should be sturdy and not exceed children's eye height to provide safe access to toys. Other furniture common to preschool classrooms includes cots, water or sensory tables, painting easels, cubbies for coats, workbenches, small tables for listening centers or science activities, kitchen and dramatic play units, and comfy chairs such as bean bag chairs or pillows.

Kindergarten and Elementary Children Kindergarten and elementary classrooms should have chairs that are 16 to 18 inches high. Tables or desks are needed to ensure that each child has a place to sit. Tables of various sizes are useful for projects and small-group activities. Other furnishings may include water and sensory tables, easels, tub-style shelving units, open shelves, bookshelves, cubbies, and lockers or coat hooks.

Confirming Furniture Safety

Furniture for children's environments must be obtained from reputable sources. Each piece should be strong and durable and free from splinters or sharp edges. No lead-based paint or other toxic products should be used in construction. Soft-surfaced furniture, such as child-sized couches and chairs, should be covered with an easily cleaned material. Furniture purchased from import suppliers should be reviewed to determine if it meets U.S. product safety standards.

Storing Classroom Supplies

Most early childhood teachers report that there is never enough storage. It seems that creative teaching goes hand in hand with collecting teaching materials. Storage must be carefully managed to avoid having materials overflow into the classroom and hallways, creating an appearance of disorganization and lowering the professional appearance of the environment. Insufficient storage can also be a safety hazard. Materials may slide off of overloaded shelves or topple as closet doors are opened.

Ideally, enough storage space should be available in classrooms for materials used on a daily basis, and there should also be common storage space for materials that are shared by several teachers. Cupboards, file cabinets, or closets should be available for the teacher's personal teaching materials.

Organizing Materials for Storage

Various storage systems are available to help teachers organize materials. Small toys and those with many pieces are less likely to be separated or lost if they are stored in boxes or transparent plastic tubs. The tubs can be labeled and children are able to see the items, which helps when returning toys to storage at cleanup time. Thoughtful storage prolongs the considerable investment that is made in curriculum materials and prevents a tripping hazard if toys are left in walkways.

What if. . .

a parent asked you to store her child's epinephrine autoinjector (EpiPen) in the classroom for emergency use, but your program's practice is to lock the EpiPen with other medications in the director's office? Is the parent's request legitimate? How would you manage this?

Storing Medications

Any medications that are to be administered to children in care must be stored in a medication lockbox or locking cupboard. These should be located so the medication is easily accessible to the teacher but out of the reach of children. A lockbox may be needed to store medications securely in the refrigerator.

Storing Cleaning Supplies

All cleaning supplies, lotions, bleach, and other potentially toxic materials must be stored outside of the children's space or in a locked cabinet (AAP et al., 2002).

Avoiding Infestation of Insects and Rodents

Teachers often use dried-food products in sensory bins such as rice or cornmeal. Food-related products and birdseed must be carefully stored to avoid spoilage or infestation by insects or rodents. Containers with tight-fitting lids are required. These materials should be discarded periodically so the bins and storage area can be cleaned thoroughly.

Controlling for Hazards

Teachers are responsible for the safety of the children's environment and, hence, must monitor all decisions about materials used in the setting that could introduce safety hazards such as plants, wall displays, electrical appliances, and recycling bins.

Selecting Plants for the Classroom

Comfortable classrooms include softening materials such as flowers and plants to enhance the welcoming environment and to add aesthetic appeal. However, not all house plants, plant material used for decoration, or class activities are appropriate for children's settings. Figure 15-6 identifies plants that are appropriate for children's settings and those that should not be used because of their poisonous properties. Teachers should monitor the flowers and plants that are brought into the class as gifts or for display. For example, a winter arrangement of blooming narcissus has a lovely fragrance, but introduces flower bulbs that are poisonous.

Managing Classroom Displays

Early childhood classrooms are typically bright with the displays of children's artwork and posters that are affixed to bulletin boards and taped to the walls. Using a large amount of paper in displays, however, can be a fire hazard. The local fire department can be a resource for guidance about the appropriate use of paper for displays. For example, many fire districts do not allow paper to be suspended from the ceiling. Bulletin, chalk, and white boards should be securely fastened to the walls and located low enough that children can see and enjoy them. Materials should be attached using tape rather than tacks or pins that can fall to the floor, to be discovered by young children.

Electrical Outlets and Appliances

A sufficient number of electrical outlets should be located at intervals around the classroom. This supports the occasional use of electrical appliances as allowed by licensing requirements and avoids overuse of electrical cords that can be trip hazards. Electrical outlets introduce danger because a curious child may poke fingers or toys into the sockets which could cause an electric shock. This can be avoided by installing outlet covers that close off the outlet when not in use.

Providing Recycling and Compost Bins

Conservation of supplies and recycling are natural topics in early childhood settings. To support recycling efforts, many teachers provide recycling bins for paper in the classroom. The bins need to be placed out of the walkways and emptied periodically to avoid creating a fire hazard. Some settings also provide compost bins for food waste. These should be located appropriately in the outdoor play area, and managed to support the composting process, yet avoid attracting rodents.

What if. . .

you were preparing to introduce recycling in your classroom? How would you set up a recycling area in your classroom? What key messages would you teach to children?

Creating Indoor Areas for Active Play

Indoor active play spaces are important to ensure that children receive sufficient opportunity to stretch and use their energy. Over time, early childhood programs have tended toward inactivity with fewer opportunities for children to play outdoors and more focus on sedentary table activities indoors (Pate, Pfeiffer, Trost, Ziegler, & Dowda, 2004). Teachers also have tended to place more restrictions on the activity level and intensity of play indoors. It is common to hear teachers say, "Remember to use your walking feet!" This needs to be balanced with plenty of opportunity for children to use their "running feet."

Figure 15-6 Safe and Poisonous Plants

Safe Plants	Safe Plants	Poisonous Plants	Poisonous Plants
USE these plants in children's settings	**USE these plants in children's settings**	**DO NOT USE these plants in children's settings**	**DO NOT USE these plants in children's settings**
House Plants	Wax plant	**House Plants**	Potato (sprouts and green parts)
African violet	Weeping fig	Bird of paradise	Rhubarb leaves
Aluminum plant	Yellow day lily	Castor bean	Tomato (green parts)
Anthurium, tailflower		Dumbcane (Dieffenbachia)	**Trees and Shrubs**
Aphelandra		English ivy	Black locust
Baby tears		Holly	Boxwood
Begonia		Jequirity bean (rosary pea)	Chokecherry
Blood leaf		Jerusalem cherry	Elderberry
Boston fern		Mistletoe	English yew
Christmas cactus		Mother-in-law	Ground ivy
Coleus		Oleander	Horse chestnut, buckeye
Corn plant		Philodendron	Juniper
Dracaena		Poinsettia	Oak tree
Emerald ripple		Rhododendron	Water hemlock
Hen-and-chickens		**Common Flowers**	Yew
Hoya		Autumn crocus	**Other Wild Plants**
Impatiens		Bleeding heart	Belladonna
Jade plant		Chrysanthemum	Bittersweet
Parlor palm		Daffodil, narcissus and jonquil	Buttercups
Peperomia		Four-o'clocks	Indian hemp
Prayer plant		Foxglove	Jack-in-the-pulpit
Rubber plant		Hyacinth	Jimson weed
Schefflera		Hydrangea	Larkspur
Sensitive plant		Iris	Monkshood
Snake plant		Lily of the valley	Mushrooms (certain ones)
Spider plant		Morning glory	Nightshade
Swedish ivy		Snow on the mountain	Poison hemlock, ivy, oak,
Velvet, purple passion		**Vegetable Plants**	sumac, tobacco
Wandering jew		Asparagus	Skunk cabbage

Source: Adapted from American Academy of Pediatrics, American Public Health Association, & National Resource Center for Health and Safety in Child Care and Early Education. (2002). *Caring for Our Children: National Health and Safety Performance Standards: Guidelines for Out-of-Home Child Care Programs* (2nd ed.). Elk Grove Village, IL: American Academy of Pediatrics; Washington, DC: American Public Health Association. Retrieved August 31, 2009, from http://www.eric.ed.gov/ERICDocs/data/ericdocs2sql/content_storage_01/0000019b/80/14/0d/14.pdf. Used with permission of American Academy of Pediatrics.

Ideally, young children will play actively for at least 60 minutes every day (National Association for Sport and Physical Education, 2002). This provides the opportunity for children to learn, practice, and gain competence in gross motor skills and to direct their energies in appropriate ways. The goal of 60 minutes per day can be met by combining indoor and outdoor active playtime. Active play is important because it may reduce the frequency of roughhousing that can lead to unsafe behaviors in the classroom. Active play is thought to enhance cognitive problem solving and educational attainment due to the increased oxygen flow in the blood, which may boost alertness (Grisson, 2005). Indoor areas for active play should support a variety of movements such as running, skipping, playing catch, riding tricycles, dancing and jumping, as well as group and individual activities. The amount of space needed varies depending on the age and number of children who will use it at a given time. Active play spaces for mobile infants are effectively created in a corner of the room with a modest barrier at the boundary. More active toddlers and older children require a larger space with more definite boundaries. When space is limited, small groups of children can be scheduled to use the active play area. Figure 15-7 describes aspects to consider when establishing safe indoor active play environments.

Figure 15-7 Attributes of Safe Indoor Active Play Areas

- The space is designated for active play with appropriate boundaries and separation from nonactive play.
- Area is clean and clear of hazards; materials are stored appropriately.
- Walls are relatively smooth; there are barriers between the play area and any cupboards, closets, tables, or any other protrusions that might have corners children could run against.
- The floor surface is relatively smooth and even.
- All windows are screened for safety.
- Area is well lighted; lightbulbs are covered to avoid danger from shattering.
- There are no entrapment or entanglement hazards.
- Equipment and other toys are appropriate for the age of the children.
- Indoor climbing equipment is positioned over safety-approved resilient surfacing mats that extend at least 6 feet beyond the structure.
- Indoor equipment has a maximum height equal to 1 foot per year of age: 2 feet for 2-year-olds, 3 feet for 3-year-olds, and so on.

Source: Based on *KidsHealth for Parents: Playground Safety*, Nemours Foundation, 2009, retrieved October 23, 2009, from http://www.kidshealth.org/parent/firstaid_safe/outdoor/playground.html.

Indoor active play spaces also need to be comfortable to use. Appropriate storage for equipment that allows children to access materials on their own should be provided. A rolling equipment cart that can be easily moved in and out of a closet is a good option. Drinking water should be offered through a water fountain or by offering a tray with cups of water.

CREATING SAFE OUTDOOR ENVIRONMENTS

Outdoor environments include play yards, playgrounds, courtyards, parks, and other spaces that bring children into contact with the world and provide space for energetic and active play. They include formally designed spaces, such as school yards and public playgrounds, as well as backyards used by family child care homes. Creating safe outdoor play spaces requires understanding the need for such settings, identifying important safety features, organizing the space, selecting appropriate play equipment, providing storage, and controlling for safety hazards.

Understanding the Importance of Outdoor Play Spaces

Outdoor environments invite children to engage in active play and exploration in ways that are not available indoors. They allow children to feel the seasons and experience the climate where they live. They bring children into contact with nature and a variety of living things (Greenman, 2005; Rivkin, 1995). For many children, access to the outdoor play area at the early childhood program or school is the only time they have the opportunity to move freely outdoors. Many neighborhoods have lost their parks and community outdoor spaces due to expansion of housing and development. Some public outdoor sites are not safe for children because they are located too close to traffic or too far from family homes (Rivkin, 1995).

Busy family lifestyles also tend to separate children from the outdoors because tired parents simply do not plan time to play outside. Outdoor spaces bring children in touch with their world and give them opportunities to gain confidence and mastery in outdoor environments. These experiences form a foundation for the child's appreciation of the natural world and the role people play in it.

In safe outdoor environments, children learn about themselves and gain confidence in their world.

Outdoor environments are extensions of the classroom, providing unique resources and tools for learning. Teachers who understand this perspective plan the space, offer developmental activities, and include outdoor play experiences in the daily schedule just as they do for the indoor environment. These opportunities allow children to develop competencies and comfort to move safely in the larger natural world (Trancik & Evans, 1995).

Understanding Attributes of Safe Outdoor Environments

Children's safety must guide the development of outdoor play spaces. A study conducted by the U.S. Consumer Product Safety Commission (CPSC) (1999) found that nearly two-thirds of children's settings have at least one safety hazard in the indoor and outdoor environments. The study noted that many safety hazards are not sufficiently covered in licensing regulations, and that often teachers and families are unaware of the safety concern. Safety regulations must guide decision making whenever play areas are being constructed or rearranged as restrictions and recommendations continue to evolve and change (CPSC, 2008). We look at various characteristics of safe outdoor play areas next.

Providing Sufficient and Appropriate Space
The NAEYC (2007) recommends that outdoor areas should provide a minimum of 75 square feet per child of usable space. The space should be open for active play and provide visibility for adult supervision.

Installing Appropriate Fencing and Barriers
The outdoor space should be fenced or have other appropriate barriers to prevent children from wandering into the street or parking lot or other unsafe location. Fences should be a minimum of 4 feet in height. Gate latches should be self-closing and childproof. Fenced areas should have at least two exits.

Clearing the Environment of Safety Hazards
The outdoor play area should have no dangerous materials such as debris, metal, or broken glass. The space should be well drained with no standing water.

Selecting Resilient Surfacing Materials
Falls are the major safety concern in the outdoor environment. This makes the selection of protective surfacing under climbing equipment one of the most important safety decisions made when creating outdoor environments. Surfacing materials include unitary surfacing materials and loose-fill surfacing materials. Unitary materials include rubber mats and tiles that are installed in place. Safety-tested rubber mats are appropriate and provide access for wheelchairs. Loose-fill materials include sand, pea gravel, and wood chips. These products are often less expensive but require more maintenance.

Each option has been tested to understand its protective features based on the height of a fall, toxicity related to the product (such as treated wood or recycled products), the minimum required fill depth of loose-fill materials, and accessibility for wheelchairs (CPSC, 2008). A listing of appropriate and inappropriate surfacing materials is provided in Figure 15-8. Sufficient loose-fill surfacing materials must be provided to offer the protection that children need. Table 15-1 describes the minimum depths of different loose-fill surfacing materials to protect children against falls from different heights. Resilient surfacing should extend 6 feet past the equipment.

Providing Safe Setbacks
Climbing equipment, slides, and swings should be installed away from other play areas with a sufficient setback from hazards such as fences and walkways. Play structures more than 30 inches high should be separated by a space of at least 9 feet to avoid overlapping danger zones.

unitary surfacing materials rubber mats and tiles used for playground surfacing

loose-fill surfacing materials small products used for playground surfacing, such as pea gravel and wood chips

Figure 15-8 **Appropriate and Inappropriate Playground Surfacing Materials**

Use These	Do NOT Use These
Any material tested to meet ASTM F1292* specification standards	Asphalt
	Carpet not approved by ASTM F1292 standards
Sand	Concrete
Pea gravel	Dirt
Shredded recycled rubber mulch	Grass
Wood mulch that has not been treated with chromated copper arsenate (CCA)	Wood mulch that has been treated with CCA
Wood chips	

*American Society for Testing and Materials (ASTM) F1292.

Source: *Public Playground Safety Handbook* (Publication No. 325), by the U.S. Consumer Product Safety Commission, April 2008, retrieved October 23, 2009, from http://www.cpsc.gov/CPSCPUB/PUBS/325.pdf.

Table 15-1	Minimum Compressed Loose-Fill Surfacing Depths	
Inches	Of Loose-Fill Material	Protects to a Fall Height of (feet)
9	Wood chips	10
9	Shredded/recycled rubber	10
9	Wood mulch (non-CCA)	7
9	Pea gravel	5
9	Sand	4

Source: *Public Playground Safety Handbook* (Publication No. 325), by the U.S. Consumer Product Safety Commission, April 2008, retrieved October 23, 2009, from http://www.cpsc.gov/CPSCPUB/PUBS/325.pdf.

Swings cause the most childhood injuries from moving equipment. They should be located away from other play areas and be made of rubber, plastic, or other soft material. Slides are also potentially dangerous. They must be appropriate for the size of children using them. They should face away from busy play areas so that children exiting the bottom of the slide do not hit others. They should also be positioned so they are not pointing directly south (or west) where sun may heat the surface, causing potential for burns (CPSC, 2008).

Providing Protective Barriers

The height of platforms and elevated walking surfaces on children's climbing equipment influences the need for guardrails and barriers to minimize the likelihood of falls. Guardrails are provided on all platforms, landings, and stairs. They reduce the likelihood of accidental falls, but do not prevent children from purposefully climbing through them. Barriers are required on any elevated walking surface above 18 inches for toddlers, 30 inches for preschoolers, and 48 inches for school-age children (CPSC, 2008). Barriers are designed to prevent intentional efforts to climb through.

Checking for Entrapment and Pinch or Crush Points

Playground equipment can introduce hazards such as head entrapment and pinch and crush points. Head entrapment can occur if a child's head becomes lodged between nonmovable objects, putting the child at risk for strangulation. Play equipment, fences, handrails, and guardrails are potential sources of head entrapment. Openings should measure less than 3½ inches or be wider than 9 inches. Equipment should also be monitored to ensure that surfaces are smooth and no pinch spots are evident that could catch fingers and clothing. Barriers are designed to prevent children from purposefully trying to climb through them.

Providing Sun and Shade

Monitoring the amount of direct sunlight children are exposed to in the outdoor environments is an important safety consideration. Overexposure to direct sunlight can cause painful sunburn and puts children at risk for developing skin cancer later in life (American Academy of Dermatology, 2005). Sun protection should begin in infancy, and babies in particular should be kept out of direct sunlight. This can be addressed by constructing covered areas that offer shade if natural shade is not available.

Offering a Variety of Textures and Surfaces

The outdoor environment should provide a range of sensory and physical experiences including textures such as hard surfaces for tricycle and bicycle pathways; sand and soil for digging; grass and other plants and trees; and flat surfaces, hills, and bumps in the landscape. Special areas should be available for infants to crawl, toddlers to roll, preschoolers to ride, and school-age children to play sports. Although variety is desirable, surfaces should transition gradually to avoid creating tripping hazards and to encourage the play of children who move with wheelchairs or crutches.

Supporting Play and Socialization

Outdoor play areas should also offer comforts that are inviting, such as places for children to rest, access to drinking water, areas for social groups to cluster, and outdoor lighting for safety if the space is used in the evenings (NAEYC, 2007).

Organizing the Outdoor Space

A well-designed outdoor environment addresses children's developmental needs, supports appropriate supervision, and provides accessible and safe opportunities for active and energetic play. These goals are accomplished by recognizing the opportunities provided by the particular site, reflecting on goals for use of the space, and designing a safe arrangement that optimizes children's ability to play (Rivkin, 1995).

Reviewing the Site

Each outdoor play space has particular attributes that contribute to an appealing play area. Some have interesting trees or slopes that can guide the arrangement of the space. Potential safety hazards need to be recognized and addressed. These include identifying the pathways children use to access the outdoor area, and understanding hazards such as nearby traffic, standing water, poor soil drainage, and exposure of the space to the sun and wind (CPSC, 2008). Creating a space use plan that depicts the assets of the area as well as hazards is useful in planning the outdoor environment.

Designating Activity Areas

Activity areas need to be thoughtfully located to avoid unnecessary conflicts or hazards. Clustering certain activities, such as climbing equipment and swings in one area and open areas for running games in another area, is desirable because it provides opportunity to address playground surfacing requirements and creates areas of focus for teacher supervision (Trancik & Evans, 1995). Activity areas also help children become autonomous because they are better able to predict the kinds of activities and behaviors that are expected or allowed in each area.

Figure 15-9 provides a list of typical activity areas for the outdoor environment. Most activity areas overlap to some degree. However, planning clear transition zones and entry and exit routes is helpful. For example, a concrete walkway that divides the grassy area from the climbing equipment, which is surrounded by wood chips, provides a physical reminder that children are moving from one zone to another.

Planning Appropriate Spaces for Each Age Group

Outdoor play environments should be appropriate for children's age and developmental capabilities and offer a series of gradually increasing challenges (CPSC, 2008). In shared-use spaces this requires separating areas to be used by toddlers from those to be used by

Figure 15-9 Activity Areas for the Outdoor Environment

Spaces to Support Developmental Goals:	Spaces to Support Program Goals	Spaces to Support Teaching
Running and jumping Climbing and balancing Building and construction Carrying and moving Riding and rolling Digging and exploring Creative and dramatic play Quiet areas	Natural area to study Vegetable garden Open active areas Group game area	Group gathering area Picnic area Rain and shade cover Storage areas

preschoolers, elementary age, and older children. This allows each age group to play actively in their area and provides safety for younger children who are easily bumped and knocked over by older children running by. Pathways, shrubs, and benches are options for separating age group play areas.

Infants Outdoor spaces designed for infants should provide many sensory experiences without overexposure to sun and wind. This can be achieved by installing nontoxic shrubs and plants in various sizes and with various colors of leaves. Planning pathway surfaces with textures that offer gentle variations adds interest as children are pushed in strollers over them. Mobile infants enjoy outdoor surfaces that are interesting and safe for crawling, such as concrete aggregate pathways that incorporate rounded stones, colored concrete, areas with rubber mat surfacing, and grassy areas.

Toddlers Spaces designed for use with toddlers should offer a variety of walking surfaces. This allows children to practice walking on regular and less regular surfaces, such as grass, concrete, or rubber mats. Loose-fill surfacing materials, such as pea gravel, wood mulch, or shredded rubber mulch, should not be used in toddler playgrounds because they introduce hazards for eating or aspirating small pieces (CPSC, 2008). Appropriate plants and shrubs offer variety in color and texture.

Preschoolers and School-Age Children Outdoor spaces for preschool and older children should also offer variety in textures and colors through surfacing materials, trees, plants, and shrubs. In addition, this age group enjoys the challenges of sloped areas for running and rolling, and hills and dips in tricycle and bicycle pathways to challenge their riding skills.

Ensuring Accessibility

Children with special developmental needs are more able to actively participate in outdoor environments that have enough space to move safely. Walkways that accommodate wheelchairs and children on crutches should be at least 44 inches wide, and the surfacing should be firm and sturdy (Rivkin, 1995). Teachers should review ramps and slopes to ensure that children can negotiate them.

   Some play structures provide interests especially designed to be reached from a wheelchair, such as steering wheels or sand and water trays. Swings are also available for wheelchair access or with seats in which children can be secured to support their special developmental needs. Sufficient space around accessible equipment should be provided for adults to assist children.

Encouraging Socialization

Outdoor play time is an important opportunity for socializing. Equipping the environment to encourage this is a natural way to bring children together. For example, a large lightweight tub with a handle on each side requires two children to move it as they collect leaves

What if. . .

your family child care has only a small space for outdoor play? How will you create play areas for children across the age range of infants to 5 years? What safety aspects should you consider?

Outdoor equipment supports social interactions as well as active play.

or pinecones. A tricycle with a carriage seat at the back brings two or three children together. A tire swing has space for two to four children, meeting the needs of a small group better than a single swing.

Children also need to learn about rules in the outdoor environment. The *Teaching Wellness* feature describes ways teachers can introduce children to the correct use of equipment and teach outdoor safety rules.

Offering Semiprivate Spaces

Children also enjoy semiprivate spaces in the outdoor environment that offer respite from the noise and action. Playhouses, tunnels, and areas under a shrub or climbing platform are examples of spaces that are visually open to facilitate supervision, and they also offer a sense of privacy for child-directed make-believe play.

Selecting Equipment for Outdoor Environments

Equipment for children's outdoor environments should invite children to try new challenges and develop new skills. Two types of equipment should be offered: *fixed equipment,* such as climbing structures, swings, and slides and *movable equipment,* such as balls, cones, and hoops. Outdoor environments that offer both fixed and movable equipment achieve the status of outdoor classrooms. Choosing equipment that is appropriate for each age group and ensuring that the equipment is durable and installed properly establishes a safe setting for young children.

Selecting Equipment for Each Age Group

Many fun and challenging options are available for fixed equipment. However, some are not recommended for use in children's settings because of the risks of impact injuries and strangulation hazards. These include trampolines, swinging gates, ropes that are not attached at both ends, heavy metal swings, rope swings, swinging rings, and trapeze bars (CPSC, 2008). Making intentional selections of fixed equipment avoids these hazards.

Play areas that are used by children of various age groups should offer sufficient equipment for each developmental skill level. This ensures that younger children are not playing on equipment that is too large for them, introducing challenges beyond their abilities (Nemours Foundation, 2009). Equipment is selected to reflect each age group's emerging skills in balance, coordination, and reaction time, as well as arm and upper body strength. Figure 15-10 provides recommendations of equipment appropriate for toddlers, preschoolers, and school-age children.

Ensuring Durability

Equipment must be durable and safe. When making selections it is important to refer to resources that provide guidance for equipment safety, such as the *Public Playground Safety Handbook* published by the U.S. Consumer Product Safety Commission (2008). In general, equipment should be constructed of materials that have been used in similar playground settings and have a demonstrated history of durability and safety. The equipment should not contain any products that are known to be toxic. Painted or coated metal options offer strength and safety. Wood used in the construction of play equipment should be naturally resistant to insects and deterioration, such as cedar or redwood, or it should be treated with an appropriate product. Equipment made from wood is resilient and natural, but is harder to maintain because of the potential to splinter. Fasteners and connectors should be secure with no protruding hardware that can cause cuts. Moving parts should be covered with shields to avoid entrapment.

Figure 15-10 Age-Appropriate Equipment

Toddlers	Preschoolers	Elementary-Age Children
• Climbing equipment no higher than 32 inches • Swings with bucket seats • Slides • Spring rockers • Ramps • Stairways • Single-file ladders	• Climbing equipment • Swings with bucket or belt seats, rotating tire swings • Slides • Stepladders • Rung ladders • Stairways • Spring rockers • Horizontal ladders	• Arch climbers • Spiral slides • Swings with belt seats, rotating tire swings • Ladders • Stairways • Overhead rings • Ramps • Fulcrum seesaws • Merry-go-rounds • Vertical sliding pole • Track rides

Source: *Public Playground Safety Handbook* (Publication No. 325), U.S. Consumer Product Safety Commission, April 2008. Retrieved October 23, 2009, from http://www.cpsc.gov/CPSCPUB/PUBS/325.pdf.

Purchasing and Installation

Equipment should be purchased from and installed by an experienced and reputable vendor. The vendor should be able to confirm that the product meets CPSC safety guidelines for children's equipment. The manufacturer's directions for assembly and installation should be strictly followed, and all instructions should be maintained on file (CPSC, 2008). The equipment should be evaluated periodically to ensure continued safety, and any problems should be corrected immediately. Teachers are in a good position to monitor playground equipment and to notice and report such problems.

Providing Safe Storage

Storage of movable equipment is important to maintain the best condition possible for safe play and to protect the investment made in the toys. Weatherproof storage sheds located near the play areas are ideal. This helps ensure that equipment made of metal, such as tricycles, does not rust or deteriorate, causing safety hazards. Storage units should be large enough to contain the equipment. They should be well organized, easy to access, and should lock securely.

Outdoor storage closets and sheds can pose safety hazards when they are overfilled. Tubs of toys positioned on shelves and tricycles hung against the wall may be too heavy for children to access safely. For this reason, these areas should primarily be used by adults. Providing child-accessible shelving such as a hinged shelving unit that opens and that can be locked when folded closed is a useful option. This allows children to be self-directed as they access the toys they need to develop their play themes.

Children are more likely to be active if appropriate toys are accessible to them.

Controlling for Hazards

Safety hazards exist in the outdoor environment. Teachers need to be vigilant and active to reduce the potential for harm to the greatest extent possible. The CPSC (1999, 2008) reported that the most frequent injuries that occur in the early childhood playground environment involve:

- Falls—from platforms, slides, swings.
- Collision—with equipment or being struck by equipment.
- Entrapment—in gaps that allow the child's head or other body part to enter.
- Entanglement—with protruding components, "S"-style hooks, and ropes or straps that children bring into the environment.
- Pinching or crushing—of fingers and other body parts.

Teaching Wellness *Let's Play Outdoors and Be Safe*

Learning Outcome Children will identify the games and equipment typically associated with outdoor play and demonstrate ways to play safely.

Infants and Toddlers

- *Goal:* Infants and toddlers will experience the sensory aspects of being outdoors.

- *Materials:* Clean and safe outdoor play area.

- *Activity plan:* Take children into the play area. Set nonmobile infants on the grass or on a blanket on the ground. Allow infants to touch the ground surface. Bring appropriate leaves near the child's hands and demonstrate touching and stroking the leaves. Allow crawling infants and toddlers to move around the environment. Focus their attention on touching. Provide descriptions and vocabulary for what they experience, such as rough tree bark, smooth grass, scratchy concrete. Talk about how the outdoors feels and smells. Identify sounds of birds, wind, people playing.

- *How to adjust the activity:* Provide squishy rubber balls and rings for children to toss. Provide paper or fabric pinwheels or blow bubbles for children to chase and watch in the breeze.

- *Did you meet your goal?* Did children touch aspects of the environment? Did they listen to the descriptions of the sensations, smells, and sounds of the outdoors? Did they repeat the words and offer other words for these sensory descriptions?

Preschoolers and Kindergartners

- *Goal:* Children will demonstrate how to play with the fixed and movable equipment available in their play yard and describe the safety rules for each kind of equipment.

- *Materials:* Fixed equipment such as swings, slides, climbing equipment, and movable equipment such as tricycles, balls of different styles, hoops, cones, parachute.

- *Activity plan:* Place movable equipment in stations located at intervals around the play yard. As a group move with children from one station to the next. Use a different style of movement as you move from station to station, such as jumping, hopping, walking backwards. At each station have children play a game with the equipment, such as rolling or tossing a ball between partners or hopping around a pair of cones. Briefly describe the safety rules for each piece of equipment. Include the fixed equipment (slides, swings, climbing equipment) in the stations. Identify safety rules: climb up the ladder and slide down the slide feet first, keep back from swings when they are moving, hold on when climbing. After visiting each station, provide free-choice playtime using the equipment. Move about the play yard and ask children to tell you about the safety rule for the equipment they are playing with.

- *How to adjust the activity:* Invite children to draw a play yard including the equipment they like to play with. As they are working, move around the children and ask them to tell you about their picture and the safety rules they have for their play yard. Offer to help them write the safety rules on their picture.

- *Did you meet your goal?* Are children able to demonstrate different ways to play with the equipment? Can they describe appropriate safety rules?

School-Age Children

- *Goal:* Children will identify equipment used in outdoor games and sports and demonstrate how to use each piece of equipment safely.

- *Materials:* A variety of movable equipment including various styles of balls, hoops, cones, parachute, disks.

- *Activity plan:* Pair pieces of equipment such as two balls and two hoops, or a parachute and a ball, or three hoops and three cones. Set them around the play yard in stations. Create small groups of three to four children. Have them run to one of the stations and make a game using the equipment at their station. Take turns having each group teach their game to the rest of the class. Ask the children to describe the safety rules for the game they have developed.

- *How to adjust the activity:* Invite an athlete to come talk about an outdoor sport. Ask them to show the equipment they use to keep their body safe. Talk about the rules of the game and how the rules improve safety.

- *Did you meet your goal?* Are children able to name equipment, games, and sports usually conducted outdoors? Can they discuss some of the safety rules?

Slides are involved in more than half of the fall injuries reported for children under the age of 2 (CSPC, 1999). Slide-related injuries include falls, collisions, and children twisting their legs while negotiating the slide. A periodic review of the outdoor environment and careful supervision are critical to protecting children from these potential hazards. Other potential hazards also need to be monitored, including selecting appropriate plants, watching for hazards that have been introduced into the setting, recognizing the effects of the seasons and climate, and conducting periodic reviews of the children's outdoor environment to ensure safety.

Selecting Plants, Shrubs, and Trees

Plants, shrubs, and trees contribute to the beauty and natural appeal of the outdoor environment. They should be selected with child safety in mind. Plants, shrubs, and trees with poisonous parts should be removed. While not all mushrooms and toadstools are poisonous, they should be removed from the play yard on a daily basis if necessary. Gloves should be worn when removing mushrooms and toadstools to avoid physical contact with the plant and to demonstrate to children that these plants may be dangerous and should not be touched.

Teachers who engage children in planting gardens should be aware of the parts of fruits or vegetables that might be dangerous. Both safe and unsafe plants can have attractive berries and seed pods that may tempt children to taste them. Children should be educated to look at but never eat any plant material that has not been served to them by their teacher or family.

Monitoring for Incidental Entry of Hazardous Materials

Teachers need to monitor the outdoor environment for hazards every day. The nests of wasps or hornets should be removed to reduce the potential for stings. If a bat is found hanging under a covered area, children should be kept at a distance until the bat is removed by an appropriate naturalist. Animal excrement should be immediately removed. Teachers should also screen the area to ensure that no garbage, beverage cups, needles, broken glass, or other hazards have been brought into the environment.

Recognizing the Effects of the Season and Climate

Children's safety can be impacted by the season or weather. Long periods of hot sun can cause drying and splintering of wooden structures. A hot sunny day can raise the temperature of the slide, making it an unsafe burn hazard. Freezes can damage trees and shrubs, causing hazards from falling limbs. Teachers need to be observant for safety problems and be ready to correct or report them.

Periodic Monitoring

Regular review of the outdoor environment and equipment is important to ensure the play area continues to meet safety expectations. A review by the CPSC (1999) found that 27% of early childhood playgrounds were poorly maintained and that 24% provided unsafe surfacing under children's equipment. This suggests that many children in care are exposed to hazardous conditions. Periodic monitoring for problems reminds teachers to correct safety hazards and improves safety for children. Table 15-2 provides a checklist that teachers and families can use to monitor the safety of the outdoor setting.

What if. . .

you identified some problems with rust and rough areas on your swing set? Whom would you contact to help you resolve this safety problem?

SELECTING SAFE TOYS

Selecting safe and appropriate toys for the early childhood environment is both exciting and challenging. A wide variety of interesting toy options are available, and rigorous marketing is as effective with teachers as it is with children. Sorting through the options and making

Table 15-2	Playground Maintenance Checklist		
Maintenance Problem		**Follow-Up**	**Initial When Complete**
☐ Surfacing under equipment is not sufficient			
☐ Crush and shear points			
☐ Entanglement or impalement aspects (protruding nuts and bolts)			
☐ Head entrapment area			
☐ Sharp points, corners, or edges			
☐ Suspended hazards (cables, ropes, wires)			
☐ Trip hazards			
☐ Garbage, debris, broken glass, other hazardous materials			
☐ Gaps in fencing or other safety barriers			
☐ Broken gate latches; latches that do not work			
☐ Toys or equipment with rust or chipped paint exposing metal			
☐ Wooden structures, tables, toys that are decayed, with splinters or large cracks			
☐ Damaged equipment or missing components			
☐ Corrosion, rust, or deterioration on equipment structural components that connect to the ground			
☐ Equipment footings are exposed			
☐ Equipment and other hardware has projections, protrusions, or is loose or worn (entanglement hazards)			
☐ Ropes or straps have been brought into the area (entanglement hazards)			
☐ Standing water; problem with drainage			
☐ Sandbox cover missing; sand not protected from animals			
☐ Cracks in plastic equipment			
☐ Other			

Source: *Public Playground Safety Handbook* (Publication No. 325), U.S. Consumer Product Safety Commission, April 2008. Retrieved October 23, 2009, from http://www.cpsc.gov/CPSCPUB/PUBS/325.pdf.

informed selections for young children is a significant aspect of safety management. Toys should be appropriate, available in sufficient quantity, and meet high safety standards.

Choosing Appropriate Toys

Toys are an important part of the young child's experience and a major component of the early childhood environment. They are children's learning tools, representing more than just a fun pastime. Interaction with interesting toys allows children to act on, construct knowledge from, and make discoveries about their world. Developmentally appropriate selections need to be made to fully take advantage of this enthusiasm. Toys should offer educational value, fit the program's goals for learning, and be useful for teaching concepts.

Providing Developmental Challenge

Children's interest in particular toys varies according to their age and stage of development. Appropriate toys should be offered that attract children's interest, invite interaction, and match children's need for challenges. Teachers work to understand children's emerging interests in order to provide the tools the children need to move from one skill level to the next. Table 15-3 describes children's developmental interests and lists toys that are good choices and those that should not be selected for children in each age group.

Toys should also promote child-directed play and self-directed learning. Characteristics of toys that provide this value include those that:

- Are self-explanatory, allowing children to explore and figure out what to do on their own.
- Offer attributes of self-correction, with pieces designed to fit in specific ways so children can understand the concept the toy presents.

Toys that promote skills in several developmental areas are ideal. For example, small blocks that encourage fine motor skills also offer exploration of spatial awareness and can be used for counting and color and shape recognition or become part of a dramatic play theme when matched with trucks or people figures.

Considering Toy Characteristics

Various attributes of toy design are important when making choices that are appropriate for the children who will use them. Toys must fit the skill, maturity, and interest needs of the age group (CPSC, 2008). A list of characteristics to consider when selecting toys is provided in Figure 15-11.

Matching the Program Philosophy

The toys that are selected to promote children's development reflect a program's philosophy of play, or beliefs about the goals and values of play and attitudes about which toys are most appropriate and most valued for their social and educational contribution to play and overall learning. Some programs lean toward traditional and classic selections, such as wooden block-shaped trucks rather than brightly colored plastic trucks, or basic baby dolls rather than more trendy options. Some programs provide toys that represent popular television characters. Others involve children in making their own toys. In all cases, teachers must ensure that each toy is safe for the children who will use it.

Using Toys to Teach Wellness Concepts

Toys are important tools for teaching wellness concepts through both child-directed and teacher-directed interaction. For example, safety concepts are naturally promoted by offering traffic signs for use near the tricycle path in the play yard. Figures and trucks that depict emergency personnel offer opportunities to discuss topics such as fire safety and people who help in emergencies. Medical equipment props for the dramatic play area encourage children to explore health care concepts. The *Nutrition Note* describes how toys and equipment teach important nutrition lessons.

> **What if. . .**
>
> parents asked you why you do not have some of the more popular fashion dolls or electronic toys in your classroom? How would you explain how toys are selected for your children's setting?

philosophy of play
beliefs about the goals and values of play and attitudes about which toys are most appropriate and most valued for their social and educational contribution to play and overall learning

Table 15-3	Selecting Developmentally Appropriate Toys

Age: Birth to 1 Year

DEVELOPMENTAL DESCRIPTION	CHOOSE:	DO NOT CHOOSE:
Children are interested in color contrast, design, patterns, and interesting sounds. Children frequently put toys to mouth to explore.	• Soft toys • Rattles • Simple musical toys • Board books	• Stuffed toys with plastic or glass eyes that could fall off • Any toy with parts that are small enough to fit inside a 35-mm film container • Any toy with lead paint or other poisonous paints

Age: 1 to 2 Years

DEVELOPMENTAL DESCRIPTION	CHOOSE:	DO NOT CHOOSE:
Children explore with their mouths, hands, and toes. Children are interested in other children. Children are increasingly interested in communicating; language develops quickly. Children are becoming more mobile, but may continue to be unstable.	• Board books • Small blocks • Shape sorting toys • Nesting toys • Take-apart toys with large parts	• Toys that can be pulled over on top of the child • Toys with sharp edges • Toys with strings • Toys that are more appropriate for older children

Age: 2 to 3 Years

DEVELOPMENTAL DESCRIPTION	CHOOSE:	DO NOT CHOOSE:
Children may be energetic and interested in many things. Children's language continues to grow. Children are more mobile; can move quickly.	• Toy animals • Puzzles with one to four large pieces • Board books and simple paper books • Rubber balls • Sturdy riding toys	• Coins, beads, marbles, magnets • Glass mirrors • Toys of metal or plastic with sharp edges • Toys with small removable parts • Riding toys for use on slopes or near streets

Age: 3 to 5 Years

DEVELOPMENTAL DESCRIPTION	CHOOSE:	DO NOT CHOOSE:
Children are eager to try new things. Children continue to become more mobile; can run and ride quickly. Children's curiosity may exceed their abilities. Children are becoming interested in cooperative play.	• Puzzles with 1 to 12 pieces • Blocks and construction toys • Dolls and child-oriented housekeeping toys • Riding toys • Manipulative and sorting toys • Toy vehicles	• Toys with metal edges • Toys that use electricity • Toys that shoot small items

Age: 6 to 8 Years

DEVELOPMENTAL DESCRIPTION	CHOOSE:	DO NOT CHOOSE:
Children have a wide range of interests; are able to explore topics with detail. Children are growing in capability.	• Board and card games • Manipulative building sets • Puzzles with 1 to 100 pieces • Sturdy bikes and scooters	• Bikes too big for child • Electrical toys without supervision • Fireworks

Table 15-3	Selecting Developmentally Appropriate Toys *(Continued)*

Age: 6 to 8 Years

DEVELOPMENTAL DESCRIPTION	CHOOSE:	DO NOT CHOOSE:
Children enjoy both social and solitary play.		• Lawn darts
		• Toys that shoot
Children may enjoy a hobby collecting objects of interest.		• Water guns that shoot more than 3 feet
Children may begin to experience peer pressure.		• Poorly made sports equipment

Source: Adapted from *Tips on Toys* (Publication No. 350-063), by Valya Telep, 1997, Blacksburg: Virginia State University Cooperative Extension. Retrieved October 24, 2009, from http://pubs.ext.vt.edu/350/350–063/350–063.html.

Figure 15-11 **Toy Characteristics Checklist**

Size and shape of parts	☐ Are the attributes of the toy safe, suitable, and appealing for the age group?
Number of parts	☐ Does the number of parts suit the ability of the intended age group?
	☐ Does the toy provide appropriate challenge?
Interlocking nature of parts	☐ Does the connection of the parts suit the interest and ability level of the age group?
Materials	☐ Are the materials the toy is made of suitable for the age group?
Developmental skill needed to play	☐ Do the motor and cognitive skills needed fit the intended age group?
Color/contrast	☐ Does the appearance of the toy invite the child to engage in play?
Cause and effect	☐ Does the toy respond in some way to the child's actions?
Sensory contribution	☐ Does the toy offer unique sensory experiences appropriate for the age group?
Level of realism	☐ Does the toy suit the maturity level of the age group?
Licensing	☐ Is the toy marketed to encourage a licensed product or character?
	☐ Does the licensing interest suit the age group and program goals?
Classic aspects	☐ Does this toy have long-lasting appeal? Will it maintain interest over time?
Robotic or smart features	☐ Does the toy have electronic or robotic appeal? Is it easy to use?
	☐ Does it encourage appropriate cognitive reasoning?
Educational	☐ Does the toy have an educational or cognitive goal that is achievable by the age group and appropriate to the program philosophy?

Source: Adapted from *Age Determinant Guidelines: Relating Children's Ages to Toy Characteristics and Play Behavior*, edited by T. P. Smith, September 2002, Bethesda, MD: U.S. Consumer Product Safety Commission. Retrieved October 24, 2009, from http://www.cpsc.gov/businfo/adg.pdf.

Providing a Variety of Toys

Toys should be provided in sufficient quantities to encourage all children into play. They should be accessible for children with special developmental needs, be reflective of cultural diversity and contribute to children's active play.

Ensuring a Sufficient Quantity of Toys

Providing a sufficient quantity of toys ensures that all children have the opportunity to be actively involved in constructive play and helps avoid undue competition for popular items (Ritchie & Weller, 2005). This is especially important for toddlers and very young children who are still learning to wait for a turn to play. Having a variety of interesting toys available allows teachers to redirect toddlers to appealing alternatives while they are waiting for a turn with the specially desired toy.

Nutrition Note

Toys That Teach Nutrition Concepts

- Play foods representative of many cultures
- Play and real kitchen equipment: measuring cups and spoons, bowls, whisks, pancake turners, pots, pans, funnels

- Occasional specialty equipment: butter churn, hand-operated food grinder, food mill, pasta maker, crank-style apple peeler
- Books with food themes

- Puzzles, matching and lotto cards with food pictures
- Posters of food, crops, children cooking, and children eating

All children can be supported in their learning through thoughtful toy and equipment choices.

Positive social interactions are promoted when several children are able to play side by side with similar toys. For example, a good quantity of blocks moves the play from a solitary activity to a more social activity as children see one another's structures, participate in give and take, and talk about what they are building. In some cases there should be enough of some equipment so that each child has one to use, such as when dancing with ribbon streamers. Offering a sufficient quantity of toys contributes to classroom safety by engaging children in appropriate play and productive interactions.

Providing Toys for Special Developmental Needs

Every child needs to be able to access the learning environment through the toys and materials that are available. To accomplish this, teachers need to recognize barriers that may keep some children from full participation. Sometimes simply providing a particular toy with a range of attributes will assist in making the activity easier or harder according to the developmental skill of the child. For example, paintbrushes with chubby handles rather than skinny ones may be easier for children whose hand strength and coordination skills are just emerging. Selecting and offering a range of paintbrush styles ensures that there is an option for each stage of development which benefits all children.

Some toy attributes are especially appropriate for children with special developmental needs:

- Toys with texture and color contrasts and realistic and recognizable designs help children focus on the object and persist with play.
- Toys with large components or raised parts are easier for children with motor challenges to grasp.
- Toys that are sturdy and have nonskid bases will hold still as children play, an attribute that supports children with coordination challenges.

MyEducationLab

Go to the Assignments and Activities section of Topic 10: Mental Health in the MyEducationLab for your course and complete the activity entitled *Supporting Children's Uniqueness*. How do developmentally appropriate toys promote safety for young children?

Some toys and materials are designed to allow the teacher to offer specific assistance, such as adaptive scissors. Adaptive scissors provide spaces for both the teacher and child to position their fingers in the scissors and to practice the cutting movements together. This helps children build hand strength and coordination, and teaches the rhythm of cutting. Adaptations are sometimes made to typical equipment to help children be successful in learning skills. Attaching a wooden block to a tricycle pedal helps a child with low muscle tone learn to push effectively against the pedal to ride the tricycle. Developmentally appropriate toys, adaptive equipment, and adaptations made to typical equipment enhance safety by fitting the challenge of the materials to the child's emerging capabilities. This allows all children to use the toys safely and appropriately.

Choosing Toys That Encourage Active Play

In order to be active, children need access to toys that encourage active play. In many early childhood settings, toys that support active outdoor play are controlled more closely than toys used indoors. Balls, rolling toys, and sports equipment are often available only when the teacher sets them out. This may be due to lack of storage or inattentiveness to arranging the outdoor environment. As a result children are not as active outdoors as families and teachers think.

Providing ready access to a variety of active play toys encourages children to choose to be active and energetic, and it may redirect them from chasing and bullying on the playground. Locating the toys so that children can use them at will ensures that gross motor development becomes part of the learning opportunities throughout the day.

What if. . .

your children's program did not have storage near the playground for mobile equipment? How would you ensure that active play toys were available to children every time they went outside?

Ensuring Toys Are Safe

Teachers are responsible to review each toy against safety guidelines. Potential choking hazards must be avoided and toys should be checked periodically to be sure they continue to be safe for use.

Meeting Safety Guidelines

Toys in the United States are reviewed by the U.S. Consumer Product Safety Commission, which is charged with establishing safety requirements and testing strategies to ensure toy safety, as well as for toy safety labeling requirements. These requirements ensure that toys do not contain lead paint, have small parts that could be swallowed, or present other hazards. In general, toys used with young children must be in good repair and durable for use in the busy children's setting. They should have smooth and safe surfaces with no sharp edges or protrusions and no splinters or chipped paint. They should be constructed of nontoxic materials.

Some imported toys are not constructed for U.S. markets and are not reviewed against the safety guidelines before they are made available for sale. Imported toys should be evaluated carefully and removed from the classroom if there is concern. In some instances imported toys have been discovered to contain lead and other materials that are toxic to young children. The CPSC provides lists of toys and equipment that have been recalled or pulled off the market due to child injury. This information can be accessed on the CPSC website (see the end-of-chapter Web Resources section). Teachers can also register to receive e-mails about toy recalls.

Toys purchased at garage sales, flea markets, and thrift shops, as well as those donated to the children's program, should be reviewed very carefully. Toys that have been recalled due to safety hazards may have been donated for sale in these settings, unknowingly putting new buyers at risk for purchasing dangerous products. In addition, older toys may not have been constructed to meet the current safety standards. Teachers need to be smart by checking any purchase against the guidelines and recall information provided by the CPSC and by carefully reviewing the condition and appearance of each toy. If the toy does not meet a high standard for safety, cleanliness, and appropriateness, it should be discarded.

What if. . .

a family brought you a gift of toys from their country for use in the classroom? You know the potential hazards, but how will you respect the generous gesture while also ensuring children's safety?

Avoiding Choking Hazards

Toys provided for babies and very young children should not have small parts that can be swallowed, causing a choking hazard. Toys commonly associated with choking include:

- Marbles, small balls, and beads.
- Toys with small parts, such as wheels on toy cars that can be chewed off.
- Coins and buttons, which are often used for sorting and counting activities.
- Balloons, often associated with celebrations or used as gross motor props; an uninflated balloon or pieces of popped balloons can cause choking.
- Small magnets, which pose a choking hazard, can also attach to one another inside the body, causing internal damage.

Choke testing devices that are designed to resemble a child's throat, are available to test toys with dangerous small parts. The CPSC tests toys and toy parts using a device that is $1\frac{3}{16}$ inches deep with an oval-shaped opening measuring approximately $1\frac{3}{8}$ inches by 2 inches. If any part of a toy fits into the testing device, the toy is considered too small for use with babies and toddlers. This includes toys and rattles that have handles or other protruding parts. If the protruding parts can fit into the space created by the testing device, they can also be inserted far into the child's mouth and cause choking.

The U.S. Consumer Product Safety Commission prohibits the sale of toys designed for use by children under the age of 3 if the toy contains small parts or is easily broken into pieces that form small parts. However, even with toy labeling laws, unsafe toys still find their way into stores. The *Safety Segment* describes how manufacturers can mislead consumers through misuse of labeling laws.

Teachers need to recognize and follow the guidance posted on toy labels. Teachers who work with a mixed-age group of children must be especially vigilant about the toys that are accessible to the very youngest children. Older children should be taught about the safety hazard and the importance of keeping toys with small parts away from the younger children.

In addition, teachers need to ensure that they do not introduce materials that pose choking hazards by creating activities that use products with small pieces. For example, paper clips or square plastic fasteners from bread bags might be used in a sorting activity. This would be inappropriate in classrooms that serve children under the age of 3. Older children should be monitored to ensure they do not put small pieces into their mouths.

Providing Clean and Sanitary Toys

Toys need to be free from germs to keep children safe from disease. However, everyday play results in toys in mouths, as well as paint on chairs, and sand and dirt sticking to sensory bin toys. Cleaning toys periodically helps keep them sanitary and safe for use and maintains their inviting appearance. Sanitizing toys is especially important for babies and very young children who naturally explore with their mouths.

Safety Segment

Toy Labeling Troubles

The U.S. Consumer Product Safety Commission requires toys designed for use by children under the age of 3 to be banned from the market if they contain small parts or are easily broken into pieces that form small parts. Toys intended for children ages 3 to 6 that contain small parts must be specifically labeled with a choke hazard warning. However, some manufacturers appear to misuse the labeling laws, allowing unsafe toys to enter the market. This is done by marking toys with the choke hazard warning for children ages 3 to 6, even though the toy is typically associated with the play of infants and toddlers. This effectively gets around the ban on small parts in toys for children under the age of 3 through "creative" labeling. For example:

- A series of small-sized children's foam books, with titles such as *I Love My Puppy* and *Dinosaur Loveables*, look like board books typically suitable for children as young as 7 months even though they are marked for children ages 3 to 6. The books have Velcro tabs that tear off easily, posing a choking hazard.
- A plastic tea party set looks suitable for children 18 months of age, but the package is marked for children ages 3 to 6. The small plastic utensils are easily broken into small parts, presenting a choking hazard.

Source: Based on *Trouble in Toyland, Attachment A: 2006 Summary of Toy Hazards and Examples of Potentially Dangerous Toys. Potential Choking Hazards.* Boston, MA: U.S. PIRG. Retrieved October 24, 2009, from http://www.uspirg.org/html/2006DangerousToyList.pdf.

Many teachers establish a "clean-me" tub, where toys that have been put into children's mouths, dropped on the floor, or otherwise soiled are placed during the day. These toys are washed and sanitized before they are reintroduced into the classroom. Plastic toys can be washed in the dishwasher (sanitizer) or washed and sanitized using a three-sink method of wash, rinse, and sanitize in a bleach-and-water solution. Other toys should be wiped with a sanitizing solution and left to air dry. Choosing toys that are easy to clean and sanitize is wise, especially for use with children under the age of 5.

Toys with attached parts that can fit in the choke testing device, such as the wheels on this train, introduce a choking hazard.

How often a particular toy should be cleaned varies according to use and the age of children who use it. Also, when a group of children is experiencing a high number of colds or other communicable illness, toys should be cleaned more often, perhaps daily. The NAEYC has identified periodic cleaning and sanitizing of toys as an emerging practice for accredited programs. This means that the importance of sanitizing toys is moving toward the level of a policy requirement.

Keeping Toys Usable

Toys should be monitored on an ongoing basis to observe for breakage and ensure that all parts are in good working order. Checking toys as they are put away at cleanup time is a good way to notice if parts are missing or if parts are coming loose, which could cause a safety hazard. Toys with missing parts and incidental lost parts should be placed in a "missing parts" tub where hopefully they will be reunited. In addition, toys with missing pieces, such as puzzles, should be removed because they deny children the full enjoyment of completion. This results in undue frustration and may even "teach" the concept of leaving a job undone. Toys that are broken, worn out, or have missing parts should be discarded.

Storing Toys Appropriately

Each toy should have a specific storage place on a shelf or in a tub in the classroom or common storage area. This sends a message of respect for the materials that children use for learning. Proper storage helps keep the parts of toys together, prolonging the usable life of the toy. Caring for toys in this way enhances safety by avoiding breakage.

Summary

Young children need safe, nurturing, and appropriate environments in which to grow, learn, and thrive. Establishing safe spaces involves recognizing characteristics that contribute to children's safety and understanding the strategies that increase security in the early childhood setting.

Teachers are responsible for establishing safe indoor spaces. Classrooms must be furnished to meet children's developmental needs, and supplies must be stored safely and carefully monitored for potential hazards.

Teachers are also in charge of creating safe outdoor environments. This requires teachers to understand the attributes of safe outdoor play areas and know how to organize the space to avoid potential hazards.

In addition, teachers must be prepared to select toys that are safe and appropriate for the children they teach. Product safety guidelines must be followed, and toys should be maintained appropriately. Broken or dangerous toys must be removed to ensure safety.

Whether the children's space is created in a family care home, a temporary care program at the gym, a child care center, or an after-school enrichment club, children rely on their teachers to create and maintain interesting, appropriate, and safe environments for learning.

MyEducationLab

To assess your understanding of how to evaluate indoor and outdoor environments to ensure safety for all children, go to the Book Specific Resources section in the MyEducationLab for your course, select *Nutrition, Health, and Safety for Young Children*, Chapter 15 of the Study Plan, and then complete the multiple choice questions and activities.

Key Terms

Review Questions

1. What aspects of a neighborhood or community have the most impact on decisions about how to create safe facilities and classroom environments for children?

2. How do environments communicate value for children and families?

3. What makes an early childhood setting "accessible"?

4. What types of security risks might impact early childhood teachers?

5. How do spaces equipped with child-sized furniture improve children's learning?

6. Why are toys described as children's tools?

7. What features of outdoor play equipment would you consider when making safe selections for the play yard?

8. How would you make your classroom culturally relevant and responsive?

9. What safety aspects would you consider in creating a safe indoor environment that supports physically active play?

10. What steps would you take to monitor safety of the early childhood environment?

Discussion Starters

1. Describe your philosophical perspective of how children learn, and discuss your opinion about how to create environments that promote children's development and learning.

2. Consider the developmental characteristics of each age group: infants, toddlers, preschoolers, and school-age children. Identify the safety hazards that must be considered for each age group and discuss ways you would arrange the indoor environment to address them.

3. Recall early childhood settings where you have worked or classrooms you have observed. Describe the potential safety hazards of each environment and how they were addressed (or not addressed) by the teacher in charge. What aspects of children's safety would you find most challenging to correct?

Practice Points

1. Identify an age group of your choice and draft a detailed space use plan for an indoor classroom or outdoor play yard.

2. Go to the U. S. Consumer Product Safety Commission's website and access the *Public Playground Safety Handbook* at http://www.cpsc.gov/CPSCPUB/PUBS/325.pdf. Use the Suggested General Maintenance Checklist in Appendix A to conduct a safety review of a playground in your community. Forward your recommendations to the school or public parks office.

3. Explore the types of toys and children's equipment that have been recently recalled due to safety hazards. Access the U. S. Consumer Product Safety Commission's website at http://www.cpsc.gov/cpscpub/prerel/category/toy.html and summarize the types of hazards that were identified in the 15 most recent toy recalls. Describe how this information helps you with your teaching.

Web Resources

Head Start Design Guide, Second Edition
www.headstartinfo.org/publications/hs_design_guide/index.htm

National Clearinghouse for Educational Facilities
www.edfacilities.org/rl/teachers_workplaces.cfm

National Resource Center for Health and Safety in Child Care and Early Education
http://nrc.uchsc.edu/STATES/states.htm

U.S. Architectural and Transportation Barriers Compliance Board, Guide to ADA Accessibility
www.access-board.gov/play/guide/guide.pdf.

U.S. Consumer Product Safety Commission
http://www.cpsc.gov

U.S. Department of Justice, ADA Standards for Accessible Design
www.ada.gov/stdspdf.htm

chapter 16 | Promoting Safe Practices through Effective Classroom Management

Learning Outcomes

After reading this chapter, you should be able to:

1. Name and describe safety routines that teachers establish in early childhood classrooms.

2. Describe safe supervision strategies and identify situations that require special attention to safety.

3. Discuss the unique safety needs of children of different age groups and describe ways to teach children to be safe.

Jean had been teaching third grade for 4 years, and was delighted to learn that this year she has been assigned to teach a full-day kindergarten class. Over the summer she organized her teaching plans, and when the school year started she was ready and her classroom was inviting. She had approached the start of school with great enthusiasm, but now 3 weeks into the year she finds herself exhausted and disheartened.

Her class of 22 students has taken a toll on her confidence. Three of the children are still having separation challenges and cry well into the first hour of the day. Two children have gotten hurt at recess. Manny has kicked children during circle time, and at one point he grabbed Sasha's hair and pulled her under the table. Candida, Olivia, and Sebastian are English learners and tend to fade into the background. Kellis and Mohammed focus well, but they finish their work quickly and tend to start bossing around the other children. Sam, who has Down syndrome, left the classroom at one point and another teacher found him sitting on the floor outside the classroom door. Yesterday, she discovered that Emma was trading her lunch with Angie, who has a food allergy. And just this morning Malcomb's mom called and said that she doesn't feel he is being challenged enough.

Jean is an experienced teacher but her class seems unmanageable and she is unsure of where to turn for help. If she contacts her principal, he may feel that she is not doing her job. Jean feels bewildered and unsure if the children are even safe, and she certainly is not making progress on her lesson plans!

Any age group of children can present teachers with a variety of individual needs and classroom challenges. How teachers such as Jean sort through these challenges, and the approaches they use to address them, determines the effectiveness of the learning environment and affects children's safety. In the opening case scenario, Jean is faced with a range of issues that cause her to question her ability to provide a safe class experience. Some are safety issues that should be her first priority; others are more educational or organizational safety concerns that require thoughtful and intentional intervention. What management approaches will assist teachers like Jean to plan and implement strategies to ensure children's safety?

In this chapter we present a variety of methods that establish safety in the early childhood setting. We start by discussing management routines that set the stage for children's safety in the early childhood setting. Next we describe supervision strategies used in the indoor and outdoor environments. Finally we discuss how teachers implement safety practices that address children's safety needs and provide strategies to teach children appropriate safety messages.

DEVELOPING APPROPRIATE SAFETY PRACTICES

Safety in early childhood classrooms is supported by familiar routines. Routines are everyday activities, rhythms, and habits that are practiced in the classroom setting. They provide organization to the classroom and allow children to practice self-help skills that contribute to their safety in the setting.

Designing Classroom Routines

Classroom routines are designed to engage children, teachers and families in regular and familiar safety activities. Greeting and checking in with the teacher at arrival, hanging up coats, and washing hands before play are examples of classroom routines. Routines should be developmentally appropriate, doable in the setting, and realistic for the number of children and teachers in the group. Examples of classroom routines that contribute to safety are listed in Figure 16-1.

Figure 16-1 Sample Daily Routine Checklist

☐ Setting up and reviewing the classroom and outdoor play area for safety
☐ Monitoring child arrival and departure
☐ Taking attendance
☐ Supervising hand washing and toileting
☐ Offering and supervising snacks and meals
☐ Monitoring cleanup
☐ Conducting transitions
☐ Supervising classroom activities
☐ Supervising outdoor activities
☐ Managing children's difficult behaviors

routines
specific repetitious and predictable rhythms of the daily schedule of activities in a particular class

MyEducationLab

Go to the Assignments and Activities section of Topic 6: Health Appraisals/ Screening in the MyEducationLab for your course and and complete the activity entitled *Comprehensive Health History*. Why do you think it is important for teachers to understand children's health histories in order to keep them safe?

What if. . .

you were arranging an orientation visit for your classroom and learned that one of your families speaks only Spanish? If you speak only English, how would you prepare for the visit? What resources are available to support you to communicate effectively? How would you present safety information?

Using Evidence-Based Safety Practices

Research on the frequency of unintentional injuries and death in young children guides teachers when establishing classroom routines for each age group. The Centers for Disease Control and Prevention (CDC) (2006) and the American Academy of Pediatrics (AAP), American Public Health Association, and National Resource Center for Health and Safety in Child Care and Early Education (2002a) use this research data to identify the most effective strategies for reducing disease, injury, disability, and death in children's settings. This information guides teachers to know what to do to keep children safe, how to do it, and why.

Most states require that early childhood teachers learn and keep current on recommended safety practices through yearly training and professional development activities. This ensures that classroom safety routines continue to address emerging issues. Teachers who understand and use evidence-based safety practices can feel confident that they are teaching in ways that are consistent with the recommendations of the field (Strain & Dunlap, 2006) and are doing all they can to ensure children's safety.

Gathering Information at Enrollment

Information gathered at enrollment provides the details that teachers need to develop appropriate safety routines and prepare to supervise children effectively. Beyond learning about the child's daily rhythms and feeding and nap schedules, teachers need to know about any situations that require special attention to safety, and how to contact the family if needed (AAP et al., 2002a). Ideally teachers will have the opportunity to review enrollment materials and meet with families before children attend so that everyone who will care for the child understands any special safety needs (AAP et al., 2002a; French, 2004). Figure 16-2 lists the kind of information that helps teachers understand how to support children's safe participation. In the opening case scenario Jean would have benefited from this information as a guide to developing supportive classroom routines.

Providing Orientation to Safety Practices

Inviting families and children to visit the classroom before classes begin is a good way to introduce classroom safety routines and helps families understand their role in supporting them (American Academy of Pediatrics, American Public Health Association, & National Resource Center for Health and Safety in Child Care and Early Education, 2003; National Association for the Education of Young Children [NAEYC], 2008). During the visit safety topics are discussed naturally. For example, the importance of staying with the group is introduced as children walk into the classroom. Teachers demonstrate routines such as washing hands at arrival, and show how to walk carefully near the sinks in case the floor is wet to avoid slipping. This is also an important time to remind families to dress children in clothes suitable for the weather and to provide appropriate shoes or bring boots so outdoor play will be safe and comfortable (AAP et al., 2003; NAEYC, 2008). Classroom and playground safety rules can also be discussed.

Families that do not speak English should be encouraged to bring a trusted family member or friend to assist if a translator is not available. This helps ensure that children understand beginning safety rules such as staying with the group and waiting in the classroom until the parent arrives. It allows families to ask questions and increases everyone's confidence about safety in the setting. When a large percentage of children in a class group speak a language other than

Figure 16-2 Enrollment Information That Supports Child Safety

---

Child Information

☐ Child's name and nickname
☐ Child's birth date
☐ Arrival and departure plan

Contact Information

☐ Contact information for custodial parent(s) or guardian(s): name, address, daytime phone numbers, e-mail
☐ Emergency contacts: at least one person who lives locally, but is not a member of the immediate family
☐ Secondary emergency contact: include a family member or friend who lives outside the community (in community-wide emergencies, local communication may be jammed but individuals at a distance may be available to contact)
☐ Names of any persons who should never pick up the child from care

Health Information

☐ Record of child's immunizations
☐ Special health considerations including allergies
☐ Food or other restrictions due to religious, cultural, or family practice
☐ Information about identified or suspected developmental needs
☐ Child's health care providers and contact information (medical, dental, other)
☐ Child's insurance provider (policy or member number)
☐ Statement of program emergency medical response plan signed by the parent

Child Comfort Information

☐ Feeding and toileting practices (especially for infants and toddlers)
☐ Child information to support transition into care:

  • Favorite toys or games
  • Child's words for routines
  • Names of siblings or close friends
  • Child's comfort strategies

☐ Other information (family information that may affect the child in care, such as illness of parent or close relative, incarcerated parent)

Sources: *Caring for Our Children: National Health and Safety Performance Standards: Guidelines for Out-of-Home Child Care Programs*, 2nd ed., 2007, Elk Grove Village, IL: American Academy of Pediatrics; Washington, DC: American Public Health Association. Retrieved August 31, 2009, from http://www.eric.ed.gov/ERICDocs/data/ericdocs2sql/ content_storage_01/0000019b/80/14/0d/14.pdf; and *NAEYC Early Childhood Program Standards and Accreditation Criteria: The Mark of Quality in Early Childhood Education*, 2005, Washington, DC: National Association for the Education of Young Children.

English, the program should, for safety and as a matter of good practice, provide at least one teacher who speaks that language (AAP et al., 2002a).

Creating Secure Arrival and Departure Procedures

Children arrive and depart from early childhood classrooms in many ways. In some settings children are delivered directly to the teacher at arrival and picked up directly from the teacher at departure. Sometimes children are transported by a bus. School-age children may travel to school on their own. Teachers need to understand the plan for each child. They need to know how and when the child will arrive, who will be bringing the child to the class, and who is authorized to pick up the child. Having this information will help teachers conduct smooth transitions and ensure that children are received and released appropriately.

Ensuring Safety at Arrival and Departure

Teachers should be present to supervise and greet children at arrival and say good-bye at departure. Clear policies are needed to support safety during this exchange (AAP, 2002a). For example:

- Young children must be delivered directly to the teacher and not be dropped off outside the building and allowed to "run in" to the classroom.
- Children may not be dropped off or picked up when the program is conducting an emergency evacuation or lockdown, except under the direction of a public safety official.
- Children may not be released to go home with other children without written consent from parents or other authorized individuals.

Planning child-directed activities at arrival and departure times helps teachers to be accessible to visit with families and to monitor for safety. For example, setting out activities such as puzzles that children can easily join as they arrive or providing books for children to look at as families arrive to pick them up help create smooth and organized transitions (Hemmeter & Ostrosky, 2008).

What if. . .

you recognized that arrival and departure times for your classroom had become chaotic as children try to find their coats and family members ask you questions? How would you ensure safety when you are balancing these responsibilities?

Signing In and Out Most early childhood settings for infants through preschool age require that children be "signed in" upon arrival and "signed out" at departure. This routine documents who transported the child and when and creates a record of the exchange if there is any confusion. Figure 16-3 provides a sample sign-in and sign-out sheet. Arrival and departure routines can be complicated, especially if several adults participate in transporting the child. A plan is needed to record arrival and departure if families arrive while the class is in the play yard or away from the classroom. Teachers might carry a small notebook in their pocket for parents to sign.

Releasing Children to Appropriate Adults Teachers are responsible for releasing children only to the custodial parent or other authorized adult. The identification of anyone who is authorized to pick up the child but is unknown to the teacher must be checked. Children should not be released to anyone who displays behaviors that could endanger the child due to debilitation by alcohol, drugs, or other impairing conditions (AAP et al., 2003). State requirements differ about how such situations should be managed. At a minimum, teachers should have a plan in place to delay the release of the child while other arrangements are made, such as calling an alternate authorized adult. Teachers may also need to contact the police for advice. Sometimes families authorize an older sibling to pick up a younger child from the classroom. Rules regarding the ages of children who are allowed to pick up children from care and the ages of children who can be released to a minor are not universal. Teachers should consult with their local child care licensing authority for guidance. In addition, teachers should have a plan in place in the event that no authorized adult comes to pick a child up. The local child protective services agency is a resource for helping design a protocol for this situation.

Monitoring Child Attendance

Taking attendance is a familiar safety routine in early childhood classrooms. Teachers need to know who is present and how many total children are in attendance at all times (AAP et al., 2003). Attendance should be recorded immediately as each child arrives and as soon as each child departs to avoid confusion. Throughout the day, teachers should periodically count the number of children to confirm that all are present. This is especially important any time the group moves from one location to another such as to and from the play yard, during an emergency drill, when the class gets on and off the bus for a field trip, or after walking down the hallway to the school restroom and back.

Figure 16-3 Arrival and Departure Sign-In and Sign-Out Sheet

Note to Families: Please include time of arrival/departure and sign or initial below.

CHILD'S NAME	Monday, October 20		Tuesday, October 21	
	Arrive	Depart	Arrive	Depart
Annette	7:50 *Alice Yates*	5:25 *Ben Yates*	7:45 *Ben Yates*	5:15 *Alice Yates*
Arturo	7:45 *Belinda Dee*	12:15 *Belinda Dee*	7:45 *Belinda Dee*	5:45 *Belinda Dee*
Maria D.	7:45 *Belinda Dee*	12:15 *Belinda Dee*	7:45 *Belinda Dee*	5:45 *Belinda Dee*
Maria M.	7:55 *Marc Mitchel*	5:15 *Mike Robinson*	7:55 *Marc Mitchel*	5:15 *Mike Robinson*
Su Lin	7:55 *Seong Yun*	5:25 *Joon Lee Yun*	7:55 *Seong Yun*	5:45 *Joon Lee Yun*

Contacting Parents about Child Absence Monitoring children's absences is also an important health and safety routine. Families should be oriented to contact the teacher in advance if planned absences are anticipated (for a doctor's appointment or trip, for example), and to phone or e-mail if a child is absent due to illness or other unexpected reason. Knowing why children have not come to school helps teachers track the spread of communicable disease and alerts teachers to potential safety concerns.

If children are absent without notification, the teacher should call the family to ask about the reason for the absence. If several children are absent due to illness, teachers know to conduct additional sanitizing and other precautions to prevent spread of disease in the classroom. If school-age children are late or absent, program or school safety policies should be in place to ensure that teachers call the family to ensure the child is safe. This is especially important for children who travel to school on their own.

Attendance should be recorded as children arrive to ensure that all children are accounted for at all times.

Tracking Midday Interruptions in Attendance On occasion, children may leave the classroom but return again before the school day is complete. For example, a child might be picked up for a dental appointment, or a child who receives speech services might be taken to participate with a small group in another room. Policies for recording midday interruptions in children's attendance are important so that teachers are able to account for each child and recognize changes in the total number of children in attendance (AAP et al., 2002a).

Transporting Children Safely

Transportation services have been provided for school-age children and those with special developmental needs for many years (Bluth, 1993). Other children's programs, such as Head Start and some child care programs, also provide transportation as part of their services to children and families (Early Childhood Learning and Knowledge Center, 2005). Teachers often supervise children as they travel between the bus and classroom at arrival and departure times or on field trips. They should have a basic knowledge about guidelines for safely transporting young children.

Understanding Child Transportation Regulations

Children are more safe being transported in school buses than any other form of motor vehicle (NHTSA, 2005). The strict requirements for school bus construction and people's familiarity with the bright yellow buses used to transport children are two reasons given for the high safety rating.

The use of vans to transport young children is highly discouraged (and in many areas is strictly forbidden) because of a variety of dangers such as fewer regulations for vehicle construction, no requirements that vans stop at train crossings, and the fact that vans do not cue other drivers that children are inside.

Although federal guidelines direct the safe transportation of young children, each state establishes the specific requirements for transporting children to and from public schools. Some state regulations identify guidelines specific to transporting children younger than 5 years of age such as (NHTSA, 2009a):

- The kinds of child safety restraint systems to be used.
- The maximum number of children who may be transported on a bus (based on age).
- The number of adult monitors required to maintain appropriate supervision and their qualifications.
- Pick-up and drop-off procedures.

Teachers can learn more about these regulations from each state's director of pupil transportation services.

Supporting Safe Transportation Practices

Teachers have an important role in supervising children's safety at bus arrival and departure times. Even though school buses are the safest way to transport children, each year, on average, 20 children are killed getting on and off school buses (NHTSA, 2009b). Most of these fatalities involve children between 5 and 7 years of age who are hit in the danger zone immediately surrounding the bus. The school bus danger zone is shown in Figure 16-4. Teachers need to be especially vigilant for children's safety as they move through the danger zone.

Teachers should also observe the program's transportation routines for problems and make recommendations for change if safety issues are recognized. Transportation regulations for young children continue to evolve as the number of children under the age of 5 who are being transported continues to increase.

child safety restraint system equipment used to seat children safely in buses, cars, and other vehicles; includes child safety seats or, for bus transportation, safety vests

Federal and state regulations guide safe transportation services for young children.

Arranging Transportation for Field Trips

Some early childhood programs provide transportation for field trips. Although transportation activities for private programs are not governed by federal guidelines, each situation requires special planning to ensure that safety is addressed. All settings that serve young children should develop appropriate policies about how children will be transported for field trips. Central to such policies should be the requirement that each child must ride in an appropriately installed child safety restraint system and that adult supervision is appropriate for the group (NHTSA, 2009b). Communication with families about transportation for field trips is also very important. Teachers need to inform families:

- When the child will be transported away from the setting.
- How the child will be transported.

- Who will be doing the transporting.
- Who will be supervising the children and monitoring the transportation activity for safety.

Ultimately, teachers carry the responsibility for managing the planning, communication, and compliance with program transportation safety rules, and must view the rules as nonnegotiable. In practice this means that if safe and appropriate transportation cannot be achieved, program activities such as field trips and excursions must be cancelled.

Figure 16-4 School Bus Danger Zone

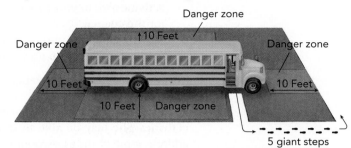

Source: From *Tip #10: School Bus Stops*, 2009, Washington, DC: National Highway Traffic Safety Administration. Retrieved October 30, 2009, from http://www.nhtsa.dot.gov/people/injury/childps/newtips/pages/Tip10.htm.

Following a Daily Schedule

A familiar schedule guides the flow of daily activities and supports an organized approach to safe group management. The schedule should offer a predictable plan of activities, provide smooth transitions, and be flexible enough to manage occasional disruptions.

Establishing Predictable Routines

A predictable daily schedule organizes the day around blocks of active and quiet playtimes, minimizing the number of interruptions that can cause confusion and potential safety hazards. Predictability helps both teachers and children anticipate what will happen next. The daily schedule should fit the age and maturity of the children. The schedule for infants is more individualized as teachers follow children's familiar eating and sleeping routines (Petersen & Wittmer, 2008). Schedules for toddlers begin to introduce longer blocks of playtime. As children mature, they are more able to accommodate a schedule that is designed for the group. Once children learn the routine of the daily schedule, they are able to be more self-directed and are competent moving through the familiar steps such as hanging up their coats after outdoor playtime, going to wash their hands, and then sitting down at the lunch table. This rhythm increases children's engagement in productive play and allows teachers to focus on supervising the group for safety (Alter & Conroy, 2007).

Creating Smooth Transitions

The term transition refers to the short periods of time where the group changes from one activity to another, such as ending free-choice play and cleaning up for snack time or getting ready to go outside to play. Transitions need to be well planned and managed as they have the potential to introduce disruption in children's behavior that may lead to confusion and increase the potential for unintentional injury (Alter & Conroy, 2007). For example, some children who are reluctant to stop their free play may respond with frustration. Others may seek to avoid cleanup time by running about and knocking toys off of tables. Some children might suddenly remember that their parent is gone and begin to cry. What was a calm group of busy children one minute can become a whirlwind the next. The safety concerns that such disruption may cause can be avoided by (Alter & Conroy, 2007):

- Keeping the number of transitions to a minimum by planning large blocks of playtime.

What if. . .

you wanted to take children on a field trip using parent volunteer drivers? Is this allowable in your state? What safety issues would you need to consider?

transition
change from one activity to another in the daily schedule

A predictable schedule empowers children to be more self-directed.

- Moving about the classroom giving small groups of children a 5-minute warning before activities are to end, providing time for them to finish what they are doing and prepare for the change.
- Moving gradually into the transition by, for example, directing small groups of children to clean up and then go wash their hands.

These approaches show respect for the importance of children's play and help keep the group on track.

In the opening case scenario, Jean may benefit from reviewing her daily schedule of activities. She may be able to discover ways to reduce the number of transitions to help address some of the classroom management challenges she is facing.

Addressing Disruptions

Interruptions to the daily schedule can come from many sources such as late lunch delivery, unplanned emergency drills, or loss of electricity. These situations disturb the flow of daily routines and can cause confusion for teachers and children. Teachers need to reassure the children while swiftly assessing the situation. Teachers need to determine the source of disruption, identify if children's safety is threatened, and sort out strategies to increase safety while the issue is being resolved. For example, teachers can read a story while waiting for lunch. Emergency lighting sources can be used while waiting for power to be restored. In some settings the loss of power may introduce a safety hazard because in some buildings power loss deactivates the emergency alarm system. Teachers need to make a judgment about how to respond: Call families to take children home or finish the day without electricity?

What if. . .

you recognized that the children in your class had developed a habit of running about when cleanup time was announced? What strategies would you implement to improve this situation?

ESTABLISHING SAFE SUPERVISION PRACTICES

Supervision is crucial to safe and effective teaching. It is the most important way that teachers ensure safe physical interactions and secure emotional environments for young children. Effective supervision decreases the possibility of unintentional injury and increases the likelihood that children will thrive in the setting. Various strategies can be used to ensure safe and appropriate supervision of children in group settings.

Understanding Appropriate Supervision

Supervising children's safety in group settings requires deliberate planning and consistent and careful attention. Teachers must supervise children by sight and sound, clarify individual teacher responsibilities, coordinate supervision with team teachers, reassure children that teachers are watching out for them, and maintain attention and focus.

Supervising by Sight and Sound

Keeping children safe and secure through attentive supervision is crucial. At the most basic level, it is what teachers *do* and what teachers *don't do* on a daily basis that makes the most difference in keeping children secure from harm. The *Code of Ethical Conduct* of the NAEYC (2005a) calls for teachers to supervise children by sight and sound:

- Infants and toddlers must be supervised by sight and sound at all times.
- Preschoolers must be supervised by sight at all times. Preschoolers may be out of sound supervision for short periods of time.
- Kindergartners, in a safe environment, may be out of sight and sound supervision for short periods of time if they are checked on regularly.

Sight and sound supervision is accomplished in different ways, depending on the age group. Infant rooms typically create spaces for sleeping, areas where diapering and feeding take place, and spaces where children play. The room arrangement needs to allow teachers to

MyEducationLab

To listen to two different program directors discuss teachers' supervisory roles during outdoor play, go to the Video Examples section of Topic 11: Safe Environments in the MyEducationLab for your course and watch the video entitled *Outdoor Safety*. Why is it important that teachers remain standing at all times when supervising children's outdoor play?

view and hear children who are participating in each activity. Spaces used by toddlers and older children are usually equipped with low shelving, allowing the teacher to monitor activity by moving about the room. Some states have specific requirements related to supervision of children when they are sleeping. For example, regulations for registered family child care homes address whether children can sleep on a different floor from where the teacher is working.

Teachers must be continually aware of whether all children are in view. They must also know how to position themselves in the space, such as (NAEYC, 2005a):

- Standing or sitting where the majority of children are easily in view.
- Being in a position to see the door to prevent a child from walking out.
- Continually scanning the environment to keep aware of the group.
- Periodically walking around the group and changing position.

Teachers also need to be alert to what they observe when they are supervising and know how to respond. Table 16-1 describes a variety of scenarios and guides teachers to assume the full range of supervision responsibilities by knowing what to do and what to avoid.

Assigning Children to Specific Teachers

Very young children require close support and supervision to ensure they are safe. Each child must be assigned to a specific teacher who carries primary responsibility for knowing where that child is and what that child is doing at all times. Ideally children are assigned to the same teacher and teaching team and the same group of children every day (NAEYC, 2008). This allows parents to communicate directly with their child's assigned teacher when there are changes in the child's care routine, reducing the potential for mistakes that might introduce safety concerns.

Infants and Toddlers For infants and toddlers, specific and consistent teacher assignments (called *continuity of care*) ensure that the child's feeding and sleeping routines are

Table 16-1	Teacher Supervision Practices
What to Do	**What to Avoid**
Keep children in direct sight and sound at all times.	Never leave children unattended.
Teach children to always stay with the group.	Don't assume that children know when and how to keep safe either within or outside of the school setting.
Understand each child's family dynamic sufficiently to recognize if there are any special considerations that would affect a child's safety (i.e., custody issues, any individual having a restraining order limiting access to the child, or if friends or family members pose a risk to the child).	Don't make assumptions about a child's family members or friends being safe people.
Know who the parent has approved to pick up their child from care.	Don't ignore issues that you read about happening "somewhere else."
Require photo identification for approved persons you do not know.	Don't release the child to anyone not previously approved in writing by the child's parent or guardian.
Know what to be concerned about. Understand the potential security risks to children in the setting. Anticipate potential security risks when traveling away from the center with children and take appropriate precautions.	Don't assume that security is being taken care of by other people.
Understand the program plan to control access to children and procedures to improve security.	Don't assume that it is all right for people you don't know to be in your classroom, the hallways, or any other part of your secure environment.
Step in immediately if you identify a person in the facility that you do not know. Ask if you can provide assistance. Escort the individual to the appropriate location.	

understood and their emotional and comfort needs are supported. Typically, in infant and toddler settings, each teacher is assigned to a specific small group of three or four children. For example, a total class group of eight infants and toddlers is led by two teachers. Each teacher is assigned to supervise four specific children. This direct teacher-to-child assignment increases the intensity of supervision and clarifies who is ultimately responsible for the care and security of each individual child.

Preschoolers Class groups of 16 to 18 preschool children are often led by at least two teachers. The teachers work together to provide consistent supervision of the class.

School-Age Children Kindergarten and elementary school class groups vary greatly in size, ranging from 18 to 24 or more children. These class groups are often led by one teacher who is responsible for providing safe class activities and consistent supervision. Teachers of school-age children plan activities and lessons that allow children to be self-directed, providing opportunities for the teacher to move about the group and attend to the needs of individual children.

Children with Special Needs Specific teacher assignments increase the likelihood that each child's special educational supports, language assistance, and allergy or other medical needs are managed consistently and safely (NAEYC, 2008). Depending on a child's particular needs, an educational assistant may be assigned to assist the child in the classroom. Educational assistants are part of the teaching team and need to understand their specific supervision responsibilities.

Temporary Groupings Some programs, such as full-day child care or before- and after-school care, create temporary groupings of children. Temporary groups bring together children of different ages and from different class groups for a short period of time, often at the beginning or end of the day. In these settings it is especially important for teachers to know who they are responsible for and understand any special safety needs.

Coordinating Supervision with Team Teachers

Groups of children younger than kindergarten age are most often led by two or more teachers, called *teaching team*. This requires a deliberate plan to be created for sharing the responsibility of supervision (Kern & Wakeford, 2007). For example, the day's activities may require direct teacher supervision at just one activity, such as the water table activity, which allows the other teacher to move about the room supervising in a general way. Identifying zones for supervision and dividing tasks to ensure that at least one teacher is observing if the other is attending to a child's need or setting up lunch are other strategies. Clarifying the supervision plan ensures that teachers focus on their assigned responsibility and prevents teachers from thinking that "someone else" is watching (Kern & Wakeford, 2007).

Reassuring Children That They Are Safe

Teachers also have a responsibility to help children develop trust in the environment and know that the teacher is there to keep them safe. Children who feel safe and secure are able to move out into the play setting and to enjoy and learn from their interactions in the environment (Bowlby, 1982). They are also more likely to seek the teacher for help if a safety issue arises.

The amount of reassurance required depends on the children's age and maturity, and need at a particular time. For example:

- Infants benefit from being able to see and hear the teacher, and know that the teacher will attend to their needs.
- Toddlers need reassurance that the teacher is nearby as a physical and emotional safety base.
- Preschool children like to know that the teacher is available to listen to their ideas and concerns and to respond when they have a need.
- School-age children like to know what the rules are and who to go to if they need help.

The reassurance that teachers provide includes being accessible (physically near and attentive) and responsive (approachable and easy to talk to). This requires that teachers position themselves physically to supervise effectively and engage with children to show they are available and ready to listen to children's safety concerns.

Keeping Focused and Alert

Maintaining attention is critical to safe supervision. This means teachers must avoid distractions such as the following (AAP et al., 2002a):

- Talking together or talking on the telephone.
- Daydreaming.
- Cleaning or performing tasks that interrupt appropriate supervision.
- Being overly involved in children's play so that group supervision is forgotten.

Teachers must learn to balance interaction with individual children with full classroom oversight. For example, when helping a toddler place shape blocks into a puzzle, the teacher should periodically look up to scan the remainder of the room, ensuring that all children are playing safely, making eye contact, and smiling at other children who are playing.

Supervising Classroom Activities

Supervising children in the classroom comprises the largest portion of the teaching day. Activities should be developmentally appropriate, and teachers should focus special attention on supervising sensory table activities, interactions with animals, and water play activities.

Planning Appropriate Activities

Careful planning is needed to balance the number of activities that require direct teacher involvement with the number of activities that children can participate in on their own (Alter & Conroy, 2007). Planning interesting activities and making materials accessible allow children to be self-sufficient. This frees teachers to move about the room observing for safety.

Monitoring Activity Areas

Teachers need to continually monitor activity areas to ensure that safety hazards are avoided and corrected. For example, manipulative toys or blocks may be left in the walkway, potentially causing a tripping hazard or blocking emergency exits. In the course of active play the sensory-bin materials such as sand, rice, or water may be spilled on the floor introducing a slipping hazard. These issues should be anticipated and avoided through careful room arrangement or by taking safety precautions such as placing safety mats under the sensory table. Safety problems that emerge should be corrected right away.

Supervising Interactions with Animals

Children are very interested in animals and pet care is a good way to introduce concepts of empathy and kindness. But special strategies should be used for the safety of children and classroom pets or visiting animals. Child care regulations may limit the types of animals that are allowed in children's settings because of safety concerns (AAP et al., 2002a). For example, birds with hooked beaks and animals that may carry salmonella (lizards, frogs, turtles, baby chicks) are typically not allowed. Any visiting animals should be healthy and not aggressive with children.

A safe way to arrange interactions between children and animals is through small-group activities. The teacher should give specific instructions to the children as they sit in a circle on the floor, saying:

> Today Sally's dog, Bess, is coming to visit. So we don't frighten Bess, we will sit in a circle while Sally introduces her to us. When Sally says it is OK, she will invite each of you to come up one at a time to pet Bess.

What if. . .

a child told you she likes being at school and always wants to be with you? What is the child expressing? How would you respond?

Safety hazards, such as spilled materials from the sensory table, should be cleared away as soon as they are identified.

This approach provides children with the information they need to understand how to behave. It communicates:

- What the rule is (sit in the circle; wait until you are called forward).
- What will happen (introduction of the pet to the children).
- How the children are to respond (come forward when invited).
- Who will get to participate (everyone).

When children know what is expected and receive confirmation that each will be able to participate, the experience is more enjoyable and safe for the children and the animal.

Supervising Activities That Involve Water

Water activities present significant safety concerns that require careful supervision to ensure safety. Water play for infants and toddlers should be offered in shallow trays to avoid the possibility of children "tipping" over into the water. Teachers should closely supervise water activities, watching for appropriate play and ensuring that the floor under the table does not become slippery.

Water play such as wading or swimming should be offered in compliance with the regulations governing child care in the local area. Some states do not allow wading pools in children's programs. The American Academy of Pediatrics (2002a) is another resource for guidance related to swimming pool safety. It is important for teachers to know how to keep children safe as well as understand the liability issues related to water play activities.

Supervising Outdoor Activities

Special attention should be directed to supervising children in outdoor play areas because injuries outdoors can happen quickly and have the potential to be severe. Children must be visible at all times, and teachers must be able to hear them to understand if they are in danger or if they are being harassed or bullied. A well-designed outdoor environment should work "with" teachers, supporting the ability for teachers to scan the near and far environments to track for safety (Kern & Wakeford, 2007). Supervising children effectively in the outdoor play environment involves recognizing that outdoor time is useful for teaching, using supervision zones, and organizing supervision in shared spaces.

Planning Outdoor Playtime

Outdoor play areas are learning spaces that must be intentionally prepared to ensure that children are involved in safe and interesting play. Teachers are responsible for:

- Providing appropriate equipment and supplies.
- Planning and implementing interesting activities.
- Using the outdoor classroom to support motor skill and social skill development.
- Encouraging children to be highly active at least part of the time.
- Supervising children for safety at all times by keeping children within sight and sound.

Giving attention to the activities that are available to children sets the stage for safe play and reduces the likelihood of bullying and rough play that may emerge due to boredom.

Using Supervision Zones

When supervising in outdoor settings teachers need to stay alert, allow children to explore and discover without undue intervention, but be ready to intervene immediately if unsafe behavior is observed. Sometimes early childhood teachers might fall into the habit of considering outdoor playtime or recess as "break time." They might cluster at the periphery of

Close supervision is needed for any water play.

the play area, supervising from a distance, but not engaging with children except when needed. These practices can be harmful. Outdoor play spaces are usually large and trees and equipment may block views, making supervision by sight more challenging. Dividing the outdoor play area into "zones" and assigning each teacher to supervise a zone is a good strategy to improve safety (Kern & Wakeford, 2007). This approach helps teachers focus their attention on the specific activities occurring in their zone and increases their attentiveness to guiding children to play appropriately.

Organizing Supervision in Shared Spaces

Some early childhood settings do not have an outdoor play area so they make arrangements to use community spaces such as parks and playgrounds for outdoor play. These are called shared spaces. Shared spaces offer valuable opportunities for programs to provide active outdoor play, but these spaces also introduce challenges. Shared spaces should be reviewed by the local child care licensing agent who can identify ways the environment can be managed to meet safety requirements.

shared spaces
indoor and outdoor spaces that are shared by the early childhood program and other groups, including public parks

The shared play space needs to be well defined and children should be taught to recognize the boundaries of the "OK to play" area. Marking the boundaries with brightly colored cones helps children remember. Supervision in shared spaces must be especially vigilant to ensure that children do not wander off to other areas and to be aware of and monitor other people who may come into the play space. Teachers may be less comfortable with children's exploration, and as a result must be cautious not to oversupervise children and limit their play.

Anticipating Potential Safety Concerns

Many situations may threaten children's safety in the early childhood setting. Teachers should anticipate these and prepare to use their professional experience and common sense to address issues as they occur.

What if. . .

you found yourself daydreaming about what you needed to purchase at the grocery store when you were supposed to be supervising children at the swings? How would you improve your supervision in this important area?

Focusing on Field Trip Safety

Even carefully planned field trips can pose challenges to children's safety. Moving out of the familiar environment into new settings has the potential to distract children's attention from teachers and other adults who are guiding and supervising them. Many aspects of the natural environment can introduce hazards such as tripping over curbs or brushing against sharp objects (bricks, fences). Teachers reduce the possibility of unintentional injury by selecting appropriate field trip destinations and by visiting the field trip site in advance to assess the setting for safety concerns. Orienting children and adult volunteers about the safety rules for the field trip is also important.

Ensuring Safety When Substitutes Are Assigned

Any change in group leadership can introduce potential safety concerns. Substitute teachers and teachers who are assigned to float from one group to another during the day may not know individual children well and must quickly adjust to the classroom schedule. Substitute or assistant teachers should gather the children together for an opening group time (if appropriate) to explain why the regular teacher is absent and to conduct introductions. This helps avoid confusion if the substitute is not known by the children and is essentially a stranger to them. The activity plan for the day should be adjusted to ensure that the majority of activities are child directed, allowing the teacher to focus on interacting with the children and supervising for safety. Teachers should have lesson plans prepared in advance to support substitute teachers.

Supervising Visitors and Occasional Volunteers

Visitors and occasional volunteers bring welcome assistance and special skills to the early childhood setting, but they can also introduce disruption to safety routines. They need to be oriented to their roles and responsibilities and to the safety routines of the classroom.

Teachers should introduce them to the children, confirming that they are "teacher-approved" members of the classroom. Visitors and volunteers should be given clear assignments, such as reading with children, filling the paint containers, or supervising the block corner. They should never be left alone with the children and teachers should supervise their interactions at all times (AAP et al., 2003).

Sometimes visitors in uniform, such as firefighters with helmets or costumed characters, may visit the children's program. Adults may see these characters as fun and interesting, but children may find them frightening. These visitors should be scheduled only if appropriate for the group. They should be oriented in advance about ways to appropriately interact with the children. Teachers should always be present to ensure children's comfort and safety.

Confronting Intruders

On occasion teachers may need to confront unknown people entering the classroom, hallway, or outdoor play area. Teachers must approach any unknown person to determine who he or she is and why the person is there. Teachers must identify the purpose and appropriateness of that person's presence and request the person to leave if necessary. A backup plan should be in place if the teacher requires assistance, such as calling in support from other teachers or the program director or principal (AAP et al., 2002a).

Guiding Family Socials

Gathering the families of young children together for social and other events is a common outreach activity of early childhood programs, yet such events can introduce disruptions that pose safety concerns. Children can become very excited about having their families with them and the larger group of people adds noise and a sense of confusion in the setting.

There may also be confusion about who is supervising the children at these events—the teacher or the family? It is important for teachers to clearly communicate the goal of the event and who is in charge of supervision. This can be accomplished in the way the invitation is extended:

- If the teacher will be responsible for supervising children, parents could be invited to "Please come watch the class dance and sing favorite songs."
- If parents are to supervise their child, the invitation could say, "Please supervise your child while you enjoy walking through the classroom art show together."

Ultimately, when family events are program or school sponsored, the teacher should continue to supervise for safety and be ready to step in to ensure that safety policies are followed.

Families need to know about classroom safety policies.

Enforcing Program Safety Policies

Sometimes teachers need to spontaneously intervene to ensure children's safety. Family members and visitors may introduce unsafe situations in the classroom through lack of information and some may show outright disregard for the program safety approach. These situations can catch teachers by surprise. Teachers cannot assume that other adults will always behave appropriately around children or understand dangers. Sometimes situations arise that require teachers to step forward, kindly but firmly stating the program safety rule that needs to be enforced. Teachers should persist until unsafe activities stop and safety is restored. Table 16-2 provides examples of situations that require teacher intervention and examples of management strategies.

Addressing Family Issues

Other challenges may occur due to complicated family situations or custody issues. A parent might report that the noncustodial parent or another adult has a court-ordered temporary restraining order and is not allowed to have contact with the child. Teachers need the support of their program or school to recognize how such issues should be handled. In some cases,

Table 16-2	Incidental Situations That Require Responsive Action
Potential Safety Hazard	**Responsive Action**
A pet is brought into the classroom unannounced.	Inform the pet owner that the pet must be kept outside. Explore the possibility of having the pet come at a scheduled time when the interaction can be planned safely.
A parent parks her bicycle in the walkway to the classroom.	Identify the bicycle as a safety hazard, and show the parent where she can safely park her bike.
A child brings potentially unsafe toys to the family care home.	Ask the child to tell you about the toys, briefly explain why they are unsafe for the setting, then show the child where the toys will need to be kept until they can be taken home at the end of the day.
Parents loiter in the child care playground after pick up; they do not monitor their children closely and do not enforce the program's safety rules.	Approach the parents and explain your concerns. Clarify the program's safety rules and request their cooperation.
A person walks by the play yard and engages in conversation over the fence with a child.	Intervene immediately to redirect the child and ask the person to refrain from interacting with the child. Review the play yard barrier to determine if it needs to be adjusted or if supervision needs to be increased, or both.
A parent sends an unfamiliar person to preschool to pick up a child.	Keep the child in care until the parent can be contacted. Ask the parent to clarify who the unfamiliar person is, and obtain verbal permission to release to the unknown adult. Require the unfamiliar person to show picture identification to confirm identify.
A neighbor offers to donate toys, some of which are unsafe, to the family child care provider.	Thank the neighbor for the kind gesture. Inform them of your need to only accept toys that meet safety standards.
A parent calls in to the class and asks the teacher to send the child out to the car where they are waiting.	Remind the parent that the child can only be released directly to the parent. Work with the parent to create a workable pickup plan.
A parent leaves a sleeping baby in the car while coming in to pick up a preschool-age child.	Talk with the parent about the dangers of leaving a sleeping child alone in the car. Explore options with the parent that will provide safety for both the infant and the child in care.
At a family social, a parent shows children how to run up the slide and encourages the preschoolers to follow.	Talk with the parent about why your program safety rule is "Climb up the ladder, and slide down the slide." Explain that young children's coordination and balance are not fully developed and that running up the slide is dangerous.

the temporary restraining order must be reviewed and the limits of the exclusion understood. This is done to ensure that the teacher does not restrict access to the child by one parent simply on the direction of the other parent.

Parents involved in custody battles might ask teachers to record observations about the other parent. Teachers need to avoid being drawn in to family disagreements. They should explain to families that the school setting is a safe and neutral area for the child. Developing a relationship of collaboration with families helps when it is necessary to communicate about difficult issues such as these (Olson, 2007).

Intervening When Families Are Unsafe

Teachers need to act decisively when they observe families using unsafe practices with children. For example, teachers may learn that a child is being transported without an appropriate car restraint seat or seat belt. Or they might observe that an infant is being left

What if. . .

you were asked by a parent to record all the times the "other" parent picked a child up late from school? How would you approach this situation?

Safety Segment

Don't Leave Children in Motor Vehicles

Leaving children in motor vehicles is a severe safety hazard. Vehicles trap sunlight and heat up like a greenhouse. It only takes 10 minutes for the heat inside vehicles to become life threatening. When parked in the sun, vehicles can reach internal temperatures of up to 131°F (55°C). Even on mildly warm days of 60°F (15°C), the passenger area of a vehicle can reach 110°F (43°C). Teach families these safety rules:

- Never leave a child in an unattended vehicle even with the windows down.
- Remind families to be careful of routines for dropping children off at child care. Have them place a needed item like a purse, lunch, or backpack in the back seat where they will see the child when they get out of the vehicle. Sometimes a sleeping child is forgotten.
- Remind families to always lock the doors of their vehicles at home so children do not enter the car and accidentally lock themselves in.
- Teach children to never play in a vehicle.
- Call 911 if you see a child left unattended in a vehicle.

Sources: *Children and Cars: A Potentially Lethal Combination*, 2009, Washington, DC: National Highway Traffic Safety Association, retrieved September 22, 2009, from http://www.nhtsa.dot.gov/people/injury/enforce/ChildrenAndCars/pages/Unattend-HotCars.htm; and *Safety In and Around Cars: Never Leave Your Child Alone*, 2009, Washington, DC: Safe Kids, retrieved October 30, 2009, from http://www.usa.safekids.org/skbu/cars/nlyca.html.

unattended in a vehicle while the parent drops off or picks up another child from the classroom. This practice has led to the deaths of many children due to heat suffocation. The *Safety Segment* provides information and reminders to families about the dangers of leaving children unattended in cars. Teachers must notify families immediately about such safety concerns and work with them to resolve the dangerous situation. Families are most often appreciative of guidance that helps them keep their child safe. If families are resistant and the dangerous behavior is repeated, teachers need to contact the police.

IMPLEMENTING SAFE MANAGEMENT PRACTICES

The early childhood years are a time of rapid change. Children grow from being vulnerable infants to active and involved young children; from being very dependent to being more independent. Greater skills and maturity help children learn from experience and from their teachers how to recognize dangers and learn to keep safe. But these increasing abilities can also introduce new dangers. This means that teachers must understand appropriate safety management practices, be attuned to the safety needs of different age groups, and be prepared with strategies to teach all children safely.

Identifying Appropriate Safety Management Practices

When children's physical skills develop more rapidly than their reasoning skills and knowledge about danger, they may unknowingly put themselves in dangerous situations. For example, once toddlers discover walking, they enjoy testing their new skills by walking up stairs or in the direction of the street—unaware of the potential dangers. It is a mistake to "blame" very young children for acting in unsafe ways simply because they are young and inexperienced. Similarly, it is not helpful to "allow" older children to behave in unsafe ways based on the assumption that they should "know better." Teachers are responsible for using management strategies that keep pace with these changes. Three functions guide appropriate safety management practices in the classroom: planning, managing, and teaching about safety.

1. *Planning for safety* includes ensuring that children are physically able to safely accomplish the activities that are made available and capable of understanding the related safety directions and effects of dangerous behavior. This requires attention to developmentally appropriate planning and supervision. For example, by about age 3, most typically developing children can understand a direction such as "Go down the slide feet first."

2. *Managing for safety* in all aspects of teaching involves considering safety when establishing the environment; modeling safe and appropriate interactions, such as how to safely put toys away or how to get ready to go outside; and guiding children to interact with the environment and one another in appropriate ways.

3. *Teaching appropriate safety messages* rounds out the spectrum of safety management approaches used in early childhood settings (AAP et al., 2002a). Safety messages are taught in a gradual and progressive way across the early childhood years. This means that each safety message is introduced in a simple way that focuses on safety rather than dwelling on danger, then is repeated with more detail as children mature, and is reinforced through practice. The *Teaching Wellness* feature activity provides an example of how safety messages are introduced and gradually reinforced across the early childhood years.

Understanding the Safety Needs of Infants

In the first year of life, children develop from vulnerable infants to enthusiastic crawling or walking explorers. Safety management should encourage and not get in the way of this normal development. The infants interests in exploration need to be encouraged because this allows the child to gain practical abilities and knowledge as well as confidence that the environment is safe and inviting.

Implementing Appropriate Safety Practices

Safety for infants is based on individualized care rhythms such as a familiar schedule for eating and sleeping, as well as a safe environment, kind and caring touch, and appropriate encouraging conversation (NAEYC, 2006). In addition, teachers in infant care settings should:

- Check the environment for safety every day to ensure clean floors, covered electrical outlets, no choking hazards, no rough or sharp surfaces, sturdy furnishings, no blinds with pull strings, no bibs except during feeding, no pacifiers on strings around necks.
- Label and store infants food, personal belongings, high chair, and crib appropriately.
- Place infants on their backs to sleep, alone in cribs with no toys, blankets, or bumper pads.
- Talk and sing to help infants associate the sound and feel of language with positive social connection and safe relationships.

Managing for Safety

Managing the behavior of infants is a basic part of the everyday teacher and child interaction (AAP et al., 2002a). Key management approaches for infant safety include the following:

- Supervise how babies interact with materials. Teachers must sanitize dropped pacifiers and toys and make sure toys that have been in mouths are not exchanged with other babies.
- Guide interactions. Teachers must help children touch without grabbing at eyes or earrings, saying, "Pat Lin-Lin's cheek gently like this."
- Teachers in family child care or mixed-age group settings must ensure that infants are protected from older and more mobile children who may be playing nearby. The guidance approach in these settings is instructive for the older children and protective for the infant.

MyEducationLab

Go to the Assignments and Activities section of Topic 2: Feeding Children in the MyEducationLab for your course and complete the activity entitled *Developmentally Appropriate Mealtimes for Infants*. What does this teacher do to assure this infant that she is safe and secure?

Babies rely on their teachers to teach them how to touch each other gently.

Teaching Wellness *Class Safety Rules*

Learning Outcome: Children will name and describe safety rules.

Infants and Toddlers

- *Goal:* Babies and toddlers will experience the safety rule of "Be kind to one another" by hearing kind words and seeing teachers model caring for people and toys.

- *Materials:* Play space, appropriate toys including people figures and toy animals.

- *Activity plan:* Place babies and toddlers in the play area with enough toys for everyone. Sit with children. As they play and interact, use words that convey caring and kindness. Say, "You are touching the toy doggie very gently. See how you can pet the toy doggie? Let's use this blanket to make a bed for the doggie. That's how we can take care of him." When children interact or touch one another, provide words to describe what the children are doing. Say, "Zack, you are being careful of Owen. That makes him happy." Redirect rough touching by guiding children's hands and modeling careful touch.

- *How to adjust the activity:* Invite children to build a tower with small unit blocks. Talk about stacking the blocks carefully so the tower does not tip over. When you are done playing, help children put toys in a tub and say, "This is how we take care of our toys."

- *Did you meet your goal?* Did children hear kind words and see the teacher modeling care for people and toys?

Preschoolers and Kindergartners

- *Goal:* Children will name two classroom safety rules and tell how the rules help keep children safe.

- *Materials:* Paper, marking pens, crayons, tape for posting pictures, poster-sized paper.

- *Activity plan:* Provide drawing materials at a table. Tell children who come to the drawing area that you are making a classroom safety poster of pictures that help children learn rules about keeping safe in the classroom. Invite the children to think of ways to keep safe. Encourage them to draw and write their ideas on their paper. Ask if they would like you to write their words on their paper. Talk about their safety rules as they work. Encourage children to tape their picture to the poster. Bring the poster to group time. Talk about each picture and the safety rule. Invite children to say more about their ideas for safety rules.

- *How to adjust the activity:* Provide additional opportunities for children to draw, write, and discuss safety rules. Guide the discussion toward specific topics such as rules for the play yard or for riding on the bus or touching animals.

- *Did you meet your goal?* Listen to children's discussion. Are they able to name safety rules? Can they provide descriptions of how the rules help keep children safe?

What if. . .

an infant in your care cried a great deal and was difficult to soothe? What strategies would you use to help the baby build trust with you and the environment?

Teaching Safety Messages

Teachers of infants convey important safety messages by establishing safe and trusting environments and teaching babies to interact appropriately. Infants learn about safety as teachers:

- Respond to the infant's needs.
- Place the infant to eat and sleep in safe positions.
- Introduce infants to gentle touching and safe sounds, helping them to experience safe and secure feelings.

School-Age Children

- *Goal:* Children will identify rules for several school settings (the classroom, the cafeteria, the bus, outdoors) and for field trips and will be able to explain the rules to others.

- *Materials:* Poster-sized paper, marking pens, tape.

- *Activity plan:* Introduce the concept of rules for keeping children safe and for respecting others. Create small groups. Have each group select a school setting and create a poster listing two to four rules for that setting. Have the children illustrate their poster. Bring the children together and have each group describe their list of rules and explain how the rules keep children safe. Invite the class to give feedback about the rules and offer additional ideas.

- *How to adjust the activity:* Display the rule posters in the hallway or school library. Have the children make safety rule "books" to share with the kindergarten class.

- *Did you meet your goal?* Are children able to name equipment, games, and sports usually conducted outdoors? Can they discuss some of the safety rules?

Petee reminds his friends to hold hands and stay together when they go on field trips.

Understanding the Safety Needs of Toddlers

The toddler years (from walking to age 3) are a time of increasingly active movement, exploration, and interest in independence. Teachers should take advantage of this enthusiasm by guiding children to participate safely in their environment and with each other.

Implementing Appropriate Safety Practices

Teachers of toddlers should address safety by recognizing that the toddlers' greater mobility may lead them to climb higher, toddle further, and engage with materials in new and inventive ways. Important safety practices for toddlers include the following:

- Review the environment for safety. For example, child safety locks should be used on cupboards and furniture should be sturdy so children can pull themselves up to a standing position by holding on to the furniture and balance without worry of furniture tipping over.
- Provide toileting supports, including potty chairs, child-sized toilets, child-accessible sinks or sturdy stepstools, and monitor children's access to toilets.
- Arrange open spaces for play and provide plenty of time for toddlers to move and explore without undue restrictions.
- Monitor toys, sensory bin materials, and food for potential choking hazards.
- Offer finger-food options that promote independence but do not present choking hazards.
- Label and store children's personal items and sleeping mat or cot.

Managing for Safety

Toddlers need close supervision. They have discovered the joys of movement and seek independence, but may have relatively limited ability to communicate and sometimes are not able to achieve the goals they are aiming for. A child might move the helpful teacher's hand away saying, "Alex do it. Alex big boy." Or a child might respond to frustrating situations through familiar toddler behaviors such as scratching or biting, behaviors that cause grief for children, teachers, and parents. The teacher should stay as close as necessary to recognize when such behaviors are about to occur, and be ready to intervene immediately to prevent the problem behavior and redirect the child to productive play. If a problem occurs, management should be clear and direct (NAEYC, 2005c):

- Firmly state what the child should do: "No biting!" or "No running to the street!"
- Briefly state why: "Biting hurts" or "Streets are dangerous!"
- Provide an alternative: "You can play with these blocks. At snack time you can bite an apple" or "Here is the safe place to run. Let's go!"

Teaching Safety Messages

Safety messages for toddlers are taught through modeling safe practices, introducing rules, and teaching words to encourage safe play. This approach helps toddlers see appropriate behavior and connect words with their meaning, enhancing understanding of the safety message. For example, the teacher might guide a child's hand to poke a tofu cube with a small fork while saying, "Use the fork to poke the tofu. No poking people." Adding facial expressions that reinforce the "yes" and "no" part of the message increases the likelihood of correct communication. The toddler might repeat back the message, "Poke fu," while nodding his head up and down in affirmation. Other safety messages taught through modeling actions and words include these:

What if. . .

a toddler you were laughing and playing with suddenly reached out and grabbed your glasses? How would you respond?

- *Use gentle touch:* Keep from poking or scratching eyes and faces, or pulling earrings.
- *Stay back from dangers:* Beware of hot stoves, fire, broken glass, unknown animals, swings, and so forth.
- *Eat and drink safely:* Sit while eating and drinking; eat slowly and remember to chew.
- *Move safely in the environment:* Watch out for tabletops that stick out at eye level; go down slides feet first.
- *Interact safely in the environment:* Say, "The flower is for touching and smelling, but not eating." Use phrases like "The window is just for looking, not hitting."
- *Play safely:* Say, "Look Jenna, hold the truck down here where it is away from Leon's eyes. Down here is the safe place for your truck."

Safety messages can be introduced to toddlers using storybooks or puppet dramas that address appropriate safety situations.

Understanding the Safety Needs of Preschoolers

Preschool children (ages 3 to 5 years) mature from playing individually or alongside other children to being highly interested in interactive play. They are increasingly able to move, run, and climb quickly and are capable of sustained involvement with activities and inventive dramatic play. Preschool children are also able to learn, implement, and teach others important safety routines. Safety management strategies should respect these increasing capabilities while also empowering children with knowledge to recognize dangers and ways to keep safe.

Implementing Appropriate Safety Practices

Teachers enhance safety for active preschoolers by creating environments where children can test their skills in appropriate ways, encouraging children to try solving problems and supporting the development of self-help skills (NAEYC, 2008). Safety practices for preschool-age children include the following:

- Review the environment to ensure that furniture is stable and toys are organized on low shelves where children can easily reach them. Large toys should be stored on the floor, not on shelves where a child could pull them down upon herself.
- Encourage the development of safe self-help skills by setting out tubs for dirty dishes so children can clear their spaces after meals.
- Label a cubby or hook for the child's coat and a cot or sleeping mat for each child's consistent use. Create labels that use the language the child speaks.
- Provide access to toileting at will, if possible. Supervise children when they are toileting.

Managing for Safety

Supervising preschool children requires teachers to anticipate potential problems. Preschool-age children move independently and quickly and are increasingly interested in social interactions. They can develop intense play themes that may introduce dangers, such as making and eating "stew" from leaves and mushrooms during outdoor play, and they may follow the unsafe behaviors of other children, such as running up the slide, climbing around equipment and barriers and jumping from high platforms. Here are some strategies for managing safety for preschoolers:

- Teach children the boundaries for activity and safety.
- Recognize and reinforce safe behaviors with a smile, a wink, or whisper.
- Guide children to recognize the effect of their unsafe actions. Say, "If you keep riding your tricycle toward the hopscotch area, someone may get hurt."
- Teach children strategies to assert and communicate their needs in unsafe settings. Say, "Tell her you don't want to do that. It is not safe."
- Supervise children's social interactions and intervene in bullying situations.
- Move actively and confidently to correct unsafe behaviors.

Teaching Safety Messages

Preschool children are growing in their ability to understand the causes and effects of behaviors and are able to understand and learn safety messages. However, teaching preschool children about dangers has the possibility of introducing worries, and ultimately such discussions may convey the message that sometimes things occur that adults cannot control. For example, teaching children to evacuate for a fire drill introduces the concept that fires might happen. Safety messages need to be presented in ways that are appropriate for the child to understand and that avoid overdramatizing worrisome events. Typical safety messages for preschool children include:

- Follow the teacher's directions to evacuate in case of emergency.
- Take cover in case of a tornado or earthquake.
- Keep away from dangerous materials (matches and lighters, paints, cleaning supplies, poisons, hot beverages), strange animals, and strangers.
- Eat only the foods given to you by your family or teacher.
- Play safely outdoors and follow the rules of games.

Safety messages can be taught through books and flannel board stories that depict children responding appropriately in potentially dangerous situations. Visits by safety officers such as firefighters and police officers, field trips to locations where safety lessons can be discussed in context such as swimming pools, and dramatic play settings that allow children to explore safety topics are also effective ways to teach about safety.

As preschool children develop greater language skills, they become more able to communicate about fears or experiences that threaten them. Teachers can support this process by helping children learn to recognize and name their emotions. Pictures

MyEducationLab

Go to the Assignments and Activities section of Topic 13: Wellness Curriculum in the MyEducationLab for your course and complete the activity entitled *Toilet Learning*. What can teachers do to help parents and children develop safe and secure toilet learning?

Preschool-age children are growing in ability to understand the causes and effects of behaviors and are able to understand and learn safety messages.

Figure 16-5 Helping Children Identify Emotions

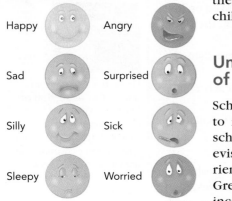

Happy   Angry

Sad   Surprised

Silly   Sick

Sleepy   Worried

showing various facial expressions, such as those in Figure 16-5, can help children to communicate how they feel. Learning to recognize and understand their own emotions and those of others is a developmental task of early childhood.

Understanding the Safety Needs of School-Age Children

School-age children (ages 5 and older) are more mobile and often are allowed to move independently in their neighborhood and travel on their own to school (CDC, 2006). This is also an impressionable age group where heroic television characters and other media-driven images are infused into their experience, potentially confusing children's understanding about realistic abilities. Greater independence can place school-age children in unsupervised settings, increasing the potential for unintentional injury. At the same time these children are capable of learning and following safety rules and telling others about safety. Teachers need to maintain attention to safety practices, while focusing more on teaching children about how to keep safe and supervising from a greater distance.

Implementing Appropriate Safety Practices

Safety practices for school-age children continue to focus on safe environments and appropriate activities. Teachers need to avoid thinking that children's greater maturity and capability suggest they know how to keep safe (CDC, 2006). Safety practices for school-age children include the following:

- Model safe behaviors and establish boundaries for movement and behavior.
- Plan activities that provide appropriate challenge as well as opportunities to learn about safety hazards and ways to keep safe.
- Ensure that children do not have access to dangerous items such as matches, lighters, harmful cleaning products, poisons, alcohol, drugs, firearms, sharp knives.
- Be aware of peer pressure and the influences of older children who may be intrigued by dangerous items; listen for interest in fire, smoking, firearms, explosives, drugs, alcohol, and other dangerous products, which may be signs of inappropriate interactions.
- Recognize when children are becoming tired and need guidance to stop and rest.

Managing for Safety

Various inappropriate and unsafe behaviors may be exhibited and boundaries may be tested with intensity during the school-age years, making managing for safety a challenge. Behaviors teachers may need to confront include children using materials inventively but unsafely, trying "daredevil" behaviors, and bullying other children and telling them they "can't play." Although these may be typical ways in which children explore and test their skills, they are also examples of times when teachers need to help children identify boundaries (Gartrell & Gartrell, 2008). Teachers should reaffirm that inappropriate and dangerous behaviors will not be allowed. Safety management strategies include:

- Focus on behaviors and provide clear messages that communicate the problem and confirm that unsafe behaviors are not allowed. Say, "That tree is dangerous to climb; you need to come down."
- Direct the industriousness and productivity of this age; provide new challenges and opportunities for children to explore.
- Help children build their leadership skills; ask them to help resolve conflicts and identify safe alternatives.

Teachers redirect unsafe behaviors by providing interesting opportunities for both individual and group activities. Planning a variety of appropriate activities that will appeal to everyone, such as crafts, hobbies, information about collecting, and photography is another useful strategy.

Teaching Safety Messages

Safety messages for school-age children focus on preventive safety themes and ways to keep safe in the future. Safety topics for this age group include:

- How to ride a bicycle safely (wearing a helmet and following the rules of the road).
- How to be a safe passenger in the car (keeping hands and head inside the car, not distracting the driver) and in the bus (how to get on and off the bus safely).
- How to call 911 for help in case of an emergency.
- How to respond if a stranger approaches and who to go to for help.
- Staying away from sick or injured animals.
- Staying away from guns, knives, and other sharp objects.
- Staying away from deep water; don't go swimming without an adult.
- How to safely use e-mail and the Internet.
- How to stay home alone for short periods of time (for older school-age children).

Preventive messages can be more abstract than with younger children because this age group is increasingly able to discuss dangers that they may not have actually experienced. For example, children are capable of learning how to stay away from matches to avoid starting a fire and how to respond using the stop-drop-roll actions and calling for help.

Group problem-solving approaches, such as classroom meetings are effective in helping school-age children gain skills to address safety issues. Teachers who hold classroom meetings regularly can use this approach when bullying or unsafe behaviors are observed. Children gather in a circle, discuss the problem, and offer solutions by following simple rules such as letting everyone speak, listening, and being respectful (Gartrell, 2006). The teacher should guide the process, providing sufficient time for children to have their point of view heard, but also moving children through the process of negotiation in an appropriate way. The use of long and drawn-out problem-solving meetings to help children resolve small-scale issues is counterproductive and often ends up with children forgetting what the issue was about. An example of appropriate steps in group problem solving is provided in Figure 16-6.

Understanding the Safety Needs of Children with Special Needs

Sometimes, due to lack of information or experience, teachers might be hesitant about how to keep children with special developmental needs safe in the classroom. The Americans

> ## What if. . .
>
> you overheard a small group of children in your class talking about a gun they had been looking at the previous afternoon? What would you do with this information?

MyEducationLab

Go to the Assignments and Activities section of Topic 5: Health Promotion/Policy in the MyEducationLab for your course and complete the activity *Health Activities for Elementary Children.* What are the safety messages that children learn through this program?

Figure 16-6 Steps in a Group Problem-Solving Process

1. Identify the issue. [Tricycles are parked in front of the door.]
2. Talk about why the issue is a safety problem. [The tricycles block the door so people cannot come in; people might trip over the tricycles.]
3. Think about ways the problem could be solved. [Not let children ride tricycles? Park the tricycles against the wall? Make signs for "No tricycle parking"?]
4. Choose one or two resolutions to try. [Park tricycles against the wall and make "No parking" signs for the door.]
5. Agree on the plan. [Heather and Connor will make signs.]
6. Implement the resolution. [Try it for a few days.]
7. Do a checkup. [Is it working?]

Health Hint

Information Teachers Need to Serve Children with Diabetes

✓ Detailed training that discusses specifics of the diabetes medical management plan such as medication administration, blood glucose testing, and diet.

✓ Training on emergency care steps for low blood sugar levels including glucagon administration

✓ Resources to contact for more information, such as those provided by the American Diabetes Association:

- *Diabetes Medical Management Plan*
- *Tips to Help Teachers Keep Kids with Diabetes Safe at School*
- *Solutions for Common Diabetes Management Concerns in the Classroom*

Sources: *Sample Section 504 Plan & Diabetes Medical Management Plan for a Student with Diabetes*, June 2007, Alexandria, VA: American Diabetes Association, retrieved October 30, 2009, from http://www.diabetes.org/advocacy-and-legalresources/discrimination/school/504plan.jsp; *Tips for Teachers of Students with Diabetes*, Alexandria, VA: American Diabetes Association, retrieved October 30, 2009, from http://www.diabetes.org/uedocuments/ten-tips-for-teachers-2007.pdf; and *Diabetes Management in Schools: Solutions for Common Concerns*, Alexandria, VA: American Diabetes Association, retrieved October 30, 2009, from http://www.diabetes.org/uedocuments/solutions-for-common-diabetes-management-cr-2007.pdf.

with Disabilities Act (ADA) guides teachers to not make assumptions about how a child will behave or what the child can learn simply because the child has an identified disability or special health care need. Instead it is important to consider children's individual needs related to the potential of the program to reasonably meet those needs. For example, children with special developmental needs may need adaptive supports or special assistance, children with food allergies or food restrictions may need special monitoring, and children with special health needs such as diabetes or seizure disorders may require special health routines. The *Health Hint* describes information that teachers need to feel confident in supporting children with diabetes.

Implementing Appropriate Safety Practices

Safety routines that may be unique for children with special needs are developed in collaboration with families, early interventionists, medical providers, and others who advise the teacher about safety accommodations (AAP, 2003). Safety routines include:

- Addressing children's physical support needs by acquiring special equipment such as adaptive scissors or chairs with seat belts for security.
- Supporting children's individual behavior needs by providing extra support and supervision during playtime, and by using a variety of communication methods such as accompanying gestures to reinforce spoken language or photographs and drawings to depict what children should do during transition time (put toys away, wash hands, sit down for snack) (Hanline, Nunes, & Worthy, 2007).
- Ensuring children with special health needs and allergies are supported by a health management plan.
- Addressing food allergies by selecting classroom menus and food-related activities that allow all children in the class to participate. A "Classroom Cookbook of Approved Recipes" helps teachers plan safe cooking activities (see the *Nutrition Note*).

Managing for Safety

Safety management for all children, including those with special needs, should address the child's maturity and ability to follow safety guidance. Management should specifically focus on behaviors that can lead to dangers, and guidance reminders should be repeated

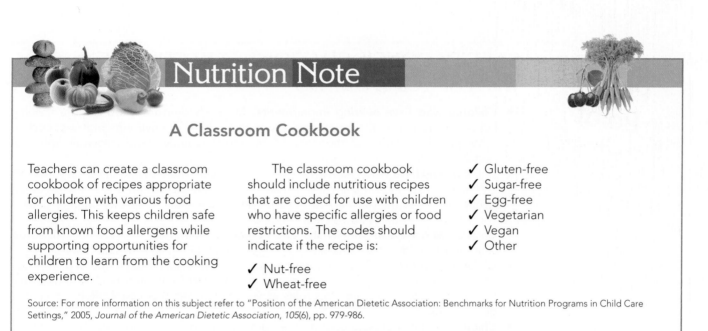

Nutrition Note

A Classroom Cookbook

Teachers can create a classroom cookbook of recipes appropriate for children with various food allergies. This keeps children safe from known food allergens while supporting opportunities for children to learn from the cooking experience.

The classroom cookbook should include nutritious recipes that are coded for use with children who have specific allergies or food restrictions. The codes should indicate if the recipe is:

✓ Nut-free
✓ Wheat-free

✓ Gluten-free
✓ Sugar-free
✓ Egg-free
✓ Vegetarian
✓ Vegan
✓ Other

Source: For more information on this subject refer to "Position of the American Dietetic Association: Benchmarks for Nutrition Programs in Child Care Settings," 2005, *Journal of the American Dietetic Association, 105*(6), pp. 979-986.

frequently and followed consistently to avoid confusion. Reminding children frequently of rules that have been discussed previously can seem frustrating to teachers, but should be done kindly and with a steady voice, remembering that for some children learning the safety rules will take longer.

Teaching Safety Messages

Safety messages for children with special needs should be appropriate for the child's developmental ability to understand and accomplish, and should be relevant to each child's special situation. The teacher also needs to be able to assess the degree to which the child can understand danger.

Here are some examples of safety messages for children's specific situations:

- It is important for children to learn how to recognize and avoid situations that are dangerous. A child with physical challenges must learn to look for uneven pavement that may cause tripping. A child who is hearing impaired needs to remember to look at the teacher when she gives safety directions, because not doing so might be dangerous. Additional examples of safety messages to teach children with special needs are listed in the *Policy Point*.
- Safety messages for children with specific health concerns include how to recognize personal safety hazards and, when age appropriate, how to monitor personal safety, such as teaching a child with asthma to wear a dust mask when sanding wood at the workbench, or guiding a child with food allergies to not eat certain foods.
- Safety messages for children who are learning English include how to recognize the words and gestures for safety, including *stop* and *dangerous*.

Using Focused Strategies

The strategies used to present safety messages should recognize the child's specific circumstances. Many strategies suitable for children with special concerns are appropriate to use with any child. Some examples are listed next.

For children with special developmental needs:

- Use direct and clear language, supplemented by gestures or photographs to communicate and reinforce sequenced responses where appropriate.
- Place danger picture codes or "Stop" signs near boundaries or areas of danger.

Policy Point

SAFETY CONSIDERATIONS FOR CHILDREN WITH SPECIAL NEEDS

- *Children who have hearing impairments:* Teach children to recognize the flashing lights or vibrations of the emergency alarm and to look for environmental cues such as other people lining up at the door. Make sure they understand crosswalk lights for pedestrians.
- *Children who have vision impairments:* Teach children where to find the emergency exit and how to recognize the smell of smoke. Practice an evacuation drill using the emergency exit. Keep the pathway to the emergency exit clear. Keep the furniture pattern consistent because this forms cues to find the exit.
- *Children who move in wheelchairs:* Ensure that the emergency exit is wheelchair accessible. Teach children how to use the emergency exit during an evacuation drill.
- *Children with ADHD:* Teach children to use visual cues such as a picture of a stop sign on the door, or for an older child, a sign that says "Wait for the teacher" to remind children what to do to be safe. Post rules where children see them easily. Rehearse emergency scenarios.
- *Children with diabetes:* Recognize the warning signs of low blood sugar levels which if untreated can become life threatening. Keep glucose tablets or gel, juice, and other emergency foods (as indicated in the diabetes medical management plan) on hand in case of low blood sugar levels.

Sources: *Safety Tips*, 2009, Seattle, WA: Seattle Children's Hospital, Center for Children with Special Needs, retrieved October 30, 2009, from http://cshcn.org/planning-record-keeping/safety-tips; and *Preventing Accidental Injury: Special Needs*, 2009, Washington, DC: Safe Kids USA, retrieved October 30, 2009, from http://www.usa.safekids.org/tier2_rl.cfm?folder_id=2020.

For children with specific health concerns:

- Clearly state the safety concern: "You have a special condition called diabetes."
- Describe the purpose of any safety measures: "We need to test your blood sugar levels and choose just the right foods for your snack."
- Help the child know what to expect: "After group time we will go into the quiet corner where we can concentrate while we test your blood. I'll wear gloves and you can sit on the story chair. Then we will join the other children at snack."
- Teach the child to explain his or her health condition to others as a way of fostering normal conversation about the child's specific health safety need.

For children who are learning English:

- Talk with families or others who can provide safety words in the child's home language. Create note cards with the directions written phonetically.
- Provide books that present safety issues and are written in the child's home language. Request that the family assist you in teaching the safety message.
- Use clearly spoken English with gestures when giving safety directions. Repeat and demonstrate what is expected. Use inviting and encouraging expressions.

Managing Challenging Behaviors

Sometimes children's behaviors are intense and dangerous to themselves or others. Challenging behaviors can threaten safety as children test boundaries and rules, such as climbing on furniture or using playground equipment in irrational and unsafe ways. Challenging behaviors can also introduce unsafe situations when children bite, hit, scratch, kick, or bully others. These behaviors can be very damaging for the child who is out of control, the child or teacher who is the target of the behavior, and all the children of the group who are at risk for feeling insecure and unsafe in the setting.

Teachers need to develop guidance strategies to help children be safe and appropriate in the social setting (Fox & Garrison, 2009). Guidance is a method of teaching that promotes children's understanding and ability to appropriately manage their behaviors. Guidance is not discipline, which tends to be associated with punitive approaches to enforce acceptable behavior. Guidance helps children avoid interpersonal conflicts or outbursts during which they might hurt themselves or others (Alter & Conroy, 2007).

Teachers should work closely with families to explore the child's behaviors and to identify guidance approaches that can be reinforced in both the school and home environments (Alter & Conroy, 2007). Such interventions help children manage their behaviors and become more able to listen to and follow directions, both of which are crucial responses in emergency situations. In the opening case scenario, Jean experienced a high level of discouragement due to a variety of child behaviors. She needed to summon the courage to reflect on her classroom management style and seek support to help her create a plan for improvement. This is a good example of the efforts that teachers make to manage safety in the group setting.

guidance
methods that teach children to control and regulate their own behaviors

discipline
methods that seek to enforce appropriate behaviors; discipline has come to be closely associated with methods of punishment and restraint

Reinforcing Safety Messages

Guiding children to be safe should be central to the early childhood curriculum. Recognizing the safety lessons in daily activities and helping children understand safety as important in their lives are ways teachers reinforce safety messages.

Recognizing Everyday Safety Lessons

Reinforcing the safety messages that are part of everyday activities helps children begin to recognize that they deserve—and can achieve—safety and security in their lives (Bales, Wallinga, & Coleman, 2005). Learning to stack blocks so the tower does not fall over teaches children about careful touch and the consequences of being rough. Learning to carry a cup of water so it does not spill is another way in which children learn through trial and error about being careful and cautious. Teachers should help children recognize the safety skills that they are developing. Observing children using toys appropriately and following play yard rules demonstrates that children are beginning to understand how to be safe.

Using Teachable Moments

Sometimes injuries can offer useful teaching opportunities. While the teacher's first response to an accident is to care for the injury and comfort the child, these situations can also be learning moments if they are handled kindly and with understanding. After administering needed first aid, the teacher could hug the child and state, "Bumping heads hurts! Next time walk slowly around the corner to keep from bumping your head." This acknowledges the hurt while offering the child a strategy to avoid the hurt in the future.

Making Safety Relevant to Children's Lives

Safety messages should be relevant to children's experiences and address their worries and concerns. Some children may experience events that make them feel unsafe, such accidents or frightening storms. Teachers can help them discover ways to address their worries such as telling their family when they are scared. Some children witness acts of violence through the media or in their neighborhoods. Storybooks that explore potentially frightening scenarios that describe how the character demonstrates strength and resilience in difficult situations can support conversations about how to keep safe.

Safety messages should also be tailored to dangers children might find in or around their home or community. Children in rural settings may benefit from safety messages that relate to farm animals, use of farm equipment, and staying away from irrigation canals. Children in urban areas should be taught about how to safely ride on the subway or use elevators.

Although teachers impart safety knowledge of many kinds, they often do not know in the long run if the safety lessons they teach will, in fact, keep children safe in the future. Teachers provide a place and a period of time where children can be secure and have a chance to learn, and where the ideas of a safe environment and safe and positive interactions are planted.

MyEducationLab
To assess your understanding of how to promote safe practices through effective classroom management, go to the Book Specific Resources section in the MyEducationLab for your course, select *Nutrition, Health, and Safety for Young Children,* Chapter 16 of the Study Plan, and then complete the multiple choice questions and activities.

Summary

Effective classroom management in early childhood settings relies on the development of practices that when used systematically, increase children's safety in the setting. Organized daily routines, a predictable schedule, and attention to transportation regulations provide a foundation for safety and offer a rhythm to the classroom day where children's safety is of primary importance.

Supervision is crucial to children's safety. Teachers must be prepared to supervise children in a variety of settings, and to use appropriate strategies, professional experiences, and common sense to anticipate and address safety concerns.

Teachers also need to understand and address the safety needs of all children. By adapting safety management strategies to fit children's developmental capabilities, and making safety relevant to children's lives, teachers guide children to establish patterns of safety that benefit them now and in the future.

Key Terms

Child safety restraint system, p. 528

Discipline, p. 549

Guidance, p. 549

Routines, p. 523

Shared spaces, p. 535

Transition, p. 529

Review Questions

1. Describe how information collected during enrollment assists teachers to plan safe classroom routines.

2. Name the two key elements of safe supervision. Give examples of how teachers coordinate classroom supervision.

3. What is meant by the term *supervision zones* as applied to outdoor environments?

4. Identify safety messages that are unique for children with special developmental or health needs.

5. Describe how safety messages can be infused in the daily curriculum.

Discussion Starters

1. Classroom safety routines are important to the development of safety habits in the early childhood setting. Identify a classroom safety routine you think is important and discuss why.

2. Parents often rely on family and friends to help them transport their children to care. Discuss what you would do if "Auntie Janet" came to pick up Meg, a preschooler in your care, but her name is not on your list of persons authorized to pick Meg up from school.

3. Supervising children for safety requires teachers to adapt their strategies to meet the changing needs of children as they grow and mature. Discuss some of the ways in which supervising preschoolers and school-age children are the same and ways that are different.

Practice Points

1. Using the Web Resources section as a guide, search the Internet for an article that discusses a current issue related to safe practices for early childhood classrooms.

2. Identify a potential field trip site for a kindergarten class. Visit the destination and make a list of potential safety hazards and explain how you would ensure children's safety at the location.

3. Draft a newsletter for families that communicates the safety rules for your classroom. Provide an explanation for each safety rule that describes how the rule improves children's safety while also allowing them to explore and learn.

Web Resources

National Association for Child Care Resource & Referral Agencies
www.naccrra.org

National Association for the Education of Young Children
www.naeyc.org

National Education Association, Promoting Effective Classroom Management
www.nea.org/tools/14367.htm

U.S. Department of Health & Human Services, Early Childhood Learning and Knowledge Center
http://eclkc.ohs.acf.hhs.gov/hslc

Zero to Three
www.zerotothree.org

chapter 17 | Responding to Emergencies

Learning Outcomes

After reading this chapter, you should be able to:

1. Define emergencies and discuss steps to take to prepare for emergencies.

2. Describe volunteer protection laws and describe the purpose of universal precautions.

3. Understand the basics of first aid, including the ABCs of airway, breathing, and circulation.

4. Explain what is meant by shelter-in-place, lockdown, and evacuation, and describe when these actions are recommended.

5. Explain appropriate response for disaster emergencies, including natural disasters, hazardous materials spills, and large-scale attacks and threats.

6. Describe how teachers can help children regain a sense of security and safety following emergencies and disaster events.

Jamal runs a small family child care program that serves five children ages 2 to 5 years. They are all outside where the children are selecting balls from a cart that Jamal rolled out into the grass. Mattie and Tristan are tossing balls across the grass and Callie and Ahmed, who are older, are running after them and rolling them back. They are laughing as the brightly colored balls bump across the yard.

Jamal smiles as he watches them. Then he hears a crash and turns to discover that 2-year-old Aidan has pulled the ball cart over on top of himself. As Jamal quickly removes the cart, he sees that Aidan has been badly cut. A bright red welt runs from Aidan's forehead across his eyebrow and cheek, and blood is pouring out of his nose and mouth. Aidan's eyes are open and staring, but he is completely silent. Jamal crouches down to assess the situation and puts on the plastic gloves that he always carries in his pocket. The other children gather about him. He calls out to Aidan saying, "Hey, Aidan. Hey, buddy! Are you ok?" Aidan blinks and looks at Jamal. Then he takes in a big breath and begins to cry and reach out to Jamal.

Jamal picks Aidan up gently and, calling for the other children to follow, carries him through to the kitchen where he has the first aid supplies stored. He shifts Aidan to his hip and directs Callie and Ahmed to entertain the younger children in the book corner. Jamal opens sterile gauze pads and presses them to Aidan's nose and mouth. He rocks his body back and forth saying, "It's ok, it's ok now, Aidan. We're going to make it better." Aidan is puffing and whimpering but settles in against Jamal. Jamal picks up the phone and calls Aidan's mother Mimi, who is at work. She says that she will come as soon as she can.

Then Jamal moves to sit with Aidan where they can see the other children playing. He continues to hold the gauze against Aidan's face and distracts him by talking quietly about the story the children are "reading." Aidan's eyes move to watch the other children, but he seems groggy and drowsy. When Mimi arrives she is alarmed by Aidan's appearance. Jamal encourages her to take Aidan to the doctor. They tape the gauze gently against Aidan's cheeks.

After they leave Jamal ties the soiled gauze and latex gloves in a plastic bag, disinfects the nearby surfaces, and washes his hands. Then he helps the other children get ready for nap time. That evening Jamal checks the ball cart and sees that a protective cover for one of the supports has fallen off. It looks like it can be repaired, but he sets the cart in the garage until later when he can work on it carefully. Then he calls Mimi and learns that Aidan needed stitches, but that he should be fine.

Early childhood teachers assume a complex range of responsibilities when caring for and educating young children. They must care for the small injuries that occur and sometimes must effectively manage more serious emergencies. In order for teachers like Jamal to respond efficiently, they need to be able to recognize when injuries are emergency situations. They need to have an emergency management plan in place and have the skills and confidence to take action if needed. In addition, teachers must be prepared for disaster situations and have a plan to supervise children until they can be released to their families.

In this chapter we discuss the planning processes that help teachers prepare to take effective action and describe the steps in basic first aid. This information does not replace the need for teachers to obtain first aid and emergency response training from credible authorities. Together emergency preparedness and periodic training assist teachers to respond effectively to keep children safe.

PREPARING FOR EMERGENCIES

Any injury to a young child is alarming. The child may be crying and vigorously moving or be unnaturally quiet and still. Blood may be spilling profusely or the child may be blanched and pale.

Such events are shocking to witness. In addition, while teachers are assessing the situation, the play of the rest of the children is likely to have been disrupted, potentially throwing them into confusion as well. In these difficult moments teachers are called on to:

- Recognize that an injury has occurred.
- Make a focused assessment of the nature of the incident.
- Respond quickly and appropriately.
- Ensure the rest of the children are safely supervised.

It can be challenging to remain calm and make decisions in such stressful situations. Even so, the moment an injury is recognized, the process of effective response begins. Teachers need to be prepared to understand when a situation is an emergency and be ready to implement an emergency response plan.

Defining Emergencies

emergency
any situation that threatens the life of the child or that presents risk for permanent injury or disability

Teachers are responsible for doing all they can to keep children safe from unintentional injury. If injuries occur, teachers need to be able to identify when basic first aid care is sufficient and when emergency help is needed. An emergency is any situation that threatens the life of the child or that presents risk for permanent injury or disability (National Association of Child Care Resource & Referral Agencies [NACCRRA], 2006).

Emergencies require the assistance of specially trained and equipped emergency medical personnel. Emergencies include:

- Medical threats caused by an unintentional injury such as a broken bone sustained from a fall.
- Hazardous situations that threaten harm to people, such as fires or disasters.

Figure 17-1 lists signs that cue teachers that a child is experiencing an emergency situation. When teachers recognize these signs, they must call for emergency assistance and immediately provide first aid until emergency medical personnel arrive.

Creating an Emergency Management Plan

An emergency management plan (EMP) is an important tool for guiding effective response in emergency situations. Such a plan describes emergency preparation activities and outlines responsibilities. Next the EMP presents the steps that must be taken to respond effectively. It lists who is responsible for administering first aid and who should call 911. Finally, the EMP directs teachers and other program personnel to document the cause of the emergency and how it was managed, and guides review and reflection of the incident to determine if additional safety precautions can be implemented to reduce danger in the future.

An emergency management plan should be created for each specific early childhood setting to ensure that the steps are relevant for the particular site and age of children and to fit the needs of the teaching team.

Figure 17-1 When Is It an Emergency?

An emergency exists if the child:

- Loses consciousness or becomes less and less responsive.
- Has trouble breathing or cannot speak.
- Has gray, dusky, or blue appearance.
- Has confusion, headache, or vomiting after a head injury.
- Has signs of a broken bone.
- Has a large or deep wound that won't stop bleeding.
- Is vomiting blood or passing large quantities of blood in the stool.
- Shows signs of shock.
- Has increasingly severe pain.
- Shows signs of dehydration: sunken eyes, lethargic.

Sources: *Caring for Our Children: National Health and Safety Performance Standards: Guidelines for Out-of-Home Child Care Programs*, 2nd ed., 2002, by American Academy of Pediatrics, American Public Health Association, & National Resource Center for Health and Safety in Child Care and Early Education, retrieved August 31, 2009, from http://www.eric.ed.gov/ERICDocs/data/ericdocs2sql/content_; and "*Handling emergencies*" by M. M. Gray, 1996, National Network for Child Care (NNCC), retrieved January 14, 2010 from http://www.nncc.org/Health/cc45_handl.emergencies.html

Identifying Community Resources

Knowing about the availability and accessibility of emergency personnel and resources when developing a site-specific EMP is important. Some areas have a rich variety of medical treatment facilities and transport options to serve children in case of severe injury or illness. Other communities may have few nearby emergency services and, thus, may have to rely on air transport to more distant medical centers. In settings where support is available and quickly accessible, teachers can focus on implementing basic emergency first aid and keeping children stable for a shorter period of time than in those settings where emergency personnel are at a greater distance or take longer to respond, or both.

Teachers working in settings where there may be a significant delay in receiving emergency assistance need to be prepared to address a child's first aid care needs and be ready with a plan to transport the child themselves or provide comfort care until medical assistance can be obtained. Creating formal arrangements with medical providers for over-the-phone consultation and guidance may be needed.

Considering Specific Site Characteristics

On-site resources vary and should be considered when drafting the plan. Child care centers and school-based programs usually have a variety of personnel who can assist with emergency response. Like Jamal, teachers in family child care or short-term child care settings may be individually responsible for the care of a small group of children and, hence, will need to plan an effective response that includes providing care for an individual child while at the same time supervising the remaining small group of children. Aspects of the site that support emergency response include having a space to care for an injured or ill child. Access to both a telephone (land line) and cell phone is advisable to provide a backup option if the electricity is out or the cell phone batteries are dead.

The EMP should also address response procedures for each aspect of the classroom day such as when children are playing inside and outside or are at lunch or napping. Steps should also be outlined for emergency management when children are on a field trip. The pattern of supervision and location of the children need to be considered as emergency procedures are planned.

Planning for Special Needs

Some children have special medical concerns that need to be addressed in the emergency plan. Special additions to the first aid kit may be needed as well as copies of individual emergency medical protocols. Medications that have been approved for administration to individual children should be readily available for teachers to access during an emergency. This may require special planning to ensure that these items are accessible to the teacher, but out of the reach of children.

> ## What if. . .
> a child in your class has a known allergy to bee stings? What extra items might you need in your first aid kit to support this child in case of an emergency?

Obtaining Emergency Response Training

Training is an essential part of preparing to manage emergencies. Infant and child first aid and cardiopulmonary resuscitation (CPR) training provide the foundation for an appropriate response. These types of training offer specific information about the injuries and emergency situations that might involve young children. The classes include opportunities to practice implementing first aid such as stopping blood flow, applying bandages, and simulating CPR procedures for adults, children, and infants.

A valuable understanding that teachers gain from this training is the importance of responding and getting past the fear of doing something wrong. In emergencies the consequence of *not* responding may be death, for example, from a blocked airway or other situation that first aid actions could have helped. Periodic training builds teacher confidence and inspires teachers to take action when needed.

Teachers may also need to participate in special training to address potential emergency needs for children with health concerns. Special emergency response training topics may include:

- Use of glucagon for children with diabetes.
- Use of epinephrine autoinjectors (EpiPens) for children with sensitive allergies.

- Special response for children with seizure disorder.
- Emergency response for children with specific developmental concerns, such as potential for choking.

Most states require that teachers maintain certification in infant and child first aid and CPR through periodic training, with the specialty trainings acquired as needed. This ensures that teachers refresh their skills and are aware of new and emerging safety practices. Sometimes well-learned lessons become outdated as new information is discovered and safety practices are improved.

First aid and CPR certification are offered through organizations such as the American Red Cross, the American Heart Association, and hospitals. Larger child care centers or schools may schedule periodic training for staff, but ultimately it is the responsibility of individual teachers to maintain their certification, which can help keep their skills current. Another way to keep informed is to learn about emerging practices such as those that are under study by the National Association for the Education of Young Children (NAEYC). The *Policy Point* describes emerging safety practices.

Assembling Emergency Supplies

An important part of emergency preparation involves obtaining the supplies needed to administer first aid. First aid kits, blood spill cleanup kits, and supplies to support children's special health concerns all need to be assembled in advance of an emergency.

First Aid Kits

The American Academy of Pediatrics (AAP), American Public Health Association, and National Resource Center for Health and Safety in Child Care and Early Education (2004) recommend that children's programs maintain at least one first aid kit at the facility and one

MyEducationLab

To listen to a preschool program director discuss emergency preparation and staff training, go to the Video Examples section of Topic 9: Emergencies and Injuries in the MyEducationLab for your course and watch the video entitled *Preparing for Health Emergencies.* Note where medications and supplies are stored out of the reach of children. What other precautions does the director mention regarding teacher training?

Policy Point

EMERGING PRACTICES

Health and safety practices continue to evolve. These are called emerging practices and include actions that are important to quality services, but are not yet widely followed in early childhood classrooms. Emerging practices include:

- *Physical environment safety:* Obtaining and documenting regular safety assessment of play equipment by a certified playground safety inspector (NAEYC Accreditation Standard 9.B.07)
- *Health—disease safety:* Taking precautions to ensure that infectious disease is not transmitted through communal water play activities (NAEYC Accreditation Standard 5.A.10)
- *Health—food safety:* Ensuring the food that comes from home to be shared with other children is either whole fruit or commercially prepared packaged food in a sealed container (NAEYC Accreditation Standard 5.B.02)
- *Health and safety—negative impact of lead exposure:* Recommending that all children are screened for lead exposure to reduce risk for low cognitive and behavioral development
- *Health and safety—environmental safety:* Requiring that programs protect children from environmental tobacco smoke by providing a smoke-free environment in the early childhood setting, and by supporting parents to provide smoke-free homes

Sources: *Health: A Guide to the NAEYC Early Childhood Program Standards and Related Accreditation Criteria,* edited by S. Ritchie and B. Willer, 2005, Washington, DC: NAEYC; *Lead Screening* (Information Memorandum ACF-IM-HS-08-07), March 20, 2008, Washington, DC: Office of Head Start, retrieved October 31, 2009, from http://www.acf.hhs.gov/programs/ohs/policy/im2008/acfimhs_08_07.html; and *Partnership with the Environmental Protection Agency* (Information Memorandum ACF-IM-HS-08-08), March 20, 2008, Washington, DC: Office of Head Start, retrieved October 31, 2009, from http://www.acf.hhs.gov/programs/ohs/policy/im2008/acfimhs_08_08.html.

to take along on field trips. The AAP and child care licensing agencies specify the first aid supplies that are required for children's settings.

Figure 17-2 provides a checklist of first aid supplies. First aid kits should be reviewed periodically to ensure they are complete. First aid kits should be labeled and easily identifiable. They should be located out of reach of children but easily accessible for teachers. A "traveling" first aid kit can be packaged in a backpack along with children's emergency contact information and any special medical protocols for children with special health needs. This kit should be positioned where teachers can easily access it when they take children on walks and field trips away from the classroom.

Blood Spill Cleanup Kits

Careful cleanup of blood spills or splashes is important to avoid possible exposure to bloodborne diseases. A well-equipped blood spill kit includes protective equipment such as gloves and goggles or other eye protection. A spray bottle or bucket should be available for mixing disinfectant products, such as the bleach and water solution used to sanitize soiled surfaces. Paper towels to absorb the spill and bags to safely dispose of soiled materials should also be included, as well as soap or antibacterial gel for washing hands after cleanup.

Children's programs need at least one first aid kit at the facility and one to take along on field trips.

In the opening case scenario, Jamal was able to quickly attend to Aidan's cut because all of the emergency supplies he needed were readily available. This supported Jamal's effective management of the injury and reduced confusion so he was better able to direct the remaining children to a safe activity.

Posting Emergency Procedures

Emergency procedures should be posted where they can be easily seen and used as a resource during the alarm and confusion of an emergency event. The emergency procedures should describe what teachers should do, provide a list of emergency telephone numbers, identify the name of the program or school, provide the address and driving directions to the location, and the telephone number of the classroom.

The information should be clear, straightforward, and printed in large bold print so that it can be read from a distance. The procedures should be written in all languages spoken by the teachers or any volunteers who might be assisting. The poster should be located where

Figure 17-2 First Aid Supplies Checklist

☐ Telephone numbers for community emergency care providers and Poison Control center	☐ Sterile gauze pads and rolls
	☐ Adhesive bandage tape
	☐ Safety pins
☐ Emergency contact information for children's families	☐ Triangular bandages
	☐ Eye dressing
☐ Guide to standard first aid care	☐ Cold pack
☐ Emergency medications for children with special medical needs	☐ Pen/pencil and note pad
	☐ Water
☐ Disposable plastic gloves	☐ Small plastic or metal splints
☐ Scissors	☐ Liquid soap
☐ Tweezers	☐ Plastic bags for disposing of soiled materials
☐ Nonglass thermometer	
☐ Adhesive-style strip bandages	☐ Cell phone

Source: *Emergency/Disaster Preparedness for Child Care Programs: Applicable Standards from "Caring for Our Children,"* American Academy of Pediatrics, American Public Health Association, and National Resource Center for Health and Safety in Child Care and Early Education, 2004. Retrieved October 31, 2009, from http://nrckids.org/SPINOFF/EMERGENCY/Emergency.pdf.

everyone will know where to look, such as on the wall near the first aid kit, and beside each telephone so the information is readily available to support teachers when making an emergency call. Figure 17-3 provides an example of an emergency procedures poster.

It is helpful to post directions for common first-aid procedures on the inside of a cupboard door where the first-aid kit is stored or on the wall where first aid care would be provided. This way the information can be a reminder for a teacher who is working quickly to put on gloves, access first aid supplies, and administer first aid. The *Health Hint* provides suggestions about how to ensure that teachers have plastic gloves nearby.

Conducting Medical Emergency Drills

Practicing for medical emergencies is a useful way to determine if the emergency response plan is realistic and workable. Practice builds teachers' familiarity with the actions that will support them in case of an emergency. Managing simulated emergency

Figure 17-3 Sample Emergency Procedures Poster

Head Teacher:

- Stay with the child at all times.
- Administer emergency first aid and CPR.
- Provide child's medical information to emergency personnel and travel with the child to the hospital if needed.
- Transfer responsibility directly to parent or other authorized adult.

Assistant Teacher:

- Call 911. Give directions. Stay on the line. If available, send an adult to stand outside and flag down emergency personnel.
- Contact other program staff for backup.
- Contact the child's family.
- Provide supervision for remaining children.

> Emergency Telephone Numbers
> FIRE - AMBULANCE - POLICE: Call 911
> POISON CONTROL: Call 9-1-800-222-1222
> Emergency Room at Good Health Medical Center: Call XXX-XXXX
> Electricity: Call XXX-XXXX Water: Call XXX-XXXX Gas: Call XXX-XXXX

Say "I'm calling from Kennedy School at 567 NW 160th Street, at the corner of 160th and Adams Boulevard. Take Main Street to Adams, turn north and travel one mile to 160th Street. The building is on the right side of the street. We are in room 107. Our phone number is XXX-XXX-XXXX."

Health Hint

Tips for Having Plastic Gloves Ready

- Install glove dispenser boxes on the wall near the emergency first aid supplies and in the diapering and toileting areas.
- Place a pair of gloves in a plastic bag and carry them in a pocket.
- Package a pair of gloves inside several plastic bags. Tape the bags at various locations around the children's indoor and outdoor spaces where they can be easily seen and readily accessed.
- Include several pairs of gloves in the traveling first aid kit.

scenarios also builds a sense of teamwork and confidence among program or school staff—qualities that can be crucial to effective response. Through practice, teachers are able to recognize aspects in their own personal or family lives that could be impacted by a medical emergency at school. Teachers may need to travel with the injured child to obtain emergency medical care and, hence, may need a backup plan for their own children and families. The plan should identify ways to communicate with their family as needed. Planning in advance helps teachers avoid being distracted by competing responsibilities.

Emergency drills using injury or medical scenarios can be done with children just as fire and tornado drills are practiced. The teacher might select a child to serve as the injured child, then move through the steps of calling for emergency assistance, conducting first aid, contacting the child's family, cleaning up after the scenario, supervising children, and completing the closing report. Questions to consider during a medical emergency drill include the following:

- Are first aid supplies and child emergency contact information easily accessible?
- Is at least one communication source available to call for emergency aid?
- Does the plan provide sufficient supervision of the remaining children?

Emergency procedures should be periodically reviewed to be sure that barriers and problems have been corrected and that all supports remain available. During an emergency is no time to learn that bandages were "borrowed" from the first aid kit for use in dramatic play.

MANAGING EMERGENCIES

Even though teachers may have a strong commitment to children's safety, taking action in emergency situations is not always easy or natural. Emergencies can be alarming, disconcerting, and stressful. Teachers may be anxious that they will cause the child pain, or may worry that they will make a mistake and be sued for trying to help. Familiarity with the volunteer protection laws, a clear understanding of the teacher's role, knowing how to assess an emergency and use universal precautions, and completing emergency response reports are all aspects that prepare teachers to respond when emergency action is needed.

Understanding Volunteer Protection Laws

Most states have laws that offer protection for rescue efforts that are provided in good faith. These are called *volunteer protection laws,* sometimes referred to as the Good Samaritan doctrine. Volunteer protection laws were designed to encourage people to help in emergencies by protecting rescuers from being sued for wrongdoing when they provide emergency help as long as the care is "reasonable and prudent and the helper uses the resources available at the time" (Medi-Smart, 2006). In order for emergency assistance to be covered by the Good Samaritan doctrine:

Good Samaritan doctrine laws designed to encourage people to help in emergencies by protecting rescuers from being sued for wrongdoing

- The help must be a volunteer act.
- The person receiving the help must not object.
- The actions of the helper must be a good faith effort to provide emergency care (Medi-Smart, 2006).

The Good Samaritan doctrine does not provide protection for rescue acts that are unreasonable, careless, or negligent. In the teaching setting, this means that teachers are expected to provide appropriate emergency first aid assistance for the child's immediate needs, but that this care is only administered as a substitute until professional emergency medical help can be obtained. Calling for medical assistance and ensuring the child receives professional care are part of the expectations of teachers under the Good Samaritan doctrine.

Recognizing the Teacher's Role

Emergencies require definite and organized action. It is essential that teachers understand their role and the activities for which they are responsible. Each teacher should know:

- Who will call for emergency assistance.
- Who will provide emergency care and stay with the child.
- Who will supervise the remaining children.
- Who will contact the child's parent or other authorized adult.
- How responsibility for the injured child will be transferred to the parent or other authorized adult.
- Who will document and report the emergency to the program director or principal, if appropriate.

In group settings teachers share emergency responsibilities. This inspires confidence among the teaching team and contributes to children's safety during emergencies. Family child care workers such as Jamal need to develop supports in advance, such as identifying a neighbor who will help during an emergency. Teachers in elementary school settings need to know who to call for backup assistance in the classroom in case of an emergency.

Assessing for Signs of Injury

The first few minutes after an injury occurs are of crucial importance to a positive outcome. Brain death, for example, begins within 4 to 6 minutes after sudden cardiac arrest if air and circulation are not restored (American Heart Association [AHA], 2005). If effective CPR is provided within minutes of cardiac arrest the chances of survival can be doubled (AHA, 2005). Even when children are under the watchful eye of the teacher, it is possible for a serious injury to occur. Teachers need to be able to do a quick and concise review of the type and seriousness of an injury, reach a reasonable judgment about the emergency response steps needed, and move quickly into a plan of action.

First, teachers should quickly scan the physical environment looking for signs of what may have contributed to an injury and anticipating the type of injury that may have occurred. For example:

- Is the child lying under climbing equipment that might suggest a fall? If so, the head or back may be injured and the child should not be moved.
- Is furniture tipped over? If so, was the child hit or cut?
- Could electricity be involved? If so, do not touch the child until the electricity is turned off.
- Are sharp objects present such as broken glass? If so, look for ways to avoid danger while approaching and assisting the child.

Next, teachers need to observe the child's physical appearance. This is done by quickly inspecting the child from head to toe looking for problems or signs of injury. For example:

- Is the child breathing?
- Is the child bleeding profusely?
- Is the child's body position abnormal or distorted in any way?

Finally, teachers need to notice the child's behavior by observing how the child is responding and looking for signs of distress and concern. For example:

- Is the child moving?
- Is the child crying?
- Does the child respond when spoken to?

This information is used to determine whether the situation is an emergency and helps teachers decide whether the child should be moved or cared for in place. Table 17-1 guides teachers to consider the context of the accident when determining what types of injuries might have occurred.

Table 17-1	Accident Settings and Potential Injuries

Setting	Types of Injuries
Climbing equipment	• Fall from equipment (head injury, broken bone?) • Climbing (pinched fingers?)
Tricycle	• Striking against objects (bumps, bruises?) • Falling over in motion (bump to head?)
General outdoor playground	• Fall (skinned knee, bumps, bruises?) • Insects (bites or stings?) • Children running (bumps and bruises from children running into each other?) • Excessive heat (heat exhaustion or heatstroke?)
Sandbox	• Sand (foreign object in the eye?)
Workbench	• Hammer, nails (cut or pierced?)
Indoor play	• Striking against objects (bumps and bruises?) • Objects falling against child (bumps, bruises, cuts?)
Craft materials	• Exposure to allergens (acute illness or anaphylaxis?)

Emergency medical personnel should be called whenever an injury is serious or life threatening. Injuries that are less serious should be carefully treated with first aid, families should be notified, and children should be monitored to ensure that underlying concerns are not overlooked. In the opening case scenario, Jamal was able to quickly recognize that Aidan's wound was the result of being struck by the ball cart and that there was low likelihood of broken bones. By the time he reached Aidan he had determined that he could move the child without worry. But even though the bleeding was managed with bandaging, Jamal encouraged the family to seek medical advice since a head injury was involved.

Using Universal Precautions

Many emergency situations involve bleeding injuries. For this reason teachers need to know and use basic universal precautions when providing emergency assistance. Universal precautions are a set of safety measures that are designed to prevent the transmission of bloodborne diseases such as human immunodeficiency virus (HIV), hepatitis B virus (HBV), and other bloodborne pathogens (CDC, 1987/1996). Universal precautions are recommended to ensure that emergency responders are not themselves harmed when they provide first aid assistance. The specific universal precautions identified by the CDC (1987/1996) and the American Red Cross (2006) include the following:

- Wear gloves at all accidents involving blood or any other body fluids containing visible signs of blood.
- Use a one-way mask when offering rescue breathing.
- Watch for sharp objects, electricity, toxic fumes, and other hazards at the site of the accident.
- Use appropriate hand washing when providing medical assistance.
- Dispose of contaminated materials appropriately.

Figure 17-4 describes the steps for properly removing and discarding gloves that have been soiled by blood to avoid contamination with potential bloodborne pathogens.

Completing Emergency Response Reports

After the immediate emergency actions have been managed, teachers still need to bring closure to the event. This includes reviewing the setting to see if a blood spill has occurred, cleaning the area safely, and disposing of any soiled toweling and gloves in an appropriate way.

universal precautions a set of precautions designed to prevent transmission of human immunodeficiency virus (HIV), hepatitis B virus (HBV), and other bloodborne pathogens when providing first aid or health care

Universal precautions include wearing protective gloves when caring for any injury that involves blood or body fluids containing visible signs of blood.

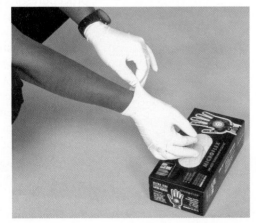

Figure 17-4 Procedure for Safely Discarding Protective Gloves

1. Grasp the palm of the left hand glove with the fingers of the right gloved hand. Pull outward and remove the left hand glove from the hand. Do not reach inside the opposite glove—let only the dirty surfaces touch each other.
2. Grasp the left hand glove in a ball inside the palm of the right hand.
3. Using a finger of the left hand reach inside the wrist of the right hand glove. Peel the right hand glove off inside out to encase the dirty surfaces of both gloves.
4. Drop the soiled gloves inside a plastic bag. Seal the bag and discard it in an appropriate location.
5. Wash your hands thoroughly.

Source: Based on *Keeping Kids Healthy: Preventing and Managing Communicable Diseases in Child Care*, 1995, Sacramento CA: California Department of Education; and Appendix D, p. 412, in *Caring for Our Children: National Health and Safety Performance Standards*, retrieved November 2, 2009, from http://nrc.uchsc.edu/CFOC/PDFVersion/Appendix%20D.pdf.

What if. . .

like Jamal in the opening case scenario, you had effectively managed an emergency in your classroom? How would you tell other families about the event when it was over? Do you think the other families will blame you for "allowing" the accident to happen?

Teachers should also make a record of the event and the emergency response actions by completing an accident report. This is important to do soon after the event so that all details about the incident and the first aid offered can be recorded while the information is still fresh. Teachers should also assess how the other children in the group are feeling and provide extra comfort so they know the doctor and family are taking care of the injured child.

ADMINISTERING FIRST AID

Injuries can, and do, occur in early childhood settings and schools. As a result teachers are likely to be involved in providing some level of first aid assistance for a variety of injuries. First aid refers to the set of actions taken to address injuries or illness (American Red Cross, 2006). First aid has three primary goals:

first aid
the actions taken to immediately address illness or injury

1. To preserve life.
2. To avoid additional injury.
3. To assist with recovery.

Obtaining formal training in first aid procedures is the most important way for teachers to learn appropriate response techniques for different kinds of injuries and signs that emergency assistance is needed. In this section we offer descriptions of injuries and provide teachers with common approaches to first aid care.

Offering First Aid

First aid in the early childhood setting usually involves uncomplicated, commonsense procedures such as cleaning and bandaging a small cut or placing a cold compress on a bump or strained ankle. These are examples of *basic first aid* that are easily performed and that in most cases do not require formal medical assistance.

Some situations are more complex, requiring advanced actions such as providing rescue breathing or wrapping a body part to immobilize an injured area in case of a broken bone. These are examples of injuries that require *emergency first aid*. If an injury requires emergency first aid, emergency medical personnel should be called at once to reduce further injury and to avoid risk of death. Teachers should obtain periodic training and maintain certification in infant and child first aid and CPR in order to be prepared to implement emergency first aid using an orderly series of steps, such as (AHA, 2006, 2008; Heller & Zieve, 2009b, 2009c):

1. *Assess the situation.* Is the child unconscious, asleep, or playing? Try to rouse the child. Say the child's name and ask, "Are you all right?"
2. *Call for medical assistance.* Quickly direct another adult or child, if needed, to call for emergency help. In most locations this is done by calling 911.

3. *Address nearby dangers.* Clear away potential dangers. Remove tipped-over furniture or sweep back broken glass. Do not move the child if there is potential for spine or head injury. Do not attempt to remove objects that may be impaled in the body.

4. *Address breathing.* Lack of oxygen is the most crucial aspect of an injury and must be addressed before any other concern to avoid brain death (AHA, 2008). Listen for sounds of breathing, look to see if the child's chest is rising and falling, and feel for the movement of breath. Pull out the lower lip and look for pink color on the inner lip. Open the airway by lifting the chin. Conduct rescue breathing and CPR as needed.

5. *Stop the bleeding.* Apply direct pressure to the wound. Use clean gauze to cover the wound. Hold the bleeding area higher than the heart to slow blood flow, if possible. Hold firm against pressure points to stop excessive bleeding if necessary.

6. *Treat for shock.* Lay the child down and elevate the feet. Keep the child evenly warm. If the child is breathing and appears stable, move the child into a recovery position by placing the child on one side. This assists with breathing and helps prevent choking if the child vomits.

7. *Stay with the child at all times.* Do not leave the child unattended. Travel with the child to the emergency medical facility if needed. Stay with the child until you can release responsibility to the child's parent or guardian.

8. *Speak calmly and reassure the child.* Let the child know you are going to stay very near.

9. *Provide the child's medical information to emergency personnel.* This information should be near at hand. It should include the child's health history, allergies, immunization record, information about any special health or medical need, the physician's name and contact information, and insurance information.

10. *Call the child's parent or guardian.* Report the cause of the accident and the first aid and medical care that has been provided. Give information about where the child is and if the child has been transported for medical assistance. Do not attempt to diagnose the situation or offer medical advice or guidance. Direct the family to the medical provider for professional assistance and follow-up.

These steps highlight the teacher's responsibility to provide immediate care, obtain emergency assistance, and stay with the child until responsibility can be transferred to the parent, guardian, or other authorized individual.

Falls

Falls are a primary cause of injury in young children. Some falls can cause significant injury. Falls from greater heights onto hard surfaces are more likely to result in a head injury or broken bone. If a fall is witnessed or suspected:

In an emergency, first aid is administered until professional medical help can be obtained.

- Do not move the child.
- Check the child to ensure the airway is open and the child is breathing.
- Notice the height of the fall and consider the surface on which the child landed. Review the child for potential head injury. Watch for unequal size of pupils; fluid draining from the nose, ears, or mouth; confusion or drowsiness (Heller & Zieve, 2009a).
- Review the child for potential broken bones. Watch for a misshapen limb and intense pain and observe if a child is favoring a limb or is unable to move a body part (Vorvick & Zieve, 2009a).
- Treat minor wounds with basic first aid.

Keep the child still and seek immediate medical help for any suspected head injury or broken bones. Inform the family of the fall, even if the injury appears minor. This way the child can be monitored for any unrecognized injuries (Nemours, 2009).

Head Injury

Any injury to the head should be considered significant, and should be reported to the child's family as soon as possible. A severe head injury can cause bleeding inside the skull, which can result in brain damage or death. Even if the child begins to play again soon after the head injury, families should be consulted so they can participate directly in determining if medical care is needed. The child should be observed carefully for the next 24 hours.

In case of head injury:

- Lay the child down, positioning the head higher than the feet.
- Observe the child's eyes, looking for unnaturally dilated pupils.
- Notice if the child is disoriented.
- Keep the child calm.

Seek immediate medical assistance if the child is unconscious or if any signs of concussion are evident such as drowsiness; nausea and vomiting; slurred speech; disorientation; fluid seeping from nose, ears, and mouth; or headache (CDC, 2004).

Stopped Breathing

Some injuries may stop children's breathing. Choking and drowning are the most common reasons a child's breathing would be stopped. First aid when a child is not breathing uses the ABC approach: airway, breathing, and circulation.

A = Airway

Check the airway. If the airway is blocked, it must be opened.

For a child (Heller & Zieve, 2009b):

- Lay the child on a flat surface.
- Lift the child's chin, letting the head tip back naturally. This lifts the tongue off of the throat, opening the airway.

For infants (Heller & Zieve, 2009c):

- Lay the infant on a flat surface.
- Lift the baby's chin and gently press back on the forehead to tip the baby's head back naturally.

If the child or baby is unconscious, these moves can often correct the cause of stopped breathing.

B = Breathing

Listen and watch for breathing. Check for pink color in the inside lower lip. If breathing does not start when the airway is opened, call 911 immediately. Start rescue breathing:

rescue breathing steps taken to offer breath, artificial respiration, when someone has stopped breathing

- Keeping the child's chin tilted upward, gently pinch the nose closed to ensure that air is guided into the child's lungs.
- Lay a one-way mask across the child's mouth and offer one rescue breath per second for 5 seconds (AHA, 2005). At each breath the rise in the chest should be visible.
- For infants, place mouth over the baby's nose and mouth. Give small rescue breaths by offering a puff-breath or small "mouthful" of air. Then check for circulation.

If a rescue breath does not go in, check that the airway is sufficiently opened and try again. If breath still does not go in, the airway may be obstructed and must be cleared before performing CPR. Perform emergency actions to clear the airway.

For children (Heller & Zieve, 2009d):

- Give 5 back blows: Have the child bend over at the waist. Using the heel of the hand, give 5 blows to the child's back between the shoulder blades. Watch and listen to see if the airway is cleared.

- Give 5 abdominal thrusts: If the airway is still blocked, give abdominal thrusts using the Heimlich maneuver:
  - Kneel behind the child.
  - Wrap arms around the child's waist.
  - Make a fist with one hand over the other.
  - Position the hands just above the navel.
  - Press hard giving 5 quick sharp thrusts inward and upward.
- Repeat blows and thrusts until the object is dislodged.

For infants (Heller & Zieve, 2009e):

- Sit down. Place the infant along your forearm facedown. Hold the infant's jaw with your fingers and the chest with your hand. Keep the head lower than the body.
- Using the heel of your hand give 5 firm thumps on the middle of the back. Check to see if the item has been dislodged.
- If not, turn the child face up on your forearm, keeping the head lower than the body. Place two fingers just below the nipple line on the middle of the breastbone. Give 5 quick chest compressions, thrusting in ⅓ to ½ of the depth of the chest.
- Continue giving 5 back thumps and 5 chest thrusts until the object is dislodged or emergency personnel arrive.

Do not give up! Your efforts may save the child's life.

C = Circulation

Circulation is the last of the ABCs. Check to see if the heart is beating and blood is circulating. Look at the child's overall color. Pull out the lower lip and inspect the color of the inner lip. Pink coloring means the heart is beating and blood is circulating. White or blue coloring means the heart is not beating and CPR is needed. CPR provides artificial circulation through rhythmic compressions that massage the heart and move blood through the body. This artificial pumping helps oxygen-rich blood circulate to the brain, keeping the brain alive. The AHA (2008) recommends giving 30 compressions plus two breaths (and repeat) for children and infants (AHA, 2005, 2008). Trained individuals are prepared to administer CPR using the general process described below.

For a child (AHA, 2008; Heller & Zieve, 2009b):

- Place the child on a hard surface such as the floor or table. Call out to another teacher or child to call 911.
- Kneel over the child, placing the heel of one hand at the midpoint of the child's breast.
- Keeping the elbows locked, apply 30 downward compressions. Press inward about 2 inches, or until resistance is felt, at a rate of 1 compression per second. Then give two rescue breaths.
- Repeat this "30 and 2" cycle for 2 minutes. Then, if you are alone, call 911.
- Continue the compression and breathing cycle until emergency help arrives.

For infants (AHA, 2008; Heller & Zieve, 2009c):

- Lay the baby on a hard surface. Call out to another teacher or child to call 911.
- Use two fingers positioned on the center of the chest just below an imaginary "line" between the two nipples to give compressions to the depth of 1/2 or 1/3 of the chest.
- Give 30 compressions at a quick rate (about 2 per second) and two rescue breaths.
- Repeat this "30 and 2" cycle for 2 minutes. Then if you are alone, call 911.
- Continue the compression and breathing cycle until help arrives.

Do not give up! Your efforts may save the child's life.

Choking

Choking occurs when a child swallows or aspirates (breathes in) a small object, such as food or a toy, that gets stuck in the throat. The blockage stops the flow of air and oxygen is cut off to the brain. First aid is required as soon as possible.

Watch for a child who is:

- Clutching the throat.
- Unable to talk or cough.
- Turning blue—look at skin, lips, nails.
- Unconscious.

Clear the airway using the techniques listed earlier (Heller & Zieve, 2009d).

Asthma

The most common symptoms of asthma attack in children are a wheezing sound when breathing and frequent episodes of coughing or coughing spasms. In some cases asthma attacks can be acute and life threatening. Watch for:

- Increasing shortness of breath or wheezing.
- Chest tightness or pain.
- High level of distress.

For children with a known asthma condition, treat according to the child's emergency medical plan using the child's nebulizer. Contact the family to report the child's condition and to have the family participate in determining a follow-up plan. Seek medical help immediately if the asthma attack is acute and resembles anaphylaxis (Kaneshiro & Zieve, 2008).

Anaphylactic Shock: Severe Allergic Reaction

Allergies can result in anaphylactic shock, a life-threatening reaction that causes respiratory distress or circulatory collapse. Severe allergic reactions may result from a wide range of causes including allergy to foods or drugs, insect venom (from bites), pollen, latex, and other possibly unknown causes (Dugdale, Henochowicz, & Zieve, 2008). Reaction can occur quickly or a few hours after exposure. Some children may have known allergies, while others have not yet shown signs of allergic reaction. Signs of anaphylactic shock include:

- Hives that spread.
- Swelling of the eyes or mouth.
- Difficulty breathing and talking.
- Dizziness or mental confusion.
- Abdominal cramping, nausea, and vomiting.

Treat anaphylaxis as follows:

- Call 911 immediately.
- Administer epinephrine injection (EpiPen).
- Lay the child down on her or his back.
- Do not offer any food or drink.
- Monitor the child carefully.
- If breathing stops, administer CPR.

Seek medical assistance immediately. Epinephrine treatment is only temporary. A second injection may be needed if signs of anaphylaxis return (Dugdale et al., 2008).

Bleeding from Cuts, Bumps, and Wounds

Follow these steps when treating a child who is bleeding:

- Wear vinyl or nonlatex gloves.
- Cover the wound with a sterile gauze pad.
- Apply direct pressure.
- Have the child sit or lay down.
- Hold the wound higher than the heart.
- If blood fills the gauze, add more layers of gauze. Do not remove the gauze because this will disturb the natural blood clot that is forming.

Seek medical help if the wound is dirty or deep, if you cannot stop the bleeding, if any blood seeps from the ears, or if the child vomits blood (Heller & Zieve, 2009f).

Nosebleeds

Nosebleeds can be quite common in the early childhood setting. Treat them as follows:

- Have the child sit down and lean forward.
- Use a sterile gauze pad to pinch the nose between the thumb and index finger. Have the child breathe through the mouth.
- Hold this position for 10 minutes or until bleeding stops.

Seek medical help if the nosebleed is the result of an injury to the head or if the bleeding does not stop (Cunah & Shieh, 2007).

Bites

Bites are one of the top causes of unintentional injury in young children. Bites may be the result of animals, humans, or spiders.

Animal Bites

Teachers should closely supervise children with any animal in the early childhood setting. If injury occurs:

- Apply direct pressure to stop the bleeding.
- Wash the wound thoroughly with soap and water.
- Cover the wound with a bandage.

Seek medical help immediately if the bite was caused by an animal with unknown immunization for rabies, if the wound is deep and the skin is torn, or if there are signs of infection (Duldner, 2008d).

Human Bites

Biting among young children is a common challenge for teachers. The human mouth can contain dangerous bacteria and viruses that present a high risk for infection.

Human bites can also transmit bloodborne pathogens. If the bite breaks the skin:

- Apply direct pressure to the wound, using a sterile gauze pad, until the bleeding stops.
- Wash the bite area with soap and water for 3 to 5 minutes.
- Apply a clean bandage.

Contact the child's family and recommend that the family seek medical advice (Duldner & Zieve, 2008a).

Spider Bites

Usually spider bites are just an annoyance, but brown recluse (violin shape on back) or black widow (red hour glass shape on back) spider bites can be dangerous. If possible, capture or try to identify the spider. To treat a spider bite:

- Clean the bite area.
- Apply a cool compress.
- Watch for signs of chills, fever, nausea, or abdominal pain, which may indicate a serious spider bite.

Seek immediate medical assistance if the bite is from a brown recluse or black widow spider or if signs of a serious bite are observed (Duldner & Zieve, 2008b)

Bruises and Bumps

Bruises are a common injury among young children. Often good comfort care is the best first aid:

- Raise the injured area.
- Wrap a cold pack in cloth; hold it against the bruised area. Do not place the cold pack directly against the skin because this may cause damage by freezing.
- Cover the bruise with a bandage only if the skin is broken and bleeding.
- Rest the bruised area.

Seek medical assistance if the bruised area is extensive or if there is sign of infection (U.S. National Library of Medicine & National Institutes of Health, 2009; Vorvick & Zieve, 2009b).

Burns

Burns are classified according to the severity of the wound:

A cool cloth and comfort care may be the best first aid for bumps and bruises.

- *First-degree burn:* The skin looks red.
- *Second-degree burn:* The skin is red, blotchy, and blistered.
- *Third-degree burn:* The skin is charred; may be black or ash white.

What to do:

- Cool the burned area under cool running water for 5 minutes.
- Do not use ice.
- Do not apply oils or ointment.
- Do not pop any blisters.
- Cover with a light dry sterile gauze bandage.
- Monitor breathing and treat for shock as needed.

Seek medical assistance for any burn on an infant. For toddlers and older children, seek medical help if the burned area is larger than 3 inches in diameter or if the burn is on the hands, feet, face, groin, or buttocks, over a major joint, or if signs of infection appear (National Institute of General Medicine Sciences, 2008). Notify the child's family as soon as possible.

Drowning

Drowning is the third leading cause of death for children in the early childhood age group (CDC, 2004). The goal of emergency response is to rescue the child from the water source and begin first aid as soon as possible:

- Remove the child from the water without endangering self.
- Check to see if the airway is open.
- Begin rescue breathing as soon as possible.

- Conduct CPR if the child's heart is not beating.
- Keep the child warm and treat for hypothermia and shock.
- Don't give up. Some children have been successfully resuscitated after being in cold water for up to an hour.

Seek medical help as soon as possible. Even if resuscitation has revived the child, medical observation is needed to ensure that infection, respiratory problems, or other complications do not occur.

Electrical Shock

If a child is severely shocked by electricity:

- Do *not* touch the child. Assess the situation.
- If possible turn off the electricity or move the electrical source away from the child and yourself using a nonconductive product such as cardboard or plastic.
- Call 911 for emergency assistance if the electrical source is a high-voltage wire or if you cannot turn off the electrical source.
- If the child is no longer touching the electrical source, observe the child for breathing and heartbeat. Restore breathing with rescue breathing. If heartbeat has stopped, call 911 and conduct CPR.
- Treat for shock: Lay the child down with legs elevated.

Call 911 for emergency assistance if the child shows signs of cardiac arrest or heart rhythm problems, stopped breathing, muscle seizure, or pain or if the child is unconscious (Heller & Zieve, 2009g).

Foreign Objects

Children are very involved with their environment and explore their world in ways that make them vulnerable to foreign objects in the eyes, nose, and mouth. The goal of first aid is to carefully remove any object without hurting the child.

To remove a foreign object from an eye:

- Wash hands carefully.
- Have the child sit down and look upward.
- Lift the eyelid away from the eye and look for the object.
- If the object is visible, try gently flushing the eye with water to wash it out.
- Do *not* rub the eye or try to remove items that are lodged in the eyeball.

Seek medical assistance if the object is not removed through tears, if the object is large, or if vision is impaired (Subramanian, 2007).

To remove a foreign object from the nose:

- Determine which nostril holds the foreign object.
- Gently pinch in the other (unobstructed) nostril and have the child blow the nose gently to dislodge the object.
- Do not probe the nose—this may move the object in deeper.

Seek medical assistance if these steps do not dislodge the object (Heller & Zieve, 2009h).

Tooth Injury

If a child's tooth is knocked out, careful treatment can sometimes restore it:

- Find the tooth.
- Gently rinse tooth in a bowl of water; do not rub or scrape it.

- Place the tooth in the tooth socket in the child's mouth; cover with gauze and hold in place or have the child bite down gently on the gauze. If the tooth cannot be replaced in the socket, then place the tooth in a cup of whole milk (Nemours, 2007).

Seek medical attention immediately at a dental office or the emergency room.

Heat Exhaustion

Heat exhaustion refers to moderate heat-related illness. It may occur when children are engaged in highly active play during very warm days. Dehydration may be a cause. Signs of heat exhaustion include dizziness, nausea, rapid heartbeat, and cramps.

What to do:

- Move child to shady area, lay child down, and remove extra clothing.
- Sponge or spray child with cool water.
- Offer cool water to drink.

Seek medical assistance if symptoms increase (Centers for Disease Control and Prevention, 2006a).

Heatstroke

Heatstroke is the most severe heat-related illness. Without aid, heat stroke can lead to death. Watch for these signs:

- Elevated body temperature (above 104°F) [40°C].
- Hot dry skin.
- Rapid heartbeat.
- Confusion, dizziness, fainting, coma.

What to do:

- Move child to a cool and shady place.
- Call 911 for emergency medical assistance.
- Lay child down and remove extra clothing.
- Cover child with moist cloth or spray with cool water.
- Offer cool water to drink if possible.

Seek medical assistance immediately (Centers for Disease Control and Prevention, 2006a).

Seizure

Seizures are the result of abnormal activity in the brain. Some children may have known seizure history and physician-suggested protocols for seizure management. For others the seizure may be a new event. The goal of first aid is to prevent the child from being hurt during a seizure. Watch for these signs:

- Temporary confusion or loss of consciousness.
- Uncontrolled jerking of arms, legs, and head.
- Staring straight ahead; no recognition.

If a seizure occurs:

- Protect the child from harm: Have the child sit or lay the child down. Place something soft under the child's head and clear the area around the child.
- Do not put anything in the child's mouth.
- Do not restrain the child.
- Let the seizure take its course.
- Call the child's family immediately to report the seizure event.

Seek immediate medical help if the seizure lasts more than 10 minutes or if the child is slow to improve (National Institute of Neurological Disorders and Stroke, 2009).

Shock

Shock is often associated with injury, but can also occur with heatstroke, allergic reactions, infections, poisoning, or other causes. Shock is a sign that the body is struggling. Watch for:

- Cool and clammy skin.
- Weak but rapid pulse.
- Faintness or confusion.

    Treatment for shock includes:

- Lay the child down.
- Raise the child's feet if this does not contribute to injury.
- Check the ABCs (airway, breathing, and circulation).
- Keep the child calm, comfortable, and warm.
- Do not give the child anything to eat or drink.
- Address any injuries.

Seek medical assistance if these actions do not resolve the concern, or if shock is associated with significant injury (Duldner & Zieve, 2008c).

Cleaning Blood Spills

Blood spills can be relatively common in early childhood settings. Skinned knees, bloody noses, and cuts, especially those to the mouth, can cause small blood spills that must be cleaned up in a safe and hygienic way. Cleaning up blood spills is important to prevent the possibility of transmitting communicable disease. The U.S. Occupational Safety and Health Administration and the *National Health and Safety Performance Standards* (AAP et al., 2002) are good sources of information for managing blood spills in the work site and early childhood setting.

Cleaning Blood Spills Indoors

Teachers should wear gloves and other appropriate protection (apron, eye covering) depending on the extent of the blood spill. Do not step on the contaminated area and avoid splashing the spill into eyes, mouth, nose, or unprotected skin. The area should be sprayed thoroughly with disinfecting solution (1 tablespoon bleach to 1 quart of water) and wiped with absorbent paper towels. This should be repeated a second time. Then the area should be washed with soap and water and wiped with paper towels. Soiled paper towels should be placed in a leakproof plastic bag, being careful to not touch the outside of the bag, and the bag should be closed securely and discarded. Teachers should wash their hands thoroughly when done (AAP et al., 2002).

Cleaning Blood Spills Outdoors

Teachers should wear appropriate protection and avoiding stepping on or splashing the spill. The grass, sand, bark, or sidewalk areas should be sprayed or flooded thoroughly with disinfecting solution (¼ cup bleach to 1 gallon of water), left to stand for 15 minutes, and then the area should be flooded with 5 gallons of water or washed with a hose (Purdue University, 2006).

Cleaning Large Blood Spills

Large spills can be cleaned using absorbent pellet materials. The pellets should be allowed to absorb the spill and then collected and discarded along with other contaminated materials.

Cleaning Upholstery and Carpeting

Upholstery and carpeting should be spot cleaned using a disinfectant product designed for fabrics. Let the solution set for 15 minutes (or as directed) and then blot the area dry. This should be repeated until the spill is no longer visible on the surface (AAP et al., 2002).

Addressing Blood Spill Splatters

If unprotected skin is splashed with a blood product, the skin should be washed with soap and water as soon as possible. If the splash is in the eyes, the eyes should be flushed thoroughly with clean water. Splashes on skin that has cuts or open sores should be washed, and the child's medical provider should be contacted for follow-up (AAP et al., 2002).

PREPARING FOR DISASTERS

Disasters are specific kinds of emergencies. Disasters are events that overwhelm available community emergency response resources and often result in widespread injury, death, and destruction of property (AAP et al., 2004; NACCRRA, 2006). Teachers of young children are responsible for taking on significant decision-making responsibilities such as evacuating to alternate locations and sheltering with children in disaster emergency situations (National Child Care Information and Technical Assistance Center, 2008). To do this, teachers need to participate in emergency preparedness activities and be ready to manage supervision of children if community resources have been disrupted and emergency personnel cannot respond to the program's needs. The Federal Emergency Management Agency and the American Red Cross (2004) recommend that programs that care for young children make specific plans to prepare for disasters:

1. Find out what disasters could happen in your area.
2. Create a disaster emergency plan.
3. Implement preparation strategies.
4. Practice disaster emergency response.

disaster
an event that overwhelms available community emergency response resources and often results in widespread injury, death, and destruction of property

Identifying Potential Disaster Threats

Disasters result from any event or combination of events that overwhelm the ability to restore safety and order in a short period of time. Several types of disasters may threaten children's safety (AAP et al., 2004; NACCRRA, 2006):

- *Natural disasters:* Caused by nature, such as hurricanes, tornadoes, wildfires, or snowstorms, these types of disasters are sometimes referred to as "acts of God."
- *Technological disasters:* These are caused by industrial sources and exposure to hazardous materials. Examples include loss of electricity or water, fires, and chemical or oil spills.
- *Attacks and threats to personal safety:* These acts of violence include threats from guns, sniper fire, bomb threats, kidnapping (missing child), intruders, and acts of terrorism.
- *Health emergencies:* These are disasters caused by severe health concerns or potentially deadly disease epidemics, such as avian flu, H1N1, or other pandemic flu illnesses.

Most geographic areas have some likelihood for natural disasters to occur and in some cases the potential for disaster can be anticipated. For example, natural disasters often occur in a rhythm related to seasons, such as tornadoes and hurricanes, or other conditions, such as fires caused by drought (NACCRRA, 2006). Some areas experience frequent threats from earthquakes or floods.

Areas with industrial plants and major transportation routes for industrial materials may experience threats from chemicals or oil spills. In addition, some types of disasters can link to one another. For example, earthquakes often cause fires, severe storms can cause mudslides and power outages, and spills of toxic materials may bring on acute illness (NACCRRA, 2006). The Federal Emergency Management Agency (FEMA) provides information about the types and dates of disasters that have been declared for each state. This information can be helpful in planning for the types of disasters that might occur.

Industrial activities can introduce technological hazards to nearby early childhood settings.

Disasters can also create barriers to effective management such as causing road closures that might slow or obstruct evacuation or stop families from being able to retrieve children from school or care. Careful planning is needed to be prepared if disaster strikes.

Creating a Disaster Emergency Plan

The disaster emergency plan outlines actions to take in case of a disaster. The plan should outline options for taking shelter or implementing lockdown at the facility or evacuating and transporting children to an alternate location. The plan should address the unique needs, resources, and challenges of the particular kind of early childhood setting.

Deciding to Shelter-in-Place

Staying in the early childhood facility and taking shelter until help can arrive is called shelter-in-place. This is an appropriate choice when the facility is essentially safe and secure, and when leaving the facility is either unsafe or not an option due to outside dangers or blocked evacuation routes.

shelter-in-place
tactic of taking shelter in the early childhood setting if the facility is secure and if leaving the facility would put children at risk

Knowing When to Implement Lockdown

Lockdown refers to sheltering with children in a secured location within the early childhood facility. Lockdown is required when danger from the outside is present and children are threatened even in their own classroom. This might occur if there is danger from gunfire. Lockdown is put into action when the threat is imminent and leaving the facility is unsafe.

lockdown
taking shelter in the children's facility while stopping the access and entry of an intruder

Deciding to Evacuate

Evacuation is required when it is not safe to remain in the children's facility. Evacuation may involve moving the children to a nearby assembly location in response to a sudden emergency such as a fire in the children's facility. The nearby location should be within walking distance and be suitable for sheltering for a short time until families can be contacted to pick children up. Children may also be moved to an evacuation site further away if the children's facility is damaged or dangerous, which can occur as a result of an earthquake or flood. This location should be suitable for taking shelter for a longer period of time. Each evacuation location should be identified in advance.

Transporting Children

The emergency plan should identify how children will be transported to the evacuation site if needed. Teachers need to consider the number of children who might need to be transported and the availability of program and private vehicles that could be used. Alternate methods of transportation might be needed, including walking or using strollers, carts, wagons, or wheelchairs. The plan should address children's special mobility needs.

Being Prepared

Disaster emergency preparedness involves taking steps to minimize the impact of likely disasters. It includes assembling emergency supplies and children's emergency information, creating a family communication plan, and participating in community emergency management planning.

Removing Potential Hazards

Disaster preparation includes reviewing the children's setting for potential hazards. Light fixtures must be well secured to the ceiling, tall furniture, must be attached to the wall, and heavy items should be placed on the floor to avoid danger of falling if an earthquake occurs.

Teachers should learn how to turn off gas, water, and electricity to avoid dangers during severe storms. Dangerous tree branches that could be blown into the children's facility should be removed. Reporting potential dangers to program or school managers is one way teachers help to improve the safety of the children's areas.

Gathering Disaster Emergency Supplies

Emergency supplies need to be available to support children's care in case the children must shelter-in-place or evacuate to another location for a period of time. Supplies should be sufficient to support extended shelter care for 48 to 72 hours. A checklist of food and water supplies to gather is provided in the *Nutrition Note* (see also Figure 8-19 Food Safety and Storing Emergency Foods). A sample checklist of disaster emergency supplies is shown in the *Safety Segment.*

Assembling Emergency Information

Certain emergency information should be readily available in case evacuation is required. Emergency records that are needed include the following:

- *Attendance roster for the day* to ensure all children are accounted for.
- *Children's (and teacher's) emergency contact information* to support communication with families or others authorized to pick up children.
- *Emergency medical plans for children and staff* to ensure that special health or medical needs are addressed appropriately.

Maintaining emergency information in a current, readily accessible, and portable format takes special attention. Teachers might copy this information on CDs, e-mail the information to a secure location so it is available electronically, or create a packet of printed materials to place in the traveling first aid kit.

Creating a Family Communication Plan

Communicating with families once children have been evacuated in disaster emergencies is crucial. To begin, teachers need to orient families to the disaster emergency plan through program orientation meetings, handbooks, newsletters, the program website, and posted emergency plans. In particular, families want to know:

- Who will care for their children during a disaster emergency.
- Where children will be sheltered in case of emergency evacuation (address and telephone number).
- How families will be contacted.

Families need to understand that teachers must give their first attention to the safe care and supervision of children in emergency situations, and that communication with families is seen as a later step in emergency management. This can sometimes be a topic of dispute. In some scenarios a family member may learn from a news report that a fire or other problem has occurred at the school or children's site before teachers have the opportunity to implement the parent communication plan. Sharing information with families is very important, but children's safety always comes first.

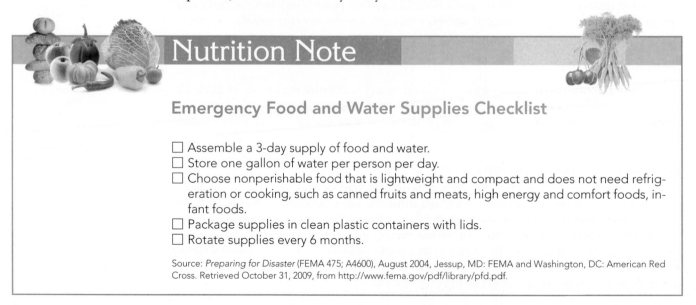

Nutrition Note

Emergency Food and Water Supplies Checklist

☐ Assemble a 3-day supply of food and water.
☐ Store one gallon of water per person per day.
☐ Choose nonperishable food that is lightweight and compact and does not need refrigeration or cooking, such as canned fruits and meats, high energy and comfort foods, infant foods.
☐ Package supplies in clean plastic containers with lids.
☐ Rotate supplies every 6 months.

Source: *Preparing for Disaster* (FEMA 475; A4600), August 2004, Jessup, MD: FEMA and Washington, DC: American Red Cross. Retrieved October 31, 2009, from http://www.fema.gov/pdf/library/pfd.pdf.

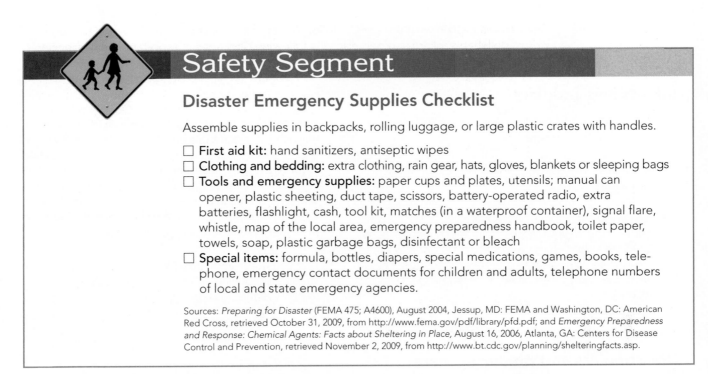

Safety Segment

Disaster Emergency Supplies Checklist

Assemble supplies in backpacks, rolling luggage, or large plastic crates with handles.

☐ **First aid kit:** hand sanitizers, antiseptic wipes
☐ **Clothing and bedding:** extra clothing, rain gear, hats, gloves, blankets or sleeping bags
☐ **Tools and emergency supplies:** paper cups and plates, utensils; manual can opener, plastic sheeting, duct tape, scissors, battery-operated radio, extra batteries, flashlight, cash, tool kit, matches (in a waterproof container), signal flare, whistle, map of the local area, emergency preparedness handbook, toilet paper, towels, soap, plastic garbage bags, disinfectant or bleach
☐ **Special items:** formula, bottles, diapers, special medications, games, books, telephone, emergency contact documents for children and adults, telephone numbers of local and state emergency agencies.

Sources: *Preparing for Disaster* (FEMA 475; A4600), August 2004, Jessup, MD: FEMA and Washington, DC: American Red Cross, retrieved October 31, 2009, from http://www.fema.gov/pdf/library/pfd.pdf; and *Emergency Preparedness and Response: Chemical Agents: Facts about Sheltering in Place*, August 16, 2006, Atlanta, GA: Centers for Disease Control and Prevention, retrieved November 2, 2009, from http://www.bt.cdc.gov/planning/shelteringfacts.asp.

Participating in Community Disaster Response Training

Teachers benefit from participating in community emergency management training events. Being involved also helps teachers learn about the resources that may be available in case of disaster. In turn, early childhood facilities and schools can be supports for the community in times of disaster by serving as potential evacuation sites or by providing child care for emergency personnel who are working to address the effects of the disaster. When teachers participate in disaster planning they also help raise awareness that children and early childhood programs are vulnerable parts of the population that should be considered in community emergency management plans (AAP et al., 2004).

Practicing Disaster Emergency Response

Disaster emergency drills should be scheduled on a regular basis. One approach is to identify a potential disaster scenario that requires teachers to determine the appropriate evacuation response and simulate putting a plan into practice. This helps teachers focus on the unique aspects related to taking shelter and offers an alternative to fire drills to teach children how to follow directions in an emergency. Practice helps children gain comfort and familiarity with emergency drills. The *Teaching Wellness* feature offers ideas about how to help children develop skills in focusing and following directions.

Practicing disaster emergency response also offers opportunities for teachers to review the emergency supplies and determine whether emergency foods and water have been rotated, batteries for flashlights have been replaced, and whether emergency information is readily available to take if evacuation is needed. These actions help ensure that disaster preparations are organized and useful.

MyEducationLab

Go to the Assignments and Activities section of Topic 9: Emergencies and Injuries in the MyEducationLab for your course and complete the activity entitled *Fire Safety*. What safety lessons did you learn from this video that you could pass on to children?

RESPONDING TO DISASTERS

Disasters can strike suddenly or may occur through a series of unfolding events. In any case, teachers must take action as soon as possible to ensure positive and safe outcomes for children. In general the goals for immediate disaster response guide teachers to:

• Recognize the source of concern.
• Identify the appropriate shelter or evacuation safety response.
• Implement the disaster emergency response plan.

Teaching Wellness   *Sometimes I Lead—Sometimes I Follow*

Learning Outcome: Children will explain what it means to follow directions (look at the teacher, listen to the words, do what is asked) and describe why following directions is important in emergencies.

Infants and Toddlers

- *Goal:* Babies and toddlers will participate in copying and following activities.

- *Materials:* Play space, colored blocks, three tubs or containers.

- *Activity plan:* Sit with individual child. Play copying games: touch your nose, then touch baby's nose. Guide the child's hand to do what you do. Play copying games with facial expressions or sounds. Follow what the baby does; then encourage the baby to follow you.

- *How to adjust the activity:* Sit with a child on the floor. Place the blocks in a pile beside the three tubs. Say, "Do this." Place a block in one of the tubs. Guide the child to place a block in the same tub. Repeat, this time placing a block in a different tub. Guide the child to do the same. Once the game is established, say, "Now it's your turn. I'll follow you." Guide the child to be the leader in placing a block in a tub. Follow the child's lead.

- *Did you meet your goal?* Were you able to engage children in copying and following play? Were you able to observe the child participating in the activity goals?

Preschoolers and Kindergartners

- *Goal:* Children will demonstrate or describe the concepts of "leading" and "following."

- *Materials:* Blocks of different sizes or colors, large beads and yarn, paper strips cut to 3.5 inches × 8.5 inches, colored marking pens.

- *Activity plan:* Set up activities during child-selected playtime. Place the blocks in an area, and the beads and yarn in another. On the first day allow children to play with the materials as they wish. On the second day add pattern cards that depict arrangement of the blocks or beads in patterns. Guide children to try copying the patterns on the pattern cards. Talking about copying: looking at the design and doing what you see. On days 3 to 5, remove the pattern cards and provide the paper strips and marking pens. Guide the children to draw block or bead patterns on the paper strips for other children to follow. Talk about being a leader. Encourage children to teach their pattern to others.

- *How to adjust the activity:* Provide additional opportunities for children to be leaders and followers. Play musical games where children sit down when the music stops (listening for directions). Play follow-the-leader games where children follow the movements of a leader (watching for directions).

- *Did you meet your goal?* Did children participate? Are children able to copy designs or movements? Do you hear children using words that show they understand the concepts of leading and following?

Various resources help keep teachers informed about emerging conditions that have the potential to place children in danger. The National Weather Service provides a Storm Watch, Warning, and Advisory map that can be accessed electronically (see the Web Resources). Community emergency personnel may be able to provide guidance if danger threatens. Alternatively, teachers must make the best safety decisions possible. This means deciding whether to take shelter or evacuate and responding appropriately for different types of disaster emergencies (NACCRRA, 2006).

Taking Action in Disaster Emergencies

Safe disaster management relies on a confident and organized response. The first steps in disaster response include the following:

- Remain calm.
- Review the facility for danger.

School-Age Children

- **Goal:** Children will explain what it means to follow directions and tell why following directions is important in an emergency.

- **Materials:** 1-inch-cube blocks; 12-inch × 18-inch tagboard pieces; current event article from the newspaper describing an emergency or disaster; paper and marking pens.

- **Activity plan:** Introduce children to the concept of following directions. Talk about the importance of looking and listening. Create stations for children to practice giving and following directions. Fold a piece of tagboard in half and stand it on a table. Sit one child on either side, each with eight blocks. Ask one child to create a structure and then give instructions for the other child to build one like it just by listening to the directions. Remove the paper to see if the child was able to build the same structure. Now link the concept to following directions in emergencies. Read a current event about an emergency. Describe what people did to evacuate for safety. Ask children to identify an emergency and talk about why children should follow the directions of emergency safety workers.

- **How to adjust the activity:** Have children make drawings of an emergency situation or disaster. Invite them to tell others why they should follow safety directions in emergencies.

- **Did you meet your goal?** Are children able to describe what it means to follow directions? Do they include looking (watching) and listening to a leader?

- Provide first aid for any injury.
- Listen to the radio for reports and guidance.
- Decide whether to take shelter, lock down, or evacuate.
- Take action.

The decision on where to shelter is dictated by the source of the threat.

Sheltering in Place

Sometimes sheltering in place simply involves staying inside the facility. In other situations special measures may be needed. For tornadoes, shelter should be sought in the lowest area in the building such as a basement or interior room. For chemical spills or other hazardous threats, children should be moved into an interior room, and the doors, windows, and any air vents should be covered with plastic and sealed shut with duct tape (CDC, 2006b). If sheltering in place is needed, teachers should:

- Assemble children inside as quickly as possible.
- Go into the identified shelter room.
- Cover windows, doors, and air vents, if necessary.
- Engage children in calm and quiet games: reading, playing with manipulative toys.
- Listen to the radio for announcements and information.
- Stay in shelter until word is received that it is safe to leave.

In most cases teachers and children need to shelter-in-place only for a few hours. However, if sheltering for a longer period is required, teachers should use the disaster emergency supplies to care for and comfort children.

Implementing Lockdown

One important goal of lockdown is to stop the access and entry of an intruder. If lockdown is needed, teachers should:

- Have a program code word or other way to signal the need for lockdown.
- Assemble children in an interior room or the children's classroom.
- Count children to be sure all are present.
- Close and lock all doors and windows and close the blinds.
- Turn off the lights.
- Call 911 to report the reason for the lockdown.
- Stay quiet and still. Read books quietly.
- Stay in lockdown until informed by emergency personnel.

Lockdown situations can be intense and unpredictable. Teachers may need to shelter with children in the setting for several hours. Locating bottled water and small comfort toys in the designated space can support teachers and children until the lockdown is lifted (Curtis, 2008).

Evacuating

Evacuation requires that children be assembled and safely moved to a previously identified location. In some cases, community emergency personnel will direct the group to an evacuation site. If evacuation is needed:

- Gather children and exit the classroom safely to the designated assembly location.
- If time permits, place a sticker label on each child's coat with the child's name, family name, address, and phone number.
- Be sure each child is assigned to an adult.
- Take first aid supplies, important records, and disaster supplies.
- Travel to the emergency evacuation spot.
- Make contact with emergency personnel if possible and follow directions.
- Listen to the radio for instructions as appropriate.

Because disaster emergencies are unpredictable, support for evacuation is hard to anticipate. In some cases, emergency responders from outside the disaster area are able to arrive quickly to help. In other situations the disaster may be widespread and emergency aid very slow to contact all those in need. Teachers may find that their informed care and management makes the difference between life and death for the children and themselves. Preparation, practice, and courage are the resources that teachers carry with them to make a positive impact in such significant situations.

Natural Disasters

Disasters can be caused by a wide range of natural causes, including tornadoes, hurricanes, earthquakes, storms, floods and fires. The plan for response is unique to each situation.

Tornadoes

Programs in areas with the potential for tornadoes should install a weather radar warning system. Teachers should listen for storm watch warnings on the radio and take action as recommended:

- Move children to shelter in an underground space or interior room or hallway away from windows.
- Take cover under tables or desks.
- If a mobile home is used for family child care, leave and take shelter in another location.
- Take a cell phone or cordless phone.
- Remain in the shelter until the warning has ended.*

MyEducationLab

Go to the Assignments and Activities section of Topic 11: Safe Environments in the MyEducationLab for your course and complete the activity entitled *Developing Safety Policies and Procedures*. Note the precautions teachers take as they evacuate children from the school. Is there anything they should do that was not mentioned?

Hurricanes

Teachers should listen for hurricane warnings and keep alert to storm watch systems on radio, TV, or the Internet. If enough time is available, try to return children to their families. If not, follow these precautions:

- Close windows and secure the facility as much as possible.
- Turn off propane tanks and unplug unneeded appliances.
- Take cover inside away from windows.
- Remain indoors until the hurricane has passed over.
- Evacuate if necessary.*

If an earthquake occurs, take cover under tables or desks or in a door frame until shaking stops.

Earthquakes

Earthquakes usually occur without warning. Teachers and children must be prepared to take cover immediately:

- Move to safest location in the room away from windows.
- Take cover under tables or desks or in a door frame until shaking stops.
- After shaking stops, evacuate the facility if it is unsafe. Be aware that aftershocks may occur.
- If outside when the earthquake occurs, move to an open area away from walls, windows, or electric wires.*

Storms

Check emergency broadcasts for storm warnings and travel advisories. Close the children's program if recommended. Return children to families if time allows. If the children must remain at the school or care facility, then:

- Move to an interior space away from windows if high winds are a concern.
- Stay in shelter until the storm is passed.
- Evacuate if needed.*

Floods

Keep aware of flood warnings. Close the facility and return children to families if time allows. If not, then:

- Evacuate from the facility if needed.
- Secure the facility: Forward electronic records to a recipient outside of the area, move equipment to a higher location, and turn off gas and utilities.*

Wildfires and Forest Fires

Keep aware of active fires in the area. Follow the guidance of emergency management personnel regarding closure or evacuation. Close the facility and return children to family if time allows. If a fire approaches near the children's setting:

- Gather all children inside.
- Close doors and windows.
- Turn off gas and electricity.
- Position sprinklers to spray water against the building and roof.
- Evacuate as soon as possible.*

---

*All lists in Natural Disasters, Technological Hazards, and Health Emergencies (pp. 578-580) are from *Is Child Care Ready? A Disaster Planning Guide for Child Care Resource & Referral Agencies.* Copyright © 2008 NACCRRA, www.naccrra.org. Used with permission.

Technological Hazards

A variety of technological hazards can introduce danger to children's settings. These include situations that disrupt utilities, chemical spills, or explosions involving toxic materials and threats to personal safety.

Disruption of Utilities

The children's program should be closed if water, electricity, heat, and the ability to communicate by telephone are disrupted for more than a short time. When utility disruption occurs without warning:

- Gather children in a secure location that has sufficient light and heat.
- Help children feel secure and comfortable.
- Contact families by cell phone or wireless e-mail to pick up children as needed.*

Chemical Spills, Leaks, or Explosions of Hazardous Materials

Assess the situation to determine a plan for shelter and then follow these steps:

- Evacuate immediately if it is safe to do so; otherwise, shelter-in-place.
- Assemble children in an interior room.
- Cover windows, doors, and air vents.
- Use cell phones or wireless e-mail to communicate with emergency personnel.
- Stay in the shelter until advised by emergency personnel that it is safe to leave.*

Attacks and Threats to Personal Safety

Attacks and threats usually occur without warning. Teachers need to be prepared to take appropriate and responsive actions, such as:

- *Explosions:* Take cover from falling debris. Evacuate quickly and calmly.
- *Fire:* Keep low. Stop-drop-roll and cover eyes with hands if clothes catch on fire. Evacuate.
- *Missing child or kidnapping:* Call 911 to report a missing child immediately. Provide information about when and where the child was last seen and what the child was wearing. Follow the guidance of emergency personnel.
- *Bomb threat:* Report bomb threats to emergency personnel immediately. Provide details about the threat. Evacuate quickly and calmly.
- *Person with firearms:* Call 911. Implement lockdown procedures. Stay in lockdown until directed.*

Health Emergencies

Health emergencies are situations where communicable disease is widespread, challenging the ability of public health organizations to administer aid to victims and to stop the spread of disease. Some health emergencies, such as pandemic flu, may unfold gradually as health professionals recognize the outbreak and monitor the spread of disease across the world. Other health emergencies are discovered as unusual numbers of people are suddenly stuck with acute illness, such as may occur with Severe Acute Respiratory Syndrome (SARS). Health emergencies impact classrooms as teachers must pay special attention to sanitizing the environment, teaching children ways to reduce the spread of disease, and monitoring children's health. Teachers themselves are threatened with contracting disease during health emergencies and must take precautions such as obtaining special immunizations. Teachers should be aware of diseases under emergency watch and be prepared to:

- Follow the guidance of medical personnel to reduce the exchange and spread of disease.
- Communicate closely with families about symptoms of disease.
- Report identified cases as directed.
- Close the children's program as directed by community health personnel.*

Teachers' resilience and courage may be tested to the extreme when disaster strikes. Following the strategies and procedures of the disaster emergency response plan helps teachers keep focused on the goals of achieving safety for children and adults: preserving life, avoiding additional injury, and assisting with recovery. Disasters are a rare occurrence. If they do happen, prepared teachers are ready.

SUPPORTING CHILDREN AFTER EMERGENCIES

When the drama of emergency events has passed, teachers face the next step in effective management: focusing on helping children cope with the trauma they have experienced. and learn to develop resilience.

Helping Children Cope

After emergencies teachers continue to guide children by being confident role models, reestablishing familiar classroom routines. and supporting children as they process their worries. If tragedies have occurred, teachers are important resources for helping children and families cope with their feelings of loss. As teachers conduct these supportive activities, they also need to recognize their own need for support.

Being a Confident Role Model

After emergency events children need to regain their confidence that things will be "all right." Children gain this assurance when they observe their teachers managing the situation confidently and with appropriate optimism. This means teachers must pay special attention to moving with confidence rather than appearing disorganized. It is also a reminder for teachers to speak appropriately about the emergency events and avoid the use of frightening descriptions when speaking to one another or when talking on the phone in the presence of children.

Teachers should acknowledge the difficulties and distress of an emergency situation by stating frankly, "That was scary, wasn't it?" But it is especially important to focus as much as possible on the actions children, teachers, and others performed to resolve the emergency situation, by moving to a place of safety until everyone could reunite with their families.

Regaining a Sense of Routine and Control

Young children derive great comfort from the routines and rhythms of their day. When these have been disrupted by injury, emergency, or disaster response, children may feel that no one is in control. Returning to familiar routines as quickly as possible is one way to begin the process of healing (MacCormack, 2008). Once children are surrounded by their familiar world, they are better able to work through the stresses of the unusual events and to regain a sense of safety and well-being.

Continuing to Monitor the Effects on Children

Each child copes with extraordinary events in unique and personal ways. Some may be very outward in their expression of worry, sadness, or dismay, whereas others may seem uninterested and unaffected by the events. Children need many opportunities to safely express their concerns. This support should be provided over a long period of time because a child may express worry many weeks after the event (MacCormack, 2008). Tips for helping children cope after distressing situations are provided in Figure 17-5. Teachers should continue to watch for signs that suggest children may need special help to resolve their worries.

Addressing Tragedies

Sometimes emergencies and disasters have tragic outcomes such as the death of a playmate or teacher. Children, families, and teachers all need the opportunity to process their feelings of loss. One approach is for teachers to invite families to join their child while the teacher explains in simple terms what has happened. Describing how much the child or teacher was loved, and talking about how the group will miss that person, offers opportunity for children and teachers to tell their stories of love and loss.

Figure 17-5 Tips for Helping Children Cope after Disasters

☐ Limit television – disaster reports can be graphic and disturbing.
☐ Pay attention to what children say – learn what they are worried about.
☐ Provide reassurance – let children know that everyone is working to keep them safe.
☐ Watch for changes that might signal emotional stress – seek professional counseling support if needed.
☐ Understand different responses – all children do not experience events in the same way.
☐ Provide children extra time and attention – be available, accessible, and close.
☐ Model positive coping – explain your feelings as appropriate and help the child recognize how you are managing your emotions.
☐ Reestablish normal routines and activities – surround the child with normal and appropriate activity.
☐ Find a way for children to provide helpful action – have them draw picture cards or send books to a damaged early childhood program.

Source: *How to Help Children Cope after the Tornadoes in the South: Ten Tips from Save the Children*, by Charles MacCormack, 2008, Westport, CT: Save the Children. Retrieved October 31, 2009, from http://www.savethechildren.org/newsroom/2008/how-to-help-children-cope.html.

Turning sad thoughts to productive actions and expressions is a positive next step. Decorating a special remembrance poster with drawings or planting a special tree "for teacher Karla" are options that allow children to express their feelings through action. Managing a sad event with children is one way to model healthy coping strategies and can be supportive for children, families, and teachers alike.

Recognizing That Teachers Need Support, Too

Teachers involved in managing emergencies also need support. They carry the dual responsibilities of emergency responder and care provider for children, which can be extremely stressful. Some teachers may feel responsible for injuries, thinking they should have protected the children in some way, or they may wonder if they made the right decisions during an emergency situation. Unsettling events may cause teachers themselves to feel unsafe in the environment. It is important for teachers to be aware of these concerns and access needed supports to help resolve their feelings and regain their sense of personal confidence and well-being.

Preparing Children to Be Resilient

Children are active participants in emergency situations and need to be prepared with knowledge and strategies to help them cope. This is accomplished by sharing information about injuries, illness, and emergencies in child-appropriate ways through what is called a "child-centered risk reduction program" (International Save the Children Alliance, 2006). Classroom activities that equip children with the knowledge that helps them be resilient include these:

Planting a tree or creating a special poster are positive actions that help children express their feelings of loss.

- Explore the topics of injury and illness through books that address these topics and provide dramatic play settings such as a doctor's office, or offer appropriate props such as firefighter hats and pieces of hose.
- Use current events to begin discussions with school-age children about emergencies that are being addressed, and focus specifically on the ways people help each other in emergency situations.
- Conduct emergency drills that teach children what to do, which helps them develop a sense of routine about evacuating the classroom.

Teachers should infuse these life lessons into everyday activities to help children recognize their competence in participating in the emergency process. Equipping children with appropriate information and skills makes them partners in keeping themselves safe and builds their resilience to face and manage the negative impacts of disastrous events.

Summary

Teaching is a dynamic profession that requires many competencies, including the ability to safely manage injuries and emergency situations when they occur. Teachers must be able to recognize the signs of injury and know how to safely assist children with appropriate first aid or comfort care. Teachers must also be able to recognize when an emergency has occurred, know how to contact emergency medical providers, and know how to administer first aid until professional help can be obtained.

Any early childhood setting has the potential to be impacted by a disastrous event. Teachers need to know what kinds of disasters might occur in their area and take steps to prepare. They must be ready to supervise children when disaster strikes, to lead children to safety, and to take shelter until the children can be released to their families.

Managing emergencies can be stressful. Teachers need to access resources to help them cope when necessary. Teachers make important contributions to children's safety by responding to injuries and managing emergencies with confidence and competence.

MyEducationLab

To assess your understanding of how to respond to emergencies and injuries, go to the Book Specific Resources section in the MyEducationLab for your course, select *Nutrition, Health, and Safety for Young Children*, Chapter 17 of the Study Plan, and then complete the multiple choice questions and activities.

Key Terms

Disasters, p. 572

Emergency, p. 554

First aid, p. 562

Good Samaritan doctrine, p. 559

Lockdown, p. 573

Rescue breathing, p. 564

Shelter-in-place, p. 573

Universal precautions, p. 561

Review Questions

1. What signs indicate that emergency medical assistance should be obtained?
2. What are the three goals of first aid?
3. What are volunteer protection laws and why are they important?
4. What is the definition of a disaster?
5. Provide examples of how teachers help children cope following traumatic events.

Discussion Starters

1. Think about a children's classroom that you have observed. Describe the setting and propose an emergency management plan for the classroom. Discuss some of the supports available for the classroom and identify challenges.

2. Consider a rural and an urban community in your state. Identify and compare some of the similarities and differences in challenges that teachers in those areas may face in accessing emergency assistance.

3. Select an age group—infants, toddlers, preschoolers or school-age children—and develop activities for teaching the children the appropriate emergency response for different disaster events.

Practice Points

1. Imagine that you manage a small child care program in a rural area. You know that first aid training is important, but you have to work every weekday, and no training is available in your small town. What other options for training can you identify?

2. Go to the Federal Emergency Management Agency website listed in the Web Resources. Review the site to learn about emergencies that have been recorded for your area. What disaster emergency management plans could you put in place to prepare yourself and the children in your class for such emergencies?

3. Create a list of emergency supplies needed to support a class group of 18 children and two adults for 3 days. Use the Web Resources to guide your planning. Draft a budget for the needed supplies. Explain how the supplies can be assembled in readiness for emergency evacuation.

Web Resources

American Academy of Pediatrics, Disaster Planning
www.aap.org/healthtopics/disasters.cfm

American Red Cross
www.redcross.org

Federal Emergency Management Agency
www.fema.gov

Mayo Clinic, First Aid Information
www.mayoclinic.com/health/FirstAidIndex/FirstAidIndex

National Oceanic and Atmospheric Administration's National Weather Service
www.weather.gov

National Resource Center for Health and Safety in Child Care and Early Education
http://nrc.uchsc.edu

Save the Children
www.savethechildren.org

chapter 18 | Child Abuse
and Neglect

Learning Outcomes

After reading this chapter, you should be able to:

1. Define child maltreatment and describe different types of child abuse and neglect.

2. Describe some of the physical and behavioral signs of child maltreatment.

3. Explain the term mandated reporter and describe the steps in reporting suspected child maltreatment.

4. Identify other sources of violence and explain their impacts on children and families.

5. Describe some of the strategies that teachers can use to reduce the effects of maltreatment and violence and assist children to build positive coping skills.

6. Discuss ways to prevent child abuse in early childhood settings and help children and families develop protective factors.

Min Jee teaches a small group of children ages 2 to 5 years, who are gathered together from several class groups at the end of the program's service day. The children are involved and busy, and she notices with pleasure that Katherine is drawing with marking pens. Katherine usually spends the end of the day in the book corner alone. Min Jee watches as Katherine carefully outlines a figure of a girl in a pink dress who has curly hair just like her own. Min Jee encourages Katherine by saying softly, "Tell me about your picture." Katherine pauses, and then speaks slowly, "This girl is a special princess. She has a beautiful dress and she likes to dance." Then Katherine looks intensely at Min Jee and says very solemnly, "But I'm dirty." Leaving her picture on the table she gets up and walks over to the book corner where she curls up against a pillow.

Min Jee is bothered by this statement but it seems to summarize the concerns she has about Katherine. The child often wears clothes that are too large. The other children do not want to sit beside her because she smells. Though Katherine is anxious to eat at afternoon snack, she struggles to chew and sometimes gives up. Min Jee and Katherine's full-day teacher agree to provide information about social service assistance. Min Jee also decides to refer Katherine's mother to a volunteer dentist, but even when Min Jee offers to help her make the call Katherine's mother responds by saying, "That girl is always causing me trouble. She's just too dumb to brush her teeth." Min Jee reflects on all of these observations and makes a decision. She calls the child protective services hotline to report child maltreatment due to neglect.

Child abuse, neglect, and violence are serious threats to children's safety. They interfere with healthful development by eroding children's trust in others and in their world. These forms of maltreatment and violence inflict cruel injuries, scarring children physically and emotionally, and can cause disability and death (U.S. Department of Health and Human Services, Administration for Children and Families [HHS/ACF], 2009). However, in spite of these overwhelming negative impacts, child maltreatment is sometimes disregarded by those who confuse maltreatment with guidance and discipline, or overlooked by those who have the notion that child maltreatment "doesn't happen here."

Young children are vulnerable, unable to defend or protect themselves, and may not know where to go for help. Teachers play an important role in keeping children safe from maltreatment and by reporting maltreatment when it is suspected. In this chapter we discuss the different types of child maltreatment, provide guidance for teachers to recognize the signs of maltreatment, and outline the steps to take if abuse or neglect is suspected. We also present strategies to prevent and reduce maltreatment and to address the effects of all forms of violence in children's lives.

UNDERSTANDING CHILD MALTREATMENT

Childhood is a unique and special time of development. Young children have the right to expect safe and kind treatment and support for their basic needs. In turn, children's "task" during childhood is to explore and experience the world and to develop the competencies that will allow them to grow in health and curiosity. Unfortunately, young children are particularly impressionable and are seriously affected by negative experiences. Many behaviors of parents, teachers, caregivers, and others enhance the child's development, but sometimes these people mistreat children. In this section we define child maltreatment, discuss the history that brought child maltreatment to the public's notice, and describe the different kinds of maltreatment, their risk factors, and impacts on individuals and their communities.

Defining Child Maltreatment

child maltreatment
a collective term that encompasses all aspects of harmful or injurious behaviors toward children, including abuse and neglect

child abuse
child maltreatment that involves harmful *acts* toward children

child neglect
child maltreatment that refers to failure to protect a child from harm

Child maltreatment is a collective term that encompasses all aspects of harmful or injurious behaviors toward children, including abuse and neglect. Child abuse specifically involves *harmful acts*, whereas child neglect refers to *failure to protect* a child from harm. A formal definition of child maltreatment was first established by the federal government as recently as 1974 through legislation called the Child Abuse Prevention and Treatment Act, and was reaffirmed through the Keeping Children and Families Safe Act of 2003. The law defines child maltreatment as follows:

> Any recent act or failure to act on the part of a parent or caretaker, which results in death, serious physical or emotional harm, sexual abuse, or exploitation, or an act or failure to act which presents an imminent risk of serious harm. (Child Welfare Information Gateway [CWIG], 2008a)

The federal definition is considered the "minimum set of acts or behaviors that define child abuse and neglect" (CWIG, 2008a). Each state is allowed to further define child maltreatment in state law. This means that the actual definition of child maltreatment may vary from state to state, and that the state definition may be stricter and more detailed than the federal definition.

Teachers must know the laws for the state in which they work. In the opening case scenario, Min Jee reviewed the statutes for her state when she began her teaching position. This helped her to understand her responsibilities related to child maltreatment. This information is available through the State Statutes Search provided by the Child Welfare Information Gateway, a service of the U.S. Department of Health and Human Services.

Understanding the History of Child Abuse Prevention

Throughout history children have been used and exploited, suffering the cruelty of forced labor, long work days, and dangerous environments. Early on, the treatment of children was considered a family matter and there was no formal recognition of child abuse or neglect. Efforts to protect children from abuse first emerged from the success of the Society for the Prevention of Cruelty to Animals (SPCA). In 1875, Henry Bergh, who had founded the SPCA, was approached about a little girl named Mary Ellen who was being severely beaten, with the hopes that his work with the SPCA could be used to help this child. He was successful in bringing the case to court. The proceedings highlighted the seriousness of the abuse, which was made real when the jurors wept aloud at the sight of the child. As a result, in 1875, the New York Society for the Prevention of Cruelty to Children was established (New York Society for the Prevention of Cruelty to Children, 2008).

The frequency and severity of nonaccidental injuries to children caused by their parents and other adults was not fully understood until Henry Kempe, a physician, changed the course of history with his articles describing maltreatment as "the battered child syndrome" (Kempe, Silverman, Steele, Droegemueller, & Silver, 1962). Subsequently the landmark Child Abuse Prevention and Treatment Act of 1974 (Public Law 93-247) was written into law. The act provided federal funding for research and a variety of prevention and treatment services that are in place today. The act also sparked greater attention to children's safety, such as protecting children from environmental hazards.

Over time child maltreatment has become better understood, leading to more specific definitions for each type of maltreatment and the expectation that state and local agencies should investigate and manage reports of abuse. However, historic tensions continue. Some people deny that child maltreatment is a concern in their community or consider it a problem of "other" economic or cultural groups. Others believe their communities are doing too little to protect children from maltreatment. Even as these tensions persist, the reports of child maltreatment continue to increase, and the ill treatment of children continues to threaten children's growth and development.

What if. . .

you were at a teacher's meeting and one of the teachers remarked that parents have the right to manage their children however they want? How would you introduce a full discussion of this topic? What points would you consider important to discuss?

Types of Child Maltreatment

Although the definitions of child maltreatment vary from state to state. Four primary types of child maltreatment are typically identified (CWIG, 2008a):

1. Physical abuse.
2. Neglect.
3. Sexual abuse and exploitation.
4. Emotional abuse.

Physical Abuse

Physical abuse includes any physical injury that is not the result of an accident (HHS/ACF, 2006). Such injuries may include welts, cuts, broken bones, sprains, burns, and bites that are inflicted on a child. Physical abuse can also include poisoning by forcing children to drink huge quantities of water or laxatives. Patterns of particular kinds of physical abuse have been assigned specific names:

physical abuse
any physical injury that is not the result of an accident

- *Battered child syndrome:* Battered child syndrome results as a pattern of abuse over a period of time. The child may demonstrate injuries at various stages of healing.
- *Shaken baby syndrome:* Shaken baby syndrome refers to injuries that result from shaking an infant violently or hitting or impacting the child's head (National Center on Shaken Baby Syndrome, 2009). Injuries associated with shaken baby syndrome include internal bleeding, blood clots, injury to the brain, blindness, and death. Children of any age can be damaged by being shaken or hit on the head.
- *Munchausen's syndrome by proxy:* This type of maltreatment occurs when the parent, usually the mother, causes the child to become ill, induces the symptoms of disease, or fabricates illness claiming the child has symptoms that do not exist. The child may undergo frequent medical procedures to address the false symptoms. This form of abuse is usually identified by medical personnel who notice variations from typical disease characteristics (Van Voorhees, 2006).

Neglect

Neglect is defined as a failure to provide for the basic needs and age-appropriate care of the child (CWIG, 2008a). When identifying neglect the focus is on what the responsible adult does *not* do to appropriately care for the child. Neglect is further clarified through four distinct categories:

neglect
failure to provide for the basic needs and age-appropriate care of a child

1. *Physical neglect:* Physical neglect refers to deprivation of the basic necessities of food, clothing, and shelter or not providing sufficient supervision such that the child's safety and health are compromised (CWIG, 2008a; HHS/ACF, 2006).
2. *Medical neglect:* Medical neglect involves failure to provide for the medical and health care needs of a child in spite of having sufficient resources to do so, or refusing care for the child when medical help is offered (CWIG, 2008a; HHS/ACF, 2006). This is the type of neglect that Min Jee recognized when she noticed Katherine's unmet need for dental care and saw how it was interfering both with her ability to eat and her overall health. Medical neglect also refers to cases where parents do not access medical care for their child due to religious beliefs. Religious beliefs are typically honored and are not considered neglect except in cases where the child's life is in danger. A checklist of signs of medical neglect is provided in the *Health Hint*.
3. *Educational neglect:* Educational neglect includes failure to provide for the basic education or special education needs of a child (CWIG, 2008a).
4. *Emotional neglect:* This category encompasses failure to act on behalf of the child's emotional needs. It includes not interacting with or being responsive to a child's needs and not protecting a child from threats, bullying, or other fearful situations. It also includes ignoring a child's use of alcohol or drugs (CWIG, 2008a).

What if. . .

you were told by another parent that a family was restricting a child's food because of religious or cultural practices such as fasting? How would you explore this with the family to learn more?

Health Hint

Signs of Medical Neglect

☐ Child has chronic and severe diaper rash or infections that are not treated.
☐ Child's injury is not cared for; for example, a child who experiences a fall or blow to the head that could typically cause a fracture or concussion is not taken for medical assessment.
☐ Child is inappropriately medicated without guidance from a medical professional.
☐ Child's special health needs, such as diabetes or allergies, are not addressed.

Sexual Abuse and Exploitation

sexual abuse and exploitation
any sexual contact with a child for the purpose of sexual gratification or financial benefit

Sexual abuse and exploitation refers to any act of a person, adult or child that forces a child under the age of 18 to have sexual contact or participate in a sexual act for the purpose of sexual gratification or financial benefit. Sexual abuse includes fondling, molesting, or assaulting a child for sexual purposes and rape. It also includes indecent exposure, exposing a child to pornographic materials, and forcing a child to witness sexual acts. Exploitation involves actions that take advantage of a child in a sexual manner such as coercion to participate in prostitution or pornography (CWIG, 2008a). Sexual abuse occurs among children of all ages including infants.

Emotional Abuse

emotional abuse
specific acts that cause injury to a child's emotional, psychological, or mental stability

Emotional abuse refers to specific acts that cause injury to a child's emotional, psychological, or mental stability. It includes verbal abuse such as threatening, ridiculing, or making demands that are beyond the child's ability or developmental level to achieve; threat of harm such as exposure to or involvement in domestic violence; patterns of terrorizing, isolating, or rejecting a child; selling a child for sexual purposes; and deserting or abandoning a child (CWIG, 2008a; HHS/ACF, 2006).

Neglect is the most frequent form of child maltreatment.

Categories of maltreatment can also overlap. For example, physical abuse and emotional neglect and emotional abuse may occur together. Some states use an "other" category to describe situations where several kinds of abuse occur in combination, and some identify additional categories such as parental substance abuse and abandonment as specific categories of child maltreatment (CWIG, 2008a).

Incidence of Child Maltreatment

The National Child Abuse and Neglect Data System collects and summarizes reported cases of child abuse and neglect and examines the findings made by state child protective agency investigations (CWIG, 2008a). This information helps teachers understand the kinds of maltreatment that may be evident among children in the classroom. In 2006, 3.6 million reports of suspected maltreatment were made, with 905,000 cases confirmed nationwide (HHS/ACF, 2006). The following trends were revealed:

- Neglect is the most frequent form of child maltreatment, accounting for more than 66% of the confirmed cases. Other causes of maltreatment included physical abuse, "other" forms of maltreatment, sexual abuse, and emotional abuse as described in the chart shown in Figure 18-1 (HHS/ACF, 2008).
- While the majority of confirmed cases of maltreatment involve children with no history of previous abuse (75%), about 25% of children suffer repeated abuse (HHS/ACF, 2009).

- Child maltreatment takes place in all communities and groups regardless of socioeconomic, racial, cultural, or religious backgrounds (HHS/ACF, 2006). This dispels myths that child abuse, neglect, and other forms of maltreatment only occur within certain groups of people.
- Child maltreatment can cause permanent disability and death. In 2007, nearly 1,600 fatalities occurred due to maltreatment (HHS/ACF, 2009). The majority of the deaths were due to a combination of types of maltreatment (35%) or neglect (34%). Physical abuse caused nearly 27% of deaths, and medical neglect accounted for 1% of the deaths due to maltreatment.
- The maltreatment and death rates vary according to age. The incidence of maltreatment is higher among older children, while death due to maltreatment occurs more frequently among younger children (see Figure 18-2) (HHS/ACF, 2009).

In spite of these sobering statistics, there is doubt about whether the magnitude of the problem of child maltreatment is sufficiently understood. Several reasons are cited for this challenge (Chalk, Gibbons, & Scarupa, 2002):

- Many instances of abuse are never reported to child protective agencies, leaving questions about how many cases go unreported.
- A small percentage of the incidents that are reported are actually substantiated due either to lack of follow-up or insufficient evidence.
- State definitions of maltreatment vary, making it difficult to compare data.

The actual numbers of children who are abused or neglected or who are at risk for maltreatment are likely to be much higher than the reported numbers. This suggests that more reliable methods of counting the incidence of maltreatment are needed.

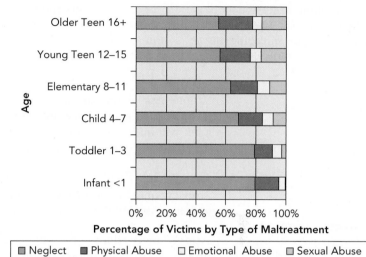

Figure 18-1 Child Victims of Maltreatment, by Age Group and Type of Maltreatment (2006)

Source: *Child Maltreatment 2006*, U.S. Department of Health and Human Services, Administration for Children and Families, 2008, Washington, DC: U.S. Government Printing Office. Retrieved November 2, 2009, from www.acf.hhs.gov/programs/cb/pubs/cm06/index.htm.

perpetrators
people who commit acts of abuse or harm children by neglecting them

Perpetrators of Abuse and Neglect

The people who commit acts of abuse or harm children from neglect are called perpetrators. Perpetrators include parents, other immediate family members, relatives, the unmarried partner of a parent, foster parents, child care providers, family friends, and other children (HHS/ACF, 2006). However, patterns of abuse and neglect indicate that those who have the most frequent contact with the child perpetrate the majority of the maltreatment. Such trends identify the following:

- Maltreatment is more often committed by the biological parent (74%), most often by the child's mother, with fewer instances by stepparents and adoptive parents (HHS/ACF, 2009).
- Sexual abuse is committed most often by a relative or the child's parent (HHS/ACF, 2006).

Figure 18-2 Incidence of Maltreatment and Death Due to Maltreatment, by Age Group (2007)

Source: *Child Maltreatment 2007*, U.S. Department of Health and Human Services, Administration for Children and Families, 2009, Washington, DC: U.S. Government Printing Office. Retrieved November 2, 2009, from www.acf.hhs.gov/programs/cb/pubs/cm06/index.htm.

What if. . .

you had experienced abuse or neglect personally? How might reading about maltreatment be difficult for you? Where might you get support if reading this information is difficult for you to handle?

MyEducationLab

Go to the Assignments and Activities section of Topic 12: Child Abuse and Neglect in the MyEducationLab for your course and complete the activity entitled *Child Abuse Risk Factors*. Have you ever suspected that someone was a victim of abuse? If so, what risk factors caught your attention?

- The racial distribution of those who perpetrate child maltreatment is similar to that of child victims. More offenses are committed by Caucasians (nearly 49%), followed by Hispanics (20%) and African Americans (nearly 19%) (HHS/ACF, 2009).
  - Child death from maltreatment is most often caused by the child's parents (70%), usually by the mother alone or by the mother and father together (HHS/ACF, 2009).

Because parents and family members are frequently the perpetrators of maltreatment, it is important for teachers to serve as healthy role models for adult and child interactions.

Risk Factors Associated with Maltreatment

Various risk factors are associated with the likelihood that a child will be maltreated, including age, gender, race, and disability. Risk factors associated with the likelihood that an adult will inflict abuse or acts of neglect include personal and situational factors and triggers that may spark acts of maltreatment.

Child Risk Factors for Maltreatment

A review of the confirmed cases of child maltreatment identifies the factors discussed next as being associated with a greater likelihood of abuse or neglect.

Age Younger children have the highest risk for maltreatment. Thirty-two percent of confirmed cases occur among children under the age of 4. An additional 24% of cases occur among children 4 to 7 years of age (HHS/ACF, 2009). The majority of children who die from maltreatment (75%) are under the age of 4 years (HHS/ACF, 2009).

Gender More than half (51.5%) of abused children are girls. However, the fatality rate due to maltreatment is slightly higher among infant boys (at nearly 19 per 100,000) compared to girls (just less than 15 per 100,000) (HHS/ACF, 2009).

Race and Culture Maltreatment occurs among all racial and cultural groups. Of the victims of maltreatment, 46% are Caucasian, 22% are African American, and 21% are Hispanic (HHS/ACF, 2009).

Disability and Special Developmental Needs Nearly 8% of children who are maltreated have a disability (HHS/ACF, 2006). Because of underreporting, some studies suggest that the abuse rate among children with disabilities is more than twice that of children who are typically developing (Cosmos, 2001). This is important for teachers to recognize. For example, Malika, a home visitor for a community Healthy Start program, thinks about this when she goes on home visits. She knows that new parents may feel particularly isolated and ill equipped to cope with the discovery that their newborn has a developmental delay.

Other Other circumstances that put children at greater risk for maltreatment include (American Academy of Pediatrics [AAP], American Public Health Association, & National Resource Center for Health and Safety in Child Care and Early Education, 2002):

- Being an unwanted child.
- Being born prematurely.
- Having colic or chronic illness.
- Displaying emotional challenges and difficult behaviors.

Table 18-1 provides a summary of the incidence of child maltreatment by age, gender, and race.

Adult Risk Factors for Maltreating Children

Risk factors common among those who commit violent acts against children include personal attributes, stresses or situations that increase the risk for abuse, and susceptibility to triggers that might set off abusive events (AAP et al., 2002). These aspects of risk can compound; that is, when more risks are evident the likelihood for maltreatment increases.

Table 18-1	Rates of Child Maltreatment by Age, Gender, and Race (2006)			
	Maltreatment		Fatalities Due to Maltreatment	
	Rate of Victimization per 1,000 Children of Same Gender, Age, and Race	Percent of Maltreatment Cases	Rate of Victimization per 100,000 Children of Same Gender, Age, and Race	Percent of Fatalities Due to Maltreatment
Age				
Infant (<1 year)	24.4	11.4%	16.7	44.2%
Toddler (1–3 years)	14.2	19.6%	12.8	33.8%
Child (4–7 years)	13.5	24.2%	1.2	11.9%
Elementary (8–11 years)	10.8	19.4%	0.5	4.8%
Gender				
Girls	12.7	51.5%	1.7	40.2%
Boys	11.4	48.2%	2.5	59.8%
Race				
African American	19.8	18.8%	2.04	29%
Alaska Native	15.4	0.8%		0.8%
American Indian	15.9	1.2%		0.8%
Asian & Pacific Islander	2.5	1%		
Hispanic	10.8	18.4%		17%
Caucasian	10.7	48.8%		43%

Source: *Child Maltreatment 2006*, by U.S. Department of Health and Human Services, 2008, Washington, DC: Government Printing Office.

Personal Risk Factors Personal risk factors are associated with negative experiences in an adult's early life as well as personal aspects that disrupt her or his ability to appropriately care for children (AAP et al., 2002). Personal risk factors include:

- Having been abused as a child.
- Having experienced punitive parenting.
- Having a negative view of self.
- Experiencing low self-esteem.
- Suffering from depression.
- Having substance abuse problems.
- Having poor control of impulses.
- Being a young or teenage parent.
- Having expectations of a child's behavior and ability that are unrealistic or not age appropriate.*

These personal risk factors reduce the adult's ability to cope with a child's behaviors or situations that, although they may be difficult, are typical aspects of caring for young children. In the opening case scenario, Min Jee might wonder if Katherine's mother suffers from depression and low self-esteem. These could be risk factors in the neglect that Min Jee suspects.

---

*Adapted from *Caring for Our Children: National Health and Safety Performance Standards: Guidelines for Out-of-Home Child Care Programs*, 2e, Copyright 2002. Used with permission of the American Academy of Pediatrics.

Situational Risk Factors Situational factors are conditions or circumstances that are common among those who commit acts of violence toward children. These include:

- Being physically or socially isolated.
- Being a single parent.
- Being a victim of domestic violence.
- Dealing with family or economics issues such as unemployment or financial concerns.
- Being an unrelated male in the home.*

Stressful circumstances such as those listed here can cause an adult to be cut off from positive social connections and social support. Limited access to advice, relief, or respite from challenging conditions may cause violent and abusive behaviors to escalate.

Triggering Factors Triggers are conditions that set off a series of events that may increase the risk for abuse. Triggers include:

- Children's challenging behaviors, such as excessive crying or misbehaving.
- Discipline that has gotten out of control, such as spanking that escalates.
- Teaching situations that have gotten out of control, such as exerting excessive pressure when toilet training.
- Adult arguments that carry over to behaviors acted out against a child.*

Understanding the Effects of Maltreatment

Maltreatment can negatively affect children, families, and society for a lifetime, if not for generations Children's Bureau, Office on Child Abuse and Neglect & DePanfilis, 2006. The impacts vary according to the characteristics of the abuse and the services available in the community to help children and families cope.

Impacts on Children

The effects of maltreatment vary according to the child's age and the type, frequency, and duration of the maltreatment. Some effects are temporary and fleeting, such as bruises, whereas other experiences cause permanent physical and emotional scars. Teachers like Min Jee recognize that abuse and neglect can interrupt children's ability to thrive and learn.

Maltreatment that is frequent and continual significantly increases a form of stress called **toxic stress**. Toxic stress disrupts the body's hormones and brain's chemical systems, which negatively impacts brain development, impairing learning, behavior, and health (National Scientific Council on the Developing Child, 2005). This is especially alarming for infants and toddlers who have the greatest risk for maltreatment and consequently are in the greatest danger for long-term damage.

Children who have suffered brain injuries, such as those seen in cases of shaken baby syndrome, may suffer permanent brain damage or death because of bruising of the brain and intracranial bleeding (Chalk et al., 2002). In addition, children who experience maltreatment are more likely to suffer as adults from depression (JAMA and Archives Journals, 2007) and physical health concerns such as allergies, arthritis, asthma, high blood pressure, and ulcers (Springer, Sheridan, Kuo, & Carnes, 2007).

Impacts on Communities

Communities are also affected by maltreatment because they must fund child welfare agencies, investigate reports, and provide social services for children and families when maltreatment occurs (Children's Bureau & DePanfilis, 2006). Other impacts include higher rates of crime, juvenile delinquency, and disability and mental illness in children who have been mistreated. For example, children who were abused are more than twice as likely to be arrested for violence as an adult (English, Widom, & Brandford, 2004).

toxic stress
persistent traumatic stress that disrupts the body's hormones and brain chemical systems. This negatively impacts brain development, impairing learning, behavior, and health

Difficult conditions can trigger acts of maltreatment.

*Adapted from *Caring for Our Children: National Health and Safety Performance Standards: Guidelines for Out-of-Home Child Care Programs,* 2e, Copyright 2002. Used with permission of the American Academy of Pediatrics.

RECOGNIZING CHILD MALTREATMENT

Teachers like Min Jee interact closely with children, observing their growth and development and building relationships of trust that allow children to bring forward their worries and concerns. Teachers must be intentional about watching for the physical and behavioral signs of maltreatment. This involves understanding cultural perspectives related to treatment of children and recognizing the difference between guidance and abuse.

Recognizing Signs of Child Maltreatment

Children display the signs of child maltreatment in various ways that astute teachers learn to recognize. The signs may be obvious and observable or exhibited through very subtle changes in the child's behavior. The behaviors of the parent may also be signs that maltreatment is occurring (Crosson-Tower, 2002).

Teachers need to consider all of the ways in which maltreatment may be evident and use this information to determine if there is reasonable cause to suspect that abuse has occurred or is occurring. For example, at a Head Start teachers' meeting Celia has just shared her frustrations about working with a child whose behavior has regressed. Some of the other teachers respond to her descriptions saying, "That sounds like neglect!" When Celia reflects on it, she decides they are right. How did she miss it? Figure 18-3 lists signs of maltreatment.

Physical Signs

Some signs of maltreatment are definite and unambiguous. Teachers are able to observe marks, movements, or other visible signs that signal abuse or neglect are occurring. Special attention should be given to details.

Observable Marks Signs of maltreatment can be clearly visible and observed during the teacher's daily interactions with children (Crosson-Tower, 2002). The marks of physical abuse may be evident in the form of bruises, burns, or scalds. They may be easily viewed on the child's face, neck, or hands; revealed on the legs and torso when changing a baby's diaper; or seen on the arms when children pull up their sleeves to play in the sensory bin. Teachers must look closely and weigh whether the marks observed seem logical for the kinds of injuries children typically experience and for the usual activities of the child (Crosson-Tower, 2002). For example, a skinned knee is a common result from a fall on the sidewalk, but a series of circular burns on the leg would be unusual to see. The teacher should watch for:

- Marks that are unusual or different from the injuries a child might logically receive during the course of everyday play.
- Marks that are patterned, such as in the shape of a hand or object or a series of striped marks caused by being hit with a strap.
- Marks in various stages of healing, suggesting the possibility of repeated physical abuse (Crosson-Tower, 2002).

For example, Mandy is alarmed to notice dark bruise-colored marks all over Krissy's arms. They look like Krissy has been poked repeatedly with a blunt object. As she studies them closely, Krissy says, "See! I was playing 101 Dalmatians last night and those are my spots. I made them with markers, but they are hard to wash off." In this case the spots are harmless.

Observable Movements When Carolyn first notices 6-year-old Ennis limping, she asks him what has happened. Looking down he answers, "Um, I fell down." Teachers may observe a child limping or protecting a sore arm, or the child might complain of a headache or other soreness. Teachers should not investigate or try to "prove" that maltreatment has occurred. However, it is within the realm of a teacher's responsibility to show sympathy for a child's injury and to ask, "How did it happen?" or say, "Show me where it hurts." Soreness and some injuries may be easily explained by overexertion or typical accidents, but a child's unlikely explanation may be a signal that maltreatment has occurred (Office on Child Abuse and Neglect, Caliber Associates, & Crosson-Tower, 2003).

MyEducationLab

Go to the Assignments and Activities section of Topic 12: Child Abuse and Neglect in the MyEducationLab for your course and complete the activity entitled *Recognizing Signs of Child Abuse.* Based on the information in this fact sheet, would you feel confident in your ability to recognize signs of child abuse?

Figure 18-3 Child and Parent Signs of Maltreatment

Physical Abuse

Child PHYSICAL Signs

✓ Bruises, welts, and marks, possibly in varying stages of healing

✓ Burns and marks in the shape of objects: cigarette, handprints, wooden spoons

✓ Bald spots from severe hair pulling

✓ Unexplained or recurrent injuries

✓ Unexplained broken bones

✓ Child reports being hit by parent

Child BEHAVIOR Signs

✓ Limping or protecting body parts

✓ Recurrent complaints of headache or belly ache or other pains

✓ Child protests when it is time to go home; seems frightened of the parent

✓ Child's behavior changes; is more withdrawn or aggressive

Parent Signs

✓ Parent cannot explain child's injuries or offers unconvincing or conflicting explanations

✓ Parent reports that child harmed self

✓ Parent shows little interest or concern for child

✓ Parent instructs teacher to use harsh discipline with child

Emotional Abuse

Child PHYSICAL Signs

✓ Unexplained delayed physical, intellectual, or emotional development

✓ Otherwise unexplained persistent habits such as rocking, sucking on fingers, head banging

✓ Self-destructive actions (hitting self)

✓ General destructive actions

Child BEHAVIOR Signs

✓ Apathy and depression: low affect, empty facial expression

✓ Fear of parent

✓ Extreme fears or phobias

✓ Extreme behavior: overly passive or aggressive

✓ Cruelty to others; laughing at others' pain

Parent Signs

✓ Parent belittles the child

✓ Parent rejects the child

✓ Parent minimizes concerns for the child

Sexual Abuse

Child PHYSICAL Signs

✓ Pain, itching, bruises, or bleeding around the genitalia

✓ Stained or bloody underclothing

✓ Discharge from vagina or urinary openings

✓ Difficulty walking or sitting

Child BEHAVIOR Signs

✓ Acting out sexual behaviors that are too sophisticated for age

✓ Asking others to do sexual acts

✓ Acting in a sexual or seductive manner

✓ Showing an inordinate fear of males (or females)

✓ Child reports sexual abuse

Parent Signs

✓ Parent is controlling and secretive

✓ Parent is isolated or secretive

Neglect

Child PHYSICAL Signs

✓ Poor hygiene such as dirty hair, skin, and clothes; smells of urine or feces

✓ Unaddressed medical or dental needs

✓ Dress that is inappropriate for the weather

✓ Failure to grow and thrive

Child BEHAVIOR Signs

✓ Begging for food

✓ Hoarding food

✓ Fatigue or listlessness

✓ Child craves attention, even eliciting negative attention

Parent Signs

✓ Parent is indifferent and uninterested in the child

✓ Parent is depressed or seems apathetic

✓ Parent does not provide age-appropriate supervision for long periods of time

Sources: *Caring for Our Children: National Health and Safety Performance Standards: Guidelines for Out-of-Home Child Care Programs*, 2nd ed., 2002, Elk Grove Village, IL: American Academy of Pediatrics; Washington, DC: American Public Health Association, retrieved August 31, 2009, from http://www.eric.ed.gov/ ERICDocs/data/ericdocs2sql/content_storage_01/0000019b/80/14/0d/14.pdf; *Child Abuse Primer for Health Care Professionals*, 2000, Bethlehem, PA: Project Child; "How Can We Recognize Child Abuse and Neglect?" by C. Crosson-Tower, pp. 8–34, in *When Children Are Abused: An Educator's Guide to Intervention*, 2002, Boston: Allyn and Bacon; and "Appendix D: Educators' Checklist for Recognizing Possible Child Maltreatment," in *The Role of Educators in Preventing and Responding to Child Abuse and Neglect*. *User Manual Series*, by Office on Child Abuse and Neglect, Caliber Associates, and C. Crosson-Tower, 2003, Washington, DC: Child Welfare Information Gateway, retrieved online October 16, 2009 at: http://www.childwelfare.gov/pubs/usermanuals/educator/educatorc.cfm.

Visible Signs of Neglect Neglect can also be observed through recognizable patterns that suggest that the parent is ignoring a child's needs. The child may be consistently hungry, dirty, dressed inappropriately for the weather (even when the family has resources for appropriate garments), or the child may have unaddressed medical or dental needs, such as Katherine in the opening case scenario (Office on Child Abuse and Neglect et al., 2003).

Child Statements A child might also clearly tell the teacher about an incident of maltreatment. Trina might say, "I don't want to go home; my mom hits me with a spoon." Dustin, her teacher, should believe what she says. Young children are considered to be very reliable sources for reporting abusive situations, and at the very minimum they are expressing worry or fear. Dustin should respond to Trina's statement without shock (Office on Child Abuse and Neglect et al., 2003). He should reassure Trina that the incident was not her fault and tell her that there are people who can help. When she returns to play, Dustin should immediately report Trina's statement to the appropriate child protective service or law enforcement agency, and make special efforts to demonstrate support and understanding to Trina.

Hiding Signs of Maltreatment Teachers should also be alert to indications that a parent or child is trying to hide the signs of maltreatment. For example, Brandie might dress her son Jacob in excessive layers of clothing to cover the marks of abuse, or William might report that he does not know how his daughter Sophia's injury occurred. In some cases a child may be coached to explain marks of abuse through unlikely stories, or the child may be threatened that if they tell what happened, their pet or a family member will be hurt. Children who have been sexually abused are often caught up in a web of secrecy and threats that lead them to hide the signs of abuse.

Child Behavioral Signs

Maltreatment can also be expressed through a child's behavior, for example, in the themes of play or by changes in the child's mood and level of activity (Crosson-Tower, 2002). Behavioral indicators can be more ambiguous and harder to connect clearly to maltreatment. These signs should be considered together with other observations of the child and parent when considering whether abuse is occurring. Some behavioral indicators are discussed next.

Communicating through Play Children sometimes reveal signs of maltreatment through play, for example, by repeatedly acting out abusive situations in the housekeeping area or doll house. Sami might hit and spank the dolls excessively or make cruel threats. Laurie may not understand the sexual abuse that she has experienced; sometimes it is not until years later when a child's greater maturity helps them understand the meaning of the actions they have experienced (London, Bruck, Ceci, & Shuman, 2005). However, Laurie may demonstrate signs of sexual abuse by inviting others to engage in secretive games that suggest awareness of sexual actions beyond her maturity (Crosson-Tower, 2002). Teachers may also find that children demonstrate their experiences by depicting the abuse in drawings or by building clay structures that communicate situations of maltreatment.

Children sometimes communicate signs of maltreatment through play.

Change in Mood Teachers should pay special attention if a child shows a change in mood. A typically happy child who suddenly becomes excessively withdrawn or sad or a typically congenial child who suddenly becomes overly aggressive, argumentative, or resistant may be experiencing abuse or neglect (Crosson-Tower, 2002).

Change in Activity Level A change in the child's typical level or style of activity should also raise concern (Crosson-Tower, 2002). For example, Madison, who is usually a leader, might suddenly prefer to play alone. Grace, who is typically rather timid and inactive, may unexpectedly begin to run constantly during recess. Or Logan, who is typically very active, may lose interest in the games he used to enjoy and appear listless and lethargic. These changes may be signs of abuse or neglect.

Parent and Family Situations

Caring for the needs of a family is a big job for which many parents are not prepared. Parents must manage the typical challenges of family life, such as balancing a budget and providing for the care of family members, but they are also often faced with a variety of situations over which they may have little control, such as finances and health. Some stressors may be chronic and ongoing; others may occur without warning. Stressors that can negatively impact the family include:

- Loss of employment or underemployment.
- Illness or disability of the parent or another family member.
- Divorce or separation.
- Lack of support due to isolation from family and friends.
- Parenting a child who has aggressive or challenging behaviors (Olson & Hyson, 2003).

When stressors such as these overlap, they can compound, increasing the potential for maltreatment. Teachers often learn of changes in a child's family life through conversation with a parent or report by a child, making it possible for the teacher to recognize that the family may be at risk. Understanding that such stressors may increase the potential of maltreatment offers teachers the opportunity to refer families to services that may help mediate the effects of such challenges. Figure 18-4 describes the risk for maltreatment among military families who face long periods of time when one parent is absent during deployment.

Parent Behaviors

The daily interactions that teachers observe between parents and their children may reveal behaviors or a style of interaction that, when consistently demonstrated, suggests risk for abuse. These include negative interactions such as (Office on Child Abuse and Neglect et al., 2003):

- Belittling the child.
- Describing the child in negative ways, such as "evil," "bad," or "worthless".
- Ignoring the child and showing lack of interest or concern.
- Not attending to child needs when they have been identified.
- Having unreasonable expectations for the child's behavior or performance.

The suspicion of child maltreatment is often based not on just one signal, but on the combination of indications including observable signs, behaviors of the child or parent, as well as interactions between the child and parent (Office on Child Abuse and Neglect et al., 2003). Teachers need to be alert to the many ways in which maltreatment is communicated and the ways it may be hidden and reflect on all they know about the child and family when determining whether there is reasonable cause to suspect maltreatment.

Considering Cultural Perspectives

Teachers must also be aware of the cultural traditions practiced among the families in their class and understand how these may impact perceptions of maltreatment. Definitions of child abuse, perspectives about the vulnerability of children, and child-rearing practices are highly influenced by culture (Roer-Strier, 2001).

Figure 18-4 Risk for Maltreatment among the Families of Enlisted Soldiers

Military families face a variety of challenges including making frequent moves, experiencing times of single parenting while the soldier parent is being trained or is on assignment, and managing the impacts of combat-related deployment.

A research investigation explored the incidence of parent-perpetrated child maltreatment among families of enlisted U.S. Army soldiers during combat-related deployment and times when the parent soldier was not deployed. When soldier-fathers were deployed, the incidence of physical abuse doubled and the rate of neglect was four times greater than when the soldier father was not deployed. To address these challenges, the army provides support services for families affected by combat deployment including assistance centers that link families to support agencies.

Source: "Child Maltreatment in Enlisted Soldiers' Families during Combat-Related Deployments," by D. Gibbs, S. Martin, L. Kupper, and R. Johnson, 2007, *Journal of the American Medical Association, 2989*(5), pp. 528–535. Retrieved October 12, 2009, from http://jama.ama-assn.org/cgi/content/full/298/5/528?maxtoshow=&HITS=10&hits=10&RESULTFORMAT= &fulltext=%22child+maltreatment+in+enlisted+soldiers%22&searchid=1&FIRSTINDEX=0&resourcetype=HWCIT.

What if. . .

you were teaching full time during the day and taking classes at the community college in the evening? How would you ensure that you have the time to appropriately reflect on the observations for the day and remain alert to the signs of maltreatment?

There is no common international standard for child maltreatment by which cultural practices are judged. For example, African American families tend to use mild physical punishment such as spanking with more frequency than European American families, but does this constitute abuse (Dodge, McLoyd, & Lansford, 2005)? A practice called "coin rubbing" is used by Vietnamese families as a traditional cure for fevers, chills, and headaches (McIntyre & Silva, 1992). Heated metal coins are pressed forcefully against the child's body, typically leaving circular bruises or scrape marks. The purpose is to enhance the child's health and, although the practice causes bruises to the child, the intent is different from what is typically considered abuse.

Some cultures allow young children more freedom and autonomy than typical Western cultures, permitting young children to move freely and with little supervision or allowing a child to stay home alone (Dodge, McLoyd, & Lansford, 2005). These might be viewed as signs of neglect. When Jessica is confused about how to interpret such behaviors in her classroom, she makes a call to the child protective service agency to discuss her concern. They clarify steps to take when the parenting practices are unfamiliar and the potential for child maltreatment is not easily understood. Being culturally sensitive is appropriate and important, but it does not mean overlooking signs of child maltreatment (McIntyre & Silva, 1992).

Recognizing the Difference between Guidance and Abuse

Some parents use spanking as a form of child guidance and discipline. In fact, 79% of men and 71% of women believe that a good hard spanking is sometimes needed (Child Trends, 2002). Others consider spanking to be inappropriate. Although not recommended, spanking is not generally defined as child maltreatment unless it is severe, for example spanking with a solid object, such as a belt or hairbrush. To identify the difference between spanking as a form of guidance and abusive spanking, these questions must be considered (CWIG, 2004a):

- How is the act conducted?
- What is the purpose and goal of the adult's behavior?
- What will the child learn from the adult's actions?

Table 18-2 provides examples that can help teachers when making judgments about the differences between guidance and abuse.

Child guidance and disciplinary practices are heavily influenced by regional, cultural, and religious perspectives. Some approaches are permissive; others are stricter than typical practices used in the early childhood classroom. Understanding the parents' perspective helps teachers to interpret the meaning behind child guidance practices and guides teachers when assessing whether the acts are considered abusive or neglectful from the family's perspective (McIntyre & Silva, 1992).

Becoming acquainted with the family provides opportunities for the teacher to discuss common goals for the child's positive development and program practices for child management. Such conversations contribute to the background knowledge that a teacher reflects on when considering whether maltreatment may be occurring.

REPORTING CHILD MALTREATMENT

It is standard practice in early childhood classrooms to observe children on a daily basis to look for signs of general health, illness, or stress. These observations may also reveal the possibility that abuse or neglect is occurring or has occurred. Teachers need to be prepared to report maltreatment as soon as it is suspected.

> **What if. . .**
> you observed a parent interacting harshly with a child and using threats that seemed to be escalating? How would you intervene to redirect the situation? How might you begin a conversation with the parent about more effective ways to gain the child's cooperation?

Parent–child interactions can provide information about the potential for maltreatment.

Table 18-2   Is It Guidance or Abuse?

It's Guidance When:	It's Abuse When:
• Adults are teaching children to change their actions to be more appropriate and to gain control of their behaviors and emotions. • The purpose and goal is to guide the child to learn ways to be appropriate and to help the child build skills they can use in the future to be an appropriate member of the group. • Actions are thoughtful, relatively calm, and are fair and appropriate to the situation. • Actions are occasional and are usually brief. • Actions include verbal reasons, descriptions, and explanations. • Actions include reasonable or logical consequences, such as taking away a toy or privileges, or requiring the child to resolve the issue by helping another child rebuild a knocked over block structure.	• Adults are conducting acts that satisfy their own needs, such as expressions of power or frustration, or as a release for anger. • The adult's behavior has no educational purpose or goal; there is no lesson to be learned. • Actions result from an outburst of emotions. • Actions are not in proportion to the situation. • Actions are occasional and brief but intense. • Actions are frequent and prolonged. • Actions are premeditated, ritual, or systematic. • Actions are not explained or based on reason. • Actions are not based on a reasonable consequence. • Consequences include removing food or shelter, or confinement.

Source: From *Talking About Touching: A Personal Safety Curriculum*, 1st edition, Grades 4–5 Teacher's Guide (pp. 35–36), by Committee for Children, 1987, Seattle, WA: Author. Copyright 1987 by Committee for Children. Adapted with permission.

Understanding Reporting Responsibilities

Reporting child maltreatment is a serious and important responsibility. Teachers, by the nature of the profession, have a legal obligation and professional and ethical duty to report suspected child abuse and neglect.

Mandatory Reporters

mandatory reporters persons who because of the nature of their employment have close and frequent contact with young children are required by state law to report suspected child maltreatment

Teachers and others employed in positions that have close and frequent contact with children are considered mandatory reporters, because their proximity to children and the large amounts of time they spend with children make them likely to become aware that maltreatment may be occurring. Mandatory reporters are required by law to immediately report their "reasonable suspicions" of child maltreatment to law enforcement or the child protective service agency in the area. Each state identifies the professions that are mandatory reporters. They typically include (CWIG, 2008b):

- Medical personnel such as physicians, nurses, dentists, optometrists, and psychologists.
- Law enforcement personnel.
- Employees in licensed child care and early education programs.
- Teachers and other school employees.
- Social workers, counselors, and therapists.
- Clergy.
- Attorneys.
- Firefighters.

Professionals such as these are responsible for making more than half (58%) of the reports of child maltreatment (HHS/ACF, 2009). Another 27% of cases are reported by nonprofessional sources such as parents, relatives, friends, neighbors, and sports coaches.

Indeed, the involvement of "everyday citizens" is important in reporting and stopping child maltreatment.

Professional and Ethical Responsibilities

Teachers have an **ethical responsibility** to protect children in their care. That is, they have a duty to take honest and moral action to protect a child from further abuse. The Code of Ethical Conduct and Statement of Commitment of the NAEYC (2005) outlines this ethical responsibility:

> Principle 1.1 - Above all, we shall not harm children. We shall not participate in practices that are disrespectful, degrading, dangerous, exploitative, intimidating, emotionally damaging, or physically harmful to children.
> Principle 1.8 - We shall be familiar with the symptoms of child abuse, including physical, sexual, verbal, and emotional abuse, and physical, emotional, educational and medical neglect. We shall know and follow state laws and community procedures that protect children against abuse and neglect. (p. 3)

By taking on the responsibility to care for and educate children, teachers also pledge themselves to advocate for the health and safety of each child by reporting suspected cases of abuse. This is an important aspect of professionalism.

Sometimes, however, teachers may struggle with their own discomfort in discussing or addressing instances of child maltreatment (Kenny, 2001; Reyome & Gaeddert, 1998). Teachers cite various reasons for having difficulty in reporting suspected maltreatment:

- Worry about retribution from the family if they learn that the teacher has made a report.
- Concern that they will disrupt the family by reporting suspected maltreatment.
- A mistaken notion that they can "help" the family better by withholding information or delaying such a report.
- Lack of trust in child protective services.
- Lack of knowledge about the signs of child maltreatment or how to report suspected abuse.
- Worry about making a mistake or being wrong especially when there are no observable signs of abuse (Kenny, 2001).

Not reporting suspected child maltreatment is harmful to children. It abandons children to the dispair of neglect and abuse and the long-term negative effects they create and may even jeopardize the child's life. Teachers can gain confidence in their ability to appropriately participate in protecting children by learning the signs of maltreatment, who to contact, and how to make a report.

Responding Appropriately When Abuse Is Suspected

When children reveal that they have been abused or when observations suggest maltreatment has occurred, teachers need to immediately reassure them that they will be kept safe. Children should be allowed to fully express worry, fear, and any other emotions that surround their experience. The teacher's response should be warm and encouraging, and it should clearly communicate that the teacher believes what is being said. It is important to avoid showing alarm or dismay. Table 18-3 provides a guide for teachers regarding what they should or should not do when a child discloses situations of maltreatment.

Reporting Suspected Abuse and Neglect

When maltreatment is suspected, teachers need to be ready to make a report and assume their responsibilities in the protective services process.

ethical responsibility
duty to take honest and moral action

MyEducationLab
Go to the Building Teaching Skills and Dispositions section of Topic 12: Child Abuse and Neglect in the MyEducationLab for your course and complete the activity entitled *Identify and Report Potential Abuse and Neglect*. As you work through the learning unit, consider the consequences of not reporting suspected cases of neglect.

Table 18-3   What Should Teachers Do When a Child Discloses Abuse?

Do this:	Do NOT do this:
Be prepared:	**Do not ignore a child's report of abuse.**
✓ Understand your responsibility as a reporter. ✓ Know your program policy about reporting. ✓ Know the signs of child maltreatment. ✓ Know who to call for help.	**Do not promise not to tell**. You must report abuse. Tell the child you will find people to help.
Take action if needed.	**Do not act shocked.** Don't correct or criticize the child's choice of words or language. Just receive the information with confidence.
Allow the child to talk or show what happened without interruption or questions.	**Do not express doubt** or disbelief or try to talk the child out of what he or she is saying.
Believe what the child says.	**Do not ask a lot of questions.** Act quickly to mobilize the system that will investigate and protect the child.
Reassure the child that it was a good thing to come to you and that you will find the right people to help.	**Do not entice the child to disclose.** Do not offer rewards or suggest negative consequences if the child does not tell.
Redirect the child to play.	
Report immediately by calling child protective services or law enforcement.	**Do not conduct an investigation.** Document the information and investigators will take over from there.
Keep the child with you unless authorities agree the child may be released to the parent.	**Do not call the child's parents.** Let law enforcement or child protective services decide at what point the parents should be involved. Investigations can be ruined and children endangered by informing family members.
Write down what the child told you as soon as possible.	
Continue to support the child.	

Making a Report

When preparing to make a report, teachers should briefly record what was observed and what the child said that led to the suspicion that maltreatment has occurred. This helps keep the details of the concern clear. The call to report suspected abuse or neglect should be made from a private location. It is important to clearly state the purpose of the report and when possible to provide basic information about the child and family. Figure 18-5 provides an example of information to share when making a protective services call. Teachers can contact the National Child Abuse Hotline (1-800-4-A-CHILD) to learn more about making a child abuse report.

Steps in Protective Service

Once a report has been made, the protective services or law enforcement agency will determine if the situation warrants investigation and follow-up. An investigation may include interviews with the child, teacher, and family (Children's Bureau & DePanfilis, 2006). Sometimes teachers are asked to participate in the interview with the child to provide familiarity and support. For example, Abby participated with law enforcement when Leon was being interviewed about injuries he obtained during a weekend visit to his dad's house. Her presence helped Leon talk about the experience. The information gathered through the assessment process determines whether there is reasonable cause to believe that maltreatment has occurred and whether there is continuing threat of harm.

When Maltreatment Is Confirmed

If it is established that maltreatment has occurred, the protective and law enforcement workers move quickly to protect the child from immediate harm. Child protection workers consider whether the child can safely remain in the family home. If it is

Figure 18-5 Steps in Reporting Maltreatment

1. Provide your name and contact information
   Say: *My name is Min Jee Kim. I am a teacher at the Northside Child Development Center. My phone number is XXX-XXX-XXXX.*

2. State the purpose for your call and what maltreatment you suspect has occurred.
   Say: *I'm calling to make a report. I suspect a child is being neglected.*

3. Give the name of child, age, and birth date if known.
   Say: *The child's name is Katherine Goss. She is four years old. Her birthday is March 4, 2007.*

4. Give the name and address of the family.
   Say: *Her parents are Lynn and Calvin Goss. They live at 3579 Canal Street, Our City and State.*

5. Tell what you observed.
   Say: *This child is consistently dirty and has severe dental needs, and Katherine told me she does not want to go home because her mom hits her when she wets her pants.*

6. Provide other relevant information.
   Say: *We referred the mom to community dental services to help the child, but she won't go. The dad recently lost his job and I think that he may have an alcohol problem. I know that toilet training has been a challenge for this child.*

determined that the child's safety is at risk, an out-of-home placement is identified and temporary shelter may be arranged with a safe relative or an appropriate foster family. Meanwhile, the child protective service agency creates a service plan with the child's family to provide support and training, addresses the issues that contributed to the maltreatment, and increases the capacity of the parents to safely care for the child's well-being in the future.

Guidance for Teachers

Teachers should not contact parents or other family members to inform them that a report has been made. This is important for several reasons (Office on Child Abuse and Neglect et al., 2003):

- Doing so may put the child in danger of retribution, especially if the child is the one who disclosed the abuse.
- The parent may flee with the child.
- The parent may try to coach the child to deny the abuse.
- There may be risk for suicide by the perpetrator following reports of sexual abuse.

The child protective or law enforcement agency will direct teachers about how to appropriately interact with families immediately following a report of maltreatment. Although reports to law enforcement and child protective services are confidential, a parent may suspect that the report came from the teacher. If approached, teachers should be prepared to discuss the situation with the parent in a calm and professional manner, explaining the teacher's responsibility to make a report if they suspect abuse.

If a discussion with a parent feels threatening in any way, teachers should know who in their school or program they can contact to provide support (Office on Child Abuse and Neglect et al., 2003). Likewise a family child care provider should have a neighbor or nearby friend or family member to call on for support. Usually, listening to the parent's concerns and treating the parent with respect helps to diffuse difficult situations such as these and can be crucial in building a relationship of support to help keep the child safe in the future.

MyEducationLab
Go to the Assignments and Activities section of Topic 12: Child Abuse and Neglect in the MyEducationLab for your course and complete the activity entitled *Reporting Child Abuse and Neglect.* How would you respond if you had received the memo in this activity?

What if. . .

you suspected that a child has been maltreated? What aspects of reporting abuse do you feel would be most difficult or challenging? How would you overcome these worries?

RECOGNIZING OTHER FORMS OF VIOLENCE IN CHILDREN'S LIVES

Violence has become a reality in the lives of many children today. It is so prevalent that some experts consider violence to be a "public health epidemic" (Osofsky, 1997; Shelton & Banchero, 2009). Zero to Three: National Center for Infants, Toddlers and Families, maintains that "the United States is the most violent industrialized country in the world" (2008, p. 1). Violence enters children's lives from various sources, putting children at risk for its negative effects.

Identifying Sources of Violence

The potential for any child to witness or be affected by violence is very high. Violence is evident in nearly every part of the environment: the home, school, and community. Although children's exposure to these sources of violence may vary, it would be difficult to find a child who has not experienced at least some source of violence.

Domestic Violence

Young children are often witnesses to violence within the home. Domestic violence includes verbal and physical abuse between parents involving insults, hitting, and fatal assault with weapons. Seven million children live in families where severe parent or partner violence occurs; 15.5 million children live in households where partner violence has occurred at least once in the past year (Family Violence Prevention Fund, 2009). Besides being traumatized by seeing and hearing the violent acts of others, children in homes where domestic violence occurs are also 15 times more likely to be physically abused or neglected (Osofsky, 1999). This compounds the potential negative impact of violence on children.

Media Violence

Nearly every child in the United States today is touched in some way by the violence depicted through media sources such as television, movies, the Internet, electronic games, and music. It is estimated that a typical child watches television 28 hours per week and by the age of 18 has seen 200,000 acts of violence and 16,000 dramatized murders (American Psychological Association [APA], 2004). Cartoons often depict more than 80 acts of aggression or cruelty an hour, which is 50 to 60 times more violent acts than adult prime-time programs (APA, 2004). This is especially damaging because most acts of violence depicted go unaddressed or unsanctioned. Even children as young as 14 months are more likely to imitate the violent and aggressive behaviors they view on TV since punishment is not shown as a consequence (APA, 2004). The sounds of violence can also pervade children's experience even when they are not watching television by the sounds of programs that adults watch when children are playing or in bed.

Research links exposure to violence from media sources with increased aggressive behaviors, fears about the world, and desensitization to both fantasy and real violence (APA, 2004; Huesmann, Moise-Titus, Podolski, & Eron, 2003; NAEYC, 1997). Increases in nightmares and sleep disturbances as well as depression have also been associated with exposure to media violence. Claire, a second-grade teacher, is passionate about encouraging families to turn off the TV. Every year she provides families with a stream of ideas about what to do besides watch TV.

Community Violence

Many children live in neighborhoods that exhibit high levels of community violence and frequent exposure to the use of guns, knives, drugs, and random violence (Osofsky, 1999; Shonkoff & Phillips, 2000). These children are able to describe witnessing shootings and beatings, and may see them as everyday and ordinary events (Osofsky, 1999). Community violence also includes the signs of aggression and vandalism that children see, such as broken windows, and the sounds associated with violence, such as yelling in the street and police sirens. Karl plays soft music from different cultures in his kindergarten class to direct children's attention away from the sounds outside.

Other Forms of Violence

Other forms of violence, such as gang violence, drug use, and assault, may be part of children's growing up experiences. These types of violence may not involve young children directly, but children may have older siblings who are involved in gang activity or drug use. Young children may witness gang violence in the neighborhood or be the unintended victims of violence associated with drug use. Children may also become involved in gangs or social groups that are founded on violence. They may be trained by older children to threaten or inflict violence on younger children. Teachers who recognize the context in which the children live are aware of the potential for these forms of violence to affect the children they teach and are better prepared to address the impacts of violence.

What if. . .

a child in your class reported that he had witnessed acts of violence and was afraid to go outside? How would you assist this child?

Recognizing the Effects of Violence

The APA (2004) identifies the negative effects of violence as measurable and long lasting. Violence impacts everyone: children, families, and teachers.

Impacts on Children

The effects of violence on very young children are just beginning to be understood. Recent research has revealed that experiencing violence directly or indirectly affects children of all ages (Shonkoff & Phillips, 2000). Even before children can talk, the negative effects of witnessing domestic or community violence are demonstrated through temper tantrums, fears, and difficulty separating from parents (Osofsky, 2004). Sleep disturbances such as fear of going to sleep, aggressive or withdrawn behaviors, and disruption in parent and child attachment are also associated with exposure to violence (Rice & Groves, 2005). Some children who witness violence in the community even show symptoms of posttraumatic stress disorder similar to the responses of those who experience violence in war zones (Jenkins, 1996).

Witnessing violence interrupts normal brain development, resulting in reduced ability to learn. Kindergarten and school-age children are able to understand the intentionality of acts of violence and often have trouble concentrating and paying attention due to fears and intrusive thoughts. Children who are not able to trust in the safety of their surroundings may withdraw and have trouble building social attachments. They may also become disassociated with their surroundings, eventually losing the ability to develop care and empathy for others (APA, 2004). For example Marion, a teacher of 3-year olds, remembers two brothers that attended her class. They had been so traumatized by violence in their neighborhood that when they first joined her class they would lay on the floor right in front of the door. They didn't cry, but they didn't play. She helped them to transition into typical play by bringing toys to them and allowing them to gain trust slowly.

Sonya uses storyboards to help her first graders review the actions of the characters in a story. She teaches words to describe inappropriate behaviors and provides opportunities for the children to offer creative alternatives for the poor decisions or aggressive actions of the characters.

What if. . .

you observed children dramatizing violent acts in their play? How would you redirect the children's play to themes of empowerment?

Impacts on Parents

Domestic and community violence traumatize parents as well as children. Parents are challenged to cope and manage their own fears while at the same time realizing that they might not be able to keep their child safe (Osofsky, 1999). Parents who have been victims of violence, or who have witnessed violence, may respond by becoming overprotective of the child and not allowing the child to be away from them, or by becoming numb to the effects of violence and experiencing extreme sadness and depression. Parents are likely to have an overwhelming sense of helplessness and hopelessness that is unavoidably communicated to their child. As a result, the parent may become emotionally unavailable and unable to be a source of comfort to the child. Over time the parent may become more irritable, talk less, and be less responsive to the child's needs (Osofsky, 1999). As a result, violence interrupts parents' ability to provide supportive care for their child, which disrupts the parent-child relationship.

Domestic and community violence disrupt a basic function of the family by challenging a mother's ability to keep her child safe.

Parents living in violent environments need to find ways to manage their own trauma before they are able to support their children. Teachers play an important role in this effort by offering information for parents about social service supports and by strengthening the parent–child relationship through positive experiences in the early childhood setting. Maria keeps a stack of information cards on her desk that provide information for social service supports in her community. Because she has these readily available, parents recognize that many people need extra support now and then.

Impacts on Teachers

Adults who work with young children who are affected by violence also experience its negative effects. Teachers need to develop strategies to help children cope with negative experiences and to manage behaviors such as children's aggression toward others, fears and clinginess, or regression in toileting or language development. Learning about the child's tragic stories can also evoke fear and anxiety.

Teachers may express the "secondhand" effects of violence through physical symptoms such as headaches and stomach upsets, as well as emotional distress, exhaustion, and sadness (Rice & Groves, 2005). Teachers may need support from their supervisors and assistance to help them manage children's needs and cope with their own stresses (Osofsky, 1999; Rice & Groves, 2005). In the opening case scenario Min Jee recognized the signs of maltreatment and knew how to make a report. However, after doing so, she might reflect on her actions and wonder if she should have noticed and addressed her concerns sooner. She might feel guilty that she could not protect Katherine from the effects of abuse and neglect. Min Jee may need to seek support from others to help her resolve her feelings about this situation and focus on planning ways to support Katherine and her mother in the future.

What if. . .

you knew that a serious case of abuse had been confirmed for a child in another class? How would you detect whether the teacher of that class was experiencing stress from the situation? How might you reach out to that teacher to offer support?

ADDRESSING THE EFFECTS OF MALTREATMENT AND VIOLENCE

A caring and supportive relationship is crucial in helping children and parents manage the effects of traumatic events. Teachers are a source of safety, caring support, and reassurance for the child and family (Office on Child Abuse and Neglect et al., 2003). They are able to create classroom environments and offer activities that help children and families cope with the effects of maltreatment and violence and build resilience.

Implementing Supportive Strategies for Children

To improve children's positive long-term outcomes after negative experiences, teachers focus special attention on supports for the child in the classroom. This includes providing continuity, focusing on children's needs, and assisting children to manage their emotions in appropriate ways.

Providing Continuity

Disruption in the child's familiar daily routine may be a consequence related to maltreatment or experiences of violence. The child may be placed in the care of a family member or foster care provider who is unaware of the child's regular schedule. By encouraging the protective service agency to continue the child's participation in the early childhood setting, teachers help support the child's familiar routine, which contributes to the child's positive coping process. Often services for children who have experienced traumatic events include positive socialization experiences such as those provided by early childhood programs (Office on Child Abuse and Neglect et al., 2003).

Focusing on Needs

Teachers help children cope with the impacts of maltreatment and violence by acknowledging children's needs and challenges. These may include the needs to:

- Overcome fear and regain ability to trust.
- Dispel a sense of helplessness.
- Regain self-esteem.
- Feel safe and supported.
- Build a sense of autonomy, or independence.
- Feel in control and competent.

These concerns can be addressed through positive classroom experiences and opportunities for the child to experience success (Office on Child Abuse and Neglect et al., 2003; Rice & Groves, 2005).

The Infant Teachers should provide extra time for holding and caring for infants. They should also smile and speak kindly and gently when playing. Special attention should be paid to the infant's cues for hunger, need to sleep, or interest in play, helping to reestablish the baby's trust.

The Toddler Toddlers need extra support and positive interactions. Allowing the toddler to play with certain toys without having to share for an extra period of time may help to build the child's sense of autonomy and control. Encouraging the child to explore a new task such as crawling and climbing through an interesting obstacle course may help the child to regain interest in play and develop a sense of competence.

The Preschooler Preschoolers benefit from opportunities to immerse themselves in positive play, where they can retreat from their fears, relax, and pursue their own interests. Interesting dramatic play settings, extended play periods in the sensory bin materials or sandbox, and positive interest from the teacher are all ways to build the child's self-esteem, sense of safety, and personal control.

The Kindergarten and School-Age Child Teachers can support school-age children in two somewhat opposing ways. On the one hand, children in this age group may be interested in expressing and discussing their fears and feelings of violation from maltreatment or abuse. Inviting children to share their concerns with the teacher at appropriate times is one approach. At the same time these children may wish to retreat from the experience and simply immerse themselves in play and exploration. In the opening case scenario, Min Jee notices that Katherine has recognized that she is dirty. Min Jee helps Katherine gain self-care skills by presenting activities in group time about how to brush your teeth, how to wash your hands and face, and how to comb your hair. Activities such as these assist children to gain a sense of control and competence.

Children who have experienced traumatic events benefit from a variety of activities that allow them to express and process their emotions.

Providing Appropriate Outlets for Expressing Emotions

All children benefit from the opportunity to express their emotions. Children who have experienced violence or have been maltreated need access to a variety of appropriate opportunities for the open and free expression of their emotions and ideas. Expressive activities can be provided across the curriculum, including:

- Providing dramatic play props that support dramatization of everyday home life, including cooking, cleaning, and shopping props.
- Creating a designated space for children to build and keep their block structure from one day to the next until the children are ready to disassemble it.

- Exploring feelings through children's literature and small-group discussions.
- Guiding children to draw, dictate, or write a story about a child solving a problem and, hence, gaining strength and confidence.
- Offering music and opportunity for children to play a rhythm instrument or to dance and move to a variety of musical styles as a method of expressing their feelings.

Reducing the Child's Sense of Isolation

Children who have experienced maltreatment or violence often feel set apart or isolated from other children. Strategies to help these children engage with others include providing activities that encourage interactive play and that build social skills such as group games, team projects, and dramatic play. For example, when Min Jee sees Katherine alone in the library corner, she invites her to join the children who are playing with play dough. Min Jee offers Katherine a basket of cookie cutters to share with others at the table.

Creating Opportunities for Appropriate Problem Solving

Children who have been victimized may have experienced feelings of being trapped or not in control. They need support to regain a sense of confidence and competence. Teachers encourage this by offering the child appropriate choices and by guiding the child through reasonable problem-solving situations that build a sense of accomplishment. Activities to accomplish this include:

- Providing new physical challenges, such as offering the toddler an interesting new target for bean bags or presenting a preschooler with a variety of appropriate challenges on the child-sized balance beam.
- Involving the preschool child in selection of the snack menu or the books for story time for the following week.
- Creating opportunities for school-age children to assist in making decisions for the classroom, such as choosing books to purchase or selecting the games for gym time.

Addressing Violence in Children's Play Themes

Children may engage in play about violence, especially if this has been a part of their experience. Children are also easily attracted to strong characters depicted in the media, such as superheroes, and are interested in the excitement of games that involve chasing others and using pretend weapons. Children use play to explore and understand events, and play involving violent themes may have value in therapeutic settings (Levin, 2003). However, in the early childhood setting teachers worry that play with violent themes may be detrimental. Teachers are concerned about play with violent themes for these reasons (Levin, 2003):

- Once violent play gets started it is hard to stop; children get out of control.
- Other children may be scared or traumatized by viewing the play violence.
- Acting out violent acts reinforces violent behaviors and may teach children to be violent.
- Playing the same fantasy role over and over may interrupt children's social connection with other children and distracts children from other skill development.

Teachers have an important role in helping children meet their needs through play, but there is no simple solution to meet children's needs and teacher concerns. Some basic strategies can be implemented for all age groups of young children (Levin, 2003).

Recognizing Violent Themes in Play Teachers should be observant and try to understand the topic children are exploring through play. Simply banning such play denies children the opportunity to process difficult topics in a developmentally appropriate way; also it rarely works, and is often counterproductive because children may respond by hiding the play themes and perhaps even lying about their play (Levin, 2003). Instead teachers should offer interesting challenges to divert interest away from violent play, and explore alternative ways to meet children's needs. For example, Noemi recognizes that Aaron and Kip tend to act out shooting themes in their play. She brings a variety of bean bags out to the play yard and helps the boys create targets for a challenge course. Later, Noemi guides the children to write creative stories and draw pictures about events that interest them. In this way Aaron and Kip are provided an active alternative in the play yard and an opportunity to explore the violent themes that interest them in ways that do not disturb the other children.

Ensuring Everyone Is Safe Children engaged in play with violent themes may frighten others. Teachers need to establish safety limits on such play and involve children in the development of rules and limits. Erika holds a group time where she talks with the children about what to say when they don't want to play the scary games.

Meeting Children's Needs Teachers need to be purposeful in planning activities that provide alternative and appropriate ways for children to explore frightening topics. Offering opportunities for children to paint, build with clay, and dictate stories helps children who have experienced trauma to outwardly express emotions in ways that are less threatening than speaking about them (Malchiodi, 2001). It is also important to rotate the toys and materials that are available for play to ensure that children have interesting alternatives and are not falling back on violent play themes as a sign of boredom.

Promoting Healthy Play Violent play themes sometimes emerge as children imitate violent actions they have experienced. This is called imitative play. Children involved in imitative play act out the same violent events and themes over and over again. For example, Warren and Kyle might persist in play where one child pretends to be waiting for a bus while the other sneaks up behind him and "shoots" him. Children engaged in imitative play seem stuck and unable to move beyond these repetitious themes.

Imaginative play, on the other hand, is play that explores a variety of scenarios, with the play partners demonstrating creative ways for keeping safe or withstanding the effects of violence. Tony, Karen, and Enrique pick up their play theme each day at recess, but the ideas and activities change. What began as play focused on police and shootings evolves to firefighters saving people and animals, and then changes to play about being a veterinarian. Teachers can encourage these empowering themes by offering ideas for resolving conflicts and giving suggestions about how the "characters" might take charge and manage the dramatic theme in appropriate ways. This approach guides children to move on to new kinds of play.

Children who persist with play themes about violence and death might benefit from the special assistance of a counselor or mental health specialist. Teachers should work closely with families to share strategies for managing a child's worries and identifying ways to reduce the child's exposure to violence.

imitative play
> play that replicates acts, including violent acts, that children have seen or experienced

imaginative play
> play that explores a variety of creative and child-developed scenarios

> ## What if. . .
> a small group of parents approached you with a complaint that they had observed children acting out violent themes in the play yard? How would you respond?

Building Conflict Resolution Skills

Learning to resolve disagreements in positive and productive ways helps children build the skills they need to cope with and resolve future difficulties. Conflict resolution approaches offer concrete alternatives to using force or violence to address problems. Activities that help children develop these skills include:

- Reading books about children who solve problems.
- Using puppets to act out a challenge, such as figuring out how to divide an apple.
- Planning activities that require problem solving, such as setting out cut-and-paste activities for four children, while providing only two pairs of scissors and two glue sticks.
- Teaching children the language of conflict resolution and modeling how to solve a problem, such as naming the problem, identifying possible solutions, and selecting a mutually agreeable result (Office on Child Abuse and Neglect et al., 2003).

Recognizing Overlooked Victims

Violence affects everyone in the family. Children may have witnessed the abuse of a sibling. They may have been required to participate in the abuse in some way, they may have been coached to cover up the abuse, or they may feel guilty that they were not able to protect the

MyEducationLab

Go to the Assignments and Activities section of Topic 12: Child Abuse and Neglect in the MyEducationLab for your course and complete the activity *Preventing Child Abuse and Neglect.* What can teachers to do provide support to children's families who are at risk of committing abuse or neglect?

What if. . .

you knew that the mother of one of the children in your class had been a victim of domestic violence? You can see that she wants to develop friendships with other parents. How would you help her to get acquainted?

resilience
the ability to cope with negative experiences

other child from maltreatment. Similarly a parent may suffer from guilt, feeling that he should have recognized and protected his child from the maltreatment of another adult. These are often overlooked victims who may need support to express and manage their emotions.

Supporting Families

Teachers are a source of support for families who have been affected by maltreatment and other forms of violence. They make a positive contribution by creating welcoming environments and offering activities such as (Office on Child Abuse and Neglect et al., 2003):

- Providing information about typical child development and positive parenting.
- Conducting activities that help families develop social contacts, reducing the family's sense of isolation.
- Encouraging families to be involved in community service projects to help develop a sense of contribution, confidence, and connection to the community in which they live.

Teachers can also help families identify their strengths and available resources. For example, Alicia tells parents about the strong points she can observe, such as picking their children up on time, and encourages families to see their friends as positive resources. Sometimes simply being friendly can offer the encouragement that families need to face the process of healing from traumatic events (NAEYC, 2004).

Building Coping Skills and Resilience

In spite of the serious effects of child maltreatment and violence, not all children demonstrate poor development. Some children who have experienced acts of violence display considerable ability to cope and are able to thrive following interventions that restore their sense of confidence. This characteristic is called **resilience** (Children's Bureau & DePanfilis, 2006). Various factors appear to be associated with a child's ability to be resilient.

Personal Characteristics

Specific aspects of the child's temperament or personality style are associated with resilience, including optimism, humor, intelligence, and positive self-esteem (Fraser & Terzian, 2005). These characteristics mediate the negative effects of maltreatment and support the child's ability to think positively and to heal from the emotional trauma.

Aspects of the Experience

The ability to be resilient is affected by various aspects of the experience. For example, resilience following maltreatment is impacted by the following:

- *Age of the child:* Younger children tend to be more resilient and more responsive to appropriate therapies following experiences of abuse or neglect (National Scientific Council on the Developing Child, 2005).
- *Relationship of the child to the abuser:* Children who know their abuser find it harder to cope with the effects of maltreatment. An extreme sense of betrayal is experienced when the abuse is perpetrated by someone the child knows, such as a parent, family member, or friend (Office on Child Abuse and Neglect et al., 2003).
- *Kind, frequency, and severity of maltreatment:* Children are better able to cope with the effects of maltreatment when it is less invasive and less emotionally involved. For example, a child who experiences a single incidence of abuse may be better able to cope than a child who has been neglected over a long period of time (Children's Bureau & DePanfilis, 2006).

Social Support Resources

Children who are surrounded by warm and reassuring environments fare better than those who are isolated or not supported (CWIG, 2004b). The extended family members, caring

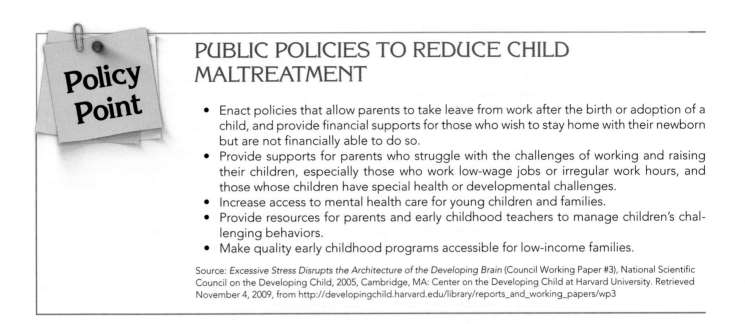

PUBLIC POLICIES TO REDUCE CHILD MALTREATMENT

- Enact policies that allow parents to take leave from work after the birth or adoption of a child, and provide financial supports for those who wish to stay home with their newborn but are not financially able to do so.
- Provide supports for parents who struggle with the challenges of working and raising their children, especially those who work low-wage jobs or irregular work hours, and those whose children have special health or developmental challenges.
- Increase access to mental health care for young children and families.
- Provide resources for parents and early childhood teachers to manage children's challenging behaviors.
- Make quality early childhood programs accessible for low-income families.

Source: *Excessive Stress Disrupts the Architecture of the Developing Brain* (Council Working Paper #3), National Scientific Council on the Developing Child, 2005, Cambridge, MA: Center on the Developing Child at Harvard University. Retrieved November 4, 2009, from http://developingchild.harvard.edu/library/reports_and_working_papers/wp3

and responsive teachers, and other positive role models can assist the child to form an optimistic vision of the future (Fraser & Terzian, 2005). For example, when Mitch teaches a child who has experienced abuse or violence, he makes the child a paper journal. Once a week he and the child sit down together, open the booklet, and each draws a picture on his side of the book. They talk and enjoy the time together.

Positive Community Influences

Aspects of the broader community also support children's resilience. These include access to health care, social service resources, stable neighborhoods, and safe schools (Fraser & Terzian, 2005). Children in communities that have accessible resources such as these are more likely to have their physical and emotional health needs met, thus reducing the long-term negative effects of maltreatment.

In spite of this knowledge, however, and the increasing scientific evidence about the long-term negative effects of child maltreatment, little is being done to systematically provide the resources or strategies needed to reduce maltreatment or address its consequences (Center on the Developing Child, 2007). The *Policy Point* provides some examples of public policies that could improve this situation.

PREVENTING MALTREATMENT AND PROTECTING CHILDREN FROM VIOLENCE

Prevention is the most effective way to reduce maltreatment. For teachers this involves understanding the risks for abuse and neglect, and taking prevention measures in the early childhood setting. Teachers are also important in helping children and families build protective skills that reduce the risk for abuse and serve as advocates for reducing maltreatment in their communities.

Prevention Measures for the Classroom

A variety of prevention activities are appropriate in early childhood settings. These include special scrutiny during the hiring process, making special arrangements in the environment, being sensitive to children's needs, and recognizing teacher risk factors for abuse.

Safe Hiring Practices

Teachers of young children must be competent and safe. Even though early education teachers themselves make up a small percentage (less than 1%) of those who abuse children (HHS/ACF, 2006), it is alarming to note that maltreatment does occur in early childhood settings. To address this, great care must be taken during the hiring process. Prospective teachers should be prepared to earnestly participate in the process, understanding that this is an important abuse prevention strategy. For example, the hiring process may involve:

- Reviewing the applicant's education and work history to clarify competency for work with young children.
- Conducting interviews that reveal personal temperament traits and dispositions that suggest a good fit for work with young children.
- Conducting criminal background checks before new teachers are hired.
- Checking references to screen for any concerns about appropriateness for hire.
- Observing applicants working with children to recognize skills.

People who have the potential to abuse children are often drawn to work in settings where they have frequent contact and access to them (Koralek, 1992). Careful screening during the hiring process helps to eliminate these concerns.

Arranging the Environment

The way the classroom or home care environment is arranged helps reduce the chance of abuse and protects teachers from claims of suspected abuse (Rice & Groves, 2005). Furniture and equipment should be positioned so there is a clear view of all of the indoor and outdoor spaces, with no hidden areas. Diaper changing and toileting areas should be open so that adults can be observed for appropriate interaction.

What if. . .

you were asked in an interview why you wanted to work with children? What would you say to communicate your appropriateness to teach young children?

Following Safety Guidelines

Program and school safety policies are designed to keep children safe and eliminate the possibility that abuse could occur. Teachers need to understand and follow these guidelines. For example, some settings may require that teachers and volunteers are never alone with children. The *Safety Segment* provides examples of program policies and practices that should be in place to ensure children's safety from maltreatment and protect teachers from potential allegations of abuse.

Safety Segment

Practices That Reduce Risk of Abuse by Teachers

- Policies allowing parents access to their children at all times.
- Procedures for diapering, assisting children with toileting, and changing clothes.
- Policies restricting teachers from taking children away from the center without a parent's permission.
- Procedures describing appropriate methods for managing challenging behaviors.
- Field trip procedures that minimize opportunities for adults to be alone with children.
- Procedures for reporting accidents and recording responsive actions to mitigate possible allegations of abuse in the early childhood setting.
- Procedures for responding if an allegation of maltreatment by a teacher or staff member is made.

Sources: *Caregivers of Young Children: Preventing and Responding to Child Maltreatment*, by D. Koralek, 1992, Washington, DC: U.S. Department of Health & Human Services, retrieved November 2, 2009, from http://www .childwelfare.gov/pubs/usermanuals/caregive/caregive.pdf; and *Building Circles—Breaking Cycles* (Publication DD2), 2004, Washington, DC: National Association for the Education of Young Children.

Touching Children Appropriately

Many early childhood settings have policies related to touching children. Some prohibit teachers from holding children on their laps or hugging a child, others may have "no touch" policies. Implementing "no touch" policies to reduce the risk of abuse is an extreme measure, especially because touch is an essential component of interaction and responsive care for very young children. More appropriate approaches guide teachers to touch children in ways that are suitable for the setting. Holding hands, patting a child on the back, or putting an arm around a child's shoulder are ways teachers can show care through safe touch. Teachers must also be mindful of cultural variations in acceptable ways to touch. In addition, it is important to recognize and respect that children always have the right to say they do not want to be touched (NAEYC, 2004; Koralek, 1992).

Recognizing Signs of Potential Abuse

On occasion even well-seasoned teachers may experience frustration and find it difficult to manage children's behaviors. Teachers who frequently exhibit frustration and poor management may show signs that they could abuse children, such as (Koralek, 1992):

- Yelling at or belittling children for mistakes.
- Responding inappropriately to challenging behaviors such as grabbing or jerking the child.
- Expressing personal frustrations to a child.
- Showing unusual or inappropriate interest in a particular child or seeking to be alone with a child.

Supervisors watch for these kinds of behaviors as signs of inappropriateness for working with children. Teachers should also be aware of their own behaviors and recognize when they may need additional supports, such as rest breaks and new strategies to ensure they can keep children safe.

> ## What if. . .
> you witnessed another teacher threatening, belittling, or yelling at a child? What would you do?

Building Protective Factors

Child abuse prevention also involves supporting children and families to develop protective factors. Protective factors are buffers that reduce the potential for abuse or neglect. These factors are associated with a decreased incidence of child maltreatment, making them important contributors to abuse prevention (CWIG, 2008b).

protective factors
buffers that reduce the potential for abuse or neglect

Protective Factors for Children

High-quality early childhood settings help children develop protective factors by providing opportunities for positive experiences within a nuturing environment. Such environments allow children to experience safety and security in a setting where all people are treated with respect and dignity (Cohen & Knitzer, 2004). These experiences help children form secure relationships, increase their interest in problem solving, and promote the development of language, healthy physical development, and positive social skills (J. Cohen, Onunaku, Clothier, & Poppe, 2006). These protective factors also provide opportunities for children to develop interests and hobbies, practice self-control, and learn to both seek help and gain independence and autonomy (CWIG, 2004b). In her classroom, Jen sets up activities that can evolve across the week. She takes pictures for the project story poster so children can reflect on how they worked through the steps of their projects.

As children grow through the preschool and elementary years, they can learn personal safety skills through appropriate and purposefully planned activities. Activities might focus on lessons such as:

- Don't go with strangers.
- Who to go to for help.
- "Good" secrets and "bad" secrets.
- Safe touch—it's ok to say "don't touch me."

The *Teaching Wellness* feature provides examples of ways to teach children about safe touch and how to say "Stop!"

Teaching Wellness *Keeping Me Safe*

Learning Outcome   The purpose of this activity is to teach children the difference between friendly and not friendly touch, and to let children know that they can choose if they want to be touched.

Infants and Toddlers

- *Goal:* Children will imitate gentle touch.

- *Materials:* Small doll or stuffed animal.

- *Activity plan:* Sit with the infant or toddler on the floor. Create play interactions between the child and the doll or animal. Hold the prop kindly and demonstrate gentle touching. Point to the eyes, ears, nose, and say, "This is how I touch gently" or "This hug is my friendly touch." Reinforce these concepts in everyday interactions.

- *How to adjust the activity:* Provide several dolls or stuffed animals and props such as a small tub for bathing or cups and spoons for feeding. Demonstrate gentle play. Provide negative response to rough touch saying, "Oh, hitting is not friendly. That hurts." Reinforce gentle touch by remarking, "You know how to be gentle. That is a friendly way to touch."

- *Did you meet your goal?* Did the child imitate the gentle touching that you modeled? Did the toddler begin to use words like *gentle, kind, friendly*?

Preschoolers and Kindergartners

- *Goal:* The child will describe friendly and unfriendly touch, and know how to respond appropriately when the child does not want to be touched.

- *Materials:* Large piece of paper, marking pen or crayon, scissors.

- *Activity plan:* Have one child lay on a piece of butcher paper while the teacher or another child draws a line around that child. Name the body parts while drawing. Use correct names for all body parts. Talk about friendly touching. Say, "Friendly touching is touch that cares for us and make us feel good like hugging or patting or giving a high-five." Talk about other kinds of touch sensations, such as hot or cold, or getting a cut or skinned knee. Identify the friendly ways that these sensations are cared for. Talk about unfriendly touching, the kind that hurts—like hitting or kicking. Tell children that unfriendly touching is not ok, and that children can stop unfriendly touching by saying, "You need to stop. That hurts!"

- *How to adjust the activity:* Play a word game using a puppet. Have the puppet ask the children "Is hitting a friendly touch?" Ask the children to respond verbally. Repeat the game, but this time ask the children to pat their shoulders if the answer is yes or touch their knees if the answer is no. Take turns using the puppet. Have children draw pictures that show friendly touch or show they are happy.

- *Did you meet your goal:* Is the child able to describe friendly and unfriendly touch? Can the child model appropriate responses to each kind of touch?

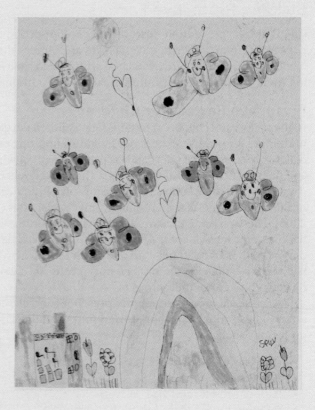

School-Age Children

- *Goal:* Children are able to describe a variety of friendly and unfriendly touches, and can articulate when a friendly touch becomes an unfriendly touch.

- *Materials:* Small pieces of paper, marking pens.

- *Activity plan:* Create game cards by having children write down different kinds of friendly and unfriendly kinds of touch on small pieces of paper. Fold the papers and place them in the middle of the group. Have the children take turns selecting and reading from one of the papers. Ask the other children to "vote," by raising their hands, whether the touch is a friendly or unfriendly touch. Ask the children to explain why they voted the way they did.

- *How to adjust the activity:* Using the same cards have the children role-play responding to unfriendly touch. Encourage a variety of polite but firm ways to say, "Stop!" Role-play situations where a child communicates that friendly touch is not welcomed by saying, "I don't want to be hugged right now." Guide children to consider when a friendly touch might start feeling like an unfriendly touch, such as hugging too hard or tickling too much. Create posters that convey friendly touch is "okay" and unfriendly touch is not.

- *Did you meet your goal?:* Are children able to define friendly and unfriendly touch? Can children demonstrate that they recognize when friendly touch begins to feel like an unfriendly touch? Are children able to demonstrate when friendly touch is not wanted?

Source: Based on *Child Abuse: Teaching Touching Safety Rules*, by B. Normand, 2009, Seattle, WA: Committee for Children. Retrieved November 4, 2009, from http://www.cfchildren.org/programs/hot-topics/abuse/touchsaferules.

Protective Factors for Families

Protective factors for families include knowing about community support resources and how to access them and building positive parenting skills. Many early childhood programs, such as Head Start, have a specific commitment to supporting families through planned parent education and family service approaches. Schools may have a family social service worker who assists families to access resources that help to bolster these protective factors, but often the early childhood teacher is seen as the most accessible and trusted resource for parents. Strategies that help families develop the protective factors that reduce the potential for maltreatment include (Children's Bureau & DePanfilis, 2006):

- Arranging times to talk with families to explore and recognize their strengths and use them as the foundation for future growth.
- Guiding families to identify their needs, recognize their current network of supports and resources, and engage in problem solving about how to address challenges.
- Linking parents to available resources and providing them with access to these supports.
- Modeling and offering guidance techniques for children's challenging behaviors.
- Helping families know who to call in times of crisis.

Knowledge of the resources in the community and familiarity with the individuals who work in those settings support teachers in this role of social support provider. Building relationships with social services providers also helps the agency be receptive to referrals from the teacher. Brenda participates in a local child and family network group. This provides a chance to meet other early childhood teachers and family services workers and to talk about community, child, and family needs. The *Nutrition Note* describes an example where collaboration with a local dietitian helps families develop protective factors, and a situation of potential medical neglect is resolved.

Nutrition Note

Community Partners Help Develop Protective Factors

Teachers play an important role in linking families to community support agencies. Programs such as the Women, Infants, and Children (WIC) program can help families access food and support them to address a child's special nutritional needs. For example, a child with an iron deficiency is at risk for poor growth and learning challenges. A parent who offers the child a vegetarian diet may not be aware of the growing child's need for an iron-rich diet, resulting in anemia. WIC dietitians teach the parent how to offer a diet that will address the child's need for iron-rich foods. This knowledge builds protective factors that reduce the potential for medical neglect.

Contributing to Community Abuse Prevention Efforts

Effective child abuse prevention relies on community efforts. However, sometimes energizing the public around the topic of abuse is difficult because it requires people to think about an uncomfortable subject. A lack of common understanding about the incidence and prevalence of abuse and disagreements about appropriate parenting practices can also hinder community efforts. Early childhood teachers are logical partners for such initiatives because they have knowledge and experience that equip them to speak strongly about the challenges that families face and the negative effects of maltreatment and violence.

A positive approach to child abuse prevention is often the best approach. This involves placing the focus on supporting and strengthening all families and raising healthy children (Washington Council for Prevention of Child Abuse, 2005). Successful child abuse prevention efforts focus on (Thomas, Leicht, Hughes, Madigan, & Dowell, 2003):

* Providing support programs for parents, especially first-time parents.
* Enhancing family relationships.
* Teaching parenting skills.
* Providing access to emergency care and shelter for domestic violence protection.

It is important to frame the actions of child abuse prevention as part of the many ways in which communities contribute to the positive growth and development of children, such as by providing libraries, parks, schools, and youth sports and recreation programs. Effective prevention messages must also be culturally relevant and appropriate, so that all members of the community participate in the goal to raise safe and healthy children (Fontes, 2005).

MyEducationLab

To assess your understanding of how to identify and report abuse and neglect, go to the Book Specific Resources section in the MyEducationLab for your course, select *Nutrition, Health, and Safety for Young Children*, Chapter 18 of the Study Plan, and then complete the multiple choice questions and activities.

Summary

Many young children suffer from harmful acts of abuse or the failure of families to protect them from harm. Teachers need to be aware of the different types of maltreatment and understand that the effects of abuse can be long lasting. Maltreatment is expressed through both physical and behavioral signs. Children may have visible marks, show the effects through play, or tell teachers about the abuse. Cultural differences must be considered when interpreting the signs that suggest abuse is occurring.

Teachers and others who work closely with young children are mandated to report when abuse is suspected. To prepare, teachers need to recognize the signs of maltreatment, know how to make a report, and understand their role in the protective service process.

Children are exposed to many other sources of violence that can negatively affect their ability to learn and thrive. Teachers need to be prepared with strategies to help children cope and to manage difficult behaviors.

Teachers play an important role in helping children who have witnessed violence to attain coping skills that help them to be resilient in difficult times. This is an important step in supporting children to build trust in people and the world.

Child abuse prevention efforts include hiring safe teachers who know how to appropriately nurture and care for children. In addition, teachers are important resources for their communities as they convey the importance of child abuse prevention in building safe communities and enhancing the development of healthy children.

Key Terms

Child abuse, p. 588

Child maltreatment, p. 588

Child neglect, p. 588

Emotional abuse, p. 590

Ethical responsibility, p. 601

Imaginative play, p. 609

Imitative play, p. 609

Mandatory reporters, p. 600

Neglect, p. 589

Perpetrators, p. 591

Physical abuse, p. 589

Protective factors, p. 613

Resilience, p. 610

Sexual abuse and exploitation, p. 590

Toxic stress, p. 594

Review Questions

1. Define physical abuse and neglect. Describe how these forms of maltreatment are different. Identify four examples of abuse and four of neglect.

2. Describe some of the physical and behavioral signs of maltreatment.

3. It is good practice to ensure that families understand that teachers are mandatory reporters of suspected maltreatment. How would you share this information with families in your class?

4. What are some of the types of violence that children experience? Name three and describe how they impact young children.

5. Provide three examples of ways teachers can support children in coping with the effects of violence.

Discussion Starters

1. Reflect on your own experiences as a child and perhaps as a parent. What is your philosophy of appropriate guidance and discipline? Is spanking an appropriate guidance strategy? Is it child abuse? How do your opinions match with others in your class and the definitions discussed in this chapter?

2. Most teachers find some children's styles or behaviors to be annoying and frustrating, such as clinging, crying, or whining, always having a runny nose, or demonstrating challenging and aggressive behaviors. Identify the style or behavior that you find most frustrating. What steps have you taken (or would you take) to learn how to better manage these frustrating behaviors? Talk with others about your ideas and supports that may be available.

3. Making reports of suspected abuse or neglect can be very stressful because it means that teachers must recognize when they have reasonable suspicion that maltreatment has occurred. What aspects of child maltreatment do you feel would be the most difficult to recognize? What would be the most difficult part of making a report for you? What agency would you call to make a report?

Practice Points

1. Refer to Table 18-1. Speculate about why the incidence of each form of maltreatment varies according to children's age. Discuss your reasoning with others. Test your thinking by exploring authoritative resources.

2. Spend time reviewing the children's television programming that is available in your area. What aspects of violence stand out to you? Are the characters performing the aggressive or violent acts punished for their behaviors? What lessons about violence are communicated in the programs that you reviewed? What activities would you implement in your classroom to reduce the impact of such messages?

3. Gather information about the incidence and prevalence of abuse and neglect in your community. Identify the resources that are available to support children who are victims of maltreatment and their families. What specific kinds of services are available to children and parents? Is there a cost associated with getting this help? Are there other barriers that might keep some families from benefiting?

Web Resources

American Humane Society
www.americanhumane.org/protecting-children

Child Trends
www.childtrends.org

Child Welfare Information Gateway
www.childwelfare.gov

Family Violence Prevention Fund
http://endabuse.org/userfiles/file/Children_and_Families/DomesticViolence.pdf

National Center on Shaken Baby Syndrome
www.dontshake.org

New York Society for the Prevention of Cruelty to Children
www.nyspcc.org

appendix

CACFP Meal Pattern Requirements for Infants and Children

Infant Meal Pattern
Breakfast

Birth through 3 Months	4 through 7 Months	8 through 11 Months
4-6 fluid ounces of formula[1] or breast milk[2,3]	4-8 fluid ounces of formula[1] or breast milk[2,3]; 0-3 tablespoons of infant cereal[1,4]	6-8 fluid ounces of formula[1] or breast milk[2,3]; and 2-4 tablespoons of infant cereal[1]; and 1-4 tablespoons of fruit or vegetable or both

[1]Infant formula and dry infant cereal must be iron-fortified.
[2]Breast milk or formula, or portions of both, may be served; however, it is recommended that breast milk be served in place of formula from birth through 11 months.
[3]For some breastfed infants who regularly consume less than the minimum amount of breast milk per feeding, a serving of less than the minimum amount of breast milk may be offered, with additional breast milk offered if the infant is still hungry.
[4]A serving of this component is required when the infant is developmentally ready to accept it.

Infant Meal Pattern
Lunch or Supper

Birth through 3 Months	4 through 7 Months	8 through 11 Months
4-6 fluid ounces of formula[1] or breast milk[2,3]	4-8 fluid ounces of formula[1] or breast milk[2,3]; 0-3 tablespoons of infant cereal[1,4]; and 0-3 tablespoons of fruit or vegetable or both[4]	6-8 fluid ounces of formula[1] or breast milk[2,3]; 2-4 tablespoons of infant cereal[1]; and/or 1-4 tablespoons of meat, fish, poultry, egg yolk, cooked dry beans or peas; or ½-2 ounces of cheese; or 1-4 ounces (volume) of cottage cheese; or 1-4 ounces (weight) of cheese food or cheese spread; and 1-4 tablespoons of fruit or vegetable or both

[1]Infant formula and dry infant cereal must be iron-fortified.
[2]Breast milk or formula, or portions of both, may be served; however, it is recommended that breast milk be served in place of formula from birth through 11 months.
[3]For some breastfed infants who regularly consume less than the minimum amount of breast milk per feeding, a serving of less than the minimum amount of breast milk may be offered, with additional breast milk offered if the infant is still hungry.
[4]A serving of this component is required when the infant is developmentally ready to accept it.

Source: From USDA Food and Nutrition Service Child and Adult Care Food Program at http://www.fns.usda.gov/CND/Care/ProgramBasics/Meals/Meal_Patterns.htm.

Infant Meal Pattern
Snack

Birth through 3 Months	4 through 7 Months	8 through 11 Months
4–6 fluid ounces of formula[1] or breast milk[2,3]	4–6 fluid ounces of formula[1] or breast milk[2,3]	2–4 fluid ounces of formula[1] or breast milk[2,3], or fruit juice[5]; and 0-½ bread[4,6] or 0-2 crackers[4,6]

[1]Infant formula and dry infant cereal must be iron-fortified.

[2]Breast milk or formula, or portions of both, may be served; however, it is recommended that breast milk be served in place of formula from birth through 11 months.

[3]For some breastfed infants who regularly consume less than the minimum amount of breast milk per feeding, a serving of less than the minimum amount of breast milk may be offered, with additional breast milk offered if the infant is still hungry.

[4]A serving of this component is required when the infant is developmentally ready to accept it.

[5]Fruit juice must be full strength.

[6]A serving of this component must be made from whole-grain or enriched meal or flour.

Child Meal Pattern
Breakfast

Select All Three Components for a Reimbursable Meal			
Food Components	Ages 1–2	Ages 3–5	Ages 6–12[1]
1 milk fluid milk	1/2 cup	3/4 cup	1 cup
1 fruit/vegetable juice,[2] fruit and/or vegetable	1/4 cup	1/2 cup	1/2 cup
1 grains/bread[3] bread or	1/2 slice	1/2 slice	1 slice
cornbread or biscuit or roll or muffin or	1/2 serving	1/2 serving	1 serving
cold dry cereal or	1/4 cup	1/3 cup	3/4 cup
hot cooked cereal or	1/4 cup	1/4 cup	1/2 cup
pasta or noodles or grains	1/4 cup	1/4 cup	1/2 cup

[1]Children age 12 and older may be served larger portions based on their greater food needs. They may not be served less than the minimum quantities listed in this column.

[2]Fruit or vegetable juice must be full-strength.

[3]Breads and grains must be made from whole-grain or enriched meal or flour. Cereal must be whole-grain or enriched or fortified.

Child Meal Pattern
Lunch or Supper

Select All Four Components for a Reimbursable Meal			
Food Components	Ages 1–2	Ages 3–5	Ages 6–12[1]
1 milk			
fluid milk	1/2 cup	3/4 cup	1 cup
2 fruits/vegetables			
juice,[2] fruit and/or vegetable	1/4 cup	1/2 cup	3/4 cup
1 grains/bread[3]			
bread or	1/2 slice	1/2 slice	1 slice
cornbread or biscuit or roll or muffin or	1/2 serving	1/2 serving	1 serving
cold dry cereal or	1/4 cup	1/3 cup	3/4 cup
hot cooked cereal or	1/4 cup	1/4 cup	1/2 cup
pasta or noodles or grains	1/4 cup	1/4 cup	1/2 cup
1 meat/meat alternate			
meat or poultry or fish[4] or	1 ounce	1 1/2 ounces	2 ounces
alternate protein product or	1 ounce	1 1/2 ounces	2 ounces
cheese or	1 ounce	1 1/2 ounces	2 ounces
egg or	1/2	3/4	1
cooked dry beans or peas or	1/4 cup	3/8 cup	1/2 cup
peanut or other nut or seed butters or	2 Tbsp.	3 Tbsp.	4 Tbsp.
nuts and/or seeds[5] or	1/2 ounce	3/4 ounce	1 ounce
yogurt[6]	4 ounces	6 ounces	8 ounces

[1]Children age 12 and older may be served larger portions based on their greater food needs. They may not be served less than the minimum quantities listed in this column.

[2]Fruit or vegetable juice must be full-strength.

[3]Breads and grains must be made from whole-grain or enriched meal or flour. Cereal must be whole-grain or enriched or fortified.

[4]A serving consists of the edible portion of cooked lean meat or poultry or fish.

[5]Nuts and seeds may meet only one-half of the total meat/meat alternate serving and must be combined with another meat/meat alternate to fulfill the lunch or supper requirement.

[6]Yogurt may be plain or flavored, unsweetened or sweetened.

Child Meal Pattern
Snack

Select Two of the Four Components for a Reimbursable Snack			
Food Components	**Ages 1–2**	**Ages 3–5**	**Ages 6–12[1]**
1 milk			
fluid milk	1/2 cup	1/2 cup	1 cup
1 fruit/vegetable			
juice,[2] fruit and/or vegetable	1/2 cup	1/2 cup	3/4 cup
1 grains/bread[3]			
bread or	1/2 slice	1/2 slice	1 slice
cornbread or biscuit or roll or muffin or	1/2 serving	1/2 serving	1 serving
cold dry cereal or	1/4 cup	1/3 cup	3/4 cup
hot cooked cereal or	1/4 cup	1/4 cup	1/2 cup
pasta or noodles or grains	1/4 cup	1/4 cup	1/2 cup
1 meat/meat alternate			
meat or poultry or fish[4] or	1/2 oz.	1/2 oz.	1 oz.
alternate protein product or	1/2 oz.	1/2 oz.	1 oz.
cheese or	1/2 oz.	1/2 oz.	1 oz.
egg[5] or	1/2	1/2	1/2
cooked dry beans or peas or	1/8 cup	1/8 cup	1/4 cup
peanut or other nut or seed butters or	1 Tbsp.	1 Tbsp.	2 Tbsp.
nuts and/or seeds or	1/2 oz.	1/2 oz.	1 oz.
yogurt[6]	2 oz.	2 oz.	4 oz.

[1]Children age 12 and older may be served larger portions based on their greater food needs. They may not be served less than the minimum quantities listed in this column.

[2]Fruit or vegetable juice must be full-strength Juice cannot be served when milk is the only other snack component.

[3]Breads and grains must be made from whole-grain or enriched meal or flour. Cereal must be whole-grain or enriched or fortified.

[4]A serving consists of the edible portion of cooked lean meat or poultry or fish.

[5]One-half egg meets the required minimum amount (one ounce or less) of meat alternate.

[6]Yogurt may be plain or flavored, unsweetened or sweetened.

references

Chapter 1

American Academy of Pediatrics. (2007). *Healthy Childcare America*. Retrieved September 13, 2009, from http://www.healthychildcare.org/about.html

American Academy of Pediatrics, American Public Health Association, & National Resource Center for Health and Safety in Child Care and Early Education. (2002). *National health and safety performance standards: Guidelines for out-of-home child care programs* (2nd ed.). Elk Grove Village, IL: American Academy of Pediatrics; Washington, DC: American Public Health Association. Retrieved August 31, 2009, from http://www.eric.ed.gov/ERICDocs/data/ericdocs2sql/content_storage_01/0000019b/80/14/0d/14.pdf

American Dietetic Association. (2005, June 8). *MyPyramid.gov: Steps to a healthier you*. Retrieved September 1, 2009, from http://www.webdietitians.org/cps/rde/xchg/ada/hs.xsl/home_4259_ENU_HTML.htm

American Psychological Association. (2009). *APA Task Force on Psychology's agenda for child and adolescent mental health: Promoting awareness of children's mental health issues*. Retrieved March 2009 from http://www.apa.org/ppo/issues/tfpacmi.html

Barker, D. J. P. (2004). The developmental origins of adult disease. *Journal of the American College of Nutrition, 23*(Suppl. 6), 588S–595S.

Blankenau, J. (2009, January). *Nutrition, physical activity, and obesity in rural America* (No. 1). Lyons, NE: Center for Rural Affairs. Retrieved August 31, 2009, from http://files.cfra.org/pdf/Nutrition-Physical-Activity-and-Obesity-in-Rural-America.pdf

Bronfenbrenner, U. (1979). *The ecology of human development: Experiments by nature and design*. Cambridge, MA: Harvard University Press.

Bronte-Tinkew, J., Zaslow, M., Capps, R., & Horowitz, A. (2007). *Food insecurity and overweight among infants and toddlers: New insights into a troubling linkage*. Retrieved December 2008 from http://www.childtrends.org/Files//Child_Trends-2007_07_11_RB_FoodInsecurity.pdf

Butte, N., Cobb, K., Dwyer, J., Graney, L., Heird, W., & Rickard, K. (2004). The start healthy feeding guidelines for infants and toddlers. *Journal of the American Dietetic Association, 104*, 442–454.

Centers for Disease Control and Prevention. (2007). QuickStats: Percentage of persons with untreated dental carries by age group and poverty status—National Health and Nutrition Examination Survey (NHANES), United States, 2001-4. *Morbidity and Mortality Weekly Report, 56*(34), 889.

Centers for Disease Control and Prevention. (2008). *Obesity and overweight: Childhood overweight: Contributing factors*. Retrieved December 10, 2008, from http://www.cdc.gov/nccdphp/dnpa/obesity/childhood/contributing_factors.htm

Centers for Disease Control and Prevention. (2009). *Vaccines and immunizations: Maps/figures 2007—Estimated coverage by state*. Retrieved September 1, 2009, from http://www.cdc.gov/vaccines/stats-surv/nis/figures/0708_map.htm

Cherry, D. C., Huggins, B., & Gilmore, K. (2007). Children's health in the rural environment. *Pediatric Clinics of North America, 54*(1), ix, 121–133.

Child Trends & Center for Child Health Research. (2004, September). *Early childhood development in social context: A chartbook*. Retrieved September 1, 2009, from http://www.childtrends.org/Files//Child_Trends-2004_09_01_ES_Chartbook.pdf

Cohen, E., & Kaufmann, R. (2005). *Early childhood mental health consultation* (DHHS Pub. No. CMHS-SVP0151). Rockville, MD: Center for Mental Health Services, Substance Abuse and Mental Health Services Administration.

Council on Sports Medicine and Fitness & Council on School Health. (2006). Active healthy living: Prevention of childhood obesity through increased physical activity. *Pediatrics, 117*(5), 1834–1842.

Cutfield, W. S., Hofman, P. L., Mitchell, M., & Morison, I. M. (2007). Could epigenetics play a role in the developmental origins of health and disease? *Pediatric Research, 61*(5, Pt. 2), 68R–75R.

Decker, W. W., Campbell, R. L., Manivannan, V., Anuradha, L. A., St. Sauver, J. L., Weaver, A., et al. (2008). The etiology and incidence of anaphylaxis in Rochester, Minnesota: A report from the Rochester Epidemiology Project. *Journal of Allergy & Clinical Immunology, 122*(6), 1161–1165.

Dey, A. N. & Bloom, B. (2005). Summary health statistics for U.S. children: National Health Interview Survey, 2003. National Center for Health Statistics, Vital health Stat *10*(223). Retrieved September 13, 2009, from: http://www.cdc.gov/nchs/data/series/sr_10/sr10_223.pdf

Dolinoy, D. C., Das, R., Weidman, J. R., & Jirtle, R. L. (2007). Metastable epialleles, imprinting, and the fetal origins of adult diseases. *Pediatric Research, 61*(5, Pt. 2), 30R–37R.

Douglas-Hall, A., & Chau, M. (2008). *Basic facts about low-income children: Birth to age 6*. Retrieved December 2008 from http://www.nccp.org/publications/pub_847.html

Federal Interagency Forum on Child and Family Statistics. (2008). *America's children in brief: Key national indicators of well-being, 2008*. Retrieved August 31, 2009, from http://www.childstats.gov/americaschildren08/index.asp

Federal Interagency Forum on Child and Family Statistics. (2009). *FAM3.A: Child care: Primary child care arrangements for children ages 0-4 with employed mothers by selected characteristics, selected years 1985-2005 and Summer 2006*. Retrieved August 31, 2009, from http://www.childstats.gov/americaschildren/tables/fam3a.asp

Fine, A., & Hicks, M. (2008, November). *Health matters: The role of health and the health sector in place-based initiatives for young children*. Retrieved September 1, 2009, from http://www.wkkf.org/DesktopModules/WKF.00_DmaSupport/ViewDoc.aspx?LanguageID=0&CID=1&ListID=28&ItemID=5000555&fld=PDFFile

Folton, G. I. (1995). Critical issues in urban emergency medical services for children. *Pediatrics, 96*(2), 174–179.

Fontaine, K. R., Redden, D. T., Wang, C., Westfall, A. O., & Allison, D. B. (2003). Years of life lost due to obesity. *Journal of the American Medical Association, 289*(2), 187–193.

Gluckman, P. D., Hanson, M. A., & Pinal, C. (2005). The developmental origins of adult disease. *Maternal & Child Nutrition, 1*(3), 130–141.

Hallam, M. K. (2009). Another piece of the language learning puzzle: Why teacher dispositions are crucial to student success. *The Language Educator*, pp. 26–29. Retrieved March 2009 from http://www.actfl.org/files/TLE_Jan09_Article.pdf

Hawley, T. (2000). *Starting smart: How early experiences influence brain development*. Retrieved December 2008 from http://www.zerotothree.org/site/DocServer/startingsmart.pdf?docID=2422

Joens-Matre, R. R., Welk, G. J., Calabro, M. A., Russell, D. W., Nicklay, E., & Hensley, L. D. (2008). Rural-urban differences in physical activity, physical fitness, and overweight prevalence of children. *Journal of Rural Health, 24*(1), 49–54.

Kaput, J. (2004). Diet-disease gene interactions. *Nutrition, 20*(1), 26–31.

Kaput, J. (2008). Nutrigenomics research for personalized nutrition and medicine. *Current Opinion in Biotechnology, 19*(2), 110–120.

Kauwell, G. P. (2008). Epigenetics: What it is and how it can affect dietetics practice. *Journal of the American Dietetic Association, 108*(6), 1056–1059.

Kindler, A. L. (2002). *Survey of the states' limited English proficient students and available educational programs and services: 2000-2001 summary report*. Retrieved August 27, 2009, from http://www.ncela.gwu.edu/files/rcd/BE021853/Survey_of_the_States.pdf

Liu, J., Bennett, K. J., Harun, N., & Probst, J. C. (2008). Urban-rural differences in overweight status and physical inactivity among U.S. children aged 10-17 years. *Journal of Rural Health, 24*(4), 407-415.

Massachusetts Institute of Technology. (2006). *Researchers provide first evidence for learning mechanism in brain.* Retrieved March 22, 2009, from http://www.sciencedaily.com/releases/2006/08/060824222608.htm

National Association for the Education of Young Children. (2005). *Code of ethical conduct and statement of commitment.* Retrieved August 31, 2009, from http://www.naeyc.org/positionstatements/ethical_conduct

National Association for the Education of Young Children. (2009a). *Developmentally appropriate practices.* Retrieved August 31, 2009, from http://www.naeyc.org/DAP

National Association for the Education of Young Children. (2009b). *NAEYC Radio presents . . . Why playful learning is more effective.* Retrieved August 31, 2009, from http://www.naeyc.org/newsroom/pressreleases/20090609

No Child Left Behind. (2001). *No Child Left Behind Act; Public Law 107-100.* Retrieved August 31, 2009, from http://www.ed.gov/policy/elsec/leg/esea02/107-110.pdf

Nord, M., Andrews, M., & Carlson, S. (2004). *Household food security in the United States, 2003* (Food Assistance and Nutrition Research Report No. FANRR42). Washington, DC: U.S. Department of Agriculture, Economic Research Service.

Office of the Surgeon General. (2000, May). *Oral health in America: A report of the surgeon general* (pp. 10-11). Rockville, MD: Author. Retrieved August 27, 2009, from http://www.surgeongeneral.gov/library/oralhealth/index.html

Ogden, C. L., Carroll, M. D., Curtin, L. R., McDowell, M. A., Tabak, C. J., & Flegal, K. M. (2006). Prevalence of overweight and obesity in the United States, 1999-2004. *Journal of the American Medical Association, 295*(13), 1549-1555.

Ogden, C. L., Carroll, M. D., & Flegal, K. M. (2008). High body mass index for age among U.S. children and adolescents, 2003-2006. *Journal of the American Medical Association, 299*(20), 2401.

Oken, E., Taveras, E. M., Kleinman, K. P., Rich-Edwards, J. W., & Gillman, M. W. (2007). Gestational weight gain and child adiposity at age 3 years. *American Journal of Obstetrics and Gynecology, 196*(4), 322.e1-322.e8.

Olshansky, S. J., Passaro, D. J., Hershow, R. C., Layden, J., Carnes, B. A., Brody, J., et al. (2005). A potential decline in life expectancy in the United States in the 21st century. *New England Journal of Medicine, 352*(11), 1138-1145.

Oregon Environmental Council. (2009). *Eco-healthy child care checklist.* Retrieved September 1, 2009, from http://www.oeconline.org/resources/publications/kitsandtipsarchive/2007EHCCChecklist

Otten, J. J., Pitzi-Hellwig, J., & Meyers, L. D. (Eds.). (2006). *Dietary reference intakes, the essential guide to nutrient requirements.* Washington, DC: National Academies Press.

Partnership for 21st Century Skills. (2004). Retrieved September 14, 2009, at http://www.21stcenturyskills.org/index.php?Itemid=183&id=195&option=com_content&task=view

Poulter, M. O., Du, L., Weaver, I. C. G., Palkovits, M., Faludi, G., Merali, Z. S., et al. (2008). GABAA receptor promoter hypermethylation in suicide brain: Implications for the involvement of epigenetic processes. *Biological Psychiatry, 64*(8), 645-652.

Rodenhiser, D., & Mann, M. (2006). Epigenetics and human disease: Translating basic biology into clinical applications. *Canadian Medical Association Journal, 174*(3), 341-348.

Sentencing Project. (2009, February). *Incarcerated parents and their children: Trends 1991-2007.* Retrieved August 31, 2009, from http://www.sentencingproject.org/doc/publications/publications/inc_incarceratedparents.pdf

Sigman-Grant, M., Christiansen, E., Branen, L., Fletcher, J., & Johnson, S. L. (2008). About feeding children: Mealtimes in child-care centers in four western states. *Journal of the American Dietetic Association, 108*(2), 340.

Sorte, J. M., & Daeschel, I. (2006). Health in action: A program approach to fighting obesity in young children. *Young Children, 61*(3), 40-48.

Strain, P. S., & Dunlap, G. D. (2006). *Recommended practices: Being an evidence-based practitioner.* Center for Evidence-Based Practices: Young Children with Challenging Behavior. Retrieved September 1, 2009, from http://challengingbehavior.org/do/resources/documents/rph_practitioner.pdf

U.S. Department of Agriculture. (2008). *MyPyramid.gov: Inside the pyramid.* Retrieved August 31, 2009, from http://www.pyramid.gov/pyramid/index.html

U.S. Department of Health and Human Services. (2000). *Healthy people 2010* (2nd ed., 2 vols.). Washington, DC: Author. Retrieved August 31, 2009, from http://www.healthypeople.gov/Publications

U.S. Department of Health and Human Services. (2003, April 29). *National call to action to promote oral health* (NIH Publication 03-5303). Rockville, MD: U.S. Department of Health and Human Services, National Institutes of Health, National Institute of Dental and Craniofacial Research. Retrieved August 31, 2009, from http://www.cdha.org/downloads/NationalCallToAction.pdf

U.S. Department of Health and Human Services. (2008). *Healthy people 2020: The road ahead.* Retrieved March 2009 from http://www.healthypeople.gov/hp2020/

U.S. Department of Health and Human Services, Health Resources and Services Administration, Maternal and Child Health Bureau. (2005). *The national survey of children's health 2003.* Rockville, MD: U.S. Department of Health and Human Services. Retrieved January 2, 2010 from http://www.cdc.gov/nchs/slaits/nsch.htm

U.S. Department of Health and Human Services and U.S. Department of Agriculture. (2005). *Dietary guidelines for Americans, 2005.* Washington, DC: Authors. Retrieved September 1, 2009, from http://www.health.gov/dietaryguidelines/dga2005/document/pdf/DGA2005.pdf

U.S. Department of Labor, Bureau of Labor Statistics. (2006). *Employment characteristics of families in 2005: Table 5. Employment status of the population by sex, marital status, and presence and age of own children under 18, 2004-05 annual averages.* Retrieved August 31, 2009, from http://www.bls.gov/news.release/archives/famee_04272006.pdf

U.S. Department of Labor, Bureau of Labor Statistics. (2008). *Table 7. Employment status of women by presence and age of youngest child, March 1975-2007.* Retrieved March 12, 2009, from http://www.bls.gov/cps/wlf-table7-2008.pdf

World Health Organization. (2009). *Global strategy on diet, physical activity and health. Physical inactivity: A global health problem.* Retrieved July 2009 from http://www.who.int/dietphysicalactivity/factsheet_inactivity/en/index.html

Chapter 2

Alemango, S., Niles, S., Shafer-King, P., & Miller, W. (2008). Promoting health and preventing injury among preschool children: The role of parenting stress. *Early Childhood Research & Practice, 10,* 2.

American Academy of Pediatrics. (2007, April). *Healthy Child Care America: Health and safety E-news for caregivers and teachers.* Retrieved August 27, 2009, from http://www.healthychildcare.org/ENewsApr07.html

American Academy of Pediatrics, Committee on Early Childhood, Adoption, and Dependent Care. (2005). Policy statement: Quality early education and child care from birth to kindergarten. *Pediatrics, 115*(1), 187-191.

American Academy of Pediatrics, American Public Health Association, & National Resource Center for Health and Safety in Child Care and Early Education. (2002). *National health and safety performance standards: Guidelines for out-of-home child care programs* (2nd ed.). Elk Grove Village, IL: American Academy of Pediatrics; Washington, DC: American Public Health Association. Retrieved August 31, 2009, from http://www.eric.ed.gov/ERICDocs/data/ericdocs2sql/content_storage_01/0000019b/80/14/0d/14.pdf

Aronson, S. S. (Ed.). (2002). Child care health consultants and trainers (pp. 114-117). In *Healthy young children: A manual for programs* (4th ed.). Washington, DC: NAEYC. Retrieved August 27, 2009, from http://www.journal.naeyc.org/btj/200403/ HealthConsultants.pdf

Bowman, B. T., Donovan, S., & Burns, M. S. (Eds.). (2000). *Eager to learn: Educating our preschoolers.* Washington, DC: National Academies Press.

Bruner, J. (1966). *Toward a theory of instruction.* Cambridge, MA: Harvard University Press.

California Childcare Health Program. (2006). *Social and emotional development of children*. San Francisco: University of California, San Francisco School of Nursing.

Center on the Developing Child. (2007). *A science-based framework for early childhood policy: Using evidence to improve outcomes in learning, behavior, and health for vulnerable children*. Retrieved August 27, 2009, from http://www.developingchild.harvard.edu/content/downloads/Policy_Framework.pdf

Goodway, J., & Robinson, L. (2006, May). SKIPing toward an active start: Promoting physical activity in preschoolers. *Beyond the Journal: Young Children on the Web*. Retrieved September 13, 2009, from http://journal.naeyc.org/btj/200605/GoodwayBTJ.pdf

Hassink, S. (Ed.). (2006). *A parent's guide to childhood obesity: A road map to health*. Elk Grove, IL: American Academy of Pediatrics.

Howes, C., Burchinal, M., Pianta, R., Bryant, D., Early, D., Clifford, R., et al. (2008). Ready to learn? Children's pre-academic achievement in pre-kindergarten programs. *Early Childhood Research Quarterly, 23*(3), 27-50.

Huffman, C. (2006, July). Supportive care for infants and toddlers with special health care needs. *Beyond the Journal: Young Children on the Web*. Retrieved September 2, 2009, from http://www.journal.naeyc.org/btj/200607/Huffman706BTJ.pdf

Mester, J. (2008). Creatively constructing a community of learners. *Early Childhood Research & Practice, 10*, 1.

National Association for the Education of Young Children. (1999). *Working together to keep children healthy*. Retrieved August 27, 2009, from http://www.naeyc.org/ece/1999/14.asp

National Association for the Education of Young Children. (2004). *Where we stand: Early learning standards*. Retrieved March 2009 from http://naeyc.org/about/positions/pdf/elstandardsstand.pdf

National Association for the Education of Young Children. (2005). *Where we stand: Many languages, many cultures: Respecting and responding to diversity*. Retrieved March 2009 from http://naeyc.org/about/positions/pdf/diversity.pdf

National Association for the Education of Young Children. (2009). *Developmentally appropriate practices*. Retrieved September 2, 2009, from http://www.naeyc.org/DAP

National Association for the Education of Young Children & National Association of Early Childhood Specialists in State Departments of Education. (2002). *Early learning standards: Creating the conditions for success*. Retrieved March 2009 from http://naeyc.org/about/positions/pdf/position_statement.pdf

National Scientific Council on the Developing Child. (2006). *Perspectives: Rich experiences, physical activity creates healthy brains*. Cambridge, MA: Center on the Developing Child, Harvard University. Retrieved September 2, 2009, from http://www.developingchild.net/pubs/persp/pdf/Physical_Activity_Create_Healthy_Brains.pdf

National Scientific Council on the Developing Child. (2007). *The science of early childhood development*. Cambridge, MA: Center on the Developing Child, Harvard University.

Retrieved September 1, 2009, from http://www.developingchild.net/pubs/persp/pdf/Science_Early_Childhood_Development.pdf

O'Connor, J. (1999). New children's health insurance program: Early childhood professional outreach efforts can make a difference. *Young Children, 54*(2), 63-65.

Piaget, J. (1929). *The child's conception of the world*. New York: Harcourt, Brace Jovanovich.

Sahn, L. S., & Reichel, A. G. (2008, March). Read all about it! A classroom newspaper integrates the curriculum. *Young Children, 63*(2), 12-18.

Schickedanz, J. A. (2008). *Increasing the power of instruction: Integration of language, literacy, and math across the preschool day*. Washington, DC: National Association for the Education of Young Children.

Shonkoff, J. P., & Phillips, D. A. (Eds.). (2000). *From neurons to neighborhoods: The science of early childhood development*. Washington, DC: National Academy Press.

Sorte, J. M., & Daeschel, I. (2006). Health in action: A program approach to fighting obesity in young children. *Young Children, 61*(3), 40-48.

U.S. Department of Education. (2007). *History: Twenty-five years of progress in educating children with disabilities through IDEA*. Retrieved July 2009, from http://www.ed.gov/policy/speced/leg/idea/history.html

U.S. Department of Education. (2009). *Building the legacy: IDEA 2004*. Retrieved August 27, 2009, from http://idea.ed.gov

Vygotsky, L. S. (1962). *Thought and language*. Cambridge, MA: MIT Press.

Vygotsky, L. S. (1978). *Mind in society: The development of higher psychological processes*. Cambridge, MA: Harvard University Press.

Wesson, K. A. (2003, November). *Early brain development and learning*. Retrieved September 3, 2009, from http://www.sciencemaster.com/columns/wesson/wesson_early_01.php

Chapter 3

American Academy of Pediatrics Committee on Nutrition. (2003). Policy statement: Prevention of pediatric overweight and obesity. *Pediatrics, 112*(2), 424-430.

American Academy of Pediatrics Committee on Nutrition. (2009). In Kleinman, R. (Ed.), *Pediatric nutrition handbook* (6th ed.). Elk Grove, IL: American Academy of Pediatrics.

American Dietetic Association. (2005a). Position of the American Dietetic Association: Fortification and nutritional supplements. *Journal of the American Dietetic Association, 105*(8), 1300-1311.

American Dietetic Association. (2005b). Position paper: Benchmarks for nutrition programs in child care settings. *Journal of the American Dietetic Association, 105*(6), 979-986.

American Dietetic Association. (2006). Position of the American Dietetic Association: Individual-, family-, school-, and community-based interventions for pediatric overweight. *Journal of the American Dietetic Association, 106*(6), 925-945.

American Dietetic Association. (2008). Position of the American Dietetic Association: Nutrition guidance for healthy children ages

2 to 11 years. *Journal of the American Dietetic Association, 108* (6), 1038-1047.

Barker, D. J. P. (2004). The developmental origins of adult disease. *Journal of the American College of Nutrition, 23*(Suppl. 6), 588S-595S.

Beard, J. L. (2008). Why iron deficiency is important in infant development. *Journal of Nutrition, 138*(12), 2534-2536.

Block, R. W., Krebs, N. F., Committee on Child Abuse and Neglect, & Committee on Nutrition. (2005). Failure to thrive as a manifestation of child neglect. *Pediatrics, 116*(5), 1234-1237.

Brotanek, J. M., Gosz, J., Weitzman, M., & Flores, G. (2007). Iron deficiency in early childhood in the United States: Risk factors and racial/ethnic disparities. *Pediatrics, 120*(3), 568-575.

Brotanek, J. M., Gosz, J., Weitzman, M., & Flores, G. (2008). Secular trends in the prevalence of iron deficiency among U.S. toddlers, 1976-2002. *Archives of Pediatric Adolescent Medicine, 162*(4), 374-381.

Brotanek, J. M., Halterman, J. S., Auinger, P., Flores, G., & Weitzman, M. (2005). Iron deficiency, prolonged bottle-feeding, and racial/ethnic disparities in young children. *Archives of Pediatrics and Adolescent Medicine, 159*(11), 1038-1042.

Butte, N., Cobb, K., Dwyer, J., Graney, L., Heird, W., & Rickard, K. (2004). The Start Healthy feeding guidelines for infants and toddlers. *Journal of the American Dietetic Association, 104*, 442-454.

California WIC Association. (2008). *New WIC foods: WIConnect*. Retrieved February 19, 2009, from http://www.calwic.org/new-food.aspx

Casey, P. H., Simpson, P. M., Gossett, J. M., Bogle, M. L., Champagne, C. M., Connell, C., et al. (2006). The association of child and household food insecurity with childhood overweight status. *Pediatrics, 118*(5), e1406-1413.

Centers for Disease Control and Prevention. (2009, January 27). *Healthy weight: Assessing your weight: About BMI for children and teens*. Retrieved September 8, 2009, from http://www.cdc.gov/healthyweight/assessing/bmi/childrens_bmi/about_childrens_bmi.html

Centers for Disease Control and Prevention, National Center for Health Statistics. (2007a). *2000 CDC growth charts*. Retrieved May 22, 2007, from http://www.cdc.gov/growthcharts

Centers for Disease Control and Prevention, National Center for Health Statistics. (2007b). *NHA NES United States growth charts—background information*. Retrieved May 26, 2007, from http://www.cdc.gov/nchs/about/major/nhanes/growthcharts/background.htm

Childhood Obesity Action Network. (2008). *State obesity profiles*. National Initiative for Children's Healthcare Quality, Child Policy Research Center, and Child and Adolescent Health Measurement Initiative. Retrieved March 20, 2009, from http://www.childhealthdata.org/content/ObesityReportCards.aspx

Coleman, K. J., Geller, K. S., Rosenkranz, R. R., & Dzewaltowski, D. A. (2008). Physical activity and healthy eating in the after-school environment. *Journal of School Health, 78*(12), 633-640.

Committee on Nutrition Standards for National School Lunch and Breakfast Programs Food and Nutrition Board. (2008). *Nutrition standards and meal requirements for national school lunch and breakfast programs: Phase I proposed approach for recommending revisions,* Stallings, V.A, Taylor, C.L. (Ed.), Washington, DC: Institute of Medicine of the National Academies, the National Academies Press. Retrieved January 14, 2010, from http://www.nap.edu/openbook.php?record_id=12512&page=R1

Committee on the Use of Dietary Reference Intakes in Nutrition Labeling. (2003). *Dietary Reference Intakes: Guiding principles for nutrition labeling and fortification.* Washington, DC: National Academies Press.

Darmon, N., Ferguson, E. L., & Briend, A. (2002). A cost constraint alone has adverse effects on food selection and nutrient density: An analysis of human diets by linear programming. *Journal of Nutrition, 132*(12), 3764-3771.

Dietz, W. H. (1995). Does hunger cause obesity? *Pediatrics, 95*(5), 766-767.

Dietz, W. H. (1998). Health consequences of obesity in youth: Childhood predictors of adult disease. *Pediatrics, 101*(3), 518-525. doi:10.1542/peds.101.3.S1.518

Dolinoy, D. C., & Jirtle, R. L. (2008). Environmental epigenomics in human health and disease. *Environmental and Molecular Mutagenesis, 49*(1), 4-8.

Drewnowski, A., & Darmon, N. (2005). The economics of obesity: Dietary energy density and energy cost. *American Journal of Clinical Nutrition, 82*(1), 265S-273S.

Drewnowski, A., & Specter, S. E. (2004). Poverty and obesity: The role of energy density and energy costs. *American Journal of Clinical Nutrition, 79*(1), 6-16.

Duyff, R. L. (2006). *The American Dietetic Association complete food and nutrition guide* (3rd ed.). Hoboken, NJ: John Wiley & Sons.

Finn, K., Johannsen, N., & Specker, B. (2002). Factors associated with physical activity in preschool children. *Journal of Pediatrics, 140*(1), 81.

Flegal, K. M., Graubard, B. I., Williamson, D. F., & Gail, M. H. (2005). Excess deaths associated with underweight, overweight, and obesity. *Journal of the American Medical Association, 293*(15), 1861-1867.

Fontaine, K. R., Redden, D. T., Wang, C., Westfall, A. O., & Allison, D. B. (2003). Years of life lost due to obesity. *Journal of the American Medical Association, 289*(2), 187-193.

Georgia State University. (2004). *New education for new Americans project: Multicultural nutrition and diabetic handouts.* Retrieved May 29, 2007, from http://monarch.gsu.edu/multiculturalhealth

Gluckman, P. D., Hanson, M. A., & Pinal, C. (2005). The developmental origins of adult disease. *Maternal & Child Nutrition, 1*(3), 130-141.

Gordon, A. R., Crepinsek, M., Ronette, R. B., & Clark, M. (2009). The third school nutrition dietary assessment study: Summary and implications. *Journal of the American Dietetic Association, 109*(2), S129.

Halterman, J. S., Kaczorowski, J. M., Aligne, C. A., Auinger, P., & Szilagyi, P. G. (2001). Iron deficiency and cognitive achievement among school-aged children and adolescents in the United States. *Pediatrics, 107*(6), 1381-1386.

Health Canada. (2008). *Canada's food guide.* Retrieved February 23, 2009, from http://www.hc-sc.gc.ca/fn-an/food-guide-aliment/order-commander/index-eng.php

Hughes, S. O., Patrick, H., Power, T. G., Fisher, J. O., Anderson, C. B., & Nicklas, T. A. (2007). The impact of child care providers' feeding on children's food consumption. *Journal of Developmental and Behavioral Pediatrics, 28*(2), 100-107.

Innis, S. M. (2007). Dietary (n-3) fatty acids and brain development. *Journal of Nutrition, 137*(4), 855-859.

Jarratt, J., & Mahaffie, J. B. (2007). The profession of dietetics at a critical juncture: A report on the 2006 environmental scan for the American Dietetic Association. *Journal of the American Dietetic Association, 107*(7), S39.

Kurtzweil, P. (1995, March). Labeling rules for young children's foods. *FDA Consumer Magazine , 29*(2) 14-18.

Lozoff, B., Jimenez, E., Hagen, J., Mollen, E., & Wolf, A. W. (2000). Poorer behavioral and developmental outcome more than 10 years after treatment for iron deficiency in infancy. *Pediatrics, 105*(4), e51.

Mayer-Davis, E. J., Rifas-Shiman, S. L., Zhou, L., Hu, F. B., Colditz, G. A., & Gillman, M. W. (2006). Breast-feeding and risk for childhood obesity: Does maternal diabetes or obesity status matter? *Diabetes Care, 29*(10), 2231-2237.

Mayo Clinic. (2007). *Lead poisoning: Prevention.* Retrieved February 27, 2009, from http://www.mayoclinic.com/health/lead-poisoning/FL00068/DSECTION=prevention

Mayo Clinic. (2008). *Multivitamins: Do young children need them?* Retrieved March 18, 2009, from http://www.mayoclinic.com/health/multivitamins/AN01406

McDonald's Corporation. (2009, January 26). *McDonald's delivers another year of strong results in 2008* [Press release]. Retrieved February 7, 2009, from http://www.mcdonalds.com/corp/news/fnpr/2009/fpr_012609.html

Mehta, N. K., & Chang, V. W. (2008). Weight status and restaurant availability: A multi-level analysis. *American Journal of Preventive Medicine, 34*(2), 127-133.

Meinke, M. (2009). *Think what you drink.* Lincoln: University of Nebraska–Lincoln Extension in Lancaster County. Retrieved September 7, 2009, from http://lancaster.unl.edu/NEP/thinkdrink.shtml

Meyer-Davis, E. (2008). Type 2 diabetes in youth: Epidemiology and current research toward prevention and treatment. *Journal of the American Dietetic Association, 108*(4), S45-S51.

National Association for Sport and Physical Education. (2009). *NASPE sets the standards.* Retrieved August 9, 2009, from http://www.aahperd.org/naspe/template.cfm?template=ns_index.html

Nead, K. G., Halterman, J. S., Kaczorowski, J. M., Auinger, P. Y., & Weitzman, M. (2004). Overweight children and adolescents: A risk group for iron deficiency. *Pediatrics, 114*(1), 104-108.

Nevin-Folino, N. L. (2008). *Pediatric manual of clinical dietetics* (2nd ed. update). Chicago: American Dietetic Association.

Office of Dietary Supplements, National Institutes of Health. (2007). *Dietary supplement fact sheet: Iron.* Retrieved March 18, 2009, from http://ods.od.nih.gov/factsheets/iron.asp

Olshansky, S. J., Passaro, D. J., Hershow, R. C., Layden, J., Carnes, B. A., Brody, J., et al. (2005). A potential decline in life expectancy in the United States in the 21st century. *New England Journal of Medicine, 352*(11), 1138-1145.

Otten, J. J., Pitzi-Hellwig, J., & Meyers, L. D. (Eds.). (2006). *Dietary Reference Intakes: The essential guide to nutrient requirements.* Washington, DC: National Academies Press.

Painter, J. R., & Lee, Y. K. (2002). Comparison of international food guide pictorial representations. *Journal of the American Dietetic Association, 102*(4), 483-489.

Pearse, A. J., & Mitchell, M. C. (n.d.). *Nutrition and childhood lead poisoning (HYG-5536-93).* Columbus: Ohio State University Extension. Retrieved September 8, 2009, from http://ohioline.osu.edu/hyg-fact/5000/5536.html

Pereira, M. A., Kartashov, A. I., Ebbeling, C. B., Van Horn, L., Slattery, M. L., Jacobs, D. R., Jr., et al. (2005). Fast-food habits, weight gain, and insulin resistance (the CARDIA study): 15-year prospective analysis. *Lancet, 365*(9453), 36-42.

Pettifor, J. M. (2004). Nutritional rickets: Deficiency of vitamin D, calcium, or both? *American Journal of Clinical Nutrition, 80*(6), 1725S-1729S.

Pinhas-Hamiel, O., Newfield, R. S., Koren, I., Agmon, A., Lilos, P., & Phillip, M. (2003). Greater prevalence of iron deficiency in overweight and obese children and adolescents. *International Journal of Obesity and Related Metabolic Disorders, 27*(3), 416-418.

Porth, C. (2007). *Essentials of pathophysiology: Concepts of altered health states.* Philadelphia: Lippincott Williams & Wilkins.

Satter, E. (2000). *Child of mine, feeding with love and good sense.* Berkeley, CA: Bull Publishing Company.

Scholtens, S., Brunekreef, B., Smit, H. A., Gast, G. C., Hoekstra, M. O., de Jongste, J. C., et al. (2008). Do differences in childhood diet explain the reduced overweight risk in breastfed children? *Obesity, 16*(11), 2498-2503.

Schwimmer, J. B., Burwinkle, T. M., & Varni, J. W. (2003). Health-related quality of life of severely obese children and adolescents. *Journal of the American Medical Association, 289*(14), 1813-1819.

Skalicky, A., Meyers, A., Adams, W., Yang, Z., Cook, J., & Frank, D. (2006). Child food insecurity and iron deficiency anemia in low-income infants and toddlers in the United

States. *Maternal & Child Health Journal, 10*(2), 177-185.

Sloan, A. E. (2008). What, when, and where America eats. *Food Technology, 62*(1), 20.

Sloan, A. E. (2009). The new super segments. *Food Technology, 63*(1), 22.

Southeastern Michigan Dietetic Association. (n.d.). *General nutrition information: Cultural food pyramids/Complementary nutrition archives.* Retrieved September 8, 2009, from http://www.semda.org/info

Spear, B. (2006). The need for family meals. *Journal of the American Dietetic Association, 106*(2), 218-219.

Story, M. (2009). The third school nutrition dietary assessment study: Findings and policy implications for improving the health of U.S. children. *Journal of the American Dietetic Association, 109*(2), S7.

Story, M., Kaphingst, K., & French, S. (2006). The role of child care settings in obesity prevention. *The Future of Children, 16*(1), 143-168.

Sweltzer, S. J., Briley, M. E., & Robert-Grey, C. (2009). Do sack lunches provided by parents meet the nutritional needs of young children who attend child care? *Journal of the American Dietetic Association, 109*(1), 141-144.

Thomas, D. R. (2007). *Undernutrition: Disorders of nutrition and metabolism.* Retrieved March 14, 2009, from http://www.merck.com/mmhe/sec12/ch153/ch153a.html

Uauy, R., & Castillo, C. (2003). Lipid requirements of infants: Implications for nutrient composition of fortified complementary foods. *Journal of Nutrition, 133*(9), 2962S-2972S.

University of California Cooperative Extension, San Luis Obispo County. (2007). *Lunch box handouts—Nutrition, family, and consumer sciences.* Retrieved February 12, 2009, from http://cesanluisobispo.ucdavis.edu/Nutrition,_Family_and_Consumer_Science208/Lunch_Box_Handouts.htm

U.S. Department of Agriculture. (2005). *MyPyramid for kids.* Retrieved June 19, 2008, from http://www.mypyramid.gov/kids/index.html

U.S. Department of Agriculture. (2009a). *Ethnic/cultural food guide pyramid: Dietary guidance: Food and nutrition information center.* Retrieved February 21, 2009, from http://fnic.nal.usda.gov/nal_display/index.php?info_center=4&tax_level=3&tax_subject=256&topic_id=1348&level3_id=5732

U.S. Department of Agriculture. (2009b). *MyPyramid for preschoolers.* Retrieved July 6, 2009, from http://www.mypyramid.gov/Preschoolers

U.S. Department of Agriculture. (2009c). *MyPyramid.gov for professionals.* Retrieved February 22, 2009, from http://www.mypyramid.gov/professionals/pdf_framework.html

U.S. Department of Agriculture. (2009d). *MyPyramid.gov: Steps to a healthier you.* Retrieved September 7, 2009, from http://www.mypyramid.gov/downloads/resource/MyPyramidBrochurebyIFIC.pdf

U.S. Department of Agriculture, Center for Nutrition Policy and Promotion. (2008). *Diet quality of low-income and higher income Americans in 2003-2004 as measured by the healthy eating index-2005.* USDA Nutrition Insight 42. Retrieved September 7, 2009, from http://www.cnpp.usda.gov/Publications/NutritionInsights/Insight42.pdf

U.S. Department of Agriculture, Food and Nutrition Service. (2009). Child and Adult Care Food Program Legislation. Retrieved October 1, 2009, from http://www.fns.usda.gov/cnd/care/Regs-Policy/Legislation.htm

U.S. Department of Agriculture, Food and Nutrition Service. (2008). School food safety program based on hazard analysis and critical control point principles: Proposed rule. *Federal Register, 73*(151).

U.S. Department of Agriculture, Food and Nutrition Service. (2009). *FNS Supplemental Nutrition Assistance Program (SNAP).* Retrieved February 19, 2009, from http://www.fns.usda.gov/FSP

U.S. Department of Health and Human Services and U.S. Department of Agriculture. (2005). *Dietary guidelines for Americans, 2005.* Washington, DC: Authors. Retrieved September 1, 2009, from http://www.health.gov/dietaryguidelines/dga2005/document/pdf/DGA2005.pdf

U.S. Department of Labor, Bureau of Labor Statistics. (2008). *Employment characteristics of families in 2007.* Retrieved January 26, 2009, from http://www.bls.gov/cps/demographics.htm#families

U.S. Food and Drug Administration. (2003a, July 9). *FDA backgrounder: The food label.* Retrieved September 8, 2009, from http://vm.cfsan.fda.gov/~dms/fdnewlab.html

U.S. Food and Drug Administration. (2003b, July 10). FDA to encourage science-based labeling and competition for healthier dietary choices [press release]. Silver Spring, MD: Author. Retrieved January 2, 2010, from http://www.newcenturyhealthpublishers.com/news_item.php?id=3

U.S. Food and Drug Administration. (2007, January 23). *Questions and answers on the gluten-free labeling proposed rule.* Retrieved September 8, 2009, from http://www.fda.gov/Food/LabelingNutrition/FoodAllergensLabeling/GuidanceComplianceRegulatoryInformation/ucm111487.htm

U.S. Food and Drug Administration. (2009). *How to understand and use the nutrition facts label.* Retrieved August 16, 2009, from http://www.fda.gov/Food/LabelingNutrition/ConsumerInformation/ucm078889.htm

Wagner, C. L., Greer, F. R., Section on Breastfeeding, & Committee on Nutrition. (2008). Prevention of rickets and vitamin D deficiency in infants, children, and adolescents. *Pediatrics, 122*(5), 1142-1152.

Waters, E. B., & Baur, L. A. (2003). Childhood obesity: Modernity's scourge. *Medical Journal of Australia, 178*(9), 422-423.

Williamson, D. A., Copeland, A. L., Anton, S. D., Champagne, H., H., Lewis, L., Martin, C., et al. (2007). Wise Mind project: A school-based environmental approach for preventing weight gain in children. *Obesity, 15*(4), 906-917.

Wright, C. M., Parkinson, K. N., & Drewett, R. F. (2006). How does maternal and child feeding behavior relate to weight gain and failure to thrive? Data from a prospective birth cohort. *Pediatrics, 117*(4), 1262-1269.

Chapter 4

Alwitry, A. (2000). Vitamin A deficiency in coeliac disease. *British Journal of Ophthalmology, 84*(9), e1075.

American Academy of Pediatrics. (2008). *Oral health initiative: Oral health risk assessment: Training for pediatricians and other child health professionals.* Retrieved September 8, 2009, from http://www.aap.org/oralhealth/cme

American Academy of Pediatrics Committee on Nutrition. (2009). In Kleinman, R. (Ed.), *Pediatric nutrition handbook* Chapter 25 Pediatric Feeding and Swallowing Disorders (6th ed.). Elk Grove, IL: American Academy of Pediatrics.

American Academy of Pediatrics Committee on Nutrition. (2009). In Kleinman, R. (Ed.), *Pediatric nutrition handbook* Chapter 18 Iron (6th ed.). Elk Grove, IL: American Academy of Pediatrics.

American Beverage Association. (2009). *School beverage guidelines: The American Beverage Association & The Alliance for a Healthier Generation.* Retrieved October 16, 2009, from http://www.ameribev.org/nutrition—science/school-beverage-guidelines/

American Dental Association. (2005). *Early childhood tooth decay (baby bottle tooth decay).* Retrieved September 9, 2009, from http://www.ada.org/public/topics/decay_childhood_faq.asp

American Dietetic Association. (2004). Position of the American Dietetic Association: Use of nutritive and nonnutritive sweeteners. *Journal of the American Dietetic Association, 104*(2), 255-275.

American Dietetic Association. (2008). *ADA nutrition care manual.* Retrieved September 9, 2009, from http://www.nutritioncaremanual.org/index.cfm?Page=Home

American Heart Association. (2006). Dietary recommendations for children and adolescents: A guide for practitioners. *Pediatrics, 117*(2), 544-559.

American Heart Association. (2008). *Know your fats.* Retrieved September 9, 2009, from http://www.americanheart.org/presenter.jhtml?identifier=532#satfat

American Heart Association & Clinton Foundation. *Alliance for a Healthier Generation healthy schools program.* Retrieved September 9, 2009, from http://www.healthiergeneration.org/schools.aspx

Ball, J. W., & Bindler, R. (2006). *Child health nursing: Partnering with children and families.* Upper Saddle River, NJ: Pearson Prentice Hall.

Benton, D. (2008). Sucrose and behavioral problems. *Critical Reviews in Food Science and Nutrition, 48*(5), 385-401.

Berg, J. M., Tymoczko, J. L., Stryer, L., & Clark, N. D. (2002). *Biochemistry*. Retrieved August 21, 2007, from http://bcs.whfreeman.com/biochem5/default.asp?s=&n=i=&v=&o=&ns=0&t=&uid=0&rau=0

Bhargava, A., & Amialchuk, A. (2007). Added sugars displaced the use of vital nutrients in the national food stamp program survey. *Journal of Nutrition, 137*(2), 453–460.

Biesemeier, C. (2006). *Food products and trans fat—staying on top of recent changes*. Retrieved August 15, 2007, from http://www.eatright.org/cps/rde/xchg/ada/hs.xsl/nutrition_9899_ENU_HTML.htm

Blossfied, I., Collins, A., & Delahunty, C. (2007). Texture preferences of 12-month-old infants and the role of early experiences. *Food Quality and Preference, 18*(2), 396.

Bowen, R. A., Austgen, L., & Rouge, M. (2006). *Pathophysiology of the digestive system*. Retrieved September 9, 2009, from http://www.vivo.colostate.edu/hbooks/pathphys/digestion/index.html

Bray, G. A., Nielsen, S. J., & Popkin, B. M. (2004). Consumption of high-fructose corn syrup in beverages may play a role in the epidemic of obesity. *American Journal of Clinical Nutrition, 79*(4), 537–543.

Burt, B. A. (2006). The use of sorbitol- and xylitol-sweetened chewing gum in caries control. *Journal of the American Dental Association, 137*(2), 190–196.

Butte, N., Cobb, K., Dwyer, J., Graney, L., Heird, W., & Rickard, K. (2004). The Start Healthy feeding guidelines for infants and toddlers. *Journal of the American Dietetic Association, 104*(3), 442–454.

California Department of Education. (2008). *Nutrition competencies for California's children—healthy eating & nutrition education*. Retrieved September 9, 2009, from http://www.cde.ca.gov/ls/nu/he/ncccindex.asp

Campanozzi, A., Boccia, G., Pensabene, L., Panetta, F., Marseglia, A., Strisciuglio, P., et al. (2009). Prevalence and natural history of gastroesophageal reflux: Pediatric prospective survey. *Pediatrics, 123*(3), 779–783.

Campbell, J. K., Canene-Adams, K., Lindshield, B. L., Boileau, T. W., Clinton, S. K., & Erdman, J. W., Jr. (2004). Tomato phytochemicals and prostate cancer risk. *Journal of Nutrition, 134*(12), 3486S–3492S.

Centers for Disease Control and Prevention. (2009, January 27). *Healthy weight: Assessing your weight: About BMI for children and teens*. Retrieved September 8, 2009, from http://www.cdc.gov/healthyweight/assessing/bmi/childrens_bmi/about_childrens_bmi.html

Centers for Disease Control and Prevention, Division of Oral Health. (2009). *Children's oral health—topics—oral health*. Retrieved September 9, 2009, from http://www.cdc.gov/oralhealth/topics/child.htm

Clark, K. (2009). *High fructose corn syrup*. Retrieved September 8, 2009, from http://www.eatright.org/cps/rde/xchg/ada/hs.xsl/nutrition_7883_ENU_HTML.htm

Daniels, S. R., Greer, F. R., & Committee on Nutrition. (2008). Lipid screening and cardiovascular health in childhood. *Pediatrics, 122*(1), 198–208.

Dee, D. L., Sharma, A. J., Cogswell, M. E., Grummer-Strawn, L. M., Fein, S. B., & Scanlon, K. S. (2008). Sources of supplemental iron among breastfed infants during the first year of life. *Pediatrics, 122*(Suppl. 2), S98–S104.

Duyff, R. L. (2006). *The American Dietetic Association complete food and nutrition guide* (3rd ed.). Hoboken, NJ: John Wiley & Sons.

Eledrisi, M., McKinney, K. S., & Shanti, M. S. (2008). Vitamin A toxicity: Overview. *EMedicine Endocrinology*. Retrieved September 9, 2009, from http://emedicine.medscape.com/article/126104-overview

Elliot, S., Keim, N., Stern, J., Teff, K., & Havel, P. (2002). Fructose, weight gain, and the insulin resistance syndrome. *American Journal of Clinical Nutrition, 76*(5), 911–922.

Fasano, A., Berti, I., Gerarduzzi, T., Not, T., Colletti, R. B., Drago, So., et al. (2003). Prevalence of celiac disease in at-risk and not-at-risk groups in the United States. *Archives of Internal Medicine, 163*(3), 268–292.

Gold, B. (2007). *Management of pediatric reflux: Distinguishing pathologic GERD from physiologic GER*. Retrieved March 26, 2009, from http://www.medscape.com/viewarticle/554385

Guandalini, S., Frye, R., Rivera, D. M., & Borowitz, S. (2006). *Lactose intolerance*. Retrieved September 8, 2009, from http://www.emedicine.com/ped/topic1270.htm#section~introduction

Hark, L., Deen, D., & Campbell, I. (2005). *Nutrition for life*. New York: Dorling Kindersley Publishers.

Harris, W. S., Mozaffarian, D., Rimm, E., Kris-Etherton, P., Rudel, L. L., Appel, L. J., et al. (2009). Omega-6 fatty acids and risk for cardiovascular disease: A science advisory from the American Heart Association Nutrition Subcommittee of the Council on Nutrition, Physical Activity, and Metabolism; Council on Cardiovascular Nursing, and Council on Epidemiology and Prevention. *Circulation, 119*(6), 902–907.

Harvard School of Public Health. (2009a). *The nutrition source: Fats and cholesterol: Out with the bad, in with the good*. Retrieved September 8, 2009, from http://www.hsph.harvard.edu/nutritionsource/what-should-you-eat/fats-full-story/index.html

Harvard School of Public Health. (2009b). *The nutrition source: Vitamins: The bottom line*. Retrieved September 8, 2009, from http://www.hsph.harvard.edu/nutritionsource/vitamins.html

Heyman, M. B. (2006). Lactose intolerance in infants, children, and adolescents. *Pediatrics, 118*(3), 1279–1286.

Horvath, A., Dziechciarz, P., & Szajewska, H. (2008). The effect of thickened-feed interventions on gastroesophageal reflux in infants: Systematic review and meta-analysis of randomized, controlled trials. *Pediatrics, 122*(6), e1268–e1277.

Holick, M. F. (2008). Vitamin D deficiency: A worldwide problem with health consequences. *American Journal of Clinical Nutrition, 87*(4), 1080s–1086s.

Hurrell, R. F., Reddy, M. B., Juillerat, M., & Cook, J. D. (2006). Meat protein fractions enhance nonheme iron absorption in humans. *Journal of Nutrition, 136*(11), 2808–2812.

International Food Information Council. (2008, November). *Sugar alcohols fact sheet*. Retrieved September 8, 2009, from http://www.ific.org/publications/factsheets/sugaralcoholfs.cfm

Jakobsen, M. U., O'Reilly, E. J., Heitmann, B. L., Pereira, M. A., Balter, K., Fraser, G. E., et al. (2009). Major types of dietary fat and risk of coronary heart disease: A pooled analysis of 11 cohort studies. *The American Journal of Clinical Nutrition, 89*(5), 1425–1432.

Kalayci, A. G., Kansu, A., Girgin, N., Kucuk, O., & Aras, G. (2001). Bone mineral density and importance of a gluten-free diet in patients with celiac disease in childhood. *Pediatrics, 108*(5), e89.

Ly, K. A., Milgrom, P., & Rothen, M. (2006). Xylitol, sweeteners, and dental caries. *Pediatric Dentistry, 28*(2), 154–163; discussion, 192–198.

Mahan, L., & Escott-Stump, S. (Eds.). (2004). *Krause's food, nutrition, & diet therapy* (11th ed.). Philadelphia: W. B. Saunders.

Malik, V. S., Schulze, M. B., & Hu, F. B. (2006). Intake of sugar-sweetened beverages and weight gain: A systematic review. *American Journal of Clinical Nutrition, 84*(2), 274–288.

McBean, L. D. (2000). *National Dairy Council: A protective effect of dairy foods in oral health*. Retrieved September 8, 2009, from http://www.nationaldairycouncil.org/NationalDairyCouncil/Health/Digest/dcd71-1Page6.htm

MedlinePlus. (2009). *Infant and toddler nutrition*. Retrieved September 8, 2009, from http://www.nlm.nih.gov/medlineplus/infantandtoddlernutrition.html

Mennella, J. A., Zeigler, P., Briefel, R., & Novak, T. (2006). Feeding Infants and Toddlers Study: The types of foods fed to Hispanic infants and toddlers. *Journal of the American Dietetic Association, 106* (1), 96–106.

Michail, S. (2007). Gastroesophageal reflux. *Pediatrics in Review, 28*(3), 101–110.

Murphy, S., & Johnson, R. (2003). The scientific basis of recent U.S. guidance on sugars intake. *American Journal Clinical Nutrition, 78*(4), 827S–833S.

National Digestive Diseases Information Clearinghouse. (2008). *Your digestive system and how it works*. Retrieved September 8, 2009, from http://digestive.niddk.nih.gov/ddiseases/pubs/yrdd

National Heart Lung and Blood Institute. (2008). *What causes a heart attack?* Retrieved September 8, 2009, from http://www.nhlbi.nih.gov/health/dci/Diseases/HeartAttack/HeartAttack_Causes.html

National Institutes of Health Office of Dietary Supplements. (2008). *Dietary supplement fact sheet: Vitamin D*. Retrieved September 8, 2009, from http://dietary-supplements.info.nih.gov/factsheets/vitamind.asp#h3

National Resource Center for Health and Safety in Child Care and Early Education. (2009).

Healthy kids, healthy care: Illness, chronic conditions and special needs. Retrieved September 8, 2009, from http://www.healthykids.us/illness.htm

Nelms, M., Sucher, K., & Long, S. (2007). *Nutrition therapy and pathophysiology.* San Francisco: Brooks/Cole Cengage.

Nevin-Folino, N. L. (2008). *Pediatric manual of clinical dietetics* (2nd ed. update). Chicago: American Dietetic Association.

Nicklas, T., Johnson, R., & American Dietetic Association. (2004). Position of the American Dietetic Association: Dietary guidance for healthy children ages 2 to 11 years. *Journal of the American Dietetic Association, 104*(4), 660–677.

Otten, J. J., Pitzi-Hellwig, J., & Meyers, L. D. (Eds.). (2006). *Dietary Reference Intakes: The essential guide to nutrient requirements.* Washington, DC: National Academies Press.

Prasse, J. E., & Kikano, G. E. (2009). An overview of pediatric dysphagia. *Clinical Pediatrics, 48*(3), 247–251.

Ramakrishnan, U., & Darnton-Hill, I. (2002). Assessment and control of vitamin A deficiency disorders. *Journal of Nutrition, 132*(9), 2947S–2953.

Rampersaud, G. C., Bailey, L. B., & Kauwell, G. P. (2003). National survey beverage consumption data for children and adolescents indicate the need to encourage a shift toward more nutritive beverages. *Journal of the American Dietetic Association, 103*(1), 97–100.

Rashid, M., Cranney, A., Zarkadas, M., Graham, I. D., Switzer, C., Case, S., et al. (2005). Celiac disease: Evaluation of the diagnosis and dietary compliance in Canadian children. *Pediatrics, 116*(6), e754–e759.

Reed, K. A., Warburton, D., & McKay, H. A. (2007). Determining cardiovascular disease risk in elementary school children: Developing a healthy heart score. *Journal of Sports Science and Medicine, 6*(1), 142.

Samour, P., & King, K. (2005). *Handbook of pediatric nutrition* (3rd ed.). Boston: Jones & Bartlett Publishers.

Shills, M., Shike, M., Ross, A., Caballero, B., & Cousins, R. (Eds.). (2006). *Modern nutrition in health and disease* (10th ed.). Baltimore: Lippincott Williams & Wilkins.

Sizer, F., & Whitney, E. (2006). The remarkable body. Chap. 3 in *Nutrition concepts and controversy* (10th ed., p. 75). Belmont, CA: Thomson Wadsworth.

Stipanuk, M. (2006). *Biochemical, physiological and molecular aspects of human nutrition* (2nd ed.). St. Louis: Saunders Elsevier.

Strathearn, L., Mamun, A. A., Najman, J. M., & O'Callaghan, M. J. (2009). Does breastfeeding protect against substantiated child abuse and neglect? A 15-year cohort study. *Pediatrics, 123*(2), 483–493.

Taylor, E. D., Theim, K. R., Mirch, M. C., Ghorbani, S., Tanofsky-Kraff, M., Adler-Wailes, D. C., et al. (2006). Orthopedic complications of overweight in children and adolescents. *Pediatrics, 117*(6), 2167–2174.

Texas Heart Institute. (2009). *Heart information center: Coronary artery disease.* Retrieved September 8, 2009, from http://www.texasheartinstitute.org/HIC/Topics/cond/CoronaryArteryDisease.cfm

University of Maryland Medical Center. (2009, June 23). *Gastroesophageal reflux disease and heartburn: Risk factors.* Retrieved September 8, 2009, from http://www.umm.edu/patiented/articles/who_gets_gastroesophageal_reflux_disease_000085_3.htm

U.S. Department of Agriculture. (2004). *USDA national nutrient database for standard reference, release 17: Fiber content of foods.* Retrieved September 8, 2009, from http://www.nal.usda.gov/fnic/foodcomp/Data/SR17/wtrank/sr17a291.pdf

U.S. Department of Agriculture. (2009). *MyPyramid.gov: Steps to a healthier you.* Retrieved September 7, 2009, from http://www.mypyramid.gov/downloads/resource/MyPyramidBrochurebyIFIC.pdf

U.S. Department of Health and Human Services and U.S. Department of Agriculture. (2005). *Dietary guidelines for Americans, 2005.* Washington, DC: Authors. Retrieved September 1, 2009, from http://www.ealth.gov/dietaryguidelines/dga2005/document/pdf/DGA2005.pdf

U.S. Food and Drug Administration. (2006). *Trans fat now listed with saturated fat and cholesterol on the nutrition facts label.* Retrieved September 9, 2009, from http://vm.cfsan.fda.gov/~dms/transfat.html

Vartanian, L. R., Schwartz, M. B., & Brownell, K. D. (2007). Effects of soft drink consumption on nutrition and health: A systematic review and meta-analysis. *American Journal of Public Health, 97*(4), 667–675.

Wagner, C. L., Greer, F. R., Section on Breastfeeding, & Committee on Nutrition. (2008). Prevention of rickets and vitamin D deficiency in infants, children, and adolescents. *Pediatrics, 122*(5), 1142–1152.

Whole Grains Council. (2009). *Whole grains 101.* Retrieved September 8, 2009, from http://www.wholegrainscouncil.org/whole-grains-101

Wolraich, M. L., Wilson, D. B., & White, J. W. (1995). The effect of sugar on behavior or cognition in children. A meta-analysis. *Journal of the American Medical Association, 274*(20), 1617–1621.

Yoshida, Y., Kameda, M., Nishikido, T., Takamatu, I., & Doi, S. (2002). Gastroesophageal reflux disease in preschool children with asthma. *Allergy, 57*(5), 529–535.

Chapter 5

Abad-Jorge, A. (2008). The role of DHA and ARA in infant nutrition and neurodevelopmental outcomes. *Today's Dietitian, 10*(10), 66.

Adler, J., & Dickinson, C. J. (2009). Thickened formula is only moderately effective in the treatment of gastroesophageal reflux in healthy infants. *Journal of Pediatrics, 154*(5), 774.

Allali, F., El Aichaoui, S., Saoud, B., Maaroufi, H., Abouqal, R., & Hajjaj-Hassouni, N. (2006). The impact of clothing style on bone mineral density among post menopausal women in Morocco: A case-control study. *BMC Public Health, 6, 135.*

American Academy of Breastfeeding Medicine. (2004). *Protocol 8: Human milk storage information for home use for healthy full-term infants.* Retrieved September 20, 2009, from http://www.bfmed.org/Resources

American Academy of Pediatrics. (2005). Breastfeeding and the use of human milk. *Pediatrics, 115*(2), 496–506.

American Academy of Pediatrics Committee on Nutrition. (2004). In Kleinman, R. (Ed.), *Pediatric nutrition handbook* (6th ed.). Elk Grove, IL: American Academy of Pediatrics.

American Academy of Pediatrics, American Public Health Association, & National Resource Center for Health and Safety in Child Care and Early Education. (2002). *Caring for our children: National health and safety performance standards: Guidelines for out-of-home child care programs* (2nd ed.). Elk Grove Village, IL: American Academy of Pediatrics; Washington, DC: American Public Health Association. Retrieved August 31, 2009, from http://www.eric.ed.gov/ERICDocs/data/ericdocs2sql/content_storage_01/0000019b/80/14/0d/14.pdf

American Dietetic Association. (2005). Position of the American Dietetic Association: Promoting and supporting breastfeeding. *Journal of the American Dietetic Association, 105*(5), 810–818.

Auestad, N., Scott, D., Janowsky, J. S., Jacobsen, C., Carroll, R. E., Montalto, M. B., et al. (2003). Visual, cognitive, and language assessments at 39 months: A follow-up study of children fed formulas containing long-chain polyunsaturated fatty acids to 1 year of age. *Pediatrics, 112*(3), e177–e183.

Avery, A. A. (1999). Infantile methemoglobinemia: Reexamining the role of drinking water nitrates. *Environmental Health Perspective, 107*(7), 583–586.

Avery, A., Zimmermann, K., Underwood, P. W., & Magnus, J. H. (2009). Confident commitment is a key factor for sustained breastfeeding. *Birth (Berkeley, Calif.), 36*(2), 141–148.

Bates, K. (2007, November 5). *Baby's IQ raised by breastmilk and genes.* Retrieved September 20, 2009, from http://www.dukenews.duke.edu/2007/11/breastIQ.html

Beard, J. L. (2008). Why iron deficiency is important in infant development. *Journal of Nutrition, 138*(12), 2534–2536.

Beauchamp, G. K., Mennella, J. A. (2009). Early flavor learning and its impact on later feeding behavior. *Journal of Pediatric Gastroenterology and Nutrition, 48* (Suppl. 1), S25–S30.

Bergmann, K. E., Bergmann R.L. von Kries, R., Böhm, O., Richter R., Dudenhausen, J.W., & Wahn, U.(2003). Early determinants of childhood overweight and adiposity in a birth cohort study: role of breast-feeding. *International Journal of Obesity, 27*(2), 162–172.

Berseth, C. L., Mitmesser, S. H., Ziegler, E. E., Marunycz, J. D., & Vanderhoof, J. (2009). Tolerance of a standard intact protein formula versus a partially hydrolyzed formula in healthy, term infants. *Nutrition Journal, 8*, 27.

Black, M. M., Siegel, E. H., Abel, Y., & Bentley, M. E. (2001). Home and videotape intervention delays early complementary feeding among adolescent mothers. *Pediatrics, 107*(5), e67.

Blossfied, I., Collins, A., & Delahunty, C. (2007). Texture preferences of 12-month-old infants and the role of early experiences. *Food Quality and Preference, 18*(2), 396.

Bray, G. A., Nielsen, S. J., & Popkin, B. M. (2004). Consumption of high-fructose corn syrup in beverages may play a role in the epidemic of obesity. *American Journal of Clinical Nutrition, 79*(4), 537-543.

Butte, N., Cobb, K., Dwyer, J., Graney, L., Heird, W., & Rickard, K. (2004). The start healthy feeding guidelines for infants and toddlers. *Journal of the American Dietetic Association, 104*(3), 442-454.

California Department of Public Health, Division of Communicable Disease Control. (2004). *When to avoid honey*. Retrieved September 20, 2009, from http://www.infantbotulism.org

Centers for Disease Control and Prevention. (2007a). *Proper handling and storage of human milk*. Retrieved September 20, 2009, from http://www.cdc.gov/breastfeeding/recommendations/handling_breastmilk.htm

Centers for Disease Control and Prevention. (2007b). Does breastfeeding reduce the risk of pediatric overweight? (Research to Practice Series No. 4). Retrieved September 20, 2009, from http://www.cdc.gov/nccdphp/dnpa/nutrition/pdf/breastfeeding_r2p.pdf

Centers for Disease Control and Prevention. (2008). *Breastfeeding report card United States, 2008: Outcome indicators*. Retrieved July 10, 2009, from http://www.cdc.gov/breastfeeding/data/report_card2.htm

Centers for Disease Control and Prevention. (2009). *Viral hepatitis: FAQ for the public*. Retrieved July 31, 2009, 2009, from http://www.cdc.gov/hepatitis/B/bFAQ.htm

Chao, H., & Vandenplas, Y. (2007). Effect of cereal-thickened formula and upright positioning on regurgitation, gastric emptying, and weight gain in infants with regurgitation. *Nutrition, 23*(1), 23-28.

Cheatham, C. L., Colombo, J., & Carlson, S. E. (2006). *n-3* fatty acids and cognitive and visual acuity development: Methodologic and conceptual considerations. *American Journal of Clinical Nutrition, 83*(6), S1458-S1466.

Children's Hospital at Westmead. (2003, June 6). *Oral facial hypersensitivity*. Retrieved September 19, 2009, from http://www.chw.edu.au/rehab/brain_injury/information_sheets/swallowing/oral_hypersensitivity.htm

Christensen, N., & Saal, H. (2005). Cleft lip and/or cleft palate and other craniofacial anomalies. In S. W. Ekvall, & V. K. Ekvall (Eds.), *Pediatric nutrition in chronic diseases and developmental disorders* (2nd ed., p. 185). New York: Oxford University Press.

Clemson Extension. (2009). *HGIC 4259 making your own baby food*. Retrieved September 19, 2009, from http://www.clemson.edu/extension/hgic/food/nutrition/food_shop_prep/food_prep/hgic4259.html

Corbet, S. J., & Poon, C. C. (2009, July 30). Toxic levels of mercury in Chinese infants eating fish congee. *Medical Journal of Australia, 88*(1), 59-60.

Cox, N., & Hinkle, R. (2002, April 1). Infant botulism. *American Family Physician, 65*(7), 1388-1408.

Dangerfield, S. D. (1998). *Human growth after birth* (6th ed.). Oxford: Oxford University Press.

Dee, D. L., Li, R., Lee, L., & Grummer-Strawn, L. M. (2007). Associations between breastfeeding practices and young children's language and motor skill development. *Pediatrics, 119*(Suppl. 1), S92-S98.

Dellwo Houghton, M., & Graybeal, T. E. (2001). Breast-feeding practices of Native American mothers participating in WIC. *Journal of the American Dietetic Association, 101*(2), 245-247.

Devaney, B., Ziegler, P., Pac, S., Karwe, V., & Barr, S. I. A. (2006). Nutrient intakes of infants and toddlers. *Journal of the American Dietetic Association, 104*(1), 14-21.

Diamant, A. (2005). *The new Jewish baby book: Names, ceremonies, & customs—A guide for today's families*. Woodstock, VT: Jewish Lights Publishing.

Duyff, R. L. (2006). *The American Dietetic Association complete food and nutrition guide* (3rd ed.). Hoboken, NJ: John Wiley & Sons.

Encyclopedia of Food & Culture. (2006). *Baby food*. Retrieved September 20, 2009, from http://www.enotes.com/food-encyclopedia/baby-food

Farmularo, C. A. (2009). Infantile botulism: Clinical manifestations, treatment, and the role of the nurse practitioner. *Journal for Nurse Practitioners, 5*(5), 335.

Fries, W. C. (2009). *Making the transition from breast to baby bottles*. Retrieved September 20, 2009, from http://www.webmd.com/parenting/baby/bottle-feeding-9/weaning-from-breast

Gale, C. R., Walton, S., & Martyn, C. N. (2003). Foetal and postnatal head growth and risk of cognitive decline in old age. *Brain, 126*(10), 2273-2278.

Gaur, A. H., Dominguez, K. L., Kalish, M. L., Rivera-Hernandez, D., Donohoe, M., Brooks, J. T., et al. (2009). Practice of feeding premasticated food to infants: A potential risk factor for HIV transmission. *Pediatrics, 124*(2), 658-666.

Gazetteers Department, Government of Maharashtra. (2006). *Ahmadnagar: The people: Rituals and ceremonies*. Retrieved September 20, 2009, from http://www.maharashtra.gov.in/english/gazetteer/Ahmadnagar/people_rituals_ceremonies.html

Geraghty, S. R., Khoury, J. C., Morrow, A. L., & Lanphea, B. P. (2008). Reporting individual test results of environmental chemicals in breastmilk: Potential for premature weaning. *Breastfeeding Medicine, 3*(4), 207-213.

Gill, S. L. (2009). Breastfeeding by Hispanic women. *Journal of Obstetric, Gynecologic, and Neonatal Nursing, 38*(2), 244-252.

Goran, M. I., & Sothern, M.S. (Eds.). (2006). *Handbook of pediatric obesity: Etiology, pathophysiology, and prevention*. Boca Raton, FL: Taylor and Francis Group.

Greer, F. R., Shannon, M., Committee on Nutrition, & Committee on Environmental Health. (2005). Infant methemoglobinemia: The role of dietary nitrate in food and water. *Pediatrics, 116*(3), 784-786.

Grummer-Strawn, L. M., Scanlon, K. S., & Fein, S. B. (2008). Infant feeding and feeding transitions during the first year of life. *Pediatrics, 122*(2), S36.

Harley, K., Stamm, N. L., & Eskenazi, B. (2007).The effect of time in the U.S. on the duration of breastfeeding in women of Mexican descent. *Maternal and Child Health Journal, 11*(2), 119-125.

Heinig, M. J., Follett, J. R., Ishii, K. D., Kavanagh-Prochaska, K., Cohen, R., & Panchula, J. (2006). Barriers to compliance with infant-feeding recommendations among low-income women. *Journal of Human Lactation, 22*(1), 27-38.

Hendy, H. M., & Raudenbush, B. (2000). Effectiveness of teacher modeling to encourage food acceptance in preschool children. *Appetite, 34*(1), 61-76.

Innis, S. M., Gilley, J., & Werker, J. (2001). Are human milk long-chain polyunsaturated fatty acids related to visual and neural development in breast-fed term infants? *Journal of Pediatrics, 139*(4), 532-538.

Irani, C., Germanos, M., Kazma, H., & Merhej, V. (2006). Food allergy in Lebanon: Is sesame the "Middle Eastern" peanut. *Journal of Allergy and Clinical Immunology, 117*(2), S38.

Irwin, J. J., & Kirchner, J. T. (2007). Anemia in children. *American Family Physician, 64*(8), 1379-1386.

Kids Health. (2009). *Formula feeding FAQs: How much and how often*. Retrieved September 20, 2009, from http://kidshealth.org/PageManager.jsp?lic=1&ps=104&article_set=45609#

Kimbro, R. T. (2006). On-the-job moms: Work and breastfeeding initiation and duration for a sample of low-income women. *Maternal and Child Health Journal, 10*(1), 19-26.

Kleinman, R. K. (Ed.). (2009). *Pediatric nutrition handbook* (6th ed.). Elk Grove, IL: American Academy of Pediatrics.

Krebs, N. F. (2000). Dietary zinc and iron sources, physical growth and cognitive development of breastfed infants. *Journal of Nutrition, 130*(2), 358.

Krebs, N. F., & Hambidge, K. M. (2007). Complementary feeding: Clinically relevant factors affecting timing and composition. *American Journal of Clinical Nutrition, 85*(2), 639S-645S.

La Leche League International. (2009). *A current summary of breastfeeding legislation in the U.S.* Retrieved July 10, 2009, from http://www.llli.org/Law/LawBills.html

Li, R., Darling, N., Maurice, E., Barker, L., & Grummer-Strawn, L. M. (2005). Breastfeeding rates in the United States by characteristics of the child, mother, or family: The

2002 national immunization survey. *Pediatrics, 115*(1), e31-e37.

Lignell, S., Aune, M., Darnerud, P. O., Cnattingius, S., & Glynn, A. (2009). Persistent organochlorine and organobromine compounds in mother's milk from Sweden 1996-2006: Compound-specific temporal trends. *Environmental Research, 109*(6), 760-767.

Lloyd, B., Halter, R. J., Kuchan, M. J., Baggs, G. E., Ryan, A. S., & Masor, M. L. (1999). Formula tolerance in postbreastfed and exclusively formula-fed infants. *Pediatrics, 103*(1), e7.

Lozoff, B., Jimenez, E., Hagen, J., Mollen, E., & Wolf, A. W. (2000). Poorer behavioral and developmental outcome more than 10 years after treatment for iron deficiency in infancy. *Pediatrics, 105*(4), e51.

Macknin, M. L., Medendorp, S. V., & Maier, M. C. (1989). Infant sleep and bedtime cereal. *American Journal of Diseases of Children, 143*(9), 1066-1068.

Mayer-Davis, E. J., Rifas-Shiman, S. L., Zhou, L., Hu, F. B., Colditz, G. A., & Gillman, M. W. (2006). Breast-feeding and risk for childhood obesity. *Diabetes Care, 29*(10), 2231-2237.

McCann, J. C., & Ames, B. N. (2005). Is docosahexaenoic acid, an *n*-3 long-chain polyunsaturated fatty acid, required for development of normal brain function? An overview of evidence from cognitive and behavioral tests in humans and animals. *American Journal of Clinical Nutrition, 82*(2), 281-295.

McDowell, M. M., Wang, C., & Kennedy-Stephenson, J. (2008, April). Breastfeeding in the United States: Findings from the national health and nutrition examination survey, 1999-2006 (NCHS Data Brief No. 5). Atlanta, GA: Centers for Disease Control and Prevention.

Mennella, J. A., Jagnow, C. P., & Beauchamp, G. K. (2001). Prenatal and postnatal flavor learning by human infants. *Pediatrics, 107*(6), e88.

Mennella, J. A., Ziegler, P., Briefel, R., & Novak, T. (2006). Feeding infants and toddlers study: The types of foods fed to Hispanic infants and toddlers. *Journal of the American Dietetic Association, 106* (Suppl. 1), S96-S106.

Moreland, J., & Coombs, J. (2000). Promoting and supporting breast-feeding. *American Family Physician, 61*(7), 2093-2100, 2103-2104.

National Association for the Education of Young Children. (2008). *Academy for early childhood program accreditation: Standard 5: NAEYC accreditation criteria for health standard*. Retrieved June 14, 2009, from http://www.naeyc.org/files/academy/file/OverviewStandards.pdf.

Nevin-Folino, N. L., Armorde-Spalding, K., & Nieman, L. (Eds.). (2008). *Pediatric manual of clinical dietetics* (2nd ed.). Chicago: American Dietetic Association.

New York State Department of Health. (2008). *Breastfeeding friendly child care centers*. Retrieved September 20, 2009, from http://www.health.state.ny.us/prevention/nutrition/cacfp/breastfeedingspon.htm

Nickerson, K. (2006). Environmental contaminants in breast milk. *Journal of Midwifery & Women's Health, 51*(1), 26-34.

Oregon Department of Education. (2009). *USDA CACFP child care center manual*. Retrieved October 22, 2009. from http://www.ode.state.or.us/services/nutrition/cacfp/center_manual.pdf

Otten, J. J., Pitzi-Hellwig, J., & Meyers, L. D. (Eds.). (2006). *Dietary Reference Intakes: The essential guide to nutrient requirements*. Washington, DC: National Academies Press.

Pak-Gorstein, S., Haq, A., & Graham, E. A. (2009). Cultural influences on infant feeding practices. *Pediatrics in Review, 30*(3), e11-e21.

Public Health: Seattle and King County. (2009). *Model health breastfeeding promotion and support policy for child care programs*. Retrieved September 20, 2009, from http://www.kingcounty.gov/healthservices/health/child/childcare/modelhealth.aspx

Ramachandran, A. (2004). *Congee: Asia's comfort food: Things Asian*. Retrieved July 31, 2009, from http://www.thingsasian.com/stories-photos/2953

Rees, L. (2005). Immunity and the GI tract. *South African Family Practice, 47*(5), 56-58.

Ribas-Fito, N., Julvez, J., Torrent, M., Grimalt, J. O., & Sunyer, J. (2007). Beneficial effects of breastfeeding on cognition regardless of DDT concentrations at birth. *American Journal of Epidemiology, 166*(10), 1198-1202.

Ryan, A. S., Rush, D., Krieger, F. W., & Lewandowski, G. E. (1991). Recent declines in breast-feeding in the United States, 1984 through 1989. *Pediatrics, 88*(4), 719-727.

Sacker, A., Quigley, M. A., & Kelly, Y. J. (2006). Breastfeeding and developmental delay: Findings from the millennium cohort study. *Pediatrics, 118*(3), e682-e689.

Samour, P., & King, K. (2005). *Handbook of pediatric nutrition* (3rd ed.). Boston: Jones and Bartlett Publishers.

Savino, F., Maccario, S., Guidi, C., Castagno, E., Farinasso, D., Cresi, F., et al. (2006). Methemoglobinemia caused by the ingestion of courgette soup given in order to resolve constipation in two formula-fed infants. *Annals of Nutrition & Metabolism, 50*(4), 368-371.

Schanler, R. J. (2007). Evaluation of the evidence to support current recommendations to meet the needs of premature infants: The role of human milk. *American Journal Clinical Nutrition, 85*(2), 625S-628S.

Shaikh, U., & Ahmed, O. (2006). Islam and infant feeding. *Breastfeeding Medicine, 1*(3), 164.

Stockholm Convention. (2009). *Fact sheet: What is the Stockholm convention*. Retrieved August 1, 2009, from http://chm.pops.int/Convention/Media/Factsheets/tabid/527/language/en-US/Default.aspx

Tanzi, M. G., & Gabay, M. P. (2002). Association between honey consumption and infant botulism. *Pharmacotherapy, 22*(11), 1479-1483.

Tarini, B. A., Carroll, A. E., Sox, C. M., & Christakis, D. A. (2006). Systematic review of the relationship between early introduction of solid foods to infants and the development

of allergic disease. *Archives of Pediatrics Adolescent Medicine, 160*(5), 502-507.

Taylor, S. N., Wagner, C. L., & Hollis, B. W. (2008). Vitamin D supplementation during lactation to support infant and mother. *Journal of the American College of Nutrition, 27*(6), 690-701.

Texas Department of Health/Nutrition Services. (1994, April). *Infant feeding: Low-birth-weight and preterm infants* (Nutrition Fact Sheet No. 7). Retrieved September 19, 2009, from http://www.dshs.state.tx.us/wichd/nut/pdf/fac7-s.pdf

University of Washington Center on Human Development and Disability. (2001). *Frequently used guidelines: Failure to thrive—Assessing nutritional status*. Retrieved September 19, 2009, from http://depts.washington.edu/nutrpeds/fug/ftt/assess.htm#diet

U.S. Department of Agriculture, Food and Nutrition Service. (2000). *Issues related to feeding infants in the CACFP*. Retrieved July 12, 2009, from http://www.fns.usda.gov/cnd/Care/Regs-Policy/InfantMeals/2000-04-20.htm

U.S. Department of Agriculture, Food and Nutrition Service. (2002a). *Child and adult care food program: Meal patterns*. Retrieved September 20, 2009, from http://www.fns.usda.gov/CND/Care/ProgramBasics/Meals/Meal_Patterns.htm#Infant_LunchSupper

U.S. Department of Agriculture, Food and Nutrition Service. (2002b, July). *Feeding infants: A guide for use in child nutrition programs*. Retrieved September 19, 2009, from http://www.fns.usda.gov/tn/Resources/feeding_infants.html

U.S. Department of Agriculture, Food and Nutrition Service. (2008, September) *Infant nutrition and feeding: A guide for use in WIC and CSF Programs*. Retrieved October 21, 2009. from: http://www.nal.usda.gov/wicworks/Topics/FG/Contents.pdf

U.S. Department of Health and Human Services. (2000). *Healthy people 2010* (2nd ed., 2 vols.). Washington, DC: Author. Retrieved August 31, 2009, from http://www.healthy people.gov/Publications

U.S. Department of Health and Human services, (2007), *Nourishing the very low birth weight infant*. Retrieved September 19, 2009, from http://depts.washington.edu/growing/Nourish/index~4.htm

U.S. Food and Drug Administration. (2009). *Infant formula: Guidance & regulatory information*. Retrieved July 13, 2009, from http://www.fda.gov/Food/FoodSafety/Product-SpecificInformation/InfantFormula/GuidanceRegulatoryInformation/default.htm

Wagnon, J., Cagnard, B., Bridoux-Henno, L., Tourtelier, Y., Grall, J. Y., & Dabadie, A. (2005). Breastfeeding and vegan diet [Abstract]. *Journal de Gynecologie, Obstetrique et Biologie de la Reproduction, 34*(6), 610-612.

Wang, R. Y., Jain, R. B., Wolkin, A. F., Rubin, C. H., & Needham, L. L. (2009). Serum concentrations of selected persistent organic pollutants in a sample of pregnant females and changes in their concentrations during gestation. *Environmental Health Perspectives, 117*(3), 1244-1249.

Wisconsin Department of Health Services. (2008). *Ten steps to breastfeeding friendly child care centers: Resource kit.* Retrieved September 20, 2009, from http://dhs.wisconsin.gov/health/physicalactivity/pdf_files/BreastfeedingFriendlyChildCareCenters.pdf

World Health Organization. (2003). *Global strategy for infant and young child feeding.* Geneva, Switzerland: World Health Organization.

World Health Organization. (2009). *Complementary feeding.* Retrieved September 20, 2009, from http://www.who.int/nutrition/topics/complementary_feeding/en/index.html

Worobey, J., Lopez, M. I., & Hoffman, D. J. (2009). Maternal behavior and infant weight gain in the first year. *Journal of Nutrition Education and Behavior, 41*(3), 169-175.

Worobey, J. M., Medina, M. M., & Martin, I. (2007). Maternal feeding style as a contributing factor to infant weight gain. *Journal of the American Dietetic Association, 107*(8), A12.

Chapter 6

American Dietetic Association. (2005). Position paper: Benchmarks for nutrition programs in child care settings. *Journal of the American Dietetic Association, 105,* 979-986.

American Heart Association. (2006). Dietary recommendations for children and adolescents: A guide for practitioners: Consensus statement from the American Heart Association. *Pediatrics, 117*(2), 544-559.

Anderson, S. E., & Whitaker, R. C. (2009). Prevalence of obesity among U.S. preschool children in different racial and ethnic groups. *Archives of Pediatrics Adolescent Medicine, 163*(4), 344-348.

Bell, K. I., & Tepper, B. J. (2006). Short-term vegetable intake by young children classified by 6-n-propylthoiuracil bitter-taste phenotype. *American Journal of Clinical Nutrition, 84*(1), 245-251.

Benton, D., & Jarvis, M. (2007). The role of breakfast and a mid-morning snack on the ability of children to concentrate at school. *Physiology & Behavior, 90*(2-3), 382-385.

Brotanek, J. M., Schroer, D., Valentyn, L., Tomany-Korman, S., & Flores, G. (2009). Reasons for prolonged bottle-feeding and iron deficiency among Mexican-American toddlers: An ethnographic study. *Academic Pediatrics, 9*(1), 17-25.

Butte, N., Cobb, K., Dwyer, J., Graney, L., Heird, W., & Rickard, K. (2004). The Start Healthy feeding guidelines for infants and toddlers. *Journal of the American Dietetic Association, 104*(3), 442-454.

Centers for Disease Control and Prevention. (2009). *What should pregnant women know about 2009 H1N1 flu (swine flu).* Retrieved October 7, 2009, from http://www.cdc.gov/h1n1flu/guidance/pregnant.htm

Centers for Disease Control and Prevention & National Center for Chronic Disease Prevention and Health Promotion. (2009). *Healthy youth!*

Local wellness policy tools & resources. Retrieved October 6, 2009, from http://www.cdc.gov/HealthyYouth/healthtopics/wellness.htm

Chatoor, I. (2009). Sensory food aversions in infants and toddlers. *Journal of Zero to Three, 29*(3), 44.

Cooke, L. J., Haworth, C., & Wardle, J. (2007). Genetic and environmental influences on children's food neophobia. *American Journal of Clinical Nutrition, 86*(2), 428-433.

Daniels, S. R., Greer, F. R., & Committee on Nutrition. (2008). Lipid screening and cardiovascular health in childhood. *Pediatrics, 122*(1), 198-208.

Ellyn Satter Associates. (2009). *The picky eater.* Retrieved October 6, 2009, from https://ellynsatter.com/showArticle.jsp?id=265&section=278

Field, A. E., Javaras, K. M., Aneja, P., Kitos, N., Camargo, C. A., Jr, Taylor, C. B., et al. (2008). Family, peer, and media predictors of becoming eating disordered. *Archives of Pediatrics & Adolescent Medicine, 162*(6), 574-579.

Fisher, J. O., Liu, Y., Birch, L. L., & Rolls, B. J. (2007). Effects of portion size and energy density on young children's intake at a meal. *American Journal of Clinical Nutrition, 86*(1), 174-179.

Food Research and Action Center. (2009). *School breakfast program.* Retrieved October 6, 2009, from http://www.frac.org/html/federal_food_programs/programs/sbp.html

Fox, M., Devaney, B., Reidy, K., Razafindrakoto, C., & Ziegler, P. (2006). Relationship between portion size and energy intake among infants and toddlers: Evidence of self-regulation. *Journal of the American Dietetic Association, 106*(1 S), 77-83.

Huber, D. (2009). Making a difference in early childhood obesity. *Child Care Exchange.* Retrieved October 6, 2009, from http://ccie.com/resources/view_article.php?article_id=5018916&keyword_id=&page=3

Hunter, J., & Cason, K. (2008). *Feeding your preschooler* (HGIC 4103). Clemson, SC: Clemson University. Retrieved October 7, 2009, from http://www.clemson.edu/extension/hgic/food/nutrition/nutrition/life_stages/hgic4103.html

Kleinman, R. K. (Ed.) 2009. *Pediatric nutrition handbook,* Chapter 6 Feeding the Child (6th ed., p. 146). Elk Grove, IL: American Academy of Pediatrics.

Knaapila, A., Tuorila, H., Silventoinen, K., Keskitalo, K., Kallela, M., Wessman, M., et al. (2007). Food neophobia shows heritable variation in humans. *Physiology & Behavior, 91*(5), 573-578.

Luitel, A. (2006), Food and eating customs differ around the world. *Silver International Newspaper.* Retrieved October 6, 2009, from http://silverinternational.mbhs.edu/v202/V20.2.05a.eatingcustoms.html

Martinez-Gonzalez, M. A., Gual, P., Lahortiga, F., Alonso, Y., de Irala-Estevez, J., & Cervera, S. (2003). Parental factors, mass media influences, and the onset of eating disorders in a prospective population-based cohort. *Pediatrics, 111*(2), 315-320.

McConahy, K., Smiciklas-Wright, H., Mitchell, D., & Picciano, M. (2004). Portion size of common foods predicts energy intake among preschool-aged children. *Journal of the American Dietetic Association, 104*(6), 975-979.

Muthayya, S., Thomas, T., Srinivasan, K., Rao, K., Kurpad, A. V., van Klinken, J. W., et al. (2007). Consumption of a mid-morning snack improves memory but not attention in school children. *Physiology & Behavior, 90*(1), 142-150.

National Association for the Education of Young Children. (2008). *Academy for early childhood program accreditation: Standard 5: NAEYC accreditation criteria for health standard.* Retrieved May 23, 2009, from http://www.naeyc.org/academy/primary/standardsintro

Nevin-Folino, N. L. (2008). *Pediatric manual of clinical dietetics* (2nd ed. update). Chicago: American Dietetic Association.

Ochs, E. S. M. (2006). The cultural structuring of mealtime socialization. *New Directions for Child and Adolescent Development, 11,* 35-49.

Oregon Department of Education. (2009, May). *USDA CACFP child care center manual.* Salem, OR: Author. Retrieved January 2, 2010, from http://www.ode.state.or.us/services/nutrition/cacfp/center_manual.pdf

Orlet Fisher, J., Rolls, B. J., & Birch, L. L. (2003). Children's bite size and intake of an entree are greater with large portions than with age-appropriate or self-selected portions. *American Journal of Clinical Nutrition, 77*(5), 1164-1170.

Rainville, A., Wolf, K. N., & Carr, D. H. (2006). Recess placement prior to lunch in elementary schools: What are the barriers? *Journal of Child Nutrition & Management, 30*(2). Retrieved October 6, 2009, from http://docs.schoolnutrition.org/newsroom/jcnm/06fall/rainville/index.asp

Rampersaud, G. C., Pereira, M. A., Girard, B. L., Adams, J., & Metzl, J. D. (2005). Breakfast habits, nutritional status, body weight, and academic performance in children and adolescents. *Journal of the American Dietetic Association, 105*(5), 743.

Roberts, S. B., & Heyman, M. B. (2000). Micronutrient shortfalls in young children's diets: Common, and owing to inadequate intakes both at home and at child care centers. *Nutrition Reviews, 58*(1), 27-29.

Rolls, B., Engell, D., & Birch, L. (2000). Serving portion size influences 5-year-old but not 3-year-old children's food intakes. *Journal of the American Dietetic Association, 100*(2), 232-234.

Rome, E. S., Ammerman, S., Rosen, D. S., Keller, R. J., Lock, J., Mammel, K. A., et al. (2003). Children and adolescents with eating disorders: The state of the art. *Pediatrics, 111*(1), e98-108.

Satter, E. (2000). *Child of mine: feeding with love and good sense.* Berkeley, CA: Bull Publishing Company.

Satter, E. (2007). Eating competence: Definition and evidence for the Satter eating competence model. *Journal of Nutrition Education and Behavior, 39*(5), S142-S153.

Sizer, F., & Whitney, E. (2006). *Nutrition concepts and controversy* (10th ed.). Belmont, CA: Thomson Learning.

Snow, C. E., & Beals, D. E. (2006). Mealtime talk that supports literacy development. *New Directions for Child and Adolescent Development*, (111), 51-66.

Stallings, V. (2009). *Nutrition standards and meal requirements for national school lunch and break programs: Phase I: Statement of Virginia Stallings*. Retrieved October 6, 2009, from http://www7.nationalacademies.org/ocga/testimony/Nutrition_Standards_and_Meal_Requirements_for_Schools.asp

Stein, M. T., Boies, E. G., & Snyder, D. M. (2004). Parental concerns about extended breastfeeding in a toddler. *Pediatrics, 114*(5), 1506-1509.

Sustainable Schools Project. (2008). *Sustainable schools project: About us*. Retrieved October 7, 2009, from http://www.sustainableschoolsproject.org/about

Tanofsky-Kraff, M., Faden, D., Yanovski, S. Z., Wilfley, D. E., & Yanovski, J. A. (2005). The perceived onset of dieting and loss of control eating behaviors in overweight children. *The International Journal of Eating Disorders, 38*(2), 112-122

U.S. Department of Agriculture. (2009a). *Healthy meals resource system*. Retrieved October 6, 2009, from http://healthymeals.nal.usda.gov/nal_display/index.php?info_center=14&tax_level=1

U.S. Department of Agriculture. (2009b). *MyPyramid for preschoolers*. Retrieved July 6, 2009, from http://www.mypyramid.gov/Preschoolers

U.S. Department of Agriculture. (2009c). *MyPyramid for professionals*. Retrieved October 6, 2009, from http://www.mypyramid.gov/professionals/pdf_framework.html

U.S. Department of Agriculture Economic Research Service. (2002, May). *Effects of CACFP reimbursement tiering: Major findings of the family child care homes legislative changes study* (Food Assistance and Nutrition Research Report No. 24). Retrieved October 6, 2009, from http://www.ers.usda.gov/Publications/FANRR24/

U.S. Department of Agriculture Food and Nutrition Service. (2009a). *Healthier US school challenge*. Retrieved October 6, 2009, from http://teamnutrition.usda.gov/HealthierUS/index.html

U.S. Department of Agriculture Food and Nutrition Service. (2009b). *National school lunch program*. Retrieved October 6, 2009, from http://www.fns.usda.gov/cnd/Lunch

U.S. Department of Agriculture Food and Nutrition Service. (2009c). *School breakfast program*. Retrieved October 6, 2009, from http://www.fns.usda.gov/CND/Breakfast

U.S. Department of Agriculture Food and Nutrition Service. (2009d). *Team nutrition homepage*. Retrieved October 6, 2009, from http://teamnutrition.usda.gov

U.S. Department of Agriculture Food and Nutrition Service. (2009e). *WICWorks resource system: WIC foods*. Retrieved October 6, 2009, from http://www.nal.usda.gov/wicworks/Sharing_Center/gallery/wic_foods3.htm

U.S. Department of Health and Human Services & U.S. Department of Agriculture. (2005). *Dietary guidelines for Americans, 2005*. Washington, DC: Authors. Retrieved September 1, 2009, from http://www.health.gov/dietaryguidelines/dga2005/document/pdf/DGA2005.pdf

U.S. Department of Health and Human Services Administration for Children and Families. (2008). *Office of Head Start legislation & regulations*. Retrieved October 6, 2009, from http://www.acf.hhs.gov/programs/ohs/legislation/index.html

Walls, A. F., Hertzler, A., & Miller, S. M. (2001). Vitamin A, vitamin C, calcium, and iron content of federally funded preschool lunches in Virginia. *Journal of the American Dietetic Association, 101*(3), 348.

Wardle, J., & Cooke, L. (2008). Genetic and environmental determinants of children's food preferences. *British Journal of Nutrition, 99*(S1), S15-S21.

Williams, K. E., Hendy, H., & Knecht, S. (2008). Parent feeding practices and child variables associated with childhood feeding problems. *Journal of Developmental and Physical Disabilities, 20*(3), 231-242.

Zeratsky, K. (2009). *Breakfast: Why is it so important to weight control?* Retrieved October 7, 2009, from http://www.mayoclinic.com/health/food-and-nutrition/AN01119

Zero to Three. (2009). *It's too mushy! It's too spicy! The peas are touching the chicken! (or, how to handle your picky eater)*. Retrieved September 6, 2009, from http://www.zerotothree.org/site/PageServer?pagename=ter_key_health_picky

Chapter 7

Addessi, E., Galloway, A. T., Visalberghi, E., & Birch, L. L. (2005). Specific social influences on the acceptance of novel foods in 2-5-year-old children. *Appetite, 45*(3), 264-271.

Affenito, S. (2007). Breakfast: A missed opportunity. *Journal of the American Dietetic Association, 107*(4), 565-569.

American Academy of Pediatrics. (2007). *AAP parenting corner Q & A: Choking prevention*. Retrieved July 7, 2009, from http://www.aap.org/publiced/br_choking.htm

American Academy of Pediatrics. (2008). *Starting solid foods*. Retrieved June 21, 2009, from http://www.aap.org/publiced/BR_Solids.htm

American Academy of Pediatrics, American Public Health Association, & National Resource Center for Health and Safety in Child Care. (2007). *Caring for our children: National health and safety standards: Guidelines for out-of-home child care* (2nd ed.). Elk Grove, IL: American Academy of Pediatrics.

American Academy of Pediatrics Committee on Nutrition. (2004). In Kleinman, R. (Ed.), *Pediatric nutrition handbook* (5th ed.). Elk Grove, IL: American Academy of Pediatrics.

American Diabetes Association. (2008). Diabetes care in the school and day care setting. *Diabetes Care, 31*(Suppl. 1), S79-S86.

American Dietetic Association. (2004). Providing nutrition service for infants, children and adults with developmental disabilities and special health care needs: Position statement. *Journal of the American Dietetic Association, 104*(1), 97-107.

American Dietetic Association. (2005). Position paper: Benchmarks for nutrition programs in child care settings. *Journal of the American Dietetic Association, 105*, 979-986.

American Dietetic Association. (2006). Position of the American Dietetic Association: Individual-, family-, school-, and community-based interventions for pediatric overweight. *Journal of the American Dietetic Association, 106*(6), 925-945.

American Dietetic Association. (2007). *Nutrition fact sheet: Whole grains made easy*. Retrieved August 25, 2009, from http://www.wheatfoods.org/_FileLibrary/Product/81/Whole_Grains.pdf

American Dietetic Association. (2008a). *Evidence summary: What evidence suggests a relationship between fruit and vegetable intake and blood pressure in healthy and hypertensive adults?* Retrieved March 2, 2008, from http://www.adaevidencelibrary.com/evidence.cfm?evidence_summary_id=250192

American Dietetic Association. (2008b). *Topic: Fruits and vegetables intake and childhood overweight*. Retrieved March 1, 2008, from http://www.adaevidencelibrary.com/topic.cfm?cat=1054

American Dietetic Association. (2008c). Position of the American Dietetic Association: Nutrition guidance for healthy children ages 2 to 11 years. *Journal of the American Dietetic Association, 108*(6), 1038-1047.

American Dietetic Association. (2009). *Executive summary of recommendations: Pediatric weight management*. Retrieved June 22, 2009, from http://www.adaevidencelibrary.com/topic.cfm?cat=3013

American Dietetic Association & American Diabetes Association. (2003). *Exchange lists for meal planning*. Chicago, IL, and Alexandria, VA: Authors.

American Heart Association, Gidding, S. S., Dennison, B. A., Birch, L. L., Daniels, S. R., Gilman, M. W., et al. (2006). Dietary recommendations for children and adolescents: A guide for practitioners. *Pediatrics, 117*(2), 544-559.

American Medical Association. (2007). Obesity: Recommendations of the treatment of pediatric obesity. Retrieved January 5, 2008, from http://www.ama-assn.org/ama/pub/category/11759.html

Anderson, J. (2009, June 11). Birthing green students. *Estacada News*. Retrieved January 13, 2010, from http://www.estacadanews.com/sustainable/print_story.php?story_id=124456510676248000

Bagnell, A., & Davies, T. *Muscular Dystrophy campaign: Nutrition and feeding in individuals with neuromuscular conditions*. Retrieved November 17, 2007, from http://www.muscular-distrophy.org/assets/0000/7842/Nutrition_and_feeding.pdf.

Birch, L. L., Gunder, L., Grimm-Thomas, K., & Laing, L., D. G. (1998). Infants' consumption of a new food enhances acceptance of similar foods. *Appetite, 30*(3), 283–295.

Butte, N., Cobb, K., Dwyer, J., Graney, L., Heird, W., & Rickard, K. (2004). The Start Healthy feeding guidelines for infants and toddlers. *Journal of the American Dietetic Association, 104*(3), 442–454.

California Department of Health Services. Cooking with children. http://www.wicworks.ca.gov/education/nutrition/kidsRecipes/cooking_w_index.htm. http://www.cdph.ca.gov/programs/wicworks/Pages/WICNECookingwithChildren.aspx.

Child Care Inc. (2001). Operating budget for child care programs. A Childcare, Inc. Resource paper, 4. Retrieved October 6, 2009, from http://www.childcareinc.org/pubs/OperatingBudgets.pdf

Code of Federal Regulations. (1998). *Title 7, Part 210.10, Nutrition standards and menu planning approaches for lunches and requirements for afterschool snacks.* pp. 16–37 Retrieved August 20, 2009, from http:// www.fns.usda.gov/cnd/Governance/regulations/7cfr210_09.pdf

Connecticut State Department of Education. (2005). *How can programs identify children's nutrition needs?* Retrieved July 5, 2008, from http://www.sde.ct.gov/sde/search/search.asp

Cooke, L. J., Haworth, C. M., & Wardle, J. (2007). Genetic and environmental influences on children's food neophobia. *American Journal of Clinical Nutrition, 86*(2), 428–433.

Dauchet, L., Amouyel, P., Hercberg, S., & Dallongeville, J. (2006). Fruit and vegetable consumption and risk of coronary heart disease: A meta-analysis of cohort studies. *Journal of Nutrition, 136*(10), 2588–2593.

Davis, M. M., Gance-Cleveland, B., Hassink, S., Johnson, R., Paradis, G., & Resnicow, K. (2007). Recommendations for prevention of childhood obesity. *Pediatrics, 120*(Suppl. 4), S229–S253.

Edwards, G. M. (2003). The health cost of soul food: Introduction. *Topics in Advanced Practice Nursing eJournal, 3*(2).

Ekvall, Shirley W. & Ekvall, Valli K. (Eds.). (2005). *Pediatric nutrition in chronic diseases and developmental disorders: Prevention, assessment and treatment* (2nd ed.) New York: Oxford University Press.

Food Allergy Anaphylaxis Network. (2007). *For the newly diagnosed: Food allergy basics.* Retrieved July 12, 2008, from http://www.foodallergy.org/NewlyDiagnosed/basics.html

Green Mountain Technologies. (2009). *Earth tub.* Retrieved June 23, 2009, from http://www.compostingtechnology.com/invesselsystems/earthtub

Greer, F. R., Sicherer, S. H., Burks, A. W., & Committee on Nutrition and Section on Allergy and Immunology. (2008a). Effects of early nutritional interventions on the development of atopic disease in infants and children: The role of maternal dietary restriction, breast-feeding, timing of introduction of complementary foods, and hydrolyzed formulas. *Pediatrics, 121*(1), 183–191.

Greer, F. R., Sicherer, S. H., Burks, A. W., & Committee on Nutrition and Section on Allergy and Immunology. (2008b). Effects of early nutritional interventions on the development of atopic disease in infants and children: The role of maternal dietary restriction, breast-feeding, timing of introduction of complementary foods, and hydrolyzed formulas. *Pediatrics, 121*(1), 183–191.

Guidetti, M., & Cavazza, N. (2008). Structure of the relationship between parents' and children's food preferences and avoidances: An explorative study. *Appetite, 50*(1), 83–90.

Harris, G. (2008). Development of taste and food preferences in children. *Current Opinion in Clinical Nutrition and Metabolic Care, 11*(3), 315–319.

Harvard School of Public Health. (2008). *The nutrition source fruits & vegetables: The bottom line.* Retrieved March 2, 2008, from http://www.hsph.harvard.edu/nutritionsource/fruits.html

Hendy, H. M., & Raudenbush, B. (2000a). Effectiveness of teacher modeling to encourage food acceptance in preschool children. *Appetite, 34*(1), 61–76.

Hendy, H. M., & Raudenbush, B. (2000b). Effectiveness of teacher modeling to encourage food acceptance in preschool children. *Appetite 34*(1), 61–76.

Hill, P. (2008). Ohio State University fact sheet: Cultural diversity: Eating in America, Asian, Retrieved August 25, 2009, from http://ohioline.osu.edu/hyg-fact/5000/5253.html

Howell, E., & National Food Service Management Institute. (2003). *Diabetes fact sheet for child nutrition professionals.* Retrieved July 13, 2008, from http://www.olemiss.edu/depts/ nfsmi/Information/Newsletters/diabetes.html

Islamic Food and Nutrition Council of America. (2008). *What is halal?* Retrieved July 14, 2008, from http://www.ifanca.org/halal

Katz, D. I., O'Connell, M. O., Yanchou Njike, V., Yeh, M., & Nawaz, H. (2007). Strategies for the prevention and control of obesity in the school setting: Systematic review and meta-analysis. *International Journal of Obesity, 31*, 1–11.

Krishnaswamy, G., Ajitawi, O., & Chi, D. S. (2006). The human mast cell: An overview. *Methods in Molecular Biology, 315*, 13–34.

Kulkarni, K. D. (2004). Food, culture, and diabetes in the United States. *Clinical Diabetes, 22*(4). 190–192.

Martin, J., & Conklin, M. (1999). *Managing child nutrition programs: Leadership for excellence.* Gaithersburg, MD: Aspen Publishers.

Mennella, J. A., & Pepino, M. Y. R., D.R. (2005). Genetic and environmental determinants of bitter perception and sweet preferences. *Pediatrics, 115*(2), e216–e222.

Mennella, J. A., Ziegler, P., Briefel, R., & Novak, T. (2006). Feeding infants and toddlers study: The types of foods fed to Hispanic infants and toddlers. *Journal of the American Dietetic Association, 106*(Suppl. 1), S96–S106.

Mier, N., Piziak, V., Kjar, D., Castillo-Ruiz, O., Velazquez, G., Alfaro, M. E., et al. (2007). Nutrition provided to Mexican-American preschool children on the Texas–Mexico border. *Journal of the American Dietetic Association, 107*(2), 311–315.

National Association for the Education of Young Children. (2008). *Academy for early childhood program accreditation: Standard 5: NAEYC accreditation criteria for health standard.* Retrieved June 14, 2009, from http://www.naeyc.org/academy/standards/standard5/standard5A.asp.

National Food Service Management Institute. (2004). Meal time memo for child care-purchasing for child care centers. University, MS: University of Mississippi. Retrieved January 2, 2010, from http://www.nfsmi.org/documentlibraryfiles/PDF/20080610015834.pdf

National Initiative for Children's Healthcare Quality. (2008). Childhood obesity action network. Boston: Author. Retrieved August 22, 2009, from http://www.nichq.org/NICHQ/Programs/ConferencesAndTraining/ChildhoodObesityActionNetwork.htm

National Resource Center for Health and Child Care and Early Education. (2009). *Healthy kids, healthy care: Illness, chronic conditions and special needs.* Retrieved August 4, 2007, from http://www.healthykids.us/illness.htm

Nevin-Folino, N. L. (2008). *Pediatric manual of clinical dietetics* (2nd ed.). Chicago: American Dietetic Association.

Nicklaus, S., Boggio, V., Chabanet, C., & Issanchou, S. (2005). A prospective study of food variety seeking in childhood, adolescence and early adult life. *Appetite, 44*(3), 289–297.

Nolan, J. E. (2008). *Ohio State University fact sheet: Cultural diversity: Eating in America, Middle Eastern.* Retrieved July 13, 2008, from http://ohioline.osu.edu/hyg-fact/5000/5256.html

Office of Head Start (OHS), Administration for Children and Families (ACF), & U.S. Department of Health and Human Services (HHS). (2008). Statistical fact sheet fiscal year 2008. Retrieved July 6, 2009, from http://www.acf.hhs.gov/programs/ohs/about/fy2008.html

Ohio State University, College of Food, Agriculture, and Environmental Sciences. (2009). *Ohioline—Food: Cultural diversity—Eating in America.* Retrieved August 25, 2009, from http://ohioline.osu.edu/lines/food.html

Oliviera, P. (2005). Connecticut child care center operating budget basics: Calculating your bottom line. Connecticut Voices for Children, retrieved October 6, 2009, from http://www.ctkidslink.org/publications/ece06operatingbud.pdf

Pilant, V. B., & American Dietetic Association. (2006). Position of the American Dietetic Association: Local support for nutrition integrity in schools. *Journal of the American Dietetic Association, 106*(1), 122-133.

Rampersaud, G. C., Pereira, M. A., Girard, B. L., Adams, J., & Metzl, J. D. (2005). Breakfast habits, nutritional status, body weight, and academic performance in children and adolescents. *Journal of the American Dietetic Association, 105*(5), 743.

Riboli, E., & Norat, T. (2003). Epidemiologic evidence of the protective effect of fruit and vegetables on cancer risk. *American Journal of Clinical Nutrition, 78*(3), 559S-569.

Samour, P., & King, K. (2005). *Handbook of pediatric nutrition* (3rd ed.). Boston: Jones and Bartlett Publishers.

Sampson, H. A., Munoz-Furlong, A., Campbell, R. L., Adkinson, N. F., Jr., Bock, S. A., Branum, A., et al. (2006). Second symposium on the definition and management of anaphylaxis: Summary report—Second National Institute of Allergy and Infectious Disease/Food Allergy and Anaphylaxis Network Symposium. *Journal of Allergy and Clinical Immunology, 117*(2), 391-397.

Satter, E. (2005). *Solving feeding problems— What if my child won't eat vegetables?* Retrieved July 1, 2008, from http://www.ellynsatter.com/$spindb.query.memo.kelcyview.17.7

Shuman, M. (2005). *Portland State sustainability —food service.* Retrieved July 15, 2008, from http://www.pdx.edu/sustainability/cs_co_food_services.html

Simons, F. E. R., Frew, A. J., Ansotegui, I. J., Bochner, B.S., Golden, D. B. K., Finkelman, F. D., Leung, D. Y. M., et al. (2007). Risk assessment in anaphylaxis: Current and future approaches. *Journal of Allergy and Clinical Immunology, 120*(1), s2-s24.

Sizer, F., & Whitney, E. (2006). *Nutrition concepts and controversy* (10th ed.). Belmont, CA: Thompson Learning.

Steffen, L. M., Jacobs, D. R., Jr., Stevens, J., Shahar, E., Carithers, T., & Folsom, A. R. (2003). Associations of whole-grain, refined-grain, and fruit and vegetable consumption with risks of all-cause mortality and incident coronary artery disease and ischemic stroke: The atherosclerosis risk in communities (ARIC) study. *American Journal of Clinical Nutrition, 78*(3), 383-390.

Stein, K. (2004). Cultural literacy in health care. *Journal of the American Dietetic Association, 104*(11), 1657-1659.

Society for Nutrition Education, Weight Realities Division. (2002). *Guidelines for childhood obesity prevention programs: Promoting healthy weight in children.* Indianapolis, IN: Author. Retrieved August 22, 2009, from http://nature.berkeley.edu/cwh/PDFs/Chi%20Obesity%20Paper%20.pdf

Tucker, K. L., Hallfrisch, J., Qiao, N., Muller, D., Andres, R., & Fleg, J. L. (2005). The combination of high fruit and vegetable and low saturated fat intakes is more protective against mortality in aging men than is either alone: The Baltimore longitudinal study of aging. *Journal of Nutrition, 135*(3), 556-561.

United Nations Department of Social and Economic Affairs Division for Sustainable Development. (2009). Initiative details page. Retrieved July 6, 2009, from http://webapps01.un.org/dsd/caseStudy/public/displayDetailsAction.do?code=

U.S. Department of Agriculture. (2005). *MyPyramid for kids.* Retrieved June 19, 2008, from http://www.mypyramid.gov/kids/index.html

U.S. Department of Agriculture. (2007). *Nutrient standard menu planning: Healthy meals resource system.* Retrieved March 25, 2008, from http://healthymeals.nal.usda.gov/nal_display/index.php?tax_level=1&info_center=14&tax_subject=234

U.S. Department of Agriculture. (2009). *MyPyramid for preschoolers.* Retrieved July 6, 2009, from http://www.mypyramid.gov/Preschoolers

U.S. Department of Agriculture, Food and Nutrition Service. (2000). *Building blocks for fun and healthy meals—A meal planner for the child and adult care food program.* Retrieved March 26, 2008, from http://teamnutrition.usda.gov/Resources/buildingblocks.html

U.S. Department of Agriculture, Food and Nutrition Service. (2001). *Accommodating children with special dietary needs in school nutrition programs—guidance for food service staff USDA.* Retrieved March 26, 2008, from http://www.fns.usda.gov/cnd/guidance/special_dietary_needs.pdf

U.S. Department of Agriculture, Food and Nutrition Service. (2007a). *Child nutrition labeling.* Retrieved March 27, 2008, from http://www.fns.usda.gov/cnd/CNlabeling/default.htm

U.S. Department of Agriculture, Food and Nutrition Service. (2007b). *Jewish schools, institutions and sponsor: Special diets: Healthy meals resource system.* Retrieved November 16, 2007, from http://desearch.nal.usda.gov/cgi-bin/dexpldcgi?qry1500512842;1

U.S. Department of Agriculture, Food and Nutrition Service. (2007c). *The road to SMI success—A guide for school foodservice directors.* Retrieved July 1, 2008, from http://www.teamnutrition.usda.gov/Resources/roadtosuccess.html

U.S. Department of Agriculture, Food and Nutrition Service. (2008a). *CACFP policy memo: Automatic eligibility for free meal benefits extended to all children enrolled in Head Start.* Retrieved June 23, 2008, from http://www.fns.usda.gov/CND/Care/Regs-Policy/PolicyMemoranda.htm

U.S. Department of Agriculture, Food and Nutrition Service. (2008b). *Child and adult care food program.* Retrieved June 21, 2008, from http://www.fns.usda.gov/cnd/Care/Default.htm

U.S. Department of Agriculture, Food and Nutrition Service. (2008c). *Schools/CN commodity programs.* Retrieved March 25, 2008, from http://www.fns.usda.gov/fdd/programs/schcnp/schcnp_eligibility.htm

U.S. Department of Agriculture, Food and Nutrition Service. (2009). *National school lunch program.* Retrieved July 6, 2009, from http://www.fns.usda.gov/cnd/Lunch

U.S. Department of Health and Human Services. (2000). *ABC's of successful menu planning: Family-style meal service. Building blocks for healthy meals.* Retrieved July 5, 2008 from http://teamnutrition.usda.gov/Resources/buildingblocks.html

U.S. Department of Health and Human Services, Administration for Children and Families. (2006). *Head Start 101.* Retrieved July 14, 2008, from http://www.headstartinfo.org/infocenter/hs101.htm#hspps

U.S. Department of Health and Human Services, Administration for Children and Families. (2007). *Head Start program performance standards and other regulations.* Retrieved June 2, 2008, from http://eclkc.ohs.acf.hhs.gov/hslc/ProgramDesign andManagement/HeadStartRequirements/HeadStartRequirements

U.S. Department of Health and Human Services and U.S. Department of Agriculture. (2005). *Dietary guidelines for Americans, 2005.* Washington, DC: Authors. Retrieved September 1, 2009, from http://www.health.gov/dietaryguidelines/ dga2005/document/pdf/DGA2005.pdf

U.S. Food and Drug Administration. (2005). *U.S. FDA/CFSAN FDA food code.* Retrieved June 1, 2008, from http://www.cfsan.fda.gov/~dms/foodcode.html

U.S. Food and Drug Administration. (2006). *Approaches to establish thresholds for major food allergens and for gluten in food.* Retrieved June 21, 2009, from http://www.fda.gov/Food/LabelingNutrition/FoodAllergensLabeling/GuidanceComplianceRegulatoryInformation/ucm106108.htm

Wardle, J., & Cooke, L. (2008). Genetic and environmental determinants of children's food preferences. *British Journal of Nutrition, 99*(Suppl. 1), S15-S21.

Wardle, J., Cookea, L. J., Gibsona, E. L., Sapochnika, M., Sheihama, A., & Lawson, M. (2003). Increasing children's acceptance of vegetables: A randomized trial of parent-led exposure. *Appetite, 40*(2), 155-162.

Wesnes, K. A., Pincock, C., Richardson, D. Helm, G., & Hails, S. (2003). Breakfast reduces declines in attention and memory over the morning in schoolchildren. *Appetite, 41*(3), 329-331.

Whole Grains Council. (2008). *The whole grains stamp.* Retrieved July 3, 2008, from http://www.wholegrainscouncil.org

WIC Works Resource Team. (2009). *WIC works resource system.* Retrieved June 7, 2009, from http://www.nal.usda.gov/wicworks

Chapter 8

Aiello, A. E., Coulborn, R. M., Perez, V., & Larson, E. L. (2008). Effect of hand hygiene on infectious disease risk in the community setting: A meta-analysis. *American Journal of Public Health, 98*(8), 1372-1381.

Alvarez, V. B., Bash, W., Cornelius, B., Courtney, P. & Knipe, L. (2007). *Ensuring safe food—A HACCP-based plan for ensuring food safety in retail establishments* (Ohio State University Extension Bulletin 901). Retrieved September 17, 2009, from http://ohioline.osu.edu/b901/index.html

American Academy of Pediatrics. (2007). *Parenting corner Q&A: Choking prevention.* Retrieved September 15, 2009, from http://www.aap.org/publiced/BR_Choking.htm

American Academy of Pediatrics, American Public Health Association, & National Resource Center for Health and Safety in Child Care and Early Education. (2007). *National health and safety performance standards: Guidelines for out-of-home child care programs* (2nd ed.). Elk Grove Village, IL: American Academy of Pediatrics; Washington, DC: American Public Health Association. Retrieved August 31, 2009, from http://www.eric.ed.gov/ERICDocs/data/ericdocs2sql/content_storage_01/0000019b/80/14/0d/14.pdf

American Red Cross. (2009). *Prepare your school and students.* Retrieved September 16, 2009, from http://www.redcross.org/portal/site/en/menuitem.d8aaecf214c576bf971e4cfe43181aa0/?vgnextoid=0dc51a53f1c37110VgnVCM1000003481a10aRCRD&vgnextfmt=default

B.C. First Nations Head Start. (2003, Summer). *Using traditional foods.* Retrieved September 15, 2009, from http://www.bcfnhs.org/downloads/sixComponents/culture/CULT_Traditional_Foods.pdf

Benton County Health Department. (2006, April 27). *Making the news in Benton County: Norwalk-like virus health alert.* Retrieved September 16, 2009, from http://www.co.benton.or.us/read_article.php?d=&p=72

Boggs, J. D., Whitwam, R. E., Hale, L. M., & Briscoe, R. P., & Kahn, S. E. (2001). Outbreak of Listeriosis associated with homemade Mexican-style cheese—North Carolina, October 2000-January 2001. *Journal of the American Medical Association, 286*(6), 664-665.

Centers for Disease Control and Prevention. (2005). *Preventing health risks associated with drinking unpasteurized or untreated juice.* Retrieved September 17, 2009, from http://www.cdc.gov/foodborne/juice_spotlight.htm

Centers for Disease Control and Prevention. (2008a). *Disease listing: Botulism general information.* Retrieved September 14, 2009, from http://www.cdc.gov/nczved/dfbmd/disease_listing/botulism_gi.html

Centers for Disease Control and Prevention. (2008b, April 14). Preliminary FoodNet data on the incidence of infection with pathogens transmitted commonly through food—10 states, 2007. *Morbidity and Mortality Weekly Report, 57*(14), 366-370.

Centers for Disease Control and Prevention. (2009). Preliminary FoodNet data on the incidence of infection with pathogens transmitted commonly through food—10 states, 2008. *Morbidity and Mortality Weekly Report, 58*(13), 333-337.

Clemson University Department of Food Science and Human Nutrition. (2008). *Differentiate between the major types of foodborne illnesses—infection, intoxication, and toxin-mediated infection.* Retrieved September 17, 2009, from http://www.foodsafetysite.com/educators/competencies/general/definitions/def5.html

Colorado State University Extension. (2006). *Sushi: Minimizing the food safety risk.* Retrieved September 15, 2009, from http://www.ext.colostate.edu/safefood/newsltr/v10n3s01.html

Federal Emergency Management Agency. (2009). *Disaster assistance for individuals and families.* Retrieved September 15, 2009, from http:// www.fema.gov

Field, C. J. (2005). The immunological components of human milk and their effect on immune development in infants. *Journal of Nutrition, 135*(1), 1-4.

Food Safe Schools. (2004). *Food safety for the local health department.* Retrieved September 17, 2009, from http://www.foodsafeschools.org/healthdepartment.php

Fraser, A. (2007, October). *HACCP in your school.* Retrieved September 14, 2008, from http://www.foodsafetysite.com/resources/pdfs/schoolhaccp/SchoolHACCPManual.pdf

Fraser, A. (2008). *Food microbiology: An introduction for food safety educators.* Retrieved September 15, 2009, from http://www.foodsafetysite.com/educators/microbiology/overview

Goodrich, R. M., Schneider, K. R., & Schmidt, R. H. (2005, August). *HACCP: An overview.* Retrieved September 14, 2009, from http://edis.ifas.ufl.edu/FS122

Hoffman, R. E., Greenblatt, J., Matyas, B. T., Sharp, D. J., Esteban, E., & Liang, A. K. H. (2005). Capacity of state and territorial health agencies to prevent foodborne illness. *Emerging Infectious Diseases, 11*(1), 11-16.

Homeland Security. (2009). *Ready America: Get a kit.* Retrieved September 16, 2009, from http://www.ready.gov/america/getakit

Hospitality Institute of Technology and Management. (2005). *AMC-HACCP publications and reports: Double hand washing with a fingernail brush HACCP.* Retrieved September 16, 2009, from http://www.hi-tm.com/Documents/Handflow.html

Imhoff, B., Morse, D., Shiferaw, B., Hawkins, M., Vugia, D., Lance-Parker, S., et al. (2004). Burden of self-reported acute diarrheal illness in FoodNet surveillance areas, 1998-1999. *Clinical Infectious Diseases, 38*(Suppl. 3), S219-S26.

Iowa State University Extension. (2007). *Implementation of HACCP in schools.* Retrieved September 16, 2009, from http://www.extension.iastate.edu/HRIM/HACCP/haccpinschools.htm

Jay, M. J., Loessner, M. J., & Golden, D. A. (2005). *Modern food microbiology* (7th ed.). New York: Springer Science + Business Media.

Jelley, K. L., & Ohio State University Extension. (2003). *Health and safety for caregivers: Preventing food borne illness in the child care setting.* Retrieved October 30, 2009, from http://ohioline.osu.edu/hsc-fact/pdf/HSC5.pdf

Jones, T. F., Ingram, L. A., Fullerton, K. E., Marcus, R., Anderson, B. J., McCarthy, P. V., et al. (2007). A case-control study of the epidemiology of sporadic salmonella infection in infants. *Pediatrics, 118*(6), 2380.

Krueger, L. (2007). *Accommodating children with special dietary needs.* Retrieved September 17, 2009, from dpi.wi.gov/fns/ppt/ms_sdn_2.ppt

Lelieveld, H. L. M., Mostert, T., Holah, J., & White, B. (2003). *Hygiene in food processing: Principles and practice.* Boca Raton, FL: CRC Press.

Lynch, M. F., Tauxe, R. V., & Hedberg, C. W. (2009). The growing burden of foodborne outbreaks due to contaminated fresh produce: Risks and opportunities. *Epidemiology and Infection, 137*(3), 307-315.

Marchiony, A. (2004). *Food-safe kitchens.* Upper Saddle River, NJ: Pearson Prentice Hall.

Marcus, R. (2008). New information about pediatric food borne infections: The view from FoodNet. *Current Opinions in Pediatrics, 20,* 79-84. Retrieved September 17, 2009, from http://info.med.yale.edu/eph/eip/publications/MOP284.pdf

Marriott, N. G. & Gravani, R. B. (2006). *Principles of food sanitation* (5th ed.). Gaithersburg, MD: Aspen Publishers.

McElhatton, A., & Marshall, R. (2006). *Food safety: A practical and case study approach (integrating safety and environmental knowledge into food studies towards European sustainable development).* Berlin: Springer.

McSwane, D., Rue, N. R., & Linton, R. (2005). *Essentials of food safety and sanitation* (4th ed.). Upper Saddle River, NJ: Pearson Prentice Hall.

Mississippi State University Extension Service. (2005). *Food safety: What do I need to consider when handling jars of baby food?* Retrieved September 15, 2009, from http://msucares.com/health/food_safety/foodfaq61.html

Monterrosa, E. C., Frongillo, E. A., Vasquez-Garibay, E. M., Romero-Velarde, E., Casey, L. M., & Willows, N. D. (2008). Predominant breast-feeding from birth to six months is associated with fewer gastrointestinal infections and increased risk for iron deficiency among infants. *Journal of Nutrition, 138*(8), 1499-1504.

Nash, C. (2002). *NEHA training: Food safety first principles.* Canada: Chadwick House Group Limited.

National Association for the Education of Young Children, Academy for Early Childhood Program Accreditation. (2009). *Standard 5: NAEYC accreditation criteria for health standard.* Retrieved May 23, 2009, from http://www.naeyc.org/academy/primary/standardsintro

National Food Service Management Institute. (2002). *Serving it safe, 2nd edition.* Retrieved September 17, 2009, from http://www.olemiss.edu/depts/nfsmi/Information/sisindex.html

National Food Service Management Institute. (2005a). *Food safety standard operating procedures (SOPs).* Retrieved September 15, 2009, from http://www.nfsmi.org/ResourceOverview.aspx?ID=75

National Food Service Management Institute. (2005b). *Mealtime memo for child care: Safe food storage.* Retrieved September 16, 2009, from http://www.olemiss.edu/depts/nfsmi/Information/Newsletters/meme2005-4 .pdf

National Food Service Management Institute. (2005c). *HACCP-based SOPs: Reheating potentially hazardous food.* Retrieved September 15, 2009, from http://sop.nfsmi.org/HACCPBasedSOPs/ReheatingPHF.pdf

National Food Service Management Institute. (2009). *Food safety fact sheet: Thawing foods.* Retrieved September 15, 2009, from http://www.nfsmi.org/documentlibraryfiles/PDF/20090319104324.pdf

National Institute of Diabetes and Digestive and Kidney Diseases. (2007). *Bacteria and foodborne illness.* Retrieved September 16, 2009, from http://digestive.niddk.nih.gov/ddiseases/pubs/bacteria/#2

National Resource Center for Health and Safety in Child Care and Early Education. (2009). *Healthy Kids, Healthy Care: Illness, Chronic Conditions and Special Needs.* Retrieved October 30, 2009, from http://www.healthykids.us/illness.htm

National Restaurant Association. (2008). *ServSafe coursebook* (5th ed.). Upper Saddle River, NJ: Pearson Prentice Hall.

Neifert, M. (2009). *Pediatric advisor 2009.1: The storage and handling of breast milk.* Retrieved October 30, 2009, from http://www.med.umich.edu/1libr/pa/pa_storage_pep.htm

New Mexico State University Cooperative Extension Service. (2004). *Food safety for home child care providers: Chill.* Retrieved September 16, 2009, from http://www.childcarefoodsafety.com/chill/chill.html

New York State Department of Health. (2006, January). *Food defense strategies—A self-assessment guide for food service operators.* Retrieved September 16, 2009, from http://www.health.state.ny.us/environmental/indoors/food_safety/food_defense_strategies.htm

Noah, N. (2009). Food poisoning from raw fruit and vegetables. introduction. *Epidemiology and Infection, 137*(3), 305–306.

Ohio State University Extension. (2003). *Health and safety for caregivers: Preventing food borne illness in the child care environment.* Retrieved September 14, 2009, from http://ohioline.osu.edu/hsc-fact/pdf/HSC5.pdf

Partnership for Food Safety Education (PFSE). (2006). *Safe food handling: Cook to proper temperatures.* Retrieved September 17, 2009, from http://www.fightbac.org/content/view/172/2/

Pennsylvania Emergency Management Agency. (2008). *PEMA: Day care planning tool kit.* Retrieved September 22, 2008, from http://www.portal.state.pa.us/portal/server.pt?open=512&objID=4625&&PageID=480221&level=2&css=L2&mode=2

Schmidt, R. H., & Newslow, D. L. (2007). *Hazard analysis critical control points (HACCP)—Principle 3: Establish critical limits; Principle 4: Monitoring critical control points (CCPs).* Retrieved September 17, 2009, from http://edis.ifas.ufl.edu/FS141

Sneed, J., & Strohbehn, C. H. (2008). Trends impacting food safety in retail foodservice: Implications for dietetics practice. *Journal of the American Dietetic Association, 108*(7), 1170–1177.

U.S. Department of Agriculture. (2006). *USDA recipes for schools.* Retrieved September 17, 2009, from http://www.olemiss.edu/depts/nfsmi/Information/school_recipe_index_alpha.html

U.S. Department of Agriculture. (2008). *About food safety and inspection service.* Retrieved September 14, 2009, from http://www.fsis.usda.gov/About_FSIS/index.asp

U.S. Department of Agriculture, Food and Nutrition Service. (2005, June). *Guidance for school food authorities: Developing a school food safety program based on the process approach to HACCP principles.* Retrieved September 15, 2009, from http://www.fns.usda.gov/cnd/CNlabeling/Food-Safety/HACCPGuidance.pdf

U.S. Department of Agriculture, Food Safety and Inspection Service. (2006). *Safe food handling: How temperatures affect food.* Retrieved September 15, 2009, from http://www.fsis.usda.gov/Fact_Sheets/How_Temperatures_Affect_Food/index.asp

U.S. Department of Agriculture, Food and Nutrition Service. (2008). School food safety program based on hazard analysis and critical control point principles: Proposed rule. *Federal Register, 73*(151).

U.S. Department of Agriculture, Food Safety and Inspection Service. (2009, May 4). *New York firm recalls ground beef products due to possible E. coli O157:H7 contamination.* Retrieved September 15, 2009, from http://www.fsis.usda.gov/News_&_Events/Recall_019_2009_Release/index.asp

U.S. Food and Drug Administration. (2009). *Once baby arrives. Food safety for moms-to-be.* Retrieved October 29, 2009, from http://www.fda.gov/Food/ResourcesForYou/HealthEducators/ucm089629.htm

U.S. Environmental Protection Agency. (2007). *Food safety.* Retrieved September 15, 2009, from http://www.epa.gov/oecaagct/tfsy.html

U.S. Environmental Protection Agency. (2009a). *Food irradiation: Radiation protection.* Retrieved September 15, 2009, from http://www.epa.gov/rpdweb00/sources/food_irrad.html

U.S. Environmental Protection Agency. (2009b). *Labeling: Radiation protection.* Retrieved September 15, 2009, from http://www.epa.gov/rpdweb00/sources/food_labeling .html

U.S. Food and Drug Administration. (2005, September 1). Prevent your child from choking. *FDA Consumer Magazine.* Retrieved September 17, 2009, from http://www.encyclopedia.com/doc/1G1-151662143.html

U.S. Food and Drug Administration. (2007a). *Bad bug book: Escherichia coli O157:H7.* Retrieved September 17, 2009, from http://www.fda.gov/Food/FoodSafety/FoodborneIllness/FoodborneIllnessFoodbornePathogensNaturalToxins/BadBugBook/ucm071284.htm

U.S. Food and Drug Administration. (2007b, March 23). *FDA finalizes report on 2006 spinach outbreak.* Retrieved September 17, 2009, from http://www.fda.gov/NewsEvents/Newsroom/PressAnnouncements/2007/ucm108873.htm

U.S. Food and Drug Administration. (2008b, September 12). *FDA issues health information advisory on infant formula.* Retrieved September 17, 2009, from http://www.highbeam.com/doc/1G1-184816822.html

U.S. Food and Drug Administration. (2008a, September 23). *FDA updates health information advisory on melamine contamination.* Retrieved September 17, 2009, from http://www.fda.gov/NewsEvents/Newsroom/PressAnnouncements/ucm161499.htm

U.S. Food and Drug Administration. (2008c). *Hazard analysis critical control point.* Retrieved September 17, 2009, from http://www.cfsan.fda.gov/~comm/haccpov.html

U.S. Food and Drug Administration. (2008d). *Irradiation: A safe measure for safer iceberg lettuce and spinach.* Retrieved September 17, 2009, from http://www.fda.gov/downloads/ForConsumers/ConsumerUpdates/UCM143389.pdf

U.S. Food and Drug Administration. (2009a). *FDA food code.* Retrieved September 15, 2009, from http://www.fda.gov/Food/FoodSafety/RetailFoodProtection/FoodCode/default.htm

U.S. Food and Drug Administration. (2009b). *Torres Hillsdale country cheese LLC announces the recall of asadero and oaxaca cheeses due to possible Listeria contamination.* Retrieved September 15, 2009, from http://www.fda.gov/Safety/Recalls/ArchiveRecalls/2009/ucm128978.htm

U.S. Food and Drug Administration, Center for Food Safety and Applied Nutrition. (2004a). *Chapter 2: Current and proposed definitions of "potentially hazardous foods."* Retrieved September 16, 2009, from http://www.fda.gov/Food/ScienceResearch/ResearchAreas/SafePracticesforFoodProcesses/ucm094143.htm

U.S. Food and Drug Administration, Center for Food Safety and Applied Nutrition. (2004b). *Food Allergen Labeling and Consumer Protection Act of 2004* (Public Law 108-282, Title II). Retrieved September 15, 2009, from http://www.cfsan.fda.gov/~dms/alrgact.html

U.S. Food and Drug Administration, Center for Food Safety and Applied Nutrition. (2006a). *Food Allergen Labeling and Consumer Protection Act of 2004 questions and answers.* Retrieved September 14, 2009, from http://www.fda.gov/Food/LabelingNutrition/FoodAllergensLabeling/GuidanceComplianceRegulatoryInformation/ucm106890.htm

U.S. Food and Drug Administration, Center for Food Safety and Applied Nutrition. (2006b). *Managing food safety: A manual for the voluntary use of HACCP principles for operators of food service and retail establishments.* Retrieved September 15, 2009, from http://www.cfsan.fda.gov/~dms/hret2toc.html

U.S. Food and Drug Administration, Center for Food Safety and Applied Nutrition. (2007). *FDA/CFSAN: Food safety for you.* Retrieved September 17, 2008, from http://web54.sd54.k12.il.us/schools/stevenson/Food_Safety_For_You!.pdf

World Health Organization. (2008). *Melamine-contamination event, China, September-October 2008.* Retrieved September 17, 2009, from http://www.who.int/environmental_health_emergencies/events/Melamine_2008/en/index.html

Chapter 9

American Academy of Pediatrics, American Public Health Association, & National Resource Center for Health and Safety in Child Care and Early Education. (2002). *Caring for our children: National health and safety performance standards: Guidelines for out-of-home child care programs* (2nd ed.). Elk Grove Village, IL: American Academy of Pediatrics; Washington, DC: American Public Health Association. Retrieved August 31, 2009, from http://www.eric.ed.gov/ERICDocs/data/ericdocs2sql/content_storage_01/0000019b/80/14/0d/14.pdf

American Academy of Pediatrics & Migrant Clinician Network. (2000). *Guidelines for the care of migrant farmworkers' children* (J. McLauring, Ed.). Elk Grove, IL: Author.

Ball, J., & Bindler, R. C. (2006). Social and environmental influences on the child and adolescent. Chap. 7 in J. Ball & R. Bindler (Eds.), *Child health nursing: Partnering with children and families* (pp. 191-199). Upper Saddle River, NJ: Pearson Prentice Hall.

Bortz, W. (2005). Policy, biology, and health. *American Journal of Public Health, 95*(3), 389-392.

Bronfenbrenner, U. (1979). *The ecology of human development: Experiments by nature and design.* Cambridge, MA: Harvard University Press.

California Dental Association (n.d.). *Dental health education resource guide: Preschool through 5th grade.* Retrieved April 2009 from http://www.cda.org/library/dentalhealthguide.pdf

Centers for Disease Control and Prevention. (2009, March 3). *Healthy youth! nutrition, physical activity, and childhood obesity: Local wellness policy tools and resources.* Retrieved April 25, 2009, from http://www.cdc.gov/HealthyYouth/healthtopics/wellness.htm

Dowda, M., Brown, W., McIver, Karin, A., Pfeiffer, J., O'Neill, C., et al. (2009). Policies and characteristics of the preschool environ- ment and physical activity of young children. *Pediatrics, 123,* e261-e266.

Emerson, E. (2009). Relative child poverty, income inequality, wealth, and health. *Journal of the American Medical Association, 301*(4), 425-426.

English, T. (2008). *Poor neighborhoods create health "double jeopardy" for minority kids.* Center for the Advancement of Health. Retrieved September 23, 2009, from http://www.cfah.org/hbns/archives/getDocument.cfm?documentID=1674

Fass, S., & Cauthen, N. (2009, June). *Ten questions about child poverty and family economic hardship.* National Center for Child Poverty. Retrieved July 24, 2009, from http://www.nccp.org/publications/pub_829.html#question7

Gehshan, S., & Wyatt, M. (2007). *Improving oral health care for young children* (Publication No. 2007-203). Washington, DC: National Academy of State Health Policy. Retrieved April 2009 from http://www.oralhealthamerica.org/pdf/NASHPImprovingOralHealthofYoungChildren.pdf

Institute of Medicine. (2003). *Unequal treatment; Confronting racial and ethnic disparities in healthcare* (B. Smedley, A. Stith, & A. Nelson, Eds.). Washington, DC: National Academies Press.

Lapin, B., & Smith, J. B. (2008). *Dental care: The often neglected part of health care.* New Haven, CT: The School of the 21st Century, Yale University. Retrieved September 23, 2009, from http://www.yale.edu/21C/pdf/2009_IssueBrief_DentalCare_updated.pdf

National Association for Sport and Physical Education. (2002). *Active start: A statement of physical activity guidelines for children birth to five years.* Reston, VA: Author.

National Center for Education in Maternal and Child Health & Georgetown University. (2008). *Bright futures.* Retrieved February 2, 2009, from www.brightfutures.org

Prilleltensky, I., & Nelson, G. (2000). Promoting child and family wellness: Priorities for psychological and social interventions. *Journal of Community and Applied Social Psychology, 10*(2), 85-105.

Ritchie, S. & Willer, B. editors. *Health: A guide to the NAEYC early childhood program standard and related accreditation criteria.* National Association for the Education of Young Children: Washington, DC: p. 21.

Spector, R. (2009). *Cultural diversity in health and illness* (7th ed.). Upper Saddle River, NJ: Pearson Prentice Hall.

Stebbins, H., & Knitzer, J. (2007, June). *State early childhood policies: Highlights from the improving the odds for young children project.* New York: National Center for Child Poverty, Columbia University Mailman School of Public Health. Retrieved September 23, 2009, from http://www.nccp.org/publications/pdf/text_725.pdf

Turner, M., & Kaye, D. (2006). *How does family well-being vary across different types of neighborhoods.* Washington, DC: The Urban Institute.

Turnock, B. J. (2004). *Public health: What it is and how it works* (3rd ed.). Sudbury, MA: Jones and Bartlett Publishers.

U.S. Department of Health and Human Services, Administration for Children and Families. (2007). *Head Start program performance standards and other regulations.* Retrieved June 2, 2008, from http://eclkc.ohs.acf.hhs.gov/hslc/ProgramDesignandManagement/HeadStartRequirements/HeadStartRequirements

Watura, J. (2002). Nut allergies in schoolchildren: A survey of schools in the Severn NHS Trust. *Archives of Disease in Childhood, 86*(4), 240-244.

Wilensky, G., & Satcher, D. (2009). Don't forget about the social determinants of health. *Health Affairs, 28*(2), w194-w198.

Wittmer, D., & Petersen, S. (2006). Infant and Toddler Development and Responsive Program Planning: A Relationship-Based Approach. Upper Saddle River, NJ: Person.

World Health Organization. (2003a). *Preamble to the Constitution of the World Health Organization as adopted by the International Health Conference, New York, 19-22 June 1946; signed on 22 July 1946 by the representatives of States (Official Records of the World Health Organization, no. 2, p. 100) and entered into force on 7 April 1948.* Retrieved July 10, 2009, from http://www.who.int/about/definition/en/print.html

World Health Organization. (2003b). *Social determinants of health: The solid facts* (2nd ed., R. Wilkinson & M. Marmot, Eds.). Retrieved July 2009 from http://www.euro.who.int/InformationSources/Publications/Catalogue/20020808_2

Chapter 10

American Academy of Pediatric Dentistry. (2009). *Frequently asked questions.* Retrieved September 29, 2009, from http://www.aapd.org/pediatricinformation/faq.asp

American Academy of Pediatrics. (2005a). *The complete and authoritative guide: Caring for your baby and young child; birth to age 5.* New York: Bantam Books.

American Academy of Pediatrics. (2005b). *The complete and authoritative guide: Caring for your baby and young child; ages 5 to 12.* New York: Bantam Books.

American Academy of Pediatrics. (2009). In L. K. Pickering, C. J. Baker, D. W. Kimberlin, & S. S. Long (Eds.), *Red book: 2009 report of the Committee on Infectious Diseases* (28th ed.). Elk Grove Village, IL: Author.

American Academy of Pediatrics Committee on Environmental Health. (2005). Lead exposure in children: Prevention, detection, and management. *Pediatrics, 116*(4), 1036-1047.

American Academy of Pediatrics, American Public Health Association, & National Resource Center for Health and Safety in Child Care and Early Education. (2002). *Caring for our children: National health and safety performance standards: Guidelines for* out-of-home child care programs (2nd ed.). Elk Grove Village, IL: American Academy of Pediatrics; Washington, DC: American Public Health Association. Retrieved August 31, 2009, from http://www.eric.ed.gov/ERICDocs/data/ericdocs2sql/content_storage_01/0000019b/80/14/0d/14.pdf

American Dental Association. (2009). *Give kids a smile*. Retrieved July 31, 2009, from http://www.aapd.org/pediatricinformation/faq.asp

Bayer, J. K., Hiscock, H., Ukoumunne, O., Price, A., & Wake, M. (2008). Early childhood aetiology of mental health problems: a longitudinal population-based study. *Journal of Child Psychology and Psychiatry, 49*(11):1166-74.

Centers for Disease Control and Prevention. (2006). *Childcare and school immunization requirements, 2005-2006*. Retrieved September 28, 2009, from http://www.cdc.gov/vaccines/vac-gen/laws/downloads/izlaws05-06.pdf

Centers for Disease Control and Prevention. (2009). *Toys*. Retrieved July 31, 2009 from http://www.cdc.gov/nceh/lead/tips/toys.htm

Centers for Disease Control and Prevention. (2009). *Recommendations and guidelines: 2009 child & adolescent immunization schedules*. Retrieved September 28, 2009, from http://www.cdc.gov/vaccines/recs/schedules/child-schedule.htm

Centers for Disease Control. (2008). *Epidemiology and prevention of vaccine-preventable diseases* (10th edition, 2nd printing ed.). (W. Atkinson, J. Hamborsky, L. McIntyre, & S. Wolfe, Eds.). Washington, DC: Public Health Foundation.

Child and Adolescent Health Measurement Initiative. (2003) *2003 National survey of children's health, data resource center for child and adolescent health website*. Retrieved September 29, 2009, from http://www.nschdata.org

Early Head Start National Resource Center. (2009). *Developmental screening, assessment and evaluation: Key elements for individualizing curricula in early Head Start programs* (Technical Assistance Paper No. 4). Retrieved September 29, 2009, from http://www.zerotothree.org/site/DocServer/FinalTAP.pdf?docID=221

Elder, J., Broyles, S., Brennan, J., Zuniga de Nuncio, M., & Nader, P. (2005). Acculturation, parent-child acculturation differential, and chronic disease risk factors in a Mexican-American population. *Journal of Immigrant Health, 7*(1), 1-9.

Farel, A., & Kotch, J. (2005). The child from 1 to 4: The toddler and preschool years. In J. Kotch (Ed.), *Maternal and child health; Programs, problems, and policy in public health* (2nd ed., pp. 159-201). Sudbury, MA: Jones and Bartlett Publishers.

Greenberg, J., Evans, A., Harris, K., Loyo, J., Ray, T., Spaulding, C., et al. (2007). Preschooler feeding practices and beliefs: Differences among Spanish- and English-speaking WIC clients. *Family and Community Health, 30*(3), 257-270.

Gupta, R. S., Pascoe, J. M., Blanchard, T. C., Langkamp, D., Duncan, P. M., Gorski, P. A., et al. (2009). Child health in child care: A multi-state survey of Head Start and non-Head Start child care directors. *Journal of Pediatric Health Care, 23*(3), 43-149.

Harley, K., Stamm, N., & Eskenazi, B., (2007). The effect of time in the U.S. on the duration of breastfeeding in women of Mexican descent, *Maternal and Child Health Journal, 11*(2), 119-125.

Heward, W. (2009). *Exceptional children: An introduction to special education* (9th ed.). Upper Saddle River, NJ: Pearson.

Ikeda, J., Crawford, P., & Woodward-Lopez, G. (2006). BMI screening in schools: helpful or harmful. *Health Education Research, 21*(6), 761-769.

Kentucky Cabinet for Health and Family Services. (2009). *The Health Insurance Portability Act of 1996 (HIPAA)*. Retrieved September 28, 2009, from http://chfs.ky.gov/dcbs/dcc/hipaa.htm

Laraque, D., & Trasande, L., (2005). Lead poisoning: Successes and 21st century challenges. *Pediatrics in Review, 26*(12), 435-443.

Mayer, G. G., & Villaire, M. (2007). *Health literacy in primary care: A clinician's guide*. New York: Springer.

National Center of Medical Home Initiatives for Children with Special Needs. (2007). *What is a medical home?* Accessed September 29, 2009, from http://www.medicalhomeinfo.org

National Conference of State Legislatures. (2009, September). *States with religious and philosophical exemptions from school immunization requirements*. Retrieved September 29, 2009, from http://www.ncsl.org/programs/health/SchoolExempLawsChart.htm

Omer, S., Pan, W., Halsey, N., Stokley, S., Moulton, L., Navar, A., et al. (2006). Nonmedical exemptions to school immunization requirements: Secular trends and association of state policies with pertussis incidence. *Journal of the American Medical Association, 296*(14), 1757-1763.

Owens, R. E., Metz, D. E., & Haas, A. (Eds.). (2007). *Introduction to communication disorders: A lifespan perspective* (3rd ed.). Boston: Allyn & Bacon.

Pickering, L., & Orenstein, W. (2008). Active immunization. In S. Long (Ed.), *Principles and practice of pediatric infectious diseases* (3rd ed., pp. 48-71). Philadelphia: Churchill Livingstone.

Prevent Blindness America. (2005). *Signs of possible eye problems in children*. Accessed September 29, 2009, from http://www.preventblindness.org/children/trouble_signs.html

Squires, J. (2003). *The importance of early identification of social and emotional difficulties in preschool children*. Retrieved September 29, 2009, from http://asq.uoregon.edu/pdf/ImportEarly_IdenCIR.pdf

Thomas, A., & Chess, S. (1977). *Temperament and development*. New York: Brunner-Mazel.

Tingley, D. H. (2007). Vision screening essentials: Screening today for eye disorders in the pediatric patient. *Pediatrics in Review, 28*(2), 54-61.

U.S. Department of Health and Human Services, Administration of Children and Families. (n.d.). *Child health record*. Retrieved July 31, 2009, from http://eclkc.ohs.acf.hhs.gov/hslc/resources/ECLKC_Bookstore/Child%20Health%20Record.htm

U.S. Food and Drug Administration. (2005). *Thimerosal in vaccines*. Retrieved July 31, 2009, from http://www.fda.gov/cber/vaccine/thimerosal.htm

U.S. Preventive Services Task Force. (2008). Universal screening for hearing loss in newborns: U.S. Preventive Services Task Force recommendation statement. *Pediatrics, 122*(1), 143-148.

Chapter 11

American Academy of Pediatrics. (2009). In L. K. Pickering, C. J. Baker, D. W. Kimberlin, & S. S. Long (Eds.), *Red book: 2009 report of the Committee on Infectious Diseases* (28th ed.). Elk Grove Village, IL: Author.

American Academy of Pediatrics, American Public Health Association, & National Resource Center for Health and Safety in Child Care and Early Education. (2002). *Caring for our children: National health and safety performance standards: Guidelines for out-of-home child care programs* (2nd ed.). Elk Grove Village, IL: American Academy of Pediatrics; Washington, DC: American Public Health Association. Retrieved August 31, 2009, from http://www.eric.ed.gov/ERICDocs/data/ericdocs2sql/content_storage_01/0000019b/80/14/0d/14.pdf

Ball, J., & Bindler, R. (2006). Infectious and communicable diseases, Chapter 19 in *Child health nursing: Partnering with children and families* (pp. 595-645). Upper Saddle River, NJ: Pearson Prentice Hall.

Bresee, J. (2008). Viral gastroenteritis, Chapter 60 in S. Long (Ed.), *Principles and practice of pediatric infectious disease* (3rd ed., pp. 383-387). Philadelphia: Churchill Livingstone.

Centers for Disease Control and Prevention. (2006). Preventing tetanus, diphtheria, and pertussis among adults: Use of tetanus toxoid, reduced diphtheria toxoid and acellular pertussis. *Morbidity and Mortality Weekly Report, 55*(RR-17), 1-33.

Centers for Disease Control and Prevention. (2007a). Guidelines for animals in school settings. *Morbidity and Mortality Weekly Report, 56*(RR05), 18-19.

Centers for Disease Control and Prevention. (2007b, October 12). *Standard precautions*. Retrieved May 14, 2009, from http://www.cdc.gov/ncidod/dhqp/gl_isolation_standard.html

Centers for Disease Control and Prevention. (2007a). *Epidemiology and prevention of vaccine-preventable diseases* (10th ed.), W. Atkinson, J. Hamborsky, L. McIntyre, & S. Wolfe (Eds.). Washington, DC: Public Health Foundation.

Centers for Disease Control and Prevention. (2009a). *Epidemiology and Prevention of Vaccine-Preventable Diseases.* (11th ed.,), W. Atkinson, S.Wolfe, J. Hamborsky & L. McIntyre (Eds.). Washington, DC: Public Health Foundation.

Centers for Disease Control and Prevention. (2008a, June 30). *Methicillin-resistant Staphy- lococcus aureus (MRSA) in schools.* Retrieved April 6, 2009, from http://www.cdc.gov/ncidod/dhqp/ar_mrsa_in_ schools.html

Centers for Disease Control and Prevention. (2008b, September 11). *National MRSA education initiative: Preventing MRSA skin infections.* Retrieved April 6, 2009, from http://www.cdc.gov/mrsa

Ford-Jones, E. L., & Ryan, G. (2004). Implications for the fetus of maternal infections in pregnancy. In J. Cohen & W. G. Powderly (Eds.), *Infectious diseases* (2nd ed.). New York: Elsevier.

Kemper, K., Vohra, S., & Walls, R. (2008). The use of complementary and alternative medicine in pediatrics. *Pediatrics, 122*(6), 1374-1386.

Kerschner, J., (2007) *Nelson textbook of pediatrics* Chapter 639 in R. Kleigman, R. Behrman, H. Jenson, & B. Stanton (Eds) Otitis media, (18 ed. pp. 2532-2545). Philadelphia: Saunders Elsevier.

Kotch, J.B., Isbell, P., Weber, D.J., Nguyen, V., Savage, E., Gunn, E., Skinner, M., Fowlkes, S., Virk, J., & Allen, J., (2007). Hand-washing and diapering equipment reduces disease among children in out-of-home child care centers. *Pediatrics.* 120(1), e29-36.

Mumcuoglu, K., Meinking, T., Burkhart, C., & Burkhart, C. (2006). Head louse infestations: The "no nit" policy and its consequences. *International Journal of Dermatology, 45*(8), 891-896.

Pappas, D., & Hendley, J. (2008). The common cold. Chapter 28 in S. Long (Ed.), *Principles and practice of pediatric infectious diseases* (3rd ed., pp. 203-206). Philadelphia: Churchill Livingstone.

Sciscione, P., & Krause-Parello, C. (2007). No-nit policies in schools: Time for change. *Journal of School Nursing, 23*(1), 13-22.

Shane, A., & Pickering, L. (2008). Infections associated with group childcare. Chapter 3 in S. Long (Ed.), *Principles and practices of pediatric infectious diseases* (3rd ed., pp. 23-32). Philadelphia: Churchill Livingstone.

Staat, M. (2008). Infectious diseases in refugee and internationally adopted children. Chapter 4 in S. Long (Ed.), *Principles and practices of pediatric infectious diseases* (3rd ed., pp. 32-37). Philadelphia: Churchill Livingstone.

Yale Center for Public Health Preparedness. (2006). Modes of transmission of infectious organisms. *Public Health News, 1*(4). Retrieved September 2006, at http://publichealth.yale.edu/ycphp/newsletters/newsletter.html.

Chapter 12

Akinbami, L. (2006, December 12). The state of childhood asthma, United States, 1980-2005. *Advance Data from Vital Health and Statistics, 381,* 1-23.

American Academy of Pediatrics, American Public Health Association, & National Resource Center for Health and Safety in Child Care and Early Education. (2002). *Caring for our children: National health and safety performance standards: Guidelines for out-of-home child care programs* (2nd ed.). Elk Grove Village, IL: American Academy of Pediatrics; Washington, DC: American Public Health Association. Retrieved August 31, 2009, from http://www.eric.ed.gov/ERICDocs/data/ericdocs2sql/content_storage_01/0000019b/80/14/0d/14.pdf

American Psychiatric Association. (2000). *Diagnostic and statistical manual of mental disorders* (4th ed., text revision). Washington, DC: Author.

American Speech-Language Hearing Association. (2009). Early hearing detection & intervention action center. Retrieved October 9, 2009, from http://www.asha.org/advocacy/federal/ehdi

Ball, J., Bindler, R., & Cowen, K. (2010). *Child health nursing: Partnering with children and families* (2nd ed.). Upper Saddle River, NJ: Pearson Prentice Hall.

Blanchard, L., Gurka, M., & Blackman, J. (2006). Emotional, developmental, and behavioral health of American children and their families: A report from the 2003 National Survey of Children's Health. *Pediatrics, 117*(6), e1202-e1212.

Centers for Disease Control and Prevention. (2005). *Preventing lead poisoning in young children.* Atlanta, CA: Author. Retrived January 3, 2010, from http://www.cdc .gov/nceh/Lead/Publications/PrevLeadpoisoning.pdf

Centers for Disease Control and Prevention. (2007). Prevalence of autism spectrum disorders. *Surveillance Summaries, 2007. MMWR, 56*(SS-1), 1-40.

Centers for Disease Control and Prevention. (2009, May 22). *Preventing dental caries with community programs.* Retrieved October 7, 2009, from http://www.cdc .gov/NCCdphp/publications/factsheets/Prevention/oh.htm

Council on School Health. (2008, May). Role of the school nurse in providing school health services. *Pediatrics, 121*(5), 1052-1056.

Data Resource Center for Child and Adolescent Health. (2008). *Who are children with special health care needs?* Retrieved June 1, 2009, from http://www.childhealthdata.org

Dennis, K., & Azpiri, T. (2005). *Sign to learn: American Sign Language in the early childhood classroom.* St. Paul, MN: Redleaf.

Descartes, M. (2007). Cytogenetics. Chapter 81 in R. Kliegman, R. Behrman, H. Jenson, & B. Stanton (Eds.), *Nelson textbook of pediatrics* (18th ed., pp. 507-509). Philadelphia: Saunders Elsevier.

Division for Early Childhood & National Association for the Education of Young Children. (2009). *Early childhood inclusion: A joint position of the Division for Early Childhood (DEC) and the National Association for the Education of Young Children (NAEYC).* Chapel Hill: The University of North Carolina, FPG Child Development Institute. Retrieved October 7, 2009, from www.naeyc.org/files/naeyc/file/positions/DEC_NAEYC_EC_updatedKS.pdf

Dopheide, J., & Pliska, S. (2009). Attention-deficit-hyperactivity disorder: An update. *Pharmacotherapy, 29*(6), 656-679.

Gallaudet Research Institute (2008). *Regional and national summary report of data from the 2007-2008 Annual Survey of Deaf and Hard of Hearing Children and Youth.* Washington, DC: Author. Retrieved October 9, 2009, from http://gri.gallaudet.edu/Demographics/2008_National_Summary.pdf

Green, J. (2007). Prenatal alcohol exposure and supporting students. *Journal of School Health, 77*(3), 103-108.

Greer, F., & Sicherer, S. (2008). Report reviews evidence on whether early dietary practices can reduce atopy. *AAP News, 29*(1), p. 12.

Haddad, J. (2007). Hearing loss. Chapter 636 in R. Kliegman, R. Behrman, H. Jenson, & B. Stanton (Eds.), *Nelson textbook of pediatrics* (18th ed., pp. 2620-2627). Philadelphia: Saunders Elsevier.

Hannah, J. (2002). The role of schools in attention-deficit/hyperactivity disorder. *Pediatric Annals, 31*(8), 507-513.

Harrison, R. (2008). Noise-induced hearing loss in children: A "less than silent" environmental danger. *Paediatric Child Health, 13*(5), 377-382.

Heward, W. (2009). *Exceptional children; An introduction to special education* (9th ed.). Upper Saddle River, NJ: Pearson.

Jackson Allen, P. (2004). Children with special health care needs: National Survey of Prevalence and Health Care Needs. *Pediatric Nursing, 30*(4), 307-314.

Johnston, M. (2007). Febrile seizures. Chapter 593.1 in R. Kliegman, R. Behrman, H. Jenson, & B. Stanton (Eds.), *Nelson textbook of pediatrics* (18th ed., pp. 2457-2458). Philadelphia: Saunders Elsevier.

Katz, L., & Schery, T. D. (2006). Including children with hearing loss in early childhood programs. *Young Children, 61*(1), 86-95.

Lagae, L. (2008). Learning disabilities: Definitions, epidemiology, diagnosis, and intervention strategies. *Pediatric Clinics of North America, 55*(6), 1259-1268.

Laraque, D., & Trasande, L. (2005). Lead poisoning successes and 21st century challenges. *Pediatrics in Review, 26*(12), 435-443.

Leslie, L. (2002). The role of primary care physicians in attention deficit/hyperactivity disorder. *Pediatric Annals, 31*(8), 475-484.

Liu, A., Covar, R., Span, J., & Leung, D. (2007). Asthma. Chapter 143 in R. Kliegman, R. Behrman, H. Jenson, & B. Stanton (Eds.), *Nelson textbook of pediatrics* (18th ed., pp. 953-970). Philadelphia: Saunders Elsevier.

Major, P., & Thiele, E. (2007). Seizures in children: Determining the variation. *Pediatrics in Review, 29*(10), 363-372.

McPherson, M., Arango, P., Fox, H., Lauver, C., McManus, M., Newacheck, P., Perrin, J., Shonkoff, J., Strickland, B. A new definition of children with special health care needs. *Pediatrics, 102*(1):137-140, 1998.

Milgrom, H., & Leung, D. (2007). Allergic rhinitis. Chapter 143 in R. Kliegman, R. Behrman, H. Jenson, & B. Stanton (Eds.), *Nelson Textbook of Pediatrics* (18th ed., pp. 949-952). Philadelphia, PA: Saunders Elsevier.

Murphy, N., Carbone, P., & Council on Children with Disabilities. (2008, May). Promoting the participation of children with disabilities in sports, recreation, and physical activities. *Pediatrics, 121*(5), 1057-1062.

Newacheck, P., Kim, S., Blumberg, S., & Rising, J. (2008). Who is at risk for special health care needs: Findings from the National Survey of Children's Health. *Pediatrics, 122*(2), 347-359.

Niccols, A. (2007). Fetal alcohol syndrome and the developing socio-emotional brain. *Brain and Cognition, 65*(1), 135-142.

Psoter, W. J., Pendrys, D. G., Morse, D. E., Zhang, H., & Mayne, S. T. (2006). Associations of ethnicity/race and socioeconomic status with early childhood caries patterns. *Journal of Public Health Dentistry, 66*(1), 23-29.

Raishevich, N., & Jensen, P. (2007). Attention-deficit/hyperactivity disorder. Chapter 31 in R. Kliegman, R. Behrman, H. Jenson, & B. Stanton (Eds.), *Nelson textbook of pediatrics* (18th ed., pp. 146-150). Philadelphia: Saunders Elsevier.

Ross, D., Holstrum, W. J., Gaffney, M., Green, D., Oyler, R., & Gravel, J. (2008). Hearing screening and diagnostic evaluation of children with unilateral and mild bilateral hearing loss. *Trends in Amplification, 12*(1), 27-34.

Schwartz, I. S., Billingsley, F. F., & McBride, B. M. (n.d.). Including children with autism in inclusive preschools: Strategies that work. *New Horizons for Learning.* Retrieved October 8, 2009, from http://www.newhorizons.org/spneeds/inclusion/information/schwartz2.htm

Selwitz, R., Ismail, A., & Tellex, M. (2007). Dental caries. *The Lancet, 369*(9555), 51-60.

Shah, P., Dalton, R., & Boris, N. (2007). Pervasive developmental disorder and childhood psychosis. Chapter 29 in R. Kliegman, R. Behrman, H. Jenson, & B. Stanton (Eds.), *Nelson textbook of pediatrics* (18th ed., pp. 133-136). Philadelphia: Saunders Elsevier.

Shah, S., Kublaoui, J., & White, P. (2009). Screening for type 2 diabetes in obese youth. *Pediatrics, 124*(2), 573-579.

Shapiro, B., & Batshaw, M. (2007). Mental retardation (intellectual disability). Chapter 38.2 in R. Kliegman, R. Behrman, H. Jenson, & B. Stanton (Eds.), *Nelson textbook of pediatrics* (18th ed., pp. 191-197). Philadelphia: Saunders Elsevier.

Stein, M., & Perrin, J. (2003). Diagnosis and treatment of ADHD in school-age children in primary care settings: A synopsis of the AAP practice guidelines. *Pediatrics in Review, 24*(3), 92-98.

Thobro, J. (2007). Addressing social and emotional issues of children with diabetes. *Northwest Public Health Newsletter*, pp. 1-4.

Turnbull, A., Turnbull, R., & Wehmeyer, M. (2010). *Exceptional lives: Special education in today's schools* (6th ed.). Upper Saddle River, NJ: Pearson.

U.S. Department of Education. (2004). *Building the legacy: IDEA 2004.* Retrieved October 7, 2009, from http://idea.ed.gov

U.S. Department of Health and Human Services. (2000). *Healthy people 2010* (2nd ed., 2 vols.). Washington, DC: Author. Retrieved August 31, 2009, from http://www.healthypeople.gov/Publications

U.S. Department of Health and Human Services, Health Resources and Services Administration, Maternal and Child Health Bureau. (2008). *The national survey of children with special health care needs: Chartbook 2005-2006.* Rockville, MD: U.S. Department of Health and Human Services. Retrieved October 7, 2009, from http://mchb.hrsa.gov/cshcn05

U.S. Department of Health and Human Services & U.S. Department of Education. (2003). *Managing asthma: A guide for schools.* Retrieved October 9, 2009, from http://www.nhlbi.nih.gov/health/prof/lung/asthma/asth_sch.pdf

U.S. Preventive Services Task Force. (2008, July). *Universal screening for hearing loss in newborns.* Rockville, MD: Agency for Healthcare Research and Quality. Retrieved October 9, 2009, from http://www.ahrq.gov/clinic/uspstf/uspsnbhr.htm

Vargas, C., & Ronzio, C. (2006). Disparities in early childhood caries. *BMC Oral Health, 6* (Suppl 1), S3.

Chapter 13

American Academy of Pediatrics. (2005a). *The complete and authoritative guide: caring for your baby and young child: Birth to age 5.* New York: Bantam Books.

American Academy of Pediatrics. (2005b). *The complete and authoritative guide: Caring for your baby and young child; ages 5 to 12.* New York: Bantam Books.

Balaban, N. (2006). Easing the separation process for infants, toddlers and families. *Young Children, 56*(6), 70-76.

Ball, J., & Bindler, R. (2006). *Child health nursing: Partnering with children and families* (pp. 1369-1403). Upper Saddle River, NJ, Pearson Prentice Hall.

Beesdo, K., Knappe, S., & Pine, D. (2009). Anxiety and Anxiety Disorders in Children and Adolescents: Developmental Issues and Implications for DSM-V. *Psychiatric Clinics of North America, 32*(3), 483-524.

Bovey, T., & Strain, P. (2008). *Using classroom activities and routines as opportunities to support peer interaction* (What Works Brief #5). Champaign, IL: Center on the Social Emotional Foundations of Early Learning. Retrieved October 9, 2009, from http://www.vanderbilt.edu/csefel/briefs/wwb5.html

Bowlby, J. (1969). *Attachment and loss. Volume I: Attachment.* New York: Basic Books.

Boyd, J., Barnett, W. S., Bodrova, E., Leong, D., & Gomby, D., (2005). *Promoting children's social and emotional development through preschool education.* New Brunswick, NJ: National Institute for Early Education Research.

Bradley, R., Houts, Nader, O'Brien, Belsky, Crosnoel. (2008). The relationship between body mass index and behavior in children. *Journal of Pediatrics, 153*(5), 629-634.

Brennan, E. M., Bradley, J. R., Ama, S. M., & Cawood, N. (2003). *Setting the pace: Model inclusive child care centers serving families of children with emotional or behavioral challenges.* Portland, OR: Portland State University, Research and Training Center on Family Support and Children's Mental Health.

Bricker, D., Davis, M. S., & Squires, J. (2004). Mental health screening in young children. *Infants and Young Children, 17*(2), 129-144.

California Childcare Health Program. (2006). *Social and emotional development of children.* San Francisco: University of California, San Francisco School of Nursing. Retrieved October 11, 2009, from http://www.ucsfchildcarehealth.org/pdfs/Curricula/CCHA/15_CCHA_SocialEmotional_0406_v2.pdf

Centers for Disease Control and Prevention. (2005). Health care and well being of children with chronic emotional, behavioral, or developmental problems—United States, 2001. *MMWR, 54*(39), 985-989.

Datar, A., & Sturm, R. (2004). Childhood overweight and parent- and teacher-reported behavior problems. *Archives of Pediatrics and Adolescent Medicine, 158*(8), 804-810.

Datar, A., & Sturm, R. (2006). Childhood overweight and elementary school outcomes. *International Journal of Obesity, 30*(9), 1449-1460.

Egertson, H. A. (2006). In praise of butterflies: Linking self-esteem and learning. *Young Children, 61*(6), 58-60.

Egger, H. L., & Angold, A. (2006). Common emotional and behavior disorders in preschool children: Presentation, nosology, and epidemiology. *Journal of Child Psychology and Psychiatry, 47*(3-4), 313-337.

Ewing Marion Kauffman Foundation. (2002). *Set for success: Building a strong foundation for school readiness based on the social-emotional development of young children.* Kansas City, MO: Kauffman Early Education Exchange.

Fox, L. & Duda, M. (2008). *What are kids trying to tell us? Assessing the function of their behavior.* Center on Social Emotional Foundations for Early Learning. Training Kit

#9 retrieved October 21, 2009, at http://www.vanderbilt.edu/csefel/trainingkits.html

Fox, L. & Smith, B. (2007, January). *Promoting social, emotional and behavioral outcomes of young children served under IDEA* (Policy Brief). Tampa, FL: Center for Evidence-Based Practice: Young Children with Challenging Behavior.

Gallagher, K. C. (2005). Brain research and early childhood development: A primer for DAP. *Young Children, 60*(4), 12–20.

Gallagher, K. C., & Mayer, K. (2006). Teacher–child relationships at the forefront of effective practice. *Young Children, 61*(4), 44–49.

Gilliam, W. S. (2005). *Prekindergartners left behind: Expulsion rates in state prekindergarten programs.* New York: Foundation for Child Development. Retrieved October 11, 2009, from http://www.fcd-us.org/resources/resources_show.htm?doc_id=464280

Ginsburg, K. R. (2007). The importance of play in promoting healthy child development and maintaining strong parent–child bonds. *Pediatrics, 119*(1), 182–191. Retrieved October 11, 2009, from http://www.aap.org/pressroom/playFINAL.pdf

Hamre, B. K., & Pianta, R. C. (2001). Early teacher–child relationships and the trajectory of children's school outcomes through eighth grade. *Child Development, 72*(2), 625–638.

Hirsch, G. S. *Attention-deficit/hyperactivity (ADHD) and anxiety disorders.* NYU Child Study Center. Retrieved January 12, 2010, from http://www.aboutourkids.org/articles/attentiondeficithyperactivity_adhd_anxiety_disorders

Homer, R. H., Albin, R. W., Sprague, J. R., Storey, K., & Newton, J. S. (1997). *Functional assessment and program development for problem behavior.* Pacific Grove, CA: Brooks/Cole Publishing. Retrieved online at: www.vanderbilt.edu/csefel/modules-archive/module3a/handouts/4.html

Katoaka, S., Zhang, L., & Wells, K. (2002). Unmet need for mental health care among U.S. children: Variation by ethnicity and insurance status. *American Journal of Psychiatry, 159*(9), 1548–1555.

La Paro, K.M., Pianta, R.C., & Stuhlman, M. (2004). The Classroom Assessment Scoring System: Findings from the prekindergarten year. The Elementary School Journal, 104 (5), 409–426.

Lucich, M. (2004, July). *The value of play* (Health and Safety Notes). Berkeley, CA: California Childcare Health Program. Retrieved October 10, 2009, from http://www.ucsfchildcarehealth.org/pdfs/healthandsafety/valueplayen_adr.pdf

National Advisory Mental Health Council (2001) *Blueprint for change: Research on child and adolescent mental health. Executive summary and recommendations.* National Institute of Mental Health, the National Advisory Mental Health Council Workgroup on Child and Adolescent Mental Health Intervention Development and Deployment.

National Scientific Council on the Developing Child. (2007). *The science of early childhood development: Closing the gap between what we know and what we do.* Cambridge, MA: Author. Retrieved October 9, 2009, from http://developingchild.harvard.edu/library/reports_and_working_papers/science_of_early_childhood_development

National Scientific Council on the Developing Child. (2008). *Mental health problems in early childhood can impair learning and behavior for life* (Council Working Paper #6). Cambridge, MA: Author. Retrieved October 9, 2009, from http://developingchild.harvard.edu/library/reports_and_working_papers/wp6

Ostrosky, M. M., Jung, E. Y., & Hemmeter, M. L. (2008). *Helping children make transitions between activities* (What Works Brief #4). Champaign, IL: Center on the Social Emotional Foundations of Early Learning. Retrieved October 11, 2009, from http://www.vanderbilt.edu/csefel/briefs/wwb4.html

Pianta, R. C., La Paro, K. M. & Hamre, B. K. (2006). *Classroom Assessment Scoring System: Manual k-3 Version.* Charlottesville: Center for Advanced Study of Teaching and Learning.

Prager, L. (2009). Depression and suicide in children and adolescents. *Pediatrics in Review, 30*(6), 199–206.

Raver, C. C., & Knitzer, J. (2002, July). *Ready to enter: What research tells policymakers about strategies to promote social and emotional school readiness among three- and four-year-old children.* New York: National Center for Children in Poverty. Retrieved October 11, 2009, from http://www.nccp.org/publications/pdf/download_108.pdf

Rimm-Kaufman, S. E. & Chiu, Y. I. (2007). Promoting social and academic competence in the classroom: An intervention study examining the contribution of the Responsive Classroom approach. *Psychology in the Schools, 44*(4), 397–413.

Schore, A. N. (2001). Effects of a secure attachment relationship on right brain development, affect regulation, and infant mental health. *Infant Mental Health Journal, 22*(1-2), 7–66.

Shore, R. (1997). *Rethinking the brain: New insights into early development.* New York: Families and Work Institute.

Shore, R. (2002). *What kids need: Today's best ideas for nurturing, teaching, and protecting young children.* Boston: Beacon.

Simpson, G., Cohen, R. A., Pastor, P. N., & Reuben, M. A. (2008). *Use of mental health services in the past 12 months by children aged 4-17 years: United States, 2005-2006.* Atlanta: Centers for Disease Control and Prevention. Retrieved October 10, 2009, from http://www.cdc.gov/nchs/data/databriefs/db08.htm

Substance Abuse and Mental Health Services Administration. (2009). *Children's mental health facts: bipolar disorder.* Accessed October 22, 2009, at http://mentalhealth.samhsa.gov/publications/allpubs/sma05-4058/

U.S. Public Health Service. (2000). *Report of the Surgeon General's Conference on Children's Mental Health: A national action agenda.* Washington, DC: U.S. Department of Health and Human Services.

Webster-Stratton, C., Reid, M., & Stoolmiller, M. (2008). Preventing conduct problems and improving school readiness: Evaluation of the Incredible Years Teacher and Child Training Programs in high-risk schools. *Journal of Child Psychology and Psychiatry, 49*(5), 471–488.

Wiles, N., Northstone, K., Emmett, P., & Lewis, G. (2009). 'Junk food' diet and childhood behavioural problems: Results from the ALSPAC cohort. *European Journal of Clinical Nutrition, 63*(4) 491–498.

Zeanah, P., Nagle, G., Stafford, B., Rice, T., & Farrer, J. (2005, January). *Addressing social-emotional development and infant mental health in early childhood systems: Executive summary* (Building State Early Childhood Comprehensive Systems Series No. 12). Los Angeles: National Center for Infant and Early Childhood Health Policy. Retrieved October 9, 2009, from http://www.eric.ed.gov/ERICDocs/data/ericdocs2sql/content_storage_01/0000019b/80/29/89/a6.pdf

Zero to Three: National Center for Infants, Toddlers and Families. (2009). *Early childhood mental health.* Available online at: http://www.zerotothree.org/site/PageServer?pagename=key_mental

Chapter 14

Agran, P. F., Anderson, C., Winn, D., Trent, R., Walton-Haynes, L., & Thayer, S. (2003). Rates of pediatric injuries by 3-month intervals for children 0 to 3 years of age. *Pediatrics, 111*(6) pp. e3683–e692.

American Academy of Pediatrics. (2001). Prevention of agricultural injuries among children and adolescents. *Pediatrics, 108*(4), pp. 1016–1019.

American Academy of Pediatrics. (2000). *Common Myths about Immunizations.* Retrieved October 23, 2009, from http://www.cispimmunize.org/fam/fam_main.html?http&&&www.cispimmunize.org/fam/myths.html

American Academy of Pediatrics, American Public Health Association, & National Resource Center for Health and Safety in Child Care and Early Education. (2002). *Caring for our children: National health and safety performance standards: Guidelines for out-of-home child care programs* (2nd ed.). Elk Grove Village, IL: American Academy of Pediatrics; Washington, DC: American Public Health Association. Retrieved August 31, 2009, from http://www.eric.ed.gov/ERICDocs/data/ericdocs2sql/content_storage_01/0000019b/80/14/0d/14.pdf

Bureau of Labor Statistics, U.S. Department of Labor, *Occupational outlook handbook: 2008-09 edition,* Teachers-Preschool,

Kindergarten, Elementary, Middle, and Secondary. Retrieved October 22, 2009, from http://www.bls.gov/OCO

Bureau of Labor Statistics. U.S. Department of Labor, 2010. *Career guide to industries,* (2010-2011 ed.), *Child day care services.* Retrieved January 13, 2010, from http://www.bls.gov/oco/cg/cgs032.htm

Centers for Disease Control and Prevention, (2006). *10 Leading causes of injury death by age group highlighting unintentional injury deaths, United States, 2006,* Retrieved October 23, 2009, from http://www.cdc.gov/injury/Images/LC-Charts/10lc%20-%20Violence%20Related%202006-7_6_09.jpg

Centers for Disease Control and Prevention. (2006). *10 Leading causes of death, United States, 2006.* Retrieved October 23, 2009, from http://webappa.cdc.gov/cgi-bin/broker.exe

Centers for Disease Control and Prevention. (2007). *National estimates of the 10 leading causes of nonfatal injuries treated in hospital emergency departments, United States, 2007.* Retrieved October 2009 from http://www.cdc.gov/injury/Images/LC-Charts/10lc%20-%20Nonfatal%20Injury%202007-7_6_09.jpg

Cohen, J., Onunaku, N., Clothier, S., Poppe, J. (2005). *Helping young children succeed: Strategies to promote early childhood social and emotional development.* Retrieved May 31, 2007, from http://www.zerotothree.org/site/DocServer/helping_young_children_succeed_final.pdf?docID=1725&AddInterest=1157

Copple, C., & Bredekamp, S. (2009). *Developmentally appropriate practice in programs serving children from birth through age 8.* Washington, DC: National Association for the Education of Young Children.

Currie, J. M., & Hotz, V. J. (2004). Accidents will happen? Unintentional injury, maternal employment, and child care policy. *Journal of Health Economics, 23*(1), 25-59.

Danseco, E. R., Miller, T. R., & Spicer, R. S. (2000). Incidence and costs of 1987-1994 childhood injuries: Demographic breakdowns. *Pediatrics, 105*(2), e27. Retrieved October 13, 2009 from http://pediatrics.aappublications.org/cgi/content/full/105/2/e27

Fiore, A. E., Wasley, A., & Bell, B. P. (2006, May 19). Prevention of Hepatitis A through active or passive immunization practices: Recommendations of the Advisory Committee on Immunization Practices. *MMWR, 55*(RR07), 1-23. Retrieved October 13, 2009, from http://www.cdc.gov/mmwr/preview/mmwrhtml/rr5507a1.htm?s_cid=rr5507a1_e

Galinsky, E., Howes, C., Kontos, S., & Shinn, M. (1994). *The study of children in family child care and relative care. Highlights and Findings.* New York: Families and Work Institute.

Helburn, S. (Ed.). (1995). *Cost, quality, and child outcomes in child care centers* (Technical Report). Denver: University of Colorado at Denver.

Maine Bureau of Insurance. (2006). *Day care liability insurance.* Retrieved October 22, 2009, from: http://maine.gov/pfr/insurance/consumer/daycare.htm

Maslow, A. (1954). *Motivation and personality.* New York: Harper & Row.

Maslow, A. H. (1968). *Toward a psychology of being* (2nd ed.). New York: Van Nostrand Reinhold.

National Association for the Education of Young Children. (1998). *Licensing and public regulation of early childhood programs.* Retrieved September 14, 2009, from http://208.118.177.216/about/positions/pdf/PSLIC98.PDF

National Association for the Education of Young Children. (2005). *Code of ethical conduct and statement of commitment.* Retrieved October 13, 2009, from http://www.naeyc.org/positionstatements/ethical_conduct

National Association for Regulatory Administration. (2005). *The 2005 child care licensing study.* Retrieved October 12, 2009, from http://www.nara.affiniscape.com/displaycommon.cfm?an[equals]1&subarticlenbr=104

National Institute of Child Health and Human Development. (2006). *SIDS: "Back to sleep" campaign.* Retrieved October 12, 2009, from http://www.nichd.nih.gov/sids

Perri, F. S. (2006). *You're being investigated... Now what?* Resources for Child Caring: Business Resources for Family Child Care Providers. Retrieved January 5, 2010, from http//www.resourcesforchildcaring.org/index.cfm?page=beinginvestigated

Pressley, J. C., Barlow, B., Kendig, T., & Paneth-Pollak, R. (2007). Twenty-year trends in fatal injuries to very young children: the persistence of racial disparities. *Pediatrics, 119*(4), e875-e884.

Ritchie, S. & Willer, B. (eds.) (2005). *Leadership & Management: A guide to the NAEYC early childhood program standards and related accreditation criteria.* National Association for the Education of Young Children: Washington, DC. (pp. 29)

Shonkoff, J. P., & Phillips, D. A. (Eds.). (2000). *From neurons to neighborhoods: The science of early childhood development* (National Research Council and Institute of Medicine, Committee on Integrating the Science of Early Childhood Development, Board on Children, Youth, and Families, Commission on Behavioral and Social Sciences and Education). Washington, DC: National Academy Press. Retrieved October 12, 2009, from http://www.nap.edu/openbook.php?isbn=0309069882

Sicherer, S. H., Muñoz-Furlong, A., Murphy, R., Wood, R. A., & Sampson, H. A. (2003). Symposium: Pediatric food allergy. *Pediatrics, 111*(6), 1591-1594. Retrieved May 2007 from http://pediatrics.aappublications.org/cgi/content/abstract/111/6/S2/1591

Wrigley, J., & Dreby, J. (2005). Fatalities and the organization of child care in the United States, 1985-2003. *American Sociological Review, 70*(5), 729-757.

Wyatt, J. (2001, September). *Just what is adequate liability coverage?* Minneapolis, MN: Resources for Child Caring. Retrieved October 12, 2009, from http://www.resourcesforchildcaring.org/index.cfm?page=adequateliabins

Chapter 15

American Academy of Dermatology. (2005). *Sun protection for children.* Schaumburg, IL: Author. Retrieved October 23, 2009, from http://www.aad.org/public/publications/pamphlets/sun_sunprotection.html

American Academy of Pediatrics, American Public Health Association, & National Resource Center for Health and Safety in Child Care and Early Education. (2002). *Caring for our children: National health and safety performance standards: Guidelines for out-of-home child care programs* (2nd ed.). Elk Grove Village, IL: American Academy of Pediatrics; Washington, DC: American Public Health Association. Retrieved August 31, 2009, from http://www.eric.ed.gov/ERICDocs/data/ericdocs2sql/content_storage_01/0000019b/80/14/0d/14.pdf

Edwards, C., Gandini, L., & Forman, G. (1993). *The hundred languages of children: The Reggio Emilia approach to early childhood education.* Norwood, NJ: Ablex Publishing.

Greenman, J. (2005, May). Places for childhood in the 21st century: A conceptual framework. *Young Children: Beyond the Journal.*

Grisson, J. B. (2005). Physical fitness and academic achievement. *Journal of Exercise Physiology, 8*(1), 11-25.

Katz, L. G., & Cesarone, B. (Eds.). (1994) *Reflections on the Reggio Emilia approach.* Urbana, IL: ERIC Clearinghouse on Elementary and Early Childhood Education.

Montessori, M. (1966). *The secret of childhood.* Notre Dame, IN: Fides.

Moore Johnson, S. (2006). *The workplace matters: Teacher quality, retention, and effectiveness* (Best Practices Working Papers). Washington, DC: National Education Association. Retrieved from http://www.nea.org/research/bestpractices/images/wcreport.pdf

National Association for the Education of Young Children. (2005). *Code of ethical conduct and statement of commitment.* Washington, DC: Author. Retrieved October 13, 2009, from http://www.naeyc.org/positionstatements/ethical_conduct

National Association for the Education of Young Children. (2007). *NAEYC early childhood program standards and accreditation criteria: The mark of quality in early childhood education.* Washington, DC: Author.

National Association for the Education of Young Children. (2008). *NAEYC accreditation standards and criteria: Standard 9:*

Physical environment. Retrieved from http://www.naeyc.org/files/academy/file/OverviewStandards.pdf

National Association for Sport and Physical Education. (2002). *Active start: A statement of physical activity guidelines for children birth to five years.* Reston, VA: Author.

National Head Start Facilities Information Services. (2002). *Region IV Head Start quality improvement center* Bowling Green, KY: Author.

Nemours Foundation. (2009). *Kids health for parents: Playground safety.* Retrieved October 23, 2009, from http://www.kidshealth.org/parent/firstaid_safe/outdoor/playground.html

New Jersey Department of Education, Office of Early Childhood Education and Office of School Facilities Financing. (2004). *Facilities: New construction and renovation guidance.* Retrieved September 2009 from http://www.state.nj.us/education/ece/archives/facilities.pdf

New, Rebecca S. (1993). *Reggio Emilia: Some lessons for U.S. educators.* Retrieved October 24, 2009, from http://ceep.crc.uiuc.edu/eecearchive/digests/1993/new93.html

Olds, A. R. (1987). Designing settings for infants and toddlers. In C. Weinstein and T. David (Eds.), *Spaces for children: The built environment and child development* (pp. 117–138). New York: Plenum.

Olds, A. (2001). *Child care design guide.* New York: McGraw Hill.

Overturf Johnson, J. (2005). *Who's minding the kids? Child care arrangements: Winter 2002* (Current Population Reports). Washington, DC: U.S. Census Bureau. Retrieved September 2009 from www.census.gov/prod/2005pubs/p70-101.pdf

Pate, R., Pfeiffer, K. A., Trost, S. G., Ziegler, P., & Dowda, M. (2004). Physical activity among children attending preschools. *Pediatrics, 114*(5), 1258–1263.

Riddell, R. (2007). Assessing your school's security needs: How to increase safety and reduce risk for students and staff. *Learning by design.* National School Boards Association. Retrieved November 9, 2009 at: http://www.learningbydesign.biz/2007/feature3.html

Ritchie, R., & Weller, B. (Eds.). (2005). *Physical environment: a guide to the NAEYC early childhood program standard and related accreditation criteria.* Washington, DC: National Association for the Education of Young Children.

Rivkin, M. S. (1995). *The great outdoors: restoring children's right to play outside.* Washington, DC: National Association for the Education of Young Children.

Savage, M. A., Kawanabe, I. T., Mejeur, J., Goehring, J. B., & Reed, J. B. (2002). *Protecting children: A guide to child traffic safety laws.* Washington, DC: National Conference of State Legislatures.

Sussman, C., & Gillman, A. (2007). *Building early childhood facilities—What states can do to promote quality* (NIEER Preschool Policy Report). New Brunswick, NJ:

National Institute for Early Education Research. Retrieved January 12, 2010, from http://www.nieer.org/resouces/research/Facilities.pdf

Tarr, P. (2001). Aesthetic codes in Early Childhood Classrooms: What Art Educators Can Learn from Reggio Emilia. *Art Education. 54*(3) 33–39.

Tinsworth, D. K., & McDonald, J. E. (2001) *Special study: Injuries and deaths associated with children's playground equipment.* Washington, DC: U.S. Consumer Product Safety Commission.

Trancik, A. M., & Evans, G. W. (1995). Spaces fit for children: Competency in the design of daycare center environments. *Children's Environments, 12*(3), 43–58.

U.S. Consumer Product Safety Commission. (1999). *Consumer product safety commission staff study of safety hazards in child care settings.* Washington, DC: Author. Retrieved October 23, 2009, from http://www.cpsc.gov/library/ccstudy.html

U.S. Consumer Product Safety Commission. (2008, April). *Public playground safety handbook* (Publication No. 325). Retrieved October 23, 2009, from http://www.cpsc.gov/CPSCPUB/PUBS/325.pdf

U.S. Department of Defense (2002). *Unified facilities criteria (UFC). Design: child development centers.* Washington, DC: Author.

U.S. General Services Administration. (2003, July). *Child care center design guide.* Washington, DC: Author. Retrieved October 23, 2009, from http://www.gsa.gov/gsa/cm_attachments/GSA_DOCUMENT/Design%20Guide_R2FD38_0Z5RDZ-i34K-pR.pdf

White, R., & Stoecklin, V. (2003) *The great 35 square foot myth.* Kansas City, MO: White Hutchinson Leisure & Learning Group. Retrieved October 24, 2009, from http://www.whitehutchinson.com/children/articles/35footmyth.shtml

York, S. (1991). *Roots and wings: Affirming culture in early childhood programs.* St. Paul, MN: Redleaf Press.

Chapter 16

Alter, P. J., & Conroy, M. (2007). *Recommended practices: Preventing challenging behavior in young children: effective practices.* Center for Evidence-Based Practice. Retrieved October 30, 2009, from http://www.challengingbehavior.org/do/resources/documents/rph_preventing_challenging_behavior.pdf

American Academy of Pediatrics, American Public Health Association, & National Resource Center for Health and Safety in Child Care and Early Education. (2002a). *Caring for our children: National health and safety performance standards: Guidelines for out-of-home child care programs* (2nd ed.). Elk Grove Village, IL: American Academy of Pediatrics; Washington, DC: American Public Health Association. Retrieved August 31, 2009, from http://www.eric.ed.gov/ERICDocs/data/ericdocs2sql/content_storage_01/0000019b/80/14/0d/14.pdf

American Academy of Pediatrics, American Public Health Association, & National Resource Center for Health and Safety in Child Care and Early Education. (2002b). *Healthy kids, healthy care: Allergies, asthma, & other chronic conditions.* Retrieved October 27, 2009, from http://www.healthykids.us/chapters/allergies_main.htm

American Academy of Pediatrics, American Public Health Association, & National Resource Center for Health and Safety in Child Care and Early Education. (2003). *Stepping stones to using "Caring for our children"* (2nd ed.). Elk Grove Village, IL: American Academy of Pediatrics; Washington, DC: American Public Health Association. Retrieved October 27, 2009, from http://nrckids.org/STEPPING/SteppingStones.pdf

Bales, D., Wallinga, C., & Coleman, M. (2005). *Teaching basic health and safety in the early childhood classroom curriculum.* Athens: University of Georgia. Retrieved October 30, 2009, from http://www.fcs.uga.edu/ext/families/ece_curriculum.php

Bluth, L. (1993). Transporting infants, toddlers, and preschool children with disabilities. *School Business Affairs, 59*(4),13–16.

Bowlby, J. (1982). *Attachment and loss: Vol. 1. Attachment* (2nd ed.). New York: Basic Books.

Carson, K. (2006). Family mealtimes: More than just eating together. *Journal of the American Dietetic Association, 106*(4), 532–533.

Centers for Disease Control and Prevention. (2006). *Web-based injury statistics query and reporting system (WISQARS).* Retrieved October 27, 2009, from http://www.cdc.gov/injury/wisqars/index.html

Early Childhood Learning and Knowledge Center (ECLKC). (2005). Office of Head Start, US Department of Health and Human Services Administration for Children and Families. Head Start Transportation Fact Sheet: United we ride. Retrieved November 13, 2009, from http://eclkc.ohs.acf.hhs.gov/hslc/Program%20Design%20and%20Management/Transportation/Safety/Policies%20%26%20Procedures/transp_art_00908_010807.html:

Fox, L. & Garrison, S. (2009). Helping children learn to manage their own behavior. *What Works Brief #7.* Center for Social and Emotional Foundations for Early Learning. Retrieved November 2009 from http://www.vanderbilt.edu/csefel/resources/what_works.html

French, K. (2004). Supporting a child with special health care needs. *Young Children, 59*(2), 62–63.

Gartrell, D. (2006) Guidance matters: The beauty of class meetings. *Young Children. 61*(6) 1–3.

Gartrell, D. & Gartrell, J. J. (2008) Guidance matters: Understanding Bullying. *Young Children. 63*(3) pp. 54–57.

Hanline, M. F., Nunes, D., & Worthy, M. B. (2007). Augmentative and alternative communication in the early childhood years. *Young Children, 62*(4), 78–82.

Hemmeter, M. L., Ostrosky, M. M., Artman, K. M., & Kinder, K. A. (2008). Moving right along . . . planning transitions to prevent challenging behavior. *Young Children, 63*(3), 18-25.

Kern, P., & Wakeford, L. (2007). Supporting outdoor play for young children: the zone model of playground supervision. *Young Children, 62*(5), 12-18.

National Association for the Education of Young Children. (2005a). *Code of ethical conduct and statement of commitment.* Washington, DC: Author. Retrieved October 13, 2009, from http://www.naeyc.org/positionstatements/ethical_conduct

National Association for the Education of Young Children. (2005b). *NAEYC early childhood program standards and accreditation criteria: The mark of quality in early childhood education.* Washington, DC: Author.

National Association for the Education of Young Children. (2005c). Biters: Why they do it and what to do about it. *Early Years are Learning Years.* Retrieved October 30, 2009, from http://www.shandonprescdc.org/public/files/docs/biters-whytheydoit.pdf

National Association for the Education of Young Children. (2006). *NAEYC accreditation classroom observation tool.* Washington, DC: Author.

National Association for the Education of Young Children. (2008). *Developmentally appropriate practice in early childhood programs serving children birth through 8.* Washington, DC: Author.

National Highway Traffic Safety Association. (1999, February). *Guideline for the safe transportation of pre-school age children in school buses.* Retrieved October 29, 2009, from http://www.nhtsa.dot.gov/people/injury/buses/Guide1999/prekfinal.htm

National Highway Traffic Safety Administration. (2005). *School bus safety Assurance Program.* Washington, DC. Retrieved November 10, 2009 from http://www.nhtsa.dot.gov/people/injury/buses/1998_2005School Bus_Recalls/index.html

National Highway Traffic Safety Administration. (2009a). *Uniform guidelines for state highway safety programs.* Retrieved online November 10, 2009, from http://www.nhtsa.dot.gov/nhtsa/whatsup/tea21/tea21programs/402Guide.html#g17

National Highway Transportation Safety Administration. (2009b). *Fatality analysis reporting system, general estimates system, 2007 data summary.* (Publication 811003). Washington, DC: Author. Retrieved October 29, 2009, from http://www-nrd.nhtsa.dot.gov/Pubs/811003.pdf

Olson, M. (2007). Strengthening families: Community strategies that work. *Young Children, 62*(2), 26-32.

Petersen, S. & Wittmer, D. (2008). Relationship Based Infant Care: Responsive, On Demand, and Predictable. *Young Children, 63*(3), 54-57.

Strain, P. S., & Dunlap, G. (2006). *Recommended practices: Being an evidence-based practitioner.* Tampa: University of South Florida, Louis de la Parte Florida Mental Health Institute.

Chapter 17

American Academy of Pediatrics, American Public Health Association, & National Resource Center for Health and Safety in Child Care and Early Education. (2002). *Caring for our children: National health and safety performance standards: Guidelines for out-of-home child care programs* (2nd ed.). Elk Grove Village, IL: American Academy of Pediatrics; Washington, DC: American Public Health Association. Retrieved August 31, 2009, from http://www.eric.ed.gov/ERICDocs/data/ericdocs2sql/content_storage_01/0000019b/80/14/0d/14.pdf

American Academy of Pediatrics, American Public Health Association, & National Resource Center for Health and Safety in Child Care and Early Education. (2004). *Emergency/disaster preparedness for child care programs: Applicable standards from "Caring for our children."* Elk Grove Village, IL: American Academy of Pediatrics; Washington, DC: American Public Health Association. Retrieved October 31, 2009, from http://nrckids.org/SPINOFF/EMERGENCY/Emergency.pdf

American Heart Association. (2005). *Guidelines for cardiopulmonary resuscitation and emergency cardiovascular care* CPR facts and statistics. *Circulation, 112*(24, Suppl. 1), entire issue.

American Heart Association. (2008). *Hands-only CPR.* Dallas, TX: Author. Retrieved October 31, 2009, from http://handsonlycpr.org

American Red Cross. (2006). *Learn Red Cross first aid and CPR. Welcome to Red Cross training online.* Retrieved October 31, 2009, from http://www.redcrossonlinetraining.org/Distance/Default.aspx

Centers for Disease Control and Prevention. (1987/1996 updated). *Universal precautions for prevention of transmission of HIV and other bloodborne infections.* Atlanta, GA: Author. Retrieved October 31, 2009, from http://www.cdc.gov/ncidod/dhqp/bp_universal_precautions.html

Centers for Disease Control and Prevention. (2004). *Web-based injury statistics query and reporting system (WISQARS).* Retrieved October 27, 2009, from http://www.cdc.gov/injury/wisqars/index.html

Centers for Disease Control and Prevention. (2006a). Frequently Asked Questions about extreme heat. *Emergency preparedness and response.* Retrieved November 15, 2009, from http://www.bt.cdc.gov/disasters/extremeheat/faq.asp

Centers for Disease Control and Prevention. (2006b). *Emergency preparedness: Chemical spills.* Retrieved November 16, 2009, from http://www.bt.cdc.gov/planning/shelteringfacts.asp

Cunah, J.P. & Shiel, W.C. (2007) *Nosebleed.* Retrieved January 13, 2009 from, http://www.medicinenet.com/nosebleed/article.htm

Curtis, N. (2008). *Emergency response planning for child care providers.* Montgomery County, MD: Child Care Resource and Referral Agency. Retrieved October 31, 2009, from http://www.acphd.org/AXBYCZ/Admin/QuickLink/Flu/documents/PF_Childcare_Manual.pdf

Dosa, N. P., Boeing, N. M., & Kanter, R. K. (2001). Excess risk of severe acute illness in children with chronic health conditions. *Pediatrics, 107*(3), 499-504.

Dugdale, D.C., Henochowicz, S.I., & Zieve, D. (2008). *Anaphylaxes.* MedlinePlus. U.S. National Library of Medicine & National Institutes of Health. Retrieved November 16, 2009, from http://www.nlm.nih.gov/medlineplus/ency/article/000844.htm

Duldner, J. E. & Zieve, D. (2008a). *Human bites.* MedlinePlus. U.S. National Library of Medicine & National Institutes of Health. Retrieved November 16, 2009, from http://www.nlm.nih.gov/medlineplus/ency/article/000035.htm

Duldner, J. E. & Zieve, D. (2008b). *Insect bites and stings.* MedlinePlus. U.S. National Library of Medicine & National Institutes of Health. Retrieved November 16, 2009, from http://www.nlm.nih.gov/medlineplus/ency/article/000033.htm

Duldner, J. E. & Zieve, D. (2008c). *Shock.* MedlinePlus. U.S. National Library of Medicine & National Institutes of Health. Retrieved November 16, 2009, from http://www.nlm.nih.gov/medlineplus/ency/article/000039.htm

Federal Emergency Management Agency & American Red Cross. (2004, August). *Preparing for disaster* (FEMA 475; A4600). Jessup, MD: FEMA and Washington, DC: American Red Cross. Retrieved October 31, 2009, from http://www.fema.gov/pdf/library/pfd.pdf

Health and Safety Performance Standards, retrieved November 2, 2009, from http://nrc.uchsc.edu/CFOC/PDFVersion/Appendix%20D.pdf.

Heller, J. L., & Zieve, D. (2009a). *Head Injury.* MedlinePlus. U.S. National Library of Medicine & National Institutes of Health. Retrieved November 16, 2009, from http://www.nlm.nih.gov/medlineplus/ency/article/000028.htm

Heller, J. L., & Zieve, D. (2009b). *CPR-child 1-8 years old.* MedlinePlus. U.S. National Library of Medicine & National Institutes of Health. Retrieved November 16, 2009, from http://www.nlm.nih.gov/medlineplus/ency/article/000012.htm

Heller, J. L., & Zieve, D. (2009c). *CPR-infant.* MedlinePlus. U.S. National Library of Medicine & National Institutes of Health. Retrieved November 16, 2009, from http://www.nlm.nih.gov/medlineplus/ency/article/000011.htm

Heller, J. L., & Zieve, D. (2009d). *Choking - adult or child over 1 year.* MedlinePlus. U.S. National Library of Medicine & National Institutes of Health. Retrieved November 16, 2009, from http://www.nlm.nih.gov/medlineplus/ency/article/000049.htm

Heller, J. L., & Zieve, D. (2009e). *Choking - infant under 1 year.* MedlinePlus. U.S. National Library of Medicine & National

Institutes of Health. Retrieved November 16, 2009, from http://www.nlm.nih.gov/medlineplus/ency/article/000048.htm

Heller, J. L., & Zieve, D. (2009f). *Bleeding.* MedlinePlus. U.S. National Library of Medicine & National Institutes of Health. Retrieved November 16, 2009, from http://www.nlm.nih.gov/medlineplus/ency/article/000045.htm

Heller, J. L., & Zieve, D. (2009g). *Electrical injury.* MedlinePlus. U.S. National Library of Medicine & National Institutes of Health. Retrieved November 16, 2009, from http://www.nlm.nih.gov/medlineplus/ency/article/000053.htm

Heller, J. L., & Zieve, D. (2009h). *Foreign body in the nose.* MedlinePlus. U.S. National Library of Medicine & National Institutes of Health. Retrieved November 16, 2009, from http://www.nlm.nih.gov/medlineplus/ency/article/000037.htm

International Save the Children Alliance. (2006). *Two years later. Rebuilding lives after the Tsunami: The children's road to recovery.* London: Author. Retrieved October 31, 2009, from http://www.savethechildren.org/publications/emergencies/savechild_tsunami_report.pdf

Kaneshiro, N. K., & Zieve, D. (2008). *Signs of an asthma attack.* MedlinePlus. U.S. National Library of Medicine & National Institutes of Health. Retrieved November 16, 2009, from http://www.nlm.nih.gov/medlineplus/ency/patientinstructions/000062.htm

MacCormack, C. (2008). *How to help children cope after the tornadoes in the south: Ten tips from Save the Children.* Westport, CT: Save the Children. Retrieved October 31, 2009, from http://www.savethechildren.org/newsroom/2008/how-to-help-children-cope.html

Medi-Smart. (2006). *Nursing legal issues: Good Samaritan statute.* Kaplan University. Retrieved October 31, 2009, from http://medi-smart.com/gslaw.htm

National Association of Child Care Resource & Referral Agencies. (2006). *Is child care ready?: A disaster planning guide for child care resource & referral agencies.* Retrieved October 1, 2009, from http://www.naccrra.org/disaster

National Association for the Education of Young Children. (2005). *Code of ethical conduct and statement of commitment.* Washington, DC: Author. Retrieved October 13, 2009, from http://www.naeyc.org/positionstatements/ethical_conduct

National Child Care Information and Technical Assistance Center. (2008, September). *Helping children cope with natural disasters.* Fairfax, VA: Author. Retrieved October 31, 2009, from http://nccic.acf.hhs.gov/poptopics/disasters.html

National Institute of General Medical Sciences. (2008). *Burns fact sheet.* Retrieved November 16, 2009, from http://www.nigms.nih.gov/Publications/Factsheet_Burns.htm

National Institute of Neurological Disorders and Stroke. (2009). *Febrile seizures fact sheet.* Retrieved November 15, 2009, from http://www.ninds.nih.gov/disorders/febrile_seizures/detail_febrile_seizures.htm

Nemours Foundation. (2009). KidsHealth. *Falls instruction sheet.* Retrieved November 15, 2009, from http://kidshealth.org/parent/firstaid_safe/sheets/falls_sheet.html

Office of Head Start (2008a, March 20). *Lead screening* (Information Memorandum ACF-IM-HS-08-07). Washington, DC: Author. Retrieved October 31, 2009, from http://www.acf.hhs.gov/programs/ohs/policy/im2008/acfimhs_08_07.html

Office of Head Start. (2008b, March 20). *Partnership with the Environmental Protection Agency* (Information Memorandum ACF-IM-HS-08-08). Washington, DC: Author. Retrieved October 31, 2009, from http://www.acf.hhs.gov/programs/ohs/policy/im2008/acfimhs_08_08.html

Purdue University. (2006). *Radiological and environmental management: Blood spill procedures.* West Lafayette, IN: Author. Retrieved October 31, 2009, from http://www.purdue.edu/REM/eh/bsp.htm#slib

Ritchie, S., & Willer, B. (Eds.). (2005). *Health: A guide to the NAEYC early childhood program standard and related accreditation criteria.* Washington, DC: National Association for the Education of Young Children.

Subramanian, M. (2007). *Eye - Foreign object in.* MedlinePlus. U.S. National Library of Medicine & National Institutes of Health. Retrieved November 16, 2009, from http://www.nlm.nih.gov/medlineplus/ency/article/002084.htm

U.S. National Library of Medicine & National Institutes of Health. (2009a). *Wounds.MedlinePlus.* Retrieved November 15, 2009, from http://www.nlm.nih.gov/medlineplus/wounds.html.

Vorvick., L. J. & Zieve, D. (2009a) *Broken bones.* Medline Plus. U.S. National Library of Medicine & National Institutes of Health. Retrieved November 16, 2009, from http://www.nlm.nih.gov/medlineplus/ency/article/000001.htm

Vorvick., L. J. & Zieve, D. (2009b) *Bruises.* Medline Plus. U.S. National Library of Medicine & National Institutes of Health. Retrieved November 16, 2009, from http://www.nlm.nih.gov/medlineplus/ency/article/007213.htm

Chapter 18

American Academy of Pediatrics. (2000, July 26). *Joint statement on the impact of entertainment violence on children* (Congressional Public Health Summit). Elk Grove Village, IL: Author. Retrieved November 3, 2009, from http://www.aap.org/advocacy/releases/jstmtevc.htm

American Academy of Pediatrics, American Public Health Association, & National Resource Center for Health and Safety in Child Care and Early Education. (2002). *Caring for our children: National health and safety performance standards: Guidelines for out-of-home child care programs* (2nd ed.). Elk Grove Village, IL: American Academy of Pediatrics; Washington, DC: American Public Health Association. Retrieved August 31, 2009, from http://www.eric.ed.gov/ERICDocs/data/ericdocs2sql/content_storage_01/0000019b/80/14/0d/14.pdf

American Psychological Association. (2004). Violence in the media – Psychologists help protect children from harmful effects. *Psychology Matters.* Retrieved November 18, 2009, from http://www.psychologymatters.org/mediaviolence.html

Center on the Developing Child at Harvard University. (2007, August). *A science-based framework for early childhood policy: Using evidence to improve outcomes in learning, behavior and health for vulnerable children.* Cambridge, MA: Author. Retrieved November 2, 2009, from http://developingchild.harvard.edu/files/7612/5020/4152/Policy_Framework.pdf

Chalk, R., Gibbons, A., & Scarupa, H. J. (2002). *The multiple dimensions of child abuse and neglect: New insights into an old problem* (Child Trends Research Brief). Washington, DC: Child Trends. Retrieved November 3, 2009, from http://www.childtrends.org/files/childabuserb.pdf

Child Trends. (2002). *Charting parenthood: A statistical report of fathers and mothers in America.* Washington, DC: Author. Retrieved November 2, 2009, from www.childtrends.org/...//Child_Trends-2002_05_01_ES_ParentReport.pdf

Child Welfare Information Gateway. (2004a). *Discipline vs. abuse.* Washington, DC: Author. Retrieved November 2, 2009, from http://www.childwelfare.gov/can/defining/disc_abuse.cfm

Child Welfare Information Gateway. (2004b). *Risk and protective factors for child abuse and neglect.* Washington, DC: Author. Retrieved November 2, 2009, from http://www.childwelfare.gov/can/factors

Child Welfare Information Gateway. (2008a). *What is child abuse and neglect?* Washington, DC: Author. Retrieved online November 17, 2009, from http://www.childwelfare.gov/pubs/factsheets/whatiscan.cfm

Child Welfare Information Gateway. (2008). *Mandatory reporters of child abuse & neglect. State statutes series.* Washington, DC: Author. Retrieved November 2, 2009, from http://www.childwelfare.gov/systemwide/laws_policies/statutes/manda.cfm

Children's Bureau & DePanfilis, D. (2006). *Child Neglect: A guide for prevention, assessment and intervention.* User Manual Series. Retrieved November 17, 2009, from http://www.childwelfare.gov/pubs/usermanuals/neglect/index.cfm

Cohen, E., & Knitzer, J. (2004, January). *Young children living with domestic violence: The role of early childhood programs.* Iowa City: University of Iowa.

Cohen, J., Onunaku, N., Clothier, S., & Poppe, J. (2006). *Helping young children succeed: Strategies to promote early childhood social and emotional development* (Early Childhood Research and Policy Report). Washington, DC: National Conference of State Legislatures and Zero to Three.

Cosmos, C. (2001). Abuse of children with disabilities. *Council for Exceptional Children Today, 8*(2), 1-2, 5, 8, 12, 14.

Crosson-Tower, C. (2002). How can we recognize child abuse and neglect? In *When children are abused: An educator's guide to intervention* (pp. 8-34). Boston: Allyn and Bacon.

Davis, J. E. (2005). *Accounts of innocence: Sexual abuse, trauma, and the self.* Chicago, IL: University of Chicago Press.

Dodge, K. A., McLoyd, V. C., & Lansford, J. E. (2005). The cultural context of physically disciplining children. In *African American family life: Ecological and cultural diversity* (pp. 245-263). New York: Guilford Press.

English, D. J., Widom, C. S., & Brandford, C. (2004). Another look at the effects of child abuse. *National Institute of Justice Journal, 251*, 23-24.

Family Violence Prevention Fund. (2009). *The facts on domestic, dating and sexual violence.* San Francisco, CA: Author. Retrieved November 2, 2009, from http://endabuse .org/userfiles/file/Children_and_Families/ DomesticViolence.pdf

Fontes, L. A. (2005). Child maltreatment prevention and parent education. In *Child abuse and culture: Working with diverse families* (pp. 176-199). New York: Guilford Press.

Fraser, M. W., & Terzian, M. A. (2005). Risk and resilience in child development: Principles and strategies of practice. In G. P. Mallon & P. M. Hess (Eds.), *Child welfare for the 21st century: A handbook of practices, policies, and programs* (pp. 55-71). New York: Columbia University Press.

Gibbs, D., Martin, S., Kupper, L., & Johnson, R. (2007). Child maltreatment in enlisted soldiers' families during combat-related deployments. *Journal of the American Medical Association, 298*(5), 528-535.

Huesmann, L. R., Moise-Titus, J., Podolski, C., & Eron, L. D. (2003). Longitudinal relations between children's exposure to TV violence and their aggressive and violent behavior in young adulthood: 1977-1992. *Developmental Psychology, 30*(2), 201-221.

JAMA and Archives Journals. (2007, January 3). Child abuse and neglect associated with increased risk of depression among young adults. *Science Daily.* Retrieved November 2, 2009, from http://www.sciencedaily.com/ releases/2007/01/070102092229.htm

Jenkins, E. (1996). *Children's exposure to community violence.* Institute on domestic violence in African American communities proceedings. Washington DC: Administration for Children and Families.

Kempe, C. H., Silverman, F. N., Steele, B. F., Droegemueller, W., & Silver, H. K. (1962). The battered-child syndrome. *Journal of the American Medical Association, 181*(1), 17-24.

Kenny, M. C. (2001). Child abuse reporting: Teachers' perceived deterrents. *Child Abuse and Neglect, 25*(1), 81-92.

Koralek. D. (1992). *Caregivers of young children: Preventing and responding to child maltreatment.* Washington, DC: U.S. Department of Health & Human Services. Retrieved November 2, 2009, from http:// www.childwelfare.gov/pubs/usermanuals/ caregive/caregive.pdf

Leventhal, J. M. (1999). The challenges of recognizing child abuse: Seeing is believing. *Journal of the American Medical Association,281*, 657-659.

Levin, D. (2003, March). *Beyond banning war and superhero play: Meeting children's needs in violent times.* Washington, DC: National Association for the Education of Young Children.

London, K., Bruck, M., Ceci, S., & Shuman, D. (2005). Disclosure of child sexual abuse: What does research tell us about the ways the children tell? *Psychology, Public Policy, and Law, 11*(1), 194-226.

Malchiodi, C. A. (2001). Using drawing as intervention with traumatized children. *Trauma and Loss: Research and Interventions, 1*(1). Gross Pointe Woods, MI: National Institute of Trauma and Loss in Children. Retrieved November 3, 2009, from http://www.tlcinst .org/drawingintervention.html

McIntyre, T., & Silva, P. (1992). Culturally diverse childrearing practices: Abusive or just different? *Beyond Behavior, 4*(1), 8-12.

National Association for the Education of Young Children. (1997). *Early years are learning years: Media violence and young children.* Washington, DC: Author. Retrieved November 2, 2009, from http:// oldweb.naeyc.org/ece/1997/05.asp

National Association for the Education of Young Children. (2004). *Building circles— Breaking cycles* (Publication DD2). Author.

National Association for the Education of Young Children. (2005). *Code of ethical conduct and statement of commitment.* Washington, DC: Author. Retrieved October 13, 2009, from http://www.naeyc.org/ positionstatements/ethical_conduct

National Center on Shaken Baby Syndrome. *Physical consequences of shaking.* Retrieved November 2, 2009, from http:// www.dontshake.org/sbs.php?topNavID=3& subNavID=23

National Scientific Council on the Developing Child. (2005). *Excessive stress disrupts the architecture of the developing brain* (Council Working Paper #3). Cambridge, MA: Center on the Developing Child at Harvard University. Retrieved November 4, 2009, from http://developingchild.harvard. edu/library/reports_and_working_papers/ wp3

New York Society for the Prevention of Cruelty to Children. (2008). *The catalyst: 1870-1874.* New York: Author. Retrieved November 3, 2009, from http://www .nyspcc.org/nyspcc/history/the_catalyst

Office on Child Abuse and Neglect, Caliber Associates, & Crosson-Tower, C. (2003). *The role of educators in preventing and responding to child abuse and neglect. User manual series.* Retrieved October 16, 2009, from http://www.childwelfare.gov/pubs/ usermanuals/educator/educatorc.cfm

Olson, M., & Hyson, M. (2003). *Early childhood education and child abuse prevention. NAEYC's perspective, research findings, and future actions.* Washington, DC: National Association for the Education of Young Children.

Osofsky, J. (Ed.). (1997). *Children in a violent society.* New York: Guildford Press.

Osofsky, J. D. (1999). The impact of violence on children. *The Future of Children, 9*(3), 33-49.

Osofsky, J. (Ed.). (2004). *Young children and trauma: Intervention and treatment.* Guildford Publications.

Reyome, N. D., & Gaeddert, W. (1998). Teachers' awareness of child and adolescent maltreatment. *Child Study Journal, 28*(2), 111-122.

Rice, K., & Groves, B. (2005). *Hope & healing: A caregivers' guide to helping young children affected by trauma.* Washington, DC: Zero to Three.

Roer-Strier, D. (2001). Reducing risk for children in changing cultural contexts: recommendations for intervention and training. *Child Abuse and Neglect, 25*(2), 231-248.

Shelton, D. H., & Banchero, S. (2009). Seeking safe passage: Curing a public epidemic. *Chicago Daily Tribune.* Retrieved October 12, 2009, from http://www.chicagotribune.com/news/ chi-youth-violenceoct07,0,7180296.story?t rack=rss

Shonkoff, J. & Phillips, D. (Eds.). (2000). *From neurons to neighborhoods: the science of early childhood development.* Washington DC: National Academy Press.

Springer, K. W., Sheridan, J., Kuo, D., & Carnes, M. (2007). Long-term physical and mental health consequences of childhood physical abuse: Results from a large population-based sample of men and women. *Child Abuse and Neglect, 31*(5), 517-530.

Thomas, D., Leicht, C., Hughes, C., Madigan, A., & Dowell, K. (2003). *Emerging practices in the prevention of child abuse and neglect.* Wayne, PA: Caliber Associates. Retrieved November 2, 2009, from http://www .childwelfare.gov/preventing/programs/ whatworks/report/report.pdf

U.S. Department of Health and Human Services, Administration for Children and Families. (2006). *Child maltreatment 2004.* Washington, DC: U.S. Government Printing Office. Retrieved November 2, 2009, from http://www.acf.hhs.gov/programs/cb/pubs/ cm04/figures_6.htm

U.S. Department of Health and Human Services, Administration for Children and Families. (2008). *Child maltreatment 2006.* Washington, DC: U.S. Government Printing

Office. Retrieved November 2, 2009, from www.acf.hhs.gov/programs/cb/pubs/cm06/index.htm

U.S. Department of Health and Human Services, Administration for Children and Families. (2009). *Child maltreatment 2007*. Washington, DC: U.S. Government Printing Office. Retrieved November 2, 2009, from http://www.acf.hhs.gov/programs/cb/pubs/cm07/index.htm

Van Voorhees, B. W. (2006). Munchausen syndrome by proxy. *Medline Plus*. Bethesda, MD: U.S. National Library of Medicine. Retrieved November 4, 2009, from http://www.nlm.nih.gov/medlineplus/ency/article/001555.htm

Washington Council for Prevention of Child Abuse. (2005). *Reframing child abuse messages*. Seattle: Author.

Zero to Three. (2009). *Research summary: children exposed to violence*. Retrieved November 17, 2009, from http://www.zerotothree.org/site/DocServer/Children_Exp_to_Violence.pdf?docID=2502

name index

subject index

photo credits

Ariel Daeschel, pp. vii, 88, 101, 149 (all), 170, 172, 183, 188 (top left, top right, bottom left), 196, 280; Shutterstock, pp. 1, 6, 9, 63, 163, 185, 234, 285, 287, 328, 341, 386, 395, 449, 568, 572; Photodisc/Getty Images, p. 2; iStockphoto.com, pp. 3, 29, 51, 98, 116, 323, 359 (top), 363, 469, 485, 523, 553; Krista Greco/Merrill, pp. 4, 40, 379, 493; T. Lindfors/Lindfors Photography, pp. 14, 190, 368; © Ellen B. Senisi, pp. 19, 126, 289, 374, 450, 552, 586; Annie Pickert/AB Merrill, pp. 21, 176, 286, 326, 425, 428, 490, 498, 499, 533, 536; Pearson Learning Photo Studio, p. 28; Frank Siteman, pp. 30, 302, 414, 452, 509, 534, 539; © Lilian Henglein/cultura/Corbis, p. 38; David Mager/Pearson Learning Photo Studio, p. 45; Michael Newman/PhotoEdit Inc., pp. 59, 152; Photos to Go, pp. 64, 97, 117, 188 (bottom right), 307, 451, 459, 590, 599, 606; Jupiter Unlimited, pp. 65, 118, 134, 135, 147 (both), 151, 154, 169, 342; © BananaStock Ltd., p. 66; Anthony Magnacca/Merrill, pp. 67, 248, 393, 529; Jeff Baker/Getty Images, Inc.-Taxi, p. 68; © Mike Goldwater/Alamy, p. 71; Bart's Medical Library/Phototake NYC, p. 73; Andersen Ross/Getty Images, Inc.-Photodisc, p. 77; Lynn Walters/Cooking with Kids, Inc./www.cookingwithkids.net, p. 96; Edward H. Gill/Custom Medical Stock Photo, Inc., p. 102; Vanessa Davies © Dorling Kindersley, p. 128; Mac H. Brown/Merrill, p. 146; Charles Gupton/Corbis-NY, p. 168; Dreamstime LLC-Royalty Free, pp. 175, 200, 246; Masterfile Royalty Free Division, p. 178; M. Bracken and C. Sorte, pp. 155, 180, 489, 504, 508; Lori Whitley/Merrill, pp. 195, 373, 519, 543; Barry Gregg/Corbis RF, p. 201; StockFood America-Royalty Free, p. 210; Dr. P. Marazzi/Photo Researchers, Inc., pp. 232, 389; Pearson Science, p. 241; C Squared Studios/Getty Images, Inc.-Photodisc/Royalty Free, p. 247; SuperStock Royalty Free, p. 253; Pearson, p. 281; Hope Madden/Merrill, p. 293; John Harris, p. 300; Arthur Tilley/Getty Images, Inc.-Taxi, p. 306; Andy Crawford © Dorling Kindersley, p. 308; EyeWire Collection/Getty Images-Photodisc-Royalty Free, pp. 309, 422; George Dodson/PH College, pp. 340, 401, 484; © Lowell Georgia/Science Source/Photo Researchers, Inc., p. 359 (bottom); © Dorling Kindersley, pp. 361, 557; Mark Clarke/Photo Researchers, Inc., p. 362; Scott Cunningham/Merrill, p. 372; Katelyn Metzger/Merrill, pp. 382, 527; 607; Eddie Lawrence © Dorling Kindersley, pp. 387, 410; Michal Heron/PH College, pp. 388, 561; Paul Miller/Merrill, p. 415; BananaStock/Jupiter Unlimited, p. 416; Thinkstock Images/Jupiter Unlimited, p. 456; Jeff Greenberg/PhotoEdit Inc., p. 477; Dallas Police Department, p. 480; courtesy of eSpecial Needs-www.eSpecialNeeds.com, p. 516; Richard Hutchings/PhotoEdit Inc., p. 522; Comstock Images/Jupiter Unlimited, p. 528; Ryan McVay/Getty Images, Inc.-Photodisc/Royalty Free, p. 563; PH College, p. 565; Corbis-NY, p. 579; Keith Weller/USDA/Natural Resources Conservation Services, p. 582; Stockxpert/Jupiter Unlimited, pp. 587, 597; David Glick/Getty Images Inc.-Stone Allstock, p. 594.